ENGLISH RECUSANT LITERATURE
1558–1640

Selected and Edited by
D. M. ROGERS

Volume 180

THOMAS FITZHERBERT

The Second Part of a Treatise Concerning Policy, and Religion
1615

THOMAS FITZHERBERT

The Second Part of a Treatise Concerning Policy, and Religion

1615

The Scolar Press

1974

ISBN 0 85967 155 0

Published and printed in Great Britain by
The Scolar Press Limited, 59-61 East Parade,
Ilkley, Yorkshire and
39 Great Russell Street,
London WC1

NOTE

Reproduced (original size) from a copy in the library of the Abbey, Fort Augustus, by permission of the Prior.

Reference: Allison and Rogers 317; not in STC.

THE SECOND PART OF A TREATISE CONCERNING POLICY, AND RELIGION.

Wherein the necessity, fruite, and dignity of Christian religion, in commonwelth, is euidently showed, with the absurdity of false religions, and the danger, and dammage, that ensueth thereof to all states; And by the way somme philosophical, moral, and politicall matters are treated: dyuers pious lessons & instructions geeuen, tending to christian perfection: many controuersyes in religion debated, and discussed: and the obiections of polityks, and heretyks answered; Finally it is clearely proued, that the Catholique Roman religiō only doth make a happy common welth.

Written by THOMAS FITZHERBERT Esquyre and Catholique priest.

Quærite primùm regnum Dei, & iustitiam eius, & hæc omnia adijcientur vobis. Matth. 6. Seeke first the Kingdome of God, and his iustice, and all these things shalbe geuen yow besydes. Math. 6.

At Douay, by IOHN HEIGHAM

With Licence of Superiors.

Anno Domini 1615.

THE PREFACE ADVERTISING DYVERS THINGES TO BE NOTED IN THE TREATISE FOLLOWING.

Sicilides Musæ paulo maiora canamus,
Non omnes arbusta iuuant, humilesq; myricæ.

O song the pastoral poet, when he meant to tune his pype to a heygher note, that is to say, to passe from treating rural, and cuntry conceits of sheppards, sheepe, goates, shrubs, busshes, hils, and dales, to sing and celebrat the prayses of Augustus Cæsar, *& his florishing Empire, by the occasion of the birth of* Saloninus *sonne to* Asinius Pollio *cheefe fauorit of* Augustus, *to whome he applyed a prophesy of* Sybilla Cumana, *which in truth concerned the byrth of our Sauiour* IESVS Christ *and his most happy empyre, and dominion ouer the soules of men.*

Therefore I being now to flye, (as I may say) a heygher pitch, then in my former Treatise, that is, to passe from handling so meane, and weake a subiect, as is the infirmity of mans wit, and humane pollicy grounded thereon, to treate of the necessity, frute, and dignity of religion in common welth, yea of that religion, and euerlasting empyre of Christ, *whereof the prophetesse* Sibilla *spake in the prophesie aforesayde (an argument much more incomparably excelling the former, whereof I treated before, then the imperial maiesty, and power of* Augustus, *excelled the poore and base quality of sheppeards, sheepe, busshes, hils, and dales (yea as much as heauen surpasseth earth, or rather all things nothing) I may with much more reason say,* multò maiora canamus, *and in steede of the* Sicilian Muses*(whose helpe the poet implored) inuocat that holy, and deuyne spirit, which is the true light of harts, & teacher of all truth, whome therefore I humbly beseech so to illuminat my understanding, and guyde my pen, that I may worthily treate of so worthy & hygh a subiect, as is the transcendent woorthines and perfection of Christian religion.*

For although my intent is not to unfould all the mysteries of the christian faith, neyther yet to handle any part thereof further, then the same may some way concerne common welth, yet for as much as I ame to proue in this treatise, that the perfection, and felicity of common welth consisteth in Christian religion, I cannot sufficiently performe the same, except I show the perfection, and incomprehensible excellency, effects, and fruits thereof, no more then if I should undertake to treate of the woorthines & felicity of man, and omit to speake of the excellency of the soule, and of the euerlasting beatitude, whereto he is ordayned, and wherein consisteth his last, and cheefe felicity.

Therefore, whereas there are ouer many at this day, who haue such a prophane conceit of common welth, and pollicy, that they think matters of spirit, altogether impertinent thereto, and expect in a politicall discourse nothing els but rules, or instructions teaching cunning practyses, sleyghts, subtiltyes, shifts (or as I may tearme them tricks of state) yea coosenages, & fraudulent deuyses, rather then prudent, and sound aduises, such being now the corruption generally growne in the world, that craft, and suotilty is held of many for prudence, the deepest dissimulation for the profoundest wisdome, and (if I may speake plainly without offence of modest eares) the fynest, and best cloked knauery for the wysest, and heyghest policy, Therefore I say to such, that if they could frame a common welth of a company of coggers, coseners, and connicatchers, tending euery one to his owne particuler proffit, or pleasur, or yet of a congregation all of sensuall men, litle better then a heard of cattle, or beasts (I meane though endued with reasonable soules, yet lead, and gouerned altogether by sence) they should haue more reason to exclude from it, all matters not only of spirit, but also of vertue, & morall honesty; but if common welth be a ciuill society of men united with the communion of lawes, for a publyk, and common good, I say of men, that is to say reasonable creatures, hauing reasonable soules created by almighty god to his owne ymage, and for his owne seruice, yea ordayned to a supernatural end, that is, to eternal beatitude, to be obtained by spiri-

tual

tual meanes, to wit by religion, iustice, pietye, and the practise of all vertue (all which I will make most euident in the ensuing discourse, nay if I euidently proue that the cheefe end, and felicity of the common welth it selfe, ys no other then the end, and happynes of euery particuler man in this lyfe, and that the same cannot otherwayse be atchiued, but by the perfect practise of christian religion, they cannot thinke it strange, or impertinent to the subiect which I handle, if I doe now and then, intermix discourses of true christian perfection, and such things as belong thereto; For seeing no common welth can be perfect without perfect vertue, nor any perfection of vertue be had without Christian perfection, nor the same be any where found but in Christian religion, as I will make most manifest heereafter, I cannot delineat a true, ciuil, & political man, that is to say a perfect member of a christian common welth, except I descrybe a perfect christian, neither yet performe that, except I also show what is christian perfection; nor that without the explication of many heygh misteries, and excellencies of christian religion.

And for as much as I cannot accomplish all this with the benefit that I wish to my reader, except I also lay doune the meanes how to attayne to christian perfection, thereby to arriue to a perfect vnion with god (which is the proper effect of true religion, and the only true felicity of man, and common welth) therefore I meane also to enterlace many spiritual aduises, and rules tending to the true vse, & practise of christian religion, lest otherwayse I may be lyke to one that should tell a sick man of a souueraigne medicin for his disease, and conceale from him the vse of it; so that my desyre, and intention, yea my obligation being (my subiect considered) not so much to show, or describe, as to make a perfect member of christian common welth, & to supply the defects of humane pollicy (whereof I treated in my fyrst part) with the perfection of christian religion (which is the subiect of this my second part) I hope no man can iustly mislike that I doe oft inculcat matters of spirit, and especially the office, and duty of a true christian man; and touch also now and then, somme poynts of the heyghest christian perfection. And whereas I shall also haue occasion to relate by the way, somme admirable, miraculous, & stupendious effects of gods grace in holly men, I dout not but the pious, and well disposed reader, will receiue greate edification thereby, noting, and admiring therein, not only the eminent dignity, and excellency of christian religion, but also the infinit power, wisdome, and bounty of almighty god towards his seruants

And as for such incredulous miscreants, as the Apostle S. Iudas *tear-*
Iude 1. *meth* animales spiritum non habentes, men altogether sensual, hauing no spirit, *who therefore doe not vnderstand (saith S.*Paul,*)* ea quę sũt spiritus Dei, those things vvhich are of the spirit of god,
1. Cor. 2. *beleeuing no more of good woorks then they see with theyr eyes, or touch with their hands, or can comprehend within their weake, idle, and addle heads, such I say, I remit partly to that which I haue discoursed in my first part against* Atheists, *and partly to the experience of gods most admirable woorke in this kind, which I shall haue occasion to demonstrat in this my second part, drawing the same from the fountayne of the holly scriptures, according to the interpretation of the Catholyke church, and deryuing it to these our dayes, by the examples and testimony of gods saints in all tymes, and ages.*

And if neuertheles they persist obstinat in their incredulity, and think with some ridiculous, and blasphemous iest, (as commonly they are wont) to elude such a sacred authority of experience both ancient, and moderne, I leaue them with sorrow, and pitty of their case, to the terrible sentence of S: Peter *pronounced of such as they.* Hi velut pecora irrationa-
2. Pet. 2. bilia &c. these being lyke to vnreasonable beasts, naturally tending to the snare, and destruction, blaspheming in those things vvhich they knovv not, shall perish in their ovvne corruption, receiuing the revvard of iniustice &c.

Furthermore for as muchas the differẽce of opiniõs in matters of religiõ at this tyme, requyreth some discussion of the truth, that thereby it may appeare who they are that truely professe the christiã religion, I do therefore think good to treate of diuers poynts in controuersy betwyxt the Roman Catholyks, & their aduersaries, thereby to show the preiudice that groweth to state by false religions, exemplifying the same especially in Lutheranisme, *and* Caluinisme, *because those sects eyther doe comprehend, or haue engendred all other, and are more generally embraced then any of the rest.*

And therefore whereas I may perhaps be censured by some as ouersharpe, and vehement sometymes in the reprehension of Lutherans, *&* Caluinists, *and their doctrin, (out of the abundance of my zeale to the catholyke faith) whereby I may also seeme to cast some aspersion of iniury (as perhaps*

perhaps it may be interpreted vppon my owne cuntrymen, I meane Protestants *and* Puritans *in* England, *I wish them to vnderstād, that although I hope to vse such due moderation towards* Lutherans, *and* Caluinists, *as not to reproue, and taxe them further then they shall iustly deserue, yet I think I may be the bolder with them, as iust occasion shall be offred, because I persuade my selfe that no* Protestant, *nor* Puritian *in* England, *can iustly take him selfe to be iniured thereby, seeing that there is none of them (for ought I know, or can imagin) that is formally eyther a* Lutheran, *or a* Caluinist, *I meane that holdeth, & professeth the doctrin of* Luther, *or* Caluin *otherways then with such additions and substractions, as euery mans priuat spirit doth suggest, and therefore whatsoeuer I shall say of* Luther, *or* Caluin, *or any of theyr progeny, I would not haue it further to be extēded then I meane it, which is only to those* Archsectaries *and such others as are content to be held, and styled for their disciples, I meaneto be called* Lutherans, *or* Caluinsts.

And as for my louing Cuntrimen who reiect some part of their doctrin, and admit the rest, I would wish them, heere by the way of aduise well to consider, what assurāce they haue more for that which they take, then for that which they leaue since they (I meane Luther, *and* Caluin*) assured them selues no lesse of the one, then of the other, pretending the warrant of holly scriptures, and the assistance of gods holly spirit equally for both; So that if they were deceiued in part, they might aswell be deceiued in the whole, especially seeing that neyther of them had any other ground of his new doctrin, but only his owne priuat sence, and vnderstanding of scriptures, for yf they had had the assistance of gods spirit therein, they could nether of them haue erred in any part thereof, and much lesse haue dissented the one from the other so much as they did, being so opposit, & cōtrary (euen in some of the most important, and essential poynts of faith) that they detested, & condemned one an other for damnable heretykes, as their follwers doe vntill this day; whereby it is euiden, that at least the one of them was mightiely deceiued, and therefore had not the spirit of god, yea & that the other also buylding vpon no better ground then his companiō, but vpon the selfe same (I meane his owne presumption to vnderstand the scriptures aright) had no more assurance of the holly ghosts assistance then he, and therefore might erre as dangerously, and absurdly as he.*

And it

And if any man grounding him selfe also vpon the same foundation, follow the one more then the other, and yet neuertheles doth approue him in part, and reproue him in the rest, he is to consider, that he may with reason feare, lest he him selfe be as much beguyled in that which he accepteth, as his maister was in that which he reiecteth, seeing he hath no more assurance for the one part, then for the other; his owne, or his maysters priuat sence of scripture, beeing the ground of both; So that we see all is buylt heere, vpon vncertainety & that no man can, by this meanes, haue any ground or assurāce of his faith; whereby we may also learne what extreame folly & danger it is for any man, to leaue the infallible iudgement of the church (which is the spouse of Christ, *and guyded by his holly spirit) to follow his owne, or any mans priuat sence in the exposition of scripture, which can proceede of nothing els but singularity, temerity, presumption, and pryde, the mother of heresy, and as I may say, the very precipice whereby infinit numbers haue fallen headlong into the pit of eternal perdition; whereof I neede not to say more heere, because I shall touch it now, and then in the ensuing discourse.*

It resteth now good reader that, I aduertise thee of some alteration of my desygnement, since I wrote my first part. For, although I was then determined to compact my whole conceit into two volumes, or parts, yet there hath since occured vnto me such abundance of matter, necessary, parly for thy proffit, and partly for thy delectation, that I ame now resolued to adde a thyrd part. And seeing that the subiect of the whole, beeing Pollicy, & Religiō, *my first part treated principally of* Pollicy, *I meane that this secōd part shall treate most of* Religion, *& the thyrd indifferently of both; wherein I also hope fully to discharge my obligation touching some particuler poynts promised in my first part, which I shall not haue opportunity to performe in this, as also to consummat the whole subiect of my first proiect, whereof there will remayne much to be accomplished, according to this my latter desygne.*

So that thou seest, good reader, it falleth out with me, as it doth with buylders, who seeldome content themselues with their first plot; and commonly spend both longer tyme, and much more money, then at the first they determined. And although I cānot presume duly to obserue the rules, and precepts of Architecture in the fabrike of this my religious pallace (if so I may tearme a woork treating of Religion) yet I will not be careles of

that

that which most importeth, and best correspondeth to the nature of such a buylding; & therefore I will not only furnish it with implements of pious lessons, and instructions of greate edification, but also erect and buyld therein an oratory, or chappel for christian contemplation; and in the very porch or entry thereof, represent unto thee a true pourtrait of the natural contemplation of the philosophers; And though I dout not, but thou wilt fynd therein excellent matter, and perhaps woonder to see such hygh and mistical doctrin in pagans and heathens, who could reach no further, then nature, and the light of reason could lead them, yet I do not recommend it unto thee for any other purpose, then to serue for a foyle to set foorth our Christian contemplation, that is, to make thee the better see, and vnderstand the excellent perfection thereof.

Yf therefore it may please thee sometymes to retyre thy selfe into this contemplatiue chappel, and there with due, and serious meditation to contemplat not so much the forme of the buylding, (which by the smale skill of the Architect, may fayle in proportion) as the matter, and furniture thereof, borowed from the holly scriptures, and most comtemplatiue fathers, I dout not but thou shalt receiue such spiritual benefit, and contentment thereby, that thou wilt say, as S. Peter sayd vpon the mount. Bonum est nos hic esse, or with the royal prophet. Quam dilecta tabernacula tua domine virtutum, concupiscit & deficit anima mea in atria Domini. Matth. 17. Psal. 83.

And for as much as in the buylding of a Palace, special care is to be had to make it fayre, and beautifull to the eye, and to grace it with variety of pictures, images, and pourtraicts of dyuers sorts, I will be carefull also to geeue thee some satisfaction in that behalfe; and therefore doe meane to paynt, and adorne this my religious buylding, with greate diuersity of moral, and political doctrin, and with store of histories, as well profane, as Ecclesiasticall, as also with the true and liuely pourtraits of the most famous, and woorthy men that haue florished in gods church since our sauiours tyme, proposing to thy view theyr vertuous, and heroical acts, in the contempt and triumphant conquest of the world, and themselues, for the loue of god; to the end that framing thy lyfe after the model of theyr example, thou mayst arriue to some degree, at least, of true christian perfection.

Moreouer, whereas there is no palace so beautifull, or magnificent that hath not dyuers retraicts, channels, sinks, and other base, and homely places (which though they be lothsome of theyr owne nature, yet are necessary for the whole buylding) thou shalt also fynd in this my religious palace matters of that quality, I meane the absurd, beastly, and impious opinions, and liues of Pagans, Mahometans, Ievves, Macchiauillians, Polityks, & Heretyks *representing vnto thee the horrour of false religion, which may serue, not only to moue thee to the detestation thereof, but also to breede in thee a greater estimation, loue, and honour of true religion.*

Finally, as nothing more importeth in buylding, then to lay a sure foundation, and to make the walles substancial, and able to resist the force, as well of wynd, and wether, as of enemies, if neede requyre, so will I haue a special care to found all this my buylding, vpon the firme, and immoueable rock of truth, and to rayse strong walls of pregnant arguments, & reasons drawne from nature it selfe, fortifying the same with the euident testimonies of holly scriptures, and ancient fathers, and with many old & moderne examples; And therefore seeing I haue benne content, good reader, for my part to be at the charges, and paynes, not only to buyld this pallace, and to make it commodious for thee, but also to present it vnto thee for thy vse and habitation, I hope thou wilt not vse it as an Inne, for a bayte, or a nights lodging, (that is, only take a superficial view of it) but make thy abode in it at least for some tyme; I meane read, and ruminat the whole woork with dilligence, and after practise that which thou shalt fynd therein fit for thy vse. For so shalt thou, of this my laboure reape the benefyte, I the comefort, and almighty God the glory, to whose grace, and holly protection I recommend thee.

Thy hartie well willer.

Thomas Fitzherbert.

A PER-

A PERFECT ANATOMY OF THIS TREATISE, SHOWING PARTICVLERLY WHAT MATTERS are handled in it, and in what Chapters.

Touching Religion only.

HAT religion is most natural to man, and most neceſſary for the conſeruation, not only of all mankind, but alſo of the whole world. Chap. 1. & 2.

How much the heathens and pagans eſteemed religion, and prieſthood, and ſome what touching the eminent dignity of chriſtian prieſthood, & of the church of Chriſt. Chap. 6.

The purity and excellency of Chriſtian religion, and the admirable force, and effects of gods grace for the repreſsion of vyce, and the reformation of mans manners. Chap. 15. & 16.

The excellency of chriſtian contemplation with the practiſe and ſtupendious effects thereof. Chap. 18. 19. 20. & 21.

That the Catholyke Roman religion hath the true imitation of Chriſt and Chriſtian perfection. Chap. 25. 26. 27. 28. 29. 31. 37. & 38.

Touching Religion, & Pollicy ioyntly.

That the end and felicity of common welth conſiſteth in religion, according to the doctrin as well of the old philoſophers, as of Chriſtian deuines. Chap. 4.

That all pollicy is to be directed by the rule of religion, and that otherwayſe it can not be good, and true pollicy. Chap. 6.

That the ciuil society, or common welth ys, by the law of nature, subordinat to the ecclesiastical society. Ibidem.

That Atheisme destroyeth common welth, & by what meanes. Ca. 8.

That the vse of taking and geuing othes, is most necessary for common welth. Chap. 8.

That all false religions are pernicious to common welth. Chap. 6. Showed in paganisme, Chap. 7. 8. & 9. in Mahometisme, and Iudaisme, Chap. 14. In Lutheranisme and Caluinisme. Chap. 28. and in the rest of the chapters vnto the end of the booke, and especially in the 30. 35. 36. and the last chapter.

That the christian religion is truely ciuil, or political, that is to say conforme to reason of state, and most behoouefull for common welth. Chap. 15. 16. & 17.

That the Catholyk Roman religion, ys the true Christian religion before mencioned, & therefore is truely ciuil, or political, and maketh a happy common welth. Chap. 25. 26. 27. 36. 37. and 38.

That the practise of the Euangelical counsels, to wit of voluntary pouerty, chastity, and obedience, or abnegation of a mans selfe, ys conuenient and necessary for common welth. Chap. 25. 28. 29. 30. 31. 34. and the last chapter num. 87. 88. 89. 90. & 91.

Certayne arguments, and reasons of Machiauel against Christian religion, out of reason of state are confuted. Chap. 24.

Other obiections of polityks against the single lyfe of priests, and religious disciplin are answered. Chap. 34.

That no political law can subdue the law of the flesh, without the help of gods grace. Chap. 15.

Touching Policy only.

How temporal goods, and commodities may serue, and auayle to the felicity of common welth. Chap. 4. and in the last chapter num. 111.

That common welth standeth by vertue, & falleth by vyce. Chap. 9.

Dyuers political obseruations, and rules taken out of *Plato* for the good gouernment of common welth. Ibidem.

That all the scyence, and practise of the Southsayers, and Augures amongst the Romans, & Grecians was absurd, and contrary to true reason of state. Chap. 8.

That *Poligamy*, or the hauing many wyues at once vsed amongst Turks, Persians, and Moores is against reason of state, and hurtfull to common welth. Chap. 14.

That many ciuil constitutions of the *Iewes* ordeyned in their *Talmud*,

are

are not only most absurd and impious, but also most repugnant to reason of state. Ibid.

Touching matters of morality, philosophy, and the philosophers.

That the felicity which wicked men imagin to be in sensuality, riches honours, and pleasures of the world is no felicity, but misery. Chap. 5.

That paynimes, and infidels could neuer arriue to the perfection of moral vertues, though many of them seemed to excell in some of the moral vertues. Chap. 16.

That the philosophers beleeued, that there is but one god, and that philosophy is the handmayde of diuinity. Chap. 3.

That the philosophers did not know the true cause of the general disseas in mans nature, and therefore laboured in vayne to cure it by their precepts. Chap. 15.

That *Aristotle* placed the felicity of man, and of common welth in contemplation. Chap. 4.

What manner of contemplation the philosophers requyred to mans felicity, & what practise they had thereof. Chap. 17.

What the philosophers taught concerning the actiue, and contemplatiue lyfe, & in what manner they thought that the common welth might be made happy by contemplation. Chapp. 22.

How much virginity was esteemed amongst the paynimes, & what meanes they taught to liue chast, Chap. 30.

Touching matters historical.

An historical relation of the religion of the Romans. Chap. 7. & 8.

Examples of dyuers florishing common welths ouerthrowne by vyce. Chap. 9.

An exact epitome of the Roman history, with the mutation & changes of theyr commonwelth, and empyre. The welth, power, and ample dominion of the Roman emperours, theyr desastrous deaths whyles they were paynimes, and an exact obseruatiou of the rigour of gods iustice from tyme to tyme vpon the Roman comon welth, and empyre from the foundation of Rome, vntill the propagation of the Christian religion vnder Constantine the greate. Chap. 9. 10. 11. 12. & 13.

An historicall relation of the religion of *Mahomet*, and the ridiculous absurdities and lyes contayned in the *Alcoran*, and his other books; Also of the *Talmud* of the iewes, and theyr absurd impiety, and folly. Chap. 14.

Examples of the admirable effects of gods grace, in the reformation of mens manners. Chap. 15, & 16.

Examples of contemplatiue, and holly kings. Chap. 23.

An historicall relation of the beginning, and proceeding of all the religious orders in gods church, from Christs tyme vntill this day. Chap. 25. & 26.

Examples of gods extraordinary fauours bestowed vppon his seruants by extases and rapts, reuelations, the spirit of prophesy, and other miraculous operations in euery age since our Sauiours tyme. Chap. 27.

Examples of emperours, kings, and other greate princes, who haue forsaken the world for the loue of god. Chap. 28.

An historical relation of the licentious lyues of *Luther*, *Caluin*, *Beza*, and other sectaries. Chap. 30. Of theyr dissentions and pryde obiected by one of them against another. Chap. 31. And of the fruit of their new ghospell, noted, and acknowledged by themselues in theyr disciples, and followers. Chap. 36.

What cuntryes haue benne conuerted to the christian faith, by religious men, with examples of many other greate benefits bestowed also by almighty god vppon princes, and theyr states, by theyr meanes: and finally, what monasteries haue benne buylt in England by the kings thereof. Chap. 34.

Examples of *Arrians, Donatists*, and other infamous heretykes, and notorious wicked men, who were professed enemies of religious men, and theyr profession. Chap. 31.

Examples of gods iustice extended vppon wicked emperours, and princes, who had made lawes against monastical disciplin, and religious men. Chap. 34.

Examples of miracles vaynely attempted, false reuelations, and diabolical illusions, happened to dyuers sectaries, namely to *Luther*, *Caluin*, *Foxe*, and others. Chap. 32.

Examples of greate austerity vsed by holly men, for the satisfaction of gods iustice, mortification of their flesh, or other pious ends, as well in the old testament, as the new, and in all ages since our sauiours tyme, in imitation of him, and of his apostles. Chap. 36.

Matters of Religion in controuersy betwixt Catholykes and theyr aduersaries, debated and discussed.

The euangelicall counsels in general, proued to haue benne taught, & practised by our sauiour and his apostles. Chap. 24.

Con-

Matters belonging to Christian perfection, and to the felicity of man in this lyfe consisting in his vnion with god.

Of

THE TABLE OF THE CHAPTERS SHEVVING THE CONTENTS OF THE SECOND PART OF THIS Treatise.

HE necessitie of religion, for the conseruation and perfection of the worlde, is proued by the reduction, and returne of all creatures to their beginning and first cause, that is to say, God their Creator. Chap. 1.

In what maner all creatures are reduced to God their Creator by religion, and by the way, the beginning, effect, vtilitie, and end of religion, is euidently declared out of the best philosophers: & consequently it is proued, that religion is so natural to man, that it can not be extuinguished, except mankind be exterminated, and the whole worlde dissolued: whereby the necessitie of religion, the prouidence of God, and the blindnes, and impietie of the politike, is euidently shewed. Chap. 2.

It is obiected, that the philosophers which haue beene alleadged in the former chapters, were Idolaters, and that therfore their testimonies, for matters of Christian religion are impertinent, and not to be vsed by Christians. The obiection is answered: and it is proued, that the religion whereof the philosophers treate, was true religion, consisting in the worship of one God, whom they acknowleged to be the author of nature. Also, that philosophie is the handmaide of our deuinitie, and to be vsed for the confirmation thereof, with certaine considerations prouing the necessitie of religion, and the ignorance, and blindnesse of politiques. Chap. 3.

To shew the necessitie of religion in common wealth, it is cleerly proued, as well by the philosophers, as by deuines, that the end, and true felicitie of euery man in this life, and of common wealthe, consisteth in religion. And finallie it is declared,

how

A conti-

peareth partly in their owne workes, and partly by the testimonies of one of them against an other. Finallie it is made most euident, that they are not only voide of all true imitation of Christ, and christian perfection, but also that they are sworne enemies of it, and therefore farre from all vnion with God, and true felicitie. Chap. 31.

VVhere as it is shewed, that the Roman Catholikes, haue all the externall signes that may be, of Gods externall vnion with them, (to wit, ecstases, rapts, and reuelations, the spirit of prophesie, visions, and apparitions of our Sauiour, his Angels and Sainctes, and the operation of manifestest miracles: (it is here examined, what our aduersaries can pretend to haue had, or to haue in this kind: and it is proued, that they haue had nothing els, but certaine counterfet miracles, which haue miscaried vnder their hands, illusions of wicked spirits, idle and phantasticall dreames, horrible visions, and apparitions of deuils, and fained reuelations. Lastly, their obiections against our miracles, are confuted, and they concluded to be wilfully blynd. Chap. 32.

For the finall conclusion of the question, concerning the Euangelicall Counsells, and religious life, the matter of religious vowes is debated, and defended against our aduersaries. Also, that the continencie of clergy men, is beneficiall to the common wealth, and that certaine wicked Emperours, who haue sought by lawes to restraine, & to prohibit monasticall life, haue bene seuerelie punished by almighty God for the same. Finallie a breefe recapitulation is made of all the premises, concerning the true imitation of Christ, and our aduersaries are thereby conuinced, to be vtterly void, aswell of all Christian perfection, as of the true felicitie of man, and common welth. Chap. 33.

Certaine obiections of the Politikes, out of the lawes of diuers Emperours and Kinges, against religious disciplin are answered, and the impietie of the said lawes is shewed, by the notable punishment of God vppon the lawe makers. VVith a breefe recapitulation, and conclusion of all the former chapters, concerning religious discipline. Chap. 34.

To proue that the Catholike religion is conforme to true reason of state, and the contrary doctrin repugnant thereto, ten points, controuersed betwixt the Catholikes, and their aduersaries, are debated by way of state: and it is euidently shewed, that the doctrin of Catholikes, leadeth to all vertue, and is therefore most conuenient for state, and that the doctrin of their aduersaries, eyther withdraweth from vertue, or inciteth to vice, and consequently is most pernicious to all states. Finally, the bad state of Lutheranisme *and* Caluinisme *in Common welth, is shewed*

by

THE SECOND PART OF A TREATISE CONCERNING POLICY AND RELIGION.

THE NECESSITIE OF RELIGION, FOR THE CONseruation, and perfection of the vvorlde is proued, by the reduction, and returne of all creatures to their beginning and first cause, that is to say, God their Creator.

CHAP. I.

SVCH is the simpathy, and correspondence betwixt the body, and the partes thereof, that whatsoeuer is conuenient, and necessary for the whole, is also necessary for euery parte, for with the whole, the partes are ioyntly conserued, or destroyed; therefore whereas I am now to shew the fruit, dignitie, and necessitie of religion in commōwelths, kingdomes, & states (which are but partes of the world) I thinke it not amisse first to shew, that religion is so necessary, for the conseruation of the whole world, that the same could not stand without it; whereby two thinges will manifestly appeare, the one, that religion is consequentlie necessarie for the conseruation of all commonwealthes; and the other, that the politikes, who reduce religion to a bare name, and matter of opinion, or fantasy. (contenting themselues with the shew, and apparance thereof in the states, where they gouerne (doe, asmuch as in them lyeth) tend to the destruction, not only of commonwelth, but also of the whole world.

2 This will easely be made manifest to any man, that hath had but any tast of Philosophy, which teacheth that the world, and all thinges therin being produced by one first cause, doe not only continually depend thereon, but also are finally reduced therto, and could not

otherwise subsist, and be conserued; which I will proue to be the especiall effect of religion.

First therefore I will treat of the reductiõ of all thinges to almighty God, their first cause and beginning: And after I will declare, how the same is wrought, and performed; Let vs heare then, the doctrin of some of the most ancient, and best philosophers.

Diogenes, Laertius Proœm. in vitas Philosopho. *Marsilius Ficin. comment. in conuiuium Plato, oratio 2. c. 1.* *Ibid.* *Mercuri. de potestate & sapient. c. 3.*

3 The *Pithagorians* who were the first that were called Philosophers (because theyr master *Pithagoras* being demaunded what he was or what he professed, answered, that he was *Philosophus*, a louer of wisedome) taught that all thinges are measured, and gouerned by almighty God with a certayne Trinity, in respect of *theyr beginninge, theyr midst, and theyr end*, for that all thinges proceede from God, returne vnto him, and are perfected in him: for which cause also *Orpheus*, *Mercurius Trismegistus* and *Plato* call him, *principium, medium, & finem vniuersi*; The beginninge, midest, and end of the world, because as all creatures, are procreated, moued, and gouerned by him, so also they are referred to him, as to theyr end, and finally haue theyr consummation in him, and by him.

Aristotle 12. metaph. c. 12.

4 Therefore *Aristotle* compareth almighty God, to the General of an army, or master of a family, and the world to the army, or family, because all thinges in the world proceeding from God, their first cause, are also finally referred to him: as all thinges (sayth he) in an army haue theyr relation to the generall, or in a family to the head thereof.

Plato in Timæo.

Plato also affirmeth, that God is the beginninge, and end of all thinges, of some thinges ymmediately, and of others by the meanes of man, which how yt ys effected, shalbe declared after a while. Hereuppon *Iamblicus* (one of the cheefe *platonickes*) sayth, that yf all thinges had not a maruelous reuolution to God (from whom, and in whom they haue theyr being) *in nihilum repentè corruerent*; *they vvould soddaynely fall to nothing*, which *Proclus* also confirmeth, saying, that all thinges haue a perpetuall recourse, and as yt were a refluxe to the fountayne from whence they first flow, that ys to say, to God.

Iambli: apud Marsilium Ficin. in compendio in Timæum. ca. 6. *Proclus in element Thelog.* *Dionys. lib. de diuin. nominib. ca. 4.*

5 *Dionysius Areopagita* a Christian philosopher, and most learned deuyne sayth to the same purpose, that euery thing in the world, *ex optimo est, & in optimum conuertitur*: is of the best (that ys to say, hath beginning and being of God) and doth turne agayne to the best; which is also conforme to our holly scriptures teaching expressely that, *vniuersa propter semetipsum operatus est dominus*, our Lord made all thinges for him selfe, and that all thinges, are *ex ipso, per ipsum, & in ipso*, of him, by him and in him, which last ys read in the Greeke εἰς αὐτόν, *in ipsum*, that ys to say

Prouerb. 16. *Rom. 11.*

to ſay *into him*, ſignifying thereby the relation, and recourſe that all thinges haue to God, in which reſpect he ys alſo called in the Apocalipſe, α. & ω. *the beginninge, and end*, and being as *Boetius* ſayth.

Apocal. 1.

Boet. de conſola. philoſo. li. 3. metro. 9.

Principium, rector, Dux, ſemita, terminus idem.

The beginning, the gouernour, the guide, the vvay, and the laſt end vvhereto al thinges tend: ſuch being his infinit bounty, and loue towardes his creatures, that he not only conſerueth thoſe thinges which he hath created, but alſo conuerteth, and turneth them to him ſelfe.

6 For (as *Dionyſius Areopagita* ſaith) the loue of God prooceeding from him, and extending it ſelfe to all, and euery one of his creatures, maketh as it were a circle returninge, and drawing with it all thinges vnto him, whereby he doth not only conſerue his creatures, but alſo conſummat, and perfitt them. For then may any thing be truly ſaid to haue conſummation, and perfection, when being returned to the beginninge, from whence it was firſt deduced, it can goe no further, as we ſee it fall out in a circle which is ended, and perfited, when the lyne is reduced to the ſame point from whence it was firſt drawne; whereto *Boetius* may ſeeme to allude, when he ſaith thus.

Dionyſ. lib. diuin. nom. ca. 4.

Repetunt proprios quæque recurſus,
Redituque ſuo ſingula gaudent;
Nec manet vlli traditus ordo,
Niſi quod fini iunxerit ortum,
Stabilemque ſui fecerit orbem.

Boëtius de conſol. lib. 3. metro. 2.

The ſence is, that all thinges do naturally deſire to returne to their beginning, and nothing doth conſummat the courſe, and order that nature hath aſſigned it, vntill it hath made à circuite, or circle, and ended where it beganne.

7 This being ſo, let vs now ſee, how this is accompliſhed, in the whole world, that is to ſay, how the world, and all thinges therein, are reduced to their beginninge. This is moſt truly, and euidently performed by the meanes of man, being *Microcoſmus*, a litle world, and participating of the nature aſwell of all heauenly, as of all earthly thinges: in which reſpect, he is called in the ſcripture, *omnis creatura*, euery creature, as *S. Gregory* noteth vppon the wordes of our Sauiour, *prædicate Euangelium omni creaturæ*, preach the goſpell to euery creature, becauſe ſayth *S. Gregory*, *Omnis creaturæ aliquid habet homo*, &c. *Man hath ſomethinge of euery creature, for he hath beinge common vvith ſtones, ſenſe vvith bruite beaſtes, and vnderſtanding vvith Angels.*

Mercuri. Tris. ad Aſclepium ca. 3.

Mar. 16.

S. Gregor. in Marc. 16. Ho. 29.

8 Thus ſayth he, beſydes that it is alſo further to be vnderſtood, that God gaue vnto man a participation, not only with all creatures

in heauen, and earth, but also with him selfe, making him to his owne ymage and likenes, to the end he might be a meanes betwixt him and his other creatures, to vnite them and the whole world with him theyr creator, for nothing is more agreable to reason, nor more vsuall, or familiar to nature, then to conioyne two extreames by the meane of some thinge tempered, and composed of the nature of both. *Omnia Domino, &c. All twoo thinges* (sayth Cicero) *doe require some meane to serue them for a bond, or knot to vnite them:* for euen as in a building or house the roofe cannot be connected with the fundation, but by the helpe and meane of some thinge in the middest (as of walls, or pillars which may extend to both) so in naturall thinges, there can be no connexion of extreames, but by some thing, which hauinge participation of theyr nature, may, as it were, touch them both and ioyne them together.

Cicero libr. de vniuersit.

9 And this is euidently seene as well in all naturall societies, as in the naturall coniunction of all other thinges. In the oeconomical society, wee see, that the wife obeying her husband, and commanding her children, and seruants, is, as it were, the bond of the family, beinge partaker of the condition of both, the highest and lowest. And in ciuil societie, wee see the like, wherein the king is vnited with his subiects by magistrates, communicating in commandement with him, and in obedience with them. Also in man himselfe, reason doth not otherwise performe her function, or doe her office in the gouerment of the body, but by the facultie, and power of sense, which hath part of both: And the like may be obserued in the motion, and progresse of nature, which doth not passe from the extreame heate of sommer, to the extreamitie of winters colde, but by the temperature of spring and Autumne, which connecting the one with the other, doth acomplish the course of the whole yeare.

10 Finally the same may be also in some sort noted in the blessed Trinitie, wherein the Father, and the Sonne, are vnited with perpetuall communication of the holy Ghost, proceeding from them both. It is therefore most requisit, that the same reason, and manner of connexion, which is seene, not only in creatures, but also in God their creator, should haue place in the whole world, that is to say, that man whom God hath ordained to bee his lieutenant vppon earth, should haue a kind of midle condicion betwixt the highest, and the lowest nature, to the end that being conioyned with both, he might be a meane to vnite, and conioyne them both. This he doth principally by the meanes of religion, as may appeare by the very etimology therof,

therof, for (whether we define religion to be *the science of seruing God* as Plutarke calleth it, or *Iustice tovvards God* whereby true worship is giuen him (as Cicero defineth it) or *a vertue vvhereby vve doe due honour, and vvorship to God*, as our deuynes say, the name of *religion* is deriued of the effect thereof, to wit, *a relegando*, of tying together (according to S. Augustine) because saith he, *it tyeth and vniteth our soules vvith God our indefitient beginning*, which Lactantius, also affirmeth saying, that religion taketh that name *a vinculo pietatis, from the bond of piety, because God doth tye vs vnto him thereby* whiles we serue him as our lord, and obey him, as our father. Thus saith Lactantius reiecting the deriuation of Cicero who in his booke, *de natura deorum* deduceth it *a relegendo*, from reading agayne, though neuertheles els where he seemeth to allude to the other etymology, speaking of the goods of Lētulus which he saith were *religioni religata*, meaning therby that they were cōsecrated to the Gods.

Plut. in vita Pauli Æmi. Cicero l.2. de nat. Deorū. D. Tho. 22. q.81. ar.5.c. Aug. de vera relig. Lactantius lib. 4. ca. 28. lib. 2. de natur Deor. Cicero orat pro domo sua.

11 But whatsoeuer is to be thought of the nature, or etimology of the word *religion* (wherof there haue bene diuers opinions) there is no doubt, but that the especiall effect thereof, is, the vnion of man with God, and the reduction of all other creatures by his meanes to the seruice of their creator; for although almightie God taking vpon him our humaine nature, did therby vnite him selfe with al mākind in generall, yet the application of this general vnion to euerie man in particuler, is principally wrought by the meanes of religion, as shall appeare in the next chapter.

In vvhat maner all creatures are reduced to God their Creator by religion, and by the vvay, the beginning, effect, vtilitie, and end of religion, is euidently declared out of the best philosophers: & consequently it is proued, that religion is so natural to man, that it can not be extuinguished, except mankind be exterminated, and the vvhole vvorlde dissolued: vvhereby the necessitie of religion, the prouidence of God, and the blindnes, and impietie of the polityke, is euidently shevved.

CHAP. II.

1 THe force, and effect of religion to vnite man with God, was curiously obserued, and exactly taught by the most ancient, and best Philosophers, and first by *Mercurius Trismegistus*, who teaching that all thinges visible, and subiect to our senses, were created by allmighty God, for the vse, and seruice of man, addeth that *God made man to his ovvne image, & as vvell of an eternall, as of a mortall nature*, to the end, he might *discharge tvvo functions*

Mercur. ad Asclep. c. 4. & 6.

ctiōs according to his diuerse natures, the one in the gouermẽt of the earth, & the other in the contemplation, and seruice of God whereby man, (whom he calleth *magnum miraculum*, a great miracle) may arriue, saith he, to such a combination, and society with God, that he may be of *a deuine nature*, and as it were a God.

Ibid. ca. 3.

Arist. ethic. lib. 10. cap. 7.

2 *Aristotle* in like sort teacheth, that there are two functions of the vnderstanding of man, whereof the one consisteth principally in the contemplation of God, and of cœlestiall thinges, the other in action. By the first, man vniteth himselfe with God, by the second, he communicateth with other creatures; and this contemplation, whereof *Aristotle* speaketh, is nothing els but religion, or a necessary part thereof, as it is euident, for that *Aristotle* placing the felicity of man therin, requireth thereto not only the knowledg of God (without the which there can be no contemplation of him) but allso the loue, and worship of him, and all perfection of vertue; and therefore concluding his disputation of the felicity of man, he saith, that the contemplatiue man is most happy, both because he is most vertuous, and also because he is most like to God, and best beloued of him, and cherished, rewarded, and benifited by him. And as for the worship of God, seeing *Aristotle* allso in his Ethicks requireth of euerie man that he honour, and worship God, so much as he possibly may, which *no man* (saith he) *can doe so much as he ought*, there is no doubt, but that he holdeth the same to be most requisit in his contemplatiue man, whome he affirmeth to be the greatest louer, and frind of God, and best beloued of him, as I haue declared. So that it is manifest, that the contemplation (whereto *Aristotle* ascribeth the amitie, and vnitie of man with God) is eyther religion, or a necessary part therof.

Arist. ethic. li. 10. ca. 8.

Ibid.

lib. 8. c. 14.

Plato in Timæo 3. & de leg. li. 4.

3 *Plato* teaching that al thinges on earth were made for the behoofe, and seruice of man, and man himselfe for the seruice of God, assigneth no other end thereof, but only that man may be vnited with him, and therefore he saieth, that we must not contemplate God, only to know him, but much more to worship, and loue him, to the end we may contract a straight amitie, and frindship with him, *for those* (saith he) *vvhich knovv God, are not gratefull vnto him, except they loue him, and those vvhich both knovv, & loue him, are not acceptable vnto him, for their knovvledg, but for their loue, for a man may knovv God, and bee his enemie, and blaspheme him, vvhich he cannot doe, and loue him.* Thus teacheth he, who also requireth that this loue of God in man, be not a superficiall, and a light affection, but a most feruent, and pure loue, correspondent to his infinit beauty, bounty, and goodnes, that is to say, a loue *sine modo aut termino*,

Vide Iauell. in Epitome in Ethic. Platon. Tract. 4. c. 2.

mino, without measure or end, due to God alone for himselfe, & to all creatures for God; by which loue man may be so linked & cōioyned with God, that they may become, as it were, both one; whereto *Plato* also requireth the worship and seruice of God, consisting in *adoration*, *vowes*, *praiers*, *sacrifices*, *oblations*, *pietie*, *modestie* and *humilitie*, all which concurring are nothing els but religion.

Plato in Phædone & Simposio. Idem in Timæo. in Alcibiade. 2. 4. de leg. in Eutiphron.

4 To *Plato* I will adde only two of his followeres, to wit *Porphyrius*, and *Iamblicus*, who teaching that man is ioyned with God by religion, doe withall, notably shew, and explicat, the reason, beginning, force, effect, vtilitie, and end thereof: whereto I wish the politikes to be attentiue, to the end they may learne of the verie paynims, that religion is not a matter of fantasie or humayne deuice, but that it floweth from the very fountaine of nature it selfe. *Porphyrius* attributing the combination, and connexion of man with God, to the only force, and effect of religion, doth vse notable reasons to teach and perswade the excellencie, and necessity thereof. Whereof the first is, that whereas God is all in all, and man but (as it were) a part of all, it is necessarie that man do conuert, and turne himself vnto God, to the end he may be conserued by him, and receyue health both of body, and soule, seing the part cannot haue conseruation or health but from the whole. The second is, that seing all humane thinges are subiect to mutation & change of good, and bad successe, it is therefore necessarie that God who guideth, and gouerneth the affaires of men, be adored and serued by them. The third reason is, that we may by the adoration, and worship of him be combyned, and ioyned with him, wherein (saith *Porphyry*) consisteth all the force, and fruite of adoration in this life. The fourth and last is, that seing we are the children of God, but seperated and as it were banished from him in this exile, and prison of the world, it is conuenient that we worship, and serue him here with all piety, to the end that being deliuered hence, we may returne to him, for otherwise we shall for euer be like to Orphanes, that are depriued of theyr Parents.

Vide Iauell. vbi supra c. 1. 2. & sequent.

Vide Marsil. Ficinū prologo in Timæo. ca. 6.

5 Thus saith *Porphyrius*, who also teacheth that there groweth such a familiarity, and vnion betwixt God, and man by the meanes of religion, when it is accompanied with puritie and sanctitie of life, that he calleth the true religious, and contemplatiue man, *a deuine man*, and the *incontaminat temple* of God: and saith further, that hauing God in himselfe, he hath an assured pledge of life euerlastinge, *& totus translatus ad Deum Iouis familiaris euadit*, and being wholy as it were in the possessiō of God, becōmeth his familiar, or fauorit; thus saith he,

Porphyrius de Sacrificijs ca. vlt.

6 Iam-

6 *Iamblicus* an other famous *Platonik*, deriuing religion, and the first instinct thereof, from no other roote, but from almighty God, affirmeth that God hauing created man to his owne likenes, doth draw, and reduce him to him selfe; for seing, that nature, saith he, flowing from God, imparteth to diuerse inferiour things a certaine simpathy, and conueniency with the superiour, whereby they haue alwayes an inclination and disposition to follow the course therof (as wee see by experience in those thinges wherin the sunne, and moone doe predominat) much more doth the father, and creator of soules, imprint in them a certaine force, or instinct, which continualy moueth, and draweth them to him, which naturall instinct *Iamblicus* calleth *tactum quēdam diuinitatis, a certayne touch of diuinity, better, and more certayne then any humane knovvledge*, and hereuppon groweth the naturall propension, and inclination in man to the adoration, and worship of God, that is to say, to religion, and Gods gratefull acceptancie thereof at mans hand, when it is duly performed.

Vide marsil. Ficinum vbi supra.

Iamblic. de mysterijs Ægyptior. §. 1.

7. Thus teacheth *Iamblicus*, and the like, or rather the very same in effect is taught by *Proclus*, *Plotinus*, and other *Platonicks*, who speake of these thinges so deuinely, and so like contemplatiue Christians (as shall farther appeare hereafter) that the Politikes, and Atheists of our times, may be ashamed of their blindnes, seing that pretendinge, as they doe, to weigh all thinges in the ballance of reason, and seeming to them selues farre wiser, and of clearer sight then other men, yet cannot see that, which these Philosophers, saw to be conforme to reason, to wit, that God made man to his owne image, giuing him a reasonable soule, capable of the knowledge of him, imprinting therein the instinct of religion, that is to say, a naturall inclination to adore, worship, and serue him, whereby man may be conioyned with him, and attaine to the greatest felicitie which may be had in this life. And this I shal not neede to confirme with the testimonies of our scriptures, and Christian Fathers, for that no true Christian man is eyther ignorant, or doubtful of it, whereof neuerthelesse I shal haue occasion to say somwhat hereafter, and therefore I wil only shew now for the present, how it foloweth vppon this coniunction of man with God, that the whole worlde is reduced to God, and combyned with him, by the benefit of mans religion.

8 For although all creatures, may truly and properly be said to returne or to be reduced to their Creator, partly because they serue him, to what vse soeuer it pleaseth him to ordaine; and partly because they glorifie him, in giuinge manifest testimonie of his infinite bountie, wis-

dome, omnipotencie, and other his diuine perfections expressed in them: neuerthelesse not only their returne, and reduction to him, but also their combination with him, is most euidently and excellently, wrought and performed by the religion of man, especially three wayes. The first, by a certaine consequence of the subordination that all earthlie creatures haue to man, and man to God. For as in a kingdome gouerned by a kinges lieutenant, or deputie, when the subiects doe obeye the lieutenant, and he the king, all the people is vnited with the king, by the meanes of the lieutenants obedience: so also, when all creatures inferior to man serue him, & he serueth & worshippeth God, they are all connected, and cõbyned with God by the religion of man.

9 The second waye is; That for asmuch as by the consideration of Gods ineffable wisdome, omnipotencie, and bountie in the creation, and disposition of all his creatures, man is induced, not onlie to know God, but also to honour, praise, and serue him, all creatures may also be said to honour, praise, and serue God in man, and by man, whereto the three children in the furnace inuited them, saying, *Benedicite omnia opera domini domino*, &c. All the workes of our lord prayse yee our lord, &c. which they doe most properlie by the religion of man. For (as *Euthymius* saith) *Laus qua ego deum laudo propter illa, eorum quoque laus efficitur &c. The praise vvhich I giue to God for them, becommeth theyrs, vvhen I take occasion by them to prayse God.* Euthim.

10 The third consideration is yet more particular, because man doth not only vse the seruice, or helpe of al creatures, for the seruice of God, but also doth by religion particularly offer, and dedicate them, vnto him for the most part, eyther vowing, or consecrating them to his honour, or applyinge them to some holy vse for his service, in sacrifices, oblations, tithes, first fruites, ceremonyes, in the buildinge, or ornament of temples, and churches, and in other acts of religion: And as for such creatures as are not fitt, for any religious act, or holy vse (as noysome beasts, serpents, poysons, and such like) such doe also glorifie God by the meanes of mans religion, by the which their natures are manie tymes tempered, and corrected, and made eyther harmeles, or els beneficiall to the seruants of God, for his greater glorie, according to the promise of our Sauiour, to such, as should beleue in him. *Serpentes tollent, & si mortiferum quid biberint, &c. They shall take avvay serpentes, and yf they drinke any poysoned thing, it shall not hurt them.* Marci. 16.

11 Finallie all creatures what soeuer in heauen, earth, or hell become at one time or other obedient, or pliable to mans will by the meanes of religion, for the seruice, and glorie of God. *Moyses* by religion tur-

Exod. cap. 7. ned the riuers *of Egipt* into blood, killed the fish therein, destroyed
Cap. 8. & 9. the *Egiptians* with froggs, flies, plague, thunder, lightning, and fiery
Ibid. cap. 14. haile, made the sea giue place, and passage to the children of *Israell*,
Exod. 17. *and turned the stone, and rocke into streames of vvater*. *Iosue* staied the course
Psal. 113. of the sunne, and moone a whole day together. *Elias* commaunded
Iosue. 10. fire to come from heauen, to deuoure the captaynes, and souldiars
4. Reg. 1. of king *Ochosias*. *Elizeus* purified the poysoned fountaine of *Hiericho*,
Ibid. c. 2. reuiued the dead, and chaunged the tast, and nature, of bitter, and pe-
cap. 4. stiferous herbes. The three children represt the force of fire, & walked
Dan. 3. securely in the burninge furnace. *Daniel* remained safe in the dungeon
Ibid. cap. 14. amongst the hungry lions. *Ionas* hauing bene in the belly of the whale
Ion. 2. three daies, and *S. Paule* in the bottome of the sea a day, and a night
2. Cor. 11. were restored to land aliue; To conclude, by religion the seruants of God commaunde deuels, triumphe ouer all infernall powers, and drawe the verie Angels, and celestiall spirites to their helpe and assistance, when the seruice and glorie of God requireth it; so that by
Apoc. 5. the religion of man, all thinges good, and bad, glorifie and serue God. In which respect *S. Iohn* in the *Apocalipse* saith that he heard, *Omnem creaturam &c. Euery creature vvhich is in heauen, vppon earth, and vnder the earth, and in the sea, say vnto him vvhich sate in the throne, and to the lambe, benedictio & honor, & gloria, & potestas in sæcula sæculorum, blessing, and honour, and glory, and povver for euer and euer.*

12 Thus then we see, how the circle (as I may terme it) of the world is consummat, and perfected by mans religion, whereby all thinges, are reduced to theyr first beginninge, that is to say, to almightie God their creator, for whose seruice they were created: wherein appeareth the infinit wisdome, and goodnes of God, his prouidence in mans affaires, and the admirable force, and effect of religion, which may therefore be tearmed the indissoluble bond of the world, or a diuine knot, or lynke, whereby man, and all other creatures, are tyed, and knit to their creator: which knot, whosoeuer seeke to dissolue (as our politykes doe) they consequentlie conspire the dissolution, and destruction of the whole world. To conclude, it is most euident by all the precedent discourse, that religion is so naturall to man, and so farr from being a matter of conceit, or opinion, or an humaine inuention (as the politikes esteeme it to be) that except humaine nature be vtterlie extirped, and mankind exterminated, religion cannot be extinguished.

It is obiected, that the philosophers vvhich haue beene alleadged in the former chapters, vvere Idolaters, and that therfore their testimonies, for matters of Christian religion are impertinent, and not to be vsed by Christians. The obiection is ansvvered; and it is proued, that the religion vvhereof the philosophers treate, vvas true religion, consisting in the vvorship of one God, vvhom they acknovvleged to be the author of nature. Also, that philosophie is the handmaide of our deuinitie, and to be vsed for the confirmation thereof, vvith certaine considerations prouing the necessitie of religion, and the ignorance, and blindnesse of politiques.

CHAP. III.

1 BVt some perhaps wil say vnto me, that these Philosophers, (vppon whose authoritie I haue hitherto relyed) treat not of true religion, for that they neuer knew it, but rather of the Idolatrie which possest the world in theyr tymes, or of some other deuise of their owne, seeing that the ancient Philosophers before Christ (as *Mercurius Trismegistus*, *Plato* and *Aristotle*) reiected the religion of the Iewes, and the other more moderne since Christs tyme (as *Porphyrius*, *Iamblicus*, *Proclus* and *Plotinus*) contemned and vtterlie condemned, the Christian religion, wherevppon it may seeme to folow, that theyr testimonyes, which I haue produced, are to no purpose for the confirmation of true religion.

2 For the satisfaction of this scruple, and the better explication of al this question concerning religion, it is to be vnderstood, that the philosophers treating of the worship, and honour of God consisting in religion, did vnderstand, that worship and seruice of God, which man is bound by the law of nature, and taught by the light of reason to yeald him alone, whome they knew, and acknowledged to be the first cause of all causes, and the author of nature, and of all natural thinges, as I haue sufficiently declared in the first part of this treatise, *In the preface.* and therfore neede not to repeate it here: only I wil add that there was none of them so simple, or senseles, but that he dispised the false gods that were worshipped in those times, *as Iupiter, Iuno, Venus, Mars, Mercury,* and the rest, whom they knew to be most wicked men, in so much, that *Socrates* was put to death by the *Athenians* for impugning them, and denying the multitude of gods.

3 Neuertheles, for as much as they knew, and confessed God, and *Rom. 1.* did not glorifie him (as the Apostle saith) but trusted wholie to their

owne wisdome, puft vp with pride of their knowledg, being (as *S. Hierome* calleth them) *base bondslaues of popular praise*, men (for the most part) most sensuall, and impure of life: (as I haue sufficientlie shewed in my first part) for this cause, I saie, they were iustlie giuen ouer by almightie God into a reprobat sense, in so much that thin-
Rom. 1. king *themselues wise* (as the Apostle saith) *they became such fooles*, that they not onlie worshipped the common gods, which they themselues derided, but allso did accomodat their bookes, and writinges in manie thinges, to the common opinion of the people, least otherwise they might incurre the penaltie of the lawes, as *Socrates* had donne, & hereuppon it grew, that (as *S. Augustine* affirmeth) *they pro-*
Augustin. li. de vera religione ca. 1. *fessed, and practised publickelie one religion with the people, and taught priuatly in theyr schooles an other*, consisting in the contemplation, and worship of the author of nature, which being considered purelie in it selfe, as voyd of all Idolatrie and superstition, was true religion, and may in some sort, be said to be the same that ours is, with this difference, that in them, it was onlie naturall, and therfore imperfect, and in vs it is not onlie naturall, but also enriched, and perfected by Gods grace, for grace doth not abolish nature, but reforme, and repayre it, illuminat, and strengthen it, enrich, and adorne it, and finallie bringeth it to that perfect felicitie, and happines whereto God hath ordeined it.

4 So that naturall religion, which the Philosophers knew, & taught, was true religion, and maie be called both theyrs, and ours, differing onlie in them and vs, as an infant differeth from himselfe afterwards, when he becommeth a man. For, if we consider the progresse, that religion hath made in mankind from the beginninge, and creation of man, it may be said, that being considered in it selfe after his fall, it was borne weake, and naked, and receyued first clothing, and growth in the law of nature, wherein it passed a kynd of infancie, and after grew to more strength, and stature in the law of *Moyses*, as in a kynd of youth, and now lastlie being augmented, and illuminated with the faith of our Sauiour Christ, and infinit giftes, and graces of the holie Ghost, it is growne to perfection.

5 Therefore seeing the religion, which the philosophers taught, and beleeued, was not only true religion, but also the same which we professe (though not in such perfection) two thinges follow thereon: the one that we may with great reason vse, & transferre their doctrine concerning religion, to the confirmation of ours. For (as *Clemens*
Clem. Alex. strom. li. 6. *Alexandrinus* saith) *philosophy was giuen by almighty God to the Gentilles, as their proper testament, to serue for the foundation of Christian philosophy*, or rather

rather (as he saith in an other place) *to serue it for a hand mayd.* In which *Clem. Alex. li. 1. strom.*
respect he compareth the philosophy of the Gentils to *Agar*, and our *Gen. 16.*
Theology to Sara, to whome *Abraham* said of *Agar. Ancilla tua in manu tua est, vtere ea, vt libet. Thy handmaid is in thy ovvne povver, vse her as it pleaseth thee.* And *Gregorius Nissenus* alluding to the law of the ould testa- *Gregor. nissin vita Moysis.*
ment (which commaunded, that no Iew should marrie any forrayne woman, whom he should take prisoner, except he did first shaue her *Deut. cap: 21 v: 12.*
head, and pare her nayles) compareth philosophie to the captyue woman, whom he saith the Christian may marrie, so that he cut of her superfluous, and extrauagant opinions, and conforme her to Christian philosophie, that is to say, to the law of Christ. And to the same purpose also, one of our latter deuines saith notably thus. *Philisophis datũ est a deo Philosophari propter nos &c. God ordayned that the Philosophers should teach theyr philosophy for vs, to the end that they might cultiuate, and till the barrayn fieldes of mens myndes, & sovv notable seedes of doctrine, vvhich vve might aftervvards reape, vvhen it should be ripened vvith the sunne, and heate of our faith.* *Hugo de S. Victore in exordio sup. Ecclsia. Hierarch.*

Thus he, following *S. Augustin*, who saith, that *all those thinges vvhich the philosophers taught, consonant to our faith, ought to be taken from them as from vsurpers, or vniust possessors, and to be applied to our vse, as Ciprian* (saith he) *Lactantiũs, Victorinus, Hilarius and others haue done.*

The other thing which I conclude vpon the Philosophers doctrin is, that those which measure all their beleefe concerning matter of religion with onlie reason, cannot with anie show of reason denie those poyntes of Christian catholike doctrin, which the most famous Philosophers were forced by the verie light of nature, and reason to confesse: As that there is one God, the author of nature, and of naturall thinges, that he made man to his owne ymage, and for his owne seruice, and that therefore he gaue him a reasonable soule, capable of the knowledge of him, and endewed with an instinct of religion, by the which he might not onlie worship, honour, and serue him, but also be most happilie vnited with him euen in this life, as I haue partlie showed alreadie, and wil doe much more amplie hereafter.

6 Seeing thẽ, that the Philosophers doe teach, not only these poynts last mentyoned, but also the finall reduction, of all creatures to their beginning, that is to say, to God their creator, and seeing also I haue proued the same to be most fullie, and euidentlie performed by the meanes of mans religion, yea, and that God is glorified in man, and all other creatures thereby, it must needes follow, as I haue noted before, that religion is most naturall, and necessarie,

not onlie for man, but alſo for the whole world, and that whoſoeuer derogateth from it, doth iniurie both to God, and to all his creatures and ſeeketh as much as in him lyeth, to breake the indiſſoluble bond, with the which God, and they are connected, and the world perfitted, and conſerued.

7 And to all this, I will yet add for the cōcluſion of this chapter, two other conſiderations of mans infinit obligation, to worship, and ſerue God. The one is, the incōprehenſible excellencie of his deuine nature: For yf men doe worthily honour, and reuerence a king, or prynce, for the only dignity of his perſon, though they be not his ſubiects, what honour, worship, and ſeruice is due to him, that is king of kings, and lord of lords, not by election, or ſucceſſion, but by nature, in whome all the ſeuerall excellencies, and perfections of all creatures are ioyntlie, infinitlie, and incomparablie ſupereminent, as in theyr firſt cauſe, being infinit in power, wiſdome, iuſtice, bounty, beauty, knowledg, veritie, nobility, maieſty, felicitie? In which reſpect the beaſtlie *Epicurians* them ſelues, though they denied the diuine prouidence in the affaires of men, confeſſed neuertheles and acknowledged the neceſſitie of religion, for the reuerence, and worship of God, in reſpect of the moſt admirable, and ineffable perfections of his deuine nature, as appeareth in *Cicero* in his bookes *de natura deorum.*

Cicero de natura deorum.

8 The other conſideration is grounded on our Chriſtian faith, teaching our duty, and obligation to the ſeruice of God, in reſpect of our creation, conſeruation, and redemption, yea and of the eternall reward due by his promiſe for his ſeruice, and eternall punishment threatned for the contempt thereof. But of theſe poyntes I shall not neede to ſay any thing now in particular, both becauſe our Chriſtian doctrine is of it ſelfe moſt euident in that behalfe, and alſo becauſe there wilbe many occaſions offred to ſpeake thereof in this diſcourſe.

To shevv the neceſſitie of religion in common vvealth, it is cleerly proued, as vvell by the philoſophers, as by deuines, that the end, and true felicitie of euery man in this life, and of common vvealthe, conſiſteth in religion. And finallie it is declared, hovv temporall commodityes may ſerue, and avayle to the felicitie of common vvealth.

CHAP. IIII.

1 HAuing shewed in the former chapters aſwell the neceſſitie, as the admirable force, and effect of religion, generally in the whole world, I wil now shew the ſame particularlie in common welth, which may appeare not onlie by the generall

generall consequence, & inference that may be made from the whole to euerie part (as that religion being necessarie for the whole world, must needes be necessarie for common welth, which is a part thereof) but much more in respect of the speciall force, fruite, and office of religion, in common welth; which I will deduce from the considera-tion, and proofe, of an infallible, and irrefragable veritie, to wit, that the cheefe end, and felicitie whereto common welth is naturallie or-dayned, consisteth in religion, that is to say, in the due worship, and seruice of God: which being declared, and proued, will serue for a most solid, and sure foundation to the building of this whole treatise, and by necessarie consequence, draw after it diuerse important consi-derations, and conclusions, which I will after prosecute for the more cleare vnderstanding of all that which belongeth to common welth.

2 Now then, to fynde out the true end and felicitie of common wealth, it shalbe conuenient to waigh the force of an argument of *Aristotle* discussing, and resoluing the same question, who sheweth euidentlie in few wordes, that the end, and felicitie of euerie particular man, and common welth, is all one; his Argument is this. Seeing, that euerie particular man in the cittie, and all the citi-zens are of one, and the self same nature, and that the felicitie of all the cittie, or common welth, doth grow of the felicitie, or happines of euerie particular citizen: it must needes follow, that the felicitie of euerie particular man, and of the whole com-mon welth is all one, as the power (saith he) to laugh is one, and the selfe same in euery man, and in all mankynd. Thus reasoneth *Aristotle*, and his argument is demonstratyue, whereby it appeareth, that to shew the true end and felicitie of common welth, it shalbe conuenient to declare, what is the end, and true felicitie of euerie man in this life.

Aristot. li. 7. polit.

And although the same is in parte performed allready in the two former chapters, where it appeareth by the opiniōs of the best philo-sophers, that God made mā to noe other end, but for his owne seruice, that is to say, to the end to worship, honour, and serue him by true religion, and to be thereby most happily vnited with him (where vpon it foloweth that both the end, and also the felicitie of man in this life consisteth in religion) though, I say, this appeareth allreadie, yet because I handled not the same of purpose to shew the end, and feli-city of man, but only touched it, by the way, vppon an other occasion, I will now more amply treat therof, as of a matter most important, and necessary to the whole subiect of this treatise.

3 First then I will beginne with the doctrine of the Philosophers. *Aristotle* and the *Peripatetikes*, being most curious, and subtile searchers of nature, obserued, that as in all thinges that haue substance, some are more excellent then other, and one substance (to wit God) most excellent of all other, whereto all other are referred, as to theire end (which therefore hath no relation to anie other thinge) so allso in the actions of men, some are better, and more noble then others, and one action the best, and most worthy of all the rest, to the which,
Aristotle. they all ought to be referred, as to theire end, and in this action these
Ethic. li. 10. philosophers placed the felicitie of man, determininge, that whoso-
ca. 6. & 7. euer arriueth to the perfect excercise of that action, is as happy as man can be in this life. And for as much as reason taught them that this best action of man, must needs proceede from the worthiest, and best part of man, and that nothinge is more worthy, and noble in him, then his vnderstanding, and againe no action of the vnderstanding
Ibid. better then the contemplation of God, they concluded by a necessary consequence, that mans felicitie in this life, consisteth in the contem-
Chap. 2. *nu.* 2. plation of God, to the perfection whereof they required not only the worship, but also the loue of God, and practise of all vertue: as I haue
chap. 2. *Idem ibid. cap.* 8. shewed before in the second chapter out of *Aristotle*, who houldeth his contemplatiue, or wise man, to be most happy, because he is most vertuous, and in fauour with God, and cherished, and benifited by him.
Idem ibid. li. 8. *c.* 14. Besides that, I haue also declared in the same place, that *Aristotle* requireth in his contemplatiue man, the worship of God in the highest degree, which concurring with the loue of God, and the true excercise of vertue, is nothing els but religion: whereby it appeareth, that the contemplation whereto *Aristotle*, and the *Peripatetikes* his folowers ascribed the end, and felicitie of man, doth principally consist in religion.

Cicero li. 4. *de finib.* 4 The like may be iustlie affirmed of the opinion of the *Stoikes*, who placed the end, and happines of man, in a conformitie of mans life to the rule, and lawe of nature, by the exact exercise, and practise of the morall vertues, whereof the cheefe is religion, which as I haue declared is, *iustitia erga Deum*, iustice towardes God, whereby his due honour is duly rendred vnto him. Besides that, nothing is more conforme to nature, then that the author of nature be duly worshipped, honored, and serued, which euidently appeareth to be the opinion of the *Stoickes*, by theyr doctrine of Gods particular prouidence in the go-
Seneca. lib. 4 *de benef. c.* 6. uerment of the world, and of the affaires of men, as is manifest in *Senica* the famous *Stoicke*, who in that respect not only condemneth, and detesteth

detesteth the ingratitude of *Atheists* towards God, in that they acknowledged to haue receyued all their particular benefites, of nature, and not of him, but also requireth a most perfect, and sincere obedience in man, and a resignation of his wil, to the will of God, in the patiẽt suffering, & willing acceptaunce, of all the calamities that it shall please God to lay vppon him in this life, as I haue amplie shewed in *Senecas* owne wordes, in the first part of this treatise: so that there can be no doubt, but that the felicitie of man, which he, and other Stoicks attributed to the exercise of vertue, according to the præscript of nature, did in theyr opinion consist in the worship, loue, and seruice of God the author of nature, that is to say, in religiõ, which is the principall vertu, & most naturall to man, as may appeare by the naturall instinct thereof most euident in all men.

Idem de prouid. c. 1. & 4. & 5.

Cap. 2. nu. 23. & chap. 25. nu. 27. & 28.

5 And as for *Plato*, and his followers, it is manifest by that which I haue signified at large in the second chapter, that he, and all they, taught expressełie, that the end, whereto man is ordayned, is religion, seeing they affirmed that he was created by almightie God to his image, and liknes, and for his seruice, that is to say, to loue, honour, and worship him, and by that meanes to be vnited with him, which they accounted the onlie felicitie of man in this life, and that the same should be consummated in the life to come, by the perfect vision and fruition of God; as though they should say with *S. Paule. Nunc videmus per speculum in ænigmate, tunc facie ad faciem, &c. Novv vve see as it vvere through a glasse, in obscuritie, then vve shall see face, to face, novv vve knovv in part, then vve shall knovv as vve are knovvne.*

Chap. 2. nu. 3. 4. 5. 6. & 7

1. Cor. 13.

6 To this perfect felicitie of the life to come, *Plato* requireth the other felicitie of this life, as the high way that leadeth therto, and consisteth, as he teacheth, in a religious wisdome: in which respect, he accounteth the speciall office, & dutie of a Philosopher, or wise man, to be, to search forth the reasons, and causes of all thinges, that he may thereby ascend to the knowledge of the diuine reason, whereby they were made (that is to say, of the deuine nature, or God him selfe) and that knowing him, he may worship, and serue him, and so finallie come to enioie him; whereto he requireth much more vertue, and pietie in a wise man, or philosopher, then science, or knowledge, though he thinke the same also verie requisit, to the end, that God (the master of all science, and the author of all thinges that are knowne) may be thereby the better knowne by him, and the more sincerelie honored, and serued.

Plato de Rep. li. 6. & 7. & in Epinom.

7 Thus teacheth *Plato* in his *Epinomis*. Where he also affirmeth, that religion is the greatest of all vertues, and that the negligence, or contempt thereof, is the cause, or mother of all vnhappie, and miserable

ignorance: whereby it appeareth, that whereas *Plato* attributeth mans felicitie ſometymes to wiſdome, he meaneth nothing els but a religious wiſdome, conſiſting both in the true knowledge of God, as alſo in the adoration, worship, and ſeruice of him. In which

Lactantius lib. de vera ſapient.

reſpect *Lactantius* ſaith of religion, and wiſdome thus. *Non poteſt nec religio a ſapientia &c. Neyther can religion be ſeparated from vviſedome, nor vviſedome from religion, becauſe God is not onlie to be knovvne, and loued (vvhich belongeth to vviſdome) but alſo to be honored, and ſerued (vvhich belongeth to religion) but vviſdome goeth before, and religion follovveth, for firſt vve knovv God, and then vve honour, and vvorshipp him: ſo that theſe tvvo names ſignifie one force, the firſt conſiſting in ſenſe, and vnderſtanding, and the other in act.* Thus farr *Lactantius*: which may alſo be confirmed out of our holie ſcriptures, wherein it appeareth, that true wiſdome concurreth euer with religion, or rather conſiſteth therein, that is to ſay, in the feare, loue, and worship of God, and in the obſeruation of his commaundements, as I haue amplie proued in the firſt part of this treatiſe.

8 The like alſo I wish to be noted aswell *in Plato*, as in the *Platonicks* and other Philoſophers, when they aſcribe mans felicitie, ſome tymes to the knowledge of God, ſometymes to a ſimilitude, or likenes of God in man, and ſometymes to the coniunction of man with God, ſeeing they vnderſtand the knowledge of God to be a part, or rather the ground of religion, and the other two, to be the effects thereof: for the knowledge of God is, as it were, the roote from whence religion, and all the fruites

Sap. 15. *Ad Aſclep. ca. 10. & 6.*

thereof doe ſpring, in which reſpect the booke of wiſdome ſaith: *Scire iuſtitiam & virtutem tuam Domine, immortalitatis radix eſt: To knovv thy iuſtice, and povver, o lord, is the roote of immortalitie*. In which ſenſe, *Mercurius Triſmegiſtus* ſaith, that the onlie felicitie of man is, *cognitio maieſtatis diuinæ*, the knowledge of the deuine maieſtie; vnderſtandinge the knowledge of God in perfection, that is to ſay, with all the fruite, and effect thereof: becauſe in the roote, is conteyned the vertue, and perfection of all the tree.

Ibidem. ca. 4. & 6. *Ibid.*

9 This is euident in *Mercurius* himſelfe, who aſcribing the felicitie of man, to his coniunction with God, requireth thereto, not onlie the knowledge and worship of God, but alſo perfect pietie, vertue, and contēpt of riches, and of all other thinges, yea of the bodie it ſelfe, & this he calleth (as in deede it is) perfect religion, and *menſuram hominis*, the *meaſure, or rule*, according to the which man ought to frame his life; And therefore the *Platonicks* doe alſo affirme, that by the meanes of religion (which ſome of them call adoration) man is not onlie made like to God, but alſo conioyned with him: wherein they place both the force of religion

gion, and alſo the felicitie of man, as appeareth by that which I haue cyted in the ſecond chapter out of *Plato, Iamblicus*, and *Porphyrius*: Beſides *Chap. 2.* that, *Iamblicus* alſo ſaith, that onlie *true adoration doth make ſoules happy, and* *Iamblicus* *reſtore them to theyr country*, that is to ſay, to heauen, and that, *no man can at-* *de miſteriis* *tayne to perfect happynes, but by the meanes thereof.* *Ægipt. in fine.*

10 Hereby we ſee, that howſoeuer the beſt Philoſophers may ſeeme in wordes to differ, and diſſent one from an other, concerning the end, or felicitie of man, yet in ſenſe and ſubſtance, they doe all notablie agree. For, whereas ſome of them do aſſigne mans felicitie to contemplation, ſome to the knowledge of God, ſome to wiſdome, ſome to vertue, ſome to the adoration or worſhipp of God, they all vnderſtand eyther religion, or ſuch a part thereof, as cannot be perfect, but when it is ioyned with the whole.

11. And this manner of ſpeach is very vſuall alſo in the holie ſcriptures themſelues, concerning aſwel mans iuſtification, as his felicitie, both which are atributed ſometymes to the knowledge of God: as when our Sauyour ſaid praying to his Father: *hæc eſt vita eterna &c: this is life euerla-* *Ioan. 17.* *ſting that they may knovv thee, the only true God, and Ieſus Chriſt vvhom thou haſt ſent*: And ſometymes agayne to the feare of God, as in the pſalmiſt: *Beatus* *Pſalm. 111.* *vir qui timet dominũ; happy is the man vvho feareth God:* And ſomtymes to hope in God, as. *Beatus homo, qui ſperat in te: bleſſed is the man, that truſteth in thee:* *Pſalm. 83.* Somtymes to faith, or beleefe in God, as: *Beati qui non viderũt, & crediderũt:* *Ioan. 20.* *bleſſed are thoſe vvhich haue not ſeene, & beleeued*: & otherwhiles to the obſeruation of gods commandements, as: *Beatus vir qui non abijt in conſilio impio-* *Pſalm. 1.* *rum, &c. happy is the man, that hath not gone in the councell of the vvicked, but his vvil is in the lavv of our lord* &c. And this I ſay, is moſt vſuall in the ſcripture, for that the knowledge, feare, and loue of God, faith, hope, charitie, and the obſeruation of his commandements (which are all requiſit, to true, and perfect religion) doe alwayes, and muſt of neceſſitie concurre, whenſoeuer mans happynes or iuſtification, is aſcribed to any of them.

12 Therefore the Apoſtle teacheth, that, *he vvhich ſaith he knovveth God,* *1. Ioan. 2.* *and doth not keepe his commandements, is a lyer*, and that, *he vvhich loueth not, doth not knovv God.* And the Preacher ſaith: *qui timent dominum non incredi-* *Eccleſ. 2.* *biles erunt* &c. *thoſe vvhich feare God, vvill not be incredulous to his vvorde, they vvil ſearch vvhat is his vvill, and pleaſure, they vvil ſanctify theyr ſoules, and keepe his commandements:* And after againe for concluſion of his whole diſcourſe, he ſaith: *finem loquendi pariter omnes audiamus, deum time, &* *Ibid. c. vlt.* *mandata eius obſerua, hoc eſt enim Omnis homo: let vs all heare the end, or concluſion of all ſpeech, feare God, and kepe his cõmandements, for this is euery man:* thus ſaith

the Preacher, giuing vs to vnderſtand that the perfection, or end of euery man, conſiſteth in the feare of God, and the obſeruation of his commaundements, that is to ſay, in religion, and that when man diſchargeth his dutie in that behalfe, he doth execute, and accomplish the proper office, whereto humane nature was ordayned.

13 This may farther appeare by that, which our holye ſcriptures alſo teach, concerninge the creation of man to the ymage of God, as the precepts giuen him in paradiſe, the miſery which followed vppon his tranſgreſſion thereof, the lawes, and commaundements impoſed vppon him, both in the ould teſtament, and the new, penalties both temporall, and eternall threatned, like rewards promiſed, examples of Gods ſeuere iuſtice vppon offenders, and of his great benefits beſtowed vppon his ſeruantes: all which, as alſo the whole courſe of the holye ſcriptures, and Chriſtian doctrine, doe denounce nothing els to man, but that he is the creature, and naturall bondſlaue of God, and that therefore the end, and proper office, or function, whereto God ordayned him, is religion. Wher-
Lactan. lib. 4. cap. 28. uppon *Lactantius* ſaith: *Hac conditione*, &c. *VVe are created or made vvith this condition, or to this end, that vve may yeld due honour, and ſeruice to God our creator:* And againe in an other place. *Yf any man* (ſaith he) *should aske a man,*
Ibid. li. 3. ca. 9. *that is truly vviſe, to vvhat end, or purpoſe he vvas created, he vvould anſvver readily, and vvithout all doubt, that he vvas created to vvorship God, vvho made vs to the end vve may ſerue him.* Thus ſaith he, of the end, whereto man was ordayned, and the ſame alſo he affirmeth of mans felicitye in this life: and therefore hauing confuted the opinions of many of the philoſophers, concerning mans cheefe good, or felicitie, he concludeth. *Summum igitur hominis bonum, in ſola religione eſt: therefore the cheefe good, or happynes of man, is only in religion.*

Ambros. de offic. li. 2. ca. 5. 14 And *S. Ambroſe* alſo confirmeth the ſame, by the authoritie of the holie ſcriptures ſaying. *Scriptura diuina*, &c. *The deuine ſcripture placeth the happynes and felicity of mans life, in the knovvledge of God, and in the fruite of*
Aug. de ciuit Dei. lib. 14. cap. 26. & lib. 19. cap. 4. *operation, and vvorking*, that is to ſay in faith, and good workes. And although *S. Auguſtine* do reproue ſome of the philoſophers, for houlding that man may be happy in this life, and therefore teacheth, that there is no true beatitude here, eyther by morall vertue, or by frendship, or by
Ibid. cap. 5. & 8. a ciuill, and ſociable life, and much leſſe by riches, honours, and dignities (in reſpect of the continual conflict that the beſt, and the wiſeſt morall men haue, partly with ſenſualitie, and vicious inclinations, & partly with the ordinarie dangers, cares, feares, detriments, ſicknes, and afflic-
Ibid. ca. 20. tions incident to the liues and ſtates of all mortall men) yet he doth not deny all kynd of happynes in this life, (eſpeciallie that, where of our

holye

holye scriptures often make mention) but that felicitie which some of the Philosophers taught, namely the *Epicurians, Peripateticks*, and *Stoicks*, of whom the first ascribed felicitie to sensuall pleasure, and the other two, to vertue, though with some difference: all which I say, he impugned for two respects, the one because they were perswaded that mā was the only worker, and cause of his owne happynes, *vvhereas*, saith he, *non facit beatum hominem, nisi qui fecit hominem. None maketh man happy, but he vvhich made man.* [*Idem. epi. 52.*] The other reason was, because they taught that man might be absolutely, & perfectly happy euen in this life, which he proueth cannot possiblely be, for the reasons touched before, affirminge neuertheles that man may, by the gift, & grace of God, arriue here to a kynd of felicitie, though in comparison of the perfect beatitude, which we are to enioy in the next life, it is no better then misery: & therefore he saith: [*Idem. de ciuitat. lib. 19. c. 10.*] *Hic dicimur beati, quando pacem habemus, quantulacunquè hic haberi potest in vita bona: VVe are here called blessed, or happy, vvhen vve haue asmuch peace, & contentment, as may be had here in a good, or godly life.* [*Ibid.*]

15 So that *S. Augustine* denieth not all kynd of happynes in this life, but teacheth two thinges concerning the same: the one that no felicitie of man dependeth on man alone, or proceedeth from himselfe (be it either from his soule, or from his body, or from both) but that it is the gift of God, and dependeth on his grace, and assistance: the other is, that there is no perfect happynes, or beatitude in this world, but that the felicitie, which by Gods grace, and gift we may enioy here, is vnperfect, and to be consummated, and perfited in the next life.

16 And so we are to vnderstand all the beatitude, or happines, which in the holie scriptures and fathers, is ascribed to mortall men, in which sense. *S. Augustine* himselfe saith: *Omnis vitæ bonæ, & beatæ via, in vera religione constituta est*; All the way & course, of good and happy life, consisteth in true religion. [*Aug. de vera religi. c. 1.*] And *S. Ambr. Certū est virtute sola vitā præstari beatā, per quam vitam, vita acquiritur æterna. It is certaine that only vertue giueth, or maketh the happy life, by the vvhich the eternall and euerlasting life is obtainted.* Thus he. [*Ambros. de offic. lib. 2. cap. 5.*]

17 Therefore I conclude that he may worthylie be called happy in this world, who liuing religiouslie in the feare, & loue of God, dwelleth as the psalmist saith, *in adiutorio altissimi &c. In the help of the highest, and in the protection of the God of heauen*, [*Psal. 90.*] by whose grace, & fauour, he enioyeth such peace of soule, & cōscience here, that he not onlie sayleth securely amidst the stormes of this tēpestuous life, tryumphing ouer all the miseries thereof, but also arryueth in the end at the port of eternal felicitie. But what manner of happynes this is, which may be had here, & what true pleasure, & delectation there is therein, I will declare amply hereafter, when [*Chap. 18. 19. 20. & 21.*]

I shall

I shall treate of Christian religion, and wil now conclude this chapter with he consideration of what is the felicity of common welth.

18 Seing then it is manifest by all this precedent discourse, that the end, and felicity of man in this life, consisteth in religion, it must needes follow, according to the argument of *Aristotle* before alleaged, that the end, and felicitie of cōmonwelth consisteth also therein, which *S. Augustine* confirmeth, saying: *Non aliunde beata ciuitas, aliunde homo, cum aliud ciuitas non sit, quam concors hominum multitudo. The common vvelth is not happy for one cause, or reason, and man for an other, seeing that common vvelth is nothing els, but a multitude of men agreeing together*: Thus he.

Aug. ep. 52. ad Maccedonium.

Aristotle. Ethic. li. 10. c. 7. & 8. Idem Polit li. 7.

19 Therefore *Aristotle* hauing in his *Ethicks* ascribed the end, and felicitie of man, to the contemplation of God (which as I haue shewed before is an act of religion) he also assigneth the same end, and felicitie in his politikes to common welth: And although he affirmeth, that there are two kindes of felicities, the one speculatiue, consisting in contemplation, and the other practical, consisting in the exercise of al the moral vertues, and calleth this latter politicall felicitie (because the common welth may then be worthily called happy, when it florisheth with the perfect practise of al vertue:) Neuerthelesse he teacheth, that this practicall felicitie is subordinate to the speculatiue, as to the end whereto it is naturally ordained, and that therefore, all politicall actions, ought no lesse to be referred to contemplation, then labour to repose, busines to ease, and warr to peace: In which respect he admonisheth the lawmaker, or institutor of the common-welth, to frame his lawes, and the maners of the prince, and subiects, rather to contemplation, then to action, by the example of nature it selfe, which being most carefull of those thinges that are most noble, and excellent, hath alwayes farr greater care of the end, then of the meanes that lead, or helpe thereto.

Idem li. 4. polit.

20 And for this cause, he assigneth priesthood for the first office in the common welth, as most important, and principally tending to the obtayning of the end, whereto common welth is ordained.

Plato 1. de rep.

Plato also teacheth the same most expressly in his booke of common welth, in his lawes, and in his *Epinomis*, in al which, it is euident, that he assigneth no other end of common welth, but the contemplation, and worship of God: And therefore he laboureth principally to make his common welth happy by a religious wisdome, consisting partly in the speculation, or contemplation of God, and partly in the worship of him: In the coniunction whereof, (which is nothing els but religion) he placeth the felicitie of man, and of common welth: and the reason is, for that the especiall effect of religion (as I haue declared sufficiently in the

Marsil. Ficin in Argum. in epinom.

the ſecond chapter)is to vnite man with God, whereuppon it alſo foloweth, that the felicitie of man, and common welth, conſiſteth therin.

21 For who can denie but that man, and conſequently all common welths, are then moſt happy, and fortunate, when they are moſt vnited with God, the fountaine, and only author of true happines, vpon whoſe will, they, and all theyr felicitie depend: Which the royall prophet ſignifieth notably, who hauing deſcribed the temporall proſperity, which wicked men ſometimes enioy by the permiſſion of God (as that *theyr children are comely, faire, and vvell decked, theyr barnes and cellers, full of prouiſion, theyr ſheepe, and theyr cattel fruitefull, theyr beefes fatt, and not ſo much as a decaying, or ruinous vvall or hedge, in theyr terrytoryes, nor any tumult, or clamour in theyr ſtreetes,*) He addeth, *beatum dixerunt populum &c: Men call the people happy vvho haue theſe thinges, but happy is the people,* or common welth, *cuius dominus Deus eius, vvhoſe lord is theyr God*, that is to ſay, who liuing in the feare, and ſeruice of God, haue him for theyr lord, and protector. *Pſal. 143.*

22 Thus ſayth the royall prophet, teaching notably that no people, or common welth, be they neuer ſo proſperous for a time, can be truly counted happy, being out of the fauour of allmighty God, whereof I shall haue occaſion to ſay ſome what more hereafter. And neuertheles I wish it here to be vnderſtoode by the way, that I doe not hereby wholy exclude temporall commodityes, from the felicitie of common welth: but that I ſignifie wherein this felicitie principally conſiſteth, acknowledging with *Ariſtotle* and other philoſophers, that the goods of fortune (as they terme welth, power, honours, & proſperity) are neceſſary to the happy ſtate of cōmon welth, ſo that they be taken, and vſed only as inſtruments, or helps thereto, and not as felicitie it ſelfe, or as any eſſentiall partes, or cauſes thereof: being rather in deed, the true cauſes of al miſery, if they be not principally referred to the ſeruice and honour of God, yea, and vſed with great moderation.

23 Therefore *Ariſtotle* and *Plato*, require the goods of fortune to the happines of common welth in a mediocrity, teaching, that ſuperfluity of riches, is no leſſe pernicious to the publicke good, then to the priuate weale of man: In ſo much, that *Plato* being earneſtly requeſted by the *Cyrenians* to giue them lawes, refuſed to doe it, by reaſon of theyr exceſſiue welth and proſperitie, which he thought would make them indiſciplinable, and not fit to be gouerned. And what he farther ordayned in his owne common welth, concerning the goods of fortune, and temporal commodityes, yt shalbe declared in the ninth chapter, where I will alſo shew by examples, what damage, and deſtruction followeth to ſtates, by the abundannce of riches, and temporall proſperitie, by reaſon *Ariſtot li. 5. politic. Plato 4. de repub. Plutar, de doctrina principis.*

of

of the great corruption and vice, that commonlie groweth thereof.

24 This is also signified in the holie scriptures, concerninge the people of *Sodome*, whose iniquity (saith the prophet) was. *Superbia, saturitas panis, abundantia & otium. Pride, saturity or fullnes of bread, and meate, aboundance, and ease*: giuing to vnderstand, that theyr sinne, and consequently theyr ruine, grew of theyr welth, plenty, and prosperitie: And *Moyses* also ascribeth the fall of the Iewes to the same cause. *Incrassatus est dilectus*, saith he, *& recalcitrauit: incrassatus, impinguatus, dilatatus dereliquit Deum factorem suum* &c. *My beloued people vvax fatt, and then they began to kick, for vvhen they grevv once to be full, vvell fed, fatted, and dilated, or amplified, they abandoned God theyr maker*. Thus prophesied *Moyses* of the future fall of the Iewes, by the meanes of theyr ouermuch ease, welth, and prosperitie, which so enwrapped, and snared them in pleasures, & worldly delightes, that as the prophet *Abacuc* saith, they forgott theyr God, and *sacrifized to the very netts* which entangled them, making idolls of theyr welth, and contentments, and placing theire end, and felicitie therein.

Ezech. 16. *Deut. 32.* *Abac. 1.*

25 So farre are temporall commodities from being any essentiall part, or cause of mans felicitie, that they rather draw him many times to all infelicitie, and misery: as shall farther appeare in the next chapter, wherein I will discouer the supposed, and false happines of wicked men, who contemning religion, and the seruice of God, frame to them selues, a kinde of felicitie in sensualitie, honours, and pleasures. Where as I will make it manifest, that be they neuer so welthy, potent, and prosperous, they haue neuer any contentment, and peace of mind, but are allwayes most miserable. And hereof I will yeald only fiue, or sixe reasons, whereby also, the vanitie of worldly welth, dignitie, and pleasure, shall suficiently appeare.

That the felicitie vvhich vvicked men place in sensualitie, riches, honours, and vvorldly delightes, is no felicitie, but miserie: and that there is no true contentment, or happines but in God. And by the vvay, the vanitie of the vvorld, and vvorldly men, is euidently shevved.

CHAP. V.

1 HThe first reason, why wicked men, neyther haue any true felicitie in theyr worldlie pleasures, but infelicitie, and misery, is, the continuall contradiction of theyr owne passions, and concupiscences, which doe miserably teare, and distract them inwardly, with such a perpetuall combat, and ciuill warre, that they can neuer

neuer haue any repose and true contentment of mind: Whereuppon *S. Iames* sayth, *vnde bella, & lites in vobis? &c. vvhence grovve vvarres, and strifes vvithin you? doe they not grovv of your ovvne concupiscences, vvhich make vvarre in your bodies?* Thus saith he: whereof the reason is, for that mens passions are so different, and diuers, that many tymes they contradict one an other, for what the flesh desireth, regard of honour sometimes admitteth not, and that which both honour, and the flesh requireth, respect of profitt otherwhiles reiecteth: much like as when a sicke man is pestred with contrary humors, or with a cold stomack, and a hote lyuer, which two as they torment, and afflict the patient, so also one of them, hindreth the cure of the other. And therefore whiles passionat men, eagerly hunt after the accomplishment of all theyr desires, and find themselues hindered with their mutuall contradiction, and conflict, they haue such a babilonicall confusion, and perpetuall garboile in the citty (as I maie say) of their owne breasts, that the saying of the Prophet *Dauid* may iustly be applied vnto them. *Præcipita Domine, diuide linguas eorum, quoniam vidi ini-* Psal. 54.
quitatem, & contradictionem in ciuitate. Cast them dovvne headlong o lord, deuide their tongues, for I haue seene iniquity, and contradiction in the citty. Thus saith the royall prophet, giuinge to vnderstand, that where is iniquity, there is contradiction, and disquiet of mind.

2 The second reason of the infelicity of the wicked, is the anguish and torment of mind, that accompanieth euery passion or vice, which will easely appeare, if for example sake, we consider the nature and condition of some three, or foure of them. And first to beginne with couetousnes, how restles, and insatiable is the hunger and thirst, that the couetous, and auaricious man hath after riches, who the more he hath, the more he desireth: and as *Valerius* saith; *Not possessing his vvealth, but being possessed by it,* Valer. Max.
is a miserable slaue of his ovvne money, to whom a man cannot wish a grea- li. 9. cap. 4.
ter harme, then that he may liue long to torment himselfe, who though he desire all, yea and haue all that he desireth, yet in effect hath nothing. For as the prodigall man wanteth many thinges, so the auaricious man wanteth all thinges, not enioying that which he hath, and thirsting after all thinges els: whereof the preacher saith thus. *Est & aliud malum quod* Eccles. c. 6.
vidi sub sole, &c. There is an other euill, or mischeefe vvhich I haue seene, or noted vnder the sunne, and the same very frequent, or common amongest men, to vvitt: a man to vvhom God giueth riches, and substance, and honour, and he vvanteth nothing of all that his soule desireth, and yet God doth not giue him povver to eate therof, but some stranger shall deuoure it, this is vanity, and great misery. Thus saith the preacher.

3 In like manner the ambitious man insatiably gaping after honours,

and dignities, is vexed with enuie at euerie other mans prosperitie, not receiuing saith *Seneca*, so much contentmẽt by seeing manie men behind him, as disgust by seeing any one before him, whereby he is drawne in

S.August.li. 8.confes.c.6. to manie dangerous practises, and attempts: and as S.*Augustine* saith. *Per multa, & magna pericula, ad plura, & maiora peruenit: by manie, and great dangers, he passeth to more, and greater,* vntill at length he runne headlong to his owne ruine, whereof wee see dailie experience, besides infinit examples of ancient times, needeles to be alleadged.

4. But who can expresse how hipocriticall, base, and ridiculous is the passion of ambition, for though the ambitious man desire nothing more, then honour, yet he would seeme most of all to contemne it, and commonlie so contradicteth himselfe in his owne actions, that euerie man discouereth his humour. And whereas he seeketh to commande all men, he is forced to be euerie mans slaue, crouching, and creeping to euerie one, fawning, and flattering, bribing, dissembling, and committing infinit indignities, to rise to dignitie. And therefore

D.Ber.ep. 126. S. *Barnard* fitlie calleth ambition, *negotium ambulans in tenebris*, as the

Psal.4. Psalmist saith, *a busines vvalking in the darke.* For *the filthy vice of ambition* (saith he) *lieth lovv, but looketh vp to the highest, and yet vvould not it selfe be seene: it is the mother of hipocrisy, it lurketh in corners, loueth darkenes, and cannot endure the light. And no meruell: for if it be once discouered, it becommeth ridiculous:* And so falleth it out to be true, which

Philip.3. the Apostle saith: *Gloria in confusione eorum, qui terrena sapiunt: Theyr glory is their confusion, vvho seeke after earthly thinges.* Thus saith S. *Barnard* in substaunce, of ambition, which also in an other place he calleth,

D.Ber. in Psal.90.ser. 6. *a subtle euill, a secrett poison, a priuy plague, a forger of lies, and deceites, the mother of enuy, the fountaine of vice, the nurse of sinne, the moth that eateth and consumeth sanctity, and piety, the blinder of hartes,* and finally such a pestilent passion, that it engendreth, and breedeth sicknes of the very medicines, and remedies, that are applied to the cure of it, corrupting, and abusing all thinges, euen the holiest, to the furtherance of her designements.

5. Furthermore, who can expresse the folly of the ambitious man, who neuer knoweth when he is well, and ventereth his life, and state many times, either he knoweth not for what, or for that which in ef-

Plutar.in Pyrrho. fect he hath already: the which *Plutark* representeth notably in *Pyrrhus* king of *Epyrus*, who hauing greatly enlarged his dominions with the conquest of the great kingdome of *Macedonie*, beganne also to designe with him selfe the conquest of *Italy*, and hauing communicated his deliberation with his great counselour *Cineas*, he demaunded his aduise:

whereto

whereto *Cineas* answered, that he greatly desired to know what he ment to doe when he had conquered *Italy*? Mary quoth *Pyrrhus*, the kingdome of *Sicily* is then neare at hand, and deserueth to be had in consideration, aswell for the fertility, as for the riches, and power of the Iland. Well quoth *Cineas*, and when you haue gotten *Sicily*, what will you then doe? Then quoth *Pyrrhus* *Africk* is not farr of, where there are diuers goodly kingdomes, which partly by the fame of my former conquests, and partly by the valoure of my souldyars, may easily be subdued. I graunt it, quoth *Cineas*, but when all *Africk* is yours, what meane you to doe then? When *Pyrrhus*, saw that he vrged him still with that question, mary then, quoth he, thou, and I wilbe merrye, and make good cheare. Whereto *Cineas* replied, if this saith he, shalbe the end of your aduentures, and labours, what hindereth you from doing the same now? Will not your kingdomes of *Epyrus* and *Macedony* suffise you to be merry, and make good cheare? And if you had *Italy*, *Sicily*, *Africk*, and all the world, could you, and I be merrier then we are, or make better cheere, then we doe? Will you therefore venter your kingdomes, person, life, honour, and all you haue, to purchase that which you haue already? Thus said *Cineas* to *Pyrrhus*, reprehending his immoderate ambition, who knew not when he was well, neither yet what he would haue, seeing in conclusion he desired no more, then that which he had already, which in the end cost him deare: for following his owne ambitious, and vnbrideled appetite, to amplify his dominions, as he gott much, so he lost much, being able to conserue nothing any time, and at length hauing entred the towne of *Argos*, by force, he was killed with a brickbat, throwne downe by a woman from the topp of a house.

6. Therefore I conclude aswell of ambitious, as of auaricious, and coueteous men, that they may well be said to be those, of whome the Psalmist speaketh, when he saith. *Errauerunt*, &c. *They vvandred vp and dovvne in the drie desert, and found not the vvay to the citty vvhere they desired to dvvell, but for very hunger and thyrst; faynted and gaue vp the ghost.* Psal.106.

7. And what shall I say of the intemperate man, whose belly, as the Apostle saith, is his God, who breatheth, and belcheth out, nothing but surfett, and sinne? Who eateth not to liue and serue God, but liueth, yea, and serueth God to eate, referring all thinges spirituall, and temporall, to the belly: more like a beast that is fedd for the shambles, then a reasonable creature: and what benefitt reapeth he thereof in the end, but infinit diseasses, and Philipp.3.

 either

either vntymely death in his youth, or a lothsome life in his age, loaden with dropsies, tormented with gouts, and consumed with cattarres, whereby he payeth the penalty of his owne excesses: In which respect, the prouerb saith truly, that *more die by surfett, then by the svvord.*

„ 8 *Seneca* describeth notably the infelicity of the riotous glutton in this „ maner. From riott saith he, and excesse in diett, proceedeth palenes of „ face, trembling of the sinewes soaked in wine, and leannesse of body „ caused by surfetts, more miserable then that which followeth of famin. „ Thence proceed the vnstaied, and staggering stepps of men, pining away „ in paine, and realing as though they were drunck. Thereof groweth „ the dropsy dispersed throughout all the skinne, the swelling of the belly „ accustomed to receyue more then it can well containe. Thence followeth „ the ouerflowinge of the gall, discoulored countenannce, consumptions, „ rotting inwardly, crooked fingers, with stiffe ioyntes, numnesse of the „ arteries, and shaking palsies. What should I speake of the giddinesse of „ the head, of the torments of the eyes, and eares, of conuulsions caused „ by enflamed braines? Or yet of the passages, by which we purge, tainted „ with inward soares, and vlcers, besides innumerable sortes of feuers, so„ me entring with violence, others creeping in by easie infection, others „ assailing with horror, and trembling of all the members? What shoulde I „ reckon vp infinit other diseases, that are punishments of riott, from the „ which those are free, who suffer not themselues to be transported with „ sensuall pleasures, and delightes.

Seneca ep. 95.

9 Thus saith he. Whereto is to be added, a Christian consideration of the eternall paine, due by the iustice of God, *to the vvorkes of darknes*, as the Apostle termeth the sinnes of intemperaunce, to wit, dronkennes, and frequent feasting, and bankettinge. *Abijciamus* (saith he) *opera tenebrarum*, &c. *Let vs cast of the vvorkes of darkenes, let vs put on the armour of light, let vs vvalke honestly, as in the day light, not in banketting, and dronkennes, not in bedding and lasciuiousnes, not in contention, and æmulation, but put vppon you our lord Iesus Christ, and doe not pamper your flesh, accordinge to your desires.* Thus saith the Apostle, who also in an other place recknoneth *commessationes, & ebrietates,* that is to say, frequent banketting, and dronkennes amongst the workes of the flesh, concluding, *Qui talia agunt, regnum Dei non consequentur. They vvhich doe these, and like thinges, shall not attayne vnto the kingdome of God.*

Rom. 13.

Gall. 5.

10. Moreouer, who can sufficiently expresse the miserable state of a sensuall, and dissolute man, who giuing himselfe ouer to beastly lust, becommeth no better then *equus, & mulus, quibus non est intellectus, a horse, and a mule vvhich haue no vnderstanding?* In which respect, the prophet *Hieremy*

Psal. 31.

saith

ſaith of ſuch men. *Equi amatores & emiſſarij facti ſunt, &c. They became like to* *Hiere.c.5.*
ſtallions, or ſtoned horſes, vvhen they are in loue, for euery one of them vvent neying after his neighbours vvife. Thus ſaith the prophet, deſcribing very aptly the inſatiable, and beaſtly paſſion of ſenſuall, and laſciuious men, who alſo as we ſee by experience, haue commonly ſowre ſauce to their ſweete meate: for beſides innumerable inconueniences, which they daily incurre (as loſſe of reputation, danger of puniſhment by law, quarrels, braules, murders, and miſcheefes) they beare the pennance of their incontinency, by ſuch horrible, and filthy diſeaſes, that many of them rotte aliue, and are no leſſe lothſome to them ſelues, then to all other men.

11. And who is ſo miſerable, or ſo mad, and frantick, as he that is ſurpriſed with the paſſion of loue, wherewith he wreſtleth, and lauguisheth day and night, conſuming himſelfe with needeleſſe cares, phrentick feares, or ielouſies, framed in the forge of his owne idle conceits, and yet he contenteth, and pleaſeth himſelfe with his owne torment, ſaying with *Phædria* in *Terence*. *Nunc me miſerum ſentio, & tædet, & amore ardeo, & prudens,* *Terent. in eunuch. act. 2. ſcen. 1.*
ſciẽs, viuus, videnſq; pereo, nec quid agã ſcio. I novv find my ſelfe to be miſerable, I am vveary and cloid, I burne in loue, and perish, vvitting, knovving, liuing and ſeeing my ruyn, and yet knovv not vvhat to doe?

12. Againe, is there any more miſerable then the enuious man, who as a poet ſaith. *Alterius rebus macreſcit opimis: grovveth leane vvith other mens fatt,* *Horat ad Lollium. epi. 1. Virgil. de liuore.*
& ſibi pœna ſemper eſt, and is alvvaiſe a puniſhment to himſelfe? In reſpect whereof we may well ſay with *Horace*.

Inuidia Siculi non inuenere tyranni
maius tormentum.

The tyrants of *Sicilly* neuer inuented a greater torment then enuy. And the like may alſo be ſaid of anger, which is nothing els, but *breuis furor* (ſaith the poet) *a short madnes*, for it depriueth the ſoule of iudgemẽt, it diſtempereth, and waſteth the body, it maketh a man vntractable, and yrkſome more like a furious beaſt, or a mad man, or a perſon poſſeſt with a ſpirit, then a man of reaſon, and vnderſtanding. In ſomuch, that (as *Plutarke* noteth) he ſpareth neither God nor man, but ſweareth, blaſphemeth, curſeth, raileth, reuileth, killeth, murdereth, and committeth all miſcheefe.

13. Therefore what felicity, quiet, or peace of mind can he be ſaid to haue, that is tyranniſed by theſe paſſions, whereof any one were ſufficient to make a man miſerable, and much more all of them, and commonly they all predominate, and reigne in wicked men: In which reſpect the prophet ſaith moſt truly; *Impius quaſi mare feruens, quod quieſcere non poteſt:* *Eſai. 57.*
The vvicked man is like to a ſvvelling ſea, vvhich cannot reſt.

14 And therefore *Plutarke* affirmeth with reaſon, that vice ſuffiſeth of it ſelfe to make a man miſerable (as I haue noted in my firſt part of this treatiſe.) And *Cicero* teacheth, that ſinne is the greateſt puniſhment, that
Cicero de God doth lay vppon man in this life for ſinne; *Tu cum furiales, &c.* When
Haruſ. reſp. thou ſaith he to *Clodius*, furiouſly crieſt out in the aſſemblies of the peo-
" ple, ouerthroweſt howſes, burneſt the temples of the gods, makeſt no
" difference betweene thy wife, and thy ſiſter, careſt not what woman
" thou corrupteſt, when thou rageſt, and reuileſt, then doeſt thou pay the
" penalty ordained by the gods for the wickednes of men: for the body,
" in reſpect of the frailty thereof, is ſubiect to manie caſualities, but the
" darts of the gods, doe ſtrick the mindes of wicked men: and therefore
" when thou art drawne by thy eies into all deceite, & miſcheefe, thou art
" more miſerable, then if thou hadſt no eies at al: Thus ſaith *Cicero*. And the like ſaith *Plutarke* of *Tigellinus*, one of *Neros* fauourits: which maie alſo
Rom. 1. be confirmed out of the Apoſtle, who ſaith, that *God gaue ouer the ould Philoſophers to a reprobat ſenſe*, permiittng them to fall into all vice and wickednes in puniſhment of their pride, and ingratitude to him: For ſinne is a iuſt puniſhment of ſinne, not onlie in reſpect of the eternall damnation, whereto it draweth men, but alſo for the torment of conſcience, vexation, and anguiſh of mind, wherewith it is accompanied: As I haue amply declared in the firſt part of this treatiſe, and therfore omitt to ſpeake further thereof in this place.

15 An other reaſon of the vnquiet, and peaceleſſe mind of the wicked is, that their appitites commonlie are ſo inordinate, and their wills ſo vnbridled, that they can endure no reſtraint, or check thereof in anie thinge whatſoeuer. In ſo much, that though they haue neuer ſo much contentment in al other thinges, yet if in ſome one, they ſee themſelues croſſed, or looſe the leaſt part of thir pleaſures, they ſo torment themſelues, that they take no pleaſure in anie thinge els: much like to litle children of a froward, and curſt nature, who if they be broken of their wills, or if, of many of their puppets, ſome one be taken from them, they crie out mainelie, and caſt away all the reſt, and ſo doe paſſionate men ſometimes for verie trifles. Whereof we haue a notable example in the holie ſcripture, in *Aman*, who abounding in honour, welth, and pleaſure, and ſeeing *Mardocheus*, the poore Iew let him paſſe without doing
Heſter. 5. him reuerence, was ſo vexed therewith, that he aſſembled his wife, children, and freindes, and after he had made them an ample relation of all his good fortunes, his riches, his magnificence, and greatnes, and of his ſamiliaritie with his king *Aſſuerus*, and *Heſter* the queene, he added that he ſhould account all that nothinge, ſo long as *Mardochæus* the Iew, ſhould

should ſit before the pallace gate, and not doe him reuerence as others did: and thereuppon ſeeking to haue his will alſo therein, and to be reuenged of poore *Mardochæus*, he was hanged on the gallowes, which he had prepared for him.

16 Loe then how impotent, & exorbitant wicked men are in their paſſions, and how miſerable they are thereby, for ſeing no man is ſo potent on earth, that he can haue his will in all thinges, but wanteth it, and is croſſed many times in his deſignements, & deſires, thoſe muſt needes be moſt afflicted therewith, who neuer vſe to reſtraine their owne wills, or paſſiōs, but alwaies giue full ſcope thereto, as wicked men cōmonly doe. Beſides that almighty God ſo diſpoſeth out of his iuſtice, for their iuſt punishment, that ſome ſecrett diſguſts doe commonly ouerway their publike pleaſures, & therefore that which the prophet ſaid of the great *Aſſyrian* king, may welbe applied vnto euery wicked man, be he neuer ſo glorious and proſperous: *Mittet*, ſaith he, *dominator dominus in pinguibus* *Iſai.* 10.
eius tenuitatē, & ſubtus gloriā eius ſuccenſa ardebit cōbuſtio ignis. Our lord the Ruler vvill extenuat his fatt, and vnder his glory ſhalbe kindled a burninge flame of fire.

17 Laſtly ſuch is the very nature, and condition of the pleaſures, and proſperity of this world, that no true happines, or contentment, can poſſibly be had therein, whereof I may make the worldlinges themſelues iudges, if they will but ponder, and duly conſider their owne experience, concerninge the contentment they haue, or can haue, in honour, riches, or any earthly delights, which are ſo farr from giuinge any true repoſe, and ſatisfaction to the mind of man, that euen when they are poſſeſſed, & had in the higheſt degree, they either kindle a greater deſire of themſelues (which breedeth a continuall thirſt, and torment) or els they cloy, & weary their poſſeſſors, & force them to ſeeke ſolace in other thinges.

18 *Xerxes*, ſaith *Cicero*, *flovving in all abundance of vvordly vvealth, honour, povver, and pleaſure, vvas ſo farre from being content therevvith, that he offered great revvards to vvhoſoeuer could inuent any nevv pleaſure, and vvhen it vvas found, he vvas not ſatisfied*; *Neque enim*, ſaith *Cicero*, *vnquam finem inuenit libido. For mans luſt could neuer yet find any end.*

19 Beſides that, if we regard the vncertainty of all worldly proſperity, and contentments, yea with what danger to all, and vtter ruine to many they are purchaſed, poſſeſſed, and conſerued, we may eaſely iudge, how litle true felicity there can be therein. Whereuppon *Valerius* ſaith admirably well. *Caduca, & fragilia, puerilibuſq; conſentanea crepundijs ſunt iſta, &c. Theſe thinges vvherein conſiſt the force, vvealth, and pleaſure of man, are tranſitory, frayle, and like to childrens puppets, they abound ſometimes vppon a ſuddaine, and are againe as ſuddainly loſt, they take no roote, nor aſſured reſt in any place, or perſon, but being toſſed to and fro, vvith euery puffe, or blaſt of fortune, hoyſe men vp on heigh*

vvhen they flovv, and aftervvards ebbing agayne, either leaue them destitute on dry ground, or drovvne them in the deapth of misery, and therefore they ought not to be esteemed, or yet to be called goods, especially seing that, besides the mischeefs vvhich they dravv vppon vs, they redouble in vs a painefull thirst of them selues.

20. Thus saith he, most truly, yea and this might be the better borne with in them, if they were not also the meanes to corrupt our mindes, and to replenish vs, with all kind of vice, and sinne. And therefore the
2.Tim.6. Apostle saith: *Qui volunt fieri diuites, incidunt in laqueum diaboli: They vvhich*
Eccles.11. *vvill be rich, fall into the snare of the deuil.* And the preacher: *Si diues fueris, non eris immunis à peccato: if thou be rich, thou shalt not be free from sinne.* In
Matth 7. which respect our Sauiour compared riches to *thornes*, and said also,
Mar.4. that it was, *as hard for a rich man to enter into the kingdome of heauen, as for a*
Luc.8. *camel to passe through a needles eye.*
Matth.19.
Mar.10. 21. This was wisely considered by *Salomon* when he prayed to almighty
Luc.18. God, to giue him neither riches, nor pouerty, but only thinges compe-
Prou.10. tent, and necessary for his maintenaunce, lest perhaps by plenty, and abundance, he might forgett and deny God, or by pouerty be forced to steale, and blaspheme him. And although he was aduanced by almighty God to the greatest honour, wealth, and glory that euer mortall man had, and became a very mirrour of humane power and prosperity, yet how litle true felicity, and happines he found therein, we may learne partly by the example of his foule fall from God by reason thereof, and
,, partly by his owne testimony. Who saith thus. I magnified my workes,
,, and built houses, I planted vineards, I made gardens, aud orchards, and
Eccl.2. ,, furnished them with all kind of trees. I made fish ponds to water my
,, wood of yong trees. I had slaues and handmaides, and a great family,
,, droues of cattell, and great flocks of sheepe, more then all that euer were
,, before me in *Ierusalem*. I stored, and heaped vp siluer, and gold, and the
,, substance, and wealth of kinges, and prouinces: I had musitians both
,, men, and women, and all the delicacies of the sonnes of men: I had
,, bowles, and goblets for wine, and exceeded all my predecessors in riches,
,, and wisdome, and I denied nothing to my eyes, that they desired, neither
,, did I restraine my hart from the vse, and fruition of all the pleasure, and
,, delectation, that could be reaped of all that which I had prepared, per-
,, swading my selfe, that it was my part (that is to saie my felicitie) to vse
,, and enioy the fruites of mine owne labour. But when I seriously consi-
,, dered all the workes which my handes had wrought, and all the labours
,, where in I had bestowed so much vaine toile, and paine, I saw vanity,
,, and affliction of mind in all, and that nothing is permanent vnder the
,, sune. Thus saith the wisest, and most fortunate king of the world that

euer

euer was, or is euer like to be, who speaking of his owne experience deserueth to be beleeued.

22. Therefore, I may iustly say with the Psalmist, to all such as put their felicitie in worldly pleasures. *Filij hominum, vsquequo graui corde, vt quid diligitis vanitatem, & quæritis mendacium? O yee sonnes of men, hovv long shall your hartes be heauy, and dull? vvhy doe you loue vanity, and seeke after lyes?* That is to say, why doe you sett your affection vppon the goods, and pleasures of the world, which are nothing els but vanitie, and lies, being not onlie vaine, and friuolous, short, transitorie, and much sooner lost then had, but also false, and fraudulent, like to the cupp of *Babylon* guilt on the out side, and full of poison within, appearinge and seeming to be profitable, pleasant, and glorious, but being indeede alwayes dangerous, and manie times most pernicious. Wherevppon *Pyndarus* the greeke poet, was wont to saie, that euerie good in this world, is accompanied with two euills, and euerie contentment seconded with a thousand sorrowes, and those farre more irkesome, and dolefull, then the pleasures delightfull: For, more are wee greeued with losse, then contented with gaine, more afflicted with sicknes, then delighted with health, more offended with iniurie, then pleased with honour, and which is worst of all, *extrema gaudij,* saith *Salomon, luctus occupat, sorrovv euer succeedeth ioy.* In which respect the Philosopher *Hermes*, or *Mercurius Trismegistus*, had great reason to giue to God, as he said, *ingentes gratias*, exceeding great thankes, that whilst he meditated vppon the nature of the true good, God did infuse into him this certaine iudgement, that *mundus est congeries malorum, the vvorld is nothing els, but a heape of euills.*

Psalm. 4. *Plutarc.* *Pro. 30.*

23. Therefore I conclude with a certaine contemplatiue man, who saith of the world, much to this effect. What els is the world but a magazin of woes and sorrowes, a schoole of vanities, a markett of deceits, a laborinth of errors, a dungeon of darkenes, a way besett with theeues, a tempesteous sea, a garden full of weeds, and poisonfull hearbes, a fountaine of cares, a sweet, and pleasant poison, and a delectable phrensy? what good is there in the world, that is not false, and counterfet? what euill, that is not truly euill? it killeth thee, to betraie thee: it flattereth thee, to deceiue thee: it exalteth thee, to cast thee downe againe: it maketh thee merrie, to redouble thy sorrow: all the ease, and comfort it giueth, is mixt with labour, and paine: the securitie it promiseth, is without foundation: the hopes vaine: the ioyes false, and fained: and the sorrowes true, and insupportable: in so much, thas (as *S. Barnard* saith) if it were not for the hope that wee haue here of the other life, there would be litle difference betwixt the world, and hell.

Ludouic. Granat. Dux pec. lib. 1 part. 3.

24. This being so, I leaue it to the consideration of any prudent, and vnpassionate man, what peace of mind, or true happines, euill men can haue in the pleasures and contentments of this world, or rather how miserable they are, euen in the verie height of their supposed felicitie, seeing it is not onlie accompanied with much miserie, but also doth wholie alienate them from almighty God, who (as I haue proued) is the fountaine of all happines, our cheefe, and onlie good, our beginning, and our end, in whome onlie we may haue true repose. For (as *S. Bernard* saith) *he made all thinges, he hath all thinges, and he is all thinges: Quodcumque bonum cupis, quodcumque pulchrum quæris*, &c. *VVhat good soeuer thou desirest, vvhat beautifull, or faire thinge soeuer thou seekest, vvhat soeuer svveet, or delectable thing thou requirest, thou shalt find, and enioy it all in him*, &c. *If thou desire povver, he is povver, if thou desire fortitude, he is fortitude, if iustice, he is iustice, if vvisedome, he is the fountaine of vvisdome, if charity, he is charity, if beauty, he is beauty it selfe, if honour, glory, peace, and contentment of mind, he is true glory, the highest honour, eternall peace, the cheefe good, and all good.* Thus he.

D. Bern. ser. de miseria human.

25. And therefore, euen as wee see, that the marriners compasse being touched, or rubbed with the load stone (which hath a naturall sympathy with the north pole) can neuer rest, or repose, vntill it looke directly northward, and that then it stayeth, and fixeth it selfe without any farther motion, or trepidation: euen so mans soule (being made to the image of God, and to the onlie end to serue him, and by the meanes thereof to be vnited with him) hath such a naturall inclination, and instinct euer mouing it to the end, whereto it was created, that it cannot haue any perfect repose, vntill it be vnited with him, and in the meane time it euer laboureth, and can neuer be fully satisfied with worldly thinges: which as *S. Bernard* saith very well, *may occupy, and possesse the soule of man, but neuer fill, or satisfy it: for nothing*, saith he, *that is lesse then God, can fill that vvhich is capable of God*. And he addeth farther, that therefore euerie man doth naturally desire. *Summum bonum*, the cheefe good (that is to saie God) and that no man can haue rest, vntill he arriue to it. But *vvicked men* (saith he) *doe miserably erre, and vvander, vvho finding not the next vvay, ambulant in circuitu* (as the psalmist saith) *goe rounde about, vvhiles they hunt after the lesser goods, desiring alvvayes the cheefe good, and neuer obtaining it, though it be nearer them*, &c. And a litle after, *vis peruenire*, saith he, *incipe transilire*, &c. *VVilt thou attaine vnto the cheefe good, beginne to leape ouer the lesser goods, for othervvise thou shalt be miserably entangled, and detained vvith the desire, and loue of earthly thinges.*

Bernar. declamatio. in verba euangel. Ecce nos reliquimus, &c.

Psal. 11.

26 Thus

26. Thus saith *S.Bernard*: shewing how it falleth out, that although all men doe naturally tend to felicitie (which is God) yet most men doe not obtaine it, because they erre in the way, or meanes that leadeth vnto it, pursuinge continually the lesser goods, in steede of the cheefe good, and thirsting after apparent goods (yea very trifles, and toyes) in steede of the true good; Like one that running a race for a prize of inestimable valew, followeth euerie butterfly that crosseth his way, till at length he fall into some deepe ditch, where he is drowned in durt, and looseth both the prize, and his life: for so doe worldly men, who hauing the incōparable ioyes of heauen, and God himselfe proposed vnto them, for rewarde of their good course in the race of this life, runne at randome (as I may saie) after euerie butterflie of worldlie pleasure, till at length they fall headlong into the pitt of eternall perdition.

27. And yet neuertheles, they might enioy both the temporall goods of this world, and the eternall, if they would not abuse the first, but vse them onlie as a meanes to the latter, that is to say, for the seruice, and honour of God, for the which they were principallie ordained: whereas they putting their onlie felicity in their worldly wealth, loose their true felicitie, liuing in a continuall obliuion of their end, and of their duty to God their creator. For euen as we see that hoggs and swyne (when their keeper doth cast downe from the tree store of accornes to feede them) doe neuer so much as lift vpp their heades, or eyes to haue any cogitation of him, but grunting, and grumling one against an other, attend onlie to their feeding: euen so these worldlinges, notwithstanding the continuall benefits, which almighty God doth most bountifully powre downe vppon them, doe neuer so much as eleuate their eyes, or mindes from the earth, and delights of this world to thinke vppō him, and much lesse to be thankefull vnto him, but grumling one against an other, and thinking all the world to litle for themselues, attend onlie to their present pleasures, fatting themselues as hoggs, and swine doe for the slaughter, that is to saie, daily encreasing, and heaping damnation vppon themselues. And though they know well that they must die, and cannot be ignorant, if they be Christians, that then they are to yeld a strait account of their life past, and of euerie idle word, yet they liue as rechles, and careles thereof, as if they were sure to liue for euer: and which is more, are content for verie toyes, and vaine trifles, not onlie to venter, and loose the eternall ioyes, but also to purchase to themselues eternall paine.

28. Therefore I conclude this point, concerning mans felicitie, with the saying of the Psalmist. *Beatus vir cuius nomen Domini spes eius, & non*

Psal.39. *respexit in vanitates, & insanias falsas. Blessed is the man vvhose hope is the name of our lord, and hath not regarded, and esteemed vanities, and false madnes,* that is to say, worldly wealth, honours, and pleasures, which so bewitch men with false shewes of transitorie delights, that they depriue them of the true felicitie of euerlasting ioyes, whereunto God created them, and draw them to the endlesse infelicitie, and miserie of eternall paine, prepared for the diuell, and his Angels.

That ciuill society is subordinat to religious, or ecclesiastical society: that is to say to the Church. And by that occasion it is declared, hovv much religion hath benne honored, and respected in profane common vvelths: and the eminent dignity of the Church of Christ *is touched by the vvay. Also certaine conclusions are dravvne out of all the precedent chapters, and some groundes laid, for the better examination of false religions, to vvit of* Paganisme, Mahometisme, Iudaisme, Lutheranisme, *and* Caluinisme.

CHAP. VI.

Plato. dialogo. 1 de rep. vide Marsil. Ficinum in Argumento dial. 1. de rep.

1. HAuing hetherto proued, that religion is the end of common welth, I thinke it conuenient, aswell for the further confirmatiō thereof, as also for the better explication of this whole question, to shew how common welth serueth, or is referred to religion, as the meane, or way to the end. Whereby it will euidentlie appeare, that religion is not ordained for common welth, but common welth for religion: and that whereas man is naturallie enclined, both to religion, and also to ciuil society, his inclination to the latter, is subordinat to the former, that is to say, that he is by nature, inclined to liue in common welth, to the end he may the better performe the acts of religion.

2. The reason of this may well be gathered out of *Plato*, who teacheth, that men are assembled, and doe liue togither in ciuil societie, to the end, that all mankind may giue that due worship to God, which euerie man oweth him, and one man alone can not sufficientlie performe, nor yet manie together, except they liue in ciuil society. To which purpose it is to be considered, that the worship which is due to God from man, cannot be so compleat, and perfect in one man, or in a few, as in manie (for

Prouer.14. as *Salomon* saith. *In multitudine populi, dignitas regis. The honour of the king, is in the multitude of his people:*) And if it be requisit, that manie shall concurre to the worship of God, then it is also necessary, that they liue in order, and be gouerned by magistrats, and lawes, for otherwaise their multi-

multitude would breede confusion: and where manie are vnited with one communion of lawes, and magistrates, there is ciuil society. Therfore seeing manie men, can not duly worship God, and performe the acts of religion, except they liue in ciuil society (which is common welth:) it followeth that common welth is most requisit, and necessarie, to the perfection of religion.

3 Moreouer, whereas the office, and acts of ciuilitie, and religion, are distinct, and different, the one from the other, and yet are exercised in one multitude, and communitie of men, there must needes be also in the same communitie, distinct and different orders, proper to the nature, aswell of religion, as of ciuilitie: that is to say, as man is, in respect of ciuil societie, gouerned, and guided for the good of common welth by lawes, and magistrats, ordained to that end: so also he must, in regard of religion be directed by other different magistrats and lawes, conuenient to the office, and end of religion: in which respect *Cicero* saith. *Sine ijs qui sacris publicè præsint, priuatæ religioni satisfieri non posse. Men cannot satisfy their priuat religion,* or deuotion, *except there be some, that haue publike charge of the things that belong to religion.* And this cannot be imagined, but in a societie, proper to religion, that in one communitie of men, we find two societies, whereto nature hath ordained vs, the one ciuil, or political, and the other religious: whereof the former is called common welth, and the other, is now by Christians properly tearmed *the Church:* both of them euidently distinguished, the one from the other, by different magistrats, and lawes in all common wealths. *Cicero lib.2. de leg.*

4 Now then forasmuch as the religious societie, or the Church, hath the seruice of God, and deuine things for her proper and peculiar end, and that the ciuil societie, or common welth doth of her owne nature, and condition, respect only humane and temporal matters, it must needes follow, that the religious societie is farre more perfect, and worthie, then the ciuil, yea, and that the ciuill societie is subordinat vnto the religious, such being the course of nature, alwaies to proceede by the inferiour to the superiour, and by the lesse perfect, to the more perfect, as by the meane to the end, and this is most euident in all thinges, which are of one kind.

5 The Elements are aswel in dignitie, as place, superiour one to an other: The orbs, and spheres in like sort are subordinat to the highest, and moued by it: The sciences are all, as it were, subiect to *Metaphisick*, which therefore, *Aristotle* calleth the godesse of *sciences,* and (to omit multitudes of examples in a matter euident) the same may be noted in the societies, inferiour to common welth: for, humane nature is led, *Aristot.lib.1. metaphys.*

 as

as it were, by degrees and passeth from the lower, to the higher, or more worthy: as from the societie of the master, and the seruant, to the familie: from the familie, to the towne, or corporation: and from thence, to some kind of common welth, as to the more perfect, for the more ease, and better comoditie of man: And therefore by the like reason, humane nature resteth not there, but tending euer to the best, and to her proper end, it passeth from all sortes of common welth, and ciuil societies, to the religious, or ecclesiasticall societie, as to the highest, and most perfect, whereby man (who was ordained for the worship, and seruice of God) may discharge his dutie towards him, and attaine to eternall felicitie.

Cæsar comment. de bello Gallico l. 6

6 Thus then we see, not onlie that religion is the end of common welth, but also that the religious societie, or the Church, is farre more excellent, and worthy, then anie ciuil societie, by the same law of nature, that the soule is superiour to the body, reason to sense, heauen to the earth, and deuine thinges to humane.

7 The force of this naturall law, and the transcendent dignitie of religion, hath benne alwayes most manifest, euen in the common wealths of the Gentils. For, although true religion, could not haue any place, and much lesse any commaunde amongst them, (whiles they were drowned in the depth of Idolatrie) yet their natural propension to true religion, appeared euidentlie in the honour and respect, that they bore to their errour, and superstition; as (to omit other manifest arguments, and proofes thereof) it was euident in the great authoritie, and dignitie of the priesthood, which was exercised in the different religions of diuers countries; whereof I thinke good to lay downe some examples.

8 We read in the Commentaries of *Cæsar*, that certaine priestes called *Druydes* (because they dwelt most in the woods) were of such authoritie amongst the *Brittaynes* in our countrie, and the *Gaules* now called *Frenchmen*, that they were, not onlie exempt from all kind of taxes, or impositions, seruice in warre, and all other greueances, but also had in their handes the education, and instruction of all the youth and the decision of all ciuill and criminall causes, and other controuersies, either publike, or priuate, punishing such as refused to stand to their iudgement, with depriuation of all participation of their sacrifices: which was held for the most greueous penaltie that might be, and he which incurred it, was reputed to be so wicked, and infamous, that no man would conuerse with him, or speake to him: and such was the power of these *Druydes*, that they made warre, sometimes

times amongst themselues, for the office of cheefe priest, when it was vacant.

9 Also amongst the *Egiptians*, priesthood was of such high estimation, that no man could be king, except he were priest: And in diuerse partes of *Greece*, as *Plutarcke* affirmeth, priesthood was held equall in dignitie, with princelie estate, or kinglie maiesty. In *Æthiopia*, the kinglie authoritie was so subiect to the priestlie power, that when the priest denounced to the king, that it was the will of God, that he should kill himselfe, he neuer refused to doe it: in so much, that for manie descentes, and generations, the kinges of *Æthiopia* killed themselues, by the sentence, or decree of the priests, preferring the reuerence, and respect of religion, before the loue of their liues. *Baptista Fulgos. lib. 1.* *Strabo.*

10 And who can sufficientlie expresse, the great care, and respect, the *Romans* had of religion? Of whom *Cicero* saith: *Nec Numero Hispanos, nec robore Gallos, &c. VVee doe not surmount the Spaniards in number, nor the French in strength, nor the Africans in craft, nor the Greekes in the sciences, but vvee goe beyond all nations in religion, and pietie.* Thus he. And this is euident throughout all the course of their common welth, and empire. *Romulus* their first king, thought it vnfit, that any other but himselfe, should haue the care, and charge of the temples of the gods, and of their sacrifices, and ceremonies. Which custome, passed also from him as hereditarie, to the kings his successors. *Numa*, who succeeded him, did not only thinke himselfe greately honoured, with the title of cheefe bishop, but also ordained all that maiesticall forme of ceremonies, sacrifices, priestlie, and pontificall dignities, which the *Romans* euer after most curiouslie obserued. And such was the priuiledge, and dignitie of their priesthood, that *Iupiters* priest was (as *Plutarcke* witnesseth) *Viuum, sacrumque perfugij simulachrum: A liuing and holly image of refuge*, that is to say, his verie person, was a sanctuarie. For, *vvhosoeuer did fall dovvne at his feete, he vvas that day free from stripes or other punishment, and if he vvere alreadie tied, or bound, he vvas presentlie loosed.* *Cicero de Haruſp. reſp.* *Onuphrius de Romana Repub.* *Plutarc. in Numa.* *Titus Liuius Dec. 1. lib. 1.* *Plutarc. in quæst. Rom. q. 111.*

11. The cheefe bishop (who was called, *Pontifex Maximus*, and had the cheefe charge of all things belonging to religion) was subiect to no man, nor accountable for his doings to any: and which is more, the supreme authoritie of the common welth rested in him, & the inferiour bishops, as *Cicero* witnesseth, saying *that it vvas most notably, and deuinely ordained, by the ancient Romans, that the Bishops should haue the cheefe commaund in matters, that pertained asvvell to the common vvelth, as to the religion of the gods.* *Cicero orat. pro domo sua.*

Thus

Thus saith *Cicero*, whereof there may be alledged diuers examples, but two, or three shall suffise. *Metellus* being cheefe bishop, forbad *Posthumius* the Consul, (who was also a prieste) to goe to *Africk* with his Army, to the end he might attend, to his priestly charge, as occasion should require: wherein the consul obaied him, and so *the cheefe dignitie of the common vvelth yelded*, saith *Valerius*, *to religion*. *Cn. Tremellius* the *Tribune* of the people, was fined, because he had so litle respect to *AEmilius Lepidus*, the cheefe Bishop, as to contend iniuriouslie with him: whereuppon *Florus* obserueth; that *sacrorum magistratuum ius potentius fuit. The authoritie of the sacred, or holly magistrats, vvas more potent*, then the authoritie of the *Tribunes*, who where held equall with the consuls, and instituted of purpose by the people to counterpeise them.

Valer. Maxim. li. 1. c. 1.

Lucius Florus epito. lib. 47.

12 I might add hereto the soueraigne, and supreeme authoritie of the *Augures*, ouer all temporall magistrats in all matters of the common welth, were it not that I shall treat of it at large, in the *eight* chapter, where I shall haue occasion to lay downe some examples thereof, and namely of the two consuls. *P. Claudius* and *Lucius Iunius* condemned to death, for disobaying the *Augures*. For such was the reuerend regard of the *Romanes* to religion, that the violation, and contempt thereof, was not only alwaies ignominious, but also sometimes capital to the greatest princes, and supreme magistrats of the common welth; In which respect, *Valerius Maximus*, saith. *Omnia post religionem ponenda semper nostra ciuitas duxit, &c. Our citty hath alvvaies thought, that religion is to be preferred before all thinges, yea euen in men of the highest dignitie, and maiestie: and therfore our Empire, hath alvvaise most vvillingly submitted it selfe, and obaied in matters of religion, esteeming, that it should in time attaine to the soueraignetie of humane gouerment, if it did vvell, and constantly, serue the deuine povver.* Thus saith *Valerius*, of the time of the *Romane* consuls, and common welth.

Chap. 8. nu. 1. 2. 3.

Valerius Maxim. li. 1. c. 1.

13 And what respect was had to religion afterwards, it may appeare sufficiently, by that which wee read of the time of the Emperour *Alexander Seuerus*: As that there was an appellation from him to the bishops, and that they reuersed his sentences, when they saw cause: And (to omit other arguments of this matter) there is in *Nicephorus*, extant a letter of *Iulian* the *Apostata* to *Arsacius*, an Idolatrous bishop, or high priest in *Galatia*, wherein he admonisheth him, to be euer mindfull of his owne dignity, and that therefore, he should not goe to visit the gouernours of the prouince, but verie seldome, nor suffer any priest to goe forth to meete them, when they should come to the cittie, nor to be seene in the theaters, nor to haunt Tauerns, nor that any souldiar, of what condition soeuer

Baptista Fulgos. lib. 1. c. 1.

Niceph. eccl. hist. lib. 10. c. 22.

soeuer he were, should goe before any priest in the temple, for *as soone*, saith he, *as any temporall magistrat doth sett his foote vvithin the dore of the temple, he becommeth a priuat man, for thou hast the cheefe authority or commaund, in the temple, as thou knovvest, and so also the deuine decrees doe require.*

14 Thus wrote the Emperour *Iulian*: Whereby we may see, what conceit the pagan Emperours themselues held, of the grauity, and dignity of priesthood, and consequentlie of the excellencie of religion. The like may also be obserued amongst the *Turkes*, where such honour, and respect is borne to the clergie, that whereas, all other sorts of men, of what dignitie, or degree soeuer they be, are counted no better then slaues to their Emperour; the priests are counted free men, and neuer pay, either taxe, or tribut, and the cheefe bishop, or patriarch (who is called *Muphty*) is of such absolut authority, that no man what soeuer (not the Emperour himselfe) intermedleth in the affaires belonging to his charge, where as he neuerthelesse assisteth, when he thinketh good, in all the counsells of state. And although the other ordinarie counsellers of the Emperour (who are commonlie *foure* in number) may be, and are ofttimes changed: yet he can neuer be changed, or excluded: yea, and if he contradict any decree of the counsell, or law of the Emperour, and affirme it to be contrarie to the *Alcoran*, or law of *Mahomet*, it is presently anulled, and held to be of no force. Finally such is the respect that the Emperour beareth him, that as oft as the *Muphty* commeth vnto him, he riseth out of his seat, and laying his hand vppon his breast, boweth his head downe to the ground to doe him reuerence. Thus much I haue thought good to note by the way, concerning the high esteeme that Infidels of all sorts, haue had of religion and priesthood.

Munster. in Cosmographia. pag. 47

Melăchton. in præfat. Alcoran.

Cispin in tractatu de Mahomete.

Theuet Cosmogra. li. 17. c. 7.

Leonclauius in pandect. hist. Turc. ca. 34.

Postel. de la iustice des Turcs.

15 Seeing then superstition, and Idolatrie hath had such power to captiuat the minds of men by reason of the natural instinct, and inclination that all men haue to religion, what may be thought of the force, and power of true religion, accompanied with the light and power of Gods grace? Shall it not be much more potent to moue men to embrace, esteeme, and honour it aboue all earthly things? And shall not the priesthood, and prelacy belonging thereto, be more worthily respected, and reuerenced, then an earthly power? This appeareth euidently in the law of God, giuen to the *Ievves* by *Moyses* in the ould testament, where it was ordained, that it should be death to disobay the commaundements of the high priest, and almighty God also said to the Prophet *Ieremy*. *Ecce constitui te hodie*, &c. *Behold I haue constituted* and ordained *thee this day aboue nations, and kingdomes, that thou maist pluck vp, and destroy, and dissipat, and build, and plant*, &c.

Deuter. 17.

Ieremi. 1.

16 What meruell then, that the priesthood of our Christian Church (which is the kingdome of *Christ*, and the pillar of *truth*, as the Apostle calleth it (whereof the prophets also foaretold, that it should in glorie exceede the sinagogue of the *Ievves*, which was but a figure of it) what meruel, I say, that in authoritie and honour, it excelleth all earthlie power, and principalitie? In which respect the holie martyr, *S. Ignatius*, disciple to S. *Iohn the Euangelist*, said of our Christian priesthood that it is *Summa omnium honorum, qui in hominibus consistunt: The cheefe of all honours, vvhich are in men*. And S. *Chrisostome* calleth it *Principatum ipso regno, &c. A principality more venerable, and greater, then the kingdome it selfe*, because the princelie power, doth not exceede the boundes of the earth, whereas the power of the Christian priest, extendeth it selfe to the heauens: and the Prince saith he, hath authority onlie ouer the body, but the priest hath power ouer the soule. Thus reasoneth S. *Chrisostome* in his excellent treatise, which he wrote of the dignity of priesthood.

Isai. 49. & 60. Agga. 2 Hieron. in Agga.

S. Ignatius ep. ad Smyrnen.

S. Chrisost. Ho. 4. & 5. de verb. Esaia vidi dominum & li. 3. de sacerdotio.

17 This then being so, it cannot be doubted, but that our Christian Church, wherein this pristhood is exercised, is that religious, and ecclesiastical society, whereto all other societies are by the law, and course of nature subordinat, and subiect, which will be more cleare then the sunne heareafter, when I shall treat purposelie of Christian religion, and of the Catholike Church in particuler: for here I speake but of religion in generall.

18 Neuerthelesse, for the conclusion of this point, I will say further heere, concerning the dignity of our Church, that if wee consider the excellent institution of it, (as that it is a most exact, and exquisit Monarchie notablie tempred of all kind of common welths) and waigh withall the deuine wisdome of the lawmaker, that is to say, our Sauiour *Christ*: the equity, and sanctity of his lawes: the terrour of the iudgements and penalties extending to the eternal punishment of body, and soule: the inestimable worth of the heauenlie, and euerlasting rewards: the dignitie, and grauitie of the magistrats: the authoritie of the supreme Senat, or Parlament: (I meane the generall councels:) the venerable maiestie of the head, and his ample power to bind, and lose: the boundes of his dominion, propagated from the east, to the west, the stabilitie, and perpetuitie thereof, which hellgates shall not ouercome (hauing alreadie continued in a perpetuall succession, of more then *Tvvo hundred*, and *forty* bishops from the Apostle *Saint Peter*, not with standing the enuie and hatred of Heretikes, and the violent impugnation of most wicked, and potent Emperours.) And if with all we consider the

Matth. 16.

Ibid.

the hollie inſpiration of the deuine ſpirit, which moueth, and gouerneth all this miſticall bodie, the giftes, graces, and miracles, wherewith it is adorned, the admirable force, and vertue of the Sacraments: the profound wiſedome, and knowledge of Doctors: the Mellifluous eloquēce of preachers: the immaculat chaſtity of virgins, the inuincible fortitud of Martyrs: the innocent life of confeſſors: and the moſt ſweet ſauour of all vertues, that redoundeth of theſe heauenly flowers: finally, if we ponder alſo, the communion that this Eccleſiaſtical ſociety hath with the heauenly *hierarchy* (whereby we become, *Ciues ſanctorum*, & *domeſtici Dei*, *fellovv cittizens vvith ſaints, and houshould ſeruants of God.*) We cannot doubt, but that it is the lady, and miſtreſſe of all ſocieties, the Queene of Common welths, and Empreſſe of all kingdomes, and Empires. In which reſpect, it his honored, & adorned in the holly ſcriptures, with moſt excellent titles, *of the houſe of God, the gate of heauen, the citty of God*, and ſuch like: whereof alſo almighty God, ſaid by the Prophet. *Ponam te in ſuperbiam ſæculorum*, &c. *I vvill place thee for a pride* (that is to ſaie, *for an honour*, and glorie) *to vvorlds, or ages, a ioy to generation, and generation, and thou shalt ſucke the milke of nations, and shalt be fedd vvith the Papp of kings*, &c.

Ephes. 2. Gen. 28. Pſal. 86. Iſai. c. 60.

19 And againe: *Filij eorum, qui te humiliauerunt, curui venient*, &c. *The children of thoſe, vvhich humbled thee, shall come crouching vnto thee, and shall adore the foote ſteps of thy feete, and thy gates shalbe open continually, they shall not be shut day, or nigth, to the end, that ſtrength of nations, and their kinges, may be brought vnto thee: for the nation, and kingdome, vvhich shall not ſerue thee, shall perish.* And in an other place: *Erunt reges nutricij tui. Kings shalbe thy foſter fathers, and Queenes thy nurſes, they shall adore thee, vvith their face bovved dovvne vppon the earth, and shall lick the duſt of thy feet, and thou shalt knovv, that I am thy lord.* Thus ſaid the prophet foretelling the dignitie, maieſtie, and glorie which now wee ſee, in the Chriſtian Church, whereof I ſhall haue occaſion to ſpeake amply heereafter, in the third part of this treatiſe.

Ibid. Idem. c. 49.

20 This therefore, is the ſocietie, whereto euerie man is by nature inſtituted, and ordained: This is the huge, and immenſe ocean, to which all the ſpringes and riuers, as I may ſay, of humane, and ciuil ſocieties, of families, citties, and common welths, of kingdomes, empires, and ſtates, doe naturally direct their courſe. This, I ſaie, is that eternall kingdome, and monarchie of our Sauiour *Chriſt*, which being ſpread ouer the whole world, doth not onlie remaine alwaiſe, one, and the ſelfe ſame (retaining her authoritie, and dignitie in all Chriſtian common welths, though neuer ſo different in their forme, na-

ture, and institution) but also comprehendeth them all, and as it were, fostreth them like a louing mother in her bosome, linketh, and combineth them in a spirituall vnion one with an other, adorneth, and perfetteth them, and finally (if they swarue not from her) bringeth them to true felicitie, conioyning them, and euerie part of them with God, by the meanes of true religion, which is found onlie in her, and is the end, for the which all common welths, and euerie particular man is ordained.

21 And now to conclude this question concerning religion in generall, thou hast seene, good Reader, that I haue hetherto treated of the necessity of religion, in common welth, in respect first of the whole world, secondly of euerie man in particuler, and lastly of common welth it selfe: and therefore I thinke good, before I passe further, to draw certaine conclusions out of the premisses, whereby the ignorance, errour, and impiety of the pollitikes, may be the more manifest.

Chap.2.& 3. 22 Seeing then, that religion floweth, (as I haue proued) from the fountaine of nature it selfe, and is the bond, or linke, wherewith man and all other creatures subiect to him, are tied, and linked with their creator, and that the vertue, and force thereof is such, that not onlie all humane thinges doe by the helpe thereof, remaine in the protection of almighty God, but also man himselfe is thereby vnited with him, and becommeth a most happie, yea deuine creature (first here in this life, by grace, and after in the next by euerlasting glorie:) what man can be so wicked, or senseles, as to thinke, that any humane, or worldlie thing, may be preferred before it, or yet compared with it? Who is so blind, that he seeth not the absurditie of those, which thinke it to be a humane deuise, consisting onlie in the opinion of men? What els may be thought that they pretend, but the destruction of man, the subuersion of the whole world, and the ruine of nature it selfe? For if there were no religion, or if all men should contemne it (as they doe) what connexion could there be of man, and of the world with God? What meanes, or way to true felicitie? Should not the world, by the breach of the common bond, fall to confusion, and man be ouerwhelmed with remediles miserie?

Chap.4.per totum. 23 Furthermore, seeing I haue also proued, that religion is the end not onlie of man, but also of common welth, and that all true political felicitie, cōsisteth principally therein: what els doe they which ouerthrow, or deface religion, but subuert common welth, and depriue it of all true happines, and consequently draw it to infelicitie, and vtter desolation? And lastly seeing the end, wherto any thing is ordained, is farre more noble,

noble,& worthie, then the meanes that leadeth to the end: it is most euident, that religion, being the end of common welth, is farre more worthie, and excellent, then all humane pollicie: and that the axiome of the law is most true, to wit; *summa ratio est, quæ pro religione facit, it is the cheefe, and highest reason, vvhich makes for religion?* Where vppon it followeth, that religion is the verie rule, whereby all policie is to be directed, and the touch stone, wherewith it is to be tried: and that when pollicie is correspondent to the rule of religion, then it may trulie be counted good, and true pollicie, because it is conforme to the end, whereto it was ordained: and when it deflecteth, or dissenteth from it, then it is bad, and false pollicie, as disagreeing from the true end, whereto all true policie tendeth. As for example, the health of man, is the end of phisicke: and therefore whatsoeuer is holesome, and good for mans healthe, the same is medicinable, and agreable to the rule of phisick: and on the other side, whatsoeuer is vnholesome, or hurtfull to health, the same is contrarie to the true rule of phisicke.

24 Therefore whereas Politikes do accomodat all religion to state (as though state or pollicie were the end, and rule of religion) who seeth not that they are as absurde therein, as the phisitian, that should not seeke principallie the health of his patient, but the commendation of his medicine, or art, and would labour to wrest his patients complexion, and disease to the nature, and operation of his medecin, and not applie the medicin to the cõplexion of the patient, or to the nature of the disease? Or are they not as wise as the shoomaker, who would seeke to fitt the foote to the shooe, and not the shooe to the foote? Or as the carpenter, who would frame his squire, and rule to his tymber, and not his tymber to his rule? Could any thing be more praeposterous, absurd, or ridiculous? No truelie; and yet so doe the politiks, in the states where they gouerne, framing religion to the rule of their state, that is to say, the end, to the meane; the sicke mans health, to the medicine; the squire, to the tymber; and the foote to the shooe.

25 Now then to proceed to the declaration of what religion it is, which is the end of common welth, and consequentlie most conuenient for state, thow shalt vnderstand, good Reader, that forasmuch as diuers religions, partlie haue bene, and partelie are professed in diuerse common welths (as *paganisme* amongst the *Greekes*, and *Romaines* in times past: *Mahometisme* amongest the *Turkes*, and *Persians*, and *Africans* at this day: *Iudaisme* amongest the *Ievves* in sundry partes of the world: *Christianisme* amongst the Christians, and lastlie the different sects of *Christians*, who haue seperated themselues from the Catholike Church in diuerse parts

of Christendome at this present) I will therefore treat seuerallie of all these, and finallie proue, that the religion, which doth vnite man, and common welth with God, and beatifie both, is the Christian faith: And that of those religions, which differentlie professe the faith of *Christ* at this daie, the ancient Catholike Roman religion, is not onlie the true religion, but also most politicall, that is to say, most agreable to true reason of state: And finallie that the doctrine of the sectaries, professing the name, and faith of *Christ*, namelie of *Lutherans* and *Caluinists*, is no lesse contrarie to true reason of state, then to the veritie of our holie scriptures.

26 To this purpose, I thinke good, first to lay downe, *tvvo infallible groundes, and positions*, whereby I meane to examine the religions aboue mentioned, and to performe in part, that which I haue vndertaken. *The one is*, that no false religion can be the end of common welth, nor vnite the same with God, nor yet benefit, and much lesse beatifie it. This may appeare, by the verie naturall instinct, that wee haue to religion: For, seeing that the religion, which is the end of man, and of common welth, is the same whereto nature moueth and inclineth vs, it must needes be, a good, and true religiō; it being euidēt, and grāted by all men, that as all naturall inclinations (such I meane as are conforme to the law of nature) are good and true, so also all those thinges, whereto they moue, and encline vs, are true, and good in like manner: For *bonum & verum*, that is to saie, *good* and *true* are inseparable, seeing what soeuer is good, the same is true, and what soeuer is true, it is also good: & if nature should encline vs to any thing that were euill, or false, it should both erre it selfe, and also induce vs to errour: which were most absurd to say, for thereuppon it must needes follow, that God the author of nature, and truth it selfe, should be the author of euill and falsity, which all philosophers deny with our deuines: and therefore *Cicero* saith of nature, that *natura duce errari nullo modo potest*: If *vvee follovv nature vve cannot erre*, whereuppon it followeth, that the religion whereto nature inclineth vs, must needes be a good, and true religion: for if it were false, it could neither be good, nor yet naturall, and much lesse the end whereto nature moueth man, and common welth.

S. Tho. 22. q. 26. ar. 6 c.

Aristot. Metaphy.

Cicero de legib. li. 1.

27 Furthermore a false religion cannot be the meanes to vnite man and common welth with God, who being veritie it selfe, and also most iust, hateth, and punisheth nothing more then falsitie, especiallie in those thinges which concerne his worship, and seruice. And therefore our Sauiour *Christ* said, that those which worshipp and adore God, ought to adore him, in *spiritu & veritate*, *in spirit and truth*: wereuppon it also followeth

loweth that all false religion,is most pernicious to common welth,both because it deuideth the same from God(vppon whom dependeth all the good and felicitie thereof:) as also for that it draweth his wrath and vengeance vppon it,no lesse then vppon particular men: as shall appeare by manifest examples hereafter in the third part of this treatise: and thus much for the first grounde.

29 *The second position* or grounde shalbe:that the religion, which consisteth either in the worshipp of a false god,or yet in precepts, customes, or beleefe inducinge to vice,and corruption of manners,must needes be a false religion,and destroy common welth. For as in the first, (I meane the worship of a false god) it impugneth the author of nature (who as I said before is veritie it selfe)so in the latter (to wit in the induction to vice)it impugneth the lawe of nature. which leadeth to all vertue: in which respect the *Stoicks*, teaching, that the felicitie of man, and common welth,consisteth in vertue,taught also, that *to liue verteously*, is nothing else,but *to liue according to the rule, and lavv of nature*. And therefore the religion which leadeth,and induceth to vice, must needes be against nature,and consequently against reason, and true pollicy, that is to saie, not onlie false,but also pernicious to state:False,because all truth is conforme to nature. Pernitious to state, because state, or common welth standeth by vertue, & is ruinated by vice,as I will euidently proue hereafter. And in the meane time, hauing laid these two infallible groundes,I will thereby examine the religions aforesaid,and first beginne with *Paganisme*, as it was professed by the *Romans*, who in their kind, were most religious, or rather superstitious, and placed a great part of their pollicy, in the exact obseruation of their religion: which neuertheles I will manifestlie shew, to haue bene both false, and contrary to true reason of state,and consequently pernicious to their common welth.

Cicero de Finib. li.4.

Chap.9.per totum.

The absurdity of Paganisme, is shevved in the religion of the aunsient Romanes, and that the same vvas no lesse contrary to true reason of state then to true religiō:not only for the vanity of their gods, and the impiety of their sacrifices, and ridiculous ceremonies:but also for the bad effectes of vice, and all kind of vvickednes, vvhich it produced in their common vvelth.

Chap. VII.

1 Being here to discipher aswell the impietie and vanitie of Paganisme, as the dammage that ensued thereof to the Roman common welth, I cannot but first make reflexion on the imbecillity,and vanity of man, when he is void of gods grace, seing that so wise a people,as the *Romanes* were, and as it seemeth, so well

so well disposed, and inclined to vertue, were neuertheles so blinde, and withall so impious, as to embrace for some hundreths of yeares, such an absurde, ridiculous, and sacrilegious religion as they did, and with such notable detriment to their common welth, as did, and must needs grow thereof. Which no man can denie, that dulie considereth the multitude, turpitude, and abiection of their gods, honoured with such detestable sacrifices, rites and ceremonies, that their beliefe, and the practise of their whole religion, could not possiblie produce in time, any other effect in their common welth, then contempt of God, and of religion, that is to say, Atheysme, and extreame dissolution of life, and manners, to the vtter ouerthrow of their state.

2 That this may euidentlie appeare, I will first treate of their gods: Secondly of their sacrifices: And lastlie of the effects of their whole religion. And first for their gods, and goddesses, what could be more contemptible then manie of them, whose names, and functions, did rather deserue derision, then deuotion, and might moue men rather to contemne them, then to reuerence them: As *Hercules* ἀπομυος scarre-flee (whose deuine office, was to dryue flies awaie: And the goddesse called *Cloacina*, because she was found in a sinke: And the rustie goddesse, named *Rubigo*, to whom they worthilie sacrificed a dogge: And the dombe goddesse, called *Muta*: Also the dungehill god *Sterquilinus*: And their sweeping goddesse *Deuerra*, who with her beesome (together with two other gods called *Pilumnus* and *Intercido*, the one armed with a pestle, and the other with an axe) defended women newly brought a bed, from the great god of the woods, called *Siluanus*: whereof the ceremonie was most ridiculous: for three men being sent about the house in the night, the first strooke the threshould of the dore with an axe, the second with a pestle, and the third with a beesome, and so shee that lay in childbed, was held to be secure from the god *Siluanus*, who, as they feared, would otherwise haue entred into the house, and donne her some great harme.

Lactant. li. 1. cap. 20. Ouid fast. 4. Lactant. de falsa relig. li. 1. ca. 20. D. Aug. de ciuit. Dei. li. 6. c. 9.

3 But what should I say of an infinit number of trifling gods, whom they worshipped, assigning a particular god, almost for euerie thing? As, *Forculus* for the god of the dore, or gate: *Limentinus* the god of the threshould: and *Cardea* the goddesse of the hinges: so that they had two gods and a goddesse, appointed to keepe one dore, which one dogg would haue kept much better. And what a number of gods had they about a maried coople? first the god *Iugatinus*, to ioyne them togither: then the god *Domiducus* to bring the bride home, then the god *Domitius*, and the goddesse *Manturna*, to keepe her at home, besides *Venus*, and

Idem ibid. cap. 7. S. August. Ibid. c. 9.

Priapus,

Priapus, and a great manie of beastly gods, and goddesses, to assist them for procreation: whose names I forbeare to relate, because they import nothing but matter of lust, and lasciuiousnes.

5 In like maner, they had a goddesse of meate, called *Edulica*: an other of drinke, called *Potina*: and for corne, they had so many, as it would be tedious to tell their names: for besides *Ceres*, and *Proserpina*, who had the cheefe chardge thereof, there was a god, or a goddesse for the eare of the corne, an other for the stalke, an other for the ioyntes, or knots, an other for the blade, an other for the graine, an other for the huskes, an other for the blouth of it, an other for the groweth, an other for the ripeninge, and to be breefe, they had in like sort, for euerie other trifle some trifling god, or goddesse. And yet if their folly had stayed there, it had bene more tollerable: but who can expresse sufficiẽtly their madnes, in that they did not onlie assigne a god, as I haue said, for euerie toye, but also made gods of the verie diseases, passions, vices, and sinnes of men: which as *S. Augustin* saith verie well, could not be called *Numina, sed crimina colentiũ*, not the gods, but the crimes of those that worshipped them: For besides the goddesse *Febris*, that is to saie, the Ague, and *Fortuna mala, & detestata*, bad, & detestable fortune to the which they dedicated temples and ordained sacrifices they had also a god called *Pallor*, palenes, and an other called *Pauor*, feare, also a goddesse of slouth, which they called *Murcia*: and, least coueteousnes might want some deuine patrons, to protect, and nourish it, they made *gold, siluer, brasse* and *money* gods, yea and worshipped pleasure, and lust, vnder the names of *Volupia* and *Libentina*: and which is more beastly, they adored the verie priuie parts of man in the ceremonies of *Bacchus*, & were also no lesse absurd, in theyr worship of their god *Pryapus*. whereof I omit to recount the particulars, and occasion, not to offend chast eares, but he that list to see it, may read *Lactantius*, in his booke, *de falsa religione*.

Ibid.li.4. c.8.

Cicero de leg.lib.2.

Arnobius li. 4.contra gentes.

D.Aug.de ciuit.li.7. cap.21.

Lactant.de falsa relig. lib.1.ca.21.

5 But what should I say of all the rest of their gods and goddesses, such I meane as had bene mẽ, & womẽ? As their great god *Iupiter, Saturne, Mars, Venus, Berecinthia*(called the mother of all the gods) *Hercules*, and diuers others, were they not all of thẽ, true patternes of impiety, & wickednes?

6 *Iupiter* hauing expelled his father, *Saturne*, out of his kingdome, married his owne sister, *Iuno*, & was also so dissolute of life, that he gaue occasion to the poets to faine of him, those monstrous tales of his excessiue lust, where with their poems are replenished, & therefore no meruaile, if his daughter *Venus* (who was also a principall goddesse of the *Romans*) were as *Euemerus* declareth the first that set vp a bordell or stewes, & taught he *Græcian* women, and specially them of *Cyprus*, to make gaine of their

Ludouic.vi-ues in Comment.in li. 4.S.August. de ciuit.Dei. c.10.

Iustin.li.22. owne bodies: whereuppon grew the custome of the *Cypriots*, whereof *Iustin* writeth, to witt, to prostitute their maides at the sea coast for some dayes before their mariage, to paie their offring to *Venus* for their chastity, all the rest of their liues.

7 And what may we thinke of *Saturne Iupiters* father? Doe not *Hesiodus*, and *Diodorus* testify, that he was also a very wicked man, and that he depriued his owne father of his kingdome, as he himselfe was after depriued of his by *Iupiter* his sonne? In like sort doe not all authors agree, that *Mars* the great God, and protectour of the *Roman* Empire, was taken in adultery with *Venus*? Which ministred to the poets ample matter, for their further fictions? Also *Berecinthia* or *Cibele*, called the mother of the gods, was not shee starke mad with the loue of *Atis*, as shalbe declared more particularlie after a while?

Ludouic. viues vbi supra ex Hesiodo. Euem. ro & Diodoro.

8 And what neede I speake seuerally of euery one of the gods? Seeing *Euemerus* a Siciliā, who wrote their history, (which he collected with great industry, out of the anciēt records of their tēples) declareth thē all to haue bene so impious, and beastly, that he was held by some in those times, for no better thē an Atheist, & an enemie of the gods, for writing the truth, & yet his history was generallie called, *Sacra historia*, the holie history.

Vide Ludouic. viuem in Commēt. in li. 6. S. Aug. de Ciuit. Dei. ca. 7

9 But perhaps some may thinke, that the *Romans* hauinge receiued those gods, and their ceremonies from *Greece*, were deceaued by the common opinion of the *Grecians*, who had adored them for gods long before, and that their owne proper gods (such I meane as they thēselues deified) were of more worth, or of better fame at least: Which neuertheles, was nothing so, as may appeare by their deification of *Romulus* their first founder, who was a parricide of his owne brother, a breaker of leagues, & all lawes, humane, & deuine, and such a tyrant, that the Senators whome he had made, killed him in the senate: and yet neuertheles, though they thought him vnworthy to liue, they held him worthy of deuine honour, & by a decree of the senat, made him a god. So also, *Tiberinus* of *Alba*, a notable theefe, and robber, being by the iust iudgement of God, drowned in the riuer *Albula* (which hath bene euer since called *Tyber*) was made a god by *Romulus*. So also, *Flora*, a common strompet, was receiued, & declared for a goddesse by the *Romans*, & honored with an image, and with such beastlie feastes, called *Floralia*, that I am ashamed to speake of the particularities thereof, which may be seene in *Lactantius*.

Euseb. de preparat. Euang li. 2. ca. 4.

Titus Liuius Decad. 1. li. 1. Plutarc. in vita Romuli.

Vide Ludouic. viuem vbi supra in li. 5 c. 23.

Lactant. lib. 1. cap. 20. Plutar. in Romulo. Vide Ludouic. viuem vbi supra in li. 4. c. 8.

10 This *Flora* was also called *Larentia*, and was nurse to *Romulus*, hauing bene so incontinent, that she was called *Lupa* (which in those daies did not onlie signifie a shee wolfe, but also a common queane) whereuppon grew the fable, that *Romulus*, and *Remus* were nourished by a shee wolfe.

Lactant. vbi supra.

11 But

11 But besides this *Larentia*, there was also an other of the same name, & quality, & honored, by the *Romans* for a goddesse, vppon this occasion, as *Plutarke* writeth. A priest of *Hercules*, saith he, being idle, and disposed to sport himselfe, inuited his god to play at dice with him, vppon cōdition, that if the god did winne, the priest should make him a great banket in his temple, and seeke him out the fairest woman that could be found, & if the priest did winne, the god should bestow vppon him somewhat of great valew, fitt for a god to giue. This bargaine being made, or at least deuised in his owne braine, he cast the dice, first for himselfe, and after for the god, and acknowledging himselfe in the end to haue lost his wager, he prepared a sumptuous bankett, and sought out *Larentia* (being famous for her beautie at that time) whome he hired to lie in the temple all night, which shee did, and they say, shee was admonished by *Hercules*, that shee should make choise of one to be her freend, whom shee should meete first in the morninge, at her going out of the temple, and so it fell out, that it was one *Tarrutius*, a verie old man, exceeding rich, and without children, who lead her home to his house, and within a while died, and made her his heire of all his goods, and possessions, which shee leaft after her death, to the common welth, in recompence whereof, shee was made a goddesse, and the feasts called *Larentinalia* were ordained for her honour, and seruice.

Plutar. in Romulo. S. Aug. de ciuit. Dei. li. 6. c. 7.

12 Whereby we may see, what manner of gods the *Romans* had, aswell of their owne choise, as by tradition from the *Grecians*: and if we consider withall, with what ceremonies, feastes, & sacrifices these gods were honored, and serued, we shall find some of them, so ridiculous, & others so impure, beastly, and impious, that wee may both wonder at the blindnes of the *Romans*, and also easily conceaue, what bad effects their religion must needes worke in their common welth.

13 As concerninge their foolish and ridiculous ceremonies, I shall not neede to produce any other wittnes, then the graue philosopher *Seneca*, who hauing derided the *Egiptian* rites, addeth: *Huic tamen furori*, &c. Yet this madnes lasteth but a while: It is tollerable to be madde once a yeare. But if you come to the Capitoll of *Rome*, and see what passeth there, you „ wilbe ashamed to see such publike folly, & fury all the yeare lōg: one stādeth there to tell *Iupiter* what a clock it is: an other to make all the other „ gods obey him: one is his seargeant, & an other is his ointer: some there „ are, whose office is to dresse the heads of *Iuno*, and *Minerua*, standing farre „ from their temples, and images, and only counterfeiting to doe it, with a „ vaine motion of their handes, & armes, whiles others hould the looking „ glasse: some also inuite the gods to their lawdayes: some present them „

Seneca apud Aug. de ciuit. Dei lib. 6. ca. 10.

,, memorialls, and enforme them of their causes: and the ould *Archepanta-*
,, *lon*, being already so discribed, that he is cleane out of date, and no longer
,, fitt for the stage, playeth his part euery day in the *Capitoll* before the gods,
,, as though they would take pleasure to behould him, whom men deride
,, and cōtemne. All kynd of tradesmen are there idle as though they were
,, entertained to worke for the gods: yet, they may be borne with, for
,, that they offer them not any vile, or infamous, but onlie superfluous ser-
,, uice. But what say you of the women that sitt in the *Capitoll*, and thinke
,, that *Iupiter* is enamored of them, & yet are not afraid of *Iunos* frowninge
,, lookes? Thus saith *Seneca*: who being himselfe a *Painym*, worthly skorneth (as you see) the childish superstition of the *Romans*, and their ridiculous religion.

14 But what? Was not also the solemne ceremonie of the *Lectisternia* most vaine, friuolous, and irreligious? When to pacifie the wrath of the gods, in time of great plague, and pestilence, they made them great bankets in their temples, and prepared beds for the gods and goddesses? Whereof *Liuy* declareth the origen, saying that there was a great plague in *Rome*, a litle before it was taken by the *Gaules*, and that for the remedy thereof, the *Romans* had recourse to the bookes of the *Sybils*, where they found (as it seemed to them) that they should appease the gods with bankets for eight dayes together, and make three festiuall beds in the temples, for *Apollo* and *Latona*, *Hercules*, and *Diana*, *Mercury*, and *Neptune*: by which meanes saith *Liuy*, the wrath of the gods was pacified, and no maruaile if their choller were asswaged after so much good cheare, and so good entertainment for so manie dayes together.

Liu.lib.5. Dec.1.an. vrbis.356.

15 But what could be either more vaine, or more impious, yea, and dishonorable to their gods themselues, then their stage playes, instituted specially for their honour, to be vsed in their greatest solēnities? Wherein nothing els was represented, but their dissentiōs, quarrels, warrs, thefts, and adulteries, & nothing heard but contumelies, railing, and reuilinge speeches against them, as though the gods (if they had bene any thing at all) could haue bene delighted with their owne shame, and reproch, or could haue thought themselues to be honoured by their dishonour?

16 Such were the playes called *Megalesia*, dedicated to the honour of *Berecinthia*, the mother of the gods, and celebrated the twelfte of Aprill: the occasion whereof, I thinke good to relate, as also the storie of the great goddesse *Berecinthia*, not much vnlike to a comedy, seeing I speake now of stage playes.

17 This *Berecinthia*, being called also *Cibele*, and *Idea*, was daughter to *Minos*, one of the most ancient kinges of *Phrigia*, who vppon a prophecy which

(which seemed to threathē him some great harme by her) exposed her, as soone as shee was borne, to be deuoured of wild beastes, vppō the mountaine called *Cibelius*, wherevppō she was afterward called *Cibele*, but being foūd there by a sheppards wife, & brought vp by her, as her owne daughter, shee grew in time, to be a woman of a very rare beauty, & falling in loue with a younge man called *Atys*, had a child by him. Afterwards her father, hauing heard the great fame of her beauty, and discouering with all that shee was his daughter, sent for her home, and when he vnder stoode that shee was corrupted by *Atys*, he caused both him, and her nurse to be killed, whereuppon she fell starke mad with sorow, and loue of her *Atys*, and ranne out of her fathers house, wandring about the country with a tabber, & pipe, and her haire about her eares, vntill shee died. And within a while after, it chanced, that all *Phrigia*, being greatly afflicted with famine and pestilence, the oracle commaunded the *Phrigians*, for remedie thereof, to worship *Atys*, and *Cibele*: which they did first vppon the hill called *Berecinthius*, where vppon shee was called *Berecinthia*: and after vppon mount *Ida*, and therefore shee was called *Idea*, and out of an erronius conceit of the people, that shee was mother to *Iupiter*, *Iuno*, *Neptune*, and *Pluto*, shee was called at length the mother of the gods. This mad gadding goddesse, was as madly serued, by as mad ministers as her selfe: for her priests (who because they vsed to drinke of the riuer *Gallus* in Phrigia, were called *Galli*) became phrentick, and madd, as oft as they dronke thereof: and with kniues, cut their owne faces, and other partes of their bodies, running vpp, and downe, and biting one, an other in honour of their goddesse, to expresse both her madnes, and their owne. But to declare how shee came to be honored of the *Romans*, it is to be vnderstood, that manie yeares, after that she was thus deified, and adored in *Phrigia*, it chaunced in the second warr of *Carthage*, that the *Decemuiri* of the *Romans*, found a prophesy in the bookes of the *Sibils*, which (as it seemed to them) promised the *Romans* great victories, and expulsion of their enimyes out of *Italy*, in case they procured that the mother of the gods should be brought to *Rome* from *Phrigia*: whereuppon Embassadors were sent to demande it of king *Attalus*, who then raigned there, and they were commaunded by the way, to passe by the oracle of *Delphos*, to enquire what hope they might haue of good speede: the oracle tould them, that they should obtaine their demaunde, and admonished them, to haue a speciall care, that the most vertuous man in all the citty of *Rome*, should be sent to meete, and receiue her. The Embassadours went from *Delphos* to *Phrigia*, and easelie obtained their request of *Attalus*, who directed them to the mountaine of *Ida*, where

Diodorus Sicul. li. 4. Bibliotheca. Vide Ludouic. viuem. Comment. in li. 1. de ciuit. Dei. ca. 4

Liuius dec. 3. li. 9.

this great goddesse had her habitation. And there no doubt they expe- cted to find some great matter, or rather some great maiestie in the mother of the gods, who they vnderstood should driue their enimies out of *Italy*, and repair their wracked common-welth, yea and should not be receiued, or entertained by any other, but by the verie best man in the citty of *Rome*.

18 But when they came thither, they found nothing els, but a huge great stone, called in that country the mother of the gods, which they tooke vp with great honour, and reuerence, and carried to *Rome*, aduertising first the Senat of their returne, where vppon *Scipio Nasica*. (who was esteemed at that time the most vertuous man in the citty) and all the matrons of *Rome*, were sent to receiue this great stone goddesse, in the name of the senate, and of the people: which was performed the twelfth of Aprill, with verie great pompe, and solemnity, in the consulat of *Scipio Africanus*, and *Publius Licinius*: and thirteene yeares after, *Iunius Brutus* dedicated a temple to her, and instituted the playes called *Megalesia*, in honour of that dedication, which playes were such, as they must needes haue irritated the gods to the destruction of *Romans* if they had not bene all as stony, stupide, and senselesse, as their mother, for not only the players vsed all kind of reprochfull tants, and iestes, towards *Berecinthia*, and her louer *Atis*, but also all the streets, and euerie house in *Rome*, during those feastes sounded fotrh nothing els but their shame, and infamie: besides that the most honest, and ciuill citizens of *Rome*, vsed all that time, to goe desguised from house, to house, and to speake most dishonestly, and filthily, all that they could deuise. *Herodian. in Comodo.*

19 Therefore to conclude this story, what could be either more ridiculous, or more impious in the *Romans*, and their religion, then to deifie, whome they diffamed, and dishonoured, and to defame, and dishonour those, whome they deified? The like also may be said of their other stage playes, whereof we haue sufficient examples in *Terence*, and *Plautus*, wherein their gods are described to be theeues, rauishers of women, adulterers, and most wicked men, which is so notorious to euerie boy in grammer schooles, that I shall not neede to saie any more thereof in this place. Neither yet doe I thinke good to speake of their most impure, and beastly ceremonies in their feastes, called *Saturnalia*, dedicated to *Saturne*, and *Fugalia*, instituted in the honour of the goddesse of mirth, which (as S. *Augustin* saith) might truly be called *Fugalia pudoris & honestatis, driuers avvay of honestie, and shamefastnes*. And no lesse beastlie were their *Floralia*, whereof I haue said some what before: and their feastes

S. Aug. li. 2. de Ciuit. Dei ca. 6.

Num. 9.

feastes dedicated to *Liber*, or *Bacchus*, of which there were two sortes: the one called *Bacchanalia*, celebrated at the first onlie by women in the day time, who hauing tipled well vntill they were dronke, ranne vpp and downe, as though they had bene surprised with some deuine fury: but afterwards men also concurred in the celebration of the feast in the night, vntill at length, such horrible impietie was practised therein, of adulteries, incest, sodomie, witchcrafts, murders, subornation of false witnesses, and diuers other mischeefes, that, the same being discouered by a Spanish woman, there were seuen thousand men, and women, either put to death, or banished, or forced to flee, and the *Bacchanalia* vtterly abolished.

Liuius. Dec. 4. li. 9.

Ibidem.

20 But the other sort of *Bacchus* feastes, called *Sacra liberi patris, the feasts of the father liber,* were neuer suppressed, though they were replenished with all kind of beastlie impuritie: and celebrated, not in secret, or priuat houses, but publikelie in townes, and abroad in the country in the high wayes, for a whole moneth together: wherein such filthie, & lasciuious spectacles were represented, & such beastlie ceremonies practised, that I am ashamed to thinke thereof, and much more should be to relate the particulars, which could not but incense, & kindle in the behoulders, vnquencheable flames of lust: though neuertheles, the most chast matrons were manie times compelled to plaie their partes therein, and as *S. Augustin* saith, *to doe that in publike, vvhich common queanes, should not be suffred to doe in the presence of matrons.*

Augustin. de ciuit. Dei. li. 7. ca. 21.

21 And therefore omitting to speake further, of the feastes, and ceremonies of that kind, I will conclude with their inhumane, horrible, and abominable rites, consisting in their bloodie ceremonies, and sacrifices of men, which *Seneca* reproued, and abhorred in them, saying: *Se ipsi in templis contrucidant, &c. They kill themselues in their temples, and pray to theyr gods, vvith their vvoundes, in such sort, that no man can make any doubt but that they vvere starke mad. And if there vvere but a fevv of them, it might be borne vvith all: but their best defence, or excuse from madnes, is their multitude of mad men.* Thus saith he. And *Arnobius* testifieth that the custome of sacrificinge men, was vsed amongst the *Romans*, euen to his time, saying that the *Romans* were then wont to sacrifice *Greekes*, and *Gaules*, of either nation a man, and woman: *Hodieque* saith he, *ab ipsis Latialis Iupiter homicidio colitur, &c. and euen at this day, Iupiter letialis is vvorshipped by them vvith the murther of men, and satiated vvith the blood of malefactors, vvhich is a sacrifice fitt for the sonne of Saturne.* Thus farr *Arnobius*. Whereby it is euident, that although such sacrifices of men, hauing alwayes before, bene most vsuall amongst the *Romans*, *Greekes*, *Cartha-*

Seneca, apud S. Aug. de ciuit. Dei. li. 6. c. 10.

Arnobius contra gentes.

Plinius li. 36. anno vrbis. 657. Sueton. in Auguſto Lactant. de falſa religio. li. 1. c. 21. Euſebius.

Carthaginenſes and *Gaules*, were firſt prohibited by a decree of the *Senate* about a hundred yeares beſore our Sauiour was borne, and afterwards againe, by an other decree of *Auguſtus Cæſar*: yet neuertheles they ceaſed not of a long time after, as it appeareth alſo by the teſtimony of *Lactantius*, and *Euſebius*: who witnes, that men were ſacrificed to *Iupiter Latialis* vntill the yeare of our lord 300. which was about the thirteenth yeare of the Emperour *Diocleſian*.

22 This ſhall ſuffice for their gods, and ſacrifices, though much more might be added, which I omitt for breuities ſake. And now to ſaie ſomewhat of the effects thereof, who can be ſo abſurde to thinke, that ſuch a religion could either be a true religion, or yet profitable to the common wealth, ſeeing it muſt needes breede in the profeſſours thereof, not onlie extreame corruption of manners, but alſo contempt of all religion, and verie Atheiſme? For firſt to ſpeake of the corruption of manners: who ſeeth not, that the more religious, and deuout the people ſhould be to ſuch wicked, and beaſtly gods as theſe, the more wicked, & beaſtly they ſhould become themſelues? Seing it is naturall to eueri one, to deſire and endeuour to imitate the deuine nature, which we truly acknowledge to be moſt happy, and moſt perfect: and cannot with any reaſon imagin any other way, or meanes, to attaine to perfect felicitie, and immortalitie, but by being like to almighty God, who is the fountaine of beatitude, and the true paterne of all perfection.

Geneſ. 3.

Iſay. 14.

23 And this the crafty ſerpent, and ancient enimie of mankind, knew ſo well, that he tooke an eſpeciall occaſion thereby, to perſwade our firſt father *Adam*, to tranſgreſſe the commaundements of God. *Eritis* (ſaith he) *ſicut dei: you ſhalbe as it vvere gods*. And by the ſame meanes alſo *Lucifer* himſelfe fell: *Aſcendam* (ſaith he) *& ſimilis ero altiſſimo: I vvil aſcend, and be like to the higheſt.* Therefore it is no meruaile, if euery one deſireth to be like the God, he adoreth, and ſerueth: ſeing it cannot be thought, that there is any euill, or imperfection at all in the deuine nature, or that God doth any thing either vniuſtly, or vnaduiſedly. Which *Lucian*, an Atheiſtical pagan, noteth verie well of ſuch as profeſſed paganiſme in his time, alleaging himſelfe for example, ſaying, that when he was a boy, and heard out of *Homer*, and *Heſiodus*, not onlie the ſeditions, and warres of the gods, but alſo their rapes, adulteries, and thefts: he beganne euen then to be greatly affected towards thoſe vices, perſwading himſelfe, that if they had bene euill, the gods would neuer haue vſed them, as I haue declared in *Lucians* owne wordes, in my firſt part, vppon the occaſion of an abſurd law of *Ariſtotle*.

Lucian in Menippo.

Chap. 8. nu. 26. Aug. de ciuit. li. 2. cap. 27.

24 Therefore *S. Auguſtin*, ſpeaking of thoſe gods of the *Romans*, and of the

of the effect that their exāple must needs woorke in the cōmon welth, saith, *Hæc ignominiosa deorū facta &c. These ignominious acts of the Gods whether* they were *shamefullie, & wickedly fained, or more shamefullie, & wickedly committed, were publikelie represented to the eies, & eares of the people, who seeing such things to be pleasing to the Gods, & cōmitted by them, easilie beleeued that they might both be offred to their seruice, and also imitated.* Thus saith he.

25 Furthermore this religion of the *Romans*, did not onlie seeme to promise to the professors thereof, a similitud, or likenes of God, but also diuinitie it selfe, by the meanes of vice, for what els could the common people conceiue, but that diuinitie was the due reward of vice & wickednes, seeing that most wicked men, & women, (namelie *Saturne, Iupiter, Mars, Bacchus, Hercules, Romulus, Tiberinus, Venus, Laurentia, Flora*, & such other, (as had benne tyrannts, adulterers, theeues, common queanes, & strumpets) were honored as Gods & goddesses, whiles on the other side *Coriolanus, Camillus, Scipio, Cato, Brutus*, & other *Romans*, famous for their vertue, were neither Deified after their deaths, nor yet could whiles they liued, long continue in the grace, and fauour of the people, but were some of them banished, others otherwaise disgraced, & some of them forced to bereaue them selues of their liues; yf then a good, & vertuous life, might seeme to merit deification, who woold not think that these vertuous men, had better deserued to be made Gods, then those notable villaines, whose filthie & beastlie sacrifices, & detestable feasts, gaue sufficient testimonie (euen to the most ignorant) of their turpitude, and impietie? who then was imbued with paganisme, and had not reason, rather to make choise to satisfie his lust, and loose the bridle to all vice, with *Iupiter, Iuno, Venus*, and the rest of those gods, and so hope in the end to be, made a god; then to liue vertuouslie with *Camillus, Scipio, Cato*, and other such, and reape no other benefit, therebie in the end, but danger, at least of banishement, or disgrace?

26 Moreouer, was not the dedication, and deification of the vices, and sinnes them selues, a wonderfull prouocation to vice, and sinne? Especiallie seeing that the corruption of humane nature ys such, that yt doth not commonly so much seeke a iust cause to sinne (which yt can neuer haue) as some apparant pretence thereof, couered with some cloake of vertue. And what better colour could anie man haue to commit notable villanies, then not onlie to doe gratefull seruice to some god, or other, but also to doe a deuine act, I meane some sinne, that was held to be a god? Who would trouble himselfe, to restraine his lust, and concupiscence; to bridle his affections, and to conquer

his passions, and to haue no god for his patron, when by satisfying his lust, and taking his pleasure, he might hope tohaue the protection of two goddesses, *Volupia*, and *Libentina?* for by those names were pleasure, and lust deified, as I haue signified before. Could any man haue a better pretence, or a greater occasion to sinne, then to serue these goddesses, to be like them, to be gratefull to them, yea, and to doe an act that was reputed to be deuine? Where vppon it must needes follow, that the more religious those were, who professed that religion, the more impious, and wicked they were, and that the common wealth, according to their religion, was then most religious, when it flowed with all intemperance, vice, and wickednes.

27 But here perhaps you will demaunde of me, whether the *Romans* were in deede so vicious, and wicked, as I presume by their religion they were, specially seeing that S. *Augustin*, greatly commendeth them for their vertue, and thinketh that in respect thereof, God gaue them the empire of the world. Whereto I answer, that although some of them did now, and then some notable acts of morall vertue, yea, and that a kind of ciuill iustice, florished in their common welth (for the which S. *Augustin* affirmeth that God rewarded them with temporall dominion, as I haue signified in the first part of this treatise) neuertheles it cannot be denied, but that they were generally most wicked, as may appeare by the testimony of *Cicero*, who pitifully lamenteth the vtter decay of vertue, and the generall corruption of manners in his dayes, imputing thereto, the fall, and ouerthrow of their common welth. *Nostris vitiis* saith he, *non casu aliquo remp. verbo retinemus, reipsa vero iampridem amisimus. VVe retaine our common welth only in name, and haue long since lost it in deede by our vices, and not by any casualty, or chaunce. Salust* also confesseth the same, complaininge exceedingly of the coueteousnes, riot, cruelty, discord, and all kind of wickednes in his tyme. And although he seeme to attribute it in some part, to the ouerthrow of *Carthage*, (the feare whereof, while it stood, was, as he thought, some bridle vnto them) yet it is manifest inough, by their owne histories, that before that time, they were generally most wicked, as may appeare by the feastes called *Bacchanalia*, suppressed at length for the abominable impiety which was excercised therein, by an incredible number of men, and women: insomuch that aboue seauen thousand, were executed or banished for the same, in the yeare 568. after the foundation of *Rome*, as I haue declared before: And this happened, forty yeares before the destruction of *Carthage*, which was razed in the yeare 608.

D. August. de ciuit. dei. li. 5. c. 15.

Cicero apud Aug. de ciuit. dei. lib. 2. cap 21.

Salust. apud D. August. ibidem. ca. 18

Liuius Dec. 4. li. 9

Num. 19.

28 And againe, aboue one hundred yeares before the prohibition of the

the *Bacchanalia*,there was diſcouered a horrible conſpiracy,amongſt the
very matrons of *Rome*, to poiſon the cittie, for the which three hun- *Liuius Dec. 1.li.8.*
dred,and ſeauenty of them, were executed, after they had poiſoned a *Eutrop. li. 2.*
great number of men of all ſorts, and qualities;Whereby it may eaſely
be gathered, how maligne,and impious the people were generally at
thoſe daies,ſeeing that the feminine ſex,naturally endued with modeſty, mildnes,pitty, and compaſſion, was ſeazed with this furious, and
extrauagant impiety,cruelty, and thirſt of humane blood,without any
other cauſe, then the malignity of their owne natures. And this paſſed, whiles the *Romans* were held to be moſt vertuous, to wit, in the
yeare, after the foundation of *Rome*, long before they had extended
theyr dominion out of *Italy*. Beſides that, if we conſider the tyranni- *An.vrb.423*
call oppreſſion of the people by the nobility,preſently after the expul-
ſion of the kinges,the continual ſeditions, where with the common
wealth was perpetually garboiled,from that tyme,vnto the Monarchy
of *Auguſtus Cæſar*, their deteſtable ingratitude towards the worthieſt
patrons,protectors,and propagators of their common welth, as *Corio-*
lanus Camillus, both the *Scipij*, *Cicero*, and diuers others, and finally the *Plutarc. in their liues.*
inſatiable ambition,and horrible cruelty, of diuerſe of their gouuer-
nours,namely of the *Decemuiri*, *Appius Clodius*,and his fellowes,of *Ma-*
rius, *Sylla*, *Carbo*, *Cinna*,and laſtly of the *Triumuiri* (of all which I omitt to *Liuius Dec. 1. li. 3.*
relate the particularities here, becauſe I shall doe it heareafter at lar-
ge,vppon an other occaſion) if,I ſay,we conſider all this, we shall eui- *Chap. 12.*
dently ſee,that all kind of wickednes reigned amongſt them in the hi- *ſub fin.*
gheſt degree, from the very beginninge of their common welth. So
that though they excelled other nations in ſome vertues, pertaininge
to the gouernement of their ſtate,and eſpecially in a kind of ciuill iuſtice,and exact military diſcipline, yet they were otherwiſe moſt vicious,and wicked: whereby yt well appeared that the politicall vertues,wherein they ſurpaſſed other people,were no true vertues, proceeding of no other ground,but of vaine glory,and an extreame deſire
of honour, ioined with a great loue to their common welth, as I shall *Chap. 13*
haue occaſion to ſignify farther hereafter. *nu.5.*

29 In the meane tyme thou ſeeſt good reader, that I haue euidently
proued in this chapter, twoo thinges: the one that their religion was
ſo abominable,that the practiſe of it could not but make them moſt
corrupt,vicious,and wicked:& the other, that the ſame was manifeſt
in them by the effect,to wit,by their notorious corruption of manners
vice,and all kind of iniquity: which will yet be much more euident,
when I shal haue proued that their religiõ cold not but produce alſo in

them meere Atheisme (that is to say, contempt of God, and of all religion) and consequently redouble their wickednes, and impiety.

30 But because this chapter ys alreadie growne long, I will remit the discourse thereof to the next, wherin I will first discouer the superstitious vaintie and absurdity of their diuinations (which were also a part of their religion) and then will shew how pernitious the same were to their state, and lastlie I will treat of Atheisme, and proue that the same must needes growe of their religion, to the inestimable dommage of their common welth.

That the profession of the Augurs, and Southsaiers amongst the Romans, and all their manner of diuination, was friuolous, vaine, and most pernitious to their common welth: Also that their religion could not but breede Atheisme in verie manie of the professors of yt, and was also in that respect, contrarie to reason of state: to which purpose yt ys declared, how Atheisme destroieth common welth.

CHAP. 8.

1 AMongst the ridiculous toies, and superstitious vanities belonging to the religion of the *Romans*, none was ether more friuolous, or preiudiciall to their state, then their southsaying, or maner of diuination, to know future euents by the flight of eagles, by the voice of birdes, by the feeding of certaine chickens, which were kept in cages, by the falling of thunderbolts, by shooting of starres, by looking vppon the intrailes of the beastes which they sacrificed, and by diuers other foolish obseruations, reduced to an art, or science, professed by those that were called *Augures*, and *Aruspices*: of whom the latter made their coniecture by the entrailes of beastes, by thunder bolts, and by all kynd of strange and prodigious euents, and the former, to wit, the *Augurs*, deuined by birdes.

And to these diuiners, there was such respect borne, and so much credit giuen, that all the cheefe actions in the common welth, depended vpon their resolution: in so much, that nothing of moment was resolued, or executed, but they were first consulted with. For when the Consuls, or other officers were to be choosen, or the magistrates to goe to their prouinces, and charges, or warre to be denounced, or peace made, or a battaile fought, or anie such important matter to be executed: if then the *Augurs*, or Southsaiers, opposed them selues, vppon pretence, that either the chickens would not eate, or that some crow had not fauourablie chanted, or that some thunderbolt had not fallen aright, or perhaps (as once it fell out) some mouse had gnawed the gold of the temple, or finallie that some strange, or vncouch matter had hapned: then, I say, neither the election of officers was held for good, nor the gouernours were to goe to their prouinces, nor the magistrates to vndertake their charges, nor warr to be denounced, nor peace to be made, nor yet battaile to be giuen, though the enemie were neuer so weake.

2 Here vppon *Cicero* saith, *that the authoritie, and power of the Augurs,* was such, that they *could ratifie or annullat the election of the highest officers, dimisse, or dissolue assemblies, depriue magistrats of their offices, ordaine, or forbid the senat to treat with the people, yea, and that, nihil domi, nihil foris, per magistratum gestum &c. nothing was done by anie magistrate, at home, or abroad, which could be ratified without their authoritie.* And hereof the experience was seene manie times. As when the frist tribunes of the souldiers were chosen, to witt, *Aulus Sempronius Atratinus, Lucius Atilius,* and *T. Cæcilius,* theie were by the decree of the *Augurs*, forced within a while to renounce their office. The like also happened to the two consuls *Scipio,* and *Figulus,* and to omit diuers other examples, which might be alleged in this kind. *P. Claudius* the consul was condemned, and executed, be cause he went to sea contrarie to the opinion, and resolution of the southsaiers; insomuch, that *Lucius Iunius* his companion, aswell in office, as in his nauigation, killed himselfe, to auoid the ignominie of like punishment.

Cicero de leg. li. 2.

Liuius Dec. 1. lib. 4.

Cicero de diuinatio. li. 2.

Valer. maxi. li. 1. c 4.

3 But who seeth not the absurditie of this? For, if there were any force, or power in byrdes, beastes, or senseles thinges to foreshow, and pronosticate the vncertaine euent of mens actions, it must needes be said, that the same proceeded, either of some natural propertie in them, or of some deuine institution, and operation aboue nature. But that this cannot be ascribed to any naturall cause, it is euident inough; seeing that those, who were most addicted to these diuinatiõs, found so litle probabilitie, or ground of naturall reason, to maintaine the reputation thereof, that they referred them whollie to a deuine operation. In which respect, there was emongst the *Romans* a solemne priesthood, and colledge of *Augurs,* who were called. *Iouis optimi maximi sacerdotes interpretes & internuncij: The priestes, interpreters, and messengers of the greatest, and best God Iupiter,* and *Diuorum Augures*, the *Augurs of the gods:* who, as *Seneca* testifieth, taught that the birds were moued by a deuine instinct to foreshew, good, or bad successe: and that the thunderbolts were cast out of the cloudes by a speciall prouidence, and disposition of the gods, to signifie future euents, good, or bad. But how ridiculous this their opinion, and doctrin was, it may appeare diuers waies.

Seneca natural. q li. 2. 45. & 46.

4 First by the fabulous origen, and begining thereof which *Cicero* re-counteth, according to the opinion, and tradition, of the greatest, and

Cicero li. 2. de diuinatione.

ancientests deuines, to wit, the *Hetrusci* or *Tuscans*, who deriued it from one called *Tages*, who they say was plowed vp out of a furrow by chaunce, as one was tilling, and plowing the ground in *Hetruria*. And this *Tages*, say they, being like a child in bignes, and shape, but like an ould man for witt, and iudgement, taught all the art of diuination, or southsaying to the people of that countrie, whereat *Cicero*, scoffeth in good earnest, and with great reason.

5 But what beginninge soeuer it had (which was most like to be some illusion of wicked spirits) the very maner of their diuination, sufficientlie bewraieth the vanitie thereof, seeing that (to omit many other impertinent toies,) they kept alwaies, chickens in a cage, and when they would know the successe, or euent of any thing, they let them out, and gaue them certaine liquide sopps to feede on, and if they refused to eate, it was taken for an ill signe, and if they fled away, it was much worse, but if they did eate greedilie, it was held for a very good pronostication, and specially if any of the sopps fell out of their mouthes vppon the ground, which was called, *tripudium solistimum*, and counted for the best, and most fortunat presage, that might be.

Idem ibid. li. 1. & 2.

6 But who seeth not the foolerie of this? For what wonder was it to see hungry chickens, eate hungerly, or that some part of the liquid sopps, fell from their mouthes vppon the ground, when they tooke more then they could swallow at once, as commonly they would doe, when they were hungry? Where vppon it must needes follow, that the diuination could not but be very good, if it were taken, when the chickens were fasting, and therefore *Flaminius*, answered well to the *Augurs*, when they forbad him to fight with *Hannibal*, because the chickens would not eate: then (saith he) I see well wee must fight only when they are hungry, and not when they are full.

Idem li. 1. de diuinatione.

7 The like folly *Seneca* noteth in their obseruation of thunderbolts, whereof they said, there were three kindes: The first of those which *Iupiter* cast alone, and those were taken for very good signes: the second were such as he cast with the counsell of twelue gods, and those were very ominous and vnfortunate: and the third were those, which certaine superiour gods cast downe of their owne accord, and that kind of thunderbolt was held to be most pernicious, and to portend some greater desaster, where vppon Seneca saith, *quid tam imperitum est* &c. *what is so foolish as to beleeue, that Iupiter, some tyme with his thunderbolt striketh trees, pillers, yea, and his owne images, and leaueth wicked men vntouched: or that he hath not witt, or iudgment inough, to cast his boults himselfe, but that he must haue the aduise of other gods: or els that those thunderbolts should*

Seneca, natural. quaestio. li. 2. c. 42 & 43.

should be counted fortunate, which he casteth alone, and those desastrous and vnlucky which he casteth with counsell, and aduise? Thus saith *Seneca.* Who neuertheles, though he reiect this kind of diuination, referring it only to the inuention and deuise of men, yet draweth out of it, a notable morall lesson for princes, whom he admonisheth by the example of *Iupiter*, to doe good alwayes by themselues alone, and whensoeuer they are to hurt any, to take the aduise of many, *Hoc discant reges*, saith he. *Let kinges learne this, that Iupiters owne iudgement suffiseth not, when he is to strike any thing with his thunderbolt.* Thus saith he drawing like the good bee, the holesome hony of a good document, out of the venemous herbe of vaine superstition. But to proceede. *Ibidem.*

8 The contrariety & repugnance of their diuinations, sheweth also euidently that there was no deuine operation in them, but that they were most fond, and friuolous: For whereas the *Greekes*, and other nations, had their *Augurs*, and Southsaiers, aswell as the *Romans*, their manner of diuination, was farr different, and many times very contrary, as *Cicero* declareth. The *Romans* held, that the thunderbolts which fell on the leaft hand were the best, where as other nations, accounted the same for the worst, and most vnfortunate, esteenning those to be the best, which fell on the right side: And the very same difference, and contrariety of opinions, may also be obserued amongst them, concerning the flying, and chaunting of birds: and what meruaile? Seeing that many times in some one consultation, the pronostications were cleane repugnāt, one to an other, as when twoo beasts were sacrificed at once, or one after an other, the entrails of the one, were very faire promising great good, & the other very foule, threatning great euill. As it fell out before the conflict, wherein the famous. *M. Marcellus* was slaine, & *Crispinus* his felow consul mortally wounded, by the souldiars of *Hannibal.* In the warr also, which the cōsul *Lucius Papirius* made with the *Samnits*, it hapned that the chickens would not eate (which signified that he should not fight) and yet at the same time a crow gaue a signe of battaile. *Cicero li. 2. de diuinat.* *Idem ibid.* *Liui. Dec. 1. lib. 10.*

9 But what neede I alleadge other reasons to proue the vanity of deuinations, seeing that experience did sufficiently shew by the vntruth thereof, that they were either alltogether casuall, or els that they proceeded from the father of lies, as it appeared in the foresaid warr, which *Papirius* had with the *Samnits*, wherein the *Augure* being consulted concerning the issue of the battaile, belied his chickens, denouncing vnto *Papirius*, *tripudium solistimum* (that is to say, telling him that the chickens had eaten so greedily, that the sopps fell out of their mouthes which

Liui. li. 1. Dec. 1. which was counted the best signe that might be.) when neuertheles they had eaten nothing at all, & yet *Papirius*, giuing battaile had a notable victory. And king *Deiotarus*, who, as *Cicero* testifieth, would doe nothing without the consent, & counsell of the Augurs, had all the fauourable presages, that could be wished, when he went to assist *Pompey* in the ciuil warres, as also *Pompey* himselfe, was assured of the victory by all the *Augurs*, & Southsaiers of *Rome*, & yet they were both ouerthrowne, & *Deiotarus* lost his kingdone, & afterwards *Pompey* his life.

Cicero de diuinat. li. 2.

10 Also a principall Southsayer, pronosticated to *Iulius Cæsar* very ill successe if he passed into *Africk* before winter, which neuertheles he did with very good fortune to himselfe, & great dommage to his enemies. And before the famous bataile at *Cannæ*, betwixt *Hannibal*, and the *Romans*, the Southsaiers promised victory to *Paulus Æmilius* the consul, who neuertheles lost his life, & almost all his army, with the greatest disgrace, and detriment to the common welth, that the *Romans* euer receiued. And *M. Attilius Regulus*, not with standinge the fauourable predictions of the Southsaiers, & *Augurs*, was ouerthrowne, taken prisoner, cruelly tormented, & murdred by the *Carthaginians*. Finally many other examples may be alleadged, to shew that many times the deuinations of the *Augurs* & Southsaiers, either had no successe, or els fell out cleane contrary to their predictions: so that it may wel be said, that when they proued true, it was either by chance, or els because almighty God for a iust punishment of the superstition of the *Romans*, suffered them to be deluded by the deuill, who being author of these deuinations, did sometimes, for continuance, & encrease of their authority, more cunningly insinuat himselfe into them: foreshewing such presages, as might be verified, with the euents, wich he foresaw, were most like to follow: whereby he drew them also very oft, into great calamities, as may appeare by the examples alleadged. And as for the meanes how the deuill may foresee, or know thinges to come, I haue sufficiently declared them, in the first part of this treatise.

Idem ibid.

Arnob. contra gentes.

Idem. ibid.

Chap. 36. nu. 8.

11 This then being so, let vs consider alitle what benefit the common welth of the *Romans*, might reape by these deuinations. Can any man with reason imagin, that it could be profitable, or conuenient to their state, that their most important consultations, and affaires of peace and warre, should depend, not vppon the mature counseil, and deliberation of wise men, and oportunities of tyme, and place, but vppon such vaine toyes, and trifles, as these were, and vppon meere chance? For seeing there was not any deuine operation in these pronostications (as it is euident) what else may be

be imagined therein, but either casualitie, and chance, for the most parte, or els otherwhiles some diabolicall illusion, as I haue said, which could neuer tend to anie good, but to miserie, ruine, and destruction in the end? And therefore trulie, if we consider how seriouslie foolish, or rather how solemlie mad, the wise *Romans*, and *Greekes* were, to gouerne their greatest affaires by thinges so vncertaine, and casual, we cannot but see, and acknowledge, how weake, and vaine al humane wit, and vnderstanding is, without the light of Gods grace: especiallie, seeing that the wiser sort, aswell of the *Romans*, as *Greekes*, saw the vanitie of those diuinations, and yet thought them conuenient to be continued in their common welths.

Cicero and *Seneca* reiected, and derided them, as you haue heard, and the Philosophers *Xenophanes*, *Dicaarchus*, *Cratippus*, and *Panatius* (as *Cicero* testifieth) did the like: and the wise *Cato* was wont to say, he meruelled that two Southsaiers, did not laugh one vppon an other, whẽ they mett, to thinke how they cosened the world. Therfore would a man thinke it possible, that anie of these should thinke it necessarie for the common welth, to retaine the vse of these diuinations, which they held to be so ridiculous? Neuertheles *Cicero*, after he had sheewed the vanitie of them, by many notable arguments, concludeth, that, *ad magnas tamen reip. vtilitates, retinendum ius augurum, & collegij autoritas: yet in respect of the great profit of the common vvelth, the right, and povver of the Augurs, and the authority of theyr colledge, is to be maintained.* and in his lawes he ordayneth thus. *Auguribus qui non paruerit, capitale esto. He vvhich doth not obey the Augurs, let him be punished vvith death.* And therefore speaking also of the consul *P. Claudius*, who was condemned, and executed, because he disobeyed the *Augurs*, he saith. *Parendum fuit religioni, nec patrius mos tam pertinaciter repudiandus. He should haue obeyed religion, neither vvas the custome of his contrie to be so obstinatlie refused.* Thus saith he.

Cicero lib. 1. de diuinat.

Idem l. 2. de diuinat.

Li. 2. de leg.

Idem de diuinat. li. 2.

But what trow you might be the great profit, and publik commodityes for the which *Cicero*, and the rest of the *Romans*, thought the vse of these diuinations necessarie? Marrie forsooth, because they were perswaded, that it might redound to the preiudice, and discredit of all their religion, yf this custome (which had bene religiouslie, and generallie obserued for so manie hundreths of yeares) should be abrogated. Which reason might haue bene of some consideration, if these graue wise men had not thought, and knowne, that the same was altogether vaine, superstitious, and consequentlie irreligious. Yea, but say you these men perhaps were Atheists, and beleeued that there was no God, and therefore holding that religion was necessarie for the common welth, only for reason of state, they had reason to permit and tolerate some such vanities, as were crept in to their religion, and generallie receiued, rather then to abolish them, with the disgrace of their whole religion. Whereto I answer that albeit this reason might passe amongst Atheists in some cases, (as when the permission of such vanities could not draw with it anie great detriment, or inconuenience to the state) yet in this case, their follie could not be excused: for that, retaininge as they did, all the vse, & practise of their faiyned religion, for the benefitt of their states, they permitted neuertheles, and vsed such thinges, as were contrarie to all reason of state, and pernitious to their common welth: as it was, to suffer their most weightie, and important matters to be gouerned, as I haue said, by chance, and, as it were, by dice-play, or drawing of cuts. seeing that the crying of a Crow, or the flying of an Eagle, or the falling of a thunderbolt, on the right side, or on the leaft, or the sacrificing of a beast, with faire, or foule entrails, or such other like thinges, where on the deuiners grounded their predictions, were no lesse casuall, euen in *Cicero* his owne opinion, then the chance of the dice, or of lots or of cuts, or such like.

13 Therefore when the *Romans* suffered their affaires to be guided by such casualties, they were as wiselie occupied, as a certein prince, who, as I haue heard, vsed for his sport, and recreation, to determine of the suits of his subiects, by playing at crosse, and pile, with his fauourits, to resolue which memorial should be graunted, and which denied: though to say trulie, the follie and fault of the *Romans*, was farr greater, then his, in respect that it redownded to the damage, not so much of perticuler persons, as of the whole common welth, and state: which was sett thereby, as a man may say, vpon six & seauen: wheras it is a knowne rule of state, and was punctuallie practised by *Tiberius Cæsar*, (as *Cornelias Tacitus* witnesseth) *Non omittere caput rerum nec se in casum dare. Not to omit the first occasions or oportunityes of things, nor to expose himselfe, or his actions to chance*, as I haue declared in the first part of his treatise, where I haue also largelie shewed how vnfit it is for a wise man, to leaue anie thing to chance, which may be assured by wisdome, and counsel.

Chap. 32. num. 11.

14 What reason then had *Cicero* to thinke, that it could be profitable to the common welth, that the election of magistrats, the resolution of peace, or warre, the giuinge of battaile, and the execution of other important designemēts, should depend vpon the casuall crying of a Crow, or the flight of an eagle, or such like? Had it bene anie profitt to the *Romā* common welth, that *Lucius Papirius*, of whom I haue spoken before being readye to giue battaile to the *Samnits*, and requested by his sonne to forbeare, because the chickens of the *Augurs* would not eate, had it, I say, bene

Liuius Dec. 1. li. 1.

bene good, or conuenient for the common welth, that he should haue forborne that battaile, wherein he slew aboue thirtie thousand enemies and tooke nintie seauen ensignes, and three thousand eight huudred & seauentie prisoners? Or had it bene good for *Cæsar*, to haue stayed his iourney to Africk all winter, as the Southsayer aduised him: whereby his enemies might haue ioyned all their forces, and strength, which he by his diligent passage preuented, to their ouerthrow, & his owne great honour, and benefit? Or was it anie profit to the common welth, that *Pompey* being most superstitious in obseruing the diuinations of *Augurs*, and Southsayers, was by their fauorable predictions, and promises of victory, encouraged, as I haue signified before, to giue battaile to *Cæsar*, by whom both he, and the common welth. were vtterlie ouerthrowne? Wherein we may well note the speciall prouidence of God, who out of his iustice permitted that this superstition of southsaying, and deuininge (wherewith the *Roman* commō welth, had bene so manie hundreth yeares infected) hould amongst manie othercauses, concurre to thevtter ruine thereof: and that *Pompey*, who superstitiouslie obserued all kind of diuinations, was ouercome, and ruined by *Cæsar*, who vtterlie despised, and contemned them. For so hatefull are those superstitious, vanities to almightie God, that he destroied the nations, which dwelt in the land of promise, partlie for the same, as he signified to his owne people in *Deuteronomy*, saing, *Quando ingressus fueris terram*, &c. *VVhen thou shalt be entred in to the lād, vvhich thy lord thy God vvill giue thee, bevvare that thou doest not follovv the abominations of those nations, and let there be none found in thee, vvho shall goe about to purge, or purifye his sonne, or daughter by fyre, or consult vvith Southsayers, or obserue dreames, or deuinations by byrds*&c. *for thy lord doth abhorre all these abominations, and vvill destroy all those nations for the same, at thy entrance.*

Cicero de diuinat. l. 2.

Idem Ibid.

Deut. 18.

15 Thus sayd almighty God to the children of *Israel*, signifying, how execrable all those kinds of deuinatiōs are in his sight: & therefore no meruaile, if the *Romans* paid some part of the penaltie thereof, euen by the meanes of the same, it being most conforme to the iustice of God, to punish sinners, by the sinnes whereby they offend him. So that we see, that the religion of the *Romans* also in this point of their deuinatiōs, was not onlie most hatefull to God, voyde of all verity, and full of superstitious vanities, and folly: but also most preiudiciall to their state.

16 Now it resteth, that I shew, how their religion also produced *Atheisme*, and consequentlie bred, in that respect, irreparable damage to their common welth. Therefore whereas it appeareth, by the discourse of the precedent chapter, that all the religion of the *Romans*, was not onlie vaine, friuilous, and ridiculous, but also absurd, and impious:

it is now further to be considered, that although in some of the simple sort of the common people, it wrought perhaps no other effect, then superstition, and corruption of manners (their simplicitie, and credulitie mouing them to the first, and the example of the vicious liues of their Gods, leading them to the latter) yet in the wiser and more considerat sort of men, it could not but breede an extreme contempt of their Gods, and auersion from all religion. Wherevppon grew those poetical fictions of the Warrs of the Gods, not amongst theim selues, (which *Homer* describeth at large) but also with men, and how they were wounded by them, as *Iuno* and *Pluto*, by *Hercules*: *Venus* and *Mars*, by *Diomedes*. Also here *Iupiter* transformed himselfe into a swan, into a bull, to a dragon, to a goulden shouwer, and to the shape of a man, to satisfie his lust with *Leda*, *Europa*, *Proserpina* (who was his owne daughter) *Danae*, and *Alcmena*, all which, & diuers others, he corrupted by such deuises, as the poets fained: who if they had not contemned both those Gods, and all their religion, neuer would, nor durst haue inuented, and published such things of them, and so reproched, & reuiled them in their poems, as not onlie the satirical and comical poets did, but also other of the grauest, as *Homer*, *Hesiodus* and *Euripides*. Wherevppon neuertheles it followed, that the common people turned the same to religion, or, as it may more truly be said, to a superstitious deuotion, conceiuing that they honored their Gods, by mocking and reuiling them. For whereas the simple people are wont to frame a conceit of other men, according to the simplicity of their owne good nature, and meaninge, and therefore cannot imagin, but that those, whom they admire for their wisdome, are also to be admired, and imitated for their vertue, and religion: it is no meruaile, though the common sort of painims referred to the honour of their Gods, all that which they vnderstood was written of them by the poets, who were held for the learnedst, and wisest men for manie yeares.

Homer. l. 20 Idem li. 5. & Pangassis apud Arnobium contra gentes l. 4.

17 Herevppon it grew, that *Timotheus* the musitian, singing the praises of *Minerua* at *Athens*, thought he praised and honoured her greatly, in saying that she was mad, furious, and out of her wits. And in like sort the plaies instituted in honour of the Gods, and to pacifie their wrath, were full of contumelious and opprobrious speeches against them (as I haue declared before): whereby it appeareth that the vanitie, and absurditie of paganisme, did breede in the wiser sort of men, nothing els but impiety, which became in time, the religion of the simple, in such sort, that scurrilitie was held for sanctitie, derision of the Gods, for deuotion, and their greatest contempt and dishonour, for their greatest honour, and seruice.

18 But

18 But what doe I speake of contempt of the gods, growing of paganisme, seeing it is manifest, that it bred in verie manie meere Atheisme. Which was well obserued by *Plutarck* in the *Egiptians*, whereby he also condemned at vnawares the religion both of the *Greekes* and the *Romans*, which he professed himselfe. The *Egiptians* (saith he) worshipping those beastes (to wit the Dogge, the Cat, the Oxe, the Ramme, the Storke, the Shornebud, the Crocodill, and other such like) did not onlie expose all religion to contempt, & derision, but also ingender in the minds of men, a certaine vehement opinion, which drew the simpler, and weaker sort of men to meere superstition, and droue the wiser headlong to beastly cogitations, & conceits full of impiety, and *Atheisme*. Thus saith he of the Religion of the *Egiptians*, and reprouing in an other place, the general and common superstition of those times, he saith, that, the ignorance, or want of true knowledge of God, meeting with a rude, and hard nature, engendreth therein impiety, and Atheisme: and falling into a more mild, and facile condition, as into a more fertill ground, breedeth superstition, and that thereof also springeth *Atheisme*, which not onlie taketh roote therein, but also excuseth, and defendeth it selfe there by: for that the ridiculous acts, affections, passions, and witchcrafts of the superstitious, moue many to thinke it better to beleeue, that there are no Gods, then such Gods, as take pleasure in such thinges. Had it not benne better, saith he, that the ould *Gaules*, should neuer haue had anie opinion, or conceit of God, then to thinke, as they did, that he was delighted with the slaughter and sacrifice of men? And had it not bene lesse hurtfull to the *Carthaginienses*, to haue receiued their lawes of *Diagoras*, and *Critias* (two notable Atheists) then of those who ordained that they should sacrifice their owne childrẽ to *Saturne*? Thus saith *Plutarke*, taxing the abuses, no lesse vsuall, and familiar to the *Romans* and *Greekes* (though he name them not) then to the *Gaules*, or other barbarous people: seeing their superstition (I meane of the *Greekes*, and *Romans*,) was most ridiculous, absurd, and impious, aswel for the inhumaine sacrifices of men, as other beastly, and abominable ceremonyes, as may appeare by that which I haue signified before, concerning the religion of the *Romans*, which neuertheles was farre more moderate in all kind of impiety, then that of the *Greekes*.

Plutarch. de superstition.

Chap. 7. nu. 21.

19 Therefore it is no meruaile, if an infinit number of *Athests*, did spring in time of *Paganisme*, out of these two fountaines, whereof *Plutarck* speaketh, to wit, ignorance of the true God, and the execrable superstition, of false, friuolous, and impious religion. Wherein it is to be noted, that I take Atheists, not only for those, who denie that there

is a God, but also for such, as denie the particuler prouidence of God in the affaires of men: who are no lesse to be counted Atheists, then the other. For he which houldeth that God is the first cause, and mouer of the heauens,& consequently of all thinges else:& yet doth not acknowledge him for his owne creator,cõseruator & Iudge,he may truly be called an Atheist,that is to say a man without a God:for though he beleeue that there is one beginning, and one first cause(that is to say,one author of nature, or one God) yet he beleeueth not in him, but graunteth a God to the heauens, and none to him selfe: confessing that there is one only God, but dening that he is his God, and so he is truly *a theos,* without a God,that is to say, an Atheist. Besides that, denying *the prouidence of God, and the communication af his grace, he denieth that vvhich is most proper to the deuine nature, and so consequntly denieth God,* as *Cicero* concludeth verie well in his booke *de natura Deorum.*

Cicero *de natur.Deorum li.* 1.

20 Thus then we see, what fruite the religion of the *Romans* must needes yeld, to wit, extreame corruption of manners, and meere *Atheisme*, and therefore now I will shew, how preiudiciall, and pernicious such a religion is to common welth, to the end, that we may know the tree by the fruite,the mother by the child,and the cause by the effect. And because corruption of manners springeth aswell from *Atheisme*, as from false religeon: I will first declare how *Atheisme* destroyeth common welth, and after speake of the other.

21 Is it possible, that the religion,which causeth the contempt of God, and *Atheisme*, should be good for common welth? No trulie. For if religion be necessary for the establishment of state,(as I haue proued,and all men confesse it to be) then the religion, which destroyeth religion, must needes be pernicious to state. Lawes are not onle conuenient, but also most necessarie, and profitable to common welth, yet the law that should ouerthrow both it selfe, and all other lawes, would also ouerthrow, and destroy common welth. For such a law, or religion might well be compared to a candle, fixed to some principall post of a house, which consuming it selfe, burneth the whole house in the end.

22 This will be euedent, if we consider what a one an *Atheist* is in a common welth, who hauing neither bridle of conscience, nor feare of God, hath commonlie no respect at all, either to his word, or to his promise, or to his oath,or to any lawes,humane,or deuine,whẽ he may with security, satisfie his owne desire, and pleasure: perswading himselfe, that the soule dieth with the body, and that consequentlie, it shall neither be rewarded, nor punished, for any thing donne in this life: as the holie Ghost signifieth notablie in the booke of wisdome, descri-

describing the opinion, & humour of *Atheists* in these wordes. Wicked *Sap. 2.*
men hauing bad thoughts, or cogitations say with in them selues, the »
time of our life is short and tedious, and there is no ease, or pleasure in »
the end of man, neither hath anie man bene knowne to haue returned »
from hell for we were borne, or created of nothing, and hereafter »
we shalbe, as though we had neuer bene borne: for our bodie shal »
be dead ashes, and our spirit shalbe dispersed like the thinne ayre. »
Therefore come, and let vs enioy the goods which we haue, and »
vse the creature without delay, as in our youth: let vs fill our selues »
with precious wine, and ointments, let vs not loose the flower of »
our time, let vs crowne our selues with roses before they wither, let »
there be no meadow, or pleasant field, which our riott shal not passe »
ouer. Let vs leaue euery where signes of our mirth, for this is our »
part, this is our lott. Let vs oppresse the poore iust man, let vs not »
spare the widow, nor the ancient man, nor beare respect to the »
hoarie haires of old age, let our strengh be the law of our iniu- »
stice, &c.

23 Thus saith the wise man, in the person of *Atheists*, and how trulie, it may appeare by the doctrine of *Epicurus*, and his disciple *Mecrodorus* (which I declared in my first part) who taught, that a wise man, should not bind himselfe to the obseruation of lawes, for respect of conscience, or feare of God, but onlie to auoid punishement: and that he should in all things preferr his priuate commoditie, and pleasure, before the publike good: wherevpon it followeth, that whereas *Atheisme* infecteth the common welth, there is no more ciuill societie amongst the parts, and members thereof, then amongst brute beastes. For whiles euerie one seeketh his owne priuate good, without respect of the publike, all become for the most part treacherous, & perfidious, one towards an other: whereby there is neither anie true friendshipp amongst them, nor care of couenant, or promise, nor respect of fidelity, nor regard of oath, nor consequently any common welth.

Plutar. cõtra Colatem. Epicureum.

24 And to the end, that this may the more euidentlie appeare, let vs consider the necessitie of oathes in cõmon welth: such being the weakenes, and imbecillitie of all humaine credit, that it needeth to be corroborated, & fortified in manie cases, with the authoritie of some thing, that is esteemed more firme & holie then it selfe. Herevppon the Apostle saith, that men vse to sweare, *per maiorem se*, by one that is greater then themselues, that is to say, by almightie God: for, the corruption of mans nature is such, and the secrets of his hart so alostruse and hidden, that in matter doubtful, one man seemeth not to de-

Hebr. 6.

ferue credit of an other, except God, the iust iudge, who feeth the harts of euerie one, and punisheth all falshood, be called to witnes, And therefore S. *Chrisostome* saith. *Iuramentum est fidei iussio, vbi mores fidem non habent. An oath is a suerty where mans manners haue no credit.* And this may also be confirmed by the frequent, and overcommon custome of swearing in common conuersation, wherein men acknowledge their owne want of credit, thinking that they cannot other wise be beleeued, except they sweare.

S. Chrysost. in alt. Apost. ca. 3. Ho. 9.

Domin. Soto de iust. & iure l. 8. quæst. 1. art. 5.

25 There fore *Dominicus Soto* doth teach with great reason, that if we had remained still in the state of innocency, there should haue bene no vse, or neede of oathes: which may allso appeare, by the custome that stil passeth amongst men, seeing that commonlie oathes are not exacted of such, as are knowne to be of sincere conscience, and entire credit. And the same, as *Soto* affirmeth, was allso exactly obserued in the law of nature: and *Plutarke* testifieth, that amongst the *Romans*, noble men were not put to their oaths, but onlie in steede of torment, as when they were suspected, and charged with some great delict, in which case, as bondemen, or slaues were tormented, so were they forced to purge themselues by oathe, whose bare affirmation was otherwise held to be of sufficient weight, and authority: whereby it appeareth, that the vse of oathes hath growne in common welth of the imbecillity of humane fidelity, or credit.

Idem ibid. artic. 10. Plutarch. in problemat. Roman. quæst. 44.

D, Tho 22. q. 89. ar. 1. Cor. Soto de iure & Iustit. l. 8. q. 1. ar. 1.

26 Further more the force of an oath is such, that it hath the authority of law, which the verie etimology of the latin word declareth: for (as *S. Thomas* geueth to vnderstand) *Iuramentum a iure dicitur.* An oath is so called (in latin) *of lavv*, because it was first introduced, or admitted as a law, and is with all holines, and reuerence to be vsed, and obserued, and therefore some of the ould lawmakers, vsed no other law to decide causes, and controuersies, but an oath, as *Plato* testifieth of *Radamanthus.*

Plato de leg. Dialog. 12.

27 And such is the authoritie, yea, & necessity of oathes, that they confirme, and perfit all lawes of nature, nations, and civil: for though the law of nature requireth that euery man obey his lawful prince, and defend his country, yet princes doe commõly bind their subiects therevnto by oath, to fortifie thereby their naturall obligation. And allthough the law of nations bind princes, aswell enemyes as freendes, to obserue leagues, confederacies, and couenants made amongst themselues, yet the same seemeth not to suffise, exeept it be cõfirmed by oath. Allso the ciuill law hath such neede, & vse thereof, that commonly it decideth no cause with out it, and holdeth it for the consummation, and end of suites, and controuersies, as the Apostle obserueth, saying: *Omnis controuersiæ finis ad*

Hebra. 6.

nis ad confirmationem est iuramentum. The end of euerie controuersie, for the confirmation thereof, is an oath.

28 Thus then we see, that *Atheists*, who contemne, and denie the authoritie of others doe ouerthrow common welth two waies: For first they take away that whereby law, (which *Plato* calleth the *Anchor and soule of the common vvelth*) is fortified, and confirmed: Secondly they destroy all humane fidelitie, and credit, which being of it selfe weake, and insufficient (as I haue declared) is strenghned, and as it were vpheoulden by the force and authoririe of oathes, so that if oathes were not in vse and force, common welth could not stand. For seeing that fidelitie, as *Cicero* saith, *is the foundation of Iustice*, and Iustice the nerues, as it were, and sinewes, which doe compact and vnite the political body in it selfe, it must needes follow, that, where there is no fidelity amongst men, there can be no iustice, and consequently no common welth, as I haue amply declared in my first part, treating of the fidelity that is necessary, aswel amongst the subiects themselues, as betwixt the prince, and them. Where I haue also shewed by manie examples, how seuerely almighty God punisheth perfidiousnes, and periurie in men; and therefore I thinke it needelesse to repeate the same in this place, and onlie wish to be noted, that the lawes of all countries, doe worthily ordaine verie rigorous punishment for periury, as most pernicious to common welth.

Plato 12. de leg.

Cicero de officijs li. 1.

Chap. 31. nu. 18. & sequ.

29 The *Aegiptians* punished it by death, and amongst the *Indians* the fingers, and toes of periured persons, were cut of. Amongst the *Romans* they were for a time cast down headlong from a rocke, and afterward it was ordeined that they should liue in coutinuall infamie, and shame, (which is worse then death) and therefore *Cicero* saith in his lawes: *Periurij pæna diuina, exitium: humana, dedecus. The diuine punishment for periurie, is destrution, the human is ignominie, or shame.* Which is also the ordinarie penaltie thereof at this time in all Christian countries.

Alexand. ab Alexandro dieb. genial.

30 Therefore no maruaile if *Atheists* (who reiect, and despise the sacred authoritie of oaths, and thereby supplant al humane fidelity,) were seuerelie punished amongst the Painimes, whensoeuer they were discouered, as may appeare in *Plutark*, testifiyng, that manie cities, and common welthes in *Greece*, made lawes against all *Epicurians*, who were held for notable *Atheists*. And *Plato* in his booke of lawes, teaching that there are two kind of Atheists, ordaineth seuere punishments for them deuiding the first kind into two sortes of men: the one of those, who though they held that there is no God at al, yet are so subtle, and craftie, that they dissemble their opinion, being neuertheles most wicked in life, and manners: whome he thinketh worthy not of one, but of

Plutarch.

Plato 11. de lege.

many deathes: The other sort of *Atheists*, is of those, who though they thinke there is no diuinitie, yea, and publikely speake and professe it, yet are of so good disposition by nature, that they liue well, and vertuously: and for such he ordaineth fiue yeares imprisonment, and if they amend not therewith, that then they shalbe punished with death. The second kind of *Atheists*, are such, as though they beleeue, there is a God, yet denie his prouidence here on earth, and for such he assigneth perpetuall imprisonment, in such sort, that no free man, may euer haue accesse vnto hem, ordaining also, that when they die, their bodies shalbe caried out of the confines of the countrie, and left vnburied.

31 Hereby we maie see, how odious *Atheists* were to the Painims, in times past, and that worthily: seing that, contemning God, as they doe, they disolue, and breake the bandes, not only of religion, but also of al humane lawes, when they can doe it with their commoditie, and securitie: Whereby they seeke (as much as in them lieth) to extirpate, and destroy al common welth, & therefore deserue to be held, for no other, then monsters of nature, & publicke enemies to mankind. For although some of them, being perhaps by nature enclined to vertue, are not altogether so pernitious to common welth, as those, whose *Atheisme* is accompanied with a vicious, & maligne inclination of nature, yet the best or rather the least euill of them, groweth in time most corrupt in manners, and consequeutly most pernicious to common welth.

32 For as *Atheisme* groweth of the extremitie of vice, (wherevppon
Pro. 18. the scripture saith, *Impius cum profundum venerit, contemnit. The vvicked man, vvhen he commeth to the depth of sinne, contemneth*) so also on the other side, extremitie of vice, and sinne, groweth of *Atheisme* (be the *Atheist* at the first, or of his owne nature, neuer so well disposed) for being giuen ouer by allmighty God, to a reprobate sense, he slideth from vice, to vice, and from sinne to sinne, vntill he fall headlong at last to the verie depth' and extremity of sinne, and therefore the psalmist saith of al *A-*
Psal. 13. *theists. Corrupti sunt, & abominabiles facti sunt in iniquitatibus. They are corrupted, and become abominable in al iniquity.*

33 Seeing then I haue alreadie declared how daungerous, and pestiferous *Atheisme* (on of the children of Paganisme) is to common welth, I will now shew the like effect, of the corruption of manners, being the issue and ofspringe of both, whereby it wil euedently appeare, that the religion of the *Romans*, being such; that it must needes fil their common welth with vice, could not but be most dammageable thereto.

That

That the corruption of manners, and the vice vvhich grevv of Paganisme could not but be very preiudiciall to the Roman common vvelth, to vvhich end, the necessitie of vertue for the conseruation of state, and the dammage that followveth of vice is declared, vvith diuers politicall obseruations, and rules out of Plato *to the same purpost: And to the end it may appeare, hovv the Roman common vvelth could stand, and encrease, to so great an empyre, as it did, vvith the exercise of that religion, it is signified, that as God out of his prouidence did conserue, and encrease their estate, to the end, that he might build his Church in tyme vppon the ruyns of their empyre: so also he punished the same most seuerely from tyme to tyme, for their impious religion, vvhich appeareth in this chapter, from the foundation of* Rome, *vntill the expulsion of their Kings.*

CHAP. IX.

1. THE dammage, and destruction, that vice bringeth to all states where it reigneth, wilbe the more euident. Yf we consider the nature, and condition of common welth, and the effects that vertue worketh therein. For seeing nothing is more requisite to common welth, then that the common & publike good be preferred before the priuate commodity of any one (which the verie name of *common vvelth* doth sufficientlie declare) & againe seeing vertue doth wholye tend to a common good, and vice, or wickednes to some priuat commoditie or pleasure, with the preiudice & damage of the weale publike it followeth necessarily, that nothing is more auailable to cōmon welth then vertue, nor anie thing more preiudiciall there to, then wickednes or vice: and therefore *Aristotle* teacheth, that the true reason of ciuill societie, or common welth, consisteth principallie, *in recte viuendi communione*, in the communion of those that liue well and vertuously, and that it was not onlie ordained: *vt simul homines viuant*, that men might lyue together, *sed vt honeste agant*, but also that they may doe vertuously. *Aristot. politic. lib. 1.*

2 This wilbe the more manifest, if we compare vertue, with vice, and consider them in men, as they are mēbers of the common welth. Therefore whereas all morall vertue, is reduced to foure heades, to wit, *Prudēce Iustice, Fortitude*, and *Temperance*: experience teacheth that the prudent, & wise man, is not onlie profitable to himselfe, but also to others, yea, and to the whole common welth: the iust man doing wrong to no man but giuinge to euery one his owne (wich is the office of Iustice) is beneficiall to all mē: the valiāt man defendeth not only himselfe, & his frinds, when occasiō serueth, but also his coūtry: the tēperate mā, being modest, meke, & peaceable towards al, & cōmaunding his owne passions in al occasiōs,

is gratefull to all men, and most sociable, & therefore most fitt for ciuill societie. So that, where all, or most men are wise & prudent, iust, valiant, and temperat, euerie one louing, comfortinge, & helping an other: there must needes be, the best, and most florishing common welth: but where on the contrary side, sinne, and wickednes reigneth in all, or most men, where, I say, magistrats, and subiects are generallie imprudent, vniust, cowardlie, auaricious, ambitious, ryotous, and lasciuious, euery one cosening, and deceyuing his neighbour, robbing, and spoiling, and seeking in all thinges his owne particular gayne, or pleasure, with the iniurie of others, there the common welth being most wicked, is with all most miserable, or rather no common welth at all.

3 Further more who knoweth not, that wickednes, & vice, is, as I may tearme it, an internall disease, or pestilence, which corrupting the common welth, doth consequently ouerthrow it, no lesse thē externall force? For euen as it may litle auaile vs to arme our selues from top to toe, to resist the attempts of our enemyes, or to decke, or trym our persons with rich Iewels, and sumptuous clothes, except we haue also care of our inward healths: so it litle helpeth anie cittie, or common welth, to be neuer so stronglie fortified against forraine force, and inuasion, or externallie beautified, and adorned with gorgeous buildings, tropheis, and triumphant arkes, if it be not also preserued from the inward sicknes of vice, and iniquitie: which the comicall poet expresseth elegantlie, speaking of a citty, which seemed to be verie strong, being, with all replenished with vice:

Plautus in Persa.

Si incolæ benè morati, pulchrum arbitror
Perfidia & peculatus ex vrbe, & auaritia si exulant,
Quarta inuidia, quinta ambitio, sexta obtrectatio,
Septimum periurium, octaua indiligentia,
Nona iniuria, decimum, quod pessimum ag gressis scelus.
Hæc nisi inde aberunt, centuplex murus rebus seruandis paruus est.

That is to say, if the people be well manered, and vertuous, if perfidiousnes, fraud, extortion, coueteousnes, enuy, ambition, detraction, periurie, idlenes, iniuries, and lastly if all kind of pernicious wickednes be banished out of the towne, or cittie, I thinke it notable well fortified, but otherwise, a hundred walls wilbe to litle to preserue it. Thus saith he.

4 For this cause, all those which haue eyther written of cōmō welth, or instituted anie, haue endeuored nothing more by their lawes, then to exclude from thence all kind of vice, and to shake away, and preuent all occasion thereof. Wherefore *Zaleucus* made a notable law, to forbid all companie, and fellowship with wicked men, which law I wish were in force,

Diodor. sicul. li. c.

force,and vre in Christian common welths: seenig experience teacheth, that vice is no lesse contagious then the plague, and that manie towardly men,and of vertuous disposition, are onlie with euill companie most pernicioussie corrupted: for, *Qui tetigerit picẽ,inquinabitur ab ea.* He which toucheth pitch,shalbe defiled with it.

5 For the same cause, *Aristotle* forbiddeth, in his written common welth,not onlie vnhonest and wanton talke,but also lasciuious pictures (as I haue declared before in the first part of this treatise):& to the same end,and purpose,lawes were ordained in times past in all good common welths,against other occasions of vice,and sinne,as against excesse in apparell,diett,playe,and al kind of delicacie, by which the gate is opened, and matter ministred to all wickednes, and as *Valerius* saith, verie Well: *Animi, & corporis vires expugnantur,The force,and strength,asvvell of body,as of mind,is beaten dovvne,in so much,* saith he,*that, it is hard to say, vvhether is more pernicious to the common vvelth,to be taken by the enimye, or to be possest by pleasure and delicacy.* And therefore King *Cyrus*,hauing with great difficultie, conquered the *Lidians*,who were a most warlike, and valiant people, drew them by litle and litle,from labour, and the excercise of armes, to ydlenes, sports, and pleasures, loose, and delicious life, and by that meanes, saith the storie: *That industrious, potent, and strong nation,grovving vvithin a vvhile effeminat,both in body,and mind,vtterly lost their old vertue,provvesse, and glorie.*

Aristot. li.7. politic.ca.17 *Chap. 8. num. 13.*

Valer. Max. lib.9.c.1.

Iustin.li. 1.

6 This was well considered by *Licurgus* the lawmaker of the *Lacedemonians*,who therefore prouided by his lawes, to take away the matter, & occasions of vice in his common welth:for he forbad all vse of gold and siluer, and equally deuided the landes of the countrie amongst the people, he prohibited bankets in priuat houses, prescribed the maner, and charges,of publike feastes: allowed to yonge men but one garment for the whole yeare,not permitting one to be better appareled thẽ an other, and ordaining that the youth of the cittie, should beat a certaine age transported in to the country,& there accustomed to continuall labour, and exercise,and to sleepe vpon the bare grounde, and not to returne in to the cittie,vntill they were men.

Idem li.1. & Plutar. in Licurgo.

7 These,and other such lawes, *Licurgus* ordained to the end,to shutt vp all the passage,and entrance to vice,& wickednes in the common welth of the *Lacedemonians*:and so long as they liued in that discipline,they florished no lesse in moral vertue,then in armes, and dominion ouer other partes of *Greece*:vntill at length,hauing ouercome,and spoiled the *Athenians*, they brought in to *Lacedemonia*, the delicacy of *Athens*, together with the riches,and welth thereof. For with the possession of riches,entred

Plutar. in Licurgo & Lisandro.

tred auarice, and couetcousnes: and of the vse thereof, grew ryot, and excesse, of auarice, followed vsurie, cosenage, and deceit, periurie, iniuries, rapine, all kind of iniustice, and lastly tumult, and sedition. Of riott, and excesse, followed droukennes, surfett, sicknes, diseases, idlenes, debt, pouerty, effeminate maners, and finallie all dissolution, and wickednes: whereby that notable common welth, fell to vtter ruine, & decay within few yeares.

8 The like may be obserued in *Liuij* of the *Campam*, a people in *Italy*, whose cheefe cittie was *Capua*, held for power, & magnificence, to be-

Liu. dec. 1. li. 7. ann. ab vrb. cōd. 412 equall with *Rome*, or *Carthage*, before the great warrs betwixt the *Romans*. and the *Samnits*. But such was the aboundant fertilitie of their territorie, and so great their owne delicacie, by the occasiō thereof that they grew in time, to be idle, & effeminate, & had neither power, nor courage to defend thēselues against the *Samnits*, their neighbours, in somuch, that they were faine, to giue thēselues, & their whole state to the *Romans*, vpō condicion, to defend them. And afterwards, when the *Roman* army, was sent

Ibid. an. 413. to *Capua*, to winter there, it was within a while so corrupted whith the pleasures, and delicacies of the cittie, and country, that it became indisciplinable, and fell to conspiracies, and rebellion. And againe afterwards

Idē dec. 3. li. 3. an. ab vr. cond. 539. when *Hannibal* possessed it in the the time of his warrs with the *Romans*, one winter in *Capua* weakened his armie, more thē all his former warrs. For as *Liui* saith, *Quos nulla mali vicerat vis, perdidere nimia bona, & voluptates immodicæ. Superfluity of wvelth, and immoderate pleasures, ouerthrevv them, vvhom no force of enimy, nor misery could ouercome*: in somuch that afterwards, *Hannibal* rather stood by the fame of his former victories, then by his present prowes. Thus saith *Liui*.

Valer. Max. li. 9. ca. 1. 9 But farr more shamefull, and miserable, was the calamitie, and fall of the *Volsinians* in *Tuscan* by the same occasion, of whom *Valerius Maximus* recounteth, that they maintained themselues many yeares in great reputation, both of vertue, and valour: vntill at lenght they opened the gate to all kind of pleasure, & consequētly to vice, whereby they fell in to the greatest, & most ignominious seruitude, that hath bene read, or heard of. For they grew to be so effeminate, that their owne slaues, tooke courage against them, & first presumed to demaunde place, and voice in their senate: and after tooke vpon them to gouerne the common welth: maryed their maisters daughters: & ordeined that no wills, oa testaments should be made without their consents, & aprobation: forbad all assemblies, but of thēselues: made a lawe, not only that adulterie should not be punished in them, but also that no maid should be maried to a free man, but that some of them should abuse her first, and finally banished their masters:

who crauing aide of the *Romans*, were after much miserie, which they had sustained, restored to their former states, & their slaues suppressed, & punished, according to their deserts.

Orosius li. 4. c. 5 an. vrb. cond. 480.

10 I omit infinit other examples of ancient times, to speake of one in the last age, to wit, of the lamentable ouerthrow, and conquest of the *Hungarians*, who hauinge florished a long time in warr', and peace, and falling at length into excesse of drunkennes, and pleasure, and of the vices that accompanie the same: did so farr degenerat, from their former vertue, that their nobilitie, and people would not leaue their banquetting, and drinking, to atend to their owne defence, against *Soliman* the great Turke: who therefore very easely subdued them, and brought them to that miserable seruitude, wherein the most part of them haue liued euer since. Whereuppon a noble man of that country, and court, at the same tyme, sayd pleasantly (as *Surius* reporteth) that he beleeued, there was neuer so mighty, rich, and potent a kingdome so merily lost, as *Hungary* was.

Sur. commēt. an. 1541.

11 Thus then we see, how pernicious to common welth those vices are, which many hold either for vertues, or at least necessarie supplemēts of humane felicitie, I meane riotous, and delicious life, and excesse of all kind of pleasure. What then shall we thinke of other vices, which all mē hold for wickednes, as fraud, & deceit, peiurie, murders, rapyns, and all kind of iniustice? Shall not they vtterly destroy, common welth? For, let vs conceyne a companie of men, cōsisting of cosenoers, periured persons, theeues, robbers, parricids, murderers, extortioners, adulterers, and suchlike, who haue no other respect, but euerie man to his owne particuler commodity, or pleasure, can there be any ciuil society amongst thē, more then amongst as many beares, & tygers, or cats, and dogs?

12 This is so euidēt to common sense, that it needeth no further proofe: therefore I thinke good to conclude this chapter with certaine political condicions, which *Plato*, requireth to the perfect establishement, and felicity of all states, whereby we may see the force, & effect of vertue, and vice in common welth.

13 First he requireth, that all the members of the common welth, aswell magistrats, as subiects, doe seeke, and possesse, three kindes of goods, to witj, of fortune, of the bodie, and of the mind, in due, and ordinate manner: that is to say, that they preferre the goods of the mind (which are religion, vertue, and knowledge) before all others: & then that they esteeme the goods of the bodie (to witt, beautie, strength, health, and suchlike) so farr forth onlie, as they may serue to aduāce the goods of the mind: and lastly, that no other acounte be made of the goods of fortune which

Plato Ep. 8. ad Dionis amicos.

which are honour,dignitie,and wealth, then as ministers, and seruantes to both the other, that is to say, so farr forth, as they may be auaileable to the conseruatiō or encrease, first of the goods of the minde,& secōdly of the goods of the body: & what law soeuer, saith *Plato* doth effectuate this,it is a good and perfect law,and maketh a happie state.

14 An other condition is, that the citizens content themselues with moderate libertie, and the magistrats with moderate commaunde, and authoritie: For,seruitude,and liberty,saith *Plato*,are both of them good, and necessarie for the common welth, so long as they are conserued in due measure: but if they grow to excesse,they are dangerous, and manie times pestiferous to state. For ouergreat seruitude,incenseth the mindes of the subiects against the prince, and state: and to much libertie, breedeth insolencie, and contempt of the lawes, and of the prince.

Ep. 8. ad amicos Dioni. *Li.3.de legib*

Li.4.de legib 15 Also that they be contented with moderate wealth,as neyther to be ouer rich,nor too poore,because great inconueniences grow to commō welth,aswell by excesse of riches,as by the extremitie of pouertie:for of the first groweth pride,ambition,effeminacie,and riot: and of the latter, proceedeth theft,robbery, discord,& seditions,which ouerthrow common welths.

Li.5. de legib 16 That they doe not apply themselues to vsury, and vnlawfull gaines, which are of their owne nature infamous, and vnworthie of mans generosity, yea,and dangerous to common welth: for that they corrupt mens manners,making them coueteous,deceitfull, & perfidious. Besides that vsury impouerisheth, and in time, beggereth the common welth, drawing the substance, and riches thereof, in to the handes of a few, to the generall damage, and discontent of all men, whereupon aryse tumults,seditions,rebellions,

Ep.8.adDionis amicos. *De leg.li.8.* 17, That euerie citizen, or member of the common welth, preferr the publike,and common good, before his owne particuler: for nothing is more contrarie to reason of state, and common welth, or sooner subuerteth it, then priuate commoditie, procured with publike damage.

Li.4. de rep. 18 That euerie man perswade himselfe,that foure vertues are most necessarie for the happy direction of his life, in respect aswell of his particuler, as of the publike good. Those vertues are *Prudence, Temperance, Fortitude*,and *Iustice*. And although *Plato* teach, that all these vertues are necessary in euery member of the common welth, yet he requireth that some of them be more eminent in some men, then in others: as *Prudence* in magistrats,and *Fortitude* in souldiars, and that there be a perfect mixture of *Fortitude*, and *Temperance* in euery man,to the end, that being balanced

Ibidem. *Li.3 de rep.*

lanced with an equal temperature of both, he may neither feare to much nor dare to much; but that by *Fortitude*, he may first ouercome him selfe (which *Plato* teacheth to be the cheefe victorie) and after repell both priuate, & publike iniuries, and by *Temperance* may abstaine from doing iniury, and that as *Fortitude* may moue him to honest, vertuous, and noble exploits, so *Temperance* may withhold him from vicious, wicked, and base actions. *Li.1.de leg.*

19 And further he thinketh, the vertue of *Temperance* (aswell in dyet, as in other pleasures of the bodie) so important for the good of common welth, that he affirmeth riotous, and lasciuious life to be a speciall cause of the destruction of Kingdomes, and states, because it consumeth both the bodies, & substance of men, and maketh them effeminate. And therefore he forbiddeth the vse of wine to magistrats, to Iudges, when they are to giue sentence, to souldiars in the campe, to slaues, and to weomen; allowing it to none, but onlie at publike feastes, and with great moderation. And further he ordaineth punishemét for the sinnes of the flesh, as for adulterie, fornication, incest, sodomie, and such like, giuinge notable rules of continencie, and chastitie, whereof I shall haue occasion to speake heare after. *Li.3.de leg.* *Li.2.de leg.* *Li.8.de leg.* *Chap.30.*

20 Moreouer he calleth the vertue of *ciuill Iustice* the solide, and sound foundation of common welth, and the principal propp, and stay, of state, for that by the meanes thereof, God is dulie honored, & the prince obeied, & euerie one hath his due: vertue is rewarded, vice punished, amity conserued, fraud and iniurie abolished, and euerie on liueth in his vocation, according to the rule, and law of nature, referring all his actions, rather to the publike, then to his own priuate good, whereby the common welth, must needs florish, in great peace, and tranquillitie. *Li.4.de rep.*

21 And therefore *Plato* aduiseth, that euerie member in the common welth, doe labour perfectly to vnderstand, and know his dutie in his degree, and vocation: to which purpose he describeth the office, or dutie of al sorts of men (as of priuate persons, magistrats, & princes, in diuers parts of his woorkes, thus in substance.

22 That priuate men ought so readily, and willingly to obay the ordinances, and commaundements of the magistras, that it may appeare, they are moued thereto onlie by their owne vertue, and not by compulsion, or necessitie of the law.

23 That magistrats ought alwayes to haue in mind, that they are not lordes, but ministers of the law, and tutors, or publike gardians of the common welth. For *the state* (saith he) *cannot stand long, vvhere the lavv is gouerned by the magistrats, and not the magistrats by the lavv.* *Li.4.de legib*

[*In Gorgia*] 24 Alſo that they endeuour to enrich the common welth, rather with the goods of the mind, then with the goods of fortune : that euerie one of thẽ attended ſeriouſly to his owne chardge, without intermedlinge in the offices of other mẽ, & all of them ſpecially reſpect, the publike good. [*Ep. ad Dionis omicos.*]

25 That euill men be not admitted to publike offices, for *he* (ſaith *Plato*) *vvho cannot gouerne himſelfe, is not fitt to gouerne others.* And laſtlie that offices be not beſtowed vppon them, that ambitiouſlie ſeeke them, or haue not ſufficient wiſdome, experience, and other talents well to discharge them. [*Li. 1. de rep. Li. 3. de leg. Li. 1 de rep.*]

26 In the prince, *Plato* requireth theſe conditions following. That he labour as much to excell all other men in iuſtice, veritie, magnificence, temperance, clemency, prudence, & religion, as indignity & authority. [*Plato ad Dionem ep. 4*]

27 That he shew himſelfe in deede ſuch a one, as he would ſeeme to be, that is to ſay, that he be truly vertuous, & not verteous onlie in shew, and appearance. [*Ibidem.*]

28 That he alwayes remember, & well conſider, that all mens eyes are fixed vpon him, and that therefore neither his vices, nor defects, be they neuer ſo litle, can be long hid, nor that he can with meane vertue, ſatisfie the expectation of all men. [*Ibidem.*]

29 That he aſſure himſelfe, that the beneuolence and loue of his ſubierts, is moſt neceſſarie aſwell for the good gouernement of them, as for his owne ſecurity, and that the ſame can neuer be gott or conſerued, but by humanitie, and clemency. [*Ibidem.*]

30 That he ſeeke to ioyne perfect prudence, and wiſdome, with the ſoueraintу of his power. For, as wiſdome is weake, or lame without power: ſo power is pernicious without wiſdome, And therefore *Plato* doth not onlie aduiſe princes, to haue alwayes wiſe men about them, but alſo exhorteth wiſe men to attend vppon princes, & to aſſiſt them with their counſell: for, *happy*, ſaith he, *is the familiaritie, or frendship that grovveth betvvixt vviſe and potent men.* But more happy is the vnion of wiſdome, and power in one man, and therefore moſt happie is that common welth, where the prince is both wiſe, and potent, or as *Plato* ſpeaketh, *vvhere philoſophers reigne, or kinges become philoſophers.* [*Ep. 2. ad Dioniſium. De rep. dial. 5*]

31 Furthermore he requireth, that the prince labour to almighty God, whoſe place, and perſon he repreſenteth amongeſt men, and this ſimilitude or likenes, he ſaith cãnot otherwayes be had, *but by iuſtice ioyned vvith prudẽce, and ſanctity of life.* And therefore he aduiſeth princes, firſt to compoſe thẽſelues, according to the modell of the deuine iuſtice, innocency, and other deuine vertues : and then to frame their families, and ſubiects, according to the ſame rule, and paterne. And furthermore he propoſeth [*Li. 7. de rep. In Theate. Li. 9. de rep.*]

vnto

vnto them, the consideration of the rigorous and seuere iudgement of God, which they are to passe after their death, & that they are to be punished for their sinnes, farre more greeuously then priuat men. *In Gorgia, & in phadome.*

32 Also, that they vnderstand, and consider well, the necessity of Gods helpe, & assistance, for the gouerment of their states, seing that no man can without it, well gouerne himselfe, and much lesse a common welth, which consisteth of so manie and different members, and partes, and is subiect to so manie casualities. *Li.7.de rep.*

33. That like to good pilots, they neuer withdraw their eie, nor their hand, from the sterne. For as in a shipp, so also in common welth, or state, a litle negligence may some tymes ouerthrow it. *li. de Ciuili, vel de reg.*

34. That they permit nothing in their states, which may breede corruption of manners, although neuer so great encrease of power or wealth, may in the opinion of men, be like to follow thereof, For as in mans bodie, so also in common welth, the internal corruption doth easily ouerthrow it, though it florish neuer so much externally for the time. *Li.4.de leg.*

34 Finally, that the scope of all their actions, & gouernement, be to procure, partly by good lawes, & partly by their owne example, that all vertue may florish in their common welths, and that their subiects doe not ouermuch esteeme the temporall and false prosperity of this transitorie life. And not so much to desire, and endeuoure, that the state may long stand, as that, so long as it standeth, it may be truely vertuous, and religious, for, *Hic finis legum est,* saith *Plato,* &c. *This is the end of all good lavves, and of common vvelth, that vve may attaine to perfect happynes, Dei cultu, & vitæ puritate, by the vvorship of God, and purity of life.* *Ibid.* *Ibid.* *In epinomide.*

36 Thus much I haue thought good to collect onlie out of *Plato*, concerning the necessitie of perfect vertue, & religion in the commõ welth, for the happie state, & gouerment thereof: whereby it may appeare, how preiudiciall, and pernicious, the religion of the *Romans* must needes be vnto their state, seeing that it could not but produce, and engender there in *Atheisme*, and all kind of vice, and wickednes, as I haue largely proued before in the twoo last chapters. *Chap.7.&8.*

37 But now, for asmuch, as there may aryse here, no small doubt, how it came to passe, that the *Roman* commõ welth grew to so great an empire, as it did, with the continuall vse of their religion, if it were so pernicious to their state, as I haue here affirmed it to be: I must therefore for the satisfaction thereof put thee (good veader) in mind of twoo thinges, which I haue ãply proued in my first part. The one is, that the prouidẽce of God disposeth of princes states, & (as I alleadged out of *Daniell* the Prophet) *Chap.17.* *Dan. 2.*

changeth times, & ages, translateth, & ordained kingdomes at his pleasure, where of I also shewed the experience, aswell in the accomplishment of *Nabuchodonosors* vision, and *Daniels* prophesye, of the foure Empires (to wit, the *Aßirians, Medians, Greekes and Romans*, which were to succeede one an other) as also in declaring the causes, why almightie God, giueth dominion, and kingdome, rather to one man, then to an other, and for what sinnes he punisheth princes, and common welths, and subuerteth their states.

Chap. 17. nu 10. & sequ.

Nu. 21. & sequent.

38 The other point, which I proued, and wishe here to be remembred, is, that almighty God, doth some times absolutely, determyne to destroy a prince, or state (as when he said of the people of *Iuda*, that though *Moyses*, and *Samuel* should pray for them, yet would he not spare them) so also otherwhiles, he determineth, as absolutely to conserue a state for a time (as when he promised to *Iehu*, that his posteritie should succeede him in his kingdome to the fourth generation) in both which cases, I shewed, that no endeuour of man, by good, or bad pollicy, could vphold or ouertrow the state contrarie to the will of God; yea, and that in the latter case (I meane when God doth absolutely determyne to conserue the state) he serueth himselfe, euen of the bad pollicyes of wicked princes, to produce the effect, which he designeth: though neuer the lesse in the meane time, he punisheth the same otherwise, both in the prince, & in the state, with warrs, plagues, famins, and other afflictions, and in the end (the time of his præordination being expired) he powreth vpon them, the extremitie of his wrath, and vengeance, to their vtter subuersion.

Chap. 36. nu. 23.

Ierem. 15.

4. Reg. 10.

Chap. 36. nu. 27.

39 This I emplified in the kingdome of *Israell*, and will now also make manifest in the *Roman* common welth, and empyre, which notwith standing the bad effects, that their absurde, and impious religion produced (to wit *Atheisme* in verie manie, and extremitie of vice in the most part) was to grow, and stand so long, as almightie god had determined to vphold it, and as it was foretold by the Prophet *Daniel*, to wit, vntil a stone should be *cut out of a hill vvithout handes*, that is to say, vntill our Sauiour Christ should be borne of the Virgin *Mary*) without the helpe of man, yea, and should haue planted the seate of his empyre, and kingdome vpon the ruyns thereof: though in the meane time, God executed his iustice vppon them for their Idolatry, and sinne, in such sort, that the continuall course of warrs famine, pestilence, seditions, & mutations, where with they were miserably, and perpetually afflicted, might haue vtterly ruyned their state sundry tymes, if God had not preserued it for the end aforesaied, as in his wisdome he had preordained.

Dan. 2.

40 And

40 And that this may appeare, let vs consider the punishement that God layed vpon them, from tyme to tyme, euen from the verie foundation of their cittie, first vnder their Kings, secondly vnder their *Consuls, Dictators, Decemuiri*, and other magistrats, and lastly vnder their Emperors, vnto the time of *Constantine* the great, whē Christian religion was generally receiued: though neuerthelesse it is to be considered, that for the first three hundreth, or foure hundreth yeares after the foundation of *Rome*, their best histories are so breife, or rather barren of matter, by reason of the great antiquity, and rudenes of those tymes, that *Liui*, and other Historiographers, complaine greatlie thereof. And therefore it is no maruaile, that we find no mention for manie yeares, of diuers great punishements of God, which appeared to be verie ordinarie afterwards, when their histories were written with more diligence, aud greater particularitie: and yet we may easely gather, by those generalities, which are mentioned, how continuate were their calamities, and miseries, euen in their verie begininges.

Liui. Dec. 1.

Dionisi. Halicar. antiq. Roman. li. 1.

41 First then, for the times of their Kings (who were but seauen in all) it is to be vnderstood, that when the two bastard brethren, *Romulus* and *Remus* (sonnes of the vestall virgin *Rhea Siluia*) had killed their great vncle *Amulius*, restored their grandfather *Numitor* to his Kingdome of *Alba*, and laid the foundation of *Rome*: *Romulus* not brooking the companie, & fellowshipp of his brother *Remus* in his new intended Kingdome, embrued his handes in his blood: and to the end he might the better people his new cittie, he offred by publike proclamation, free accesse, and habitation to all the malefactors, that would repaire thither, from anie place what soeuer, whereby it was replenished with in foure, or fiue yeares, with theeues, murderers, outlawes, and the outcasts of all *Italy*, and then partly by force, and partly by fraude, he spoiled the *Sabins*, and other his neighbours of their daughters, contrarie to all lawes humane, & deuine, hauing inuited them together with their parents, to certaine publike feastes, celebrated in *Rome*, in honour of their Gods. Where vppon he had bloudie warrs some yeares with the *Ceninenses, Antennates, Crustumiami*, and the *Sabyns*, of whome he ouercame the three first, but the last, to wit, the *Sabins* entred *Rome*, beseeged, and tooke the *Capitoll*, gaue battaile to *Romulus*, greuiouslie wounded him, and slew a great part of his armie, when the daughters of the *Sabins*, which were maried to the *Romans*, interposed themselues betwixt the two armyes, & procured them to come to composition: whereby it was agreed, that the *Romans* and *Sabins*, should ioyne not onlie in amitie, but also in the societie, and fellowship of one common welth, and that *Tatius* the King of the *Sabins*, should reigne

Liuius Dec. 1. li. 1.

Plutar. in vita Romul.

An. vrbis Romæ 1.

An. vrb. 5.

reigne ioyntlie in *Rome* with *Romulus*.

Plutarc. in Romulo. 42 But within a while *Tatius* was slaine (not without the priuity, and consent of *Romulus*, as it was thought) and shortly after (as *Plutark* testifieth,) there fell a prodigious raine of blood in *Rome*, pronosticating, as it seemed, a most cruell famine, and strange plague, which presently followed, and killed great numbers of men, and women suddenlie to the *An. vrbis 16* astonishment of all men: and during this plague, the *Camerini* also made warr vpon the *Romans*, and after them the *Vesentes*, though *Romulus* had *Idem ibid.* the victorie in both: whereby he grew so insolent, and proud, that he became an insuportable tirant, which moued the senators in the end, *Ann. vr. 37.* to conspire his death, and to kill him in the senate, & to institute a new forme of gouerment of tenne men, who ruled by turnes, euerie owne *Ann. vr. 38.* fiue daies, which also gaue so litle repose, and contentment to the people, that it lasted but a yeare,

Liuius Dec. 1. li. 1. Plutarc. in Numa. 43 After this *Numa Pompilius* was chosen king, who though he reigned fortie three yeares in continuall peace yet being most supersticious, and faning to haue familiarity with a certaine Nimph, or godesse called *Ageria*, introduced infinit superstitions into the *Roman* common welth, deuising all that forme of religion, which they obserued euer after: and thereby infected them with a spirituall plague, farr wors then any temporall, seeing it exposeth them to the continuall wrath of God, which neuer ceased to scourge, & afflict them after his daies. In so much, that whereas he ordained, that the temple of *Ianus* should be allwayes shut in time of peace, it could neuer after, for the space of six hundred yeares be closed, but onlie once. And during the raigne of the kings his successors who were but fiue in number (to wit *Tullus*, *Hostilius*, *Ancus Martinus*, *Tarquinius Priscus*, *Seruius Tullus*, and *Tarquinius superbus*) the *Roman* state was perpetually garboyled with no lesse then a ciuill warre: seeing that fight was with their neere neighbors, yea their allyes, and kinsemen, I meane the cities so neare adioyning vnto them, that they contracted mariages, & kindred with them.

44 This may appeare by the warre betwixt the *Albans* & the *Romans*, vnder *Tullus Hostilius*, wherein vpon agreement of both armies, the decision of their quarrel, being remitted to a combat betwixt three bre- *Liuius Dec. 1. li. 1.* thren, called *Horatij* on the *Romans* part, and three other brethren called *Curiatij* on the part of the the *Albans*, and the victorie falling to the *Romans*, for that one of the *Horatij* (his two brethren being slaine) killed al the *Curiatij*, the victor *Horatius* returning triumphantly to *Rome*, slew his owne sister publickly in the streete, because shee wept for the death of one of the *Curiatii*, to whom shee was fianced, & promised in mariage

whereby

whereby, I say, it may appeare, how ciuil, & domestical these their warrs were, which continued alwayes more or lesse, for the space of twoo hundreth fourty foure yeares, to wit, vntil the expulsion of the kinges. *Eutrop.li.1.*
In al which time, they could neuer dilate their dominion fully sixeteene mile from *Rome*, so that their warres were euer at their owne gates (and consequently accompanied with continuall effusion of their blood, extreame cares, feares, and sorow for the losse of parents, children, brethren, knisfolke, andfreendes) which yet had bene more tolerable, if ambition amongst themselues, & the vnfortunate end of their kinges, had not ministred further matter to the encrease of their domestical calamities.

Plutarc. in vita Numæ.
45 For of the fiue Kings, which succeeded *Numa*, three came to the gouernement by intrusion, and all fiue as *Plutark* testifieth, died either violentlie, or at least in banishement: though others affirme it onlie of foure of them, that is to say of *Tullus Hostilius*, *Tarquinius Priscus*, *Seruius Tullus*, and *Tarquinius Superbus*, of whom *Tullus Hostilius* in a time of great plague was burnt in his owne pallace, which was sett on fire from heauen with a thunderbolt. *Tarquinius Priscus* being made by his predecessor *Anius Martius*, tutor to his children, and hauing afterwars defrauded them of the kingdome, was killed by a sheaphard in reuenge thereof. *Seruius Tullius* hauing cuningly intruded himselfe into the gouerment, was in the end depriued thereof, and also of his life by his sonne in law *Tarquinius Superbus*, with the consent of his owne daughter *Tullia*, who caused her chariot to be driuen ouer her Fathers dead body, as it laie cast forth in the markett place, and finallie *Tarquinius* being the fourth of the aforenamed, & the last king of the *Romans*, was for his tiranie, and his sonnes (who rauished *Lucretia*) expelled the citty, and died after in exile in *Tusculum*, within twelue miles of *Rome*. And such was the hatred, that aswell the people, as the senate had conceiued against kingly authority, for the tirannie of their former kinges, that they vtterly abolished the same, and instituted twoo consuls.

Ann.vr 113. Liuius Dec. 1. li. 1. *Ann. vr 175* *Ann.vr.219* *An. vr.244.*

46 But what? did they enioye thereby anie more happines, peace, or rest then before? Nothing at all: for, such was their miserie afterwards, & so continual the entercourse, or counterchange of externall warrs, ciuill seditiōs, plague, famins, and other strange kinds of calamities, that the punishment of God was most euident vpon them. And therefore seing the *Roman* histories are from this time forward, more particular, cleare, and abondant of matter, then in the former ages vnder the kings, and still the further they goe, the more particular, and plentifull: and that I find also such a perpetuall connexion, and concatenation of calamities, throughout

throughout the whole state of the *Romans* vntill the time of *Constantine*, the great, that I may by the relation thereof, with some litle addition of circumstances, now, and then, giue thee (good reader) a perfect *epitome*, of all the Roman historie, and imagining that I shall doe therein a worke gratefull, vnto thee, whether thoú hast read the *Roman* histoires or noe, (for if thou hast read them, thou maist perhaps be content to renew the memorie of them, by a breife suruey of the substance of the whole, and if thou hast not read them, I make account thou wilt be glad to see in two, or three chapters, the summe of the most notable and remarkable matters, which the Historiographers of the Romans relate in large volumes, for the space of aboue eight hundreth yeares) vppon this conceit, I say, I am content for thy pleasure, and profitt, to take the paine to giue thee an abridgement of the Historyes of the *Romans* during that tyme.

47 Neuertheles, I thinke good to auertise thee, that if thou be not so much delighted with historicall matters, and desirest to take a shorter course, then to read these three chapters following, thou shalt find the conclusion thereof, in the fourth chapter, from this (which is the thirteenth of this booke) wherein thou shalt see, not only the inferenees, that I meane to draw out of the whole, but also the substãce of the same breefely touched, to present vnto thee, the course of the deuine prouidence, in conseruing, encreasing, and aduancing the Roman common welth, on the one side, and his iustice on the other side, in scourging, and afflicting it from time, to time, with such continuall, and exemplar punishements, as the like perhaps hath not bene read, or heard of in anie state, that hath still stode, & beene conserued, and much lesse in any that hath bene so much amplyfyed, and encreased, as the *Romayne* empyre was.

A continuation of the same matter, to shevv the seuerity of Gods iustice in punishing the Romans, *from the expulsion of the Kinges, vntil the first vvarr of Carthage, vvith a perfect* Epitome, *or abridgement, of the Roman history during that tyme.*

Chap. X.

1. THE verie first yeare of the cõsuls was no lesse, vnfortunate to them, then to the common welth. For *Iunius Brutus*, who expelled the tyrant, and was one of the first two consuls, put to death two of his owne sonnes, and two of his wiues brethrẽ for conspiring the reduction, and restitution of the tyrant. He also depriued

ued *Lucius Tarquinius Collatinus* his companion in the consulat, and forced him to depart out of the cittie, only because his name was *Tarquinius*, whereas he him selfe was nephew to the tyrant (to wit his owne sisters sonne) and in steed of *Lucius Tarquinius*, was chosen *P. Valerius Publicola*: Finallie *Iunius Brutus* being slayne the same yeare in battaile, by *Aruns Tarquinius*, the tyrants sonne (whom he also slew) *Spurius Lucrecius* succeded him in his office, and died within a few dayes, in whose place *Marcus Horatius* was chosen. *Liuius Dec. 1. li. 2.* *An. vrb. 245*

2 So that there were fiue consuls in one yeare, of whome one was killed in battaile, an other depriued, and the third died in his consulat. Besides that the same yeare, there begāne an other most cruel warr, betwixt the *Romans*, & the tyrant *Tarquinius*, who was supported by *Porsenna* King of the *Clusins* in *Hetruria*, (now called *Tuscan*) & by the *Satyns*, which warr continued at the very gates of *Rome* three yeares, with so great danger to the *Romans*, that *Liuij* saith, *Non vnquam alias ante tantus terror Senatum inuasit: The senate vvas neuer before that time seazed vvith so great feare.* *Liui. ibid.*

3 And in this warre passed the famous acts of *Horatius Cocles*, and *Mutius Scæuola*, of whome the first defended the entrance of a draw bridge, against all *Porsenna* his armie, vntill the bridge was cut downe behind him and then he lept into the water, and swamme to land. The other, to wit, *Mutius Scæuola*, entered into the campe of *Porsenna*, killed his secretarie in steede of him, and being taken, & threatned with torment, put his owne hand voluntarie in to the fire, and there held it vntill it was consumed, to shew how litle he feared torments, or death it selfe, protesting also, that three hundred yong *Romans* had vowed to attempt the death of *Porsenna* in like manner. Wherevppon *Porsenna* being strooken with admiration of his vallours dismissed him, and made peace with the *Romans*: for assurance whereof, manie hostages were geuē him, amongst whom were diuers maides of accoūt, and namely the famous *Clælia*, vnder whose cōduct all the other maydes escaped away ouer the riuer of Tyber through the enemies army, and although she was restored to *Porsenna* vppon his demaunde, yet for the great admiration he had of her courage, and other good partes, he not onlie dismissed her againe, but also at her request, dischardged al the bardlesse youthes that were amongst the ostages, for the which the *Romans* honoured her with an image, representinge her on horsebacke. And thus ēded their warre with king *Porsenna*. Presently after, there ensued no lesse dangerous, and bloudy warres with the *Sabins*, *Aequi*, *Volsci*, and the *Arunci*, & though the *Romans*, had diuers victories, yet they bought them with much more blood on their owne part, and especially in their warre, with the *Arunci*, who miserably spoiled all the *Idem ibid.* *An. vrb. 248* *Idem ibid.* *An. vrb. 25[illegible]*

Roman territorie, ouerthrew their armie, and almost killed one of their Consuls. Besides that certaine townes that were colonies of the *Romans*, rebelled against them, and yelded to their enimies.

Ibidem. 4 And thus continued their dangers, feares, & troubles, vntill the same were redoubled by a new league of thirty principall cities against them, in fauour of their former king *Tarquinius*, in so much, that they were for-
An. vrb. 253. ced to make a *Dictator*, (that is to say, one soueraigne gouernour for the space of six monethes) which they neuer did, but in some extreame danger of their state. And though in this warre also the *Romans* had the victorie in the end, yet they had so litle repose thereby, that they were
An. vrb. 260 faine in respect of new dangers, to make a new *Dictator* within a while, & in the meane time, the people also being consumed with pouertie, and oppressed with debts, grew to be tumultuous aboue measure. For, whereas they had vntill that time, serued in all the former warrs vpon their owne charges, and by reason of the continuance thereof, and the ordinarie plagues, and famins had bene forced to borrow much money of the noble men, or Senatours, and not being able to pay either the vsurie, or the principal, were miserablie afflicted with imprisomēts, giues, and fetters, yea and some with whipping, & torments (their bodies being adiudged by the magistrats to their creditors for satisfaction of their debts) they assembled themselues on the holie hill three miles from *Rome*
Idem ibid. or as some writte vppon mount *Auentin*, within *Rome*, & there fortified thēselues. And although *Menenius Agrippa*, being sent vnto them frō the senate, pacified them with a fable, which he told thē (of a muteny & conspiracy of all the partes of mans bodie against the belly, wherby the whole bodie pined away) yet the senate was faine to grant them, fiue *Tribunes*, to be chosen out of the people themselues, to serue them for a coūterpeyse against the Cōsuls, & to defend thē against the Senators who oppressed thē, wherevpon there grew afterwards many great incōueniēces, & continuall troubles in the common wealth, as shall appeare hereafter.

5 This seditiō being appeased, there followed the very next yeare, an o-
An. vrb. 261 ther much worse, accōpanied also with an extreame famin, in which seditiō, the people banished the worthy *Martius Coriolanus*, notwithstāding
Ibid. his great seruice donne to the cōmon welth, & his famous victories: who fled to the *Volsciās*, & being made by thē their captaine generall, beseiged *Rome* with a great armie, whereby the *Romans* were so terrified, that first they sent the priests of the cittie, & afterwards *Veturia* his mother, & *Volumnia* his wife, with a great multitude of matrons, and other women to appease him, by whom he was entreated at last to raise his seige.

6 And before two yeares were fullie past (the warrs still continuing

6 And

with the *Volsci, Aequi*, and *Hernici*) there arose new seditions, not onlie
betwixt the senatours, and the people, but also betwixt the two Consuls *Ann.vr 263*
Proculus Virginius, & *Sp. Cassius*, of whome the latter aspired to a tiranny, by
the propositiõ of a law called *Agraria*, (for the deuision of laudes amõgst *Idem ibid.*
the people) & was notwithstãding afterwards condemned, & executed.
And yet neuertheles new tumults grew euery yeare for a lõg time, by the
meanes of the Tribunes, feeding the humour of the people, & irritating *An.269.*
them against the Senat, with the propositiõ of that law: & though some
times they were forced to intermit their domesticall diuisiõs, & animosi-
ties, to attẽd to their defence against the forraine enimies (as in the cõsu- *An. 270.*
late of *Lucius Aemilius*, & *Caeso Fabius*) yet within two yeares after, their se- *Ibid.*
ditions so reuiued, that *Liuy* saith. *Non segnior discordia domi, & bellum foris
atrocius fuit: The discord at home vvas no lesse, then it vvas vvont to be, and the
vvarre abroad farre more cruell.*

7 In these warrs, which they had some yeares with the *Volsci, Aequi*, and
Vejentes, first their consul *Marcus Fabius*, & after three hundred, & six *Fabij* *An.274.*
(al of one familie hauing obteined of the Senate to be emploied in that *An.277.*
warre were al in one battail slaine by the *Vejentes*, assisted by the *Hetrusci*, *Ibidem.*
who made warre at the verie gates of *Rome*: and hauing taken the mount
Ianiculus, so spoiled the coũtry round abount, that the *Romãs* were almost
famished, vntill their consul *Sp. Seruilius*, & *A. Virginius* after much losse,
& diuers foiles, slew the greatest part of their enemies, & put the rest to *An.vr.278.*
flight. This warr was no sooner ended, & their famine releeued, but the
Tribunes beganne againe to make new stirres, propounding the law *A-
graria*, aboue-mencioned, & irritating the people, not only against all the
Senatours in generall, but also against euerie on of them in particuler: in
so much that they caused *T. Menenius*, who had benne Consul, to be
wrongfullie condemned, & accused also *Sp. Seruilius*, consul the yeare before, who hardly escaped. *Ann.vr.279*

8 This domestical storme being somewhat appeased, there arose an o-
ther the same yeare from abroad, by a new warre of the *Vejentes, Sabini,
Volsci*, & *Aequi*, & presently after, the next yeare, the discord, & seditions, *Ann vr 280*
betwixt the Tribunes, & the Cõsuls, & betwixt the people, & the senate, *Ibidem.*
grew to such violẽce, that the officers of the Cõsuls were abused the ensignes of Iustice brokẽ, the Consuls thẽselues forced to saue thẽselues by
flight, & the senat cõstrayned in the end, after 2 yeares tumultuous contẽ-
tiõ, to exclude thẽselues from the election of the Tribunes, & to grãt the
same wholy to the people, to the ẽd they might prouide for the defẽce of
the cõmon welth, against the *Volsci*, & *Aequi*, who renewed their former
warrs, wherin the *Romãs* receiued a most shameful ouerthrow, vnder the *An.vr. 283.*

Consul *Appius Claudius*.

9 And such was the entercourse of warre abroad, & sedition at home, that if I should vndertake to make particular relation thereof, I should doe nothing els, but write the whole story of the *Romans*; seing that whensoeuer there was anie litle peace, or repose, the same was (saith *Liuij*) *semper solicita certamine patrum, & plebis*. Alwayes full of care, and trouble, by reason of the contention betwixt the Senate, and the people, and as *Dionisius Halicarnassus*, saith, *Sic in orbem redibant vicissitudines, &c. Such vvas the course, and counterchange of vvarre, and sedition, that they vvent round, as it vvere in a vvheele, in so much, that peace bredd sedition, & vvarre brought them againe to composition*; which was also (as *Eutropius*, & *Orosius* note) so intermixt with frequent pestilence, that their truces, which were verie rare (saith *Orosius*) were made either by reason of some great plague, or accompanied with it, whereby infinit numbers perished, as in the consulate of *Q. Seruilius*, and *Spurius Posthumus*, when (as *Eutropius* saith) a great part of the people died of the plague. And againe foure yeares after, not onlie the most part of the souldiarrs, and a great number of the common people, but also the two Consuls *T. Ebutius*, and *P. Seruilius*, and verie manie Senators, died in like maner of the same contagion: though during these times, they had also great warrs, with their ancient enimies, yea, & with their owne slaues, and fugitiues, who being conducted by *Herdonius* the *Sabyn*, assayled *Rome*, burnt the *Capitoll*, and killed *Valerius* the Consul, whiles neuerthelesse the Tribunes of the people, continued their wonted furie (as *Liuij* witnesseth) in stirring the people to sedition, and incensing them against the Senate.

Ibidem. *Dionisi. Halicar. antiq. Roman.* *Oros. l. 2 c. 12* *Eutrop. li. 1.* *An. vr. 288.* *Eutrop. ibid.* *Ann. vr. 291* *Ann vr 294* *Liuius Dec. 1. li. 3.*

10 And the next yeare after, as *Eutropius* and *Orosius* say, (though according to *Liuij* it should be twoo yeares after) the *Aequi*, & *Volsci*, discomfited a great armie of *Minutius* the Consul, and beseiged him within twelue miles of *Rome*, vntill *Q. Cincinnatus* (being fetcht from the plough) was made *Dictator*, who releeued him, when he was brought to great extremitie: whiles also in the meane time they had benne miserably distracted, and deuided in *Rome*, by their turbulent Tribunes, seeking to extinguish, or at least to diminish, the authoritie of the Consuls. Besides that, they were terrified with most prodigious accidents of terrible earthquakes, strange noyses, and horrible sights in the ayre, and showers of great peeces, or gobbets of flesh, whereof part was seased on by the birds, ere they fell to the grounde, and the rest that fell lay many dayes vncorrupted: all with prodigious signes, and diuers others, which I omitt (threatninge as the deuines denounced ruin to the common welth for their seditions) being also seconded with famin, and continuall danger of forrein.

Ann. vr 296 *Idem ibid.*

reine warrs, ſuffiſed not neuertheles to temper, and intigate the mindes of the Tribunes, who propounded new lawes in fauour of themſelues, *Ann.vr 298* incenſing the people continuallie againſt the Senate,& Conſuls. Whereuppon their tumults ſtill encreaſing, & new contentions dailie growing (concerning the validitie of the new lawes) to the manifeſt,& extreame danger of the common welth: it was at laſt agreed,to ſend embaſſadours to *Athens*,to fetch a coppy of *Solons* lawes, and other ordinannces of the *An. 300.* *Grecians*,whereby they might reforme theirs. And although during the *Ibidem.* abſence of their embaſſadours (which was not aboue two yeares) they enioyed ſome repoſe,aſwell from tumults at home,as warrs abroad; yet their affliction ceaſed not,for as *Liuij* ſaith: *Duo ſimul mala ingentia exorta,* *Ibidem.* &c. Twoo great miſcheifes grew amongſt them,at once,to wit,famin, and peſtilence,wherewith infinit numbers, not only of men, but alſo of *An.301.* catle were conſumed,in ſo much,that.*Vrbs*,ſaith he,*aſſiduis exhauſta funeribus,multæ & claræ lugubres domus,multiplici clade fædatus annus,The city vvas* *Ibid.* *exhausted vvith continuall deaths, manie noble houſes vvhere replenished vvith mourninge, and all that yeare vvas diſgracefull,by reaſon of manie calamities.*

11 The next yeare, which was the three hundreth, and two, after the foundation of *Rome*, the embaſſadours being returned from *Greece*, the *An.302.* *Romans* changed their forme of gouerment,choſing in ſteede of two Cōſuls, tenne gouernours called *Decemuiri* to whoſe chardge it was committed,both by the Senate,& people,aſwell to make new lawes, as alſo *Idem ibid* to adminiſter iuſtice, euery one of them in his turne, euery tenth day; who conſpiring together the ſecond yeare of their office, and binding themſelues by oath to mantaine one an other,oppreſt the commō welth two yeares,and vſed great tirannie, committing all kind of iniuſtice: in *An. 305.* ſo much that one *Virginius* publikely ſlew his owne daughter, to deliuer her from *Appius Claudius* one of the *Decemuiri*, who,to the end he might deflower her, had not onlie cauſed a dependant of his owne to claime her for his ſlaue, but alſo had giuen ſentence againſt her. Wherevppon there aroſe ſuch a tumult of the people, and ſouldiars, that the *Decemuiri* *Ibidem.* were forced to leaue their office,and two Conſuls were choſen after the old maner,and *Appius Claudius* being committed to priſon, killed himſelfe:an other of the *Decemuiri* died alſo in priſon, & the reſt were baniſhed,and their goods confiſcated.

12 During this tirannicall *Decemuirat*, the *Sabins*, and *Aequi* making warre in the territorie of the *Romans*, gaue them two ſhamefull ouer- *An.306.* *Ibid.* throwes, and put the citie of *Rome* in no leſſe danger,then feare.

13 And if I should proceede in this manner,to recount particulerlie, al their domeſticall diuiſions,& other calamities enſuing thereof,(where-

with they were continuallie afflicted, whensoeuer they had anie litle truce, or surceasse from forraine warrs) I should occupie, and imploy the whole volume of this treatise in the relation thereof, & therefore I wish it for the present to be noted, that from the time of this *Decemuirat*, to the verie ouerthrow of their commõ welth, by *Iulius Cæsar* (which was foure hundreth yeares after) their ciuill tumults, & consequently their afflictions grew dayly greater, by reason that the Senate, after the deposition of the *Decemuiri*, were forced, for the further satisfaction of the people, not onlie to renew their former officers called Tribunes, but also to encrease their number to Tenne: yea, & with in a while also to grant, that in stede
Ibidem. of the two Consuls (who were chosen onlie out of the ancient nobility) there should be other magistrats, called Tribunes of the souldiars, who should haue the authoritie of Consuls, and be chosen partlie out of the
An.310. plebeians, and partly out of the patricians.

And so seditious, and furious commonlie were the Tribunes of the people, in stirring thẽ vp against the *Senat*, that the Senatours, were faine to seeke some times, the most dangerous remedies that might be, to wit, the occasion of some great warr, euen at their owne gates (I meane with
Dec.1. li. 4. their next neighbours not manie miles from *Rome*) *Adeo vel infœlix bellum*, saith *Liuij*, *ignominiosæ paci præferebant. So farr they vvere faine to preferr an vnfortunate vvarre, before an ignominious peace.* Which neuertheles suffised not mannie times, to quiet the turbulent humours of the people, and their Tribunes: in so much that otherwhiles, when they were most pres-
Ibid. sed by their enimies, they had, as *Liuij* saith, *Plus belli domi, quam foris.* More warre at home, then abroad, whereby the senate was constrained to endure manie indignities.

14 This therefore being vnderstood, to haue passed continually in the *Roman* state, not onlie before the election of the *Tribuni militum*, (which was in the yeare of three hundred and tenne, after the foundation of *Rome*) but much more euerafter, I will henceforth for breuities sake, touch
An.310. onlie their most notorious calamities, and afflictions, whereby it shall sufficiently appeare, how seuere, and continuall was the scourge, and punishment of God vpon them for their wickednes.

15 These Tribunes of the souldiars, being chosen, and composition made thereby for the present, betwixt the people, and the *Senate*, (to the end they might attend to the defence of their state against the *Aequi*, *Volsci*, and *Vejentes*) the said warrs were no soner ended with good successe to
An. 315. the *Romans*, but succeded the vnfortunate Consulat of *Proculus Geganius*
Dec. 1. li. 4. *Macerinus*, and *L. Menenius Lanatus*, *Notorius*, saith *Liuij*, *for the manifold calamities, dangers, famin, seditions, and almost perpetuall losse of liberty*, in so much

(saith

(saith he) that if there had bene anie externall warre at that time, *Vix ope Deorum omnium res sisti potuisset. All the Gods could hardly haue conserued the state.* The occasion was, that there being so great a famin, that manie drowned themselues in *Tyber*, to auoid the torment of hunger, *Sp. Melius*, hauing at his owne charges, greatlie releeued the people with corne, & victuall: aspired to make himselfe Kinge, and had so farr gained their good wills thereto, that the Senat was compelled to make *Lucius Quintus Dictator*, by whose meanes (with the helpe of *Quintus Seruilius* Master of the horse) *Sp. Melius* was in the end slayne, and the peo- *Ann. vr 316*
ple pacified.

16 The yeare following beganne a most dangerous warre, by the rebel- *An. 317.*
lion of the *Fidenates*: who were not aboue eighteene miles from *Rome*, & had at the instance of the *Veientes*, rebelled against the *Romans*, and killed foure of their Embassadours, which were sent vnto them, to vnderstand the cause of their defection. In so much, that the Senate (*vt in trepidis rebus*, saith *Liuij, as their custome vvas in time of feare, and danger*) made a *Dictator*, to *Idem ibid.*
wit *Mamercus Aemilius*, and though he ouerthrew his enimies, and had a notable triumph, yet his victorie was counterpeised, with such terrible earthquakes, and plagues, that the *Romans* were in feare of *Eutrop. li. 1.*
vtter desolation, aswell to the cittie, as to the countrie: besides new warrs presentlie after with the *Fidenates*, and *Vejentes*, who *An. 317.*
approched with a great armie to the walls of *Rome*, wherevppon, *& 318.*
trepidatum, saith *Liuij*, *non in agris magis, quam in Vrbe, There vvas no lesse feare in the cittie, then in the fields abroad.* And therefore they made *An. 320. Liuius Dec.*
a new *Dictator*, to wit *A. Seruilius*, who repelled the enimie and toke *1. li. 4.*
the cittie *Fidenæ*.

17 And other warrs arising the next yeare (wherevppon they were also *An. 321.*
forced to make a new *Dictator*) there followed an other pestilence, which *An. 322.*
made great destruction both of men, and cattle, in the cittie, and country. *An. 327.*
And within foure, or fiue yeares after, the *Veientes* made new warrs, which were also accompanied with extreame drought, wherevppō followed verie great contagion, & death of men, and beastes: and shortlie *An. 329.*
after, the *Veientes* gaue an ignominious ouerthrow to the three Tribunes of the souldiars, who gouerned that yeare: and *Rome* it selfe was in such *Ibidem.*
feare, that it kept watch, and ward vppon the walles, and was, as *Liuij* *An. 331.*
saith, *more like a campe, then a cittie*: and within three yeares after the Consul *Sempronius* was also shamefullie ouerthrowne, by the *Volsci*. *An. 337.*
Not long after againe, an other armie of the *Romans* was defeated by the *Lauricani*, and *Aequi*, and the wonted seditions growing daily greater at *An. 342.*
home, passed also frō the people in the cittie, to the souldiars in the cāpe *An. 343.*

who

who killed *M. Posthumius* their generall; and presently after followed a great pestilence, and famine, whereby the citie was for a time left as it were, desolat, and desert whiles the common sort perished, and the Senatours and others of wealth & account, went abroad to seeke remedie against the hunger and contagion.

18 And thus continued for some yeares this successiue change of seditions, plagues, famine, and warre (where in also the *Romans* amid some victories, receiued many disgraces, and ouerthrowes) vntill the great, & long seige of *Vejentum*, which dured tenne yeares, winter, and sommer, after seauenteene yeares warre, that it had made against the *Romãs*: who, though they tooke it in the end (to wit in the yeare three hundreth fiftie nine) vnder the conduct of *M. Furius Camillus*, yet had bene foyled, disgraced, & beaten by it, not onlie oft before, but also diuers tymes during the seige; in which time also they were pestred with almost cõtinuall warrs, by other their neighbours, and with seditions at home more then euer, and finally with that notorious pestilence, which happened in the yeare three hundred fifty six, whereof I haue spoken in the seuenth chapter, for remedy whereof, they made their first *Lectisternium* to pacifie the wrath of their gods.

An. 350. *Idem Dec. 1. li. 5.* *An. 356,*

19 And how pernicious their ciuill dissentions, and seditions in *Rome* it selfe, were also to the common welth, it appeared shortlie after, when the famous *Furius Camillus*, was wrongfully banished by the *Tribunes* of the people: in punishment whereof, *Plutark* supposeth, that God sent the *Gaules* to *Rome*, who the next yeare after, ouerthrew *Fabius Ambustus*, & his whole army, not farr from *Rome*, with great slaughter of the *Romans*, and entred the citie, sacked, spoiled, and burnt it, killed a great number of Senatours in their owne houses, and put all to the sword, except such as fled to the *Capitol*, which they also beseiged, though they were in the end expelled, & ouerthrowne by *Camillus*, who being banished (as I haue declared) releeued, and repaired the wracke of his vngratefull country.

An. 364. *Plutarc. in Furio Camil* *An. 365.*

An. 366. 20 This dangerous, and terrible tempest being ouerblowne, new stormes of warrs presently arose from the *Volsci*, *Aequi*, *Satrini*, & *Prænestini*, of whom some encamped themselues at the verie gates of *Rome*, wherevpon saith *Liuij*, *Ingens in vrbe trepidatio: There was exceeding great feare, and trembling in the cittie.* And although the *Romans* ouerthrew, & conquered them all in the end, by the valour of *Furius Camillus*, and *T. Quintus Cincinnatus* (whereby also they enlarged greatly their dominions in *Italy*) yet they were in the meane time continuallie molested, and vexed with their wonted calamities: as some times with disgraces in warres, some times with

Liuius Dec. 1. li. 6.

with plague and famine, and otherwhieles, or rather continually, with *An.*372.
domesticall diuisions, and tumults? partlie by reason of the pouerty of
the people, loden, and opprest with debts, and partlie byt he ambition, *An.vrb.*369
first of *Marcus Manlius*, who aspiret to make himselfe King, and after
of *Licinius Stolo* and *L. Sextius* Tribunes of the people, who for fiue yeares *An.*379. 380.381.
togeter, hindred the election of all other magistrats, but them selues 382.383.
and forced the Senate in the end, to graũt that one of the Consuls, should
for euer after be a Dlebeian, and yet before this dissention could be
fully composed, the *Gaules* returned againe with a huge army and came
within foure mieles of *Rome*, destroynig all the country roundabout, *Ann vr.* 388
but were within a while defeated by *Turius Camillus*.

21 Shortly after there grew a strange plague, of contagious diseases, *Liuius Dec.*
which continued some yeares, and destroyed infinit numbers of people, 1.*li.* 7.
and amongst the rest, there died *Turius Camillus*, three Tribunes of the *An.vrb.*390
people, a *Censor*, and an *Ædil*, for remedy wherof, they absurdlie brought
in vse, their filthy staghe plaies, to pacifie the wrath of the Gods, as I haue
signified in the seuenth chapter.

22 Within twoo yeares after or somewhat more, the earth opened vn-
to the verie bowels thereof, in the midest of the greatest market place in *An.* 393.
Rome, and so remained some dayes, to the extreame terrour of all men;
their deuines cõcelled them to throw in what soeuer was most precious *Idem ibid.*
in the cittie, wherevppon the matrons cast in all their Iewells, but nothing auailed, vntill *Marcus Curtius* being armed on horsebacke cast himselfe into it, which being donne it closed within a while; and before the
yeare was fully ended, L. *Genutius* the Consul was ouerthrowne & slaine
by the *Hernici*.

23 From this time forward, vntell the warr of the *Samnits*, that is to
say, for the space of twentie two yeares, the *Romans* were so contiunaly *Ibid.*
distressed, either with rebellions of their subiects, or defections of their
freendes, and confederates, or new inuasions of the *Gaules* (who gaue thẽ
an other bloody battaile, at the verie gates of *Rome*) or finallie with their *An.* 395.
ciuill discord amongst themselues, that they were forced almost euerie
yeare, to make a *Dictator*, in respect some times aswell of Domesticall, as *An.*405.
of foraine dangers: and although they had manie notable victories, yet
they receiued with all so manie disgraces, with such losse of blood, and *An.*394.
such spoile of their territories, and such oppression of the people, that 395.367.
it may trulie be said, they liued all that while in continuall affliction &
miserie, the particularities whereof, where to long to recount, & therefore I wil passe to the warre of the *Samnits*.

24 In the yeare after the foundation of *Rome* foure hundred & twelue, *An.*412.

Ibid. the *Romans* denounced warre to the *Samnits* in fauour of the *Campani*; who not being able to defend themselues against the *Samnits*, gaue to the *Romans*, not onlie their cittie, *Capua*, (which was then held equall in greatnes, or magnificence with *Rome*) but also themselues, and their whole state, vpon condition that the *Romans* should defend them.

25 The *Romans* therefore vndertaking this warre in defence of the *Campani*, as of their owne subiects, had prosperous successe, and notable victories, for three, or foure yeares, aswell against the *Samnits*, as the *Latins* their neighbours, who breaking their ancient league, made warre vpon them: in which time passed those famous actes of the two Consuls

An. 415. *T. Manlius Torquatus*, and *Publius Decius*: of whome the first, to conserue the authoritie, and integritie of militarie discipline, put to death his owne sonne, for accepting an importunate chalēge of combat without his order, though he valiantlie slew the enimie: and the other Consul *Decius*,

Liuius Dec. 1. *li.* 8. seeing his armie put to the worse, and like to be ouerthrowne, vowed, and with manie ceremonies (which *Liuy* declareth) consecrated himselfe as a sacrifice to the gods, to obtaine the victorie, which his armie obtained, though he himselfe was slaine.

An. 416. 26 But the next yeare after, one of their consuls being a Plebeian, and the other though a Patrician, yet disgusted with the Senat (because it

Idem Ibid. would not grant him a triumph) cōspired together in fauour of the Tribunes, and people, and making one of themselues *Dictator*, ordained such lawes, that, as *Liuy* witnesseth, their common welth receiued more detriment, by the malignitie of their seditious Consuls, and *Dictator* at home, then good happ, or felicitie by their victories abroad. And these warrs cōtinuing yearelie, they were also infested with strange plagues, & mortalitie, especiallie in the foure hundred twentie and third yeare, after the

An. 423. foundation of *Rome*, at what time, an incredible, and most horrible conspiracie of the matrons of *Rome*, to poison the cittie was detected, by one

Ibidem. of their women seruants, after that verie manie principall men, and a great number of the meaner sort, had bene made away, dying strangelie, and suddainelie all after one manner: besides infinit others, who being more able to resist the force of the poison, languished miserablie, and pined away, vntill the matter being discouered (as I haue said) and examined, three hundred and seauentie matrons (as *Orosius*

Oro. l. 3 *c.* 10 and *Eutropius* witnesse) were condemned, and executed for it: no o-

Eutrop. li. 2 ther motiue, or cause of their wicked act being euer discouered, but onlie a phantastical, and malicious madnes, which had surprised them.

27 A few

27 A few yeares after this, the warre with the *Samnits* being renewed, the *Roman* armie conducted by the twoo Consuls *T. Veturius* and *Sp. Posthumius*, was driuen to such a straite; that they were forced to saue their liues, with losse of their honour, passing vnder the yoke (as it was termed) that is to say, vnder three lances set vp in gallowswise, spoiled of their armes, and clothes, with such conditions also of peace, as it pleased their enimies to impose vpon them: for the assurance whereof, six hundred *Roman* Gentlemen were left for hostages. And this the *Samnits* held for a greater victorie, then if they had put them all to the sword, as they might haue done, if they would.

An. 431. *Liuius Dec. 1. li. 9.*

28 And from this time forward, they had continually for many yeares, verie cruel and bloudie warrs, partly with the *Samnits*, and partly with other their neighbours, and though they had diuerse notable victories, yet they bought them manie times so deare, that they had small cause to reioyce thereat: partlie by reason of their owne losses, and partlie for the frequent plagues which occurred. In so much, that *Eutropius* speaking of these times saith thus; *It is to be vnderstood, that the peace, and repose of the Romans, vvas euer interrupted vvith externall vvarrs, and the vvarres againe vvith infectious, and contagious plagues, so that they vvere on euerie side miserablie molested.* Thus saith he, vpon the occasion of a most greuous pestilence, which ensued a victorie, that *Quintus Fabius Maximus*, had against the *Samnits*, and *Gaules*, though with the losse of seauen thousand *Romans*, and of his fellow Consul *P. Decius*, sonne to the other *P. Decius*, who vowed, and dedicated himselfe, as a sacrifice to the Gods, in a battaile against the *Latins* (as I haue signified before) whose example his sonne also followed in this battaile, and with his death purchased the victorie for the *Romans*, as they were perswaded.

Eutrop. li. 2.

An. 458. *Liuius Dec. 1. lib. 10.*

Num. 25.

29 The same yeare, this plague, and warre was also accompanied with manie prodigious euents, as that it rained earth, and manie were slaine in the armie of the *Romans* with thunderbolts: besides that the *Gaules* also intercepted, and slew a whole legion of the *Romans*, whereof not one man escaped, and the warrs with the *Samnits*, stil continuinge with great losse on both parts (though the *Romans* commonly had the victorie) there fell within three yeares after such a plague in *Rome*, and such a murrein, and destruction of catle in the countrie, for three yeares together, that (as *Liuy* witnesseth) it was *portento similis*, like a monstrous wonder. And during the same time, the *Samnits* also ouerthrew the Consul *Q. Fabius Gurges*, who saued himselfe by flight, hauing lost three

An. 461. *Liuius Dec. 1. li 10.*

For the remidy of this Esculapius *vvas fetcht from* Epidaurus.

 thousand

*An.*463. thouſand of his ſouldiars, though within a while (after fortie nyne
Eutrop.li. 2. yeares warres, and manie bloudy battailes as *Eutropius* witneſſeth) they
ſubdued the *Samnits*, & deſtroyed their cheefe cittie called *Samnum:* And
about the ſame time, alſo grew ſuch a ſedition in *Rome*, that the people
tooke armes, and rebelled, requiring that plebeians might be admitted
to marry with the nobilitie.

30 Preſently after, there followed new warrs with the *Sabins*, & then
*An.*470. with the *Lucani, Brutij, Toſcani*, and *Galli*, with whom the *Samnits*, had made
league, with intent to rebell: and the *Romans* thinking to withdraw the
Gaules from them, ſent Embaſſadours vnto them, whom the *Gaules* kil-
led, and ſhortlie after diſcomfited alſo an armie of the *Romans*, and ſlew
*Epitome T. Liuius li.*12. their general *Cecilius* the Prætor, ſeauen Coronels, and manie noble men,
beſides twentie eight thouſand common Souldiars, as *Oroſius* teſti-
*Oro.l.*3.*c.*22 fieth.

31 The next yeare after, they beganne an other warr with the *Taren-*
*Eutrop. li.*2. *tins*, who had alſo aſſailed, and ſpoiled a nauie, of theirs, killed their
*Oroſ li.*4.*c.*1 Captanes, and their moſt ſeruiceable ſouldiars, ſould the reſt, and abu-
An 471. ſed alſo their Embaſſadours, who were ſent to complaine of the iniurie.
And this warr ſo preſſed them, that they were faine to arme their *Pro-
letarij*, who being of the pooreſt ſort, were ſuch as had benne before ex-
empted from warre, to the end they might ſtay at home, and attend to
procreation for encreaſe of the common welth.

*Epi.Liu.l.*12. 32 By the occaſion of this warr, the *Tarentins* called *Pyrrhus* King of *Madonie*, and *Epyrus*, into *Italy*, to aſſiſt them againſt the *Romans*, betwixt
whome there paſſed three cruell, and bloudie battailes, whereof the *Romans* loſt the firſt, after a whole daies fight, vnder the *Conſul*, *Leuinus*,
though the ſlaughter of their enimies was ſo great, that *Pyrrhus* ſaid, *That*
Ibid.li. 13. *ſuch an other victorie, vvould ſend him home vvithout ſouldiars.* The *Romans* loſt
*An.*473. *Plutarc. in Pyrrho.* in that battaile fourteene thouſand, eight hundred & fourescore footemen, and two hundred forty ſix horſe, beſides eight hundred and twoo
horſe and fote, which were taken priſoners, and thoſe which eſcaped by
flight, were ſtrangelie terrified, with horrible, & prodigious thunder, and
thirtie foure of them killed with thunderbolts, and twentie two left
halfe dead, in ſo much, that it ſeemed the verie heauens fought againſt
them.

*An.*474. 33 The *Romans* wanne the ſecond battaile, and ſlew twentie thouſand
of their enimies, with the loſſe of fiue thouſād of their part. In the third
Idem ibid. battaile, the famous Conſul *Fabricius* (who diſcouered to *Pyrrhus* the trea-
*An.*475. ſon of his phiſician which had offred to poiſon him) ouerthrew him:
And then *Pyrrhus* being called into *Sicily* to aſſiſt *Agathocles* king thereof,
depar-

departed for a time,and returning againe afterwards, was ouerthrowne by the Consul *M.Curius Dentatus*, and forst to leaue *Italy*, fifteene yeares, after his first arriuall there,as *Eutropius* testifieth. *Liui.li. 14. in Epito. An. 479. Eutrop.li. 2.*

34 And in the meane time also,the *Romans* were cruelly infested, in the second consulat of *Fabius Gurges*,with a verie strange plague, which killed the children in their mothers wombes,and yong cattel in like sort in their dames bellies,so that it was feared (as *Orosius* witnesseth) that the succession, and offspring both of men, and beastes, would haue vtterlie failed, *An.477. Oros.li.4.c.2*

35 There followed shortlie after, new warres with the *Tarentyns*, who rebelled with the helpe of the *Carthaginenses*, not withstanding that the said *Carthaginenses*,where then in league,with the *Romans*. But the *Romans* ouerthrew thē both,which the *Carthaginenses* reuenged afterwards with manie yeares warre,as shalbe declared after a while. *Idē ibid.ca 3. An.482.*

36 The next yeare after this warr with the *Tarentins*, a whole legion of the *Romans*,hauing cruellie murdered all these people of *Regiū* (to whose succour they were sent) and possessing themselues of the towne, were beseeged by the rest of the *Roman* forces,taken, and sent to *Rome*, where they were al put to death,so that the *Romans* themselues killed so manie of their owne souldiers, that if they had bene slaine by the enemie, it would haue bene held for a publike,and common calamitie. *An.483. Idem Ibid.*

37 Presentlie after,followed manie prodigious signes,and amongst the rest, a maruelous eruption of fire out of the ground, which burned for three daies together, consuminge the corne,and trees neere about it,and the yeare following,there passed a most bloudy fight, betwixt the *Picentes*,and the *Romans*,notwithstanding that when they were ready to ioyne battaile, there was vpon a suddaine, such a horrible earthquake, with such a roringe noise (which issued out of the earth) that as (*Orosius* and *Eutropius* doe witnes) it might well be thought,that the earth it selfe trēbled,& mourned,for the aboūdance of humane bloud,that was presentlie to be shed in that battaile, wherein neuertheles, the *Romans* had the better. *An.484. Oros.l.4.c.4 Eutrop.l.2. An.485.*

38 The verie next yeare after, there were other no lesse prodigious signes,as to omitt diuerse others, aboundāce of bloud flowed out of the earth,pretēding no doubt,the bloody warrs,which presentlie folowed. First with the *Salentini* and *Brundusini*,and shortlie after with the *Carthaginenses*. Besides that,the *Romans* were also about the same time, miserably afflicted with twoo yeares pestilence, which did so depopulate the cittie,and country,that afterwards, when it ceased, they made a cense, saith *Orosius*, not so much to see how manie were dead, as how many re- *Idem Ibid. Circ.an.487 Oros.l.4.c.5.*

mained aliue.

39 But ſeing we are now come to the firſt warrs of *Carthage*, and that this chapter is alreadie growne long, I will proſecute the reſt in the chapter followinge, and touch only the moſt important matters, to auoid prolixitie.

The epitome of the Roman *Hiſtorie is continued, and the exemplar puniſhment of God vppon the* Romans, *further obſerued, from the beginninge of the firſt vvarre of* Carthage, *vntill the ouerthrovv of their common vvelth, & the birth of our Sauiour Chriſt, vnder* Auguſtus Cæſar, *the firſt Roman Emperour.*

CHAP. XI.

1. THE *Romans* hauing paſſed, (as I may tearme it) an eſſay of their warre with the *Carthaginienſes* in *Italy*, by the occaſion of the *Tarentins*, (as I haue already ſignified) beganne afterwards to play their maine prize in *Sicily*, in the conſulat of *Appius Clau-*
An. 483. *dius Pulcher*, and *Quintus Fuluius Flaccus*, in the foure hundreth eighty third yeare after *Rome* was built, as *Eutropius* affirmeth, though according to
Eutrop. li. 2. *Glareanus* (whoſe exact chronologie I rather follow) it was the yeare
Oroſ. li. 4. c. 7 foure hundreth eighty eight. The occaſion was, that the *Mamertini*, a
An. 488. people of *Sicily*, whoſe cheefe cittie was *Meſsina*, craued the ayde of the *Romans* againſt *Hieron* King of *Syracuſa*, aſsiſted by the *Carthaginienſes*, whom the *Romans* ouerthrew in two great battailes, and the warre ex-
An. 493. tending it ſelfe, firſt into *Sardinia*, and within foure, or fiue yeares, from land to ſea, the *Romans* were forced, to build, and furniſh a nauie, of
Eutrop. li. 2. on hundred and thirtie shipps, which they did with incredible ſpeede, to wit in threeſcoore dayes, but *Cornelius Aſina* the Conſul, who had the chardge thereof, was taken priſoner, & ſlaine by the elder *Annibal*, with the pretence of a falſe treatie of peace, which was preſently after reuenged by the other Conſul *C. Duillius*, with the ſlaughter of three thouſand men, and with an other ouerthrow, which *Caius Florus*, and *Lucius Corneli-*
An. 494. *us* gaue them alſo by ſea, the yeare followinge.

2 But this their good fortune, beganne preſentlie to be checked, with a moſt dangerous conſpiracy of three thouſand ſlaues, confederat with ſo
Idem ibid. manie ſailers, who had ſurpriſed *Rome* (which by reaſon of theſe great warrs was deſtitute of al gard) if the conſul had not in time diſcouered, & preuẽted it. Whereby it may appeare, how much the *Romãs* were preſſed, and greeued with this warre, notwithſtanding their good fortune therein, ſeeing that *Rome* it ſelfe was drawne ſo dry of ſouldiars to defẽd it,

it, that so few slaues durst attempt to surprise it.

3 And within two yeares after, *M. Attilius Regulus* the Consul, hauing passed into *Africke*, and slaine in battaile eighteene thousand of the *Carthaginienses*, and taken by composition fourescore and two cities, was taken prisoner himselfe by them, with the helpe and conduct of *Xantippus* King of *Lacedemony*, at what time also thirtie two thousand of the *Roman* armie were slaine, and fiue hundreth principall men taken prisoners. *An. 496.* *Oros li. 4. c. 9* *Eutrop. li. 2.*

4 This is that *M. Attilius Regulus*, whose memory is so highlie celebrated by *Cicero*, and other *Roman* autors, for returning to *Carthage*, to dischardge his oath, whereby he was bound, either to procure the liberty of the *Carthaginians* that were prisoners, or els to returne himselfe to prison, which later condition he willingly performed, hauing himselfe disswaded the senat to deliuer the other, for the which he was cruellie slaine at his returne. *Cicero 2. de finib. & li. 3. officio. & de senectute. Valer. Max. li. 1. ca. 1. li. 2 cap. 4.*

5 And albeit this great disgrace of *Attilius Regulus*, was presently after recompensed, with two great ouerthrowes giuen to the *Carthaginienses* by sea, wherein they lost 134. ships, and 44. thousand men, and afterwards also 20000. were slain by the Consul *Metellus* by land, yet the two Consuls *Aemilius Paulus*, and *Seruius Fuluius*, returning into *Italy* with their victorious nauie of three hundred saile, loaden with the spoile of the *Carthaginienses*, made a miserable shipwracke, and lost two hundred and twentie of their ships, and hardly saued the rest, with casting ouerbord all their goods. And the like fortune had two other Consuls *Cn. Seruilius Cæpio*, and *Sempronius Blæsus* shortlie after, who hauing also made a prosperous voyage by sea, and gott a great spoile of the *Carthaginienses*, were in their returne cast vpon the rockes, and lost a hundred and fiftie ships of great burthen, whereupon *Orosius* saith verie well. *Apud Romanos numquam diuturna felicitas erat* &c. *The Romans vvere neuer long together fortunate, but euerie good successe of theirs, vvas presently ouervvhelmed vvith a heape of vvoes.* *Eutrop. li. 2. Oros. l. 4. c. 9.* *An 498.* *An. 500.* *Oros. l. 4. c. 9*

9 This appeared to be true at this time, whereof I now treat, for, the prosperous scccesse, whereof I haue spoken, was seconded with diuers disgraces, and calamities, as with the ouerthrow of an other *Attilius Regulus* surnamed *Caius* and *Manlius Volso*, both of thē Consuls, with their nauie of two hundred saile, and foure legions in it, and of an other nauie of a hundred and thirtie saile the yeare followinge, vnder the Consul *Claudius*, who hardly escaped with thirtie ships, the rest being either taken, or drowned, with eight thousand souldiars slaine, and twenty thousand taken, besides that *Caius* or *Lucius Iunius* the other Consul, lost also his whole fleete by shipwracke the same yeare. *Idem ibid. cap. 10* *Eutrop. li. 2.* *An. 503.* *An. 504.* *Ibidem.*

7 And

An. 505. 7 And the yeare following, a fleete of the *Carthaginienses* passed in to *I-*
Idem ibid. *taly*, and spoiled diuers parts thereof, & thus continued these warrs with
harde varietie of fortune, and inestimable losses to both parties, vntill
Luctatius the Consul, had a notable victorie some foure, or fiue yeares af-
An. 511. ter in *Sicily*, where he ouerthrew *Hanno*, the Generall of the *Carthaginien-*
Eutrop. li. 2. *ses*, slew foureteene thousand souldiars, and tooke thirtie two thousand
prisoners, whereby the *Carthaginienses* were so broken, and discouraged,
Oros. l. 4. c. that they were forced to demande peace, which was granted them,
10. & 11. and so ended the first Punicke warre, after it had lasted twentie three
An. 512. yeares.

8 But was the ioy of this victorie, and peace (thinke you) cleare to the
Romans, without their wonted counterchange of calamitie? No truly, for
An. 513. the very next yeare after, as they were preparing for their triumph, there
Eutrop. li. 2. was such an inundation of the Riuier of *Tiber*, and it lasted so long, that
it destroyed al the lower part of the citie, and presently after, a fire also
which tooke in the higher partes of the cittie, (no man knew how) consumed not onlie innumerable houses, and the temples of the Gods, but
also a great number of men, and such store of riches, and welth, that, as
Oros. l. 4. c. 11 *Orosius* saith. *Many forraine victories could not recompence the losse that the Romans*
receiued thereby,

An. 513. 9 In this meane while, there arose new troubles of warrs from the *Fa-*
lisci, the *Gaules*, and the *Sardinians*, who rebelled by the sollicitation of the
Idem ibid. *Carthaginienses*, which warrs lasted some fiue, or six yeares, with so litle
cap. 12 gaine to the *Romans*, especiallie against the *Gaules*, that though they had
Eutrop. li. 2. the victorie, yet their losse was so greate with al, that the Consul *Valerius*
An. 514. could not obtaine the honour of triumph: but in the end, all those tumults being appeased, and the *Carthaginienses* vppon humble suite, by di-
uers embassages pardoned, there was such an vniuersall peace, that the
Temple of *Ianus* was shutt vp the first time, after *Numa Pompilius*, that is
An. 518. to say, after foure hundreth & threescore yeares of continuall warre, be-
Oro. l. 4. c. 12 sides the other afflictions of plagues, domestical diuisions, and other miseries, wherewith they had bene many times brought almost to vtter
desolation, as I haue signified before,

10 This peace continued only one yeare, which being ended, there arose
new quarrels, and cruell warres with the *Illirici*, for killing certaine embassadors of the *Romans*, & presently after with the *Gaules*, in punishmét
Oros l. 4. c. 13 (as *Orosius* and *Eutropius* note) of a most inhumane sacrifice, which the
Eutrop. li. 3. *Romans* made of two *Gaules*, a man, and a woman, whome they buried a-
liue together, with a *Gracian* woman, after which there followed with
in a while, such an inundation of the *Gaules*, aswel of those which dwelt
in *Italy*

in *Italy*, as also of the others beyond the *Alpes*, that the *Romans* were forced to arme eight hundred thousand men, vnder the cōduct of their two Consuls, *Publius Valerius Flaccus*, and *Caius Attilius Regulus*, of which huge host, fourescore thousand were slaine by the *Gaules*, with the Consul *Attilius*, and all the rest put to flight; though neuertheles afterwardes, the *Romans* ouerthrew them in three battailes vnder diuerse Consuls, & lastlie killed their King *Viridomarus*, and tooke *Millan*, the cheefe cittie of the *Gaules*, called *Cisalpini*. But how much bloud these three victories cost them, it may easily be imagined, & ere that warre was fullie ended, they were forst to prepare for an other against the *Istri*, whom also they subdued ere long, but *multo Romanorum sanguine*, with much bloud of the *Romans*, as *Orosius* witnesseth. *Oros. ibidem* *An. 527.* *Eutrop. li. 3.* *An. 532.* *Oros. vbi sup* *An. 533.*

11 But now, who can sufficientlie expresse the miseries, and calamities, that fell presentlie vpon them by the second Punicke warre, when *Hannibal*, seeking occasion to breake peace with them, beseiged the cittie of *Saguntum* in *Spaine*, which was their confederat, and so faithfull vnto them, that hauing endured extreame famine some moneths, & seeing no possibilitie of succour, refused *Hannibals* offer of capitulation, and burnt their cittie, with all their goods, and themselues. And warr being therevppon denounced by the *Romans*, against *Carthage*, *Hannibal* marched towards *Italy*, with a hundred thousand footemen, as some write, and twentie thousand horse, leauing also his brother *Asdrubal*, with great forces in *Spaine*. And passing the *Alpes* with incredible difficultie, and speede, to wit, in fifteene dayes (notwithstanding that he was forced to open his way through the maine rocks, with great industry, dissoluing them with vinager, and fire) he descended into the champian countrie about *Turin* in *Piemont*, where encountring with the Consul *Scipio*, he ouerthrew him, and killed almost all his armie, and *Scipio* himselfe being greueously wounded, escaped hardly by the valorous helpe of yonge *Scipio* his sonne. *An. 535.* *T. Liui. Dec. 3. li. 1.* *Vide Plutar. in vita Hannibal.* *An. 536.*

12. And shortlie after this, *Annibal* gaue an other ouerthrow to *Sempronius* the other Consul, by the riuer called *Trebbia*, with no lesse losse, & disgrace to the *Romans*, then in the former, for the consul lost the greatest part of his armie, and hardlie saued his owne life by flight. And though *Hannibal* being wounded in that battaile, & so distressed afterwards with the extreame could of the winter, that he lost one of his eyes, and great number of his souldiars, yet he gaue an other battale in the beginninge of the spring to *Flaminius*, the Consul, whom he killed, with twenty fiue thousand *Romans*, and tooke six thousand prisoners, neere to the lake called *Thrasimenus*, not farr from *Perugia* in *Tuscan*. *Liuius Dec. 3. li. 1.* *An. 537. Idem Ibid. li. 2.*

An.538. 13 After this againe followed the famous battaile at *Canna*, where *Han-*
Idem ibid. *nibal* slew the consul *Paulus Aemilius*,& forty foure thousand foote, three
Plutar. in thousand, fiue hundred horse, twẽty of the most principall personages of
Hannibal. *Rome*, who had bene Consuls, & thirtie Senators, with three hundred o-
ther men of mark, either slaine, or takẽ: & the other consul *Terentius Var-*
ro, saued himselfe by flight, with only fiftie horse. And finally, such was
the slaughter of principall men, that *Hannibal*, sent to *Carthage*, (as *Orosius*
Oro.l.4.c.16 witnesseth) three bushels of gold rings, taken from the hands of the *Ro-*
man gentlemen which were slaine, & such was the astonishmẽt, & fright
of the *Romans* by this ouerthrow, that if *Hanniball* had followed his victory, & gone directly to *Rome*, he had by al likelyhood surprised it, and
Oros.ibidem vtterly ouerthrowne the *Roman* state. For al *Campania*, or rather as *Orosius*
saith, almost al *Italy*, yelded to him, & the Senators thẽselues were in such
despaire, that many of them deliberated to leaue *Italy*, and had donne it,
T.Liui.Dec. but that yong *Scipio* being then a Coronel, drew his sword, and protested
3.li.2. that he would kill whosoeuer should consent vnto it, & procured in the
end, that they all tooke an oath with him to defend their country.

14 Furthermore, such was the want of souldiars, for the maintenannce
of the warre, that *Iunius Decius* being made *Dictator*, was faine to follow
Oro.l.4.c.16 the example of *Romulus*, and to grant impunity to al malefactors, that
would come, and serue in that warre, whereby he shortlie assembled six
thousand men, and further made vp foure legions of tag, & rag, giuing libertie to such slaues as were thought most seruiceable, taking armes out
of the verie temples to furnish them, and the common treasure was so
exhausted, that the *Romans* were forced to supplie with new contri-
butions.

15 And though both before and after this, *Hannibal* receiued some ouer-
Liuius Dec. throwes, namely by *Fabius Maximus*, before the battail of *Canna*, and af-
3.li.2.
Idem Ibid. terwards by *M. Claudius Marcellus*, yet he gaue manie more, as to *Sempro-*
li.7. *nius Gracchus*, to *Centenius Penula*, to *Gneus Fuluius* the Prætor, whom he
An.542. put to flight, and slew fifteene thousand of his men. And lastlie to the
An.546. two Consuls *Crispinus*, and the afore said *Marcellus*, both whome he slew
by a traine. And comming once within three mile of *Rome*, to the great
An.543. terrour of the *Romans*, he presented them battaile twice, and as they were
ready to fight, there fell both times such a terrible storme of raine, and
haile, that both the armies were forced to returne into their camps, in so
much that *Hannibal* himselfe ascribing it to the will, and worke of God,
Oro.l.4.c.17 retired himselfe, saying. *That God did not giue him some times the vvill, and some
times the povver to assaile Rome*: wherein I note by the way, that which I
wish to be obserued throughout al this discourse, concerning the *Romãs*,
to wit,

to wit, on the one side the seuere iustice of almightie God, in punishing them for their horrible idolatrie, and impietie: and on the other side, his maruelous prouidence, in preseruinge, and augmenting their state, to so great an empire, as after he gaue thē, to the end it might serue for a foundation to the biulding of his Church.

16 But to conclude concerninge *Hanniball*, he remained in *Italy* for the space of sixteene yeares, to the incredible affliction, and molestation of the *Romans*, for as *Polibius* testifieth, he gaue order to his souldiars, that they should spare neither man, woman, nor child, but put all to fire, and sword, which they executed with al rigour, and destroyed nineteene notable, and famous cities, and killed also in that time, aboue two hundred thousand of al sorts of people, as may appeare by the censes made before and after. *Polib. li. 3.*

17 And this continued, vntill at length *Scipio* (who was called afterwards *Africanus*) hauing ouercome *Hanno*, and *Asdrubal* in *Spaine*, and subdued it wholy from the *Pyrené* mountaines, vnto the *Ocean* sea, was made Consul, and passed by order of the senat into *Africk*, thereby to draw *Hanniball* out of *Italy* to the defence of his owne country, and such was his successe, that *Hanniball* after fourteen yeares warre, which he had made in *Italy*, was forced to returne to *Carthage*, to defend it, and was shortlie after ouerthrowne by *Scipio*, wherevppon the *Carthaginienses*, craued peace, and obteined it with hard conditions, as that their nauy of fiue hundred saile, should be burnt, which was performed, and so ended the second *Punick* warr, and *Scipio* remained with the honorable title of *Africanus*. *Oros. l. 4. c. 18 & 19.* *An. 549.* *Liuius Dec. 3. li. 8.*

18 And yet I cannot omitt to note, that in this meane time, the *Romans* had also great losses, and disgraces otherwere, as by the *Gaules* who killed *Lucius Posthumius* the designed Consul, and all his armie of twentie fiue thousand men, the yere after their ouerthrow at *Cannæ*. Besides that the two *Scipioes* father, and vncle to *Africanus*, were slaine in *Spaine* by *Asdrubal*, *Hannibals* brother, who afterwards passing into *Italy*, to the succour of his brother *Hannibal*, was killed himselfe in battaile with sixty three thousand *Africans*, *Spaniards*, and *Gaules*, by the two Consuls, *Caius*, *Clodius Nero*, and *M. Liuius Salinator*. *An. 539.* *Oro. l. 4. c. 18* *Ibidem.*

19 Also the *Romans* were forced during these their afflictions, and miseries in *Italy*, to maintaine warres in *Macedonie*, against *Philip* king thereof, and in *Sardinia*, and *Sicilie*, where there passed also in this time, the surprise of *Syracusa*, by *M. Claudius Marcellus*, who was afterwards slaine by *Hannibal* (as I haue already declared) and this seege of *Syracusa*, was famous by the notable endeuours of the great *Geometrician Archimedes*, *Num. 19.* *Plutarc. in Marcel.*

who with his admirable engins, defended the citie a long time againſt *Marcellus*, ſo that it is hard to ſay, whether the *Romans* were more to be pittied for their diſtreſſed, and miſerable ſtate, or to be admired for their courage, and power in that they were able to ſuſtaine, and paſſe through ſo great, and continuall calamities, and doubtles they could neuer haue done it, if God had not, as I haue ſaid, verie particularlie protected, and aſſiſted them, for the erection of their Monarchie, to the which his deuine Maieſtie beganne now at this time (I meane at the end of the ſecond warre of *Carthage*) to open a great gate: propagating greatly their dominion in diuers parts, and yet ſo, that their ſcourge, and puniſhment euer accompanied, or ſpedelie ſeconded their good ſucceſſe, and encreaſe of empire, as ſhall appeare throughout all the enſuing diſcourſe.

20 Now then, a few moneths after the end of the ſecond warre of *Car-*
An.554. *thage*, firſt the Conſul *Seruius Sulpicius Galba*, and ſhortlie after *T. Quintius*
Flaminius, were ſent into *Macedonie*, where, with manie cruel battailes,
An. 556. and great loſſe of his owne ſouldiarrs, *Flaminius* conſtrained *Philip* the
King to craue peace, which he graunted him with hard conditions, as
Oro.l.4.c 20 to render all his galleis to the *Romans*, except fiftie, & to pay them foure
Eutrop.l.4. thouſand weight of ſiluer, for tenne yeares ſpace. And by this meanes he
deliuered alſo the *Grecians* from the oppreſſion of King *Philip*, and reſto-
Plutarc. in red them to their ancient liberty, for the which he gained great honour,
Quin Flam and fame in *Greece*, and had afterwardes a glorious triumph in *Rome* for
An 557. his victorie.

21. But this good fortune was counterpoyſed with the great diſgrace,
that an other *M. Claudius Marcellus*, receiued preſentlie after of the *Boij* in
An.558. *Toſcan*, who ouerthrew him, and killed a great part of his armie, though
afterwards they were alſo vtterly vanquiſhed by him, and by his fellow
Oro.l.4.c.20 Conſul *L. Furius*. And about the ſame time, *Sempronius Tuditanus* was diſcomfited in *Spaine*, and ſlaine with al his Army, beſides that *Rome* it ſelfe,
and diuers partes of *Italie*, were greatly infeſted with frequent earth-
An.561. quakes, and inundations, eſpeciallie in the yeare fiue hundred ſixtie one,
Boz. de nouo at what time *Bozius* affirmeth, (according to the opinion of diuerſe, as he
& ant. Ital. ſaith) that the great deluge happened, whereof *Pliny* ſpeaketh, which
Plin. natur. drowned twenty three townes in a part of the *Roman* territorie called
his li.3. c.5. *Pontinum*, and that *Rome* was greatly endammaged the ſame yeare, with
Bozius ibid.
num.91. twelue ſeuerall inundations.

22 The yeare before, to witt fiue hundred and threeſcore, beganne the
An.560. *Sirian* warr, by reaſon that *Hannibal*, vnderſtāding that the *Romans* ſought
to haue him deliuered into their handes, fled from *Africk* to *Antiochius*

King

King of *Syria*,& perſwaded him to paſſe out of *Aſia*, into *Europe*, to make warre vpon the *Romans*, and *Antiochus* after diuers bloudie battailes (in *Oro.l.4.c.20.* one of the which the Conſul *M. Accilius Glabrio* put to flight, and ſlew fortie thouſand of his ſouldiars) was finallie ouercome both by ſea, and *An.563.* by land, by *L.Cornelius Scipio*, with the helpe of his brother *Scipio Africanus* who was content to be his liuetenant generall in that warre. For which victories *Lucius Scipio* had the title of *Aſiaticus*, as his brother had of *Africanus*.

23 And during this warre, the *Romans* had alſo other warres, with the *Ligures* in *Italy*, and with the *Celtiberians*, and other people in *Spaine*, but not with like good ſucceſſe. For *Publius Digitius* the Prætor, loſt almoſt al *Idem ibid.* his armie in *Spaine*, & *Lucius Aemilius* the Proconſul, was not onlie ſlaine himſelfe, by the *Luſitanians*, but alſo all his armie cut in peeces. And *Lucius Bebius*, paſſing towards *Spaine*, was alſo killed by the way, with his whole armie, by the *Ligures*, in ſuch ſort, that there remained not one man of them aliue, to carrie the newes to *Rome*, where it was firſt vnder- *An.568.* ſtood from *Marſilia*, and *Quintus Martius*, the Conſul thinking to be reuẽged of the *Ligures*, for the ſlaughter of *Lucius Bebius*, was put to flight, with the loſſe of foure thouſand men, and hardlie ſaued himſelfe, and the reſt of his armie.

24 At this time alſo was detected, the beaſtly, and abominable abuſes of the *Bacchanalia*, (which as I haue declared in the ſeauenth chapter) *Num.19.* were certaine feaſtes celebrated in the night, by men, and women, in honour of the God *Bacchus*, wherein Adulteries, Inceſt, Sodomie, Mur- *Liuius Dec.* ders, and al kind of miſcheefe, were partelie executed, and partlie con- *4.li.9.* triued, and of this confraternitie were diſcouered aboue ſeauen thou- *An.568.* ſand in *Rome*, of whome verie many both men, and women were put to death, and the reſt fled.

25 And here I cannot forbeare to put thee in mind, good Reader, of an other calamitie, wherewith (as I haue declared before) the *Romans* were continuallie vexed, more or leſſe, though I haue not ſpoken thereof in theſe latter times, to witt their domeſticall diuiſions, which at this time, whereof I now treat, grew to ſuch extreame malignitie, that the famous *An.567.* *Scipio Africanus* (nothwithſtanding his great meritts, was falſely accuſed, *Liuius Dec. 4.li.8.* to haue defrauded the common welth, and forced by the malice of calumniators, to lead a baniſhed life, at *Linternum*, where he died three yeares after, to wit, the ſame yeare, that *Hannibal* his competitor in mar- *An.571.* tiall glorie poiſoned himſelfe, fearing that *Pruſia* King of *Bithinia*, would *Idem ibid.* deliuer him to the *Romans*. And in like manner, the other *Scipio* his bro- *Valer. Max.* ther, called *Aſiaticus*, was condemned to priſon vpon pretence, that he *li.5.*

alſo had defrauded the common welth, for his owne priuat commodity.

An.572. 26 The next yeare after the death of *Scipio Africanus*, and *Hannibal*, there
Liuius Dec. fell in *Rome* a prodigious rayne of blood two dayes together, beſids di-
4.li.9. uers other feareful preſages of ſome future calamity, which as it ſeemeth
Idem ibidem foreshowed a moſt cruel plague that preſently followed, aſwell in *Rome*,
li.10. as ouer all *Italy*, & laſted a boue three yeares, in which time it almoſt diſ-
An.574. peopled the cittie, and cuntry, and amongſt others, died the Conſul *Ca.*
Calpurnius Piſo, and manie woorthy, and notable men, to the greate dam-
Eutrop.l.4. mage of the commō welth. Neuertheles it may be obſerued here, that as
An 574. almighty God punished the *Romans* at home at this time, ſo he dilated, &
Oro.l.4c.20 amplified their empire abroad, namely in *Spaine* where *Fuluius* the *Prætor*
An. 575. ouerthrew in battaile 23. thouſand men, & tooke 4000. of thē priſoners,
Liuius Dec. *Lucius Poſtumius* defeated 40 thouſand, and *Gracchus* the *Prætor* tooke 200.
4.li.10. tounes, and citties, and ſlew 22. thouſand *Celtiberians*.

27 With in a few yeares after ſucceded one of the greateſt warrs that the *Romans* euer had for the time it laſted, to wit the ſecond warr of *Macedony*
An.586. againſt king *Perſeus*, who gaue the *Romās* many great ouerthrowes, both
Liuius Dec. by lād, & ſea, ſlew greate numbers of them, ſould many of thē for ſlaues,
5.li.4.& 5. & kept many in captiuity, and ſeruitud in *Macedony*, though in the end he
Oro.l.4c.20 was ſubdued with incredible facility, & ſpeede, by *Paulus Aemilius*, who lead him, and his children priſoners to *Rome*, and triumphed there moſt magnificently, hauing not onlie made *Macedonia* a prouince of the *Romans*, but alſo much encreaſed their treaſure by the ſpoile thereof, in ſo
Plutarc. in vita Pauli Aemil. much, that the people had no neede to pay any tribut (as in former times they were wont to doe) vntil the cōſulat of *Hircius*, & *Panſa*, in the beginning of the raigne of *Auguſtus Cæſar*, which was about a 100 yeares after.

28 And now vpon this occaſion I can not forbeare, good Reader, for thy further ſatisfaction to repreſent vnto thee the forme of a *Roman* triūphe, & to exemplify the ſame in the triumph of this *Paulus Aemilius*, which laſted three dayes with no leſſe pompe, and magnificence, then varietie of gratefull showes and ſpectacles in this manner.

Plutarc. ibid 29 The firſt day, there were lead through the citie, 200 fifty carts, or waines, loadden with moſt excelent images, & pictures of all ſorts, brought from *Macedony*, which were ſo manie, that al that day was ſpent in their paſſage. The ſecond day there paſſed in like manner al the richeſt, & faireſt armour of the *Macedoniās*, notably wel furbished, together with their bucklers, shilds, targets, ſwordes, pikes, quiuers of arrowes, *Thracian* hatchets, & other weapōs, tied looſely together, in ſuch ſort that they made a horrible noiſe with their motion, & the shock of one of them againſt an other, thereby to repreſent the terrour, & horrour of warre, aſwell to the

the eare as to the eye. And after followed alſo the ſame day, ſeauen hundred fiftie veſſels, euery one capable of three talents, wherein was caried an admirable quantity of coined money, & ſiluer medals, by 3. thouſand mē, that is to ſay foure to euery veſſel, which they bore vpō their ſhoulders, beſides that others carried in their handes, ſiluer cupps, goblets, bowles, baſins, and ewers, no leſſe remarkable for their ſundry ſtrange faſhions, then for their quantitie, and greatnes.

30 The third day earely in the morninge, there paſſed al the trumpets of the army, ſounding after the manner of warre. And after them a hundred & twentie bulls, with their hornes gilt, & gardlands vpon their heades, were lead, by as manie gallant yong men to be ſacrificed, and others bare the bowls, and cups of ſiluer, and gold, which were vſed in ſacrifice, and preſently after followed three hundreth, and eight men, bearing ſeauentie ſeauen great veſſels full of gold coine, (foure men to euerie veſſel) in the ſame manner that the ſiluer was caried the day before, and after this there was caried a cuppe, dedicated by *Paulus Aemilius*, to the gods, which coſt tenne talents of gold, being richly ſett with gemmes, & precious ſtones; and next after went all the rich plate of gold, that King *Perſeus* had taken from *Antigenus Seleucus*, and other princes, and was wont to vſe in his moſt ſumptuous bankets.

31 Then followed the chariot, & armour of King *Perſeus*, together with his royall crowne, and after went his children, lead priſoners, being two boyes, and a girle, but ſo yonge, that they had no apprehenſion of their owne miſerie, and therefore moued the behoulders to greater compaſſion: with them went alſo a multitude of their officers, ſchole-maſters, and ſeruants, all of them turninge on euerie ſide towards the people, as they went, and houlding vp their handes to them in forme of ſuppliants, which they alſo made the Kinges children to doe.

32 After them followed King *Perſeus* himſelfe on horſback, reueſted in his royall robes but ſo diſmaied, and aſtonished with the conſideration of his owne miſerie, that he ſeemed to haue loſt his witts, being accompanied with a dolefull troope of his cheefe nobility, counſellours, freendes, & fauorits, houlding downe their heads, & yet caſting other whiles ſuch pitifull glanſing lookes vpon their King, that they ſeemed more to lament his fortune, then their owne. And after al this, there were caried foure hundred crounes of gold, which had bene ſent, and preſented by ſeuerall citties to *Aemilius* to congratulate his victorie, who followed the ſame himſelfe vpon a moſt ſumpteous chariot appareled in purple, embrodered with gold, carying in his right hand a bough of bayes, or lawrel, & ſecōded with al his army, crowned with garlands of bayes,

who

who being deuided into ſquadrons, followed his charriot, ſinging his praiſe with all ioy, and exultation, whereto the people applauded with incredible contentement.

33 Thus ended the triumph of *Paulus Aemilius* in whom *Plutarck* obſerueth notablie the inconſtancie of al humane felicity, in that his triumphant glorie, was checked with the death of his two ſonnes, of whome the one died fiue dayes before his triumph, and the other three dayes after, which neuertheles he bore with admirable conſtancie, & patience, aſſembling the people after the buriall of his ſecond ſonne, and vſing vnto them a moſt prudent, and magnanimious ſpeach, wherein he admoniſhed them of the frailty, and inſtabilitie of all humane thinges, ſignifing vnto them, that from the beginninge of his *Macedonian* warr, he had greatlie ſuſpected the extraordinarie ſucceſſe, firſt of his proſperous paſſage into *Macedony*, and after of the incredible ſpeede of his victorie, hauing taken the king, and his children priſoners within fifteene daies, after his arriual there, in which reſpect he euer feared, as he ſaid, ſome frowne, or check of fortune, which might obſcure the glorie of his conqueſts, with ſome publike diſgrace, but now ſeeing, that the diſaſter was fallen onlie vpon himſelfe, and his owne familie, he hoped that the felicitie of his victory would remaine cleare, ſtable, and aſſured to the common welth, which he would hold for a ſufficient comfort, and recompence of his priuat calamitie. Thus ſaith this wiſe, and magnanimious *Roman*, which I could not omitt to touch by the way, to ſerue for a holeſome document, of the ſmall truſt that ought to be repoſed in humane happines.

Plutar. ibid.

34 And now to proceede. After this immediatlie followed a moſt dangerous warre with the *Celtiberians* in *Spaine*, which was ſo terrible to the *Romans*, that no man durſt vndertake to goe thither, either as a ſouldier, or as Embaſſadour, vntill at length, yonge *Scipio*, who afterwards razed *Carthage*, offered himſelfe to the enterpriſe, and happilie performed it, whiles neuertheles in the meane time, *Sergius Galba* the prætor, loſt his whole armie in a battaile with the *Luſitanians*, and verie hardlie eſcaped himſelfe with a few.

An. 603. *Idem ibid.*

35 Then followed the third, and laſt warre with the *Carthaginienſes*, vpõ breach of couenaunts on their part, wherevpon the *Romans* beſeeged *Carthage*, which was twentie miles about, and defended it ſelfe foure yeares with great bloudshed on both partes, and great diſgrace to the two *Roman* Conſuls *L. Cenſorius*, and *M. Manlius*, whom the *Carthaginienſes* defeated. But the fourth yeare *Scipio*, (who was therefore called *Africanus*, no leſſe then the former) partlie burned it, and partly razed it, and the

An. 605. *Oroſ. ibid. c. 22. & 23.* *Eutrop. li. 4.*

the very same yeare the *Romans* also tooke and destroyed the famous cittie of *Corinth*; And during all these great warres in *Macedony*, *Syria*, *Spaine*, and *Africk*, they had also diuerse other with the *Etolians*, *Histrians*, *Galle-græcians*, or *Gallathians*, & the *Illirians*, al which warres so farr from home, with what great paine, & difficultie, extreame charges and oppression to the common welth, and continuall losse of blood they were sustained amidst so many great ouerthrowes, and disgraces, as I haue signified, anie man may easely iudge.

36 Neuertheles these former times may seeme verie tollerable in respect of those, which are to follow, for presentlie vpon the destruction of *Carthage*, I meane the very same yeare in the consulat of *Lucius Cornelius*, and *L. Mumius*, one *Viriatus*, a *Lusitanian*, or *Portugues* (as now we call them) being basely borne, first beganne to robb vpon the high wayes, and after assembling other theeues, infested whole prouinces, and within a while grew so strong, that he was able to make warre vpon the *Romans*, & presumed to beare the ensignes of the Consuls of *Rome*, ouerthrew *Caius Vetilius* the prætor, and killed almost al his armie, and then discomfited *Caius Plautius* in manie battailes, and shamefully disgraced *Claudius Vnimanus*, with the slaughter of al his army, wherein cōsisted the greatest force of the *Romans* at that time. Finallie he continued to molest, and trouble the *Roman* empire, for foureteene yeares together, vntill at length he was slaine by his owne souldiars, hauing killed in warre aboue threescore thousand *Romans*, as *Florus* testifieth.

An. 908. Oros. l. 5. c. 4. Eutrop. li. 4.

Florus li. 3.

37 Also at the same time, *Appius Claudius* the Consul, receiued a great disgrace by the *Gaules*, with the losse of tenne thousand of his souldiars, and the next yeare followinge, *Rome* was visited in the old manner, with a most strange, & horrible plague, which made such destructiō of people therein, that there were not men inough aliue, to burie the dead, nor heires to be found to enherit ample, and great patrimonies, and finallie the stinch of the dead bodies, & the corruption of the aire was such, that no man could endure of a long time to come neere the cittie.

An. 611. Oros. l. 5. c. 4. Eutrop. lib. 4. An. 612. Idem ibid.

38 The next yeare after, beganne the warr with the cittie of *Numantia* in *Spaine*, which resisted all the force of the *Romans* foureteene yeares, with only foure thousand men, and first ouerthrew the Consul *Q. Pompeius*, & after *C. Hostilius Mancinus*, forcing them to make two dishonorable, and shamefull peaces, though *Mancinus* had in his armie thirtie thousand mē, and albeit the senate allowed the first peace, yet they refused to admit the latter, & therefore caused their consul *Mancinus* to be deliuered to the *Numantins* naked, with his hands bound behind him, who was left so by the *Romans* before the towne of *Numancia*, a whole day together, and yet

An. 617. An. 613. Orosius & Eutrop. ibid.

the *Numantins* would not receiue him. In concluſion the towne being af-
Oroſ. lib.5. ca.6. terwards long beſeiged by *Scipio Africanus*, & the inhabitants finding thẽ
ſelues not able longer to reſiſt, they burnt themſelues, and their towne,
in ſuch ſort, that no one of them could be taken priſoner, to be caried in
triumph to *Rome*. About the ſame time *Lepidus* the proconſul, receiued a
shameful ouerthrow of the *Vaccei*, a people in *Spaine*, & loſt 6000. *Romãs*,
in puniſhment as it may be thought of the iniuſt warre, which he made
vpon the *Vaccei*, againſt the expreſſe order of the Senat: But this diſgrace
was recompenſed in an other part of *Spaine*; with the victorie of *Brutus*,
who ſlew in battail 50. thouſand *Gallitians*, & took 6. thouſand priſoners.

An.619. 39 In the meane time there aroſe in *Sicily* a great rebellion of ſeauentie
Oroſius li.5. c.5. thouſand ſlaues, who foiled diuers great armies of the *Romans*, & by their
exãple, many thouſands alſo of ſlaues tooke armes in diuerſe other pro-
Eutrop. li.4. uinces, who in the end were either killed, or crucified. And in *Rome* there
grew the famous ſedition, of *Tiberius Gracchus* Tribune of the people, who
to be reuenged of the ſenat, for that it charged him to be ſome cauſe of
the shamefull peace made with the *Numantins*, ſtirred vp the people to
ſedition, with the propoſition of new lawes for the equal diuiſion of the
An. 622. legacy, which *Attalus* the king of *Pergamus*, had giuen to the common
Oroſ.l.5.c.8. welth of *Rome*, in which ſedition *Tiberius Gracchus* was ſlaine with two
thouſand of the people, that tooke armes in his defence.

An. 623. 40 And preſently after this, the Conſul *P. Licinius Craſſus*, being aſſiſted
Oroſ.li. 5. ca. 10. with the forces of the kings *Nicomedes* of *Bithinia*, *Mithridates* of *Pontus*, &
Armenia, *Ariaratus* of *Capadocia*, and *Philomenus* of *Paphlagonia*, was ouer-
Eutrop. li.4. throwne, & a great part of his army ſlaine by *Ariſtonicus* brother to the
king *Attalus* in *Aſia*, and *Craſſus* himſelfe flying was killed by a *Thracian*,
whom he chaũced to ſtricke in the eye with his riding rod, whoſe death
An. 624. and diſgrace was after reuenged by the conſul *Perpenna*, & *Ariſtonicus* taken, & ſent to *Rome*, where he was ſtrangled in priſon. And the yeare fol-
An.625. lowing the famous *Scipio Africanus*, (who deſtroied *Carthage*) hauing bene
forced to plead publikelie for his honour, and life, in anſwer of certaine
calumniations impoſed vpon him, by the malignitie of his aduerſaries
was found the next day in the morninge dead in his bed, which *Oroſius*
Idem ibid. and *Eutropius*, do reckon amongſt the other infelicities of the common
welth, and for an example of the great ingratitude of the *Romans*, and a
lamentable effect of their ciuill diſſentions.

Oroſ.l.5.c.11 41 About this time alſo there came flying into *Africke*, ſuch innumera-
Eutrop.li. 4. ble ſwarmes of Locuſts, that they deſtroyed all the fruit of the earth, and
there followed ſuch an vniuerſall peſtilence in all thoſe parts, that there
died thirty thouſand *Roman* ſouldiars, who were in garriſon at *Vtica*, and
there

there about for the guard of the country, besides a million and eighty *An.629.* thousand of all sorts of people in *Africk*.

42 Shortly after followed in *Rome*, the sedition of *Caius Gracchus*, brother *An.633.* to *Tiberius*, who following his brothers example, made the like, or rather *Oros.l.5.c.12* a greater tumult, & was slaine with aboue two hũdred & fifty of the peo- *Eutropius li.4.* ple, which tooke his part, besides that *Opimius* the cõsul did put to death, *Orosius cap.* for the same cause 3. thousand others, of whome manie were innocent. *13. & 14.* About the same time *Metellus* subdued the Ilands of *Maiorica* & *Minorica*: *Gneus Domitius* slew 20000. *Sauoyans*, and *Fabius* the Consul, ouerthrew a huge armie of *Bituitus* king of a part of *France*, in which battaill 50000. *Gaules* were partly slaine, and partly drowned.

43 Ere long after beganne the warre of *Iugurthina* king of *Numidia* in *An.643.* *Africk*, who hauing ouerthrowne *Aulus Posthumius*, & his armie of forty *An.644.* thousand men, drew al *Africk* from the obedience of the *Romans*, & being confederat with *Bocchus* king of the *Moores*, was after many bloudy con- *Orosius eod. l.c.15.* flicts with *Caius Marius*, put to flight, with his confederat *Bocchus*, who *Eutrop. ibid.* betrayed, and deliuered him to the *Romans*.

44 This warre was not ended, when the *Cimbri, Tentones, Tigurini,* and *Ambroni* people of *Gallia* (now called *Fraunce*) & of *Germany*, conspired together to assaile *Italy*, to ouerthrow the *Roman* state: And being encoun- *An. 649.* tred by *Caius Manlius* the consul, killed him, his two sonnes, & a hundred *Orosius ibid* twentie thousand of his men, in so much that there was but only tenne *c.16.* left aliue of all his armie, which filled al *Rome* with no lesse sorrow then *Eutrop.li.5. an.653.* feare. But in the end, the Consul *C. Marius*, hauing had two yeares doubtfull and bloudy warre with them, killed three hundred and forty thousand of them, and tooke a hundred and forty thousand prisoners, besides an innumerable company of women, who fought no lesse then the men, & rather then they would be takẽ aliue, killed thẽselues, & their childrẽ.

45 But who can sufficiently expresse, the calamities, that presently followed vpon this victorie, when *Caius Marius* being returned triumphãt to *Rome*, & chosen Consul the sixt time, conspired with *Saturninus* the Tri- *An.654.* bune of the people, and *Glaucia* the prætor, against the worthy *Metellus* *Oros.l.5.c.17* *Numidicus*, whom they banished to the great discontent, and sorrow of al *Eutrop.li.5.* good men, and after fell to variance amongst themselues, *Marius* taking part with the bettet sort against *Saturninus*, wherevppon there grew a great warre in the citty, and horrible slaughter of a great number of the people, and manie principall senators, and amongst the rest, of *Saturninus* and *Glaucia*, with diuers others their friends.

46 After this succeded such prodigious things in diuers parts of *Italy*, that all men were astonished therewith, and did easilie pronosticat, *An.663.*

some great miserie to the common welth : for to let passe many other thinges, two mountains in the territory of *Modena* ranne one against the other diuers times, with a terrible noyse, and in the end retired to their places againe, whilst also in the meane time, great flames of fire, and aboundance of smoke issued from betwixt them, and with this conflict of these two hills, diuers villages, and great store of cattle, which were betwixt them, were ouerwhelmed, and destroyed in the sight of manie *Romans*, and other passingers, who at the same time were traueiling that way. Also all kind of cattle, and beastes, aswell domesticall, as other fell mad, and ranne howlinge, and roaring vp, & downe the fields, & woods, not suffering anie man to approach them. All which was seconded with a generall league of the *Picentes, Vestini, Marsi, Peligni, Marrucini, Samnites*, and *Lucani*, who tooke armes to deliuer themselues from the dominion of the *Romans*. *Pompey* the *Prætor* being sent against them by the senate, was ouerthrowne by the *Picentes*. *L. Iulius Cæsar*, was likewise put to flight by the *Samnits*, and his armie cut in peeces. *Rutilius* the Consul was himselfe slaine by the *Marsi*, with many noble men, and eight thousand *Romans*. *Cæpio* with his whole armie, had the like successe, by an ambushment of the *Vestini*, and *Marsi*, al which caused such lamentation, & feare in *Rome*, that the senators, and all the citizens put on mourning apparell, and although in the end, all those confederats were vtterlie vanquished by *Marius, Silla, Cn. Pompeius, Porcius Cato*, and other *Roman* Captaines, yet the citie of *Rome* was reduced to such penurie and necessitie, that they were forced to take from the *Augures, Bishops*, and *Flamins*, many houses, and possessions, which they had about the Capitoll, and to sell them, to buy corne for the publike prouision.

Plinius natural. hist. li. 2. cap. 83. *Oros. l. 5. c. 18* *Eutrop. li. 5.* *Idem Ibid.* *An. 664.* *Ibidem.*

47 And before this warre was ended, beganne not only the warrs, with the great King *Mithridates*, but also the ciuil warrs betwixt *Marius*, and *Silla*, whereof it would be to long to relate the occasion, with all the lamentable effects, but to say some what of both. It being vnderstood in *Rome*, that *Mithridates* King of *Pontus*, and *Armenia* the lesse, did not onlie make warre vppon *Nicomedes* king of *Bithinia* (who was confederat with the *Romans*) but also had in one daie caused a hundreth and fiftie thousand *Roman* citezens to be killed in *Asia*, where they partlie dwelled, and partlie negotiated, and traueyled as passengers, it was resolued by the senat, that the Consul *L. Cornelius Silla*, should goe against *Mithridates*, and he being already on the way with his army, but somewhat detained in *Campania*, to end the foresaid warre of the confederats (whereof there was yet some relicks there) he vnderstood, that *Marius* in *Rome* practised to be made Consul, the seauenth time, and to haue

An. 666. *Oros. l. 5. c. 19* *Eutrop. li. 5.*

to haue the honour and charge of the warre against *Mithridates*, where oppon *Sylla* returned in furie with his armie to *Rome*, and being resisted, and encountred by *Marius*, and his freinds, put *Marius* to flight and then marched forward into Greece against *Mithridates*, *Marius* flying in the meane tyme, and being taken escaped out of prison, assembled a great number of fugitiues, and ioyning him selfe with *Cinna*, who was then one of the Consuls, and with *Sertorius*, and *Carbo*, ouerthrew *Plantius*, and his whole armie, and spoyled diuers cittyes, and committed horrible crueltyes in theyr way towards *Rome*, and *Pompey* being in the meane tyme called by the senat to ioyne with *Cn. Octauianus*, the other consul, and hauing had an vnfortunat conflict with *Sertorius*, was killed with a thunderbolt, and all his armie consumed with the plague. *An. 667.*

48 *Marius*, and *Cinna* entring *Rome*, filled the city with blood, and killed, saith *Florus*, all the nobility, delighting and recreating themselues with the horrible spectacle of the heads of the senatours, which they caused to be brought into their banketts and sett vp in diuers parts; and so barbarous was their crueltie, that it suffised for the death of any man yf *Marius* did not offer him his hand to kisse, or gyue him good countenaunce, when he came to salute him, which the souldiars obserued, as a signe, or watchword, for the slaughter of manie noble men, whereupon those few senatours which escaped fled into *Greece*, with *Sillas* wife, and children to craue his ayde for the defence of the common welth, whiles in the meane time, *Marius* (hauing made himselfe consul, the seauenth tyme, with *Cinna*) died, and *Cinna* hauing also satiated himselfe with the blood not onlie of the good, and innocent, but also of the eight thousand fugitiues (which came to Rome with *Marius*) was killed by his owne souldiars. *Florus l. 86. an. 668. Oros. lib. 5. ca. 19. Eutropius li. 5.*

49 *Silla* hauing ouerthrowne *Archelaus* captaine of *Mithridates*, in three battayles, and killed in the first aboue a hundred thousand of his enimyes, with the losse of only thirteene souldiers of his owne, and in the second battaile, fiftie thousand, and in the last the whole armie of *Archelaus*, forced *Mithridates*, to craue peace, which he graunted, to the end he might bend his forces, against yonge *Marius* sonne to the other, and *Carbo* who being then at *Rome*, and both of them consuls, sent forth their captaines to encounter *Silla*, and to hinder his passage, who vanquished them with great bloodshed, and when he came to *Rome*, he fought a most cruel, and bloudie battaile with yong *Marius*, wherein were slaine on the part of *Marius* fourescore thousand men, and entering into the cittie he killed, three thousand, some say foure thousand, which had yealded them selues vnto him, vpon his promise of security. And so ge- *Orosius li. 6 c. 2. An. 672. Oros. li. 5. ca. 20. Strabo. li. 5.*

nerall was the ſlaughter which he made there, of good, and bad, innocent, and nocent, that nine thouſand of his owne freendes were killed amongſt the reſt.

50 Then followed the moſt infamous, and cruel proſcriptions, or outlawries, that euer were heard of, for, aboue foureſcore thouſand men in *Rome*, and abroad, were proclaimed outlawes, their goods to be confiſcate, and themſelues to be ſlaine, which was alſo executed vppon as manie of them, as could be found, yea, and great ſlaughters were committed in diuers parts, and eſpecially in *Preneſte*, and *Sulmo*, in both which cities, all the citizens were condemned by *Silla* to be ſlaine, as though they had bene but one man, which was alſo performed, and the citties ſacked by the ſouldiars, onlie becauſe they had fauoured *Marius*. In like manner, he vtterlie deſtroied the cheefe cittie of the *Samnits*, and manie other in their iuriſdiction, and deuided diuerſe parts of Italie amongſt a hundred tenne thouſand of his ſouldiars, partly killing, and partlie expelling the ancient inhabitants.

Eutrop. li. 5. *Oroſius li. 5. c. 21.* *Flor. li. 89.* *Appian. li. 1.*

51 To conclude, yt is noted by the hiſtoriographers, that in the ſpace of tenne yeares, to wit, during theſe laſt two warrs of the confederats, and this ciuill warre, there were ſlaine aboue one hundred fiftie thouſand *Roman* ſouldiars, twentie foure principall men, that had bene conſuls, ſix that had bene prætors, threeſcore which had bene *Ædils*, and almoſt two hundred ſenatours, beſides an infinit number of people throughout *Italy*.

Oroſ. ibid. ca. 22.

52 So that I thinke a greater miſerie of a countrie cannot be imagined, eſpeciallie if yt be conſidered withall, that the fyre of this ciuill warre, was but, as yt were, raked vp for a while in ashes, and shortlie brake forth againe into new flames, which burned manie yeeres, for *Silla* hauing of his owne free will, to the wonder of all men depoſed his dictatorshipp, and ended his daies in a priuate ſtate, whereas he might eaſilie haue made himſelfe monarch (which no doubt he did not becauſe the time, which God had prefixed for the erection of the monarchie was not yet expired) certaine freendes of *Marius*, namelie the conſul, *Lepidus Brutus*, and *Sertorius*, made new broyles, and although the two former were in one ſommer ſuppreſt (but with much bloodshed) yet the laſt, to wit *Sertorius*, held warres in *Spayne* againſt *Metellus*, and *Pompey* eighteene yeares, and gaue them manie great diſgraces, and ouerthrowes, vntill at laſt he was killed by his owne men.

An. 675. *Idem ibid.* *Idem c. 23.* *Eutrop. li. 6.*

An. 681. 53 In the meane tyme, there aroſe foure other great warrs, to wit, in *Macedony*, *Dalmatia*, *Pamphilia*, and the infamous warre of the fugitiues

vnder

vnder *Spartacus* the Gladiator or fensor and his companions *Chrisso*, and *Tinomao*, who being in prison in *Capua* with seauenty one other of their profession, brake out, and assembled so manie rogues, vagabonds, and malefactors, that first they put to flight *Clodius* the prætor, and spoyled his campe, and after procuring aide of the *Gaules*, and *Germans*, ouerthrew *Gneus Lentulus* the consul, and after that againe defeated both the same *Lentulus*, and the other consul *Lucius Gellius* his companion, and in their fourth battaile they killed *Caius Cassius* the proconsul, and discomfited, all his armie, with no lesse terrour to the *Romans*, as the *Historiographers* report, then when *Hannibal* made his approach to *Rome*: and finallie ranging vp, and downe *Italy* three yeares, they committed infinit cruelties, spoyles, rapes, and all kind of mischeefe, vntill at last hauing giuen seauen ouerthrowes to the *Romans*, they were cut in peeces by *M. Licinius Crassus*, who in three battailes killed, and tooke prisoners, a hundred thousand of them, and their confederats, of whome thirtie thousand were *Gaules*, and *Germans*.

Oros. li. 5. c. 24. Eutrop. li. 6. An. 682. Oros. li. 5. ca. 24. Eutrop. li. 6. An. 684.

54 And yet whiles the *Romans* were thus miserablie vexed in *Italy*, they were faine to maintaine those other great warrs (whereof I spoke before) in *Spayne*, *Macedony*, *Dalmatia*, and *Pamphilia*, and ere the warre in *Macedonie* was ended, *Mithridates*, also broke peace with them, and renewed his former warrs, with redoubled forces to the great terrour, and danger of the Roman state, all which neuertheles was after a few yeares prosperouslie ended, by *M. Lucullus*, *Publius Seruilius*, *C. Scribonius*, *Lucius Lucullus*, brother to *Marcus*. And finallie by *Gneus Pompeius*, surnamed the great, of all which the two last left eternal memorie of their prowesse to all posterity; for *L. Lucullus* gaue manie notable ouerthrowes to the two potent kings, *Mithridates*, and *Tigranes*, aswell ioyntlie, as seuerallie. He put *Mithridates* to flight, and cut in peeces all his armie at the citie *Cyzicum*, and ouerthrew him againe in *Pontus*, and slew sixty thousand of his souldiars, he discomfited also *Tigranes* king of the greater *Armenia*, and put to the sword a hundred thousand of his footemen, and almost all his horse, with the losse of onlie fyue of his owne men, though he had not the twentith part of his enimyes forces: finallie he put them both to flight in *Armenia*, with an incredible slaughter of their huge armie, and had vndoubtedly subdued them both, and fully ended that warre, if a great mutinie of his owne souldiars had not hindred the prosecution of his victory.

Oros. li. 5. ca. 23. Oros. l. 6. c. 2. Plutar. in vita Lucull.

55 But what wanted on his part, was after supplied and performed

by

Idem in Pompeio. by *Gneus Pompeius*, who succeeding him in his charge, vtterly vanquished them both, and depriued them of a great part of their states, and kingdomes, and made them tributorie for the rest to the *Romans*. Besides that he subdued also twentie other kings, and tooke aboue a thousand castells, and fortresses, nine hundred cities, and eight hundred saile of shipps, to the great glorie of the *Romans*, and encrease of their dominions ouer all *Asia*, and manie other countries (eastward, as also *Iulius Cæsar*, had the like successe in fiftie battailes which he fought with the *Gaules*, *Heluetians*, and *Germans*, of whom a million, and a hundreth ninetie, and twoo thousand were slaine by the *Romans* vnder his conduct.

Cæsar in cōmen. belli gal. li. 1. 3. 6. &c. Plut. in Iulio Cæsare. Eutrop. li. 6.

56 For now the tyme approching, which almighty god had in his infinit wisdome and deuine prouidence, appointed for their advauncement, to the monarchie of the world (according to the prediction of the prophets), he gaue them a continuall course of victorious conquests, for the propagation of their empire, fiffeteene yeares together, I meane, from the warre of the fugitiues, which ended in the yeare sixe hundred eightie foure. vnto the second consulat of *Pompey*, and *Crassus*, which was in the yeare sixe hundred nintye nine.

Dan. 2. *An. 684.*

57 Wherein neuertheles yt may be noted, that the execution of Gods iustice, was no lesse notorious in their punishment at home, then the effects of his prouidence in their prosperitie abroad. For ere foure yeares were fully past, after the warres of *Spartacus*, and the other fugitiues, there brake forth the warre of the pirats, who being but a few in the beginning of the ciuill warrs betwixt *Marius*, and *Silla*, grew by litle, and litle, to such number, strength, and audatious pride, that they not onlie spoyled all passengers without exception, but also tooke whole Ilandes into their possession, and manie townes, and cities vppon the sea coast, to the number of foure hundred, whereof they fortified manie, hauing their *Arsenals*, and different nauyes, in different parts, mounting to the number of a aboue a thousand sayle.

An. 688. *Plutarc. in Pompeio.*

58 And such were their riches, and pompe, that they had golden masts, oares of siluer, and sayles of purple, their insolencie, and impietie was such, that they committed all kind of villanies in rapes, murders and sacriledge, hauinge spoyled a hundred, and seauenteene of the most principall, and famous temples of the gods, that were in those dayes. Finallie they made so litle account of the power of the *Romans*, that they tooke their *Prætors*, and magistrates prisoners, and put them to ransome, abusing them, and all the *Romans* which fell into their handes, with great indignities, contempt & derision, to the incredible disgrace & detriment of the *Roman* state, wherupon *Cneus Pompey* being then of the greatest fame,

Idem ibid.

and

and reputation in *Rome*, and newlie returned from the *Spanish* warrs, was chosen Generall against them: and within three moneths vtterlie ouerthrew them. *An.*681.

59 Within two, or three yeares after, *Cicero* being Consul, discouered the conspiracie of *Catelin*, which was already growne to that ripenes, & danger to the common welth, that *Catelin* being expelled out of *Rome*, by *Cicero*, gaue battaile to *Caius Anthonius*, the other Consul, who slew him, and ouerthrew all his armie. *An.*691. *Oros.l.*6. *c.* *Eutrop.l.*6.

60 Furthermore the old disease of the *Roman* common welth (I meane their domesticall diuisions, betwixt the Senate, and the people, yea and betwixt the Senatours themselues) was now growne to be so exorbitant that all good order in the election of magistrates, and the exercise of Iustice, was turned vpside downe: in so much, that neither vertue, nor wisdome, nor great merits, towards the common welth were respected in anie man, as might appeare by the banishment of *Cicero*, at the suite of the wicked *Clodius*, and by the wounding of *Cato*, when he resisted the violent election of *Pompey* and *Crassus* to their second consulat, which they procured with the terrour of armed men, and lastly by the league, which *Pompey*, and *Crassus* made with *Iulius Cæsar*, deuiding the prouinces, and publike charges amongst themselues, and their freendes. *An.*698. *Plutarch. in Cicerone.* *Idē in Pompeio & Crass.* *An.*699. *Idem in Iulio Cæsare.*

61 And thus continued this feuer, as I may tearme it, of dissention with dailie encrease of dolefull effects, and mortall signes, of a remediles ruine speedelie to follow, vntill the flame of ciuill warres growing of *Cæsars* ambition, ruined the common welth, whereto the ouerthrow, and slaughter of *Crassus*, and his whole armie by the *Parthians*, serued for a lamentable preamble: besides that, the casuall burning of a great part of *Rome* shortlie after, was a pittiefull presage, or pronostication thereof. *An.*700. *Idē in Crasso.* *An.* 702. *Eutrop.lib.*6. *Oro.l.*6.*c.*14.

62 And now to come to the vpshot, I meane the vtter ouerthrow of the *Roman* common welth, and change thereof into a *Monarchie*, it is to be vnderstood, that *Iulius Cæsar*, returning from *France*, with his victorious armie, and being vpon the suspicion of his ambitious designements, prohibited by the senate to come to *Rome*, except he dismissed his forces (yea and *M. Antonius*, and *P. Cassius*, tribunes of the people, being also, for the fauour they bore him, suspended from their offices, and fled to him from *Rome*) he marched forward with his armie, pretending onlie to restore his freendes the tribunes to their offices, wherewith the senate was so terrified, that they departed from *Rome* towards *Greece*, recommending the protection of themselues, and the common wealth to *Pompey*, whereVppon *Cæsar* arriuing at *Rome*, made himselfe *Dictator*, and possessing himselfe of the publike treasure, which he tooke by force (because it was *Plutarc. in Iulio Cæsar.* *Oros.l.*6.*c.*15 *Eutrop.lib.*6 *An.*704. *An.*705.

denied to be deliuered him) departed thence shortly after to make warr against *Pompey*, who was not onlie himselfe in armes, but also had sent his captaines with forces to all parts of the *Roman* empire, for the conseruation thereof. But *Cæsar* after manie bloodie victories, which he gained against *Pompeis* freendes in diuerse partes, addressed his forces against *Pompey* himselfe, with whome he fought two battailes, and being ouerthrowne in the first, gained the latter, wherein he slew fifteen thousand souldiars, and forced *Pompey*, to abandon the field, who flying to *Alexandria* in *AEgipt*, was there slaine by the order of yonge King *Ptolomeus*.

Idē Autores vbi supra. *An.707. Plutarc. in Pompeio.*

63 And although *Cæsar* found afterward great difficulty, and resistance, aswell by the same *Ptolomeus* in *AEgipt*, as also by *Pompeys* children in *Spaine*, and his other freendes in *Siria*, and *Africk*, yet he ouercame them all in the end, contrarie euen to his owne expectation. For first in a conflict with *Achillas*, captain of King *Ptolomæus*, he was put to flight, and forced to escape away by sea, and to saue his life by swimminge: and againe in his last battaile with *Pompeys* children, at a towne called *Munda* in *Spaine*, he was brought to such an exigent, that his ould souldiars beganne to fly, and he himselfe was in great feare to be ouerthrowne, and taken, in so much that he was once resolued to kil himselfe, when presentlie his enimies beganne to runne away, and leaue him both the field, and the victorie, which he prosecuted, vntill he had slaine *Sextus Pompeius*, *Titus Labienus*, and *Accius Varus*, with thirty thousand of their souldiars.

Oro.l 6.c.16 Eutrop.li.6. *Idem ibid.*

64 This battaile was fought iust the same day foure yeares, that *Pompey* fled with the senat out of *Rome*. And *Cæsar* returning thither shortlie after, tooke vpon him the title of perpetual *Dictator*, and the absolute gouerment of the common welth. For the which he grew so odious to the senate, that *Brutus*, and *Cassius* with two hundreth sixty Senators, and Knights of *Rome* conspired to kill him, which they performed in the senat it selfe, giuing him twenty three wounds.

An.709. *Plutarc. in Iulio Cæsare. Eutrop. li.6. Orosius li.6. c.17.*

65 And although the senatours aspiring now to their former libertie, meant to shake of the yoke of seruitude, and therefore beganne againe to take vppon them the gouerment of the common welth, yet the time being come, that God had ordained for the erection of the monarchy, al their endeuour serued to no other purpose, but to redouble their owne calamities, & to produce those effects, which God had in his infinit wisdome præordained. For whereas *M. Antonius*, being then one of the most potent in the *Roman* state, had, of his owne priuat authoritie, assembled an army to beseige *Decius Brutus* in *Modena*, for reuenge of priuat quarrels

An.710. *Oros. ibid. ca.18.*

betwixt

betwixt them, the ſenate ſent not onlie the two Conſuls *Hircius*, and *Panſa*, but alſo yonge *Octauianus Cæſar*, nephew, and heire to *Iulius Cæſar*, with equall authoritie to repreſſe the inſolencie of *Antonius*. [*Eutropius li.7. An.711.*]

66 And ſo it fell out by Gods ſpecial prouidence (no doubt) that though *Antonius* was defeated, and put to flight, yet the battaile was ſo bloudie on both parts, that *Hircius* one of the Conſuls was killed, and *Panſa* the other conſul died shortlie after of a wound, whereby the legions which [*Oroſ.l.6.c.18 Eutrop. li.7*] ſerued vnder them both, came to the cōduct of *Octauianus Cæſar*, who hauing enherited no leſſe his vncles ambition, then his goods, and being alſo deſirous to reuenge his death, determined to auaile him ſelfe of the oportunitie offred him, and of the great forces, that he had then in his hands. And for as much as *Antonius* was then fled to *Lepidus* (who had ben one of *Iulius Cæſars* moſt confident freendes, and by him placed in the gouermēt of *Fraunce*) *Octauianus* reſolued to make freendship with them both, which he performed, and vppon conference, they agreed not onlie to deuide the *Roman* empire amongſt them, but alſo to proſcribe, or outlaw almoſt all the Senat, ſelling the liues of their neareſt kinſfolkes, or deareſt freendes one to an other, to the end, that euerie one of them [*Idem ibid.*] might be reuenged on his enimies. And therefore *Antonius* yelded to the [*Plutarc. in M.Antonio.*] proſcription of his owne vncle, and *Lepidus*, of his brother, and *Octauianus* of his tutor, *C.Toranius*, and of *Cicero* his greateſt friend, whome he vſed to call father, in reſpect that he had bene the ſpeciall meanes of his aduancement.

67 And this being ſecretlie determined amongſt them, they came to *Rome* with all their forces, and without reſiſtance vſurped the gouerment of the common welth, vnder the name of a *Triumuirat*, beginninge preſentlie to put in execution their barbarous proſcription, or outlawry, with greater crueltie, and bloodshed of the *Roman* nobility, [*Plutarc. in M.Antonio.*] then had paſſed vnder *Marius*, or *Silla*: for, three hundred ſenatours were [*Petro Mexia in vit.Imper in Auguſto.*] put to death, and their landes, and goods confiſcat, and two thouſand other principall *Romans*, were alſo expoſed to the like crueltie, and yet neuertheles they commanded by publick edict, that al men shuld reioyſe and show publike ſignes of ioy, as *Dio* witneſſeth. [*Dio in Aug.*] Wherein I thinke good to note by the way, that, which I haue vpon diuers occaſions repreſented in the firſt part of this treatiſe, to wit the courſe of Gods ſecret, & iuſt iudgement, in the execution of his iuſtice, vpon the ſenat by a groſe errour of the ſenatours thēſelues, in that they gaue ſo great power, & authoritie, as they did, to *Octauianus Cæſar*, in whom they might with great reaſon ſuſpect, and feare, that either the deſire to reuenge his vncles death, or els his ambition (ſeconded with the confidence of a ſtronge

party, by his vncles friendes) might moue him to seeke, for the soueraignety, if euer opportunity should be offered him.

68 And whereas perhaps, they thought him sufficientlie counterpeised, with their two Consuls, it may appeare hereby how short is the sight of the wisest men some times, and how easilie God dissipateth their counsels, & designements, by accidents neuer dreamt of, as he did in this case, by the death of both the Cõsuls, whereby all their power, yea, & the force of the senate, and common welth, fell into the handes of *Octauianus*, contrarie to their expectation, and turned to their vtter ruin, and to the establishment of his Monarchie, though it pleased God to dispose, for the greater affliction, and iust punishment of all the *Roman* state, that there passed first twelue yeares of most bloudie and cruell ciuill warre, which *Octauianus*, and his twoo Collegues made in diuers parts: first
Oros.l.6.c.18 with *Brutus*, and *Cassius*, who were the cheefe conspiratours against *Iu-*
Eutrop.li.17 *lius Cæsar*: secondlie with *Lucius Antonius*, who being Consul in *Rome*,
Ibidem. sought to ouerthrow their *Triumuirat*: thirdly with *Sextus Pompeius*, who had possest himselfe of *Sicily*: and lastlie amongst themselues, in which warre *Lepidus* being abandoned by the most part of his souldiars, submitted himselfe vnto *Octauianus*.

An.720. 69 About the same time as some suppose, a towne called *Pisaurum* (a colonie of *Antonius*) was whollie swallowed vp by the earth, neere vnto
Plutar. in Anton. the place, where *Pesaro* (called also in latin *Pisaurum*) now stãdeth, which prodigious, and disastrous accidẽt, was shortlie after seconded with the vtter ouerthrow, and ruine of *Antonius*, whom *Octauianus* defeated in a
Idem ibidem nauail battaile at *Actium*, and pursued to *Alexandria* in *Aegipt*, & there
Oro.l.6.c.19 ouerthrew him againe by land, wherevppon both *Antonius*, and also
Eutrop.li.7. *Cleopatra* Queene of *Aegipt*, killed themselues, and all *Aegipt* became subiect to the *Romans*, who then began their empire, as it was foretold by
Zachar.6. *Zacharias* the Prophet, when he said, that *the pyde, and strong horses* in the
Vide Riberã in 6.c.Zach. fourth chariot, (signifiing the *Romans*) *vvent forth into the South*, that is to say, into *Aegipt*, giuing to vnderstand the fourth Monarchie (to wit the *Roman* empire) should then beginne, when the Kingdome of the *Grecians* (that is to say all the successors of *Alexander* the great) should be vtterly ouerthrowne, which was fullie accomplished at this time, when *Octauianus Cæsar*, made *Aegipt* a prouince of the *Romans*, by the ouerthrow, and death of the Queene *Cleopatra*, who was the last that the *Romans* subdued of all the successours of *Alexander*, whereby the empire of the *Grecians*, was vtterlie extinguished, and the Monarchie of *Augustus Cæsar* began.

70 For after this victorie, *Octauianus* returning triumphant to *Rome*,

was

was with the common consent, and vniuersall applause of the senat, saluted by the name of *Augustus*, which he euer after retained, and transmitted to his successors, remaining from that day foreward sole emperour, and Monarck of the *Roman* empire, which he gouerned for thirtie yeares, with such crueltie, and tirannie, that verie manie principall men were forced to kill themselues: and to the end he might the better discouer practises against himselfe, he vsed to corrupt mens wiues by adulterie, as *Suetonius* testifieth, & finally deuided a great part of *Italy*, amongst his souldiars, with the destructiō, or banishmēt of the inhabitans thereof, as *Dion* witnesseth. Whereto also the poet alludeth in his pastorall Eclogue, representing the lamentable complaint of the husbandmen, that were expelled from their ancient dwellings.

An.725. Oro l.6.c 20 Eutrop.li. 7. Sueton. in August. c. 69 Dio in Aug. Virg. Eclog. 1

At nos hinc alij sitientes ibimus Afros,
Pars Scithiam, & rapidum Cretæ veniemus Oaxem
Et penitus toto diuisos orbe Britannos, &c.
Impius hæc tam culta noualia miles habebit?
Barbarus has segetes. &c.

71 And notwithstanding this crueltie of *Augustus*, almightie God did also laie his heauie hand vpon the *Romans* diuerse wayes, during the same time, partlie by great inundations of *Tiber*, partly by fire (whereby a great part of the cittie of *Rome* was consumed) and partlie by stormes, and tempests, whereof *Horace* seemeth to speake, when he saith.

Iam satis terris niuis, atque diræ
Grandinis misit Pater, & rubente
Dextera sacras iaculatus arces
Terruit vrbem, &c.

Horat. li. 1. Ode 2.

Besids that the plague was so great in *Rome*, and throughout *Italy*, that the ground was generallie left vntilled for some time, wherevppon also followed great famin: And finallie in these first yeares of *Augustus* his raigne (to wit the sixt of his Monarchie which was the seauen hundreth twentie and nine yeare after the foundation of *Rome*) a huge armie of the *Romans* perished in *Arabia*, by a maruelous strange disease which tooke them in the heades, and suddenlie killed them.

Solinus ca. 2. An. 729. Dio in Aug.

72 And thus continued the scourge of God vpon the *Romans*, vntill it pleased his deuine maiesty, to take vpon him our humanitie, and not onlie to be borne in the *Roman* empire, but also to be registred for a citizen of *Rome*, and a subiect of *Augustus*, whose latter daies were therefore blessed, with a speciall priuiledge of prosperitie, and peace, our Sauiour ordaining out of his deuine prouidence, that the same should be vniuersall at the time of his birth: and therefore *Augustus* hauing then subdued

An.751.

Oros. lib.6. ca.21.& 22. Eutrop. li.7. dued the *Asturians* and *Cantabrians* in *Spaine*, and conquered many fierce, and warlicke people in *Germany*, laid downe armes, and shut vp the temple of *Ianus* in signe of an vniuersall peace, which cōtinued for the space of twelue yeares. And no maruaile if the author, giuer, and prince of peace, vouchsafing to come into the world, brought with him both tēporall, and spirituall peace, imparting the temporall to all nations in generall, and the spirituall to his elected seruants, according to the heauēlie proclamation published at the time of his birth by the Angels, when *Luc.2.* they song; *Gloria in excelsis Deo, & in terra pax hominibus bonæ voluntatis. Glory be to God on high, and in earthe peace to men of good vvill.*

73 But seeing I am now come to the birth of our Sauiour *Christ*, and the establishmēt of the *Roman* Monarchy vnder *Augustus Cæsar*, I thinke good to prosecute the rest of his raigne, and of the pagan emperors his successours, in an other chapter.

A prosecution of the same matter, vvith a continuation of the abridgement of the Roman *Historie, from* Augustus Cæsar, *vntill the empire of* Constantine *the great, the first Christian emperour. Also the extreame tirannie of the pagan Emperours, their persecutions of the Church, hovv long euerie one of them reigned, and in vvhat manner, and yeare they died, and finallie the horrible calamities, and miseries inflicted by Gods iustice vpon them, and the* Roman *empire during their raigne.*

CAP. XII.

1. THOV hast hetherto seene, good Reader, the manifold afflictions, and calamities of the *Romans*, for the space of seauen hundred, aud fiftie yeares, that is to say, from the first foundation of their cittie of *Rome*, vntill the birth of our Sauiour *Christ*, and the change of their gouerment from a popular state, to a monarchie, vnder *Augustus Cæsar*: wherein I doubt not, but thou hast obserued the concurrence of Gods iustice in their continual punishment, and of his prouidence in the amplification of their dominion, and empire: & therefore now it resteth, that I procede to manifest vnto thee, the course of Gods seuere iudgements vpon the Emperours and the empire, for the space of 300. & eighteene yeares, which passed frō our Sauiours birth, to the time of *Constantin* the great, after the ouerthrow, & death of *Licinius*.

2 And first to make an end of the raigne of *Augustus*, I haue already declared, how cruell, and tirannical he was, for thirtie yeares, & although he became afterwards a most clement, and benigne prince, & was ther fo

fore greatlie honoured,and beloued of the people, and held for,*Pater pa-* *Sext.Aureli.*
triæ, the father of his country , yea, and that our Sauiour,as I haue ſigni- *Victor in*
fied before , bleſſed him , and his empire with extraordinarie peace for *Auguſto.*
ſome yeares, yet it cannot be denied, but that aſwell the *Romans* his ſubiects , as alſo he him ſelfe in his owne perſon , paid continuallie the penaltie of their idolatrie,and abominable impietie diuerſe wayes.

3 As firſt,for the *Romans.Dio Nicæus* witneſſeth,that they were much af- *Dio Nicæus*
flicted with earthquakes,in the yeare ſeauen hundreth fiftie ſeauen,after *in Auguſt.*
the foundation of *Rome*,which was the ſeauenth yeare of our Sauiour,& *An.vr.757.*
thoſe earthquakes cauſed, as *Caßiodorus* in his chronicle affirmeth , great *An.Domi.7.*
deſtruction of houſes,& people in *Rome*,for eight dayes together:beſides *Caſſiodorus in Chron.*
that *Tiber* made ſuch an inundation, that al the lower parts of the cittie *Dio in Aug.*
was nauigable, for ſeauen dayes. There was alſo great famin about the
ſame time,and a miſerable ſlaughter of *Quintilius Varus*,and his whole army,in *Germany* , where with *Auguſtus* was ſo afflicted, that he ranne his
head againſt a wall,and cried out,*Quintilius,reſtore me my legions:*& where- *Eutrop.li. 7.*
as al men were ſurpriſed with ſuch feare,that no man would be preſt for *Sextus Aur.*
a ſouldiar to ſupplie the loſſe , he cauſed euerie fift man , that was vnder *Victor in Auguſto.*
the age of thirtie fiue yeares , and euerie tenth man aboue that age, to be *Dio in Aug.*
drawne out by lot , and to be ſpoiled of his goods , and made infamous,
& put manie to death for the ſame cauſe. Alſo he had in pay at the ſame
time,three and twenty ſeueral armies,to the great oppreſſion of the people,impoſing vpon them great extraordinarie taxes for the maintenance *Idem ibid.*
thereof.Beſides, that *Eutropius* teſtifieth, that there was neuer before that
time , greater damage donne by caſuall fire in *Rome* , then in the yeare , *Eutrop.li. 7.*
ſeauen hundreth and ſixtie , which was the tenth yeare after our Saui- *An.vr.760.* *An.Do.10.*
ours natiuitie : in ſo much,that *Auguſtus* was forced, to contribute largely out of his treaſure,to the reparation of the damage:& in this meane
while alſo,there was ſuch a cruel famin throughout *Italy,* that great nũ-
bers of people were baniſhed *Rome* , and forced to depart almoſt a hundreth miles from the cittie, for the eaſe, and releefe thereof , and of the
countries adioyning.

4 Finally,the *Dalmatians* greueouſlie infeſted al the ſea coſt of *Italy*,from *An.vr.764.*
the yeare ſeauen hundreth fifty eight , vntill the yeare ſeauen hundreth *An.Do. 14.*
ſixty foure , that is to ſay , vntill within two yeares before the death of
Auguſtus,which was ſeconded,ſaith *Solinus,* with an extreame dearth, & *Solin.ca.2.*
penurie of all thinges.

Thus much for the calamity of the *Romans* in the laſt yeares of *Auguſtus.*

5 And as for his owne perſon,it is to be conſidered,that beſides his continuall affliction of a ſickly bodie , he was moſt vnfortunate both in his *Ibid.cap.3.*

iſſue,

Sueton. in Auguſto.

iſſue, and alſo in his end, according to the opinion of ſome) for although he had foure wiues, yet he had no other children, but only one daughter, called *Iulia*, who was alſo infamous for her diſhoneſt, & laſciuious life, & though ſhee was maried thrice, & had ſonnes by her ſecond huſband *Agrippa*, yet two of them died before *Auguſtus*, and the other called *Agrippa*, ſo much diſliked him, that he baniſhed him, and adopted for his ſonne, and ſucceſſor *Tiberius*, the ſonne of his wife *Liuia*, and maried his daughter *Iulia* to him. And *Liuia* vnderſtanding afterwards, that he was determined to recall *Agrippa* from baniſhment, & fearing leaſt it might turne to the preiudice of *Tiberius* her ſonne, haſtened the end of *Auguſtus* as ſome authors affirme, by poiſoned figgs in the fiftie ſeauenth yeare of his empire, whereof he had reigned twelue yeares in companie of *Lepidus* and *Antonius*, and fortie foure yeares alone. Thus much concerning *Auguſtus*.

Vide Sextum Aurelium Victorem in Auguſto. An. ur. cond. 767. An. Dom. 17

6 But now who can ſufficientlie expreſſe, the miſerable ſtate of the *Romans*, from his time vntill *Conſtantin*, through the extreame tirannie of their emperours, I meane not in reſpect of the cruell perſecutions raiſed by a eleuen of them againſt the Chriſtians, (for that ſome of thoſe perſecutors, were held by the Painims for good emperours, as *Traian*, *Marcus Aurelius*, *Decius*, and *Diocleſian*) but in reſpect of their extreame crueltie towards all men, and eſpecially towards the ſenate, and men of the greateſt vertue, for the which the Paynims themſelues held them for moſt barbarous, and cruell, as *Tiberius*, *Caligula*, *Claudius*, *Nero*, *Galba*, *Vitellius*, *Domitian*, *Hadrian*, *Commodus*, *Septimius Seuerus*, *Caracalla*, *Macrinus*, *Heliogabalus*, *Iulius Maximinus*, *Gallienus*, *Aurelianus*, *Carinus*, *Maximianus*, *Maxentius*, *Maximinus* ſurnamed *Iouius*, and *Licinius*.

Dio in Tibe.

7 And to ſay ſomewhat breefelie of the crueltie, and other enormities of euerie one of theſe. It is written of *Tiberius*, that he killed ſo manie of the ſenate, and other men of worth, that for lack of fitt men to employ in the offices, and charges of the common welth, he was faine to continue the Prætor three yeares, and the Conſuls ſix in their offices, which were wont to be annuall, beſides that he condemned whole families, ſuborned accuſers, againſt many principal men, and aſſigned rewards for ſuch as would accuſe any man, and ſometimes alſo for witneſſes. All teſtimonies were admitted, all offences made capitall, no day ſo holy, that it was free from the puniſhment, torment, and ſlaughter of men, whereof ſuch particulers are declared by the hiſtoriographers, that it is lamentable to read, which I omitt for breuities ſake.

Sueton. in Tiberio c. 61

8 And to ſpeake a word, or two of his coueteouſnes, and exceſſiue rapins, he killed manie rich men, onlie to haue the ſpoile of their welth, he confiſca-

confiſcated the goods of diuers princes in *France, Spaine, Siria*, and *Greece*, for ſuch trifles, and with ſuch an impudent manner of calumniatiõ, that ſome were charged with no greater fault, then that they had a great part of their wealth in ready money. *Sueton. in Tiberio c.49*

9 And whereas *Veno* the King of *Parthia*, being by them expelled from his Kingdome, came to *Antioche*, with exceeding great wealth, putting himſelfe into the protection of the *Romans*, he cauſed him to be ſpoiled, & ſlaine. His life was alſo moſt vile, & vicious, in ſo much, that *Dion* ſaith, he was oppreſt with the ſhame and infamie of his luſt, and loue of women, & boyes, taking them by force from their parents, or freendes, whẽ he could not winne them, by entreatie, or corrupt them with gifts. To conclude, finding himſelfe to be moſt odious to al men, he leaft the empire of purpoſe to *Caius Caligula*, becauſe he knew him to be monſtrous in all kind of wickednes, and crueltie, hoping thereby, either to extinguish, or at leaſt to qualifie the ignominie of his owne impietie, and tyrannie. Thus much touchinge *Tiberius*. *Idem ibid.* *Dio in Tibe.*

10 His ſucceſſour *Caius Caligula*, exceeded him no leſſe in ſecret murders, then in the publike ſlaughters of innocent men, and could not be ſatiſfied, except he ſaw men tormented, boweled, and quartered, and ſo inſatiable was his thirſt of blood, that he wiſhed, that all the people of *Rome*, had but one head, that he might cut it of at one blow. And ſome time when there wanted condẽned men to be deuoured of beaſtes (with the ſight whereof he was much delighted) he cauſed his ſouldiars to take ſome of the ſtanders by, & behoulders, to caſt them to the beaſtes to continue his ſport. *Sueton. in Caligula.ca. 28.29.30. 31.32.* *Dio in Calig*

11 Furthermore, hauing leuied a huge army of two hundred fifty thouſand mẽ, he killed moſt of them within a while, & hauing cauſed a great number of the worthieſt *Romãs* to be ſlaine, partly in ſecret, (ſommoning them afterwards to the Senate, as though they had bene ſtil liuinge) and partly publikly for fained crimes, he determined at laſt, to deſtroy all the principal ſenatours, & noble men, & ſo to remoue from *Rome* to *Alexandria*, & had performed it, if he had not bene preuẽted by his owne death. Alſo his rapins, & extortions, were ſuch, that, as *Dion* ſaith, when he had cõſumed al the money of *Rome & Italy*, he went into *France*, of purpoſe to ſpoile it, and *Spaine*, where (ſaith the ſame author) it was made a publike crime to be rich. His impoſitions, tributes, & new deuiſed exactiõs, were innumerable, whereof I omit the particularities, for breuities ſake, as alſo his deteſtable inceſts, with his owne ſiſters, & adulteries, & many other execrable acts of his, related by *Suetonius, Dion*, & other graue authors, all which, I ſay, I omitt, & will conclude with his abominable, & *Luciferian* *Idem ibid.* *Ibidem.* *Sueton.c.24* *Dio in Calig*

Idem ibidem pride, in that he made himselfe a God, erecting a temple with his image in it, ordeining priests, and most costlie sacrifices, to be offered there to himselfe, and faining great familiarity with *Iupiter*, he vsed to talke some times with his image, and sometimes falling out with him, he threatned to send him away into *Greece*, and yet afterwards seeming to be pacified againe, he would be content, that their images might stand together: finallie he grew to that excesse of vanitie, and extrauagant impietie, follie, and madnes, that he vsed to make loue to the moone, when it was at the full, as though it had bene a woman. And thus much concerning him.

Dio. in Clau. 12 *Claudius* succeeded him, who being accustomed, saith *Dion, to glut himselfe vvith the blood of men*, committed manie suddaine, and rash murthers, at the suggestiō of the wicked *Messalina* his wife, & of his fauourits, who when they would haue the life of any mā, vsed to terrifie him with some practise, & deuise of a fained cōspiracy, whereby they drew him to yeeld to the death of whom soeuer they would: & such was their power saith *Victor* and authority that, *Stupris, exilio, cæde & proscriptionibus omnia fædabant*. They filed all things with fornications and adulteries, banishments, slaughters, & proscriptions, or outlawries.

Victor in Claudio.

Dio in Nero. 13 *Nero*, as *Dion* testifieth, held vertue, riches, and nobility for no lesse thē publike crimes, and therefore manie rich, noble, and vertuous men, were either killed by his instruments, or forced to kill themselues. And *Eutropius* affirmeth of him, that, *Infinitam partem Senatus interfecit, & bonis omnibus hostis fuit. He killed an infinit part of the Senate, and vvas enemie to all good men*. And he did not content himselfe, saith *Tacitus*, with the death of manie notable men, but sought in the end to destroy vertue it selfe in *Barea, Soranus*, and *Thraseas Petus*, and amongst others he caused the famous philosopher *Seneca*, his master, yea, and his owne mother, to be slaine, and made her after to be opened in his owne presence. Besides that he desired saith *Dion*, to see the destruction of the Roman empire, and of the cittie of *Rome*, and therefore caused the cittie to be set on fire, whereby. *Innumerabiles incendio perierunt*. An infinit number of men perished. And in the meane while he stood on the topp of a tower to see it burne, singing the destruction of burning *Troie*, and such was the damage done by fire, that of foureteene regions, saith *Tacitus*, whereinto *Rome* was deuided, onlie foure were free, the rest either wholy consumed, or pitifullie defaced, and afterwards he almost destroyed all the empire with exactions, to repaire the cittie, and such were his extortions, throughout the greatest part of his reigne, that *Dion* saith. *Omnem terrarum orbem expilauit. He robbed and pilled all the vvorld.*

Eutrop. li. 7. in Nerone. Tacitus l. 16 Dio in Nero. Tacitus l. 16 Dio in Nero.

14 Mo-

14 Moreouer, his custome was, to runne vp and downe the streets in the night with his souldiars, rauishing women, and boyes, spoiling, striking, wounding or killing all those that he mett, neither could any man (saith the same author) be safe in his owne house. *Nerone in domos, & officinas insubtante. For that Nero vsed to breake into mens houses, and shops.* And to conclude concerning him, he was so exorbitant in al kind of vice, and wickednes, that it appeared sufficientlie in him, how detestable may be the effects of a vicious, & tirannical nature, when it is ioyned with soueraignty. And therfore no maruaile, if that he was the first, who generally persecuted the Christians, and embrued the cittie of *Rome*, & the *Roman* empire, with the bloude of infinit martirs, & amōgst others the glorious Apostles *S. Peter*, and *S. Paule*: which how it was punished in him, shall appeare after a while, when I shall speake of the ends of all the Emperours, and the continuance of their reigne, for here I touch nothing, but their tirannicall crueltie, or other impietie. And now to proceede.

Idem. *Baron. To. 1. An. Dom. 69*

15 *Galba*, was infamous for his intemperaunce, coueteousnes, dissolute life, and especiallie for the abominable sinne of *Sodomy*, and his crueltie. He dismanteled diuers citties in *Spaine*, and *France*, and put to death their gouernours, with their wiues, and children, because in his rebellion against *Nero*, they did not yeeld vnto him, at the verie first. He made away manie noble men, vpon very light suspitions, without anie triall of their cause, & hauing ordained that a great number of sea souldiars (who had in former time bene sailers, or rowers) should be casht, & returne to their old trade, he caused them to be decimated, that is to say, euery tenth man of thē to be killed, because they made great instāce to the cōtrary. Finally he suffered himselfe to be so wholy lead, & gouerned by three fauorits (who were extreamely arrogāt, couetous, & vicious,) that he was worthily hated of al men, no lesse for their auarice & cruelty, then for his owne.

Suetonius in Galba c. 12. & 22. *Idem c. 14.* *Idem ibid.* *Sex. Aurel. Victor in Gal.* *Io. Ba. Egnat in Galba.*

16 *Vitellius* was, saith *Suetonius, prone to the slaughter, and torment of euery man, for euerie trifle*, and killed manie of the nobilitie (who had bene his ould friends, and companions) *vario genere fraudis*, with diuers kinds of deceit, & was so cruel, that he made men to be murdered in his presence, saying that he would feede his eyes, and commanded two to be killed, for that they entreated him for the life of their Father: he caused a great number of the common people to be slaine in a publike feast, because they were clad in greene, which colour was vsed by those, that were of a faction called *Prasina*, he being addicted to the contary called *Veneta*.

Sueton. in Vitel. c. 14. *Idem ibid.*

Finally, whosoeuer was but accused to be an astronomer, was presentlie executed, though it were not proued, and in this cruelty he continued during the short time, that he raigned, which shalbe declared hereafter.

Sext. Aureli. Victor in Domitiano. 17 *Domitian*, as *Victor* teſtifieth, was more like a ſauage beaſt, then a man, for his crueltie towards all kind of men: and to maintaine his extreame prodigalitie, he killed many of the richeſt, and principall men of the Senat, onlie that he might haue their goods, of whome, ſome were made away by poiſon, others by other ſecret meanes, & many conuict of *Dio in Dom.* falſe crimes. And he cauſed ſo many to be ſlaine, one way, or other, that *Dion* ſaith, *no man could tell the number of them.* He confiſcated the goods, aſwel of the dead, as of the liuinge, vpon euery light accuſation, or pretẽce of crimes, eſpecially of matter of ſtate, in ſo much that it ſuffiſed, that the *Suetonius in Domitiano ca. 11. & 12.* leaſt deede, or word in that kind, was but ſo much as obiected againſt anie man. He claimed manie rich mens goods, after their death, as their heire, ſuborning witneſſes to proue it: he cauſed manie to be killed, and others to be baniſhed, onlie becauſe they ſtudied philoſophie, or were more vertuous, and learned then other men. And finallie, ſo intolerable was his pride, that he ordained by publike edict, that in all writtings, wherin he should be mẽcioned, vpõ any occaſiõ, he should be called *Dominus Deus. Lord God*, & therefore no maruel, though he was withal a moſt cruel perſecutor of the Church, & raiſed the ſecõd perſecutiõ after *Nero.*

Idem ibid. Spartian. & Dio in Adri. 18 *Adrian* (as *Spartianus* & *Dio* witneſſe) killed a great number of principal perſonages for very trifles, & the moſt notable mẽ of al arts, & ſought to extinguish the memory of *Homer*, & a litle before his death, he baniſhed, or killed, all moſt all his old friendes, and thoſe which he himſelfe had aduanced.

Lamprid. in Commodo. 19 *Commodus* after his death, was called by a decree of the ſenat, *Sauior Domitiano, qui omnes occidit*, more crüel then *Domitian*, who killed all men, & *Carnifex Senatus*, the butcher of the ſenat, for he killed an infinit number of all ſorts of men, and women, ſome for their great nobilitie, ſome for their wealth, ſome for their excellẽt learninge, or other vertues, ſome *Dio in Com.* for their beauty, or cõlines of their perſon, ſome for fained cõſpiracies, or light ſuſpitions, ſome for hyre, ſelling mens liues to their enimies for money: and finally ſome times he killed one for an other, whiles alſo in the meane time he was otherwaies for his life abominably diſſolut, ſpẽding al his time in bankets, & feaſts with 300. concubins, & boies choſen for their beautie, aſwel out of the nobilitie, as of the communaltie. And hauing in the end after infinit other ſlaughters, reſolued to kil a great nũ- *Herodianus in Commod.* ber of the cheefe, and principall perſons, that were ſtil liuinge, he made a liſt of their names, for his better remembrance, which being found by *Martia* his concubin (who was one of the number that was contained in it) moued her, and the reſt to ſeeke their owne ſecuritie, by his death, as *Num. 56.* shalbe declared hereafter.

20 *Septimius Seuerus*, (as *Dio*, and *Spartianus* do testifie) killed very manie of all sorts of men for fained crimes, or verie small occasions, and amōgst them, one and fortie senatours were put to death (saith *Dion*) without anie cause, either proued, or obiected. Besides that he suffered his father in law *Plautianus*, to make away a great number, aswell of magistrats, as of priuat men, to haue the spoile of them, and farther to pill, and robb all the citties, and prouinces of the empire. Finally *Seuerus* murdred verie manie noble men, *Spaniards*, *Gaules*, *Romans*, and whosoeuer he thought to be fitt to gouerne, fearing that the souldiars might preferre them before his children after his death, in so much that he was compared with *Marius*, for his crueltie, and the last counsell that he gaue to his children, when he died, was, *Locupletate milites cæteros omnes contemnite. Enrich your souldiars, and contemne all other men.* Spartian. & Dio in Septim. Seuero. Idem in vita Pescenny.

21 *Antonius Caracalla* his sonne, exceeded him in crueltie, in which respect he was called by a decree of the senat after his death, *Interfector senatus, & populi. The murtherer of the senat, and people.* He killed his brother *Geta*, in his mothers armes, and twentie thousand, saith *Dio*, or as *Spartianus* saith, innumerable others, of his brothers friends and wellwillers, some as they were at table, others in the bathes, and where soeuer els they were found, he made away by one meanes, or other, all those whom his father speciallie fauoured, or loued, and amongst the rest, he put to death his fathers phisitians, because they would not consent to kill his father, as he earnestlie requested thē to doe: and after infinit other murthers of all sorts of men, being greatlie offended with the people of *Alexandria*, because they misliked his crueltie, he inuited manie of thé to a bāket, and caused others to be shut vp in houses, and all of thē to be slaine, and to conclude, *Dion* saith of him, that, *Romam bonis omnibus spoliauit, & mutilauit*, He lamed *Rome*, and spoiled it of all good men. Iulius Capitolin. in Macrino. Dio & Spartian. in Caracalla. Herodian. in Seuero. Dio in Caracalla.

22 *Macrinus*, as *Dion* testifieth, put to death a great number of the senatours, and noble men of *Rome*, for fained crimes, and made away all those whome he suspected, to mislike his election, he deuised new, and strange punishmēts, tying men aliue to dead mē, to the end, they might languish with the horrour, and stinke of the dead carkases, and vsed to close some vp with walls aliue, and so to let them pine away, and perish, and *Iulius Capitolinus* calleth him. *Hominem omnium vitiorum, superbum, & sanguinarium, &c. A man of all vice, proude, and bloody.* And further saith, that his house was alwaies full of blood, like a butcherie, by reason of the continuall slaughters of his seruants, in respect whereof, manie would not call him *Macrinum*, but *Macellinum*, the *Butcher*. Idem. in Macrino. Iul. Capitolinus in Macrino.

23 *Heliogabalus* his successor, was most hatefull, and horrible for his cruelty, he vsed by the counsell of Magicians, to sacrifice children

Iulius Capitolinus. Herodian. Lampridius in Heliogabalo.

which were ſpeciallie choſen throughout all Italie, for their nobility, and beauty, and ſuch as had both father, and mother liuing, and then made his deuinations by looking into their bowels. He baniſhed all the ſenate, ſaith *Lampridius*, out of *Rome*, and killed manie of them, and diuers other notable men, he was more monſtrous for all vice, and villanie, then anie that euer was before, or after him, in ſo much, that whenſoeuer he remoued out of *Rome*, he caried with him ſix hundreth chariots, and horſe-litters full of ſtrumpets, and boies, and all to litle, ſay the hiſtoriographers, for his vnſatiable luſt, for that he neuer had the companie of anie aboue once. He made manie times aſſemblies of hoores, and baudes wherein he vſed to make ſolemne orations vnto them, calling them, *commillitones*, fellow-ſouldiers, and treated with them of all the moſt beaſtlie matters, and acts that could be imagined.

Idem ibid.

24 Furthermore, ſuch was his prodigality in the furniture of his pallace, and perſon, coſtlie bankets, yea, and his ordinarie diett (nothing contenting him which was not of exceſſiue price, and farre fetcht) that the reuenue of the empire could not ſuffice for the ſame: for as *Lampridius* teſtifieth, euerie ordinarie meale, ſtood him in two thouſand fiue hundred crownes (after our account) and manie times he ſpent at ſome one ſupper 75000. crownes.

Herodian. Lamprid.

25 Moreouer he ordained ſuch toyes, that yt may be wondred, how the grauitie, and maieſty of the Roman empire, could brooke, and endure them, for he erected a ſenat of women, to the end they might treat and conſult, of their owne buſines belonging to their apparell, and dreſſing, and decreed that ſuch thinges, as are accuſtomed to be done in the day, ſhould be done in the night, and therefore he vſed to goe to bed in the morninge, and to riſe at ſunne ſetting, and then was ſaluted with good morow. I omit manie other ridiculous acts of his, which might ſeeme vncredible, but that they are teſtified by the graueſt hiſtoriographers, and by this which I haue ſignified, may well appeare the infelicity of the *Romans*, and of their empire, gouerned ſo childiſhlie by a boy, for ſo *Heliogabalus* was, being but fourteene yeares ould when he was choſen, and not fullie eighteene when he was killed, of the manner whereof I ſhall haue occaſion to ſay more heareafter.

Iulius Capitolin. Herodian. in Maximino.

26 *Maximinus*, was for his cruelty called *Cyclops*, *Buſiris*, *Scirron*, *Phalaris*, and *Tiphon*, he ſpoiled, baniſhed, and murdred manie innocent, and worthie men, which had bene conſuls, and all the noble men that were about him, eſpeciallie thoſe, who knew anie thing of his baſe birth, and linage. Finallie he killed all ſorts of men without accuſer, witnes, or iudge, and ſo much thirſted after blood, that hauing put to death foure

thouſand

thousand in the three yeares that he raigned, yet he could not, saith *Capitolinus*, be satisfied. *Iulius Capitolin. in Maximino.*

27 *Gallienus*, was no lesse pernicious to the Roman empire, by his dissolute, and wicked life, and his extreame negligence in gouerment, then the former were for their cruelty, and therefore *Trebellius Pollio*, saith of him, that he seemed to be borne for nothing els, but for his bellie, and his pleasure, and that spending his whole time, both day, and night in wine, and women, *perdidit orbem terrarum*, *he destroyed the whole world.* Thus saith he; for that in the greatest troubles of the *Roman* empire (which in his time was extreamelie afflicted with the inuasion of barbarous nations, and the vsurpation of manie tirants) *deseruit rempublicam*, saith *Orosius*, *he forsooke, and abandoned the common welth*, and gaue himselfe whollie to lust at *Milan*. Besides that, his cruelty was also such towards his owne souldiars, that he killed three thousand, and sometimes foure thousand of them in one day, which if yt had benne done by the enemie, would haue benne counted a great infelicity to the *Roman* empire. *Trebellius Pollio in Gallieno.* *Oros. c. 22.* *Pollio in Gallieno.*

28 *Aurelianus*, is termed by *Victor*, and *Eutropius*, *sæuus*, and, *sanguinarius*, cruell, and bloudie, he fained crymes of conspiracies, against manie senatours, and principall men, and put them to death for the same, besides manie others whome he also caused to be killed, for very small matters. *Vopiscus. Sext. Aurel. Victor. Eutrop. l. 10.*

29 Of *Carinus*, it is testified by *Pomponius Lætus*, and *Vopiscus*, that he was. *Piorum sanguine madefactus, totius vbique iuuentutis corruptor, homo omnium contaminatißimus &c. Embrued with the blood of good men, a corrupter of youth euery where, the most impure, and wicked man that lyued*, and *one*, saith *Vopiscus*, *that not only abused all yong men, but also suffred him selfe to be abused contrary to his sexe.* He filled his pallace with iesters, queanes, ribalds, ruffins, and bauds, he bore great respect to all wicked men, and made them bankets, and feastes, and was euerie way so abominablie impious, that his father *Carus* the emperour, with whome he raigned, hearing of his manner of life, swore that he was none of his, and determined to kill him: neuertheles when *Carinus* heard that his father was dead, he was, say the histories, farre more beastlie, and brutish in all kind of villanie, and what became of him in the end, shalbe declared hereafter. *Pomponius Lætus Vopiscus in Carino. Sext. Aurel. victor.* *Flauius Vopiscus in Carino.*

30. To conclude the other foure emperours, which remaine of the one and twenty aboue named, (to wit *Maximianus*, *Maxentius*, *Maximinus* surnamed *Iouius*, and *Licinius*, were no lesse cruel, and wicked, then most of the former, as I will declare more particularlie after awhile: whereby it may appeare, how miserable was the state of the empire, partlie by reason of their monstrous cruelty, and wickednes, and partlie by the afflictions that God also layd vppon the *Romans* otherwayes from tyme to tyme,

tyme, during the reignes, not onlie of these, but also of all the other Emperours, from *Augustus Cæsar*, to *Constantin* the great.

31 And to the end, that this may be the more euident, I will touch euery one of them by name in order, as they raigned. And first I will speake of the seauen first Emperours after *Augustus*, declaring breeflie, how they came to the empire, how long they reigned, how they died, and finallie I will add thereto, what notable punishments God laid vppon the Roman empire, during their gouerment.

32 *Tiberius*, (the first of the wicked, and tirannical Emperours of whome I haue spoken before) was sonne in law to *Augustus Cæsar*, aswell by the mariage of his daughter *Iulia* (then a widow, by the death of *Agrippa* her former husband) as also because he was sonne to *Liuia*, wife to *Augustus*, whom he succeeded in the empire by adoption. And hauing raigned, or rather tirannized, twenty three yeares, was poisoned, and as some write smothered by his owne nephew *Caius Caligula*, whome for want of issue he had adopted for his sonne, and ordained for his successour, being great graundchild to *Augustus*, to wit, sonne to *Agripina*, daughter to *Iulia*, by *Agrippa* her former husband.

Sueton. in Tiberio. c. 7. & 15. An. Do. 39. Idem ibid. ca. 73.

33 This *Caligula* being most monstrous for his wickednes, and cruelty (as I haue alreadie declared) was slaine by his owne guards (who were called, the *Prætorian* souldiers) when he had reigned but three yeares, and tenne moneths, and the senat being determined to extinguish all the race of the Cæsars, for the detestation of him, it chaunced that his vncle *Claudius*, hauing for feare hid himselfe in a verie secret place of the palace, was found by one of the prætorian souldiers, who came thither to ransacke, and spoile it, and was first by him saluted Emperour, and after by the rest of the souldiars, who also forced the senate to approue their election of him.

Sueton. in Caligula c. 58. An. Do. 43. Dio in Claudio. Eutrop. li. 8.

34 This *Claudius* (one of the tirrannical emperours, mentioned by me before) was also descended of the familie of *Augustus Cæsar* by his mother *Antonio*, neece to *Augustus*, being daughter to his sister *Octauia*, and to *M. Antonio* the *Triumuir*. His infamous reigne dured fourteene yeares; and not long before his death, hauing killed the wicked *Mestalina* his wife, he maried *Agrippina*, his owne sisters daughter, being the widow of *Domitius Nero*, by whome shee had a sonne of the same name, and though *Claudius*, had a sonne of his owne, called *Britannicus*, yet he adopted her sonne *Nero* for his successour, and within a while after was poisoned by her, who concealed his death, vntill shee had caused the souldiars to accept, and proclaime her sonne *Nero* Emperour, which the senat also approued.

Sueton. Claudio. c 1. Idem c. 26. 39. 43. & 44. An. 56. Ibid. c. 45.

35 Nero

35 *Nero* (of whose barbarous, and incredible crueltie, I haue spoken already) hauing plagued the world, as many yeares, as his predecessour (to wit foureteene) was worthily condemned by the senate as a publike enemie to the common welth, and being there vpon abandoned of all men, killed himselfe, with the helpe of one of his slaues, and in him ended the race, and familie of the *Cæsars*, which had possessed the empire about ninty eight yeares.

Dio & Sueton. in Nero. c.49.

An.70.

36 After *Nero*, succeeded *Galba*, whome I haue also numbred amongst the wicked, and tyrannicall Emperours. He in *Neroes* time, was his luietenant Generall in *Spaine*, and Gouernour thereof, and rebelling against him, was first declared Emperour by his owne souldiars, and presentlie after *Neroes* death, confirmed by the Senat: and within seauen monthes, killed by a conspiracie of *Otho*, who succeeded him.

Sueton. in Galb. c.9. & 10. Ibid. c.23.

An.71.

This *Otho*, though I haue not reckoned him amongst the tirannical Emperours, yet was most infamous, for his wicked life, as hauing benne a great fauorit of *Nero*, and an instrument of his wickednes, and being chosen emperour by the prætorian souldiars, and shortly after ouercome by *Vitellius*, he slew himselfe, hauing reigned but three moneths, and fiue dayes.

Plutarc. in Othone. Sueton. in Othone c. 2. 3. & 11.

An.71.

37 About the same time that *Otho* was chosen Emperour in *Rome*, *Vitellius* being Generall of an armie in *Germanie*, was also proclaymed Emperour by his owne souldiars, and hauing ouerthrowne *Otho* neere to *Rome*, succeeded him in the empire, which neuertheles he enioyed but eight monethes, and tenne dayes; for *Vespasian* being also at the same time chosen Emperour by his owne army in *Iudæa* (where he was emploied to appease a rebellion of the *Ievves*) sent some of his Captaines, with a great part of his forces to encounter *Vitellius*, who being ouerthrowne, and taken prisoner, was drawne with a halter about his necke along the streetes, halfe naked, to a market place, where after manie outrages donne vnto him by the people (for the hatred of his tyrannicall crueltie, and beastly impietie) he was killed, together with his brother, and cast into the riuer *Tiber*.

Sueton. in Vitellio ca. 9.

Ibidem. c. 15.

Ibidem c.17.

An.72.

38 Thus ended the seauen first Emperours after *Augustus*, and in the meane while (I meane during their reignes) God laid his heauie hand vppon the empire diuerse wayes. As in *Tiberio* his time, *Rome* suffered exceeding great dammage twice by fire, and by twoo inundations of *Tyber*, and twice by famin.

Euseb. in Chron. Tacit. li.1,

Dio.li.58. Tacit.li. 4. Idem.li.2. And in *Fidenæ*, fiftie thousand men were partlie slaine, and partlie maimed, by the fall of an *Amphitheater*, besides, a horrible earthquake which in one night ruined thirteene cities in *Asia*.

Idem.li.12. 39 Also in the tyme of *Claudius*, *Crebris terræ motibus*, saith *Tacitus*, *prorutæ domus*, &c. Howses were ouerthrowne in *Rome* by frequent earthquakes, wherewith all men were so terrified, that whiles they hasted to seeke some places of refuge, and securitie, verie manie of the weaker sort were oppressed, and styfled amidst the confused throng of the people, and in his time also was the great generall famin ouer the whole world, which is spoken of in the acts of the Apostles. Acto.11.

Plin.li.2. ca.83. Dio. in Nerone. 40 In *Neros* raigne, the earthquakes were so horrible, that as *Pliny* testifieth, whole fields were remoued out of their places, and *Dion* affirmeth, that it seemed the whole earth woulde be shaken in peeces, and dissolued; *In so much*, saith he, *that yt vvas thought, that the soules of those, vvhome Nero had murthered, did insult and rise against him.* And in his tyme also, the *Brittans* being cruellie oppressed, rebelled against the *Romans*, and slew seauentie thousand of them, and of their confederats; besides most strange, and noisome tempests, whereof *Tacitus* maketh mention, and a most cruell plague in *Rome*, which plague saith he, *Omne mortalium genus depopulabatur. Destroyed all kind of mortall creatures.* Tacit.li.16.

Sueton.in Galba.c.18. 41 Finallie in the beginning of *Galba* his raigne, a most prodigious earthquake, accompanied with a horrible roaring sound, shooke both the cittie of *Rome*, and the Emperours pallace, and in those few monethes, that *Otho*, and *Vitellius* reigned *Rome* receaued incredible dammage, not onlie by a most pitifull inundation of *Tyber*, (the greatest, saith *Plutark*, that had euer bene seene before) but also by extreame dearth, and famin, all which *Tacitus* lamentablie describeth, besides the great bloudshed in *Rome* it selfe, betwixt *Galba*, and *Otho*, and much more afterwards both in *Rome*, and abroad betwixt *Vitellius*, and *Otho*, who fought a most bloudie battaile, at *Cremona*, wherein were slaine fortie thousand men on both sides, and the souldiers of *Vitellius*, hauing the victorie, miserablie spoiled, and ransaked all the countrie. Plutar.in vita Othon. Tacit.li.17. Dio in Othone.

42 And within a litle more then three monethes after *Othos* death, there passed two cruell, and bloudie battailes betwixt *Vitellius*, and *Vespasian*. First at *Cremona*, and after at *Rome*, in which battailes a hundred thousand men were slaine, and *Cremona* spoiled, and ruined, and all this bloudshed hapned within a yeare, and twentie daies after the death of *Nero*, so that if we adde these afflictions of Idem in Vitellio.

of the *Romans*, to the continuall tirannie of their Emperours, we shall easelie see, that they had not one day, or houre of ease, or repose, from extreame miserie, vntil the raigne of *Vespasian*, that is to say, for the space of the first fiftie fiue yeares after *Augustus*.

43 And now to proceede with the rest of the Emperours in like manner. Although I doe not number *Vespasian*, amongst the cruell tyrants, yet his gouerment was in some sort so tyrannical, that he may also be counted an instrument of Gods iustice vppon the *Romans*, *Dio in Vespasiano.* in respect of his extreame coueteousnes, and the most greueous exactions, and impositions, which he layd vppon all men, inuenting taxes and gabelles neuer vsed, or imagined before, and employing in the greatest offices, and charges, the greatest extorcioners, that he could find, whom he also vsed, as it was commonlie said, *Like spunges, filling them vvhiles they vvere dry, and crushing out theyr licour vvhen they vvere full*, *Sueton. in Vespasiano. ca.16.* that is to say, spoiling them when they were rich. Whereto also may be added the crueltie of his sonne *Titus*, who commanding all vnder him, killed so manie noble men vppon light suspitions, *Idem in Tito ca.6. & 7.* that he was helde, as *Suetonius* affirmeth, for an other *Nero*. *Vespasian* raigned tenne yeares, and died of a fluxe, leauing two sonnes, *Titus*, and *Domitian*: and *Titus*, succeeding him in the gouerment, *An. Do. 81.* notwithstanding his crueltie in his fathers time, proued to *Ibidem &c. 8. 9. &c.* be one of the best Emperours, that euer the *Romans* had, whose raigne neuertheles was so short (to wit onlie twoo yeares, and some moneths) that the ease which they had vnder him, seemed to serue, for no other purpose, but to make them feele the more the tirannicall crueltie of his brother *Domitian*. And although most authors agree, that *Titus* died naturallie, yet some write, that there was great suspition, and fame that his death was eyther procured, or hastened by *Domitian*. *Dio in Tito. An. Do. 83.*

44 But did the scourge of God vppon the *Romans* cease during those two yeares, of the good gouerment of, *Titus*? No trulie. For in that tyme, euen in the verie first yeare of his raigne, the hill in *Campania* called *Vesuuius* in the kingdome of *Naples*, cast forth such in- *Dio in Tito.* credible heapes of fierie ashes, and with such violence, that two notable cities named *Pompeij*, and *Herculanum*, were ouerwhelmed, and the *Amphiater* in *Rome* filled therewith, yea, and the ashes were also cast into *Greece*, *Siria* *AEgipt*, and *Africk*. Wherebie it may be ghessed what dammage the same did, not onlie in *Rome*, but also in those partes of *Italy*: besides that there presentlie followed such a pestilence, that *Victor* saith, the like was almost neuer seene before, and there was

Sext. Aureli. Victor in Tito. withall such trembling, and roaring of the earth, and such obscuritie, and darkenes at noone dayes, that men imagined, that the whole world would perish, as *Dion* amplie declareth.

45 The yeare following there was such a fire in *Rome*, for three dayes together, that all the famous biuldings of *Augustus*, with his library, and the baths of *Agrippa*, the theater of *Galba*, the temples of *Iupiter Capitolin*, *Isis*, *Serapis*, *Neptune*, and that of all the Gods, called *Pantheon*, the stage of *Pompey*, and diuers other principall partes, and great ornaments of the cittie, were consumed therewith, whereby it may also be coniectured, how generall and lamentable was the detriment, and losse otherwayes throughout the whole cittie. *Dio in Tito. Sueton. in Tito cap. 8.*

46 After *Titus*, succeeded the cruell *Domitian*, being his Brother, and next heire, he raigned, or rather raged fifteene yeares, and fiue dayes, and was killed by a conspiracie of his owne seruants. *Dio in Dom. An. Do. 98.*

47 His next successor *Cocceius Nerua*, being chosen by the Senate, was a notable Emperour, and a great freend to Christians, and recalled from banishment, all those who were banished by *Domitian*, amongst whom was *S. Iohn* the *Euangelist*, but he raigned not aboue a yeare and a few moneths, and died his naturall death, as none of the Emperours his predecessours had done before him, except *Vespasian*, and *Titus*, though there was great suspition, as I haue signified before, that *Titus* was murdred by *Domitian*. *Idē in Neru. Baro. an 99. An. Do. 100*

48 After *Nerua*, followed *Traian*, whom he had adopted, and ordained to succeede him. This *Traian*, though he be counted a verie good Emperour for his clemencie, and iustice, yet he was otherwayes verie vicious, and persecuted the Christians for a time. And albeit the *Romans* bore not their wonted yoake of tirannie during his reigne, yet he, and they felt otherwayes the heauie hand of almightie God, as may appeare by the pittifull narration which *Pliny* maketh, at large, of the excessiue dammage donne in *Rome*, and in all the territorie thereof, not only by the inundations of *Tiber*, and other riuers, but also by most violent tempests, and stormes, which caused a miserable desolatiō throughout the whole country. *Dio in Neru. Plini. l. 8. ep. ad Macrin.*

49 Also during the time of *Traian*, the wonted punishment of God, fell not onlie vppon *Rome* by pestilence, and fire (kindled partlie by thunderbolts, and partlie by other casualities) but also vppon the whole empire, by most terrible earthquakes, especiallie at *Antioch*, whiles *Traian* himselfe was there, where the greatest part of the cittie was destroyed, trees pulled vp by the rootes, and the verie birdes of the aire fell downe dead: and such were the lightnings, thunders, *Plini. li. 36. cap. 15. Dio in Traiano.*

ders, and fier that fell from the heauens, that manie men were burnt, and consumed therewith, and great feare conceyued, that the whole worled would be set on fire. After which followed, an extreame, and intollerable heate, and such a generall dust raised euerie where, that men could not see one an other, and manie were stifled therewith; besides that, the earthquakes were also, at the same time, so generall, that sundry citties in *Greece*, and diuerse partes of *Asia* were wholy subuerted, infinit numbers of men killed, mountaines sunck into the ground, and riuers dried vp.

50 And shortlie after this, the *Ievves* which then inhabited seuerall parts of the world, made great commotions all at once, wheresoeuer they dwelled (as though they had beene all seazed with one frenzy, and especially throughout *Africke*, where they almost exterminated al the inhabitants, in so much, that *Adrian* the Emperour, who succeeded *Traian*, was forced to send many new colonies thither, to supply the wāt of people in those partes: and they did the like also in *Egipt*, and in the Iland of *Cipirus*, where they killed two hundreth thousand persons, wherevppon *Traian* sent great forces into all those partes, and ordained, that all the *Ievves* inhabiting there, should be put to the sword, which was executed most rigorouslie, with the slaughter of incredible numbers of them. *Idem ibid.*

51 Finallie I hold it for no small infelicitie of the *Romans*, at that tyme, also that *Traian*, to entertaine the people, and make them sport, (according to the custome in those dayes) gaue them tenne thousand gladiators, or fencers, to fight to death, and kill on an other in their presence. He raigned nineteene yeares, six monethes, and a halfe, and died naturallie, as most authors affirme, though as *Dion* testifieth, he himselfe suspected that he was poisoned. *Dio in Traiano.* *An.Do.119.*

52 After the one and twenty yeares, of the good Emperours, *Nerua*, and *Traian*, succeeded the cruell *Adrian* by adoption, or as some affirme, by the practise of *Plotina*, *Traians* wife, who concealing her husbands death some dayes, and shewing to the Prætorian souldiars a counterfet instrument, or writting of adoption (as though *Traian* had in his last sicknes adopted *Adrian* for his sonne, and successour) procured his election, first by the acclamation of the souldiars, and after by the approbation of the senat: His crueltie, and tirannie (whereof I haue spokē before) was accompanied with great famin, and pestilence, inundations, and earthquakes, whereby exceeding great dammage was donne aswell in *Rome*, as in diuers parts of the Roman empire. And in the end *Adrian* *Ælius Spartian. in Adr.* *Dio in Adri.* *Num.18.*

receiued alſo euen in this life, ſome part of the punishment due to his crueltie, aſwell towards Chriſtians, as towards all others, being moſt miſerablie tormented in all his limmes, in ſuch ſort, that he ſought by entreatie, perſwaſions, and gifts, to moue his fauorits, and friendes to kill him, and when he could not obtaine it at their handes, nor die of his torments, he reſolued to forbeare to eate, and ſo famished himſelfe as ſome write, or, as *Dio Nicæus* ſaith, vſed of purpoſe vnholſome meates, wherevppon he died, when he had reigned one and twenty yeares, and eleuen months.

[*Pero Mexia in Adriano. Baron. To.2 An.Do.140. Dio in Adri.*]

53 *Adrian*, adopted for his ſonne, and ſucceſſour, the famous, *Antonius Pius*, ſo called for his great pietie, as he well deſerued, whoſe empire God bleſſed, no doubt, with great peace and proſperitie, for the great fauour that he shewed to Chriſtrians, after many cruell perſecutions, which they had ſuffered vnder his predeceſſors: for he forbad vpon greueous paines, that no man should accuſe them for their religion, which he acknowledged to be the worship of the immortall God, affirming alſo, that the great earthquakes, and ſuch other calamities, wherewith the empire was afflicted, proceeded of the iuſtice of God, for the iniurie donne to them, as may appeare by the copy of the edict, related by *Eutropius*, and therefore we may well ſuppoſe, that God rewarded him with greater felicitie, then anie pagan emperour, had either before, or after him, though neuertheles, beſides the earthquakes, which he mentioned in his edict, we reade of extreame dearth, and famin in *Rome*, great loſſe by fire, and inundations of *Tiber*. He raigned twentie two yeares, ſeauen moneths, and ſix dayes, and died his naturall death.

[*Eutrop.l.10.*] [*Ibidem.*] [*Sext.Aurel. Victor Capitolin.in Antonino Pio. An.Do.162.*]

54 There followed him, by his adoption, an other good emperour for his gouerment, though he perſecuted the Chriſtians for ſome time, to wit, *Marcus Aurelius*, called the Philoſopher, who made *Lucius Verus* his companion in the empire. But how ſeuere the punishment of God, was vpon the *Romans*, in the time of *Marcus Aurelius*, it appeareth by that which *Sextus Aurelius Victor*, a pagan author writeth briefly thereof. *Ab armis*, ſaith he, *quies nunquam erat*, &c. *There vvas neuer anie reſt, or repoſe from armes, the vvarres throughout Italy, France, and all the eaſt partes, vvere continuall, beſides earthquakes, vvith the ſubuerſion of citties, inundations of riuers, murrein amongſt cattell, and fields deſtroyed vvith locuſts, yea, and there is almoſt no kind of calamitie, that can either be named, or imagined, vvhich did not abound during his raigne*. Thus ſaith he. And *Eutropius* affirmeth, that the empire was ſo miſerablie infeſted, and vexed with warres in all partes, that all the *Roman* armies, were ouerthrowne, and that the plague was ſo violent euerie where, that the greater part of men, & almoſt al the ſouldiars died thereof. Ne-

[*Epito. Sexti Aure.Vict.in Marco Ant.*] [*Eutrop.li.10*]

of. Neuertheles he had a notable, and miraculous victorie against nine hundred thousand *Marcomanni*, *Quadi*, and other barbarous people in *Germany*, by the prayers of his Christian souldiars (as I haue declared in the 15.chap. of the first part of this Treatise) and in respect of that victory, he ceased his persecution of the Christians, and made edicts in their fauour: His companion *Lucius Verus*, died suddenlie in the eleuenth yeare of his raigne, and he hauing reigned eighteene yeares, died his naturall death.

Chap.15. Num.2.

An.172.

An.181.

55 Though the raigne of this emperour was most vnfortunate, for infinit calamities, and miseries, which oppressed the empire in his time, yet he left behind him a greater plague to the world, then euer had benne in his dayes, I meane his sonne *Commodus*, who besides the cruel persecutions which he raised against Christians, vsed all barbarous crueltie towards all sorts of men, as I haue declared before; but after he had reigned twelue yeares, and eight moneths, he was killed by his Concubin, who as I haue also signified before, finding by chance, her owne name, with a great number of others, of most principall personages designed for the slaughter, in a list written with his owne hand, thought to preuent him with poison, which shee gaue him, & seeing him after he had receiued it, vomit so freely that she feared he would cast it vp againe, she called in one, whose name was also in the list, & betwixt them both they dispatched him.

Num.16.

Num.eod.

Herodian.in Commodo.

An.Do.194.

56 Besides this cruel tiranny of *Commodus*, and the affliction ensuing thereon to the Roman empire, there was such horrible contagion, and pestilence in his time, that (as *Dio* saith who was then liuing) he neuer knew anie so great, whereby there died in *Rome* two thousand in one day. There was also in his raigne so great dearth, and famin, that the people falling into furie, killed *Cleander* one of his greatest fauourits. Also a great part of the cittie, and manie principall ornaments thereof, were twise burnt during his reigne. The first time by a thunderbolt, which fired, and burnt the *Capitol*, the librarie, and all the houses about it: and the later, by a casuall fire, wherewith his owne pallace, the famous temples of *Vesta*, and of *Peace*, with no small part of the cittie, were consumed to the verie ground, which euerie man held to be a iust punishment of God for his wickednes, as *Herodian* testifieth.

Dio in Com.

Herodian.in Commodo.

Idem ibid.

57 But that which may be iustlie counted the greatest calamitie of the *Roman* empire, both at the time whereof I now treate, and also continuly after vntill *Constantins* time, was the licentious libertie, and ambitious presumption of the souldiars, not onlie of those which were called *prætoriani milites*, (and were the guards of the Emperours) but also of the other legions, that were dispersed throughout the empire, for the defence

thereof.

thereof. For such was the insolencie, first of the Emperours gards in *Rome*, and after of the other souldiars abroad, by their example, that they tooke vpon them to make emperours, and chãge them at their pleasure, whereby the emperors themselues, and al the empire was brought to a miserable seruitude.

58 This appeared presently after *Commodus*, vpon whose death, the prætorian souldiars made election of his successor, and chose the worthie Captaine *Pertinax*, whome the senate partlie for feare, and partlie also for the regard of his great merits, easily approued. But within lesse then three moneths, to wit, eightie fiue dayes, they killed him, by the practise of one, who sought to make himselfe emperour, though he failed of his purpose. For the souldiars sett the empire on sale, making proclamation, that they would giue it, to whosoeuer would giue most: and whereas, there were two competitors (to wit *Sulpicianus*, and *Didius Iulianus*, both which offered largelie for it) they preferred *Iulianus*, partlie because the other was father in law to *Pertinax* whom they had slaine, and partly because *Iulianus*, gaue them readie money, wherevppon, they forced the senat to accept him.

Herodianus in Pertinace An. 195. Iulius Capit. & Herodia. in Iuliano.

59 And the other legions abroad, taking also the like libertie to themselues, at the same time, made emperours in diuers parts: for, the ordinary legions, that were in *Siria*, made choise of the viceconsul *Pescennius Niger*, who gouerned there, and the legions in *Germanie*, chose *Septimius Seuerus*, who hasting with his forces to *Rome*, was admitted by the senate, and *Iulianus* being abandoned of all men, was killed in his pallace, by the senats order, before *Seuerus* arriued, within lesse then seauen moneths after his election: And *Seuerus* shortlie after ouercame *Piscinnius*, the other emperour, though with so great bloodshed on both sides, that the ditches of water, where the battaile was fought seemed to be all bloud, & againe ere it were long, one *Albinus* was made Emperour in *Britannie* by his souldiars, & ouerthrowne also, and slaine by *Seuerus* in no lesse bloodie a battaile at *Lyons* in *France*. Whereby it may be iudged, how miserable were these times by insolencie of the souldiars, which encreasing dailie, grew within a few yeares after, to be so greate, that there were thirtie emperours made by the armies, in diuers parts in the space of fifteene, or sixteene yeares, by meanes whereof, the empire was pitifully rent, & torne with ciuil warrs, and opprest with infinit calamities, and verie many of the emperours themselues killed by the souldiars, which had chosen them, as shall farther appeare hereafter.

Idem ibid.

An. Do. 195. Ibidem.

60 So that it is hard to say wether the Senat, and people were more tirannized by the emperours, or the emperors by the souldiars: but howsoeuer

ſoeuer that was, it is euident, that both the Emperours, and ſouldiars, were inſtruments of Gods iuſtice, not onlie one vppon an other, but alſo vppon all the Roman empire, and that the ſouldiars alſo executed Gods iuſtice vppon them ſelues, who to maintaine their different elections of emperors in diuers places, came cōmonlie in the end to ſpill each others blood, with infinit ſpoile, dammage, and debilitation of the Romã empyre, and this continued more or leſſe, from the tyme of *Commodus*, vntill *Conſtantin* the great, as will euidentlie appeare, by the further proſecution of this hiſtorie.

61 Therefore now to returne to *Septimius Seuerus* (of whoſe enormious crueltie I treated before) he choſe for his companion in the empire, his ſonne *Antonius Caracalla*, and gouerned together with him eighteene yeares, and in that tyme beſides his other exorbitant cruelties, he extreamlie perſecuted the Chriſtians (which is counted the fift general perſecution after *Nero*) and though he had manie victories, yet they coſt him, and the empire ſo deare, that *Oroſius* worthilie attributeth the ſame to Gods iuſt punishment for his perſecution of Chriſtians: whereto may alſo be added his miſerable end, being extreamlie tormented not onlie with the gout, and intollerable paines throughout all his bodie, but alſo with greefe, and anguish of mind, hauing diſcouered his ſonnes determination to poiſon him, after he had failed to kill him, with his ſword, where vppon he ſought to poiſon himſelfe, and being hindred by his ſeruants, he killed himſelfe by a voluntarie ſurfett, eating ſuch a quantitie of groſe meate, that his ſtomake was not able to diſgeſt it: which hapned in England at Yorke, after he had appeaſed a great rebelliō there, and built (as *Victor* ſaith) a famous wall from ſea to ſea, in the north parts, to hinder the incurſions of the *Scotiſh*, and *Picts*, though *Polidore Vergil* holdeth it for more certein, that the ſame wall was built twoo hundreth yeres after *Seuerus* his time, in the reigne of *Theodoſius* the Emperour, by certein capteins ſent by *AEtius* with forces to aſſiſt the Britãs againſt the *Picts* and Scottish.

Nu.20. *Oroſ.li.7. ca. 17.* *An. do. 213. Sext. Aurel. Victor in Septim. Seuero.* *Polydor. Vergil. hiſt. Angl.li.2.*

62 *Antonius Caracalla* his ſonne, exceeding him in bloodie crueltie, and all impietie, as I haue alſo declared before, reigned after him in companie of his brother *Geta*, whom he ſlew within a yeare, and when he had reigned alone fiue yeares, he was killed of his owne gard; and although he left a ſonne called *Antonius Heliogabalus*, yet the ſouldiars choſe for his ſucceſſor *Macrinus* prefector captaine of the gard (of whoſe crueltie I haue alreadie treated) and he preſentlie made his owne ſonne *Diadumenus*, his companion in the empire: But within foureteene moneths after the election of *Macrinus*, the ſouldiars, who

Nu. 21. *An 215.* *An.219.* *Dio & Spartian. in Caracalla.* *Nu. 22.*

Iulius Capitolin. in Macrino. An. do. 220. had chosen him, grew so wearie of him for his tirannie, that they forsooke him, in fauour of *Heliogabalus* afore said, sonne to *Caracalla*, being not aboue foureteene yeares of age, by whose souldiars *Macrinus*, and *Diadumenus*, his sonne, were both slaine.

63 I haue sufficientlie declared before, how monstrous, this *Heliogabalus* was, in crueltie, and all kind of vice, and therfore will onlie add here concerning his end, that when he had rioted, and reuelled, rather then raigned foure yeares (or as some say six) the prætorian souldiars, being his owne garde, slew him, and most ignominiouslie drew his bodie throughout the streetes in the dirt, and after threw him into the riuer *Tiber*, with stones about his necke, calling him *insatiable bitch*, in respect of his effeminat, and most dissolute life. *Lamprid. Herodian. Sext. Aurelius Victor An. do. 224.*

64 And here I wish thee, good reader, to note by the way, how incessāt the tirānie of the emperours were from *Marcus Aurelius*, vntill the death of *Heliogabalus*: for although the good emperours *Pertinax*, and *Didius Iulianus* gouerned in this meane time, yet forasmuch as they were both killed, and raigned not a full yeare betwixt them both, and twoo other emperors chosen also in the meane tyme as I haue declared, I count not their raigne for anie interruption of the tirannie, and of the intollerable oppression of the common welth vnder the fiue forenamed emperors, to wit, *Cōmodus, Septimi⁹ Seuer. Caracalla, Macrinus, & Heliogab.* which fiue most miserablie afflicted, and oppressed the empire, for the space of 42. yeres. *Nu. 58. & 59.*

65. And although the souldiars, chose the good emperour *Alexander Seuerus*, to succeede the wicked *Heliogabalus*, yet so wicked also were they, that they could not endure his vertue, but killed him within thirteene yeares, and chose an other, to wit, the monstrous Tirant *Maximinus*, who imparted the imperiall title, and dignitie to his sonne called also *Maximinus*. And in this meane time (I meane in the raigne of *Alexander*) the legions in the east chose one *Taurinus*, and declared him emperour so much against his will, that he drowned himselfe in the riuer *Eufrates*: and after *Alexanders* death, and the election of *Maximinus* in *Germany*, the legions also of *Afrik* made an other emperour, called *Gordian*, together with his sōne of the same name, which electiō being approued by the senat (for the hatred they bore to *Maximinus*, in respect of his crueltie) the yonger *Gordian* was ouercome and slaine in battaile, by a captaine of *Maximinus*, where vppō his father hanged him selfe, for sorrow, and feare, and *Maximinus* marched towards *Rome*, to be reuēged on the *Romans*, for approuing the electiō of *Gordian*, and therefore the senat chose for their defence two other ēperors, *Pupienus* (who was called also *Maximus*) and *Balbinus*, and as they marched with their forces to meete with *Herodian. Lamprid. Anno 237. Iulius Capitolin. in Maximinis. Sext. Aurel. Victor in Alexandro Seuero. Iulius Capitolin. in Gordianis. An. do. 239. Idem in Maximo & Balbino.*

with *Maximinus*, God executed his iustice vppon him, by the meanes of his owne souldiars, who being alreadie growne to detest him for his crueltie, killed him, and his yonge sonne, saying, that of *so ill a race, there vvas not to be kept so much as a vvhelpe*, and this was within three yeares after they had chosen him.

Herodian. & Sext. Aurel. Victor in Maximino. An. do. 240.

66 And although the emperours gards at *Rome* (called as I haue sayd *Prætoriani milites*) seemed to allow for a while, the election of *Pupienus*, and *Balbinus*, yet within twoo yeeres, they killed them both: besides that, they had also before that time, during the raigne of *Maximinus*, miserablie spoiled, sacked, and burnt *Rome*, in a sedition which fell out betwixt them, and the people, whereby the greatest part of the cittie was burnt, as *Herodian* witnesseth.

Pomponius Lætus. An. do. 242. Herodianus.

67 After they had killed *Pupienus*, and *Balbinus*, they chose yonge *Gordiã*, grandchild to that other *Gordian* who hanged himselfe in *Aphrick*, and within three or foure yeares after, suffred him to be killed, by one *Philip*, to whom they had before graunted the imperial title to raigne with *Gordian*. And ere six yeares passed, they killed also *Philip*, and his sonne, whom his father had made his companion in the empire, whereas an other armie of souldiars, being sent against the *Gothes* (who at the same time inuaded the *Roman* empire) made emperour their general *Marinus*, and within a while after, falling in dislike with him, killed him with no lesse facilitie and leuitie, then they had chosen him.

Iul. Capitolinus, & Pomponius Lætus. An. 246. Oros. lib. 7. c. 20. An. 253 Iidẽ autores. Eutrop. li. 10

68 And here I cannot omit by the way to make mention of a most strãge, punishment of God vppon the *Roman* empire, in the raigne of *Gordian* aforesaid, by a most terrible, and generall earthquake, whereby the earth opened in diuers places, and whole citties with their inhabitants, were swallowed vp. For the which great sacrifices were made, not onlie in *Rome*, but also ouer all the world (as *Capitolinus* testifieth: and shortlie after in the raigne of the two *Philips*, *Rome* receiued great detriment by fyre, and although *Philip* was at the later end of his raigne a Christian (or as some write, dissembled to be so, to haue the helpe of the Christians against *Decius*) yet it is sure, that he was before, most wicked, and cruell, in so much that he is numbred by some amongst the tyrants, yea, and cõpared by *Vopiscus* for cruelty with *Maximinus*, whereof the particulars are not knowne, because there is litle written of his life, in which respect I haue not nũbred him amõgst the tyrannical emperours. But to proceede.

Iulius Capitolin. in Gordiano. Pero Mexia in Philippo. Vopiscus in Aureliano.

69 The souldiars hauing slaine the two *Phillips*, chose *Decius* emperour, who declared also his owne sonne for his companion in the empire. And the second yeare of his raigne he was ouerthrowne, and his sonne slaine, and his whole army cut in peeces by the *Gothes* and *Scithians*,

Pomponius Lætus.

Sext. Aurel. Victor in Decio. An. do. 253. Oros. li. 7. ca. 21.

the treason of *Gallus* a captaine of his owne, and being hardlie pursued by his enimies, he lepte with his horse into a deepe ditch of water, and mudde, wherein he was drowned, and neuer no more seene, or heard of. A iust punishment no doubt, for the great persecution which he had raised against the Christians, and in his time also, great hurt was done in *Rome*, by fire, in so much that the *Amphitheater* was burnt.

Idem ibidē. An. do. 256.

Sext. Aurel. Victor in Virio Gallo. Eutrop. in Æmiliano li. 10.

70 *Decius* being dead, the souldiars gaue the imperiall title to the traitour *Gallus*, and his sonne *Volusianus*, and within twoo yeares, slew them both in fauour of *AEmilianus*, who being sét by *Gallus* against the *Gothes*, and hauing giuen them a great ouerthrow, was by his souldiars saluted emperour, and in this meane time also, *Hostilianus Perpenna*, being chosen emperour by the senate, died of the plague, and *AEmilianus* (who as *Eutropius* saith) being baselie borne, gouerned the empire as baselie, was within foure moneths after his election, slaine also by his souldiars.

Pomponius Latus, in Treboniano Gallo.

71 But to speake a word, or two more of *Gallus*, who succeeded *Decius*, it is to be vnderstoode, that the *Gothes*, who ouerthrew, *Decius*, hauing first forced *Gallus* to make a shamefull peace with them, with condition to pay them a great yearlie tribute, broke the peace presentlie after, and entred againe into the confines of the empire, and destroyed all *Macedonia*, *Misia*, *Thessalia*, and possessed them selues of a great part thereof, and of all *Thracia*, and the *Persians* did also the like in *Mesopotania*, and *Armonia*, and remained in the possession thereof.

Oros. li. 7. c. 21. & 27. Eutrop. li. 10

72 This affliction was also accompanied with a generall, and most violent plague, which infested all the Roman empire, infecting the verie water euerie where, in so much that, *Orosius* saith, it destroied both men, and beasts, and that there was neither prouince, cittie nor familie, which was not almost consumed there with, and this no doubt was a iust punishment of God, for the persecution of the Christians, continued by *Gallus* after the death of *Decius*.

Idem ibid. Eutrop. li. 10

73 *Gallus* being slaine as I haue signified, and *AEmilianus* chosen emperour, by the souldiars of them both, certaine other legions in the *Alpes*, who were vnder the conduct of *Valerian*, dislikingthe election of *AEmilian*, made choise of their generall *Valeriā* to succeede *Gallus* in the gouerment of the empire, where vppon the souldiars of *AEmilian* slew him, and passed to *Valerian*, whose election also the senat admitted.

An. do. 256 Aurel. Victor in Licinio Valeriano.

74 This *Valerian* being, as *Victor* saith, a foole, a dullard, and altogether vnfit, either to counsell, or to execute, chose his sonne *Galien* for his companion

companion in the empire, and within a few yeares was taken prisoner in warre by *Sapores* king of *Persia*, who vsed to make him his foote-stoole, when he mounted vppon his horse, and in the end caused him to be fleyed, and salted alyue: which was, no dout, a iust iudgement of God vppon him, for his cruel persecution of the Christians, which he still continued after *Decius*, and *Gallus*. And allthough *Galien* his sonne raigned some fifteene yeares, yet the empire endured the greatest miserie in his time, that euer was read, or heard of, partlie by the licentious libertie of the souldiars (whereby thirtie seueral emperours were chosen in manie partes of the empire) and partlie by the inuasion of the *Gothes*, *Scithians*, and manie other northen people, who destroied a great part of *France*, and *Italie*, and came as farre as *Rauenna*: and partlie by famins, and most horrible plagues, which in his time were vniuersall, and so cruell aswell in *Rome*, as in other parts, that fiue thousand died thereof some times in one daie, and this saith *Zozimus* seemed to be some releefe of the other extreame miseries, which were such, that those who were strooken with then plague, thought themselues happie to be rid thereby out of the world.

Oros. lib. 7. c. 22. Pero Mexia Agato. orat. Constantini apud Eusebium. Trebellius Pollio. Sext. Aurel. Victor. Oros. li. 7. ca. 22. Pomponius Latus. Zozimus.

75 For besides the former calamities, there was a most prodigious darkenes, for manie dayes together, and such horrible roaring noises heard out of the earth with such earth quakes, that the ground opened in manie places, and swalowed vpp manie houses, with the inhabitants, and the sea-water was found in ditches farre within the land, yea and in some places, the sea it selfe brake in, and drowned manie cities: all which being added to the continuall spoyles, sackes, and bloodshed, which happened euerie where throughout *Galiens* raigne, by the ciuil warrs of the thirtie tyrants abouesaid, and the inundations of barbarous strangers, may manifest the seueritie of Gods iust, and rigorous iudgement vppon the Roman empire, and vppon *Galien* himselfe, who also hauing lead a most brutish, and beastlie life, for fifteene yeares (as I haue declared before) was killed in battaile by *Aureolus* one of the vsurping tyrants, and with *Galien* were slaine his brother *Valerianus*, and his owne sonne *Saloninus*, both which were emperours also, and reigned with him, the former, two yeares, and the latter, a yeare before his death. Besides that, he had imparted also the imperiall dignitie, and title before to *Odenatus*, one of the thirtie tyrants, who had possessed himselfe of all the east parts of the empire, and was afterwards trayterouslie slaine, by a cosen germaine of his owne. So that during these fifteene yeares reigne of *Galien*, there were fiue emperours which might be counted lawfull: to wit, *Galien* himselfe, his father *Valerian*, his brother *Valerian*,

Trebel. Pollio. Eusebius eccles. hist. li. 7. Pompon. Latus in Galieno. Iornandes. An. Do. 270

his sonne *Saloninus*, and *Odenatus*, though the last was first an vsurper, and after emperour, by composition with *Galien*.

76 And at the time of *Galiens* death, *Aureolus*, who ouerthrew, and slew him, possessed *Milan*, and gouerned also all *Sclauonia* by his captaines. And in like manner one *Tetricus*, an other of the tyrants, had impatronized himselfe of all France, and of the greatest part of Spaine, and Germanie; And *Zenobia* widow of *Odenatus*, commaunded all the east parts, with the name of empresse. And finallie, the *Gothes* had in their possession, a great part of *Thracia, Macedonia*, and manie prouinces both in *Europe*, and *Asia*, which I signifie the more-particularlie, to shew the miserable distracted state of the *Roman* empire at that time.

Trebellius Pollio in decem Tyrannis.

77 After the death of *Galien*, the souldiars chose *Claudius*, the second emperour of that name, who was a notable captein, but a great enimie of the Christians, whom he persecuted, and within two yeeres died of the plague, which in his short raigne was very violent, & vniuersal, besids great famin, and the other calamities, that must needes accompanie the continuall warrs he had with the *Gothes*, and other barbarous nations, who also in his time inuaded the empire, first with three hundreth twentie thousand men, and after with two hundred thousand, all whom he prosperouslie ouerthrew, and slew also *Aureolus* the tyrant, and recouered that part of the empire that was in his hands.

An.do. 272. Trebel. Pollio. Eutrop li.10 Pompon. Latus.

78 He was no sooner dead, but the souldiars in *Italie*, chose for emperour his brother *Quintilius*, who had gouerned there in his absence, and was presentlie admitted by the senat. But the victorious armie of *Claudius* in *Germanie*, elected an other called *Aurelianus*, whose fame for his great valour, and prowes was such, that *Quintilius* dispaired to be able to hold the empire, and therefore within seauenteene daies after his election, killed himselfe, as some say, or as others affirme, was slaine by some of his souldiars, as *Aurelianus* also was in the end, through a practise of his owne secretarie, whome he had threatned. This *Aurelianus* reigned six yeres onlie, and during that time gouerned most cruellie, as I haue declared before, though in the meane while, he ouerthrew *Zenobia*, *Tetricus*, and all the other tyrants, and recouered for the empire, all that which they had for some yeares vsurped: neuertheles both he, and the whole empire, receiued not only great disgrace, but also incredible dammage, by the irruptions of the *Alnians* and *Marcomans* into *Italie*, which they spoyled, and destroied pitifullie, and gaue the *Romans* such a bloudie ouerthrow, neere to *Placentia, ut pene solueretur imperium*, that *the empire*, saith *Vopiscus*, *was almost dissolued, and ruined.*

Oros.lib.7. ca.22. Eutrop. li.10 Vopiscus in Aureliano. An.do. 272. An.do. 278. nu. 28. Vopisc. in Aureliano.

79 *Aurelian* being slaine, *Tacitus* succeeded by election of the senat,

after

after ſix moneths vacancie of the empire, for that the ſouldiars were then ſo courteous, as it chanced, that they remitted the choiſe of the emperour to the ſenate, and the ſenators were on the other ſide ſo reſpectiue of the ſouldiars, and ſo fearefull to offend them, that they refuſed it, vntill at lenght, after many embaſſages and replies too and froo, they yeelded to chooſe *Tacitus*; Whereby it may appeare, in what ſeruitude the ſenat was at that time, and how abſolute was the commaunde of the ſouldiars.

Idem in Tacito.

80 But *Tacitus* died within leſſe then ſix moneths, or as *a* ſome write was ſlaine by the ſouldiars, who alſo within two moneths after, killed *b Florianus* his brother, though they had choſen him emperour before, and the reaſon was, that the legions in the eaſt, had elected at the ſame time *Aurelius Probus*, a man of rare, and ſingular valour.

a *Ioan. Bapt. Egnat. in Tacito. An. do. 279.* b *Vopiſc. in Floriano.*

81 This *Probus*, though he was for the ſhort time he raigned, one of the moſt worthy and fortunate emperours in warre, that euer the Roman empire had, hauing recouered *France* from the *Germãs*, with the ſlaughter of 400. thouſand of them, beſids the ſuppreſſion of three tyrants, *Saturninus*, *Proculus* and *Bonoſus*, and many notable victories againſt diuers barbarous nations, yet was killed by his ſouldiars the fift yeere after his election. And in his time, *Rome* was miſerablie ranſacked by certaine *Gladiatours*, who breaking priſon to the number of foureſcore, and aſſembling a great number of other loſt companions, ſpoyled, and ſacked the cittie, with the ſlaughter of manie.

Idem in Probo, Saturnino Bonoſo & Proculo. An. do. 283. Pomponius Lætus.

82 After the death of *Probus*, the ſame ſouldiars, that ſlew him, choſe *Carus* (who was prefect, or capteine of the emperours gards) and he declared his two ſonnes *Numerianus*, and *Carinus*, for his companions in the empire. *Carus* was within leſſe then twoo yeares killed with a thunderbolt, and *Numerianus*, who gouerned in the eaſt partes, was alſo ſhortlie after ſlaine by *Arrius Aper*, his father in law, hoping to make himſelfe emperour, though he failed thereof: for the ſouldiars in place of *Numerianus*, elected *Diocleſian*, who ſlew *Arrius Aper* with his owne hãd, in reueng of *Numerianus* his death. *a* And finally *Carinus*, who gouerned in the weſt partes, being a moſt vicious, & cruell tyrant (as I haue declared) was after diuers bloudie conflicts, ouerthrowne, and killed by *Diocleſian*, in a moſt cruell battaile in *Frãce* within leſſe thẽ three yeares after his electiõ.

Vopiſcus in Probo, & Caro. An. do. 284. Idem in Caro & Numeriano. An eodem. Idem in Numeriano & Carino. Pomponius Lætus. a *Nu 29. An. do. 286.*

83 This *Diocleſian*, within two yeares after he was choſen emperour declared *Maximian*, ſurnamed *Herculeus* for his companion, in the empire, whome I placed amongſt the tyrãnicall emperours. for that he was moſt cruell, and bloudy, as *Victor*, and *Eutropius* doe witneſſe, and executed not only his owne tyrannicall aſſignements, but alſo the rigorous councels

Nu. 6. & 30. Sext. Aurel. Vict. in Galerio Maxim.

and

and proiects of *Dioclesian*, who craftelie dissembling his owne crueltie, made him, and others the instruments, and ministers thereof.

Oros. lib. 7. ca. 25. Eutrop. li. 10 Pompon. Latus in Diocletiano.

84 These two reigned both together twentie yeares. *Dioclesian* in the east parts, and *Maximian* in *Italie*, and all the west parts, and for eighteene yeares, they, and the whole empire, were miserablie afflicted, with continuall, and most cruell warrs, partlie by the incursion of the *Scithians*, *Gothes*, *Sarmati*, *Alani*, *Carpi*, *Cati*, *Ouati*, and other barbarous nations, and partlie by the rebellion of the *Quinquegentiani*, in *Aphrick*, and the irruptions of the *Almans* into *France*: and partlie also, by the inuasions of *Narseus* king of *Persia*, and lastlie by ciuill warrs, with diuers vsurping tyrants, who were made emperours by the souldiars, in sundrie partes of the empire, as *Carausius* in *Brittanie*, *Achilleus* in Ægipt, and *Iulianus* in *Italie*, by which meanes, all the Roman empire, was for eighteene yeares together, as I haue said, pitifullie distressed, vexed, and spoyled, though in the end, *Dioclesian* and *Maximian*, with the two *Cæsars* (whom they chose to assist them, to wit, *Constantius Chlorus*, and *Galerius Maximianus*, surnamed *Armentarius*) subdued them all, and put the empire in peace.

Oros. li. 7. ca. 25. Euseb. eccles. hist. li. 8. c. 1. 2. 3. &c. An. do. 304. Idem ibid. c. 26. Eutrop. li. 10 An. 307.

85 But in the meane time, God extended also his wrath vppon the empire, by a terrible earth quake, where with manie thousands of men perished, and in conclusion, *Dioclesian*, and *Maximian*, hauing raised the most cruell persecution against the Christians, that euer was in the Church, renounced the empire of their owne voluntarie wills, and retired themselues to a priuat life, and yet neuertheles in the end, they bore the penaltie of their crueltie, aswell toward the Christians, as towards all other.

Sext. Aurel. Victor in Dioclesiano. & Galerio Maximiano An. 316.

86 For *Maximian*, attempting afterwards to recouer the empire, was taken, and strangled, at *Marsels*: and *Dioclesian* hauing receiued some yeres after, a threating message, or letter, from *Constantin* the great, poisoned himselfe for feare.

Sext. Aurel. Vict. Eutrop. li. 11. An do. 306. Euseb. eccles. hist. lib. Oros. lib. 7. ca. 28. Eutrop. li. 11.

87 These two left the gouerment, and imperial title to the twoo Cæsars, *Constantius Chlorus*, and *Galerius Maximiamus* surnamed *Armentarius* (because he had ben a drouier) of whom the former, succeeding *Maximian* in the west parts, died within two yeeres after at *Yorke* in *Britanie*, and the latter, to wit *Galerius Maximianus* succeeding *Dioclesian*, no lesse in his persecution of the Christians, then in the gouerment of the east parts, felt and acknowledged the heauie hand of God vppon himselfe for the same, being extreamelie tormented, not onlie with an vlcer in his priuie partes, but also with such a horrible disease, proceeding of an inward putrifaction, that he cast aboundance of stinking wormes, out

at his mouth, and hauing put to death manie of his phisicians, because they could not cure him, he conceiued at last, that it was a punishment of God for his persecution of the Christians, and therefore recalled all his former edicts against them, made new in their fauour, yea, and commended himselfe to their praiers, and finding in the end no ease of torment, he killed himselfe, as *Orosius*, and *Eutropius*, testifie. *Idem ibid. An.do.* 311.

88 And now to end this chapter, and matter, with the three last bloudie tirants, *Maxentius Maximinus*, and *Licinius* (of whom I made mention before amongst the tirannicall emperours:) it is to be vnderstood, that *Constantius Chlorus*, being as I haue signified, dead at *York* in *Brittanny*, *Eutrop. li.* 11. and his sonne *Constantin* (after surnamed the great) succeeding him in the gouerment of the west parts of the empire, by the election of the souldiars, *Galerius Armentarius*, who stil gouerned in the east, gaue the title, and dignitie of *Cæsar*, to his nephew *Maximinus* the same yeare, and *Maxentius*, also sonne, or rather as *Baronius* saith, sonne in law to the emperour *Maximian* aforesaid (according to the inscription of an old coyne *Baron. An.* 307. latelie found) being at the same time in *Rome*, declared himselfe emperour, by fauour of the prætorian souldiars, and became within a while, the most wicked, and cruell tirant, that euer was in Rome.

For as *Eutropius* saith, he made the wiues of the senatours, and of the other noble men to be brought him by force, and after he had rauished, *Eutrop. li.* 11. and dishonored them, he sent them backe to their husbands, who durst not make so much as anie demonstration of sorow, for that he killed manie, not so much for anie offence taken against them, as for his pleasure, and delight. And such was his barbarous crueltie, that sometimes he commaunded his souldiars to goe into the streetes, and to kill all that they met, of what age, sex, or condition soeuer they were, whereby an infinit number of people, saith *Eutropius*, was murdered. He caused the *Ibidem.* senators (speciallie such as were rich) to be falselie accused, condemned, and executed, to the end that he might haue the spoile of their goods: *Euseb. eccles. hist. li.* 8. *c.* 26. and being giuen to the art *Magicke*, and gouerned wholie by *Magicians*, he vsed to open the bellies of women with child, and to make his deuinations by looking into the intrailes of their infants, whom he also opened for that purpose, and to all this, he added also a most cruell persecution of the Christians.

89 Finallie, such was the feare conceiued of his tirannie, not onlie in *Rome*, but also in all the cities, and townes in that part of *Italy*, that most *Idem ibid.* men abandonned their dwellings, and hid them selues, some in caues, and some in the deserts, where vppon followed extreame famin in *Rome*, and thereabout, for lacke of tillage of the ground. For remedie of all

which miſerie,the ſenat ſent to *Cōſtantin*,and craued his aſſiſtaunce,who marching towards *Rome*, had that heauenlie viſion of the croſſe in the aire at midday,and of our Sauiour in his ſleepe, by the which he was made a Chriſtian: and after ſome bloodie battailes,ouerthrew the tirant
Eutrop.li.11. *Maxentius*, who flying into *Rome* to ſaue himſelfe, and being ſo hardlie purſued, that he was forced to enter vppon a falſe bridge of boats,
Euſeb. Eccl. (which he had made of purpoſe,to entrap *Conſtantin*) *Incidit*, as the pſal-
hiſt. l. 9.c.8. miſt ſaith, *in foueam quam fecit.* He fell into the pitt which he made him-
An. do. 312. ſelfe,for the bridge brake vnder him, and he fell into the riuer *Tyber*, where he was drowned. Thus much concerninge *Maxentius*,and the miſerie of the *Romans* vnder him, for the ſpace of ſixe yeares,for ſo long he reigned, or rather tiranniſed.

90 No leſſe miſerable was the eaſt part of the empire,at the ſame time, and for two yeares after,vnder *Maximinus* ſurnamed *Iouius*, who gouerned there, firſt as *Cæſar* for the ſpace of fiue yeares,vnder *Galerius Armentarius*, and after his death,as emperour for three yeares.

Euſeb. Eccl. 91 This *Maximinus*,was, as *Euſebius* affirmeth, not onlie a great freend,
hiſt.l.8. c.27 and as it were a ſworne brother of *Maxentius*, but alſo verie like him in condition,yea,and more wicked in all reſpects then he; for beſides that he was a mortall enimie,and perſecutor of Chriſtians, moſt libidinous, giuen to the art magicke,a notorious drunkard, and cruell aboue meaſure, he oppreſſed alſo all the prouinces of the eaſt part, ſubiect to his gouerment,with moſt cruell exactions,impoſitions, mulcts, and penalties, he ſpoiled the richeſt men to enrich his flatterers, and finallie, he gaue his ſouldiars ſuch free leaue, to vſe all kind of rapin, and to ſack, ſpoile,and ranſacke euerie where throughout his dominions, that they ſeemed to be no leſſe abſolute in tirannie then he. And this generall calamitie was much augmented,with diuers ſtrāge diſſeaſes, and the moſt
Idem ibid. pitifull famine, and plague, that euer was heard of, as appeareth by the
li.9 c.7. lamentable deſcription thereof,made by *Euſebius*, who liued in the ſame time,and was an eye witnes of it.

92 Here alſo may be added the bloudie warrs, which *Maximinus* had, partlie againſt the *Armenians*, who defeated him with great ſlaughter of his armie, and partlie againſt *Licinius*, who being made *Cæſar* ſome yeares before, by *Galerius Armentarius*, gouerned alſo the eaſt parts of the empire together with *Maximinus*. And ſuch was the ambition, and
Idem ibid. intollerable pride of *Maximinus*, that he could endure no companion,
ca. 8. or equall, and therefore ſought to ſuppreſſe *Licinius*, who neuertheleſſe ouerthrew him, and ſlew the greateſt part of his armie, and in fine God alſo exacted of *Maximinus*, the penaltie due to his iuſtice, for his impie-

tie, and

tie, and wickednes: for after theſe other diſgraces, and afflictions, he fell ſicke with ſuch extreame paſſion, and paine in his entrails, that he could neither eat, drinke, nor ſleepe, but caſt himſelfe diuerſe times out of his bed, vppon the ground, and ſo violent was his torment, that his *Ibidem.* eies leapt out of his head, and in the end, after manie daies anguiſh in this manner, he died, confeſſing, that God did puniſh him, for his per- *An. do. 314.* ſecution of the Chriſtians.

93 Now it reſteth onlie, that I ſpeake a word, or twoo of *Licinius,* who by the death of *Maximinus,* was the onlie Collegue, and companion in the empire, of Conſtantine the great, whoſe ſiſter *Conſtanza* he had maried, hauing now vnder him, all the eaſt parts, as *Conſtantin* had the weſt.

94 This *Licinius,* was not onlie a perſecutor of Chriſtians, but alſo, as *Eutrop. li. 11.* *Eutropius* affirmeth, moſt vicious, and coueteous, and ſuch an enimie of learning, that he called it, *the poiſon and plague of common vvealths.* And finallie he was, as the ſame author affirmeth, paſſionat, and cruell in all extremitie, and therefore when he had ſerued fifteene yeares for an inſtrument of Gods iuſtice vppon the empire, he himſelfe receiued the due puniſhment of his wickednes, through his owne fooliſh ambition, and *Euſeb. in vita Conſtantini li. 2. c. 15. 16. 17. 18.* the enuie he bore to *Conſtantius* great glorie, not with ſtanding their affinitie, and therefore, firſt ſeeking to poiſon *Conſtantin,* and after making open warr vppon him, he was ouercome by him in two cruel battailes, *An. do. 318.* and in the end alſo put to death, by his order, whereby *Conſtantin* remai- *Sext. Aurel. Victor in Conſtantino.* ned ſole emperour: as almightie God, had in his eternall wiſdome, and prouidence ordained, for the extinction of Idolatrie, and the propagation of Chriſtian religion.

95 Therefore, hauing now paſſed through the whole courſe of three hundred, and eighteene yeares after our Sauiours birth, and the raigne of all the pagan emperours, from *Auguſtus* to *Conſtantin*, as I promiſed, I will therewith end this chapter, and reſerue for the next, certaine obſeruations, and concluſions, which I meane to draw out of the premiſſes, for the confirmation of my principall intention, and the further ſatisfaction (as I hope) of my Reader.

The conclusion of the foure former chapters, concerning the religion, common vvelth, and empire of the Romans, and first of the amplitude of their dominion, their great vvelth, and povver, and the meanes hovv they attained vnto it is breefly signified, vvith a compendious recapitulation of their calamities, vvhich are proued to be farre greater then the miseries, and calamities of Christiãs haue bene at any tyme. And finally it is declared, hovv their great povver, and ample dominion, serued for the propagation of the faith, and Church of Christ*: vvhereby it appeareth, hovv his prouidence in the conseruation and amplification of their state, for the good of his church, concurred vvith his iustice in their seuere punishment, for the abominable impiety of their religion.*

Chap. 13.

1. BEing now to conclude all this former discourse cõcerninge the Roman Empire, I thinke good, for the better satisfactiõ of my curious Readers (and to make my *Epitome* of the Romã historie more cõpleat) to add first a word, or two, touching the amplitude, welth, and power of the Roman Empire. Yt is therefore to be vnderstood, that although, it be commonlie said, yea, & auouched, by the ancient historiographers, that the Romans had all the world vnder their dominion (and therefore *Dionisius Halicarnasseus* saith. *Romana vrbs imperat toti terræ* &c. *The citie of Rome commaundeth all the earth vvhere soeuer it is accessible, and habitable, as also all the seas that are nauigable*,) neuertheles there was a great part, aswell of *Europe*, northward, as of *Asia*, and *Africk* towards the east, and south, which was not subiect to the *Roman* Empire. But that which may trulie be said concerning the amplitude of their dominion is, that they commaunded, an gouerned the greatest and best part of the world, which was then knowne to be habitable, or rather, as *Lipsius* affirmeth, as much thereof, as they thought worth the cõquest, and conuenient to be kept, and therefore whereas, *Traian*, subdued the contries beyond the riuer *Euphrates* eastward, to the riuer *Tigris* (as *Armenia*, *Arabia*, *Mesopotania*, and *Assiria*) and made them prouinces of the *Roman* empire, *Adrian* his successor gaue them ouer againe, and reduced the empire to the former limits; which were, eastward the riuer *Euphrates*, the mountaine *Taurus*, and the countrie of *Armenia*; towards the west, the furthest part of Spaine, and Portugal; towards the south *Æthiopia*; and northward the riuer of *Rheyn*, and *Danuby*: and further they had in their subiectiõ, all the mediterranian sea, and the Ilãds thereof, & *Brittany* in the northerne sea, so that, as *Appianus*, & *Polibius* affirme, they possessed more, almost by the one halfe, thẽ all the other monarches before them, to wit, then the *Assirians*, *Medes*, *Persians*, and *Greekes*.

Dionis. Halicar: antiq. Roman. li. 1.

Iustus Lipsius de magnitudine Romana li. 1. c. 3.

Festus Rufus

Appianus in procemio hist. Lybica.

Polybius.

Further-

2 Furthermore they had, as *Appian* teſtifieth, alwaies in pay, twoo hundred thouſand footemen, fortie thouſand horſe, three hundreth fighting elephants, three thouſand armed chariotts, and three hundred thouſand of all ſorts of armes in their armories, for the ſupplie of neceſſities. Their power alſo by ſea, was correſpondēt to their land-forces, for they had twoo thouſand ſayle of shipps, a thouſand fiue hundred gallyes, and foureſcore great gallions, with their pupps, and prows guilt, for oſtentation of the maieſtie of the *Roman* empire, and for the ſeruice of their emperours, and generalls, as occaſion should require; And for all this nauie, they had alwayes double prouiſion in readines. *Appian. in proœmio hiſt. Lybica.*

3 Finallie their yearlie reuenew, was as (*Lipſius* gathereth out of their ordinarie tributs, rents, gabels, and taxes) aboue a hundreth and fiftie millions, and the readie, money, which they commonlie had in ſtore, in diuerſe parts, for their prouiſion of warrs by ſea, and land, was (as *Appian* affirmeth) ſeauentie fiue thouſand *Ægiptian* talents, which according to our accompt, mounteth to ſix hundreth millions of crownes, which might ſeeme incredible, if it were not affirmed by a graue author, and alſo conforme to their greatnes in other reſpects, eſpeciallie ſeeing wee reade, that the yearelie rent of *Craſſus* in the time of the Conſuls, was eſteemed at ſeauen thouſand and a hundred talents, which after our accompt, mounteth almoſt to a eleuen millions. And the riches of *Marius*, as *Plutarke* teſtifieth, was ſuch, that it might haue ſufficed manie kings. Alſo *Iulius Cæſar*, whiles he was a priuate man, was able to giue nine hundred thouſand crownes at one gift, to *L. Paulus*, to withold him for bearing armes againſt him, and to *Curio* a greater ſomme, ſaith *Suetonius*, to winn him to his partie, and much more to his ſouldiars, by diuers donatiues, and eſpeciallie at his triumph, at what time he gaue them (as appeareth in *Dio*, and *Appian*) fifteene millions; Beſides that *Auguſtus Cæſar*, and *Antonius*, in their warres againſt *Brutus*, and *Caſſius*, gaue to their ſouldiars for one donatiue, aboue a hundreth, and fifty millions, as *Lipſius* gathereth out of *Appian*; And *Nero* being reprehended by his mother, for ordaining two hundreth and fiftie thouſand crownes to be giuen to the ſouldiars of his gard, commaunded the monie to be all brought, and laid out before him, and when he ſaw it, he ſaid, he thought it had not beene ſo litle, and ordained them as much more, and beſtowed, at one other time vppon *Tiridates*, king of *Armenia*, partlie in his entertainement at *Rome*, for nine moneths, and partlie for his returne, aboue ſeauen millions, and a halfe. Finally to omit diuerſe others, the emperour *Adrian* beſtowed, vppon his ſouldiars, and the people in donatiues, and playes, tenne millions in the feaſts which he made, when *Lipſius de magnitud. Romana. li. 2. c. 3. Appian in proœmio hiſt. Lybica. Plutarc. in Craſſo. Idem in Mario. Sueton. in Iulio Cæſare Dio in Iulio Cæſare. Appian. de Ciuil. Rom. bellis li. 4. Iuſtus Lipſius de magnit. Romana li. 2. c. 12. Sueton. in Nerone ca. 30. Ælius Spartian. in Adriano.*

he adopted *Ceionius Commodus.*

4 And all this may be the better beleeued, seeing *Zonaras* testifieth, that a greeke emperour of *Constantinople*, to wit, *Pasilius Porphyrogenitus* (who had but a part of the Roman empire) had in his treasure, a thousand, and two hundred *Millions* of crounes, besides an infinit wealth in gould and siluer plate, and in precious stones. Whereby it may be gathered, how excessiue were the riches, and power of the *Roman* empire, whiles it was entire.

Circa. an. Do. 800. Zonaras, Annal. To.3.

5 And if thou desire good Reader to know, by what meanes they arriued to so great power, wealth, and dominion, thou shalt breeflie vnderstand, that almighty God hauing determined, out of his eternall wisdome, and prouidence, to aduaunce them to the Empire of the world, disposed them thereto, by sixe politicall vertues wherein they excelled other nations, (though they were otherwaies most vicious, and wicked, as I haue declared before.) The first was, an exceeding loue to their countrie, and common welth. The second, a strict obseruation of ciuil iustice, aswell towards their enimies, as towards their confederats and subiects. The third was, an inuincible fortitude, and courage euen in their greatest calamities. The fourth, a singular clemencie, towards their subiects, and those that yealded themselues vnto them. The fift was, notable prudence in gouerment. And the last, an excellent discipline of warre, most exactlie obserued.

Chap.7. nu.27. & sequen.

6 Now then to come to the conclusion of all the discourse concerning the *Romans*, I must first put thee in mind, good Reader, what hath bene my principall intention, and drift therein, whereby thou mayst the better iudge, of the inference that I am to draw thereof. Thou maist remember, that I amplie proued before, in the seauenth, and eight chapters, that the religion professed by the *Romans*, was most ridiculous, absurd, and impious in it selfe, and produced two bad effects, the one *Atheisme*, and the other extreame corruption of manners: wherevppon it consequentlie followed (as I also signified there) that it must needes be most pernicious to their common welth, not onlie because *Atheisme*, and vice, are most contrarie to true reason of state: (which I proued at large, in the eight and ninth Chapter but also because false religion of it selfe, draweth the wrath, and vengeance of God, vppon the states, that are infected there with.

Chap.7. & 8. per totum.

Chap.8. & 9.

7 And whereas there might grow hereuppon a great doubt, how the common welth, and empire of the *Romans*, could so long stand, and florish, as it did, in the profession, and exercise of their religion, if it were so hatefull to almightie God, and consequentlie so preiudiciall to their state,

ſtate,as I preſumed it to be,I tooke vppon me,for the ſatisfaction of this doubt,to proue the veritie of my aſſertion, by the experience of their owne hiſtories,and to ſhew throughout the whole courſe thereof,that, as on the one ſide,almightie God did,out of his prouidence,aduance thẽ to the monarchie,& empire of the world (to make thereby the way to the building of his Church) ſo alſo on the other ſide,he moſt manifeſtly executed his iuſtice vppõ thẽ,in puniſhing thẽ ſeuerely frõ time to time, for their wicked religion, and the abominable fruit that it yealded.

8 This hath firſt appeared euidentlie in the *Roman* ſtate, from *Romulus*, to *Augustus Cæſar*, by their continuall afflictions, and neuer ceaſing calamities. I meane their cruell, and bloudie warrs,both ciuill, and forreine, their horrible plagues, and famins, their frequent inundations, dammages by fire, and domeſticall diuiſions, beſides other moſt rare, and ſtrange puniſhments of God, which either vexed, and infeſted them with a continual counterchange,and entercourſe one after an other (as they neuer failed to doe) or els afflicted,and oppreſſed them all at once (as manie times they did) in ſuch ſort,that it may be euidẽt to anie man, who ſhall conſider the particulers related by me before,that the Roman common welth,growing of ſo poore,and baſe a beginninge, as it did, could not poſſiblie haue reſiſted ſuch torrents of miſeries, and much leſſe, haue arriued to ſuch a height of empire, if the ſpeciall prouidence of God had not conſerued,amplified, and aduanced it.

9 This, I ſay, I haue ſhewed ſufficientlie in the ninth, tenth,and eleauenth chapters,from the foundation of *Rome*, to the erection of their monarchie : and the ſame is no leſſe euident alſo in their monarchie it ſelfe, by that which I haue diſcourſed in the laſt chapter, and may the better appeare by theſe few obſeruations following.

10 Yt is manifeſt by the ſcriptures themſelues,that one of the greateſt puniſhments, that God laieth vppon anie kingdome, or countrie, is to giue it into the handes,of a wicked, and tirannicall prince, and therefore our Lord threatned the ſame to the *Ievves*, as a ſpeciall ſigne of his extreame wrath, and indignation, ſaying, *Dabo eis regem in furore meo. I vvill giue them a king in my fury.* And againe by the prophet *Iſay. Dabo pue-* *Iſay. 3.*
ros principes eorum, & effeminati dominabuntur eis. I vvill giue them children for their princes, and effeminat men, shall rule, and gouerne them. And the ſame is alſo ſignified by *Iob*, when he ſaith, that *God maketh the Hypocrit to* *Iob. 34.*
raigne, Propter peccata populi. For the ſinnes of the people.

11 This thẽ being ſo,it muſt needes be grãted,that the puniſhmẽt of the Roman empire in this kind,during the time of their Paganiſme, was exceding great, aſwell for the nũber of the wicked,& tirãnical emperours, as for

as for their excesse in wickednes, and tirannie, seeing it appeareth in the last chapter, that they were twentie two in all (*Augustus Cæsar*, being counted for one, during one and fortie yeares of his raigne) all of them most cruell, and tirannicall, and the farre greater part of them (I meane fifteene, of the two and twentie) verie monsters, not onlie for crueltie, but also for all kind of vice, and wickednes, being euerie one of them, so voyde of all vertue, or good inclination, that it may well be said, they were not men, but verie sauage beastes, or infernall furies, reuested in the habit, and shape of men, ordained for no other end, but for the scourge, and plague of the whole world.

12 And although, there were also during the same time of Paganisme, one and fortie other emperours, who were counted either good, or indifferent, or at least not so bad, as the others, yet if we consider, the time that the twentie two raigned, we shall find, that in continuance, and length of dominion, they farre exceeded the other. For whereas, *Augustus*, who was the first, beganne his tirannie in the yeare seauen hundred, and eleauen after the foundation of *Rome*, and *Licinius* who was the last, was ouerthrowne by *Constantin* in the yeare one thousand seauentie seauen, there passed in the meane while, three hundred, sixtie six yeares, of which time, the tirannicall emperours, raigned at one time, and other, two hundred thirtie fiue yeares, and the other of the better sort, but one hundred thirtie one yeares: so that the twoo and twentie tirannicall emperours, had aboue a hundred yeares vantage of fortie one good, or tollerable emperours, in the space of three hundreth yeares, raigning twise as long as they. Wherein it is also to be noted, that although the good emperours were intermixed with the bad, yet there was commōlie small intermission of tirānie, especiallie for the first hundreth yeares, whereof nintie eight were wholie spent in the affliction, and oppression of the common wealth, excepting onlie the last foureteene yeares of *Augustus*, and the first fiue yeares of *Nero*, before he beganne to tirānize.

13 And although after these nintie eight yeares, succeeded *Vespasian*, and his sonne *Titus* (of whome the first may be counted tollerable in respect of his predecessours, and the second, to wit *Titus*, was one of the best emperours, that euer the Romans had) yet they raigned but twelue yeares betwixt them both, and the latter of them but two yeares, and presentlie after, followed the cruell *Domitian*, whose tirannie lasted fifteene yeares.

14 And whereas after *Domitian*, suceeeded two other of the good emperours, to wit *Nerua*, and *Traian*, for the space of one and twentie yeares, the same was counterpeised with the crueltie of their successour

Adrian,

Adrian, who reigned, as manie yeares, as they both. And the thirtie six yeares raigne of the two notable emperours (*Antonius Pius*, and *Marcus Aurelius*, who succeeded *Adrian*) was ouerwaighed with the twoo and fortie yeares tirannie of *Commodus*, *Septimius Seuerus*, *Caracalla*, *Macrinus*, and *Heliogabalus*, all which fiue succeeded *Marcus Aurelius*.

15 The like also may be obserued in the ensuing times, vntill *Constantin*. For although the good *Alexander Seuerus* (who succeeded *Heliogabalus*) raigned thirteene yeares, and the cruel *Maximinus* his successour but three yeares, yet cōsidering the state of those times, we may well say, that what wanted in the raigne of *Maximinus*, for the tirannical oppression of the common welth, was supplied with the tirannie of the souldiars, who oppressed (especiallie at that tyme) the emperours, and senat, and the whole empire, and slew successiuelie fiue emperours after *Maximinus*, within nine yeares, to wit, *Pupienus*, *Balbinus*, yong *Gordian*, and the two *Phillips*, the father, and the sonne, of which, the two last were held equall in barbarous crueltie with *Maximinus* (as I haue declared before) *Vopiscus in Aurelian.* and reigned fiue yeares, whereas the three other good emperours, reigned but foure yeares amongst them all.

16 And presentlie also, ensued the disgracious deaths of six other emperours, in the foure yeares that immediatelie followed, to wit, of *Decius*, and his sonne, of *Hostilianus Perpenna*, *Gallus* with his sonne, *Volusianus*, and *Emilianus*, which three last were killed by their souldiars, and although I haue not put them in the list of the tirannicall, and wicked emperours, yet they might wel be counted of their crew, being very pernicious to the empire, in respect of their bad gouerment, for the short time they reigned, which was but two yeares, as I haue declared before: so that I count not their raigne for anie intermission, but rather for a continuance, or increase of the infelicitie of the Roman empire. Whereto is also to be added the fifteene yeares calamitie that presētlie followed, during the infamous raigne of *Valerian*, and *Gallien* his sonne, who next succeeded *Emilian*. And though after *Gallien*, followed the good emperour *Claudius*, & his brother *Quintilius*, yet the former raigned but two yeares, and the latter but seauentie daies, whereas the cruel *Aurelian* who succeeded them, continued his reigne six yeares. And albeit there followed after him fiue good emperours, to wit *Tacitus*, *Florianus*, *Probus*, *Carus*, and *Numerianus*, yet they reigned not aboue six yeares amongst them all, and for twoo yeares of the six, the wicked *Carinus* reigned together with *Carus*, and *Numerianus*, and ouer-liuing them more then a yeare, had for his successors *Dioclesian*, and *Maximian*, whose seuere, and cruell gouerment, lasted thirtie yeares, and was, within two

yeares after, seconded with the tirannie of *Maxentius*, and the crueltie of *Maximinus*, and *Licinius*, who were the last pagan emperours.

17 Thus then we see, that those wicked, and tirannical emperours, were by the prouidence of God, so distributed from time to time in the *Roman* empire (for the iust punishment thereof) that there was neuer anie great intermission of tirannie, and otherwhiles the most cruell, and continuall oppression that euer was heard, or read of, in anie countrie, for so manie yeares together. And thus much for the first obseruation.

18 The second may be Gods iustice, and seuere iudgment vppon the emperours themselues, being, as I haue said, sixtie three in all (I meane such onlie as were acknowledged, for emperours by the senat) who died all of them violentlie, except tenne, to wit, *Augustus*, *Vespasian*, *Titus*, *Nerua*, *Traian*, *Antonius* surnamed *Pius*, *Marcus Aurelius*, *Lucius Verus*, *Tacitus*, and *Constantius*. Of which tenne neuertheles some write, that *Augustus*, *Titus*, and *Traian* were poisoned, as I haue signified in the last chapter, and that *Tacitus*, who liued not a yeare, was killed by his souldiars; so that of sixtie three, there were but onlie six of whose naturall, and peaceable death the authors agree, the rest ending their daies vnfortunatlie, either by the treacherie of their souldiars, seruants, or by their enemies in the field, or by their owne handes, or els by the manifest hand of God; whereto I ascribe, not onlie the miserable end of *Maximinus*, and *Galerius Armentarius*, who died of most strange, and horrible diseases, but also the vntimelie death of the emperour *Claudius*, who hauing reigned, but twoo yeares, died of the plague, in a most cruel, and general contagion, which miserablie afflicted the empire in his dayes, and therefore as *Victor* signifieth, *Claudius* finding in the fatall bookes that the first, or principal man must die, for the expiation of the common wealth, and hearing *Pomponius Bassa*, make offer of his life for the publike good, said that no man was to be preferred in that point, before himselfe being emperour, and so saith *Victor*. *Vitam dono reipublicæ dedit. He gaue his life for a gift to the common vvelth*, and therefore was honored with an image of gold, which was placed by the image of *Iupiter*, so that in the opinion of the paynims themselues, he died vntimelie by the iudgment of God, as a sacrifice for the remedie of the publicke calamities.

Pero Mexia in Traiano, & Tacito.

Sext. Aurel. Victor in Claudio.

19 And it is also further to be obserued, that so ordinarie, and continuall was the punishment of God vppon the *Roman* emperours, that from the death of *Augustus* vnto *Vespasian*, which was the space of fiftie fiue yeares, seauen emperours successiuelie died violentlie; And againe afterwards from the death of *Marcus Aurelius* (who died in the yeare of

our Lord,one hundreth eightie one) the ſame iudgement, and puniſhment of God neuer failed in anie of them, for the ſpace of one hundreth twentie nine yeares,to wit, to the death of *Constantius Chlorus*, who was a great fauourer of Chriſtians, and died naturallie in the yeare of our Lord three hundreth, and tenne: during which ſpace of a hundreth twentie nine yeares,no one emperour,died his natural death, and after *Constantius*, thoſe three pagan emperours, which ſucceeded in the eaſt, and weſt,to wit, *Maxentius*,*Maximinus*, and *Licinius* died diſgracefullie, all three in the ſpace of eighteene yeares, as I haue declared: whereto may alſo be added the like diſgracious,and miſerable end of all the reſt, that tooke vppon them the title of emperours (though they were not allowed by the ſenate, and therefore not held as lawfull) who being aboue fortie in number at one time,and other,were all of them, except ſome two,or three,ſlaine by their owne ſouldiars,or by their enimies in the field,or els they made away themſelues,in ſo much, that of aboue a hundred emperours, lawfull,and vnlawfull, there cannot be reckoned aboue tenne,that died a naturall death.

20 Moreouer, it may alſo be noted,what diuerſities of diſaſters, and diſgraces befell them in their deaths, for that ſome were poiſoned, as *Augustus*, and *Claudius* the firſt: ſome died of the plague, as *Claudius* the ſecond,and *Perpenna*: ſome were drawne like doggs vp, and downe the ſtreates, as *Vitellius*, and *Heliogabalus*: ſome were killed in battaile, as the yonger *Gordian*,*Gallien*,and *Carinus*: and others were ſlaine by their owne ſouldiars,or gardes,as *Caligula*,*Pertinax*,*Alexander*,*Seuerius*,*Pupienus*,*Balbinus*,and diuers others.

21 *Tiberius*, was ſmothered with a quiſhon: and *Decius* drowned in a durtie ditch: *Maxentius* in the riuer *Tiber*: *Carus* killed with a thunderbolt: *Valerianus* fleied, and ſalted aliue: *Nero* cut his owne throat: *Otho* ſtabbed himſelfe: *Quintilius* and *Florian*, let them ſelues blood to death: *Adrian* famiſhed himſelfe: *Septimius Seuerus*, killed himſelfe purpoſelie with a ſurfett: The elder *Gordian* hanged himſelfe: *Diocleſian* poiſoned himſelfe: *Galerius Armentarius* rotted inwardlie aliue,and caſt out at his mouth aboundance of ſtinking wormes,vntill he died: and finallie *Maximinus* ſurnamed *Iouius*, died in ſuch extreame torments, that his eyes leapt out of his head. So that almightie God executed his iudgements, vppon thoſe emperours, by all kind of miſerable death, to make them liuelie examples of his iuſtice,and a true ſpectacle, and mirrour to the world of humane infelicitie,and miſerie.

22 And to this purpoſe alſo it is to be conſidered, that nine and twentie of the emperours aboue named,did not raigne amongſt thē all,aboue

fiue and twentie yeares and od moneths, and yet seauenteene of those nine and twentie, raigned aboue two and twentie yeares of that time, (two of them three yeares, as *Maximinus*, and his sonne, and the rest a yeare, or two a peece) so that there remaineth not aboue three yeares, and od moneths for the raigne of the other twelue emperours, of whom none enioyed his title, aboue seauen, or eighte moneths, and some but two, or three moneths a peece, and some of them but a few dayes, in so much, that *Rome* had once fiue emperours in litle more, then a yeare, to wit, *Nero*, *Galba*, *Otho*, *Vitellius*, and *Vespasian*, one succeding an other. Whereby it may appeare, what hauock was made of the emperours in those daies, and how vnfortunate a thing it was, to attaine to the highest fortune, I meane to the soueraigntie of the *Roman* empire, which was so well noted, by those, that were not wholie blinded with ambition, that when, after the slaughter of the emperour *Pertinax*, the souldiars, who had killed him, set the empire on sale, there were but two, who would offer anie money for it, as I haue declared: and after that againe, *Audentius* refused it flatlie, when it was offered him by the souldiers, and *Pupienus*, being chosen emperour by the senate, togither with *Balbinus*, tould him that they had small cause to reioyce, for it would cost them their liues err yt were long, and so it did, for the souldiars killed them both, within twoo yeares. Yea, and *Taurinus*, being elected by the souldiars, and forced to accept the title of emperour, drowned himselfe for sorow, as I haue signified before, so miserable was the state, and condition of the emperours in those daies, that the wisest men, tooke it to be the greatest miserie, and to be eschewed euen with voluntarie death, which no doubt, must needes be attributed to the speciall iudgement, and iustice of God, not onlie vppon the emperours themselues, but also vppon the whole empire, which was miserablie afflicted by the tumults, ciuill warrs, sacks, spoiles, and lamentable desolation, which either accompanied, or necessarilie followed the frequent slaughters, of so manie emperours, and the great innouations, which ensued thereon throughout the Roman state.

Chap. 12. Nu. 58.

Chap. 12. Nu. 65.

23 But what shold I say of the insolencie, and tirannie of the souldiars, which was for the most part, the cause of the former calamitie of the emperours, and of the perpetuall miserie of the empire? For though the emperours had the title, and dignitie of cheefe gouernours, yet the souldiars gouerned, and tirãnized in effect, not onlie making, depriuing, killing, and changing the emperours at their pleasure, but also being the instruments, ministers, and maintainers of their crueltie, seeing that

without their assistāce, the tirānicall emperours neither durst, nor could haue executed their tirannie. Besides that, all the bloodshed, rapes, pillages, disorders, and infinit calamities, that ensued of the frequent ciuill warrs, wherewith the empire was infested, sprong from no other roote, *Ibid. Nu. 84.* but from the vnbrideled insolencie, and exorbitant passion of the souldiars, as I haue sufficientlie declared before.

24 So that, it being true, as *Aristotle* saith, that where passion, and sensualitie predominateth, there a beast ruleth, it may trulie be sayd, that the Roman empire, being almost continuallie gouerned by the passions, and caprichious humours of the souldiars (who were at that time raked, as I may say, out of the sinkes of all nations) was ruled by a beast of manie heades, the most vile, and sauage that could be imagined. Whereby it may also be easelie coniectured, how iustice was administred, or rather how it perished, how vertue was suppressed, and vice exalted, how litle securitie men had of their landes, goods, or liues; and finallie, how lamentable was the state of the whole empire, during this tirannie of the emperours, and souldiars, gouerning for the most part, not according to the rule of reason, conscience, and law, but according to their owne sensuall, and beastlie appetits. *Aristot'e.*

25 And if to all this, we add the frequent, and most cruell contagions, conflagrations, famins, inundations, earth quakes, subuersion, and desolation of cities, and prouinces, & such other strange calamities, which abounded euerie where, during the raigne of these emperours, we must needes confesse, that the *Roman* empire, was but a verie theater, or stage, whereon was acted the most doleful, and bloodie, tragedy, that euer was heard of, representing the height of humane infelicitie, in the persons of the Roman emperours, senat, and people, to manifest the terrible effects of Gods seuere iustice, in the due punishment of false religion, Idolatrie, tirannie, and all kind of iniquitie, and with all, to discouer the vanitie of humane pride, welth, honour, and glorie, and the follie of those princes, who reposing more confidence in gards, armies, and power of men, then in vertue, and in the protection of God, seeke rather to be feared, then beloued, and are themselues miserablie tirannized, by the instruments, ministers, and vphoulders of their tirannie.

26 All this I say, manifestlie appeareth, in that which I haue discoursed in the last chapter, concerning the Roman emperours, & empire, from *Augustus Cæsar*, to *Cōstantin* the great. And although almightie God, hath also seuerelie punished sinne in all times, and still doth, euen in these our daies, as euerie man seeth, yet, if we compare the calamities of the *Romans*, and their empire, in the time of Paganisme, with the

 afflictions

afflictions of the ensuing ages, in the time of Christian religion, we shall euidentlie see, that his deuine maiestie, punished the former with all rigour as his professed enimies, and chastiseth the latter, with all mercie as his children, and seruants: which I would make most euident, with an exact comparison of the punishments inflicted on both sorts, but that I haue spent alreadie so much time in the abridgement of the Roman historie, that I am forced to hast to the prosecution of matter more necessarie, for the performance of that which I principallie intend in this treatise.

27 Therefore I will content my selfe in this point, and desire thee also, good Reader, to be contented with the iudgment of others, who haue amplie handled the same subiect, aswell in former, as in these later times, and proued clearelie, that God extended his iustice, in farre greater rigour vppon sinners, in the time of paganisme, then he hath done since the conuersion of the world to the Christian faith. Which point is notablie, though verie breeflie handled by *Tertulian* in his Apologie for the Christians, against the Painims, who attributed all the calamities of their time, to the demerit of the Christians, and their religion. For the confutation whereof, *Tertulian* mentioneth diuerse horrible pnnishmẽts of God vppon Pagans, and such as neuer had benne heard of, from the comming of Christ to his daies, which was the space of twoo hundred yeares; As to omit others, that the citie called *Hierapolis*, and the Ilands of *Delos*, *Rhodos*, and *Goos*, were sonke, and swalowed vp by the earth, or sea, and that not onlie the townes of *Sodome*, and *Ghomorra*, but also the cities of *Vulsinium*, and *Pompeij* in Italie, were destroied by fire, the one from heauen, and the other from the moũtaine *Vesuuius*, which cast out firie flames vppon yt.

Tertul. in Apologet.

28 This same argument, is also most amplie, and learnedlie treated by *Saint Augustine*, and *Orosius*, against the Painimes of their time, who affirmed that the Christian religion was the cause of the seige, and sack of *Rome* by the *Gothes*, and of all the other calamities of those daies; whereas the authors aforenamed, notablie proued the contrarie, shewing that the miserie of former ages in time of Paganisme, farr exceeded the afflictions that God laid vppon the Christians, as may appeare in *Saint Augustins* most learned worke, intituled *de ciuitate Dei*, and in the historie of *Orosius*, which were purposelie written vppon that occasion. Wherein, amongst other things they declare, that the citie of *Rome*, receiued nothing so much dammage by the *Gothes*, as it did in times past, by *Silla*, *Marius*, and *Nero*, and other of her owne gouernours, yea, and that the *Gothes* spared the Christian temples, and all those who fled thereto: in so much

August. li. 1. de ciuit. Dei. c. 1. & l. 2. c. 1. & l. 3. c. 29 Oros. li. 7. ca. 39.

much that manie Painims tooke sanctuarie there, together with the Christians, and so escaped the furie of the enimie, whereby it was euident, say they, that the common affliction was much more moderat, and tollerable euen to the Painims themselues, by the benefitt of Christian religion, and by the mercifull prouidence of our Sauiour *Christ*.

29 And *Orosius* further obserueth, how almightie God, out of his infinit mercie so disposed, that the great inundation also of the *Vandales*, *Alans*, *Hūnes*, and other barbarous nations into the Roman empire at that time, was not onlie much more tollerable, then the like former irruptions of forreine natiōs, had bene in time past, but also turned in the end to Gods greater glorie, whereof he yealdeth three reasons. First for that it lasted but two yeares, whereas in the time of *Galien* the emperour (to omit the former ages) the empire was continuallie spoiled, and ransacked by the Northerne people, for almost twelue yeares together. Secōdlie although they possessed themselues of a great part of *Spaine*, and other parts of Christendome, yet they vsed farr greater clemencie towards the inhabitants, then the other barbarous nations had done in like occasions. Thirdlie that the Church of *Christ*, was thereby greatlie augmented by their couersion, to the Christian faith shortlie after: where vppon the same Author saith, that the mercie of God was greatlie to be praised, and extolled, in that he ordeined by that meanes, that infinit number of infidels, should receiue the light of the true faith. *Quam inuenire vtique nisi hac occasione non possent. VVhich they could not otherwaise haue found, but by this occasion.* Thus saith he.

Idem ibid. ca. 41.

30 But he that list to see this matter, concerning the seueritie of Gods iudgments vppon the Paynimes, copiouslie, and fullie handled, let him read *Bozius*, a late writer, who in two, or three seueral workes of his, hath largelie, and curiouslie treated thereof, and proued, that the punishments of God, were without all comparison, more seuere vppon the infidels, thē euer they haue bene vppon the Christiās, which he sheweth by manie examples, after the floud of *Noe*, and the confusion of tongues in *Babilon*: as by the famous deluge of *Deucalion*, which destroied not onlie all *Greece*, but also *AEgipt*, and great parts of *Italy*. The great conflagration also in *Italy*, which burned the greatest part thereof, and ministred to the poets, occasion of the fable of *Phaëton*. The horrible crueltie of the Giants, called *Lestrigones*, of whome there yet remaine most huge bones to be seene in *Puteolanum*. The absortion, or swallowing vp, of the towne *Archippe* in *Italy*, with all the inhabitants, by the opening of the earth. The destruction of the towne *Amiclæ*, by serpents. The cōtinuall, and most strange pestilence, and famin, which afflicted the *Pelasglans* in

Bosius de signis eccle. li. 1. ca. 10. & li. 15. ca. 17. Item li. 6. de ruin. Gent. ca. 2. & de Italia statu per totum.

Italy,

Italy, for seauentie yeares together, and forced them in the end to abandon their dwellings, and to passe into *Greece*. The fourteene seuerall irruptions of forraine nations into *Italie*, who possessed it before *Rome* was built. And lastlie, the innumerable and vnspeakable calamities, and desolations, not onlie of particuler cities, but also of whole countries, and prouinces, by earth quakes, and inundations of the sea: as, when *Sicily* was deuided from the continent of *Italy*, whereto it was ioyned, and when *Prochita*, ouer against the countrie of *Campagnia* in the kingdome of *Naples*, and the *Ilandes* of *Caprea*, and *Phitecusa*, were in like sort seperated from the firme land, at seuerall times, by earth quakes, which opened the earth, and swallowed vp all the land in the midway that now the sea possesseth. And finallie when the great Iland called *Atlantica* in the *Ocean* sea, was wholie absorpt, and drowned, with all the inhabitants, being as bigg as all *Asia*, and *Africk*, which hapned, saith *Plato*, by a most terrible earthquake, continuing a whole day, and a night, with the which also, great numbers of people perished at the same time in *Greece*.

Strabo. li. 1. *Plin. li.* 2. *ca.* 92.

31 All which, if they be added to the like strange, and terrible earthquakes, drowning, and swallowing vp of townes, running together of hills, darkenes for manie daies, and such other prodigious punishments of God, vppon the *Romans*, whereof I haue spoken before, the same, I say being added to these, and compared with the afflictions of Christian people, either in these daies, or in former times, may sufficientlie testifie the great, and remarkable difference of Gods iudgements, vppon the one, and the other. To which purpose *Bozius*, hath diligentlie gathered, all the plagues, famins, inundations, earthquakes, dammages by fire, crueltie of tirants, irruptions of forraine, and barbarous nations, and such other calamities, as are mencioned in the histories, to haue hapned either to Christians, or to painimes, and infidels, and sheweth euidently, that those stupendious accidents of sinking, and swallowing vp of townes, and such other of like qualitie, haue neuer hapned in time of Christians, and that the other ordinarie afflictions of plagues, famines, warrs, and such like, which are common both to Christiãs, and Painimes, were neuerthelesse without all comparison, more greueous, and frequent for the space of three hundreth, or foure hundreth yeares onlie in time of Paganisme, then they haue bene in one thousand three hundreth yeares, of Christianitie, I meane, since the raigne of *Cõstantin* the great, whereof I omitt to lay downe the particulers to auoid prolixitie, hauing spent alreadie much more time in this matter, then at the first I meant to doe.

Bozius li. de nouo & antiquo Italiæ statu.

32 Now then, to come to the conclusion of this discourse, concerning the

the *Romans*. As it cannot be denied, but that all humane miseries, and calamities, are effects of Gods iustice, for the punishment of sinne, and no sinne so hainous in the sight of God, as idolatrie, and false religiō: it must needes be graunted, that those extraordinarie, and stupendious punishments, which God inflicted, vppon the *Romans* from time to time, during their Paganisme, was the due penaltie of their idolatrie, abominable superstition, and impietie, as *Tertullian*, boldly signified to the Painimes in his time, in his Apology for the Christians, affirming that they were, *Rei publicorum incommodorum. Guilty of all the publike harmes, and incommodities,* and that, *they drevv all mischeefe vppon the vvorld, by meanes of their idolatry,* and contempt of the true, and onlie God, *for it is most credible*, saith he, *that he is more angry, vvho is contemned, then those that are vvorshipped, and serued, or els truly they are more vniust, if for the Christians sake, they hurt their ovvne vvorshippers.* Thus saith he, worthilie, ascribing all the miseries of that time, to the idolatrie of the Painimes, who falselie ascribed the same to the desart of the Christians. *Tertulian in Apologetico.*

33 This then being so, it euidentlie appeareth, that the false religion of the *Romans*, was most pernicious to their state, and caused infinit calamities therein, though in the meane while almightie God cōserued, & augmented their empire, vntill the time prefixed in his diuine wisdome, and foretold by the prophet *Daniel*, was expired, to witt, vntil the stone was cut out of the hill without handes, & grew to be that mighty moūtaine which filled the earth, that is to say (as I haue also signified before) vntill our Sauiour *Christ*, being borne of the blessed Virgin, without the helpe of man, extēded, and dilated himselfe ouer the whole world in his mistical body, which is the Christiā Catholike Church, whereto the amplitude, and great power of the *Roman* empire serued notablie, as *S. Leo* teacheth expresselie, affirming, that the diuine prouidence, gaue to the Romans such a potent, and ample Monarchie. *Vt citò*, saith he, *peruios haberet populos prædicatio generalis, quos vnius teneret regimen ciuitatis. To the end that the generall preaching of the gospell might haue the more speedy passage throughout all people, and nations, vvhich should be vnder the gouerment of one citty.* *Daniel. 2.* *Augustin concione ad cathecum.* *S. Leo serm. 1. in natali Apost. Petri & Pau.*

34 Thus saith *S. Leo*, who also addeth further, to the same purpose, that when the Apostles had receiued of the holy Ghost the gift of tongues, & deuided the world amongst them, for their more cōmodious preaching of the gospell. *Beatissimus Petrus*, saith he, *princeps Apostolici ordinis* &c. *The most blessed Peter, the prince of the Apostolicall order* &c. *VVas destinated to the head of the Roman Empire,*) that is to say, to *Rome*) *to the end that the light of truth vvhich vvas reuealed for the saluation of all nations, might the more effectually spread it selfe from the head, ouer all the body.* *Ibidem.*

35 And againe in the same place, the same holie Father making an elegant *Apostrophe*, to *Rome* it selfe, and speaking of the glorious martirdome of the holie Apostles, *S. Peter*, and *S. Paule*, who shed their blood there, saith thus. *Isti sunt* &c. *These are they, o Rome, vvhich haue aduanced thee to this glory, to the end that thou becomming a hollie nation, an elect people, a priestly, and kingly citty, and (by the holy seat of Peter) the head of the vvorld, shouldest haue further, and more ample commaund by the meanes of deuine religion, then by earthly dominion: for although thou art increased by manie victories, and hast extended thy right, and povver of empire farre, by sea, and land, yet that vvhich thou hast subdued by force of armes, is lesse then that, vvhich Christian peace, hath made subiect vnto thee.*

Ibidem.

36 Thus saith this holie, and ancient Father, shewing how the amplitude of the Roman Monarchie, and the great celebritie of the citie of *Rome*, whiles it was Pagan, serued to the propagation of the Christian faith, and to the glorious exaltation of Christes Church.

37 But because, I shall haue iust occasion in the third part of this treatise, to speak more amplie, of the great power, and glorie of the Roman Church, and of the cheefe pastor thereof, I will say no more of that matter in this place, and haue onlie touched it here, thus breeflie as you see, partlie to shew the accomplishment of *Daniels* prophesie, foretelling the rysing of Christes kingdome, in the time of the Roman Empire: and partlie, to yeald some part of the reason, why almightie God, out of his deuine prouidence, conserued, and amplified the said empire, vntill his Church was planted, propagated and exalted. As also on the other side, I haue shewed, that out of his iustice, he punished the *Romãs*, and their empire, most seuerelie from time to time, for their false, impious, and absurd religion, as euidentlie appeareth throughout the three precedent chapters. And therefore this shall suffise concerninge the *Romans*, and their religion.

The absurdity not only of Mahometisme, *(vvhich the* Turkes, Persians, *and* Africans *professe) but also of* Iudaisme *(as it is novv at this day professed, and practised by the* Iewes*) is amply declared; vvith the ridiculous lyes, falsities, and errours, taught in the* Alcorã *of* Mahomet, *& in the* Thalmud *of the* Iewes, *no lesse contrary to reason of state, then repugnant to the veritie of religion.*

CHAP. 14.

1. THe desire, I haue had (good Reader) to giue thee ample satisfaction, and contentment, concerning aswell the temporall state, and empire of the *Romans*, as their religion, hath drawne me so farre beyond, the limits, which at the first I prefixed,

prefixed,to my ſelfe,for the handling of that matter, that I muſt now be much breefer, then perhaps thou maieſt expect, touching *Mahometiſme*, and *Iudaiſme*: eſpeciallie, ſeeing there reſteth to be handled alſo here after, ſuch aboundant, and important matter, concerning our Chriſtian religion,and manie other pointes belonging to the ſubiect of this treatiſe,that if I enlarge my ſelfe much in the diſcourſe of the two religions aforeſaid, I ſhalbe forced,either to be much more ſhort,and ſkant,then were conuenient, in that which more importeth,or els farre to exceede the boundes of my deſire and purpoſe,in the proportion of this volume, and therefore I deſigne this chapter onlie for thoſe two pointes, and meane alſo to be as breefe therein, as I conuenientlie may. Firſt then touching *Mahometiſme*,I thinke good to lay downe the beginning thereof,with the qualitie,and condition of the Author, before I treate of the abſurdities that it teacheth.

2 The author of *Mahometiſme*, was *Mahomet*, an *Arabian* of baſe parentage,whoſe father was a *Painyme*, or *Heathen*,and his mother a *Ievv*. And being after his fathers death,entertained by a wealthie widow to keepe her camels,he maried her in the end,and growing thereby no leſſe ambitious,then rich,deſired to make himſelfe king in that countrie; And not finding ſufficient power in himſelfe,or diſpoſition in the people, to effectuate his deſire,he beganne to giue himſelfe out for a prophet, faining reuelations,and rapts by the occaſion of the falling ſicknes,wherewith he was oft troubled,which he cloaked with the pretence that he had in his fitts,communication with God,and his Angels. And beſides diuers other ſleights, and deuiſes of his owne, to delude the ignorant people of the countrie,he had alſo the helpe,and aduiſe of one *Sergius* an heretical monke, profeſſing the *Neſtorian*,and *Arian* hereſie,who being for his bad life,expelled from his couent in *Conſtantinople*, fled to thoſe parts, where *Mahomet* liued,and falling acquainted with him,perſwaded him to become a Chriſtian,according to the profeſſion of the *Neſtorians*, and *Arrians*, who denie the diuinitie of *Chriſt*, in which beleefe he baptiſed him,as ſome write.

Theophanes Cedrenus, an.21.Heraclij Imper. Anaſtaſius Bibliothec. apud Baron. an.630. Pomponius Latus in Compendio Rom. Hiſt. in Heraclio. Pero Mexia in Silua varia lection. li.1.c.13.

3 This infection of hereſie ſo diſpoſed *Mahomet* to *Atheiſme*, and all impietie,that within a while he beganne,with the aduiſe of *Sergius* his apoſtaticall maſter,to ſett abroach a new religion,whereto he had alſo the helpe of certaine renegat *Ievves*,who informed him,not onlie of the doctrine and ceremonies of the ould law, but alſo of the abſurd fables of their *Thalmud*, whereby it came to paſſe, that his *Alcoran* (which is his booke of ſcripture) was patched vp of manie hereſies of the *Chriſtiās*, diuers rites,ceremonies,and opinions of the *Ievves*, and a number of

Ibidem.

fabulous dreames, and mad, or rather monſtrous fictions of his owne, with the which he mingled alſo ſome cuſtomes of the Pagãs, to the end that his law, or religion, hauing ſomewhat of all other religions, might be the more plauſible, and pleaſing to all ſects, and ſorts of men.

4 So that adding alſo, to this, all libertie of ſenſualitie, and carnalitie, (as shall appeare hereafter) he eaſelie drew ſuch an infinit number of people, to follõw him, that he preſumed after a while, to take vppõ him, the title, & dignitie, aſwel of a king, aſ of a prophet. And by reaſon that the Roman empire, was then much decaied (I meane in the time of *Heraclius* the Emperour, which was about the yeare of our Lord ſix hũdreth and thirtie, he eaſelie ſubdued all *Africk*, and a great part of *Aſia*, and planted there his new ſect of religion. And for as much, as he could not confirme it either with miracles, or yet with arguments, and reaſon, he publiſhed, that as in former times, God gaue the power of miracles to *Moyſes*, and to *Chriſt*, ſo alſo he had giuen to him the power of the ſword, and commaunded him to plant his doctrin therewith: in which reſpect alſo, he vtterlie forbad, not onlie the ſtudie of philoſophy, but alſo all manner of diſputatiõ, about his *Alcoran*, ordaining the penaltie of death for the tranſgreſsion thereof, thereby to depriue the profeſſours of his religion, of all meanes to diſcouer, the abſurditie, and impietie of it.

Circa an. 630.

a *Dion. Carthuſ. contra Alcoran.*

5 And now to giue thee good Reader, ſome taſt of the doctrin, taught in his *Alcoran*, & of the practiſe thereof (at leaſt ſo farre forth, as ſeemeth to me conuenient for my purpoſed breuitie) thou shalt vnderſtand, that though he teach with the Chriſtians, that there is but one God, yet he denieth with the a *Sabelliãs*, the Trinity of perſõs; & with the b *Macedoniãs*, the dignitie of the holie Ghoſt (whome he maketh but a creature) and with the c *Arriãs*, the diuinitie of *Chriſt*; teaching him to be but pure mã, yet borne of a virgin, and free from ſinne, full of all wiſdome, vertue, & ſanctitie, calling him alſo d *the ſpirit, the vvord, the povver of God, the Meſſias promiſed to the Ievves in the lavv of Moyſes*, and affirming finallie, that the Iewes were forſaken by almightie God, becauſe they would not receiue *Chriſt* their *Meſsias*, e & that by the occaſiõ thereof, the Apoſtles preached the ghoſpell, and faith of *Chriſt*, to the Gentils, whereto alſo the practiſe of the *Turkes* (who profeſſe *Mahomets* religion) is cõforme, euen vntil this day, for that they admit no *Ievv*, to be a *Turke*, except he firſt cõfeſſe, that *Chriſt*, the Sonne of the virgin *Mary*, was the true *Meſsias* promiſed by almightie God, to the patriarks, and foretold by the prophets.

b *Pero Mexia in ſilua var. lect. l. 1. c. 13. Hiſpanicè.*

c *Galiel. Reginal. in Caluino tur. li. 2 ca. 3.*

d *Theodorus Bibliander in præfat. Alcorani. pag. 3.*

e *Dion. Carthus. Dialo. contra perfid. Mahom. art. 3. Poſtel. de la religion des Turcs. pa. 43*

6 Furthermore he teacheth, with the *Manichees*, that *Chriſt* was not put to death by the *Ievves*, but that God deliuered him, from their handes, & that they crucified onlie his forme, & shape, & that *Chriſt* himſelfe aſcended

S. Ioan. Damaſcen. de Hæreſib. in fine.

ded corporally into heauen,and is there to remaine vntill the cōming of *Antichrist*,at what time (he saith) *Christ* shall returne againe, kill *Antichrist*,& conuert the *Ievves*. Also he teacheth the resurrectiō of the dead, and approueth the law of *Moyses*, the psalter of *Dauid*,and the ghospel of *Christ*. Affirming,that both *Christ*,and *Moyses*,gaue testimonie of him , and that though the Apostles taught Christs doctrine truly, yet their successors corrupted it,& falsified both the ould testamēt,&the new,all which he pretendeth to reforme by his *Alcoran*. And though he seemed vtterly to cōdemne Idolatrie,yet to cōtent the *Painims*,he ordained the worship of a starr,called *Cubar*, which we commonlie call *Lucifer*. *Theodor. Biblian. in præfat. Alcora. Cusanus in cribratione Alcorani.*

7 Moreouer he commaundeth Circumcision,abstinence from swines flesh,and wine, and maketh his saboath day vppon friday , to the end his followers might differ both from the *Ievves*,and from the *Christians*: neuertheles they cease not from worke, on those daies , but vse more praier after their manner,then at other times . And whereas the *Ievves* turne towards the west , when they pray , and the *Christians* towards the east, they turne towards the south , and pray in their *Mosquees*, (which are their temples) fiue times in foure, and twentie houres : the first at the sunne rising , the second at midday , the third , towards the euening , the fourth , at sunne setting, and the fift after supper in the night. *Euthym in Panoplia par. 2. Tit. 24. Cuspinian. de religione Turcarum. Septem castrens. de fide & religi. Turcar. Vide Caluinoturcis. li. 2. ca. 3. Christophorus Richerius li. 2. de morb. Turcar.*

8 They vse also frequent lotions , or washings of their hands , faces, bellies , the soles of their feete , and their armes to the elbow , for the expiation , and remission of their sinnes , and if they be,where water wanteth, they rubb their faces ouer with dust.They haue also a kind of Lent, to witt,a moneths fast euerie yeare,abstayning from all kind of meates, drinke, and women all the day, which being ended , they eate, and drinke freelie, what they list, and spend the night in all riott, vntill sunne rising the next day , and at the end of their moneths fast, they celebrat, their paschal feast, wherein they visit certaine memories of the dead , and after that they haue prayed , and eaten such meates, as they bring with them thither,they kisse on an other,and say *Baaran*,that is to say, *God giue you a good feast*. And threescore daies after this paschal feast, they celebrat an other in like manner, because at that time , their pilgrimes make their perigrinations to *Medina* , and *Mecha* , which are their principal places of deuotion, and especiallie *Mecha* , where *Mahomets*, tombe is kept with great solemnitie, and visited by all the Turkes of the east parts. *Ijdem autores vbi supra. Laonic. li. 3. de reb. Turcic. apud Baron. an. 630.*

9 Also, they vse to sacrifice beastes, though they doe it most commonlie in discharge of some vow, and the fourth part of the sacrifice is

Septem caſtrenſ.c. 13. & alij apud Reginald. in Caluinoturciſsimo.li. 2. ca.3.

giuen to the prieſt, an other to the poore, and the third to the neighbours,& the laſt remaineth to him that made the ſacrifice. Their prieſts are maried, and for the moſt part vnlearned, no greater knowledge, or learning being required of them,then to vnderſtand, and litterallie to expound the *Alcoran*,which *Mahomet* left in the Arabical tongue, and ſo it remaineth.

Vide Reginaldum in Caluinoturciſ.li.3.c.20.

Poſtel. de la iuſtice des Turcs. Belforeſt Coſmograph li.2.c.9. To.2.

10 They haue alſo certaine religious men, who liue ſingle,and vnmaried. They hold all mad men for ſaincts,or holie men,eſteeming them to be ſurpriſed with a deuine fury. They burie no dead bodies in their temples,but in certaine places aſſigned for that purpoſe,whither they carry their corſes,with waxe cādells in their handes,accompanied with their prieſts,and religious mē. And although *Mahomet* left the office of cheefe prieſt, or bishop annexed to the regal dignitie (as he exerciſed both him ſelfe) yet in time, his ſucceſſours being deuided amongſt them ſelues, the dignities alſo eccleſiaſtical, and temporall came to be ſeperated in ſuch ſort,that the prince obeieth the cheefe Bishop,in all things belonging to religion,and therefore the Emperour of the *Turkes*, beareth ſuch reſpect vnto the *Muphti* (for ſo is the cheefe prieſt, or bishop called) that he riſeth out of his ſeate as oft, as the *Muphti*,cōmeth to him,laying his hand vppon his breaſt,and bowing his head downe to the ground to doe him reuerence.

Alcoran Azoar. 8. & 32.

11 But to returne to *Mahomet*, and his *Alcoran* (and to shew withall his beſtialitie,and the abſurd impietie of his law) he ordained that his followers shall marie twoo, three,or foure wiues, except they feare, that they cannot keepe ſo manie in peace one with an other:and in that caſe, they may marrie ſo manie vnder the number of foure (*ſaith the Alcoran*) as their handes can chaſtiſe. And further he alloweth them to haue the companie of as manie ſeruant women, as they are able to keepe, and to repudiat, and diſmiſſe their wiues,and to marrie others,or the ſame againe,at their pleaſure,ſo that they doe not repudiat, or remarrie one wife aboue three times.

Pero Mexia. ſilua. var. lect.par.4.c.1 Italia ex ipſo Alcorano. c. vacca. & c. elnaſa.

12 And although *Mahomet* ordaine,that he which committeth adulterie with an other mans wife,shalbe ſtoned to death, together with her, and that he who is knowne to haue the companie of an other woman, except his owne wife, ſeruants,and ſlaues, shall haue *Foureſcōre* blowes with a cudgel: yet he alloweth,the deteſtable ſinne, which is tearmed, *Peccatum nefandum* (the ſinne not to be named,commonlie called *Sodomy*) either with men or women,ſo that it be with ſuch as profeſſe his law. And albeit, he graunteth, but foure wiues at once to other men, yet ſo extrauagant, and exorbitant was his owne luſt, that he had at once ſeauenteene

seauenteene wiues, besides manie concubins, pretending to haue a speciall priuiledge from almightie God, for the same, as also to abuse other mens wiues, and his owne kinswomen, at his pleasure, as appeareth by certaine constitutions in his *Alcoran*, which he fained to haue made by especiall order, and commission from almightie God.

13 And whereas some of his wiues, hauing once taken him tardie with a yonge woman, called *Maria*, murmured greatlie thereat, and seemed to wonder how his adulteries could stand with the sanctitie, and hollines of a prophet of God, and why God dispensed with him alone in all these cases, he assembled all his wiues, and hauing read vnto them the foresaid constitutions of his *Alcoran*, and called to witnes the Archangels, *Michaell*, and *Gabriel*, he tould them further, that they ought to repent, for that they were out of the right way, and threatned them also, that if they were obstinate, God would seperate them from him, and giue him better wiues, who should be *rich, faithfull, penitent, wise, virgins, and should praise, adore, and serue God.* Which when his wiues vnderstood, seeing them selues in danger to be diuorced from him, they seemed to be sorrie for their fault, and suffred him afterwardes to doe what he listed.

Ca. 271. Vide Pero Mexia par, 4. c. 1. silua var. lect. Italia.

14 Lo then what a hollie prophet, this *Mahomet* was, and what a hollie religion he leaft to the world, which yet may the better appeare, if wee consider what reward he asigned in the next life, for his followers, which was nothing els, but sensuall pleasures, and such beastlie carnalitie, that I am ashamed to set downe the particulers thereof, and therefore I thinke good to remit thee, good Reader, to the authors quoted in the margent, his owne *Alcoran*, and an other worke of his called *Zuma*, where it euidentlie appeareth, that his law, and religion, is more fit for hoggs, and swine, then for reasonable creatures, such being the verie nature, and condition of the sensuall pleasures of the body (as *Cicero* well obserueth) that if anie man be a litle more addict thereto, then ordinarie (so that he be not *ex pecudum genere*, of the kind of beastes, *for some men*, sayth he, *are men in name only, and not in deede*) he dissembleth, and hideth as much as he may his appetite, and desire of these pleasures, euen for verie shame, whereby (saith *Cicero*) it appeareth, that the pleasures of the flesh are not to be accounted worthie of the excellent dignitie of man. Thus saith he, concluding such men, as are giuen wholie to lust, and sensualitie, for no better then beastes, and to be vnworthie of the name of men.

Bellonius des. singularites l. 3. c. 7. Caluino turcis. l. 4. c. 20. Silua di varia lection. Italia par. 4. c. 1. Alcoran. c. 1. 54. 65. 66. & 97. Cicero offic. li. 1.

15 Therefore, what shall we say of *Mahomet*, who was so farre transported with his owne beastlie lust, that he not onlie abandoned himselfe wholie thereto, but also placed the end of his religion, and felicitie

Alcor. Azoara 97. of man therein, calling it. *Optimam Dei remunerationem.* The best reward of God, and making paradise, no better then a bawdie house, or stewes? Doth he deserue to be called the prophet of God, seeing that in *Cicero* his opinion, he deserueth not the name of a man? Or can his doctrin merit to be called a religion, which all Painimes, no lesse then Christiãs, agree to consist in vnion with God, as I haue sufficientlie declared before, out of the opinion of the best philosophers? *Chap. 2. & 3*

Auicenna li. 9. 18. sua metaphis.

16 No meruell then, that *Auicenna* hauing benne nourished in *Mahomets* law from his infancy, grew in the end by the very study of Philosophie, to contemne and reiect it, and therefore he saith. *Lex quam dedit Mahametus &c. The lavv vvhich Mahomet gaue, doth only shevv the felicity, or misery of the body, but vvise deuines*, that is to say, *true philosophers, doe much more aspire to true felicity, then to the happines of the body, vvhich, though it vvere graunted them in the highest degree, yet they vvould litle esteeme, in comparison of the true beatitude, vvhich is conioyned, vvith the first truth*, that is to say, with God. Thus saith he, being himselfe a *Mahometan*, by education and profession, who neuerthelesse witnesseth, as you see, that *Mahomet* in his law, neither taught nor sought, the true felicitie consisting in vnion with God, but onlie the false or supposed happines of the bodie, where vppon it must needes follow, that his carnall, and sensuall law, deserueth not the name of religion, not hauing so much, as anie pretence of the true end of religion.

17 But how vaine, and impious, both he himselfe, and his pretended religion was, it may yet further appeare by manie ridiculous, and absurd lies, auouched by him in his *Alcoran* for serious, and religious truths, whereof I will relate some twoo, or three, to the end thou maist, good Reader, the better iudge thereby of the spirit, that possest this great prophet, and inspired him in the institution of his law.

18 Thou shalt therefore vnderstand, that though he sometimes exclude Christians and all others, that doe not professe his law, from his imagined paradise of pleasure, designing them to hell, and eternall damnatiõ, yet as he is in manie other thinges, full of contradictions, (which sufficiently bewraieth his lying spirit) so he is also in this, allowing a place in his paradise to *Christians, Ievves*, and *Samaritans*, albeyt he assigne them verie meane offices there. As to *Christians*, and *Ievves*, to be woodcarriers, to make fires (for belike there wil be cold winters, as well there, as in earth) and the *Samaritans*, he saith, shall carry out the dong, and ordure, which otherwise might make that plesant place vnsauorie. And amõgst manie other glorious things, which he promiseth in his paradise, he describeth goodlie riuers, some of honie, some of milke, and others of

Euthimius in panopia par. 2. Titu. 24.

Aromatical wynes, and telleth of Angels, whoſe heads are ſo great, that one of their eyes, ſtandeth a daies iourney from the other, and no moruaile, ſeeing he alſo ſaith, that there are certain other Angels, which ſuſtaine, and ſupport the ſeat of God, hauing ſuch ample, and ſpacious necks, that if a bird ſhould flie continuallie a long by them, ſhee ſhould skantlie be able in a thouſand yeares, to arriue from one of their eares, to the other.

Pero Mexia ſil. var. lect. par. 4. ca. 1. Italicè. Dionyſ. Carthu. in ſert. Mahom. l. 3. art. 8.

19 But if this may not paſſe currāt, for a lie, I hope, that of the nex there wilbe leſſe difficultie, he thanketh God greatlie in his *Alcoran*, for conuaying him once from his oratory in *Mecha*, firſt to *Hieruſalem*, and from thence to the ſeat, and throne of God in heauen, with incredible ſpeede, which iourney, he relateth in this ridiculous manner.

Alcoran. c. 150.

20 He ſaith, that one night as he was at his praiers, the Angel *Gabriel* came vnto him, and tould him, that God would haue him to come preſentlie to ſpeake with him, and that he mounted out of hand, vppon his truſty, and wiſe ſteede, called *Alborac*, which could ſpeake as well as he, and beganne to diſpute with him, and would not ſett forward, vntil he had promiſed him, to pray to God for him, and not to leaue him at heauen gates, but to take him in with him.

Bellonius des ſingularites li. 3. ca. 7. Vide Caluinoturcis. li. 4. ca. 20.

21 This doughty beaſt, was, as he deſcribeth him, like an aſſe, but ſomewhat bigger, and yet leſſe then a mule, and of ſuch velocitie, that in the ſpace of an houre, he would make a iourney of fifty thouſand yeares: in ſo much, that in the twinkling of an eie, he went from *Mecha*, to *Hieruſalem*, from whence he paſſed forwards the reſt of his voyage, through ſeuen heaues, or ſpheres, whereof the firſt was made of ſiluer, the ſecond of gold; the third of a certaine precious ſtone, that hath no name, the fourth of ſmaragdus; the fift of diamant; the ſixt of Carbuncle; and the ſeauenth, of a deuine light, & that euery one of theſe heauẽs, had a gate, whereat *Gabriel* knocked a good while, and could not be let in, till he had told, that the prophet *Mahomet* came with him.

22 In all theſe heauens he deſcribeth diuers formes of angels, ſome like mẽ, orhers like oxen, others like horſes, ſome like cockes, and ſome like other birdes, all which he ſaith, doe pray for creatures of their forme, and he himſelfe prayed for them all.

23 He ſaw alſo in thoſe heauẽs, innumerable ſtarrs made of ſiluer, & tied with goldẽ chaines, leſt otherwiſe, they might fall out of their places, & to theſe ſtarres (beſides the ornament, which they giue to heauẽ) he aſſigneth alſo a particuler office, to wit, to keepe watch, & ward, againſt deuils, which doe vſe to goe to heauẽ, to hearkẽ, & ſpy, what is done there: whome they driue away with firebrāds. And in the laſt heauẽ, he ſaw an

Pero Mexia in ſil. par. lect. vbi ſupra.

infinit number of Angels, euery one of them infinitelie greater then the world, hauing seauentie heads a piece, and in euerie head, a million of mouthes, and in euerie mouth, seauentie thousand tongues, which praised God, with seauen hundreth thousand thousands of languages. And amongst the rest he saith, there was one Angel, who wept bitterlie for his sinnes, for whom he praied, as also he had done before for *Moyses*, and diuers other of the old patriarkes, and prophets, whom he saw in his iourney, in diuers heauens, though when he mett with *Christ*, (who was in the seauenth heauen) he saith, he praied not for him, as he had donne for the rest, but recommended himselfe to his praiers.

Ibidem.

24 To conclude, when he came to almightie God, he found him sitting in a magnificent throne, though he could not be suffred to approch him, by two bowshot, in all which space the flooer was couered with rich tapestrie, and there, he saith, God commaunded him to ordaine, that his people should say fiftie praiers euerie day, and yet afterwards, he obtained, as he saith, dispensation for all those praiers, except fiue, by the counsell of *Moyses*, who being in the fourth heauen, and vnderstanding at *Mahomets* returne, what God had ordained, aduised him to goe back to God, to procure dispensation thereof, which he saith, cost him fiue iourneis from the fourth heauen to the last, obtaining euerie time, release of some part of the praiers, and when *Moyses* would haue had him, to returne to God the sixt time (assuring him, that the people would not say so much as those fiue praiers which remained) he saith, he was so wearie, that he would goe back no more, but went on his iourney to *Hierusalem*, and from thence to *Mecha*, and all this long voyage, and important negotiatiō was performed, saith he, in the fouretenth part of one night.

25 Now then I doubt not, good Reader, but that thou wilt take all this tale, for some dronken dreame, or phantastical conceit, of a crazed braine, or els for a fable of some one that lied for a wager, or a whetstone, rather thē for a religious historie, or a propheticall vision, seeing it containeth such absurd, and ridiculous matter, as thou hast heard, of which sort his *Alcoran*, and other workes are so full, that it may well appeare, what manner of men they are, who beleeue, & follow his law, to wit, most ignorant idiots, of brutish, and beastlie condition.

26 For who is he that hath but anie principles of ordinarie learning, or knowledge, that will not presentlie discouer the absurd foolerie of these, and diuers others his prodigious fictions, as that the moone was once equall in brightnes with the sunne, vntill the angel *Gabriel*, passing in hast to heauen, chanced to rubb vppon it with his wings, and to put out a great deale of the light of it, and that there vppon grew the diffe-

Dionys. Carthus. in sect. Mahom. li. 3. ar. 8.

rence

rence betwixt day, and night. Also that the sunne euerie night goeth to wash it selfe, and so riseth againe, verie pure, and cleare in the morninge: And that the sunne is in a warme fountaine, and the fountaine in a snake, and the snake in a great space, and the space in the hill called *Kaff*, and the hill *Kaff*, in the hand of an Angel, which houldeth vp the world vntill the day of iudgement: and that the heauen was made of smoke, and smoke of a vapour of the sea, and the sea of the hill *Kaff*, which inuironeth all the world, and holdeth vp the heauens.

Euthym. in Panoplia. par. 2. Tit. 24. Dionys. vbi supra. Idem ibid. art. 6. & Pero Mexia par. 4. ca. 1. silua &c.

27 What man, I say, is there of vnderstanding, who will not take this to be an idle discourse of some mad bedleme, or frentick man, of which sort also he hath manie others touching some of our histories, of the old, and new testament, whereof he taketh such part as it pleaseth him, to serue him, as it were, for a plaine song to deskant vppon, after his ridiculous manner, grounding thereon manie loud, and lewd lies. As when he saith, that the blessed virgin *Mary* (whom he maketh to be sister to *Moyses*, and *Aaron*) being neare her time of trauaile, sate downe by a palme tree, and wished shee were dead, and that vppon a suddaine *Christ* sate downe by her, and comforted her, and finallie, that God bad her shake the palme tree, and eate of the fruit to strenghten her selfe therewith &c.

Euthym. in Panoplia vt supra.

Idem li. 2. ar. 39.

28 He telleth also of *Salomon*, that he gathered a huge armie of Angels, deuils, men, birds, and beastes, and that he came to a great flood of Ants, or pismires, where of one perswaded her fellowes to goe into their holes lest *Salomon*, and his souldiars should kill them, and when shee had said so, she smild. And that *Salomon* died leaning vppon his staffe, and stoode so, a long time, in so much, that the diuels, which were vnder his commaund, did not know, that he was dead, vntil at length the stafe, being eaten, and consumed by a worme, brake, and his bodie fell to the ground, which when the deuils saw, they went away, and did much mischeefe to men.

Silua var. lect. par. 4. ca. 1.

29 Manie such fond, and impious fictions, he hath of *Adam*, *Abraham*, *Moyses*, *Iacob*, *Ioseph*, *Dauid*, and the old patriarks, which I purposelie omit, fearing to cloy thee, good Reader, with such impertinent toyes, and trifles. And for as much as the absurditie thereof is euident to common sense, and that all his religion is built vppon such vanities, lies, and monstrous heresies, that it needeth no other confutation, then the bare relation thereof, I will passe further to examine breeflie, how the same agreeth with policie, to the end it may appeare that this his law, or religion, is not onlie false, and irreligious, but also contrarie in diuers things, to reason of state.

30 First then, whereas the principall benefit, and cheefe end of true religion in common welth, is to vnite the same with God, and thereby to make it happy, (as I haue proued here to fore at large) it is manifest, that there can follow no such effect of *Mahometisme*, but the cleane contrarie, seeing it is false, vaine, impious, and absurd, as I haue declared, and therefore abominable in the sight of God, and consequentlie most preiudiciall to common wealth, which dependeth wholie on the will, and fauour of God.

Chap. 2. & 3.

31 Secondlie, his ordinance of *Polygamy*, or the pluralitie of wiues, is against the true reason of state, because it is contrarie to true *Oeconomy*, that is to say, to the good gouernment of families, with out the which no common welth can stand, seeing that particuler families, are as I may say, the elements, or letters, wherewith all common wealths are composed. And that, *Poligamy*, is against good *Oeconomy*, it is euident, for that it impugneth two of the speciall ends of matrimony, whereof the one is, the peaceable societie of man, and wife, and the other the remedie against concupiscence, not onlie in men, but also in women.

32 And to say some what breefelie of both, and first of the former, *Aristotle* teacheth that man, and woman, are by the law of nature, cõioyned in mariage, not only for procreation, but also for alouing, and socieable cohabitation, to the end, they may ioyntlie, gouerne their familie, according to the diuersitie of their sexes (for some things, saith *Aristotle*, doe properlie belong to the administration of men, and others to the care, and charge of women.) And here vppon the wise man saith. *Stabilimentum domus, vir, & mulier, bene consentientes. The stay, or assurans of a house, or family is, a man, and a vvoman, agreeing vvell together.* But this louing, and peaceable cohabitation, cannot stand with the pluralitie of wiues, for it is skantlie possible, that the husband can loue diuers wiues, all alike, where vppon there must needes grow enuie, ielosies, contention, and discord, not onlie amongst the women themselues, and their friends, but also betwixt them, and their husbands, and consequentlie amongst their children, and seruants, euerie one, taking part with those, which he most affecteth, as *Aristotle* obserueth notablie well, saying, that *vvhere the husband, and vvife, agree vvell together, there friends reioyce, and their enimyes are afflicted, and vvhen they disagree, their friends also fall at debate.*

Arist. li. 8. ethic. ca. 12.

Ibidem.

Eccl. 25.

Arist. Oeconom.

33 And this in the houses of great personages, may breede much inconuenience, not onlie to the families themselues, but also to the common wealth, by reason of partialities, and enmities, which by the occasion of

sion of the women discontented, may arise also abroad betwixt their kinsfolkes, and breede, tumults, seditions, yea, and ciuil warrs, to the great danger, and ouerthrow of the state, as may appeare by that which I haue discoursed in the first part of this treatise, where I haue declared the great danger of seditions, growing verie oft vppon smale occasions, euen betwixt women, or children, whereof I alleadged there diuers examples, and therefore do remit my Reader thereto, concluding for the present, that seeing peace, concord, and amitie, are most necessarie to the good estate aswell of the whole common welth, as of euerie particuler familie, and that loue, and amitie cannot be conserued in priuat families, and is also probablie endangered in the whole common welths, by the pluralitie of wiues, it must needes follow, that the ordinance, and vse thereof, is both against good *Oeconomy*, and also against reason of state.

Chap. 7. Nu. 14 15. 16. 17. 18. 19. & 20.

34 The other end of mariage, which is empeached by the pluralitie of wiues, is the remedie, against concupiscence, which on the behalfe of the woman, is litle, or nothing atall remedied, where manie wiues, haue one husband, and the greater that the number of wiues, and concubins are, the lesse is the remedie, which they haue thereby, as it is euident inough in it selfe, without further proofe. Besides that, it is a certaine iniquitie, and iniustice, that euerie woman should, by contract, giue herselfe wholie vnto one husband, and he deuide, and part himselfe amongst manie wiues, especiallie, seeing our apostle teacheth, that the husband hath not power of his owne bodie, but his wife, whereby it appeareth, that although in matters touching the gouerment, and direction of the familie, the wife is inferiour to the husband, and ought to obey him, yet for the bedd, there is equalitie betweene them, not onlie because she equallie concurreth with him to the procreation of children, but also because she hath as much neede of remedie against concupiscence as he, yea, and more in respect, that shee is weaker, and more fraile then he, and therefore the law of *Poligamy*, prouiding a superfluous, and excessiue remedie for the man, and verie litle, or none at all for the woman, but rather a greater incentiue, and prouocation to lust, is most vniust, and iniurious to all woman kind, and consequentlie, to the on halfe of euerie common welth, or rather of the whole world, in which respect it is not onlie against reason of state, but also contrarie to the law of nature.

35 And this is also cleare, by the verie first institution of mariage, where vppon our Sauiour said, that *God made man at the first, one man, and one vvoman, & propter hoc*, saith he, *relinquet homo patrem* &c. *and for this,*

Matth. 19. Mar. 10.

a man shall forsake his father, and mother, and adhere to his vvife, and they shalbe tvvo in one flesh, and therefore novv they are not tvvo, but one flesh. Thus saith our Sauiour, signifiing plainelie, that according to the first institution of mariage, one man can haue but one wife at once, nor one woman, more then one husband at once, as it is manifest, not onlie by his maner of speach, speaking of man, and wife, in the singular number, but much more by the inference, and conclusion, saying; *therefore novv they are not*
Ibidem. *tvvo, but one flesh*, which cannot be verified, but betwixt two.

36 But perhaps you will aske, how then it came to passe, that the old
Gen. 16. patriarks had more wiues then one at once, as *Abraham*, *Iacob*, *Dauid*,
& 30. &c. Whereto I answere, that although from *Adam* to *Lamech* (who was
1. *Regum.* the first that maried two wiues, being a wicked man, as the scripture
*ca.*25. testifieth) there was not anie alteration of the first institution of mariage
*Gen.*4. of one man with one woman, (which custome had continued aboue a thousand yeares) yet afterwardes almightie God, hauing not onlie extin-
*Gen.*7. guished all mankind (except *Noe*, and his familie) but also much abbreuiated the liues of men, dispensed with them, to haue manie wiues for the more speedie reparation and encrease of mankind, to the end that the world might be the sooner replenished. Neuertheles this custome of *Poligamy* ceassed generallie, no lesse amongst the *Ievves*, then amongst the *Gentills*, before Christs time, not onlie because the reason, and cause of the dispensation ceased, (the world being sufficientlie multiplied) but also, by reason of the inconuenience, that men generallie found therein. And as for the *Ievves*, it is euident inough, that they had no vse of *Poli-*
Matth. 19. 22. & 27. *gamy*, in Christs time, as may appeare first, by the verie phrase, and speech
Mar. 10. of the scripture of the new testament, where the *Pharisees*, or who
& 12. els soeuer had occasion to speake of wiues, vsed alwaies the singu-
*Luc.*1. 3. 14. lar number, speaking of a wife, and not of wiues; secondlie for
16. & 20. that there can be no example alleadged of anie, that had two wiues, at
*Act.*5. & 18. 1. *Cor.*7. once, at that time, whereas the contrarie seemeth to be euident in *Za-*
*Luc.c.*1. *chary*, who hauing a barraine wife (to wit *Elizabeth*) neuer maried other, but liued continuallie with her alone without children, vntill they were
Aul Gellius both old.

*li.*18.*ca.*6. 37 And as for the *Gentills*, though in more ancient, and rude times *Poligamy* was admitted in some countries, yet it was neuer generallie recei-
*Arist.polit.*7 *oeconom.* ued, yea, and grew in the end to be generallie excluded out of the best, and most politike common welths, as may appeare both by *Aristotle*, (who ordaineth *Monogamy*, that is to say. the vse of one wife onlie) in his *Politiks*, and *Oeconomiks*: and also by the ancient ciuil law of the *Romãs*, wherein those were held to be infamous, & punished also other waies, who

who had more wiues then one, at once. And there is no doubt, but that aswell this law of the *Romās*, as also that other of *Aristotle*, had no other grounde, then the verie law of nature, and reason of state, in respect of the great inconuenience that they obserued to grow both to priuat families, and to the whole common welth by pluralitie of wiues; wherevppon I conclude, that *Mahomets* law, not onlie allowing, but also commaunding pluralitie of wiues, and multiplicitie of concubins, is absurd, and contrarie aswel to reason of state, as to the primitiue, and naturall institution of Mariage.

F. de his qui notantur infamia. lege 1. Item c. de incest nuptijs neminem, & ad leg. Iuliā de Adulterijs lege eum qui.

38 Yet here perhaps, it may further be demaunded, why pluralitie of wiues should not be necessarie for multiplication, and encrease of the people, as also for a remedie against fornication, and adulteries, seeing we see, that some women are barrein, and some more fruitfull then others; and that no woman, after that shee hath conceiued, is fit for further procreation, vntil shee be deliuered, whiles at the same time, one man may haue diuers children, by diuers womē, and hauing manie lawful wiues, may haue also meanes to auoid fornication, whiles some of them are sick, or lye in childbed, or haue other impediments.

39 To this I say, first concerning procreation, if this were the onlie or cheefe end of man, it might be said, with the more reason, that *Poligamy*, were most conuenient for him, and necessarie, for common welth, but seeing that God hath giuen to man, the appetit, and power of procreation, not to place his end, or felicitie therein, but to the end that mankind being propagated thereby, may continuallie serue God, and be vnited with him (wherein consisteth mans felicitie) it followeth, that procreation is so to be vsed, that on the on side, mans felicity be not hindred thereby, and one the other side, mankind may be sufficientlie propagated, that is to say, seeing that the excellencie, and perfection of man, consisteth in his soule, and not in his bodie, and that therefore the body is inferiour, and subordinat to the soule, and sensualitie, to reason, it followeth that the appetits, and pleasures of the bodie and senses, are no further to be allowed, or vsed, then they are ruled, and guided by reason, and may serue, or auaile to the end, and felicitie of man, consisting in his vnion with God, whereto the propagation of mankind, and all humane actions, are speciallie to be referred.

40 Wherupon I inferre, that the procreation which is conuenient, and necessarie for the multiplication of mankind, ought to be such, as may not hinder the cheefe operation of the soule, that is to say, contemplation, whereby man is vnited with God, and made happy, both here, and eternallie.

41 But

41 But is there anie thing that doth more hebctat, dull, and offuscat, the vnderstanding, or as I may say bestialise, the soule of man, then the excesse of the pleasures of the flesh.

This all philosophers doe vniformelie teach, who require nothing more, in a contemplatiue man, aspiring to a perfect vnion with God, then that by all meanes possible, he abstract himselfe, from his bodie, and senses, and from all the delights, and pleasures thereof; as shall appeare farther hereafter, when I shall treat of philosophicall, and Christian contemplation, and therefore now in this place I will content my selfe, with the onlie testimonie of the philosopher *Auicenna*, a *Mahometan* in profession, who speaking of true felicitie, taxeth by the way, the bestialitie of the *Mahometans*, saying, thus. *VVe can haue no feeling of the true felicitie in our bodies, because vve are drovvned, and ouervvhelmed, vvith the filthy pleasures thereof.* Thus saith he, and verie trulie, so farre forth as concerneth *Mahometans*, who following the ordinance of their lawmaker, and false prophet, are so drunke, and drowned in the brutish delights of the flesh, that they haue no more tast, or imagination, of the pleasures of the soule, and true felicitie of man, then the verie bruite beasts, as may sufficientlie appeare, by that which I haue signified before concerning *Mahomets* paradise, and the felicitie that his followers expect in the next life.

Auicenna li. 9. sua metaphys.

42 Therefore, the procreation which is conuenient for the end of man, and consequentlie for the propagation of mankind, ought to be conforme to the excellencie of humane nature, that is to say, moderat, void of all excesse, and balanced with reason, such I meane, as that mankind may be sufficiently encreased, and yet other inconueniences avoyded, which must needes folow vpon Mahomets poligamy, & concubinage, as I haue declared before.

43 But perhaps, you may aske me, how it chaunced then, that poligamy, hindred not contemplation in the Patriarks, who were great contemplatiues, and familiar with almighty God? Whereto I answer, that as God dispenced with thē to vse *poligamy* vpon iust causes (which I haue declared before) so also he gaue them, an extraordinary grace, to vse it with great moderation, as it is euident in *Abraham*, whome *Sarai* his wife (seeing her selfe to be barrein) intreated to take *Agar* her handmaid also, to the end he might haue some issue by her. And when, (saith the scripture,) he yealded to her request, shee deliuered *Agar* vnto him, *in vxorem*, for a wife. Whereby we may see, how reserued, and temperat, this great contemplatiue patriark was, in the vse of *Poligamy*.

Gen. 16.

44 And now to say some what concerning the pretended necessitie of

Poligamy,

Poligamy, for the multiplication of the world. Cannot the world be sufficientlie multiplied, except *Poligamy* be admitted? Were not the commõ welths of the *Romans*, and other Gentils, most populous, not withstanding their continuall warres, and great mortalitie by plagues, and other accidents, whiles neuertheles they excluded *Poligamy*, yea, and greatlie esteemed the vertue of continencie, and chastitie, as I will declare hereafter? And are not our Christian common wealths at these daies, most numerous, and aboundant of people, though not onlie *Poligamy*, is prohibited, but also single, and chast life, embraced of an infinit number of both sexes? *Chap. 30. Nu. 32. & 33.*

45 And who knoweth not euen by common experience, throughout all the course of mans life, how true it is, which the Apostle saith. *Neque qui plantat est aliquid, neque qui rigat, sed qui incrementum dat Deus. Neyther he vvhich planteth is any thing, nor he vvhich vvatereth, but God vvhich giueth the increase?* Who knoweth not, I say, that it is no lesse true in regard of mans fructification, then in the encrease of all other things, seeing that fecunditie, and fruitfulnes, aswel, in men, as women, as in all other creatures proceedeth principallie of Gods benediction, who as the royall prophet saith. *Facit sterilem in domo, matrem filiorum lætantem. Maketh the barren vvoman in her house a glad, and ioyfull mother of children?* Whereuppon it followeth, that a plentifull ofspring, and issue, proceedeth of Gods blessing, and prouidence, and not of pluralitie of wiues, or concubines. *1. Cor. 3.* *Psal. 112.*

46 Ys it not often seene, that some one man, hath more children, by one lawfull wife, then others haue by many concubines? Hereof *Mahomet* himselfe, may serue for a witnes, who hauing seauenteene wiues, besides concubines, without number, had neuertheles no other childrẽ, but one only daughter (as I haue signified before) which I ascribe to the particuler prouidence of God, who to check, and frustrat, aswell his wicked law, as his exorbitant lust, and to shew the vaintie of the law, euen in the law maker, gaue him some issue (to wit one child) to the end it might appeare thereby, that he was not by nature barraine, and suffred him to haue no more, contrarie to all humane expectation, to the end, that his deuine iustice might be euident in the punishment of him.

47 Therefore I cõclude, that *Poligamy*, is not of necessity, for the increase & multiplication of the world, & that the moderate vse of one wife, is not onlie most coueniẽt for good *Oeconomy*, but also cõforme to the tẽperãce that is requisit to humane nature, & to the first institution of mariage, wherewith Gods benedictiõ hath speciallie concurred in all ages,

and still doth, for the sufficient propagation of mankind, and conseruation of common welths. Wheras Mahomets *Poligamy*, and the vnbrideled libertie, which he giueth to the flesh, is, as I haue declared, no lesse contrarie to the law, and rules of true *Oeconomie*, then to the verie law of nature in the first institution of mariage, yea, and obscureth the vnderstanding of man, oppresseth the spirit, and wholie hindreth the cheefe operation of the soule, which is the contemplation of God, and consequentlie maketh men more like beastes, then reasonable creatures, and depriueth them finallie of the true felicitie of man, and common welth.

48 So that, though there be also in *Monogamy* (that is to say, in the mariage of one wife onlie) some inconueniences some times (as natural sterilitie, or impediment of conception by sicknes, or such like, redownding to the hindrance of procreation) yet forasmuch as no earthlie commoditie, is without some discommodity, & that the least euil, is alwaise to be chosen, where all euils cannot be auoided, yea, and that in this case, the inconueniences that accompanie *Monogamy*, doe happ but sometimes, and concerne particuler persons, whereas the detriments of *Poligamy*, are farre more generall, and doe preiudice, the publike weale, as I haue signified before; therefore I say, the vse of *Monogamy*, is to be retained in common welth, and *Poligamy*, excluded, and much more such a profuse, and inordinate concubinage, as *Mahomet* ordaineth. Thus much concerning the supposed necessitie of *Poligamy*, for procreation.

49 And now to say some what to the other part of the obiection, touching the remedie against concupiscence, in case of the wiues siknes, or other impediments. The satisfaction of this doubt, wilbe nothing difficult, to them, that shall dulie consider the office, and dutie of a man, that is to say, of a reasonable creature, in whom roason ought, to predominat, and commaund the inferiour powers of the soule, wherein man speciallie differeth from brute beasts, which are caried headlong with sensualitie, and therefore no vertue is more proper to man, or more requisit in him, or more political, and necessarie for common welth, then *Temperance*, which bridleth sensualitie, and represseth the heat, and furie of lust. In which respect, *Plato* treating of the vertues, that are most fitt, for euerie member of the common welth, though he require some one vertue rather in one man, then in an other (as prudẽce in the magistrats, and fortitude in the souldiars) yet he holdeth *Temperance* to be so necessarie in euerie man, of what degree, or condition soeuer he be, that without it, saith he, no man can be a good member of his common welth.

Plato li. 3. de Rep. & li. 4. de leg.

So that

So that he, who hath so litle stay of himselfe, that he can neuer forbeare the companie of women, when he feeleth himselfe stirred, or moued thereto, is vnfit, and vnworthie to liue in anie ciuil societie of men, being no better then a verie bruite beast, yea worse then a beast, seeing that beastes doe not vse copulation, but with moderation, at certaine times, and conuenient seasons, as experience teacheth.

50 Therefore *Plutarke* with great reason, highlie commendeth a law, of *Solon*, concerning the repression of choller, whereby he ordained punishment, for those who quarreled, or fell out with anie man, either in the temple, or in the princes palace, or in the theaters. For it seemed to *Solon*, (saith *Plutark*) that although (the ordinarie possibilitie of men and their infirmitie considered) it were not to be expected, that men, should neuer be transported with choller, yet neuer to be able to bridle it at anie time, or in anie place, proceedeth of such exorbitant passion, that it is rather bestial, then humane, and deserueth punishment by the lawes. Thus saith he. *Plutarc. in Lolone.*

51 And the like I say in this our case, that although humane frailtie being considered, it cannot with reason be expected, that euerie man should alwaies liue continent from women, (without the special grace of God, whereof I treate not here,) yet he that will neuer doe it, is rather to be counted a beast, then a man, and worthie to be chastised. And therefore as God hath ordained mariage in respect of mans infirmitie, for a lawful remedie, against the temptation of the flesh, (to be taken, and vsed with moderation, so also both deuine, and humane lawes, iustly punish adulterie, and fornication, in respect of the dominion, that euerie man is bound, by the prescript, and law of humane nature, to haue ouer his pasions, and sensual desires.

52 Further more, who knoweth not, that the way to quench the flames of lust, is not to loose the bridle vnto it, by the inordinat, and excessiue vse thereof (which though it seeme to represse it for a while, yet doth in deede so incense, and kindle it that it becommeth inextinguible, and draweth men, as experience teacheth, to most horrible sinnes against nature) but the remedie to conquer it, is to striue against it, no lesse then against other bad affections, and pasions of the mind, which by diligent resistance, are either wholie ouercome, or much tempered, and qualified, for, he that will not fight at all with his enemie, must needes liue in continual subiection, seruitude, and captiuitie, and doe what soeuer his enemie will command him, whereas he which wrestleth, and fighteth, though he cãnot ouercome, yea, & doe receiue perhaps manie woundes, yet he looseth not the mastrie of himselfe, but remaineth free, from

violence, and tirannie, and abateth both the furie, and force, of his enemie; and therefore the meanes to moderate, or ouercome concupiscence, is to impugne, and resist it, yea, and to forbeare to satisfie it sometimes, euen in things that are lawfull.

Arist. Oeconomic. 53 For this cause, *Aristotle*, treating of the fidelitie, that ought to be inuiolable, betwixt, man, and wife, and obiecting the difficultie to performe it in case of long absence of the one from the other, giueth a notable aduise, to be obserued of maried folkes, and verie pertinent to the matter, which I now handle, to wit, he counselleth man, and wife, to vse such moderation, and abstinence, from their carnall delights, whiles they are together, that the custome thereof may make the same easie vnto them, in their absence. So farre was this pagan philosopher, from allowing one man, to haue manie wiues, to satisfie his lust, that he aduiseth the temperate, and moderate vse, euen of one wife, and frequent abstinence from her. Not vnlike to the aduise, *1. Cor. 7.* which our Apostle giueth in greater perfection. *Vt qui habent vxores, sint tanquam non habentes. That those vvhich haue vviues, should be as though they had none.* And this now you see, is a rule, not onlie of Christian religion, but also euen of moral philosophie, taught, and practised by the Gentils, as belonging to the office, and dutie of man.

54 But vppon what good ground, thinke you, doth *Mahomet* build this law of *Poligamy*. Forsooth, vppon this foundation, that it is impossible for anie man, to forbeare the companie of women, for so he teacheth in his *Alcoran*, and saith, that God knoweth it to be true, and *Alcor. c. 2. apud Dionys. Carthus li. 1. art. 12. contra Alcoran.* therefore no marueile, that as the *Italian* prouerbe saith, *Chi malamente, funda, peggio fabrica. He that laieth a bad foundation, buildeth vvorse*, whereof I will say no more, in this place, because, I shall treat further of the same point hereafter, against *Luther*, and his followers, who vppon the same beastlie, and absurd ground of *Mahomet*, build the like brutish doctrine to his, in manie pointes, and open a wide gate, *Chap. 30. Nu. 8. &c.* to his *Poligamy*, as shall most euidentlie appeare heareafter.

55 Therefore I conclude for the present, that neither the necessitie to conserue, and multiplie mankind by procreation, nor the consideration of the remedie, against the temptations of the flesh, can iustifie *Mahomets* law of *Poligamy*, and much lesse make it political, or good for common welth.

56 But what shall I say, of an other law of his, mentioned also before, more beastlie, brutish, and absurd then the former, I meane the permission of the sinne, worthilie called, *Peccatum nefandum*, a sinne not to be named, that is to say, the sinne of *Sodomy*, which he alloweth in his followers,

followers, either with their owne wiues, or with men, or boyes, so that they be of his religion? Hath it not bene alwaies held, to be abominable against nature, and pernitious to common welth, not onlie amongst Christians (who punish it with death) but also amongst the verie painimes? where vppon *Plato*, seuerelie forbiddeth it in his lawes, ordaining that those which were conuinced to haue committed it, should euer after be held, for most infamous. *Plato 8. de legibus.*

57 In like maner, what can be more vniust, and iniurious, then this law of diuorce, ordaining that a man, may repudiat his wife, for anie cause what soeuer? Which was held for so great iniustice amongst the Paynimes, that the *Romans*, had no vse, or knowledge of diuorces, for the space of six hūdreth yeares after *Rome* was built, though afterwards, the law of diuorce crept into their common welth, with much other corruption of their ancient disciplin, and manie vices, as *Tertulian*, noteth verie well. But how vniust that law of *Mahomet* is, it may appeare by diuers reasons. *Tertul. in Apol. ca. 6.* *Ibid.*

58 First, whereas mariage was instituted by the law of nature, not onlie for the procreation of children, but also for their conuenient education, it is manifest, that it is most necessarie, that man, and wife, remaine together during their liues, to the end they may haue, a common, and equall care of the children, which pertaine equallie to both, and cannot be so well prouided for by stepmothers. *Aristot. Oecon.*

59 Secondlie, whereas the husband, and wife, doe giue by their mariage, power of their owne bodies, the one, to the other, it must needes be vnderstood, that the obligation is for life, for if it were but for a time, there were no difference betwixt a contract, with some concubine, or queane, and a lawfull mariage.

60 Thirdlie, this law, giueth licentious, and wicked men, both great libertie, and also ample occasion to abuse faire women, with a pretence of mariage, meaning onlie to deflower them, and then to dismisse them, when they haue dishonored them, and made them contemptible to others.

61 Lastly, it is most pernicious to good *Oeconomy*, giuing occasion to the wife, not only lesse to loue, & esteeme her husband, but also to haue lesse care of the family, yea, & to robb, & steale secretly, what shee can of her husbãds goods, to the end shee may prouide for her selfe, in case shee be dismissed: so that, this law of diuorce is most vniust, as being iniurious to wiues, and their children, and against the reasõ of good *Oeconomy*, besides diuers other inconueniences, which I omit, for breuities sake. Whereby it appeareth, how iustlie our Sauiour reprehended the like

custome amongst the *Ievves*, when he reduced the law of mariage, to
Math.19. the first institution, declaring man, and wife, *to be one flesh*, and inseperablie ioyned by almightie God, and therefore he concluded. *Quod Deus coniunxit, homo non separet. Let no man seperat that vvhich God hath ioyned.* And although there follow inconueniences, sometimes to particuler persons vppon the indissolubilitie of mariage, yet the same is recompensed with manie commodities, and with the publike, and generall good, which all good lawes doe principallie and directlie intend, rather then the benefitt of priuat persōs, as also we see, that almightie God houldeth the same course in the gouermēt of the world, ordaining manie thinges, for an vniuersall good, which neuerthelesse, are in diuers cases, incommodious to particuler men, and thus much for *Mahomets* law of diuorce.

62 I could ad to these, diuerse other absurd, and ridiculous constitutions of *Mahomet*, were it not, that I hast to say somewhat also of the *Ievves*, in this chapter, which beginneth alreadie to grow ouerlong. Neuertheles, I cānot but in a worde, or two, touch one other law of his, in respect of the euident preiudice it must needs bring to cōmon welth, if it be put to practise. For he commaundeth in his *Alcoran*, reuenge of
Alcoran. cap. 2. iniuries, with the law of *Talion*, that is to say, with the like measure. But this must needs be, against reason of state, which requireth, that all reparation aswell of priuat, as publike, wrongs, be in the arbitrement, & power of the magistrat, according to the prescript of the law, least otherwaies, the insatiable appetite of reuenge, may transport the wronged, beyond all limits of reason, and breede implacable, and mortall quarrels, deadlie foods, and consequentlie seditions, tumults, and ciuil warres, to the manifest danger, and damage of the common welth, where vppon it followeth, that the contrarie law of our Christian religion, commaunding the remission of iniuries, is most political, as I will
Chap. 15. Nu. 26. & chap. 24. Nu 10. 11. 12. & 13. make most euident hereafter, when I shall treat of the effects of Christian religion in common welth, in which respect, I may well be the breefer here.

63 Now then to conclude, concerning *Mahomet*, and his religion, thou hast seene, good Reader, how sutable they are, the one to the other, and no meruaile, that such a beastlie monster as he was, inuented such a monstrous, and beastlie religion, which neuertheles hath through the iust iudgement of God, ouerflowed a great part of the world, for the due punishment of sinne, and speciallie of heresie, and schisme, as I will shew hereafter, in the third part of this treatise, whē I shall treate of the fruit, and effects of false religion in common welth, and now in the meane

time I

time I will onlie admonish thee, good Reader, that thou doe not attribute the prosperitie, & power of *Mahometā* princes, (I meane the Turke, and such others) to anie merit of their religion, but to the sinnes of the Christians, which God iustlie scourgeth by them, making them the instruments of his iustice, as the *Aßirians*, and *Babilonians*, were in the conquest of *Samaria*, and *Iuda*: in which respect almightie God called *Sennacherib*, *his staffe*, & *the rodd of his vvrath*, yea, and so exact is his iustice, that he may wel be thought to giue the more temporal prosperitie, and encrease of dominion, to these wicked infidells, euen for the seruice which they doe him in the execution of his iustice vppon bad Christiās, as he rewarded *Nabuchodonosor* an Idolater, with the knigdome of *AEgipt*, for the seruice which he had donne him, though vnwittinglie, in the expugnation of *Tyrus*, as I haue more amplie declared in the first part of this treatise, when I signified the causes, why God giueth kingdomes, and prosperitie to wicked men. And this shall suffise, touching *Mahomet*, and his law.

4. Reg. c. 17. & 25. Isay. 10.

Ezech. 29. chap. 26. nu. 19. & 23. & chap. 17. nu. 15.

64 Yt resteth now, that I say some what in this chapter, of the religion of the *Ievves*, I meane not, that which is conteined in the old testament. and called the law of *Moyses*, and was professed by the people of God, from the time of *Moyses*, vntil the comming of our Sauiour *Christ*, (for that the same is now no where exercised, and was when it florished, with out all doubt, a most holie, exquisite, and exact law, and religion: not onlie for the morall, and ceremonial, but also: for the Iudicial part thereof, pertaining to pollicie, and gouerment, and no maruaile, seeing that the author of it, was God himselfe,) but my meaning is, to treate breefly of that religion which the *Ievves*, now professe, consisting partlie in some ceremonies, and customes of the *Mosaycal* law, and partlie of manie traditiōs, and inuentiōs, of their *Rabbins*, deliuered in their bookes called the *Thalmud*, which signifieth a doctrin, or disciplin, deliuered after the maner of an ordinarie glose, which doctrin was gathered aswell out of ould *Rabbins* workes, before our Sauiour Christs birth, as out of manie others, which liued within the first foure hundreth seauentie yeares, after his passion, during which time, the bookes of the *Thalmud* were collected, and especiallie at three seueral times.

Sixtus Senensis Biblioth. sancta li. 2.

65 The first collection was made by *Iudas*, the sonne of *Simon*, a hundreth, and fiftie yeares after the last destruction of *Hierusalem*, and this was called *Misna*.

Idem ibid.

66 The second was composed by *Rabbi Ioannam*, *Rab*, and *Samuel*, who augmented the *Misna*, with new additions, and called it. *Thalmud Hierosolymitanum*, because it was collected in the ruynes, which were then

remayning

remaining of *Hierusalem*, and this collection was made a hundreth, and fiftie yeares after the former.

67 The third, and last was gathered by the Rabbins *Asse*, and *Hammai*, and their two sonnes, *Mair*, and *Asse*, in *Babilon* of *AEgipt*, now called *Cayrus*, about the yeare of our Lord, foure hundreth seauentie seauen, & is therefore called *Thalmud Babylonicum*, in the which is contained all the *Misna*, and the other *Thalmud Hierosolomitanum*, with all the traditiōs, statutes, and expositions of Moyses his law, gathered out of all the former *Rabbins*, deuided into six orders, or principal partes, containing sixty bookes, or treatises, in the which there are fiue hundreth thirtie two chapters, and by the doctrin, deliuered in this huge worke (tenne times bigger then our bible) all the sinagogues of the *Ievves*, that liue in the profession of their law, are gouerned vntill this day, accounting the same to be of no lesse truth, and authoritie, then the ould testament, and therefore it is written in the preface of the *Thalmud*, that *vvhosoeuer denieth the contents thereof, denieth God himselfe*: and in the worke it selfe, the paine of death is ordained for those, who denie anie thing, that is taught therein.

Petrus Galatin de arcan cathol. verit. li. 1. ca. 5.

Sixt Senen. in Bibliothe. sancta li. 2.

68 And forasmuch as these Thalmudical volumes, are refersed, and stuffed, not onlie with manie blasphemies against our Sauiour *Christ*, & the verie law of *Moyses*, which they professe (yea, against the dietie it selfe) but also with infinit other points of execrable doctrine, and precepts, contrarie to the light of reason, and the law of nature, and nations, I will therefore breefelie lay downe some few articles thereof, whereby it shall euidentlie appeare, that the lawe which the *Ievves*, now hold for their religion, is no lesse absurd in regard of policie, and reason of state, then in respect of the veritie requisit to true religion, wherein thou shalt also see, good Reader, how notablie *Mahomet*, and the authors of the *Thalmud* simbolyzed in ridiculous follie, beastlie turpitude, and the spirit of errour, lies, and blasphemy against the maiestie of God.

Ordine 1. Tract. 4. distinct. 3. vide Bibliothe. sanct. Sext. Senens. li. 2.

First then concerning almightie God, they teach, that before the creation of the world, he exercised himselfe in making manie worlds, and destroying them againe, vntill at length, he learned by long practise, to make this world, which we now see.

Ord 2. Tra. 1 dist. 14. Vide symbolū fide: Fr. Ludoui. Granat part. 4. tra. 2

That he spendeth the first three houres of the day, in reading *Moyses* law, and the three next houres, in teaching litle children, that die verie yonge, and three other howres, in iudging the world, and the three last howres, in sporting, and solacing himselfe, with a great dragon called *Leuiathan*, and that in the night he rideth vppon a verie swift *Cherubin*, and

and viſiteth 18000. worlds, which he hath made.

That *Moyſes* going vp once to heauen, found God writting, accents, or titles in the holie ſcripture. [*Ord.5.tract.6.diſt.5.*]

That God hath a certaine place of retrait, whither he retireth himſelfe at certaine times, and weepeth bitterlie, becauſe, when he was angrie with the *Ievves*, he deſtroied their temple, and gaue them into captiuity; and that ſometimes he roreth like a lion, for ſorow, and that, as oft as the *Ievves*, enter into their ſinagogues to pray, he teareth the heare of his head, and ſaith, *Happy is the king, that is thus glorified by his ſubiects, but vvoe be to the father, that hath made his children ſlaues.* [*Ord.2 diſt 5 & ord.1.d.7 Vide etiam Granat.in ſymbolo.par.4.tract.2.*]

That God is angrie once a day, and that then the combes of cocks, waxe pale, and the cocks ſtand vppon on legg, and if at the ſame time, anie man chance to curſe an other, he that is curſed dieth preſentlie. [*Ord.1.tract.1.*]

That once when certaine *Rabbins*, diſputed againſt *Rabbi Eleezer*, God gaue ſentence from heauen in fauour of *Eleezer*, and that therevppon, the *Rabbins* being highlie offended, did excommunicat God, and he ſmiling ſaid, *My children haue ouercome me.* [*Ord.4.tract.2.diſt.7.*]

That God tould a lie, to make peace betwixt *Abraham*, and *Sara*, which they ſay, to proue, that peace is a thing of verie great importance. [*Vide Granatens vbi ſupra.*]

That God commaunded the *Ievves*, to offer the ſacrifice of expiation euerie new moone, to ſatisfie for the ſinne whith he committed, when he vniuſtlie tooke the light from the moone, and gaue it to the ſunne. [*Ord.4.tract.6.diſt.1.*]

69 I omitt manie other ſuch impious, and abſurd blaſphemies, againſt almightie God, whom they depriue as you ſee, of his omnipotencie, of his wiſdome, of his veritie, and truth, and of his iuſtice, and ſanctitie, making him ſubiect to infirmitie, to vanitie, to ignorance, and errour, to lies iniuſtice, and ſinne, whereby they alſo depriue him conſequentlie of his diuinitie, and therevppon it followeth, that the doctrin, and beleefe, which they profeſſe, is no religion, but verie Atheiſme.

70 This may yet further appeare by other ridiculous articles of their Thalmudical diſciplin. As that they teach the tranſmigration of ſoules, from one body to an other, and that the ſoules of vnlearned men, shall not receiue their bodies againe in the generall reſurrection. [*Ord.4.tract.2. & alibi paſſim. Ord.3.tract.2. charta. 3.*]

Alſo, that the Archangel *Gabriel*, hauing committed a verie hainous ſinne, was by Gods commaundement whipped, with a firie ſcourge. [*Ord.2.tract.5.diſt.8.*]

That two *Rabbins*, did euerie weeke vppon the friday create or make two calues, and eate them vpp euerie iote. [*Ord.4.tract.4. diſt. 2. chart.65.*]

That if a man pray with his face, to the ſouth, he shall obtaine wiſdome, if he pray Northward he shall haue riches. [*Ord.4.tra.3.diſt.2.*]

Ordo. 2. *tract.*1.*dist.*6 That whosoeuer eateth thrise, vppon the saboath day, shall haue life euerlasting in the other world.

Ordo 4. *tract.* 10. *dist.*2. Finallie, that if anie man passe vnder the bellie of a camel, or betwixt two camels, or two women, he shall neuer be able to learne anie thing of the *Thalmud*.

71 Who is there now, that shall read this, and will thinke them well in their witts, that either teach, or beleeue these ridiculous toyes? Yet these are part of the Thalmudical doctrin, and commaũded to be beleeued vnder paine of death, both temporal and eternal.

72 But let vs heare some what more, that we may see, how wel they agree with the law of *Moyses*, the law of nature, good disciplin of life, & common honestie, to the end thou maist, good Reader, discouer the falsitie of this Talmudical, & Iewish religion, by the turpitud, and beastlines of it; and this I say the rather, because in the first part of this treatise, *Chap.* 9. *Nu.*19. I promised to make it euident in this, that dissolution of life, and filthie carnalitie, is an inseperable propertie of false religion, which I haue alreddie in part performed, treating of the two former false religions, to wit *Paganisme*, & *Mahometisme*. And therefore, as I meane also to performe the like hereafter, when I shall treate of the sects amongst Christians at this time, so now I cannot but wish it to be obserued by the way, in these Thalmudists, & the Iewes their disciples, who doe not õly allow the abominable sinne called *Nefandum*, (not to be named, as I haue signified before, when I treated of *Mahomet*) but also affirme that it was practised by *Adam*, and *Noe*, where of I forbeare to declare the particulers, for the verie horrour of them; besids that they also teach, that if a man marrie his owne sister, or daughter, he doth an act, verie gratefull to god, though the same (as also the other detestable sinne aforesaid) is expressely forbidden vnder paine of death, by the law of *Moyses*, which they professe to keepe.

*Ord.*3.*tract.* 1.*dist.*6. *Ord.* 4. *tract.*4. *Ord.* 2. *tract.* 2. *Leuit.*20.

73 Also wheras God expresslie forbad in the old law, all maner of Idolatrie, and particularlie that no man should giue anie of his children to be consecrated, and offred to the Idol *Moloch*, (which was done by the ministerie of the Idolatrous priests, (who vsed to passe men through the fire, before the Idol,) they teach, that it is no sinne, for the father, to consecrat his owne child to *Moloch*, so that he doe not giue him to the priest to be offred, or consecrated by him.

*Exod.*20. *Leuit.ca.*20 *Ibid.* *Canhedrin. ca. Abramitor.*

74 In like maner, God forbiddeth in the law of *Moyses*, to curse father, or mother, vppon paine of death, but they allow a man to curse either of both, so that he name not some of the proper names of God in his malediction. And no marueile if they permit this, seeing they teach also,

Leuit. 20. *li.Sopu. c.* 5.

that a

that a man may curſe God himſelfe, ſo that he name not one ſpecial name of his, to wit, *Semhamephoras*.

Cadhedrin cap. Arbamiot.

75 The law of *Moyſes* alſo forbiddeth wilfull murther, as all other lawes doe, but they teach that if a man tie, an other mans hands, and feete, and leaue him ſo to periſh by famin, or that he caſt him to a lion, he is not to be puniſhed by the law, though if he expoſe him to die by cold, or heate, they hold him guiltie of his death, and to deſerue puniſhment. And if in like ſort, tenne men doe kill one man with tenne ſtaues, they hold them all for guiltles. But can anie thing be more abſurd then this, or more contrarie to all lawes deuine, and humane? whereby it may alſo appeare, how political is the law of the *Thalmud*, and how conuenient for common welth, which is one ſpeciall point, that I am here to conſider, and therefore I will omit, diuers other impious, and abſurd opinions of theirs, to conclude with a few, concerning matter of gouerment.

Exod. 20. *Leuit.* 24. *Canhedrin ca. Ellu.*

76 Yf a malefactor, ſay they, being accuſed before diuers iudges, be condemned to death, by the ſentence of them all, he is to be ſett free, becauſe it is abſolutelie neceſſarie (as they thinke) that the iudges be of different opinions, and that the priſoner be condemned, or abſolued by pluralitie of voyces.

Li. ſuprin Canhedrin ca. 9.

Alſo they ordaine, that if a man be condemned to death, by falſe witneſſes, and the falſitie be not diſcouered, whiles the partie liueth, the witneſſes ſhall not be puniſhed for their falſe teſtimonie, or periurie.

Ordo. 4. *tract.* 4. *vide ſix. ſenens. in bibliothe. vbi ſupra.*

Yf a man, ſay they, find a purſe, and vnderſtand that the party which loſt it, hath no hope to recouer it, he is not bound to reſtore it.

Ord. 4. *trac.* 2. *diſt.* 4.

Moreouer, they teach, that if a *Rabbyn* (that is to ſay, one that is a maſter, or doctor amongſt them) doe not hate his enemie to death, and doe him what miſcheefe he may, he is not worthie of the title, and name of a *Rabbyn*, whereas neuertheles the law of *Moyſes* ſaith. *Non quæras vltionem, nec memor eris iniuriæ ciuium tuorum. Doe not ſeeke reuenge, nor keepe in mynd the iniurie that is donne thee by thy neighbour.*

Ord. 5. *tract.* 1. *diſt.* 2. *Leuit.* 19.

77 Alſo they teach that God cōmaunded the *Ievves*, to take the goods of *Chriſtians* by fraud, force, vſurie, theft, or anie other meanes whatſoeuer, and to eſteeme all *Chriſtians*, for no better then bruite beaſts, and ſo to treat, and handle them in all occaſions.

Ord. 1. *tract diſt.* 4. *Ord.* 4. *tract.* 8.

That if a *Ievv*, meaning to kill a *Chriſtian*, do chance to kill a *Ievv*, he deſerueth to be pardoned.

Ord. 4. *tract.* 4. & 9.

That if a *Ievv*, ſee a *Chriſtian* in a place of danger, where he may precipitat him, or caſt him, downe headlong to breake his necke, he is bound in conſcience to doe it.

Ord. 4. *tract.* 4. & *in lib. Iorodea c.* 158.

Finallie, they haue a conſtitution, whereby euery *Ievv*, and eſpeciallie

Ord.1.tract. 1.dist.4. theyr priests in their sinagogues, are bound thrise euerie day, to pray to God, to exterminat all *Christians*, with their kinges, and princes, in hatred of *Iesus* of *Nazareth*.

78 Lo heere, good Reader, some part of the deuilish doctrin of the Iewish *Thalmud*, contradicting most euidentlie, the lawes of God, of *Moyses*, of nature, of nations, & all iustice, charitie, and humanitie, whereby we may manifestlie see, the exemplar punishment of God, vppon that miserable people, not onlie in the vnspeakeable calamities, which they haue so manie hundreth of yeares endured, & still doe throughout the world (as I haue verie amplie declared in the first part of this treatise) but also in their peruerse, and wilful blindenes, which is such, that they haue lost the verie light of naturall reason, in matters pertaining to their saluation, according to the malediction of the prophet, when he said. *Excæca cor populi huius. Blynd o Lord, the harts of this people.* And the prophetical prediction of *Moyses*, when he thereatned them, saying. *Percutiet te Dominus amentia &c.* Our Lord will strike thee with madnes, blindnes, and furie of mind &c.

Chap.19.per totum.

Isay.c.6. Deut.

79 This, I say, we see euidentlie fulfilled in the *Thalmudists*, and the *Ievves* their disciples, who farre exceede both *Paynimes*, and *Mahometans*, in grosse, and palpable ignorance, and errour, and in ridiculous, and absurd impietie, or rather in most impious, and blasphemous Atheisme, masked with the vizard of the Mosaycal law, and religion, whereof they haue nothing leaft, but the bare pretence, or shadow, and yet with how litle reason, or rather how much against reason, and euident truth, they pretend the continuance thereof, it shall sufficientlie appeare, in the ensuing chapters, wherein I will proue, the veritie, and sanctitie of Christian religion, which being proued, it must needes follow, that the *Mosaycal*, law ceased by the comming of our Sauiour Christ, who hauing bene fouretould, and promised by the prophets, and represented by the signes, figures, ceremonies, and sacrifices of the law, was the full accomplishment, consummation, perfection, and end thereof, being the verity, which was prefigured, and the *Messias* promised therein, where vppon he said himselfe. *Non veni soluere legem, sed adimplere. I came not to breake the lavv, but to fulfill it.*

Matth.5.

80 Well then to conclude this chapter, I hope good Reader, thou remainest satisfied, concerninge the absurditie of *Paganisme*, *Mahometisme*, and *Iudaisme*, aswel in respect of their falsitie in matter of religion, as of their errors in matter of state, and politicall gouerment, and therefore I will now passe to treate of Christian religion, and will proue the irrefragable veritie, the incontaminat puritie, the

eminent

eminent dignitie , and abſolute neceſſitie thereof,to the felicitie of man, and common welth, the diſcourſe whereof,will draw me to the diſcuſſion of manie excelent queſtions , and important matters, neceſſarie to be knowne, and dulie conſidered of euerie Chriſtian man, in which reſpect, I craue thy fauourable attention, for thy owne ſpeciall benefit.

Of the verity, dignity, fruit, and neceßity of Chriſtian religion in common vvelth, in reſpect aſvvel of the purity, and excellency of the doctrine, as alſo of the admirable force, and effects of Gods grace, vvhich it giueth for the repreßion of vice, and reformation of manners. And by the vvay, it is declared, hovv vainely the philoſophers laboured, to reforme the diſeaſes in mans nature.

Chap. 15.

1. IF I should vndertake, good Reader, to lay downe all the arguments, and proofes, of the veritie of Chriſtian religion, I should take vppō me to write a whole volume of that onlie matter, as diuers great learned men haue donne, not only in the primitiue Church, (to wit *Arnobius, Clemens, Alexandrinus, Euſebius, Lactantius, S. Auguſtin*, and others, but alſo ſome of latter times, as *S. Thomas*, in his learned booke againſt the Gentils, and now in our daies, *F. Levvys* de *Granada*, in his excellent treatiſe, intituled de *Symbolo*, beſides diuers others who haue written more breefelie thereof.

2. But for aſmuch as my principal intention is to treat of the veritie of Chriſtian religion, ſo farre forth onlie, as it may concerne common welth, I will therefore (as alſo for breuities ſake) make choiſe of a few points, which may directlie proue, both that the Chriſtian religion is the onlie true religion: and alſo, that it is moſt politicall, that is to ſay, moſt neceſſarie, and behoofeful for the gouerment of common welth.

3 I omitt then to ſet downe the particuler propheſies, aſwell of the *Ievves*, as *Gentils*, foretelling the cōming of our Sauiour Chriſt, & giuing moſt euident, & vndoubted teſtimony of his *a* miraculous incarnatiō, & natiuity, of his wonderful *b* miracles, of the very *c* time, & *d* mãner of his paſſiō, & death, of his *e* reſurrection, *f* aſcenſion, and *g* ſending the holie Ghoſt to his diſciples, and finallie of the amplitude, dignitie, and glory of his *h* Church, all which were clearelie foretould, not onlie by the ould prophets, amongſt the people of God, but alſo by the *Sibyllæ*, amongſt the Gentils, who made particuler mention, euen of his

Arnob. cōtra gentes Clem. Alexandr. li. ſtromat. Euſebi. de præparat. & demonſtrat. euangel. Lactant. diuin. inſtitit. S. Aug. de ciuit Dei. S. Tho. contra gent. F. Ludouic. granat. de ſymbolo fidei.

a *Eſay.* 7. & 9.
b *Idem* 35.
c *Dan.* 9.
d *Iſay.* 50. & 53.
e *Oſee.* 6.
f *Pſal.* 67. & 46.
g *Iohel.* 2.
h *Eſay.* 2. 49 54. & 60. *Miche.* 4.

Apud Lactãtium li. de vera Sapiẽt. li. 4. ca. 15. 16. 17. 18. & 19. verie miracles, as of his raising the dead, his curing the blind, deafe, and lame, his feeding fiue thousand in the wildernes, with two fishes, and fiue loaues, his commaunding the sea, and windes, his walking vppon the watter, and that he should be apprehended, buffeted, spit at, scourged, and crowned with thornes, that vinager, and gall, should be giuen him to drinke, that he should die to giue vs life, that the sunne should be darkened three houres, that the veile of the temple should be torne, and finallie that he should within three dayes rise againe. Of all which, *Lactanc. Ibid.* the particularities may be seene in *Lactantius*, who alleadgeth the greeke verses of the *Sibyllæ* concerning these points, whereof *S. Augustin*, also *August. li. 18 de ciuitat. ca. 23.* maketh mention, and addeth, other verses of *Sibylla Erithræa*, touching the day of iudgement, and the resurrection of our bodies, in which verses, the first letter of euerie verse, being put all together, doe expresse the name of our Sauiour, and make this sentence. *Iesus Christus Dei filius, saluator. Iesus Christ the sonne of god, the sauiour.*

4 But I omit, I say, further to particularise these prophesies, as also to speake of the reprobation of the Iewes, and their most euident punishment, euen vntil this day, for their infidelitie, and crueltie towards *Christ*, *Chap. 19.* whereof I haue spoke amplie in my first part.

5 Also, I let passe the vocation of the Gentils, and miraculous conuersion of the world, to the Christian faith, by simple, and ignorant fishermen, and other men of occupation, preaching a doctrine, which seemed *Chap. 24. nu 33. 34. & 35.* no lesse repugnant to reason, then to mans nature, and sense, and confirming the same, with such wonderfull, and stupendious miracles, that as *S. Augustin* saith, who soeuer shall now refuse to beleeue, without *Aug. de ciuit Dei l. 22. c. 8.* new miracles, he may be held for *magnum prodigium*, that is to say, *a great, and prodigious vvonder.*

6 I forbeare also to treate at this present, of the wonderful, and miraculous manner, how the Church of *Christ* hath bene encreased, and propagated to that greatnes, which now we see, not withstanding the opposition, first of manie Pagan emperours, and since of diuers Heretical, and Schismatical kings, and princes, seeking to exterminate the same, of which point, I shall haue occasion to speak amplie, in the third part of this treatise; I omit also to treat of the ouerthrow, and extinction of Idolatrie, by the faith of our Sauiour *Christ*, as also of the power which he left to his Church to commaund deuils, of the inuincible constancie of innumerable martirs, and finallie of the honour donne to the Crosse of *Christ*, and to his poorest seruants after their death, yea, to their verie *S. Chrisost. li contra gẽtiles de S.* reliks (which *S. Chrisostome* vrgeth against the Pagans, for notable, and euident argũments, of the diuinitie of *Christ*) all these, I say, I forbeare to prosecute,

prosecute, meaning onlie to handle two pointes, pertaining no lesse to pollicie, then to religion. The one is, to proue, that all perfection of vertue (be it theological, moral, or political) is contained onlie in Christian religion. The other is, that the end of man, and of common welth, (which I haue shewed before to be both one) is also to be obtained only therby, which two points being proued, it wilbe most cleare, that Christian religion, is both true religion, and also most political, and fit for gouerment of common welth. *Babyla. & li. quod Christus sit Deus. To. 5.*

7 For the first, it is to be vnderstood, that as all false religions being vtterlie voide, of Gods grace, haue for the most part, either some mixture of absurd doctrin, contrarie to the verie light of natural reason, or at least, some inducement to vice, and impietie (as I haue alreadie declared, in the false religions of the *Pagans*, *Turkes*, and *Ievves*) so also on the other side, the Christian religion being most pure, and deuine, in doctrin, leadeth to all perfection of vertue, admitting no kind of impietie, or impuritie, reforming the manners of wicked men, & conuerting them from vice, to vertue, from errour to truth, and from darkenes to light, from sinne to sanctitie, and all holines of life, for as the psalmist saith. *Lex Domini immaculata, conuertens animas* &c. *The lavv of our lord is immaculat, conuerting soules, and the testimony, or commaundement of God, giueth vvisdome to children*, as shall appeare by all the ensuing discourse. *Chap. 7. 8. 9. & 14.* *Psalm. 18.*

8 This was foretold long before our Sauiour Christ was borne, by the prophet *Isayas*, who hauing signified, that he should cure the lame, the dumme, the deafe, and the blind, addeth that, *the dry ground, should be changed into lakes, and fountaines of vvater*, and that, *in the dennes of dragons, there should grovv greene rishes*, and *that the same should be a path, and a vvay, vvhich should be called holy:* Giuing to vnderstand, by all these metaphoricall speeches, that the *vvater* of Gods grace should flow, and abound in the *desert*, and dry soules of sinners, and that *of dennes for dragons*, that is to say, of habitacles for sinne and wickednes, they should become receptacles of vertue, and santitie. And againe in an other place, he saith in like maner, that after the comming of our Sauiour. *The vvolfe should dvvell vvith the lambe, the leopard vvith the kid, the calfe, and sheepe, vvith the lyon, and that these fierce, aud vvild beasts, should become so domestical, that they should, doe no hurt in all the holy mount. Quia repleta est terra*, saith he, *scientia Domini. Because the earth is filled vvith the knovvledge of our lord.* *Isay. 35.* *Isay. 11.*

Thus saith the prophet, signifiing that proud, & wicked men, asfierce, and cruel as lions, or wolues, should by the vertue, and power of Gods grace, become as meeke as lambes, and not disdaine the companie of the most humble, and simplest seruant of God.

9 The

9 The experience of this admirable conuerſion of ſinners, appeared
7. Luc. 37. preſentlie after our Sauiours comminge, not onlie in thoſe whome he
5. Luc. 27. called to his faith (as *Mary Magdalen*, termed in the ſcripture *Peccatrix*,
19. Luc. 2. the *ſinful vvoman*, *Mathevv*, and *Zacheus*, the publicans, and *Saule*, the per-
9. Actor. 4. 5. ſecutour,) but alſo in infinit others, who in the primitiue Church receiued the Chriſtian faith, by the preaching of the Apoſtles, and their ſuc-
ceſſors, whereby Idolatry, and the kingdome of the diuel, was ouerthrowne, and ſuch a change wrought in the liues, and minds of men,
that the world ſeeing it, in it ſelfe, admired it.

10 For, whereas all corruption, & beaſtlie abomination of vice, pride,
S. Hieron. malice, dronkennes, ſurfetts, and licencious life, had ouerflowed the
in ca. 2. E- world (in ſuch ſort that, as *S. Ierome* ſaith, publike ſtewes of boyes, were
euerie where allowed, and that the greateſt philoſophers of Greece,
were no leſſe ſubiect, to that vice, then other men) ſuch was the change
of mens manners by Chriſtian religion, that infinit numbers of all ſorts
of people, reformed their liues, and became exemplar for humilitie,
contempt of the world, loue towards their neighbour, temperance,
continencie, and caſtitie, in ſo much, that *AEgipt*, it ſelfe, which had
benne the cheefe ſeat of Idolatrie, and the verie ſinke of ſinne, floriſhed
incredibilie in all vertue, as may appeare, by the notable relation writ-
Pallad. de ten by *Palladius* of his pilgrimage, to viſit the monaſteries of *AEgipt*,
vita SS. Pa- where he found in one citie called *Oxirnico*, tenne thouſand monkes, &
trum. ca. 5. religious perſons, and twentie thouſand virgins, who had all forſaken
the world, and dedicated themſelues wholie, to the ſeruice of God, and
to the mortification of the fleſh.

11 In an other place called *Nitria*, they found fiue hundred monaſteries,
not farr a ſunder one from an other, deuided into fifteene bourgs, yet ſo
vnited, ſaith the ſtorie, in loue, and charitie, that they had all, as it were,
one ſoule, and one hart. And not farr from the citie *Thebes*, they ſaw a monaſterie, which had in it a thouſand monkes, beſides that there were three
thouſand others, in other monaſteries not farr from thence, men admirable for abſtinence, ſilence, humilitie, and all vertue. In an other place,
there were vnder the holie man *Serapion*, twelue thouſand monkes in
diuers monaſteries, and in a deſert they found ſo manie cells of Hermits,
that the place was therevppon called *Cellia*. And finallie, in the territory
of *Memphis*, and *Babilon*, there was an innumerable multitude (ſaith the
ſtorie) of monkes, endued, and adorned with diuers graces, and gifts of
the holie Ghoſt. And this wonderful reformation of mens liues, and
mãners; was not onlie in *AEgipt*, but alſo in all other parts of the world,
where Chriſtian religion floriſhed, as *Theodoretus* teſtifieth, of *Greece*, and
other

other countries knowne vnto him, to wit, *Palestina*, *Pontus*, *Cilicia*, *Syria*, *Asia*, and all *Europe*, where saith he, there were innumerable monasteries of holie virgins, which he attributeth to the force, and grace of Christian religion, saying, that *after our Sauiour vvas borne, nature yealded and brought forth the fayre, and fresh fields, or meadovves of virginity, and offred to our Creator, these faire flovvers, vvhich neuer fade, or perish.* Thus said he, aleuen hundreth yeares agoe, of the fruit of Christian religion in his time, which might be confirmed by infinit testimonies of ancient historiographers, and Fathers, if I thought it needeful. Besides that I shall haue iust occasiō to say somewhat more of this matter hereafter, when I shall treat of matters in controuersie, and therefore now for the present, I thinke good to declare the excellēt meanes whereby this mutation, & change of mind, and manners is wrought in Christian religion.

Theodoret. histor. sanct. patrum. ca. 30. in Domnina.

Chap. 25. & 30.

12 The first is, the puritie, and excellencie of Christian doctrin, tending to all perfection of vertue, and exclusion of vice, or sinne, not only in act, or intention, but also in word, and thought, in which respect our Sauiour taught, that we are, *to yeald an account for euery idle vvord*, and that he, which *doth but desire, and lust after a vvoman, only in his hart, is guiltie of the sinne of the flesh.* And therefore also he placed one of the eight beatitudes of man, in cleanes of hart. *Beati mundo corde*, saith he, *Blessed are the cleane in hart, for they shall see God.* Besides that, he requireth in vs such a pure, *a* and feruent loue of God, such *b* confidence, in his mercie and prouidence, such *c* charitie towards our neighbour (yea our verie enemies,) such *d* an acknowledgement of our owne infirmitie, such *e* contrition, and hartie sorrow for our sinnes, such *f* chastitie, such *g* humilitie, such *h* mansuetude, and meekenes, such *i* cōtempt of honours, riches, and vanities of the world, such *k* mortification of our passions, and affections, such *l* patience in aduersitie, such a *m* coniunction of simplicitie with wisdome, such *n* obedience to our magistrats, and superiours, such *o* truth in word, and deede, and finallie such *p* hate, not onlie of vice, and all euil, but also of all shew, or *q* appearance of euil, that nothing can be imagined in his doctrin wanting to the consummation, and perfection of all vertue, in so much, that who soeuer fulfilleth his precepts, leadeth rather an Angelical, then a humane life.

Matth. 12.
Matth. 5.
Ibid.
a *Matth. 22.*
b *Ibid. 6.*
c *Ibid. 22. & 5.*
d *2. Cor. 3.*
e *Luc. 13.*
f *1. Cor. 6.*
g. h *Matth. 11. & 5.*
i *Philip. 3.*
k *Matth. 16.*
l *Luc. 21.*
m *Mar. 10.*
n *1. Pet. 2.*
o *Coloss. 3.*
p *Rom. 12.*
q *1. Thess. 5.*

13 Furthermore, what shall I say of the meanes, & motiues, that he leaft to draw, & lead vs to this perfectiō? First he gaue vs an *r* assurāce aswell of eternal reward, for the performāce of his cōmaūdemēts, as of eternal punishment for the contempt thereof. Secondly he encouraged vs with his owne *s* example, performing, and accomplishing, all that which he

r *Matth. 19. Luc. 10. Matth. 25.*
s *Ibid. 16.*

a *Matth.* 18. *Act.* 20. *Ephes.* 4. b 2. *Tim.* 3. c *Mar* 16. *Ibid.* 14. *Luc.* 22. *Ioan.* 20. d *Ibid.* 14. *Matth.* 11. e *Ibidem.*

commaunded vs. Thirdly he ordained that his spouse the *a* Church, guided by his holie spirit, and furnished with Apostles, doctors, and pastors should instruct, direct, admonish, and correct vs, as occasion should require. Fourthly, he left his hollie *b* scriptures to teach, strenghten, and confirme vs, aswell in matters of maners, as of doctrin. Fiftlie he instituted holie *c* sacraments, to purifie, cleanse, sanctifie, and iustifie vs. Lastly he made vs an irreuocable *d* promise of the assistance of his grace, if we dulie seeke it, whereby, as he himselfe said, his *e* burthen should become light vnto vs, and his yoke sweete. And in this respect, the Christian religion is called the law of grace, and thereby distinguished from the law of *Moyses*. For although the seruants of God were also iustified, and saued by grace, in the law of *Moyses* (for with out grace, there could be neither iustification, nor saluation,) yet that grace was not giuen them, eyther by their law maker, or together with their law, or afterwards, by vertue of their law, or of the obseruation thereof, but by the merits of our Sauiour *Christ*, in whom they beleeued, as in their redeemer to come, no lesse then now we beleeue in him alreadie come, as *S. Augustin*, teacheth amplie: so that those which were iustified, and saued in the ould law, did belong to the new law, being iustified, and saued by the merits of our Sauiour *Christ*, who being not onlie God, and man, and a law maker, but also a Redeemer, Iustifier, and Sauiour, giueth grace together with his law, which he imprinteth, in our hartes as I will declare hereafter, whereas *Moyses*, being onlie man, & a law maker, gaue but the bare letter of the law, and therefore the Euangelist saith. *Lex per Moysen* &c. *The lavv*, of the ould testament, *vvas giuen by Moyses, but grace, and verity, is made by Iesus Christ.*

S Aug. in Psal. 118. & *Sem.* 20. *de monomachia Golia & Dauid. c.* 8. *Idem de Catechizandis rudibus c.* 19 & *de patiētia c.* 20. & 21. *Ioan.* 1.

Exech. c. 36.

14 This was prophesied long before Christs time, by *Exechiel, Hieremy*, and the royal prophet *Dauid*, *Exechiel*, hauing prophecied of our Christian baptisme, speaking in the person of God in these words. *Effundam super vos* &c. *I vvill take from you, your stony hart, and vvill giue you a hart of flesh, and vvill sett my spirit in the middest of you, and make you vvalke in my precepts.*

Hieremy. c. 31.

15 Also the prophet *Hieremy*, distinguishing expresslie, the old law from the new, saith, thus. *Ecce dies veniunt* &c. *Behold the dayes doe come, that I vvill make a nevv league, vvith the house of Israel, and the house of Iuda, not according to the couenant that I made vvith your fathers, vvhen I tooke them by the hand, to lead them out of the land of Ægipt: but the couenant, vvhich I vvill make, vvith the house of Israel, after those dayes, saith our Lord, is this, I vvill giue them my lavv in their bovvels, and vvrite it in their hartes, and I vvilbe theyr God, and they shalbe my people.* Thus farre *Hieremy*.

16 And in like maner the Roial prophet, speaking of the continual

progresse in vertue, that the faithfull seruants of God in the new testament, should make by the helpe of grace, saith. *Etenim benedictionem dabit legislator, ibunt de virtute in virtutem, videbitur Deus deorum in Sion. For the lavv maker,* (that is to say *Christ* our Sauiour) *vvill giue them the benediction of his grace,* by the meanes whereof, *they vvill proceede, from vertue to vertue,* and at last *come to see the God of gods in Sion.* Thus saith the psalmist. *Psum. 83*

17 And with these prophets agreeth the doctrin of our Sauiour himselfe, and his Apostles, and therefore he said to his disciples. *Sine me, nihil potestis facere. VVithout me you can doe nothing. Et sicut palmes &c. As the brach can beare no friut, except it remaine in the vine, so neither can you, except you remaine in me.* And inuiting the Samaritan woman to drinke of the fountaine of his grace, he signified with all the admirable effect thereof, saying. *Qui biberit ex aqua, &c. He vvhich shall drinke of this vvater, vvhich I vvill giue him* (that is to say of the water of my grace) *he shall neuer thirst, but the vvater that I shall giue him, shall become in him a fountaine, or spring continually flovving to life euerlasting.* In which words, our Sauiour signifieth notablie, the most excellent, and wonderful propertie, & effect of his grace, as that the same being infused into the hart of man, cannot be conteined, within the limits thereof, but alwais boyleth, as it were, and lifteth vp both it selfe, and mans hart withal towards heauen, to ioyne him with his first beginninge, and to reduce him to the fountaine, from whence it selfe floweth, that is to say, to God, the author, and giuer of all grace, and goodnes. *Ioan. 15.* *Ioan. 4.*

18 I omit for this time, other testimonies concerning the effect of grace in Christian religion, both because I am to speake thereof more amplie hereafter, as also for that the same sufficientlie appeareth by these alreadie alleadged. Therefore I conclude for the present two things, the one, that our Christian religion is the most perfect, and true religion, in respect of the meanes that it giueth for the attaining of true, and perfect vertue, that is to say, not onlie for the puritie, and excellencie of the doctrin, and of the rites, and ceremonies which it deliuereth vnto vs, but also in respect of the grace of God, which accompanieth the same, and enableth vs to performe the precepts, & rules thereof, and to excell in all vertue, which is the speciall, and proper effect of grace, and not to be obtained without it, as shall appeare more fullie, after a while. For heitherto I haue thought good, onlie to touch breefelie this point, to giue some light, to an other conclusion, which I am to draw out of the premisses, to wit, that our Christian religion is trulie political, and most necessarie for gouerment of state. *Chap. 16. nu. 22. & sequent.*

19 This may appeare, by that which I haue shewed alreadie, touching

 the

the puritie, and excellencie of Christian doctrin, and the effects of Gods grace, whereby it is euident, that the Christian religion, hath the most excellent, or rather the onlie meanes to attaine to true, and perfect vertue, and to obtaine the fauour, and protection of almightie God, in which two points consisteth the establishment, and felicitie of all states. And to speake first of the meanes, to vertue. Yt cannot be denied, but that the Christian faith being taught, and infused by almightie God, and accompanied with his grace, (as I haue alreadie declared) not onlie sheweth the way to perfect vertue, but also giueth force, & strenght to performe & exercise, the acts thereof in all perfection: wherevppon it followeth, that whosoeuer is a true, & perfect Christian, is, and must needes be, *bonus ciuis*, a good citizen, as *Aristotle*, tearmeth a good member of a common welth.

Euseb. li. 3. eccles. hist. ca. 27.

20 This was so euident to the paynimes thẽselues, when they cõsidered the Christiã doctrin & practise, without passiõ, & partialitie, that *Pliny*, the secõd, being procõsul of *Asia*, vnder *Traiã*, the emperour, ackowledged the same in an epistle, to the said *Traian*, writtẽ in fauour of the persecuted Christians in his iurisdiction, testifiing of thẽ, that they were an innocent, and harmeles people, whose custome, and exercise was to assemble themselues in the night, to sing certaine hymnes, and praises to *Iesus Christ*, whom they adored as their God, and that they promised, & vowed to commit no offence, or to doe anie hurt to other men, not to steale, or robb, nor to cõmit adultery, or periury, not to breake promise, and such like; vppon which testimony, *Traian* ordained, that no Christiã should be further punished, or enquired of for his religion, except he were accused, and his successor *Adrian* vppon the like suggestion, and information giuen by a noble man called *Serennio Graniano*, gaue order to *Minutius Fundamus*, his proconsul, that the Christians should not be punished, at all for their religion.

Ibidem li. 4. ca. 8. & 9.

21 Thus ordained they, knowing onlie some pointes of Christian doctrin, whereas if they had fully vnderstood, the whole, & knowne withall, all the wonderful effects of Gods grace in the reformatiõ of mẽs manners, they not only would haue permitted it as tollerable, or not vnprofitable to the common welth, but also haue held it as absolutelie necessarie to the perfect establishment, and conseruation thereof.

22 For the true Christian, inspired by the holie Ghost, and following the rules, precepts, and examples of our Sauiour *Christ*, loueth God aboue all thinges, and his neighbour as himselfe, doth iniurie to no man, pardoneth all iniuries donne to him, esteemeth, and honoureth euerie one, according to his degree and meritt, represseth all concupiscence,

piſcence, and vnlawful deſires, obeyeth magiſtrats, ſuperiors, and
lawes,as the ordinance of God (*Non propter iram, ſed propter conſcientiam,* Rom.13.
Not for feare of puniſhment, but for conſcience ſake.) Yealdeth to euerie one
his due, to *Cæſar, that vvhich is Cæſars, to God that vvhich is Gods*, and finallie Matth.22.
preferreth in all thinges the publike weale, before his priuate commo- Mar. 12.
ditie. Where vppon it followeth, that in what ſtate ſoeuer he liueth, Luc.20.
he is humble,meeke, peaceable, obedient, temperate, liberal,iuſt,reli- Ro.3.& 13.
gious,and conſequentlie a good, and excellent member of his common welth,in ſo much that if the precepts of Chriſtian religion,were
ſincerely followed,and obſerued,there ſhould neede no political law,
which as the Apoſtle ſaith. *Poſita eſt iniuſtis, & non ſubditis. Ys ordained for* 1. Tim. 1.
the vniuſt, and diſobedient, whereas perfect Chriſtians, *ſibi ipſi ſunt lex,* Rom.2.
are a lavv to them ſelues, who hauing the law of God written in their
harts, (as the prophet foretold) are themſelues liuelie *temples of the* Hierem.31.
holie Ghoſt, which moueth,directeth, guideth, and enableth them to 1.Cor. 6.
doe their dutie to God, and man, repleniſhing their harts with ſuch
charitie, that is to ſay, with ſuch feruent loue to God, and their neigh- 2.Cor.1.&3.
bour, that the vnanimitie, and amitie,which *Ariſtotle* affirmeth to be, Ariſtot.
Maximum bonum ciuitatibus, The cheefeſt good for citties, or common Polit. li.2.
welths (that is to ſay, moſt neceſſarie,for the conſeruation thereof)is ca.2.
both commaunded, and practiſed amongſt ſincere Chriſtians, in all
perfection, nothing being more requiſite to the conſeruation, eyther
of the miſtical body of *Chriſt*, or of the political bodie of the common
welth,thē the vniō,& perfect agreemēt of the parts, & mēbers thereof,
no leſſe then of the parts of mans natural bodie,which is thereby conſerued,and maintained,as on the other ſide,by the diſtraction,and ſepe-
ration of the parts, the whole is diſſolued,and periſheth.

23 Therefore, I ſay, this harmonie,and vnanimitie,being moſt neceſſarie,and eſſential to a perfect common welth, is moſt excellent, and
eminent amongſt true,and perfect Chriſtiās,for whom our Sauiour obtained it,by his moſt affectionat,and effectual praier to his Father, whē
a litle before his paſion, he praied that *thoſe vvhich ſhould beleeue in him*
might be all one, as he,and his Father are one. Tu pater, ſaith he, *in me, & ego* Ioan.17.
in te,& vt ipſi in nobis vnum ſint. Thou father in me,and I in thee, and that they
may be one in vs. And therefore alſo he recommended nothing more, or
oftner vnto his diſciples,then that they ſhould *loue one an other*,calling it
his new commaundement. *Mandatum nouum*, ſaith he, *do vobis* &c. *I giue* Ioan.13.
you a nevv commaundement, that you loue on an other as I haue loued you, thereby
all men ſhall knovv, that you are my diſciples, if you loue on an other. Thus ſaith
our Sauiour.

24 And this loue, and vnion of mindes, was alſo ſo recommended to all
Rom. 13. Chriſtians by the Apoſtles, that they inculcated nothing more, then the
neceſſitie thereof, in ſo much, that *S. Paule*, attributed thereto all the perfection of Chriſtian religion, ſaying. *Qui diligit proximum legem impleuit.*
He vvhich loueth his neighbour, as he ought to doe, *fulfilleth the lavv*, and
ſuch was his owne loue to his brethren, that he deſired to be himſelfe,
Rom. 9. *ſeperat from Chriſt* (meaning, if it ſo should be for Gods glorie) rather
then they should periſh.

25 And *S. Iohn* in like mãner ſaith, that our loue to our brethren ought
Ibid. Ioan. 3. to be ſuch, that we *should giue our liues for them*, after the example of our
Sauiour *Chriſt*. And the ſame holie Euangeliſt, at the time of his death,
exhorted his diſciples to nothing els, but to loue one an other, and when
vppon his continual repetition thereof, they asked him, why he ſo oft,
and onlie ſpoke of that one point, marie ſaith he, *it is the precept of our lord,*
S. Hieron. li. de ſcriptoribus eccleſ. *vvhich being performed is ſufficient*. And how exactly this precept is practiſed, and performed amongſt true, and perfect Chriſtians, may appeare by
the loue, and vnion that was amongſt them in the time of the Apoſtles,
Act. 4. which was ſuch, that the ſcripture, ſaith. *Erat credentium cor vnum, & ani-*
ma vna. The faithful had all one hart, and one ſoule. And the ſame may no
doubt be ſtill ſaid of all thoſe, that ſincerely profeſſe, and practiſe the
Chriſtian religion, whereby it appeareth how political it is, and what a
notable effect it worketh in a common welth, where it is embraced, and
practiſed in ſinceritie.

26 And the like I ſay, of an other precept of our Sauiour, to wit, the
remiſſion of iniuries, which is ſo political, that happie were the common welth, where it should be generallie receiued, and practiſed. For
as the reuenge of iniuries is the ſourſe, and ſpring of quarrels, garboyls,
ſeditions, and tumults (whereby ſtates are often ouerthrowne) ſo on
the other ſide the remiſſion of wrongs (which Chriſtian religiõ preciſe-
lie ordeineth) is the mother of peace, and tranquilitie, whereby the
common welth is conſerued, and floriſheth. But for as much, as I am to
a Chap. 22. ſpeake more of this point hereafter (aſwel to shew in what caſes and a
how this precept of our Sauiour bindeth, as alſo to anſwer certaine impertinent obiections of *Macchiauel*, & the politikes his followers, againſt
b Chap. 24. Chriſtian b manſuetude, and patience) I forbeare to enlarge my ſelfe further concerning the ſame in this place.

27 Moreouer, although I haue alreadie declared, how neceſſarie Chriſtian religion is for the planting of vertue in common welth, by reaſon
aſwell of the excellencie, and puritie of the doctrin, as alſo of the admirable force of grace, which accompanieth it, as a proper effect thereof.
Neuertheles

Neuertheles to shew further the necessitie of Gods grace, to the perfection, and felicitie of common welth, I will now proue, that nothing els but grace (which is onlie to be had with true religion) can eradicat, and roote out vice, out of the mind of man, and make a cōmmon welth trulie vertuous, and happie.

28 For this purpose, I laid certaine groundes in the first part of this treatise, whereof I must now refresh the remembrance, because they are most pertinent, and necessarie to the explication, & proofe of the matter in hand. I made it manifest there, that no humane lawes, nor industry, can suffise to represse *the lavv of the flesh,* which as the Apostle saith, *doth impugne the lavv of the mind,* and predominat in the corrupt nocture of man. And first I shewed, that humane lawes, haue no other meanes to doe it, but either by precepts, or by prohibitions, or by reward, or els by punishment; and proued euidentlie, that none of these meanes, nor all of them together, can extēd their force to reforme secret vices, & sinnes, and much lesse to cure the cause of euil, and sinne in man, (that is to say, his vicious habits, and bad inclinations,) but onlie to restraine some effects thereof, to wit, some external actions, and yet not in euerie man, but onlie in such as are of a vertuous nature, and disposition, or els such as haue no power, or other meanes to resist, or auoid the penalties of the lawes, which as I there signified, are auoided, or excluded manie times, eyther by the power of the delinquent, or by the princes pardō, & fauour, or by corruption of officers, or by their negligence, in so much, that manie not withstanding all the rigour of lawes, doe wallow in all kind of vice, and wickednes.

Chap. 9. per totum.

Rom 7.

29 Further more I also declared, that the law of the flesh, hath her precepts, and her prohibitions, her rewardes, and her punishments, her proctors, and her aduocats, her orators, philosophers, princes, magistrats, and common welths, where it absolutelie gouerneth, yea, and that it hath religions, with doctors, and peachers, to defend, preach, and teach it, all which being compared with the other meanes, ordained by political law, doe farre surmount them, and are much more powerful, to draw a man of a malignant nature to vice, then the other are to diuert him from it, and to incite him to vertue. And although it may be said, that lawes are good helpes, to make the subiects vertuous, or at least to with hould manie of them from publike scandalls, and offences, yet I proued plainelie, that they are no meanes at all to reforme a vicious, & wicked prince, if he be of a corrupt, and peruerse nature, by whose vice, and wickednes, the commō welth may be subuerted, be the lawes neuer so good, and the subiects neuer so vertuous.

30 And

30 And whereas,it may seeme, that good order being taken for the good education of youth,the common welth may by the helpe of good lawes, become vertuous,I also made it cleare, that no industrie of man, or careful education of youth, in prophane common welths (I meane such as are void of true religion, and consequentlie of grace) can suffice, though with the helpe of humane lawes,to exterminate vice, and plant true vertue therein,by reason of the impediments, which will vndoubtedlie occurre,either by the negligence,bad example,or euil instructions of wicked parents, or by the pouertie of manie, or because their estate may require,that their children be emploied in trades,and occupations, or by the peruerse, and incorrigible natures of manie of the youthes themselues, or by humane frailtie (whereby manie after good education, fall dailie to vice,) or by the insufficiencie, corruption, or euil example of their masters, and teachers (who in prophane common welths, cannot be trulie vertuous themselues, and much lesse teach true vertue to others. For the proofe whereof,I shewed euidentlie, that *Aristotle, Plato,* and all the old philosophers (who tooke vppon them to reforme mens maners, and to cure their exorbitant, and vicious passiõs) were themselues most vicious,and of all this, I promised to yeald further reason, in this second part, and thereby, to declare the necessitie of Gods grace, for the extirpation of vice, and planting of true vertue in common welths, which now I meane to performe,with as conuenient breuitie as the matter will permit.

Chap.10.

31 Therefore to the end,that the whole may be the better vnderstood, it shall be first conuenient to treat of the cause of this great disease in mans nature, before we come to consider of the remedie,which wholy dependeth vppon the knowledge of the cause, and therefore when the philosophers saw all other creatures but man,liue according to theprescript,and rule of nature,and to tend directlie to the end whereto nature ordained them,and that he onlie being lord of this lower world, and endued with the light of reason, declineth most commonlie from the same, and feeling also in them selues a continuall conflict, betwixt reason,and sense,the filthie motions of concupiscence,the violence of passions,the remorse of conscience,accusing,and condemning them of errour, and sinne; and perceiuing their vnderstanding to be obscured with ignorance, their will depraued, and corrupted, with malice, their reason subdued manie times, and conquered by sensualitie, which ought to obay it; and finallie obseruing the infinit calamities, and miseries whereto man is subiect, they acknowledged a great disease,corruption, and miserie in humane nature, but could not imagin whẽce it proceded;

and therefore some of them deuised verie absurd reasons for the same, as *Anaxagoras* who perswading himselfe, that all creatures were made at first out of a Chaos, wherein all thinges were disordered by reason of the confused mixture of contrarieties, thought that nature framed euery thing els but man, verie well, to wit of such substances, and qualities, as were conforme, and agreable one to an other, and that shee erred in making of man, compacting him of two substances, of repugnant, and discordant qualities, which remaining still in their owne nature, as they were in the Chaos do cause, said he, all the conflict that is in man. Thus dreamed he. And others in like maner had their particular fantasies, if not altogether, so absurd, yet at least as vntrue, as that other. Here vppon it grew that *Empedocles*, & *Heraclitus* held that nature hath nothing in her pure, or sincere being but a continual warre & contradictiõ, breeding daily destruction, which is not otherwaise repaired but with new ruins; Thus said they, & others also complained greatly of her, that shee was a mother to all other creatures, and a stepmother to man. And therfore *Homer* (as *Plutarke* witnesseth) hauing considered the state, and nature of all things, and compared them together, exclaimed, and said, *that amongst all the creatures that breath, and creepe, or craule vppon the earth, none is more miserable then man.*

Iacob. de valentia in Cant. in solut. q. est. finalis ad ar. 1.

Plutar. vtrũ animant. terrest. an aquat. plus rationis habeant.

Cicero de repub. li. 3. ap. d D. August. contra Iul. li. 4.

Plutar. vtrũ grauiores sint animi, quam corporis morbi.

32 Againe some other of thẽ acknowledged a corruptiõ in mãs nature, & that it was declined from the first integritie, & therefore vsed to recall men by the example of brute beastes, to the law of nature, from which they thought man to be degenerat, which as *Plutarke* saith verie wel, was nothing els, but *a familiar accusation of the corruption of mãs nature.* For which cause also *Cicero* lamenteth greatlie, that *the light of nature, is almost extinct in man.* So that those philosophers, and we fullie agree, concerning the corruption, and disease in humane nature, but this is the difference, betwixt vs, and them, that we hauing learned by the veritie of holie scriptures, that it is a punishment inflicted vpon our first fathers, for their auersion, and fall from God, haue withall learned the onlie true remedy thereof, that is to say, our conuersion and returne to God, by the helpe of his grace, where as the philosophers being altogether ignorant of the cause of this sicknes, could neuer know the true meanes to cure it, wherein neuertheles it is to be considered, that both the cause of our euil, and the remedie which we assigne, are so conforme to reason, that they cannot with reason be denied.

Plutar. li. quod bruta animal. ratione vtantur.

Cicero Tuscul. quest. li. de rep. li. 3.

33 For seeing no man doubteth, but that reason ought, according to the law of nature to haue the rule, and gouerment of all the inferiour powers of the soule, and yet that it is not so absolute, but that it is

it selfe subiect to a higher power, that is to say, seeing that, as the appetite is naturallie subiect to reason, the bodie to the soule, and all earthly creatures to man, so also man himselfe, his soule, and reason is subiect to almightie God his creator. And againe seeing it is no lesse euident, that man is to God, no otherwaise, then as a slaue to his lord, and so dependant on his will, and gouerment, that if he withdraw himselfe from his direction, he must needes commit manie errours, in which respect *Aristotle* comparing all the world to a house, or familie, gouerned by one lord, maketh such difference, betwixt the celestiall, and terrestial creatures, that he likeneth the heauens, and intelligences to children, which doe in all thinges their fathers will, and men to bondslaues, who doe litle, or nothing for the good of the familie, if they be not moued, and directed by their lord (for otherwise saith he, they are commonlie misled by their owne sensualitie, and doe manie things contrarie to reason) seeing, I say, all this is confessed by the philosophers themselues, what can be more probable, and consonant to reason, then that the rebellion of our inferiour powers against reason, and reasons impotencie, and imbecillitie, and all the confusion that followeth thereof in man, is a consequent of some disobedience of man to God, by the meanes wherof reason being destitute of Gods direction, and gouerment, is not able to gouerne her inferiour powers, as otherwise she might vndoubtedlie be, if shee were not for some offence of man forsaken, and abandoned by almightie God.

Arist. metaphi.12.

34 Whereby we may see, how conforme to reason our Christian doctrin is, which teacheth, that the first two parents of man kind being made to the image, and likenes of almightie God, endued with vigour, and light of reason, and with rectitude of will, balanced, as it were, with the equalitie, and peaceful concord of motions, and affections (by the benefit of Gods grace, and of original iustice where with they were adorned) did vngratefullie transgresse his commaundement, and so were not onlie worthilie depriued of his grace, and the hope of euerlasting ioye, whereto they were ordained, but also became subiect euen in this life to all miserie, as well of soule as bodie.

35 For the principal powers of the soule (which are the subiects, or seates of vertue) were both weakened, and corrupted; reason obscured, & blinded, the will disordered & peruerted; the other inferiour powers fraught, and opprest with passions, and perturbations; the bodie incensed with flames of lust, and concupiscence; and finallie the bridle of Gods grace, and original iustice (which fortified reason, and kept all the inferiour powers in obedience to it) being taken away, they all ranne headlong

headlong to their obiects with such violence, that euer since, they draw most commonlie both reason, and the will after them, by the iust iudgment of God, ordaining as *S. Augustin* teacheth, that the defection, and rebellion of reason in man against God his creator, should be punished with the like rebellion of her owne subiects, I meane the inferiour powers, which are ordained by nature to obay her, and in all thinges to be guided by her, and so we see how true it is which the Preacher saith, that *Deus fecit hominem rectum, & ipse se immiscuit infinitis questionibus. God made man righteous, and iust, and he entangled himselfe vvith infinit trouble, and garboyles.*

Aug. To. 7. de peccat. meritis & remis.

36 This the philosophers found, and tried in them selues to be true, so farre forth as concerneth, the disease and wound of humane nature, that is to say, the effects, and sequels of mans fall, and yet seeing, and feeling withal some relickes of former health, I meane some sparkes of vertue, and the light of reason, not extinguished, but onlie darkened, and obscured, they perswaded themselues, that mans disease was not so desperate, but that there might be hope of his recouerie, and therefore they vsed all endeuour, & gaue manie good precepts to that end; but not knowing the true cause of his sicknes (as I haue said) they erred in all the course of the cure, especiallie in that they expected the remedie from mans owne labour, and endeuour, thinking themselues able to arriue to the perfection of moral vertue, without the grace of God, which was impossible, seeing that mans reason, being for his offence depriued of the conduct of grace, cannot possiblelie exercise her function in the due gouerment, and direction of the inferiour powers, except shee returne to the obedience of her owne superiour, and be guided by him, no more then the will, when it is alienat from reason, can well gouerne either it selfe, or the sensitiue appetit, which is subiect vnto it. And therefore *S. Augustin* saith. *Quam libet videatur animus* &c. *Hovv laudably soeuer the soule may seeme to rule the body, and reason rule vice, yet if the soule, and reason it selfe, doe not serue God in such sort, as he hath commaunded, they can neuer vvell rule, or gouerne either of both. For hovv can the soule that knovveth not the true God, and is not subiect vnto him, but lyeth open to the temptation, and corruption of the diuel authour of all vice, hovv can it, I say, be ladie, and mistres of the body, or represse vice?* Thus saith *S. Augustin.*

D. Tho 1.2. q. 109. ar. 8.

S. Aug. li. 19. de ciuit. Dei ca 25.

37 And for as much also as the will of man, is no lesse alienated, and auerted from God, then his reason, by the fall of *Adam*, and that it is requisit for the reparation of his corrupt nature (and consequentlie for the perfection of morall vertue) that his will be conuerted againe to God, and guided also by his grace, it followeth, that no man can attaine

to the perfection of moral vertue, without his ſpeciall aſſiſtance: and the reaſon is, becauſe the conuerſion of mans will to God, is not in his owne power, but proceedeth principallie from Gods grace, which *S.Thomas* proueth verie learnedlie thus.

D.Tho. 1.2. queſt. 109. ar.6.

Seeing that, ſaith he, euerie agent, or cauſe worketh for an end, it muſt needes follow, that euerie cauſe conuerteth her owne effects, vnto her end, and therefore, when there are diuers, and different ends, the order
» of thoſe ends is to be conſidered, according to the order of the cauſes,
» wherevppon it followeth, that man is conuerted to his laſt end, by the
» motion of the firſt agent, or cauſe, that is to ſay of almightie God, and
» that he is moued, to his next end, by ſome ſecondarie, or inferiour agent:
» as for example, the ſouldiar is moued to ſeeke victorie, by the motion of
» his general, and to follow the particuler collours of ſome band, or com-
» panie, by the motion of his Captaine, or Coronel. Therfore, for as much
» as almightie God is the firſt mouer, he himſelfe is the cauſe that all things
» are finallie conuerted vnto him, according to the nature of euerie one, whereupō *Dioniſius Areopagita*, ſaith. *Deus conuertit omnia ad ſeipſum. God turneth all thinges to himſelfe.* Thus ſaith *S.Thomas*, cōfuting learnedlie, & ſoūdelie, not onlie the philoſophers, but alſo the heretikes, *Valentinus*, *Baſilides*, and *Pelagius*, who taught that mans corrupt nature, had ſufficient force, and power in it ſelfe to repaire, and rectifie it ſelfe, without the helpe of Gods grace.

Dioniſ. li. de diuin. nomin. ca.4.

38 Well then, ſeeing all the perfection of morall vertue, dependeth only on the reparation of humane nature, corrupted by the fall of our firſt father, and that the ſame cannot be purchaſed, or procured by any humane meanes, or induſtrie, without the cōcurrēce of Gods grace, it followeth, that the perfection of moral vertue, is onlie to be had in the Chriſtian religion, which (as I haue ſhewed before, and will ſhew more amplie hereafter) is the law of grace, and onlie able to heale the wound in mans nature, to illuminat his reaſon, to rectifie his will, to repreſſe ſenſualitie, and to pacifie his paſſions, and conſequentlie to enable him, to doe the acts of perfect moral vertue, and to eſchew all vice, where vppon I conclude, that Chriſtian religion is moſt political, and fit for gouerment of ſtate.

Yt is obiected that many Paynimes, and Infidels haue excelled in the moral, and ciuil vertues, though they vvere vtterlie void of grace. And for satisfaction of the obiection it is proued, that though they might haue, and had some vertues, yet they could neuer vvithout grace, arriue to the perfection of morall vertue. Finally for the further proofe of the necessitie of grace, to the repression of vice, many examples are alleadged of the notable effects of grace, in the suddaine, and miraculous conuersion of sinners, and reformation of mens maners.

CHAP. 16.

1. BVt here perhaps, some may demaund, how then it came to passe, that not only the Philosophers, but also many vnlearned men, yea & women amongst the Paynimes, left an eternal memorie of their rare vertues. For who can denie, but that *Furius Camillus* the *Roman*, left a memorable example of excellent iustice, when beseeging the *Falisci*, he caused a scholemaster (who had betraied, and deliuered into his handes, all the children of the cheefe nobilitie) to be stripped naked, and whipped back into the towne, by the children themselues, wherevppon his enemies were strooken with such admiration of his vertue, that they yelded themselues, and their towne vnto him? And no lesse notable was the iustice of the senate of *Rome*, which hauing warre with king *Pirrus*, sent embassadours to admonish him, to take heede of his phisitian, who had offered them to poison him. And no lesse commendation deserued *Lucius Crassus*, for his moderation towards *Carbo* his notable enimie. For whē a slaue of *Carbo*, brought him a deske of his masters, wherein were all his secret papers reserued, amongst the which he might be sure to find sufficient matter to ouerthrow *Carbo*, he would not open it, but sent the slaue backe to his master, with a seruant of his owne, and the deske vnopened.

Tit. Liui. Dec. 1. li. 5.

Plutar. in Pirro.

Valer. Max. li. 6. c. 5.

2 And to speake of other vertues, how famous was the continencie, & liberalitie of *Scipio*, who hauing taken in warre, a virgin of rare beautie, not onlie deliuered her inuiolat to a noble man (though an enemie) to whom she was espoused, but also gaue her, for her dowrie, the money which was paid for her ransome?

T. Liui. Dec. 3. l. 6. in fine.

3 And how admirable was the fortitude of *Horatius Cocles*, who whē the *Hetrusci* assailed the cittie of *Rome*, by a draw bridge, defended it himselfe against their whole armie, vntil it was cut downe behind him, whereby he fell into the riuer, and escaped, and as *Valerius* saith, drew the Gods themselues to such an admiration of his valour, that they conserued him from the danger both of water, and also of his enimyes.

Idem Dec. 1. li. 2. Valer. li. 3. ca. 2.

[*T. Liui. Dec.1.li.2.*] To whome may be added also diuers other *Romans*, no lesse exemplar, then the former for their valour, fortitude, and pietie to their country, as *Mutius Scæuola*, who hauing failed to kill king *Porsenna*, when he beseeged *Rome*, put his right hand into the fire, in the kings presence, and there held it vntill it was burnt, partlie to take reuenge of it, for missing the blow, and partlie to shew, how much he contemned all the tormēts, [*Idem. Dec.1. li. 3. & 10.*] which were threatned him. And the two *Decij*, the father, and the sonne, seeing their armies in danger of ouerthrow, vowed, and solemnely (after their fashion) consecrated themselues, as sacrifices to their Gods, to obtaine the victorie, as I haue declared in the tenth chapter, where I haue [*Idem Dec.1. li. 7. Valer. Max. li.1. ca. 1. Cicero de offic. li.3.*] also made mention of the famous acts of *Marcus Curtius*, and *Marcus Attilius Regulus*, memorable to all posteritie, aswell for their notable resolution, pietie to their countrie, and contempt of death, as for the fidelitie, and iustice of the latter, in obseruing his oath to his enimies, with the losse of his life.

4 What should I say of the prudence of *Socrates*, esteemed by the testimonie of the oracle of *Apollo*, to be the wisest man liuing, or of his patience, and fortitude, who being wrongfullie condemned to death by the *Athenians*, his cuntrimen, and hauing the cup of poison in his hand readie to drinke, praied for the prosperitie of his enimies, and for his vn- [*Cicero Tusq. li.1.*] grateful countrie, with such constancie, and alacritie, that, as *Cicero* saith, he spoke rather, like one, that was going triumphantlie to heauen, then one condemned to die miserablie like a malefactor?

[*Diogenes laert. in vitis eorum. Plutar. in Aristide. Idem in vit. eorum.*] 5 And what neede I speake of the excellent vertue of *Plato*, called euen vntill this day, the deuine? Or of other philosophers, as of *Bias*, *Anaxagoras*, *Democritus*, and *Crates*, whose names were greatelie celebrated amongst the Greekes, for the contempt of riches, and worldlie honours? Or of *Aristides* in *Athens*, for his rare vertue surnamed the iust? Or of *Epaminundas*, a famous captaine in *Thebes*? Or of *Timoleon* in *Corinth*, or of *Dion* in *Sicily*, or of the two *Catoes* amongst the *Romans*, and diuers others, who no lesse excelled in martial prowesse, and ciuil prudence (being great gouernours in their common welths) then in the exercise of all moral vertue? What neede I (I say) speake of them, seeing there may be alleadged infinit examples of notable women, who haue bene also mirrours of all kind of vertue? For who can sufficientlie admire the libera- [*Liui. Dec. 3. li. 2.*] litie of *Busa*, an Italian Matron, of whom tenne thousand Roman soul- [*Liui. Dec.1. li 1. Valer. Max. li.6. ca. 1.*] diars escaping from the battaile of *Cannæ*, were receiued, and maintained sometime at her owne charges? Or the chastitie of *Lucretia* the Roman, and of *Hippo* the Grecian, of whom the first killed her selfe, because she was rauished by *Tarquinius*, and the other being taken at sea by enimies,

enimies,drowned her selfe,least shee should be violated? In which two neuertheles,it is to be noted,that their vertue consisted not in that they killed themselues (which was an vnlawfull,and sinfull act) but in their greate loue of chastitie,and regard of their honour, and reputation, for the which their memorie is still celebrated in all histories.

6 The which also,is to be vnderstood of the coniugal loue of the Indian women, who vsed to burne themselues most ioifullie with the bodies of their husbandes and of *Cato*,his daughter called *Porcia*,who being maried to *Brutus*,and hauing vnderstood of his conspiracie against *Cæsar*, the verie night before it was to be executed, gaue her selfe a greeuous woũd with a knife,to trie how she could endure to kill her selfe, in case her husbands designement should not succeede well,and afterwards vnderstanding,that he was ouerthrowne in battaile, and had killed himselfe,and seeing herselfe by the careful diligence of her friends depriued of all other meanes to make her selfe away,swallowed downe hoat burninge coales,vntil shee was stiffled,and chooked therewith.

Valer. Max. li. 4. c. 6.

7 But I omit to touch other particulers, of the vertues of Pagan women,seeing that *Plutark* wrote a whole tract of that subiect, wherein he recounteth notable examples of them in all kind of vertue,so that it may seeme,that moral vertues may be had,and practised in great perfection in prophane common welths,whithout anie assistance of Gods grace.

Plutar. de claris mulierib.

8 To satisfie,this obiection,it is to be considered, that there is great difference betwixt doing the acts of vertue, and being trulie vertuous. For,not onlie children,which haue not yet the vse of discretion,but also mad men,and bruit beastes may doe the acts of vertue,though they cannot be said to be vertuous,seeing it is requisit to true vertue (as *Aristotle* teacheth) that vertuous acts be donne well,and vertuouslie,that is to say, with due circumstances of time, place, measure, order, and especiallie with due election of the end In which last point, the actions of Pagans for the most part failed of true goodnes,and vertue, because they were not referred to God, the author of all vertue, and goodnes, but most commonlie to vaine glorie, or els to some priuate, or publike commoditie,or at least to vertue it selfe, without anie further relation to God at all.

Aristot. Ethic. li. 3. ca. 1. & 2.

9 This was notablie obserued,by *S. Augustin* in the famous, and worthie acts of the first *Brutus*,*Camillus*,*Torquatus*,*Fabritius*, the two *Decij*, *Mutius Scæuola*,*Marcus Curtius*, and generallie of all other *Romans*, whom he sheweth euidentlie to haue had no other scope, or end in their actions, but either the loue of their common welth,or a desire of honour. Where vppon it is to be inferred,that neither their acts,nor anie other of Gẽtils,

D. Aug. de ciuit. li. 5. c. 12. 18. 19. & 20.

referred to the same end, could be trulie vertuous. For as *S. Augustin* saith; *Non est vera virtus, nisi quæ ad eum finem tendit, vbi est bonum hominis, quo melius non est. It is not true vertue, vvhich tendeth to anie other end, then that, vvherein is the best, and cheefe good of man*, that it to say, almightie God, or his seruice.

Ibid.

10 And this is euident by the verie nature of vertue, whereto nothing is more requisit, then to make a good election of the end, of euerie actiõ (and therefore *Aristotle* teacheth, that no moral vertue, can be without prudence, whereto the choise of the end in all vertuous actiõs, especially belongeth.) Where vppon it followeth, that seeing reason teacheth, that God is not onlie the first cause, and creator, but also the natural end of all creatures, it must needes be the office of true prudence, to direct all humane actions, first and principallie to him, and secondarilie to other lawful ends in which respect the action which is not finallie, & cheeflie referred to God, cannot be prudent, nor consequentlie trulie vertuous.

Ethic. li. 10. cap. 8. D. Tho. 1. 2. quest. 57. ar. 5.

11 And although it is not altogether vnprobable, that some few amõgst the Paynimes, I meane the philosophers (or at least some of them,) might haue, or perhaps had, some relation in their actions, to the authour of nature, (that it to say to God) either in particuler, or in general, neuertheles, it cannot be said, that they could arriue to anie perfection of moral vertue, because there is requisit thereto, not onlie to make a good choise of the end of euerie action, and to performe the same with due circumstances, but also to haue a perfect connexion, of all the morall vertues, and to perseuer in the continual vse, and practise of them, yea, and to eschew all maner of vice (as *Aristotle*, and all other philosophers teach expressie) which no paynime euer did, nor is anie way possible for mans weake, and corrupt nature, except it be repaired, and cured by grace.

Ethic. li. 1. c. 10. & li. 10. ca. 5.

12 For although, when mans nature was sound, and vncorrupt (as it was in *Adam* before his fall) he might doe all thinges, which were proportionable to his nature, and consequentlie performe all the acts of morall vertue, yea and perseuer in the exercise thereof, yet now his nature being so weakned, and corrupted as it is, he cannot doe either of both of himselfe, and yet neuertheles being not wholie corrupted, (his reason retaining still some superioritie ouer his inferiour powers) he hath so much force, and power left, that he may with diligent præmeditation, and heede, doe some particuler acts of vertue: euen as a sick man, may performe some acts, of a whole and sound man, but not all that which a sound man can doe vntill he be perfectlie cured, and healed.

D. Tho. 1. 2. q. 109. ar. 2. c.

13 Further-

13 Furthermore,great difference is to be noted betwixt the power,and habilitie to auoid all vice, and to eschew anie one particular vice, or sinne. For those two powers, do depend on diuers causes, and therefore must needes be verie different betwixt them selues.

The power to auoid anie one sinne,proceedeth of a particular cause, that is to say, of the natural subiection of the appetit to reason, and of the libertie of mans will, whereby he may (not withstanding the corruption of his nature) resist,as I haue said, some light temptations, and auoid some particuler sinnes,but the power to eschew all vice, or sinne dependeth on an vniuersal cause, that is to say, on the due subordination, and subiection of all the inferiour powers of the soule to the superiour (to wit to reason, and to the will) and that they be subiect to God, and gouerned and moued by him, as I haue signified before. For although a man may,by the libertie of his will, withstand some motions, or tēptations, which he forseeth,or expecteth,keeping due watch vppon himselfe,yet as long as his will is alienated from God, and all the inferiour powers of his soule so prone, and headlong to their obiects, and so rebellious against reason (as in our corrupt nature they are) he cannot still perseuer in his watch of himselfe, but shalbe often caried away with the vehement, and suddaine temptations of the world, the flesh, and the deuil, especiallie seeing that (as *Aristotle* saith) in suddaine motions, a man commonlie followeth his habite and inclination, rather then his pręmeditate purposes. Besides that the motions, and temptations of sinne,are often times so manie at once, that he cannot haue sufficient præmeditation,against them all, but by seeking to auoid one,he shall fall into an other,except he be supported by some supernaturall helpe.

Chap.15. nu.33. & sequent.

D.Tho.1.2. q.109.ar. 8.

Arist.li. 3. Ethic.

14 Where vppō it followeth,that the Paynims,or Infidels could neuer of themselues,attaine to the perfection of moral vertue,but were contaminated with manie vices,& foule sinnes,before they could come to get any one vertuous habite. And therfore the nature of sinne being such, that when it hath once got possession of the soule of man, it draweth still into it more corruption, and infection, except it be cleansed by grace, it is no maruaile that they, being void of grace, were so depressed with the weight of their owne sinnes, that they could neither raise themselues to the perfection of vertue, nor yet withhould themselues from horrible vices. For, euen as a bowle, or stone cast downe a hil, gathereth still force, as it goeth, and runneth euer the longer, the faster, vntill it come to the bottome: euen so a sinner not reclaimed, or staid by Gods grace, falleth com-

 monlie

monlie frō sinne to sinne, and euer the longer the worse, vntil he come,
S. Greg. in c. (as the wise man saith) *in profundum*, into the depth of sinne; where vp-
34. Iob. c. 9. pon, *S. Gregory* saith, that the sinne, which is not washt away with repentance, draweth a man, with the weight thereof to other sinnes. And
Psal. 90. the psalmist saith to the same purpose. *Via impiorum tenebræ, & lubricum. The vvay of the vvicked is darke, and slippery*, because being destitute of the light of Gods grace, he slideth still from one sinne, to an other, which also the prophet *Hieremy*, affirmeth of *Hierusalem*, and of all sinners. *Pec-*
Hierem. Thren. 1. *catum*, saith he, *peccauit Hierusalem, & propteria instabilis facta est. Hierusalem hath sinned a sinne, and is therefore become vnstable*. And *S. Chrisostome* expresseth the same, with a notable example, or similitude saying; that euen as a shipp which lacks a sterne, cannot goe, whither the pilot will, but whither the storme, or wind driueth it: so also the man, that is void of Gods grace, is carried away with vice, and sinne, vntill he runne vppon the rocks of all wickednes. Finallie this may be confirmed by the experience, that hath bene had, of the bad, and vicious liues of the best philosophers, notwithstanding their doctrin, and vaine ostentation of vertue, as I haue shewed sufficientlie in the first part of this treatise.

15 Therefore I conclude vppon all the premisses, first, that although some of the Gentils did some notable acts of moral vertue, some in one kind, and some in an other (whereby, as I signified in my first part, a few in manie ages were counted vertuous) yet none of them euer arriued to anie perfection of moral vertue, or were trulie vertuous, partlie because they neuer had that connexion of all the vertues, which in the opinion of all the philosophers is requisit, to the perfection of moral vertue, and partly because they were all of them vicious, and wicked in some kind of vice, or other: and lastlie, because they were void of Gods grace, which is the onlie meanes to repaire the corrupt nature of man, and to enable him, to doe all that, which is necessarie to perfect vertue.

16 Secondlie, I conclude, that seeing the perfection of moral vertue, is requisit to the perfection of common welth, and that the same cannot be had without the grace of God, and againe that Gods grace is (as I haue shewed in the last chapter) proper to Christian religion, it must needes follow, that Christian religion is most political, and necessarie for gouerment of common welth.

17 All this wil be yet more euident, if we cōsider more particularlie, the maruelous, or rather miraculous effects of Christiā religiō, in reforming the mindes, & māners of mē. For although I haue said somewhat therof
Chap. 15. alreadie, yet I thinke it conuenient to add also somewhat more concerning the same point, to the end, it may be as cleare, as the sunne. Therefore

fore *Lactantius* endeuoring to shew, how vainelie the philosophers laboured to reforme the mind, and manners of men, by their morall philosophie, teacheth that the remedie of mans infirmitie and corruption, ought to be such (in respect both of the priuat, and of the publike weale of man) that it may extend it selfe to euerie man, of what degree, state, or vocation soeuer he be. For as euerie man participateth of the disease hereditarie to humane nature: so it is reason, that euerie man also may participat of the remedie. In which respect, some of the philosophers, (as namelie the Stoicks) thinking the knowledge, and practise of philosophie, to be absolutelie necessarie for the perfection, and felicitie of man, taught that all sorts of men, and women, rich, and poore, bond, and free, ought to be philosophers, wherein, (as *Lactantius*, noteth verie wel) *Conati sunt facere, quod veritas exigebat, sed non potuit vltra verba procedi.* They endeuored to doe that which veritie, and truth required, but could goe no further then to wordes.

Lactant. li. 3. c. 25.

Idem ibid.

18 Thus saith he, and most trulie, for two reasons before declared. The one for that their philosophie could not reach to the roote, and cause of mans disease: and the other because none could attaine to the knowledge, and practise of it but onlie a few, such I meane as had habilitie, & leisure from other emploiments, to attend to the studie thereof, which (as it is euident) the greatest part of the common welth by farre cannot doe, and if they could, yet verie manie haue not sufficient capacitie to learne, and studie it, and therefore *Cicero* saith. *Philosophia est paucis contenta, iudicibus, multitudinem consulto ipsa fugiens. Philosophy contenteth it selfe vvith the iudgement of a fevv, and purposely flieth from the multitude,* that is to say, from the common sort of men. Where vppon *Lactantius*, cōcludeth verie well, that therefore philosophie, is not true wisdome, as the philosophers affirmed, and taught it to be. *For if vvisdome,* saith he, *be giuen by almightie God for the benefit of mankind, he gaue it to the end, that euery man may be partaker thereof, but these philosophers doe vsurpe this common, and publike benefit to themselues, as though they vvould hoodvvinck, and blindfould all other men, and that no man but they should see the same,* &c.

Cicero Tusculan. q. li. 5.

Lactant. li. 3. c. 25.

19 *Therefore seeing the nature of man is capable of vvisdome, it is conuenient, that husbandmen, artificers, vvomen, and men of all sorts, and vocations, be taught it, to the end they may become vvise thereby, vvhich is an euident argument to proue, that philosophy is not true vvisdome, the mistery vvhereof, hath more ostentation in a long beard, and a cloake, then good effect in vvorkes, and actions.*

20 Thus saith *Lactantius*, signifiing notablie, the defect, and insufficiēcy of philosophie and other humane meanes, for the reparation of humane nature, and the reformation of mens manners, which he teacheth also to

be the true, and proper effect of Christian religion in these wordes.

Idem ibid. 21 That which the philosophers, by the instinct of nature, thought cõueniẽt to be donne, & yet could neuer doe thẽselues, is performed by the heauenly doctrin (of Christiã religion) which onlie is true wisdome. For can the philosophers perswade anie man, who could neuer fully perswade themselues? Or can they represse anie mans passions, temper anie mans wrath, or restraine other mens lust, when they themselues are ouercome with vice, & therfore must needs acknowledge the force of their owne corrupt nature? Whereas dailie experience sheweth, whãt power the cõmaundements, or the law of God haue in the mindes of men. For let a man be neuer so colerick, or furious, and with a few words of God, I will make him as meeke, & quiet as a lambe; let him be coueteous, auaricious, or nigardlie, I will make him liberal, & to giue his money freelie with his owne handes; let him be neuer so timerous, and fearefull of torments, or death, he shall contemne gallowes, fire, and the bull of *Phalaris*, let him be libidinous, adulterous, and riotous, you shall straight see him, chast, and continent; let him be cruell, and bloudie, his furie shall suddainlie be changed to clemencie; let him be vniust, a foole, and a sinner, he shall become iust, prudent, and innocent; for with one onlie washing (that is to say of Baptisme) all his malice shalbe abolished, &c. And was there euer anie of the philosophers, that euer did, or was able to doe these thinges, who when they had spent all their liues in the studie of philosophie, could neither make them selues, or anie man els, the better, if nature did neuer so litle repugne? Therefore all that their wisdome could performe, was to hide vice, and not to reforme it, wheras the commaundements of God, doe so wholie change a man, and cast him in such a new mold, that you will not know him to be the same mã. Thus farre *Lactantius*, declaring his experience, aswel cõcerninge the philosophers which liued in his time, as also touching the effects of Christiã religion in the Gentils, who were dailie conuerted in his daies, which was in the time of *Constantin* the great, to whome he wrote.

22 This mutation of mind, and manners, whereof *Lactantius* speaketh, is (as I haue said) a special effect of Gods grace, infused into the soule of man, *per Spiritum sanctum qui datus est nobis, by the holie Ghost vvhich is giuen vnto vs*, whereof, *S. Ambrose* saith *Cui adest spiritus gratiæ, nihil deest, & cui spiritus Sanctus infunditur magnarum plenitudo virtutum est. He that hath the spirit of grace, vvanteth nothing, and vvhosoeuer hath the holie Ghost infused into him, hath the plenitude, or perfection of great vertues.* That is to say, of the three vertues, called Theological, to wit, Faith, Hope, & Charity, wherby mans vnderstanding is illuminated, and his will not onlie inflamed

Rom.5. D. Ambros. in Euang. Luc.c.1.

with

with the loue of God, but alſo drawne, moued, and diſpoſed to the execution of his commaundements, and the inferiour powers of his ſoule
are made obedient to the ſuperiour, and conſequentlie to the law of
God, which (as I declared before out of the prophet,) *is vvritten in the* *Chap.15.*
harts of the faithful, in ſo much, that thoſe things which before ſeemed, *nu.14.15.*
and were to mans corrupt nature impoſſible, (as the perfect practiſe, *& 16.*
and exerciſe of the morall vertues, and the obſeruation of Gods commaundements) became afterwards, not onlie poſſible, but alſo eaſie to
be performed.

23 This the prophet foretold, when ſpeaking of the comming of *Chriſt*, *Eſay.46.*
and the vocation of the Gentils, he ſaid. *Erunt praua, in directa, & aſpera in*
vias planas. The crooked ſhalbe made ſtraight, and the rough vvaies ſhalbe made
euen, and plaine, that is to ſay, the peruerſe, and crooked natures, and
conditions of men ſhalbe rectified by grace, and the way of vertue, and
of Gods law, which before was full of aſperitie, and difficultie, ſhal
be come facil, and eaſie, yea, ſweete, and pleaſant, and therefore the
Royall prophet ſaith, of the commaundements of God, that they are.
Dulciora ſuper mel, & fauum. More ſvveete then the honie, and the hony combe. *Pſal.18.*
Of which point I will ſpeake more particulary, and amply after a while, *Chap.17.18*
when I ſhall treat of the end, and felicitie of man, and common welth. *19.20.&*

24 And although almighty God for the humiliation of his ſeruants, & *21.*
their greater merit, giueth them manie times his grace by degrees, yea, &
permiteth them to haue great, & long cõflicts, with their owne peruerſe
natures, before they can ouercome them (ſuffering them to fight, & aſsi-
ſting them therein, and giuing thẽ in the end both the victorie, & crowne, for their fight) neuertheles, for his owne greater glorie, and our cõ-
forts, he beſtoweth manie times his grace in ſuch abundance, & worketh
ſuch ſodaine conuerſions of men from Infidelitie to his faith, & frõ vice
to vertue, that it cannot iuſtlie be aſcribed to anie other meanes, then to
the force of his grace, though Infidels, & wicked men, who haue not had
anie experience, or taſt thereof in them ſelues, ſo litle vnderſtand it, that
Porphiry the philoſopher, and *Iulian* the *Apoſtata*, taxed either our holie
ſcriptures of vntruth, or the Apoſtles of leuitie, and follie, for that they
followed our Sauiour *Chriſt* at the firſt call; which cauil *S. Hierome* anſwe- *D.Hiero.l.1*
reth notably well ſaying, that *if there be ſuch force, (as vve ſee) in Iett, and the* *comment. in*
loadſtone, to dravv vnto them ſtravv, and yron: hovv much more vvas the lord of *Mat.c.9.*
all creatures able to dravv vnto himſelfe, thoſe vvhom it pleaſed him to call. Thus
ſaith *S. Hierome*, whereto I add, that if the Apoſtles were fooles for following *Chriſt* at his call, then many greate philoſophers, yea, & the whole
world conuerted by thẽ. & by ſuch other, had leſſe reaſon to be Chriſtiãs

then they,and may farre more worthilie be noted of follie.

25 But no meruaile,that almightie God wrought ſuch ſuddaine, and ſtrange mutations in men by his owne Sonne, whiles he was here one earth,ſeeing he hath donne the like euer ſince in all ages,and daily doth, both by his ſeruants,and alſo by other meanes,through the merits of his ſaid Sonne,our Sauiour,as appeareth in our holie ſcriptures, by the ſuddaine conuerſion of three thouſand ſoules, at *S.Peters* firſt ſermon; and of the Eunuch by *Phillip* the diſciple, with onlie one conference, and of *Saul*,who of a perſecutor ſuddenlie became an Apoſtle, and of the great philoſopher *Dioniſius Areopagita*, conuerted alſo by one ſermon of the ſame Saul,then called *Paul*;as alſo of diuers others,which I omit, to the end I may alleadge a few examples out of other hiſtories of later times, thereby to ſhew the admirable effects, and operation of Gods grace in Chriſtian religion from time,to time.

Act.c. 2. Act. c.8. Ibidem c. 9. Ibid.c.17.

26 We read in *Euſebius*,and diuers other authors, that *S. Iohn* the *Euangeliſt*,hauing recommended a yong man,to the care, and inſtruction of a certaine Biſhop,and vnderſtanding after ſome yeares,that the yong man had not onlie abandoned the Biſhop,and the Chriſtian faith, but was alſo become a captaine of common theeues and murderers, he would needs goe ſeeke him,where he vſed to robbe, and ſpoile the paſſengers, & falling firſt into the hands of his cōpanions, he deſired to be brought to their captaine,who,as ſoone as he ſaw him, beganne to runne away, but *S. Iohn* cried vnto him to ſtay, telling him that he deſired nothing at his hands,but his eternal good,offring to pawne his owne ſoule for his ſaluation, where vppon the yong man returned, and with aboundance of teares craued pardon,of God,and him, ſubmitting himſelfe vnto his direction,and ſo entire,was his repentance,and conuerſion, that ſhortly after *S. Iohn* made him Biſhop.

Euſeb.li 3. c.17. Chriſoſt. ad Theodor. lapſum. Ioan. Caſſian.collat. 24. c.21. Baron.an.

27 We reade alſo of an other ſtrange,and ſuddaine conuerſion of a great philoſopher to the Chriſtian faith,in the firſt general councell of *Nice*. This philoſopher diſputing with Chriſtian Biſhops, could not be gained,and conuerted by way of arguments,or other meanes, vntil at laſt, an vnlearned,but a verie holie Biſhop called *Spiridion*,propoſed vnto him ſimplie our Chriſtian doctrin of Chriſt incarnat,and crucified,and asked him,whether he beleeued it,or no,whereto he anſwered, that he beleeued it and confeſſed himſelfe to be ouercome, gaue him great thankes, and proteſted publikelie,that by an vnſpeakeable,and deuine power,he was alreadie conuerted to the Chriſtian faith.

Sozo. eccleſ. hiſt.l 1.c.17. Ruffin.li.1. ca.3.

28 *S. Auguſtin*; alſo recounteth an admirable effect of Gods grace,in two companions of his friend *Potitianus*,at *Treuers* in *Germany*, the empe-

D.Aug.l.cōfeſſ.8.c.6.

rour being there. The storie is thus. *Potitianus*, and three other secular men walking abroad, in an orchard, two of them, seuered themselues from the other, onlie to talke together more priuatelie, and passing too, and fro, found by chance a poore cottage, or cell of some religious persons, where there was a booke of the life of *S. Anthony* the famous heremit, which the one of them (who was a man of account in the emperours court) beganne to read, and was within a while, so inflamed with the loue of God, by the example of that holie man, that he cast his eies vppon his freend, and said. *Tell me I pray you, vvhat doe vve pretend by all our labours in the court? Doe vve seeke ought els, or can vve hope for greater happ, then to haue the emperours fauour? And if vve obtaine it, hovv fickle a thing, and full of danger is it? And by hovv many dangers doe vvee tend to greater danger? VVhereas, if vve vvill seeke to haue Gods fauour, and friendshipp, vve may haue it presently, vvith security.* Thus said he, and pawsing a while, told his friend that he was resolued to leaue the court, and the world, at that verie instant, and to remaine there to serue God during his life, asking him, what he would doe, who being no lesse moued by his example, then by his reasons, but most of all by Gods grace, which moued, & guided them both, determined also wholie to renounce the world, and to stay with him there.

29 Towards the euening *Potitianus*, and his other companion, seeking all about for them, found them at last in that poore cell, and vnderstanding their firme resolution, and being requested by them, not to molest them, in case they would not take the same course themselues, tooke their leaues of them, with manie teares, and (as *S. Augustin* saith) *Trahentes cor in terra, abierunt in palacium. Dravving their hartes after them vppon the earth, vvent backe to the emperours palace*, whereas the other two hauing, saith *S. Augustin, setled, and fixed their harts in heauen, remained in the cell*, hauing bene both of them handfast, and betrothed, to two maids, who hearing of their resolution, dedicated also their virginitie to God. This was related in this manner by *Potitianus* himselfe to *S. Augustin*, who also declareth a notable, and strange operation, of Gods, grace in his owne conuersion, which I thinke good to touch breefelie, seeing I haue had this occasion to speake of him.

30 *S. Augustin*, hauing forsaken the companie, and heresie of the *Manichees*, and yet neither being baptized, nor reclaimed, from his former dissolute life (which still withheld him frō Baptisme, and the perfect profession of Catholicke religion,) he felt one day, such motions of Gods grace, and thereby had such a conflict with himselfe, that he burst forth into aboundance of teares, and cast himselfe prostrate vppon the ground, where *D. Aug. li. 8. confes. c. 12.*

where after a while he heard a voice, as it were of a boy, or a girle singing these words, *tolle lege, tolle lege, take vp, and read, take vp, and read*, and not seeing anie likeliehood, that it could proceede from anie child, or other mortal creature, he perswaded himselfe, that almightie God admonished him thereby to take a booke, and to note for his owne instructiō, that which he should first chaunce to cast his eie vppon, as he had vnderstood the like of *S. Anthony*, the Heremit, who opening the new Testament, by chaunce, and lighting vppon the words of our Sauiour. *Goe, and sell all that thou hast, and giue it to the poore*, &c. tooke the same as spoken vnto him, and there vppon determined to abandon the world. With this conceit *S. Augustin* opened the booke, of the new Testament, wherein that which first occurred to his sight, was these words of *S. Paul*, to the *Romās*. *Honeste ambulemus, non in commessationibus* &c. *Let vs vvalke honestly, not in bāquetting, and dronkennes, not in bedds, and lasciuiousnes, not in contention, and æmulation, but put vppon you our lord Iesus Christ, and doe not pamper your flesh in concupiscences* &c. Which when he had read, he shut the booke being fullie satisfied; for hauing read but so farr, he felt presentlie, as he saith, such a light of securitie infused into his hart, that all obscuritie, and further doubt, was cleane expelled, in so much, that he affirmeth of himselfe, that from that time forward, he determined to liue chast, and to haue no further hope, or care of this world, resoluing to become a perfect Christian, and to dedicate the rest of his life, wholie to the seruice of God, which he after performed to Gods glorie, and to the great good of his Church.

Matth. 9. *Rom. 13.*

31 I cannot omit, the strange conuersion of the famous *Pachomius*, founder of the religious monkes of *Ægipt*, called *Tabennesiotæ*. This *Pachomius*, being a Gentil, and prest for a souldiar, in the warrs betwixt the emperour *Constantin*, and *Licinius*, passed by *Thebes* in *Ægipt*, where there were manie deuout Christians, who of their ordinarie charitie to all strangers, releeued greatelie *Pachomius*, & his companie, being all in great necessity, for lacke of victuals, wherewith *Pachomius* being much moued, demanded what maner of men, and of what profession they were, that vsed such extraordinarie pietie, and curtesie to strangers, and being told that they were Christians, and that it was one speciall point of their profession, to vse great charitie towards all men in necessitie, he was presentlie illuminated, saith the storie, in his vnderstanding, and enflamed with the loue of God, and of Christian religion, in such sort, that his hart being withall full of ioy, he went a litle aside, and after feruēt praier to almightie God, vowed to become a Christiā, & when that warre was ended, was baptised, and became, a man of great fame, for his miracles, & austerity of monastical

Metaphas. 14. May. Baron. an. 316.

monaſtical life,hauing vnder his gouerment ſeauen thouſand religious diſciples,as *Paladius* teſtifieth. *Pallad. de vita SS. Patrum.c.38.*

32 An other conuerſion no leſſe ſtrange,and admirable,then anie of the former,hapned in Fraunce,by the miniſterie of *S.Bernard*,in *vvilliā* Duke of *Aquitany*,& earle of *Poytou*,a man no leſſe famous for the huge greatnes, ſtrenght, and valour of his perſon,then infamous for his wicked, and vicious life,being giuen ouer to all vice,and wickednes, and a great protectour,and defendour of the Antipope *Peter Leon*, againſt the true pope *Innocentius*,the ſecond. *Theobald. apud Suriū, 10.Febru.*

This duke being excommunicated for his ſchiſme,and great perſecution of good men,was manie times ſolicited by *S.Bernard*,and others, to change his courſe of life, and to reconcile himſelfe to the Church, but all in vaine, for he ſhewed him ſelfe dailie more obſtinate, raging, threatning, and blaſpheming, vntill at length in an aſſembly of the nobilitie,and clergie, *S.Bernard* (moued no doubt by the ſpirit of God) brought the bleſſed ſacrament to him in preſence of all the people, and ſaid, I, and manie other ſeruants of God, haue entreated thee in Gods name,to haue care of thy owne ſoule,& no longer to trouble the vnion, and peace of the Church,and thou haſt contemned vs,and thy owne ſaluation, now, thy Lord, and God himſelfe commeth to entreate thee, behold him heere,the Sonne of the virgin,and the Lord, & head of that Church,which thou perſecuteſt,in whoſe name the knees of all creatures,in heauen,& earth, and hell doe bow,thy Iudge, in whoſe hand,and power thy ſoule is,& euer ſhalbe to be puniſhed,& rewarded eternally, wilt thou then deſpiſe him,as thou haſt deſpiſed his ſeruants? The duke hearing this,trēbled,& fell to the groūd before the Bleſſed Sacramēt: at the feete of *S. Bernard*, and would not ariſe vntil the holy man,bad him ſtand vp to heare his ſentence, which was, that he ſhould ſubmitt himſelfe to the Biſhop of *Poytou* there preſent, whom he had in former time violentlie driuen out of his Church, and that from thenceforth, he ſhould be obedient to *Innocentius* the true pope,and his ſupreame paſtor, which he preſentlie performed, crauing pardon of the Biſhop,and promiſing obedience to pope *Innocentius*, and ſo aboundant was Gods grace in him, that he not onlie preſentlie reformed his wicked life, but alſo ſhortlie after gaue ouer his Dukedome, diſtributed his goods vnto the poore, retired himſelfe from the world, and ſpent the reſt of his dayes in moſt religious, and auſtere penance. He died in the yeare of our Lord, one thouſand one hundreth fiftie ſix. And it pleaſed God to glorifie himſelfe in him by ſo manie notable miracles, both during his life, and after his death, that he was *Bernardus Abbas Boneual. in vita S. Bernardi. Baronius Tom. 12. anno.1135.* *Obijt.an. 1136.*

canonized, and is worthilie honored in the Church as a Sainct.

33 I omit for breuities sake manie wonderfull conuersions,aswell of Infidels,as wicked Christians, to speake of one amongst diuers other wrought by the praiers of *S.Caterin* of *Siena.* There was in that city, a wicked,and desperat yong man called *Nanni di Seruanni*, by profession a souldiar,who had mortall quarrels with diuers for one cause, or other, and being requested as well by them, as by others to make peace, and composition with them, he could by no meanes be induced vnto it, but remained resolute to doe them some mischeefe, as oportunitie should serue, where vppon some good men his freendes, by great importunitie persuaded him onlie to speake with. *S. Caterin of Siena* (who was then liuing in the cittie,and famous for her holie life) by whose meanes they hoped, that God might impart his grace vnto him, but he assured them, that though he went vnto her it should be but in vaine, for he was resolued to be reuenged,and afterwards hauing talked with her to satisfie his friends,he told her, that nothing in the world but the blood of his enimies,should be able to make peace betwixt him, and them, and so would needes depart. Where vppon she being moued with great compassion of his desperate state, eleuated her mind to God,crauing the assistance of his grace,for the yong mans conuersion, which through Gods goodnes, wrought such effect,that he staied vppon a suddaine,as it were amazed & exclaimed saying,o Lord,what is that which tieth,& holdeth me, that I cannot depart?and presentlie fell downe at her feete,and with manie teares promised to doe what soeuer she would haue him. Behould then saith shee,how merciful God is towards you, I spoke to you for your owne good, and you would not giue eare vnto me, I haue spoken to God for you, & he hath heard me, whereby you may see, how much you are bound to his deuine maiestie. And so with manie good lessons she dismissed him verie repentant,and he proued afterwards a verie charitable,and good man.

Raimund. de Capua in vita B. Catar.l.3. c.14.

34 Diuers other suddaine, and miraculous conuersions of great, and greueous sinners,by the praiers of that holie woman,are also witnessed by graue authours,who liued in the same time,which I let passe, to conclude with the relation of the like strange effects of Gods grace in the mutation of mens minds,by the praiers,and endeuours of a holie man in these our daies,to wit father *Ignatius Loyola*, founder of the holie societie of *Iesus*,who whiles he remained in *Rome*, laying the foundation of his societie,had no lesse contradiction therein,then other founders of holie orders haue had heretofore, by the malignitie of the diuel, & especially in the yeare one thousand fiue hundred thirtie eight, at what time, amongst

Ribadeneira in vita B. Ignatij.

amongst diuers other (who by the malice, and practise of euil men were incensed against him) the Cardinal *Domenico de Cuppis*, deane at that time of the colledge of Cardinals, was so farre transported with false reports, that he laboured to alienat from him, and his brethren, one of their greatest benefactors called *Quirinio Garzonio*, in whose house father *Ignatius* lay, but *Quirinio* being often admonished, and solicited by the Cardinal to abãdon the father, beseeched him at last, that he would talke with him, and admit him to his purgation, for such things, as were laied to his chardge; the Cardinal was content he should come, and bad *Quirinio* bring him vnto him, saying that he would handle him, as he deserued. The father came, and was with him two houres in his chamber alone, in which time almightie God wrought such alteration, and change in the Cardinal, that, as he after told himselfe to *Quirinio*, he cast himselfe at the fathers feete, demaunding pardon of God, and him, for the euil opinion he had informer time conceiued of him, & the wrong he had donne him, in reporting euil of him, and in conclusion, ordained presentlie a great almes to be weekelie giuen to him, and his companie, and was euer after during his life, one of their greatest patrons, and protectors.

35 And no lesse force God gaue also to the same fathers words, and perswasions, not onlie for the conuersion of sinners (as may appeare by very many, whom he suddainelie drew to repentance, and change of life) *Idem ibid.* but also in appeasing the troubled consciences of manie in temptation, as (to omit diuers other examples,) was most euident in a Iew called *Isaac*, who being conuerted to the Christian faith, and remaining with other conuertits in the house of the fathers to be instructed, and prepared for Baptisme, had one day such a violent temtation, that he was vpon a suddaine as it were distracted, and out of his wits, crying out to haue the dore opened, that he might be gone, being fully determined, as he said, not to be Baptized, & no request, or perswasion of the other fathers would serue to appease his fury, vntil father *Ignatius* himselfe came, who saying no more to him, but onlie, *Restate con noi Isaac*, Stay with vs *Isaac*, wrought such a change in him (through the operation of the holie Ghost concurring therewith,) that he presentlie returned to his former tranquilitie, and peace of conscience, and after receiued the holie sacrament of Baptisme.

36 These few examples shall suffise to shew the great force, and notable effects of Gods grace, in the suddaine change of mens minds, and mãners, whereby it may appeare, whence proceedeth all the perfection of the moral vertues, consisting in the perfect commaund, and gouerment of mans pasions, and affections, wherto some men attaine sooner, and

ſome latter, according to the meaſure of Gods grace, mouing their wills, and cooperating together with them, in which reſpect the Apoſtle ſaith. *Non ego ſed gratia Dei mecum. Not I but the grace of God vvith me,* whereof I shall haue occaſion to ſpeake more amplie els where.

Cor. 15.

37 Therefore I conclude, that ſeeing the perfection of common welth, dependeth vppon the perfect vertue of the members thereof, and that the perfection of vertue proceedeth onlie from grace, which cannot be had, but by Chriſtian religion, it followeth not onlie, that Chriſtian religion is neceſſarie for common welth, but alſo that no common welth can be perfect without it: which would yet be much more euident, if I should treat particulerlie of the moſt effectual, and excellent meanes, whereby God giueth his grace in Chriſtian religion, to wit of the holie ſacraments, praier, faſting, mortification, pious, and holie workes, whereof I omit to ſpeake here, becauſe I muſt neceſſarilie treat thereof in the third part of this treatiſe.

38 And therefore this shall ſuffiſe for the preſent, touching the neceſſitie of Chriſtian religion in common welth (ſo farr forth, as concerneth the perfection of moral vertues) which was the firſt of the two points, that I promiſed to handle. And now I will come to the other, and proue the dignitie, and neceſſitie of Chriſtian religion in common welth, becauſe the felicitie of man in this life, and conſequentlie of common wealth, conſiſteth therein: which point I hould to be ſo neceſſary, and important for euerie man to know, and well to ponder, that I muſt craue thy patience, good Reader, whiles for thy ſpeciall benefit, I enlarge my ſelfe ſome what in the diſcourſe, and diſcuſion thereof, and of manie notable conſiderations incident thereto.

The neceßitie of Chriſtian religion, for the good gouerment of ſtate is further proued by the end, and felicity of man, and common vvelth, becauſe the ſame cannot be obtained but by Chriſtian religion. And for as much, as it is declared before, that aſvvel the Pagan philoſophers, as our Chriſtian deuines, place the felicity of man, and of common vvelth in contemplation (vvhich is an act of religion,) it is here diſcuſſed vvhat maner of contemplation, the philoſophers required to this felicitie, vvhat practiſe they had of it, vvhat delight they taught to be in it: and laſtlie, vvhat experience they had of that vvhich they taught concerning the ſame.

CHAP. 17.

1. BEing now to shew that the end, and felicitie of man in this life, and of common welth consisteth onlie in Christian religion, I am to put thee in mind, good Reader, of two thinges, which thou must haue obserued before. The one is, that when I treated of religion in general, and of the happines of man consisting therein, I proued my intent by the testimonie, aswell of the ould Philosophers, as of holie Scriptures, and Fathers. The other is, that although *Aristotle*, and *Plato*, with their followers the *Peripateticks*, and *Platoniks*, as also *Trismegistus*, and other philosophers, seemed now and then to dissent in words, concerning the end, and felicitie of man in this life, yet they agreed all in effect, placing the same in the contemplation of God, requiring thereto the loue, and worship of him, with the continual exercise of all vertues, all which concurring, is nothing els but religion. *Chap. 4.*

2 Therefore now, being to applie all that former discourse of religion in generall, to Christian religion in particuler (whereto it serued, but for a preamble) I will prosecute the same course, that before I held, confirming our Christian doctrine, with the testimonies of the philosophers, shewing also, as occasion shalbe offred, how farr they had knowledge of the truth, and in what they erred concerning matter of religion. And for asmuch, as I proued euidentlie in the fourth chapter, that the happines of man in this life, and of common welth, consisteth principallie in the contemplation of God, and seeing also that manie doe not know either what contemplation is, or how it may beatifie man, and common welth, neither yet perhaps doe beleeue, or conceiue, that there is anie such sweetenes or delectation therein, as may make it worthy to be counted felicitie; I hould it necessarie to treat aswell of philosophical, as of Christian contemplation, and to shew wherein they agree, and how they differ, what the philosophers required to theirs, what delectation they taught to be therein, what sight, or knowledge of God, or what vnion with him they had, or could haue by the practise thereof: as also what Christian contemplation is, what is requisit thereto, how notable, and necessarie is the vse and practise of it. Lastlie, how incomparable is the delectation, and benefit thereof, whereby it shall manifestlie appeare, that the onlie true felicitie, which man in this life, and common welth may possiblie obtaine, consisteth therein. In all which discourse,

I hope thou shalt find (good Reader) diuers things, as well for thy instruction, as for thy edification, and euidentlie see the great dignitie, and excellencie, not onlie of Christian contemplation, and religion, but also of a Christian common welth, wherein true Christiā religion florisheth. In which respect, I hould this subsequent discourse of contemplation, most pertinent, and necessarie to this treatise, seing it belongeth no lesse to common welth it selfe, then to religion, and hath not benne treated in our tongue, for ought I know.

3 First then I will speake of philosophical contemplation, which is nothing els, but a knowledge of God, got onlie by humane reason, and discourse, iudging of the cause by the effects, and ascending by creatures, as it were, by degrees, to the consideration, or speculation, of their creator, whose *sempiternal, and inuisible povver and diuinity is* (as the Apostle saith) *vnderstood, and seene, per ea quæ facta sunt, by those thinges vvhich are made.* Whereuppon *Cicero* saith, *quis tam vecors est, qui cum in cælum suspexerit, Deum esse non senserit?* Who is so sencelesse, that beholding the heauens, doth not thereby perceiue, that there is a God? And as there is nothing, which is not partaker of the deuine goodnes, so also there it not anie thing, wherein the same appeareth not some way, or other. Whereuppon *Trismegistus* saith notablie thus. *Deus totius inuidiæ expers* &c. *God being void of all enuy, doth shyne, and shevv himselfe euerie vvhere, in euerie litle part, or particle of the vvorld, and doth manifest himselfe vnto vs, that vve may not onlie vnderstand him, but also, as I may say, handle him vvith our handes, for his image, doth on euery side present, offer, yea and inculcat it selfe into our eyes.* Thus saith he.

Rom.1.
Cicero de Aruspic. responsis.
Mercurius Trismeg. in Piman. c.5.

4 But for as much as all naturall, and philosophical contemplation of God, is grounded vppon a weake foundation, the same must needes also be weake in it selfe. For the knowledge of God, which is had onlie by his creatures, and all the reach of natural reason, whē it is void of grace, is subiect to so manie ambiguities, doubts, and difficulties, that it is also accompanied with obscuritie, and vncertantie, as may appeare, by the infinit errours of the philosophers, and their dissensions, touching God, about whome they held no lesse then three hundreth seueral opinions, agreeing all in this, that there is a God of infinit wisdome, power, and goodnes, and differing almost in all other things concerning the deuine nature.

Socrat. eccl. Hist. li.4. cap.27.

5 Therefore the more weake, and vncertaine is the knowledge of God, the weaker also and more vncertaine must needes be the effects, that it produceth. For whome we know lesse, him we loue lesse, and whome we loue lesse, him also we worshipp with lesse reuerence, and affection: whereuppon it followeth, that all philosophicall contemplation and religion,

religion,being built vppon ſuch weake,and feeble groundes, is conſequentlie it ſelfe,ſubiect to great weaknes,and imperfections.

6 Neuertheleſſe ſuch was the delectation,that the philoſophers partly found in the contemplation of God,and partlie ſaw by reaſon muſt neecdes follow of it, that they worthilie held it for the greateſt felicity of man in this life; as shall further appeare after a while, when I shall firſt haue ſignified the meanes which they vſed,to attaine to the perfection thereof.

7 Firſt then,they conſidered a ſubordination of all thinges, in heauen, and earth,whereby they aſcended,as it were by degrees, from the loweſt to the higheſt,and ſo to their Author,and Creator,whoſe infinit,and incomprehenſible wiſdome,power,and goodnes,they noted in the admirable order,diſpoſition,conuexion,conueniencie,beautie,vtilitie,operation,multitude,magnitude,and infinit diuerſitie of his creatures, ſome corporall, other ſpirituall,ſome terreſtiall,others cæleſtiall, ſome ſenceles,others ſenſitiue,ſome onlie vegetable,others reaſonable, and finallie others purelie intellectual; in all which, they noted different degrees of perfection,and yet that the moſt perfect,was in ſome degree vnperfect, as hauing motion,multiplicitie,and a participation, and dependance of a ſupreame and moſt perfect eſſence: and therefore by the orderlie motiō of the heauens,and all creatures,they conſidered the omnipotencie, and wiſdome of a firſt mouer,and Creator,by their multiplicitie,his vnitie, by their participation and dependance,his ſimple,independant,and eternal eſſence,by their goodnes his bountie,by their beautie and excellent properties,the infinit,and ſuperminent excellencie of his perfections,according to the axiome of *Ariſtotle. Quod eſt cauſa alijs vt alia ſint, ipſum eſt maxime tale.*

Mercurius Triſmeg. in Pimandro ca. 5.

Proclus. de anima & dæmone.

Ariſtotle Metaph. l. 2.

8 Theſe conſiderations were common to all the Philoſophers, and though for the moſt part,they tended to nothing els thereby, but onlie to the knowledge of God,the author of nature,yet ſome of them (who were more contemplatiue then the reſt) extended the ſame further, drawing from thence reaſons,and motiues,to incite them ſelues to the loue of God,whereby they might be vnited with him, and therefore *Plato* teacheth in his *Epinomis*,that the office,or part of a philoſopher,and wiſe man,is to conſider Gods workes in the world,to the end, that finding out the deuine reaſon thereof, he may be kindled and inflamed, with the loue of their author,and conſequentlie may worship and ſerue him,and ſo come to enioy him,firſt in this life,and after in the next (as I haue declared before more amplie in the ſecond, and third chapter:) and to this end,he amply proueth in *Parmenides*, the neceſsitie of one beginninge,

Plato in Epinomide.

Idem in Parmenide.

beginninge, by the multiplicitie of creatures, according to the like consequence of the necessitie of an vnitie in *Arithmetick*, concluding, that as there could be no number, if there were not a vnitie (which is the beginning of number) so there could not be manie things, and creatures in the world (as we see there are) if there were not one beginninge, from whence they were produced.

9 To the same end also he, and his followers teach their contemplatiues, to eleuat their mindes to the speculation of the deuine nature, by the cõsideration of musicke, wherein they proceeded from the sensible harmonie, consisting in sound, to the intellectuall, and from thence to the authour, and fountaine of all conueniencie, harmonie, and delectation.

Proclus de anima & dæmone.

10 Also from the beautie of the bodie, they passed to the consideration of the beautie of manners, from thence to the beautie of the sciences, & then to the beautie of the mind, or soule, and from thẽce to the contemplation of beautie it selfe, which is God.

Idem ibid. Plato in Cõuiuio vide Comment. Marsil Ficini in Conuiui. orat. 6. c. 18.

11 And in like maner they vsed to the same end, the helpe of the sciences, and especiallie of the *Mathematikes*, and *Metaphisick*, whereof the first doe accustome the vnderstanding of man, to abstract it selfe from corporall thinges, and consequentlie dispose it to the speculation of the intellectual and deuine, and the latter, to wit *Metaphisicke*, leadeth directlie to the contemplation of God. Therefore *Plato* hauing taught that the foundation of all true happines, is wisdome, pietie, and vertue, and that the speculatiue sciences, are also most necessarie to the perfection of wisdome, addeth, that except those sciences, being diuers, and manie, be referred to one deuine end (that is to say, to the knowledge of God) they are but vaine and friuolous, but being referred thereto, they are thereby connected, and vnited amongst them selues, and helpe to raise the mind of him, that possesseth them, to the contemplation of God, and to that vnion with him, wherein consisteth the happines of man in this life.

Idem ibid. Proclus vbi supra.

Plato in Epinomide.

12 And to omit some other pointes (for it were to no purpose to lay downe all) they taught a numerical meditation, to ascend to the onlie one, and true vnitie, by certaine degrees of numbers, whereof some were called, *sonantes numeri*, some, *occursores*, some *progressores*, others *sensuales*, others *memoriales*, other *iudiciales*, and some *artificiales*, which I forbeare to explicat, as conteining matter of more curiositie then profit. Neuertheles, he that desireth to see more thereof, may read *S. Augustin*, in his booke de *Musica*, where following the doctrin of the *Platoniks*, he treateth amplie of all these differences of numbers, and of the vse thereof.

Aug. li. 6. de musica.

13 To conclude, all these contemplatiue philosophers, thaught vniformelie two other points, most necessarie to attaine to the perfection of contempla-

contemplation. The one was, to transcend at last all corporall things, & other creatures whatsoeuer, clearing the vnderstanding of all imaginations, and phantasies, to the end, it might contemplat God, whom they called, *Bonum per se, pulchrum per se, & ipsum vnum. Goodnes it selfe, beautie it selfe, and the only one*, being such a simple, pure, and perfect essence, that no conceit, imagination, or phantasie, can be framed of him.

Plotinus Enneadis 5. li. 6 c. 11. Mercur. Trismegis. in Pimandro ca. 4. & 5. Plato in Timeo in Conuiuio, Hippia, Phadro & parmenide.

14 The other point, which they thought absolutelie necessarie to the perfection of cōtemplatiō, was a singular *a* puritie of hart, & sincerity of conscience, whereto *Trismegistus* addeth the *hate of our owne body, & a most pure loue of God, for it is impossible*, saith he, *to attend to both at once*, such being the difference betwixt thinges corporal, and spirituall, mortall, and immortal, humane, and deuine, *that he which adhereth to the one, looseth the other.* Thus saith *Mercurius*, who also representeth the same vnto vs, with a most pathetical exhortation, which I thinke good to sett downe in his owne wordes, for they are notable to this purpose, and verie admirable, the author considered.

Plotin. Ennead. 6. li. 7.
a Porphir. de abstinentia animalium.
Mercur. Tris. in Piman. ca. 4.

15 *Quo ruitis*, saith he, *mortales ebrij*? &c. Wither doe you runne, or fall headlong, you drunken mortall men, who haue drunke vp the wine of ignorance? Seing your heads are not able to beare it, cast it vp againe, » become sober, and behould with the eyes of your soules, and if you » cannot all of you doe it, yet doe it at least so manie of you as may. » The plague of ignorance ouerthroweth all earthlie men, it corrupteth » the soule, which is shut vp in the prison of the bodie, and doth not » suffer it to take the way of saluation: suffer not your selues, to be drowned in the lake of corruption, and death, breath a while, and runne » to the fountaine of life, that is to say, to God, who will lead you into » the secrets of his temple of truth, where shineth cleare light, without » anie mixture of darkenes, where none that entreth doteth with dronkennes but are all sober and awake, and with the sharpe sight of their » soules see him, who wilbe seene, & can neither be heard with eares, nor » seene with bodilie eyes, nor expressed with speech, but you must first cast » of the garment, which you carrie about you, and is nothing els, but a » garment of ignorance, a foundation of wickednes, a bond of corruption, a liuing death, a sensitiue carkas, a mouing sepulcher, a domesticall theefe, which while it flattereth you, both enuieth, and hateth you, for such an enemie, is the shadowed veile wherewith you » are compassed and couered, which draweth you downe to it selfe, least » perhaps you might come to hate it, and perceiue the deceits of it, if » you should cast vp your eyes to see the comlines of truth, and the true » good, which is neere you, and therefore it dulleth, and darkeneth »

Mercur. Trismeg. in piman. ca. 7.

the light of the interiour senses, making them drunke with an abominable, and fastidious delight; to the end you may neuer heare, or see those thinges, which are worthy to be heard, and principallie to be seene.

16 Thus farre *Mercurius Trismegistus*, exaggerating the impediment which the soule receiueth in contemplation, by the bodie; In which respect other philosophers also call the bodie, *pestem animæ, the plague of the soule*, and compare the mind of a carnal, and passionat man, to a heauie, and grosse vapour, which cannot eleuat it selfe, vntill it be purified. And *Socrates*, *Plato*, and all their followers, whose doctrin tended cheeflie to contemplation, as the perfection, and consummation of philosophie, taught principallie the correction of manners, and suppression of passions, for that God cannot be perfectlie knowne, or contemplated, but by pure, and cleane mindes, purged from all filth of earthlie, and carnal affections, to which purpose *Plato* saith, that the soule of man being defiled with sinne, is no more capable of true wisdome (which he held principallie to consist in the knowledge, and contemplation of God) then the aire being obscured with clouds, is capable of the light of the sunne, as I signified, vppon an other occasion, in the first part of this treatise.

Plutar. in Catone & in Romulo. Aug. de ciuit. dei. li. 8. *c.* 3. *Porphyrius de abstinentia animalium. Plato in Theagene. & in ep. ad Syracusanos.* Chap. 28. nu. 6.

17 And further he affirmeth, that the felicitie of man, which may be had in this life, cannot be obtained, but by those onlie, *vvhich are in the bodie, as it vvere out of the bodie*, and liue to God rather then to themselues; in which respect also the *Pithagorians*, and some *Platonicks*, namelie *Porphirius*, prescribed to those which aspired to perfect cõtemplation, a stricke abstinence, and frequent fasts from meates and drinkes, to the end, that the bodie being extenuated, and weakened, the soule might more clearelie speculat, and the more easelie abstract it selfe from the bodie, which is the special office of a philosopher; Wherevppon, *Cicero*, calleth the philosophers life, *Mortis commentationem, the meditation of death, for vvhen a man*, saith he, *doth vse to vvithdravv, and abstract his mind* or vnderstanding, *from his body, and sences* (as philosophers doe) *vvhat doth he els, but learne and accustome himselfe to die.*

Plato in phædro. phædone, & rep. vide argument. Marsilij Ficini in Epinomidem. Porphiri de abstinentia animal. Cicero Tuscul. q. li. 1.

18 *Iamblicus* and *Proclus*, require in a contemplatiue man fiue thinges, which serued as it were, for as manie stepps, and degrees, to mount vp to the perfection of philosophical cõtemplation; the first is, the knowledge of God, and of his deuine nature, and proprieties; the second, a conformitie to almightie God, in puritie, and sanctitie of life: the third, an earnest endeuour, and eleuation of the mind, aspiring to the contemplation of him, and of heauenlie thinges; the fourth, the influence of the deuine light into the soule, to dispose, and enable it, to know, and contemplat his deuine nature; the fift, and last is, an vnion, and coniunction of the soule

Iambli. de mister. Ægip. vide Marsilium Ficin. in Compendio in Timæum. ca. 6. ex mente Iamblici & Procli.

soule with God, whereby it shall receiue true happines.

19 Furthermore they teach, that by the frequentation, and continual vse of this contemplation, our cogitations, and actions, shalbe reformed, our vnderstanding purified, and perfected, our soules purged from the corruption that they contract of the bodie, the loue of God encreased in vs, we made capable, and partakers of the deuine light, and become not onlie disciples of God, but also his familiar freinds, and lastlie, that we shalbe no longer our owne, but his, and being abstracted from the loue of all other things, shall remaine wholie rauished, and absorpt in his deuine light.

Iamblic. in mister. Ægipt. vide etiam Marsil. Ficin. vbi supra.

20 Thus teach *Iamblicus* and *Proclus* in substance, concerning not onlie the contemplation, but also the fruition of God, euen in this life, whereof *Plotinus*, yealdeth this reason. Forasmuch as God is both the beginninge, and the end of all creatures, and the cheefe obiect of our loue (in respect that he is the cheefe good) our desire cannot naturallie rest, or be satisfied, but onlie in him: and as our appetite, and desire is euer naturally moued, and inclined to our cheefe good, so also it is requisit, that we may attaine thereto (for other waies our inclination were vaine) yea, & that we may haue a natural fruition of it, that is to say, that we may enioy it, not onlie in imagination, or by knowledge, but in deede, not by an external application, or touching, but by such an intrinsecal coniunction, & vnion, that we may be made all one with it, whereof wee see, saith he, the like experience in our bodie, and senses, which desiring naturallie conseruation by the meanes of meates, and corporal sustenaunce, are cōserued not onlie by a real, and perfect coniunction of meate with the bodie, but also by the conuersion thereof into the substance of the bodie. Thus discourseth *Plotinus*, to shew that our fruition of God (who is our end, and cheefe good) consisteth in a real, and perfect vnion with him, which shalbe further declared, and explicated, when I shall treate of Christian contemplation.

Plotinus li. 9. Enneadis 6. de bono vel vno c. 9.

21 And now for the present to returne to *Iamblicus*, I wish it to be noted, that he requireth to contemplation, in the place before alleadged, the influence of a deuine light, that is to say, Gods grace, to dispose, and enable the soule of man, to contemplat the diuine nature, which seemeth also to haue beene the opinion of *Plato*, and all his followers, teaching that adoration, sacrifice, praier, and other acts of religion, are necessarie to the acquisition of the cheefe good, besides that, *S. Augustin* gathereth out of *Porphirie* (who was a platonick (that he acknowledged the necessitie of Gods grace, to the knowledge, and contemplation of God.

Marsil. Ficin. ex mēte Plotini. li. 9. Ennead. 6. de bono. c. 9. Aug. l. 10. de ciuit. dei. c. 29.

22 But of all other philosophers, *Mercurius Trismegistus*, teacheth it most expresselie, adding also thereto, the necessitie of praier, to obtaine the same, saying notably thus. *Vnicum id ingenitum incomprehensibile, phantasia* &c. That which is the onlie vnbegotten, & vncreated (that is to say God) is incomprehensible to the phantasie of man, and as all things haue their beautie, and light from him, so he also sheweth himselfe, and shineth in all thinges, and appeareth speciallie to those, to whome it pleaseth him to communicat the knowledge of himselfe, and therefore (my sonne *Tatius*) pray thou deuoutelie to our Lord, and Father, that thou maist be worthie of his mercie, for so shalt thou be able to know, and vnderstand him, if some beame of his light, shine vppon thy vnderstanding. Thus saith he, whereby we may perceiue, that besides the knowledge of God, by the meanes of his creatures, and the puritie of mind, and conscience (which all philosophers held most requisit, & necessarie to cõtẽplatiõ) some of them acknowledge, & taught expresselie, the necessitie of Gods grace, and of mans humble, and deuout praier to obtaine it.

Mercur in Piman. c. 5.

23 And now to say some what, of the great delectatiõ, & ioy, which they held to be in the vse, & exercise of it, I will content my selfe with the testimonie of two, or three of them: as first of *Mercurius*, who discourseth verie strangelie thereof in this manner. You are not (saith he) to thinke, that the sight or vision of the true good, that is to say of God, doth like the sunne beames corrupt, or blind the eyes of the behoulders, but that it cleareth, and illuminateth them, with a farr greater measure of light, according to the capacitie that euerie one may haue, to receiue the influence of that intelligible splendor. Those who being yet in their bodies, haue any plentiful participation thereof, are oft times cast, as it were, into a slepe, by the excessiue beautie of that which they see, as were *Cælius*, and *Saturnus*, our progenitours &c. The true knowledge thereof consisteth in a deuine silence, or quietnes, and an earnest, or vehement application thereto of all our powers and parts: he which vnderstandeth it, can thinke of nothing els, he which behouldeth it, can see nothing but it, he which heareth it, can heare nothing after it, nor moue the members, or parts of his bodie, but is, as it were, loosed, and dissolued from his senses, and all affections, for he which giueth light to all thinges els, doth fullie irradiat, and illustrat the mind, and abstracteth the soule from the bodie, and transformeth it whollie into the essence of God, for it is not possible, that the soule lying in the dreggs of the bodie, should take vppon it the deuine forme, neither can anie man see the beautie of God, except he be first reformed vnto God.

Mercur. in Piman. c. 10.

24 Thus farre *Mercurius*, more like a contemplatiue Christian deuine, then a

then a Pagan philosopher : who also affirmeth els where, that he which in contemplation shall arriue to the sight of the infinit good (which is God) will despise all bodilie, and earthlie thinges, and thinke this life which we liue here, to be miserie. But how true that is like to be, which he affirmeth of *Cælius* and *Saturnus* (to wit that they saw God in their rapts) or what sight of him, or vnion with him these philosophers had, or might haue, in their contemplations, I will declare after that I shall haue added, a testimonie or two more of the philosophers, concerning the exceeding delectation, which they taught to be in contemplation. *Ibid. c. 4.*

25 *Plato* hauing declared, how a man may ascend from the speculation of one faire, and beautiful thing, to an other, and then to other more beautifull, and by degrees, to the contemplation of beautie it selfe, addeth that when he shall come to behold that pure, and simple beautie, he will esteeme all gold, rich apparel, and corporal beautie, to be but trash, and concludeth, that therefore the life of the contemplatiue man is admirable, and happie, and that he is partaker of solyd, and true vertue, beloued of God, and immortal, if anie man in this life may so be called. *Plato in conuiuio. vide Cõmentar. Marsil. Ficini in conuiuium Platonis ca. 18. orat. 6.*

26 To *Plato*, I will onlie add one of his followers, to wit *Plotinus*, by whome we may perceiue the doctrine of the rest, he therefore treating of the onlie one, and true good, teacheth, that by the contemplation thereof, the soule is translated, and turned into a deuine nature, and made God, being wholie Gods, and made one with him : And of what infinit delight the same is, he also signifieth, saying : *Id igitur quisquis videt* &c. Whosoeuer, saith he, seeth it (that is to say true goodnes, and beautie) how wonderful is the loue wherewith he is inflamed? how great the desire he hath, to be ioyned, and vnited with it? how admirable is his delight? seing nature hath so ordained, that he which doth not yet see it, doth desire it, as the true good, and he which seeth it, is infinitelie delighted with it, as with true beautie, being replenished with ioy, and contentment, astonished with a pleasant, and holsome stupiditie, affected with a true, and extreame loue, and therefore, he scorneth, all other loues, and affections, and contemneth all other beauties, enioying true beautie it selfe, which makes her louers trulie faire, and louelie, *quam quisquis assequitur, euadit felici visione beatus* &c. Which whosoeuer obtaineth, he is blessed with a happie, vision, or light, as on the other side, he is most miserable, that looseth it, for the onlie gaine whereof, all the kingdomes, and empires of the world ought to be reiected. *Plotin. li. [illegible] Ennead. 6. de bono, vel vno c. 9. & 10.* *Idem li. de pulchritudine c. 7.*

27 Thus farre *Plotinus*, with much more excellent matter to the same purpose; Whereby we may see, what was the iudgement, and doctrine of the philosophers, concerning mans felicitie in this life, consisting as they taught, in his vnion with God, by the meanes of contemplation. And yet neuertheles it is not to be thought (as before I haue said) that they had the practise, and experience, of all that which they wrote: for although they might by the light of reason know, that God is of such

Plato in cōuiuio. infinit goodnes, beautie, and perfection, that he is, as *Plato* saith, to be beloued, *amore infinito, & sine modo, & termino*, *vvith an infinit loue, & vvithout measure, or limit*, and that man being his image, and ordained to serue him, and capable of his knowledge and loue, might euen in this life, be thereby vnited with him, and consequentlie enioy true contentment, & pleasure: yet it was not possible, that by anie force of nature, and light of reason, they should arriue to anie other vision of him, then speculatiue, such I meane, as they might haue of the nature of the heauens, or of the Angels, by onlie speculation, without anie supernaturall vnion with him, or sight of him, which could not be had without grace.

S. Chrisost. ho. 5. de incomprehensibili natura Dei. *S. Greg. Nazianz. orat. 42 quæ est 2. in pascha.*

28 Therefore, whereas some of the philosophers held, that man may see God, by the force of humane nature (against whom both *S. Chrisostome*, and *S. Gregory Nazianzen* did write notably,) and some others againe, taught the necessitie of grace, to the vision of God, and vnion with him, as may appeare by that, which I haue alleadged out of *Mercurius Trismegistus*, & the *Platonicks*, I wish it here to be vnderstood, that when I speake of philosophical contemplation, I meane not a contemplation of God, assisted and perfited by his grace (for so the contemplation of the philosophers and of the Christians, may be all one) but I meane a contemplation, restrained within the boundes, and limits of nature onlie, and of humane vnderstanding: For it is not to be denied, or doubted, but that manie amongst the Gentils, and consequentlie some philosophers, might haue the helpe and assistance of Gods grace, aswell for the better, and more cleare contemplation of God, as also for their saluation, seeing we read in holie scriptures, that *Iob*, and his three friendes, being Gentils, before the law of *Moyses*, were not onlie greate seruantes of God, but also

Dionys. Cælesti Hierar. ca. 9. great philosophers, as I may tearme them, and deuines. And *S. Dionisius Areopagita* witnesseth, that manie amongst the Gentils were induced, & brought, to the true knowledge of God, by the ministerie of Angels, which he exemplifieth in *Melchisedech* king of *Salem*, whose priesthood, prefigured the priesthood of our Sauiour.

29 Therefore, that which I affirme of the philosophers, and their contemplation, is, that neither these, whose testimonies I haue here produced, (to

ced (to wit *Triſmegiſtus*, *Plato* and the *Platonicks* his followers,) did euer arriue to that vnion with God, or that happie ſight of him, wherof they write, neither could anie other, by the onlie force of nature attaine thereto, it being euident, as *S. Thomas* ſaith, that whoſoeuer is raiſed, and eleuated, to anie thing exceeding the nature thereof, muſt be firſt diſpoſed thereto by ſome ſupernatural diſpoſition, in which reſpect, he alſo teacheth, that no man can ſee God, but he muſt be firſt diſpoſed thereto, either by the light of glorie (as are the glorified ſoules in heauen) or by the light of grace, whereby a farr more liuelie repreſentation, and ſimilitude of God, may be framed in the vnderſtanding and conceit of man, then can poſſiblelie be framed by nature. *S.Tho.1 p.q. 12 ar.5 in Cor.*

30 To which purpoſe it is to be vnderſtood, that the ſoule of man, whiles it is in the bodie, can not ſee, or vnderſtand anie thing though preſēt, but by the meanes of ſome kind of image, or ſimilitude repreſented (as *Ariſtotle* teacheth) partlie by the ſenſes, and partlie by the matter it ſelfe, neither yet can it haue anie vnderſtanding, or conceit of a thing abſent, and vnknowne, but by ſome kind of shape, or image, framed in like maner, in the imagination, and taken from ſome thinges, ſeene, or knowne before which neuertheles, how vnlike they are to the thinges themſelues, it plainlie appeareth, when a man commeth to ſee that, which before he conceiued, and imagined: wherevppon it muſt needes follow, that ſeeing almightie God, is a moſt pure, and ſimple eſſence, voyd of all matter, and ſo farr ſurpaſſing all capacitie of man, that not ſo much as anie true opinion, conceit, or imagination, can naturallie be framed of him (as I haue ſufficientlie declared before) it is not poſſible, that man should haue anie viſion, or perfect knowledge of him in this life, except he be diſpoſed thereto, by ſome ſupernatural light. In which reſpect, the Apoſtle ſaith of God, that *habitat lucem inacceßibilem, quem nullus hominum vidit, ſed neque videre poteſt. He dvvelleth in an inacceßible light, vvhome no man hath euer ſeene, nor yet can ſee*, that is to ſay, by the force of nature. And the *Pſalmiſt* alſo ſaith, to the ſame purpoſe, *vvith thee o Lord, is the fountaine of life, and in thy light vve shall ſee light.* And laſtlie *S. Iohn*, ſpeaking of the ſocietie of the bleſſed, or glorified ſoules in heauen, ſaith. *Charitas Dei illuminabit illam*, the clearenes or brightnes of God shall illuminat, or enlighten it. *Ariſt.3 de anima.* *1.Tim. 6.* *Pſalm. 35.* *Apoc.c. 21.*

31 Yt cannot therefore be imagined with anie reaſon, that anie Pagan, or Gentil, could by the force of philoſophical contemplation, and by the light of reaſon, haue anie viſion of God, and much leſſe ſuch a perfect vnion with him, as the philoſophers aboue named treat of, and require to the felicitie of man in this life, of whome I may alſo boldlie affirme, that

that they neuer arriued thereto, either by the light of reasō, or by grace; seeing it is manifest, that they were all of them wicked men, whereas, not onlie our deuines, but also they themselues teach, that puritie of mind, and conscience, is absolutelie necessarie to the vision of God, and vnion with him, and therefore our Sauiour said. *Beati mundo corde, quoniam ipsi Deum videbunt. Happie are those vvho are cleane and pure of hart, for they shall see God,* and all the most learned philosophers, aswell *Peripateticks*, and *Stoicks*, as *Platonicks*, require integritie of life, and perfection of vertue, to the felicitie of man, as I haue declared before, besides that I haue signified at large, in the first part of this treatise, how vicious, and wicked both *Aristotle*, and *Plato* were, and generallie all the philosophers, not withstanding their profession of vertue, & the excellent precepts which they gaue thereof, it being also manifest, that they were all of them impious Idolaters, as appeareth no lesse in *Trismegistus*, then in all the other, whose workes we haue at this day: where vpon it followeth, that they were most abominable in the sight of God, and no way participant, of anie vision of him, or vnion with him, which is the greatest reward, and blessing that he bestoweth vppon his dearest seruants, and best beloued friends.

Matth. 5. *Chap. 28. num. 6. & 7. Chap. 10. per totum.*

32 But then perhaps you will aske me, how these philosophers came to know, and treate of rapts, and of the great delectation of contemplation, in such sort as they doe. Whereto I answer, first concerning rapts, that I doe not hold it impossible, or improbable, that they might haue some kind of extasis, or rauishment of mind, in the exercise of their contemplation, seeing that experience teacheth, that the speculatiō of some liberal science, may so occupie the vnderstanding of a man, that his senses, and inferiour powers, may remaine tied, and bound for the time, in such sort, that they cannot execute their functions, and in the meane while, the mind be replenished with delight.

33 This was euident in *Archimedes*, the great geometrician, who was so transported with the delectation of his science, that commonlie he forgot to eate, or drinke, except when he was put in mind thereof, or sometimes compelled thereto, and therefore being other whiles caried by his seruants by force to the bathes, to be annointed, and washed (as the vse then was) he occupied himselfe in nothing els, whiles he was in the bath, but in drawinge geometrical figures with his finger, in the oyle that was vppon his bodie. And finallie the citie of *Syracusa*, where he dwelled, being surprised by *Marcellius* the *Roman*, he was so attentiue to the triall of certaine geometrical conclusions, at the sea side, in the sand, that he was not aware of the surprise of the towne, till at last he was found

Plutar. in Marcello.

found by a souldiar, and commaunded to come to *Marcellus*, but he so litle regarded what was sayd vnto him, that the souldiar thought himselfe, and his generall to be contemned by him, and in a rage killed him, wherewith *Marcellus* was greatlie greeued, for the great fame he had heard of him, and the experience he had also seene of his skill, by his admirable engines, wherewith the towne had benne a long time defended against the Roman armie.

34 But much more meruellous is that, which *S. Augustin* recounteth of a priest called *Restitutas*, who could so recollect his mind, and vnderstanding, and sequester it from his senses, when he listed, that he remained as it were dead, not onlie without motion, and breath, but also without sense, or feeling of pricking, or burning, or anie other violēce donne vnto him, & yet neuertheles, he could (as he said) heare the voice of men, when they spoke to him aloude, though it seemed a farr of. And the like also *Cardanus* reporteth of himselfe, who saith, that when he listed seriouslie to contemplat of anie difficult point of philosophie, or other learning, he could cast himselfe into a traunce, and that although then his bodie was senseles, yet his mind did speculat, & find out great secrets of nature, and this he said he vsed often to doe, to auoid the paine of the goute, whereto he was much subiect; and that during his extasis, or traunce, he had no feeling thereof, nor of anie thing els, that was donne vnto him.

Augustin. de ciuit. dei. li. 14. ca. 24.

Cardanus de varietate

35 Whereby it may appeare, how great may be the force of contemplation, and that it may withhould, and diuert the vnderstanding of mā, from all communication with the senses: the reason whereof is, for that the vitall spirits doe wholie retire themselues, to the inferiour powers of the soule, weakened by the diuersion of the vnderstāding from them, such being the propertie of nature, to draw aswell the spirits, as the humors of the bodie to the succour of the weakest, and most affected partes, as we see in those, which are suddainelie taken with some extreame feare, whose face groweth pale, and bodie trembleth, because the spirits and blood, doe retire from the exteriour parts, to strenghten the hart, that laboureth, and is distressed.

36 And this retrait of the spirits, to the inward parts, and the alienation thereof from the senses, commōlie happeneth, when mans vnderstāding fixeth it selfe vppon some high, and mistical matter, that moueth him to admiration, and especiallie, when his will, and affection, is also moued with some extraordinarie, & exceeding delight, as it may be obserued in the musick, which *Aristotle* calleth *Enthusiasticam*, vsed by the priests of *Iupiter Olimpicus*, in their sacrifices, wherewith the hearers were so

Aristot. Politic. li. 8. c. 5.

rauished, that they loſt the vſe of their ſenſes, and remained in a trance for ſome time.

37 Therefore,ſeeing there is nothing which may either more occupy, and aſtonish the vnderſtãding,or potentlie moue the affection of a well diſpoſed mind,then the contemplation of God,whom (as the philoſophers confeſſed,and taught)neither the vnderſtanding can comprehend, nor the affection ſufficientlie loue,of whom there cannot be framed naturallie,ſo much as an opinion,conceit,or imagination as he is in himſelfe,(who though he be all in all,yet is nothing of all that, which we either know,or can conceiue)it is no maruaile, if the contemplator of ſuch an infinit maieſtie,and incomprehenſible bountie,and beautie, not being able to penetrat the leaſt of his deuine perfections, remaine ſuſpended in the ſpeculation thereof.

38 And thus farre the contemplation of thoſe philoſophers,whoſe authorities I haue alleadged,might extend,though (as I haue ſaid) it is not probable,that they had,or could haue,anie ſuch viſion,or ſight of God, or ſuch vnion with him, as they pretended, whereof neuertheles they might ſpeake,or write probablie,and trulie,partlie by reaſon of the traditions,that remained from time to time of the doctrin, and extatical contemplations,of the ould patriarkes and prophets,and of manie other faithful ſeruants of God amongſt the Gentils, and partlie by the knowledge,which manie of them had of the ſcriptures,of the ould teſtament (as S. *Auguſtin* affirmeth of *Plato*, concerning manie pointes of his doctrin agreeing with ours:)beſides that all the latter philoſophers ſince Chriſts time, eſpeciallie the *Platonicks*,had the ſight,not onlie of the old, and new teſtament, but alſo of the writings of the firſt Fathers of the primitiue Church,by the which they learned manie things,aſwel concerning the deuine nature, as other miſteries of our Chriſtian faith, and ſo came to writ farre more excellentlie of contemplation, then their predeceſſors.

S. Aug. de ciuit. Dei li. 8. ca. 11.

39 This hath bene notablie well obſerued, and acknowledged, by a great *Platonick* in the laſt age,to wit, *Marſilius Ficinus*, who ſaith thus. *Ego certo reperi* &c. *Truly I haue found,that the cheefe miſteries in Numenius, Philo, Plotinus,Iamblicus,*and *Proclus,vvere taken by them out of S.Iohns goſpel,S.Paule, Hierotheus,and Dioniſius Areopagita,for vvhatſoeuer they vvrite magnificentlie of God,the Angels,and other thinges,belonging to Theologie, they manifeſtlie vſurped,and tooke from them.* Thus ſaith he.

Marſil. Ficin. li. de religione Chriſtiana. c.22.

40 Finallie,it is alſo verie probable,that almightie God, did illuminat their vnderſtanding in manie thinges, for the inſtruction, and good of others,and to ſerue for ſome diſpoſition of the Gentils to Chriſtianitie, for

for which cause he also inspired the *a Sibilla*, and *b Balam* the gentil, with the spirit of prophesie.

a *S. Aug. de ciuita. Dei. li. 18. ca. 23.*
b *Num. 22. & 23.*

41 Therefore vppon this precedent discourse, I conclude three thinges, concerninge philosophical contemplation, and the philosophers themselues. The first is, that so long as philosophical contemplation, doth not exceede the limits of nature, though it may cause some extasis, or rauishment of mind, yet it cannot bring a man to anie certaine, and perfect knowledge of God, and much lesse to anie vision of him, or vnion with him. Secondlie, that although some philosophers amongst the Gentils, might by the exercise thereof, and with the concurrence of Gods grace, haue some supernatural vision, and knowledge of God, and be most happilie vnited with him in this life, yea, and finallie be saued, yet none of these, whose authoritie I haue here alleadged, and whose workes are now extant, did euer attaine to either of both, being all of them wicked men, and therefore farre from all vnion with God, or vision of him: wherevppon also it followeth, that they neuer had the experience of that which they wrote, of the admirable delight, that the contemplation of God yealdeth, but that they knew it, either by tradition from others, or by reading our holie Scriptures, or other Christian authors, or els by discourse of reason, by the which it is euident ynough, that the contemplation of God, must needes produce such effects, whensoeuer it is had in perfection, as in like sort also, *Plato* and the *Platonicks* taught expressely our Christian doctrin, concerning the felicitie of man, (to wit, that it is imperfect in this life, and shalbe consumated, and perfited in the next) though they themselues neuer had, nor could haue anie experience thereof.

Plato in Epinomide. Porphyrius Plotinus. Iamblicus. Proclus.

42 Thirdlie, whereas *Mercurius Trismegistus*, writeth of *Cælius*, and *Saturnus*, that they saw God in their rapts (as I haue signified before) it is to be vnderstood, that either he fained it, to authorize his doctrin, or els that liuing in *Ægipt* (where the memorie, as well of the rapts of the people of God, during their captiuitie there, as also of manie points of their doctrin, might still remaine) he ascribed the same to *Saturnus*, and *Cælius*, of whose diuinitie he, and the superstitious people of that time, had a conceit, and beleefe, especiallie seeing their custome was, to celebrat the famous acts of Gods seruants, vnder the names of their false Gods.

Nu. 23.

43 For, so we reade, that they called *Noe*, *Ianus*, painting him with two faces, the one looking backward, and the other forward, because he had seene, as it were, two worlds, the one before the flood, & the other after. And in like manner the *Ægiptians*, honored *Moyses* for a God, vnder the

Genebrard chron.

[Eu]seb. de præpar. Euang. li. 4. c.9. *Act. c.4.* *Clem. Alexand. li.6. stromatum. ca.1.* *D. Basil. in orat. super Euang. in principio erat verbum.*

name of *Mercury*, as *Artapanus*, an ancient greeke historiographer doth testifie. And we read also in the Acts of the Apostles, that the people of *Lystra*, seeing the miracles of *S. Paule*, and *S. Barnabas*, called the one *Mercury*, and the other *Iupiter*, and would haue done sacrifice vnto them. And *Clemens Alexandrinus* sheweth by manie examples, that the gentils did not onlie steale from the patriarks, and prophets, manie notable points of doctrin, but also transferred manie of their miraculous workes to themselues, disguising them with the addition of diuers fabulous circumstances, wherevppon also *S. Basil* saith. *Furatur nostra diabolus, & suis ea largiri conatur. The diuel doth steale from vs those thinges vvhich are properly ours, and seeketh to giue the possession thereof to his ovvne children, and seruants.*

Philostrat. in vita Apolonij. *Plutarc. de defectu oraculorum in fine.*

44 Therefore it is not improbable, that *Trismegistus* attributed to *Cælius*, & *Saturnus*, those thinges which he had heard, and held for most admirable, amongst the faithful people of God, though also it is not to be doubted, but that manie amongst the gentils, being Magicians, were partlie deluded by the deuil, and partlie helped to delude others, pretending to haue great communication, and familiaritie with God in their contemplations. In which kind, verie admirable thinges are written by *Philostratus*, of the rapts or trances of *Apollonius Thyaneus*, a most famous Magician (in the time of *Domitian* the emperour) though by professiō a *Pithagorian* philosopher: as also the same was euident, in the last *Pithonissa*, which serued in the temple of *Apollo*, and gaue the oracles at *Delphos*, imitating the extatical gestures, & actions of the holie prophets of God, vntil at lēght, she appeared manifestlie, to be possessed with a deuil, crying out so hideouslie, & horriblelie, that not only certaine strangers, who were come to haue answer of the oracle, but also the priests of the tēples, that were present, fled away for feare, & shee her selfe being terriblelie tormēted, and distracted of her senses, died within a few dayes after, as *Plutark* recounteth in his treatise intituled, *vvhy the oracles ceassed.*

Chap. 14.

45 Also *Mahomet* the false prophet of the *Turkes*, being much troubled with the falling sicknes, made the people beleeue, that the Angel *Gabriel* vsed to appeare vnto him, so resplendant, and bright, that he could not endure the sight of him, but was bereaued of his senses for the time, and that then, during those transes, he had manie strange visions and reuelations, as I haue declared more amplie before in the 14. chapter. But howsoeuer it is, it cannot be douted, but that the extaticall visions of God, whereof wee read in the philosophers, were eyther mere fictions, or els perhaps, true effects of the contemplation, of gods seruāts, ascribed by the gentils to them selues, for the reputation of their doctrin, & religion. Thus much concerninge philosophical contemplation.

Of Christian

Of Christian contemplation vvhat it is, hovv it serueth it selfe of philosophical contemplation, and hovv it differeth from it, vvhat excellent meane it hath to attaine to perfect vnion vvith God, in the vvhich consisteth the end, and felicitie of man, and common vvealth: Also of three vvayes practised by contemplatiue Christians, to arriue to the perfection of contemplation, to vvit, the Purgatiue *vvay, the* Illuminatiue *vvay, and the* Vnitiue *vvay: and first some practise is shovved of the* Purgatiue *vvay, verie necessarie for beginners, and for the conuersion of sinners.*

CHAP. 18.

1. THou hast seen, good Reader, what the philosophers beleeued and taught concerning their contemplation, and therfore I will now passe to treate of the contemplation of Christians: wherein first is to be considered, that though there be great difference betwixt it, and the former, as wil appeare hereafter, yet the difference consisteth not in anie contrarietie, or exclusion of the one from the other, but that Christian contemplation admittinge the philosophicall, and seruinge it selfe thereof, as of her handmaid, excelleth it in all kinde of perfection, and as I may say, hiteth the marke wherat the other shott, and arriueth at the port, whereto the other directed her course, though shee could neuer attaine vnto it: for, the contẽplation of the philosophers, hauing no helpe of gods grace, nor other ground, as I haue signified, but the knowledge of god by his workes, and creatures, was irremediablie distracted with inextricable difficulties, doubts, and ambiguities, whereas our Christian cõtemplation, is grounded vppon the solid, and sure foundation of faith, which beinge infused by the grace of the hollie ghost, is not onelie more certaine thẽ anie humaine knowledge, or sight of our senses, but also doth illuminate our vnderstanding with a deuine sight, whereby wee doe the more clearlie conceaue, and speculate the abstruse, and incomprehensible properties of the deuine nature. Therefore the prophet *Isay* saith, according to the 10. interpreters: *nisi credideritis, non intelligetis: except you beleeue you shall not vnderstand:* And *S. Thomas* teacheth, that the light of grace, both fortifieth the light of nature, and also frameth in our imagination farr more pure, and significant phantasies, or images representinge the deuine nature, then those which nature, and sense can afford: besides that the misteries of our faith, are like to the flinte stone, for if they be strooken, as I may tearme it, with

Isay 7.
S. Tho. 1. p. quæst. 12. ar. 13.

the steele of serious consideration, they yeeld firie sparkes of the loue of God, which falling into a well prepared, and purified soule, doe kindle therein great flames of pure deuotion, and heauenlie consolation, as shall appeare manifestlie hereafter.

D. Tho.2.2. q.180. ar. 3.

Albert. in paradiso anima c. 33.

2 But to declare, before I proceed further, what *Christian contemplation* properlie is, and what are the effects thereof, *S. Thomas* defineth it to be: *A simple, and pure sight, or speculation of the eternal truth, vvithout varietie of discourse vvith the help of Gods grace, and greate affections of admiration, and loue*; or as *Albertus magnus saith, it is a recollection of the affections, and of all the povvers of the soule, to knovv vvith admiration and delight, such things as belong to the deuine nature, or to his secret iudgements and most holie vvill.* Thus doe they define *contemplation*; the effects whereof are, to vnite the soule of man with his cheefe good, to make him like to Angels, and to God himselfe, to perfect the two principall powers of his soule, that is to say, to illuminate his vnderstanding with true wisdome, and to kindle in his will, the fier of charitie, which is the loue of God, where vppon proceedeth also the loue of his neighbours, feruour of spirit, sweetnes of deuotion, puritie of hart, and integritie of all his actions.

Albert. mag. in paradiso anima c. 33.

S. Aug. l. 15. de Trinitate.

3 Furthermore, wheras *cogitation*, *meditation*, and *speculation* being acts of the vnderstandinge, haue some affinitie with *contemplation*, and are necessarie thereto, it is to be vnderstood how they differ from it, and how they helpe to the perfection thereof; It is therefore to be considered, that in *cogitation*, the minde wandreth without labour, or fruict; in *meditation* it pondereth, discourseth, and searcheth, both with labour and fruict; in *speculation*, it considereth, and seeth, (though some what obscurelie, *& tanquam per speculum*, as through a glass) yet without labour, & with fruict; in *cōtemplatiō* it beholdeth farr more cleerlie, not onlie without labour, but also with admiration, astonishment, vnspeakeable fruict, and delight.

S. Bonauent. de 7. itinerib. aeternit. sect. 3. dist. 3.

4 For *contemplation*, is then in perfection, when all the powers of the soule are collected in themselues, and vnited with God, enioying, him, admiring, his deuine perfections, and wholie reposing in him, with ineffable contentment, and ioy; whereto *cogitation*, *meditation*, and *speculation*, doe make the way, being as it were, stepps & degrees to mount thereto; For first we cogitat, or thinke, of what we would meditate, speculate, & contemplat, from *cogitation*, we passe to *meditation*, to find out by discourse the truth, which we would speculat, and hauing found it, wee then, as it were behould it, with the eye of our vnderstanding, pondering, and consideringe it by *speculation*, from the which wee passe to *contemplation*,

5 For although *speculation*, and *contemplation*, are manie times cōfounded, and

and vnderstood to signifie one thing (and sometimes also *speculation* is taken for a degree of *contemplation*, before it arriue to perfection) yet if wee will consider them, as they may be distinct in this exercise, we may obserue this difference betwixt them, that the speculation of God, may be said to be onlie an act of the vnderstanding, as it considereth the deuine nature, without the concurrence of the affection, but in the contemplation of God, the vnderstanding, and the affection concurre, so that the contemplatiues both know God, by an assured faith, and loue him by a most feruent, and perfect charitie, whereby they arriue to perfect vniō with him, as shalbe declared further heareafter. *Idem ibid.*

6 And for as much, as it is also requisit, that all the three powers of the soule, to wit, the *memorie*, *vnderstanding*, and *the vvill*, be euerie one of thē, emploied in this exercise, according to their seuerall functions, not onlie in the meditation, and speculation of hollie, and deuine thinges, but also in spirituall, and mentall conferences with almightie God: Therefore it is conuenient, that I also declare heere, what are the proper offices, and functions of these three powers in the exercise of contemplation. *B. Ignatius in primo exercit. prim. hebdom.*

7 The first (to wit the *memorie*) is emploied, not onlie in remembring the matters & points, whereof we meane to meditate, but also in representing to the eyes of our soule, the presence of almightie God, his wisedome, mercie, bountie, iustice, and other excellencies, our sinnes past, and all other thinges necessarie to be remembred, according as matter is ministred, and occasion offred in our meditation. *P. Luyz. de la Puente. Introducion de la oracion mental.*

8 The office of the *vnderstanding*, is to discurre vppon the points of our meditation to ponder them dulie, and to draw out of them, hollie motiues of the feare, and loue of God, and of the true knowledge of our selues, and to represent the same to the *vvill*, to the end it may thereby be moued to exercise the function and acts, which properlie belong to it: as sorrow for our sinnes, contempt and hate of our selues, the true loue of God, confidence in his mercie, due praises, and thankes for his benefits, humble petition of his grace, good desires, and firme purposes to amend our defects, resignation to his hollie will, and franke offer of our selues, to doe, or suffer, whatsoeuer it shall please him to ordaine: and to the stirring vp of these affections (which are the acts of the *vvill*) tendeth all the discourse of our *vnderstanding* in meditation. *Idem ibid.*

9 And because, all the acts of these three powers, are properlie mentall (in respect that in this exercise of meditation, they are for the most part, conceiued onlie in the mind, and not expressed, with the voice) and that also, there passe therein manie spirituall, and mentall conferences with almightie God, wherein the soule offereth to him praises, and thankes, bewaileth *Idem ibid.*

bewaileth her infirmities, vnfoldeth her greefes, confesseth her sinnes, and craueth pardon, remedies, graces, and fauours, therefore the whole exercise, and practise thereof, is called *mentall praier*, whereby the cōtemplatiues, doe with the inward voice of their soules, treat familiarly with almightie God, negotiat the releife of their necessities, and obtaine pardon, grace, and all vertues, aspiringe, and mounting vp, to the eternall tabernacles, where, *replentur in bonis domus Dei, they are filled vvith the goods, or pleasures of Gods house*, being vnited with him by deuotion, and loue, in which vnion consisteth the perfection, and end, of all Christian *meditation*, *praier*, and *contemplation*.

Psal. 83. Psal. 64.

10 Herein neuerthelesse this difference is to be noted, betwixt the philosophers, and vs Christians, that the philosophers tended in their contemplations, onlie to the perfection of their owne knowledge, that is to say, to know perfectlie the deuine nature, in which respect, they placed for the most part, the perfection of mans contemplation, and felicitie, in the *vnderstanding*, but the Christians tend principallie to the loue of God, aspiring to the true knowledge of him, to the end, they may sincerelie loue him, and be beloued of him, & therefore they place in the *vvill*, the perfection of contemplation in this life. And whereas the philosophers taught, that the exact knowledge of all the sciences, is absolutelie necessarie thereto (in so much that *Plato*, and his followers, held, that it is not possible for anie but philosophers, and men of great learninge, to attaine vnto it (and of them also, verie few) Christians both teach, and trie by experience, that all the perfection of true contemplation proceedeth, rather of pietie, then industrie, of charitie, and not of knowledge, of Gods grace, and assistance, and not of mans witt, or iudgement. And therefore we see that amongst Christians, the most ignorant man, assisted by Gods hollie spirit, may trulie say with the royall prophet: *Quoniam non cognoui litteraturam, introibo in potentias Domini: Because I knevv no kind of learninge, I vvill enter into the povvers of our Lord*, that is to say, for asmuch, as I am alltogether ignorant, and void of humane science, I will wholy relie vppon the confidence of Gods grace, and the light of his hollie spirit, and so make no doubt, to enter, into the consideration, or contemplation, of his great, and woundrous workes, and of his deuine power.

Albertus magnus de adhærendo deo. ca. 9. S. Tho. 2. 2. q. 180. ar. 1. Plato in Epinomide. Psal. 70.

11 So were the Apostles of most rude, and vnlearned fishermen, made great doctors, and deuines, so *the poore became preachers*, after the cōminge of our Sauiour, and so also, (I meane by the light, and helpe of grace) not onlie simple, and ignorant men, but also women, may be, and are amongst Christians, most perfect contemplatiues, as may appeare by that hollie *Marie*, in whome the contemplatiue life is represented in the Gospell,

Matth. 4. Luc. 9.

cospell, and of whome our Sauiour said, that shee *had chosen the best part,* Luc.10.
whereof also there hath béne manie notable examples in Gods Church, in hollie contemplatiue women, and great Saintes of God, as *S. Brigett, S. Clare, S. Gertrude, S. Caterin* of *Siena*, and diuers others, both in former times, and in this present age, of whom I shall haue occasion to speake heareafter. Chap.27.

12 Neuerthelesse, we doe not so farre presume vppon grace, that we vtterlie reiect, all helpe of humane science, or of the knowledge of God by his creatures (which is the ground of philosophicall contemplation) and much lesse doe wee neglect the light, and gifts of nature, all which, though they are not so absolutelie necessarie for Christian contemplation, but that the want of them may be, and is, in manie supplied by grace, yet they are so conuenient thereto, that they facilitate the same, and helpe greatelie to the perfection thereof, when they concurre with grace, and are guided thereby, for grace doth not abolish nature, or reiect humane cooperation, but admitteth, and perfitteth both, & therefore *S. Thomas* teacheth, that the images, or representations framed by grace, in the phantasie of the contemplatour, are so much more excellent, and cleare, by how much the light of nature is stronger in him. D.Tho. 1. p. quest. 12. ar.13.

13 And *S. Hierome*, also vppon the same reason obserueth in *S. Paule*, that though he had the gift of tongues, by the grace of God, yet he was allwaies more eloquent in the Hebrew (which was his owne naturall tongue) then in the other languages, which he had by infusion. And the like is also to be said of humane industrie, and indeuour in contemplation, for although of it selfe, without grace, it can effect nothing (as neither doth grace commonlie worke without it) yet how much greater humane diligence, and endeuour is, so much more excellẽt, are the effects of grace, and therefore though *S. Paule* say: *Gratia Dei, sum id, quod sum, & gratia eius in me vacua non fuit: by the grace of God, I am that, vvhich I am, and his grace, hath not bene vaine, or vvithout effect in me*, yet he addeth, *sed abundantius omnibus laboraui, non ego autem, sed gratia Dei mecum, but I haue laboured more aboundantlie, then they all, not I truelie* (alone) *but the grace of God vvith me.* S. Hieron. quest.11. ad Hedibiam To. 3. 1.Cor.15.

14 In like sort, the Christian contemplatiue, doth not neglect the knowledge of God by his creatures, and workes, but vseth the same in his contemplation, no lesse then the Philosophers did, and with farre greater fruit, then they: and therefore he saith, with the Royall prophet. *Meditatus sum in omnibus operibus tuis, & in factis manuum tuarum meditabar: I haue meditated on all thy vvorkes, and on those thinges, vvhich* Psal.142.

S. Athanas. in vita S. Antonij.

thie handes haue vvrought. And *S. Anthony*, the notable cōtemplatiue Hermit, being demaunded in the wildernes, what bookes he had for his instruction, shewed the heauens, and the whole world, saying, these are the bookes wherein I dailie contemplat, the infinit wisdome, power, and goodnes of almightie God.

15 Therefore, the difference in this point, betwixt the philosophers, & Christians, is, that whereas the philosophers, being guided onlie by the light of nature, had no other meanes to know God, but by his workes, and creatures (which kind of knowledge, as I haue declared before, is accompanied with manie doubtes, and difficulties, and consequentlie is vncertaine, and obscure) we Christians haue not onlie the same meanes, which they had, but also others, farre clearer, surer, more potent, and effectual, to wit, the light of gods grace, and the helpe of infused vertues, as of *faith*, *hope*, and *charity*, of the which, *faith*, being infused by almightie god, and therefore not possiblie subiect to falsitie, or errour, serueth for a most solid, and sure foundation to all the building: and *hope*, proceeding from the sound, and sure ground of *faith*, raiseth, as I may say, the strong walls of our contemplation to the heauens, that is to say, to the speculation of heauenlie things, with a most comfortable confidence of Gods mercie: and lastlie *charity*, *diffusa in cordibus nostris, per spiritum Sanctum, qui datus est nobis*, being *diffused, and spred in our harts by the holly Ghost, vvhich is giuen vs*, doth consummat, and perfect the whole building, vniting our soules with almightie God, as I will make manifest after a while.

Rom. 5.

16 Furthermore these vertues, and especiallie *faith*, doth not onlie fortifie, and assure in vs the knowledge of God, which we haue by his creatures, but also doth discouer vnto vs therein, diuers abstruse, and hidden secrets of his deuine nature, whereof the philosophers neuer had, nor could haue anie knowledge, or beleefe; as namelie of the high misterie of the blessed Trinitie, whereof we find a notable representation, in manie things, especiallie in the verie soule of man, wherein the *memory vvill*, and *vnderstanding*, being three seuerall powers, and but one substāce, are consequētlie an expresse image of almightie God, who though he be three distinct persons (to wit the Father the Sonne, and the hollie Ghost) yet is but one deuine substance, and essence.

D. Ber. de interiori. domo c. 67.

17 This *S. Bernard* explicateth notablie in this manner. Consider, saith he, o soule, thy owne nobilitie, for as God is whole euerie where, geuing „ life to all things, mouing, & gouerning them, so thou art whole in euery „ part of thy bodie, giuing life vnto it, mouing, and gouerning it, and as „ God is, liueth, and knoweth, so thou also after thy manner, art, liuest, and knowest,

knowest,and as in God there are three persons,the Father,the Sonne, & ,,
the holie Ghost,so thou hast in thee three powers,thy vnderstanding,thy ,,
memorie,and thy will,and as the Sonne is begotten by the Father, and ,,
the holie Ghost,proceedeth from them both,so thy will is engendred of ,,
thy vnderstanding,and thy memorie proceedeth from them both; And ,,
as the Father is God,and the Sonne God,and the holie Ghost God, and yet ,,
all three but one God,and three persons,so thy vnderstãding is thy soule, ,,
thy will is thy soule,and thy memorie thy soule, & yet not three soules, ,,
but all one soule,and three seueral powers. Thus saith *S. Bernard.* ,,

18 So that when we behould the cleare light,and shining sunne of the deitie,not onlie through the obscure,and fallacious clouds of philosophical contemplation,but also in the true glasse of our faith,yea,and add there vnto the consideration of the other misteries of our Christian religion,to wit,of the incarnation,natiuitie, life, passion, and death of our Sauiour *Iesus Christ* (as that he,being the Sonne of God,equall, and consubstantiall with his Father,*seipsum exinaniuit*, did as it were emptie, and annihilat himselfe, take flesh of a virgin,and liue here on earth, for the *Philip. 2.* space of three and thirtie yeares,enduring hunger, cold, pouertie, contempt,infinit iniuries,slanders,blasphemies,and finallie a most shameful, and paineful death vppon the crosse for our sakes, the innocent for the nocent,the iust for the vniust,the lord and master, for his seruants and slaues,that is to say,omnipotent God for most wretched, and vngrateful sinners,to the end he might redeeme vs being lost,and of his slaues, yea enimies,make vs his friends,brethren,the adopted children of God, and coheires with him,) when I say we well waighe these so great, and euident arguments of his bountie,mercie,& loue towards vs, and the ineffable benefits,that grew to vs thereby,how can wee choose, but be replenished with exceeding comfort,and ioye,and feele in our selues,most effectuall,and forcible motiues to pietie, and deuotion? How can we choose,but be inflamed with the feruent loue of God, and say with the prophet; *concaluit cor meum intra me,& in meditatione exardescit ignis; my heart is heated vvith in me,and there burneth a fire in my meditation?* *Psal. 38.*

19 Furthermore,this flame of deuine loue being kindled in our harts, what wonderful effects must it needs worke in vs,of praise,and thankes to God,of sorrow,and contrition for our sinnes,and of holie desires, and firme purposes of amendment? For when we shall consider Christ on the one side,and our selues on the other, who he is, and what we are, comparing his omnipotencie,with our infirmitie,his maiestie, with our basenes,his all,as I may say,with our nothing,his bountie, and goodnes, with our malice,his loue to vs,with our ingratitude to him, the great-

nes, and worthines of his innumerable benefits, with the turpitude, enormity, and infinit number of our sinnes, his humility, with our pride, his pouertie, with our superfluitie, his meekenes, with our wrath, his patience, with our peruersitie, his fasts, with our surfets, his teares, with our dissolute laughter, and finallie his painefull passion, with our sinfull pleasures, shall we not be confounded in our selues, and say with the
Psal. 6. royall prophet: *Sana me Domine, quoniam conturbata sunt ossa mea, & anima mea turbata est valde: Heale me o Lord, for my verie bones are troubled, and my soule is greatlie afflicted?* Shall we not *labour, and trauel* (as the same pro-
Ibid. phet saith) *in our sorrovv, and mourning, and vvash our beds vvith teares?*
Gal. 5. yea, and *crucifie our flesh, and concupiscences vvith Christ*, to the end *vve may die to sinne, and rise vvith him to life*, and not onlie loathe our former ingratitude, but also shew our selues more thankefull, hereafter? shall we not then be ashamed, to appeare emptie handed in the sight of our
Psal. 115. Lord, and say with the prophet, *Quid retribuam Domino pro omnibus quæ retribuit mihi, vvhat shall I render to my Lord, for all that vvhich he hath giuen*
Ibid. *me?* shall we not then take, *calicem salutaris, the cup of saluation, and call vppon the name of our Lord?* that is to say, shall we not offer to him the most holie, and dreadfull sacrifice of his most blessed bodie, and blood, instituted by himselfe, *in memoriam mirabilium suorum, for a memorie of all*
Psal. 110. *his maruails*, or wondrous workes, for a remembrance, and representation of his passion, for the remission of our frequent offences, and for the dailie foode of our soules? whereby we may not onlie be most gratefull vnto him, but also most admirablie vnited with him? For who can sufficientlie expresse, the admirable coniunction, and vnion, that we haue with God, by the participation of that blessed sacrifice, receiuing
Hilar. de Trinit. l. 8. the ineffable *sacrament of vnity* (as *S. Hilary* calleth it) wherein vnder the formes of bread, and wine, we trulie eate the verie bodie of our Sauiour *Christ*, and drinke his blood, wherevppon there groweth (as *S. Hilary* also
Idem ibid. amplie testifieth) a natural vnion betwixt *Christ*, and vs, we being (as
S. Cyril. Ierosol. catheche. mistagog. 4. Irenæ. li. 4. aduers. hæres. ca. 34. *S. Cyril* also saith) *concorporei consanguinei eius*, made one bodie, and one blood with him, and not onlie our soules adorned, and filled with his grace, but also our bodies fedd with his flesh, and nourished to immortalitie.

20 Who then seeth not what pregnant, and potent meanes, the Christian contemplatiue hath to arriue, euen in this life, to that vnion with God, which is the end of contemplation, and the true felicitie of man? And this will yet further appeare, if we consider, both the most excellent doctrin, and also the exquisit practise of our contemplatiues, in the vse, and exercise of three waies, whereby the soule of man is raised, and eleuated, as

uated, as it were, by degrees, to perfect contemplation, and a most happy vnion with God.

21 The first way is called *Purgatiue*, by the which, the soule is purified from the filth of sinne. The second is called *Illuminatiue*, whereby it is illustrated, and enlightned with the light of truth, encrease of grace, and disposed to receiue all perfection of vertues. The third is tearmed *Vnitiue*, whereby the soule is vnited, and ioyned with God, by feruorous loue, and affection, which three waies, are most aptlie applied and accommodated, to three sorts, and states of men, as shalbe declared heareafter.

S. Bonauentura in paruo bono. Dionisius Carthus. li. de via purgatiua. Essercitio della vita spirituale P. Luyz. de la Puente en la introducion de la oració mentall. B. Ignatius in Annotationibus annotat. 10.

22 Of all these three wayes, and the practise thereof, I thinke good some what to enlarge my selfe, in respect aswell of their excellencie, as of the fruit that I hope, the Reader may by the way reape thereby. For seeing that the subiect, whereon I speciallie treat, doth exact of me in this place, a full declaration of the nature, and dignitie of Christian contemplation (because the end, and happines of man, and common wealth consisteth therein:) and forasmuch as the same cannot be so well vnderstood otherwaise, as by the exercise, and practise of it (such beinge the nature of spirituall, and deuine thinges, that they cannot be fullie knowne, and conceiued, except they be first tasted, and tried, in which respect the psalmist, speaking of the sweetenes of God, saith. *Gustate, & videte, tast and see:*) for this cause, I say, I hold it conuenient, to lay downe some practise of our Christian contemplation, thereby to make thee (good Reader) the better to conceiue, what it is, and to moue thee with all, not onlie by reading it, the more to esteeme it, but also by practise, to make some triall of it, that so thou maiest come, to tast how sweete our Lord is, and reape the vnspeakeable fruit thereof, first here in this life, and after eternallie.

Psal. 33.

23 And I am the rather induced thereto, in respect of the benefitt, that I hope, may grow thereby, to such as doe not vnderstand Latine, and forraine lãguages. For although there are manie notable treatises, in all tõgues, concerning the practise of contẽplation, as will appeare heareafter, and diuers excellent bookes written by Catholikes in our owne language, touching meditation, and other matters tending to this exercise, yet I haue not seene, or heard, of anie in our tongue, that treateth of all the partes thereof, or giueth anie method for the practise of the whole, thereby the better to vnderstãd it, & therefore not knowing whither to remit such, as are vnlearned, for their satisfaction in this behalfe, & imagining also, that the learned thẽselues (such I meane as vnderstãd the latine

and other tongues, and yet haue no knowledge of this exercise) may rather desire to see somewhat of it presentlie, then to be differred, and remitted to others (especiallie seeing, that with a few leaues, more, or lesse, I may hope to giue them some contentmēt therein, or at least more effectuallie moue them to search out other authors, for their further satisfaction) I haue therefore, I say, resolued to vndergoe this labour, hoping to performe it, with as great perspicuitie, and breuitie, as the difficultie, importance, and worthines, of the subiect may permit, meaning rather to giue thee (good Reader) some tast of this misticall Theologie, then anie full instruction, which would require not onlie a larger discourse, then were conuenient for this time, and place, but also farre more knowledge, and practise of it, then I can iustlie challenge to my selfe.

24 Now then to come to the matter; Yt is to be cōsidered, that whereas I signified before, that the whole practise of contemplation, is deuided into three waies, to witt, *Purgatiue*, *Illuminatiue*, and *Vnitiue*, and the same appropriated to three sorts of men, the *Purgatiue* (whereof I am first to treate) is speciallie applied to those, who hauing led a wicked life, or benne verie negligent in Gods seruice, are moued by his grace, to rise out of the suds (as I may say) of their former sinnes, and to purge their soules from the filth thereof. And this way consisteth, in the due meditation of such thinges, as may moue them to a perfect knowledge, or contempt of themselues, to the feare of Gods iustice, and to the consideration of their owne ingratitude, towards his deuine maiestie, and of the lamentable sequell thereof, in respect of the punishment, both temporall, and eternall, iustlie due to them for the same; by which meanes they may be induced to hartie sorrow, and contrition for their sinnes, and so through the merits of our Sauiours passion, obtaine remission thereof, and iustification, which is the end of the *Purgatiue* way.

Eccl. 18.

P.Bartholomeo Ricci. instruct. de medit. par. 1. c. 8.

a Chap. 19. from the 4. numb. to the 51.

b Itē Chap. 20. from the 4. numb. to he 25.

25 And now to come to the practise; The hollie Ghost aduiseth vs, in *Ecclesiasticus*, alwaies before we pray to prepare, & dispose our soules conuenientlie thereto, lest otherwise, wee *be like to a man, vvhich tempteth God*, and therefore whereas there are manie thinges requisit, to the due disposition, and preparation of our selues (whereof I will treate amplie hereafter, when I shall come to speake of the *a* illuminatiue and *b* vnitiue way) I thinke it conuenient in this place to lay downe onlie one, which is, not onlie the immediate, but also the most necessarie preparatiue to all meditation; to wit, that those, which are to meditate (hauing chosen a fitt time & place of retrait, whereof I will also say some what hereafter) doe lift vp their hartes, and all the powers of their soules to almightie God,

God,& with the eies of a ſtrong faith,behould him preſent, ſaying with the Royall prophet. *Meditatio cordis mei in conſpectu tuo ſemper. The meditation of my hart is alvvaiſe in thy ſight*, aſſuring themſelues,that he ſeeth,and heareth them, yea,and ſearcheth into euerie corner of their conſciences,and that therefore they ought,as in the preſence of his deuine maieſtie, to bow the knees,not onlie of their hart (as the ſcripture ſpeaketh)but alſo of their bodie,either proſtrating themſelues,vppon the ground,or kneeling(if they be not hindred,by ſome corporall weakenes,and infirmitie) and ſo to adore him *in ſpirit, and truth*, acknowledging him to be theyr Lord,their God,their Creatour,and Father of infinit power, & maieſtie, offering vnto him their ſoules, bodies, liues, and all other actions, and particularlie whatſoeuer they shall think, ſay, or pray in their preſent meditation,moſt humblie beſeeching him to ordaine,& direct the ſame, whollie to his owne eternall glorie,and the profit of their ſoules, for the merits of our Sauiour Ieſus Chriſt.

Idem ibid. ca.11. P.Ignatius in exercitijs hebdo.4. Pſal.15. P. Ricci vbi ſupra. 2.Paral. ca. vlt. Ioan.4. P.Luyz.dela Puente en la introduct.de la orat.mental.

36 And this praier they may addreſſe,not onlie to the bleſſed Trinitie, that is to ſay,to the three deuine perſons iointlie,but alſo particularly to euerie one of them,offringe the ſame,firſt to God the Father, beſeeching him to vnite,and incorporate,their praier and meditation, in the praier of his Sonne our Lord,and Sauiour, and to accept it for his ſake, and merits.

Iidem authores. ibid.

37 And then they may turne their cogitation,to the Sonne of God (our ſaid Sauiour,and redeemer) crauing of him with all humility,that ſeeing he,being eternall God,equall,and conſubſtantiall,with the Father, vouchſafed,out of his infinit goodnes,to take our fleſh,and become our Mediatour in his humanitie,it may pleaſe him,not onlie to pray with them, and for them to his Father,but alſo to heare,fauour,and aſſiſt them,with his grace,as their Lord,and God,for his owne merits,and mercie.

38 Laſtlie, they may direct their praier to the hollie Ghoſt,acknowledging him to be alſo their Lord God,equall,and coeternall with the Father,and the Sonne,the light of hartes,and giuer of all good giftes, and then confeſſing their owne ignorance, and infirmitie, they may humbly beeſech him to illuminate their vnderſtanding,to moue,guide,and direct their will,to quicken,and refresh their memorie,to ſtay their wandring fancie,and to recollect their ſcattered thoughts, to the end, they may meditat,and pray with due attention,and reuerence,penetrat the miſteries whereof they are to meditat,ſee,and dulie bewaile their ſinnes paſt, make hollie purpoſes,and reſolutions of amendement, and afterwards performe the ſame,with his deuine helpe,and aſſiſtance.

39 And here by the way it is to be noted, that they shall not neede to continue

continue this preparatiue praier, anie longer then for the ſpace of a *Pater noſter*, an *Aue*, and a *Creede* at the moſt, except they find ſome extraordinarie conſolation, and ſweetnes therein, in which caſe, it ſhall not be amiſſe to reſt vppon it, turning the preparation into meditation, ſo long as the deuotion, and conſolation continueth, according to the aduiſe of the ancient contemplatiue, *Iohannes Climacus*, who giueth this generall rule to be vſed, throughout all the courſe of mentall praier. *Cum in orationis verbo*, ſaith he, *vel dulcedine perfundi, vel compungi te ſentias, in eo perſiſte, tunc quippe cuſtos noſter nobiſcum orat:* whenſoeuer thou feeleſt thy ſelfe, either moued with ſweetenes, or with contrition, in anie word, or part of thy praier, perſiſt in it, for then our keeper praieth with vs. Thus he.

Iohannes Climac. de orat. gradu 28.

40 This preparation being made, they may enter into a ſerious conſideration of themſelues, what man is, of what ſubſtance he was made, and what he hath of him ſelfe, as that he is the creature of God, conſiſting of ſoule, and bodie, both of them created of nothing (for though the bodie of our firſt father *Adam*, was framed of earth, and clay, yet the ſame was firſt made of nothing:) wherein is alſo to be conſidered, the infirmitie, and weakenes, of a humane bodie, the loathſome filth, that floweth frō it, the innumerable ſickneſſes, miſeries, calamities, and death, whereto it is ſubiect, and that it endeth in a carreine ſtinking carcaſe, which putrefieth, and is finallie diſſolued into duſt.

41 The due, and frequent conſideration whereof, may ſerue for a notable antidot, againſt the poiſon of pride, vaine glorie, and all worldlie vanities. Beſides that, it is alſo further to be conſidered, that the ſoule of man, though it be created to the image of God, and is immortall, capable of the knowledge of him, and of eternall glorie, yea, and was in our firſt fathers, adorned with wiſdome, and excellent gifts of grace, yet it is now ſo wounded, weakened, and corrupted, partlie by their fall, and partlie by euerie mans proper, and particuler ſinnes, that it is vtterlie deformed, blinded, and repleniſhed, with ignorance, & errour, vntill it pleaſe God, to reforme, renew, and illuminat it, with the light of faith, and giftes of his grace: ſo that if we trulie diſtinguiſh, betwixt that which is Gods, & that which is our owne, we ſhall eaſelie ſee, that wee are nothing, and worſe then nothing: for yealding to God, that which is his (to wit, not onlie the giftes of his grace, but alſo our wiſdome, our knowledge, our ſubſtance of ſoule, and bodie, our beautie, our ſtrenght, our breath, and life) there remaineth nothing to vs, but blindnes, ignorance, errour, infirmitie, filth, miſerie, death, and finallie nought els, but the nothing, whereof we are firſt made, nothing I ſay, except ſinne, which is worſe then nothing: all which being well waied, then may the meditators,

eleuat

eleuat their mindes to almightie God,& yeld him all due praise, honour, & glory, hūbling thēselues most profoūdlie in his sight,acknowledging him to be all in all & thē selues to be nothinge,to know nothing,and finally to deserue nothing of thēselues,but cōfusion,shame,& eternall dānation;whereby they may lay in their soules,the foūdatiō of true humilitie,which is the roote of all vertue,& the groundeworke,whereon the true contēplation of God is to be built.For as *S.Bernard* saith, *nisi super humilitatis stabile fundamentum, spirituale ædificium stare non potest. No spirituall building can stand,but vppon the stable,and sound foundation of humility.* *D. Bernard. supra cant. serm. 36.*

42 This being dōne,they may passe further,& profoūdlie pōder the end, for the which God created & ordained thē (which was no other,but his seruice,& their eternall saluatiō)& then cōsider the worthines,& excellencie of this end,the obligation that mā hath to almightie God for the same,the extreame follie,& madnes of those,that neglect it,yea, & how litle care they themselues haue had thereof;as,that being created to the most excellent image of God,they haue deformed thē selues by sinne, & made thēselues images,& slaues of the diuell;how they haue to the great offence of God abused,not only al the powers of their soules,their senses, all the partes of their bodies, and all the creatures of God, but also God himselfe,contēning his iustice,presuming to offēd him,the rather for his mercy,& patiēce:distrusting his prouidēce,preferring their owne wills, before his will,reiecting his hollie inspiratiōs,disobeying his ministers, and his spouse the Church,breaking all his, and her commaundements, and finallie abusing most iniuriouslie his deare Sonne, our Sauiour *Iesus Christ*,recompensing his vnspeakeable desire,and care of their saluation, with extreame negligence,and contempt of his seruice, and with intollerable ingratitude towards him. *Rom.6. Cassian. collat. 4.& 5.*

43 To all which,they may also add,the cōsideratiō of Gods rigorous, & iudgemēt,in punishing sinne,remēbring *S.Peters* admonitiō,and inferēce. *Si iustus vix saluabitur* &c. *Yf the iust man,shall hardly be saued, vvhere shall the vvicked man,and sinner appeare*,and againe? *Si Deus Angelis non pepercit* &c. *Yf God spared not the Angels,vvhich transgressed his commaundements,but cast thē dovvne to hell,to be eternally tormented,hovv can vniust & vvicked men, expect to escape, the like iudgement?* To which purpose,they may also consider,that *Lucifer*,and his fellowes, were condemned for one sinne of pride,cōmitted onlie in thought,whereas they haue cōmitted innumerable sinnes, aswell in the same kind,as in all other, not in thought only, but also in woord,& deede,whereby it may appeare,what seuerity is due to thē,yea, & the better to discouer,the horrour of sinne,they may sett before their eies,our Sauiour *Christ* crucified,in whō they may behould the rigour of *2. Pet. 4. Ibid.ca.2.*

Gods iustice, in punishing their sinnes in him, being his owne Sonne, & thereby conceiue how greeuous a penaltie they shall pay for the same themselues, if they doe not repent, and amend their liues in time.

44 And this being well pondered, then may they reflect vppon themselues, and their owne miserable state, considering the seuere punishmēt due to them for their sinnes, which they haue multiplied (as the psalmist saith) *super capillos capitis, more then the haires of their head*, or as king, *Manasses*,
Psal. 39. 2. Reg. 17. said, *aboue the sandes in the sea*, whereby they may haue iust occasion, to admire the wonderfull patience of almightie God, and his infinit mercie towards them, in suffring them so long, especiallie seeing that there are an infinit number of soules in hell, which haue not committed so manie sinnes as they, and manie perhaps who were condemned for some one, or a few mortall sinnes, whereas theirs are innumerable.

45 Therefore, let them lift vp their hartes to almightie God, and with a most reuerent, and trembling feare of his iustice, humblie thanke him, for his ineffable mercie towards them, not onlie in sparing them so long, but also in giuing them grace, now to see, and consider their danger, and detestable ingratitude towards him, most humblie crauing pardon of him for the same, through the merits of our Sauiour *Iesus Christ*, and purposing fullie to amēd their liues heareafter, with the assistāce of his grace.

46 This prayer being ended, they may then proceede, with their meditation, and ponder maturelie their owne mortalitie, how certaine their death is, how vncertaine the hower, and place, and the manner thereof, how manie die suddainelie euerie day, some by water, some by fier, some by sword, or sicknes, and of those which die in their beddes, how few haue their senses, and remembrance to the last, how stronglie the diuell will tempt them at that time, how weakelie they are likelie to resist, when they shalbe miserablie distracted, and afflicted, partlie with bodily infirmitie, partlie with torment of conscience, and the temptation of the diuell, drawing them to dispaire, and partlie by the feare of gods iudgements, and the extreame greefe, that then they are like to haue, to leaue their wealth, substance, and worldlie pleasures.

47 Lastlie they are to consider, how litle all their strenght, beautie, friendes, riches, dignities, and delightes of the world, shall then auaile them, their bodies being to become woormes meate, and their soules to yeald a straight accounte, for euerie idle word, euil thought, and negli-
Psal. 74. gēce committed in this life, before a rigorous Iudge, who as the psalmist saith, *iustitias iudicabit, vvill iudge*, and seuerelie examin, not onlie the bad workes of the wicked, but also the *good vvorkes of the iust*, whether they
Sophon. 1. had anie imperfection in them or no, and finding but anie one mortall sinne

ſinne vnrepented in this life, will condemne them to eternall fire, and *Matth.8.*
paines of hell, *ubi erit fletus*, ſaith our Sauiour, *& ſtridor dentium*, *vvhere* *Luc.13.*
there shall be, vveeping, and vvailing, and gnashing of teeth. And as *Iob* ſaith. *Iob.10.*
Nullus ordo, ſed ſempiternus horror. No order, but ſempiternall horror. Where the
neuerdying worme of conſcience biteth & gnaweth perpetuallie, where
ſaith *S. Bernard*, *the tormentors are neuer vvearie*, and *the tormented neuer die*, *S.Bernar.*
where *the fire ſo conſumeth, that vvithall it preſerueth*, where *nothing is heard, but* *Meditat.*
vveeping & vvailing, & gnashing of teeth, vvhere nothing is ſeene, but the hideous *ca.3.*
faces of the tormentors, to wit, *ouglie, and monſtrous diuells*, where *the ſorrovv, &*
paine is intollerable, the feare horrible, the ſtinke abominable, and the death both of
ſoule, and body ſempiternall, vvithout anie hope of pardon or mercy. Thus ſaith *S.*
Bernard, with much more to the ſame purpoſe, which I omit to auoide
prolixitie.

48 Who then is to deſperatlie wicked, that shall well way, and ponder all this, and will not bewaile his owne lamentable caſe, and wonder at his owne follie, yea and ſay to himſelfe; how haſt thou benne ſo blinded, and bewitched with ſenſualitie, and ſelfe-loue, to offend thy Lord God ſo oft, and hainouſlie, as thou haſt donne, and thereby expoſe thy ſelfe to the danger of ſuch endles, and vnſpeakeable torments, being ſo vncertaine as thou art, of the time, that thou maiſt be caſt headlog thereinto, which may befall thee, and is by Gods iuſtice due to thee, yea & hapneth to one or other euery day, and houre? Ys it ſelfe-loue that hath ſeduced thee? how canſt thou be ſaid to haue loued thy ſelfe, or to haue had reſpect to thy owne good, when thou haſt ſo greeuouſlie offended the onlie authour, & geeuer of all good, and ventred thy owne eternal ſaluation, for tranſitorie trifles, and vaine delites, yea for nothing?

49 Couldeſt thou commit greater follie, & madnes, then like *Eſau* to
ſell thy primogeniture, or inheritance, for a meſſe of pottage, that is to *Geneſ.25.*
ſay, heauen for earth, and euerlaſting felicitie, for short, & friuolus pleaſures, mixt with much infelicitie, and miſerie? Where was thy wit, thy iudgement, thy prouidence, & the care of thy ſelfe, which thou art wont ſo carefullie to employ in euerie trifle, that neuer ſo litle cõcerneth thee; whiles neuertheles thou haſt been moſt careles, and negligent, or rather ſenſeles in that which moſt importeth thee? Could all the world if it should conſpire againſt thee, doe thee halfe ſo much harme, as thou haſt donne thy ſelfe, by making him thy enemie, from whoſe power, no power can free thee, and who being thy Lord, & iuſt Iudge, will punish, or reward thee eternallie?

50 Call therefore thy wits to thee, and conſider what an extreame preſumption it is for ſuch a baſe, vile, and wretched woorme, as thou art,

to offend the infinit maiestie of God thy creatour, yea & to make warre vppon him with his owne weapons, that is to say, with the gifts that he geeueth thee, wherein truelie thou maist wonder at his bountie, and pacience, in that he doth not denie thee the ordinarie concourse of his helpe, euen in those things wherein thou hast offẽded him, expecting still thy repentance, though how long he will doe it, thou art vncertaine, and therefore reflect vppon thy owne danger, and say vnto him, out of an humble, and sorrowfull hart.

51 Eternal God my creatour, behold me wretched sinner thy poore creature, prostrat at the feete of thy mercie, crauing pardon most humbly of thy diuine maiestie for my horrible ingratitude towards thee, in that being made by thee of nothing to thy owne image, and ordained to enioye thee eternallie, I haue made no account of thee, but preferred euery trifle before thee, and heaped sinne vppon sinne with extreame cõtempt of thy iustice, and abuse of thy mercie, longanimitie, and paciẽce; Therefore how admirable hath thy clemencie benne towards me, in that thou hast forborne to powre downe thy vengeance vppon me, to strike me with suddaine death, and to cast me headlong to hell, as thou hast donne manie others, not so greeuous sinners as I, whiles neuertheles thou hast spared me. But seeing it hath pleased thee, out of thy infinit goodnes, now to open my eies, and to discouer vnto me, both the horrour of my owne conscience, and the bottomles pit, whereinto I was reddie to fall, vouchsafe, I beseech thee, to consũmat, & perfect thy owne good woork in me, geuing me an humble, & contrit hart, that my eies may be cõduits,
Psal. 118. & foũtaines of *vvater* to bewaile my sinnes, that my *teares may be my bread*
Psal. 41. *day, & night*, that I may doe the *vvorthy fruits of penãce*, & (through the me-
Matth. 3. rits of thy deare Sonne my Sauiour) yeeld some part of satisfaction to thy iustice in this life, whereby the ineuitable and dreadfull houre of my death, may serue me for a happie, & sure passage to those euerlasting, and incomprehensible ioyes, whereto thou hast out of thy infinit mercie ordained me.

52 Thus may they say, or some what els to the same purpose, either mẽtallie, or vocally, whereby they may with the helpe of Gods grace excite, & stirre vp thẽ selues to a confusiõ, & shame for their ingratitude, to the feare of Gods iustice, to cõtritiõ, & sorrow of their sinnes, to an effectual desire, & purpose of amẽdment, & to a true mortification of them selues,
Matth. 3. *by doing the vvorthy fruits of penance*, and vsing the meanes which our Sauiour *Christ* hath left vs in his Church, for the reconciliation of sinners, that is to say, the holly sacraments, whereby the merits of his passiõ may be applied vnto thẽ for their iustification, which is the end of the purga-

tiue way: whereof alſo the ſpeciall office is, to purge the ſoule, & diſpoſe it to receiue the light of grace, & the infuſion of Gods gifts, to rectifie the will, & cleanſe it of inordinat deſires, to purifie the vnderſtanding of errours, the memorie of culpable negligence, and forgetfullnes, the appetit of paſſions, the ſenſes of ſuperfluities, and finallie the ſoule of all vicious cuſtomes, and habits, which neuertheles the purgatiue way cannot of it ſelfe fullie accompliſh, and performe, without the helpe of the illuminatiue way, whereof I am now to treate.

Of the Illuminatiue *vvay, and the practiſe of it, vvith certaine obſeruations for the remedy of dictractions, and ſpirituall deſolation or ſterrility of ſpirit, vvhich may occurre in the exerciſe thereof. Alſo certaine meditations, to be practiſed by thoſe, that deſire to profit in the ſeruice of God, and in the vvay of vertue, and to arriue to the perfection of contemplation.*

Chap. 19.

1. THis way hath certaine degrees, according to the degrees of charitie, which as *S. Auguſtin* obſerueth, hath her *infancy, encreaſe*, & *perfection*, whereof the two firſt are proper to the *Illuminatiue* way, & the third to the *vnitiue*. The firſt, to wit, the infācy of charitie, belōgeth to thoſe that are newly iuſtified, & deſire to encreaſe, and augment their iuſtification, according to the ſaying of *S. Iohn, qui iuſtus eſt, iuſtificetur adhuc, he vvhich is iuſt, let him be iuſtified yet*, to whom the maſters of contemplatiue doctrin, applie the meditations of the miſteries of the incarnation, natiuity, circumciſion, preſentation, and infācie of our Sauiour Chriſt, drawing out of the ſame notable motiues, & conſiderations, aſwell for the proſecution, and perfection of the *Purgatiue* way (by the mortification of inordinat paſſions) as alſo for the beginninge of the *Illuminatiue* way, by ſowing in the ſoule, the ſeeds of all ſuch vertues, as are moſt requiſit for the ſtate, and condition of euerie one, as I will ſhew more particularlie after a while.

D. Aug. trac. 5. ſuper. 1. canonic. Ioan. D. Tho. 2. 2. q. 24. ar. 9. Apoc. 22.

P. Luyz. de la Puente To. 1. 4. introduc. de la oracion mental.

2 The ſecond ſtate, or degree of charitie (to wit encreaſe, & growth of grace) is proper to thoſe that haue alreadie made a good beginninge, & doe proceede, and dailie profit in the way of vertue, & mortification, tēding a pace to perfectiō, to which kind of men, are applied for matter of meditation, the miſteries of Chriſts life, as his baptiſme, his going to the deſert, his faſting, preaching, & miracles, his laſt ſupper, & laſtly the particuler points, & circumſtāces of his paſſiō, & death: the due cōſideration whereof, together with the former miſteries of his incarnatiō, natiuity, and infancie, may worke in anie pious mind foure effects, neceſſarie for

Idem ibid.

euerie Christian man. The first, a perfect vnderstãding, & a high esteeme of the inestimable worthines of our Sauiours person. The second, the knowledge of our obligation, and dutie to him. The third (proceeding of the two former) a feruent affection, and loue to him, aswell in respect of his infinit dignitie, and excellencie, as of his loue, and benefits to vs. The fourth, an earnest desire, and endeuour, to imitate his vertues, which euerie man is bound to doe, more or lesse, according to his vocation, and state.

3 But forasmuch, as it happeneth, not onlie to Nouices, or younge beginners, but also to the greatest contemplatiues, to feele sometimes great ariditie, and desolation in their soules, and sometimes againe, to be molested with distractions, by the meanes of vaine phantasies, and cogitations, therefore I thinke good, before I proceede further, to giue some aduertisements to yonge beginners, cõcerning the causes of distraction, and desolation, and the remedies of both.

P. Bartholomeo Ricci instruc. di meditare p.3.c.2.

4 *Distraction*, growing of wandring cogitations, and thoughts, which hinder our attention in meditation, proceedeth for the most part, either from our senses, drawne to their obiects, or from our phantasie, framing chimeraes, and building (as a man may say) castles in the aire, or from the passions of anger, enuie, loue, feare, or sorrow, and such like, mouing vs to thoughts conforme to their natures, and to some occasions ministred before: or els it proceedeth, from some serious busines, or perhaps from some earnest studie, wherewith we were latelie occupied: or lastly from the suggestion of the diuel, who serueth himselfe of all these meanes, and manie other to distract, and molest vs in our meditation, and praier.

Ioan. Cassian. Collat. 10. ca 14.

5 The remedie against distraction, proceeding from our senses, and phantasie, is to vse preuention, which may be donne diuers waies. The first is, to accustome our selues ordinarilie, aswell out of praier, as in praier, to restraine our senses, as much as may be, from their obiects: for the lesse, that the soule scattereth it selfe abroad by the senses, the more it is recollected within it selfe, and able to performe the worke of contemplatiõ, whereof we haue a notable example in *S. Bernard*, who being a yeare in a cell, could not tell so much, as what kind of roofe it had, neither yet whether there was more then one window in a Church, which had manie windowes, though he had gonne thither dailie for a long time: besides that passing a whole day by the great lake of *Losanna*, either he saw it not at all, or els tooke so litle heede of it, that at night he remembred it not, so obseruant, and heedefull was he in the vse of his senses, that he applied them to nothing, but to what necessitie required, retyring

P. Bartholo. Ricci. instruc. di. meditare.

Combattimento spirituale.

retyring himselfe alwaies with in himselfe, whereby he easelie, and spedelie became a most perfect contemplatiue.

6 And the like is written of a holie man in our daies, called *F. Pedro de Alcantara* a Spaniard, of the holie order of *S. Francis.* This Father was three yeares in a couent, and knew none of his brethren by sight, for that he neuer lifted vp his eies, and when he was to goe anie whither abroad with the rest, he neuer looked vp but followed them, and in manie yeares he neuer beheld anie woman, by which meanes he arriued to admirable perfection of contemplation, and sanctitie of life, whereof I shall haue occasion to speake more heareafter. *M. Teresa nella vita sua ca. 27.*

But because this kind of remedie cannot be practised, either by seculer men, or such religious as embrace the mixt life, which is both contemplatiue, and actiue (as was the life of our Sauiour, and his Apostles, and is of the greatest perfection, as I will declare more amplie hereafter) therefore to such, I say, that they must seeke to preuent the distractions in praier, which proceede of the fantasie, and senses (not so much by flight, or auoiding all occasions, which in their course of life is not possible) as by the way of combat, and victorie, vsing preuention in the practise of two things. *Combattimento Spirituale.*

7 The one is, that they vse to draw spiritual lessons, and documents, out of all that which representeth it selfe to their senses and phantasie, obseruing therein, either the power, or the wisdome, bountie, mercie iustice, or iudgements of God, according to the nature, or qualitie of the things, or matter represented vnto them; and further to seeke to glorifie God in all his creatures, and by all mens actions, be they good, or bad, taking occasion by all thinges that occurre to their senses, or imagination, to praise God, to thanke him, for his gifts, or to craue his grace; as for example, when they perceiue their senses to be ouermuch fixed vppon anie creature, let them seeke presentlie, to penetrate the same with the inward eye of their faith, & to see in it almightie God, who created, and conserueth it, and say vnto him (at least in their soule) Thou o Lord, art in all thy creatures more present, then they are to them selues, and yet I vngratefull, and carelesse wretch, doe not thinke vppon thee, doe not loue thee, nor honour thee, as I should. *Ibid. ca 13.*

8 And when they note in an other man, either power, or wisdome, iustice, bountie, or anie other perfection, let them lift vp their mind to God, and say in their soules, behold the riuers that flow from the increated fountaine, and from the bottomlesse sea of the deuine perfections, and then considering, how incomprehensible the same are in his deuine essence, let them stirre vpp themselues to reioyce, and ioy therein, yea more,

more, then if they were their owne. And if they find themselues at anie time to be ouer much drawne, and delighted with the beautie of anie creature, let them passe presentlie to the consideratiō of the deuine beautie, and say, when shall I, o Lord, place all my delight in thee, and see the incomprehensible beautie of thy glorious face?

9 Also they may in other manner, represse the excesse of anie vaine delight, that shall offer it selfe vnto them in anie creature, if they consider, that the infernall serpēt lieth hid vnder the same delight, readie to sting, and strike them to death, and therefore they may say. O cursed serpent, how craftilie liest thou lurking in Gods creatures to kill me? And then raising their mind to God they may say vnto him: Blessed art thou my Lord, that hast discouered vnto me the deceipt of my enemy, who might otherwise haue ouerthrowne me.

10 Moreouer, in the varietie of all humane accidents, that may happen vnto them, or to anie other, they are to consider the eternal prouidence of God, thereby to moue themselues, to take cōsolation in that his holly will is fulfilled, and the effects of his infinit wisdome, bountie, iudgements, and iustice shewed therein, be it in sicknes, health, heate, cold, good, or ill successe of busines, or what soeuer happeneth to men in this life.

11 Finallie, whensoeuer they shall haue, either these, or anie other good thoughts, they ought to acknowledge the same, as a speciall grace, and fauour of his deuine maiestie, and most humblie to adore him in their soule, and thanke him for it. For if the custome, and practise of these aduises, grow once to an habit, it will follow, that whatsoeuer occurreth to the senses, or is suggested by the diuell to the phantasie in time of praier, it shall at least minister matter, and occasion of good, and meritorious thoughts to his confusion.

12 The other meanes to preuent distraction, is, that when their phantasie is not occupied with some necessarie busines, they vse to frame to themselues imaginations, either of our Sauiours person, life, and passion, or of his glorie in heauen, and other heauenlie things, to the end, that such cogitatiōs, being by custome become vsuall, and familiar with thē, may not onlie alwais easelie occurre, but also exclude idle thoughts, and vaine imaginations, and stirre the soule to deuotion, and to the loue of God: for he that vseth to feede his fancie with toies, and vaine cōceits, shall not be rid of them when he would, & therefore to be free of them in time of meditation, we must not admit them at other times: as he that will not be bitten, and troubled with gnats in the night, must keepe his windowes shut in the day, for when they are once entred, it is to late to expell

expell them, in which respect *Caßianus* aduiseth vs, to be such out of the time of praier, as we would be in praier. *Cassianus colloq. 10. ca. 13.*

13 The like preuention is also to be vsed against the distractions that rise by the passions of the mind, to wit alwaise to combat with them, & to labour to resist, & represse them, accustoming our selues, when they molest vs, to ruminat, & meditat seriouslie vppon the houre of death, the seuere and terrible iudgements of God, and the horrour of hell, and eternal damnation; whereto I will add two notable, and necessarie remedies. *P. Ricci instructione di meditare p. 3. ca. 3.*

14 The one, to accustome our selues, as soone as wee feele their verie first motions, to lift vp our harts to God, & to say with the psalmist, either vocallie, or mentallie; *Miserere mei Domine quoniam infirmus sum; haue mercy vppon me o Lord for I am vveake*? or, *Adiutor & liberator meus es tu Domine, ne moreris: thou art my helper, and deliuerer, O Lord, doe not stay, or make delay*: and if the assalts continue, or be violēt, then to say: *Domine, vim patior, responde pro me: O Lord, I suffer violence, ansvvere thou for me*: or, *Saluum me fac Deus, quoniam intrauerunt aquæ vsque ad animam meam: Saue me, o Lord, for the vvaters haue entred euen into my soule*, or such like. *Psal. 6.* *Psal. 69.* *Esay. 38.* *Psal. 68.*

15 The other remedy is, by way of preuētiō: first, most earnestly to craue of almightie God euerie day in our mornings meditatiōs, his grace, & assistance against those passions, whereto we are most subiect: secondly to stand, as it were, vppon our gard, & to keepe watch vppon our selues all the day, that we be not ouertaken with them: Thirdlie if by frailtie we fall into them, to doe some kind of penāce, either presentlie (if it may be dōne with out note,) or els as soone after, as may be, as for exāple, to saie some verse of a psalme, or short praier, or to gieue some almes: or if the fall be greater then ordinarie, to depriue our selues of some part of our dinner, or supper, or of the whole, and neuer to dispence with our selues in this custome, which will make vs euerie day be more warie then other, and almightie God seeing our good desire, and endeuour, will, vndoutedlie, help vs with his grace. *P. Pinelli nella breue instructione al lettore nel principio delle meditationi sopra li sette peccati &c.*

16 And it shall not be amisse to vse this exercise, principallie against some one passion, for 10. or 15. daies together, and then to passe to an other, for as manie daies more, and after to an other, and so to returne againe to the first: as, to combat in this manner against pride, and vaine glorie, for 10. or 15. daies, and then against enuie, for as manie, and in like mãner against euerie imperfection: which practise, no doubt, will in short time aduance vs to greate perfectiō, especiallie, if we seeke not onlie to roote out these vices, but also to plant in our soules the contrary vertues: as for example, when we combat against the vice of pride, *Idem ibid.*

not onlie to craue in our praiers the vertue of humilitie, but also to determin with our selues, to doe euerie day during those 10. or 15. daies, some acts of that vertue, and euerie euening to examin our selues, whether we haue donne them, or no; and if we haue, then to thanke God for it, but if we haue not, then to doe some penance, (as is a foresaid) especiallie if we haue wilfullie omitted, and neglected to doe it, when some good occasion hath benne offred: and for conclusion of this practise, I would thinke it conuenient also, to receiue the blessed sacrament once within 10. or 15. daies, of purpose to demaund Gods grace, and assistance for the exclusion of the vice, and the infusion of the vertue: And I dout not but whosoeuer shall dulie practise this, he shall within a while, with Gods helpe, free himselfe from the tirannie of his passions, & peruers affections, not onlie in the time of meditation & praier, but also in all other occasions, with vnspeakable contentment, and peace of soule. Thus much concerning the distractions that grow of our passions in meditation.

17 In like maner, the distractions that rise by the occasion of worldlie busines, may be in great part preuented, and remedied, by the obseruatiō of these points following, to wit, that we neuer vndertake anie busines, but that it may be some way for Gods glorie, that we referr all our endeuours, and negotiations thereto, calling the same to mind oft times, or rather continuallie (as much as our frailtie may permit) that we neuer suffer the affection, or loue of anie worldlie affaire, so to possesse our soule, that we doe not principallie affect and attend to our cheefe busines, which is the seruice of God, and our owne saluation; and that therfore we accustome our selues, amidst all our negotiations, to eleuat, and lift our mindes often to almightie God, with manie holie aspirations, & iaculatorie praiers, praises, and thankes to him, crauing his grace, and assistance as occasion shall require; and finallie that we accustome our selues, to consider in all our temporal negotiations, how vaine, fraile, and casual, are all the affaires of mortall men, & all other worldlie thinges, whereby we may be moued in all occasiōs, to contemne the world, and all the vanities thereof; where vppon two speciall commodities will follow, the one, that God will giue the better successe to our busines, and the other, that the loue of temporall affaires, shall neuer take such roote in our soules, but that the loue of God shall euer predominat, and easilie expell it, especiallie in time of recollection, and praier.

18 And such wilbe the fruit of this exercise, that whosoeuer doth duly practise it, he shall not onlie meditate, and pray, but also conuerse with men in all kind of affaires, without much distraction, and shalbe, as it

were,

were, retired, and alone, euen amongst milliōs of men, as *S. Bernard* signi- S. Bernard
fieth notablie, saying. *O sancta anima sola esto* &c. *O holy soule be alone* &c. *sepe-* super cant.
rat thy selfe from companie, I meane, not in body, but in soule, in intention, in deuo- ser. 40.
tion, in spirit &c. *thou art alone, if thou doest not occupie thy mind vvith ordinary co-*
gitations, if thou doest not set thy affection vppon present, and vvorldly things, if thou
despisest that vvhich most men admire, if thou dost loath that vvhich all men desire
&c. *For othervvise thou art not alone, though thou be neuer so solitarie, so that thou*
seest both hovv thou maist be alone amongst many, and amongst manie vvhen thou
art alone. Thus saith *S. Bernard*. And the verie like saith *S. Gregory*, conclu- S. Greg.
ding, that the highest perfection of *mental solitud*, that is to say of contem- Moral. li. 30.
plation *is to be attributed to those that liue in conuersation*, meaning those that ca. 12.
leade the mixt life (partlie contemplatiue, and partlie actiue) and yet
haue true solitud and recollection of mind in action and negotiation.

19 An other meanes to preuent distractions, growing by busines, is, that we passe not immediatlie from anie serious negotiation, or earnest studie to mental praier, but to interpose some time betwixt the one, and the other, and to dispose, or prepare our minds to meditation, either by some vocal praier with conuenient attention, or by reading some spirituall booke, for reading concurring with meditation, and praier, is the most speciall meanes to attaine to perfect contemplation, as a certaine contemplatiue father witnesseth, saying, that *reading doth minister*, as it were, *meate to our mouthes, meditation doth ruminat, and chevv it, praier obtaineth the tast of it, and contemplation is the svveetenes it selfe, vvhich recreateth, & delighteth*, and this (saith he) our Sauiour may seeme to haue insinuated in these wordes, *quærite, & inuenietis, pulsate & aperietur vobis*, that is to say, *seeke* by reading, *and you shall find*, by meditation, *knock*, by praier, *and it shalbe opened vnto you*, by contemplation. Thus he. (Scala parad. inter opera Aug. To. 9.) (Matth. 7.)

20 But forasmuch as there are some, who for want either of health or of natural habilitie, and capacitie cannot discourse with the vnderstanding, and meditate, or vse mental praier, I think good to aduertise them by the way, that they doe not discomfort themselues therewith, as though they were excluded thereby from the effect, & fruit of contēplation, for almightie God who expecteth not, or desireth more of vs then we haue habilitie to performe, is wont out of his infinit bountie, to supplie the natural defects of such as doe their best endeuour, and aduanceth them manie times to a heigher degree of contemplation in a short time, then men of greater talent in manie yeares. (Padre Luis de la Puente introduction a la orat. mental §10.)

21 Therefore such as cannot meditate or pray mentallie, may content themselues with the serious reading of some deuout prayers, or spiritual matter, with due ponderation of the sence, & frequent eleuatiōs of their

P. Ribera nella vita di. M. Teresa.l.4.c.8. Camino de perfection.

mind to God, as the matter may minister occasion vnto them, and if they cannot read, they may vse onlie their vocal praier, with greate attentiō, and desire of deuotion: for, this being accompanied with continual diligence, and endeuour to mortifie their passions, & affections, (which in this exercise most importeth) may suffise to raise them to the perfection of contemplation, and vnion with God, whereof the experience hath bene seene in such, as could neuer in their liues, say other praier then their *Pater noster.*

Ibid.

22 Furthermore it is a special helpe against all kind of distractions, to retire our selues in time of praier to some solitarie place, for as the prophet witnesseth, *Sedebit solitarius &c. the solitary man shall sit, & hold his peace, because he vvill raise, or eleuat him selfe aboue him selfe*, and the Prophet *Osee*, saith, *ducam eam in solitudinem, & ibi loquar ad cor eius, I vvill lead her,* (that is to say a contemplatiue soule) *into the desert, and there I vvill speake to her hart.* And this our Sauiour *Christ* both aduised, and practised, who, not onlie counselled vs to enter into our chamber, and to shut the dore when we pray, but also vsed to retire him selfe oft vnto the mountaine, where he passed whole nights in praier, & though, a litle before his passiō, whē he wēt into the gardaine, he tooke with him three of his disciples, yet he with drew himselfe frō thē, (saith the scripture) *a stones cast*, to the end he might pray alone, & this he did onlie for our example, being himselfe alwaise so recollected within him selfe, that no cōpanie, or occasiō could distract him from the highest, & most perfect contemplation.

Thren.3. Osee 2. Matth.6. Luc.6. Matth.26. Luc. 22.

23 It is also a soueraine remedie against distractions to frame in our imaginations the forme, and manner of the actions persons, and places whereof we are to meditat, which being well printed in our minds at the first, and after renewed, as occasion is offred, doth helpe greatelie to entertaine, and stay the phantasie from wandring to other matters. Therefore *B. Ignatius* (founder of the hollie societie of *Iesus*, and an exact maister of contemplatiō,) was wont before he went to meditation, stedfastlie to behold some Image or picture, representing some such misterie of our Sauiours life, or passiō, as he meant to make the subiect of his meditation, to the end that it might rest the better setled, & engrauen in his phātasie. And this being well practised in our mornings meditatiōs, will serue for a notable entertainement of our soule, and an excellēt remedy against distractions in our praiers all the day after, especiallie if we seeke now & then to renew the imagination thereof, whereby we shall also easilie remember all the good purposes which we made therein, and be the more reddie to execute them, as occasion shall be offred.

P. Bartolom. Ricci in vita Christi ex euang. præfat ad lecto.

24 Also it importeth greatelie for the auoiding of distractiōs, that the matter of our meditation be well disposed, ordered, and deuided into points,

points,which being committed to memorie,afford sufficient matter of discourse to the vnderstanding, and motiues to the will to exercise her acts of deuotion,and loue to God: For although we are not so to tie our selues to anie certaine matter,or method in meditation,that we may not take hold of anie other that shall be ministred vnto vs in time of praier by inspiratiō of almightie God,(whose impulse,& motiō,as it is the special cause of this holie woorke, so ought it principallie to be regarded therein)neuertheles such is the ordinary course of his deuine prouidēce, that he then cōcurreth most with our actions, when we vse the greatest diligēce on our part,& therefore it cōmonly falleth out that our meditatiō is so much the more currēt,& fruitfull vnto vs,by how much better it is disposed,& prepared before hād,wherby our mind may be the more easily staied,& freed frō distractions,which we can hardly auoid, when for lack of sufficient preparation, we are forced to seeke matter whiles we meditat,by wandring,& leaping from one thing to an other, which is of it selfe a distraction,and therefore ought to be preuented.

P.Luys de la Puente meditat. de los misterios &c.ca. 5. To. 1.

25 Finally it specially importeth against all kind of distractiōs,most hūbly,& seriously to implore the assistāce of the holy Ghost, & to craue the illuminatiō of the holy angel,our keeper,& gardiā,& the prayers of the blessed virgin *Mary*,& of all the blessed saints,not only in the beginning of our meditation, and mental praier, but also through out the whole course thereof,as oft as we find our selues much molested;& if neuertheles the molestation of the distractions doth still cōtinue, it is to be borne with patience,& acknowledged, as a iust punishment for our sinnes,and former negligences, with such other considerations, as I will presently signifie for the remedies of desolation, whereof I am now to treate.

P.Ricci instructione di meditare, p.3.c.5.

26 *Desolation* comprehēdeth all kind of spiritual sterilitie,ariditie, or drines of soule, & obscuritie of vnderstanding, besides manie violent temptations which manie times concurre.

B.Ignat. exercit.Reg.ad motus &c. reg.4.

27 And this happeneth,now & then euen to the greatest cōtēplatiues,& dearest seruāts of God,as the royal prophet signified of himselfe, saying, *Cor meū conturbatū est* &c. *my hart is troobled,my vertue*,or force *hath abādoned mē,& the very light of my eies is not vvith me*,& againe he cōplaineth that his enemie persecuted his soule,that he was placed in obscurity,& darknes, *Sicut mortui sæculi,like the dead mē of the vvorld,that his spirit vvas full of anxiety*, & *that his soule* was *sicut terra sine aqua,like earth vvithout vvater*, that is to say steril,& dry,needing,& expecting some influēce ,or inundation of Gods grace. Thus lamented the royal prophet his owne desolation,& the like hath occurred to the holyest mē in all ages,as to omit other examples, we read of saint *Francis*, that he had greate desolation, and ariditie of soule for two yeeres and a halfe.

Psal.54. Psal. 142. Psal. 142.

F. Bartholo. da Saluthio nel paradiso de cōtēplat.

28 Of these desolations, diuers causes may be giuen, for some times they may proceede in great part of some indisposition, and infirmitie of the bodie, loaden, and opprest with melancholie, or perhaps with other humors, where vppon the deuil taketh the aduantage to tempt, & afflict vs, which the meditatour ought curiouslie to search, and examine in himselfe, for in that case, it were not good for him to striue to much with his owne weakenes, least perhaps he may oppresse nature, but rather to leaue his meditation for that time, and to take some other exercise of vocal praier, or reading some spiritual booke with great attention, pausing vppon such passages, and places as he findeth to moue, and stirre him most to deuotion.

29 Secondlie, desolation may grow of Gods iustice, punishing vs either for some negligence in his seruice, or for some ingratitude in refusing his holie inspirations, or for some inordinat delight in earthly thinges, or for some vaine glorie, and spiritual pride, or perhaps to preuent our fall into these, or some other sinne, wherevppon *S. Bernard* saith: *superbia inuenta est in me &c. pride hath bene found, or discouered in me, and there vppon hath growne my sterility of soule, my want of deuotion, my lacke of compunction and teares, in so much, that I haue nether delectation or tast in reading, nor in praier, nor in my wonted meditations, no inebriation of spirit, no serenity of mind, no ioy or peace in the holy Ghost.* Thus saith he. And a litle after he addeth, that although our conscience doe not accuse vs of pride, or vaine glorie spirituall, yet we may well feare, that God either findeth it in vs, and of his iustice correcteth it, or els foreseeth, that we would shortlie fall into it, and of his mercie preuenteth it, by shewing vs our owne infirmitie.

S. Bernar. ser. 54. in cantica.

30 Thirdlie almightie God, not onlie prooueth his best beloued seruants, but also purgeth, and as it were refineth them by this fire of spiritual tribulation, to their farre greater merit, and encrease of their vertues, by the exercise of their humilitie, patience, faith, hope, and charitie; for in their desolation they serue him onlie for pure loue, without their wonted pay, and reward of present consolations, with no lesse confidēce of his loue and mercie towards them, then when they receiued the greatest fauours, which now they euidentlie see proceedeth of his meere bountie, and liberalitie, and not of anie merit in them, yea and fearing least for some offence, or neglicence on their part, God may vtterly abandon them, they redouble their resignation, penance, & mortification, to the exceeding benefit of their soules, and therefore it commonlie falleth out, that after the greatest desolations, God giueth them the greatest cōforts, and illustrations, according to the saying of the royall prophet. *Secundum multitudinem dolorum meorum &c. According to the multitude of my*

Psalm. 37.

sorrowes thy consolations. O Lord, *haue giuen ioy to my soule.*

31 Thus I say, it fareth now, and then, with the greatest cōtemplatiues, and most faithful seruants of God. But it falleth out manie times much otherwise with others, for some serue God with great feruour, so long as they feele sweetenes, and sensible deuotion in their praiers, yea, and conceiue otherwhiles that they are alreadie growne to a great perfection of hollines, in so much, that they expect reuelations, or some miraculous operations in them selues, or to be donne by their meanes, and when afterwards they fall into some desolation, and find themselues depriued of all sensible comfort, they are vtterlie dismaied there with, & become so impatient, that they leaue their wonted exercise of praier, and meditation, & within a while doe vtterlie loose their spirit, shewing thereby that they serued not God for him selfe, but for his giftes, and sought not him, but them selues, and their owne delight; and finallie that they are those, who (as our Sauiour said) *doe take no roote in his seruice, but beleeue for a time, and in time of temptation forsake him.* *Luc. 8.*

32 Therefore, I will for the remedie hereof, sett downe some points to be considered and practised by yong beginners, in time of spiritual desolation, whereby they may receiue some comfort, and the better continue their exercise of meditation, vntill it please God to restore them to their former serenity.

33 First they are to consider, that the perfection of contemplation doth not consist in sensible deuotion, and spiritual sweetenes, or delectation (which is manie times rather a natural, then a spiritual affection) but in a strong faith, profound humilitie, true resignation of will, to the will of God, contempt of the world, pure, and feruent loue of God, and a desire to suffer for him, and further more that it pleaseth him sometimes, to withhold all spiritual comefort from his seruants, and as it were to hide himselfe from them, euen within themselues for a time, to appeare more glorious vnto them afterwards, to their farr greater comefort, as to omit manie other examples, it appeared in *S. Katherin* of *Siena*, when once, in time of great desolatiō, she was exceedinglie tempted and afflicted with impure, and filthie thoughts: for afterwards when our Sauiour appeared vnto her, and comforted her, and shee complained vnto him of the great affliction which shee had endured, yea, and asked him, where he was during her conflict, he answered, that he was in her hart: how could it be, quoth shee, that thou wast in my hart, whiles it was so full of filthie thoughts? But didst thou, said he, consent vnto them? And when shee answered, no, then said he, thereby thou maiest vnderstand, that I was there, for otherwise thou couldest not haue resisted. The like also

M. Teresa nella vita sua. c. 11. Blosius vbi supra, & in institut. spirit. c. 7.

P. Ribadeneira en la vida de S. Katerina.

passed,

S.Athanaſius in vita S.Antonij.

paſſed with S.Anthony, and other holie men, whom God exerciſed, and proued in that manner, ſeeming to leaue them to them ſelues for a time, though neuertheles, he did not abandon them, but gaue them ſufficient grace to reſiſt the temptations of the enimie, to their great encreaſe of meritt.

Lodouic. Bloſius.

34 But how ſoeuer God ſuffereth this in his beſt beloued ſeruants, and men of the higheſt contemplation, onlie for their probatiō, yet younge beginners ſhall doe well to perſwade themſelues (as with great reaſon they may) that their deſolation, is a iuſt puniſhment for their ſinnes, and therefore let them take occaſiō thereby, to enter into a deepe, & ſerious examination of themſelues, by what ſinne, negligence, or ingratitude, they haue deſerued it, and finding the cauſe thereof, let them labour by contrition, penance, and mortification, to ſatisfie the iuſtice of God, and to amend what they haue done amiſſe; and though their conſcience accuſe them of nothing, yet as S.Bernard aduiſeth, let them feare the rigour of Gods ſecret iudgement, and rather impute it, to ſome hidden fault of theirs, then thinke that God onlie prooueth them thereby for their greater merit, let them I ſay, humble themſelues moſt profoundlie in the ſight of God, acknowledging with the royall prophet, that they are nothing els, but *vanity*, and as Iob ſaith, *folium quod vento rapitur*, a leafe caried away with euerie wind, of vaine cogitations, *ſtipula ſicca*, *a dry ſtravv*, and as the Apoſtle teacheth, *not able to thinke a good thought of themſelues, as of themſelues, but that all their ſufficiency is of God.*

S. Bernar. ſer:54. ſuper Cantica.

Pſal.38. Iob.13. Ibid. 2 Cor.3.

35 Furthermore, they may alſo conſider that they ought to hould it for ſufficient honour, and a ſpecial fauour for them, to be but *abiects in the houſe of God*, and admitted into his familie, though it be but to digg, and delue in his garden, all the daies of their liues, rather for loue, then reward, for dutie, and not for intereſt: and therefore let them ſay with the prodigal child, *Fac me quaſi vnum, ex mercenarijs tuis, &c. make me*, o Lord, *one of thy vvoorke men*, or hyrelings, *for I am not vvorthie to be called thy child:* and let them offer themſelues as his creatures, to ſerue him in what ſort, or condition ſoeuer it ſhall pleaſe him, though it be to no other end, thē to beare his burthens like a packe horſe, ſaying with the pſalmiſt, *vt iumentum factus ſum apud te, & ego ſemper tecum*, *I am become thy packhorſe*, *or bearing beaſt, and vvill alvvaies be vvith thee*, to beare thy burdens, and carry thy croſſe after thee, let them I ſay, offer themſelues to ſerue him, with what diſguſt, paine, or penaltie ſoeuer, ſo that it may pleaſe him to graunt them perſeuerance.

Pſal.83. P.Ribera nella vita di M. Tereſia li.4.c.8. Luc.15.

Pſal.72.

36 Moreouer, they may call to mind how manie ſuters in princes courtes, are not admitted to the ſpeech of ſome meane officer, and after many

repulſes,

repulses, and some yeares trauaile, loose all their labour, and expectation, whereas they on the other side, haue free accesse to the king of kinges, and Lord of lords, being sure to be heard without scorne, or contempt, and not to be affronted, or wronged by officers, and seruants, or excluded by porters, or pages, but fauoured, and furthered by holie angels, and saincts, and all the celestiall court (whose aide and assistance, they may therefore boldlie craue) assuring themselues, that though it seemeth to them, that they are neglected, and contemned, yet they are but onlie delaied for their greater good, and better dispatch in the end, if they haue patience and perseuerance. Therefore let them take the wordes of the psalmist, as spoken to them selues. *Expecta Dominum, viriliter age, confortetur* Psal.26.
cor tuum, & sustine Dominum. Expect thy lords leasure, play the man, and be of courage, comfort thy hart, and beare, or sustaine thy Lord. Let them say to their Psal.41.
owne soules. *Quare tristis es anima mea &c. VVhy art thou sad my soule, vvhy doest thou trouble me? hope in God, for I vvill still cōfesse him.* And with *Iob; Etiamsi* Iob.13.
me occiderit sperabo in eum. Though he kill me, I vvill hope in him.

37 And if they haue had anie speciall fauours, and spiritual consolations from almightie God in former times, let them now remember it in their desolation, and say with *Iob. Si bona de manu Domini suscepimus*, &c. Iob.2.
If vve haue receiued good things from the hand of God, vvhy shall not vve also, be content to receiue euill? Dominus dedit, Dominus abstulit &c. *Our Lord gaue them, our Lord hath taken them avvay, the name of our Lord be blessed*, Yea, and considering Gods infinit mercy, and that it is he, *qui mortificat, & viuificat, vvho* 1.Reg.7.
mortifieth, and reuiueth, let them comfort them selues with hope of faire weather after this storme, saying also with *Iob. Rursum post tenebras* Iob.17.
spero lucem. After this darkenes, of desolation, *I hope againe to see the light of* consolation.

38 Furthermore one speciall remedie against desolation is, to be furnished not onlie with these considerations before mētioned, but also with diuers examples and places of the holie scripture, whereof the remembrance and meditation may at that time yeld them comfort, and help to reduce them to recollection; as for example. They may remember the Luc.2.
desolation of the blessed virgin *Mary*, & *S. Ioseph*, when they had lost our Sauiour, and went vp and doune seeking him amongst their frends, *dolentes*, saith the scripture, being full of sorrow 3. daies together, vntil they found him at length in the temple; And with this cōsideration they may seeke to moue them selues to a louing and deuout compassion of their sorrow and affliction, and to accompanie them therein, recommending also their owne affliction to them, & beseeching our sweet Sauiour, for the merits of his blessed mother & hollie *S. Ioseph*, to giue them grace to

ſeeke him with ſuch ſorrow, diligence and deuotion, that they may find him in the temple of their owne ſoule.

39 Let them remember how the bleſſed Apoſtles, being in a ship at ſea, when our Sauiour was abſent from them, were toſſed wit winds, and waues, the greateſt part of the night, vntil at length he came to them, walking vppon the water, and appeaſed the storme and comforted them with his heauenlie voice, ſaying. *Ego ſum, no lite timere. It is I, be not afraid.* Let them I ſay, humblie beſeech him to behold their trauaile, and danger, in this his abſence from them and to giue them the grace of perſeuerance, and ſtrength, to con tinue their labour, vntil it may pleaſe him, to returne vnto them and with the comfort of his bleſſed preſence, and aſſiſtance to appeaſ the ſtorme that toſſeth, and tormenteth them.

Matth.14.

Mathevv. 15. Mar.7.

40 Let them call to mind the woman of *Cananea*, who ſtill per ſeuered crying after our Lord, though as the ſcripture ſaith, *he an ſvvered her not avvord*, and when at the ſuite of his Apoſtles, h ſpoke at laſt vnto her, and gaue hard language (comparing her to dogge) ſaying, *that it vvas not fit to giue the bread of children to dogges* shee had neuertheles ſuch confidence in his mercie, that she lai her ſelfe proſtrat at his feete, crauing but the crumes that fell fro his table, by which humilitie, and perſeuerance, shee obtained he ſuite. Let them therefore in like ſort crie out after him, and ſa with her, *Miſerere mei Domine, fili Dauid* &c. *O Lord, the ſonne of Da uid, haue mercy vppon me, for my daughter*, that is to ſay my ſoule, i terriblie vexed: and acknowledging themſelues to be no better the dogges in his ſight, let them craue but ſome few crumes of his hea uenlie comfort, onlie to enable them, to beare their burthen, ſ long as it shall pleaſe him to ordeine.

Ibid.

Ibid.

41 Let them alſo conſider our Sauiours conflict in the garden when he ſweate water and bloud, and recommend vnto him thei affliction, in the vnion, and merits of his agonie, crauing of him that as he, hauing then neede of conſolation in his humanitie, wa comforted from heauen by an angel, ſo alſo it may pleaſe him to graun them comfort in their diſtreſſe, ſaying neuertheleſſe with him. *Non ſicu ego volo; ſed ſicut tu vis, fiat voluntas tua. Yet not as I vvill*, o Lord, *but as tho vvilt, thy vvil be donne.*

Matth.26. Marc.14.

42 Let them alſo remember his deſolation vppon the croſſe, wher for our encouragement, and comfort, he was content to be leaſ ſo comfortles, that he ſaid, to his Father. *Deus, Deus meus, vt qui dereliquiſti me? My God, my God, vvhy haſt thou forſaken me.* And fo aſmuch

Matth.27. Marc.15.

asmuch as the perfection of a Christian man, consisteth in his conformitie with Christ, no lesse in suffering with him, then in imitating his vertues, and seeing that his great desolation in the garden, and vppon the crosse, was no doubt the greatest of all the paines that he suffred for vs, let them take comfort in that it pleaseth him, to giue them some tast of what he suffred therein whereby they may haue also the more conformitie with him; and therefore let them not desire to be eased thereof, further then it shall please him, but onlie say with the psalmist. *Ne derelinquas me vsquequaque. Doe not o Lord, forsake me altogether.* Vppon which wordes, *Cassianus* noteth, that the prophet *Dauid* knowing well, that it was not inconuenient, but profitable for him, that God should sometimes withdraw himselfe from him, to make him see, and know his owne weakenes, did not absolutelie desire that God should neuer leaue him in anie sort, but that he would not vtterlie, or altogether abandon him. *Psal.118.*

43 They may therefore say with the same psalmist. *Ne proijcias me a facie tua. Doe not quyte cast me of, from thy face: spiritum sanctum tuum ne auferas a me: doe not take from me thy hollie spirit: Redde mihi lætitiam, salutaris tui &c. restore vnto me the ioy,* and gladnes *of thy saluation*. Let them also inuocat the holie spirit of God with that most excellent Hymne. *Veni sancte spiritus, & emitte cælitus, lucis tuæ radium* &c. pondering euerie sentence of it with special attention, which may greatlie helpe; aswell to recollect their distracted thoughts, as also to reuiue in them some heate of the deuine loue. *Psal.50.* *Robertus rex franciæ.*

44 Finallie, let them beseech almightie God, that if it please him, not to giue them recollection, and peace of soule, yet at least he vouch safe to graunt, that their distraction, and desolation, be not offensiue vnto him, or an occasion to withdraw them from his loue, and so no doubt, he will giue them, either present consolation, or els the grace of longanimitie, patience, and perseuerance, with farre greater merit, especiallie if they add to these former meanes some mortification, and penance for the loue of him, and punishment of their sinnes.

45 I will conclude concerning this point, with an aduise of *Ecclesiastes*, worthie to be considered, and practised of all those, that aspire to vnion with almightie God by contemplation. *Sustine*, saith he, *sustentationes Dei, coniungere Deo, & sustine, vt in nouissimo crescat vita tua. Beare the burdens of God, be vnited, or ioyned vvith God,* *Eccles.3.*

and beare vvith patience, that thy life may grovv in the end. Thus ſaith the preacher, giuing to vnderſtand, that the vnion with God in this life, doth not free, or exempt vs from temptations, and afflictions, but rather is infalliblie conioyned therewith, and that the patient ſuffring thereof, is the aſſured meanes, to bring vs to an inſeperable, and eternal vnion with him in the end: and this is to be vnderſtood, aſwell of the deſolations, and ſpiritual temptations (whereof I haue hitherto ſpokẽ) as alſo of all kind of corporall, and temporall afflictions, whereto the ſeruants of God, are, by his mercifull prouidence, expoſed in this life, for their euerlaſting good,

46 And as for deſolation (whereof I ſpeciallie treate at this preſent) it is further to be conſidered, that the ſame is manie times, farre more ſecure for the ſoule, and conſequentlie more to be deſired, then conſolation, and ſenſible ſweetenes, for two reſpects: the one, becauſe in deſolation there is no danger of ſelfeloue, or ſpiritual pride, but rather occaſion of humilitie, and of the true knowledge of our owne weakenes, whereas ſenſible delectation, and ſweetenes in praier, doe breede manie times the moth (as I may ſay) of ſelfeloue, and vaine glorie, which if it be not remedied in time, will depriue vs of all the fruite of our deuotion, and of Gods grace in the end.

B. Ignatius exercit. Reg. alia vtiles &c. reg. 4. 2, Cor. 11. Bloſius Can. vita ſpirit. ca. 26.

47 The other reſpect is, the danger of diabolical illuſions, which in the deſolation, & ariditie of the ſoule, is not much to be feared, but may well be doubted in ſpiritual delectation, for that the deuil (who ſometimes *transformeth him ſelfe into the angel of light*) doth otherwhiles ſeeke to worke, and procure falſe conſolations in a deuout ſoule, thereby to draw it firſt to vaine glorie, and after to certaine ſingularities, & by litle and litle, vtterlie to ouerthrow it, if it be not preuented in time.

48 Therefore, ſeeing that thoſe which giue themſelues to the exerciſe of contemplatiue diſciplin, had neede to beware of illuſions, and that it would require a farr larger diſcourſe, then this place will permit to ſett downe rules for the diſcerninge of ſpirits, I wish one general rule to be obſerued, which is moſt neceſſarie for all ſuch, as vndertake the exerciſe of contemplation, and may ſuffice alone, if it be dulie practiſed: to wit, that no man preſume to be his owne guide, and directer therein, but that he make choiſe of ſome expert maſter (if he be not by regular obedience bound to anie) and open freelie to him, without reſeruation all the ſecrets of his ſoule, and motions, good, and bad, and that he follow his direction in all humilitie, aſſuring himſelfe that his obedience, and reſignation therein, wilbe ſo gratefull to almightie God, that he will not ſuffer him to be miſled.

49 This

49 This is the aduiſe of all the Fathers, that haue written of this matter and therefore *S.Baſil* ſaith, that euen as God hath ordained that faith, which is his gift, is to be obtained by hearing: ſo alſo he hath decreed, that the doctrin of Chriſtian perfection (which is built vppon the foundation of faith) shall not otherwaiſe be learned, but by the voyce of a maſter, or teacher. *S.Gregory* alſo teſtifieth, that *he vvhich ſo farr preſumeth vppon the aſſiſtance of the holie Ghoſt, that he refuſeth to be a diſciple, or ſcholler of men, becommeth a maſter of errour.* *S.Bernard* ſaith elegantlie, that *he vvhich vvilbe his ovvne ſcholler, shall haue a foole to his maſter.* And *Ioannes Caſſian* affirmeth, that the deuil doth not anie way ſooner, or more dangerouſlie deceaue thoſe, which giue them ſelues to the contemplatiue life, then by perſwading them, to truſt to them ſelues, and to neglect the aduiſe, and directiō of a ſuperior, by which meanes, ſaith he, diuers haue greueouſly falne, both in ancient, and latter times.

D. Baſil. regul. breu. q.1
D.Greg. li.1. dial.c.1.
D. Bern. epiſt.87.
Ioan.Caſſian. collat. 2.ca.11.

50 Alſo *Ioannes Climacus*, teacheth that one onlie errour lurketh, and lieth hid in the courſe, or way of contemplatiue diſciplin, to wit. *Cum quiſque ſibi idoneus* &c. *VVhen anie man thinks him ſelfe fit to* rule, and gouerne him ſelfe, *vvhich errour,* ſaith he, *vvhoſoeuer can auoid, he shall arriue to thoſe thinges vvhich are good, and ſpirituall, and moſt gratefull to God, almoſt before he beginne, obedientia enim eſt* &c. *for true obedience is neuer to beleeue, or truſt our ſelues, during our liues, no not in thoſe thinges, vvhich ſeeme beſt vnto vs.* Thus ſaith he.

Ioan Climac. de obed. gradu. 4.

51 Finallie, that holie and bleſſed man, Father *Ignatius*, admonisheth, all thoſe that tend to perfection, to conſider, that the diuel will labour for nothing more, then to procure, that they conceale his ſuggeſtions, & temptations, and that if he can winne but ſo much at their handes, he will eaſelie deceiue them. In which reſpect, it is moſt expedient, that all ſuch as practiſe cōtemplatiue diſcipline, doe not onlie reſigne themſelues wholie to the direction of a ſuperiour, but alſo that they lay open vnto him their ſoules, and all the ſecrets thereof, to the end that they may be guided, and directed by him, and he that holdeth this courſe walketh ſecurelie, whereas otherwiſe there is greate danger of diabolicall illuſions, and errours, growing of ſelfeloue, and ſingularitie.

Reg.13. de diſcernendis ſpirit.
S.Greg.li. 1. 1.Reg.c. 1. in fine.
Caſſian de inſtitutis renuntiant.li. 4.c.9. & 37. Item collat. 16.c.11.

52 Now then, to returne to the practiſe of the *Illuminatiue* way, and to ſett downe ſome examples of the meditations belonging thereto. I will breefelie runne ouer ſome principall points, to be conſidered in our Sauiours Incarnation, ſuch onlie I meane, as concerne himſelfe, for bearing for breuities ſake, to touch manie moſt excellent, and notable points of ſingular edification, which may be obſerued in the ſtrong faith, the immaculat chaſtitie, the exemplar modeſtie, the profound humilitie, and

 reſignation

resignation of his most worthie mother, the blessed, and incontaminat virgin *Mary*, aduanced to the ineffable dignitie, not onlie to be called, but also to be indeede, the mother of God, in respect of her Sonnes hipostatical, or personal vnion with God himselfe, with whom also part of her, is by the same meanes, personallie vnited, for which cause, almighty God endewed her with incomparable graces, gifts, and priuiledges, and made her a mirrour of puritie, pietie, and all vertue, and therfore shee was worthilie called by the Angel *Gabriel*, *full of grace*, *and blessed amongst all vvomen*; by *S. Irenæus*, *the aduocate of Eue*; by *S. Athanasius*, his *mistresse*, his *lady*, his *queene*: and by *S. Ephrem*, the *peace*, the *ioy*, the *health*, and *comfort of the vvorld*; by *S. Chrisostome*, *the incontaminat mother of our God*, *more honorable*, *then the cherubyns*, and *incomparably more glorious then the seraphins*: by *S. Grigory Nazianzen*, the *light of virgins*, the *queene of the vvorld*, & *the ioy of mortal men*: by *S. Epiphanius*, the *mother of all those that haue spiritual life*: by *S. Fulgentius*, the *vvindovv of heauen*, *by the vvhich God gaue true light vnto the vvorld*: *and the heauenly ladder vvhereby God descended to the earth*, *and men clyme vp to heauen*: by *S. Bernard* (to omit manie others) the *mother of mercy*, the *ladder of sinners*, *his hope*, *and the hope of all Christians*: and lastlie *by all generations*, to the worlds end (as shee prophecied of her selfe) *she shalbe called blessed*, and be honored, and serued. But I forbeare, I say, for breuities sake, to obserue manie notable points, which occurre concerninge her, in the meditation of our Sauiours Incarnation, and will touch onlie some few, amongst innumerable others, which concerne aswell his diuinitie, as his humanitie.

Luc. 1. Iren. l. 5. contra hæres. Athanas. ser. in Euãg. de annun. Ephrem. orat. de laude Dei paræ. Chrisost. in liturgia. Greg. Naz. Traged. Christo passo. Epiph. hær. 78. G. Fulgent. ser. de laud. Mariæ. Bernard. 1. serm. de Assumptio. & in serm. de Aquæduct. Luc. 1.

53 First then, herein may be considered his *infinit goodnes*, as he was God, in that hauing manie other meanes, which he might haue vsed for the satisfaction of his iustice, & mans redemptiõ, yet he would vse no other, but the best, most honorable, and most profitable to man, that might be, that is to say, by taking our flesh, & making himselfe man, wherein also he discouered the infinit excellency of all his perfections, & deuine vertues: For first he shewed therein his *infinit bounty*, in communicating to man, not only his gifts, and graces, but also himselfe, by a personal vnion of himselfe with man: wherein he also shewed his infinit charity, & loue towards him, vniting his deuine nature, and the humane with such a straight bond, and linke, that one & the selfe same person, was both God & man: he shewed also his *infinit mercy*, in comming himselfe personally, not onlie to remedie our miseries, but also to participat of them, thereby to assure vs, that he would haue the more compassion of vs.

S. Thom. 3. par. quest. 1. ar. 1. ex S. Damascen. li. 3. orthodoxæ fidei c. 3. 1. Ibidem.

54 He shewed his *infinit iustice*, in that he made himselfe passible, to pay the penaltie of our sinne, which his iustice required: he shewed his *infinit vvisdome*,

Ibidem.

wisdome, in finding out such a wonderful meanes, to ioyne together things so distant, and different as God, and man, eternal, and temporal, impassible, and passible, mercie, and iustice, both of them in the highest degree, without the preiudice of either: he shewed his *omnipotency*, in doing for man the vttermost he could doe, making himselfe man, which was the greatest, and most wonderful worke, that euer he did, he shewed his *sanctity, hollynes*, and all his *vertues*, imprinting them in the humanity which he tooke vppō him, to the end, that the same might serue for an example, and paterne for all men to imitat, in all which, nothing seemeth more admirable, then that whereas *Adam* rebelled proudlie against God himselfe, seeking to vsurpe his diuinitie (for the which he deserued that his nature should be annichilated) almightie God, did not onlie pardon him, but also humble, & as it were annichilat himselfe, to exalt him, and his progenie, that was his rebellious enemy: yea and most liberallie bestowed vpon him, that which he had so presumptuouslie affected, to wit, his diuinitie and Godhead it selfe.

Ibidem.

Ibidem.

55 This then being well considered, with our infinit obligation to almighty God for the same, we may passe to the serious ponderation of the worke it selfe, of our Sauiours Incarnation, as that when the blessed virgin *Mary* had giuen her consent to the Angel, the holie ghost, by his deuine, and omnipotent power, framed in her sacred wombe, a most perfect bodie of her purest bloud, and created withall a most excellent soule, vniting not onlie the one with the other, but also both of them, with the person of the eternal word, the Sonne of God, in such a personal vnion, that, as I haue touched before, man became God, and God became man, and the deuine nature remained, as it were, insepe-rably wedded to our humane nature. Wherevppon ariseth this considera-tiō (besides many other which I omit) no lesse fruiteful, thē comfortable to vs, that euery one of vs, is by this meanes, perpetually, allied with almighty god, & that therfore we ought not only to loue, praise, & thāke him incessantly for the same, but also to take hart, and courage, amid the infirmities, and miseries of this life, & firmely to purpose (as *S. Leo* saith) to demeine our selues like the kinsmen, and allies of so great a king, and to doe nothing vnworthie of such a worthie, and noble alliance.

Leo serm. 1. de natiuitate.

56 And to the end we may the better vnderstand, and know, the inestimable excellencie of our Sauiours humanitie, we may consider, that whereas God giueth to men graces and giftes, with a certaine measure, that is to say, to no man all, but some to one man, and some to an other, he gaue all to him, without measure, or limitation, which neuertheles may be reduced to these heades following.

57 The

57 The first was, an incomparable innocencie, puritie, and cleanes of heart, without all kind of imperfection, or possibilitie to erre, or sinne, as it was conuenient for the most *innocent lambe, vvhich should take* Ioan. 1. *avvay the sinnes of the vvorld.*

58 The second was, the grace, or gift of a supereminent sanctitie, wherby he had all vertues in perfection, in respect whereof, he is worthylie called, *Sanctus Sanctorum, tho Holy of Holyes.* Dan. 9.

59 The third was, the full, and perfect vision of the deuine essence, whereto he was personallie vnited, which from the verie instant of his creation, he saw farre more clearelie, then all the angels, or the soules of men euer did, or euer shall doe, whereuppon also followed in him in like proportion, an vnmeasurable loue to God, and infinit ioy, in which respect the holie Ghost saith of him in the psalme. *Vnxit te Deus, Deus tuus,* Psal. 44. *oleo letitiæ præ consortibus tuis. God thy God, hath annointed thee, vvith the oile of gladnes, and ioy aboue all thy companions.*

Coloss. 2. 60 The fourth was, an immense, and inestimable treasure of deuine wisdome, and knowledge of all things, past, present, or to come.

61 The fift was, vnlimited power to doe miracles, when, where, and how it should please him, whereby he might raise the dead, commaund Luc. 4. the winds, sea, elements, and all creatures.

62 The sixt was, the power to remit sinnes, to conuert sinners, to or-Mathevv. 9. & vlt. daine, and institute sacrifices, and sacraments, to bestow graces, and supernatural gifts vppon men.

63 The seauenth was, to be head of his mistical bodie the Church, as-Ephes. 1. well the militant here in earth, as the triumphant in heauen, being the cheefe, and most worthie of all creatures in heauen, and earth, *Rex Regū,* Apoc. 19. *& Dominus dominantium, the king of kings, and Lord of lords* (and as the pro-Isay. 55. phet saith) *Dominus nominatus in signum æternum, & non auferetur ab eo. Called Lord for a sempiternall signe, vvhich shall not be taken from him.*

64 The eight was, to be the first, and principal of all the predestinat, for whose sake God did also predestinat all the rest, to the end he might Rom. 8. haue manie companions in glorie, or, as the Apostle saith *many brethren like to himsefe*, aswell in giftes of grace, as in nature.

65 The ninth, that he should be the redeemer, and Sauiour of mankind, and the onlie mediator, betwixt God, and man, who hath recon-1. Tim. 2. ciled vs to his Father in his bloud, through whose merits, all other mediation in heauen and earth, hath force and effect, be it either of Angels or Saints for men, or of one man for an other.

Apoc. 1. 66 The tenth, that he should be, *primogenitus mortuorum*, the first man that should rise from death, and enter into heauen, and open the gates thereof,

thereof, to the end that we might enter after him, and enioy the ſight of God, and eternal beatitude by his meanes, and merits.

67 The eleuenth, and laſt was, that he ſhould be iudge of the quicke, & the dead, and reward, or puniſh, euery man according to his deſerts. *Matth.24.*

68 Now then, in the conſideration of theſe moſt excellent preroga- *Apoc.22.* tiues, and priuiledges of our Sauiours humanitie, we may entertaine our ſelues, pondering euerie one a part, reioycing, and congratulating with him for the ſame, praiſing, magnifiing, and adoring him, offring our ſelues to his ſeruice, and crauing ſuch part of his graces, and vertues, as it may pleaſe his deuine maieſtie to beſtow vppon vs, ſeeing that out of his plentie, or rather *his plenitude*, and fulnes, *all men* *Ioan.1.* *are ſtored.*

69 Furthermore, all this being conſidered, we may waigh with our ſelues, the heroyical acts of vertue, which the moſt bleſſed ſoule of our Sauiour exerciſed towards God, in the firſt inſtant that he ſaw the deuine eſſence, wherewith he was vnited, who behoulding on the on ſide the infinit maieſtie of God, and on the other the innumerable benefits, that he had receiued of him (as that he was created of nothing, and exalted to ſuch an incomprehenſible dignitie) performed fiue moſt notable effects, which euerie man may, and ought to imitat.

70 The firſt was, a feruent loue to God. The ſecond, a moſt thankefull gratitude, in the acknowledgement of his benefits. The third, a moſt profound humiliation of himſelfe, conſidering he had nothing of himſelfe, but all by the infinit liberalitie, and bountie of God. The Fourth, a moſt prompt and readie offer of a moſt exact, and perfect obedience to Gods holie will, in all things whatſoeuer. The fift was, a moſt earneſt deſire of Gods glorie, and reſolute purpoſe to procure, and aduance the ſame, by all meanes poſſible; which fiue points we may applie alſo to our ſelues, practiſing the like loue, gratitude, humilitie, renunciation of our owne will, offer of our ſeruice, deſire of Gods glorie, with a firme reſolution, and endeuour, to procure it to our power, and finallie we are moſt humblie to craue the aſſiſtance of the holie ſpirit, through our Sauiours merits, for the performance thereof.

71 Afterwards, we may occupie our ſelues in the conſideration of the moſt exellent acts of vertue, which our Sauiour at the firſt inſtant of his creation exerciſed alſo towards his neighbours, to wit, the ineffable ſorrow which he conceiued, when he ſaw the moſt lamentable ſtate of the world drowned in ſinne, and the ingratitude of men (his

brethren by nature) towards God, his, and their Father, and Creator, whose honour, and glorie he infinitlie desired, and knowing withall, that his Father had ordained him for the remedie of the world (hauing giuen him a passible, and mortall bodie, to the end he might offer himselfe in sacrifice, suffer torments, and die, for the satisfaction of his iustice, and the redemption of mankind) he receiued vnspeakeable ioy, that such an occasion was offered him, to shew both his obedience to his Father, and his loue to his brethren, and accepted the same most willinglie, saying to his Father (as the Apostle noteth of him out of the

Hebra.10. Psal.39. psalme) *Seeing thou vvouldest not accept the sacrifices, and oblations of the lavv, for the remission of mans sinne, corpus autem aptasti mihi, but hast framed me a bodie*, to be offred in sacrifice for the same, *Ecce venio, vt faciam Deus voluntatem tuam, behold I come o God to doe thy vvill.*

72 Moreouer, it may be considered, that though he had a most perfect knowledge, and liuelie apprehension at the same time of all the contempt, ignominie, paines, & torments, that he should suffer throughout the course of his painefull life, and death, yea, and of the horrible ingratitude of his owne brethren towards him (whereby he begane euen then, and continued euer after for three, & thirtie yeares, to drinke the bitter cup of his passion, vntil he had dronke it all vp) neuertheles such was his loue to man, and obedience to his Father, that he was readie to suffer much more, if neede were, not onlie for all mankind, but also for euerie particular man, rather then that anie one of his brethren should perish: out of all which may be drawne, not onlie most notable motiues to the loue of God, gratitude to our Sauiour *Christ*, hate of sinne, and sorrow for our owne particular offences, but also an excellent, and necessarie document, of the charitie and loue, which we owe to our brethren, in the imitation of our Sauiour, who so loued vs all; whereto I add, that in the course of all this meditation, one special thing is to be practised, to wit, most firme purposes, and resolutions are to be taken, to imitat our Sauiour, with the helpe of his grace, in the exercice, and practise of all these vertues, and afterwards all diligent endeuour is to be vsed, for the performance thereof, in the occasions that shalbe offered, which is the speciall fruit, and effect of meditation, and the end of the Illuminatiue way.

73 But if I should prosecute all such thinges, as our contemplatiues teach to be obserued, and practised in the meditation of the Incarnation of our Sauiour, I should make a whole volume of this matter, and much more, if I should proceede in like sort with the rest, of his natiuity, life, doctrin, miracles, passion, and death, seeing that euerie word of his

of his, ſerueth for our inſtruction, and euerie act, either for our example, or our edification: and therefore it ſhall ſuffiſe, that I haue for
examples ſake, touched theſe few points in particuler, and for concluſion of that which I meane to ſay, concerning the Illuminatiue way, I
will onlie add certaine conſiderations in general, whereby thoſe that
tend to the vnitiue way, may more eaſilie attaine thereto, following our
Sauiour as their guide and captaine, whoſe doctrin, and example, may
both arme them againſt all the aſſaults of their ſpiritual enemies, and
adorne them with all kind of vertues.

74 And therefore againſt the temptation of coueteouſnes, pride, ambition, wrath, and reuenge, they may arme themſelues, with the conſideration of his voluntarie pouertie, humilitie, obedience, patience, contempt of riches, of honours, and of dignities, waying with them ſelues,
his rare examples in theſe kinds, as, that he made choiſe of a poore mother, a poore countrie (in reſpect of manie others) a poore [a] ſtable to be a *Luc.1.*
borne in, a poore cratch, or manger, for his cradle, poore sheapheards
for the firſt witneſſes of his birth, a poore offring at his [b] preſentation in b *Luc.2.*
the temple, a poore [c] trade to liue by, vntil he beganne to preach, & that c *Mar. 6.*
afterwards he [d] liued of almes, and had not ſo much as a poore [e] cottage d *Luc. 8.*
to put his head in. Alſo, that he choſe poore [f] diſciples, conuerſed with e *Matth. 8. Luc. 9.*
poore people, fled [g] honours, and popular praiſe, hiding himſelfe from f *Matth. 4.*
thoſe which meant to make him king, and shewing humilitie, & [h] obe- g *Ioan. 6.*
dience in all things which he beganne to doe, euen whiles he was in his h *Luc. 2.*
mothers wombe.

75 For when *Auguſtus Cæſar*, for oſtentation of his power, and large *Luc.2.*
dominion, commaunded by publicke edict, that the world should be
deſcribed, and that therefore all his ſubiects should repaire to certaine
places, aſsigned for that purpoſe, and there regiſter their names, and pay
tribute, our Sauiour being then not borne, and yet meaning to diſcouer
to the world, how different are the *vvaies of God, from the vvayes of men*, and *Eſay. 55.*
the cogitations of earthlie kings, from the cogitations of the king of
heauen, tooke occaſion vpon the Emperours ambitious vanitie, & pride,
to shew his owne profound humilitie, both in paying tribute, as a
ſubiect of *Auguſtus*, as alſo in being borne by the ſame occaſion in a *Luc.1.*
poore ſtable, for lacke of a better harbour.

76 The like humilitie, & obedience, he shewed throughout the courſe i *Matth. 3.*
of his life, humbling himſelfe to receiue [i] baptiſme, at the hands of *S.* k *Ioan. 13.*
Iohn Baptiſt, in the companie of ſinners, to [k] wash the feete of his apoſtles, l *Luc. 22.*
to be amongſt them as their [l] miniſter, or ſeruant, to be obedient to *Moy-* m *Ibid. c. 2.*
ſes law, in his [m] circumciſion, [n] preſentation, and the [o] obſeruation of n *Ibid.* o *Ioan. 10.*

a *Luc.2.* feasts, and ceremonies, obedient to his a mother, and supposed father (to whome the scripture saith, *he vvas subiect*) obedient to temporal b *Matth.17.* lawes, and magistrats, paying tribut to b *Cæsar*, obedient to his very c *Philip.2.* enemies, submitting himselfe to their vniust iudgement, lastlie, c *obediens vsque ad mortem, mortem autem crucis, obedient euen to death, yea to the opprobrious death of the crosse*, hauing first with inuincible patience, endured without contradiction, infinit slaunders, blasphemies, scofs, and scornes, buffeting, scourging, crowning with thornes, and innumerable indignities, and yet was so farre from seeking reuenge of his enemies, that he freelie pardoned them, excused them to his Father, praied *Luc.23.* for them, and shed euerie drop of his most precious bloud, to redeeme, and saue them.

77 Who then is there so hautie, and proude, that would not by the due consideration hereof be moued to stoupe, and to humble himselfe, seing the king of glorie, so hūble, & obedient? Who hath not cause to be sorry for his impatience, wrath, and reuenges, seing his Lord, and maker so meeke, patient, & charitable to his enemies? Who should not be induced to contemne riches, & honours, seeing the Lord of all so poore, & abiect? Who canne with anie reason, thinke much to be cōtemned, or wronged, seeing the king of heauen, & earth endure so many wrongs, outrages, & indignities? Who ought not to be ashamed to liue at ease, and pleasure, seing his Lord, & master in torment, and paine? Finally what Christian is there, who should maturelie consider, that his kinge, & creatour, partlie did, and partlie suffered all these things, not onlie for his redemption, but also for his example (to the end he might follow his stepps) and would not seeke to frame himselfe, to the imitation of such a heauenlie master, and guide, that by the participation of his vertues here, he might be partaker hereafter of his glorie?

78 But let vs heare a litle, what one of our contemplatiues meditateth vppon this matter. *Quid tibi*, saith *S. Bernard*, *dirum vel durum esse poterit?* &c. What can be either terrible or difficult to thee, when thou shalt *Ber. ser. de quadruplici debito.* remember what he is, who, being the spenldor, and figure of the sub-,, stāce of God the Father (that is to say God himselfe) vouch safed to come ,, to thy prison, to thy clay and durt, and there to be sett fast, (as the *Psal.68.* psalmist saith) vp to the verie elbowes, in the profound, and bottomeles ,, mud of thy basenes? What shall not be sweete to thee, when thou shalt ,, remember all the bitternes, that thy Lord, tasted, & suffred for thee, as the ,, necessitie of his infancie, his labours in preaching, his wearines in his ,, iourneis and trauailes, his temptations in his fasting, his watching in ,, praier, his teares of compassion, the deceits vsed to entrapp him, his

his continual dangers by false brethren, the contumelies, spitting, buffets, whipping, derision, mocks, and scofs, that he endured, and finallie the nailes that pearced his hands, and feete, and such other thinges which he partlie did, and partlie suffred, for the saluation of mankind, during the space of three, and thirtie yeares, that he liued here amongst vs?

79 O how vndue on his part, and vndeserued on ours was his mercie? How farre beyond all expectation was his clemencie, and what a stupendious sweetenes may wee conceiue in the consideration of this inuincible mansuetude, and meekenes, that the king of glorie would be crucified, for a most contemptible slaue, & wretched worme? Who euer saw, or heard the like? For hardlie, saith the Apostle *VVill any man* [*Rom.* 5.] *dye for a iust man*, but he died for the vniust, yea for his verie enimies, banishing himselfe willinglie from heauen, to carrie vs to heauen. *VVhat then shall I render to my Lord, for all this that he hath giuen me*? [*Psal.*115.] For if I giue him all that I may, and all that I am, is it anie other then a starr to the sunne, a dropp of water to a riuer, a peble stone to a mountaine, or a litle graine to a great heape of corne? I haue but two litle mites to wit, a bodie, and a soule, or rather but one mite, that is to say, my will, and therefore shall I not giue it, and resigne it wholie to his will, who being such, and so great a Lord, hath so much preuented me with such incomparable benefits, yea, and gaue himselfe wholie to purchase, and buy me wholie? For if I remaine, and keepe my will to my selfe, with what face, or with what mind, and conscience, shall I haue recourse to the bowells of his mercy? Or how shall I presume, or dare to draw to my selfe (I will not say) the drops, but the flouds of his precious bloud, which flow from the fiue parts of his bodie, for my redemption?

80 Thus saith this deuout, and contemplatiue father, with much more to the same purpose, which for breuities sake I omit, & I will conclude this matter & chapter with a breefe, though most deuout consideratiõ of [*S. Ephram de passione Domini. To.*3.] the anciẽt, & holy Father *S. Ephraem*. *Contẽplaris*, saith he, *O homo* &c. Doest thou behold o man, thy most immaculat, & vnspotted Lord, hanging vpon the crosse, & darest thou impudẽt, & wicked creature, spẽd thy daies in delicacy, sport, & pleasure? Doest thou not know (o shameles wretch) that thy Lord, which was crucified for the, will one day exact an account of thee, of all thy negligences, and contempts? And yet now when thou hearest these thinges, thou art so carelesse, and retchles, that thou contemnest, and laughest, and sports thy selfe amidst thy delights? But assure thy selfe, a day will come, a terrible day, a day of punishment, and re-

uenge, when thou shalt morne, waile, and cry out, for euer in endeles torment, and fire, when no man shall answere thee, nor haue compassion on thee.

81 These are the words of the *holy Ephrem*, worthie to be written in letters of gould, and engrauen in euerie mans hart, to the end we may alwaies haue in our remembraunce, not onlie what our Sauiour suffred for vs, but also what we owe to him for the same, and how deare our negligence, and ingratitude will cost vs, if we doe not repent in time.

And trulie one of the greatest reasons, why so few men proffit in the way of vertue, and so manie soules daillie perish, is, for that they doe not often, and dulie ponder, and way these, and such other thinges, & make particuler reflexion vppon our Sauiours life, and passion, to the end they may imitate his deuine vertues; which point our contemplatiues doe performe in most excellent manner, dailie, and most deuoutlie ruminating vppon our Sauiours actions, and euerie part of his passion, drawing thence notable instructions, and documents, for their owne vse, and practise, mortifiing their passions by the example of our Sauiour, purging the relicks of old sinnes, and continuallie crauing the assistance of Gods grace, through our Sauiours merits, whereby they proceede dailie, *de virtute in virtutem*, from one vertue to an other, and kindle withall in themselues such a fire of the feruent loue of God, that they enter into the *Vnitiue* way, whereof I am to speake next. *Psal. 83.*

Of the Vnitiue *vvay, and the practise of it, vvith rules to be obserued in the exercise thereof and meditations belonging to it.*

CHAP. 20.

1 THe *Vnitiue* way (belonging as I noted before, to the third state, or degree of charitie) is so called, because the soule of man, is thereby vnited with God, such being the force of perfect charitie, that as *S. Iohn*, saith, *Qui manet in charitate manet in Deo, & Deus in eo. He vvhich remaineth in charity remaineth in God, and God in him.* Which may the better be conceiued, if we consider the nature, and force, of perfect loue to be such, that it cannot suffer any obstacle, or impediment, betwixt the obiect that it loueth, and it selfe, nor euer resteth vntil it be conioyned, & coupled therewith, in so much that *Plato* and his followers the *Platonicks*, teach, that loue hath the force, & power, not onlie to vnit the louer with the beloued, but also to transforme the one into the other, and make them both one, hauing but one will, *1. Ioan. 4.* *Plato in Symposio.*

will, one desire, one sorow, one ioy, and, as it were, one soule in two bodies, in which respect, it is commonlie, and trulie said, that *magis est anima vbi amat, quam vbi animat, the soule is rather vvhere it loueth, then vvhere it liueth, and giueth life*, and how this is verified betwixt God and man, shall appeare after a while.

S. Bonauentura in Soliloquijs.

2 Those therefore that would walke in the vnitiue way, are to consider, that though the end whereto they tend (which is a perfect vnion, and coniunction with God) is a matter of that worth, and dignitie, that they cannot hope to attaine vnto it, by anie merits of their owne, or by humane endeuour, or by the obseruation of rules, and precepts, but by the mercie, and grace of almightie God, through the merits of our Sauiour *Iesus Christ* (for, to thinke otherwise, were nothing els, but to make an art of Gods grace, and to reduce, or tye his giftes to the inuentions of men, which were not onlie great follie, but also extreame impietie) neuertheles they may greatlie helpe, and further themselues therein, by their diligent endeuour in preparing, and disposing themselues conuenientlie thereunto, such being the course of Gods prouidence, and proceeding with men, euen in matters pertaining to their soule, and saluation, that he not onlie admitteth, but also requireth their endeuour, and cooperation with his grace, as I haue signified before.

F. Pedro de Alcantara nel trattato dell' oratione & meditat. ca.11.

Chap. 9. num.24.

3 It being then presuposed, that by the vse, and practise of the illuminatiue way, they haue alreadie obtained puritie of hart, integritie of conscience, and feruent loue to God, true mortification of their passions, and affections, hate of sinne, and contempt of the world, and of themselues for the loue of God, and lastlie a habit of all vertue, it is further requisit to the practise of the vnitiue way, that they vnderstand, & obserue certaine precepts, concerning meditation. For, although meditation is a special helpe, and as it were, the principal ladder to mount to contemplation, yet it may be sometimes a hinderaunce thereto, if it be not vsed with discretion. Therefore according to the doctrin of some great contemplatiues, fiue thinges are to be obserued therein, by those which practise this vnitiue waie.

4 The first is, that they auoid ouermuch speculation of the vnderstanding (especiallie when they meditate vppon the deuine misteries) & that they rather labour to employ their will, and affection, seeking to draw out of their meditation, motiues, and feelings of loue, admiration, or ioy, and yet not so, but that they may also reflect vppon such points of good instruction, and edification, as may occurre, yea, and recommend to almightie God, the necessities of their owne soules, and other mens (as occasion and matter shalbe ministred in their meditation) so that they principally

F. Luyz de Granada li. de meditat.

F. Pedro de Alcantara nel trattato dell' orat. & meditat. ca.11.

principallie ſeeke,and moſt inſiſt vppon motiues of loue, which are the proper foode of a contemplatiue ſoule, and the high way to a perfect vnion with God, for otherwiſe (I meane if they endeuour to occupie their vnderſtanding, more then their affection) they ſhall rather ſtudie, then pray,or contemplat, and perhaps find themſelues more dry, and void of deuotion in the end of their meditation, then they were in the beginning, contrarie to the nature & condition of true praier,whereof

Ecclef.7. the ſcripture ſaith, *Orationis melior eſt finis quam principium*,the end of praier is better then the beginning.

Ibidem. 5 The ſecond point is, that though they ought to ſeeke to ſtirr vp in them ſelues affections of loue, as I haue ſaid, yet they are to vnderſtand that the ſame is to be donne with moderation,which I ſay,for that ſome thinke to procure it, as it were, by force, and ſtriue ſo much with exceſſiue ſighes,and coacted ſorrow, to moue themſelues to teares of compaſſion, and loue, in the meditation of our Sauiours paſſion, that they doe nothing els, but hurt their healths as *Caſſianus* well obſerueth.

6 Such therefore are to conſider, that it ſuffiſeth to doe on their part, what they conuenientlie may, that is to ſay, that repreſenting our Sauiours ſuffring before the eyes of their ſoule, they behould the ſame, with a quiet, and louing compaſſion,and a tender hart, being willing, and readie to receiue anie impreſſion of ſorrow,that it ſhall pleaſe him of his mercie to giue them,crauing it at his hands, if they haue it not,

F.Pedro de Alcant. & F.Luyz de Granada vbi ſupra. and not afflicting themſelues,if it doe not pleaſe him to giue it them(for that he knoweth what is conuenient for them) deſiring nothing more in his ſeruants,then a good will,with a conuenient endeuour; whereto he will giue the effect, no leſſe then he gaue the good will, when he ſhall ſee his time.

7 The third point,which they are to obſerue in meditation is,that they

Idem ibid. vſe it onlie as a meane to contemplation, and not as the end,that is to ſay, that they meditat,vntill they haue kindled fire of loue in their ſoules, and that then they ſeeke to enioy the fruite of their labour, I meane the repoſe of contemplation; For euen as the nauigation ceaſeth when we arriue at the port, ſo ſhould our meditation ceaſe, when we arriue at the port of contemplation, that is to ſay, when we find our ſelues wholy enflamed with the loue of God, for then is the time to practiſe

S.Dionyſ.Areopag. de myſtica Theolog. ca.1. that which the greateſt contemplatiues aduiſe,to wit,to cleare, and free our ſelues from all phantaſies,& imaginations of all creatures(as though there were nothing els in the world but God,and we) ſtaying our vnderſtanding from further diſcourſe, & retiring our ſelues within our owne ſoules,there to behould God in his owne image, fixing our memorie

wholie

wholie on him, occupying our affection intyrelie, in louing, admiring, and praising him, with ioy, and exultation, not presuming to eleuat our selues to a curious search of his deuine nature, further then it shall please him to raise, and lead vs thereto, but to content our selues rather to know him, by feeling him, through the influence of his loue, & grace, then to vnderstand the particularities of his perfections, which are infinit and incomprehensible, for when almightie God, seeth a deuout soule in this state, then he is wont to communicat him selfe vnto it in an ineffable manner, and with vnspeakeable delectation, yea, and sometimes to ympart vnto it, the inscrutable misteries of his deitie.

S. Bonauentura de mystica Theolog. Blosius in institutione spirituali. c. 12. Albert. Magnus de adhærendo deo. c. 7. & 8. Blosius in Enchirid. paruulor. c. 10. Idem vbi supra.

8 And thus I say, we may forbeare to meditat, so long as this heate of loue, and gods merciful visitation continueth, and when the same cooleth, and relenteth, then we may returne to our former exercise and blow againe the bellowes of meditation, to reuiue the decaied flames of loue, to the end we may participat of such further fauours, as it shall please God to bestow vppon vs.

9 The fourth point is, that although in the case aforesaid, it be conuenient to surcease from meditation, to enioy the fruit of contemplation, yet it may also import sometimes to practise the contrarie, to wit, to leaue contemplation, to passe to meditation, namelie when the affection is ouer vehement, & excessiue, as it hapnẽth manie times to those, who being inuited, and drawne with the sweetenes of this exercise, become as it were so passionat therewith that they cannot containe themselues within the limits of discretion, but seeke to satisfie their insatiable desire, and thirst, by drinking more of the deuine wine, then humane nature can support, and beare, to the great debilitation of their bodies, and damage of their healths. Therefore for such, I say, it shall not be amisse otherwhiles, to temper the heate of their feruent contemplation, with some meditation, which may moue, and excite them to some other holie affection, meditating vppon the sinnes, and miseries of the world, or the howre of death, or the paines of hell, or such like, whereby they may ease their harts with a spiritual diuersion, and change of exercise, which in that case would be more grateful to God, then their contemplation without discretion: for discretion is the mistres of all vertues, and the salt wherewith all good actions are seazoned, in so much, that without it, vertues lose their vertue, and nothing can be acceptable to God.

F. Pedro de Alcant. vbi supra F. Luyz de Granada.

10 Finallie, they are to obserue diligẽtlie, when almighty God doth offer his grace and communication, either in time of meditation, and praier, or out of it, to the end, they may be answerable thereto on their part,

F. Pedro de Alcant. ibid. F. Bartolom. Saluthio, nel paradiso de contemplat. c. 65. F. Luiz de Granada. vbi supra. Cant. 5.

and gratefull for the same, least in punishment of their negligence, and ingratitude, God doe iustlie deny it them at other times, when they shall seeke for it, which is notablie signified in the *Canticles*, where the bridgroome knocked at the spouses doore in the night, and she refused at the first to rise, and afterwards, when shee arose to let him in, shee found him not there. *surrexi*, saith shee, *vt aperirem dilecto meo* &c. *I arose to open the doore to my best beloued, and he vvas gonne avvay.*

11 Neuertheles it is to be vnderstood, that this rule is to bepractised with some restriction, & cautel, especiallie by such asaxe wont, or apt to haue anie notorious excesse of mind in praier, or meditation, as abundance of teares, extases, or rapts, or anie other external alteration, which may be seene, or noted by others, for such men, I say, had neede to be ware, how they admit, and nourrish in publike anie such extraordinarie motions of sensible deuotion, which may cause in them, the foresaid effects, especiallie at such time, as they are to performe anie office of obligation, which may be hindred thereby.

12 For when sensible deuotion tendeth to the hindrance of obedience, or of agreater good, it may well be suspected to haue some temptation, and not to proceede of God, it being of farre greater merit, and more importing vs to discharge our duty in matters of obligation, then to be rauished with the sweetenes of contemplation, yea and to seeke, or desire the later, which preiudice of the former, were nothing els but to seeke our selues, and to prefere our owne contentment, and pleasure, before the seruice of God, and therefore it must needs be offensiue vnto him, who (as he witnesseth himselfe) esteemeth *obedience, more then sacrifice.*

1. Reg. 15.

13 Moreouer, such notorious excesses of mind, as hap in publick, are dangerous in respect of the temptation of vaine glorie, that doth commonlie ensew thereof, in which respect, though they should be diuine visitations, yet out of humilitie, and the regard of our owne weakenes, and vnwoorthines, we may securelie seeke to preuent, or auoide them, acknowledging our selues to be most vnworthie to receiue any such fauours of almightie God, especiallie in publick, where by anie man may haue occasion to think that we are anie thing more then other men, and therefore we may in such case, say with *S. Peter*, *exi a me Domine* &c. *Goe from me o Lord, for I am a sinfull man*, and with the good *Centurian*, we may refuse to receiue him into our house, saying; *Domine non sum dignus* &c. *Lord, I am not vvorthie* &c. For seeing that they (I meane *S. Peter*, and the *Centurian*,) beholding him present said this, and refused to admit him without offence, and with greate merit for their humilitie, how much more may we securelie doe the like, out of the like humilitie, whiles we

Blosius in Canone vitæ spiritual. ca. 26.

Luc. 5.

Matth. 8. Luc. 7.

are yet vncertaine, whether it be hee that offreth to fauour vs, or our enemie that seeketh to delude vs?

14 And therefore the safest way is in such cases, to make strong resistance, for if our sensible deuotion, and extraordinarie motions, shuld chance to be of our enemie the deuil, we shall no dout, thereby sufficientlie preuent his malice, and if they be of God, we shall not neede to feare, but that he will do that which he shall see to be most conuenient for his owne glorie, and our good, much the rather for our humilitie, & desire to discharge our dutie in his seruice, and thus much for the fiue points, or rules a boue mencioned concerning meditation.

15 Furthermore, they are to consider that as all kind of discreete mortifications are conuenient for the practise of true christian life, so none is more proper, or necessarie for the exercise of contemplation, then moderat abstinence, and fasting, aswell to render the bodie subiect to the spirit, as also to cleare the eyes of the soule from the grose vapours of sensual and carnal affections, the which saturitie, & superfluitie of meates, and drinks, doth continuallie euaporat, whereby the vnderstanding is so obscured, that it is not capable of the true light of contemplation, in which respect manie of the contemplatiue philosophers both vsed, and prescribed to their followers great abstinence (as I haue declared *a* before) and not onlie our Sauiour himselfe, but also *b Moyses*, *c Elias*, *S. d Iohn Baptist*, & all the ould Hermits, accompanied their contemplation in the desert with fasting, and *S. Augustin* saith of *Moyses*, that *quia ieiunauit Dominum vidit*, *he savv our Lord because he fasted*, and *Daniel* also witnesseth of himselfe that after his three weekes strict, and rigorous fast, he saw the great vision, and receiued the admirable reuelation, which he recounteth concerning the kingdome of *Persia*, *Egipt*, *Greece*, and *Siria*. Finallie Ecclesiastes testifieth, how necessarie abstinence is to contemplation, saying. *Cogitaui in corde meo* &c. *I thought, or determined in my hart, to abstaine from vvine, to the end I might giue my selfe to vvisdome, and auoid follie, vntill I should discouer, vvhat vvas profitable, and conuenient for the sonnes of men.* To conclude, *S. Leo* speaking of the benefitt of fasting, saith notably thus. *Quamuis sine anima* &c. Although without the soule the flesh desireth nothing, receiuing sence from thence from whence it hath also motion, yet is it necessarie for the soule, to deny some thinges to the body, which is subiect vnto it, to the end it may be the more free from corporall, & sensuall desires, and giue itselfe to the studie of deuine wisdome, and retiring itselfe from the noise of all earthlie eares, may ioy in holie meditations, and abound in eternall delights, Thus saith *S. Leo.*

a *Chap.* 17. b *Exod.* 34. c 3. *Reg.* 19. d *Matth.* 11. *Augustin. sermo. de temp. in Do* 1. *quadrag. ser.* 2. *Daniel.* 10. 11. & 12. *Eccles.* 2. *S. Leo ser.* 8. *de ieiunio.* 10. *mensis.*

16 Moreouer, it shall not be amisse for them to accustome themselues

ſerioullie and often, to recollect themſelues, to conſider, and behould the image of God in their one ſoules, whereby they may the more eaſily with the helpe of Gods grace, raiſe themſelues to the ſpeculation of him, who is repreſented therein, & dwelleth there, as in his temple, yea, and reigneth there as in his kingdome; *templum Dei eſtis vos*, ſaith the Apoſtle, you are the temple of God, *& regnum Dei intra vos eſt, the kingdome of God is vvithin you*, and therefore the prophet ſaith. *Audiam quid loquatur in me Dominus. I vvill heare vvhat my Lord vvill ſay in me*

D.Ber.de domo interior. c.13. 2.*Cor.6.* *Luc.17.* *Pſal.84.*

17 Herevppon *S.Bernard* ſaith. *Aſſueſcam ſola intima cogitare &c. I vvill accuſtome my ſelfe, to thinke only vppon internal, or invvard things, only to loue them, and to repoſe in them, to the end I may heare vvhat my Lord God vvill ſay vvithin me.* And againe in an other place. *Beata illa animi &c.* Bleſſed is that ſoule, which being recollected within it ſelfe; is not diſſolued, or ſcattered abroad into the pleaſures of the fleſh, for ſuch a ſoule doth inwardlie poſſeſſe all her delighrs, and being at full peace, and reſt within it ſelfe, and deſiring nothing out of it ſelfe, doth by the loue of God enioy internal repoſe, and contentment, whereby it is reformed to the image of God, which it reuerenceth, and worſhippeth in it ſelfe, ſuch a ſoule is often viſited, and honored by angels, & archangels, as the temple of God, and the habitacle of the holie Ghoſt.

D.Ber.de interior. domo. c.46. *Idem ibid. cap.3.*

18 Thus farr *S.Bernard*; who alſo ſpeaketh els where of the practiſe of this recollection in this manner. *Fruſtra cordis occulum erigit &c. He lifts vp the eye of his hart in vaine to ſee God, vvho is not fitt to ſee himſelfe.* For firſt thou muſt learne to know the inuiſible things of thy owne ſpirit, before thou canſt be fit to know the inuiſible things of God, and if thou canſt not know thy ſelfe, neuer preſume to know other things which are aboue thee. And a litle afterwards: No man, ſaith he, can euer attaine to the grace of contemplation, by his owne induſtrie, for it is the gift of God, & not the merit of man, but without doubt he ſhall receiue it, who abandoneth the care of the world, and taketh care of himſelfe, & laboureth to know what he himſelfe is. Therefore enter into thy owne hart; and diligentlie examine thy ſelfe, conſider whence thou commeſt, whither thou tendeſt, how thou liueſt, what thou doeſt, what thou art, what thou oughteſt to be, what thou waſt by nature, what thou mayeſt be by grace to what good, or euil thou art moſt inclined, what paine, or reward thou art to expect for the ſame, what diligence thou vſeſt to bewaile thy ſinnes paſt, to auoid the preſent, & to preuẽt the future. Finally how much, thou profiteſt euerie day, & how much thou declineſt, with what cogitations, affections, & tẽptations thou art moſt aſſaulted, & moleſted by the diuell, & whẽ thou ſhalt fullie know (as much as is poſſible)

Ibid.c.12. *Ca.65.*

the

the ſtate,and habite, aſwell of thy inward,as thy outward man, and not onlie what a one thou art, but alſo what a one thou ſhouldeſt be, then maieſt thou frō the knowledge of thy ſelfe,be eleuated to the contēplation of God. But now perhaps,thou wilt ſay,that thou art already entred into thy owne hart,but let not that ſuffice thee,learne to dwell there,& howſoeuer thou ſhalt be diſtracted,or drawne frō thence, make haſt to returne thiter,& without doubt, by much vſe, & practiſe thereof, thou wilt find great delectation therein,in ſo much that withoutany difficulty,thou maiſt be continually there,or rather it wilbe a paine vnto thee to be anie where els. Thus ſaith *S. Bernard*, who for his experience in matter of contemplation deſerueth to be beleeued.

19 This recollection,or retrait of the ſoule with in it ſelfe, *S. Auguſtin* practiſed, as he ſignifieth, and ſaw with the eye of his vnderſtanding, *lucem Domini incommutabilem*, the immutable or vnchangeable light of God, who did irradiat the infirmitie of his ſight, in ſuch ſort, that, *contremui* ſaith he, *amore, & horrore*, I trembled with loue, and horrour.

Aug. confeſ. li.7. cap. 10. Ibid.

20 To theſe former aduertiſements, I add further (according to the aduiſe of a great maſter of contemplation) that whereas perfect vniō with God (which is the end of the vnitiue way) is ſpeciallie atchiued by the meanes of a pure ſincere,& feruent loue of God,inducing a contēpt,and holie hate of the world,& of our ſelues,it behoueth thoſe,which tēd to this vnion,to endeuour by al meanes poſſible to attaine vnto the higheſt degree of charity,& to that end,to accuſtome thēſelues to referre & direct,all their words,works, and thoughts to the loue of God, to hate all things that may deuide thē frō it,& not only to draw out of all their meditations,yea out of all things in heauen & earth,conſiderations,which may ſtirre them therto (conſidering his infinit bountie,& benefits general & particuler) but alſo moſt humblie & inceſſantlie to beſeeche him, to enflame their harts with the fire of ſuch a burning charitie, that they may become furnaces of his deuine loue, which may conſume in them all their ſelfe loue, peruerſe affections, and other imperfections, and make their ſoules true holocauſtes, or burnt ſacrifices moſt acceptable to him: and finallie breede in them ſuch an vnquencheable thirſt, and inſatiable deſire of him, that they may trulie ſay with the royall prophet. *Quemadmodum deſiderat ceruus ad fontes aquarum* &c. *As the ſtagg deſireth or thirſteth after the fountaines of vvater, ſo doth my ſoule thirſt after thee o God*, and *inflamatum eſt cor meum*, &c. *My hart is inflamed, and my reynes are changed*, or as the ſpouſe ſaith in the Canticles, *fulcite me floribus, quia amore langudo, vnderprop me vvith flovvers, for I languish vvith loue.*

Dioniſius Carthuſian. de laude vitæ ſolitariæ ca. 35.

Pſal. 41.

Pſal. 72.

 21 And

21 And to this end it shalbe conuenient for them (as much as they possiblie may) to print, and graue in their phantasie, our Sauiour Christ crucified and the whole course of his passion, and to haue him alwaies, as it were before their eies, to which purpose S. *Bernard* hauing proposed manie other motiues to the loue of God, saith, *Sed est quod me plus mouet plus vrget, plus accendit* &c. *But there is an other thing vvhich more moueth, vrgeth, & kindleth, or inflameth me, for aboue all things, (svveete Iesu) the cupp vvhich thou didst drink for me, I meane the vvoorke of our redemption maketh thee most amiable, and louelie vnto me; This doth dulie chalenge to itselfe all our loue, This, I say, is that vvherby our deuotion is most svveetely allured, most iustly exacted and most vehemently affected.* Thus he. Therefore I say, let them procure, to haue alwaise in mind our Sauiours passion, to the end, that by the continual consideration of that infinit loue, which he shewed towards them therein, they may with the helpe of his grace, kindle in themselues the fire of loue, which may neuer cease to cast out flames of feruent affection, and holie desires of his vnion, and moue them to esteeme him, in their harts, & call him, their onlie hope, their cheefe delight, their eternall good, their ioy, their glorie, their life, the spouse of their soule, their refuge, their stay, their strenght, their end, their felicitie, their Lord, their God, their all in all: for such is the infinit bountie, and goodnes of God to his creatures, and speciallie to the soule of man; that he cannot forbeare to communicat himselfe thereto, when he seeth it surprised with his loue, and thirst after him alone, and therefore he saith to such a soule in the *Canticles. Vulnerasti cor meum, soror mea, sponsa. Thou hast vvounded my hart, my sister, and spouse, veni coronaberis, come thou shalt be crovvned.*

S. Ber. ser. 20 in cantica.

Cant. 4.

22 Furthermore, those which are entred into the *Vnitiue vvay*, and do beginne alreadie to tast how sweete our Lord is, are to vnderstand, that although he doe, of his infinit goodnes, bestow ineffable consolations vppon his seruants, in the exercise of cōtemplation, yea sometimes rapts, reuelations, the spirit of prophesie, and apparitions of our Sauiour, and his Saincts, as shall appeare heareafter, yet they ought not to seeke or desire the same, no not so much as sensible deuotion, except it be onlie to the end, that they may by the meanes thereof, become more feruent in his loue, and be more vnited with him. And although I haue spoken of this point alreadie, yet I thinke good to add further here (for it can not be to oft aduised) that nothing is more dangerous to a contemplatiue soule, thē spirituall gluttonie, if I may so tearme it, I meane a greedy desire of spirituall delectation, for the soule that is once infected therewith, & seeketh to mixe the dung of her owne delights, with the sweete, precious balme, of Gods grace, will within a while grow to loue Gods

Blosius in institut. Spirituali c. 7.

Chap. 19. nu. 33. & 47.

Idem in Canone vitæ spiritualis ca. 25.

Gods gifts more then himselfe, and serue him rather for hire, then for loue, yea, and lie open to all kind of illusions of wicked spirits, as I haue signified before.

23 And as this is to be feared in the inordinat desire of sensible deuotion, so it is much more to be doubted in the expectation, and desire of rapts or reuelations; For although they be euident tokens of Gods mercifull assistance (when they are of God) yet being extraordinary, and not necessarie to saluation, they can hardlie be desired, without vaine curiositie, or presumption, in which respect God permitteth manie times, that the diuell (*transforming himselfe into the Angel of light*) doth worthily delude those which curiouslie, or presumptuouslie seeke, and expect them: and therefore, as we ought not to desire them, so we also doe well not to admit them easilie, but rather to resist, and reiect them, vpon consideration of our owne vnworthines (except it be with the aduise and warrant of our spiritual father) for therevppon it will follow, that if they be illusions, they shall not deceiue vs, and if they be deuine fauours, almightie God (who giueth them) will in respect of our humilitie not onlie afford vs sufficient light to discerne, and know them for his, but also increase them in vs with gifts of his grace, as I haue more amplie signified before vppon an other occasion.

Idem ibid. ca. 26.

2. Cor. 11.

Idem ibid. M. Teresa de Iesus nella vita sua. c. 23. & 24.

Nu. 11.

24 And to omit other meanes how to examin them, whether they be of God, or no, on speciall rule may be, to consider what effect they worke in our soules, for if they be of God, they alwais leaue behind them great comfort, light, peace of soule, and profound humilitie, but when they are of the diuell, they worke the cleane contrarie effect, for howsoeuer they please, and content for the time, yet they discouer their poison in the end, leauing the soule drie without deuotion, troubled, and replenished with vaine glorie, and presumption. But the best, and surest way to preuent, and auoid illusions, is (as I [a] haue declared before) to [b] discouer them, and all other temptations, to some learned, and discreete spirituall father, and to follow his direction, with all due obedience, and abnegation of our selues, for the pure loue of God, for no way in this life is so secure, and gratefull to God, as the way of true obedience (as shall appeare most manifestlie hereafter, when I shall treate of the euangelicall, and Christian perfection) And this I dare be bold to say, further, that it was neuer yet seene or heard of, that anie man remaining in the vnitie of the Catholike Church, and submitting himselfe to the directiō of a superiour, with true abnegation of himselfe, was either anie long time deluded, or yet did finallie perish in the practise of contemplation.

a Chap. 19. nu. 48. 49. 50. & 51.

b Cassian. li. 4. de instit. monachor. li. 4. c. 9. & 37. Item collat. 1. c. 11. S. Greg. li. 1. in 1. Reg. c. 1. in fine. B. Ignatius reg. 13. de discernendis spiritib.

25 To conclude, there is nothing more requisit to our perfect vnion

with

M. Teresa in vita sua ca.11. Blosius in Appendice ex Thauler. c.1.

with God (which is the end of the vnitiue way, whereof I now treate) then the perfect, and true resignation of our will to Gods will, without all reseruation, to doe or suffer what soeuer it shal pleas him, yea though it were to endure the paines of hell vntill the day of iudgement; for if we expect that God shall geue himselfe to vs, it is great reason, that we first freelie, and wholie giue our selues to God, and most happie are we, if wee can make that change, that is to say, purchase heauen for earth, God for our selues, all things for nothing.

26 Now then this disposition being made, the matter, and subiect of their meditation may be, either the glorious misteries of our Sauiours resurrection, apparitions, ascension, and sempiterdal glorie in heauen, or the attributs of almightie God, as his infinit power, wisdome, bountie, beautie, iustice, sanctitie, and other ineffable properties of the deuine nature, which fill a well disposed, & prepared soule with such admiration, and loue of the incomprehensible excellencies, and perfections of God, that manie times it leoseth it selfe, being, as it were, ingulfed, and drowned in a sea of heauenlie delights, tasting euen in this mortall state, the inspeakeable ioyes of immortalitie, as I will make manifest after a while.

27 In the meane time, I wish it to be obserued, that whereas I haue here mentioned two kindes of meditation, the one cōsisting in the consideration of Christs humanitie, as it was passible here in earth (which belongeth to the illuminatiue way) and the other concerning his glorified bodie, and diuinitie in heauen (which is proper to the vnitiue way) the royall prophet seemeth to allude to both, when he saith. *Montes excelsi ceruis petra refugium herinacijs. The high hills are the habitation of stagges and the rocks, or rockie caues, are the refuge of hedge hoggs,* that is to say, (as *Cassianus* an ancient, and notable contemplatiue noteth) those that walke in the vnitiue way, and haue alreadie arriued, to the perfection of contemplation, mount vp like staggs, and feede vpon the highest mountaines, that is to say, the high misteries of Christs glorie, and dietie, whiles in the meane time, those that are still in the illuminatiue way, that is to say, enuironed with the pricks of imperfections, like hedgehoggs, haue their refuge to the rocke of our Sauiours humanitie, in whose sacred woundes they repose, as *in foraminibus petræ, the holes of the rocke,* wherof the booke of Canticles speaketh: and hereto may also the saying of the prophet *Isayas* be applied, where he saith. *Ingredere in petram, & abscondere in fossa humo a facie timoris Domini. Enter into the rocks, and hide thy selfe in the caues of the earth, from the face of Gods vvrath,* that is to say, consider the multitude of thy sinnes, and haue thy refuge to Christ, who is the

Psal.103. P Luyz de la Puente, introduct. de la orat. mental. §.4. Cassian. collat.10. c.10.

rocke

rocke, and hide thy selfe from the rigour of his iustice, in the sacred woundes of his humanitie. And this, as I sayd before, is most proper to those that walke in the illuminatiue way, whose speciall exercise is to represent continuallie to themselues the humanitie of our Sauiour Christ, and to haue him alwaies in their memorie, to conuerse with him by spiritual conferences, and iaculatorie praiers, and to condole with him for his paines and trauailes, to acknowledge, and bewaile their owne ingratitude, and infirmitie, to craue pardon for their sinnes, and grace to imitate his vertues, whereto speciallie tendeth all their endeuour.

28 Neuertheles, it is to be vnderstood, that the most perfect contemplatiues, and most vnited with God, doe also make greate vse, and profit, aswell of the misteries of Christs life, and humanitie, as of the meditations which belong, to the purgatiue way: for although, they are most commonlie so eleuated with the wings, as I may say, of a seraphical charitie, that they transcend all creatures whatsoeuer, and mount to the high misteries of the diuinitie, wherein they soare like spiritual, and high flying falcons, and solace themselues, as in their proper pitch, yet they stoupe manie times to all sorts of inferiour meditations, and serue themselues thereof in most excellent manner, and with exceeding greate fruite. For euen as in the three degrees of the soule (to wit, vegetatiue, sensitiue, and reasonable) the last being superior to the other two, doth not onlie doe her owne functions, but also theirs in farr greater perfection then they themselues can doe: euen so it faleth out in the three states, or sorts of men, which giue themselues to the contemplation of God, for those which haue alreadie beganne, and made some good progresse therein, doe exercise the meditations of nouices, or young beginners, with farre greater benefit then they, and those which are come to the state of perfection, doe vse the meditations of both the other, farre more excellentlie then they both, according to a farre greater measure of Gods grace wherewith they are endewed.

P. Luyz de la Puente vbi supra.

29 And therefore the most perfect contemplatiues, doe often returne to the verie first groundes of the purgatiue way, that is to say, to the remembrance and consideration of their former sinnes, & bad life (though past neuer so manie yeares before,) aswell to renew, & reuiue in thẽselues, a gratefull memory of Gods mercy towards thẽ, & of their obligatiõ to him, for deliuering them frõ the same, as also continually to retaine a true knowledge of themselues, & of their owne infirmitie, which is, as I may tearme it, the daylie bread, wherewith the greatest daynties

P. Ribera nella vita di M. Teresa li. 4. c. 8.

Idem ibid. of the contemplatiue life; are to be eaten, and spiritual health maintained, for no man is so great a giant (I meane of such strength, and high perfection in contemplation) but that he had neede manie times to returne to be an infant, that is to say, to consider his owne weakenes, or rather his owne nothing, humbling and annihilating himselfe in the sight of God, who exalteth the humble, and raiseth manie times his dearest seruantes and friendes, from the lowest consideration of their owne basenes, and infirmitie, to the highest contemplation of his diuinitie, imparting vnto them so much more grace, light, and true knowledge of him, by how much better, and more trulie they know themselues.

M. Teresa nella vita sua ca. 13.

30 The like also may be said of the meditations belonging to the illuminatiue way, to wit, of the blessed humanitie, life, passion, and death of our Sauiour Christ, as that they are the ladder, by the which the most perfect contemplatiues, clime vp to the speculation of his diuinitie, and to perfect vnion with him, finding in him infinit causes, not onlie of excessiue loue, as I haue touched before, but also of wonderfull admiratiō, and astonishment, in which respect he was figured in the ould law, by the propitiatorie ouer the arke, and two Cherubins were made behoulding the same, & also looking one vppon an other, as though they were amazed, and astonished.

Exod. 25.

31 For what can be more stupendious, then to consider in our propitiatorie (that is to say in our Sauiour Christ) a most perfect coniunction of the highest, with the lowest, of the most simple, with the most compounded, of the Creator, with the creature, of God, with man, and that, as there is in the blessed Trinitie three persons, & one substance, so there is in him one person, and two substances, one perfect consent, & agreement of two different wills, one adoration of diuers dignities, and one dominion of diuers powers. Furthermore that he is both our Creator, and our companion, our God, and our neighbour, our Lord, and our brother, our king, and our friend, our iudge and our aduocate, our beginning, and our end, vncreated, and yet incarnat and the sonne of man, without the helpe of man, and that he being omnipotencie, it selfe, was oppressed being bountie it selfe was reiected being perfect, and true beautie was deformed, being true light was obscured, being true wisdome was held for a mad man, and treated like a foole, being infinit maiestie was outraged, being immensitie, was measured, & abridged, being iustice it selfe, was condemned, being true felicitie was tormented, and finallie that being eternitie, and life it selfe, he died: wherevnto if we add, that all this was an effect of his infinit loue, to those that were his vngrateful creatures, and slaues, rebellious subiects, disobedient, and

Ber. de consid. li. 5.

vnnatural

vnnatural children, to remedie their miseries, to supplie their defects, to honour them, to exalt them, to glorifie them, and that to this end, he not onlie imparted to them all his owne good, yea himselfe, but also tooke vppon himselfe their miserie, & the verie penaltie of their sinnes, making himselfe mortall, and miserable with them, to make them immortall, and deuine with him; what admiration, exultation, and deuotion, will the attentiue meditation of all this, worke in a well disposed soule, I meane a soule purified by Gods grace from sinne, and enflamed with his pure loue, for of such I speciallie speake now?

32 Therefore such a soule, doth not stay it selfe here, but aspiring to the contemplation of the deitie it selfe, passeth further to the meditation of the glorious resurrection of our Sauiour Christ, and of his apparitions, and other actions whiles he remained here in earth: whereof I forbeare for breuities sake, to say anie thing in particular, to the end I may the more amply treate of some pointes, concerning his glorified bodie in heauen, his Angels, and Saincts, the ioyes of his kingdome, and lastlie of the most excellent, and incomprehensible perfections of the deuine nature. In all which neuertheles, I will be mindfull aswell of my purposed breuitie, as also of mine owne insufficiency to treat of such high misteries, and therefore, I will endeuour rather to giue some tast to the reader of these pointes, then anie complete instruction for the meditation thereof, which I leaue to those that purposelie treat of this mistical Theologie, and haue more habilitie both of skill, and practise thereof, then my selfe.

33 The contemplator, meaning to meditate vppon the pointes before mentioned, may propose to himselfe our Sauiours ascension into heauen, and accompanie him thither in cogitation, behoulding there, with what triumph the Angels receiued not onlie him, but also the blessed soules of the patriarkes, prophets, and other iust men of the ould testament, which attended on him thither, and how excessiue was their contentment and ioy, to see the celestiall court augmented, and peopled with new colonies of such worthie inhabitants, vnder the conduct of such a glorious captaine; who though he was of infinit power, euen whiles he was here on earth, and fought against both the infernall, and terrestiall potentats, yet would not vse his force, but ouercame them by infirmitie, conquering them, and death it selfe by his death, and being enriched with their spoyles, *led captiuity it selfe captiue* with him to heauen, where he tooke possession of his Fathers kingdome, and reigneth with him eternallie in incomparable maiestie, and glorie, enioying a name (as the Apostle saith) aboue all names, whereat, *all the knees in* *Ephes. 4. Psal.67.* *Philip.2.*

1. Pet. 1. *heauen, earth, and hell* doe bowe, whose glorie (saith *S. Peter*) the Angels *desire, and delight to behold*, for the inspeakeable splendor, and brightnes thereof, he being, as *S. Iohn* in the Apocalipse calleth him, *Lucerna*, the lampe, or torch which giueth light to the heauenlie *Ierusalem*, with the consideratiō whereof, we may excedinglie comfort our selues. For who would not infinitelie reioyce, to see anie friend of his, and much more his Sauiour, and redeemer, so glorious after a most painfull life, and ignonimious death suffred for him, especiallie seeing we may also consider, and behold our owne nature infinitelie exalted, and glorified in our Sauiour, whereby we may haue a firme hope through his merits, to be hereafter partakers of his glorie, aswell in bodie, as in soule.

Apoc.21.

34 Furthermore, being now mounted with our Sauiour into the heauenlie tabernacles, we may consider the inexplicable greatnes, and magnificēce thereof, whereof the prophet saith. *O Israel, quam magna &c. O Israel hovv great is the house of God, and hovv vnmeasurable is the place of thy throne? It is great, and hath no end, it is high, and immense.* Thus saith the prophet, and no meruel, if almightie God, that made the world, so greate, huge, and beautiful, as we see, for the vse, and habitation of men, made also for himselfe and his Angels, a dwelling worthie of himselfe, and of his omnipotent maiestie, for the remuneration of his elect, and the eternal manifestation of his power and glorie, where (saith the prophet *Daniel*) *thousands of thousands doe daily, serue him, and tenne times a hundred thousand of thousand of thousāds assist before his throne.* In which words the prophet expresseth, after the manner of the scripture, a certaine number, for an vncertaine, that is to say, for a number that is incomprehensible, and infinit to men, being such (as *Dionisius Areopagita* testifieth) that it exceedeth the number, not onlie of all the men that euer haue bene, are, or euer shalbe, but also of all the materiall, or corporal thinges in the world. And therefore *Iob* saith, *Nunquid est numerus militum eius*, is there anie number of his souldiars?

Barac.3.

Dan.7.

Dionys. cælest. Hierar. ca.9.

Iob.25.

35 And these infinit numbers of Angelical spirits (who alwaies attend to doe the will of God) are deuided into three *Hierarchies*, euery *Hierarchy*, containing three distinct orders, as the *Seraphin, Cherubin, & Throin* in the first *Hierarchie*. The *Dominationes, principatus*, and *Potestates*, in the second. The *virtutes Archangeli, & Angeli*, in the third. I which three *Hierarchies*, the Angels are no lesse different amongst themselues in degree of glorie, then in function, being subordinat euerie order, & each *Hierarchie*, one to an other with admirable order, and proportion, of whose gradual distinction, names, and seueral functions, *S. Bernard* discourseth

Dionys. de cælesti Hierar. c.7.8. & 9. S.Greg. ho. 34. in Euāg. ante mediū. S.Tho.1.par. q.108. per totum.

discourseth notablie, teaching that the *Angels* are those which are employed in the protection, helpe, and custodie of men, and are called our proper Angels.

S Bernar. li. 5. de consider. ad. Eugen.

36 That the *Archangels* are those which being superiour to *Angels*, are sent by almighty God to reueale the most important, and highest misteries to men, as the *Archangel Gabriel* was employed in the message to the blessed virgin for the incarnation of our Sauiour.

37 The *Vertues* are those, that haue the power, and office to doe miraculous, and prodigious workes for the glorie of God, and the admonition, terrour, and conuersion of sinners.

38 The *Potestates* are such, as represse the power, and malice of wicked spirits, and the malignitie of the aire, & elements, which would otherwise many times, be more noysome to mankind, then they are.

39 The *Principatus* are those, by whose wisdome, & ministery al principalitie in earth is guided, limited, transposed, or changed.

40 The *Dominationes* ar those, who haue presidence, & rule ouer al the aboue named, & by whome al their operations ar ordered, & disposed.

41 The *Throni* are those, in whome almighty God sitteth as in his throne of maiestie, imparting vnto them, and to others by them, tranquilitie, peace, and stability.

42 The *Cherubin* are those, which drawing a flud of knowledge, out of the fountaine of the diuine wisdome, doe communicat the same to the inferiour orders of Angels, & other seruants of God.

43 Lastlie the *Seraphin* are those, that being wholie enflamed with a deuine loue, doe kindle the same in other Angelical spirits, & also in men, when it pleaseth God so to ordaine.

44 And to conclude, *S. Bernard*, alluding to the seuerall offices of all the foresaid orders, saith, that in the *Seraphin*, God loueth as *Charity*, in the *Cherubin*, he knoweth as *truth*, in the *Throni* he sitteth as *equitie*, in the *Dominationes*, he ruleth as *Maiesty*, in the *principatus* he gouerneth as the *beginninge or first cause of all thinges*, in the *Potestates* he preserueth, and defendeth as *Health*, or *saluation*, in the *virtutes* he worketh miracles, as *vertue*, or power, in the *Archangels* he reuealeth as *light*, and in the *Angels*, he assisteth as *piety*. Thus saith *S. Bernard*, giuing to vnderstand, that almightie God, not onlie dwelleth continuallie in these holie spirits, but also worketh, and effecteth, all their seueral vertues, and operations in them, and in other his creatures, by their ministerie.

S. Bernar. vbi supra.

45 And here may verie well enter in consideration, the excellencie of the Angelical nature, most eminent in power, and wisdome,

beautie, agilitie, obedience to the will of God, and prompt execution thereof, being as the psalmist saith *potentes virtute* &c. *Mighty, and potent in vertue and povver to doe, or execute that vvhich God commaunded them*, and therefore to their charge is committed the motion of the heauens, and spheres (according to the opinion of all the philosophers, and *a* manie deuines) the *b* protection of the Church of God, the *c* gard, and defence of kingdomes and prouinces, the *d* tuition of euerie particular man (aswell to defend him from wicked spirits, and other corporal dangers, as to illuminat, and direct him for his saluation) the *e* execution of Gods decrees, both in the temporal *f* punishment of sinners, and also in the temporal *g* reward of the iust, the *h* operation of miraculous, and wonderful workes, the *i* reuelation of his misteries, and secrets to his seruãts, the *k* intimation of his will, and messages, when occasion requireth. The *l* presentation, & oblation of our praiers, and good workes to God, the *m* transport of our soules to euerlasting ioy, *n* and lastlie the seperation of the good from the bad at the day of iudgement; all which if the contemplator dulie consider he cannot but vnderstand withall, the obligation he hath to yeld them (as *o* *S. Bernard* aduiseth) *deuotion for their beneuolence, loue, and confidence, for their care of him, and due reuerence for their presence*, and *continual assistance*: in regard whereof the Apostle also commaundeth, that *vvomen be decentlie couered in the Church, p propter Angelos*, in respect of the presence of the Angels. And *q* *S. Bernard, caute ambula*, saith he, *vt cui adsunt angeli, vvalke vvarely as hauing alvvaies Angels present vvith thee*, and then he addeth further, *in quovis angulo, angelo tuo* &c. *In euerie corner doe reuerence to thy Angel, darest thou doe that in his presence, vvhich thou durst not doe in mine?* Thus saith *S. Bernard*.

46 And with these considerations, we may styrrup in our selues, a gratefull remembrance of our dutie to honour, loue, and serue the blessed Angels, and speciallie our owne proper Angel, and to recommend our selues to his speciall care, and protection, crauing most humblie pardon of him, for our ingratitude towards him, in hauing so oft times reiected his holie suggestions, and had so litle regard, and respect of him, as to offend God most abominablie in his presence. Finallie we may also here consider how much we are bound to praise, and thanke almightie God for his merciful prouidence, and loue towards vs, not onlie in geuing vs such noble, potent, wise, louing, and faithful gardians to keepe vs, as the *r* psalmist saith *in all our vvaies*, but also in exalting vs to the participation of their glorie, as our Sauiour testifieth speaking of the reward of the iust in heauen. *s* *Et sunt* (saith he) *sicut Angeli, and they* are

Psal.102.
Aristot. 8. Phys. text.52. & 12. metaphys. text.43. Plato 1. de leg.
a *S. Aug. l.83 quæstionũ, q. 79. S. Greg. l.9. Moral. c. 10. D. Tho. opusc. 10. ar. 3. & opusc. 11. ar. 2. & S. Bonauent. in 2. dist.14. ar.3. q.2.*
b *Hebr.1. & D. Ambros. in Commẽt. in Apoc. c. 5.*
c *Daniel.10. & D. Basil. l. 3. contra Eunomium.*
d *Genes. 48. Matth. 18. Act.12.*
e f *4. Reg.19. Act.12.*
g *Tobiæ 5. vsque ad 12. & Genes.19.*
h *Ioan. 5. S. Bernard. l.3. de cõsiderat. ad Eugen.*
i *Daniel. 9. & 10. & Genes. 18.*
k *Luc. 1. Matt.1. & 2.*
l *Tob. 12. Apoc.8.*
m *Luc.16.*
n *Matth.24.*

o *S. Bernard ser.12. in Psal. 90.* p *1. Cor.11.* q *Idem ibid.* r *Psal. 90.* s *Matth. 22.*

are like to the Angels, whereof resulteth also an other consideration, of our infinit obligation to his deuine maiestie.

47 For whereas *Lucifer*, and innumerable other Angels, were cast downe into hell for their sinne, and man created to fill their ruines (as the scripture saith) (who also fell from God, deseruing eternal damnation) it pleased his deuine maiestie, to giue a redeemer to man, and not to the Angels, to the end he might (not withstanding his transgression) supplie the places of the spirits that fell: whereby we may receiue ineffable consolation, if we consider therein, aswell our owne benefits, as other mens, and that an infinit number, and amongst others manie of our owne ancestors, parents, and friendes, do alreadie enioy the blessed fellowship of Angels, being ranked some with the *Seraphins*, some with the *Cherubins*, others with the *Thrones* or *Dominations*, and other inferiour orders, there being, as our Sauiour taught, *manie mansions in the house of his Father*, wherein one soule differeth in glorie from an other, as one starr doth in light from an other with such a glorious varietie, that the verie sight thereof, is no smale encrease of the accidental glorie, of Gods Saincts, distinguished amongst themselues, with diuersitie of rewards, according to their diuerse vocations, and merits here in this life, where some were Apostles, some Patriarkes, some Prophets, some Martires, other Confessors, other virgins, besides an innumerable companie of other saued soules of all sorts, and vocations, and of all nations, and people, all triumphing now ouer the malice, and miserie of the world, in the sight, and fruition of God their Creatour, in whom they see, and know, not onlie all the secrets of nature, and all naturall causes, but also what els they desire to know, yea, the abstruse misteries of his most blessed diuinitie, and Trinitie, wherein consisteth their essential glorie and mans finall, and true felicitie.

Isay.14. Psal.109. Genes.2. & 3.

D.Greg. Hom.de 100 ouibus. Ioan.14. 1.Cor.15.

48 Here then may we congratulate with all the blessed soules, for their incomprehensible ioyes, and happines, but especiallie with the most glorius virgin *Mary*, the mother of God, exalted both in bodie, and soule, not onlie aboue all the soules of men, but also aboue all the Angels, being as *S. Chrisostome* saith *incomparably more glorious then the Seraphins, and more beautifull and vvorthie then all the vvorld*, and therefore worthilie called by *S. Iohn Damascen. Domina omnium creaturarum, the lady and mistres of all creatures.* In which respect, aswell the Angels, as the glorified soules, excedinglie reioyce to see her glorie, neuer ceasing to praise, and magnifie her for the inestimable benefits, that both heauen, & earth receiueth by her, wherein we ought also to concurre with them, saying with saint, *Cyril. Salue Sancta Deipara* &c. *All hayle holy mother of God, the notable ornament*

Chrisostom. in litur. & ho. 1. in 1.c. Matth. Iohan.Dam. orth.li.4.

Sanct. Ciril Alexan. Hom. contra Nestorium Ephesi. Habita in concil. Ephesino. To. 6. Ephesini cōcil. c. 6. S. Athanas. in Euangel. de Santiss. deipara.

ornament and honour of the vvole vvorld. All hayle the inextinguible, or vnquencheable lamp, the crovvne of virginity, the scepter of the true Christian faith, the indissoluble temple of God, vvhich contained him, vvho cannot be conteined, or comprehended anie vvhere &c. Or vvith S. Athanasius thus. Exaltamus te magna & Canora voce &c. we, exalt or extol thee, vvith a hygh and loud voyce saying, hayl full of grace our Lord is vvith thee, pray for vs, o mistres, lady, queene and mother of God &c.

a Genes. 15. b & 22. c Iob. 1. d Num. 12. e Psal. 131. f Rom. 9. g Matth. 26. h Luc. 7. Psal. 141. Aug. de. verdo. ser. 64. Idem manual. ca. 17.

49 Thus may we say with these ancient and holie Fathers, recommending our selues to her intercession, and protection, as also to the praiers of all the blessed companie of Saints, and especiallie of those which are our particuler patrons, setting before our eies, the examples of all their rare vertues, desiring, and determining by the helpe of their praiers, to imitate the same, as the *a* faith, and *b* obedience of *Abraham*, the *c* patiēce of *Iob*, the mansuetude of *d Moyses*, and *e Dauid*, the burning charitie of *f S. Paul*, both towards God and his neighbour, the teares, and repentaunce of *g S. Peter*, and *h S. Mary Magdalen*, the inuincible constancie of the martirs, the immaculat chastitie of the virgins, the profound humilitie, resignation, and true contempt of the world, of all the blessed Apostles, Anchors, hermits, & religious, to the end, that following their stepps here in this life, we may in the next be partakers of their felicity, *in terra viuentium*, in the land of the liuing, which they alreadie possesse, where the ioy is so vnspeakeable that (as *S. Augustin* saith) it is more easie to tell what is not there, then what is there, where there are no dangers, no feares, no enuie, no wrath, no ambition, no temptation, no hunger, no thirst, no wearines, no neede, of sleepe, or rest, no pouertie, no sicknes, but life without death, youth without age, light without darkenes, ioy without sorrow, peace without discord, and eternal glorie, which as *S. Anselme* saith, is nothing els, but *a perfect accomplishment & consummation of the vvill, and desire of the iust, a ioy of all ioyes, a contentment, & pleasure of all pleasures, and a good of all goods vvithout anie mixture of euil, or sorrovv, and vvith euerlasting securitie.*

S. Ber. ser. 4. de ascensione domini.

50 Thus may we entertaine our selues, with no lesse fruit, then spirituall contentment, in the meditation of the heauenly court, and the inestimable ioyes thereof. And therefore S. *Bernard* exhorting vs thereto, saith. *Quid concupiscere poterit in hoc seculo nequam &c. VVhat can he desire in this vvicked vvorld, vvhose eye doth alvvayes behould, bona Domini in terra viuentium, the goods of our Lord in the land of the louing &c. VVho is there that doth vse to meditate, vppon the ioyes, the pleasure, the beatitude, and the eternal glory of the children of God, and vvill not out of the abundance of his invvard consolation, breake forth into the vvords of S. Peter, and say, bonum est nos hic esse, it is*

good

good for vs to dvvell here? Thus ſaith *S. Bernard*, with much more to the Matth.17
ſame purpoſe, to ſhew the fruit, and benefitt that followeth of theſe meditations, which muſt needes breede in our ſoules, a true contempt of this miſerable world, with a feruent loue, and deſire of heauenlie thinges, whereuppon the Apoſtle himſelfe ſaith. *Si conſurrexiſtis cum Chriſto &c. If you be riſen againe vvith Christ, ſeeke after thoſe* Coloſſ.3.
things, vvhich are aboue, vvhere Christ is ſitting on the right hand of his Father, take a taſt, and feeling of ſupernal, or heauenlie things, and not of thoſe things, vvhich are vppon the earth. Thus ſaith the Apoſtle. And therefore the royall prophet, being inflamed with the loue of heauen, by the frequent meditation thereof, exclaimeth. *Quam delecta tabernacula tua Do-* Pſal.83.
mine &c. Hovv louelie are thy tabernacles, o Lord, my ſoule fainteth in me for the feruent deſire I haue to be in the courts of our Lord?

Of certaine other meditations proper, to the Vnitiue vvay, and of the exceſſe of ſpirit, called by the contemplatiues Ecſtaſis, and of rapts, and the diuerſity of deuine fauours, and the ineffable conſolations, vvhich God imparteth to his ſeruants in the perfect practiſe thereof; vvhereby it is euident, that true vnion vvith God, and conſequentlie the cheefe felicity of man in this life, and of common vvealth, conſiſteth in Chriſtian contemplation.

CHAP. 21.

1 WHen we haue in this ſort taken, as I may ſay, ſome view or the celeſtiall kingdome, and of the glorious inhabitants thereof, we may with due reuerence, humility, & reſignatiō of our ſelues, inſinuat our ſelues further to the contemplatiō of the diuine nature, not with intention to ſound the bottomles profunditie, of that vaſt, and vnmeaſurable ſea, but with a deſire, onlie to conſider ſome part of the deuine attributes and excellencies, to the end we may excite our ſelues the rather to the admiration, praiſe and loue of our Creatour, acknowledging all, and euerie one of his diuine perfections, to be ineffable, infinit, and incomprehenſible. For who can cōceiue the moſt admirable proprietie of the deuine eſſēce, which being moſt pure, ſimple, & abſolute of it ſelfe, depēdeth on nothing, but giueth eſſence to all things, and being whole aſwell within all thinges, as without all thinges, is as it were, both their center, & their circumference, or rather as I may ſay, an intelligible ſphere, whereof the center is euerie where, and the circumferent no where, for being in all places, he is contained in no place, being in all things, he is included in nothing, & being

without all things, he is excluded from nothing, but is more present, and inward to euerie thing then anie thing is to it selfe, and though he be onlie, and simplie one, yet he is most manifold in operation, yea all
1.Cor.8. in all *of vvhome by vvhome, and in vvhom* (as the Apostle saith) all thinges are, or haue their being. And againe who can comprehend, or sufficiētly admire, the infinit excellencie of his deuine attribuits, and proprieties,
Psal.35. as of his *povver, vvisdome, bountie and iustice*, of the which euerie one is, *Abyssus multa, an inscrutable deapth and profunditie.*

2. For first to say somewhat of his power, who can conceiue how vnmeasurable it is, seeing it extendeth it selfe, as farre as his will, which is infinit: for although he will not doe all that he can, yet he can doe all
Psal.113. that he will, and therefore as *he hath made, and done all*, saith the psalmist, *that he vvould in heauen, and earth*, so also he could, if he would doe infinitelie more, yea, and in an instant annihilat all things in the world, with the like facilitie that he made them, to witt, with his only word, or will.

3 Furthermore his omnipotencie sufficientlie appeareth, not onlie in the huge immensitie of the world, and infinit multitude of his creatures in generall, but also in euerie creature in particuler, euerie one of them being a miracle in it selfe, though the dailie sight of them diminisheth the wonder, it is no lesse miraculous, that one graine of corne sowed in the ground, is multiplied into so manie graines, for the sustenaunce of
Matth.24. man, as wee dailie see, then that our Sauiour Christ, multiplied two fishes, and fiue loaues, to feede fiue thousand men, it is no lesse maruelous, and miraculous to create, and giue life to so manie soules, as God dailie doth, then if he should dailie reuiue as manie dead men. Finallie there is not so litle, and contemptible a creature vppon earth, which could haue bene at first created, or could be still conserued, and multiplied, without an infinit power in God the Creator, and therefore he is worthilie called omnipotent, or almightie, omnipotent in that he created all things of nothing, omnipotent in their conseruation, omnipotēt in their multiplication, omnipotent in their disposition & gouerment, omnipotent in punishing, omnipotent in pardoning and rewarding, from whose omnipotent power, is deriued all the power in heauen and earth, the power of Angels, good and bad, the power of the elements (which farre exceedeth all humane power) the power of princes, and
Rom.13. magistrats, the power of armies, and finallie all strength, and power of men, and of all other creatures, which, I say, floweth from the maine sea of his omnipotencie, and returneth thither againe, seeing that all created power is ordained, for no other end, but for his seruice.

4 Therefore

4 Therefore, we may here applie all this particularlie to our selues, and acknowledge, all the power, force, strength, and authoritie that we haue, to be of God, praising, and thanking him most humblie for it, crauing not onlie his grace, that we may alwaies vse it to his seruice, but also pardon for all our former abuse thereof. Also we may humblie beseech almightie God, that seeing all power, and authoritie is from him, it may please his deuine maiestie to giue vs grace, to obey our superiours with all humilitie, and due obedience, acknowledging his deuine power and authoritie in theirs. Finallie we may consider how great cause of feare all wicked mẽ haue, seeing they haue such a powerfull enemie, whose omnipotent will nothing can resist, as also that good *Rom.9.* men haue no lesse cause of confidence, and ioy hauing such a potent patron, friend, and father, to protect, and defend them, for *si Deus nobiscum,* *Rom.8.* *quis contra nos, if God be vvith vs, vvhat neede vve care vvho is against vs?* Thus much for the deuine power.

5 In like maner, how infinit is his wisdome, which knoweth not onlie all things in generall, but also euerie thing in particular, & all the partes nature, vertue, & power thereof, & (as the preacher saith,) he knoweth *Eccl.1.* the number of the starres, of the sands of the sea, of the drops of rayne, and of the daies of the world, all thinges past, present, and to come, not by discourse, but all at once. Moreouer his wisdome searcheth the very harts, and reines of men, it knoweth not onlie our future actions, but also our future cogitations, he foresaw, saith *S. Augustin,* the denial of *S. August. in Psal.140.* *Peter* in the heart of *Peter,* though then it had no cause, as it was a sinne (either in the will of God, who neuer willeth anie sinne) nor in the will of *Peter,* who as then determined the contrarie, and therefore the psalmist saith, *intellexisti cogitationes meas de longe, thou hast vnderstood my cogita-* *Psal.138.* *I.b.31.* *tions a farre of, omnes vias meas prauidisti, thou hast foreseene all my vvaies, & gressus meos,* saith, *Iob, dinumerasti, thou hast numbred all my paces*: whereby we may iustlie conceiue, aswell feare to doe euil, euen in the least thought, or cogitation (seeing it cannot be hid from him) as also desire to doe well, seeing our most secret good workes, thoughts, and intentions, are all manifest to him, and shalbe rewarded by him.

6 But what tongue, or pen can expresse, or vnderstãding comprehend, the wonderfull wisdome that God hath shewed in the creation, and conseruation of the world, consisting of contrarieties, which combat continuallie one with an other, and yet are conserued by his wisdome with a most admirable equalitie, order, beautie, vtilitie, and benefit to all his creatures, which he also guideth, & disposeth by his prouidence, extending the same particularlie to euerie thing, and speciallie to his

 seruants,

uc.21 seruants, yea to euerie *hayre of their heads*, whereof he saith, *no one shall perish*, working neuertheles in man, and in all thinges els, according to their owne natures, with such sweetnes, that he seemeth sometimes to haue no operation therein, or eare thereof, yet drawing alwaies good out of euil, and neuer permitting euil, but for a greater good, and turning all thinges in fiue, yea the euil wills of the wickedest men, to the execution of his owne will, and to his glorie, for the which he created man, and all things els? And therefore the psalmist iustlie exclaimeth with the admiration of the wisdome of
Psal.103. God in all his workes. *Quam magnificata sunt opera tua Domine, omnia in sapientia fecisti?* &c. *Hovv magnificent are thy vvorkes, o Lord, thou hast made, or donne all thinges in vvisdome?*

7 And what shall I say of the inscrutabilitie of his iudgements, proceeding also from the bottomles depth of his wisdome? For who can giue anie reason, why he rather chose the Iewes for his people, then the Gentils? Why he ordained the conuersion of the parts of the world so
Reg.12. soone, and of the Indians so late? Why hauing taken from *Roboam* part of his kingdome for his Fathers offence, he gaue it to *Ieroboam*, a wickeder man then he? Why one man is borne lame, or blind, and an other with all his limes, and eyes? Why one man is poore, and miserable, and an other rich, and prosperous, and such like? Whereof, and of all such other his deuine iudgements, in the disposition of mens affaires, the reason is no lesse iust, then certaine though reserued, and locked vp (as I may say) in the secret cabinet of his profound wisdome, to be made manifest at the latter day, at what time we shall exclaime with
Rom.11. the Apostle. *O altitudo diuitiarum, sapientiæ, & scientia Dei* &c. *O hovv high, and profound are the riches of Gods vvisdome, and knovvledge! Hovv incomprehensible are his iudgements, and vnsearcheable are his vvayes!*

8 Here then may we consider, that all wisdome of men, is but, as it were, a litle beame of light, cast forth from the sonne of Gods infinit
Sap. 1. wisdome, that therefore it is the particular gift of God, not possible to be procured by humane industrie, other then by humble praier, in which respect let vs humblie craue it of almightie God, saying with the psalmist. *Illumina tenebras meas Domine.* O Lord, illuminat my darke-
Psal.17. nes, and with the wise man. *Da mihi Domine* &c. *Giue me o Lord the*
Sap.9. *vvisdome that assisteth thy seat, to the end it may be vvith me, and labour vvith me, that I may knovv, vvhat is acceptable to thee.* Lastlie, let vs acknow-
1.Cor.3. ledge with the Apostle, that *all vvorldly vvisdome is more folly*, and say with *Iob. Ecce timor Domini* &c. *Behold the feare of God is true vvisdome, and to*
Iob. 28. *eschevv sinne is true vnderstanding.*

9 Moreouer

9 Moreouer how can the infinit bountie or goodnes of God, be eyther comprehended, or sufficientlie commended, seeing no creature in heauen, or earth hath anie goodnes at all, but onlie by participation thereof, being good, because he is good, and made all his creatures good, communicating his owne goodnes to them, from the highest to the lowest. From whence proceedeth all the benefits, that man receiueth by heauen, and earth, but from his bountie? Whence is mans beautie, his strength, his health, his welth, his ease, his honours, his vertues, whence I say, doe they flow, but from the fountaine of his deuine goodnes? How bountifull is he not onlie to his seruants in protecting, comforting, cherishing, pardoning, and rewarding them, but also to his verie enimies, in conseruing them, in expecting them to repentance, in offering them his grace, and in reconciling them to him, if the fault be not in themselues?

10 How admirable was his bountie in his Incarnation, whereby he communicated vnto vs, all his owne good, yea himselfe, and tooke vppon himselfe our humanitie, mortalitie, and miserie? How stupendious was his goodnes in our Redemption, as also in the deuine sacraments, and spirituall power left in his Church, and speciallie in feeding vs with his owne blessed bodie, and bloud, all I say, stupendious for the manner, for the effects, & for the fruit, & benefit to mākind, as I haue sufficiently declared diuers times before? How bountifull, & liberal is he in rewarding his owne gifts, & graces in vs seeing he rewardeth vs for that which he geueth vs; first imparting his grace vnto vs, to the end we may merit, and then rewarding our merits farre aboue our merits, recōpensing our transitorie, vnperfect, & weake workes with temporall, spiritual, and euerlasting rewards, surpassing all vnderstanding & imagination of man? The due consideration whereof, cannot but moue vs to two things, the one to loue, and praise him, for his infinit bountie and mercie, saying with the psalmist, *confitemini Domino, quoniam bonus, quoniam in seculum misericordia eius*; *Confesse ye our Lord, for he is bountifull, ond good and his mercy is for euer.* The other is to pray continuallie for his grace, that we may imitate his deuine bountie, communicating to our neighbours, the gifts, graces, goods, and talents which he hath bestowed vppon vs.

Psal. 105.

11 Furthermore what shall I say of his iustice, which is no lesse ineffable, & incōprehensible then the former, whether we consider it, as he punisheth, or as he rewardeth; seeing he is no lesse exact in the one, then in the other, punishing all sinne whatsoeuer without exception of persons, times, or places, from whose hand no man can escape, frō whose eye no

man can be hid, who searcheth most curiouslie into euerie corner of mans conscience, which is more cleare to him, then the sunne, and serueth him for an vnreprouable witnes against euery sinner. *Scrutabor* saith
Sophon.1. he, *Hierusalem in lucernis. I vvill search Hierusalem vvith candels, and torches,* meaning that he will sift, and straightlie examine, the hearts, and consciences, of his owne seruants. Therefore how much more narrowlie will he sift the consciences, and actions of his enimies?

12 And so seuer is his iudgement, that those sinnes, which seeme to man but light, and are, as we call them venial, deserue in his sight most rigorous punishment, as may appeare by the sinne of *Moyses*, consisting
Numer. 20. in a litle distrust, for the which neuertheles he was excluded from the
3.Reg.13. land of promise, as also a prophet, in *Samaria*, was killed by a lyon, because contrarie to the commaundement of God, he did eate a litle in the way, being deceiued by an other prophet, who pretended, to haue had, a latter reuelation to inuite him to eate, what then may we thinke of his rigour, and seueritie in the punishment of mortall sinnes, which he punisheth not onlie corporallie, and by desolation of whole kingdomes, and countries, by famins, plagues, warre inundations, fire from heauen, serpents, and such like, but also eternallie, by vnspeakeable torments? Lastlie so terrible is he in his iustice, and iudgements, that his verie elect seruants, and freends are aduised by *the Apostle to vvorke their saluation, cum*
Philip.2. *timore, & tremore, vvith feare, and trembling,* what terrour then, and horrour ought the wicked to haue, who dailie deserue the extremitie of his wrath, and vengeance?

13 But what? is not his iustice also as complete in rewarding? For although he be our Lord, and creatour, and therefore oweth vs nothing for our seruice, in respect of it selfe, yet hauing out of his bountie, and liberalitie promised vs reward for the same, and for euerie good worke, he hath thereby made himselfe our detter, if we serue him, and is of his iustice so exact in the performance of his promise, that he leaueth no good act (be it neuer so litle) nor good thought vnrewarded, yea and recompenseth sometimes the seruices of his very enimies, yea though they serue him vnwittinglie. He aduanced the Romans, as *S. Augustin*
Aug. de ciuit. saith to the monarchie of the world for their morall vertues, & recom-
dei. li.5. c.15. pensed *Nabuchodonosor* king of *Babilon*, for the seruice which he did him
Ezech. 29. vnwittinglie in the expugnation of *Tyrus*. How then will he reward his seruants, for good workes proceeding of his grace, and directed to his seruice?

14 Therefore the Apostle most confidentlie expected the crowne of iustice, for the *good course*, which, as he saith, he had *runne* here in his seruice,

seruice, *quam reddet mihi Dominus* (saith he) *in illa die iustus iudex, vvhich* 2 Tim.4.
crovvne our Lord being a iust iudge, vvill render vnto me in the day of iudgement,
and no maruaile seeing he rewardeth euerie *cupp of cold vvater* giuen *in* Matth. 10.
his name, whereby his seruants may receiue infinit comfort, seruing such an omnipotent, wise, bountifull, and iust Lord, who accepteth, and rewardeth such small seruices, yea, and for one teare, or sigh of true repentance, giueth in recompence his owne euerlasting kingdome, and the eternall fruition of himselfe. To conclud we are to consider, that as he is infinitlie to be admired, praised and beloued of vs, for his mercie, bountie, & iustice, in rewarding vs: so also we ought no lesse to admire, praise, and loue him for his iustice in punishing vs, saying alwais with the psalmist, *Iustus es Domine & rectum iudicium tuum; thovv art iust o Lord, and thy iudgement is right.* Psal. 118.

15 I omit for breuities sake manie other things, which might be considered, aswell concerninge his iustice, as other his ineffable vertues, and will touch onlie a further consideration of the three former attribuits (the power, wisdome, and goodnes of God) whereby we may be lead to some speculation of the inscrutable misterie of the most blessed Trinitie, acknowledging in the omnipotencie of God, the person of God the Father, in his wisdome, the person of God the Sonne, and in his bountie, or goodnes, God the holie Ghost.

16 For although all the three persons (being of one substance, and equall one with an other) are like omnipotent, wise, and bountifull, neuerthelesse these attributes may be particularlie, and seuerallie applied, rather to one of them, then to an other, in respect of certaine properties belonging to their seuerall persons, as omnipotencie is applied properly to God the Father, as to the beginninge, or roote from whence the other two persons spring; And wisdome is peculierlie applied to God the Sonne (who is called *sapientia Patris, the vvisdome of the Father*) because he is produced by the vnderstanding of his Father: And lastie goodnes or bountie, is attributed to the holie Ghost, because goodnes proceedeth principallie from the will, as the holie Ghost proceedeth from the will of the Father, and the Sonne, being their loue, and as it were the linke whereby they are eternallie vnited. S. Aug. li. de Trinitate ca. 15.

17 Moreouer we may also by the further consideration of the infinit goodnes of God, receiue some further light for the better vnderstanding of some other misteries, belonging to the diuine nature; For seeing that God is infinitelie good, and therefore most communicable, I meane, that seeing it is most requisit to his infinit goodnes, that he communicate himselfe to some one or other infinitlie, and with the greatest communication

nication that may be (that is to say) that he giue, and impart not onl[y] his giftes, and proprieties (as he doth to his creatures) but also his who[le] essence, nature, and substance (for other wayes he doth not communi[-] cate so much as he may) it must needes follow, that there is a distinctio[n] of deuine persons, to whom the diuine nature is communicated, wh[o] consequentlie hauing the same deuine nature, and essence, must neede[s] also be infinitlie good, & consubstantial, that is to say, of one substance, [a]nd nature, and therefore also coequal, and one God, which when w[e] haue considered, let vs then lay all reason aside, and haue recourse t[o] faith, and by the light thereof consider, and admire the rest of our Christian doctrin, concerning the three deuine persons, and their deuin[e] proprieties, without further curiositie, to penetrate, that impenetrabl[e] misterie, least by searching *into maiesty*, (as Salomon saith) *vve be oppre[st] vvith glory*, for what created vnderstanding can conceiue how the vniti[e] of one God can stand with a Trinitie of persons and their equalitie wit[h] a paternitie, filiation, and procession, how the Father behoulding, an[d] knowing himselfe from all eternitie, begate the worde his Sonne; how the holie ghost proceedeth from them both; and lastlie how euerie person is distinct, and yet hath the other two persons in him-selfe.

Prouerb. 25.

18 Therefore that which our contemplatiues aduise to be done in th[e] speculation of these incomprehensible verities, is, to humble our selues in the presence of God, to acknowledge our owne weaknes, basnes, & vnworthines, to *captiuat our reason, and vnderstanding to faith*, to admire praise, and magnifie the deuine nature, and to exult, and reioyce with all ioy and iubilation, that our Lord, and Creator is of infinit perfection maiestie, and glorie, and finallie to resigne our selues wholie into hi[s] hands, as his creatures and bondslaues to be disposed at his pleasure which being donne with a pure hart, a liuelie faith, and a feruent loue, what maruaile is it, if we be so suspended in the most sweete, and delectable speculation of beautie, and bountie it selfe, that our soule do melt, as I may say, with the heat of his loue? Or rather what maruell is it if almightie God being infinitlie good, and seeing a soule created by himselfe to his owne image, clensed by his grace from sinne, purified, and purged from passions, and peruerse affections, adorned with his giftes, wholie resigned into his handes, thirsting after him, *as the stagg doth after the fountaints of vvater, languishing in his loue*, wayting, and attending, *in atrys eius, in the courts of his pallace*, to haue some sight of him, and saying with the psalmist *Exquisiuit te facies mea &c. my face hath sought thee, o Lord, and I vvill seeke to see thy face*, (not out of a presumption, or a conceit of my owne worthines, but out of a pure loue, and a desire to behould thee, the more.

Blosius in institut. spirituali c. 8. & in speculo spirituali. c. 10.
2. Cor 10.
Psal. 41.
Cant. 5.
Psal. 83.
Psal. 28.

more to loue prayse, and admire thee) what maruaile, I say, is it, if as the loadstone draweth the yron, or the sonne the vapours of the earth, so also his diuine maiestie draw vnto him such a soule, embrace it, cherish it, yea, and be, as it were, enamored of it, and say vnto it, as he saith in the Canticles. *Surge amica mea, & veni. Aryse my loue, and come vnto me. Quam pulchra es amica mea? Hovv fayre art thou my loue? Veni sponsa mea. Come my spouse, &c.*

Cant. 2. & 5.

Ibid. ca. 4.

19 For so tender, and feruent is the loue of God to a cleane, and pure soule, that he contracteth an indissoluble matrimonie with it, vniting himselfe vnto it, or rather as the contemplatiues speake, transforming it into himselfe: For as yron put into the fire, and made red hoat, though it changeth not, nor looseth the substance of yron, yet becommeth fire: euen so the soule of man, conioyned, and vnited with God, by a pure, and sincere contemplatiue loue, is as it were, deified, and becommeth deuine, *being made one spirit vvith God*, and though it doe not yet see him, as he is in his glorie, yet it learneth by experience, how sweete he is, and that his deuine nature, and perfections doe infinitelie surpasse all that which can be said, written conceiued, or imagined of him, yea and more certainelie knoweth him, by an inward touch, and feeling of him, then we can see, or know; the visible sunne, by the sight of our corporall eyes, and yet as a certaine contemplatiue saith. *Præ cognitione fit, quasi sine cognitione, &, in sapienti quadam ignoranti constituitur. It knovveth so much of the deuine nature, that it knovveth as it vvere nothing at al, but is reduced to a kind of vvise ignorãce*, knowing only that God (whome it now feeleth, enioyeth and desireth to see and know) passeth all humaine knowledge and vnderstanding, and that the surest, and easiest way, to come to the knowledge of him, is (as *S. Dionysius* teacheth) to abstract from him, al those thinges, which man either seeth, or knoweth, or can conceiue, and therefore the same authour denieth him to be *a substance, or a soule; or a spirit, or a life essence, or æternytie* (meaning in such sort, as man can vnderstand, or conceiue them to be) for that hee incomparablie, ineffablie, and infinitlie exceedeth and excelleth all created substance or essence, or whatsoeuer can be conceiued or imagined by anie creature.

Blosius in specalo spirituali. ca. 11.

1. Cor. 6.

Blosius vbi supra.

Idem ibid.

li. 7. de deuin. nomin. lib. de mystica theolog. c. 5.

20 And this the *Caligo*, that is to say, *the obscuritie or darkenes*, whereof the contemplatiues speake, according to the royall prophet. *Nubes & caligo in circuitu eius. Clouds and darkenes doe inuiron him.* And therfore allso *Dionysius* saieth. *Diuina caligo est lux inaccessabilis in qua Deus habitare dicitur &c. The diuine darknes is the inaccessable light vvherein God is said to dvvell.* In which respect, *Aristotle*, saith verie well and trulie,

Psal. 96.

Dionys. ad dorotheum.

1. Tim. 6.

Metaphys. li. 2. tex. 1. that the vnderstanding of man is no more able to conceiue those thinges which are most manifest in nature (that is to say those thinges, which belong to the diuine essence) then the eye of the owle, can behold the beames of the sunne. But now who can expresse the ineffable ioy, and consolation, that the soule of man feeleth when being eleuated by grace aboue all force, and power of nature, it is lead by almightie God, *in cellam vinariam* (as the Canticles say) *into the vvyne cellar*, where it drinketh of the fountaine of life, and is filled with a torrent of pleasure, and as the royall prophet also speaketh, *inebriatur ab vbertate Domus Dei, is made drunke vvith the abundant, and svveete plenty of Gods house*, reposing, and sleeping (as I may say) in the contemplation of almightie God, who is so carefull to conserue the repose of such a soule, that he saith in the Canticles. *Adiuro vos filiæ Hierusalem* &c. *I adiure you, ye daughters of Hierusalem, that you doe not disquiet, nor avvake my beloued, vntill she alist to aryse*; whereupon *S. Bernard*, expounding this text, calleth this sleepe, *excessum mentis, an excesse of mynd*, or the supernaturall eleuation of a soule rauished with the sweetenes of contemplation, and this excesse is commonlie called *Ecstasis* when it worketh anie extraordinarie effects, in the bodie, as it doth diuerslie, in some more, and some lesse.

Cant. 2. Psal. 36. Ibidem. Cant. 2. S. Ber. ser. super cant. 52.

21 For sometimes it forceth a man to expresse the internal iubilation of the soule, with the externall voyce, and to sing as *Saul* did when the spirit of God fell vppon him in companie of the prophets. And the like we read of one *Richardus*, a learned, and holie English hermit, who (as he writeth himselfe) was continuallie replenished with such sweetenes of a heauenlie melodie in his soule, that he could not forbeare to sing, praise and giue, thanks to almightie God all the day.

1. Reg. 19. Richard. Pãpolitan. de incendio amoris.

22 Sometimes againe it maketh a man exult, and leape for ioy, and contentment, as the royall prophet did before the Arke, who also saith of himselfe *Cor meum & Caro mea* &c. *My hart, and flesh exulted, or lept for ioy in the lyuing God*, & of this we haue had a notable example in our daies in B. Fa. *Philip Nerio* an Italian, and founder of the congregation called the *Oratory*, or *Chiesa noua* in *Rome*, who was commonlie so transported with deuine consolations (as oft as he said masse) that he could not stay his bodie from continuall motion, and exultation, in which respect he was forced for the most part to say masse priuatelie.

2. Reg. 6. Psal. 83. Antonius Gallonius in vita eius.

23 Sometimes also it eleuateth, or abstracteth the soule from the senses in such sort, that the bodie remaineth, as it were senseles, or dead for the time, as the prophet *Daniel*, & *S. Iohn the Euangelist* testifie of themselues: and the like may be thought of the excesse of spirit, which happened to the Apostle *S. Peter*, when he saw the vision of the sheete, full of all kind of beastes.

Dan. 10. Apoc. 1. Haymo in Apoc. Act. 10.

of beastes. And such no doubt, was the extasis, or excesse of *S. Paule*, when he was, *raptus in tertium cælum, rapt into the third heauen*, not knowing as he saith whether he was in his bodie, or out of his bodie; and of this kind of *Ecstase*, or excesse of spirit, I shall haue occasion heareafter, to alledge manie examples both ancient, and moderne. *2.Cor.12.* *Chap.27.*

24 Finallie the eleuation of the soule, otherwhiles is such, that it violentlie draweth vp the bodie after it into the aire, and then it is most properlie called *raptus*, a *rapt*, whereof I omit to lay downe examples here, because I shall doe it verie amplie hereafter. *Chap.27.*

25 And therefore that, which I wish to be noted further for the present, concerning the effects of contemplation, is, that as there are diuerse degrees of perfection therein, so also, there are diuers degrees of spiritual consolations, and heauenlie fauours, which God dailie bestoweth vppon his seruants, in the vse & exercise thereof.

26 For some attaine onlie to the vnion of the will with God, and receiue thereby ineffable consolation (not withstanding, that their vnderstanding, memorie, and phantasie remaine at liberty.) And some haue their vnderstanding aswell vnited with God as their will, with farre greater cōsolation then the former, though their memorie, & phantasie being free, doe somewhat importune them, and interrupt the integritie of their repose. And some others againe, haue all their powers so combyned, and vnited with the deuine essence, that they remaine ingulfed, and absorpt in the contemplation thereof, some more some lesse, whereupon follow sometimes these admirable rapts, whereof I haue partlie spoken alreadie, and will speake more heareafter. *Camino de perfecion. M.Teresa nella vita sua c.14.15.16.17.18.19 & 20.*

27 But the highest degree of contemplation, is to be perfectlie vnited with God in soule, and to receiue extraordinarie, and continuall illustrations of the vnderstanding, and other deuine consolations, without suffring anie ecstase, or rapt, in such sort, that the soule be wholie occupied, and fixed in the contemplation of God, and yet neither the actions, or functions of the bodie, nor anie pious, or lawfull negotiation be hindred thereby, so that the comefort of contemplation, and the merit of action do concurre in the highest degree; which kind of contemplation the humanitie of our Sauiour Christ, had continuallie in the highest perfection, and it hath pleased him also to impart the same in a high degree to manie of his seruants, especiallie to his [a] blessed mother as it may be well presumed, his Apostles, besides manie others in latter times, as to [b] *S. Hildegardis* a holie woman, who had such vnion with God, and thereby such a continuall illustration of spirit, that her soule dilated it selfe into farre countries, and saw what passed there, whether shee slept, *Bozius de sig.eccle.li. 9. c.13.sig.37. Henric.Harphius de mystica Theolog.li.3.par.4.c.30.* *a Vide Lodouic. Blosium in Append. institut.spiritual.c.2.ex Thaulero.* *b Bozius vbi supra.*

or waked, and yet neuertheles, she had no alienation of her soule frō her senses, or alteration in her bodie; And the like may be said of *B. Fa. Franciscus Xauierus*, of the societie of *Iesus*, in these our dayes, who whilest he preached in the east *India*, saw in spirit, a battayle, which passed betwixt the *Portugueses*, and the infidels, and recommended the *Portugueses* to the prayers of his audience, in respect of the great danger wherein they were at that tyme, as afterwards it proued to be true. And to these may be added manie hollie men and wemen in the church of God, who haue excelled in the spirit of prophesie, and haue had also continual or verie frequent illustrations of soule, at such tymes as they had no extase or rapt, as the holie Abbots S. Hylarion and S. Benet *S. Francis of Paula S. Brigit*, *S. Katherin* of *Siena* and many others, whom I omit to auoyd prolixity.

P. Ribadeneyra, in vita eius.

28 But of these diuers degrees of deuine fauours in contemplation, *S. Bernard* treateth notablie in his sermons vppon the *Cantilces*, where he saith that the same is signified by the diuersitie of the *Aromatical oyntements*, whereof the yong wemen, which accompanie the spouse, make mention, saying. *In odorem vnguentorum tuorū currimus. VVe runne*, o Lord, *to the svveete sauours, aud smell of thy oyntments.* And the like he also obserueth in the same place, by the occasion of diuers *cellers*, whereto the king led his spouse. *Introduxit me rex*, saith shee, *in cellaria sua. The king brought me into his cellars.* Whereuppon *S. Bernard*, saith, that the king or bridegroome, hath manie different cellars, manie chambers, and mansions, whereto euerie contemplatiue is not indifferentlie admitted, but that euerie one hath a place of pleasure, or consolation assigned him, *pro diuersitate meritorum, according to the diuersitie of his merits*; wherein he giueth to vnderstand, that euerie one feeleth in his soule a different sweetenes, and delectation, according to the different measure of his desert, so that he may say (saith *S. Bernard*) *secretum meum mihi, my secret is to my selfe.* And further he saith, that the accesse to the cabinet, or secret closet of the king, is reserued onlie for the spouse her selfe, that is to say, for a soule enflamed with such a pure seraphical loue of God, that it pleaseth him to contract, as it were, a coniugal vnion, or matrimonie with it, whereby it is perfectlie vnited with him, and as I signified before, transformed into him, and yet neuertheles, saith he, the spouse her selfe cannot in this life attaine *ad omne quod vult secretum, to all the secret that shee desireth*, meaning that perfect fruition, and sight of God, wherewith she shalbe eternallie beatified in the life to come.

D. Ber. super cant. ser. 23. *Cant. 1.* *Cant. 1.* *S. Bernard. ibid.* *Isay. 24.*

29 Thus doth this great master of contemplation, signifie the diuerse degrees of spirituall comeforts, which God imparteth to his seruants, in the exercise thereof. Though whosoeuer arriueth to the least, or lowest

degree

degree of vnion with God, findeth such inestimable consolation, that he may trulie say with the royal prophet. *Quam magna est multitudo, &c. Hovv great*, o Lord, *is the multitude of thy svvetenes, vvhich thou hast hidden, or laid vp in store for them, vvhich feare thee.* As *S. Augustin* witnesseth of himselfe, and his mother, both of them replenished with such a heauenlie cōfort, & ioy at *Ostia* not farre from *Rome*, that they detested all earthly delights, and as it seemed to thē, did for the time participat of eternall beatitude.

Psal. 30.

Aug. conf. ss. li. 9. ca. 10.

30 Hereuppon also *S. Bernard* saith. *Quæ anima semel à Domino didicit, &c. The soule vvhich hath once learned of almightie God to enter into it selfe, and there diligentlie te seeke his presence, and face, I knovv not vvhether it vvould thinke the paines of hell more horrible, and insupportable for a time, then after the tast of this spiritual delectation, to goe out againe to feele the alurements or rather the molestation of the flesh, and the insatiable curiositie of the senses.* Thus saith *S. Bernard*, not of the highest kind of contemplation, nor yet of that which allienateth the soule from the senses, but of that which is ordinarie amongst those that practise the contemplatiue discipline, though worldlie men (who are drowned in the beastlie delighes of the world, and the flesh) doe neither know, nor beleeue it, neither yet can conceyue it to be true, for the Apostle saith. *Animalis homo non percipit ea quæ sunt spiritus Dei. The sensual man hath no feeling of those thinges vvhich belong to the spirit of God*; and yet reason may teach them, that as the soule in dignitie, farre excelleth the bodie, so also the proper pleasures and delectations thereof doe farre exceede all corporall delights, and that therefore the true felicitie of man in this life, must needs cōsist therein and be so much the more pure and perfect, by how much lesse the soule doth participat of any bodilie pleasure or delectation of the senses: for which respect the philosophers themselues called the boddie the plague of the soule, and held it for the greatest impediment of mans felicitie, as I haue amplie declared before in the seuēteenth chapter where I treated of philosophical contēplatiō.

D. Ber. super Cantica. ser. 35.

1. Cor. 2.

Plutar. in vita Catonis

31 This shall suffise for this time, touching the practise of our christian contemplation, & although I may perhaps seeme to some to haue bene ouer long, yet the importaunce of the matter considered, I hope the discreet, and deuout Reader, will not think anie thing superfluous, that I haue said, considering that for breuities sake, I haue omitted verie manie thinges, which otherwaies had bene verie necessarie to haue bene handled for the better explication thereof, as those which are exercised in matters of contemplation will easelie perceiue.

32 And therefore to the end that such as desire to vnderstand more of the practise of contemplation, may not only know where to find it, but also receaue further satisfaction concerning as well the importāce, as the

continual vse, and custome of it in Gods Church, I thinke it not amisse for the conclusion of this chapter, to set downe diuers learned and approued authors, both auncient and modern, who haue either purposelie treate, or by the way handled this subiect: I say diuers authors, for if I should take vppon me to lay downe all those that haue written thereof, I should be no lesse tedious to the Reader, then to my selfe, in respect of the incredible multitude of them, besides that I should vndertake more then I could performe, or perhaps anie man els, for that manie haue written of it in many languages, in which respect I will content my selfe with these that follow, noting in the margent the times when they floreshed

a *S. Paules disciple conuerted by him at Athens. act. 17.*

a S. Dionysius Areopagita de mysteca theologia. c. 1. 2. & 3. *& de diuinis nominibus* ca. 4. where he treateth admirablie of the perfection of contemplation, that is to say of a perfect vnion with god by the meanes of an extaticall loue.

b *Aboute the yeare of eur lord.* 340.

b Ioannes Climacus, in scala paradisi. wherein he leadeth his reader to the height of contemplation, by 30. steps or degrees.

ç *Anno Domini.* 370.

c S. Basill in his monasticall constitutions. ca. 1. & 2.

d *Anno* 437.

d Ioannes Cassianus in collationibus patrum, wherein he teacheth amplie the perfect practise of the contemplatiue life, geuing notable rules and precepts for the same.

e *Anno Do.* 590.

e S. Gregory the greate in diuers parts of his woorkes, and especiallie Ho. 16. & 17. in *Ezechielem.* Also li. 5. ca. 14. in 1. *Reg.* & li. 5. *Moral.* ca. 22. 23. 25. & 26. li. 6. ca. 27. & 28. & li. 23. ca. 13.

f *Anno. Do.* 1140.

f S. Bernard de vita actiua, & contemplatiua: In parabola de nuptijs filij regis: In scala claustralium. In his sermon *de conuersione ad clericos* cap. 21. & 22. *In serm. 5. de assumptione:* In his treatise *de interiori domo*, especiallie, a ca. 4. ad c. 21. and afterwards *ibidem* ca. 48. and 49. and lastlie in his sermons vppon the *Canticles* especiallie ser. 23. 31. 33. 35. 49. 52. & 62.

g *Anno. Do.* 1140.

g Richardus de Sancto victore, in his two bookes intituled *Beniamin minor & Beniamin maior*, wherein he treateth no lesse notablie, then amplie of the preparation to contemplation, and of the admirable effects of it.

h *Anno* 1260.

h Albertus magnus in his treatises *de paradiso animæ, & de adhærendo Deo.*

i *Anno* 1270.

i S. Thomas Aquinas in a particuler treatise *de beatitudine*, and in 22. q. 180.

k *Anno* 1274.

k S. Bonauenture in diuers treatises, to wit *de mystica Theologia De parno bono, siue de incendio amoris: de itinerario mentis ad Deum: de stimulo amoris, de 7. itineribus æternitatis*, and *de 7. gradibus contemplationis.*

l *Anno* 1410.

l Ioannes Gerson de mystica Theologia: de monte contemplationis: de meditatione: de oratione, & eius valore: and in diuers other notable treatises, which I pretermit.

Dionysius

m *Dionysius Richel*, (commonlie cailled *Carthusianus* because he was a m *Anno* monke of the charter house) li.2. *de vita, & fine solitarij*, & li. *de laude vitæ* 1460. *solitariæ*, ca.8.35.36.37. and in other particuler treatises n *de contemplatione*: *de meditatione, & de oratione*, to whome I might add (if I thought it need- n *Anno* full) a doozen at least of the same order: who haue written most excel- 1460. lentlie of contemplation, and meditation.

o Finallie in the last age there wrote diuers learned and holie men o *Circa an.* verie notablie of the same subiect, as *Lodouicus Blosius*, a holie abbot of the 1540. order of saint *Benet in canone vitæ spiritualis*, especiallie from the 14. chapter to the end. Also *in speculo spirituali*. ca.10.& 11. *institutione spirituali, & tabella spirituali*: and *in speculo Mona chorum*.

Henricus Harphius of the order of *S. Francis de mystica Theologia*: *B. P. Ignatius de Loyola*, founder of the Societie of *Iesus in exercitijs spiritualibus*, and to omitt manie others, *P. Rosignol*, of the same Societie yet liuing, who hath latelie written *de perfectione, & de actibus virtutum*.

All these haue written in latin of Christian contemplation, besides manie others, whome I purposelie omit for breuities sake: And those which vnderstand the spanish, and Italian toung may read certaine modern authors, who haue also written of it most excellentlie in those languages: as in spanish *F. Luyz de la Puente* of the Societie of *Iesus* in two tomes intituled. *Meditationes de los misterios de nuestra sancta fe, con la pratica de la oracion mental*.

F. Luyz de Granada, of the order of *S. Dominick de la meditacion M. Teresa* (a holie and admirable woman, of the order of the (*Carmelits*) *del camino de la perfecion*, and in the storie of her life, which she wrote by the commaundement of hir ghostlie father.

Also *F. Pedre de Alcantara* of the order of *S. Francis* in a litle treatise intitled *Tratado de oracion y meditation*.

And lastlie *P. Ribera* of the Societie of *Iesus* in the life of *M. Teresa* aforesaide, which he wrote after her death.

And these 4. bookes last mencioned, being written first in spanish, are translated into Italian, in which language there be also manie other excellẽt woorkes concerning the same matter, as *Essercitio della vita spirituale*, withoute name of author translated out of latin.

Instruttione di meditare del padre Bartolomeo Ricci della Compania di Giesu. Paradiso de' contemplatiui del P. F. Bartolomeo da Saluthio minore osseruante, and diuers other woorkes in the Italian tongue, and in other languages which I pretermit for that these may suffice for the full instruction of anie man that shall desire to see the important, and necessarie practise of contemplation.

It is

It is obiected that to make a common vvealth happy by such a christian, contemplation as hath been discribed, all the Citizens must be religious men, such as haue abandoned the vvorld. The obiection is ansvvred; & it is proued that euery member of a Christian common vvealth (of vvhat degree, state, or vocation soeuer he be) may be a perfect contemplatiue: and happie in his vocation: Also vvhat is the perfection vvhich Christ requireth in euery Christiā man: & by the vvay, some vvhat is said of the actiue *and* cōtemplatiue *life, according to the opinion, as vvell of philosophers, as of our deuins.*

CHAP. 22.

But now perhaps some will say, that to make a common wealth happy by such a contemplation, as I haue heere described (according to the opinion of either *Aristotle* and *Plato*, or yet of our deuines) wee must imagin and frame a common wealth either of philosphers or Monkes, & Friers, and other religious persons, seeing that none could in the opinion of *Aristotle* & *Plato*, be happie by philosophicall contemplation, but philosophers, & that to other Christian contemplation, & the felicitie consisting therein, are necessarily required abnegation of will, pouertie of spirit, and contempt of the world, which are proper to such as professe religious perfection, whereas all common wealths doe, and must needes consist of men (as I may say) of an other mould, to wit, princes, noble men, magistrats, souldiars, men of occupation, and of such other vocations, as seeme not to be compatible with the contemplatous, and religious life.

2 Hereto I answere, first concerning the opinion of *Aristotle* and *Plato*, that they required not to the perfection of common wealth, a barren, and fruiteles contemplation, without action, but a concurrance of the contemplatiue and actiue life, and therefore they taught, that the vnderstanding of man, is partlie speculatiue, and partly practicall, & that as it is speculatiue, it doth contemplat God, and heauenlie things (which is properlie the act, or office of wisdome) and that as it is practicall, it attendeth to matters of action, that is to say, to worke, as occasion requireth, either for our priuate, or for the publicke weale (wherein consisteth the speciall force, and office of prudence) and that of these two, the first parte is by nature farre more worthy, and noble then the other, aswell for the dignitie, and worthynes of the obiect (which as God, and his æternall truth) as also for the vnspekeable delectation, that it yeal-

it yeeldeth, besides many other reasons alleadged by *Aristotle*, which I omit for breuities sake.

3 And in this respect, these philosophers taught, that the practical vnderstanding, is subordinat to the speculatiue, as to the most worthy, & to the end whereto it is naturally ordained, and that all action is in like maner referred to speculation, no lesse then warre to peace, busines to repose, and labour to ease, and rest: whereupon it also followeth, that although these philosophers place the felicitie of man and of common wealth, principally in speculation, or contemplation, yet they require also to the perfection thereof, the practise of all the morall vertues, as the meane to the end.

Aristot. li.7. pol. D. Tho. in eundem. lec. 2. Ibid. c. 11.

Polit. li. 7. ca. 11.

4 And therefore whereas *Aristotle* teacheth, that there are two felicities aswell of common wealth, as of euery man, the one consisting in speculation, and the other in action, he farre preferreth the first, and houldeth it to be then most perfect, when it is seconded with the latter: in which respect he declareth also, how all vertues are necessary helpes to the speculatiue felicitie: As first that wisdome is requisite, because the speculation, or contemplation of God, is the propre act thereof: Secondlie that the habits of naturall knoledge are also necessarie, for that we are by the meanes of them, ledd to the knowledge and cõtemplation of God: Thirdlie that those vertues which restraine the passions of the mind (as temperance and mansuetude) doe in like maner helpe thereto, for that without them, men should be wholie withdrawne from the contemplation of God, to the delights, and pleasures of the senses, and to sensible thinges, yea, and would hould them for their felicitie: Lastly al the vertues whereby we either get, or conserue temporall goodes, are in like sort requisit to contemplation, for that without some mediocritie, and sufficiencie of temporall commodities, neither contemplation, nor yet the life of man can subsist. Whereby it appeareth, that the practise of al vertues, and consequentlie the practicall & political felicitie, is necessarie to the speculatiue, and that they tend thereto, as to the end whereto nature hath ordained them. And therfore *Aristotle* saith. *Non vacamus, vt vacemus*, we doe not rest, to the end we may repose, that is to say, we exercise, and practise vertue, to the end we may rest in the contemplation of God.

Ethic. li.10.

5 Now then for asmuch as the concurrence of both these felicities, practicall and speculatiue, is requisit to the perfect happines of common wealth, and that the practicall is subordinate to the speculatiue, as the meanes, and way thereto (in which respect *Aristotle* aduiseth the lawmaker to frame, and ordaine his lawes in such sort, that the prince,

and people may by the exercise of vertue, tend speciallie to contemplation, therefore it seemed to those philosophers, that all the common welth, might worthilie be counted happie, if it did generallie practise the moral vertues,& thereby tend to the contemplatiõ of God, though neither all, nor yet the greatest part thereof, but onlie the principall members should attaine thereto: and therefore *Aristotle* speciallie required contemplation in the prince, and magistrats; and *happie* saith *Plato*, is the kingdome, *vbi philosophi regnant, vel reges philosophantur: where either philosophers raigne, or kinges become philosophers.* For as the bodie of man is trulie said to liue, though all the parts thereof, haue neither life, nor yet feeling alike (both life, and sense resting speciallie in the vitall parts, and principallie in the hart) and as an vniuersitie instituted for learning, may worthilie be counted learned, if there be therein eminent men in all faculties, and the rest tend also thereto by dilligent studie, and obseruation of the statutes: euen so also the common welth instituted for contemplation, may iustlie be counted contemplatiue, and consequentlie happy, if the magistrats, and other principal men, ioyne contemplation with action. Though the farre greater number being the inferiour sort, doe not arriue to that perfection, but rest onlie in action, which is the way to the other.

Aristo. li 10. *Ethic. c.* 8. *Plato de rep. Dialo.* 5.

6 And such a common welth, I say, the philosophers counted happie, because it should be both well, and wiselie gouerned by the prince, and magistrats, and also protected by almightie God, the authour of happines, in respect of the vertue, aswell of the people, as of the princes: so that we see how in the opinion of the philosophers, the common welth becommeth contemplatiue, and happie, partlie by the practise of vertue which is the high way to contemplation and felicitie, and partlie by the merit of the principal members thereof, which being happie by the vse, aswell of the contemplatiue, as the actiue life, doe communicate both political, and speculatiue felicitie to the whole common welth, as the hart, head, and other principall parts of mans bodie, do impart the influence of humour, and life to the whole. Thus much for the opinion of the philosophers.

7 And now to answere the other part of the obiection, concerning the contemplation of Christians. Yt is first to be vnderstood, that our Christian contemplation doth not exclude action, but admit it in the highest degree of perfection; which being declared, it will consequẽtlie appeare, not onlie that our contemplatiõ is most necessarie for common welth, but also that euerie man in a Christian common welth, of what degree, or vocation soeuer he be, may be a perfect contemplatiue, and

vnited

vnited with God, and consequentlie as happy, as man may possiblie be in this life; which point being fullie explicated, I hope the difficultie pro posed wilbe fullie satisfied. For first it is to be considered that there are in Christian religion, three kind of liues dedicated to the seruice of God, in the which, or in any one of them, a Christian man, may as *S. Augustin* teacheth, doe his dutie, and be saued.

Aug. de ciu. Dei. li. 19. ca. 19. paulo post principium.

8 The first is, an Actiue life, wherein a man doth employ him selfe, and his talents in external workes, or actions for the pure loue of God, and the benefit, either of his owne soule, or of his neighbours, or of both.

9 The second is, a Contemplatiue life, wherin a man giueth himselfe wholie to the internal workes of the knowledge, and loue of God, by the continual exercise of reading, meditation, praier, and contemplation.

10 The third is a life mixt, and compounded of both the other, to wit, both of the actiue, and of the contemplatiue life, when our action is ioyned with contemplation, in such sort, that neither our neighbour, is depriued of the benefit of our labours, nor we our selues of the swetenes of contemplation.

11 Of these three kinds, the two first, are distinguished, by *S. Bernard* thus. *The actiue life, saith he, consisteth in the innocencie of Good vvorkes. The contemplatiue in the speculation of heauenlie thinges. The actiue life is common to manie, the contemplatiue life but to fevv; the actiue vseth vvell earthlie thinges, the contemplatiue renouncing the vvorld, liueth onlie to God. The actiue feedeth the hungrie, instructeth the ignorant, correcteth or amendeth those, that erre, reduceth the proud to the vvay of humilitie, reconcileth enemies, visiteth the sicke, burieth the dead, redeemeth the captiue, and prouideth that vvhich is necessarie for euerie one, but the contemplatiue retaininge vvholie in mind, perfect charitie tovvards God, and our neighbour, ceaseth from external action, to the end it may vvholie attend to the desire, and loue of our creator, and vvith contempt of the vvorld feruentlie aspire to the vision of his face, and sing praise vnto him eternallie, amidst the quiers of Angels, &c. Finallie the actiue life is good, but the contemplatiue is much better.* Thus saith *S. Bernard.*

S. Bernard ad Sororem de modo bene viuendi ser. 53. paulo post principium.

12 These two kindes of life, are figured and represented in the hollie scripture in the twoo sisters, *Martha*, and *Mary*, of whome the one, to wit *Martha*, represented the actiue life, being as our Sauiour said: *occupata & turbata, erga plurima:* busied, and troubled about manie thinges, and therefore hee also said vnto her, *porro vnum est necessarium*, but one thinge is necessarie, signifiyng that the multiplicitie of thinges, and our ouer great attention thereto, doth diuert vs from vniting our selues with God, our true, and onlie good. The other sister: to wit *Mary*,

Luc. 10.

represented the contemplatiue life, sitting still at Christs feete, and feeding her soule with the heauenlie foode of his deuine worde, and therfore our Sauiour said of her. *Maria optimam partem elegit, quæ non auferetur ab ea. Mary hath chosen the best part, vvhich shall not be taken from her.* wherein two thinges are to be noted, the one, that of these two kinds of liues, the life of *Mary* (that is to say the contemplatiue life) is the most worthy, and not to be left, for that of *Martha*, which was onlie actiue; for contemplation doth not onlie vnit vs with God, and make vs like him, as I haue signified before, but doth also giue perfection to our externall actions, communicating vnto them integritie, swetenes and feruour, which make them more acceptable to God, and profitable both to our neighbours, and our selues.

Ibib.

13 The other thing, that may be gathered of our Sauiours words, is, that the third kind of life, composed of both, is to be preferred, before either of the other, which our Sauiour signified in calling the life of *Mary*, *partem*, a part, giuing to vnderstand, that the perfection of Christian life, consisteth of two parts, to witt *action* and *contemplation*, whereof *Mary* had chosen the better, which neuertheles was but a part, and therefore not to be compared with the whole, that is to say, with the third kind of life, composed of both, which being most excellent, and perfect, our Sauiour Christ chose for him selfe, ioyning contemplation with continuall action, in preaching, and labouring to gaine soules, as also S. *Iohn Baptist*, and the Apostles did, besides innumerable other great saintes of God.

14 This perfection of the mixt life, proceedeth of the excellency, and perfection of charitie, which inclineth vs no lesse to desire, and seeke the good of our neighbour, by our labour, and action, then our owne benefit, and repose of spirit by contemplation. And therefore *S. Augustin*, saith. *Otium sanctum quærit Charitas veritatis, & negotium iustum suscipit necessitas charitatis. Charitie, or the feruent loue of truth* (that is to say of God) *doth seeke the holie repose of contemplation, and the necessitie of charitable loue tovvards our neighbour, doth moue vs to vndertake iust negotiation, or action.* Thus saith he, and hereuppon there groweth in Gods most zealous seruants, a counterchange of action, and contemplation, as *S. Bernard* noteth notablie vppon the Canticles, where we reade, that the bridegrome hauing giuen chardge, that none should disquiet, or awake his spouse from her sweete sleepe of contemplation, neuertheles raised her himselfe after a while, saying: *Surge, propera amica mea, &c. Arise, and make hast my loue.* Wheruppon *S. Bernard* saith: *Agnoscite vicissicudines, &c. Behould the mutual succession, or counterchange of hollie contemplation, and necessarie action; for vvhen*

Aug. li. 19. de ciuitat. Dei. ca. 19.

Cant. 2.

D. Ber. super can. serm. 58.

the

the brydegrome hath suffred his spouse to repose in his bosome for some time, he inuiteth her againe to those thinges vvhich are more profitable for his seruice, not forcing her against her vvill, but dravving her thereto, by giuing her a desire of good vvorkes, to the end shee may fructifie, and be profitable to him, vvho is her life, and for vvhome she houldeth it her lucre, and gaine to die. Idem. Ibid.

15 Thus farre *S. Bernard*, and in an another place: *As oft* saith he, *as a* serm. 51. *pious, and deuout soule leaueth contemplation, so oft it repaireth to action, to the end, that from thence it may the more spedelie, and familiarlie returne againe to contemplation, as from one neere neighbour, to an other; for these tvvo (to vvit the actiue, and contemplatiue life) are as it vvere chamberfellovves, and dvvell togither, as* Martha, *vvas* Maries *sister.*

16 Thus saith he, whereby we may see, that our Christian contemplation, when it is perfection, is still seconded with most excellent action, and fruit, in respect that the pure and feruent charitie of our contemplatiues, doth kindle in them such a zeale, & sincere loue towards their brethren (in whom they acknowledge the true image of God) that they loue them for Gods sake no lesse, or rather more then them selues, being readye euen to giue their liues for them, in imitation of our Sauiour Rom. 9. Christ, yea, and to say with S. *Paule. Opto esse Anathema a Christo pro fratribus meis. I desire to be seperated from Christ for my brethren, rather then they should perish.*

17 Seeing then our contemplation doth not exclude action, but admit, and require it in the highest degree of perfection, for the benefit of all men, it foloweth, that it is most necessary for common wealth, wherein euery man ought to desire, and seeke rather the publicke good, then his owne: in so much, that whosoeuer is a perfect contemplatiue, must needes be *bonus ciuis*, a good citizen, or member of the common wealth, aswell for his sincere loue towards all the other members, and parts thereof, and his endeuour to aduance there good, as also for his perfection in all kind of vertue, wherein a perfect contemplatiue doth excell, as may appeare by all the former discours concerning contemplation, whereuppon it also foloweth, that Christian contemplation, is most requisit in euerie member, or part of the common wealth, & that therefore it may stand with the state of euerie man, of what lawful profession, or vocation soeuer he be, vppon which point, I will somewhat enlarge my selfe, as a matter verie important, and considerable for manie respects.

18 First then, I wish it to be considered, that Christian contemplation, is nothing els but the perfect practise of Christian religion, inducing and leading vs to a perfect vnion with God, as it appeareth euidentlie in the

last chapter whereuppon two thinges are necessarilie inferred. The one is that whosoeuer is a perfect christian, he is also a perfect contẽplatiue, for that being a perfect christian, he is perfectlie vnited with almightie God. the other is, that seeing in a christian common wealth, euerie man may, and ought to be a perfect Christian, euerie one also may yea, and ought to be a perfect contẽplatiue, of what state, degree, or condition, soeuer he be.

And to the end, it may be vnderstood what is the perfection, which I require in a perfect contemplatiue, or a perfect Christian, it is to be considered that as there are two kindes of perfection in euerie thinge, the one, necessarie for the accomplishment of the nature of it, and the other necessarie for the ornament of it: as for example, a man that hath a body, & a soule is a perfect man (so farr forth as concerneth the nature of man) though hee bee crooked, simple and vnlearned, but when he is withall beautifull, wise, and learned, he hath then an other perfection, which maketh him perfect in a higher degree.

19 So also a Christian man may be considered to haue two perfections, the one which is necessarie to make him a true Christian, that is to say, the sonne of God, and inheritour to the kingdome of heauẽ (which perfection consisteth in faith, and the obseruation of our Sauiours commaundements: for other waies:) Christ were not a good lawmaker, if his law suffised not to make the keeper of it, a perfect Christian) and the other perfection, is necessarie for his encreas of merit heere, and glorie, in the other world, which kind of perfection, censisteth in the obseruation of the Euangelical counsels.

20 Of the first of these two perfections, the Apostle speaketh, where he saith to the *Corinthians*. *Fratres gaudete, perfecti estote* &c. *Brethren reioyce, be perfect* &c. And to the *Phillippenses*. *Quicunque ergo perfecti sumus, hoc sentiamus. Therefore vvhosoeuer of vs is perfect, let vs thinke this.* Also *S. Iames* of the same kind of perfection. *Patience hath a perfect vvorke, to the end you may be perfect, and intire, failing in nothinge.* that is to say, obseruing all that which pertaineth to the dutie of a true Christian man. This I say is a perfection, consisting in the exact obseruation of the commaundements of God. But of the other kind of perfection (consisting in the obseruation of our Sauiours counsels) he spake him selfe when he said to the rich young man. *Si vis perfectus esse* &c. *If thou vvilt be perfect, goe and sell all, and giue it to the poore, and thou shalt haue a treasure in heauen.* Of which kind of perfection, I shall treate amplie heareafter, as also of the Euangelicall counsells, wherein the same consisteth.

2. Cor. 13. *Philip. 3.* *Iacob. 1.* *Matth. 19.*

21 Therefore it is to be vnderstood, that the perfection necessarie to make euery mã a perfect Christiã or cõtemplatiue, is not the later (which

is not in deed compatible with the ſtate,&vocation of euery one)but the former,which may ſtād with euery mās ſtate, be he rich or poore, maried or ſingle,noble or ignoble, prince or ſubiect,maſter or ſeruant,a perfection I meane conſiſting in the obſeruation of thoſe thinges, which euerie man without exception may performe in his vocation.

22. For our Sauiour Chriſt, when he came into the world,ment not to infring,& breake the law of nature,or any thing that was agreable therto, but to adorne & perfect it. And therefore,whereas it is conuenient, yea, & naturall to common wealth to be compoſed of diuers vocations, qualities, and conditions of men,it is to be vnderſtood,that our Sauiour Chriſt meant not by Chriſtian religion to prohibit, the lawfull ſtate, or condition of any man,but to make euery man more perfect in his vocation, & more profitable to his common welth: As that the prince by being a Chriſtian, should be perfect in his degree, the magiſtrates in thers,the ſouldiars in thers, the lawer,phiſition,merchant,artificer, maried man,bachiler,maſter,ſeruant,& al other of what lawful quality, or condition ſoeuer,should euery one of them be perfect in his degree, and vocation,(as may appeare by the precepts of our Sauiour & his Apoſtls, in the holie ſcriptures for men of al degrees,&ſtats)ſo that he is to be accounted a perfect Chriſtian, or contemplatiue, who arriueth to the perfection of Chriſtian religion in his ſtate,and vocatiō, though others in a more perfect ſtate of life, may be more perfect,and merit more then he.

23. Terefore,it is now to be conſidered wherein conſiſteth chriſtian religiō,& the duty of a true chriſtian:for the which wee shal not neede to ſeeke any other maſter, or teacher, then ourSauiour Chriſt himſelfe, in his deuine ſermō vpō the moūtaine,wherein as *S. Aug.* ſaith,he taught *perfectum vitæ Chriſtianæ modo,* the true & perfect maner of Chriſtian life, whē he firſt publiſhed his admirable doctrin,cōſiſting in pouerty of ſpirit,in purity of hart,in remiſſiō of iniuries,in ſuffring perſecution, in the loue of our enimies, in perfect patience, in truſt in his prouidēce,& in all perfectiō of life: & aftarwards againe when he aſſembled thepeople, & preached vnto them perfect abnegatiō of their parēts,childrē,& of them ſelues for the loue of him, & finally, the daly & cōtinual caraig of the croſſe,in al which,what taugh he but our chriſtiā religion, & theduty of euery chriſtiā mā without exceptiō? And therfore he cōcluded his ſermō vpō the mountain with this notable ſimilitude. *Euery man* ſaith he that *hereth theſe my vvords & doth thē not,is like vnto the foole that built his houſe vpō the ſand,& the raine fel,& the lād fluds came,& the vvind blvv,& ouerthrvv it,& the ruine of it vvas very great.* Thus ſaith our Sauour, not only thoſe who were preſēt at his ſermō,but alſo of al ſuch as should eitherheare it by prea-

Aug. lib. de ſerm.dom.in monte ca.1.

Matth.5. & 6.

Marc.8. Luc. 14.

Matth. 7.

by preaching, or read it in the holie scriptures, and especially of such as should professe the Christian faith: and in like maner when he preached to the people, the abnegation and hate of our selues before mentioned, hee admonished them to cast their account, and to consider well, what they should take vppon them by following him, and therefore he proposed vnto them two similitudes: the one of a man that meaning to build a tower sate downe, & seriously waighed with him selfe, what it would cost him: and the other of a king, who meaning to make warre with an other prince, did first dulie consider, how he should be able to maintaine it, and concludeth: that euen so euerie man should maturelie ponder, & waigh with him selfe, that except hee renounce al those thinges, which he possesseth, he cannot be his disciple.

Luc. 14.

24 But heere perhaps some may thinke, that this doctrin of our Sauiour cannot be practised generally of all men in a common wealth, without the ouerthrow thereof, for if euerie man renounce, and forsake all he hath, what forme of common wealth may be imagined, where noe man can haue anie thinge in possession, for the maintenaunce either of him selfe, or of the common wealth: and if euerie man must forgiue his enimies, without seeking reparation of wrongs, then the whole common wealth, is also bound by the same precept, to suffer it selfe to bee oppressed, and ouerthrowen, and can neuer defend it selfe, against forrayn enimies, nor seeke restitution: Besides that it seemeth to bee aboue the power of our corrupt nature, to loue our enimies, and that the continuall cariage of the crosse (which our Sauiour seemed to commaund) was but a counsell, and that therefore it bindeth onlie those which take vpon them a state of religious perfection, and belongeth not to secular men, of whome a common wealth in great part consisteth.

25 To all these doubts, I will answer particularlie, and breefelie: And although I make no doubt, but that some part of our Sauiours doctrine before mencioned, is vnderstood by some, and according to the rigour of the letter may wel be thought, rather to pertaine to his counsels, then his precepts, yet the same is interpreted by the holy fathers, that it toucheth al men alike, and may, yea and ought to be performed by euerie man, of what degree or state soeuer hee be.

26 As first for the renounciation of welth, and possessions, our venerable S. *Bede* saith notablie thus. *Distat renunciare omnibus, & relinquere omnia,* &c. *There is difference betwixt renouncing all things, and leauing, or forsaking all thinges, for it belongeth but to a fevv and them men of great perfection, to forsake, and abandon all thinges, as to lay a side all care of the vvorld, and to thirst onlie after eternall, and heauenlie thinges: but it belongeth to euerie man,*

Beda. in 14. Luca.

vvhich

vvhich professeth the faith of Christ,to renounce all thinges,that is to say, so to hould, and possesse the commodities of the vvorld, that he be not detained in the loue of the vvorld by them: to haue temporall thinges onlie in vse, and eternall thinges in desire, and so to deale in matters of the earth, that he may tend vvith all his mind, & affection to heauenlie thinges. Thus saith S. *Bede.*

27 In like sorte *S. Augustin* teacheth that the renounciation of riches, which our Sauiour requireth in his desiples, that is to say in Christians, reformed not onlie by those who forsake all that they haue and giue it to the poore, but also by him *Qui plus diligens Christum* &c. *vvho louing* D. *Aug. ep: 86.*
Christ more then his riches, doth traunsfer his hope from them to him, & doth vse them in such sort, that he bestoeth and giueth them freelie, and thereby laieth vp a treasure in heauen, and is redie to forsake them, as also his parents, children, brethren and vvife, vvhensoeuer the cast, or exigent shall be such, that he cannot enioy them, except he fersake Christ. Thus saieth *S. Augustin*, who interpreteh in like manner, that other commaundement of our Sauiour. *If anie man* *Mathevv.5.*
stricke thee one the right cheeke, turne to him the left, and if anie man contend vvith *Aug. li. de.*
thee for thy coate, giue him thy cloake, vvhich precept (for so *S. Augustin* calleth *ser. Do. in*
it) *is to be vnderstood*, saith hee, of the promptitude, and preparation of *monte.ca.1.*
harte (to suffer all kind of iniuries, and not of the execusion of it, in al cases. For that sometimes it is necessarie aswell for iustice sake, as for the repression of wicked men, that reparation of wronges bee sought and procured, so that the partie wronged do for his owne parte, remit the iniurie fullie in his harte, and say with the prophet. *Paratum cor meum* *Psal.5.6.*
Deus, paratum cor meum: My harte is redie o Lord, my harte is readie, too suffer this, and much more: and therefore *S. Augustin* concludeth thus. *August. vb*
In his ergo omnibus generibus iniuriarum, &c. *In all these kindes of iniuries, our* *supra.*
Sauiour teacheth vs, that the mind of a Christian ought to be most patient, mercifull, and readie to suffer more.

28 Thus he. who also answereth to the same effect, concerning the common wealth, teaching how it may obserue this Christian precept of patience, and yet make warr aswell to defend it selfe, as to offend an enemie. and to recouer anie thing that shallbe vniustlie taken away, and detained from it, *sunt autem*, saith he, *icta præcepta patientiæ* &c. *These pre-* *August. ad Marcelli*
cepts of patience, are euer to be kept in the præparation and disposition of the harte, as *num ep. 5.*
also the good vvill neuer to render euil, for euil, is alvvaies to be fulfilled in vvill, & desire. Though manie thinges may and must be done, euen against the vvill, for the iust punishment, and correction of vvicked men, and so if earthlie, or temporall common vvealths obserue these precepts of Christ, they shal make vvarr euen vvith beneuolence, for the maintenance of pietie, and iustice in a peaceable societie, and for the benefit of their verie enemies, in chastising, yea, and ouercomming them, for

he is ouercome to his ovvne good, vvho is thereby depriued of libertie to sinne, seeing that nothing is more vnfortunate, then the felicitie of sinnes, vvhereby their impunitie is nourished, and continued, for their further punishment, and their euil vvill, (vvhich is their invvard enemie) is still strengthned, & augmented. Thus farr *S. Augustin.*

29 Hereto I add further, that the precept of our Sauiour being vnderstood, according to the rigour of the letter, bindeth onlie in some cases, and this our Sauiour himselfe taught vs by his owne practise (as *S. Augustin* also obserueth:) for although he receiued diuerse contumelies, and iniuries without any contradiction, offring himselfe still to receiue more (according to his owne precept) yet being strooken on the face before *Annas*, he offred not his other cheeke to receiue an other blow, but expostulated the matter with the striker, saing. *If I say ill, beare vvitnes of the euil, If I say vvell, vvhy doste thou strike me,* so that discretiō (which is the mother of all vertues) is specially to be vsed, in the practise of this precept, as to consider when, and how farre it may be conuenient to fulfill it, for that it cannot be presumed that our Sauiour meant it should bind to the hindrance of a greater good.

Aug. Ibid.

Luc. 18.

30 Therefore to declare, in what case, it ought to be obserued, & when not, it is euidēt that when a priuat man receiueth an iniurie, the sufferāce whereof may bee to the glorie of God, and edification of others, without preiudice of the common wealth, or of anie other person but himselfe, then he may with greate merit, and is in christian perfection bound to yeald so much of his owne right, as not to demand reparation of the wrong: but when the tolleration of the iniurie, may redound either to the dishonour of God, or to the dammage of the weale publike, or of any third persone, yea or to the encrease of the offenders insolencie and offence (whereas by his correction, and chastisement, there might be hope of his amendement) the wronged ought not to dissemble the iniurie, but to seeke a lawfull reparatiō by way of iustice, & yet so, that he do it with out all rancour, or desire of reuenge, & with a pious compassiō of his aduersaries offence & punishment: And this I doubt not but manie good Christians doe fullie performe, as all men may, and are bound to doe in like case, aswell for the publike good, which must needs redound thereof to the common wealth, as for the discharge of euerie mans dutie towards God, and his neighbour, in regarde of our Sauiours precept, especiallie, seeing the remission of our sinnes, dependeth thereon, according to the expresse wordes of our Sauiour, who therefore taught vs to pray to him, to bee forgiuen as we forgiue.

And

And thus it appeareth, that this precept of remiſſion of iniuries, being practiſed in this ſort, as I haue here declared, is not onlie moſt pious, but alſo moſt politicall, and neceſſarie for the common wealth, of which point I haue alſo ſaid ſomewhat before, and meane to treate more amplie hereafter, for the confutation of certaine friuolous obiections of *Macchiauel* touching our Christian manſuetude. *Chap.24.*

31 And now to ſay ſomewhat, concerning the precept to loue our enemyes *S. Hierome* ſaith thereof thus. *Multa præcepta Dei*, &c. *Many men vvaighing the precepts of God by their ovvne imbecillitie, and not by the ſtrength of good, and holye men, thinke them impoßible to be obſerued, and ſay that it ſuffiſeth to vertue, not to hate our enemyes, and that vvhereas vve are commaunded to loue them, the precept exceedeth the povver of mans nature, it is therefore to be vnderſtoode, that Chriſt commaundeth not impoßible, but perfect things, ſuch as Dauid performed tovvards* a *Saule, and* b *Abſalon; and* c *Steuen the martyr tovvards his perſecutors; and* d *Paule deſired to be ſeperated from God, for the ſaluation of thoſe vvhich perſecuted him, and* e *Ieſus himſelfe, both taught, and practiſed the ſame, ſaying father pardon them, for they knovv not vvhat they doe.* Thus ſaith *S. Hierome*, which may bee confirmed out of *S. Chriſoſtome*, explicating notablie how this precept is fulfilled. *Hieron. in 5. ca. Matth.* a *1. Reg. 23.* b *2. Reg. 18.* c *Act. 7.* d *Rom. 9.* e *Luc. 23.*

32 *Sicut quod dictum eſt*, ſaith he, *non concupiſces*, &c. *As that vvhich is ſaid in the commaundemeut, thou shalt not couet, vvas not ſaid to the flesh, but to the ſoule, ſo alſo, it is to bee vnderſtood of this precept (that it vvas giuen to the ſoule, and not to the flesh) for our flesh cannot loue our enemy, but our ſoule may, and the reaſon is, that the loue or hatred of the flesh conſiſteth in ſenſe, but the loue, or hatred of the ſoule is in the vnderſtanding; therefore vvhen, being hurt, or vvronged by any man, vve feele in our harts, a hatred tovvards him, and deſire of reuenge, and yet forbeare to execute it, then our flesh hateth our enemy, and our ſoule loueth him.* Thus ſaith *S. Chriſoſtome*, to whome I will add a notable diſcourſe of *S. Gregory* concerning the ſame precept. *Inimici autem dilectio*, ſaith he, *veraciter custoditur*, &c. *Chriſoſt. in ca. Matth. 5.* *D. Gregor. li. 22. moral. 6. 10. & 11.*

„ The loue of our enemy is trulie kept, or performed, when we neither are ſorrie for his riſing, nor glad of his fall, and yet it may manie times ſo fall out, that we may with charitie reioyce at his ruyn, and without enuie be ſorrie for his aduancement, as when we beleeue that by his fall ſome good men will ryſe to Gods glorie, and by his riſing ſome others may vniuſtlie bee oppreſſed; but in this point wee had neede to examine our ſelues diſcreetelie, leaſt wee bee deceiued, and vnder the collour of other mens hurt, or profit, giue way to our owne hatred, and therefore we must well waigh what mind wee ought to beare concerning the punishment of an offender, and the iustice of the punisher, for when almighty God doth strike and punish a wicked man, we ought not onlie to reioyce at the iustice of the iudge, but also to haue compation of the miserie of him, that is punished. Thus saith *S Grigorie*: And thus wee see, how our Sauiours precept of the loue of our enemies, may with the helpe of Gods grace, easilie bee fullfilled by anie man of what state, or condition soeuer hee bee.

Chrisost.ho. 36. Theoph. autor.op. imp.ho.26. 33 And now to conclud with the cairage of the crosse. *S. Chriostome, Theophilactus*, and some others expound, that precept to be vnderstood of the redie preparatiõ of our will to die for Christ, when occasion shall require, to the end we may allwayes truly say with *S. Peter. Domine tecum paratus sum &c. Lord I am redie to goe vvith thee to prisone, yea to death.* Though *S. Hillarie Eutyhmius*, and others extend it further, to wit, to the continuall mortification of our selues, in such sort, that wee may say with the Apostle. *mihi mundus crucifixus est & ego mundo. The vvorld is crucified to me, and I to the vvorld.* And how necessarie this is to euerie Christian man, the same Apostle teacheth also saing. *Qui Christi sunt, carnem suam crucifixerunt cũ vitÿs & concupiscentys suis. Those vvhich are Christs, haue crucified their flesh vvit their vices & concupisences.* so that he onlie may make account to be Christs (that is to say a perfect christian) who crucifieth his owne passions, affections, and concupiscences, practiseth perfect patience, remitteth iniuries, and is readie to abandõ parents, wife, children, frindes, lands and goods, yea and his one life, rather then to offend God in the least thing in the world, and from this abnegation no man is excepted, be he prince or subiect, publike, or priuat person, rich, or poore, and whosoeuer dischargeth his dutie in this behalfe, performeth, that which is requisit to the christian perfection, whereof I now speake, which as I haue said, doth not of necessitie require of seculer men, anie other renounciation, or contempt of honours, dignitie, substance, and wealth, but such as may stand with the lawful vse & possession of them: To which purpose the psalmist saith. *Diuitiæ si affluant nolite cor apponere. If your riches abound do not sett yeur harts thereon*: and the Apostle in like maner aduiseth maried men to haue wiues, *tanquam non habentes, as though they had none*, and rich men to enioy the commodities of the worlde, *tanquam non posidentes as though they possessed them not*, and to vse the world it selfe, *tanquam non vtantur*, as that they had no yse of it at all, hauing alwaies befere their eyes, the instabilitie, frailtie, and deceitfull casualitie thereof.

Luc. 22. Hilar. in cap. 10. Matth. Euthym. in cap. 14. Luca Gal. 6. Ibid. 11. psalm. 61. 1. cor. 7.

34 And this, the very philosophers required in some sort, not only of their wise, and contemplatiue men, but also of euery man, and therefore, *Seneca* saith of riches, thus. *No man is vvorthy of God, but he vvhich despiseth riches, vvhereof, I doe not deny thee the vse, but only vvould haue thee to possesse them vvith quietnes of mynd, vvhich thou shalt doe in some sort, if thou persvvade thy selfe, that thou mayst liue happely vvithout them, and dost regard them, as thinges that are transitory, and shall perish.* And agayne, *it is*, saith he, *a great, and rare matter not to be corrupted vvith the vse of riches, and he may be counted a great, and notable man, vvho in riches is poore, but he is most secure that hath them not.* Senec. ep. 18. Idem ep. 20.

35 Thus saith, *Seneca*, teaching, as we Christians doe, not only contempt of riches, and a certayne pouerty of spirit in the aboundance of worldly wealth, but also the great danger, that doth accompany them, and the security of a poore, and meane estate. Though neuertheles, this difference is to be noted, betwixt our doctrin, and his, that he requireth the contempt of riches to auoyd partly the distraction, & vexation of mynd, and partly the corruption of manners, which commonly groweth of the inordinat loue thereof; and we require it, not only for those reasons, which are indeede very important, but much more for the loue of God, and to imitate the volontary pouerty of our Sauiour *Christ*, and that we may the better, and more easily obserue his commaundements, who therefore compareth riches to thornes, which chooke vp the seede of Gods word in the harts of men, and not only assigneth pouerty for the first beatitude, but also saith of rich men (such I meane as place their confidence, and felicity in riches) that *it is as hard for them to enter into the kingdome of heauen, as for a camel to passe through the eye of an nedel.* Marc. 4. Math. 5. Luc. 6. Matth. 19.

36 Now then to come to the more particuler answere of the obiection wherein it was supposed, that the state of princes, noble men, rich men, souldiars, merchants, maried men, & such others, cannot stand with contemplation: I say, that as all lawfull states, or conditions of life in common wealth, admit the perfect practise of Christian religion, so also they consequently admit contemplation, which (as I haue signified sufficiently before) is nothing els but, the perfect practise of Christian religion, consisting in prayer, accompained, with the feruent loue of God, and charitie towards our neighbour, puritie of conscience, resignation of will, and other Christian vertues, from the vse and practise whereof, no man is excluded, and therefore, as any man may be a perfect Christian in any degree, or lawfull vocation, so also he may be a perfect contemplatiue as *S. Gregory* teacheth expresly in these woords, *contemplationis gratia &c. The grace of contemplation is not geuen to the highest or greatest, and not to* S. Gregor. in Ezechi. li. 2. Ho. 17.

 the least,

,, the least, but oft times to the highest, and oft to the lowest, and some-
,, times to the maried men, though it is most frequent in those that are
,, remoued or sequestred from the world: if therefore noe state, or voca-
,, tion of the faithfull, bee excluded from the grace of contemplation, it
,, followeth that whosoeuer hath his hart recollected within himselfe,
,, may bee partaker of the light thereof: Thus saith *S. Gregory*: hereof there is dailie experience, and alwaies hath bene, as shall appeare in the next chapter.

To proue that anie Christian man may bee a perfect contemplatiue in anie lawfull vocation, diuers exampls are alledged of holie, and contemplatiue Kinges, VVherouppon it is inferred, that meaner men, vvho haue lesse occasion to diuert them selues from contemplation, may bee perfect contemplatiues.

Chap. 23.

1 Although manie fearing the danger, which doth commonly accōpany worldly welth, honours & busines, do retire themselues wholie frō the affaires of the world, & abandon all the commodities, and pleasures thereof, to the end, they may the more easilie be vnited with God by perfect loue, & contemplation, neuertheles there may be, & euer hath bene great contemplatiues of men, of al sorts, degrees, & conditions in euerie cuntrie, and common wealth, yea, of those whose stats seeme most incompatible with contemplatiō, by reason of there aboundance of all wordlie honours, welth, pompe, & pleasures, and of their continuall occupation in affaires & busines, I meane kinges and princes, of whome, I will alledge some few examples, partlie of those who liuing, either vnder the law of nature, or law of *Moyses*, beleeued in Christ, that then was to come, and partlie of Christians, that haue professed the faith of Christ, since his comming.

Iob. 29
Vide Bed. in comment. in Iob. c. 29.
Theophanes ep. 2. de patientia.
Isidor. de vita & morte Sanctor. Cæsarius dia. 3.
Vide Pinedā in Iob.
Iob. ca. 1. 29. 30. & 31.

2 The first shallbe *Iob*, who being king of *Edom*, & flowing in prosperitie, and worldie welth, was replenished with al those vertues, which are requisit to the perfection of contemplation, in a man of his estate, as true humilitie, contempt of the riches and honours wherein he abounded, mansuetude, patience, charitie, and pittie to the poore, coniugal chastity, iustice, puritie of hart, and the feruent loue of God, as appeareth in the holie scriptures, which make him a verie mirrour of all vertue, besids that *S. Bernard* proposeth him for a perfect patterne both of the contemplatiue, & the actiue life, gathering the same out of his owne words, when he said. *Si dormiero dicam quando surgam, & rursus expectabo vesperam*

If I sleepe or repose, I vvill say vvhen shall I rise, and then againe, I vvill expect the euening: meaning saith *S. Bernard*, that when he had reposed in the euening or night of contemplation, he desired the morning, that he might arise to action, & then againe expected the euening, to the end hee might returne to repose of contemplation: Thus saith *S. Bernard*, and what heauenlie contemplations, *Iob* receiued in his contemplatiue exercise, & praier, it may be gathered by the reuelations, and gift of prophesie which hee had, euen in his affliction, and by the fauour which almighty God did him to speake to him, yea & to appeare vnto him, as it seemed by the words of *Iob, saying. I haue heard thee o Lord vvith my eares, and novv my eies also see thee.*

Ibid. 7. *D. Bern. ser. de cantico. regis Ezech.* *Cap. 42.*

And who may be counted, or was in deede more contemplatiue then *Moyses*, being so vnited with God, and so familiar with him, that God called him. *Fidelissimum in omni domo sua. The most faithfull seruant in all his house*, and talked with him *face to face*, and shewed himselfe vnto him, not as he did to others, by representations, and figures, but *palàm* saith the scripture, *manifestly*, in so much, that some of the Fathers hold, that he saw the verie essence of God: And yet neuer anie man had more cause of distraction from contemplation then he, hauing the conduct of such peruerse people, so mutinous, and rebellious, through so manie dangers, in the desert, for so manie yeares together, that if we should measure him by the humor, and custome of worldly men, we might thinke he should haue litle liste, and lesse leasure to attend to contemplation, but he being endewed with heauenlie wisdome, & grace, and knowing that al states stand principally by the protection of God, sought the assurance of his state, & the good successe of his actions, by the meanes of contemplatiō, assuring himselfe that his vnion with God, would be a meanes to vnite the people with God and him, & therefore he ioyned together the contemplatiue, and actiue life in al perfection.

Num. 12. *Ibid.* *S. Aug. de Symbolo ad Catecumenos li. 4. c. 3. & in Genes. ad litter.* *D. Tho. 22. q. 174. ar. 4. c.*

4 This *S. Gregory* obserueth saying of him, that *he vvent cōtinually in & out of the tabernacle*, & that whiles he was there, *he vvas rauished in cōtemplation*, & whiles he was abroad, *he attēded to negotiation*, & that in the tabernacle, *he did contēplat the heauēly secrets of almighty God*, & abroad, *he bore the heauy burthē of his earthly charge*. And how auaileable his contemplatiō was to his state, & to al his subiects, it appeareth sufficiently by their victory against the *Amalecits*, obtained by his praiers, vpon the mountaine, whiles *Iosue* and his army fought, as also by his frequēt pacificatiō of Gods wrath towards thē whē God had determined other waies to distroy thē for their sinnes.

D. Gregor. de past. cura. par. 2. c. 5. *Exod. 17.* *Exod. 31. & 32. num. 14. & 21.*

5 In like manner, was their euer a greater cōtemplatiue then king *Dauid*, seeing that neither the pompe of his royal dignity, nor the plentie of his princely

princely wealth, nor the prosperous course of his victories, nor yet his serious occupation in publike affaires, could with hould him, from the continuall and exact exercise of contemplation? For, as he testifyeth of himselfe, he vsed to *a meditat on all the vvorkes of God, to b svvepe, and clenze his spirit*, or conscience by diligent examination, *to c vvash his bed euery night vvith teares, to d prayse God seauen times in the day*, and *to e ryse at midnight to confesse him*, and further, that in this *f meditations*, he felt *a burning heat*, and such aboundant consolation, that he inuiteth all men to the triall, and tast thereof by his owne experience, saying. *g Gustate, & videte, quoniam suauis est Dominus. Tast, and see, for our Lord is svveete*; and so feruent was his loue to God, (which is most requisit to contemplation) that he compared it to a continuall Thirst. *h Citiuit*, sayth he, *anima mea ad Deum fontem viuum*; *My soule hath thirsted after God, vvho is the liuing fountaine*; yea, and so vehement, was his burning, and languishing loue to God, that his very soule fainted, and, as it were, melted there with: *Concupiscit*, sayth he, *& deficit anima mea in atria Domini*: that is to say, so ardent, and feruorous is my loue to my Lord, and so excessiue my desire of the ioyes of his kingdome, that my soule fayneth, and fayleth me, in the contemplation thereof. Thus sayth he, signifying the Extases, or rapts which he had, no doubt, many times in his meditations, no lesse then the other Prophets of God, in whom the same were ordinary. If therefore kings, and princes were so contemplatiue in the law of nature, and the law of *Moyses*, what may they now be in the law of grace?

a. Psal. 142. b. Psal. 76. c. Psal. 6. d. Psal. 118. e. Ibidem. f. Psal. 38. g. Psal. 39. h. Psal. 41. Psal. 83.

6 This may appeare by many notable *Christian* princes in all countryes, who haue excelled in Christian contemplation, and haue bene so vnited with God thereby, that their memory remayneth glorious in the Church, which hath canonized very many of them for Saints, as namely *Henry* duke of *Bauyer*, the first Emperour of that name, twoo Wenceslai kings of *Boemia*, *Levvis* king of France, *Lucius*, *Sebbi*, *Sigbert*, *Osvvald*, *Osvvyn*, *Edmond*, and the two *Edvvards*, the Martyre, and Confessour kings of England, *Canutus*, king of *Denmarke*, *Levvis* the ninth king of *Fraunce*, *Stephen* king of *Hungary*. *Cazimirus* king of *Polonia*, *Henricus* king of *Slauonia*, *Olaus* king of *Norvvay*: *Pelagius* king of *Spayne*, and diuerse others whom I omitt for breuities sake, whose liues were so exemplar to the world, & acceptable to almighty God, that his deuine Majesty glorified them with notable, and euident miracles, partly whiles they liued, and partly after their deaths, where vppon followed their canonization by the holy Church, to the greater glory of God, and their eternal honour, as wel in earth as in heauen.

S. Beda eccles. hist. gentis Angelic. Bosius de sig. Eccle. li. 11. c. 1. sig. 50. To. 1.

7 *Henry* the Emperour aforenamed, was no lesse renowned, & famous for his

for his prowes in warre,then for his iustice,and religious pietie in peace, whereby he greatlie aduanced the christian faith, for he subdued first the *Vandals* and *Boemians*(who being then infidls,infested greatlie the christiã empire) and after expelled the *Saracins* out of *Italy*, in which warres and diuers others,hee shewed more confidence to God, then in his owne force, and therefore hee allwayes made his whole army communicate, and receiue the Blessed Sacrament before hee gaue battaile, and vsed also him selfe verie great and extraordinarie deuotions, wherebyhe had sometimes, miraculous victories, being assisted by Angels, Whome hee saw other whiles goe before his armie together with *S.Lavvrence*,*S.George* and *S.Adrian*,to whome hee had perticular deuotion. And such was his care and desire to aduance by al meanes,the glorie and seruice of God,& the propagation of christian religion, that hee procured the conuersion of the *Hungarians*,in so much,that he was called by many their Apostle. Besides that he was so pious towards the Church,that he partly founded and partlie restored,and repared manie monasteries, & Cathedral Churches,being withall most liberall to the poore, and wounderfully addict to all workes of pietie, which hee accompaned with such feruour of deuotion,that he was no lesse contemplatiue in frequent, or rather continuall praier, then actiue in procuring the good of others: in so much, that it is written of him, that he passed sometimes whole nights in contemplation in diuers Churches,and places of deuotion,and that also hee receiued there verie greate and particuler fauours, and consolations of almighty God, by visions,and reuelations, and sometimes by raps,and as *Rubertus* witnesseth: hee neuer determined, or attempted anie matter of importance concerning him selfe,and others, but he first disposed himselfe thereto by praier, and almes, *vt mens eius* saith he, *& actus cælesti regimine gubernarentur, to the end,that his mind, and actions might be gouerned by heauenlie direction.*

Bonfin. de reb.Hung. des.2 li 1. Baron. an. 1022.

Rupert in vit.S.Hereberti.

8 Furthermore, amongst manie other most excellent vertues,which he had in great perfection, one was most singular, and rare in a man of his state,to wit,such contenencie, and intire chastitie of life, that although hee was maried manie yeares,to satisfie the importunitie of his subiects, who pressed him thereto,yet both hee and the Empresse, his wife(called *Cuneguntis*)by mutuall consent, liued chast all their liues, as appeareth at his death, at what time hee said to her friendes, in her owne presence, that he restored her vnto them a virgin as he receiued her of them,which was sufficientlie testified to be true, by her owne vertuous life, both before his death,and after,whereby shee merited, to be canonized also for a Saint,aswell as he.

Baron.an.1024.ex Leone ostensi. li.2.c.47.

6 And ſuch was his religious humilitie, and reuerent reſpect to the clergie, that being preſent in a Sinod of Biſhops at *Francford*, he proſtrated himſelfe vppon the ground, before he would ſpeake vnto them, and would not ariſe vntill *VVillegiſus* Arch-Biſhop of Mentz, lifted him vp, as *Ditmarus* biſhop of *Meresburg* (who was preſent) teſtifieth. Alſo when *Romualdus* the Abbot of *S. Emeran* died, and was to be buried, the Emperour would needes helpe to carrie him to his graue, and ſo did, bearing parte of the beere on his ſhoulders. Finally being by the euil counſel, & calumniations of ſome abuſed for a time, and wholie auerted from the holie biſhop of *Colen Herebert*, and admoniſhed at length by a viſion in his ſleepe, of the biſhops innocency, and ſanctitie, he went vnto him, and laid himſelfe proſtrat at his feete, crauing pardon of him for the wronge opinion which he conceiued of him.

Baron. an. 1006 *Ditmarus. in Chron.* *Baron. an. 1007.*

10 And to conclude, though to auoyde prolixitie, I am forced to lett paſſe manie notable thinges which might be obſerued in this life, I cannot omit one, to ſhew by his example, the benefit which groweth of the continuall meditation, and expectation of death, which is moſt proper to the contemplatiue life.

Surius in vita S. Henreci. 14. Iulij. vide Baron. an. 1007.

This *Henry*, before hee was Emperour being one night long at his deuotions in *Ratisbone*, in the Abbay, and at the tombe of *S. Emeran*, vnderſtood by reuelation that there was a writing in a wall neare to the ſepulchar of *S. VVolfgang* which he was admoniſhed to take out, & reade, and therein he found onlie two wordes, to wit, *poſt ſex, after ſix*, which when he ſaw, he imagined that it might be ſome forewarning of his death to enſue within ſix daies, whereupon he prepared himſelfe, to die, with all care, and diligence, and ſeeing the ſix daies paſſe without the effect, which he expected, he perſeuered in his former preparation, for ſix weekes, and when he ſaw his expectation alſo deceiued therein, he continued the ſame firſt for ſix months, and after for ſix yeares, which being expired, it pleaſed God to fulfill the propheſy, though not as hee expected, for vppon the firſt day of the ſeaueuth yeare, he was choſen Emperour, hauing in the meane time laid ſuch a ſound foundation of vertue, by meanes of his continuall preparation for death, that his imperiall honours could neuer change his manners, in ſo much that for the two and twentie yeares, which after the count of the *Germans* hee raigned moſt proſperouſlie, hee ſtill continued his former courſe, of true pietie, and vertue: Whereby we may ſee, how true it is which the Preacher ſaith. *Memorare nouiſſima tua, & in æternum non peccabis*. Remember alwayes thy laſt, that is to ſay thy end, and thou ſhalt neuer ſinne.

Eccleſ. 7.

11 Thus

Thus much for the emperour *Henry*.

11 The other two of whome I haue promiſed to treate, shallbe of our owne countrie, the one a Martire, & the other a Confeſſor, to wit, *S. Oſvvald*, and *S. Edvvard*, *S. Oſvvald* being firſt a Pagan, and conuerted to the chriſtian faith in *Scotland*, whiles he was banished there, came, by the death of his brother *Eangfred*, to bee king of *Northumberland*, and was ſo eminent in all vertue, that it is hard to *Beda. hiſtor* ſay, whether he excelled more in the contemplatiue, or in the *Anglic. li. 3* actiue life: For firſt to ſpeake of his contemplation, *S. Bede* witneſ- *c. 1.* ſeth that his deuotion was ſuch, that from the time of mattins (which was at midnight) hee continued verie oft in praier vntill *Beda. hiſtor* it was day, and that being acuſtomed alwayes to hould vpp his hands *Anglic. li. 3.* towards heauen, when he praied, he got ſuch a habit by the fre- *c. 12.* quent vſe thereof, that whenſoeuer he ſate, he held his handes vpright.

12 And of this his deuotion proceeded no doubt the feruour, and zeale hee had to pious actions; and to all workes of charitie, as firſt to gaine ſinners to God, wherein hee laboured notablie: For hauing procured the bishop *Aidan* to come from *Scotland* to preach to his people, who were then Pagans, and vnderſtood not the *Scottish* tongue, he was content to be the bishops interpreter, expounding in the Saxon tongue that which the bishop preached in *Scottish*, whereby hee conuerted them ſpeedilie to the chriſtian faith, and calling into *England* manie religious men to labour in that harueſt, and vineard of almightie God, hee beſtowed liberallie for their maintenance, and built manie Monaſteries, and Churches, in ſo much, that within a while, the Chriſtian religion floriſhed notablie in his dominion, which therefore it pleaſed almightie God to enlarge in such ſorte, that within a few yeares, all the princes of *Britanny* (which as *S. Bede* witneſſeth were then deuided into foure tongues, to wit *Britons*, *Picts*, *Scots* and *English*) became ſubiect vnto him, and yet neuertheleſſe ſaith hee *pauperibus, & perigrinis ſemper humilis, benignus, & largus fuit*, *hee vvas* *Ibid.* *alvvayes humble, benigne* and liberall towards the poore, and ſtrangers: whereto *Polidore* addeth, that *Mira fuit in homine ſanctitas &c. His ſanctity* Polid. Virgil. *or holines vvas vvonderfull, & his loue to piety, for he neuer rendred euil for euil,* *li. 4.* *but follovving the example of our Sauiour Chriſt, the king of kings, vviſhed vvell to his verie enemies, & to thoſe vvho had done him iniurie, deſiring to doe good to all men, he viſited & cōforted the ſicke; he releaſed priſoners, he paied the debts of ſuch as vvere poore, & not able to pay them,* he defēded widowes, & punished their

 oppreſ-

oppressors. Finallie his pietie, and liberalitie to the poore, was such that vnderstanding once whiles he was at dinner, that there were manie poore folkes at the court gate, he caused a siluer platter full of meate to be caried vnto them from his owne table, and not onlie the meate, but also the dish, to be distributed amoungst them, which when the holie bishop *Aidam*, who dined with him saw, he tooke him by the right hand, and said. *Nunquam putrescat hæc manus. God grant this hand may neuer rot.* Whereof, *S. Bede* noteth a notable effect, witnessing, that his arme, and hand, being cut of from his bodie by the Painims, when he was slaine, and after recouered by his successour, remained incorrupt vntill his time, who also addeth that. *Loculo inclusæ argenteo in ecclesia Sancti Petri seruantur & digno a cunctis honore venerantur. they are kept* saith he, *enclosed in a siluer case, in the citty called Bella, and the Church of S. Peter, vvhere they are vvorthilie reuerenced of all men.* Thus saith *S.Bede.*

Beda.histor. Anglic.li.3. ca.6.

Idim.Ibid. & Polid. verg.li.4.

13 Moreouer this great charitie, and deuotion of this holie king in time of peace, was accompanied with noe lesse valour in time of warr, as may appeare by the great ouerthrow he gaue to *Caduallo Britons*, whõe he slw, and a great part of his huge armie, deliuering the *English* nation from the most fierce, and potent enemie, that they had of manie yeares, in which warrs he also shewed the great pietie, and confidence in God, which concurred with all his other actions. For being come to the place of battaile, hee cased a crosse to bee made, saith *S. Bede*, with all speede, and a hole to be digged, wherein he sett it, with his owne hand, and held it vp vntill it was fastened there by his souldiars, which being donne, he commaunded all his armie to knele downe with him, and to pray to God for victorie, in respect that their warr, and quarrell was iust, and so saith *S. Bede*, the next morning setting vppon their enimies, *Iuxta meritum suæ fidei victoria potiti sunt: According to the merit of his faith, they obtained the victorie.* And *S.Bede* further addeth, that in the same place of his praier. *Innumeræ virtutes sanitatum, noscuntar, esse patratæ, ad indicium videlicet, & memoriam fidei regis, There are* saith he, *innumerable miracels done vpon the diseased in the recouerie of their health, in token, and memorie of the kinges faith.*

Beda.li.3. ca.2.

Idem.Ibid.

14 And this deuout valour, or valerous deuotion, hee shewed also in the like occasions, and specially in the last battaile which he gaue to the Pogan king of the *Mercians* called *Penda*, against whome he made warre for the defence of Christian religion, in which battaile it pleased God, to suffer him to be slaine to giue him the crowne of Martiredome. For, his armie being discomfited, and he himselfe so inuironed with his enemies, that he saw he was presentlie to die, such was his charietie, that hee

was more carefull for the soules of his souldiars, then for his owne, in so much that he was slaine praing for them: whereuppon their grew this prouerbe. *God haue mercy on their soules, quoth King Osvvald, vvhen he vas killed himselfe. And hovv great* (saith *S. Bede*) *vvas his faith to God, and his deuotion, it appeareth after his death by manie miracles, for in the verie place, vvhere he died fighting against the Painimes, manie diseased persons, and sick cattle doe still recouer their health.* Thus saith *S. Bede*, who recounteth amplie, and particularlie verie manie euedent, and famous miracles, which it pleased God to shew aswell at his tombe, as at the place where he was martired, and this shall suffise for king *Osvvald.* Wherein I wish thee good Reader, to note by the way of what religion he was, and others in our cuntry, in that our primitiue Church, seeing he sett vpp crosses, and praied for the dead, and that relickes of Saints, were so reuerenced in those daies, which was a thousand yeares agoe.

Beda. hist. Anglic. li.3. ca. 12.

15 And now to say somewhat of king *Edvvard*, commonlie called the *Confessor*, The fame of his great vertue, and deuotion, and the testimonie, that God gaue thereto, by manie manifest miracles, is so notorious, that it connot bee doubted, but that hee was a most perfect contemplatiue, greatlie vnited with almighty God, and highlie in his fauour: & therefore *Polidor vergil*, obserueth verie well of him, that God gaue him a continuall and prosperous peace, for ninteene yeares together, to the end he might the better, and more fullie satisfie his holie disire in the contemplation of heauenlie thinges, which was, saith he, all his studie, and delight, and therefore *Mathevv of VVestmister* calleth him. *Regem pacificum, Angliæ decus, indagatorem solertissimum: A peaceable king, the ornament of England, and a most diligent searcher of the heauenlie secrets.*

Polid. Verg. hist. Anglic. li. 8.

Math. VVest. an. 1065.

And although he was counted simple (being so humble and meeke, that he could not be angrie, and therefore was held at the first to be vnfit to gouerne) yet as *VVillam* of *Malmesbury* writeth of him, hee was wonderfull reuerenced of his subiects, and greatlie feared of his enemies, *&* *fouebat* saith he, *eius simplicitatem Deus, vt posset timeri qui nesciret irascy*, and God fostered, and protected his simplicitie, to the end he might be feared, who could not be angrie. Thus saith *VVillam* of *Malmesbury*, who liued in his time, or presentlie after. And further testified of him, that amid the busines, ind affaires of his kingdome he lead an Angels life, being affable, and courteous euen to the poorest, liberall to all good, and religious men, an enemie of exactions, spare of diet: And though hee was rich, and sumptuous in his royal robes, vppon festiuall daies (as was fit for the dignitie of his person) yet it euedentlie appeareth, that he rather sought Gods glorie therein, then his owne delictation: His onlie warldly recrea-

Guliel. Malm.

recreation, was hunting, and hawking, whereto neuertheles he would neuer attend, saith the same authour, vntil he had heard deuine seruice; his loue to his people was singuler, as appeareth both by his remission of the great and grieuous impositions laid vppon them, by his predecessors, as also by the care he tooke of the administration of

Alred. in vit. Eduuar. Iustice, and of the ordinance of good lawes; his chastitie was admirable, insomuch, that hauing marryed a faire and beautifull Ladie at the earnest suite, and request of his nobilitie, he persuaded her to make a vow of chastitie, and so they liued both of them continent during their liues: And so he was (as *Alredus* writeth of him) humble towards priests, pitifull to the poore, a father of orphanes, a pa-

Ared. in vit. Ed. var. tron of widowes, and a contemner of riches. Finallie his puritie of conscience, and feruour of deuotion in praier, and contemplation was such, that God imparted vnto him exceeding fauours, of visions, reuelations, and the spirit of prophesie, besides manie famous miracles

Guliel. Malmesbur. which God wrought by him, both in his life, and after his death, as all the authours that write of him do testifie, and is euident also by

Polid. Virg. hist. Anglic. li. 8. the hereditarie gift or grace of God giuen to his successors to heale the disease, called the *Kings euil*, and to blesse rings for the crampe, and falling sicknes, which was practised by the kinges of *England* from

Ibidem. his time, so long as Catholike religion remained there.

16 Now then of these examples I inferre two thinges, the first concerning kings and princes, to wit, how erroneous, and impious is the suggestion that sicophants commonlie vse to whisper into their eares, that the deuotion, and religious pietie, which I call contemplation, is more fit for cloisters, then for courts, and better beseeming monkes, or priests then princes: whereas it appeareth, by the foresaid examples, and manie others which might be alleadged, that neither the princes power, nor his dignitie, and maiestie, nor his lawfull recreations, nor the defence of his state, and person, nor yet the iust offence of his enemies, is anie way hindred by his integritie of conscience, and religious deuotion: but his power increased by the assistance of the deuine power, his dignitie, and maiestie augmented, his recreations made more sweete, and pleasant, his state assured, his enemies daunted, his name eternised, and his kingdome, or dominion translated in the end, from earth to heauen, and from miserie to immortalitie, and euerlasting glorie.

2. Reg. 6. 17 And therefore when *Michol* daughter to king *Saul* dispised, and derided king *Dauid* her husband, for dauncing in Leuits attire before the Arke of God (when it was remoued from the house of *Obed-Edom*

vnto

vnto the citie of *Dauid*) he said vnto her, that seeing God had chosen him, rather then her father, or anie of his house, to be king of his people, he would the more humble himselfe in his owne sight, to giue honour, and praise to God, not doubting but he should by that meanes be more glorious euen in the sight of men: and how much the irreligious vanitie of *Michol*, displeased almightie God, the scripture, declareth, signifying that in punishment thereof she became barrein. *Ibid.*

18 This religious humilitie, and feruent deuotion of king *Dauid*, seemed to *S. Gregory*, more laudable and admirable, then his great valour and victories in warr, and therefore he saith notablie thus. „ *Let vs consider*, saith he, what great giftes, and vertues *Dauid* receiued of al- „ mightie God, and how humble he was withall, for who would not „ haue benne extolled in mind, if he had broken the iawes of lyons, „ dismembred beares, and ouerthrowne a giant, as *Dauid* did? Or if „ being a priuat man he had bene annoynted king in steede of one al- „ readie in possession, and in the end obayed of all without contradi- „ ction, as *Dauid* was? And yet when the Arke of God was remoued to „ *Hierusalem*, he daunced before it amongst the common people, as „ though he had bene no better then they, and so he, whom God „ had preferred before all men, contemned himselfe for the loue of God „ and matching himselfe with the meanest, neither remembred his „ princelie power, not yet feared, that by dauncing before the Arke, „ he should be lesse esteemed of his subiects, but acknowledged him- „ selfe, as meane as the meanest, to render honour to God, who had „ so highlie honoured him. What other men thinke of his act, I „ know not, but for my part I more admire him dauncing then figh- „ ting, for when he fought he subdued his enemies, but when he „ daunced before the Arke of God, he ouercame himselfe. „

D. Greg. expos. moral. li. 27. in c. 37. Iob.
1. Reg. 16. 17.
2 Reg. 3.
2. Reg. 16.

19 Thus saith, *S. Gregory*, giuing therein a notable document to princes, co consider by the example of king *Dauid*, how honorable it is for them to humble themselues in matters that appertaine to the honour and seruice of God, thereby to acknowledge of whom they hould their honour, and state, and to shew themselues gratefull to him for the same: as not onlie king *Dauid* did when he daunced before the Arke, but also our good king *Osvvald*, when he was content (as I haue signified before) to be interpreter betwixt the Bishop *Aidan*, and his people for their instruction in the faith, and erected a Crosse, holding it vp, with his owne hands, vntill his souldiars had fastned it in the earth. And the like also may be obser-

be obserued in that which I signified of the holie emperour *Henrie.* who helped ro cary on his shoulders, the body of *S. Romoald*, to his buriall, and laid himselfe prostrat before the Bishops in a Sinod at *Francford.* Whereto I may add a rare example of religious humilitie & piety, in king *Edvvard* the Confessor, not mentioned before, to wit, that hee disdained not to carry on his backe, an Irish criple, borne lame, and strangelie deformed, from his pallace at *VVestmister*, vnto *S. Peters* Church, for that the criple humbly requested the same of him, hauing had as hee said, a reuelation, that he should recouer his leggs, if the king would doe him the charitie to beare him one his backe to the Church: And it pleased God to glorifie himselfe in the humilitie, and charitie of this holie king, that the criple was cured of his lamnes in the sight of all the people, whiles he was vppon the kings backe.

Alred. in vit. Edvvard.

Baron. an. 628.

20 But most nitable in this kind, was the example of *Heraclius*, the Emperour, who hauing recouered out of *Persia*, the holie Crosse, whereon our Sauiour suffred (which the *Persians* had before taken away from *Hierusalem*) caried it vpp to the mount *Caluary*, vppon his owne shoulders bare footed, and simplie appareled, hauing attempted before to carry it in his ryall robes, which he could not doe, nor so much, as remoue one foote with it, vntill he had put them of. Whereby almightie God taught him, and all princes to humiliat themselues in his sight, and to consider, that though they are more potent, and mighty then other men, and worthylie honoured, obaied, and serued of their subiects, yet before him, they are but *terra & cinis*, *earth and ashes*, that is to say, made of the same mould, that other men are, and as subiect to him, as the meanest. Thus much for the first point, which I wish to be obserued in the example before alleaged.

21 The other is that for as much as the greatest emperours, and kinges, may be perfect contemplatiues, without preiudice, yea, and with incomparable benefit to themselues, and their states, it cannat be denied, but that inferiour persons, of what degree, or state soeuer they be may also arriue to the perfection of contemplation, seeing they haue lesse cause of distraction, and that nothing is required thereunto (as I haue amply shewed alreadie) but the grace of God, and the perfection of Christian religion, which doth stand with euerie mans state, & vocation & is the onlie meanes to perfect the same.

22 Therefore although in respect of the infirmitie, and malignitie of mans nature, it cannot be expected, that euerie one in the common wealth, shallbe contemplatiue, or trulie religious, yet it is euident, by al this former discourse, that euerie one may be, and that the greater is the num-

number of contemplatiues in the common welth, the more happy it is, and consequentlie, that the true felicitie of common wealth consisteth in christian contemplation, not onlie in respect of the ineffable consolations spirituall, and tast of immortalitie, which euerie member thereof, may euen in this life receiue thereby (as I haue proued at large in the 21. chapter) but also of the temporall fauour and protection of almightie God, redounding thereof both to the whole state in generall, and to euery one in particular, as I will proue more particularlie in the third parte of this treatise, when I shall treat of the different fruit of true, and false religion in kingdomes and states.

Certaine friuolous obiections of Macchiauel *against Christian religion are answered, and his impietie, and ignorance discouered.*

Chap. 24.

1 HAuing hetherto proued the excellency, & necessitie of christian religion, for the perfection of cōmon welth, I thinke it conuenient to answer here two folish and impious obiections of *Macchiauel*: the one, that our Christian religion teaching as it doth, all humilitie, mansuetude, patience, contempt of the world, pouertie of spirit, and remission of iniuries, maketh men base minded, cowerdlie and timorous, in which respect, he preferreth the religion, and valour of the Painimes before ours, for such reasons, as shall be declared, and examined hereafter. *Macchia. li. 2. de discorsi sopra Tito Liuio. c. 2.*

2 The other obiection is, that our christian names taken from Saints, are not so fit for common wealth as the names of *Cæsar*, *Pompey*, & other Pagans, renowned greatlie for their valour, by Whose example, men might bee stirred vpp to the execution of famous, and valarous acts.

3 Thus teacheth, or rather trifleth this Atheisticall politicke, no lesse absurdlie, then wickedlie, bewrayng aswell his owne ignorance, & folly, as his notable impietie. And first concerning the first obiection, what can bee more absurd, then to thinke that the vertues, of humilitie, mansuetude, patience, and remission of iniuries should anie waies hinder the magnanimitie, valour, and fortitude of men? would anie man teach this, that knoweth what belongeth to the nature of these vertues? For who knoweth not (if he haue but anie tast of morall philosophy) that no one vertue can be had in perfection, but with a connexion of all the rest (if not of the acts, yet at least of the habits) whereby a man that is trulie vertuous, shalbe sufficientlie disposed, and able to doe all the acts of ver-

tue,as his estate,time, place and occasion shall require? and therefore although on the one side magnanimitie doth raise, aud eleuate the mind of man to worthy, and great actions,aud one the other side humilitie doth as it were, depresse him to a lowlie,and base conceit of himselfe, and to acts correspondent thereto: yet by reason of different respects, they are oposit,and contrarie the one to the other, but one man may haue the habits, and performe the acts of them both, when iust occasion shallbee offred: yea it may rather be trulie affirmed that without true humilitie no man is trulie magnanimious, but a coward and slaue to his owne passions,and by them hindred to practise true magnanimitie.

4 For as magnanimitie inciteth a man to vndartake great,and honorable actions vppon the consideration of the high, and worthy end whereto God hath ordained him, (and in respect of the dignitie of gods image

S.Thom.22. q.129.ar.3. ad 4.

in him, and of other good gifts, and fauours receiued at gods hands) so also humilitie,respecting the defects,and imperfections in man, moueth him to haue a true cōceit of his owne infirmitie,or rather of his owne nothing,and to shew it in due time, place,nd occasion by eternall acts: so that a magnanimious Christian, will not onlie doe generous and honorable actions when it seemeth to him conuenient for the honour, and seruice of God,but also will deiect himselfe to all offices, and actions of humilitie,when like iust occasion shall require it. And therefore whereas al morall vertues are reduced to foure heades, (to wit,*Prudence*,*Iustice*, *Fortitude* and *Temperance*, which are therefore called the foure Cardinall vertues) it is to be vnderstood, that *humilitie* and *magnanimitie*, are so farr from being opposit, or contrarie the one to the other, or yet to *Fortitude*, that *S.Thomas* accounteth them both as potentiall parts of *Fortitude*,redu-

D.Tho.virt. q.1.12.26.

cing them thereto,as to their head.

5 And forasmuch as *magnanimity* is as *Aristotle* saith, *decor & ornamentum virtutum*,a beautie, grace, and ornament to all other vertues,and tendeth

Aristot. Ethic.li.4. c.3.

alwaies to perfection in the exercise and practise of them (that is to say, when it concurreth to the operation of anie other vertue, it maketh the act most excelent and perfect) thereuppon it followeth, that when a magnanimious man doth the acts of humilitie, he surpasseth all other men therein,performing them in the highest degree of perfection: And noe maruaile seeing that he which is trulie magnanimious, being withall trulie prudent (for otherwaies hee could not bee trulie vertuous) and esteeming euerie thinge according to the true worth, and valew thereof, hath such a base conceit, of al earthlie and humane thinges (in respect of the heauenlie and deuine) that no man contemneth them so much as he, when occasion requireth.

6 Ther-

6 Therefore *Cicero* teacheth expresslie that *magnanimitie* is: *Animi cum ratione magnificentia humanas res, vt decet, contemnens: A magnificence, or greatnes of the mind ioyned vvith reason, contemning all human thinges, as it is conuenient*. And further he saith, that the magnanimious, and valiant man, is. *Constans, sedatus, grauis, & humana omnia premens.* Constant, sober, quiet, graue, and one that treadeth all humane thinges vnder his feete. So that although he be inclined to honour and glorie, yet it is with such moderation, and due regard of his owne desert, that he is neither vaine, glorious, nor presumptuous, nor ambitious, waying al his deserts, and actions in the balance of reason (for otherwise, he should loose the commendation of his vertue, and fall into vice) and therefore whensoeuer he seeth the respect of humane honour, glorie, or earthlie commodities, encountred with the consideration of Gods honour, and glorie, or of heauenlie, and euerlasting ioyes, he so much despiseth the former in respect of the latter, that he treadeth them vnder his feete, and triumpheth ouer them by true humilitie, contemning yea, and abandoning both them, and himselfe, for the glorie, and seruice of God, saing with *S. Paule: omnia arbitror, vt stercora, vt Christum lucrifatiam. I hould all thinges for no better then dung, and dirt, that I may gaine Christ.* Whereby it appeareth that *magnanimitie* is not empeached by Christian humilitie, and that the true magnanimious Christian, may trulie say with the same Apostle: *Scio, & humiliari scio & abundare &c. I knovv hovv to be humble, I knovv hovv to abound, I am framed, and disposed euery vvhere, and in all occasions to be full, to be hungrie, to abound, to suffer pennry, yea, I can doe all thinges in Christ, vvho strenghtneth me.* Thus saith the Apostle, who was a true mirrour, aswell of perfect *magnanimitie*, as of true *humilitie*, and all other vertues.

Tuscul. q. li. 4.

Philip. 3.

Philip. 4.

7 The like is also to be vnderstood of the concurrence of Christian mansuetude, or meekenes, with true Fortitude, seeing that no man can bee trulie, and perfectlie valiant, if hee bee not withall, mansuit, benigne, and meeke.

For whereas mansuetude, or meekenes, is the vertue which properlie represseth the excesse of anger, and desire of reuenge, it is euident that no man can haue perfect Fortitude, without mansuetud, for he that is transported with choller, anger, and an appetit of reuenge, is rather to bee counted temerarious, or furious, then valiant, seeing that true valiour neuer draweth a man beyond the bonds of reason, for as *Cicero* saith. *Non est vlla fortitudo, quæ rationis expers est. It is not anie fortitud, at all vvhich is vvithout reason.*

Cicero Tuscul. quæst. li. 4.

8 Therefore the *Lacedemonians*, who were a most valiant people, were accustomed alwaie before their battailes, to sacrifise to the *muses*, to the

Plutar. opusc. de Ira reprimenda.

end they might be able (as they thought by ſome good influence, or inſtinct of theirs) to moderat their paſſions, and vſed alſo to temper the exorbitant choller of their ſouldiars in warre, with the ſound of ſoft, & ſweete inſtruments, and ſpecially of flutes. And *Plutarck* commendeth greatlie the valour of *Chryſantus* (of whome *Xenophon* maketh mention) for that he had ſuch abſolut commaund ouer his paſſions, and was withall ſo obedient, and obſeruant of militarie diſciplin, that hauing lifted vp his ſword to ſtrike his enemy, & hearing the ſound of a retraite, he withdrew his hand, and forbare to ſtrike out his blow.

Idem. in cõparat. Marcel. & Pelopida.

9 Seeing then the proper office of Chriſtian manſuetude, is no other, but to reſtraine, and repreſſe the furius exceſſe of anger, in ſuch ſort, that we may be maſters thereof, and vſe it as a whetſtone to valour, and fortitude (that is to ſay, onlie to ſharpen it in due manner, time, place, and occaſion) who ſeeth not the ignorance and folly of *Macchiauel* in that he holdeth Chriſts precepts, and counſels of perfect meekenes, benignitie, & patience, to be preiudiciall to true valour, and conſequentlie to common wealths: as though it could be with anie reaſon imigined, that the meaning of our Sauiour Chriſt, was to bind vs to the performance thereof with the publicke detriment of common welth, or the priuat iniurie of anie third perſon, or the diſhonour of God, which were not vertue, but vice, and an offence to God, as I haue declared more particularlie, in the 22. chapter, where I haue alſo ſignified out of *S. Auguſtin*, how chriſtians may, and doe iuſtlie make warre, notwithſtanding our Sauiours precepts of ſufferance of wronges, & remiſſion of iniuries.

Chap. 22. nu. 28.

10 Furthermore who knoweth not that the pardon of iniuries, when no third parſon, nor the common welth, is damnified thereby, proceedeth of true generoſitie, and magnanimitie, & is an euident ſigne of moſt excelent vertue: And therefore *Ariſtotle* diſcribing the vertue of the magnanimious, and valiant man, ſaith that he is nether *vindex iniuriarum, vindicatiue, or a reuenger of iniuries*, nor yet *memor earum, nor ſo much as mindfull of them*, but both forgeueth and forgitteth them. And *Plato* teacheth that *Neque vlciſci decet &c. A man ought not either to reuenge anie iniurie donne vnto him, nor to hurte anie man vvhat vvronge, or dammage ſoeuer he hath receiued of other men.* And *Cicero* ſpeaking of the clemencie of *Iulius Cæſar* in pardoning his enemies, preferreth it before all his famous conqueſtes, and victories yealding thereof this notable reaſon: that his exploitis and victories in warre were not ſo entirelie, and wholie his owne but that his armies, and ſouldiars, yea fortune, and chance might challenge parte of his praiſe, whereas the praiſe of the victorie, and conqueſt which hee got ouer his owne paſſions, and himſelfe, when he perdoned his enemies, was holie his owne, and not to be communicated with anie other.

Ariſtot. li. 4. ethic. c. 3. & li. de virtut.

Plato. li. 8. de rep.

And finally he concludeth notablie thus. *Animum vnicere &c. To conquer a mans ovvne mind, to represse anger, and passion, to be moderate in victorie, and not onlie to raise a potent, and noble enemie, vvhen hee is falne, and ouerthrovvne, but also to amplifie, and encreas his former dignitie, he that doth this, I vvill not compare him vvith the vvorthiest men, but I iudge him to be most like to God.* So he. *Cicero pro M. Marcel.*

11 We read also, that the remission of iniuries was notablie practised by manie other eminent men amongst the Paynimes, as by *Licurgus* the lawmaker of the *Lacedemonians*, who hauing one of his eies strooken out by a young man, that meant to haue killed him, not onlie pardoned him, but also tooke him into his house, and taught him philosophy, thereby to correct his manners, and made him in time a notable subiect, and member of his common welth. *Plutar. in Licur.*

12 Also *Phocian*, a famous captaine of the *Athenians*, being most vniustlie, and vngratefully condemned to death by his common welth, charged his sonne, both to forgiue, and forgot it

13 And *Seneca*, highlie commendeth *Augustus Cæsar*, for pardoning a great noble man called *Cinna*, who had conspired his death, which clemency, hee saith, wrought most notable effects, not onlie in *Cinna* himselfe (who euer after remained most affectionat, and faithfull to *Augustus*) but also in all other men. For whereas *Augustus* hauing in former times bene most cruell, & vnidicatiue, was neuer free from conspiracies, *nullis amplius insidiis* saith *Seneca*, *ab vllo petitus est: he vvas neuer after endaingered by the treasonable attempts of anie man.* And of this point, manie other examples might be alledged, which I omit, seeing it is euident inough, that our Sauiour Christ commaunding remission of iniuries, ordained no more for the substance of the act, then that which the Painimes themselues both highlie praised, and most prefitablie practised, though the end and motiue which moued them thereto, was no other but either some vaine glorie, or els the desire to gaine mens affections, by the reputation of clemencie, or perhaps to auoyde the anguish, and torment which accompaned the passion of anger, and desire of reuenge, whereas wee Christians, remitting iniuries, for the pure loue of God, and our neighbour, doe gaine not onlie worldlie honour, ease, & contentment of mind, and the loue of men as the Painimes did, but also the loue of God, & our assured hope of a heauenlie, & euerlasting reward. *Seneca. li. 1. de clement. ca. 9.*

14 What then can be imagined in Christs doctrin of humilitie, mansuetude, and remission of iniuries, either contrary, or anie way preiudiciall to true fortitude? Was there euer anie man more meeke, and humble, or that more freelie pardoned his enemies, then king *Dauid*, in whome our Sauiours ineffable mansuetude, humilitie, and charitie was prefigured? And *1. Reg. 24. 2. Reg. 16. & 18.*

yet there was neuer anie man either more valiant or victorious thē he.

15 And the like may be said of *Moyses*, who was not onlie, most valiant, but also as the scripture saith. *Mitissimus omnium &c. The most meeke, and gentle of all men that liued vppon earth.* And such were also the other two Christian, and contemplatiue kings aboue named, to wit *Henry* the Emperour, and our king *Osvvald* of *England*, in whom singuler valour, and military fortitude, notably concurred with perfect humility, mansuetude, and true Christian simplicity.

Num. 12.

16 And of this concurrence of all the moral vertues in Christians, *Machiauel* could neuer haue bene ignorant, if he had not bene so gracelesse, as not to consider the effects of Gods grace, & that the same only giueth perfection of morall vertue, as I amply proued before. Besides that he euidently shewed either his ignorance in history, or his malice in dissembling that which he had read, seeing he ascribed want of valour, and cowardise to Christians, whose valorous acts, and victorious conquests, are celebrated by the histories of all countries, by the which it is manifest that christians are much to be preferred before Paynimes, for martial prowes, and military valour, as may appeare by the famous victories of our Christian Emperours, *Constantin Theodosius*, and *Charlemayne* all three surnamed *Magni, the great*: in respect of their most famous, and worthy exployts in warre, of whom the last, to wit *Charlemayne*, twice ouerranne, and conquered all *Germany*, which neither *Iulius Cæsar*, nor all the force of the Roman Empyre could euer subdue before his tyme: to whom may be added *Charles Martel*, and his sonne *Pipin* king of *France*, *Pelagius, Froila, Ranimirus*, and three *Alfonsi*, all kings in *Spayne*, and *Ferdinand* count of *Castil*, and many others who with smale forces in respect of their enemies, ouerthrew infinit numbers of *Painymes, Saracens*, or other Infidels.

Eginard in vita Caroli. Baron. an. 772. & 804. *Paul. Æmilius. in Carolo Magno & Carolo Martello. Baron. an.* 731. *Ioan. Vasæus in Annalib. Hispan.*

17 I omit to speake of the great prowes, and valour of many other inferiour princes & Christian captaynes, renowned in all histories, a *Aetius* b *Bellisarius*, c *narses*, d *Godfroy* of *Bullen*, e *Franciscus Sfortia*, our two English Captaynes, f *Talbot*, and g *Aucut*, the former terrible in *France* euen vntil this day, and the latter famous in *Italy*. Besides h *Consaluus* surnamed the great captayne, and many others euen in our daies, whose valorous acts I omit, not to trouble thee (good Reader) with a needles proofe of common experience, which is as cleare in it selfe, as the day light, or sunne shyne: and therefore it may be wondred how *Machiauel* could be so bewitched, or rather dronke with the dreggs of Atheisme, as to teach that our Christian religion maketh men cowardly, and base mynded.

Baron. an. a 451. 8. 530. c. 553. d. *Paul. Æmil. in Philip.* 1 *Baron. an.* 1098. e. *Nancler. gener.* 49. f. *Polydor. Vergil. li.* 23. h. *Guicciard. li.* 5. & 6.

18 But now let vs examine breefely the validity of the reasons, which moue him to preferre the Paynimes before Christians, for *Magnanimity*,

and valour. The first is because the Paynimes placed their felicity in worldly honour, dominion, and victories, and therefore directed al their actions thereto: whereas Christians doe place it, saith he, in pouerty of spirit, humility, and contempt, of the world, in which respect he supposeth them to become base minded, and cowardly. Wherein I beseech thee good Reader, to note his malitious folly, in that he maketh Christian humility, and contempt of the world, the end, or felicity of Christian religion, whereas it is but the meanes to the end: for who knoweth not, if he be a Christian, as *Machiauel* professed to be, that the felicity which Christ promised, and the Christians expect, is to be vnited with God, first in this life, and after eternally in euerlasting blisse: and that the same is to be obtayned by pouerty of spirit, contempt of the world, and other vertues, and yet so, that no lawful vocation in any good common welth nor any mans duty towards his country, nor the lawful desire, or possession of riches, and honours, nor the execution of valorous, and magnanimious acts either in warre, or peace, is hindred thereby, but all the same perfited in the highest degree, as I haue sufficiently proued already in all this former discourse concerning Christian religion, and especially in this, and the two last chapters.

19 Whereby the malice of *Machiauel* may appeare, in that he not only craftily dissembleth our Christian doctrin, concerning aswel mans felicity, as the meanes to obtayne it, but also idly compareth the end (which the Paynimes proposed to themselues) with some part of the meanes that Christians vse to arriue to their end, and therefore he maketh not his opposition, and comparison, betwixt the desire of honour (which was the end of the Paynimes) and mans vnion with God, and euerlasting ioye, (which is the end; and felicity of Christians) but with humility, pouerty of spirit, and contempt of the world, which our Christian religion teacheth, as the way to our end.

20 Yf therefore we compare our end, and true felicity, with that other end, and supposed happines of the Paynimes, and examine whether of both may be more forcible, and potent to moue men to acts of magnanimity, and valour, we shall easely see *Machiauels* absurdity extreame ignorance, and folly.

21 For first, who is so simple that knoweth not, how farre the assured hope, and expectation which Christians haue of eternall ioyes, and felicity, ouerwayeth all temporall respects of transitory honour, pleasures, or commodities? Which is euident in common experience, seeing that, infinit numbers amongst Christians in all tymes, and ages since our Sauiour Christ, haue abandoned all worldly welth, honours, delights, yea their

very

very liues for the loue of God, and the hope of heauenlie ioyes, and life euerlasting.

22 Secondlie who knoweth not also, that the true Christian is no more debarred, or excluded from the lawfull desire, acquisition, and possession of welth, honour and dignitie, then the Painim, yea, and that Christians both may, and doe possesse, and enioy all worldlie honour, and commodities no lesse then anie Painim euer did, and with so much more contentment, and securitie, by how much more they referr the same to the honour, and seruice of God, and vse it onlie as a meane to obtaine eternall

Matth. 6. felicitie: according to our Sauiours precept. *Primum quærite regnum Dei,* &c. *First seeke the kingdome of God, and the righteousnes, or iustice thereof, and all thinges shalbe added vnto you.* Where vppon it followeth, that the Christian, hath not onlie the end, and temporall happines, that the Paynimes sought (to wit honour, welth, and dominion) in greater perfection then they: but also the assured hope, and expectation of euerlasting ioyes, which being added to the other, and incomparablie exceeding it in estimation and valew, must needes be of farre more force to moue men to the acts of valour, and euerie way to dischardge their duties to their prince, and common welth, then the bare, and onlie hope, or desire of any temporall, and transitorie felicitie, as for example.

23 Let vs put the case, that a Paynim, and a Christian goe together to the warre to fight for their countrie, and that the Paynim hath this onlie hope, that if he behaue valiantlie, and escape death with victorie, he shall haue great honour, and temporall reward, and if he be slaine, he shall leaue behind him an eternall fame of his valour. And on the other side the Christian hath not onlie the same hope of temporall honour, fame, and reward (whether he liue, or die) but also an assured expectation of eternall felicitie; who then seeth not that the Christian hath both greater aduantage of benefits, and also a farre greater motiue, and spurre to valour then the Paynim? Besides that, it cannot be denied, but that he, who putteth his felicitie in wordlie thinges, wilbe loth to leaue them, and consequentlie loth to die, and therefore the wise man

Eccl. 41. saith verie well, and trulie. *O mors, quam amara est memoria tui, &c. O death hovv bitter, is the memorie of thee, to a man, that hath peace, and contentment in his substance?* That is to say, that placeth his felicitie in the world, and in worldlie thinges.

24 Whereuppon it followeth, that such a one is commonlie timorous, fearefull, and loth to venter his life in any occasion: whereas he, which according to our Christian doctrin, esteemeth the world, and all the honour thereof, to be no better then traslie, and holdeth death to be both

and end of humane miseries, and the way, or dore to eternal felicitie, and saith with the Apostle. *I desire to be dissolued, or to die, and to be vvith Christ.* *Philip.1.* such a one I say, willinglie, and ioyfullie, ventereth his life in anie iust occasion, and therefore is trulie valiant, which is so euident of it selfe, that it needeth no further proofe. So that I may well conclud, that if *Machiauell* had not bene either extreemelie ignorant, and blind in not knowing the end, and felicitie of Christian religion (being himselfe by profession a Christian) or els most malitious in dissembling his knowledge thereof, he could neuer haue bene so absurd to affirme that Painimes, were more valiant, and magnanimious then Christians, by reason of the end, and felicitie which they proposed to them selues. And thus much for his first reason.

25 His second reason is that though Christiās do esteeme Fortitude, for a vertue, yet they place it, principallie in suffring, and not in doing, or attempting, which as he supposeth, maketh them more patient in suffring iniuries, or torments, then couragious in assailing their enemies, and in that respect hee houldeth them to bee lesse valiant then the Painimes. Wherein he also notably bewrayeth his ignorance, concerning the nature, and office of true Fortitude, seeing that *Aristotle*, and all the Painim philosophers, requiring thereto specially two thinges: the one patience to suffer, and the other, courage to attempt, doe principally place it in the former, and not in the latter, as appeareth manifestlie, not onlie in the *Ethics* of *Aristotle*, but also in the Tusculan questions of *Cicero*, who giuing diuers diuinitions of Fortitude out of the philosophers, al to one purpose, and effect, concludeth it to be according to *Crisippus. Scientiam rerum perferendarum, the science, or knowledge to suffer thinges, or affectionem animi in patiendo, & preferendo, humanæ legi parentem, an affection of the mind, obeying the highest, and cheefe law, in bearing, or suffring with patience.* And againe, in an other place, he saith, that as Fortitude, *is most proper to man, so it consisteth principally in the contempt of death, sorrow, or payne.* And finally *Seneca* affirmeth that the highest, and most perfect part, or vertue in man, is to suffer all maner of trouble, and aduersitie with alacritie. Whereby we may see, that although courage to assault, or offend an enemie, in a iust cause, is verie requisit to fortitude: yet the speciall commendation, and praise thereof, consisteth in he contempt, and patient suffring of death, or paine: it being most euident, that it is not onlie farre more difficult, but also more contrarie to our infirme nature, to sustaine, and suffer death, or torment then to assault an enemie: and the reason why cowards dare not encounter or assaile other men, or vndertake great attempts, is the feare they haue of death, or of some paine, and harme, and he which is resolut ta endure, and, suffer death

Aristotle. Ethic.li. 3.c. 6.7.8.& 9.
Tuscul. quest.li.4.
Ibid.li 2.
Seneca. praefect.li.3. natural. quest.

cannot want courage to aſſault, or attempt, and conſequentlie hee hath both the conditions requiſit to fortitude.

26 And in this reſpect, our Sauiour Chriſt (who was the maſter, & true mirrour of al vertue) chooſe rather to ſhew his moſt eminent fortitude in ſuffring, then in attempting, wherein alſo the glorious Martirs of his Church haue imitated him, and thereby excelled all other ſorts of men in the vertue of fortitude, ſeeing, as I haue ſaid, it is moſt manifeſt, that thoſe who haue courage, and force to endure vnſpeakeable torments. and cruel death, that our Marters (as well women and children, as men) haue ſuffred would haue bene as readie to attempt anie thinge whatſoeuer poſſible to man, or to aſſaile whole armies of men, if reſpect of concience, and their dutie had required it: whereuppon it foloweth that Chriſtians, who by *Machiauels* owne confeſſion doe place fortitude, rather in ſuffring, then in attempting, and ſhew farre greater reſolution, and courage therein, then euer the Painimes did, doe not onlie conceiue trulie of the nature, & office of that moſt excellent vertue, but alſo haue it in the higheſt degree, and greateſt perfection that may be, whereby it appeareth that *Machiauels* ſecond reaſon, againſt the valour of Chriſtians, ſerueth for no other pur, poſe, but to diſcouer his ignorance, and to proue the Chriſtians to be farre more valiant, then the Painimes, which he abſurdlie denieth.

27 It reſteth now, that I examine a third reaſon, which he giueth to the ſame purpoſe, affirming that the ancient Painimes were more valiant, thē the Chriſtians are, becauſe they were more diſpoſed thereto by the vſe of bloudy repreſentations, and ſpectacles, as of the continuall ſlaughter of beaſtes, which were dailie ſacrifized euerie where, and of the combats of the gladiators, vſed ordinarilie amongſt the *Romans*, in ſight and preſence of all the people.

28 But if this reaſon were good, it would folow, that butchers, & thoſe which dwell neere about the butchery, or ſhambles, and barber ſurgeōs, which vſe dailie to let men bloud, yea, and hangmen, or other mineſters of iuſtice, who are accuſtomed to kill, and quarter men, should bee verie valiant, and eſpecially the people of *Mexico* in the weſt *Indye*; before they were conquered by the Chriſtians, should alſo by this reaſon, haue excelled in valour, and fortitude, ſeeing they vſed to ſacrifice men in ſuch aboundance, that ſometimes fiue thouſand were ſacrifized in *Mexico* in one day, and yet neuertheles *Hernando Cortes* the Spaniard with a handfull of men, I meane ſome ſix, or ſeauen hundreth, ouerthrew manie thouſands of them in diuers battayles, and in the end conquered their country.

Acoſta; Hiſto. India occid.

29 And no maruaile, ſeeing that the vſe, & cuſtome of shedding bloud, doth rather induce men to a beaſtlie ferity, fiercnes, and cruell, then to

true

true valour, for which cause butchers, and hangmen, and such other ministers of iustice, are in our countrie, excluded from Iuries of life, & death, as cruell, and merciles men, who may consequentlie, bee presumed to bee cowardlie, and fearefull, and therefore farre from true valour, seeing that cowardise, and cruelty doe commonlie concurre: which *Mauritius* the Emperour, obserued, and iustlie feared in *Phocas*, who after slew him, and his children: for when *Philippicus* tould *Mauritius* that *Phocas* was cowardlie, and fearefull, then saith *Mauritius*, hee is cruell, and bloudie, as I haue signified more at large, vppon an other occasion, in the [g] first part of this treatise.

Zouar. Annal. to. 3. Nicephor. li. 18. c. 41. Baron. an. 602. Paul. Diacon. li. 16. in fine. & alij.

30 So that whereas true valour, and magnanimitie (which neuer passe the limits of reason) are according to the doctrin of all philosophers, allwaies accompanied with humanitie, and pietie, and compassion: this Archpoliticke *Macheauel*, imagineth a kind of valour, fraught with beastlie inhumanitie, and bloudie cruelltie, and disposeth men thereto, by horrible, and inhumane spectacles of murdring combats, & effusion of bloud, the custome whereof, though it may seeme some way to mitigate, and temper the exorbitance of feare, yet prouoketh, and draweth men in the end to feritie, and cruelltie, which as I haue said, is commonlie, seconded, with temiditie, and cowardise, and can neuer accompanie true valour, and fortitude.

g *Chap. 35. nu. 30.*

31 But what should I say of his other fond deuise, in reiecting, our Christian names, and preferring the names of Painimes, as more fit for common welth? As though *Alexander* the great, or *Iulius Cæsar*, *Pompey*, or *Brutus*, or anie other Infidle, may be compared with our Christians in vertue, seeing I haue made it manifest, [a] heretofore, that though some Painimes had the fame, and commendation of some one, or a few vertues, yet none of them had euer anie perfection of vertue, and that the same, cannot bee had but onlie by Gods grace, which is proper to Christian religion: In which respect our Christians, following the example, & doctrin of our Sauiour Christ, and being assisted with his grace, and holie spirit, arriue to the highest perfection of vertue, that humane frailtie, may possiblie attaine vnto: wherevppon it foloweth, that the vse of our Christian names, is most politicall, seeing they are motiues to draw vs to imitat the most holie, and vertuous exampls of those blessed Saints, whose names, we beare, and so to bee excellent members of our common welth, by practise of all vertue: besides that they doe also admonish, & moue vs to craue their helpe, and succour, and to obtaine Gods mercifull assisttance, by their intercession, for our selues, and for the common wealth, with exceeding great benefit to both: as I would shew heere by manie

First part. 10 chap. nu. 11. 12. 13. 14. 2. part. chap. 15. & 16.

reasons, and examples, were it not that I haue sufficientlie performed it alreadie in the a first part of this treatise, when I treated of miraculous victories, and shewed by euident examples, not onlie that true valour, & fortitude, is the speciall gift of God, and that all good successe, and victorie in warre proceedeth of gods will, and fauour, but also that manie townes, and citties, whole prouinces, countries, kingdomes, and armies haue bene verie oft defended, and concerued, miraculouslie by the patronage and protection of Angels, and Saints. As the citty of a *Sergiopolis* deliuered from the seege of *Cosdroes* king of *Percia*, by *S. Surgius*: b the armie of the kinges *Theodobert*, and *Theodorik* in *France*, assisted against *Clotarius* by an Angel: and an c other armie of *Ariulphus* duke of *Spoleto* in *Italy*, protected, and helped against the *Romans* by *S. Sabinus*: besides the like benefit, and miraculous victorie which d *Pelagius* king of *Spaine* had against the *Sarazens* by the assistance of the blessed virgin *Mary*: as also king e Pepin of *France*, had the like by *S. Swibert*: king f *Alured* in *England*, against the *Danes* by *S, Cutbert*: g *Ronimirus* king of *Leon* in *Spaine*, against the *Moores* by *S. Iames*: h Pope *Iohn* the tenth against the same people in *Apulia*, by *S. Peter*, and *Paule*: i *Zimisces* Emperour of *Constantinople*, against the *Scithians*, by *S. Theodorus* the martir: k *Godfroy* of *Bullen* against the *Turkes*, *Sarizens*, and *Persians*, by an apparition, and admonition of *S. andrew*: l *Alphonsus* the eight king of Castil, against the *Sarizens*, by the blessed virgin *Mary*, m The knights of the *Rhodes* against the *Turkes*, by a Saint, or Angel, who fought for them in the aire: n The king of *Congo*, a Christian in *Ethiopia*, against his brother an Infidel, by the inuocation of the holie name of Iesus, and of *S. Iames*: o The towne of *Guintium* in *Hungary* against *Solymon* the Emperour of the *Turkes* by an Angel, who appeared, and fought on horsebake in the aire: and finally that the p castle of *S. Elmo* in *Malta*, was defended against a potent army of the same *Soliman* in the last age, by the glorious virgin *Mary*, *S. Paule*, and *S. Iohn Baptist*: Of all which examples I declared the particuliers in the fifteene chapter, of the first part of this treatise, and therefore content my selfe to haue onlie touched the same breefflie here in this place, to the end it may appeare what soueraigne benefit wee Christians and our common welth, haue by the protection of Angels, and Saints. whereuppon I conclude, that seeing the vse of their names may animat vs, not onlie to emitate their most excellent vertues, but also to seeke, and procure their helpe, and succur, as well in our publike, as our priuat distresses it followeth that the same are without comparison more behouefull vnto vs, and fit for common welth, then the

Chap 15. per totum

a *an.* 544. *procopius de bello Goth.*

b *an.* 601. *Aimon. li.* 4. *c.* 87. & 88.

c *an.* 602. *Paul. Dicon. li.* 4. *c.* 5.

d *an.* 718. *Rodericus Toletan. l.* 4. *c* 2. *vassaus. chro.*

e *an.* 749. *Baron. to.* 9. *hoc anno.*

f *an.* 880. *Polidor. Vergil. li.* 5. *Guliel. Malmesb. li.* 2. *ca.* 4.

g *an.* 825. *Vassæ. in annal. Rodericus li.* 4. *c.* 13.

h *an.* 915. *Sigonius de regno Ital. hoc anno. Luitprandus li.* 2. *c.* 14.

i *eod. Seculo. Ioan. Curopal. hist.*

k *an.* 1098. *Paul. Æmil. in Philip.* 1. *Baron. hoc anno.*

l *an.* 1212. *Roderic. Toletan. l.* 8. *c.* 10

m *an.* 1480. *Naucler. in Chron. Generatio.* 50

n *eod. Seculo. Maffæus histo. India.* o *an.* 1532. *Surius comment. hoc anno.* p *eod. Seculo. Pietro Gentile di Vandonio of the Siege of malta.*

names, of Pagans, and Infidelles, who neither after their deathes can releeue vs, nor in their liues could leaue vs anie example of true, and perfect vertue, but onlie a shadow of some good parts (for so I may rather terme them, then vertues) and those for the most part stained, if not ouerwhelmed with notable vices.

32 For who seeth not, that he which shal propose to himselfe the example of *Alexander* the great (who was held for a mirrour of valour, and fortitude) shall rather become vicius, then trulie valorous, or vertuous, seeing his vices were so manie, and such, that they not onlie drowned his supposed, vertues, but also drew him to his vntimelie death, making him so odious to his best frindes, that they poysoned him? And what true vertue was there in *Iulius Cæser* and *Pompey*, whose prowes, and valour tended to nothing els but to satisfie their insatiable ambition, which in the end distroyed both them, and their common wealth? whereas the volour of Gods fathfull seruants, and saints (as of *Moyses*, *Iosue*, *Gedeon*, *Dauid*, the *Machabees*, and of our christian souldiars, and captaines, *S. Mercury*, *S. George*, *S. Sebastian*, *S. Martin*, *S. Mauritius*, *S. Eustachius*, and manie others) was accompanied with all vertue, with true christian charitie, mansuetude, patience, and humilitie, and neuer tended to other end, but to the seruice of God, and to the good of their countrie? Who then can deny but that the names, and examples of these, are more fit to animate men to perfect magnanimitie, valour, and vertue, then the names and examples, of Painimes, who had neither true valour, not any other vertue in perfection?

33 Now then to cõclude concerning these obiections of *Machiauel*, & his reasons, I doubt not but thou seest good Reader what a graue, and learned doctour the world hath got of this Archpolitike, who to make good his new doctrin (which was deuised, no dout by the diuel for the destruction of men, and common welths) not onlie impugneth, the Christian religion, Which he him selfe professed, but also frameth an other morall philosophy, then hath hetherto bene heard of in the world, all tending to the establishment of an inhumane barbarous, and tirannicall pollicy, which howsoeuer it is admired of sensuall, and ignorant men, yet being waighed in the balance of reason, and tried with the touchstone of true, and solied learning, presentlie bewrayeth both the ignorance, and the malice of the forger, or author thereof. And this shall suffise touching him vntill an other occasion be offred.

That the Christian religion which geueth true felicitie to common welth, is no other, but the Catholike Roman *religion, because the same onlie hath the true Christian, and Euangelicall perfection, consisting in the imitation of Christ: and that consequentlie it hath the onlie meanes to vnit man with God.*

Chap. 25.

1 I Hope, good Reader, thou hast alreadie sufficientlie seene in the precedent discourse, aswell the veritie of Christian religion as also the dignitie, excelencie and necessitie of it in common wealth, seeing I haue euidentlie proued the admirable effect thereof in vniting man with God, wherein consisteth not onlie the perfection of religion, but also the true felicitie of man, and common wealth. And therefore I will now accomplish the rest of my promise, & shew that the christian religion whereof I haue hitherto treated, is no other but our Catholik religion, so called to distinguish it from the sects that professe also the fayth of Christ in these dayes. And this I shall performe sufficiently, if I proeue, as I hope to doe, two thinges, properly belonging to this subiect, The one is, that no other religion but the Catholike Roman hath the meanes before declared to vnite man, and common welth with God. The other is, that all the sects of these dayes, doe hold, and teach many poynts of doctrin, repugnant both to the verity of Christian religion, and also to true pollicy wherein neuertheles I meane not to treat particulerly of the opinions of euery sect (for it would require a larger discourse then can stand with, my present intention) but only to touch principally *Lutheranisme*, and *Caluinisme*, concerning those poynts only where in they, and all other sects for the must part agree, amongst themselues, and dissent from the Church of Rome, and therefore prouing my intent in them I shall proue yt in all the rest.

2 Now then to speake of the meanes that are in our Catholike Roman Religion to beatify man, and common welth, thou mayst remember, good Reader, that I haue amply proued three thinges, both by philosophy, and diuinity. The first is, that the end, and felicity both of man in this life, and
Chap. 4. 20. & 21. of common welth, consisteth in mans vnion with almighty God specially by the meanes of contemplation. The second is, that in this vnion with
Chap. 17. & 21. God there is such ineffable sweetenes, and delectation, that it may worthily be counted mans felicity in this life. The third, that the only way and meanes for man, and common welth to attayne to this vnion with God, and felicity, is the perfection of Christian religion, consisting in true

true faith perfect charity, contempt of the world, abnegation of our selues, pouerty of spirit, chastity, and purity of heart, mortification of our passions, & affections, the continual vse of the sacramens of Gods Church, and finally meditation, and mental prayer, all which concurring together, doe make that true Christian contemplation, which I haue proued to be the end, and felicity of man in this life, and of common welth. And therefore, if I shew that all this concurreth in most excellent manner in our Catholike religion, and that no other hath any vse, or true knowledge thereof, it cannot be denyed, but that I proue the same, to be that true Christian religion, wherein the happynes of man, & common welth consisteth. *Chap.18.19. 20.& 21.*

3 This I hope to proue clearely by euident reasons, and by manifest experience, both which doe couince that the Euangelicall perfection which our Sauiour taught, as well by his example, as by his doctrin is, and alwayes hath bene practised only in the Roman Church. Therefore whereas the perfection of Christs doctrin consisteth partly in his Precepts, partly in his Counsels (as I will make it manifest heareafter) I will now declare for the present; first, what were the Counsels of our Sauiour, Secondly that not only his Apostles, but also infinit other Christians in theyr tyme, obserued the same, Thirdly that there vppon grew the contemplatiue, and religious life, instituted first by the Apostles themselues, and after propagated throughout all Christendome, and deryued to our tyme by the most worthy, and famous men that haue bene in the Church of God: And lastly, that the Roman Catholikes hauing the true practise of our Sauiours Counsels in religious disciplyn, haue also the true meanes to arryue to perfect vnion with God, which is the end, and felicity of man and common welth.

4 For although not only religious men, but also euery man of any lawfull state, or vocation, may be a perfect Christian, and vnited with God (as I haue amply proued in the 22. and 23. chapters) yet, for as much, as there are two kyndes of perfection, and diuers degrees therein, if I proue that the highest degree of Christian perfection consisteth in the obseruation of the euangelicall Counsels, and that the Catholike Roman Church, hath the true vse, and practise thereof, yt must needes be graunted, that the same Church, hath the highest degree of Christian perfection: which being proued, it will also follow, that it hath all the inferiour degrees subordinate thereto, and consequently that it hath all the perfection of Christian religion.

5 The Counsels of our Sauiour (which comprehend in them selues all the perfection of his precepts) consist principally in three things, to wit,

voluntary

voluntary pouerty, *chastity* and *obedience*, which are called his Counsells, to distinguish them from his Precepts (to the obseruation whereof, euery man is bound (where as no man is bound to obserue his Counsels, farther then he list to bynd himselfe, and therefore our Sauyour inuited and encouraged vs thereto, with the proposition, and promise of extraordinary rewards: for as we see in all well gouerned common welths, that extraordinary remunerations are giuen to those, that doe heroycall acts whereto, they are not bound by the law (as amongst the *Romans* besydes, the ordinary pay ordayned for euery souldyar there were dyuers crownes, and other particuler honours appoynted for such as shewed extraordinary valour, and did notable seruices, beyond theyr obligation) so also our Sauiour ordayned in his law singuler, and specall rewards for those which shal performe the heroycal acts of his Counsels, whereto he bound no man.

6 And although yt may perhaps be expected that before I passe further I should proue, the same more amply, as also that there is a distinction to be obserued in the scriptures betwixt our Sauiours Counsells, and his Precepts (which our aduersaryes deny) yet because I meane to performe both the one, and the other, very fully hereafter when I shall treat of euery euangelical Counsel in particuler (which I intend to doe only in generall) I will therefore content my selfe for the present, to shew the groundes in the holy scripture, from whence we deduce our Sauiours Counsels, and then proceede to declare how they were performed by the Apostles, and other Christians in theyr tyme, and deriued from them to vs by a continuall succession of doctrin, and practise.

7 The first euangelical Counsel whereof I spoke, was *voluntary pouerty* which our Sauiour counselled, when he sayd, to the rich yong man. *Si vis perfectus esse, &c. Yf thou wilt be perfect, goe, and sell all that thou hast, and giue it to the poore, and thou shalt haue a treasure in heauen.* (*Matth.19.*) The second, which was *chastity*, he aduised, when speaking of the theree kynds of Eunuchs, and particulerly of those who held themselues for the kingdome of heauē (by volūtary chastity) (*Ibid.*) he added, *qui potest capere capiat, he that can take it, let him take it.* The third (which was *obedience*) or rather al three together he counselled, when he sayd. *Qui vult venire post me abneget semetipsum, tollat crucem suam, & sequatur me. He which wil come after me, let him deny himselfe take vp his crosse and follow me.* (*Matth. 16. Marc. 8.*) In which words he included al religious perfection consisting in the imitation of him, in his perfect obedience to his voluntary pouerty, in his most chast and single life, in the abnegation of himselfe, and in the cariage of his crosse wherin is added in *S. Luke*, *quotidie, euery day*, (*Luc. 9.*) giuing to vnderstand, that he which will follow our Sauiour Christ, as he aduiseth must not onlie beare with patience,

the crosses and afflictions which now ,and then may by chaunce fall vppon him,or bee laid one him by others, but also must dailie cary his owne crosse, that is to say *crucifie his owne flesh*;as the Apostle saith,*with the concupiscences thereof*,mortifiyng his passions and affections,with continuall penance,and austeritie of life. Gal.5

7 These were the Counsels of our Sauiour,which not onlie he himselfe,but also his Apostles practised, and performed, as appeareth by that which *S. Peter* said to him,*Ecce* saith he, *reliquimus omnia, & secuti sumus te,quid ergo erit nobis? Behould Lord, wee haue forsaken al that we had & haue followed thee, what therefore shal we haue?* In which words of *S. Peter*, are included these three pointes of perfection before mentioned, as the two first (to wit,*pouertie and continency*) in that he said we haue forsaken all thinges, whereby as *S. Ierome* noteth against *Iouinian*, it is signified, that such of them as were maryed, had leaft their wiues,aswell as their parents, and substance (for otherwaise they leaft not all) and this hee also confirmeth by the answere of our Sauiour to *S. Peter*, wherein hee made mention of wiues, saying.*whosoeuer shall forsake his house,or brethren, or sisters, or father, or mother, or wife, or lands, for my name, he shall receaue a hundreth fold,and haue life euerlasting.* Matth.19 D'Hierom.li 1.in Iouin. Matth.19.

8 Also *S. Hierome* affirmeth, that though some of the Apostles,were maryed before their apostelship yet afterwardes, they had no vse of their wiues. And in an other place he saith,that al the *Apostles were either virgins, or post nuptias continentes, continent after their mariage..* Hieron.vbi supra. & Apol.ad. Pam.

9 Furthermore their *obedience* was also signified in that *S.Peter* said. *Secuti sumus te, wee haue folowed thee.* Meaning that they had resigned them selues wholie to him, to obey him as their Lord, obseruing exactlie his commaundements, and instructions, as his disciples, subiects,and seruants.

10 And these vertues were not practised onlie by the Apostles, but also by innumerable other Christians,in their time,partlie seuerallie,& partlie ioyntlie: for we read in the acts of the Apostles, that verie many of the first Christians in *Hierusalem*,liued in common,hauing sold all their possessions,and goods, and laid the price thereof, at the Apostles feete, and that Ananias, and *Saphira* were both of them punished by *S. Peter* with suddaine death, for retaining part of the price of that which they had sold. We read also, that manie vsed in the same time, not onlie to abstaine from mariage and liue continent, but also to bind themselues thereto by vow, as the widowes did, which were receiued to the ministerie or office of women Deacons, of whome *S.Paule* saith, that they had *a will to marry, hauing damnation because they had broken their* Act.4. bidem.c.5. Timoth.5.

first faith, that is to say, their vow of continency, and chastitie, as shall be decleared further hereafter.

11 Also the acts of the Apostls doe testify, that *Philip* the Deacon had foure daughters virgins who (as yt appeareth by the testimony of *Policrates*, alleadged by *Eusebius*) remayned virgins all theyr lyues. And *Martialis*, a disciple of our Sauiour, saith of himselfe, that he perswaded *Valeria* the virgin, to vow her chastitie to God. And *Abdias* witnesseth that *S. Mathew* the Apostle, did consecrat *Iphigenia*, the daughter of a king in *Ethiopia*, to the seruice of God, that is to say, hee did veil her (as the custome is still in the Church) to serue God in virginitie. And *S. Ambrose*, *S. Epiphanius*, and diuers others testifie, that *Thecla* being conuerted to the Christian faith by *S. Paule*, did by his instruction, and persuasion, forsake her spouse, to whome she was handfast, and remained a virgin. And no maruaile that *S. Paule* moued her thereto, seeing hee exhorted all men, and women to a single, and continent life, after his owne example, *volo*, saith hee, *omnes esse sicut meipsum. I desire that all men may be as I am*, that is to say vnmaried, and continent, of which point I shall haue occasion to speake more amplie heareafter, for here my meaning is, but to insinuat these thinges concerning the Euangelicall Counsel of *Chastitie*, leauing the further discourse, and proofe thereof to other occasions, which willbee offred heareafter, as I haue signified before.

12 Therefore to proceede; not onlie *pouertie and continency*, but also *obedience* was practised ioyntlie with them in the Apostles time in a retired religious, and contemplatiue life, consisting in the practise of those three vertues, and in all kind of mortification, as appeareth euidentlie by that which diuers ancient Fathers, and other approued autours doe testifie of great numbers of Christians, embracing that maner of life, vnder *S. Marke* the *Euangelist*, at *Alexandria* in Egipt, where hee was bishop.

13 And for as much, as all Christian perfection (consisting in the obseruation of our Sauiours Counselles) was exercised in that kind of life, at that time, I will relate some perticulers thereof, out of an eye witnes of the same, though hee was himselfe no chirstian, to wit *Philo*, the *Iew*; who in his treatise *de vita contemplatiua*, discribeth the maner of life which the first Christians led at *Alexandria* vnder *S. Marke*; For which cause *S. Ierome* placeth him in his catalouge of our ecclesiasticall writers, *quia librum*, saith he, *de prima Marci &c. because hee wrote a booke of the first Church of S. Marke at Alexandria wherein he greatlie commended our Christians, and signified that they liued not onlie there, but also in diuers other*

Act.21. Euseb.li.3. Eccle.hist. c.30. Martial. ep ad Tholosa. c.8. Abdias in vit.S. Matthei. Baron.in Martyrologio 21.die Septemb. Gregor.Nissen. ho.4. in cant. Ambros.li. 2. de virgin. Epiphan .hæres.78. vide. martyrol. Baron.die.23 Septem. 1.Cor.7. S.Hierom. de script. Ecclesiast. Euseb. Eccl. hist.li. 2.ca. 16. Cassian. li.2. ca.5.& collat 18.ca.5. Philo. de vita.contemplat. S. Hieron.de scriptor. ecclesiast.

other prouinces, and called their houses monasteries. Thus saith *S. Hierome*, and addeth further, *ex quo apparet &c. whereby it appeareth, that the first Church of the faithfull was such, as our monkes doe now desire, and endeuour to bee &c.* *Euseb. eccles. hist. li. 2. c. 16.* *Eusebius* also affirmeth the same of the first Christians in *Alexandria*, alleadging out of the same booke of *Philo*, that those which professed the contemplatiue life in diuers parts, and especially about *Alexandria*, renounced all their possessions, and the care of worldlie busines, that they retired themselues from townes, and cities into the fieldes, and solitarie places, vnder certaine particular heads, or gouernours: That they had a holy place, or dwelling called *Monasterium*, a *Monastery* where they liued, and celebrated their misteries of holie life. That they laid the foundation of continency in their soules, to build other vertues vppon it. That none of them did vse to eate, or drinke, before the sunne was sett, that some of them did not so much as thinke of meate, once in three daies, yea that some abstained six daies together. That their refection was commonlie bread and salt, and their drinke water, and that those which were more delicat then the rest, added somtimes hissop to their bread. That there were also amongest them, ancient and ould women, professing chast life, and contemning the pleasures of the body, who in their congregations, were seperat from the men. That they had the same exercises of reading the holie scriptures, of singing himnes, and psalmes, of fasting, and watching (especially about the time of our Sauiours passion) the verie same saith *Eusebius* that were *Idem ibidem.* vsed in his daies, and finallie, that certaine men, to whome the charge of the ecclesiasticall ministery was committed, gouerned the rest.

14 This with much more, which for breuities sake I omit, is related by *Eusebius* out of *Philo* concerning the contemplatiue, and monasticall life, of the Iewes, conuerted to the Christian faith about *Alexandria*, & diuers other places of *Egipt*, which booke hee intituled, *de vita contemplatiua supplicum, of the contemplatiue life of suppliants*, or those whose speciall office was to pray, and praise God; whome he also calleth in the same booke *Therapeutas*, that is to say, worshippers, giuing to vnderstand, that their contemplation (which he also called philosophie) consisted principallie in praier, and such other thinges as belong properlie to the worship of God.

15 And although *Philo* doth not name those of whome hee writeth *Ioseph. li. 2. de bel. Iud. c. 7. & antiquit. li. 18. ca. 2.* *Christians*, but *Essai*, and therfore may seeme to treat of a sect of the Iewes called by *Iosephus Esseni*, whose institut in some thinges resembled our Christian religion (for so doe our aduersaries say, to answer vs

concerning this testimonie of *Philo*) yet it is to bee vnderstood, first that those *Esseni* which *Iosephus* mencioneth, were farre different from the *Essæi* of whome *Philo* treateth, for that they vsed manie erronious and superstitious thinges, which are not ascribed by *Philo* to the *Essæi*. Secondlie, that there were three different sorts of men, whereof two were called *Esseni*, and the third *Essæi*, or *Iessæi*. The first were *Samaritans*, called *Esseni*, of whome *S. Epiphanius* maketh mention in his booke of heresies. The second were *Iewes*, called also *Essæni*, of whome *Iosephus* treateth largelie in his booke *de antiquitatibus*, *& de bello Iudaico*. The third were *Christians* called *Essæi*, or *Iessæi* (as *S. Epiphanius* readeth it in *Philo*) so named either of *Iesse Dauids* father, or of *Iesu*, because (saith *S. Epiphanius*) they proceeded from him, and beleeued in him, to which purpose hee also noteth, that the faithfull, who first beleeued in *Iesus* Christ, were called *Iessæi*, before they had the name of *Christiani*, which was first giuen then at *Antioch*. And of these *Iessæi* saith *S Ephiphanius*, *Philo* wrote who celebrating their praises, and treating of their monasteries *circa Mariam paludem*, about the marsh, or lake called *Maria non de alijs*, saith he, *narrauit quam de Christianis*, *treated of no other sort of men but of Christians*.

Epiph. de. hæres. hær. 10. li. 1. *Iosephus. vbi supra.* *hæres. 29.* *Act. 11.* *Epipha. vbi supra.*

16 Thus saith *S. Epiphanius*, who was him selfe a *Iew* by birth, and very learned in their lawes, and ceremonies, and therefore could well ynough distinguish betwixt their sects, and the Christians. Besides that not onlie *S. Hierome*, and *Eusebius* (as I haue declared before) but also *Sozomenus*, *S. Bede*, and *Nicephorus* doe plainlie affirme, that the *Essæi*, whose contemplatiue, or monasticall life, *Philo* describeth, were the Christians who liued in *Alexandria*, vnder *S. Marke*: so that no man can denie the same, except he will be so shamlesse to oppose himselfe to the vniforme consent of so manie ancient, and learned Fathers of the Church; and he that list to see further proofe thereof, let him read Cardinall *Baronius* in his first tome, an. 64. where hee handleth this matter amplie, and learnedlie.

Sozom. li. 1. c. 12. Beda. in prologo sup Mar. Niceph, li. 2. c. 16. *Baron. To. 1. an. 64.*

17 Therefore it is euident that monasticall life was instituted by the Apostles themselues, seeing it cannot with anie reason be imagined, that *S. Marke* the holie euangelist, ordained it in *Egipt*, without the consent, or rather the expresse order of *S. Peter*, who conuerted him to the faith of Christ, and loued him so dearelie, that he called him his sonne, and made him bishop of *Alexandria*, and gaue him all his instructions for the writing of his gospell. Besides that it appeareth in *Philo*, that there were the like monasteries, and places designed for Christi an contemplation in diuers parts at the same time aswell in *Greece*, as other coun-

1. Pet. 1. *Philo de vita Contemplat.*

countries, where the Christian faith was receiued, which could not be so generall in the Apostles time amongst Christians, if they (I meane the Apostles) had not bene the cheefe authours thereof.

18 And all this will yet bee much more cleare, if we consider that *S. Dionisius Areopagita*, *S. Paules* disciple, not onlie wrote an Epistle, *ad Demophilum monachum*, to *Demophilus the monke* (wherein he signifieth that he made him monke with his owne hands) but also in his booke of the *ecclesiasticall Hiearchy*, hee deriueth the institution of monasticall life, and the verie name of *Monke*, from the Apostles themselues saying *Diuini preceptores nostri &c. Our deuine masters, or teachers* (for so hee calleth the Apostles) *would haue them to be named partlie Therapeutas*, that is ta say *worshippers, and partlie Monachos, Monkes, by reason of their pure worship, and seruice of God, and of their solitarie, and vndeuided life, whereby they become one, by the holie coniunction of thinges deuided, to the end they may attaine to perfection, gratefull to God, and to a deuine vnion.* Thus saith he, and afterwardes hee describeth, and explicateth the rites, and ceremonies, whereby the monkes of that time were consecrated, and dedicated to the seruice of God. *Dionis. ep. ad demo, hil. monachum.* *Dion. de eccl Hierar. ca. 10*

19 For first hee saith, that the priest standing before the Aultar, pronounced a prayre fit for that purpose, and the same being finished, approched to the partie that was to be professed, and asked him, whether he was fully resolued to renounce his secular life, and to seperate himselfe wholie from it; and when the partie had made a full promise, and couenant thereof (for so signifieth the greeke word) the priest declared vnto him, that most perfect manner of life, which he was to vndertake, admonishing him that he ought from thence forth to excell the common sort of men in life and manners, being now to become of the highest, and most perfect order of men, and that being a monke, or religious man, he might not doe manie things, which be lawfullie donne by men of the inferiour order, because his end, and intention was to be ioyned, and vnited with almighty God: And after this *S. Dionisius* sheweth how the preist signed the partie with the signe of the crosse, & cut of his haire, calling vppon the blessed Trinitie, and that then he tooke of his clothes, and vested him anew, and finallie, that when all those which were present had saluted him, and congratulated with him, the priest gaue him the holie Communion.

20 And this being declared, by *S. Dionisius*, then hee explicateth the reason of these ceremonies, geuing to vnderstand that he which was to be professed, was signed with the crosse, to signifie that he was to die, to concupiscence, crucifiyng, and mortifiyng in himselfe all carnall

desires :and that his haire was cut of, to the end, he might vnderstand that he was from thence forth, to cast of all humane, and earthlie ornaments, and to labour to make himselfe acceptable to God, by the onlie beautie of his soule: that his change of garment did signifie the change of his mind, and admonished him, that asmuch as his habit did differ from the common habit, so much ought hee to differ in manners from the common sorte of men: That the congratulations of the assistants, did represent vnto him the ioy which as our Sauiour said, the Angels in heauen haue for a soule that is ioyned with God: and lastlie that hee communicateth of the blessed body of our Sauiour Christ, to the end hee might vnderstand for what cause principally that institute of monasticall life was ordained, to wit, to the end that man might thereby arriue to perfect coniunction & vnion with almighty God.

21 Thus much I haue thought good to alleadge out of *S. Dionisius*, & whereas our aduersaries (or at least manie of them, not knowing how to answer him otherwayes) doe denie his workes, as not writen by him (because *Eusebius*, and *S. Hierome* make no mention of them) it may appeare, how little reason they haue, if we consider two thinges: the one that both a *Eusebins* & b *S. Hierome* do acknowledg that there were many authours before their time, whome they had not seene: and the other, that not onlie diuers ancient Fathers, but also the c sixt generall Counsel hath aleadged, and highlie esteemed them. For d *S. Cyril* bishop of *Alexandria* who liued, & florished in *S. Hieromes* time, citeth his workes, as *Liberatus* testifieth e *S. Greg.* the great, who also wrot about a 1000. yeares agoe, alleadgeth him, and calleth him *an ancient, and venerable Father.* f *S. Iohn Damascen.* g *Euthymius*:, & other verie learned, and ancient authours, doe also cite his workes: Besides that diuers of our aduersaries themselues doe partlie alledge him, & partlie acknowledge him for a verie ancient writer of the primitiue Church: For h master *Fulk* thinketh that this *Dionisius*, whose workes wee haue vnder the name of *Areopagita*, liued in *Origens* time, which was longe before *Eusebius*, and *S. Hierome.* i M. *Sutlif*, calleth him *the most ancient, and best witnes of antiquitie.* k Doctor *Humphrey* confesseth that *Gregorius Turonensis*, & *Michaell Singelus* (who wrote aboue a thousand yeares agoe) and *Suydas* did beleeue that *Dionisius Areopagita*, *S. Paules scholler*, was author of the *cælestis, and ecclesiastica Hiearchia*: out of the which this testimony concerning Monkes is taken. Also my Lord of l *Canturbury* writing against the Puritans, alleadgeth *Dionisius Ariopagita de cælesti Hierachia.* Besides others of our aduersaries mentioned together with these before named, by the learned authour of the Apology of the Roman Church, an excellent

worke

a *Eusebius. eccle: hist. li. 5. c. 26.*
b. *S. Hierom. in Catologo. scriptor.*
c. *sinod. Constantinopol. 6. Act. 4.*
d. *S. Cyrill Alexandrin apud Liberat. in Breuiario. ca. 10.*
e. *S. Greg: ho. 34. in euangel.*
f. *S. Ioan. Damascen. li. 1 de fide orthod. ca. 15.*
g. *Euthimius in Panoplia. par. 1. tit. 2.*
h. *Fulk against the Remish testament in. 2. Thess. 2 sect. 19.*
i. *Sutlif de presbyterio. ca. 13.*
k. *Doctor Humphrey in Iesuitis. par. 2. rat. 5. pag. 513.*
l. *In his answver to the admonition. pag. 105. sect vlt. see the Apology of the Romā Church. sect. 3. nu. 4. & num. 13.*

worke latelie published. And if anie man desire to be further satisfied, touching these workes of *S. Dionisius*, let him read the second tome of Cardinall *Baronius* anno. 109 with the appendix belonging thereto, where he clearelie proueth them to be his, and fully answereth whatsoeuer can be said to the contrary.

Baron. anno. 104.

22 Yt is therefore euident in this most ancient, & famous Father, that contemplatiue, & monasticall life was ordained by the Apostles themselues, and that the perfection of Christian religion consisteth therein by reason of the vnion with God, which is obtained thereby, in respect whereof hee calleth men of that profession, not onlie *Therapeutas* or *cultores*, as *Philo* doth, but also *Monachos*, *Monkes*, because (as he saith, they forsake all multiplicitie, to vnite themselues to the true vnity, that is to say, to God himselfe. And both hee, and *Philo* doe also call monasticall discipline, *philosophy*, because religious men, who professe the same, doe hould the same place amongst the Christians, that the Philosophers held amongst the Gentills, professing contempt of the world and the study of wisdome: & therefore *S. Chrisostome* commonlie calleth *Monkes* or religious men, *Philisophers*, and *Nilus* writting of monasticall life, intituled his booke *de Christiana Philosophia*, of Christian Philosophy, because it is the consummation of the philosophy of the Gentils, which tending to the contemplation of God, and vnion with him, by the exercise of the morall vertues (as I haue declared) cannot possiblly arriue thereto, without the helpe of this Christian philosophy, consisting in the heauenlie doctrin of our Sauiour Christ: who being wisdome it selfe, infuseth into the soules of his seruants, both true knowledge, & true vertue, and so both teacheth, and giueth the meanes to attaine to the perfection of vertuous life, and consequently to that perfect vnion with God which is the end of all true philosophy.

Dionis. Areop. vbi supra. Philo de vita contemplat.

Chrisostome. ho. 17. ad pop. Antio. ho. 11. in Act. & li. 3. contra vituperat. vita monastica. Nilus de Christ. philosophia. Chap. 17.

23 To conclud this point concerning the first institution of monasticall discipline, and religious life, all the ancient Fathers of the Church, do referr it to the time of the Apostles, yea and that *S. Chrisostome* called it *philosophiam a Christo introductam*, *a philosophy brought into the world by Christ*: and saith also, that Monkes in his time, did liue as all the faithfull liued in *Hierusalem*, in the beginning of the Church, and that the Apostles performed all that, which those monkes did practise, and this no doubt they did in the highest degree of contemplation, and Christian perfection. *Ioannes*, *Cassianus* also saith, that *Cænobitarum disciplina, a tempore prædicationis apostolicæ sumpsit exordium*. The discipline of monasticall, or religious men, began in the time, that the Apostles preached.

Chrysos. ho. 17. ad Pop. hom. 11. in Act. li. 3. cant. vituperat, vita. monast.

Cassian. collat. 18. c. 5.

The same is also affirmed, not onlie by *S. Ephiphanius*, *S. Hierom*, *Eusebius*

S.Epiph. har. 29. S.Hieroni. de script. eccles. in philone. Euseb.li.2. ca 16. Sozom.li 1. ca.12. Aug. ser 2.de commun. vit cleric. Possid.in vit Augustini. Isidor.li.2. de offic.ca.15. Nicephor. li. 2.ca.16.

Eusebius and *Sozomenus* (as may appeare by that which I alleaged out of them before) but also by *S. Augustin*, *Possidonius*, *Isidorus*, *and Nicephorus*, to omit manie other later then they.

24 Well then seeing, that the perfection of this our Christian philophy, consisteth, as I haue shewed in the exercise of our Sauiours counsells, that is to say, of *voluntarie pouerty, chastitie, and obedience*, and that the same was practised in all perfection, not onlie by our Sauiour himselfe and his Apostles, but also by innumerable Christians in their times, yea and that euen then began the practise of this contemplatiue, and monasticall life, tending to a perfect vnion with God: it resteth now, that I proue, and make it euident, that onlie the Roman Catholikes haue at this day (as euer hetherto they haue had) both the perfect exercise of this Christian philosophie, and also that perfect vnion with God, wherein consisteth the hapines of man: of both which points, I shall not neede to produce anie other proofe, then experience. First then I will speake of the first point, and after of the second, and shew that the Roman Catholikes haue them both in all perfection, and afterwards I will make it cleare, that their aduersaries haue neither of both in any sorte.

Dionis.eccles. Hierar.c. 10.

25 And to the end it may appeare, aswell in this matter, as in others, which I shall handle hereafter, that our catholike religion, is deriued by a continuall course, and succession of doctrin, and practise from the time of the Apostles, and that therefore it is that true christian religion which they taught, and deliuered vnto vs, I will deduce the exercise of this contemplatiue, or religious life from their time, to these our daies, though in diuers orders of religion, yet all agreeing in substance, that is to say, in the obseruation of our Sauiours counsels aforesaid.

Damas.in vita Telesphо. an. 117. 20.q.c 1.c. virgines. an. 147. Soter.ep.2. an. 161. Hierom. catal.scriptor. Eccles.an.193 Tritemius de script eccl.

26 I haue alreadie shewed, that the contemplatiue, or religious life, was instituted in the first age after Christ (as *S. Dionisius* affirmeth) by the Apostles themselues, who hee saith named those religious persons (whose solemne profession he describeth) *cultores, & Monachos worshippers and monkes*. And there is no doubt, but that the same manner of life, was continued both in men, & women, during al the time of the primitiue Church, whereof we find sufficient testimonie. For wee read, that *S. Telesphorus*, who was pope in the second age, whiles *S. Dionisius* liued, was an *Anchor*, or *hermit*, before he was pope, and that the popes *Pius*, & *Soter*, who liued also in the same age, made certaine decrees, concerning Nunnes, or religious women, consecrated, and dedicated to the seruice of God: and that *Serapion* bishop of *Antioch* also in the same age, professed religious disciplin.

27 This

27 This also further appeareth in an epistle of *S. Ignatius* disciple to *S. Iohn* the Euangelist, who writing to the *Tarsenses*, commaundeth them to honour the virgins that were dedicated to God, and exhorted the virgins themselues to remember, and acknowledge to whome they were consecrated: and in his epistle to the *Phillippenses*, maketh mencion of colledges of virgins: Also S. *Iustin* the Martyr, *Clemens Alexandrinus*, & *Origen*, doe write of religious virgins in their dayes, which was also the second age. *Ignat. ep. ad Tarsens. Idem. ad Philip. ep. 8. S. Iustin. in Apolg. 2. Clemens. Alex. li. 2. stromat. Origen. ho. 17. & 19. in Lucam.*

28 In like manner *Tertullian* in the same age wrote a treatise, yet extant, *de velandis virginibus, of veyling virgins* (that is to say, of consecrating them to the seruice of God) distinguishing them from secular virgins, and declaring their obligation, to serue God in perpetual chastity, and in the habite which they had taken vppon them: For, speaking of some who had presumed to bereeue them of their religious habite, he exclaimeth against them, and saith, *O sacrilegæ manus &c. O sacriligious hands, which could take of the habit dedicated to God!* And after againe, he maketh expresse mention of their vow of continency, and giueth to vnderstand, that they made *an oblation* to God *of body, & soule*, & that they *consecrated their whole substance, and essence vnto him:* and lastlie he saith, that *they were maried to Christ, and had deliuered their flesh to him*: And the like saith *S. Cyprian*, in the third age, in his booke intituled *de disciplina, & habitu virginum, of the disciplin, and habit of virgins. Quæ* saith he, *se Deo dicauerint & a carnali concupiscentia recedentes tam carne, quam mente, se Deo vouerint, who haue dedicated, and vowed themselues to God, abstayning from al carnal concupiscence of body, and mynd.* Thus saith *S. Cyprian* of the religious virgins in his time. And in the same age *S. Dionysius* the pope, and martyr, was a monke before he was bishop of *Rome*. Besides that, wee read that in the persecution of *Dioclesian* and *Maximian*, monasteries of men, & religious women were subuerted, & some of the virgins sent to the stewes, whose chastitie God preserued, and defended miraculously. *Tertuli. de velan. virgin. Ibid. ca. 11. Ibid. c. 13. S. Cipryan. de discipli. & habitu. Virginum. Damas. in vita Dionis. Baron. an. 301*

29 And *S. Athanasius* witnesseth, that Monkes liued in monasteries in the fields, not farre from townes, and cityes before *S. Antonies* time (who was borne in the yeare two hundreth and fifty) and that the said *S. Antony* being yong, and desirous to dedicat his life wholie to the seruice of God, tooke example, & instructions of those monks, and especially of an old man, who from his youth had professed monastical life: Whereby it appeareth, how false it is which the *Magdeburgenses*, in their historie affirme, to wit, that *S. Antony* began monasticall disciplin, seeing that hee learned it of old monkes, when hee himselfe was very young, though indeede it pleased God greatlie to amplifie and *S. Athan. in vita Anton. Magdeburg. cent. 4. ca. 6.*

propagat religious, and monaſticall profeſſion vnder him, who being but eighteene yeares of age, and hearing in the goſpell our Sauiours
S. Athanaſ. in vita.S. Anton.
Counſell to the rich yong man (that if he would bee perfect he ſhould ſell all hee had, and giue it to the poore) ſould the greateſt part of his poſſeſſions, and beſtowed the mony in almes: and ſhortlie after, hearing againe by an other place in the goſpell, that our Sauiour commaunded vs not to be ſollicitous, or ouer carefull for to morow, he ſould all the reſt, and gaue the money to the poore, and retyring himſelfe into the deſerts of *Egipt*, grew to bee of ſo great fame for his rare vertue, and drew vnto him ſo many diſciples, that at laſt he peopled the deſerts, not only of *Egipt*, but alſo of *Armenia*, and *Nitria*, with monaſteries, of Monks, and Nunnes.

30 Alſo *S. Hilarion* by the example, and inſtructions of *S. Antony*, replenished *Siria*, and *Paleſtina*, and all the eaſt parts with monaſteries, as may appeare by that which I haue alleadegd before in the fifetenth chapter, out of *Palladius*, & *Theodoretus*, when I treated of the admirable
Chap.15.
effect of gods grace in Chriſtian Religion: where alſo it may be ſeene in what ſanctitie, mortification, and abnegation of themſelues, they
Auguſt.de moribus.eccl.
liued, practiſing (as before I haue ſignified) the vertues, of *voluntarie pouerty, chaſtity, & obedience*, in all perfection, wherevppon *S. Auguſtin* ſaith to the *Maniches* in his treatiſe, *de moribus eccleſiæ*: Behould ſaith he,
“the excellency of perfect Chriſtians, the pouertie of their liues, and
“their ſingular continency, and chaſtitie. But you cannot bee ignorant
“of that which I am about to tell you, for who knoweth not what a
“multitude of moſt religious Chriſtians is diſperſed throughout the
“world, and eſpeciallie in the eaſt, and in *Egipt*. I ſpeake not of thoſe
“which dwell in Hermitages in the deſert, but of them who being wor-
“thy of al admiration, and praiſe, doe diſpiſe al the pleaſures, and de-
“lights of the world, and aſſemble themſelues into monaſteries, where
“they liue, and employ their time in holie exerciſes, and prayer. Thus
“farre *S. Auguſtin*

D.Chrſ.in ea 2. Math. ho.8.
31 *S. Chriſoſtome* alſo ſpeaking of the Monkes of *Egipt* in his time, ſaith thus. *Si quid nunc &c. If anie man now doe come to the deſerts of Egipt, hee shall find them more worthy then anie paradiſe of pleaſure, and shall ſee innumerable companies of Angels shine in mortall bodyes &c.* And a litle after. *Non ita varys &c. The heauens doe not ſo gliſter with varietie of ſtarres, as the deſerts of Egipt are beautified, & illuſtrated with innumerable habitacles, or manſions of Monkes, and Virgins.S.* Thus ſaith *S. Chriſoſtome*.

32 In like maner, *S. Hierome*, calleth the monaſticall order of Monks,
Hieron.pe.
and virgins. *Florem quendam, & precioſiſſimum lapideminter eccleſiaſtica ornamenta.*

namenta. A certaine flower, and most precious stone amongst the ornaments of the Church. And describeth also the notable manner of life of the religious, aswell women, as men in his time. *li.2. ep. 8. ad Marcellam.*

33 To conclude, *Sozomenus* saith of the religious men of those times, & of their profession (which hee calleth *an admirable philosophy*) that they *dispised all worldly glorie, and resisted manfully all the assaults of passions: that they had their understanding fixed one God their creator, whome they did contemplat day, and night: that they exercised themselues all their liues in patience, mansuetude, and humilitie, approching by contemplation to the deuine Maiesty, as neere as it was possible for humane nature.* Thus saith *Sozomenus* in substance, with much more to the same effect, which I omit for breuities sake, *Hierom. ad Eustochi. in Epitapluo Paulæ. Sozom. histo. Trip. li. 1. ca. 11.*

A continuation of the same matter, to proue the continuall discent of religious disciplin, from the first 300. yeares after Christ, untill our time, by the occasion whereof, the beginnings, and authours, of al the different professions, and order of religions in Gods Church, are declared: with the reasons, and causes, why it is conuenient, that there should be so many different orders in the Church of God, and that his mercifull prouidence, and bountie euidentlie appeareth therein: finally that the most holie learned, and famous men in Gods Church, haue professed, or alowed religious life, and that the later orders of religion, doe not differ either in matter of faith, or in substance of religious disciplin, from the first monkes, or religious of the primatiue Church.

Chap. 26.

1 HEitherto I haue shewed, that the contemplatiue, and monastical life, containing the perfection of Christian religiō, was instituted by the Apostles, & continued in the Church of God, for the first three hundreth yeares, and then greatlie augmented, and propagated by *S. Antony*, and his imitators, in the raigne of *Constantine*, the great: And now to proceede to the ensuing ages presentlie after the death of *S. Antony*, *S. Basil* instituted an order of religious men, or Monkes in *Greece*, differing from those of *S. Antonyes* institution, in two thinges especially: The one in that hee laboured more to ioyne the actiue life with the contemplatiue, & therefore ordained, that his monkes should draw nearer to citties, and townes, to the end they might aswell by their example, as instruction, gayne more soules to God: The other was, that whereas in former times, the superiours of monasteries, gouerned them for the most part, according to their owne iudgement, and wisdome, without any prescript, *Circa. an. 360. S. Basil. 63. & 79. S. Gregor. Nazianz. orat. in laudem Basilij. Platus. de bono status religiosi. li. 2. ca. 22.*

a *S. Basil. constitut. monast. & regula breues. & Ascetica. Item de institutionib. monacho.*
b *Baron. an 363.*
c *Circa an 340.*
d *Baron. hoo anno.*
e *Hieron. ep. li. 3. ad Principiam. ep. 16.*
Circa an. 386.
f *S. Aug. li. 8. confessi. ca. 6.*
g *S. Sulpitius Seuerus de vita S. Martini.*
h *Beda. eccl. histo. Anglor li. 2. ca. 2.*
i *Circa an. 390.*
Baron. an. 395.
k *Possidius. in vita Aug.*
l *Platus. de bono stat. religiosi. li. 2. ca. 23.*
m *Aug. ser. 1. de commun. vita. cleric.*
n *Possid. in vita Aug.*
o *D. Ambros. ep. 82.*

prescript of written lawes, or statuts, hee wrote certaine rules for the gouerment thereof, a prescribing a certaine time, and manner for the probation of nouices, before they should bee professed, and other statuts for their direction after their profession, all tending to the better obseruation of our Sauiours Counsells, consisting (as I haue oft said) in the vertues of *pouertie*, *chastity*, and perfect *obedience*: which rules of *S. Basil* are extant in his workes, & vntill this day obserued by the monkes in *Greece*, b and haue serued for a forme, and paterne to al others, that since his time haue instituted new orders of religion.

2 Some yeares before the institution of *S. Basils* order (to wit about the yeare 340) monasticall discipline passed into the west parts by the occasion of c S. *Athanasius*, and other priests of *Alexandria*, who being banished thence, and flying for succour to *Rome*, taught it to d *Marcella* a holy woman, and first beganne to professe it her selfe, and drew so many other, both men, and women to follow her example, that there were shortlie after (as e *S. Hierom* affirmeth) many monastaries of women, and an innumerable multitude of monkes, in, and about *Rome*: besides that we read, f that *S. Ambrose*, in the same age, maintained a monasterie of religious men at *Milan*, and that g *S. Martyn* erected others in *France*, and about the same time (as it is likely) the *Britons* receiued their first monasticall disciplin (conforme to that of *Egipt*) either from *Italy*, or from *France*, seeing that the monkes which were in the monastery of h *Bangor*, at the conuersion of the *Saxons*, liued all by the labour of their hands, as the monks of *Egipt* did, as may appeare in *S. Bede*.

3 Also about i the yeare of our Lord 390. *S.* k *Augustin* erected a monastery in *Afric*: l And because he builded it in a solitary place, those that followed the institut which he ordained therein, were called Hermits, & though they were manie yeares after commaunded by pope m *Innocentius* the fourth, to liue in townes, to the end that their holie conuersation, might be more profitable to their neighbours, yet the said *Innocentius* ordained, that they should retaine their old name of Hermits, whereby they are distinguished no lesse, then by their habit, and rule, from an other order instituted also by n *S. Augustin*, who whiles he was bishop of *Hippo*, made a monasterie within his owne house, as hee had also made an other ioyning to the Church before hee was bishop, wherein he and other priests liued al in common, hauing nothing proper, imitating therein (as o *Possidius* his disciple writeth in his life) the communitie vsed in the time of the Apostles p, and from this roote are sprong the diuers orders of Chanon regulers, obseruing the rule of *S. Augustin* at this day.

4 And the first of them that went from *Africk* into other parts, were for ought I haue read to the contrarie, *Gelasius*, and certaine companions of his, who came to *Rome*, by reason that *Hippo* was destroyed, and *Africk* ouerrunne by the *Vandals*, and *Gelasius* being within a while after chosen pope, assigned the Church of S. *Iohn Lateran*, to his former companions, whose successors remained there almost *eight hundreth yeares*, vntill pope *Bonifacius* the eight remoued them, and put secular cannons in their places, distributing to euerie one of them a portion of the rents, which the regular cannons had enioyed in common.

5 And it is likelie, that as *Gelasius*, and his companions, so also others of the same order of S. *Augustin*, passed from *Africk* into other parts at the same time, vppon the irruption of the *Vandals*, whereuppon it folowed, that all Christendome was afterwards replenished with Cannon regulers, of *S. Augustins* order, besides that many founders, and autors of other religious orders since his time, haue built the same vppon the foundation of his two rules, of *Hermits*, and *Chanons*, in so much, that some haue noted, about *thirty* seuerall orders of religious men, and women in diuers partes of Christendome, obseruing the rule of *S. Augustin* in substance, whereof I shall haue occasion to name some hereafter.

F. Paulo. Morigia. hist. dell orig. delle religioni.

6 But to returne to the time of *S. Augustin*, & to shew the progresse of monasticall or religious life in other orders vntill our daies. There liued in the next age after him *S. Benedict*, or *S. Benet*: a man most famous in Gods Church, and admirable for his vertue, and sanctitie, as may appeare by his life written by S. *Gregory* the great. This holie man gaue a most excellent rule, which hee practised himselfe at *Subiaco* 40. miles from *Rome*, and after in his famous monasterie of *Casinum*, in the kingdome of *Naples*, from whence it spred exceedingly in a short time, into other parts of *Italy*, and *Scicily*, and then into *France*, and other places, in S. *Benedicts* owne daies, and afterwards throughout all Christendome, as may appeare by the infinit number of monasteries of *Benedictins*, which are to bee seene, euen at this day in all the Christian cuntries of *Europ*: besides that many orders are sprong also from him at diuers times, either imitating his rule, or restoring it to the first integritie in some places where it was decayed, or els adding there to some more religious constitutions of their owne, all tending to the more perfect obseruation of our Sauiours Counsels, whereupon their folowers were distinguished from *Benedictins* by a new name, taken either from the Authours of the reformation, and additions aforesaid, or from the monasteries that were reformed.

S. Greg. li. 2. dialog. an. 520. Ibid. c. 36.

Paul. Morigia. Platus.vbi ſupra.ca. 22. an.913. 7 Such were the *Cluniacenſes*, ſo called of the Abbey of *Cluny* in *France*, reformed by *Odo*, the Abbot thereof, in the yeare of our Lord *Nine hundreth and thirteene*, whoſe example was followed, by ſo manie zealous Abbots at the ſame time in *Italy*, *Spayne*, *England* & *Germany*, that there were in a short time two thouſand monaſteries reformed, and reſtored to their ancient ſeueritie of diſcipline, from which they were much declined.

An.1000. Idem.ibid. 8 About *eighty ſeauen yeares* after this, the Hermits called *Camaldulenſes*, were inſtituted by *S. Romoaldus* vppon the *Apennin* hills in *Italy*, where they ſtill remaine, obſeruing for the moſt part S.*Benedicts* rule, with additions of greater auſteritie, fit for the heremiticall life which they lead, to the great admiration, & edification of al thoſe that viſit their holy cells.

an.1073. Idem.ibid. Hiſt. di Giouan.in villani.li.4.c. 16. 9 And ſeauentie three yeares after them, there aroſe alſo an other order in thoſe parts, called *de valle Ombroſa*, vnder a holy man named *Ioannes Gualbertus* a Florentin, vppon this occaſion. This *Gualbertus* being a ſingular man, and hauing a determination to kill one, who had ſlaine his brother, and meeting him one day at ſuch a time, and in ſuch a ſort, that hee had him at his mercy, was content neuertheles to forgiue him, yea, and to make a firme frindship with him, becauſe he deſired him to pardon him for the loue of our Sauiours paſſion. And it chanced the ſame day that *Gualbertus* wēt into a church, & praied before a crucifix, which miraculouſly bowed the head towards him, as it were acknowledgeing the charitie he had shewed towards his enemy, for our Sauiours ſake, wherewith hee was ſo moued, that hee preſentlie Baron.an. 1051. reſolued to forſake the world, and to become religious, and was afterwards ſo examplar of life, and famous for his miracls, that hee drew very many to imitate and accompanie him, whereuppon hee erected diuers monaſteries vnder the rule of *S. Benedict*, with ſome conſtitutions of his owne, tending to more ſeueritie, and rigour of monaſticall diſciplin, and becauſe his cheefe monaſtetie was in a place called *valle Ombroſa*, all thoſe of his inſtitution tooke the name thereof.

An.1098. Baron.hoc anno. Paulo.Morigia nella hiſt.dell origine delle religione. 10 After theſe beganne the *Ciſtercienſes*, about the yeare of our Lord *a thouſand ninty eight* vnder *S. Robert*, Abbot of *Moliſme* in *France*, who hauing noted, that the monaſterie where hee liued, was much declined from the auſteritie of *S. Benedicts* rule, found meanes to erect a poore monaſtery, firſt in *Moliſme*, and after in *Ciſters*, in which two places, hee began a notable reformation, and after, within a few yeares, *S. Bernard* proſecuting the ſame, brought it to ſo great perfection, and increaſe, that hee himſelfe founded a hundreth, and threeſcore reformed monaſteries

nasteries, of *S. Benets* order, and in respect thereof, as also of his great fame, and wonderfull sanctitie (which the whole world admired) the religious of those couents, following his rule of reformation, are called aswell *Bernardini*, as *Cistercienses*.

11 Besides these holy men aboue named, who were properly children of *S. Benet*, there haue bene also diuers other great seruāts of God, who vppon the mould, or paterne of his institut, haue framed others of singular edification, and rare perfection. The first was *Bruno*, a great doctor of *Paris*, who being present at the exequyes of a cannon of our Ladies Church, and seeing his dead body raise it selfe from the hearce three times, and say first, that he was accused, and after that hee was iudged, and lastlie that hee was iustlie condemned, was moued therewith to abandon the world, and with six companions, retired himselfe into the desert of *Grenoble* in *Daulphine*, & there beganne the most holie contemplatiue, and religious order of the *Carthusians*, called commonly in *England* in times past, the *Charter house Monkes*, famous euen at this day, for their solitude, contemplation, silence, perpetual abstinencè from flesh, and continuall prayer, accompanied with the exact disciplin of monasticall profession, and no where more then in the monasteries of our English *Carthusians* at *Mechlyn* in *Flaunders*, who being as it were the ofspring, and succession of the famous couent of their order in *England* called *Sheen* (dissolued in the beginning of the late Queens raigne) haue euer since vpheld, and conserued that religious body, and for their most holie, and contemplatiue life, are notable ornaments, aswell of our country, as of the Church of God.

Idem. ibid. Platus de bono stat. relig.

Baron. anno. 1086.

12 About *a hundreth, and twenty yeares* after the institution of the *Carthusians*, there began an order of Cannon regulars, founded by a holy man called *Norbert* Archbishop of *Magdeburg*, in a place named *Premostre*, in the bishopricke of *Laon* in *France*, whereuppon they were called *Præmostratensi*, and such hath bene the encrease of that order in *France*, *Spayne*, and other countries, that they haue aboue *a thousand fiue hnudreth* monasteries in one place, & other. Their rule is of S. *Augustin*, though with some litle difference.

an. 1120.

Baron. an. 1120. ex Hugone de vita Norberti.

13 In the same age also was instituted an order dedicated to the blessed *Trinity*, by two holie men, the one called *Ihon of Malta*, and the other *Felix* an Anchorit: & besides their rules common to al other religious, they bind themselues to goe into *Turky*, and other countries of the Infidels, to redeeme Christian captiues, which they do yearely, procuring the deliuery of many. They are called the order of the *Trinity*.

an. 1197. Paul. Morgia. vbi supra. Sabellicus Ennead. 9. li. 5.

14 Within three yeares after the foundatiō of this order, the religion of the

an.1200. of the *Carmelits* came first into *Italy*, and from thence dilated it selfe into other parts of Christendome, hauing bene instituted long before in
Idem. ibid. the yeare of our Lord, *foure hundreth aud twelue*, by *Iohn* patriarke of
Paulus. Morigia. & Platus. vbi supra. Tho. VValdensis. de Sacramentis. tit. 9. 84. *Hierusalem*, or as some graue authors say, but only restored then by him, for that it was (as they suppose) extant in the time of the Apostles, vppon the mount *Carmelus*, whereof they say, the whole order tooke the name, and that being afterwards spread ouer al *Palestina*, it was cast out by the *Sarazens*, when they subdued that country: this order being very examplar for pouerty, and all perfection, florished in times past in our country, aswell in learning as vertue, vnder the name of the white Friars, by reason of their white habit.

an.1212. 15 Within *twelue* yeares after that the *Carmelits* came into *Italy*, it pleased God to raise two new orders of Friars (as wee commonlie call
Platus. vbi supra. Paulo. Morigia. them) vnder S. *Francis*, & S. *Dominicke*, two lights of the world, shinyng in miraculous workes, and excelling in all the religious vertues, but making speciall profession of a most exact, and euangelicall pouerty, aboue al the religions of former times, with whome it pleased almighty God to cooperat wonderfully in the conuersion of sinners, and increase of their orders, in so much, that *S. Francis* holding a generall Chapter at *Assisio*, assembled *fiue thousand* of his order, and admitted thereto *fiue hundreth* more, before the chapter broke vp, and within a while after, all Christendome was replenished with them, who are now deuided into three orders, to wit, *Conuentuals, Obseruants,* & *Capuchins*, vnder three seueral generals.

an.1216. Idem. Ibid. Platus. vbi. supra, 16 And the like also may be said, of the propagation, and incrase of the holie order of S. *Dominicke*, which in very short time was spreed through christendome, & because his speciall institut was to preach for the conuersion, aswell of the heretikes *Albigenses* (of whome hee himselfe conuerted great numbers) as also of all sorts of sinners, those of his order were called the Friar preachers, though in our country they were best knowne by the name of black Friars, by reason of their vppermost weede which is black, though they weare white vnder it.

17 Although the same time also (to wit within *sixteene* yeares after)
an.1232. Idem. Ibid. began the order of the *Serui* or *Seruitæ* at *Florence*, by the occasion of seauen riche and noble gentlemen' who retyring themselues to a hille not far from thence, to doe penance, grewe within a while, to be so exemplar, and famous for their holie life, that very many ioyned themselnes
Paulo. Morigia. with them, who daylie multiplyinge, were at last deuided into diuers monasteries, vnder the name of *Serui della B. virgine, seruants of the B. virgin Marie*, in respect of theire particular deuotion to hir, and diuers apparitions

paritions of her to them. They obserue the rule of *S. Augustin*, with some litle difference, wherby they ar distinguished from the *Augustins*.

18 In the same age, about *thirtie* yeares after, there began in *Spaine* an order of religion, called *de la Merced, of the redemption*, whose obligation is like to that of the order of the *Trinitie* before named, to wit, to redeeme Christian captiues. This order was instituted dy *Don Iayme* king of *Aragon*, according to the rule of *S. Augustin*, but do weare a white weede with an escuchon vpon their habit, hauing in it a white crosse in a read field, with the armes of *Aragon* vnder it.

an.1264. Idem Ibid.

19 About *tenne* yeares after this, a holy man caled *Pedro Moron*, hauing liued many yeares in a desert, grew to be so famous, partly for his holy life, and partly for his greate miracles, that many resorted to him out of all partes, and submitted themselues to his direction, for theire maner of life, to whom he prescribed religious rules, and so many were his disciples in a few yeares, that he was faine to procure diuers monasteries for them, and his rule beinge confirmed by the sea Apostolicke, and he himselfe some yeares after chosen pope, and called *Celestinus* the fift, those of his institution were named *Celestini*.

Circa.an 1274. Idem ibid Platus. vbi supra. Sabellicus ennead.9 li.7.

20 And to passe ouer the rest briefly, seeinge all tende to one end (to wit, to contemplatiue life, and the perfect obseruation of our Sauiours councells) the *Oliuitani*, had their begining of a holy man caled *Bernardus Ptolomeus*, who professing the studie of philosophy in *Sienna*, withdrew him selfe with two companions, in the yeare *a thousand three hundreth and twentie*, to a mountaine, not farre from thence called *Oliuetus*, where they passed their time in such feruour of deuotion & penaunce, and drew so many to follow their example, that there grew a particular order of that name.

Paulo Morigia. Platus. an.1320.

21 Also not long after (to wit in the yeare *a thousand three hundred fiftie six*) there began in the same citie of *Siena*, an other order of religious men caled *Iesuati*, because they had euer the name of *Iesus* in their mouthes. Their firste founder, was a gentleman called *Ioannes Columbinus*, a man of singular perfection, and austerity of life, who out of his great humilitie ordayned, that none of his order should be priestes, for the reuerence he bore to the dignitie of priesthood, for which respect also *S. Antony*, *S. Hilarion*, *S. Benit*, *S. Francis*, and very many relgious men in auncient times forbore to bee priestes. Neuertheles now very lately, it hath seemed good to the popes holines to ordaine, that the *Giesuati* shal haue priestes, as other religious haue. These also of this order, doe vse to get their liuing with their labour, and therfore employe themselues commonly in the distillation of all kind of holsome waters, for the be-

An.1356. Platus. vbi supra. Paulo Morigia.

of the sick, and in diuers other thinges, besides their obligation of Pouerty, chastitie, obedience, muche prayer, and many mortifications, which they haue common with al other religious orders.

an 1381. Idem ibid.

22 And within a few yeares after this, one *Pedro Ferdinando* a Spaniard abandoning the court and fauour of his prince, *Peter* king of Castil, renewed the rule instituted about *twelue hundred* yeares agoe, by S. *Hierom* in Bethleem, which is now obserued by the *Hieronimits* in Spaine, and Portugal, with exceeding great edification for their notable discipline, and perfection of monastical life.

Idem ibid. Sabellicus. ennead.9. li.6.

23 In like maner the *Crucigeri*, hauing first their begining from a company or congregation, instituted by S. *Cletus*, the second bishoppe of Rome after S. *Peter*, to receaue, and asiste poore Christian pilgrimes or trauellers, which should come thither, and being by reason of the great persecutions vnder the pagan Emperours dissolued, were restored firste by pope *Vrbanus* the *second*, with the addition of the name of *Crucigeri*, at the same time that *Godfrey* of Bullen recouered Hierusalem from the *Sarazens*, and afterwardes they were augmented, by the popes *Innocentius* the third, *Alexander* the third, and *Pius* the second, which latter also in the yeare *a thousand four hundred* and *sixty*, and in a general counsell helde at *Mantua*, changed their habit from ashe colour, to blew.

an.1460.

circa.an. 1450. Platus.vbi supra. Paulo Morigia.vbi. sup

24 About the yeare of our Lord *a thousand four hundred & fifty*, the holy order of the Friars caled *Minimi*, which is of singular edification in the Churche of God at this present, was instituted by the famous Father, *Francisco de Paula*, a man for austerity of life and vertu of miracles, helde inferiour to none of the founders of the auncient orders.

an.1528. Idem.ibid.

25 Lastly to conclude this point concerninge contemplatiue and religious life, two other orders of religious priestes are sprong in the memory of man yet liuinge, to wit, the *Theatins*, and the society of *Iesus*, commonly caled Iesuits, whereof the first was instituted by pope *Paule* the fourth, before he was pope. And because he had bene Archbishop of *Theata*, and was stil so caled when he began that order, they were caled *Theatins*, who though they are not spread out of *Italye* (for ought I knowe) yet their life is so exemplar, and of such edification, that they are of no smale profit in the Church of God, in those places where they liue,

Idem ibid. Platus.li.2. ca.23. an.1540.

26 The other order of regular priestes, was founded by *Ignatius de Loyola*, a Spanish gentleman, whose straunge vocation, from a secular and military state, to all religious perfection, and to so greate a woorke as was the institution of the societie of *Iesus*, sufficiently appereth to haue proceeded from the special operatiō of the holy Ghost, not only for the

strang

strang maner thereof,& his admirable vertues (which I haue not now time to relate) but alſo for the notable effects & fruit which the ſaid ſociety hath wrought, and daylie doth worke, in the conuerſion of ſouls from Infidelity, hereſie, and ſinne, thoroughout the whole world euen in the eaſt and weſt Indie, where they haue notablye propagated the Chriſtian faithe: beſides theire continuall labours and indeuours in all parts of Chriſtendom, in the inſtruction of youth in al kind of learneing and vertu, which is one ſpecial end of their inſtitut, as alſo to ioyne the actiue, and the contemplatiue life together in al perfection, in imitation of our Sauiour *Ieſus* Chriſt, to whoſe holye name, their order or ſocietie, is ſpecially dedicated, by the occaſion of his apparition to Father *Ignatius* their founder, as he, and two of his companions (F. *Fabro* and F. *Laynez*) were going to Rome. In which voyage our Sauiour appeared vnto him, with his croſſe vpon his ſhoulder, and ſaid with a louing and gratious cheere. *Ego vobis Romæ propitius ero. I wil be fauorable vnto you in* Rome.

Riba deneyra. in vita Ignat. l. 2. ca. 11.

27 This shal ſuffice, concerning the propagation of religious orders, though I might ad many which ar in particular cities, not diſperſed or yet knowne abroad in other places, of whom ſome haue care of hoſpitals, others of orphanes and poore children, and other of other workes of charitie and pietie. Beſides that, I might alſo ad hereto, if I thought it needful (diuers holy orders of religious women, by whom our Chriſtian philoſophy and contemplatiue life, hath beene alwayes exerciſed in all perfection, euer from the Apoſtles tyme vntill theſe our dayes, as may apeare by thoſe religious women, who (as I haue declared befor) were in the Church of Alexandria, in the firſte age vnder *S. Marke* the Euangeliſt, and thoſe other vayled and conſecrated virgins, mentioned by *Tertulian*, and *S. Ciprian*, in the ſecond and third age, and innumerable others in the fourth, fifth, and ſixt age, in Egipt, Paleſtina, Hieruſalem, and Italie, or rather ouer al Chriſtendom, as I haue ſufficientlye proued already out of the Fathers who liued in thoſe ages, and from that time forward, I thinke no man doubteth, but that there hath bene a continual deſcent and ſucceſſion, of monaſticall diſcipline, as well in women as men, vnder the rules of *S. Auguſtin, S. Benedict, S. Francis, S. Dominick*, the *Carmilits*, and laſtly of the bleſſed *S. Brigit*, who being deſcended of the royal race of the kinges of Sweden, and maried to *Vlpho* prince of Nericia, did not only hir ſelfe, embrace a religious life after his death, but alſo induced and drewe many others thereto, and finallie left an excellent order, of religious men and women of hir owne inſtitution, whereof there is at this day, a notable monaſtery of our country

Philo. de vita contemplat. Euseb. eccles. hiſt. li. 2. c. 16.

Tertul. de veland. virgin. S. Cypri. de diſcipli. & habitu. virginum.

Ludouic. Bloſius. in appendice. monilis ſpiritualis. Paulo Morigia. dell origine delle religione.

try women in Portugal, being as I may ſay, the daughter of the famous couent of Sion, which in the begining of the laſt queenes raigne, paſſed into voluntarie baniſhment, and now after great variety of fortune by ſea and land in diuers countries, is ſeated in Lisborne.

28 Whereto I may alſo ad, other couents of religious women of our nation in Flaunders, profeſſing monaſtical diſciplin vnder diuers rules to wit, of *S. Auguſtin*, S, *Benit*, the *Carmelits*, commonly called *Tereſians* (becauſe the holy mother *Tereſa* reformed that order, as I shal haue occaſion to declare more particularly in the next chapter:) & laſtly of the holy virgin *S. Clare*, who being in Aſſiſio in Italy, as *S. Francis* alſo was & liuing there in the ſame time that he did, receiued hir rule of him. And ſo exemplar are the liues of al theſe our religious country women, aſwel in Portugal as Flaunders, that I may wel ſay, they shine like as many ſtarres in the perfect practiſe of contemplation & mortification, beinge true patterns of all religious perfection, beſides that many of them are no leſſe remarkeable and eminent, for the nobilitie and worthines of their linag, then venerable for their vertu, being moſt of thẽ gentlewomen of good houſes, and ſome of them of the moſt noble and honorable familyes in England, and this I could not omit to touch by the way, partly in reſpect of their great merit, and partly for Gods greater glorie, to the end it may appeare how powrful is his grace and vocation in them, ſeeinge that nether the weakenes of their ſex, nor the delicacie of their education, nor the natural loue to their country, parents, and friendes, nor the difficulties and dangers of the ſea or lande, could diuert them from ſo hard a choiſe, as it ſeemeth to be to flesh & blood to vndertake a voluntarie baniſhment, and to leade a religious and monaſtical life in a forreine country. In which reſpect I may boldly ſay, that euery one of them, far better deſerueth to be honored with a *ſtatua*, or image, for an eternal monument of theire valour, then that Roman *Clælia* (mentioned by me before in the epitome of the Roman hiſtory) who receued the like honor in Rome, for that being an hoſtage in the handes of king *Porſenna* when he beſeeged the cittie, shee eſcaped away together with hir companions, ouer the riuer Tiber, beeing moued and drawne therto by the loue of hir liberty, country, parents, and friendes: wheras theſe religious and holy women, haue vndergone infinit dangers by ſea and land, with the loſſe of libertie, frendes, and al worldly comodities, to performe the moſt heroical act that may be, that is to ſay, to tread and trample vnder their feete, al the honours and delights of this life, for the pure loue of God.

Tit. Liuius. Dec. 1. li. 1.

29 Wel then, by al the former diſcourſe in the laſt chapter and this, it

appea-

appeareth, first, that the practise of contemplatiue and monastical life began in the time of the Apostles, and by theire institution. Secondly, that it hath beene euer since continued in the church of God without interruption, aswel in women as in men. Thirdly, that the propagators, and practisers thereof since the apostles time, haue beene of the most famous men for vertu and miracles (and very many of them also for learninge) that haue bene in Gods church, as those which I haue mentioned, to wit, *S. Antony, S. Hilarion, S. Basil, S. Athanasius, S. Hierom, S. Martin, S. Augustin, S. Chrisostom, S. Benedict, S. Ggregory* the great *S. Bernard, S. Romuald, S. Gualbert, S. Francis, Dominick, S. Petrus Celestinus, S. Francis de Paula*, to omit other not yet canonised, though of immortal fame for their exemplar life, and singular vertu.

30 Fourthlie it is to be considered, that although there haue bene, & are different rules, in the different order of religious men, and women, yet all of them tend to one end, that is to say, to the perfect obseruation of our Sauiours Counsels (consisting as I haue said, in *voluntary pouerty, chastitie* and *obedience*, whereto they all bind themselues) as also that the reformations, or restitutions of religions decayed, and all mutations, or additions of rules, which haue bene at anie time in the said orders since the Apostles time, haue had no other end, but the further augmentation of the aforesaid vertues, and of the perfection of Christian contemplation, thereby to attaine to a perfect vnion with God, which is the end of al religion, and giueth true felicity to man, and common wealth.

31 Fiftly the great prouidence of almighty God, and his mercifull goodnes towards his Church, may be noted, in the multitude of religious men, and in the varietie of their orders: for euen as in the different *Hierarchies*, and diuers orders of Angels, and in the whole course of nature in heauen and earth, hee hath ordained that there shall bee multitude, and varietie, to the end he may communicate his owne perfections, the more amply to his creatures, for their greater good, and his greater, glorie: so also he hath most mercifully disposed, that there shallbe the like in his church, to the end, that the endles treasure of his grace, may be the more aboundantly distributed amongst his children, and seruants, to their greater benifit, and the more euident manifestation of his bountie: whereby also his spouse the church is maruilouslie adorned, and beautified, being as *S. Bernard* saith. *Circumamicta varietatibus.* Reuested, and clad al ouer with *variety*, like the *Queene* mentioned in the psalme. *S. Bernard. in Apol. ad Guliel. Psal. 44.*

32 Besides that the admirable force of his grace, and the veritie of

christian religion, is also euidentlie seene therein, seeing that so many of both sexes, are contented to abandon the world, and all the delights thereof, yea, and themselues also, for the loue of him, to the end, they may imitate him in cariage of his crosse, during all their liues: which being a thinge so contrarie to mans corrupt nature, as it is, can not bee ascribed to anie other cause, then to the wonderfull force of Gods grace, and is so much the more glorious to our Sauiour Christ, by how much greater is the multitude and number of those which follow him, with so much worldlie discomoditie, and bodily affliction to themselues.

33 Againe, the variety of these religious orders, testifieth his prouidence and bountie, in that he so mercifully prouideth for the different necessities of his church, by the different orders of religions. For as in cities and common welths, it is conuenient for the publike, and common good, that there be diuers trades, and occupations to supply al the temporall necessities thereof: so also in this spirituall citty, or common wealth of the church, it is no lesse conuenient, that there bee many, and different professions of religious orders, to serue, and supply, the spirituall necessities of the faithfull, and therefore some orders apply them selues to prayer (recommending to God the necessities of the church, no lesse then their owne:) others excell in mortification of the flesh, & austeritie of life (aswell to pacifie the wrath of God for the sinnes of men, as to excite others to penance by their example:) some also employ themselues most in preaching and teaching (to instruct the ignorant, and to gaine them to God) and though al religious orders haue the practise of al the christian vertues in a high degree, yet to the end that euerie vertue may bee the more specially recommended, and the more eminent in the eyes of men, for their example, and Gods glorie, diuers orders, doe diuersly excell in prticuler vertues, some in obedience, some in pouertie, some in contemplation, and some in action, so that euerie man may by this varietie, receiue verie particuler edification, instruction, and example, according to the neede, or want, he may haue more of one vertue then of an other.

34 Moreouer the goodnes of God, and his infinit wisdome appeareth wonderfully, in that hauing speciall consideration of mens habilities, yea, and of their different humours (whereby they are moued euen in spirituall matters, some to take one course, and some an other) he hath mercifully prouided such different professions, and orders of religions (some more straight and hard, and others more easie, and yet all tending to perfection) that euerie man may find some order, or other, as-

well to his humour, and liking, as also fit for his strength, wherein hee may to his contentment, dedicate himselfe to the seruice of God, and attaine to the highest perfection of Christian life: besides that he hath no lesse mercifully, and prouidentlie ordained, that new orders shall springe in his Church from time to time, not onlie to succeede others, which by humane frailty doe in time fall to decay, but also to serue for medicins, and remedies, against the new diseases, which grow manie times in faith and manners, and to renew in men the decaied feruour of deuotion, by their feruorous endeuours, furthred not a litle, euen with verie noueltie thereof, seeing that noueltie, is euer of it selfe grateful to mans nature, and potent to moue him, either to good, or bad: so that wee see how mercifully, almighty God doth vse to accomodate his vocatiõ of vs, to our owne infirmitie, inuiting, & drawing vs to perfection sweetelie, euẽ with respect of our owne humours & dispositiõs.

35 Finally the prouidence, and bountie of almighty God towards his seruants, appeareth admirably in the sustentation, and maintenaunce of such an innumerable multitude of religious men, who haue forsaken the world, and all the welth thereof, to serue him in pouertie, in so much, that we euidentlie see therein, the accomplishment of our Sauiours promise of, *Centuplum in hac vita*, a hundreth fould in this life, e- *Marc.10.*
uen in temporall commodities, besides the spirituall, and heauenlie *Math.19.*
consolations, whereof I shall speake amplie hereafter.

36 For as *S. Chrisostome* obserueth notablie in the Apostles, that they re- *S. Chrisost.*
ceiued *a hundreth fold* tẽporally in this life (who insteede of their poore *in ca.19.*
netts, and angle-rods, which they leaft for Christ, had all the goods of *Math.ho.65.*
the faithfull laid at their feete, yea, and their persons at their deuotion) so may wee say of all religious men (as *Ioannes Caßianus* noteth a thousand two hundreth yeares agoe) for in recompence of some one, or two, or a few houses of their owne which they sell, or abandon for Christs sake, they haue as manie houses, as there are monasteries of their order: and for a father, and a mother, or a few brethren, & frindes (and them manie times vnkind, vnfaithfull and ingrat) they haue as manie true and sincere friends, brethren, fathers and mothers (for sincere affection) as there are true religious of their order, yea, or as there are good men in the world, whose goods and riches, are alwayes at their deuotion, rather then they should want, as euidentlie apeareth in the plentifull almes daylie giuen to religious men, by the good, and vertuous people, in such aboundance, that manie worldly and vncharitable men, exceedingly repine and murmur thereat.

37 So that we see, it is truly fulfilled iu the religious, which S. *Paule*

1.Cor.3. said to the *Corinthians*. *Omnia vestra sunt, siue mundus, siue præsentia, siue futura. All thinges are yours, whether it be the world, or thinges present, or thinges to come*, and as *Salomon* saith, *fidelis viri totus mundus diuitiarum, all the riches in the world, belonge to the faithfull man*. Wherein as I haue said, manifestlie appeareth the singular prouidence, and infinit bountie of almightie God: besides that it may also serue for an encouragement to al the faithfull, to follow the counsell of the psalmist, who saith. *Iacta curam tuam*
Psal.54. *super Dominum, & ipse te enutriet*. Cast thy care vppon our Lord, and hee will nourish thee. Thus much I haue thought good to say breefly, concerning the multitude and variety of religious orders in Gods church.

38 Furthermore, I wish it also to bee noted by the way, that as the contemplatiue, and religious life, hath descended from the Apostles time to this, so also the true Christian religion, hath in like maner descended therewith, seeing it is euident, that all the aforenamed propagators of religious life (who were also the lights of the church in their tymes) haue bene all of one religion, and of the selfe same that our religious now professe, For otherwayse, let it be shewed, how *S. Antony* differed in fayth from the monks of whom S.*Dionisius* speaketh, or how *S. Basil*, *S. Augustin*, or *S. Hierome*, differed from *S. Antony*, or what difference there was in faith betwixt *S. Benet*, or any of these aforenamed, and *S. Bernard*, *S. Fraunciss*, *S. Dominick*, or the monks, and religious, that obserue theyr rule, or lastly, betwixt these of our dayes, and theyr predecessors, let it I say be shewed, how they differ in faith, and beleefe, one from an other? But this cannot be shewed by any meanes, it being most euident that the succession of religious disciplin in the church of God, hath bene alwaies accompanied with the succession of one, and the selfe same fayth, as will most euidently appeare heareafter, by the discussion, and examination of matters in controuersy betwixt the protestants, and vs,

39 Therefore I wil conclude for the present vppon all the premisses, that for as much, as I haue made yt manifest before, first, that the felicity of man and common welth, consisteth in a perfect vnion with almighty God, by the meanes of Christian contemplation: And secondly, that the true practise and exercise of this christian contemplation, is the special subiect of religious disciplin: And lastly, that the same religious disciplin hath descended to our tyme from the Apostles, without interruption, therefore it must needes follow, that the Roman Catholikes (who haue the true practise of the contemplatyue, and religious life) haue also the true meanes to arryue to a perfect vnion with God, and consequently to the true felicity of man, and common welth: where

where vppon it alſo followeth, that they haue the veritie of chriſtian religion, al which shall be yet more euident in the next chapter, where I will shew the ſame by manifeſt experience.

That God hath in all times and ages, giuen teſtimonie of his vnion with religious men, by manie extraordinarie fauours beſtowed vppon them, as by exſtaſes, and rapts, by viſions, reuelations, the ſpirit of propheſie, and the operation of miracles, whereof examples are alleadged in euerie age, from the primitiue church, euen vntill this day: And thereuppon it is concluded, that the Roman Catholikes, hauing the true imitation of Chriſt in religious diſciplin, and all the externall ſignes of Gods internall vnion with them, haue not onlie the perfection of Chriſtian religion, but alſo the cheefe felicitie of man in this life, and of common wealth.

CHAP. 27

1 THou haſt ſeene good Reader, in the laſt chapter, not onlie the antiquitie of religious life, but alſo the end, and fruit thereof, which as I haue shewed, is noe other but a perfect vnion with God, and noe maruaile, ſeeing therein is contained the perfect practiſe, and exerciſe of chriſtian contemplation, conſiſting, as I haue often ſignified, in meditation, and mental prayer, accompanied with the true loue of God, contempt of the worlde, abnegation of a mans ſelfe, chaſtitie, pouertie, obedience, and the perfection of all vertue: Al which being the ſpeciall effects of Gods grace, doe diſpoſe the ſoule of man, to the perfect vnion with God, which not onlie wee that bee chriſtians, but alſo the pagan philoſophers, doe teach to bee the end of contemplation, as I haue amplie declared in the ſeauententh, eightenth, nintenth, twentith, and one and twentieth chapters, where I haue proued that almighty God (whoſe *ſpeciall delight is,* as he himſelfe ſaith, *to be with the ſonnes of men*) doth of his infinit bounty ſo communicate himſelfe to a contemplatiue ſoule, purifieth with his grace, and enflameth with his loue, that he vniteth it with himſelfe, & (as the holie ſcriptures doe ſpeake) eſpouſeth it, imparting ſuch ineffable conſolations vnto it, that it remayneth manie times abſorpt in his loue, and alienated from the ſenſes of the bodie, wherevppon enſue thoſe admirable rapts, whereof I ſpake in the aforeſaid chapters, and promiſed to ſpeake further afterwards, which I will now performe.

Chap. 17. 18. 19. 20. & 21. *Prouer. 8.* *Cant. 4. & 9.*

2 Neuertheleſſe, I thinke good, first to aduertiſe thee good Reader,

 that

that it is not my meaning to shew here, that there is no vnion of man with God, but in rapts, or alienation of the soule from the senses, seeing I haue sufficientlie declared before, that almighty God vniteth himselfe with his seruants diuersly, according to the different capacity of euerie one of them: For euen as the sunne doth perfectly illuminate the ayre, when it is pure, and cleare from clouds, and at other times also doth imparte so much light vnto it, as the multitude, or thicknes of the clouds doth permit, and entreth into euerie house, more or lesse, according to the capacitie of the windowes, holes, or slifters, whereby it
Ioan.1. may passe: euen so almighty God being *lux vera*, the true light, as the euangelist saith, and true goodnes, doth impart the light of his grace, and communicate himselfe to his seruants, according to the puritie of their harts: so that when he findeth in them no cloudes of passions, or worldlie affections, he vniteth himselfe with them in great perfection, and neuer faileth to enter into euerie deuout soule, more or lesse, according to the disposition he findeth therein: which disposition neuertheles, is to bee vnderstood to proceede also from his grace, with-
2.Cor.3. out the which, *we cannot thinke as much as a good thought.*

3 And although the effects of his presence, and vnion, are for the
Esay.24. most part so internal, and secret, that his seruants, who enioy the same, may say with the prophet, *secretum meum mihi*, *my secret is to myselfe*: yet it hath pleased his deuine maiestie in all times, and ages, for the encouragement and example of others, and for his owne greater glorie, to giue testimonie thereof to the world by externall signes, and demonstrations, as some times by extases, or rapts, some times, by visions, and apparitions of our Sauiour Christ, or his Saints, sometimes by reuelations and the spirit of prophesie, & other whiles by the aboundance of teares, proceeding either of hartie contrition, or of feruēt loue, and deuotion, and some times also, by an euident redoundance of the internall and spirituall comforts, to the externall, and corporall parts (as
Exod.24. it appeared in *Moyses*, whose face was so glorious, vppon his conference with almighty God, that the children of *Israell* could not behould it) and finally by miraculous workes, which manifestly witnes his supernaturall assistance.

4 Therefore I intend to make it manifest here, that the Roman Catholikes haue alwayes had, and at this day haue, this externall testimony of Gods internall vnion with them, such Catholikes I meane, as
Chap.22. & 23. practise true christian contemplation in religious life, not that I tye these extraordinarie graces and fauours of almighty God, onlie to cloysters, and religious houses (for I haue shewed sufficientlie before by

diuers

diuers examples,that ſecular men of al ſtates,and vocations, may be ſo
mortified, that they may alſo participat thereof) but becauſe the ſecular ſtate (eſpecially in ſuch as are maried, and haue care of children,and familie)is ſo ſubiect to the diſtraction of worldlie cares, and
buſines,that it verie rarelie admitteth true mortification, and the exerciſe of perfect contemplation, therefore I ſay, it is ſeldome ſeene,
that ſecular men attaine thereto in ſo high a degree, as religious men
doe,who hauing abandoned the world, and giuen themſelues wholie
to the ſtudie ,and practiſe of true chriſtian contemplation, doe with
greater facilitie arriue to the perfection thereof,and receiue in al aboundance, that *Centuplum,* or *hundreth* fold which almightie God promiſed to giue euē in this life to thoſe,which ſhould forſake the world *Matth.19.*
for his ſeruice, ſuch being his bountie towards them, that hee giueth
them (as *S. Bernard* ſaith) not onlie eternal life for their reward in the
end,but alſo ſpiritual ioyes, and conſolations for their entertainement
in the meane time, *for ſo,* ſaith hee, *men are alſo wont to giue their worke-*
men meate whiles they worke, and their hire, or wages,when they haue finiſhed *Bernard. ſer.*
their worke,&ſo ſouldiars haue their pay whiles they ſerue,and a greater donatiue, *ecce nos re-*
or gift in the end,and ſo alſo the children of Iſraell were fed with manna in the de- *linquimus*
ſert,and arriued in the end to the land of promiſe. Thus ſaith *S. Bernard,* who *&c.*
alſo addeth further , that this is notably ſignified vnto vs,in the booke
of wiſdome, where it is ſaid, that *God will giue to the iuſt the reward of*
their labours,and in the meane time *lead them, in via mirabili, in a mer-* *Sap.10.*
*uellous way,*and this way ſaith he, is *that wherin the pſalmiſt ſaith he was de-* *Pſal.118.*
lighted,ſicut in omnibus diuitijs, as in al riches: whereby we may ſee,that the
way which God leadeth his ſeruants, is both pleaſant,and maruelous,
and therefore the pſalmiſt doth not onlie ſay, that *God is ſweete,* but alſo *Pſal.33.*
that he is *mirabilis in ſanctis ſuis,maruelous in his ſaints,*and no meruaile,ſee- *Pſal.67.*
ing he is ſo meruelous,and wonderful in all his workes.

5 What wonder then is it, that carnall and fleſhlie men,who haue
not ſo much as anie taſt of matters of ſpirit, and commonlie beleeue
no more,then that which they ſee,know,or feele with their hands, do
not beleeue nor can conceue the wonderful, and ineffable manner of
almighty Gods proceeding, with his ſeruants here in earth,nor the in-
trinſical familiaritie that hee vſeth towads a deuout contemplatiue
ſoule,wherwith he is vnited? Which I will now make euident, by the
experience that hath benne ſeene of Gods extraordinarie fauours, and
the externall ſignes of his internall vnion, imparted to religious men,
and women ſince our Sauiours time, to ſhew thereby aſwell the veritie and continual ſucceſſion, of Catholike religion in religious pro-

 feſſion:

fession: as also the vnspeakeable consolation, and true felicity, which it affordeth to those that embrace, and practise it in perfection, whereby it shall also appeare (as before I noted out of the psalmist) that *Deus est mirabilis in sanctis suis. God is maruellous in his saints.* *Psal. 67.*

6 In the *One and twentith* chapter, where I treated amply of the internal vnion of man with God, by the meanes of christian contemplation, I spoke sufficiently of some special effects, and externall signes thereof, aswell in the prophets of the ould testament, as in S. *Peter*, S. *Iohn*, the euangelist, and S. *Paule*, to wit, their reuelations, and rapts, mentioned in the holy scriptures. And I further signified, that the same was not peculiar, and proper only to them, but also common to others of the faithful in the new testament; concerning which point, I now say further, that the same appeareth sufficiently in S. *Dionisius Areopagita*, S. *Pauls* disciple, who maketh mention not only of his owne reuelations, touching the deliuery of S. *Iohn* the *Euangelist* from his banishment in *Patmos*, but also of a very strange vision, and reuelation, which S. *Carpus*, a bishop in *Creta*, had in his prayers, of whome also, he saith that for the purity of his soule, he was, *aptissimus ad dei speculationem*, most fit to speculat, and contemplat God, and that therefore he had alwaise some holly, and fauourable vision, before he *celebrated the deuine misteries* (that is to say before he said masse:) and further he also signifieth, that S. *Hierotheus*, was illuminated with holy inspirations concerning the misteries of the christian faith, *patiendo diuina*, suffring deuine things, meaning the excesse of spirit, which he suffred by the abundant influence of Gods gratious visitations, whereby he arriued saith S. *Dionisius*, to that mistical vnion, & faith, that the Apostles them selues had, which could not be taught, or obtained by human industry.

Chap. 21.

S. Dionis. de misti. theolog. & de diui. nomin. Idem ep. ad S. Ioan. Euang. Idem Epist. ad Demophilum monachum. Idem de diuin. nomin. c. 2. per. 1. in fine.

7 Seeing then this learned father, acknowledged these deuine fauours, and external signes of gods vnion in himselfe, and others in his time, it cannot be with any reason denied, but that he thought, and knew the same to be most proper to religious men, seeing he taught, that the vnion of man with God, is the special end, and effect of monastical disciplin, as I haue proued out of him in the last chapter. *Chap. 26. nu. 20. 22. & 24.*

8 And the same no doubt, would haue benne manifest to vs in the monks or religions of that time, if their liues had bene particulerly written as were the liues of the *Hermits*, and religious, which liued shortly after, namely of S. *Paule* the *Hermit*, and S. *Antony*, both which florished in the very next age after S. *Dionisius*. For whereas he died in the second age after Christ, (to wit in the yeare a hundreth and nineteene) they were borne in the third age, and S. *Paule*, who was a few

yeares

yeares more ancient, then *S. Anthony*, began his heremitical life, about the yeare of our lord, two hundreth and fifty, at what tyme also S. *Antony* was borne, who, as I signified before, replenished the deserts of *Egipt*, with monasteries, and learned monastical disciplin of an old monke, which had professed, and obserued it from his youth.

9 Let vs then see, what is testified by approued authours, concerning the spiritual fauours, and consolations imparted to these two, whose lyues were written by twoo of the most famous Fathers of Gods church, to wit, S. *Athanasius*, and S. *Hierome*, who liued in their tyme, and S. *Athanasius*, was familiar with S. *Anthony*, of whom he also learned so much, as the church of God hath hetherto knowne of the life of S. *Paule* the hermit, and witnesseth of them both (as also S. *Hierome* doth) that hauing liued many yeares in one wildernes, they vnderstood one of an other by deuine reuelation, and that there vppon S. *Anthony* going to seeke, and visit S. *Paule*, they saluted each other by their owne names at their very first meeting, and that where as a crow had for threescore yeares together, brought to S. *Paule* halfe a lofe of bread, for his dayes allowance, shee brought him at that time a whole lofe, with diuers other things concerning S. *Paule*, which testify how highly God fauoured him.

S. Athanas. in vita S. Anton. *S. Hieron. in vita S. Pauli.*

10 And the like appeareth concerning S. *Antony*, by that which S. *Athanasius* writeth of him, as that he had such heauenly consolations in his prayers, and meditations, that many times he continued them whole nights throughout, and complained of the light of the morning sunne, that it disturbed him, and depriued him of the true light, which he had beheld in his contemplations. Besides that he ad many apparitions of our Sauiour, many rapts, and reuelations, and did such wonderfull miracles, that all the world admired him, as may be seene in the history of his life, which was most famous in *S. Augustins* tyme, and wrought wonderful effects in them who heard, or read it, in so much, that *S. Augustin* confesseth of himselfe, that he, and *Alipius*, were maruelouslie moued, and amazed when they heard it first related, before he was conuerted. *Stupebamus*, saith he, *audientes* &c. *VVe were astonished to heare things, so maruelous in the true faith, and in the Catholick church, tam recenti memoria, & prope nostris temporibus, testatissima, which were so fresh in memory, and most manifestest almost in our tyme.*

S. Athanas. ibidem.

S. Aug. li. 8. confess. c. 6.

11 Thus saith, *S. Augustin*, and further recounteth the strange effect that the reading of *S. Antonies* life wrought in twoo great courtiers, who suddenly there vppon forsooke the world, and entred into reli-

Chap. 76. gion, whereof I haue declared the particulers already, when I treated of the suddayne, and admirable effects of gods grace. Thus
Obiit. an. 361. much concerning *S. Antony*, and the fauours which he receyued of almightie God, in the exercise of contemplatiue, and monastical life.

12 With him I will ioyne a disciple of his, to wit, *S. Hilarion*, who also greately encreased monastical disciplyn (as I haue declared
Chap.25.nu. 32. before) whose continuall penance, mortification, meditation, and prayer, *S. Hierome* amply declareth, and signifieth with all, many
S. Hieron. in vita S. Hilario. notable miracles, which he did, and the deuine illustrations, and reuelations which he had, euen in the presence of many thousands of
Obiit. an. 383. people, who came to see him in the wildernes.

13 There liued also in the same tyme, to wit, in the *forurth age*, two
S. Ephr. in orat. in laud. Basil. notable men, and great pillers of the church, *S. Basil*, surnamed the great, and *S. Ephræm*; the first a *Grecian*, and the other a *Syrian*, both of
Obiit. an. 370. them religious men, great friends the one to the other, and glorious for their miracles, reuelations, and other heuenly fauours, in so much
S. Greg. Nazian. orat. in laud. Basil. that *S. Ephræm* compareth the miracles of *S. Basil*, with those of *Elias*, and *Elizeus*, and testifieth, that as he him selfe was admonished by a deuine vision, to goe seeke saint *Basill* to the end he might receiue spi-
Amphil. in vit. eius. ritual comfort of him:) so also S. *Basill* knew of his comming to him,
Theod. li. 4. c. 17. by deuine reuelation, besides that the miracles, prophesies, and rapts of *S. Basil*, are witnessed partly by *S. Gregory Nazianzen*, partly by *S. Am-*
Zonar. in valente. *philochius*, and partly by *Socrates*, *Theodoretus*, and *Zonaras*, in their histories.

Baron. To 4. 14 And such was the fame, and estimation of *S. Eprhems* learning, and holy life, that his homilies were publikely read in churches, next
S. Hieron. de Scriptor. eccl. after the scriptures in *S. Hieroms* tyme, as he testifieth, who liued in the same age, and died not many yeares after *S. Ephræm*. Besides that, we
Platus de bono stat. relig. li. 3. ca. 7. also read, that he was wont to feele, such an inundation of sweetenes in his prayer, and contemplation, that his hart seemed to him ready to burst with the aboundance thereof, in somuch, that he often said to
Obiit. an. 370. almighty God. *Recede a me domine* &c. *Goe from me o lord, for the infirmity of my vessel, is no longer able to endure this.*

15 And no lesse admirable was *S. Martin*, at the same time, who hauing benne a monke, before he was bishop of *Tours*, would not alto-
S. Sulpit. Seuer. in vita S. Mart. gether leaue his monastical life afterwards, but liued for the most part in a monastery, with fourscore other monkes his disciples. And it appeareth in the history of his life (written by *S. Sulpicius* who liued with him) that he had very many apparitions of Angels, and some of our

Sauiour

Sauiour himselfe, and that he had the spirit of prophesy; in admirable maner, and did so many stupendious miracles, euen in raising the dead, that he conuerted thereby infinit numbers of Gentils to the Christian faith, and was held ouer all christendome for an apostolicall man.

Obiit. an. 402. Baron. eod. n. a

16 *S. Hierome*, also liued both in the *Fourth*, and *fift* age, who led a monastical life in *Bethlem*, and affirmeth of himselfe (calling God to witnesse of it) that whiles he liued in the desert, and passed whole dayes, and nights in contemplation, fasting, prayer, and teares, he had such heauenly meditations, visitations, and spiritual comeforts, that it seemed to him very oft, that he was amongst squadrons of Angels, and did ioyfully sing the verse of the canticles; *post te in odorem vnguentorum tuorum, curremus. VVe will runne after thee, to the sweete sauour of thy ointments.*

S. Hieron. ep. 22. ad Eustochium.

Cant. 1. Obiit. an. 420.

17 We read also in *Cassianus*, who liued at the same time, to wit in the *fift* age, and died within a few yeares after *S. Hierome*, that an Abbot of a monastery in the desert of *Scithia*, who had led before an heremitical life, was oft times in the desert so rauished, and abstract from his senses, with the sweetnes of contemplation, that he knew not at night, whether he had eaten any thing that day, or yet the day before, and that therefore his allowance of bread for the whole weeke was giuen him at once, by seauen equal portions, to the end he might know, aswell at the weekes end, as euery eueninge, whether he had eaten his daies allowance, or no: And the same authour also writeth vppon his owne knowledge, diuers other notable, and strange things, of the heauenly contemplation, of many other religious men, which I omit for breuities sake.

Ioan. Cassia. col. 19. c. 14. a. Obiit. an. 435.

18 In like maner *Palladius*, a bishop of *Capadocia* (who wrote a history of his owne peregrination, wherein he visited the monasteries in the deserts of *Egipt*) recounteth most admirable things, not only of the seuere disciplin, and angelical life of the religious there, but also of the great graces which almighty God bestowed vppon them, in the operation of miracles, the spirit of prophesy, rapts, and cælestial consolations, namely of the famous *Macarius*, who he saith, was almost continually rauished in spirit: And the like he affirmeth, of one *Isidorus*, who was so contemplatiue, that he fell many times into his rapts, whiles he was at meate amongst his brethren. And if I should confirme this point further by the examples of *S. Augustin*, *S. Chrisostome*, *S. Gregory Nazianzen*, and others (who were religious men, and great ornaments of Gods church, in the *Fourth*, and *fift* age) and also add thereto, many admirable things which might be alleadged to the same purpose,

Palladius hist. lausiaca, vel sanctor. patrum

Idem in Macario. Idem in Isidoro.

purpose, out of *Theodoretus* in his history, of the religious liues of holy Monks, and Nunes in his time (which was the *sixt* age, to wit about the yeare of our lord, fiue hundreth, and fifty) I feare, I should be much to tedious, and therefore I will omit, not only those examples but also many other, no lesse admirable in the ensuing ages, contenting my selfe from henceforth with some one, or two in euery age.

Theodoret. histor. religiosa. an. 550.

19 Therefore to proceede, in the *sixt* age, florished S. *Benedict*, founder and patriarke of the holy order of the *Benedictins*, who being a true mirrour of monastical disciplin, was highly fauoured by almighty God, with the spirit of prophesy, with deuine reuelations, with most wonderful miracles, whereby he raised twoo dead men, besides other thinges no lesse miraculous, testified by S. *Gregory* the great, who liued in the same age and wrote his life, and may also serue for an example of this matter, hauing benne himselfe a monke, and an abbot of a monastery before he was pope. And how much he was fauoured by almighty God, yt may appeare, in that being chosen pope, and fied from *Rome*, to hide himselfe in a rock, he was discouered from heauen, by a bright pillar, which hanged ouer him in the ayre, whereby he was found, and brought back to *Rome*: besides that, he had also diuers apparitions of our Sauiour, and of Angels, and did notable miracles, recounted by *Iohannes Diaconus* in his life, wherein it is also witnessed that petrus *Diaconus*, who liued familiarly with S. *Gregory*, saw diuers times, the holy ghost vppon his head in forme of a doue.

Obiit. an. 519.
S. Greg. in vita. S. Benedict.
Ioānes Diacon. in vita S. Greg.
Baron. To. 8. an. 590.
Obiit. an. 604.

20 In the seauenth age, died the blessed Monke *S. Augustin*, our Apostle, sent by *S. Gregory* aforesaid, into our countrie, to conuert the same from paganisme, to the faith of Christ, which hee performed, giuing sufficient testimonie of his vnion and familiaritie, with almighty God, not onlie by the notable effect of his Apostolicall preaching, in the conuersion of King *Ethelbert*, and his subiects, but also by his prophesie of Gods punishment vppon the monks of *Bangor*, for their refusall to preach to the *Saxons*: as also by the miracle which he did, in restoring sight to a blind man by his prayers, as *S. Bede* our famous country man testifieth. And therefore I cannot but note here by the way, how much England is behoulding to monks & religious men, seeing it receiued the light of christian faith from them.

Beda. li. 2. histor c. 2.
Obiit an. 609.

21 Wee read likewise in *S. Bede*, that *S. Cutbert*, who liued also in the seauenth age, being disposed once whiles he was verie yonge, to spend a whole night in prayer, had such heauenlie consolations and visions, that he determined presently to leaue the world, saying to himselfe, if with one nights praier, I haue obtained so great a fauour at Gods handes,

S. Beda in vita S. Cuthberti. c. 4.

des, what may I expect if I bestow al my hole life in prayer, and contemplation? And so repayred presentlie to a monasterie, where he entred into religion, and had afterwards, manie visions of Angels, and glorified God greatlie, by manie notable miracles, both before & after his death, whereof *S. Bede* writeth verie particularly. *Idem ibid. ca. 5. 6. 7. 8. &c. obijt. an. 88.*

22 In the *eight* age, *S. Iohn Damascen* (who was also a monke) flo rished in al vertue, and learning (as appeareth by his notable works yet extant) and how acceptable he was to almightie God, and how effectual were his prayers, it is euident inough by the famous miracle of the restitution, and healing of his hand, cut of by the commaundement of a king of the *Saracens*, which great grace and fauour hee obtained of almightie God, by his prayers to our blessed Lady, who appeared vnto him in his sleepe, and restored his hand, and reunited it to his arme, as testifieth *Iohn* the Patriarke of Hierusalem in the historie of his life. *Ioan. patria arc. Hierosolim. in vita S. Damas. obijt. circa. an. 730.*

23 In the age following, which was the *ninth*, there was an Abbot, called *Ioannicius*, who as *Metaphrastes* witnesseth, so exceeded in contemplation, that hee was often eleuated into the ayre, whiles he was in his prayer: besides that hee was verie eminent for the spirit of prophesie, and manie miraculous workes, which I omit for breuities sake. *obijt. an. 846. Metaphras. in Ioannicio.*

24 In the *tenth* age, liued and died S. *Dunstan* Bishop of *Canterburie*, who was a monke before hee was bishop, and after built forty eigh monasteries, and had throughout the course of his life, manie celestiall comforts, rapts, visions, apparitions of Angels, and conference with them, and excelled also in the operation of miracles, and prophetical predictions, testified by al our ancient historiographers, which write of his time. *obijt an. 988. Osbert. in vita Dunsto. apud Surium. 19. maij. Matth. vvestm. an. 979. Polid. histor. Ang. li. 6.*

25 In the next age, S. *Romualdus*, founder of the Hermits of *Camaldola*, was famous throughout al christendome, for his holie life, his miracles, his reuelations, his spirit of prophesie, his illuminations, and heauenlie visions, related by the famous Cardinal, *S. Petrus Damianus*, who wrote his life, within fifteene yeares after his death, whiles the fame, and knowledge thereof, was yet fresh in euerie mans memorie. *obijt. an. 1027. S. Petrus. Damian. in vita S. Romualdi. Baron. an. 1027.*

26 In the same age, liued the famous *Hildebrand*, who being first a monke in the Abbey of *Cluny*, and afterwardes pope, called *Gregory* the seauenth, was so contemplatiue, and had such deuine illuminations, that he was some times rauished in spirit, amidst his temporal negotiations, and had frequent rapts in his priuat deuotions: besides *Baron. an. 1073.*

that hee had manie reuelations euen in mens thoughts, and visions of Angels, and the spirit of prophesie, as testifieth *VVilliam of Malmesburie*, an historiographer of ours, who vnderstood some strange particulers, which he writeth of him, by the relation of the Abbot of *Cluny*, who knew him, and witnessed the same vppon his owne knowledge, and experience.

Guliel. Malmesb. de gest. reg. Angl. l. 5. Baron. an. 1061.

27 In the age following, died our notable prelate, S. *Anselmus*, who was first monke, and after Abbot of *Beck* in *Normandy*, and lastlie bishop of *Canterbury*, famous throughout the christian world, for his great vertue & learning, whereof sufficient testimony remaineth vntill this day, by his learned bookes: of whome *Edinerus* (who liued with him, & wrote his life) witnesseth that he had manie notable reuelatiōs, visions, & rapts in his praiers, & that a globe of fire, was once seene about his head, whiles he was at his deuotions, and finally that almighty God wrought by him wonderfull miracles, whereof he recounteth very manie.

Edinerus. in vita Anselmi.

obijt. an. 1109.

28 In the same age, liued and died S. *Bernard*, the honour of religious men, of whose stupendious and continual miracles, al the histories that treat of him, & his time, giue ample testimonie: besides that his vnion & intire familiaritie with almighty God, abundantly appeareth by his prophetical predictiōs, & by the innumerable soules which he conuerted to God, with his sermons & conferences, in so much that women were faine manie times to shut vp their children, & diuert their husbāds from hearing him, least otherwise they would forsake the world, as his father, vncle, brethren & sisters, & verie manie others had donne, & dalie did by his example, & perswasion, of whose great grace in the operation of miracles, I shall haue so iust occasion to speake amply hereafter, that I thinke good to omit it heare.

29 After him in the next age, three Apostolical & Euangelical men, were of singular fame in Gods church, to wit, S. *Francis*, S. *Dominick*, & S. *Thomas Aquinas*. Of the first (who instituted the holie order of the grey Friars) the famous S. *Bonauenture* witnesseth in the historie of his life, that besides the vertue of miracles, which hee had in wonderfull manner, he had also manie deuine visions of our Sauiour, manie reuelatiōs, & verie frequent rapts, & the same some times most stupendious, being raised, & eleuated into the aire, as high as the clouds. Lastly that in one of his rapts, two yeares before his death, the marke of our Sauiours most sacred wounds, were printed in his handes, feete & side, and that they remained there during his life, whereof there were innumerable witnesses, & amongst others, *Pope Alexander* the fourth, who in a sermon

S. Bonauent. in vita S. Francisci.

obijt. an. 1226.

ſermon(whereat *S. Bonauenture*, as he writeth was preſent) teſtified that he had ſeene them himſelfe.

30 *S. Dominick* alſo (who was the founder of the holie order of the black Friars, or Friar preachers) was no leſſe admirable for his miracles, and namelie for reuiuing the dead, then for his reuelations, prophetical predictions, and moſt ſtrange rapts, whereby hee was ſometimes eleuated, and detained in the aire, a cubit aboue the ground. And the verie like wee read of *S. Thomas Aquinas*, who was a *Dominican* Friar, and no leſſe fauored by almightie God, then his founder *S. Dominick*, with deuine viſions, reuelations, & admirable rapts, in ſo much that he was alſo ſometimes eleuated in the aire, beſides diuers miracles, which it pleaſed God to worke by him, aſwel in his life, as after his death.

obijt. an. 1221. S. Antonin. hiſt. tit. 23. c. 4. parag. 7. In vita eius. apud Suriū. 4. Auguſti. Obijt. an. 1271. Ibid. 7. mar.

31 And although I haue for breuities ſake, omitted heretofore diuers notable women, whoſe miraculous workes, reuelations & rapts, shewed euidently their great vniō, & familiarity with almightie God (as namely S. *Gertrud*, S. *Mechtild*, *S. Clare*, *S. Elizabeth Abbeſſe* of *Spalbec*, al of them admirable for rapts, & reuelations, & ſpecially the two laſt, of whom we read, that *S. Clare* was verie oft a whole month together, rauished in ſpirit without anie vſe of her ſenſes: and S. *Elizabeth* of *Spalbec*, was cōmonly ſeauen times a day abſtracted from her ſenſes in ſuch ſort, that shee had neither ſence, nor breath, but was ſtife & cold, as if she had bene ſtarke dead:) though I ſay I haue omitted theſe, & diuers other famous contemplatiue women, yet I cannot lett paſſe two, which ſucceeded in the next age after *S. Thomas*, to wit, *S. Brigit* & *S. Katerin of Siena*, of whome the firſt being deſcended of the royal race of the kings of *Sueden*, as I haue ſignified before, and maried to a prince called *Vlpho*, gaue her ſelfe after his death, to monaſticall and contemplatiue life, wherein shee profited and excelled ſo much, that beeing ofttimes rauished in ſpirit, shee had verie manie apparitions of our Sauiour, who amongſt manie other thinges, reuealed vnto her, the holie rule which shee leaft to thoſe of her order (whereof I haue alſo ſpoken before:) beſides that hee imparted vnto her ſo great a grace, and ſuch a hate and horrour of ſinne, that if anie man that was in mortall ſinne came to her preſence, shee could not endure the ſauour of him, but was faine, ether to ſtop her noſe, or to depart from the place.

Lodouicus Bloſius in Apolog. pro Thaulero ca. 2. Idem in monili ſpirituali ca. 2. Paulo Morigia dell' origine delle religioni. Obijt. an. 1373. Bloſius in moni. li. ſpirit. Chap. 26. nu. 27.

32 *S. Katherin* of *Siena*, dedicated her ſelfe to the ſeruice of God, and to religious life, euen from her infancy, and afterwards taking the habit of *S. Dominick*, became as I may ſay, the wonder of the world in her time, for the infinit fauours she receiued of almighty God, & the ineffa-

Obijt. an. 1380.

F. Raimund. de Capua. in vita S. Katerina Senensis.

familiarity she had with him, which appeared in her supernatural gifts, of more then humane wisdome and prudence, her most miraculous workes, her prophesies, frequent rapts, continuing ordinarily two, or three houres, after she receiued the blessed sacrament, and once three daies together, during which time, she had no vse at all of her senses, and some times in these rapts, shee was drawne vp into the aire; and finally in one of them, shee receiued of almighty God the same fauour, which *S. Frauncis* did, hauing the signes of our Sauiours fiue blessed wounds, printed in her hands, feete, and syde, all which is testified, not only by two most religious, and graue personages, who liued with her, and wrote her life, but also by pope *Pius* the second, in his Bul of her canonization, vppon due and euident proofe thereof.

P. Stephanus Carthus. P. Raymundus Dominic. Obiit. an. 1463. Frācis. Pena, & pietro Galesino in his life.

33 In the next age, liued *S. Diego de Alcala* in *Spaine*, a lay brother, of the holy order of *S. Francis*, a man of such rare vertue, and so highly contemplatiue (though altogether vnlearned) that he was seene many times, eleuated into the aire in his rapts (as before I haue also signified of diuers others:) and so many were the miracles donne by him, not only in his life, but also after his death, that he was after due examination and proofe thereof, canonized by pope *Sixtus* the Fift, in the yeare *a thousand fiue hundreth eighty eight*, at the sute of *Philip* the second last king of *Spaine*, vpon the miraculous recouery of his sonne *Charles*, who being in *Arcala* at the point of death, and giuen ouer by the phisicians, had an apparition of S. *Diego*, and there vppon recouered his health. The life, and Miracles of S. *Diego*, were written by a very learned man, called *Francisco Penia*, auditor of the *Rota*, at this present, and by *Pietro Gallesino, pronotario Apostolico*, and others.

34 In the same age, liued also S. *Frauncis de Paula*, founder of the holly order of the *Minimi* (whereof I haue spoken before) and so famous was he for his sanctity, and holly life, his many, and wonderfull miracles, his prophesies, and reuelations, his infused, and supernatural wisdome, that *Lewis* the eleuenth king of *France*, procured that pope *Sixtus* the Fourth, commaunded him to passe from *Calabria* in the kingdome of *Naples* into *France*, for the said kings consolation, and in what admiration he was there held, it may appeare by the testimony of *Philip* de *Comines*, vppon his owne knowledge, affirminge that he had heard him oft times discourse so wisely, and deuinely in the presence of king *Lewis*, of king *Charles* his sonne, and of all the peeres of *France*, that it seemed that the holy Ghost inspired him, and spake by his mouth (as I haue signified in the first part of this treatise:) and further the same auth or saith, that in his opinion he neuer saw so holly a man, and that

Phil. Comin. du Roy. Louis. c. 130.

he

he forbeareth to speake more particulerly of him, because he was then liuing. His passage into *France*, was about the yeare of our lord, *a thousand foure hundreth eighty*, and he died in the beginning of the next age following, to wit in the yeare *a thousand fiue hundreth, and seauen,* *Obiit. an.* being *Ninety one* yeares old, hauing liued an hermits life, from the age 1507. of *twelue* yeares, as *Philip* de *Comines* also witnesseth.

35 Being now come to the last age, whereof the greatest part doth not passe the memory of man, I will conclude with the examples of certaine holy personages, knowne to many yet lyuing. The first shalbe the blessed Father *Ignatius* de *Loyola*, founder of the holy society of *P. Ribadenieyra della vita del. P. Ignat.* *Iesus*, of whome I haue also spoken sometimes before. Of him it is written, by a reuerend and learned graue man yet aliue (who was intrinsecal with him) that after he had fully abandoned the world, and giuen himselfe wholy to the seruice of God, yea, and passed some greueous temptations (as commonly all those doe which tend to perfection of life) he had exceeding great consolations from almighty God, in his meditations, and prayers: As for example, being one day in S. *Dominicks* church in *Manresa*, saying our Ladies office, as he daily did, he was suddenly illuminated in his vnderstanding, and had such a liuely representation therein of the blessed Trinity, with such an inward ioy and heauenlie comefort, that he burst out into teares, which he could not stay for a long time, and all that day after, could not talke, or discourse of any thing els, but of that blessed misterie, which he explicated admirablie, to the astonishment of those which heard him; and though at that time he had studied nothing at all, neither had any ability of learning, but only to write, and read, yet he wrote presently a treatise of the blessed Trinity, of *eightie*, sheetes of paper, and euer after during his life, had particuler consolation, and swetenes, in the meditation of that profound misterie.

36 The like light he also receiued at diuers other times, concerning diuers other articles of our faith, and was sometimes wholy rauished, *Idem ibid.* and transported with the contemplation of heauenlie thinges, and speciallie once most admirablie at *Manresa*, where he had a rapt, which continued eight daies, in such sort, that no life appeared in him, but only by his pulse, and a litle panting of his hart, which this author saith, was related to him, and others, by them who were eye witnesses of it. And so aboundant was the sweetenes, and spiritual comefort which he commonlie had in prayer, that the aboundance of his teares, proceeding thereof, had almost made him blynd. Finallie his great vnion with almightie God, appeareth also sufficientlie other waise,

aswell by diuers apparitions which he had of our Sauiour, our blessed Lady, and other Saints, as by his reuelations and propheticall predictions of things to come, which may be seene in the historie of his life, and proued by other sufficient testimonie of men, yet liuing; besides many notable miracles donne by him, and his intercession to God, both since, and before his death, whereof autentical informations, and profes haue benne for some time, and are daily taken by order of the sea Apostolike.

Obiit. an. 1556.

37 In like maner, the Blessed Father *Franciscus Xauerius*, one of the first companions to Father *Ignatius* in his holy institut, and sent by him afterwards in to the *east India*, was also most admirable, not only for his reuelations, prophesies, and miracles (which he did in the conuersion of the Indians, and namely for reuiuing fower dead persons:) but also for the abundance of spiritual consolations in his prayers and deuotions, wherein he passed, and spent whole nights many times before he was aware: and so insupportable was the sweetenes which he felt therein, that he hath bene ouer heard to say to almightie God. *No more o lord, no more, this is ynough take me o lord, vnto thee or doe me not this fauour, for it is intolerable to feele thee, and not to see thee.* Thus was he some times heard to say in his priuat, and secret deuotions; besides that, he was so transported, and absorpt many times with his heauenlie meditations, that when he went any iourney (which he did alwaise on foote) he lost his way, and went into the briers and brambles, before he was aware. And to conclude concerning him, his apostolical vertues, and vnion with God, are further sufficientlie testified, by the fruites of his holy labours, *in Capo de Camorin* (where he built aboue forty churches) and in *Mazane* (where he conuerted twoo kings and a great number of their subiects) and in *Malacha*, the Ilands of *Molucche*, the Iland of *Moro* (where the people were most sauage, fierce, & barbarous: & lastly in *Giapone*, in which places he conuerted an innumerable multitud of soules to the christian faith, cured the sick, healed the lame, restored sight to the blind, and life to the dead, as I haue said: besids that his body remained a long time after his death vncorrupt, and fresh (as it still doth, for ought is yet knowne to the contrary) of all which, *Don Iohn* the third of that name, king of *Portugal*, caused autentical, and publike testimonie to be taken, in those parts where he had preached.

P. Petrus Ribaden. in vita eius & Horatius Tursellin. in vita B. Xauerij li. 2. c. 7.

Platus de bono status relig. li. 3. cap. 7.

Obiit. an. 1552.

38 To these twoo, I cannot omit to add twoo others of the same society, the one father *Fraciscus Borgia*, and the other father, *Lewis Gonzaga*,

Gonzaga, both of them princes of birth, to whome almightie God, imparted his fauours aboundantlie, in prayer, and meditation. The first to wit, father *Borgia*, being duke of *Gandia* in *Spaine*, and much esteemed of the Emperour *Charles* the fift, abandoned his estate, and dignities, and tooke the habit and name of the societie, in the yeare of our lord *a thousand fiue hundreth fifty, and one*, and within a short time, made so great progresse in contempt of the world, and mortification of himselfe, that he was admired of all that knew him, and after some yeares, was made general of the societie: and (to omit other particulers of his admirable vertues, and Gods great fauour towards him) the heauenlie consolation, and visitations which he had in prayer were such, that he was very oft depriued of all sence, and feeling for a time: and it chaunced once in the colledge of the society at *Medina del Campo*, that the Rector called Father *Ruis Portillio*, entring into his chamber vppon a suddaine, whiles he was at his prayers, found him all enuironed with a heauenlie light, and his face casting out beames like the sunne. As also an other time, a doctor called *Ayala*, comming suddenlie to him in the night at *Berlanga*, whiles he was praying without candell or fire, found all his chamber full of light, proceeding as it seemed to the doctor, from the fathers face, and eyes. I omit for breuities sake his prediction of diuers things to come, and knowledge of thinges donne, in places remote, and other his miraculous workes, which may be seene in the historie of his life, written in latine, by Father *Andrews Schottus*, and in Spanish by Father *Ribadeneira* yet liuing.

P. Pedro Ribaden. en la vida del P. Francis. Borgea.

Andreas Schottus in vita eius.

Obiit. an. 1572.

39 Father *Lewis Gonzaga*, eldest sonne to the Marquesse of *Castiglione*, of the house of *Mantua*, being but twelue yeares of age, had wonderfull illuminations of almightie God, and such grace of prayer, and contemplation, that euen then, he gaue himselfe wholie to deuotion, and by importunate suite to his parents, obtained after a few yeares, leaue to renounce his right in their state to his yonger brother, and to enter in to the societie of *Iesus*, and within a while grew to be so contemplatiue, and recollected in himselfe, that he comonlie passed whole houres of meditation, without any distraction in the world of other cogitations, in so much that if any entred into his chamber, during the time of his ordinarie prayer, he had no vnderstanding, or knowledge thereof: and such was the sweetenes, and celestial comfort he felt in his soule, & so feruent his loue of God, that commonly his hart melted, as it were, into streames of teares: and he had these heauenly motiōs of Gods loue not only in his meditatiōs but also

P. Virgil. Seppa[r]ine la vita del P. Luigi Gonzaga.

also in his ordinarie vocal prayer, not being able many times, to vtter the wordes thereof, insomuch that his superiours were forced to allow him double time to that which others had, for the saying of his office. Yea and which is more, it fell out very oft in common conuersation, that when there was any speech in his presence of our Sauiours passion, or of his loue to man, he grew to such an agony, and pang of deuine loue, that his hart would swell, and beate, as though it would breake, or leape out of his body, in which respect many did forbeare to speake of such matter, whiles he was present: and such was withall his puritie, and innocencie of life, that he was held of all that knew him, for a very saint on earth, though he was in the flower of his youth, being not aboue *twenty three yeares* of age when he died, which was but sixteene yeares agoe: sithence which time, it hath pleased God, to glorifie his owne name, and to giue testimonie to the great vertue of his seruant, by many notable, and manifest miracles, done as well here in *Rome* were he died, and is buried, as also in diuers other parts, and namely vppon the Duke of *Mantua* his kinsman, who hauing benne here not past three yeares agoe, in the yeare *a thousand sixe hundreth and fiue*, and returning backe to his state by *Florence*, was suddainely deliuered from most greeueous paines, and diseases, with the only application of a relick of Father *Lewis*, to the affected parts: whereof he presently after, aduertised by his letters, the *Marques* of *Castiglione*, yonger brother to father *Lewis*, and embassadour for the Emperour at that time here in *Rome*, as he also is at this present, which letters are printed with the historie of Father *Lewis* his life, and the relation of aboue seauenty notable miracles, and of the autentical proofes thereof.

Obiit an. 1591.

40 I omit to speake of twoo notable men, who died but a few yeares past, partly for breuities sake, and partly because they were not professed of any order of religion, though ecclesiastical persons, and liued most religiouslie, I meane the famous Cardinal *Carolo Boromeo*, Archbishop of *Millan*, and father *Philippo Nerio*, the institutor of the congregation of priestes, called the *Oratory* in *Pozzo Bianco*, or *Chiesa noua*, both of them highly fauoured by almightie God, with the gift of contemplatiue prayer, accompanied with many euident miracles, both in their life, and also since their death, which I omit, I say, to the end, that I may say somewhat of a notable, and holy woman, called Mother *Teresa de Iesus*, who died in *Spaine*, not past *fiue and twenty yeares* agoe.

41 This mother *Teresa*, being a *Carmelitan* Nunne, and the first authour of the late, and notable reformation of that order, aswell of the

the men as of the women, receiued admirable graces, and giftes of almightie God, to his great glory, and the edification of his church. For she had not only the ſpirit of propheſie, frequent rapts, and ſome-times eleuations in the aire, in the ſight, and preſence of her religious ſiſters, but alſo ordinarie apparitions, and moſt louing, and famlliar viſitations of our Sauiour, and conferences with him, wherein he comforted, aduiſed, and directed her in matters aſwell concerning the reformation of her order (which as I haue ſaid, ſhee notablie reformed, and reduced to the firſt perfection) as alſo for her owne ſpi-ritual comefort, and the direction of others in matters of ſpirit, and contemplation, whereof she wrote moſt deuinelie by the inſtruction of our Sauiour himſelfe, as appeareth in the hiſtorie of her owne life, which shee ſett downe by the commaundement of her ghoſtlie fa-ther, in ſuch ſort, that whoſoeuer readeth it, may eaſelie ſee, that it farre ſurpaſſeth the capacitie of a woman, yea, or of any man els, without the ſpeciall aſſiſtance of the holy Ghoſt: and in confirmation of all former fauours, which almightie God beſtowed vppon her, and others by her meanes in her life, it pleaſed him alſo, to honour her body after her death, with moſt ſweete and fragrant ſauours, which it caſt forth, to the admiration of all that were preſent, and not only her body yelded the ſame fragancie, but alſo all the clothes that shee vſed in her ſicknes, had, and retained the ſame a long time after: Be-ſides that the body being alſo viſited *ſix* yeares after, was ſtill vncor-rupted, retaining that fragrant ſauour, and communicating the ſame to all thinges that touched it, as the graue and learned father *Ribera* (who wrote a moſt excellent coment vppon the leſſer prophets) wit-neſſeth in the hiſtorie, which he wrote of her life, affirming the ſa-me vppon his owne knowledge, deſcribing the maner how he ſaw her body ſtand vpright vncorrupt, and breathing forth a moſt ſweete odour, in the yeare *a thouſand fiue hundreth eightie eight* (which was *ſixe* yeares after her death:) and further he declareth, the great ſuite in law, which was betwixt the townes of *Alua*, and *Auila* for her body, and how pope *Sixtus Quintus* decided the controuerſie, by his ſentence in fauour of the towne of *Alua*, in the yeare *a thou-ſand fiue hundreth eightie Nyne*, beſides diuers notable miracles, which he affirmeth to haue bene done by her relickes.

P. Ribera in vita M. Tereſa.

42 And foraſmuch as this holy woman, in her notable booke aboue mentioned, relateth certaine admirable things, concerning a religious man of her acquaintance, I wil ſet downe ſome part thereof, becauſe

it also partly concerneth her selfe, and is very pertinent to the matter, which I now treat.

43 This holly father was a Spaniard, called *F. Pedro de Alcantara*, who liuing in the austere rule of the *Franciscans*, called *Obseruants*, added therto an incredible austerity of penance, and mortification, for the space of *Forty seauen yeares*, whereof shee recounteth many strange particulers, which I omit, because I treat not of matters of that kynd, but of spirituall fauours, and consolations, accompaning the exercise of christian contemplation, to which purpose shee testifieth, that his prayer, and contemplation was such, and so continuall, that sometimes he passed eight daies without meat, by reason of his frequent, or rather continual rapts (whereof shee her selfe was once an eye witnesse:) and that a yeare before he died, he appeared to her in a vision, being many leagues distant from her, and that when his end approched, he called for all his brethren, and hauing made them a notable exhortation, he began the psalme, *Letatus sum*, &c. And as soone, as he had ended it, kneeled downe, and gaue vp the ghost, and appeared to her presently, saying, that he went to repose, which shee told to some at the same time, and within eight daies after, the newes came, that he was dead. Finally shee also witnesseth, that he appeared vnto her afterwards in great glory, and said vnto her amongst other things, that it was a happy penance, which he had donne in this life, seeing it was so highly rewarded. Thus much concerning her, and him.

44 And hauing had now this occasion to speake of this holy man, of *S. Francis* his order, I will add *two*, or *three* others of the same profession, for the deuotion I haue to that great Saint, and the honour I beare to those that obserue his rule. And although there is no printed testimony extant, of that which I meane to relate, concerning these holly men of whome I am to speake, yet I haue vnderstood the same by so good, and certaine relation, of men worthy all credit, and respect, that I make no doubt of the truth thereof.

45 Father *Antonio da monte Cicardo*, an *Italian*, professing the rule of *S. Fraunces*, in the holy order of the *Capuchins*, was a man of wonderful perfection of life, eleuation of spirit, and feruour in mentall prayer, wherein he receiued very many heauenly visitations, and deuine consolations, and had withall so great a grace of miracles, that he not only miraculously cured, and healed very many sick men in diuers places, but also raised a dead child at *Ascoli* in the kingdome of *Naples*.

46 Also Father *Antonio Corso*, a man of great austerity of life, and mortification, was so wholy giuen to mentall prayer, that he spent commonly

commonly the greateſt part of the night in the church, and of the day in the woods. And other whiles he was ſo abſtract in contemplation, that he paſſed ſome daies without meate, or drynke, and had withall a notable grace, and gift of miracles, as to giue ſight to the blynd, to heale the ſicke, and to caſt out deuils, and after his death a blind man receiued ſight, by putting on his ſpectacles.

47 In like maner, an other holly *Capuchin* in *Italy*, called *F. Giouanni Spagnolo* (becauſe he was a Spaniard) was ſo contemplatiue, that moſt commonly after maſſe, he paſſed eleauen or twelue houres together in mental prayer, and many times had great rapts, and notable reuelations, which he would neuer vtter for humilities ſake, but only when Father *Franciſco da Ghieſi*, the general of his order, commaunded him to doe it vppon obedience, for the edification, and comefort of his brethren. He foretold, that he should be martired, as afterwards he was: for, hauing got leaue of his generall to goe into *Barberie*, to preach vnto the *Mores*, he was killed by them, and as it is conſtantlie reported, his head being cut of, as he was preaching, continued his ſpeech almoſt an howre after. All theſe three *Capuchins*, died neere about one time, to wit, about the yeare of our Lord, *a thouſand fiue hundred ſixty ſix*.

48 I will now conclude theſe examples, with twoo religious women, whereof the one died, in *Siena* the 30. of Iuly, in the yere of our Lord 1606. and was called *Suora Caterina*, who hauing benne in her youth, of a very diſſolut life, and falling into affliction became ſo repentant, that shee proued an other *Mary Magdalen*, and after she had ſome yeares liued very retired, and ſo mortified with continual penaunce, that shee grew admirable to all that knew her, she entred into the monaſtery of the cõuertites in *Siena*, where shee daily encreaſed in feruour of deuotion, and arriued in time to ſo high a degree of contemplation, that shee was very oft abſtracted from her ſences, and wholy abſorpt with the ſwetenes of her inward conſolations: and this hapned oft times, not only in her priuat prayers, but alſo in her ordinarie conuerſation with others. And further shee had the grace, and ſpirit of propheſie, and did many miraculous things, which were alſo confirmed by other miracles, as well at the time of her death, as afterwards, whereof the truth may eaſelie be knowne, by ſuch of our countrie men, as trauell into theſe parts, as many yearelie, doe, whom I remit to their owne information, as occaſion shalbe offred.

49 The other holy woman, was called *Maria Magdalena di Pazzi*, who

died in *Florence*, the *fiue and twentith* of *May*, in the yeare following,
an. 1607. to wit, *a thousand sixe hundred*, and seuen. And although there passed in the course of her religious life, many admirable things worthie to be recounted, yet I will content my selfe for breuities sake, to touch a few only, which may suffise to shew the stupendious effects, of Gods vnion with a contemplatiue soule, enflamed with his loue, which in her was so abundant, that shee did often in her meditations exclaime. *My sweete Iesus, I can no longer endure this, I die, I burst, this my vessel of earth cannot suffer so great a flame*, with such other like wordes. And this was also verified, by diuers other strange effects, proceeding from the heat, and flame of Gods loue, which being kindled in her soule, had such a redundance to her body, that shee was faine oft times in the deapth of winter, to cast whole buckets of cold water into her owne bosome, in so much that shee might truly say with the Psalmist.
Psal. 38. *Concaluit cor meum intra me, & in meditatione mea exardescit ignis. My heart was heated within me, and in my meditation there burned a fire.*

50 And albeit this is very rare, and may seeme maruellous to such, as
Psal. 67. doe not consider *how meruelous God is in his saints*, yet the like hath bene also experimented in these our daies, in a holy yong man, a *Polac* of the societie of *Iesus* (called. *B. Stanislao*) who for the same cause, was very oft forced, to apply to his naked breast, linnen clothes wet in cold water, and often renewed, to delay, and temper the heat that redounded from his hart to his external parts, in so much that the phisitians being consulted, concerning the cause thereof, determined that it was supernatural: which also sufficientlie appeared by many other signes concurring therewith, all testifiing that his heart being, as I may say, a very furnace of deuine loue, caused those externall, and miraculous inflammations in his breast, whereof there are many witnesses yet liuing: besides that the wonderful miracles wrought by almightie God, through his merits, both before, and since his death, doe notablie confirme the same, as appeareth in the historie of his life.

51 But to returne to the holy woman of whom I spake before. This strange effect, and diuers others, happened vnto her many times vpon, the meditation of these words of the Euangelist. *Verbum caro factum est. The word was made flesh.* Whereby she was commonlie replenished with an extraordinarie loue of God, and drawne into frequent and wonderfull rapts, wherein her face did cast out such beames of light, that the eyes of those which did behould her, dazeled therewith. And in these rapts she continued some times, *foure and twenty houres*, and sometimes three, or foure daies and nights together, and

once

once from Whitson eue, vntill the feast of the blessed Trinitie, which was eight daies, excepting only two houres euery day, during which time shee came to her selfe, and tooke some litle refection of only bread and water, and without any other sleepe then, as it were, a silent repose vppon her knees, and leaning vpon her armes some part of those two houres.

52 And at these times, shee receiued most admirable illustrations, concerning the incomprehensible misterie of the blessed Trinitie, and many deuine impressions of most heauenlie, and saraphical conceipts, which shee vttered oft times in very good latin, though shee neuer learned the latin tongue, and applied many obscure places of holly scripture very aptly to her purpose. Finallie, so many and meruelous were her speeches in this kind, that some quires of paper remaine written thereof, being sett downe at the same time, and in the same manner that shee vttered them.

53 Shee had also the spirit of prophesie in great abundance, and frequent visions, and apparitions of our Sauiour, of his blessed mother, and of other saints: besides that, it hath pleased almightie God (for the confirmation of his other fauours towards her, and his owne greater glory) to worke many notable miracles by her, aswell in the expulsion of Deuils, as in the cure of incurable diseases, and diuers other admirable thinges, not only in the time of her life, but also since her death, euen vntill this day, as will shortly appeare in print vnder publick authoritie, with such autentical proofes of the particulers thereof (as also of all that which I haue here related) that I may be bould to say, curiositie it selfe may rest satisfied therewith.

54 This I haue thought good to set downe, concerning the contemplatiue and religious persons of our time, omitting to speake of many others, no lesse admirable then they, because I hould these sufficient. And I forbeare also to speake of diuers, liuing at this day, because no man yet knoweth how they will perseuer, for such is the mutability, and frailty of man, that the holly Ghost aduiseth in *Ecclesiastes. Ante mortem ne laudes quenquam: praise no man before his death.* yet this I may bouldy affirme, that there are amongst the Catholikes very many in in religion, to whom almightie God communicateth himselfe in no lesse familiar manner, then he hath donne heretofore to most of these others, of whom I haue here spoken: and further, I make no doubt, but that there are innumerable other catholikes, partly religious, and partly secular, who doe participat of such celestiall sweetnes in prayer, that they find how true it is, which God

Eccles. 11.

promised to the faithfull, by the prophet *Esay*, saying. *Adducam eos in montem sanctum meum & lætificabo eos in monte orationis meæ. I will bring them in to my holy hill*, meaning his church, *and I will make them glad, and ioyful in the mountaine of my prayer.* Thus saith the prophet, giuing to vnderstand, the great consolation, that God promised, and giueth many times in prayer to his seruants: whereof all those I say, which are true members of his catholike church, and withall truly contemplatiue (of what state, or vocation soeuer they be) haue sufficient experience, tasting, and drinking now, and then of that heauenly wine mentioned in the *Canticles*, whereof I haue spoken amply before, and will now conclude with *S. Bernard*, saying. *Orando bibitur vinum lætificans*, &c. *In prayer we drinke the wine that maketh vs merry, that is to say, a spirituall wine, which maketh vs dronke, and causeth in vs an obliuion of all carnall pleasures.* Thus he, who had sufficient experience thereof himselfe.

Esay. 56.

Bern. ser. 18. in Cant.

55 How then can it be denied, that the true contemplatiue man, who receiueth such inestimable fauours of almighty God, is most happy euẽ in this life, though in the meane tyme, he should endure neuer so great affliction, & torment? For if the pagan philosopher (of whome *Cicero* maketh mention) being extreamely afflicted with the goute, could say to his paine: *nihil agis dolor, paine thou preuailest nothing at al*, that is to say, thou art not able to shake, or trouble the constancy of my mynd, or to depriue me of the comfort of my vertue, how much more truly may the contemplatiue christian say the same, to all the torments, and miseries of the world, seeing he hath not only true peace of conscience, much more, then any pagan could haue, but also a supernaturall swetenes of deuine consolations, which so replenish, and fortifie his soule, that the comfort, and strength thereof, redoundeth also to the very body, making the same partaker in some sort, of heauenly felicity?

56 We may vnderstand, how true this is, by the example of *Arnulphus*, who being perswaded by *S. Bernard* to forsake the world, and to abandon the great wealth, and pleasures wherein he liued, vndertooke a religious life in the Abbey of *Clareual*, where hauing passed some yeares in great austerity, he was withall miserablie vexed with the torments of the Collick, and hauing one day, endured such an extreame pang thereof, that he had bene long without speech, or sence, he came at last to himselfe, and suddainelie exclaimed, saying. *All is true, o Lord, which thou hast said:* which he so oft repeated, that those who were present greatelie wondered thereat, and asked him the cause why he said soe, and when he still repeated the same words, and answered

Vide Platum de Bono status religiosi li. 3. c. 13. ex histor. ordinis Cisterciens.

answered nothing els, but *that all is true which our lord said*, they were perswaded that he spooke idlie, and knew not what he said: no saith he, I know well, what I say, for our Lord hath said in his gospel, that if any man renounce his riches, kinsfolkes, and freendes for his sake, he shall receiue an hundreth fould for it, euen in this life, which I now proue to be most true; for in these verie torments, which I endure, I find such sweetenes, in respect of gods mercy, that I would not want them, for all the wealth which I haue forsaken, no, though it had benne a hundreth times greater then it was. Therefore if I that ame a wicked, and sinfull wretch, do receiue such contentment, and ioy of these my afflictions, that they are a hundreth times more sweete to me, then were all my worldlie pleasures, what may be thought of the contentment, which the good, and feruent religious men, receiue of their spiritual ioyes, and consolations?

57 Thus said he to the great admiration of all those which were present, whereuppon I conclude, that hereby it appeareth, that the opinion of the Stoicks (to wit, that a good, and wise man, is happy euen in corporall torments, and miserie) is trulie verified in perfect christians, and especially in those that liue in perfection of religion, who by the assistance of gods grace, and holie spirit, doe *glorie*, as the Apostle saith, *in tribulationibus*, in their tribulations and afflictions, and feele swetenes in sorrow, pleasure in paine, and felicitie in corporal miserie, being in soule vnited with their cheefe good, aud the autour of all felicitie: and therefore *S. Ambrose*, speaking of the beatitude, or felicitie of a perfect christian, saith. *Non frangitur doloribus corporis, &c. He is not dismaied with the paines of the bodie, nor with other discommodities, and miseries of this life, which cannot any way impaire his happines, or diminish the sweetenes, and pleasure thereof.* Thus saith he.

Rom. 5.

Ambros. li. 1. de Iacob. & vita beata. ca. 7.

58 And this shall suffise for contemplatiue, or religious life, and the experience that there is at this present, and hath benne in all ages, of Gods extraordinarie fauours towards those, who liue in the perfect exercise thereof. And what I will further inferre thereon, shall appeare in the next chapter.

That the aduersaries of the Roman Church at these dayes, haue no perfect imitation of Christ, and therefore no perfection of Christian religion, nor vnitie with God, and consequentlie, no true felicitie either for themselues, or for the common welth. And for this purpose it is proued, that they haue no practise of the Euangelicall Counsels of our Sauiour: and first touching voluntary pouertie, the practise whereof, is deduced from our Sauiours example, and expresse words, besides the authority, and vniforme consent of all the ancient Fathers: and by the way, the distinction betwixt our Sauiours precepts, and counsels (denied by our aduersaries) is clearelie proued, the shifts and false gloses of Luther, Caluin, *and their fellowes, discouered, and confuted.*

CHAP. 28

1 YT is manifest by that which I haue handled hitherto in this treatise. First, that the felicitie of man in this life, and of common welth, consisteth in mans vnion with God. Secondly, that the same is to bee obtained, specially by the highest perfection of christian religion (consisting in the performance of our Sauiours Counsels, that is to say, in *true pouertie of spirit, chastitie, obedience,* and the perfect mortification, and abnegation of a mans selfe. Thirdly, that the said Counsels of Sauiour, were practised and performed, not onlie by himselfe and his Apostles, but also by verie manie christians in the Apostles time, in the exercise of religious life. Fourthlie, that religious disciplin hath benne deriued from the Apostles time, to this our age, by the approbation, and practise of the most famous, learned, and godlie men, that haue benne in the church of God. Fiftly, that God hath euidentlie concurred with the true and perfect professors thereof, by al the externall signes, that he is euer wont to shew of his internal vnion with man, to wit, by reuelations, by the spirit of prophesie, by rapts, by a corporall participation of spirituall comforts, & by miraculous workes. Lastlie, that the Roman Catholikes, which liue at this day, haue not onlie the same practise of our Sauiours Counsels, and religious life, but also that they haue in like manner, al the externall signes of internall vnion with him, as euidentlie appeareth in the last chapter.

2 Now then, all this hauing benne sufficientlie proued, I inferre thereon two thinges. The one, that the Roman Catholikes, haue aswell the perfection of christian religion, as also the effect thereof, which is true vnion with almighty God, and consequentlie the true

felicitie

felicitie of man, and common welth. And the other is, that their aduersaries, namelie the *Lutherans*, and *Caluinists*, haue none of these, that is to say, they haue no perfection of christian religion, nor vnion with God, and consequentlie no true felicitie, eyther for them selues, or for common welth.

3 And because, the former of the two inferences, which concerneth only the Catholikes, haue bene partly proued already, & wilbe much more cleare hereafter, I will now treate of the latter, concerning *Lutherans*, and *Caluinists*, and make it manifest, that they haue not any perfection of christian religion. And forasmuch, as they not only deny, that christian perfection consisteth in the obseruation of those euangelicall councels (whereof I haue hetherto treated) but also teach that there is no distinction at all of our Sauiours councells, & precepts (interpreting the scriptures which we alleadge for the same, farre otherwise then wee doe,) I will therefore, first clearely deduce the euangelical councells, out of those words of our Sauiour, which I alleaged, to that end, in the *fiue and twentith*, chapter, and wil confirme our interpretation thereof, aswell by the circumstances of the places themselues, as also by the authoritie of the most ancient, and learned Fathers of the church.

4 Secondlie I will proue, by the same authoritie of Scriptures, & Fathers, that the euangelical counsels, are necessarie to the perfection of christian religion: & lastly I will make it cleare, that the sectaries of this time, haue no practise thereof at all, where vppon it must neede follow, that they haue no true christian perfection. In all which discourse, I will also by the way euidentlie shew, the distinctiō of our Sauiours counsells, & precepts, & both discouer, & also confute the shifts, & cauils of our aduersaries, concerning the interpretation of those places of scriptures, wheruppon we ground our Cath. doctrin.

5 Therefore, to the end, that the whole discourse hereof may be the more cleare, I will treate of euery one of the euangelical counsels a part, and first I will beginne with *voluntary pouerty*, vndertaken for the loue of God, which how grateful it is to him, and necessary to christian perfection, may easely be iudged, aswell by the example of our Sauiour Christ, as by his doctrin, seeing he not only preached it, but also practised it himselfe, for our example, as may appeare by the course of his life, which I laid downe breefely out of the holy scriptures, when I treated of contemplation.

6 For he chose to be borne of a poore mother, & in a poore stable, to be visited, first by poore sheppards, to make the poore mās offring

at his presentatiō in the tēple, & to be brought vp in pouertie. He liued in his youth (as may be gathered in the scripture) by *Ioseph* his supposed fathers trade (in which respect, it may be thought, that he was called *faber*, the *carpenter*:) and afterwards when he preached, it appeareth, that he liued by almes, whereof *Iudas* was the purse-bearer, *qui habens loculos*, saith the euangelist, *ea quæ mittebantur portabat, who hauing the purse, caried those things, which were cast in*, that is to say, he had the chardge of the almes, which was giuen by good people, for the maintenance of Christ, and his disciples: besides that, the holly women, which accompanied him from *Galilæa* (as the Euangelist also testifieth) *ministrabant ei de facultatibus suis, did minister vnto him*, that is to say, did assist, and helpe him with their goods; and yet neuertheles when tribute was demaunded of him, he was not able to pay it of his owne store, but commaunded *S. Peter*, to take it out of a fish, which *S. Hierome* noteth for an euident argument of his pouertie, saying that he was so poore: *Vt vnde tributa pro se, & Apostolo redderet, non haberet that he had not where with to pay the tribute, for himselfe, and his apostle*: and then addeth further, that if any man, will obiect, that *Iudas* had money in the purse, which he caried, *respondebimus*, saith *S. Hierome*, *rem pauperum in vsus suos cōuertere nefas putauit, we will answer, that Christ held it, for a wicked act, to conuert the goods of the poore to his owne vse*, so he: giuing to vnderstand, that Christ had not so much as any part of the common almes in particuler, and therefore would not employ it to his owne priuat vse.

Marc. 6. *Ioan. 12.* *Matth. 17.* *S. Hierom. in Matt. 17.* *Matth. 8.* *Luc. 10.* *Matth. 10.* *S. Aug. de de consensu. euang. li. 2. c. 30.*

7 Moreouer he had not, as he witnesseth himselfe, so much as a poore cottage to dwell in. *Vulpes foueas habent*, saith he, &c. *Foxes haue their holes, and birds their nests, but the sonne of man, hath not where to lay his head*. Also he chose poore disciples, and sent them to preach with expresse order to cary neither *gold*, nor, *siluer*, nor so much as a *purse*, *wallet*, or *scrippe*, nor to weare *shoes*, but *sandals* (as S. Augustin affirmeth:) and so it also may be gathered out of *S. Marke*, which *sandals* were a kind of *shoe*, or slipper, hauing only a sole without vpper leather: and the same sort of shoe, it seemeth also Christ vsed himselfe (if he vsed any) being other waise barefoote, as it appeareth in the holly scripture, for that *Mary Magdalen*, could not haue washed, wiped, and annointed his feete, as he was at meat, if his feete had not beene bare, at least on the vpper part.

Mar. 6. *Luc. 7.* *S. Bonauen. opus. see S. Hierome epist. 22. ad Eustoch. Lira in 1. Io. Replicator. Mar. 1. Abulens. q 68 in 3. Math. Suarez de vita Christi Tall. in 1. Ioan. annot. 61.*

8. Furthermore, he did inculcat nothing more vnto his disciples, and hearers, then the contempt of riches, comparing them to thornes, that choake vpp the good seede, representing the dangerous state of rich men, affirming it to be as hard for thē to *enter in to the kingdome of heauen*,

Math. 19.

as

as for a *Camel to passe through a needles eye*, councelling them also to sell all that they had saying, *vendite quæ possidetis , & date elemosinam*, *sell those thinges which you possesse and giue almes* : & after againe to the rich yong man : *si vis perfectus esse vade, & vende omnia quæ habes &c. if thou wilt be perfect, goe and sell all that thou hast, and giue it to the poore.* Luc.12. Matth.19.

9 This then being so, to what purpose did he both practise such an exact pouerty, and also preach, teach, and councell it, but to the end that some at least, should imitate his example, and follow his councell? And therfore although he would not bynd any man thereto by precept, or vnder paine of sinne, and punishment, yet he inuited, and encouraged euery one thereto, by the promise of extraordinary, and eternal rewards, as to a special point of christian perfection. And this is most manifest, by that which he said to the rich yong man, who demanded of him, what he might doe to obtaine life euerlasting, whereto our Sauiour answered, that he should keepe the commaundements, and when he replied that he had kept them from his youth, and desired further to know, what he yet wanted, our Sauiour added: *If thou wilt be perfect, goe, and sell all that thou hast, and giue it to the poore, and thou shalt haue a treasure in heauen, and come, and follow me*: thus said our Sauiour. And now because the sence of his wordes, and doctrin therein, is much controuersed betwixt our aduersaries, and vs, let vs see what some of the most learned, ancient, and holly Fathers of the church vnderstand thereby. Ibid.

10 S. *Ambrose*, hauing notablie declared the difference, betwixt a precept and a councell (saying, that *where there is a precept, there is a law, and where there is a counsell, there is grace*, and that a precept is giuen to recall men to the law of nature, by terrour of penaltie, and a counsell giuen to stirr men, and prouoke them to good woorkes, with the proposition, and promise of rewards) hauing I say taught this, and much more to the same purpose, he proposeth an example of the one and the other in Christs words, to the rich yong man, saying. *Vt intelligas distantiam præcepti, atque consilij*, &c. To the end thou maist vnderstand, the difference betwixt a precept, and a counsel, remember him to whom it was præscribed in the gospel, that he should not commit murther, or adulterie, or beare false witnes (for there is a præcept, or commaundement, where there is a penalty of sinne) but wheu he said, that he had fulfilled the precepts of the law, then councell was giuen him to sell all he had, and to follow our lord, *hæc enim non pro præcepto dantur, sed pro consilio deferuntur* : *For these are not giuen as a commaundement, but as a councel.* *Ambros. li. de viduis vltra medium.*

11 Thus saith *S. Ambrose*, wherein twoo things are to be obserued against our aduersaries, the one is, the distinctió of our Sauiours, precepts, & counsels noted by *S. Ambrose* expressely; the other is that our Sauiour counselled to the yong man voluntary pouerty, aduising him to sell all he had, & to giue it to the poore: where vpon also diuers other things must needes be inferred, as first that voluntarie pouertie vndertaken for the loue, & seruice of God, is most grateful to him, & shalbe highly rewarded by him, seing he councelled it, as *S. Ambrose* teacheth & expressely promised, *thesaurum in cælo, a treasure in heauē*, for the performance of it: secondly it also followeth, that voluntary pouerty is necessary to the perfection of christian religion, seing our Sauiour not only said, *if thou wilt be perfect, goe, & sell all thou hast* &c. but also added, *& veni, sequere me, & come follow me*: signifying that voluntary pouerty, is necessary to the perfect imitation of Christ, wherein consisteth the perfection of christian religion: thirdlie, it must needes also be vnderstood, that this counsel of our Sauiour, was not giuē only to the yong man (as some of our aduersaries affirme, namely *Peter Martyr*, & *Osiander*) but also to all men in general, and therefore *S. Ambrose* alledgeth those wordes of our Sauiour, to proue the difference of precepts and councels giuen to all men alike, and not to particuler persons: besides the very circumstances of the text make the same most cleare, for, as when our Sauiour said, *if thou wilt enter in to life euerlasting, keepe the commaundements*, he gaue to vnderstand, that the obseruation of the commaundements, was a necessarie meane for all men to attaine to saluation: so also when he added, *if thou wilt be perfect, sell all thou hast*, &c. he signified, that pouertie is a necessarie meane for all men to arriue to perfection.

Petrus Mar. li. de Cælibatu & votis.

12 This appeareth also most manifestlie, by that which followeth in the text, for after that *S. Peter*, had heard our Sauiours words, and saw the yong man goe away sadd, as *Origen* noteth, he said: *behold we haue leaft all that we had, and followed thee what then shall we haue?* as who would say, we haue done that which thou hast counselled this yong man to doe, we haue abandoned all that we had and followed thee, what then shalbe our reward? whereto he answered, not that his words were to be vnderstood, as spoken to the yong man only, but to the end they might vnderstand, that he spoke also to them, and to all men els, he said, that they, (to wit the Apostles) which had leaft all, and followed him, should sit vppon twelue seats, and iudge the twelue tribes of *Israell*, and added

Origenes in ca. 19. Matt. ho. 9.

further, whosoeuer shall forsake eyther brethren, or sisters, father, mother, wife, children, or possessions for my name, shall receiue a hundreth fold for it, and possesse life euerlasting.

13 Thus said our Sauiour, giuing plainely to vnderstand, that both the councell of voluntarie pouertie, which he gaue to the yong man, and also the promise of euerlasting reward for the same, was general to all men: whereby also it appeareth, how friuolous is the euasion of *Caluin*, to auoid the force of this place, who saith, that where as the yong man had said to our Sauiour, that he had kept the commaundements from his youth, our Sauiour meaning to signifie that he had lied therein, proposed vnto him, that he should then sell all he had, and giue it to the poore, as if a man, saith *Caluin*, should boast that he knew all things, it might be said vnto him, then tell me how many graines of sand there are in the sea coast: but that this euasion, I say, of *Caluin*, is most vaine, it is euident by our Sauiours answere, to *S. Peter*, promising the reward of eternal glory, yea and an hundreth fold in this life, to whosoeuer should performe that counsell of his.

Caluin li. 4. Instit. ca. 13. ss. 13.

14 Therefore *S. Augustin* expounding this same place, calleth the counsel which our Sauiour gaue to the yong man. *Grande, & præclarum perfectionis consilium, de vendendis rebus suis. A great, and notable counsel of perfection for the selling of his goods:* and further addeth, that those which haue not receiued, or followed his counsel, and yet shalbe free from mortall sinne, *non sedebunt*, saith he, *cum Christo sublimiter iudicaturi: they shall not sitt with Christ to iudge in sublimity, or dignity* (as he promised to his apostles) *sed ad ipsius dextram stabunt misericorditer iudicandi: but shall stand on his right hand to be iudged mercifullie.* Thus saith he, signifiing thereby the eminencie, and excellencie of their reward, who follow our Sauiours counsel of perfection, in comparison of those, who are otherwaise good men, and doe not follow the same: and therefore, the same holy Father saith also in the same place: *Magister bonus mandata legis ab ista excellentiore perfectione distinxit.* Our good master, or teacher (that is to say our Sauiour) distinguished the commaundements of the law, from this more excellent perfection: *ibi enim dixit* &c. *for there he said, if thou wilt come to life, keepe the commaundements, and here he saith, si vis perfectus esse, vende omnia, if thou wilt be perfect, sell all.*

Aug. epist. 39. q. 4.

D. Chrisost. in locum Apostoli ad Rom. salutate Priscam, paulo post principium.

15 Also *S. Chrisostome*, noting the difference of a precept, & a counsell in the same words, of our Sauiour saith, *whereas he said, if thou wilt be perfect* &c. *he spoke it by the way of counsell, and admonition, & it is not all*

one to giue a councell, and to make a law, for he which maketh a law, will haue that which he ordaineth to be fully performed, but he which counselleth, and exhorteth, leaueth yt to the iudgement, and will of the hearer, to choose what he will, of that which is said vnto him, and so, faciendorum dominus, lord, or master of those things which are to be done. Thus farre *S. Chrisostome,* who also in an other place, noteth the like difference of a counsell, and a precept, in those very words of our Sauiour to the yong man, whereof I here speciallie treate. *In diuite,* saith he, *alia pracepit, alia permisit, libero animi arbitrio* &c. *In the rich man, he commaunded some things, and leaft some other to the free will of the mind, for he said not sell all thou hast, but if thou wilt be perfect, sell all.* &c.

Idem ho.21. in 1.Cor.19.

16 These are the words of *S. Chrisostome,* wherein it is also to be noted, that he vnderstood not those words of our Sauiour, as spoken to the yong má only, (as *Peter Martyr* affirmeth) or as of a thing which he did not wish, should be performed (as *Caluin* teacheth,) but as spoken, and counselled to all men in the person of the rich man, and therefore, *S. Chrisostome,* doth not say, *diuiti alia pracepit, Christ commaunded some things to the rich man,* but *in diuite, in the rich man,* meaning that in his person he commaunded some things to all men, as the obseruation of the commaundements (when he said vnto him, *if thou wilt enter into life keepe the commaundements,*) and left some other things to their free wills, as namely voluntarie pouertie, when he said, *if thou wilt be perfect, sell all* &c.

Petrus Martyr. & Caluinus vbi supra.

17 In like manner S. *Hierome,* expounding the same words of our Sauiour, saith. *In potestate nostra est* &c. *It is in our power, whether wee wilbe perfect, or no, but whosoeuer wilbe perfect,* he ought to sell all that he hath. And in an epistle to *Demetrias* the virgin, hauing said, that *it is a point of apostolical, and perfect vertue, to sell all, and to giue it to the poore,* he addeth, *si vis inquit perfectus esse non cogo, non impero* &c. *If thou wilt be perfect,* saith our Sauiour, *I doe not compell thee, I doe not commaund thee, but doe only propose vnto thee the prize, and shew thee the reward, it is in thy hands, to choose, whether thou wilt be crowned for the victory in the combate.* Thus saith *Sainct Hierome,*

S. Hiero. in ca.19 Matt. Idem ad Demetriadem ep.8. de ser. virginit. circa medium.

18 Loe then how clearelie S. *Ambrose, S. Augustin, S. Chrisostome,* and S. *Hierome,* deduce the distinction of precepts, and counsels of our Sauiours owne words, & how euident it is, that he counselled voluntarie pouertie, as a special meanes to the perfection of christian life, yea, & promised a farr greater, & more excellent reward for the same, then for the only obseruation of his commaundements, and lastly

how vaine, and absurd are the shifts of *Caluin*, and *Peter Martir*, in the exposition of this place, seeing they contradict therein, not onlie the sence, and doctrin of the Fathers, but also the verie circumstances of the text it selfe.

19 Besides that the impudency of *Caluin* may bee wondred at, in that he sticketh not to affirme in his Institutions, that *omnes veteres, vna voce clamant nullam voculam a Christo emissam esse, cui non sit necessario obtemperandum*, that al the ould Fathers cry out with one voyce, that there is no one little word vttred by Christ, which must not of necessitie be obeyed: as though the Fathers affirmed, that Christ counselled nothing, but commaunded all thinges, whereas you see, these Fathers manifestlie teach the contrary, distinguishinge clearelie betwixt his precepts, and his counsells, as also all the rest doe, that haue iust occasion to handle that matter, as shall further appeare in some of them, when I shall treat of the next euangelicall counsell, and in the meane time for breuities sake, I remit my reader to the places cited in the margent, out of a *Origen*, *S.* b *Ciprian*, c *Eusebius*, S. d *Basill*, *S.* e *Hierom*, *S.* f *Gregory Nazianzen*, g *Theodoretus*, *S.* h *Gregory* the great, and i *Theophilact*, to omit many others, or rather al other ancient Fathers, who to vse *Caluins* owne wordes, *vna voce clamant, doe cry out with one voyce*, that our Sauiour commaunded some thinges, which must of necessitie be obserued, and counselled some other thinges which hee left to our choise, and therefore *Origen* in the place before cited, calleth the latter, *supra debitum*, *thinges aboue our dutie*, or more then we are bound to, or more then is commaũded, which is also signified by the worde *supererogare*, to bestow or giue more then is due, as *S. Augustin* and *S Paulinus* obserue in the wordes of our Sauiour, speaking of the good *Samaritan*, who hauing giuen to the osteler two deniers to cure the wounded passenger, said vnto him, *quodcunque supererogaueris reddam tibi*, whatsoeuer thou shalt lay out, or bestow ouer and abone that which I haue giuen thee, I will render it vnto thee: which wordes of our Sauiour, the Fathers aforesaid apply to the performance of his Counsels, as surpassing the bounds of duty, wherevppon groweth the phrase, or manner of speech which Catholikes vse, of workes of supererogation, vtterly reiected and derided by our aduersaries, though waranted by the ancient Fathers, and grounded vppon the veritie of the holy scriptures.

20 It being therefore most euident, by that which I haue said alreadie, that our Sauiour counselled voluntarie pouertie, not onlie to the rich young man, but also to euerie man, and a speciall meanes to attaine to christian perfection, let vs now examin what practise the *Lutherans*,

a *Origen. in c.15. ad Roman.*
b *Cipri. de discipli. & habitu virg.*
c *Euseb. li.1. euang. demonst. ca.8.*
d *Basil. li de virg.*
e *Hieron. li. 1. in Iouin.*
f *Grego. Nazian. orat. & in 1. lib.*
g *Theodor. in 7.1. ad Cor.*
h *Greg. li. 15. moral.*
i *Theophil. in ep. ad Titum.*
S. Aug. li. 1. de adulter. coniug. c.14. & li. 2 quæst euan. ca. 19.
S. Paulin. ad Seuerum Sulpitium. ep. 4.

or

or *Caluinists*, haue thereof? Was it euer seene, that anie of them sold, or forsooke all that he had for Christs sake, to giue it in almes, and to imitate our Sauiour and his Apostles in pouertie? Nay doth not the doctrin of their masters, *Luther*, and *Caluin* teach the contrarie, as that it is vnlawfull, and superstitious for a man to make himselfe poore, with intention to please or serue God thereby? Wherein they reuiue the ould heresy of *Vigilantius*, who taught that it were much better for a man to keepe his goods, and to giue almes thereof by litle and litle, then to sell the same out right, to giue the mony at once to the poore: to whom *S. Hierom* ansuereth thus. *Non a me*, saith he, *sed a Domino respondebitur &c. It shal be answered not by me, but by our Lord, if thou wilt be perfect, goe & sell al thou hast, and giue it to the poore: wherein our Lord speaketh to him that desireth to be perfect, who forsaketh his father, shipp and net, as the Apostles did, whereas this other degree, which thou (Vigilantius) dost praise, and commend* (to wit, to keepe a mans goods, to giue almes thereof) *is but the second and third degree which we also allow, so that it be vnderstood withal, that the first & highest degree, is to be preferred before the second and third.*

S. Hieron. contra Vigilan. circa fine.

21 Thus saith *S. Hierome*, wherein I wish two thinges specially to bee noted. The one that hee vnderstandeth no lesse then the Fathers before alleadged, that those words of our Sauiour to the rich yong man, were a general and serious counsel, or aduise giuen to al men, and not spoken to him alone, or onlie to confound him, as *Peter Marter* & *Caluin* would haue it.

22 The other is, that voluntarie pouertie vndertaken for Christs sake, is both most acceptable and gratefull to God, and also a point of the highest perfection of christian life, and consequentlie to be performed, not onlie to auoyd the care & danger, that acompanie worldly wealth, or for the better commoditie, of study, and contemplation, as the philosophers did, or yet to the end, we may preach the gospell more freely, (for which respect the aduersaries seeme some times to admit it) but for the pure loue of God, and the true imitation of our Sauiours pouertie, which were the motiues which induced, not onlie the Apostles to forsake all they had, but moued also the faithfull in their time, to sell their goods, and to lay their money at the Apostles feete.

23 For I would gladlie know, what other cause moued so manie at that time to embrace pouertie? was it to the end they might the more freely preach the ghospell? How can that be vnderstood, either of manie of the common people, whose office, or hability was not to preach, or els of women, who might not so much as speake in the congregation? And yet aswell women as men of all sorts, sold their goods and

liued after in common. Therefore, what els could induce them thereto, but that they vnderstood, that Christ did not only liue himselfe a poore life, to giue vs example, but also that he promised the kingdome of heauen, to all those that would forsake their riches, and possessions for his name, that is to say, for the loue of him? In which respect *S. Bernard*, treating of *S. Peters* words to our Sauiour (*behold we haue leaft all, and followed thee*) and of our Sauiours answer to him, saith. *Hæc sunt verba* &c. *These are the words, which haue throughout the whole world, persuaded men to the contempt of the world, and to voluntary pouerty. These haue filled cloisters with monkes, and deserts with hermits, these doe spoile Egipt, and carry away the vessels thereof, this is the liuely, and effectuall speach, which conuerteth soules, with a happy desire of holly life, & veritatis promißione fideli, and with the faithful promise of verity.*

S. Bernard in verba euang. ecce nos reliquimus, paulo post principium.

24 Thus saith *S. Bernard*, ascribing as you see, all the practise, and exercise of our Sauiours counsel, touching voluntary pouerty, to the force of his words, and promise of eternal reward, which *S. Bernard* calleth, *fidelem promißionem veritatis*, the faithfull promise of verity, or truth, that is to say of Christ who is verity it selfe, and yet how potent soeuer his example, words, and promise haue benne in the world, from his time, vntill this day, yet they haue not had the power to make any *Lutheran*, or *Caluinist* (for ought that euer I haue heard) to sell his substance, and to giue it to the poore for Christs sake, whereas some of all sorts of men (be they neuer so riche, and powerful, neuer so noble, neuer so wise, or learned doe amongst the Roman Catholikes, abandon their worldly welth, power and nobility, renounce, and resigne their wills, wisdome, learning, and themselues wholy to serue God in religion, for the loue of him, which *S. Hierome*, also acknowledged, and admired in his time, saying. *Nostris temporibus Roma possidet* &c. *Rome hath and possesseth, that in our time, which the world knew not before, for in times past, it was rare to see wise, potent, and noble monkes.* Thus saith *S. Hierome*, which hath also appeared to be true in all ensuing ages, euen vntill this day, whereof infinit examples might be alleadged, but for breuities sake, I will content my selfe only to name some Emperours, kings, and princes, that haue bene moued with the words of our Sauiour, according to S. *Bernards* obseruation, to change their imperial, royal, and princely dignities, states, and riches, with religious pouerty.

S. Hieron. ep. 26. ad Pamachium: paulo post principium.

25 So did in *Grece* the emperours a *Isaacius Comnenus*, and b *Ioannes Brena*,

a *Zonar. Annal. To. 3. Baron. an. 1059.*

b *Vide Platum de bono status religiosi.*

Brena, wich latter being both emperour of *Constantinople*, and king of *Hierusalem*, tooke the habit, and profession of the poore *Franciscan* Friars, vppon an apparition, which he had in his prayers of *S. Francis* offring him his habit, wherin he died within a few daies after. c Also the greek emperour *Theodorus Lascaris* the second of that name, tooke a monasticall habit in his last sicknes. And in our west parts d *Lotharius* hauing ben Emperour *Fitfteene* yeares, abandoned the empire, and all worldly honours and pleasures, to serue God in religion.

c. *Nicepho. Gregor. li.* 3.
d. *Baron. an* 855.

26 Of kings there hath bene such a number, that I cannot reckon them all. and no where more, nor so many, in any one country (for ought I read) as in ours, after the comming in of the *Saxons*, as g *Sigibertus*, h *Ethelredus*, i *Chenredus*, *Offa*, k *Inas*, l *Ceolulfus*, and *Egbertus*. In other countries there haue bene very many, as m *Rachisuis* king of the *Lumbards*, n *Pipinus* king of *Italy*, o *Bamba*, p *Veremundus*, q *Ranimirus* king of diuers parts of *Spaine*, and r *Carlomanus* king of *Austratia*, and *Sueuia* in *Germany*, of whome it is written in the chronicle of the famous abbey of *Cassinum* (where he was monke of the holly order of *S. Benedict*) that being sett by *Petronace* the abbot, to keepe the sheepe of the monasterie, he was so diligent in his office, and carefull of his flock, that once, when one of his sheepe was fallen lame, and could not goe with the rest, he tooke her vp, and caried her vppon his shoulders to the fold.

S. Beda. & Polidor. Virgil. hist' Angli.
g *An.* 640.
h *An.* 704.
i *An.* 710.
k *An.* 740.
l *An.* 737.
m *Baron. an.* 750.
n *An.* 805.
o *An.* 674.
p *An.* 786.
q *An.* 1150.
r *Baron. an.* 747.

27 Furthermore to these may also be added, a *Trebellio* king of *Bulgar* in the age following, b *Hugo* king of *Italy*, and of latter times, c *Sigismund* king of *Burgundy*, *Henry* king of *Cyprus* (who was famous for his miracles) and finally d *Iohn* king of *Armenia*, which twoo last, chose to serue God in the poore habite, and religion of the Franciscan Friars, who lyue altogether vppon almes. These emperours, and kings, besides diuers others, whome I haue not named, and many more Empresses & Queenes (whome I purposelie omit for breuities sake) haue for the loue of God, voluntarilie, and ioyfullie, forsaken their imperiall, and royall riches, and dignitie, to embrace religious pouerty.

Vide Platum de bono stat. religio. li. 2. *ca.* 26.
a *Platus ibidem.*
b *Baron. an.* 945.
c *Platus vbi supra.*
d *Ibidem.*

28 And if I should take vppon me, to sett downe the names of all other princes, who haue in like maner abandoned the world, and betaken themselues to religion, I meane all those, who though they had not the title of kings, were neuertheles descended of royall race, or otherwise eyther absolute princes, or of princely state, and dignitie, I feare, I should be ouer tedious, seeing that I haue obserued in the histories of our owne country, aboue sixty sonnes, or daughrers, nephewes, or neeces of kings, who ended their daies in monasticall, and

religious

religious life, whereby it may be iudged, how many such may haue benne in all other countries. I will therefore let all other passe, and mention only some men of great wealth, title, and state, who haue taken the same course in these our daies, as *Don Francisco Borgia*, Duke of *Gandia* in *Spaine*, who entred into the society of *Iesus*, and was general thereof, as I haue signified before. And the duke of *Ioyeuse* in *France*, who some yeares agoe, tooke vppon him the poore habit, and religious rule of the *Capuchins*, and hauing benne here in *Rome*, at the chapter general of his order this last sommer, died in his returne to *France*, leauing behind him an eternal memorie, of his most religious, and exemplar life.

Obiit 1572.

Chap.7. nu. 38.

29 In *Spaine*, also there are at this day, foure heires of the most honorable, and ancient family, of the Earles of S. *Agadea*, and *Buendia*, (best knowne abroad by the title of the *Adelantado* of *Castile*) who one after an other, renounced their estates, and inheritance, to serue God in religion, of whom the eldest, to wit *Don Antonio Padillia*, being in possession of his estate, vnmaried, and hauing no brethren, resigned it to his eldest sister, and entred himselfe into the society of *Iesus*, wherein he still continueth, with great fame of learning, and vertue: and his sister after shee had a while possessed her state, gaue it ouer also to her yonger sister, retiring her selfe into a monasterie, where shee became religious, and so liueth vntill this day. And although her yonger sister, was by the importunitie of her friends, forced much against her will, for the maintenaunce of her house, to marry one of her owne name, and family, neuertheles after her husbands death, shee entred into religion, resigning her whole estate to her eldest sonne, who died without issue, not past two yeares agoe, his second brother (to whome the state then belonged) being newly entred into the societie of *Iesus*: and although he was then but a nouice, and had not made his profession, yet he could not by any meanes be persuaded to returne to the world, but continueth in his former purpose, and religious profession, hauing passed ouer his title, and states to his yonger brother.

30 I omit father *Lewis Gonzaga*, sonne, and heire to the Marques of *Castiglione*, of the house of *Mantua*, in *Italy*, who died in the society of *Iesus* some yeares agoe, and (as I haue declared before) hath benne no lesse glorious for miracles, then he was admirable in his life for his exceeding great vertue, and sanctity. I also let passe many yonger sonnes to princes, and dukes, who are at this present in diuers orders of religion. As namely two sonnes of the present viceroy, or gouer-

nour of the kingdome of *Naples*, who entred a few yeares past, the one into the society of *Iesus*, and the other, into the order of *S. Dominick*: to whom I might add, *Don Inigo de Mendosa*, heyre apparant to his brother the marques of *Mondexar* (one of the grandies of *Spaine*) which *Don Inigo*, hauing serued the catholik king some yeares, in diuers honorable emploiments, and lastly in the embassage of *Venice*, abandoned the world, and died a nouice in the society of *Iesus*, *seauen or eight* yeares agoe. But on these, I say, and diuers others of like quality, I meane not to insist, to conclude with *Don Inigo de Gueuarra Duke of Bouina*, and great marshall of the kingdome of *Naples*, who hauing had many yeares the possession of a great estate, leaft the same three yeares agoe vnto his sonne, bestowing also great somes of money in pious workes, and entred into the society of *Iesus* here in *Rome*, where I heard him protest, whiles he was in his Nouiship, that he could not imagin before he tried it, what true pleasure, and contentment God giueth to his seruants in religious life, and that he had written to his friends, and kinsfolkes, that they litle knew the comfort that he, and others receiued in *S. Andrewes* (for so is called the Nouiciat for the society in Rome) where he then liued, since which time, he hath sometimes for his better mortification, begged for the prisoners, vp and downe *Rome*, with a wallet on his back, according as the nouices of the societie, other whiles vse to doe.

31 This I haue thought good to signifie, concerning such great personages, as in my owne knowledge haue in these our dayes, accounted all the wealth, honour, glory, and delights of the world, for no better then *detrimenta, & stercora, detriments, and dong*, for the loue of Christ, insomuch that we may say, as *S. Bernard* said of such in his time. *Legeram &c. I haue read, saith he, that God hath not chosen many noble men, nor many worthy wise men, nor many potent men, but now contrary to that rule, a wonderful number of such are conuerted to God, through his admirable power, for now the present glory of the world is contemned, the flower of youth troden vnder foote, generosity dis-esteemed, wisdome of the world reputed folly, flesh, and blood not regarded, the affections, and loue of parents, knisfolkes, and friends renounced, the fauours, honours, and dignities of the world, held for no other then dyrt, or dong, to the end that Christ may be gained.*

S. Bernard. ep. 109.

32 Thus saith *S. Bernard* of his time, as also *S. Hierome* said the like before, as you haue heard of the time wherein he liued, and the same may we say still of the Roman Catholikes in these daies, wherein

euery

euery man may see, how much God is glorified, shewing continually such admirable effects of his grace, in the Catholike Roman church, to the vndoubted testimonie of the truth which is taught, and deliuered therein, whereas the *Lutherans, Caluinists*, and other sectaries, haue so litle experience, or knowledge thereof, that very many amongst them, or rather the most part of them in our country (where no publike exercise of catholike religion ys permitted) are vtterly ignorant, that any such things passe in the world abroad: whereby they are depriued, not only of the good example, that such men giue by their contempt of the world, but also of the consolation, that we catholikes receiue, by seeing the great glory of God dayly augmented, by such a manifest demonstration, of the force, and power of his grace, to the confusion of the diuill, and the conquest of the world, and the flesh. Where vppon I conclude, concerning the euangelical counsel of voluntary pouerty, that as the sectaries haue no vse, or practise thereof, so also consequently they haue no perfection of christian religion, which partly consisteth therein, as I haue sufficiently proued, and therefore I will now passe to an other euangelical counsel, to wit, single, and continent life, which shall be the subiect of the next Chapter.

Of the Euangelical counsel of Chastity, *grounded vppon our Sauiours example, and expresse wordes, according to the interpretation of the ancient Fathers. Also the cauils, and peruerse gloses of our aduersaries, are detected, and reiected.*

CHAP. 29.

1 THe Euangelical counsel, of single, and chast life, is deduced, as I haue signified before, out of these wordes of our Sauiour to his Apostles. *Sunt Eunuchi qui de matris vtero* Matth. 19.
&c. *There are Eunuchs, wich are borne so from their mothers wombe, and there are Eunuchs which are made by men, and there are Eunuchs, which haue guelded themselues for the kingdome of heauen, he which can take it, let him take it.* Thus saith our Sauiour: wherein it is to be obserued, that he did not commaund, but counsel continencie, in that, hauing said, *there are Eunuchs which haue guelded themselues for the kingdome of God*, he added, *qui potest capere, capiat, he which can take it, let him take it:* for so doe all the ancient Fathers vnderstand by those wordes,

S.Ciprian de discipli. & habi: virgi. and therefore *S. Ciprian, speaking of voluntarie Eunuchs,* which gueld themselues for the kingdome of heauen, addeth. *Nec hoc iubet dominus, sed hortatur. God doth not commaund this, but exhort vnto it.* Also *S. Augustin*, hauing distinguished plainely betwixt a counsel, and a precept *Aug. serm. 61. de tẽpore.* (saying, *aliud est consilium, aliud praeceptum, a counsel is one thing, and a precept is an other*:) exemplifieth the counsell of virginitie in those wordes of our Sauiour: *Qui potest capere capiat: he which can take it, let him take it.* *Hieron. in ca.19. Math.* *S. Hierome* also expounding the same words, saith. *Hortantis domini vox est, & milites suos ad pudicitiae praemium concitantis. Yt is the voice, or saying of our lord, encouraging his souldiars to the reward of chastity.* And againe, hauing alledged the same wordes of our Sauiour against *Iouinian*, he *Idem contra Iouinianum li. 1.* saith thus. *He proposeth a reward to his champions, he inuiteth them to the course, he houldeth the prize of virginity in his hand, he sheweth the most pure fountaine, and crieth, he which thirsteth, let him come, and drinke, &c.*

S. Chrisost. ho. 63. in Matth. 2 Also *S. Chrisostome*, interpreting the same woords of our Sauiour, saith, that forasmuch as he knew, that it would seeme greueous to exhort men to virginitie, he therefore sought to draw them to the desire thereof, by representing vnto them the necessitie of the law, concerning the indissolubilitie of matrimonie, and then to shew also, that virginitie was possible, he said, that there were Eunuchs, which were borne so, of their mothers, and others made by men, & others againe, which haue gelded themselues for the kingdom of heauen; *quibus verbis*, saith he, *latenter eos ad eligendam virginitatem inducit, dum eam virtutem possibilem esse astruit: in which wordes, he doth secretly induce them to make choice of virginity, whiles he affirmeth yt to be a vertue possible to be obtained.*

3 Thus gathereth S. *Chrisostome* of our Sauiours words, and after- *Ibidem.* wards concludeth, that whereas our Sauiour added, *he that can take it, let him take it*, he propounded the possibilitie of virginitie, together with the difficultie thereof, *vt voluntatis studium plus augeatur, to the end that the desire of mans will, might be the more encreased, and stirred vp to seeke it.* In all which is to be noted, that *S. Chrisostome* teacheth not only, that Christ counselled virginity, but also that he shewed with all, the possibilitie of it, of which point, I shall haue further occasion to speake amply heareafter.

4 But what neede I produce the testimonie of the Fathers of the church to proue virginity, and continency, to be an euangelical counsel, seeing that the Apostle also, ledd with the spirit of his master our Sauiour Christ, so expresly, and seriously counselleth the same, that it may be wondred that any christian man will denie it. *Bonum est*, saith he *1.Cor.7.* *mulierem non tangere, it is good not to touch a woman*, & againe: *Art thou free?*

or loose from a wife? Then doe not seeke a wife. Also *I say to those that are vnmaried, and to widdowes, it is good for them if they remaine so, as I doe.* And againe *I haue no precept of our Lord, concerning virgins, but I giue counsel, as one that haue obtained mercy of God to be faithfull.*] In which words he giueth to vnderstand, that the counsell which he gaue in this behalfe, was not humane, but deuine, seeing he saith, that hee gaue it as *a faithful minister of God*, which he signifieth also most euidentlie afterwardes as S. *Hierom* noteth, when hauing said, that the widow may marrie when shee will, he addeth. *Shee shal be more blessed or happy, if shee remaine so still* (that is to say a widow (and *I thinke that I haue also the spirit of God.* S.Hieron. li. 1. aduersus Iouinian.

5 Behould then how seriously the Apostle exhorteth to continency, ascribing his counsel to the holie Ghost in so much, that the impudency of *Luther* may be wondred at, who is not ashamed to say that *S. Paule* doth not counsel, but disswade continency in that epistle to the *Corinthians*, for that he speaketh also there (as *Luther* supposeth) of the necessitie of matrimonie, because hauing said: *It is good for a man not to touch a woman*, he addeth immediately, *propter fornicationem autem vnusquisque suam habeat vxorem: let euerie man haue his wife to auoyd fornication*: as though he should say (saith *Luther*) I would exhort al men to continency, were it not for one thinge, to wit, for the danger of fornication, for in respect thereof, let euerie man marrie. And this is also the opinion of *Caluin*, and other sectaries, as shall appeare more amplie hereafter.

6 But to the end, it may be seene, how these new Gospellers peruert the sence of the Apostle in this place, contrarie to the circumstances thereof, and to the interpretation of all the ancient Fathers of the church, it is to be vnderstood, that the *Corinthians*, being troubled with the erroneus doctrin of false apostles and preachers (who amongst other thinges, taught that maried men being conuerted to the christian faith, ought to abstaine from their wiues, or vtterlie to leaue them) wrote to *S.Paule*, to haue his resolution concerning the same, who therefore ansewred: *De quibus scripsistis &c. As for the matters whereof you wrotte vnto me, bonum est homini mulierem non tangere, it is good for a man not to touch a woman*, meaning his wife, as some of the Fathers vnderstand it, & as it is more plaine in the greeke where the word *Ginaicos*, signifieth a wife aswell as a woman, and therefore *S. Hierom* readeth it, *it is good for a man not to touch his wife*: so that the sence is, according to that exposition, that it were good that euen maried folkes, would abstaine from the act of matrimonie: and then the Apostle addeth: *propter fornicationem autem: but to auoid fornication* (whereinto the one, or both might Loco.cit.

fall,

fall, in case they should continually abstaine the one from the other) let euerie one of you haue *vxorem suam*, his wife, as *S. Hierom* vnderstandeth it, that is to say, the wife that he had before he was conuerted to the christian faith.

Hieron. li.1. cōtra Iouin. post princip. 7 This I say, is the interpretation of S. *Hierom*, who in his booke against *Iouinian* saith thus, *Non dixit* &c. The Apostle saith not, *let euerie man to auoid fornication marie a wife, but let euerie one haue his wife, suam inquit habiat, sua vtatur quam habebat antiquam crederet. Let him haue saith he, & vse his wife, which hee had before he beleeued: quam bonum erat non tangere &c. VVhom it were good for him not to touch, but after the faith of Christ to know her as his sister onlie, and not as his wife, were it not that the feare of fornication doth excuse it.*. Thus saith S. *Hierom*, concluding that the question expounded by the *Corinthians*, and answered by the Apostle, concerned onlie those who were maried before they were conuerted to the faith, and the same also S. *Ambrose* affirmeth in his commentary vppon this epistle.

S. Ambros. in c.7. ep.1. ad Corin.

8 And although some other Fathers doe vnderstand, that *S. Paule* speaketh generally of all men, aswell of the vnmaried, as the maried, (and so it may bee verie well vnderstood) yet none of them euer so much as dreamed of that which *Luther* auoweth, to wit, that the Apostle diswadeth from virginitie, and exhorteth to mariage, yea some of them teach expresly, that hee not onlie exhorteth to virginitie, but that also in some sort, hee disswadeth from mariage, which is flat contrarie to that which *Luther* affirmeth.

S. Chrisost. de virginitate. 9 This is euident in *S. Chrisostome* and *S. Augustin*, two principall pillers of the Greeke, and Latin Church. S. *Chrisostome*, alleadging the wordes of the Apostle: *propter fornicationem* &c. to auoyd fornication, let euerie one haue his wife, &c: addeth, *in quo videtur &c. wherein hee seemeth to giue a reason, why mariage is graunted or allowed, but indeede he doth secretlie praise and extoll continency.* Thus hee, and alitle after he saith, that the apostle representeth to the *Corinthians*, the inconueniences of maried folkes (as their mutuall subiection, and seruitude the one to the other) like a fisher, that couereth his hooke with his bayte, *eo consilio* saith he, *vt illo ipso sermone de nuptijs deterreat: with the intent to withdraw them from mariage, by his verie speach, and discourse of mariage.* And againe afterwards, yealding a reason, why the Apostle did not inuite the *Corinthians*, to the loue of virginitie, by the hope of heauenlie rewards, and ascribing it to their incapacity of heauenlie thinges, hee concludeth. *Idcirco* &c. *Therefore by the relation of earthlie, visible & sencible thinges hee both exhorteth them to virginitie, and diswadeth them from mariage.*

10 Thus

10 Thus saith S. *Chrisostom.* And the same also S. *Augustin* obserueth, *S. Aug. de*
in the Apostles manner of writing to the *Corinthians. Hoc modo* saith he, *sancta vir-*
exhortatur ad virginitatem, continentiamque perpetuam, vt aliquantulum, *ginitate. ca.*
etiam a nuptijs deterreret. He exhorteth them so to virginitie, that hee did some- *16*
what disswade them from mariage. Thus saith this holie and learned Father, litle imagining that an apostata from his order (for so was *Luther*, being an *Augustin* frier) should *a thousand two hundreth yeares* after him, teach expressely the contrarie. And if perhaps the sectaries do say (as sometimes they doe not stick to doe) that these Fathers, and wee folowing their doctrin, doe condemne mariage, I beseech thee, good Reader, suspend thy iudgment therein, for a while, and thou shalt heare them anon answer, both for themselues, and vs. In the meane time thou seest, that whether the wordes of the Apostle, be to be vnderstood of those only, who were maried before they were conuerted, or of all men in generall, our aduersaries exposition thereof, is cleane contrary to the sense that the holie Fathers deliuered, who made noe other construction of them, but that it is better for euerie man (that hath not bound himselfe voluntarilie to single and chast life) to marie then to commit fornication, and this they also gathred out of that which foloweth afterwardes, to wit. *Qui se non continent nubant. Those which doe not* *1.Cor.7.*
containe, or liue chast, let them marie. Melius enim est nubere, quam vri. For it is better to marie then to be burnt. Not vnderstanding by the word, *vrio*, to be tempted (as our aduersaries will needes haue it to be vnderstood) but to be ouercome by temptation, which is also manifest, partly by the next wordes before: *Qui se non continent. Those which doe not liue chast,* and partlie by the verie nature of the word *vri, to be burnt,* which signifieth a consumption, or a detriment, and dammage receiued by fier, and therefore gold which endureth and resisteth the flame, though it bee made neuer so hoat, cannot properly be said to be burnt, but straw or wood or such other matter as suffreth dammage, and is consumed thereby, in part or in all, and therefore iust men, who resist temptations, are compared in the scripture to gold which is tried in the fier. *S.Hieron. in*
11 Herevpon *S. Hierom* saith. *Si autem se continere non possunt &c. If they can-* *apol.l.contra*
not containe themselues, and wil rather quench the fire of lust with fornication, then *Iouinian.*
with continency, it is better to marrie then to be burnt, that is to say, it is better to marie, then to commit fornication. thus saith he.

12 Also *S. Augustin. Yt seemeth to me,* saith he, *that now at this time, those*
onlie should marie who doe not liue chast, according to that sentence of the Apostle, *S.Aug. de*
those which doe not containe themselues, let them marie, for it is better to marie, *bono cõiug.*
then *ca.10.*

S. Ambros. in 1. Cor. 1. *then to be burnt.* In like manner, *S. Ambrose* vppon the same wordes. *VVhen the will,* saith he, *consenteth to the heate of the flesh, it is burnt: for to suffer desires* (that is to say temptation). *and not to be ouercome, is the act of a worthy, and perfect man.*

13 And *Theodoretus* in like manner, obserueth, that the *Apostle, doth not call burning, cupiditatis molestiam, the trouble of desire or of temptation, sed animæ mancipationem, but the seruitude, and slauery of the soule:* that is to say, when the soule is tyrannised, and ouerthrowne by the temptation of the flesh. So that we see, that the Apostles meaning, (as the Fathers teach) is not to diswade men from single, and chast life, or to perswade them to marriage, as *Luther* dreameth, nor that euery one who is strongly tempted, or may feare fornication, should marry, but that such only as fall into fornication, and will not doe their endeuour, by prayer, o other meanes to resist the temptation, that such, I say, should vse the remedy which God hath ordained, that is to say, take a wife, *propter fornicationem, to auoide fornication.*

14 Furthermore it is euident, that the Fathers vnderstand the Apostles counsell, or permission of mariage, not to belong to those, who haue by vow bound themselues to chastity, and therefore *S. Ambrose*, saith to a professed virgin, who was fallen from her vow: *Dicit aliquis* &c. *But some doth say, melius est nubere, quam vri, it is better to marry then to be burnt, but this saing of the Apostle, doth belong to such a one, as is not yet promised, and hath not receiued the holy veile, but she which hath promised her selfe to Christ, is already married, and ioined to an immortal husband, and if shee will marry, according to the common law of marriage, shee committeth adultery, and becommeth the hand mayd of death.* Thus saith he. And in the same place a litle before, he saith. *Nescio an poßit ei condigna mors aut pæna cogitari.* I know not wheher there can be imagined a sufficient death or punishment for such a one.

S. Ambros. ad virginem lapsam ca. 5.

15 And *Theodoretus*, saith of those wordes of the Apostle. *Non peccat si nubat, shee sinneth not if shee marry. Hoc non peccat,* saith he, *dicit de iis* &c. These wordes, *shee sinneth not, he speaketh of those, who haue not made, pacta, conuenta, seu vota virginitatis, pacts or bargains, couenants or vowes of virginity.*

Theodoret. Epitome diuin. decreto. cap. de virginit. prope finem.

16 And in like sort *S. Chrisostome* distinguishing, betwixt the widow, that hath made no vow, and an other that hath consecrated her selfe to God, saith that the Apostle giueth liberty to the first to marry, but to the latter, saith he. *Non his ergo sed illis dixit, qui se non continent nubant. Not to these but to those he saith, those which doe not liue chast, let them marry.*

S. Chrysost. li. de virginit. c. 39.

Thus

Thus farre *S. Chrisostome.*

17 To whome I will adde, the learned, and holly Father, *S. Ephræm,* most famous in the church of God, euen in his owne dayes, for learning, eloquence, and purity of life, who being demaunded, to whom doe properly belong, these wordes of the Apostle. *Yt is better to marry then to be burnt,* not only satisfied the demaund, but also by the occasion thereof, expounded notably diuers other places of the Apostle, according to our catholike doctrin. *Audi,* saith he, *Apostolum dicentem* &c. Heare the Apostle saying, *I desire, that all men, should be as I am, but euery man hath a proper gifte of God, some in one sort, and some in an other:* for he neither forbiddeth men that are at liberty, lawfully to marry, neither doth he deliuer those which haue renounced the world, from the law of continencie, for to them that are free, and at liberty, he graunteth marriage, saying: *To auoid fornication, let euerie one haue his wife,* and againe: *Marriage is honorable in all, and the bed immaculat, and God will iudge fornicators and adulterers,* but to those, who haue renounced the world, he commaunded continencie, when he said: *Euery one that contendeth or striueth for the maistry, doth abstaine from all things* &c. Therefore to secular men, he permitted lawful marriage, but he would that religious men should liue continent, for if those wordes, *it is better to marry, then to be burnt,* should concerne, or belong to euery one, no man would haue exercised that vertue of continencie, neither *Helias Thesbites,* nor *Elizeus,* nor *Iohn,* nor those that haue guelded themselues for the kingdome of heauen, and haue conserued their flesh chast vnto God, neither would the Apostle himselfe haue liued continent, if he had not had respect to the reward. Thus farre *S. Ephræm.*

S. Ephræm to. 1. paulo post princ. in Resp. ad fratrem sciscitatẽ ad quem hoc dictum pertineat. melius est nubere quam vri.

18 The like is also taught by a *S. Augustin,* b *S. Hierome,* c *S. Epiphan.* d *S. Gregory,* e *Theodoretus,* f *Theophilactus,* g and *Oecumenius,* whose wordes I forbeare to alleadge, because that which I haue said already, may suffice for this point, besides that I shall haue further occasion to touch the same hereafer, when I shall treate more particularly of vowes. In the meane time it appeareth manifestly (if I be not deceiued) that *Luther* and his progenie, doe shamefullie peruert the sense of the holy scriptures, concerning virginitie, and matrimonie, contrarie to the interpretation of the most ancient, and learned Fathers of the church, which yet wilbe much more manifest, when I shall haue examined an other shift of theirs, touching the counsell of virginitie, which *S. Paule* giueth so euidentlie, that they cannot

a *S. Aug. li. de bono viduitat. c. 8.*
b *S. Hierom. lib. 1 in Iouinian.*
c *S. Epihan. hær. 61.*
d *S. Gregor. pastor. li. 3. admonit. 28.*
e *Theodor.*
f *Theophil.*
g *Oecum. in 1. cor. 7.*

possibily deny it, with any apparence or shew of reason, and therefore graunting much against their willes, that hee at least praised, and commended it, they find this euasion, that though he allowed it for temporal respects (because virgins, and continent men, are free frome the troubles of mariage, for so saith *Luther*) yea, and for some kind of spirituall consideration, as to attend the more freely to preaching, and prayer, (for so saith *Peter Martyr*, and *Melanchton*:) yet by no meanes say they, it is to be applied to the worshipp of God, as a thing gratefull to him for it selfe, or meritorius of the kingdome of heauen.

Peter. Mar. in verb. Apost. bonum est homini mulierem nō tangere. *1. Cor. 7. Melanch. in loc. 15. c. de castitate.*

19 I will therefore proue, that the Apostle commended, and counselled virginitie, and single life, not only for temporal commodity, or to the end we may preach, or pray the more freely, but much more for respect of the eternal reward, which is due to chastity, as to a thing most acceptable to God, and therefore to be dedicated to his honour, and seruice.

20 For this purpose our Sauiours owne woords (whereof I haue alreadie treated amply before) are first to be considered, who inuiting to virginitie (when he spoke of voluntary *Eunuchs*) specified the cause, why they geld themselues, saying. *Castrauerūt se propter regnum cælorum. They haue guelded themselues for the kingdome of heauen.* Signifiing, not only that he would reward it with euerlasting life, but also that it is to be vndertaken for the loue of him, to the end we may thereby eternally enioy him, and be vnited with him: and this he signified also plainelie, when he said, to his disciples, whosoeuer shall forsake his wife, *propter nomen meum*, saith he, *for my name* (that is to say *for the loue of me*) *he shall receiue in this world a hundreth fold, and life euerlasting in the next.*

Matth. 19.

Ibidem.

21 Therefore *S. Augustin*, worthily taxeth *Iouinian* the heretike, and and others his followers, of extreame folly, in that they taught (as *Luther*, and other Sectaries doe in these daies) that virginitie was not necessarie for the obtaining of heauen, but for temporall respects. *Mirabiliter* saith he, *desipiunt* &c. *They are notable fooles, who thinke that the vertue of continency, is not necessary for the kingdome, of heauen, but for this present world.* And in an otherplace, *Quæcunque mandat Deus*, saith he &c. *VVhat soeuer God commaundeth, (of which sort this is, thou shalt not commit fornication, or adultery,) and whatsoeuer he commaundeth not, but specially counselleth, or disswadeth (of which sort this is, it is good for a man not to touch a woman) it is then well performed, when it is referred to the loue of God, and of our neighbour in this world, and in the world to come.* Thus farre,

Aug. de sancta virginit. ca. 13. *Aug. in Enchiridio. ca. 121.*

farre, S. *Augustin*, teaching that virginity, and chastity, was not only speciallie counselled, and aduised by our Sauiour, but also that it ought to haue the same scope, and end which all other vertues, and good workes haue, that is to say, both the loue, and seruice of God in this world, as also the euerlasting sight, and fruition of him in the next, whereby we may reigne eternallie with him, and this is properlie that, which our Sauiour signified, when he said, *propter regnum cælorum, for the kingdome of heauen.*

S.Hilarius. in 19 Matth. paulo post. princip.

22 And therefore also *S. Hilarius*, vnderstandeth those wordes of our Sauiour, not as *Peter Martyr* doth, to be spoken of those who are content to liue single, and chast, to the end they may the more freely preach the gospell, but of those that doe it, *spe regni cælestis, for the hope of the heauenly kingdome*, which *S. Hierome* also signifieth plainely, when he saith. *Istis* (Eunuchis) &c. *To this third kind of Eunuches, there is a reward promised, but to the other, whose chastity proceedeth of necessity, and not of their will, nothinge is due.*

S.Hieron. 19.Matth.

S.Cipri.li.de habitu virg. prope finem.

23 Also *S. Cyprian*, alluding to those wordes of our Sauiour, conforteth virgins, representing vnto them, that wheras there ar many different habitations, or mansions in the kingdome of heauen, our Lord shewed vnto them the better sort, and then addeth. *Carnis desideria castrantes, maioris gratiæ præmium in cælestibus obtinetis. VVhen you do gueld or cut of the desires of the flesh, you obtaine the reward of a greater grace in heauen.* And againe in the same treatise, he exhorteth virgins, to study to please only their Lord, from whom they expect the reward of virginity, seeing he himselfe saith, that there are *Eunuchs, which haue guelded themselues for the kingdome of God.* And thus you see, that *S. Cyprian*, also teacheth, that the kingdome of heauen, whereof our Sauiour spoke, is to be vnderstood, as promised by him, for the reward of virginity.

S.Chrisost. ho.63.in ca. 19. Matth.

24 *S. Chrisostome*, in like maner, expounding our Sauiours words, saith to the voluntary *Eunuch. Gratias agas Deo &c. Giue God thankes, for thou shalt haue, magna præmia, & rutilantes coronas, great rewards, and glittering crownes.* In which words, he giueth to vnderstand, what our Sauiour meant, when he said, *propter regnum cælorum, for the kingdome of heauen.*

25 Furthermore, the same may be confirmed, out of the prophesie of *Isayas*, who in the person of God, promiseth to the Eunuchs which shall keepe his law, a place in his house: *Et nomen melius a filiis & filiabus, nomen æternum quod non peribit: A better name then to sonnes, and*

Isay.ca.56.

daughters, an euerlasting name, which shall not perish. Which wordes of the prophet, S. *Basil*, S. *Ambrose*, S. *Hierome*, S. *Cyrill*, S. *Augustin*, and S. *Gregory*, to omit others, doe vniformelie vnderstand, to be spoken of the *voluntary Eunuchs*, of whom our Sauiour spoke in the same place before alleadged. And for asmuch as *Iouinian*, and some other his followers, did in derogation of virginity, interpret those wordes of the prophet, as spoken only of true *Eunuchs*, which are either borne so, or made by mans hand (as also the *Lutherans*, and *Caluinists*, make the like construction thereof in these daies) S. *Augustin* obserueth notablie, that though any man would contend, that the prophet speaketh of true *Eunuchs*, yet the dignitie and merit of virginitie is confirmed thereby. *For if there be*, saith he, *greater glory promised, to Eunuchs who liue chast, whether they will or no, then to the iust maried men, it must needes follow, that much rather the same is promised to voluntary Eunuchs, who liue chast, when they might doe otherwise.* Thus reasoneth this worthy Father, with great reason, and saith further in the same treatise. *Quid tergiuersaris, impia cæcitas* &c. *Why doest thou seeke shifts, wicked blindines, why doest thou promise only temporal commodity to the continent, or chast saints, and seruants of God? Nomen æternum dabo eis. I will giue them an euerlasting name*, &c. And a litle after. *This euerlasting name*, saith he, *what soeuer it is, shall not be common with many, though in the same kingdome, and in the same house, for that it signifieth a certaine proper, and excellent glory, and therefore perhaps it was called, nomen, a name, because it distinguisheth them to whome it is giuen from others.*

S. Basil. de vera virgin. S. Amb. in exhort ad virgin. S. Hieron. & S. Ciril. in hūc locum. S. Aug. de virgin. c. 24. S. Gregor. 3. par. pastoral. c. 29. Petrus mart. li. de calib. & votis. S. August. de sanct. virginit. c. 24. Ibid. 25.

26 Thus farr S. *Augustin*, wherein he teacheth twoo thinges out of the prophet, which make euidently against our aduersaries. The first is, that the prophet speaketh not of true *Eunuchs* (as our aduersaries affirme) but of voluntarie *Eunuchs*, who as our Sauiour said. *Gueld themselues for the kingdome of heauen.* The second is, that it is impiety, and blindnes in any to teach (as *Luther*, and other sectaries doe) that virgins, and others that liue continent, and chast, are to expect no other benefit, or reward thereof, but that which is temporall, and to be had in this life, seeing, that God promised by the prophet, *an eternall name*, which S. *Augustin* interpreteth, to be a certaine peculier and excellent glory, that shall not be common with many other saints, as it is manifest in the plaine words of the prophet, saying. *Dabo eis nomen melius, a filiis & filiabus. I will giue them a better name, then to sonnes, and daughters*, that is to say, to other children, and seruants of God, that are not voluntarie *Eunuhcs*.

27 Therefore

27 Therefore I cannot omit, to note alſo here by the way, the abſurditie of *Peter Martyr*, who to auoid the force of this place of the prophet, doth interpret the Eunuchs there mentioned, to be ſuch Eunuchs, as did liue well, and iuſtly amongſt the Iewes, whom he ſaith, the prophet in the perſon of God comforteth, for their natural infirmitie, promiſing to eſteeme, and hould them more deare, *then ſonnes or daughters*, meaning other *Iſraelites*, who should not keepe his law, as though the wicked *Iſraelits*, who did not obſerue Gods law (and therefore were children of the diuel) could be called the children of God. Beſides that, it is euident, that the prophet promiſeth to thoſe *Eunuchs*, of whom he ſpeaketh, *an eternall name*, which whether it be vnderſtood of eternal glory in heauen, or of a temporal name, and fame in earth, it ouerthroweth the opinion of *Peter Martyr*, and our aduerſaries: For if they take it for heauenlie glory, then they muſt acknowledge with vs, that the kingdome of heauen is due to virginitie, and continencie, which they flatly deny: and if they ſay, that it is to be vnderſtood of temporall fame in this world, then we are to demaund of them, in what true Eunuchs amongſt the *Iſraelits*, the ſame hath bene fulfilled, and who they were, that were ſo famous, as the prophet promiſeth (whereof I thinke they can shew very few examples) whereas on the other ſide, we can shew an infinit number of holy virgins, and voluntarie *Eunuchs*, whoſe names, and fame remaineth glorious in Gods church vntill this day, and will doe to the worlds end.

Petrus mart. in li. de cælibatu & votis.

28 Therefore the true ſenſe thereof is, that ſuch as being voluntary Eunuchs, and doe with all liue well and iuſtly, shall haue a higher place, and greater glory in heauen, then other good men that are maried, which alſo the Apoſtle himſelfe teacheth, when he preferreth virginitie before mariage, ſaying, *that he which marieth his virgin doth well, but he which doth not marry her doth better*. And counſelling the widow to remaine vnmaried, he ſaith. *Beatior erit ſi ſic permanſerit*, *shee shalbe more happy or bleſſed* (that is to ſay, ſaith *S. Ambroſe*, *dignior in futuro ſeculo*, *more worthy in the world to come*) *if shee remaine ſo ſtill*. And the ſame is, in like manner inferred by *S. Hierome*, vppon our Sauiours parable, concerning the good ground, whereof one part yealdeth, *a hundreth for one*, an other *threeſcore*, and the other *thirty*, wherein ſaith he, is ſignified, the difference of the three ſtates, of virginity, widowhood, and mariage, & that by the *hundreth for one*, is vnderſtood the excellent dignity, and merit of *virginity*, by *threeſcore*, the *widowhood*, and by *the thirty* the *maried ſtate*. I omit to alleadge his wordes, both becauſe I hould

1. Cor. 7.

S. Ambr. in hæc verba Apoſtoli.

S. Hierome pro libris cõtra Iouinian. apolog. ep. 50.

hould it needeles, & for that he hath written expresly vppon the same point against *Iouinian*, who taught at that time, to the wonder of the world, that mariage is equal with virginitie, for which opinion amõgst others, hee is registred in the catalogue of heretikes by *S. Augustin* in his treatise of Hæresies, who also in his booke of Retractions, calleth it, *hæresim Iouinianam*, the hæresie of *Iouinian*, and saith further of him. *Huic monstro sancta ecclesia quæ ibi est fidelissimè, ac fortissimè resistit. The holly church which is there*, that is to say *at Rome, doth faithfully, and strongly resist this monster*. Finally this holy Father, wrote also his learned treatise, *de bono coniugali*, specially to confute that heresie of *Iouinian*.

S. August. retractat. li. 2. ca. 22.

29 And now to add, a word, or twoo more, concerning the cause why virginity is principally to be vndertaken, and the end whereto it is to be referred, the Apostle himselfe doth sufficiently declare it, when he saith, that the virgin, and vnmaried woman: *cogitat quæ domini sunt vt sit sancta, & corpore & spiritu: thinketh of those things, which belong to God, to the end she may be holly both in body, and soule*. Whereby we may vnderstand, that single, and chast life, was not counselled by our Sauiour, and the Apostle, only to the end that we may the more freely attend to prayer, as *Peter Martyr, and Melanchton* say, but also, that we may be sanctified thereby, and please almighty God: in which respect S. *Hierome* saith vppon the same wordes of the Apostle, that *pure virginity is, hostia Christi*, the *sacrifice of Christ*, signifiing that God is worshipped, and serued thereby, and againe. *Grandis fidei est &c. It is a point of great faith, and of great vertue, to be the most pure temple of God, and to offer our selues wholy for an holocaust*, or burnt sacrifice, *to our lord, and to be, according to the wordes of the same apostle holly, both in body, and soule*.

1. Cor. 7.

S. Hieron. cõtra Iouin. li. 1. circa medium. Ibidem. Ante mediũ libri.

30 Lo then how this most learned Father, vnderstandeth by the wordes of the Apostle, that God is worshipped, and serued by virginitie, as by a most acceptable, and grateful sacrifice, in which respect also the most ancient Fathers, *Tertullian*, and S. *Cyprian* doe say, that virgins *do wholy dedicat, consecrat, and vow themselues to God, and make oblation to him of their soules, and bodies, consecrating their whole nature vnto him*. Which is also sufficiently testified, by the solemne manner of veiling virgins, vsed from the very apostles tyme to this day, signifiing their renunciation of the world, and dedication of their virginity, to the seruice of God, as appeareth in the places before alleadged, out of *S. Cyprian*, and *Tertulian*, of whom the first, wrote a treatise *of the habit, and disciplin of virgins*, and the other, *of veiling* virgins.

S. Cyprian de disciplina & habitu virgin. Tertul. de veland. virginib.

31 Finally S. *Augustin* (besides the places, which I haue alleadged out of him,

of him before (teacheth our Catholike doctrin in this point, expreſſelie in his booke *de ſancta virginitate*, ſaying, virginitie is not honored, becauſe it is virginitie, *ſed quia deo dicata eſt*, but becauſe it is dedicated to God, which though, it be kept in the fleſh, yet it is kept with the religion, and deuotion of the ſpirit, and therefore the virginitie of the body, which pious continencie doth vow, and keepe, is alſo ſpiritual. Thus ſaith *S. Auguſtin* of virginitie, when it is vowed, and dedicated. So that it is euident, both by Scriptures, Fathers, and the very practiſe of the church, from the Apoſtles time to this, that virginal, or ſingle life, is to be vndertaken not only for temporall reſpects (as *Luther* ſaith) or for the better commoditie of prayer (as *Peter Martyr* affirmeth) but principallie to honour God, by conſecrating our ſelues wholly, aſwell body as ſoule, to his ſeruice, and for the kingdome of heauen, as our Sauiour himſelfe expreſſely taught. *Matth. 19.*

32 This then being moſt manifeſt, how can it be doubted, but that this Euangelical counſell, of ſingle life, and chaſtitie, is moſt requiſit to the perfection of chriſtian religion, eſpeciallie ſeeing I haue proued, that it was not only counſelled by our Sauiour, but alſo recommended by his owne example, and by the example of his mother, and of his Apoſtles, beſides the particuler reward, which God promiſed by his prophet *Eſay* to virgins. *Nomen melius à filiis, & filiabus.* A better name, then to ſonns, and daughters, as I haue ſignified before: *Eſay 56.* whereto may be added, the teſtimonie, of the Euangeliſt *S. Iohn*, in his *Apocalypſe*, where he witneſſeth, that the hundreth, forty and foure thouſand virgins, who followed the lambe where ſoeuer he went, had a particular reward, and different glory from the reſt, in that, he ſaith, they ſong a canticle, or ſong, which none could ſing, but they, and then addeth. *Hi ſunt qui cum mulieribus non ſunt conquinati, virgines enim ſunt.* Theſe are they who haue not benne defiled with women, for they are virgins. *Apo. 14.*

33 And although our aduerſaries, ſeeke alſo to draw this ſaying of *S. Iohn*, to a miſticall ſence, as to be vnderſtood of thoſe who had not benne poluted with Idolatrie (which is called the fornication of the greate hoore of *Babylon*) yet it is euident by the very wordes themſelues, that they cannot be ſo vnderſtood. For *S. Iohn* doth not ſay that they were not cõtaminated, *cum muliere, with the woman* (as he wold haue ſaid, if he had meant the hoore of *Babylon*) but *cũ mulieribus, with women.* Beſides that it is manifeſt, that the farre greater part of the ſaints, were free from Idolatry, whereas thoſe virgins, whereof *S. Iohn* ſpeaketh, were but few in reſpect of al the reſt, who he ſaith, were ſo many, that

Tertul. li. de resurrect. ca. 27. S. Hier. cont. Heluid. in fine. S. Aug. de virgin. ca. 2. S. Greg. part. 3. pastor. ad. 29. S. Bede. S. Anselme Primas. Oecum. in hunc locum.

no man could number them. Lastly, *Tertulian*, *S. Hierome*, *S. Augustin*, *S. Gregory*, *S. Bede*, *S. Anselme*, *Primasius*, and *Oecumenius*, doe all of them expound that place of true virgins: and to omit what the rest of them say hereof, *S. Hierome* alleadging the same place against *Iouinian* saith, that the *one hundreth forty foure thousand*, of whome *S. Iohn* speaketh, are such of the twelue tribes of the *Iewes*, as shall beleeue in Christ, and be virgins with all, and further gathereth the preeminence of virginitie, before widowhood, or mariage, out of these wordes that folow in the same place. *Hi sunt primitiæ Dei, & Agni: for if virgins*, saith he, *be the first fruites to God, and the lambe, then widowes, and maried folkes, shalbe after the first, that is to say, in the second, and third degree*. Thus saith *S. Hierome*.

S. Hier. pro libris contra Iouinian. Apolog. ad Parumachiũ epist. 50. & in Psal. 80. ad finem.

34 And now for as much, as the sectaries, are wont to cry out against vs, and to say, that we are those of whom *S. Paule* gaue warninge, when he said, that some should come in time, and forbid to marry, and to eate the meates, which God hath created to be taken with thankes giuing. The ancient Fathers, shall answer both for themselues, and vs.

S. Chrisost. de virginitate non longe a principia.

35 *S. Chrisostome* forseeing, that some would peruerslie interpret his high commendation of virginitie, to be a prohibition of mariage, preuenteth that cauill by the way of preoccupation, saying. *Qui prohibeo connubiũ* &c? How doe I forbid marriage, who doe not reprehend those which doe marry, and doe seuerely punish fornicators, and adulteries, with suspension from the sacraments, and from the communion of the " church, where as I doe yeald perpetual praise to those that lead the ma- " ried life, so that they doe it chastly, &c. He which dispraiseth marriage, doth wholy take away the glory of virginitie, and he which commen- " deth, and praiseth it, doth make virginitie much more admirable &c. " *Bonum est connubium* &c. Marriage is good, and therefore virginitie is to be admired, because it is better, then that which is good, yea, and so " much better, by how much the master of the shippe, is better then the " sailers, and rowers, the captaine then the souldiars &c. Heauen then earth, and Angels then men. Thus saith *S. Chrisostome*.

S. Hieron. cõtra Iouin. in principio.

36 *S. Hierome*, in like sort, preuenteth the like obiection against himselfe, in his learned confutation of the heresie of *Iouinian*, saying. *Neque nos Marcionis & Manichæi dogma sectantes*, &c. Neither doe wee derogate " from marriage, following the opinion, or doctrin of *Marcion*, & *Manichæus*, neither doe we thinke, that all maner of carnall copulation, " is filthy, or abominable, for we are not deceiued with with the errour " of *Tatianus*, who was the cheefe, and head of the *Encratitæ*, and condemned not only marriage, but also the meates, which God hath crea- " ted to be vsed. Thus farre *S. Hierome*, who also being afterwards calum-

niated

niated by *Iouinians* friendes, wrote an Apologie for himselfe, and for his booke against *Iouinian*, wherein amongst many other notable thinges, he saith in his owne defence. *Erubescat calumniator meus* &c. Let my calumniator be ashamed to say, that I condemne the first mariages, seeing he may read in my booke, *non damno bigamos, & trigamos, & si dici potest octogamos* &c. I doe not condemne those, that haue bene twise maried, and thrise maried, nor if I may so say, those that haue benne eight times maried: it is one thing not to condemne, and an other thing to praise, it is one thing to giue leaue, and an other to recommend a vertue &c. We reprehend *Tatianus* the head of the *Encraticæ*, who reiecteth matrimonie &c. It is the propertie of heretikes, to condemne mariage, and a litle after. *Ecclesia non damnat matrimonia, sed subiicit.* The church doth not condemne matrimonie, but make it subiect, that is to say, it preferreth virginitie before it. Loe then, how *S. Hierome*, not only defendeth him selfe against his calumniators, but also teacheth it to be the heresie of *Tatianus*, *Marcion*, and *Manichæus*, to condemne mariage, & sheweth also, what was the doctrin of the church in his dayes, concerning matrimonie, and virginitie, to wit, the same that wee stil hould, and defend against the sectaries, who haue in these dayes reuiued the dead heresie of *Iouinian*.

Idem Apologia pro libris cōtra Iouin. Paulo, post princip.

37 In like manner *S. Augustin*, to signifie how farre he was from condemning mariage, though he farre preferred virginitie before it, wrote his notable booke, *de bono coniugali*, of the good of marriage, and gaue it that title, as he witnesseth, because *Iouinians* friendes, bragged that no man could answer him, with the praise, and commendation of mariage, but with the dispraise, and reiection of it: and therefore he giueth the due praise to christian matrimonie, commending it not only for diuers other respects, but also for the sanctitie, and hollines of the sacrament, which he acknowledgeth therein, saing. *In nostrarum nuptiis plus valet sanctitas sacramenti, quam fæcunditas vteri.* In the mariage of our women, the holines of the sacrament, is of more worth and valew, then the fecunditie, or fertilitie of the wombe. And againe: *Bonum nuptiarum* &c. The good of mariage, saith he, throughout all nations, and amongst all men, consisteth in the cause of generation, and the fidelitie of chastitie, but for asmuch as belongeth to the people of God, it consisteth also in the holines of the sacrament. Thus saith *S. Augustin*, in his booke *de bono coniugali*, wherein neuertheles, he farre perferreth the excellencie of virginitie before marriage, notablie confuting *Iouinians* heresie, throughout al that learned treatise.

Retract. li. 2. ca. 22.

S. August. de bono coniugali c. 18.

Idem Ibid. ca. 24.

38 Finally it is also euident, that though wee Catholikes at this day,

doe with *S. Augustin*, *S. Chrisostome*, S. *Hierome*, and all the other Fathers, yea with the Apostle himselfe, teach virginitie to be farre morre worthy in the sight of god then mariage, yet we are so farre from condemning mariage, that we honour it, much more then our aduersaries, the sectaries doe, seing that we acknowledge it, for one of the sacramēts of the church, & that it giueth grace, & is also indissoluble, all which *three* pointes the sectaries, especially *Luther* & *Caluin* deny. For *Luther* teacheth, that neither any signe was instituted in matrimony by almightie god, nor promise of grace annexed thereto. And *Caluin* affirmeth, that there is no more reason of a sacramēt in matrimony, then in husbandry or in the trade of the shoomaker, or the barber, so cōtemptibly do they speake of Matrimony, & what their opinion is cōcerning the indissolubility of it, shal appeare in the next chapter. So that it is hereby manifest, with how litle reason they may obiect, either against the Fathers, or vs, that they or we condēne matrimony, because we preferre virginity before it.

Luther, li. de captiuit. Babilon. *Caluin l. 4. Institut. cap. 19. 34.*

39 Now then, to come to the conclusion of this question, and chapter, we see by al the premisses, that the holly Fathers in all ages, haue not only held, and taught, our Catholike doctrin concerning virginitie, & chastitie, but also grounded the same, euen as wee doe vppon our Sauiours counsell, and expresse scriptures, in which respect also, they alwayes accounted it for a most special point of christian perfection, as may further appeare by that which followeth.

40 a *S. Martial*, one of the disciples of our Sauiour, recounting *three* degrees, or states of christian life, excelling one an other, to wit, *marriage, widowhood, & virginity*, calleth the last, *excellētem gradum, perfectum, & per omnia similem Angelicæ puritati: an excellent, and perfect degree, and most like to the Angelicall purity, whereto* saith, he, *our Sauiour inuited vs saying. Non omnes capiunt verbum hoc, sed qui potest capere capiat, all men doe not take, or receiue this word, but he that can take it, let him take it*

41 b *S. Cyprian* saith, that virgins are: *Illustrior pars gregis Christi. The more worthy part of the flocke of Christ, and that no necessity, or* precept doth compell to virginitie, *sed perfectionis suadet consilium, but the counsel of perfection doth moue, or perswade vnto it.* c *S. Athanasius* calleth virginitie. *An indeficient welth*, or treasure, *a neuer decaying garland, the temple of God, the habitation of the holy Ghost, a precious Iewell, the ioy of prophets, the glory of the Apostles, the life of Angels, and the crowne of Saints.* d *S. Hierome* writing to *Heliodorus* the monke saith, *that when he leaft the world, and guelded himselfe for the kingdome of heauen, quid aliud*, saith he, *quam perfectam secutus es vitam? VVhat didst thou els but follow the perfect life,* e *S. Gregory Nazianzen,* saith

a Martial. ep. ad Tolosanos. Matth. 19. *b S. Ciprian. de habitu. virg. & de discip. & bono pudicit. & ser. de. natiuit. Christi. in fine.* *c S. Athan. l. de virginit. in fine.* *d S. Hieron. ep. ad Heliodor. circa. medium.* *e S. Greg. Nazianz. in illud dictum euang. cum consumasset. Iesus.*

saith also of the virgins life. *Nonne planè Angelicum est* &c. *Is it not truly an angelical thing, for one that is tyed to the bonds of the flesh, not to liue according to the flesh, but to be more higher, and more eminent, then nature it selfe*, besides that he also wrote verses in the prayse of virginitie, wherein he extolled it with singuler, and rare commendation.

42 Furthermore, f *S. Sulpitius* disciple to S. *Martin*, saith that, *Nihll virginitati est comparandum. Nothing is to be compared to virginity.* g S. *Cyrill* calleth it. *Angelicam coronam, & supra hominem perfectionem. An Angelical crowne, and a perfection more then humane.* h S. *Ambrose*, saith that it is no marueile, *si Angelis comparantur, quæ Angelorum domino copulantur. Yf virgins be compared to Angels, who are coopled, or maried with the Lord of Angels.* And i S. *Augustin* exhorteth virgins saying. *Pergite (virgines Dei) viâ sublimitatis, pede humilitatis. Proceede yee virgins of God in the way of sublimity, with the foote of humility*: and in his booke, *de moribus ecclesiæ*, he saith. k *That the perfect christians, doe not only praise, but also vndertake, summam castitatem, the highest kind of chastity*, giuing to vnderstand, that virginitie is a speciall part of christian perfection. To which purpose, I might alleadge also many other testimonies, aswel out of him, as out of all the rest of the ould Fathers, if I thought it needefull, hauing sett downe these the more particularly, and in the greater number, to the end, that thou maist, good Reader, confront with them the doctrin of *Luther*, & his fellowes, which I shal haue occasiō, to lay open vnto thee in the next chapter, & therfore I beseech thee, to beare them in mind.

f *S. Sulpitius de virtut. monachor. orient.*
g *S. Ciril. Hierosolem. catach. 12. in fine.*
h *S. Ambr. li. 1. de virginibus paulo post principium.*
i *S. Aug. de sancta virginit. ca. 52.*
k *Idem de moribus eccles. c. 31*

To the end it may appeare, that our aduersaries neither haue, nor accordinge to their principles can haue, anie practise at al of the euangelical counsel of Chastity, *their Mahometical doctrin (teaching an impossibilitie to liue chast) is amplie, and particularlie declared out of their owne workes, and proued to be most absurd, in respect both of reason of state, and also of experience, and common sense, yea, sufficiētlie controwled, and confuted by the Painimes and Infidels. Also the bad and beastlie effects of that doctrin, are testified by the licentious liues of their cheefe masters, or teachers. Finallie diuers of their friuolous obiections, and vaine cauils concerning this point, are fullie answered.*

Chap. 30.

1 Hauing proued by the authoritie of the holie scriptures, and ancient Fathers, that single and chast life, is an euangelical counsel, necessarie to the perfection of christian religion, and hauing discouered by the way, the vaine shifts and euasions of *Luther*, *Caluin*, and their felowes, and followers in their peruerse, and faulse interpretations of the holie scriptures, concerninge

those pointes, I wil now examine how this euangelical counsel is obserued, and practised by *Lutherans* and *Caluinists*, and to this purpose I will first lay downe the doctrin of their masters, concerning single life and virginitie, whereby it will euidentlie appeare, what practise they haue, or can haue thereof, if they stand to the groundes of their profession.

Luther to. 5. de matrimonio fo. 119.

2 *Luther* in a certaine sermon of his concerning matrimonie, saith that. *Crescite, & multiplicamini, encrease and multiplie*, is not a *precept*, but *more then a precept*, that we *cannot hinder, nor omit it*, but that it is *as necessarie as to eate, drinke, spit, purge, sleepe, and wake*, and as *it is not in mans hand, to be other then a man*, so it is not *in his power to be without a woman &c.* And againe in a nother place, if of a maried couple, saith he, the one refuse to yeald the dutie of mariage to the other (as there are manie froward, & obstinate women, which though their husbands should commit adulterie ten times, are nothing moued there with) then is the time for the husband to say, if thou wilt not, an other will: if the wife will not, lett the waiting maid come, yet so that the husband admonish his wife thereof, two or three times, yea and make others priuie of her obstinacie, to the end it may be manifest, and shee publikelie reproued. And if shee will not then yeald, dismisse her saith hee, marie *Hester*, and put away, *Vasthi*, as king *Assuerus* did. For the wife hath not power of her owne bodie, saith *S. Paule*, but her husband, and so one the other side, he saith of the man, therefore when anie of the parties denieth to yeld the dutie of mariage to the other, it dissolueth the matrimonie. Thus saith he. Who teacheth also, that if the husband bee impotent, the wife may either marie an other, or els with his consent lie secretlie with his brother, or some other man.

Idem in colloquiis germanicis c. de matrimonio.

3 Behold then how *Luther* maketh no bones, to teach adulterie to be lawful, vpon pretence of necessitie, to satisfie a mans lust. But lett vs here some more of his good doctrin. As no man saith he, can liue without meate, or drinke, so no man can abstaine from a woman &c. The cause is, that wee are conceiued in a woman, and nourished there, and borne of a woman, fedd, and bred by a woman, and therevppon it followeth, that wee cannot bee by anie meanes seperated from women. Also in the same booke he saith thus. *S. Hierome* writeth manie thinges, of the temptations of the flesh, ah a small matter, a woman in a mans house, may remedie the disease, *Eustochium*, might easelie haue helped, or relieued *Hierome* in that case. Thus saith he, and could anie shamelesse ribald, speake more shamefullie of Gods seruants, and holie Saints? And againe in an other place, he saith. As God did seuerelie commaunde

unde thou shalt not kill, thou shalt not commit fornication, or adulterie, so in the same manner, and much more it is commaunded, thou shalt marie a wife, thou shalt take a husband.

Idem præfatio in Oeconomiam Menij.

4 Finallie in an epistle to *VVolfgangus Reisembuchs*, he teacheth that a single man, who meaneth to liue chast, doth vndertake an impossibilitie, and fighteth with God. That to liue chast, is no more in our handes, then to to doe miracles, that he which meaneth to liue continent, must lay a way the name of a man, and make himselfe an Angel, or a spirit, for that God doth not graunt it to mā, by anie meanes. Thus saith he, and much more to the same purpose, his hart, being so full of filthie lust, that hee belcheth it forth euerie where most beastlie as you see.

To.4. Germanic. fo.463. Luther.ep. ad VVolfgāg Reissembuchs.

5 *Caluin*, though he be not altogether so extrauagant in his manner of speach, yet is absurd in effect, saying that these wordes of S. *Paul. Bonū est homini mulierem non tangere*, it is good for a man not touch a woman, are like as if a man should say, it were good for a man not to eate, nor to drinke, if it could be, but because it cannot be with out a miracle, therfore let euerie man eate and drinke. Thus saith *Caluin*, inferringe a necessitie for al men to marrie, because no man can liue chast, but by miracle.

Caluin. in comment. huius loci.

6 Also vppon our Sauiours wordes. *Non omnes capiunt verbum istud*, he teacheth that al men ought necessarily to marie, or that otherwise they are impious, and wicked, except onlie to those whome God hath reuealed, that they are able to liue continet, and chast. And further hee affirmeth in his *Institutions*, that it is not our part, to haue hope or confidence to obtaine at Gods handes such a special gift, as continency, or chastitie is,

Idem. com. in.19. Matt.

Idem. li.4. in Statut. cap. 13.55.17.

7 In like manner *Huldericus Zuinglius* saith, that we must looke to the instruction of God, and marrie in good time, except wee be certaine, that God hath otherwayes determined of vs. And *Conradus Pellicanus*, addeth, that no chastitie possible to man, is greater then that of mariage neither is more profitable euen to holie men, except they know certainely, that they haue a special grace, and vocation of God, and hee signifieth further, that there is a manifest law, and institution of God against single life, ordaining that men and women ought to marie.

Zuing. in 1. c. Matth. Conrad. Pellican. cap.1. Matth.

8 Finallie *Bucer* also teacheth the verie same, and addeth that those, which transgresse or neglect Gods law, and ordinance of marriage, to chose a finge life, full of danger, shal be greueously punished for their temeritie, and arrogancie, and that no man ought to demaund, or request of God the gift of continencie, except he surelie know, that God will giue it him. Whereby it appeareth, that these masters, and reformers.

Bucer. in ca. 1. Matth.

Bucer. in ca. 19. Matth.

mers of the world (for such they would seeme to be) doe not onlie impugne cotinencie, which our Sauiour, and his Apostles counseled, and practised, but also seeke to depriue themselues, & al there followers, of the meanes to obtaine it, teaching that it ought not to be so much as craued and requested of almighty god. All which absurd doctrin, they ground vppon Mahomets beastly principle, to wit, that it is impossible to liue chast, as may appeare in the Fouretenth chapter, where I treated of *Mahomet*, and his *Alcoran*.

Chap.14.nu.

9 But now let vs consider a litle, what must needes follow of this their *Mahometical* doctrin. Yf therefore it be no lesse necessarie for euery man to haue the company of a woman, then to eate and drinke, nor more possible for him to containe, then to doe miracles, and againe if it be presumption in any man, to hope that God wil giue him the gift of continencie, & much more to demaund it, then it must needes follow, first, that fornication, in those which are iustly hindred from mariage (as any man may be at least for some time) is no sinne, seing it is vnpossible for him to be continent. As put the case, that a batcheler, or a widower, being desirous to marry to auoid fornication, can find none that will marry him, in respect either of his pouerty, or of some notable deformitie, or of his bad conditions, what shall this man doe? He cannot by their doctrine containe, neither can he, or ought he, to hope for the grace or gift of continency at gods hands, must not he then of force commit at least fornication, if not some greater sinne of the flesh? And therefore, seeing it is in the opinion of these men, impossible for him, to containe, it were absurditie for them to thinke, that it were any more sinne, then to eate, drinke, or sleepe, which no man can continuallie forbeare without miracle.

10 Furthermore, put the case, that a man doe vse the only remedy for fornication, which these men assigne, to wit, that he is maried, and that his wife haue some long sicknes, or lieth in childbed, or that he himselfe hath necessarie occasion to be from home for some time, what remedie hath he? For according to their opinion, he cannot liue continent, and therefore must perforce commit adulterie. Besides, what a wonderfull gappe is opened to ielousies, and suspitions betwixt man and wife, to their continual torment, and to the breeding of endles brawles, and iarres, and consequentlie to the dissolution of mariages, and of whole families? For he that is perswaded in his conscience (as by this doctrin euery *Lutheran*, and *Caluinist* must be) that no man, or woman can liue chast, how can he forbeare to suspect his wife of incontinencie, if he be sick, or

neuer so litle from her, whereby he shall also grow to suspect bastardy in his children, and what inconuenience is like to follow thereof, to the whole familie, any man may iudge.

11 Moreouer, how reprochefull is this doctrin to all the vnmaried women, that professe the same, seeing it followeth thereof, that there cannot be an honest woman amongst them, if she can possiblie haue any meanes, or oportunitie to satisfie her lust? Yea and for what els doth it serue but, as I may say, for bellowes to blow the fire of concupiscence, and to kindle in mans corrupt nature, an inextinguible flame of lust? For he that is persuaded, that he cannot possiblie suppresse his concupiscence, must needes thinke it vaine and labour lost, to striue against it, and by that meanes, he must needes resolue to lose the bridle to lust, and giue himselfe wholy vnto it, which if it were general in all men, and women (as it should be if this religion were generallie receiued) it could not but worke most brutish, and beastly effects in common welthe, as shall partly appeare after a while, by the fruits thereof in the professors of it, whereof I shall haue occasion to say some what heareafter.

12 But what will you say, if the necessitie of mariage, which these men imagin and teach as a deuine precept, driueth them to allow not only adulterie, but also *poligamy*, or hauing of many wiues at once, which is the worst kind of adulterie? whereto, not only their doctrin, but also their practise, tendeth. First therefore I will shew, how they allow adulterie.

13 This may appeare partly by the diuorce, which as I haue signified alreadie, *Luther* ordaineth in case the wife be obstinate, and will not render the duty of mariage, and partly by the decrees of the *Geneuian*, and *German* churches, wherein it is determined, that if a woman depart from her husband, either for wickedenes of life, or for dislike of him, that then her husband may cause dilligent inquirie to be made after her, and demande of the minister letters of prouision, and cause her to be proclaimed in the church three sundayes, and if shee cannot be found, or appeare not within six weekes, that then her husband may take an other wife.

Canon. Geneuenses. an. 1560.

14 In like manner if a yong woman haue a husband, that is long absent, though it be by reason of some long sicknes, shee man cause him to be proclaimed, and cited, and if he appeare not, then shee may present her selfe vnto the minister, and demaunde a deuorce, and the minister must graunt it her, and the former husband, though he returne afterwards, and find her maried, shall neuer more enioy

Corpus doctrinæ christ. Germanicæ in Repetit. confess. August. ca. de coniugio.

her. Also if a man goe a long voyage, then his wife must expect him for a yeare, liuing continent, and recommending her selfe to God in the meane time, but if he stay longer abroad, and that it be thought needfull for her, to haue the company of a husband, then shee may haue licence to marry an other. Thus is it decreed, and practised amongst *Lutherans*, and *Caluinists*, in *Germany*, and *Geneua*.

15 But here I would be glad to know by the way, how this last decree can stand, eyther with their owne doctrin, or with our Sauiours? For whereas they ordained, that the wife for a yeare, shall recommend her selfe to God, and liue continent, and chast, in case that her husband be absent, how may shee demaund continencie of God, seing that, according to their opinion, shee neither knoweth whether he will giue it her, neither yet ought to presume it? Could shee liue so long without meat, drinke, or sleepe, which they say, is as possible as the other? And if they graunt, contrary to their former groundes, that she may by recommending her selfe to God, containe for a yeare, may shee not also, by the same meanes liue continent, twoo, or three yeares, or more if neede be? For if God assisted her one yeare, had shee not more reason to hope, that he would continue his assistance still, then to seeke to dissolue a matrimonie, which by Christs owne doctrin is indissoluble? For howsoeuer they may pretend at least, some shew of scripture, for the dissolution of a true mariage, in case of fornication, by reason of our Sauiours wordes in the fift of *S. Matthew* (to wit, *whosoeuer dismisseth his wife, except it be for fornication, and marieth an other, committeth adultery*, &c. which wordes neuertheles they interpret contrarie to the plaine and litteral sense of other texts, in *S. Marke, S. Luke*, and the Apostle, and against the vniforme consent of all the ancient Fathers, and the continuall practise of the Church, as Cardinal *Bellarmin*, and others do proue:) yet they haue not so much as any shew of scripture, to dissolue, contrarie to those expresse wordes of our Sauiour, a ratified, and true mariage, when no cause or pretense of fornication occurreth. And yet they admit, not only a diuorce, but also a new mariage for *Eight* other respects, which our learned contriman *M. VVilliam Reinolds*, setteth downe particularly, in his worthy treatise intituled, *Caluinoturcismus*, whereto I referre thee good Reader for breuities sake.

Matth. 5.

Reginald. li. 2. ca. 10.

16 But to returne to *Luther*, what els doth he, by his doctrin, but prepare the way to Turkish *poligamy*, or pluralitie of wiues? nay will he make any scruple thinke you, to allow a man many wiues at once? No truly, and this is manifest in his owne workes, where treating of the

of the *Bigamy* of bishops, he saith, that the *Poligamy* of the *Iewes* (to whom it was lawful to haue many wiues at once) is neither commaunded to christians, nor forbidden, but leaft to their choice, and the same also he confirmeth els where, adding further, that as he would not introduce such a new custome, so neither would he forbid it.

Luther de bigamia. Episcop. proposit.62. Idem in Genes. ca. 16. Ienensi.

17 Therefore it is no marueile, that one of his broode, namelie *Ochinus*, insisting vppon his groundes, directlie teacheth the pluralitie of wiues to be lawfull, inferring the same vppon *S. Paules* wordes to *Timothy*, where he ordained, that a *bisoph should be the husband of one wife*, wherein the Apostle meaneth (as the Catholike church both vnderstandeth and practiseth) such a one, as hath benne but once maried) as all the ancient Fathers of the church, doe also vnderstand it. But *Ochinus* following the interpretation of *Luther*, *Beza*, *Caluin*, *Peter Martyr*, and the rest of the sectaries, (who expound it to be meant by such, as haue but one wife at once,) argueth; that seeing *S. Paule* forbad many wiues at once to Bishops, and Deacons, he did consequentlie allow them to all other men. *Pauli mens haec est*, saith he, *vt christianis plures vxores habere liceat, ac episcopis singulas, ne multitudo vxorum, eos a populi salute procuranda auocaret.* The meaning of *Paule* is, that it may be lawful for christians, to haue many wiues (at once) and to bishops, only one, least the multitude of wiues, may withdraw them from procuring the saluation of the people.

1.Tim.3.

Ochin. Dialogo. li. 2. dialo. 21. pag. 200. & 204. vide Caluino Turcis. li. 2. c. 10.

18 Thus saith he, and yet a litle after, he alloweth also to bishops, more wiues then one at once, and teacheth that they are only forbidden to haue many wiues, as kinges were prohibited in ould time, to haue many horses, (not because they might not haue more then one, but least hauing a great number, they might put more confidence in them, then in God:) euen so also, saith *Ochinus*, the prohibition to Bishops of many wiues, is to be vnderstood, *de immodica vxorum multitudine*, of an immoderat multitude of wiues.

Vbi supra pag. 204. & 205.

19 Behould then how these men vse the holly scriptures, wresting them to serue their turne, for the maintenance of their sensualitie, and lust, whereby also you may see, how dangerous a thing it is to leaue the common sense of scriptures, giuen by the church (which is the piller of truth) to follow any mans priuat, and particuler interpretation, by which meanes all the heresies, that haue hitherto benne in Gods church, haue bene bred, and maintained, and by the same meanes haue sprong so many sects from *Luther*, as we see at this day, euery one of them building vppon his groundes, and foundations,

what he thought good, and interpreting the holy scriptures by his example, according to their owne fancies, whereby the *Anabaptists* fell first to the plurality of wiues, and after to a communitie of women, whereto *Luthers* doctrin of the necessitie of copulation, and his libertie in the interpretation of the scriptures, opened the gate, as euidentlie appeareth, in the historie of the first *Anabaptists*, in *Munster*, whereof I omit to recount the particulers for breuities sake.

20 And this shall suffise concerning the doctrin of *Lutherans*, and *Caluinists*, touching mariage, and single life, wherebie it may easely be imagined, what practise they haue of our Sauiours counsel of virgipitie, and continencie, seeing it is euident, that the seede of this doctrin, being sowed in the harts of men, and watered with the daily dew of our bad inclination, and ripened at length with the heat of concupiscence, can produce no other fruit, but corruption of manners, dissolute life, fornication, adulterie, all enormitie, and extremitie of vice. Wherebie it may easelie be iudged that the enemy of mankind, hauing alreadie ouerthrowne christian religion in the east parts of the world, by the sensual, and carnal doctrin of *Mahomet*, hath also attempted now in these latter times, to worke the like effect in the west parts, by the like sensualitie of *Luther*, *Caluin*, *Beza*, and such others, who hauing prostituted themselues, both soule, and body, to all lust, and carnalitie were the fittest instruments that he could find, to helpe him to deflower, as I may say, the virginal purity of the Catholike faith, instilling heresie into the mindes of men, together with the plausible, and pleasing doctrin, of all sensual libertie.

21 Therefore we may see, how true is that which I insinuated in the first part of this Treatise, and promised to shew more amply here, to wit, that the law of the flesh (which I proued there to be farr more potent, then ciuil, and political law) hath not only her procters, and aduocats, but also her preachers, and doctors, and a religion of her owne, as appeareth euidentlie in this doctrin, of these sectaries, and shall farther appeare by their vicious liues, whereof I am now to treat.

1. par. chap. 9. num. 19.

22. For if any man do doubt, whether their liues were correspondent to their doctrin, he may be sufficientlie resolued, by reading partly what *Luther*, and some others of them write of themselues, and partly what one of them writeth of an other. *Luther* signifieth, that in the beginning of his ghospelling, (before his sacrilegious, and incestuous mariage, with *Katherin Bore* the Nunne) he was almost mad with the heat,

Luther in in colloquiis mensalibus vide Caluinoturcismũ Reginaldi li. 2. ca. 11.

heat, and vehemencie of luſt, and the loue of women. And in his comment vppon the wordes of *Salomon*, where he praiſeth a good matron, he addeth this marginal note, *nothing is more louely, and ſweete vppon earth, then the loue of a woman*, and this he ſaith he learned of his hoſteſſe at *Iſemack*, and knew it to be true by his owne experience. Beſides that he writeth, that matrimonie is moſt worthy to be called, *a ſpirituall, heauenly, and deuine ſtate, and that the nature thereof is ſuch, as it moueth, vrgeth, and inciteth a man to the higheſt and moſt ſpirituall worke, that is to ſay, to faith.* whereby it appeareth that he was ſo drunke with the filthy delights, and pleaſures of the fleſh, that he placed all his felicitie therin, as the *Mahometans* doe.

Annotatio Lutheri in ca. prouerb. 31.

Luther to. 5. comment. in 1. Cor. 7 fol. 100. & 107.

23 As for *Caluin*, *Conradus Schluſſelhuſius*, a *Lutheran*, teſtifieth of him, that he was marked with a hot Iron, at *Noyon* in *France* for *Sodomy*, and that for ſhame thereof he ſold his benefice, and went into *Germany*. And *Hieronymus Bolſec*, who had benne a phiſition at *Geneua*, and liued with him there, witneſſeth alſo the ſame in the hiſtorie of his life, which he wrote afterwards being conuerted to the Catholike faith, and he addeth, that a gentleman called *Iacobus* de *Burgundia*, was perſuaded by his wife to remoue from *Geneua*, to *Berne*, for the great inſtance, that *Caluin* made to corrupt her, and that he oft abuſed an other mans wife, as it was confeſſed by her maid.

Conrad. Schluſſ. Calui.

Hieron. Bolſec in vita Caluini.

24 Theſe, with diuers other particulers, are alſo witneſſed by the learned biſhop *Lindan*, vppon the common fame thereof. *Non deſunt*, ſaith he, *plurima* &c. There want not many ſignes, and tokens of *Caluins* publike adulteries, with thoſe his faire and fine ſhee-diſciples who were wont to come vnto him, with their bibles vnder their armes, to be reſolued of their doubts in the ſcriptures, hauing only ſome litle child in their companie of two, or three yeare ould, which diſciples of his he vſed to catechize with the doores and windowes ſhut. And in like maner it is conſtantlie reported, that he was wont often towards the euening, to goe out of *Geneua*, to viſit a mans wife in her husbands abſence. Beſides that our contriwoman *Ealeſia*, was forcſt to remoue with her husband, from *Geneua* to *Berne*, becauſe he importunatelie ſollicited her to marry him, vppon pretence that her husband was weake, and ſickly, as ſhee her ſelfe was wont oft times to teſtifie to her friendes. Finallie, he cannot deny his inceſt, with a Nunne of the monaſterie of *Veilmur*, who being runne out of her cloiſter, was at his requeſt, maintained with a publike ſtipend of twoo crownes a moneth, by the towne of *Geneua*, to ſerue him for a chamber maid to make his

Lindan in ſua christomachia vide Staniſlaum Reſchium li. 1. de Atheiſmis euangelicor. c. 9.

bed for fiue yeares together, vntill at lenght he got her with child, and when shee was foure months gonne with child, hee married her to a certaiue apostaticall cannon, who liued at *Losanna*. Thus farre *Lindan*, and this shall suffise concerning *Caluin*.

25 Of *Beza*, there needeth no other testimonie of his lasciuiousnes, then his owne filthy Epigrammes, which *Tilmanus Hesshius* a Lutheran, calleth *sacriligum carmen*, *a sacriligious verse, or poeme*, wherein saith *Tilmanus*, he song to the world, his owne abominable loue, his fornications, and filthy adulteries, and amongst the rest, there is yet there to be seene, a most beastlie Epigrame concerning a boy, caled *Audebert*, and *Candida* a taylors wife, wherein hee debateth, whether of them he should preferre before the other. And *Hieronimus Bolsec*, writeth also in his life, that the true name of *Candida*, was *Claudia*, and that in the end, *Beza* entised her away from her husband, and fled with her to *Geneua*, where hee kept her as his wife. Finally, *Conradus Schlusselhusius*, the Lutheran aforesaid, witnesseth that *Beza*, spent his whole life in lust and lasciuiousnes, in so much, that the same authour saith, hee was transformed in *Meretricum lenam & cinedum*, which I am ashamed to explicate in English, but bee it true or false, so saith one of his brethren in the Ghospel.

Hieron. Bolsec. in vita Beza. Conrad. Schlus. Caluinist Theologia. li. 1. fo. 92.

26 Furthermore, *Huldericus Zuinglius*, of whome the sect of Sacramentaries called Zuinglians, take their name, confesseth plainlie of himselfe, and other ministers, in an epistle which hee wrote in their name and his owne, to the *Suyssers*, that the workes of the flesh, and heate of concupiscence, had made him and them, *infames coram ecclesys*, *infamous in the sight of their church*, or congregations. And in an other epistle to the bishop of *Constancia*, whereto diuers other principall Euangelists subscribed, he affirmeth of himselfe, and them, that they had so burned with lust, that some amongst them, *of forty yeares of age, had donne manie thinges vnseemely*.

Zuinglius. alijque euangelici. to. 1. fol. 115. Vide Caluinotur. li. 2. ca 11.

Vbi supra. fol. 129. Caluinotur. ibid.

27 Also I cannot omit to say somewhat of that which *Villagagnon*, a French man, writeth of his owne experience touching the vnbridled, and exhorbitant lust of certaine euangelical ministers, and preachers, who went with him by the order of *Caluin*, *Beza*, and the magistrates of *Geneua*, to *Noua Francia* in *America*, with designement to plant the ghospel there, of whome *Villgagnon* testifieth, that as soone as they came one land, they did not onlie preach manie thinges different and repugnant one to an other, but also that some of them, who had leaft theire wiues at *Geneua*, maried againe, and that other of them, were so monstrous for their dissolute life, that euen those barbarous people.

Villagagnon. contra. artic. Richer.

after

after a while abhorred them, for their brutish intemperance, and their *Sodomy*, in so much that one amongst the rest, rauished his owne sisters sonne, and when some would haue had him, and the rest punished, *Richerus* (who was cheefe minister there) excused him, and them, saying, that consideration must be had of mans infirmitie, for that, as the Apostle teacheth. *Diuisiones sunt gratiarum*, there are diuisions of graces, and so no iustice was donne vppon them.

28 Thus writeth *Villagagnon*, who was present, and cheefe commaunder in the voyage, being then a Caluinist, though afterwards he was conuerted to the Catholike faith, and wrote against certaine Articles of *Richerus* aforesaid, in which booke he testifieth this, which I haue here related.

Villag. cōtra articul. Richeri. li. 1. c. 90.

29 Seing then the doctrin of *Luther*, and his fellowes, wrought this effect in themselues, who had the verie first fruits of the Euangelicall spirit, and the puritie of it (if there were anie puritie in it) what may we thinke of the common sort of people, that followed their instructions, and example?

30 The truth whereof appeareth in a *German* writer, called *Czecanouius*, who bewailing greatelie the lamentable state of *Germanie* saith, that the sinne of the flesh, was neuer in former times so inordinate, and excessiue in those partes as in this age, for *now*, saith he, *the doctrin of Luther (that a man can no more liue without the companie of a woman, then without meate) is held for a deuine law, and so published euery where, that it is thought impossible for any yong man or maid, to abstaine, when they beginne once to be ripe*. And hereuppon (as not onlie *Czecanouius*, but also, *VVigandus* affirmeth) it followed in *Germanie*, that boyes, and girles committed great enormities, pretending for their excuse this doctrin of *Luther*, and that therefore their parents were forced to marry them so yong, that there could not but grow great inconuenience thereof to their common welth, by their vntimelie procreation.

Czecanouius de corruptis moribus vtriusque partis. Caluinoturr. li. 2. c. 11.

VVigandus. de bonis, & malis German.

31 Lo then, what is the fruite of *Luther*, and *Caluins* doctrin, whereby it appeareth euidentlie, that it serueth for no other purpose, as before I said, but to blow the coales of concupiscence, and to kindle an vnquencheable flame of lust, in all those that embrace it, seeing it teacheth an impossibilitie to liue continent, contrarie to the light of reason, and the common experience, not onlie of Christians, but also of the verie paynims, who though for the encrease of their common welths, they commonlie moued men to mariage, yet they held chastity for a great vertue, which they would not haue donne, if they had not thought, yea and knowne it, to be possible.

32 This

Plato.8.de leg.

32 This may appeare in *Plato*, who in his lawes ordaineth punishment for adultery, fornication, and the sinne against nature, prouing the equitie of his law, and the possibilitie of continency by experience, as namelie of the wrestlers and champions in the games of *Olimpus*, who were wont to liue most continent, during al the time of those exercises, onlie for the desire of victorie, and the loue of honour, whereupon he saith: *And shal not then other young men be able to containe themselues to the end they may gaine a greater victorie*, that is to say, *vt voluptate victa feliciter viuant, that by the conquest of pleasures, they may liue happilie?* Thus reasoneth he vppon common experience, and further saith, that if by the helpe of good lawes and other meanes, there were a firme opinion & conceit bred general in the mindes of men, that fornication, adulterie, and other sinnes of the flesh, were odious to God and man, it would make men as continent from other women, as they are from their sisters and daughters, from whome al men, be they neuer so wicked, abstaine for the verie horrour that is commonlie conceited thereof. Moreouer, he also perswadeth the equitie of his law, and possibilitie of continency, by the example of birds and beastes, which doe procreat with great moderation, onlie in due time and seasons, and therefore saith he. *It is a great shame that resonable men should be worse, and more incontinent then brute beastes.* Finally he concludeth, that the furie of lust may be tempered, and chastitie preserued, by the vse of continuall labour, and trauell.

Thus discourseth *Plato*, purposelie to proue that continencie is possible, contrary to the opinion of some dissolut men in his time, with whome he also confuteth *Luther* and his fellowes, yea and concludeth them to be worse then beasts.

Onuphrius in Coment. reip. Rom. de ciuit. Rom.

33 But what? Had not the Painims also their virgins, whome they held in great estimation? We reade, that the *vestall* virgins amongst the *Romans*, were so respected and honored, that whosoeuer mett them in the way (yea thoughe he were consul and supreme magistrate) gaue them place: and if a malefactour being lead to excecution did chaunce to meet them, hee was freede from death, besides manie other honorable priueldges which they had by the Roman lawes. And whereas it was ordained that they should be buried aliue, in case they were incōtinent, was it not an euident argument that the lawmaker & magistrats thought continencie to bee possible? For otherwise their law had benne vniust, neither would anie woman haue vndertaken that kind of life, if they had perswaded themselues that it was impossible, as these sectaries teach now a dayes. How manie notable virgins doe wee read

of

of, in prophane histories, whose memorie, and fame was highly celebrated, and recommended to all posteritie? whereof many particulers may be seene, in *S. Hieroms* most excellent bookes against *Iouinian*, whose heretical opinion, concerning the equality of mariage, and virginitie he confuteth, and sheweth by the way how much virginitie was prized, and honored amongst the very Painims. To which purpose he mentioneth *Atalanta* of *Calidonia*, *Harpalice* of *Thracia*, *Camilla* queene of the *Volsci*, *Chalchaus*, *Iphigenia*, the Tenne *Sibillæ*, *Cassandra*, the virgins that serued in the temples of *Diana*, *Tauricia*, and *Vesta*, who he saith, were innumerable. Also the daughters of *Phido* in *Greece*, who drowned them selues to saue their virginitie, and fifty *Lacedemonian* virgins, who suffered death, rather then they would consent to be corrupted by the *Messenians*, as also *Stimphalides* an *Orchomenian*, an other of *Thebes*, and seauen *Milesian* virgins, who saued their virginitie with losse of their liues. Besides that diuers others whom he nameth slew themselues, because they were rauished against their wills: As the two daughters of *Scedasus*, and a *Theban* maid, who in the reuenge of the iniurie donne vnto her, first slew him, that forced her, & after slew her selfe, being loth, saith *S. Hierome*, either to liue after the losse of her virginitie, or to die before shee had reuenged it. Finally he concludeth with the daughter of *Pithagoras* (who was prefect, or gouernesse of a company of virgins, and read them a lecture of chastity) to whome he also addeth fiue daughters of one *Diodorus*, who were of such singuler commendation, partly for their learning, and partly for their chast life, that the Philosopher *Philo*, master to *Carneades*, wrote a large historie of them, so that wee neede no deeper diuinitie, to confute this brutish doctrin of these late sectaries, then the experience of Painimes and Infidels.

S. Hieron. Contra Iouinian. li. 1. versus finē.

34 For although it cannot be denied, but that they had some extraordinary, and speciall helpe of almighty God, as some times the wickedst men may haue, to do some moral workes (which *S. Augustin* obserueth in *Polemon*, who being a very riotous man, became very sober & temperate vppon a suddaine, by the doctrin and persuasions of *Xenocrates*, with the special helpe of God, for otherwise saith *S. Augustin*, it could not be:) yet it must needes be graunted, that seing God of his infinit mercy, assisted them in the preseruation of their virginity, who had no intent to honour him therein, he is, and euer wilbe much more ready, to assist his faithfull seruants, that shall humbly craue his grace, to that end, with desire to honour and serue him, and to follow the example, not only of Christ himselfe, his mother, *S. Iohn Baptist*, and of all the

S. August. ep. 130. To. 2.

Apostles after their vocation, but also of diuers holly men in the ould law, for as *S. Hierome* saith. *Virgo Elias, Helizeus virgo, virgines filij prophetarum, Hieremiæ dicitur, & tu ne accipias vxorem. Elias was a virgin, Elizeus was a virgin, the sonnes of the prophets were virgins, and it was said to Hieremy the prophet, and doe not thou take a wife.* Thus saith *S. Hierome*, whereto may be added the chast widowhood of *Iudith*, and *Anna* the prophetesse, who as the Gospel witnesseth, hauing benne maried but only *seauen* yeares, *remained widow seruing God in the temple to fourescore, and foure yeares of her age.*

S. Hiero. ep. 22. ad Eustochium circa medium.
Iudith. 1.
Luc. 2.

35 But now if we consider the experience, that is, and euer hath benne, since our Sauiours comming, of the most continent, chast, and pure life of innumerable christian virgins, and other religious persons of both sexes, we may wonder at the absurditie of the new ghospellers, who measuring other mens integritie, by their owne corruption, and dissolution, do impudently deny that, which infinit numbers of men, and women in the catholike church, haue for so many ages experimented, and do daily try in them selues, as appeareth by the wonderfull multitude of virgins in the primitiue church, throughout all the east partes, as I haue amply shewed already out of the Fathers, and historiographers, of the first fiue hundreth yeares after Christ; whereto I will only ad heere, that *S. Ambrose*, speaking of the churches of *Africk*, of *Alexandria*, and of the east in his time, saith. *Pauciores hic homines prodeunt, quam illic virgines consecrantur. Fewer men appeare in these partes, then virgins are consecrated there.* Besides that, he also signifieth the great concourse of virgins to *Millan*, to be veiled there, not only out of other partes of *Italy*, but also from the furthest boundes of *Mauritania*. And what infinit numbers of holly virgins, & other religious women there haue benne euer since, and are at this day throughout all christendome, no man can be ignorant, so that the experience, euen of our owne time conuinceth, that continencie is not only possible, but also easy, with the assistance of Gods grace, for otherwise such multitudes of the weaker sex, neither would so willinglie vndertake religious life, as they doe, neither could so happilie performe it. But so blind, and absurd is heresie, that it teacheth many times thinges repugnant, not only to the light of reason, but also to common sense, and experience.

S. Ambros. li. 3. de virgin.
Idem. li. 1.

36 Therefore can any man with any reason imagin, that these men learned this their absurd doctrin out of the holy scriptures, as they pretend? Let vs then breefelie examin their groundes, to see of what validitie they are. They teach out of the scripture (and that very truly) that

continencie

continencie is the gift of God, for so saith, *Salomon. Non possum esse con-* Sap.8.
tinens, nisi deus det. I cannot be continent, except God giue it. And our Sauiour in like sort, speaking thereof, saith. *Non omnes capiunt verbum istud,* Matth. 19.
*sed quibus datum est. All men doe not take this word, but those to whom it is gi-
uen.* And lastly the Apostle, hauing exhorted all men to lead a single, &
chast life, like to him, added. *Sed vnusquisque proprium donum habet ex* 1.Cor.7.
*deo, alius quidem sic, alius vero sic. Euery one hath a proper gift of God, one in
this sort, and an other in that.* Vppon which places, and such other to the
like effect, they inferre, that seing continencie is the gift of God, it is no Caluin.li. 4.
more in mans power to be continent, then to be a prophet, or to doe Instit.c.13.
miracles, yea, and that it were no lesse presumption to pray for the gift Bucer in ca.
of continencie, then for the gift of prophesie, as I haue signified a be- 19.Matth.
fore. a Num.6.& 8.

37 But who seeth not the absurditie of this inference? Ys it not euident that there is great difference in Gods gifts, and that some of them may iustly be said to be in our power, & other not? For although some thinges are giuen vs by almighty God, without our cooperation, or any endeuour of ours (as the giftes of tongues, of prophesie and such like,) which therefore are no way in our power, yet to other gifts of God, is required our cooperation, and diligence, to obtaine the same, which are promised vnto vs, in case wee seeke them duly by prayer, & such other meanes, as God hath ordained, & such are the gifts, not only of continency, but also of faith, hope, and charitie, and all other vertues, which therefore may iustly be said to be in our power, because we may assuredlie haue them, if wee wil vse the due meanes to obtaine them.

38 And betwixt these twoo sortes of gifts, this difference is also to be noted, that those of the first sort, (as the gift of tongues, prophesie, & such like) are not necessarie either for our saluation, or for our perfection, but only are giuen by almightie God extraordinarilie, to some particular persons, at some times, and in some places, as to his infinit wisdome seemeth most conuenient for his owne glory, whereas the other giftes of the latter sort (to wit continēcie faith, & other vertues) are necessarie, either for euery mans saluation, or at least for that perfection whereto our Sauiour inuited, & counselled euery man, in which respect he is euer ready to bestow them vppon vs, whensoeuer we doe duly labour for them, and humbly craue them at his handes, as he promised when he said. *Petite & accipietis, pulsate & aperietur vobis. Aske, and* Matth.7.
you shall receiue, knock and it shalbe opened vnto you.

39 For were it not ridiculous to thinke, that our Sauiour, or his

Apostles, would so seriouslie exhort vs to continencie (as I haue proued they did) but that God will giue it vs if wee doe humbly, and duly demaund it of him? Did they euer counsell vs to doe miracles, or to prophesie, or such other things, as God giueth without any endeuour of ours? Againe are not faith, and charitie giftes of God (as I haue said) as well as continencie? *Vobis datum est*, saith the Apostle, *vt in eum credatis. It is giuen to you*, that is to say, it is Gods gift, *that you beleeue in him. Also, non omnium est fides, beleefe is not euery mans.* And againe, *Nemo potest venire ad me nisi quem pater traxerit. No man can come to me, but he that my Father drawes.* And in like maner, the Apostle saith of charitie, *that, diffusa est in cordibus nostris per spiritum sanctum qui datus est nobis. It is spred, or powred in to our harts by the holly Ghost which is giuen vs.* Neuer thelesse, forasmuch as the obtaining of these vertues, dependeth in part vppon our selues, we are exhorted in the scripture to beleeue, and to loue God, and our neighbour, which exhortation (as I haue signified before) were vaine, if it were not in our power to performe it, with the helpe of Gods grace, which he promiseth to giue to those which demaund it.

Philip. 1. *2. Thess. ca. vltimo.* *Ioan. 6.* *Rom. 5.*

40 Therfore it followeth not, that because continencie is Gods gift, therefore it is not in our power, for so should neither faith, nor charity, be in our power; where vppon it would also follow, that no man should iustly be damned for want of faith, or charitie, for no man can be iustly punished, because he wanteth that which he cannot by any meanes compasse, or procure. And therefore although almightie God doth punish no man because he doth not prophesie, and doe miracles (which are not in our hands, or power) yet he iustly condemneth Infidels, for want of faith, and bad Christians, for want of charitie, adulterers, and fornicators, for lacke of continencie, and for the same cause also iustly punisheth those, which breake vowes of chastitie, as the Apostle testifieth of the yong widows, who he said had, *damnation, for that they brake their first faith:* and the reason is because they might haue liued chast, if they would haue donne their due dilligence, and vsed conuenient meanes to obtaine the grace, and gift of chastity at Gods handes.

1. Tim. 5.

41 But let vs heare what the ancient Fathers say concerning this matter, I haue shewed before, that *S. Chrysostome* expounding those very wordes of our Sauiour, which these men peruert to their purpose, (to wit, *non omnes capiunt verbum istud* &c. teacheth expresselie, out of the circumstances thereof, not only that our Sauiour did seriously exhort vs to continencie therein, but also that he encouraged

S. Chrysost. Tom. 2. Ho. 63. in ca. 19. Matth.

vs

vs thereto, by proposing vnto vs partly the worthines, and greatnes of the vertue, and partly the possibilitie of it, and then he maketh this objection against himselfe. But if *this*, saith he, *be a matter of our election, why did our Sauiour say in the beginning of his discourse, that all men do not take, or receiue this word, but those only to whome it is giuen? Mary this he said, vt singulare certamen esse discas, non vt sorte datam necessitatem suspiceris. To the end thou maiest learne, that it is a single combat, and not a necessitie giuen by lot,* (that is to say, that it is a thing, which any man may haue, if he will fight for it, and not that some men haue it, as it were by lot, and that others can not haue it:) *his enim datum est qui sponte id eligunt, for it is giuen to them, who choose it willingly, and therefore (our Sauiour) said so to signifie vnto vs, that if wee will haue the victorie in this combat, we haue neede of helpe from aboue, which helpe is readdy for all those that craue it.* Thus saith he. And a litle after. *Si supremæ solummodo donationis est* &c. *Yf* (chastity) *be only the gift of God, and that those who conserue themselues in perpetual virginitie, doe not seeme to conferre, or contribute any thing at all thereto, the kingdome of heauen is promised them superfluously,* or without cause, *neither doth (our Sauiour) worthilie distinguish them from other Eunuches.* *Idem ho. 63. in c. 19. Matth.*

42 Thus saith *S. Chrysostome*, notablie confirming our Catholike doctrin, out of our Sauiours owne words, and confuting aswell the interpretation that our aduersaries make thereof, as also their doctrin of the impossibilitie of continencie, which he proueth to be possible for euery one (that will dulу labour for it) because our Sauiour exhorted, and encouraged vs vnto it, with promise of eternall reward, which promise, saith he, had benne superfluous, if it were only Gods gift, in such sort, that it did not also partly depend vppon our selues, that is to say, vppon our owne diligent endeuour, aswell in seeking the helpe of Gods grace, as also in vsing such mortifications, as are requisit to the repression of concupiscence.

43 For the same reason also *Tertulian*, rehersing the same wordes of our Sauiour, saith. *Elige quod bonum est, si non potes, quia non vis, posse enim si velis ostendit, quia tuo arbitrio vtrumque proposuit &c. Choose that which is good, if thou canst not, because thou wilt not, for he showeth, that thou maist if thou wilt, seeing he leaueth it to thy choise, thow must depart from him, whose will thow wilt not doe.* So he: alluding to the rich man, in the ghospel, who went away from our Sauiour, because he wold not follow his counsel, in selling his goods and geuing the money to the poore. *Tertul. li. de Monogamia prope finem.* *Matth. 19.*

44 Also *Origen* in his commentary vppon that Ghospel, and the same wordes, saith. *Qui vult capere verbum* &c. *He which will take the word of* *Origen. in ca. 19. Matt.*

S.Hieron. in 19. ca. Matt. *our Sauiour concerning chastitie, let him craue it, beleeuing him that said it, and shall receiue it, not doubting of that which was said* (by him) *omnis qui petit accipit, euery one which asketh receiueth*. Thus saith *Origen*.

45 And with these agreeth *S. Hierome*, who expounding the same woords saith. *Hu datum est* &c. *It is giuen to them, who haue craued it, who would haue it, and haue laboured to receiue it*. To conclude all the Fathers of the church, which haue occasion to treate of virginitie, doe vniformelie hould, & affirme the same that these doe, amongst whom, *S. Augustin*, and *S. Basil* (who were twoo of the most famous for learning, and holly life) doe expressly, and amply teach, that continency is so possible to all men, that euen those may, and doe obserue it, who are forced against their wills, (as many times it happeneth) to vndertake some condicion, or state of life that requireth chastity, though they neuer determined it, or thought of it before.

S. August. li. 2. de adulter. in coniugiis ca. 10. 13. & 20. S. Basil. in lib. virginitate vltra medium.

46 Therefore whereas some of these Fathers before aliedged, doe seeme sometimes to speake of some, that cannot liue chast, or exhort those to chast life, who cannot performe it, they are not to be thought to contradict themselues, and to deny that any man may haue the gift of chastitie, who will vse the due meanes to obtaine it, but it is to be vnderstood, that supposing the corruption of many mens wills to be such, that they will not vse such prayer, and mortification, as were conuenient to the obtaining of it, the Fathers vse sometimes that manner of speach, as though some men could not be continent, supposing I say, that they will not doe their endeuour thereto: as in like maner we see, that some sick man, being willed to take a potion that might cure his dissease, hath such a loathing to it, that he saith, he possiblie cannot, and will rather be sick still, or perhaps die, then take it, though neuertheles he might take it, if he would, & cannot, because he will not, and in that case the phisitian may well say vnto him (supposing his determinat will and resolution) that seing he cannot take medicin (which is the only meanes for his cure) there is no remedy, and in the same sort and sence, the Fathers speake some times of some that cannot liue chast.

S. Hieron. in Apologia. pro lib. contra Iouiniā.

47 This appeareth euidentlie in *S. Hierome* who hauing said. *Si autem se continere non possunt. If they cannot be continent*, addeth presentlie, *and will rather quench the fire of lust with fornication then with continencie, it is better for them to marry, then to be burnt*. So that *S. Hierome* explicateth sufficientlie, what he meaneth by saying, *if they cannot conteine*, vnderstanding that they will rather commit fornication, then labour to be continent.

48 And

48 And the like alſo may be ſaid of other ancienc Fathers , who treating ſometimes of mans cōtinencie, may wel vſe the words, *can*, or *cannot*, in the ſame ſenſe, to wit, with ſuppoſition of mans will, either to labour dulie for it, or no, for that thoſe which will vſe conuenient prayer to God, and mortification, may liue chaſt, and thoſe which will not vſe thoſe means connot And thus much I haue thought good to note by the way, to eaſe our aduerſaries of the labour, to ſeeke out ſuch manner of ſpeach in the Fathers, whoſe meaning can be no other then that which heere I haue ſett downe, except they will make them moſt abſurdlie contradict themſelues.

49 Thus then thou haſt ſeene good Reader, the different doctrin of *Luther*, *Caluin* and their followers one the one ſide, and of the moſt ancient, learned, and holie Fathers of the Church one the other ſide, as repugnant and oppoſit, as blacke and white, as light and darkenes, as errour and truth, that is to ſay, as hereſie and Catholike religion: and therefore whether of theſe are to be beleeued and followed, I leaue it to the iudgment of anie indifferent man.

50 And what trow you doe our aduerſaries anſwer to the vniforme conſent of the Fathers againſt them in this point? Marie ſaith *Peter Martir* *Petrus Martir. li. de cælibatu & votis in fine.* their tiſtimonies are but humane, and it is againſt the dutie of a chriſtian man, yea iniurious to the holie Ghoſt, to appeale from the ſcriptures of God, to the iudgment of man. But who ſeeth not how ridiculous is this anſwer? Firſt, are the teſtimonies of the Fathers humane, and the other of *Peter Matir* and his followers deuine? And if the Fathers were men, as in deede they were ar theſe other, trow you ſuch celeſtial creatures, that, they may attribute more to themſelues then to thoſe greate ſeruants of God, and ſaintes, whoſe greate learning and moſt holie life, al the chriſtian world hitherto hath admired, and God himſelfe hath oft times approued, by notable and euident miracles, which cannot be denied to bee true, without the impudent deniall of the teſtimonie of all antiquitie? Whereas one the one ſide, thoſe others haue no teſtimonie at all, for the confirmation of their doctrin, either from antiquitie, or by their owne good life, and much leſſe from almightie God by miracles. For the teſtimonie of antiquitie, as you ſee condemneth them. Their looſe and ſenſual liues (whereof I haue partlie ſpoken alreadie, and will doe more hereafter) bewraieth their bad ſpirit. And ſo farr of are they, from hauing anie miraculous approbation from almightie God, that they are faine for the want thereof, to denie the vndoubted experience that the worlde hath at this day, and euer hath had of miracles, as ſhall appeare more amplie heareafter. *Num. 22. 23. 24. 25 26. &c. Chap. 31. num. 34. 35. 36. &c. Chap. 28.*

51 Yea

51 Yea but, say they we haue the scriptures, and to appeale from them to the Fathers, is iniurie to the holie Ghost. As though the Fathers had not the scriptures, aswell as they, yea and more then they? Doe not their most learned and notable commentaries (I meane of the Fathers) vppon all the ould and new testament, and the confirmation of al their doctrin by the frequent, plentifull, and continuall allegation thereof, wittnesse sufficientlie their knowledge, esteeme, and reuerence of the holie scriptures? Nay which is more, in this question which now wee handle, concerning the counsels of our Sauiour, and particularly touching the possibilitie and dignitie of virginitie, haue you not seene that the Fathers confirme their Catholike doctrin and ours, aboundantlie with expresse scripture, confuting the same opiniōs that our aduersaries hold, partlie with the verie circumstances of the texts, that are now controuersed betwix them and vs, and partlie with the conference of one text with an other? Doe we then appeale from the Scriptures to the Fathers, or is the question betwixt vs and them, whether we or they alledge the scriptures, or rather who vnderstandeth them aright? For as we doe not denie that they cite scriptures for their opinions (as the diuel did to Christ, and the *Arrians*, and all heretikes haue euer donne, yea maniē times more aboundantlie then they) so they cannot deny, but that we also plentifully alleadge them for our Catholike doctrin. But herein is the difference, that we vnderstand the same scriptures, not accordinge to our priuat and particular fancies (as they and al sectaries and heretikes doe) but according to the sense that the greater number of the most ancient, learned and holie Fathers of the church deliuered thereof, aboue a thousand yeares agoe, before these last controuersies arose betwixt them, and vs.

Matth. 4. *Luc. 4.*

52 Therefore I say, I leaue it to the iudgment of anie indefferent and vnpassionate man, who hath care of his soule, and a desire to know and embrace the truth, whether it bee more secure for him to follow those Fathers, in their vniforme interpretation of the scriptures, then the sense that our aduersaries draw thereof, to the maintenance of the most sensual, and carnal doctrin that euer was heard of amongst men, professing the name, and faith of Christ, as sufficientlie appeareth by that which I haue alleadged before, out of their owne workes, wherein through the iust iudgment of God, they notablie betray their owne spirits, powring forth out of the aboundance of their harts, such sensual and carnal paradoxes as you haue heard. Whereby it may easelie be iudged, that al the rest of the euangelical libertie, which they preach, proceedeth from the same groūd of beastlie carnalitie, which is an inseperable companion and vndoubted marke,

marke, of the impure spirit of heresie: as on the contrarie side purity of life and chastity, is a special badge, and an infalible signe of the spirit of God, and truth of Christian religion.

53 Therefore the prophet *Zachary*, foretelling the comming of Christ, and the speciall fruites, and effects of his grace in his elect, saith. *Quid enim bonum eius est, & quid pulchrum eius, nisi frumentum electorum, & vinum germinans virgines? VVhat is the good, and faire which he giueth, but the wheat of the elect, and wine which bringeth forth virgins?* By which wordes *S. Hierome* vnderstandeth the admirable force, and effect of the blessed sacrament of the *Eucharist*, working in Christians the puritie of virginal and continent life, as a special fruit of christian religion.

Zachar 9.

S. Hieron. in 9. ca. Zach.

54 Thus then we euidentlie see, that *Lutherans*, and *Caluinists*, neither haue, nor can haue, any practise of this euangelical counsel of continencie, no not so much as the very Paynims had, amongst whome, some at least liued continent: whereas amongst these none doe, neither yet can doe, if they eyther beleeue their masters doctrin, or follow their example. And the like I will also shew concerning the abnegation of our selues, which is the third Euangelical counsell, whereof I determined to treate, and because this chapter is alreadie growne to be long, I will remit it to the next.

Of the third Euangelical counsel, to wit, perfect Obedience *and abnegation of our selues, deduced out of the expresse doctrin of our Sauiour, and confirmed by the testimonie of the Fathers, and examples of Gods miraculous approbation thereof, in diuers cases. Also that our aduersaries haue not so much practise thereof, as the very painimes had, nor so much as any disposition thereto: and this is proued by the intollerable pride of their cheefe masters, which appeareth partly in their owne workes, and partly by the testimonies of one of them against an other. Finally it is made most euident, that they are not only voide of all true imitation of Christ, and christian perfection, but also that they are sworne enemies of it, and therefore farre from all vnion with God, and true felicitie.*

CHAP. 31.

WHen I spoke of the Euangelical counsells in generall, I deduced the counsell of *Obedience*, out of those wordes of our Sauiour. *Si quis vult venire post me, &c. Yf any man will come after me, let him deny himselfe, and take vp his crosse, and follow me.* In which wordes it may be noted, that our Sauiour doth not commaunde, but counsell perfect obedience, and the abnegation of our selues, for that he spake conditionallie, referring it to the will of the hearer,

Matthevv. 16.

as I haue also shewed the like before, by the exposition of the Fathers, in his counsell of voluntarie pouertie, which as *S. Chrisostome* noteth, he propounded with the like condition, saying. *Yf thou wilt be perfect, goe and sell all* &c.

2 Therefore, whereas there are twoo kindes of obedience, the one absolutely necessarie for our saluation (that is to say, to obey not only almightie God, but also our parents, and all lawfull magistrats, spiritual, or temporall, whereto euery man is bound by precept,) and the other, to obey such as we shall voluntarie choose to commaunde vs, for our direction in Gods seruice (whereto no man is bound, further then he list to bynd himselfe, by vow, or promise:) it appeareth that our Sauiour in this place speaketh of the latter, inuiting vs to an extraordinarie obedience, for his more particuler seruice, and our greater perfection, consisting in the perfect imitation of his obedience, and abnegation of himselfe, and the cariage of his crosse.

3 These twoo kinds of obedience (the one absolutelie necessarie, & the other voluntarie) may also be noted in the ould testament. To the first kind may be referred the obedience, vsed in the obseruation of the commaundements, which no man could without sinne and punishment, refuse to obey. To the later kind, may be referred the voluntary obedience of the *Rechabits*, who were praised, and commended by almigtie God, for abstaining from wine, and not tilling, and sowing their groundes, and dwelling only in tents, which they did to obey the commaundement of their father *Ionadab*, for the which they were also rewarded, as appeareth in the prophet, who signifieth vnto them from almightie God, that their race, and succession should not faile, *pro eo quod obedistis*, saith he, *præcepto Ionadab patris vestri* &c. *because you haue obeyed the commaundement of your father Ionadab* &c.

Deut. 17.

Ierem. 35.

4 Wherein, it is to be vnderstood, that this obedience of theirs was voluntarie, seing no man, that is alreadie arriued to the full yeares of discretion, & able to gouerne himselfe, is bound vnder paine of sinne, to obey his parents in matters of that qualitie, especiallie after his parents death, and much lesse can a whole posteritie be bound thereto, if they doe not willinglie bind themselues, by the voluntarie acceptance of such a commaundement. And therefore it is manifest, that this perpetuall obedience of the *Rechabits*, which almightie God so highlie cõmended, & rewarded in them, was at the first voluntarie on their parts, & depended of their owne wills, as *Rabanus* noteth very wel, who in his cõmentary vpon the same place geueth to vnderstãd that the childrẽ of *Ionadab*, did more in that behalfe, thẽ the law of God cõmaunded thẽ.

*Rabanus in ca.*35. *Hieremia.*

5 Further

5 Furthermore, the ſame difference may be obſerued, concerning theſe two kindes of obedience, in the ould teſtament, which the Fathers (whom I haue before alledged) obſerue betwixt the precepts, & counſells of the new: as that in the former a penaltie is propoſed, & in the latter a reward promiſed, yet with this diſtinction betwixt the ould law, and the new, that the rewards of the ould law were temporall, and belonging only to this life, whereas as wel the rewards, as the puniſhments proper to the new law, are eternal, & pertaine to the world to come, to wit, euerlaſting damnation for the breach of precepts, and eternal ſaluation in heauen, for the obſeruation of the counſells, as appeareth euidentlie, in that which I haue alreadie diſcourſed cōcerning the twoo former Euangelicall counſels of *pouerty*, and *chaſtity*, and may in like maner be inferred, touching this counſell of *obedience*, conſiſting in the perfect imitation of our Sauiours abnegation of himſelfe, beeing a thing ſo difficult, & contrarie to mans nature, that it muſt needes be a worke of no leſſe merit, then perfection.

S. Ambroſ. li. de viduis vltra medium.

6 For as *S. Gregory* ſaith. *Minus eſt abnegare quod habet, valde autem multum eſt abnegare quod eſt. Yt is a leſſe matter, or more eaſy to deny, and renounce that which a man hath* (that is to ſay his wealth, & ſubſtance) *but it is a very great matter*, or of great difficultie, *for a man to deny, or renounce that which he is*. Thus ſaith, *S. Gregory*, whereuppon it followeth, that ſeing the vertues of voluntarie pouerty, & chaſtity, are ſo gratefull to almighty God, and meritorious, as I haue before proued them to be, it cannot be denied, but that true religious obedience, is of farre greater excellency, and merit then they: for whereas voluntarie pouertie, doth offer to God only externall, and temporall goods, and chaſtitie depriueth the body, only of ſenſuall pleaſures for the loue of God, religious obedience doth ſacrifice to him the internall goods of the ſoule, which oblation, or ſacrifice muſt needes be ſo much more worthy, then the acts of the other two vertues, by how much the goods of the ſoule, excell the goods of the body, or of fortune.

Greg. Hom. 32. in Euāg.

7 And therefore, for aſmuch, as our Sauiour propoſed and promiſed great rewards (as I haue proued already) to thoſe which renounce, and abandon their ſubſtance, and depriue themſelues of their bodilie pleaſures for his ſake, it muſt needes follow, that he will giue farre greater, and higher rewards, to thoſe that renounce, abandon, and deny themſelues for the loue of him.

8 For ſeeing that all our life in this world is nothing els but, as *Iob* ſaith, *militia ſuper terram*, *a warfare vppon the earth*, and that God giueth the higheſt crowne, to him that fighteth moſt valiantlie, and hath the

Iob. 7.

greatest victorie, it is euident, that no man shall haue so great a crowne, as he who by true abnegation of himselfe (which religious obedience includeth) doth fully conquer himselfe, which is the hardest and greatest conquest, that may be, whereby he doth not only subdue his sence, his appetit, and his passions, but also ouercome the pride of the world, and the malice of the diuel, and by true humilitie, triumph ouer them all, yea ouer himselfe, giuing his owne libertie and (as I may say) the scepter of his owne dominion to an other, for the pure loue of God, wherein he obtaineth not one, but many victories, and therefore the saying of the wise man, may be wel applied vnto him. *Vir obediens lo-*
Pro. 21. *quetur victoriam. The obedient man may speake of his victory.*

9 Moreouer if the obedience of *Abraham*, in resoluing to sacrifice
Gen. 22. his sonne *Isaac* vppon Gods commaundement, and the obedience also of *Isaac*, in yelding himselfe to be sacrificed, was so gratefull to almightie God, as the scripture declareth, it must needes be graunted, that true religious obedience, is much more gratefull vnto him, & that it surpasseth the obedience of them both: for whereas *Abraham* resolued to sacrifice his sonne, the true religious man doth by his obedience, sacrifice himselfe. *Isaac* only suffred himselfe to be bound by his father, but the religious man, by his vow byndeth himselfe. The obedience of *Abraham* was vppon commaundement, and therefore of necessitie, and due by obligation, but religious obedience procedeth only of our Sauiours counsell, and is therefore before the vow voluntarie, and cōsequentlie more acceptable then the other. The obedience both of *Abraham*, and of *Isaac*, consisted only in will, and resolution without performance of the act, but religious obedience, consisteth not only in will, and resolution, but also in action. Finally, their obedience was exercised but in one act, and only once, but the obedience of the religious man, extendeth it selfe to infinit acts, to wit, to all such lawfull acts, as his superiours shal commaund him, according to the institute of their rule, and this not for once, or twise, but during his life, imitating therein (as much as humane frailtie man permit) the continuall obedience, and resignation of our Sauiour, and his perpetuall abnegation of him selfe, who throughout the whole course of his life, did voluntarilie, and willinglie obey, not only his Father in heauen, his mother, and supposed father in earth, and the temporall magistrats, but also in some sort, his very enemies, that crucified him, resigning himselfe wholy into their handes, conforming his will to theirs, and deliuering himselfe vnto them, to be bound, and tied, haled, pulled, scorned, buffeted,
Philipp. 2. scourged, and finallie crucified, *factus obediens vsque ad mortem, mortem*

autem

autem crucis, being made obedient, euen to death, yea the death of the crosse. Where vppon it must needes follow, that as his voluntarie obedience and abnegation of himselfe, was of such infinit perfection, and merit, that as the Apostle saith. *God did therefore exalt him, and gaue him a name, super omne nomen, aboue all names*, so also the exact imitation thereof, must needes be of exceeding, and singuler merit, and perfection, in his seruants.

Ibid.

10 Therefore, for asmuch as the oportunitie is not alwayes offred vs, to follow, and imitat his humilitie, and resignation, in giuing our selues to our enemies hands, or our liues either for him, or for our brethren as he did, it hath pleased him out of his deuine prouidence, so to dispose, that there shalbe alwayes meanes in his church, whereby we may if we will, practise the perfect abnegation of our selues, and imitat him in most excellent manner, renowncing our owne wills, & iudgements for the loue of him, and giuing our selues wholy to the will, direction, yea to the correction, & chastisement of a spirituall master, to be guided by him in the way of perfection, to the seruice, & honour of God, & good example of others, all which is most excellentlie performed in religious disciplin, the perfection whereof consisteth in the cariage of our crosse, or rather in crucifiing our selues with Christ, by perfect obedience, and abnegation of our selues: for as *Cassianus* saith, the true religious man, is like one that is crucified, wherby it may be vnderstood, that he is so fast nailed, & bound by obedience, to the will of his superiour, representing to him the person of God, that he hath no motion, or operation of himselfe, but moueth and worketh, only according to his superiours commaundement.

Ioan. Cassi. li. 4. de instit. cænob. c. 35.

11 Therefore *Ioannes Climacus*, giueth certaine notable definitions of *religious obedience* saying, that it is, *a perfect abnegation of our selues, shewed by the ministery of the body, or els the mortification of the body, in a liuing soule: or lastly a motion without examination, or discussion, a willing and voluntary death, a life voide of curiositie, a secure danger, an immediat excuse before God, a safe nauigation, and a iourney made sleeping.*

Ioan. Climacus gradu. 4. de obedient.

12 Finally after much more to the same purpose, he concludeth that he which is truly obedient, will neuer whiles he liueth beleeue himselfe, or trust his owne iudgement in any thing whatsoeuer, though it seeme neuer so good vnto him. Thus teacheth he, and with great reason: For the true religious obedience, and abnegation of our selues, which our Sauiour counselled, requireth not only conformity of will, to the will of our superiour, but also resignation of iudgement to his iudgement, when the euidence of a knowne truth, dot not conuince

the vnderstanding, and force it to iudge otherwise, in which case it is neuertheles requisit, that the will obey, and presentlie yeald to the execution of the commaundement, when it is free from sinne.

13 And to this conformitie and resignation, euerie religious man is bound, for els his obedience, and abnegation of himselfe is not perfect, and sincere, seeing that a vowe of true religious obedience, is as *S. Gregory* calleth it, an *holocaust* or burnt sacrifice, wherein a man doth offer, and as it were immolat himselfe wholie to God in the fire of charitie, in which respect he must deny, and resigne himselfe, and all that is in him, without reseruation: for otherwise his resignation is not entire, but like to the oblation of *Ananias*, and *Saphira*, who hauing promised all their goods to almightie God, gaue him but a part thereof: or rather like to the offrings of those wicked *Iewes*, who gaue the worst to God, and kept the best to themselues, which God detested, and worthilie reprehended by the prophet *Malachias*. And the like I say, doth that religious man, who hauing promised his whole soule to God, giueth him but an inferiour part thereof (to wit his will) reseruing to himselfe the cheefe, and best part, which is his reason, and vnderstanding. Therefore I conclude, that this resignation of iudgement, is not only most necessarie to the perfect abnegation of our selues, which Christ counselled, but also most gratefull vnto him, both because it is (as I haue said) the best, and principall part in man, and also in respect of the difficultie that man hath, to captiuat, and submit his reason, and iudgement, in all things to the iudgement of an other.

Greg. 35. Moral. Cap. 10. & in Ezechiel. ho. 20.

Malach. 1.

14 But now let vs see, what the ancient Fathers teach concerning religious obedience, and the practise of it. *S. Basill* amply discourseth thereof in his monasticall institutions, and teacheth it by the example of the Apostles, who though our Sauiour said vnto them, that he sent them like sheepe amongst wolues, yet went most willinglie exposing themselues to all dangers, contumelies, crosses, and death it selfe, and the same obedience, saith *S. Basill*, ought the monk to yeald to his superiour: *Siquidem discipulos*, saith he, *Christus in hoc elegit* &c. *For Christ chose his disciples to this end, that they following this institute, or kind of life, might remaine for a paterne to the ensuing posterity.* Thus saith *S. Basill*, affirming also, that the superiour of religious men, representeth the person of Christ, and that they ought to be so resigned to his will, that they doe not so much as examine what he commaundeth them, so that it be not a sinne, and that they should be vnto him, as sheepe to their sheapeard, and the toole to the workeman,

S. Basill. in monast. instit. c. 23.

man, who is to vse it, and that otherwise they cannot serue God, and be saued in their profession.

Vide S. Basil. vbi supra.

15 S. *Hierom* in like sort, writing to *Rusticus* a monke, describeth notably the institutions and customes of the Monkes in his time, aduising him amongst manie other thinges, to liue in exact obedience to his superiour, for his diet, sleepe and apparel, yea and bodilie labour, concluding. *Præpositum monastery timeas, vt dominum &c. Feare the præfect, or superiour of the monasterie as thy lord, loue him as thy father, and beleeue that whatsoeuer he commaundeth thee, is good for thee, without taking vppon thee to iudge of his ordinaunce, or will, it being thy part to obey, and to performe that which is commaunded thee. S.* Thus saith *Hierom.*

S. Hieron. ad Rustic. ep. 4.

16 Also *S. Seuerus Sulpitius,* treating of the monkes of the east parts, in the time of *S. Martin* (whose disciple he was) saith. *Precipua ibi virtus, & prima est obedientia &c. The cheefe and first vertue there, is obedience, and none is receiued into the monasterie vppon other condition, but first to passe his trial, and that he refuse not to execute whatsoeuer is commaunded him by the Abbot, though it seeme neuer so difficult, or base, and vnworthy to bee suffred.* so saith hee.

S. Sulpit. in dialogo. 1. de virtut. monacho. 4. orientaliū. c. 12.

17 In like manner *S. Augustin* saith of the monkes, and their superiours in the same age. *Hi patres,* saith he, *nulla superbia &c. These Fathers doe prouide for those whome they call their children, without all pride, with great authoritie on their part in commaunding, and with great will and promtitude of the others in obeying.*

S. Aug. de morib. eccl. l. 1. ca. 31.

18 *S. Iohn Damascen,* in his historie of *Barlaam* and *Iosaphat,* speaking of some that lead a religious life, saith that they liued vnder the gouernment or commaund of one prefect, & did quite cut of their owne wills, with the sword of obedience, in such sort, that *they esteemed themselues, no other then slaues, bought for mony, not liuing to themselues, but to him, to whom they had submitted themselues for the loue of Christ.*

S. Ioan. Damas. in hist. Barlaam.

19 Thus doe the ancient and holie Fathers treat of religious obedience, vndertaken and performed for the loue of our Sauiour Christ, & in imitation of his perfect abnegation of himselfe: In which respect, *S. Ephræm* saith. *Beatus qui vera &c. Happy is he who is endewed with true & vnfained obedience, for hee is the imitator of our best master, who was obedient to death, and therefore he is trulie happy, that is trulie obedient, who imitating and following our Lord, is also made his coheire, or partaker of his inheritance.* Thus saith he.

S. Ephræm. de vertut. & vit. ss. ca. de obedient.

20 And now to shew by euident examples, how acceptable this religious and monasticall obedience is to almightie God, I will relate some two, or three histories, of Gods most miraculous approbation

thereof,

thereof, recounted by most holie and learned men, aboue a thousand yeares agoe.

S. Seuerus. Sulp. Dial. 1. de. virtutib. monacho. oreint. ca. 13.

21 *S. Seuerus Sulpitius*, who florished about the yeare of our Lord *foure hundreth*, witnesseth, that one who had resolued to be religious, came to an Abbot of a monasterie in *Egipt*, desiring to be receiued there. The Abbot after manie difficulties proposed, asked him whether hee was determined to be obedient, in whatsoeuer should bee commaunded him: And when he promised to obey in al thinges without exception, the Abbot sticked downe in the ground a dry wand or rodd, which he had in his hand, & cōmaunded him to water the same euerie day, vntill it should grow, the yong nouice vndertooke it, fetching water euerie day from the riuer *Nilus*, which was almost two miles distant from the monasterie, and continued his labour two yeares, without hope of anie other fruit, or effect thereof, then the reward of his obedience at Gods handes, when neuertheles the third yeare it pleased God, that the dry sticke tooke roote, and within a while grew to bee a little tree, which *S. Seuerus* saith, he himselfe had seene in the courte of the monaerie, *where it remaineth* saith he, *as it were for a testimonie of the merit of obedience, and of the force of faith.*

Idem ibid.

22 The same holie Father, recounteth also an other no lesse strange to the same purpose, which happned in the same monasterie, and vnder the same Abbot, as that when an other craued to be receiued for a nouice, and promised with extraordinarie confidence, to refuse nothing that shoud be enioyned him, the Abbot suspecting that his franke offer rather proceeded of presumption then humilitie, commaunded him to enter into a hoat furnace, or ouen, which then was heating to bake bread, whereat the nouice repined nothing at all, but entred into it presentlie, and as *S. Seuerus* saith. *Superata natura est, fugit incendium &c. Nature was ouercome, the fire fled him, and hee insteed of being burned, was refreshed in the midst of the furnace, with a heauenlie dew: and whereas* (saith *S. Seuerus, he was put to trial, being taken to be weake, he was found to be perfect, the verie first day: merito fælix, merito gloriosus, probatus obedientia, worthily happy, & worthylie glorius, being proued by obedience.*

S. Greg. Dial li. 2 cap. 7.

23 Heereto I will add one other out of *S. Gregorie* the great, as that *S Maurus*, beeing a monke vnder *S. Benedict*, and commaunded by him to goe to succour *Placidus* (who was then a child, and fallen into a riuer, & caried by the streame a bow-shot from the shore) was so cōfident vpon his superiours commaundement, that without respect of danger, hee ranne to the riuer, and walked firmelie vppon it, and drew out *Placidus*, without being himselfe wetshod, *which* (saith S. *Gregory*) S. *Benedict did*

wholy

wholie attribute to the great merit of Maurus *his obedience.*

24 I might, add hereto, if I thought it needefull, what *Ioannes Cassianus* testifieth, of a most famous Abbot called *Iohn*, who for his greate obedience, was rewarded by almightie God with the spirit of prophesy. As also what *Dorotheus* writeth vppon his owne knowledge, of a religious man, whome he saw sudainelie, and miraculouslie transported ouer a torrent, or furious streame, which he would needs venter to swimme ouer, out of an obedient desire, he had to be at home, at the time appointed him by his superiour, which was related by *Dorotheus*, a thousand & a hundreth years agoe, *to shew* saith he, *tantam esse obedientiæ, & abnegatæ, voluntatis vim, vt a morte quoque hominem liberare possit. That the force of obedience, and of a resigned wil is such, that it may also deliuer a man from death.*

Ioan. Cassiā. li. 4. de instit. renunt. *Dorotheus. doctrina. vi. de Coccium. li. 4. de vita. monastica.* *Idem.*

25 By these and diuers examples, which most graue authours doe witnes, we may learne how acceptable to almighty God is true religious obedience, and the abnegation of our selues, and no meruel, seeing the same proceedeth from a most pure and feruent loue of God, and a profound humilitie, whereby we doe trulie imitate and follow our Sauiours humilitie, obedience and abnegation (as much as is possible for men to doe) and also sacrifice our selues wholie to him, offring and yealding our soules, renouncing our owne wills, vnderstanding, and iudgment, for the pure loue of him: And therefore S. *Gregory* saith, *longe altioris meriti est &c. It is a matter of farr greater merit, to subiect our owne wills alwaies to an other mans will, then to wast our bodies with fasting, or secretlie to sacrifice our selues by compunction &c. And hee which hath learned perfectlie to fullfill the will of his master, excelleth, and is preferred in the kingdome of heauen, before those that fast, and weepe for their sinnes.*

S. Greg. in 1. Reg. c. 15. li. 6.

26 Thus saith S. *Gregory*, not vnlike that, which *Samuel* the propeth said to king *Saule*. *Melior est obedientia, quam victima. Obedience is better then sacrifise:* where vppon I conclud, tha the Roman Catholikes, practising this counsel of our Sauiour in monasticall life, doe imitate his obedience, humiltie and resignation, in as excellent sort, as mans frailtie, and imperfection doth permit, and doe performe therein a notable point of christian perfection, which cannot be imagined to consist in anie other thinge, then in the perfect imitation of the most excellent, and perfect vertues of Christ

1. Reg. 15.

27 Let vs now consider, what exercise, or practise *Lutherans*, or *Caluinists* haue of this euangelical counsel, and how they imitate Christ in the perfect abnegation of themselues, and wherein they may, but so much as pretend, the obedience, or resignation of their will, iudgment, and vnderstanding, in all which it will appeare, that the verie Panims,

and Infidels, partlie matched them, and partlie excelled them.

28 Well then, they will say perhaps, that they are as obedient and resigned as is conuenient, in that they obey their magistrats, spirituall and temporal, and that therein, they exercise the obedience of the will: as also that they practise the obedience of their vnderstanding, in captiuating the same, to the faith of Christ, and that therein they abnegat, and denie themselues. Whereto I answer, first, that this is farr from the sense of our Sauiours wordes, and the perfection that hee required in his disciples, seeing that hee spoke not of matters of faith or beleefe, but of the imitation of him, speaking expreslie of those which would

Matt.16. folow his actions, & course of life, saing. *If anie man wil come after mee, let him denie himself.* And then to shew whereto this abnegatiō of our selues should tend, he added, *let him take vpp his crosse and folow me*, that is to say, let him denie himselfe, as I did in my passion, mortifiyng, and as it were, crucifiyng his owne wil, and affections in such sort, that hee haue no more vse, or commaund of them, then he should haue of his owne bo-

Num.10. dy, if he were crucified and nailed fast to a crosse, as I noted before out

Ioan.Cassiā. of *Ioahnnes Cassainus*, who applieth these wordes of our Sauiour, most

l.4.de instit properly and aptly, to monasticall obedience.

Cœnob.c.35. 29 And this also S. *Peter* doth verie wel insinuat, when he saith. *Christus passus est pro nobis &c. Christ suffred for vs, to leaue you an example to follow*

1.Pet.2. *his footstepes*, that is to say, to imitate his profound humilitie, obedience, abnegation of himselfe, and mortification, which vertues doe most excellentlie, & eminentlie appeare in al the course of his life & passion, and therefore are to bee exactlie followed, of such as pretend to arriue to the highest perfection of christian religion. Of which kind of obedience, and perfect resignation, consisting in action, there is no exercise at all amongst *Lutherans*, and *Caluinists*, as euerie man seeth, and knoweth.

30 For as for their obedience to their magistrats, what great perfection of christian religion, may we imagin to bee therein, seeing that euerie pagan, and infidel, may, and doth performe it, aswel as we? And if they will pretend to captiuat their vnderstanding to the faith of Christ, and so in some sort to denie their owne iudgment, and consequentlie to obserue his counsel, in the abnegation of themselues, it will easilie appeare, that it is farre otherwise. For were there euer anie, professing the name of Christ, who lesse renounced their owne iudgments in matters of faith then they? This euidentlie appeareth, not onlie in some important points of christian religion, whereto the obedience, and resignation

reſignation of the vnderſtanding is moſt requiſit (as namely in the matter of the holly *Euchariſt*, and in all kind of miraculous workes) but alſo in the interpretation of the holy ſcriptures, which euery one of them vnderſtandeth, according to his owne particuler iudgement, and fancy, where vppon haue growne about *twoo hundred*, and *ſeuenty* ſects, ſince *Luthers* tyme, whereas from Chriſts time to his, there cannot be reckoned aboue *a hundred eighty one*, ſo that there haue riſen more ſects in theſe laſt 100. yeares, then there aroſe in *a thouſand fiue hundreth* yeares before. Beſides that, ſo different haue bene their interpretations of the ſcripture, that they haue made amongſt them, *foureſcore and foure* ſeuerall expoſitions, of theſe few wordes of our Sauiour. *Hoc eſt corpus meum.* This is my body: yea, and *Oecolampadius* a ſacramentary, noteth amongſt the *Lutherans* only, *ſeauenty ſeauen* mutations, and changes in their expoſition of ſcriptures, and their other phantaſies, as he tearmeth them.

Vide Stanislaum Reſchium, in cẽtur. Euang. ſectarum.

Vide Claudiũ de ſainctes de veritate Eucharis. repetitione 1. c. 10. Matt. 26. Oecolamp. in Æqua reſponſ. ad præfat. Lutheri.

31 Therefore they are ſo farr, from ſubmitting their iudgement, and vnderſtanding to faith, that they doe ſubiect all authoritie, humane and deuine (I meane of Fathers, Councels, Scriptures, and the Church) and conſequentlie all the Chriſtian faith, to their owne iudgements. For though they talke of nothing but of ſcripture, and continuallie appeale thereto, yet for as much as they preſume, to make themſelues the only iudges of the true ſence thereof, they reduce in concluſion, the reſolution of all queſtions and controuerſies, and the ſcriptures themſelues, to their priuat iudgement. I meane not the iudgement of them all in generall (as the reſolution of the whole *Lutheran*, or *Caluiniſticall* congregation) but the fancy of euery one of them in particuler: for that euery cobler, & tinker amongſt them, preſumeth to haue the ſpirit of God in ſuch plenty, and ſo at his commaunde, that he taketh vppon him to vnderſtand, and interpret the holly ſcriptures at his pleaſure; where vppon it followeth, that they of all other men, can leaſt pretend with any ſhew, or collor of reaſon, to renounce their owne iudgements, yea much leſſe then many Infidells haue donne.

32 For we read of the ſchollers of *Pithagoras*, that they ſo much eſteemed and reuerenced the opinion, and iudgement of their maſter, that his word ſtood for a law, and was held for an oracle, and an infallible truth, in ſo much that it ſuffiſed for the deciſions of all queſtions, and the reſolution of the greateſt doubts amongſt them, to ſay only, *ipſe dixit, Pythagoras ſaid it*: whereas theſe ſectaries are, *nullius addicti iurare in verba magiſtri*, men that cannot endure to follow any maſter, or teacher, and therefore though they all come out of one ſchoole, yet they are ſo

Cicero. li. 1. de natura deorum. Horat. ep. 1 ad mecænatem.

so deuided amongst themselues, & subdeuided into many seuerall sects, (as I haue signified before) and those also of euery sect, so addict euery one to his owne opinion, that they hold and condemne each other for heretikes, railing one vppon an other, in most shamefull and spitefull manner, as it is most euident in the writings, not only of the *Caluinists* against the *Lutherans*, and againe of these against them, but also of the *Puritanes* in *England*, against the *protestants* there, whom they chardge with *intollerable errours, manifest defection from Christ, impious contempt, and prophanation of the sacraments,* and call the bishops, *reliques of the seede of Antichrist, and sworne enimies of the church of Christ*: though neuertheles they all pretend alike, an assurance, and infallibilitie of their doctrin, grounded as they all say, vppon the scriptures, and inspiration of the holy Ghost. But by this their difference, and dissention, it is more cleare then the sunne, that they haue not the spirit of God, but that they falsly baptize, their owne phantasticall conceits, and priuat iudgements, with the name of Gods spirit: wherebie also it euidentlie appeareth, that they doe not captiuate their iudgements and vnderstanding to faith, but measure all their faith by their owne conceit, and iudgement, calling it the spirit of God. Whereupon I conclude, that they haue not amongst them, in any sort, that true obedience, and abnegation, which our Sauiour counselled, but rather that they are such as S. *Peter* describeth. *Qui dominationem contemnunt, audaces sibi placentes, sectas non metuunt introducere, men which despise to be gouerned, or directed, audacious, standing in their owne conceits, and feare not to introduce, or bring in new sects.*

Puritani Angli in secunda admonitione ad parlamentum. Vide Stanislaum Reschium in Ministromachia.

2. Pet. 2.

33 But perhaps they will say, that it sufficeth for the abnegation which Christ requireth in a christian man, to performe it only in preparation of will, and readines to doe it when occasion shall require, (as it is also to be said, concerning our Sauiours counsel, of perfect patience in suffering iniuries, and of the hate of our owne liues:) whereto I answer, that although this preparation of mind and will, may suffise for the saluation of euery particular man (if he bind himselfe to no more) yet it sufficeth not, to the perfection of the church of Christ, and of christian religion, whereto it is requisit that there be some continual and publike practise thereof amongst christians, as I will declare further after a while: and in the meane time, I wish it to be considered, that there is great reason to thinke, that they haue not so much as any true preparation of will, to the perfect abnegation of themselues, which I say for diuers respects. First, because they haue no exercise or practise thereof at all amongst them, whereby

it may

it may well be thought, that they haue no sufficient disposition thereto: whereas amongst Catholikes, very many doe practise it, and performe it notablie in religious life, by whose example also, other catholikes are moued to dispose, and prepare their wills, and mindes, to the performance of it, when occasion shall require. Secondlie, it cannot be otherwise thought, but that they, who hould, and teach, that the commaundements of God are vnpossible to be kept, doe thinke it much more impossible, to obserue the counsells, and specially this of perfect abnegation, which is the most difficult, in which respect, it may be well presumed, that they doe thinke it but labour lost, to dispose, and prepare their mindes, to accomplish it when occasion shalbe offred, for no man is so simple, to dispose himselfe to doe a thing, which he thinkes impossible.

Luther. in resp. ad dialog. Syluestri prierat. Melanch. ad cap.4. ep. ad Rom. editione 1. Caluin. li.2. Instit.c.7. vide Cocciũ in Thesauro de Iustif. li.3. ar.2.

34 Lastly, it seemeth that they are farre from that profund humility, which is the ground of all true obedience, and resignation, as it may sufficiently appeare in their cheefe Apostles, *Luther*, *Caluin*, and other their ringleaders, whereof wee neede no other testimonie, then their owne writings, wherein they accuse each other of intollerable pride, presumption, and contumacie: and against *Luther* a better witnes cannot be desired, then his owne bookes, as namelie that which he wrote against king *Henry* the *Eight* of *England*, wherein he affirmed, that he himselfe was so good, and holly a man, *coram mundo*, euen in the sight of the world, that all the Popes, Cardinals, Princes, Bishops, and Monkes, *were vnworthie, calceamenti corrigiam soluere, to vntye the string of* his shoe, and that he cared not, *for a thousand Ciprians, or a thousand Augustins*. And in his booke intituled, *against all the false ecclesiasticall order of bishops*, he saith thus. *En appello me ecclesiasten Dei gratia* &c. *Behould I call my selfe Ecclesiastes*, or preacher by the grace of God, *I haue adorned my selfe with a title, whom you* (he speaketh to all bishops) *doe with whole waine-loades of reproches call an heretike: And I take the title of Ecclesiastes vppon me, with great contempt of the diuel, and you all.*

Luther cõtra regẽ Angliæ.

Idem li. aduersus falso: nominat. Ecclesiast. statũ Papæ. & Episcoporum.

35 Thus saith he, and addeth, that he might also call himselfe an *Euangelist*, and that he doubteth not, but Christ would allow it as he is sure, that he holdeth him for his *Ecclesiastes*. And further he saith, that he signifieth plainelie to the Bishopps, by that writing of his, that from thence forth he would not doe them so much honour, or beare them so much respect, *as to vouch safe to submit himselfe, or his doctrin, to the iudgemẽt eyther of them, or of any Angel in heauen*. And in the prologue of the same booke he saith. *Doctrinã meam ego nolo iudicari* &c. *I will not haue*

Ibid.

Apud Suriũ in comment. an. 1522.

my doctrin to be iudged by any mā, or by al the Angels, for seeing that I am assured of it, I will be iudge, not onlie of you (he meaneth the pope and the bishops) *but also of the angels &c.* Thus worte he.

Vide Thesaur. Coccij. li. 8. de Sig. eccl. de Lutheranorum &c. Corruptelis. Surius. an. 1530.

36 And being once aduertised from a frind of his, that his aduersaries tooke great aduantage against his German translation of the new testament, for that he had added the worde, *sola*, in the third chapter of the epistle of *S. Paule* to the *Romans*, making him say, *sola fide iustificari*, to be iustified by onlie faith, whereas the Apostle hath not the word *only*: he wrote in answer thereof, that if he had knowne, that al the Papists put together, could haue translated onlie one chapter of the deuine scripture aright in the German tongue, hee would haue craued their aduise in his translation of the new testament: and againe alitle after, he saith.

Cocc[illegible]us. vbi supra.

Si Papista tuus &c. If thy Papist will still wrangle about the worde sola. I answer him presentlie, that Doctor Martin Luther will haue it so, and that a papist and an asse is al one. Sic volo, sic iubeo stat pro ratione voluntas &c. So I wil, and so I commaund, my will or pleasure standeth for reason, for we will not be disciples or schollers, but masters, and iudges of the Papists, Luther will haue it so, and saith that he is a Doctor aboue al the Docters in the whole papaltie. Thus hee, who addeth further for the conclusion of the whole, that he was sorrie he had not added two other words, to wit, *omnibus & omniū, to operibus legis, that so the text might haue bene, sine omnibus operibus omnium legum. VVithout al workes of al lawes.*

37 Furthermore writing in his vulgar tongue, a gainst adecree made by the Emperour *Charles*, and al the princes of the Empire, at *Augusta*, he calleth them al *traytors, wicked and vaine knaues*, and compareth them to swine, and addeth further, concerning his owne doctrin of iustyfiyng faith. *Dico ego Doctor Martinus Lutherus, Domini nostri Iesu Christi indignus Euangelista &c. I Doctor Martin Luther, the vnworthy Euangelist of our Lord Iesus Christ doe say, that the Emperour of the Romans, the Emperour of the Turkes, the Emperour of Tartary, the Emperour of Persia, the Pope, all Cardinals, Bishops Priests, Monks, Nunnes, Kinges, Princes, Lords, yea all the world, with all the diuels thereof, ought to suffer this article* (*to wit, onlie faith without all good workes doth iustifie before God*) *to stand firme, and inuiolat, and that they shall furthermore haue the fier of Hell vppon their heads, and no thankes at all. Hic esto meus Docteris Luteri instinctus, a spiritu Sancto, verumque, ac sanctum Euangelium. Let this goe for the instinct, which I Doctor Luther haue from the holie Ghost, and for the true and holie ghospell.*

Idem ibid. ā. 1531.

Stanisla. Resch. in ministromach. ex Iohanne. Spangenberg.

38 Thus bewraied hee his most insolent, and luciferian pride, which was also sufficientlie noted and taxed, by those that sprong from him.

and professed his doctrin, as the Lutherans of the vniuersity of *VVittenberg*, who beginning to discent from him in tenn or eleauen points of doctrin, gaue him amongst many other opprobrious epithets, the name of *Philauton*, one that attributeth much to himselfe, and stood highlie in his owne conceit: and called him also, *Philonicum* and *Eristicum*, one that would by scoulding, defend al his owne sayings, and doings whatsoeuer, and *Doctorem Hyperbolicum*, an *Hyperbolical Doctor*, that vsed to make a camel of a gnat, and boasted of thousands, when he had skant fiue: *Polipragmonicum*, one that intruded himselfe into all mens busines: and finally to omit the rest, *ingenij ostentatorem*, one that sought to make a vaine ostentation, and shew of his owne witt.

39 Thus say his owne disciples of *VVittenberg*, who knew him best, for that he liued for the most part amongst them, & lieth buried there. In like manner *Conradus Gesnerus* (who was also of his brood) saith, that hee was a man, *so vehement and impatient, that hee could not indure anie man, which did not agree with him in all thinges*. And further he beseecheth God to graunt, that he (I meane *Luther*) *did not in the end, hurt his church as much with his contention and impudency, as he had furthred it in the beginning*. And the *Tigurin ministers* wrote of him thus. *Lutherus sua quærit, pertinax est, & insolentia nimia effertur. Luther seeketh his owne commoditie, and is obstinat and ouer insolent*.

Conrad. Gesner. in vniuersa. bibliotheca.

Tigur. ministri. in resp. ad li. inscript. contra Zuinglium.

4 Thus is *Luther* censured for his pride by the *Tigurin ministers*, whereto all the *Sacramentaries* and *Zuinglians* doe willinglie subscribe, who terme him, *a presumptious and obstinat fellow, a new pope, and cosen german to Antichrist: in cuius moribus* say they, *superbia factus, & intollerabilis prope ambitio deprehendatur: in whose manners may be discouered, pride, arrogancy, and almost an intollerable ambition:* and to conclud concerning *Luther, Conradus Riss*, saith of him, *that God did take from him the true spirit, for his pride, and gaue him insteede thereof, an angrie, proud, and lying spirit*,

apud Stanisla. Resch. in ministromachia. In charta quadam. Zuinglian. edit. an. 1527.

41 I omit manie other testimonies of sectaries concerning *Luthers* pride, to add two or three touching *Caluin*: of whome his master *Bucer* (a man of no smale reputation amongst the sectaries, especially in *England* in King *Edwards* time (affirmeth that he was *transformed into an Idol* and that hee would by his good will, bee honored throughout all *Fraunce* with sacrifice: In so much that those, saith he, who were called in times past *Idololatræ*, might be called *Caluinolatræ*, that is to say, worshippers of *Caluin*. And *Theomorus* a *Caluinist*, amongst other notable vices, which hee laboureth to excuse in *Caluin*, though they were obiected against him, by men of his owne sect (reckneth, *ambition*

Stanisla. Reschius. in ministromachia. ex Edero.

Ibid. ex Sainctio. & Edero.

and

and *deſire of tyrannie, bloudy crueltie, implacabilitie, immoderat choller*, and *anger* &c.

42 Alſo *Heßhuſius* a *Lutheran*, chargeth him with the like, and with contempt and diſdaine of others, beſides diuers other *peccadillos*, which I omit, be cauſe I ſpeake ſpeciallie of his pride and preſumption.

Heshuſ. in defenſione ſua.

43 So that we neede not to make any doubt, of the truth of that which *Hierome Bolſec* (his diſciple in *Geneua* for ſome yeares, though after a Catholike) wrote of him out of his owne knowledge, to wit, that many times in his ſermõs, he would breake forth into theſe wordes. *I am a prophet, I haue the ſpirit of God, and if I erre, it is thou o God, that for the ſinne of this people doſt caſt me into errour, and deceiue me, I cannot erre*, and ſuch like: and the ſame authour alſo witneſſeth, that he was ſo vaine glorious, that he would ſometimes *ſett forth letters, and like treatiſes in print, vnder fained names, wherein he publiſhed his owne praiſes, his worthines, and great merits towards the church.*

Hieron. Bolſec in vita Caluini.

Idem. Ibid.

44 Lo then, what good diſpoſition and preparation of mind, thoſe men had to that profound humilitie, obedience, mortification, and abnegation of themſelues, which our Sauiour councelled. Whereuppon I inferre, that ſeeing as our Sauiour ſaid: *Diſcipulus non eſt ſuper magiſtrum. The diſciple is not aboue his maſter*, it were againſt all reaſon to thinke, that their diſciples, I meane thoſe, that profeſſe their doctrin, ſhould more profit in humilitie therebie, then they themſelues, who had the firſt fruits of the euangelical ſpirit.

Matth.10.

45 And to the end, that the matter may not depend altogether vppon my coniecture, I wiſh thee, good Reader to conſider what their followers write, one of an other, concerning this point of their pride, I meane not the pride of particuler men amongſt them, but of their whole ſects. *Caluin* obiecteth againſt *VVeſtphalus*, and all his fellow *Lutherans, that they were puffed vp with a diabolical pride, and that they had no reſpect to the iudgement of God, or his Angels*, and therefore, he calleth them *Cyclopes, Gyants*, and *phrentick barkers*. *Ochinus* in his Dialogues, calleth *Caluin* with all his *Geneuian*, and *Tigurin* miniſters. *Sectam terrenorum deorum, ſiue paparum. A ſect of earthly Gods, or popes*, meaning that out of an intollerable pride, they tooke vppon them to be popes, or rather to be Gods. And in like maner *Caſtalio*, tearmeth the *Caluiniſts: ſuperbos feroces, inflatos: proud, fierce*, and *ſweld or puft vp with pride:* and beſides many other vices (which I omit) he chargeth them with *Tyranny*, and *obſtinacy*, which are the inſeperable companions, or rather the daughters of the higheſt pride.

Ioan. Caluinus in vltima admonitione ad Ioachim vveſtphalum.

Ochinus Dial. contra ſectam terre. Deorum.

Checouicius apud Staniſla. Reſchiũ. miniſtromach.

46 I let paſſe for breuities ſake, many other ſuch like teſtimonies, which

which oft occurre in their writings, and inuectiues of one against an other, for by this, which I haue said, it sufficientlie appeareth, that *Lutherans* and *Caluinists*, persisting in the doctrin, and spirit of their euangelical masters, can haue no due disposition to perfect obedience, resignation, and contempt of the world, and of themselues, which our Sauiour counselled, and required in his followers, and is with all endeuour sought, and practised by Catholikes, in monastical disciplin.

47 Seeing then it appeareth euidentlie, that they haue no vse or practise at all, either of perfect abnegation of themselues, or of the euangelicall counsells, preached, and practised by our Sauiour, & his Apostles (as I haue clearelie proued before:) it must needes follow, that they haue not the perfection of christian religion, which cannot consist in any thing els, but in the perfect imitation of our Sauiour Christ, and his Apostles, and therefore *S. Paule* said to the *Corinthians. Imitatores mei estote sicut ego Christi. Be you followers of me, as I am of Christ.*

Chap. 28. 29 & 30.

1. Cor. 4.

48 And *S. Peter* said to Christ, in the name of all the Apostles, *secuti sumus te, wee haue followed thee*, not meaning thereby, that they had gonne vpp, & downe the country after him, but that they had obeyed him, and imitated, or followed the example of his pouerty, chastitie, obedience, and mortification. Besides that also, an infinit number of christians in the Apostles time, imitated our Sauiour, and them, in the perfect exercise of the same vertues, in monasticall and religious life, as I haue shewed amply before. In which respect, *S. Dionisius*, *S. Basil*, and S. *Gregory Nazianzen*, call the monasticall profession. *Vitam perfectissimam. The most perfect life.* And *S. Chrisostome*, tearmeth it. *Perfectionis culmen, virtutisque fastigium. The height of perfection, and toppe of vertue. S. Hierome* saith to *Heliodorus* the monke. *Perfectum te fore pollicitus es* &c. *Thou hast promised to become perfect.*

Mat. 19.

S. Dionisius Ecclesiast. Hierar. c. 6. par. 2.

S. Basil. de monast. constit. c. 19.

S. Greg. Nazianz. orat. de obitu S. Basil. S. Ioan. Chrisost. li. 3. aduersus vituperat. vitæ monast.

S. Hieron. ep. ad Heliodorum.

49 Furthermore *Eusebius* declareth notablie, the difference betwixt the perfection of religious life, and the laudable, & good life of other christians, in these wordes. *In Ecclesia Dei duo modi viuendi instituti sunt* &c. Two manners of life, are instituted in the church of God. The one exceeding our nature, and the common course of men, not requiring mariage, children, substance, or wealth, & wholy addicted to the worshipp and seruice of God, for the vnmeasurable loue of heauenly things. The other kind of life, is more remisse, and humane, being occupied with the care of familie, with mariage, and with the procreation of children, prescribing also rules, for those which make iust warre, and not neglecting possessions, and wealth, and merchandize, so farr as the respect of religion may permit, and this is the second degree

Euseb. li. 1. de monast. Euang ca. 8.

Ooo of

of piety. Thus saith *Eusebius* of these two kinds of life, attributing, (as here you haue seene) the perfection of christian religion, to the former, consisting in the exercise of Christs counsells.

D. Ber. de vita solitaria ad fratres de monte Dei.

50 To conclude *S. Bernard*, writing to certaine religious men, whom he calleth *fratres de monte Dei*, saith thus. *Altissima est professio vestra* &c. *Your profession is most high, or excellent, it passeth the heauens, it is like to the purity of Angels, for you haue not only vowed all hollynes, but also all perfection of holynes, yea and the very end of all consummation, or perfection* &c. *Yt belongeth to other men to serue God, but it is your part to adhere vnto him, or to be vnited with him: other men ought to beleeue in God, to loue him, to reuerence, and worshipp him, but you ought to tast him, to vnderstand him, to know him, and to enioy him.* Thus saith *S. Bernard*, of religious perfection.

51 Seeing then, this is the doctrin of all the ancient Fathers, grounded vppon the holly scriptures, and most conforme to reason it selfe, it were absurd to say, that any religion professing Christ, should be a true, and perfect religion, that should not haue this christian perfection. For although no man is bound, to the obseruation of the Euangelicall counsels, except he bind himselfe, and that therefore the christian perfection which consisteth therein, is not of necessitie required in euery member, or part of Christs church: yet it is so necessary for the whole, that it cannot be perfect without it, as wee see also in other societies, that many things are requisit to the perfection of the whole, which are not necessarie in euery part. Yt is conuenient for the perfection of an vniuersitie, that there be deuines therein, yet neither is any man bound to professe diuinitie, except he list himselfe, neither is it necessarie that euery man should be a deuine. Also it is requisit, that in a perfect common welth, there should be all trades, and occupations, and yet it is not necessarie, that euery man should professe some trade, neither is any man bound to it, further then he thinketh good to bynd himselfe.

52 Also in the church it selfe, wee see, that it is most necessarie to the perfection thereof, that there be priests therein, and yet no man is bound to take the order of priesthood (if he doe not bind himselfe) neither is it necessarie that euerie man should be a priest. Euen so also, though it be not requisit to the perfection of the church of Christ, and of christian religion, that euery man keepe the Euangelical counsells, yet it is necessary that some doe obserue them. For seeing that the perfection of christian religion, must needes consist in the perfect imitation of Christ, (as I haue said) and that he did not only practise the ver-

tues,

tues, of *pouerty*, *chastity*, and *abnegation of himselfe*, throughout the whole course of his life, but did also counsell and inuite vs to imitate him therein, it were absurd to thinke, that there shall not be alwaise some in his church, who shall make publike profession to follow his example, in as high a degree of perfection, as may stand with humane infirmitie: for whereto tended all his actions, his continuall mortifications, his austeritie of life, his humilitie, pouertie, and obedience, but to giue vs an example, which we might imitat? The least dropp of his most precious bloud, suffised for our redemption, which also he might haue shed without so much paine, ignominie, and contempt, as he suffred in his passion, and without such pouerty, humilitie, and mortification, as he practised throughout the course of his life, but only that he would thereby, giue vs example, and encourage vs to follow him, in the exercise of those vertues. So that it cannot otherwaise be imagined, but that his meaning was, to haue alwayes in his church some publike state, and profession of life, wherein his most excellent vertues, should be imitated and exercised for his glory, and the example of the weaker sort of men. For as it was necessarie, that there should be a most liuely paterne, and example of christian perfection, in his church in his owne time, not only in himselfe, but also in his Apostles, and other his disciples: so also it is conuenient, that there be the like, continuallie in his church, to the worldes end, to serue as it were for a marke, whereat all sorts of christian men may shoote.

53 Therefore as almighty God, out of his ordinarie prouidence, alwaies stirreth vpp some in all common wealths, to professe all kind of trades, necessarie for the publike good thereof, and euer moueth some in his church to be priests, though he bind no man thereto: so also out of the same prouidēce, he hath alwaies moued infinit numbers of both sexes, to imitate him in the practise of his counsells in religious life, for his greater glory, shewing therein the wonderfull force, and effects of his grace, and bounty, and imparting thereby to his church, such other graces, and benefits, as I haue signified before, when I deli- *Chap.26.* uered the causes, and conueniencie of the multiplicitie, and varietie of religions.

54 Therefore I conclude, that seeing *Lutherans* and *Caluinists*, haue not within the whole latitude of their congregations, and religion, any exercise at all of the Euangelicall counsells, preached and practised by our Sauiour, by his Apostles, and by the christians, aswell in the primatiue church, as in all ensuing ages, euen vntill this day, it followeth

of necessitie, that they haue neither perfection, nor truth of christian religion.

55 But what may we thinke of their spirit, seeing they are not only void themselues of this perfection, but are also such professed enemies of it, that they seeke to hinder it in all others. Yea to supplant, and exterminat it out of the christian world? As may appeare, by the implacable hatred, and malice, they beare to all religious persons, whose life and profession, consisteth in nothing els, but in the exercise of the euangelicall counsels, against whom they proclaime open warr, wherein they doe notablie simbolize, with the *Arrians, Donatists*, and other famous, or rather infamous, heretikes of former ages.

Circa an. 373. Ruffinus li. 2. c. 3. Socrat. li. 2. ca.17.

56 For we read in the ecclesiasticall histories, that *Lucius* an *Arrian* bishop, *turned* saith *Ruffinus, the Armes of his fury against monasteries, and made warr with aboue three thousand religious men, that were dispersed throughout the desert, whither he sent tropes of armed men, vnder coronells and captaines, as though they had benne to fight with some barbarous enemies, and when they came there, they found a new kind of warre, for their enemies did but offer their neckes to the swoord, and say nothing els, but as Christ said to Iudas. Amice, ad quid venisti? Friend, to what end art thou come.* Thus farre *Ruffinus*, and the same is also testified by *Socrates*.

Socrat. li. 2. c.17. An. 370. Hieron. in chroni. An.38.

57 Wee read in like manner in *S. Hierome*, that the wicked *Arrian* Emperour *Valens*, did so hate all monkes, and religious persons, that he made a law, that they should either be souldiars, or els be beaten to death with clubbs.

Optat. li. 2. contra Donat. An. 390. Hieron. contra Vigilant. An. 400. S. Aug. cōtra Petilian. li. 3. ca. 4. S. Damascen. de heres. An. 700.

57 The *Donatists* also, as *Optatus Milleuitanus* witnesseth, did vse to vnueil holly virgins, and nunnes, therebie to vndoe their former profession. And *S. Hierome* writeth of *Vigilantius*, that he diswaded men from monasticall life. And *S. Augustin* affirmeth, that *Petilianus* the heretike (against whome he wrote) did raile vppon Monkes, and inueigh bitterlie against monasteries, reprehending also, *S. Augustin* himselfe, because he had instituted an order of religion. *S. Iohn Damascen*, maketh mention of certaine heretikes, called *Lampetiani*, who taught that monkes might liue as they list, both for their diet, apparell, and all other thinges.

Theocteri. in orat. funeb. in S. Nicetā. An. 890. Constitutio Theophi. Imperator.

58 The wicked, and hereticall Emperour *Constantinus Copronimus*, labored for nothing more, then to extinguish all monasticall orders. And the Emperour *Theophilus*, who was also a Tyrannicall heretike, and a magician, profaned monasteries, and religious houses, and forbad Monkes to come into townes, or citties, and would not suffer them,

to liue any where in peace, and rest.

59 And how well the spirit of *Martin Luther*, and *Iohn Caluin*, agreeth with all these former heretiks, it may appeare by their owne writings. *Luther* saith. *Cupio eradicata & abolita esse vniuersa monasteria* &c. *I wish that all monasteries were rooted out, extinguished and abolished, and I would to God that they were destroyed from heauen, with fire, and brimestone, like Sodome, and Ghomorrha, so that there might be no memorie at all least of them.* And *Caluin* calleth *monasticall vowes, the netts of Sathan*, and monkes, *hoodded sophisters*, & saith that *they haue giuen themselues wholy to the deuil.* So that to imitate the life of our Sauiour, that is to say, his *pouerty, chastity, mortification and abnegation of himselfe*, is in the opinion of these men, *to giue a mans selfe wholy to the deuil*, and deserueth no lesse, *then fire, and brimstone from heauen*: and therefore wee see also, that their followers doe destroy all monasteries, and seeke to extirpate, monasticall life, wheresoeuer they commaund, or haue power to doe it.

An. 1520. Luther de votis monasticis.

Ioan. Caluin li. 4 instit. c. 13.

60 And although they pretend commonly, that the euil life of religious men, is the cause of their hatred towards them, it is euident by the doctrin of *Luther, Caluin*, and their followers (which I haue declared) that it is the perfection of religious life, which they cannot brooke, because it is flat contrarie, aswell to their loose liues, as to the principles of their doctrin.

61 And as for the euil life of some religious men, wee mislike, and lament it no lesse, and more then they, yea and wee say with *S. Augustin*, that as there is none better then the good religious, so there are none worse then the bad, whereof *Luther* himselfe, and the other Apostatas his companions, may serue for examples. Wherein also it may be noted for an infallible truth, that the worst and most dissolute men of all others in religion, are those that become sectaries, leauing the straight rule of monasticall disciplin, and religious mortification, to the end they may amongst the sectaries, giue free scope, and libertie to the flesh, without controle, as shall be declared more particulerly hereafter.

S. August. de opere monachor. ca. 28.

Chap. 36.

62 Neuertheles, it is no reason for the offence of some, to punish or destroy all, nor to take away the good vse of any thing, because some doe abuse it, seeing there is nothing so holly on earth, but it is sometimes misused, neither is there any company, or congregation of men so vertuous, but some amongst them, may serue for an example of humane infirmitie, as wee see by experience in the very colledge of the Apostles, and therefore whosoeuer is so vnaduised, and vncharitable, as to make more reflection vppon the bad, then vppon the good it is

no marueile though he be scandalized: whereas, if he were so carefull to note the vertues of the best, to follow their example, as to obserue the vices of the worst, to haue matter to carpe at, he should not only be greatelie edified, but might also make himselfe within a while, an example and paterne of vertue.

63 But such is the mercifull prouidence of almightie God, in the gouerment of his church, that besides the ordinarie endeuour vsed by his pastors, to reforme such religions, as decline from their former integritie, he also inspireth many religious men, to reduce, and restore their owne decayed orders, to their primitiue perfection, and stirreth vp many others, to beginne, and institute new rules, to supply the decay of the ould, thereby to continue alwaise in his church, the true, and perfect imitation of our Sauiours life, and deuine vertues, as I haue sufficiently declared before, and common experience sheweth to be true. Therefore I conclude, that seeing *Lutherans*, *Caluinists*, and other sectaries of our time, are professed enemies of christian perfection (consisting in the imitation of Christ by the obseruation of his counsels) they haue neither the perfection, nor truth, of christian religion, nor consequently that vnion with God, from whence proceedeth the true felicitie of man, and common welth, which also wilbe yet more manifest in the next chapter, wherein I will examin, what externall signes they haue of internall vnion with God.

VVhere as it is shewed, that the Roman Catholikes, haue all the externall signes that may be, of Gods externall vnion with them, (to wit, ecstases, rapts, and reuelations, the spirit of prophesie, visions, and apparitions of our Sauiour, his Angels and Sainctes, and the operation of manifestest miracles:) it is here examined, what our aduersaries can pretend to haue had, or to haue in this kind: and it is proued, that they haue had nothing els, but certaine counterfet miracles, which haue miscaried vnder their hands, illusions of wicked spirits, idle and phantasticall dreames, horrible visions, and apparitions of deuils, and fained reuelations. Lastly, their obiections against our miracles, are confuted, and they concluded to be wilfully blynd.

Chap. 32.

1 HAuing shewed alreadie in the twenty seauenth chapter, that almightie God hath approued the vse and practise of religious disciplin, and euidenthe tistified his internal vnion with the professors thereof, by the externall, and manifest

nifest signes of reuelations, visions, apparitions, rapts, and the gifts of miracles, in all ages, and times, euen vntill this day, I will now breefelie examine, what the sectaries can pretend to haue in this kind, to proue the perfection of their religion, and their vnion with God.

2 Therefore, whereas the deuine fauours aforesaid, are speciall effects of the contemplation of God, and of his vnion with man, I may bouldly affirme, that the sectaries, our aduersaries, neither are, nor can be partakers thereof, being vtterly void of the meanes to obtaine them at Gods hands, to wit, of true humilitie, mortification, and abnegation of them selues, whereof they haue no practise at all, nor so much as any true disposition thereto (as I haue proued in the last chapter:) Besides that, they haue neither vse nor knowledge (for ought that appeareth in their liues, or in any of their workes) of one speciall meanes, wherebie our contemplatiues arriue to a perfecte vnion with God, I meane mentall prayer, and frequent meditations of the life, and passion of our Sauiour, to the end to imitate his deuine vertues: which exercise doth not only breede in a contemplatiue soule, contrition, humilitie, and true mortification, but also kindle in it such flames of deuine loue, that it remaineth ingoulfed, and absorpt many times, in the aboundant delectation thereof, and is thereby disposed to receiue those heauenlie visitations and fauours, whereof I haue hitherto treated.

3 For if we consider the notable effects, that the serious, and frequent meditation of our Sauiours life, and death, must needes worke in any true christian man, it cannot be denied, but that it is a most excellent meanes to raise, and eleuat him to a most perfect vnion with God. For first it fortifieth, and feedeth our faith, it nourisheth, and encreaseth our hope, it kindleth, and enflameth our charitie, it breedeth a shame, and hatred of sinne, it ministreth examples of all vertue, it conforteth the soule in affliction, it strenghtneth, and encourageth it in infirmitie, it sheweth the high way to perfection, it armeth it against temptation, and finallie it serueth (as I haue said els where) for a ladder, to mount immediatelie to the contemplation of our Sauiours deuinitie, seeing that the ineffable perfections of his diuine nature (as his iustice, wisdome, bounty, liberalitie, and longanimity) were printed, and represented in his humanitie, as in a most liuely image, or cleare glasse, and expressed, no lesse in his actions, then in his doctrin, throughout the whole course of his life, and death. In which respect he may welbe said to be *the booke*, that the prophet *Ezechiell*

Ezechiel.2. chiell saw written *within*, *and without*, which whosoeuer doth dilligentlie read and study, and eate it with the prophet (that is to say inwardlie receiue the substance and doctrin of it, printing in his hart the internall vertues of our Sauiours humanitie) he shall find it to be as sweete as honny, as the prophet did.

4 Therefore the greatest contemplatiues, who haue benne most vnited with God, and receiued the greatest fauours of him, haue not only vsed to meditate continuallie vppon the life and passion of our Sauiour, but also to prescribe the vse, and practise thereof to others, as wee see by experience in the Apostle, who shewing whereon his cogitations were most fixed, saith. *Absit mihi gloriari* &c. *God forbid that I*
Gal.6. *should glory in any thing els, but in the Crosse of our Lord Iesus Christ*. And
Hebra. 12. writing to the *Hebrewes*, he taught them and vs, the continuall meditation thereof, and aduised vs to accompanie him therein, *beholding*, saith he, *Iesus the authour and consummator of faith, who though ioy was proposed vnto him, sustained, or bore his crosse, contemning confusion, or shame*. And addeth further. *Recogitate eum* &c. *Thinke againe, and againe* (or seriouslie meditate) *on him, who suffered such contradiction against himselfe, at the hands of sinners*. Thus farre the Apostle, teaching notablie and expresselie as you see, the frequent, or rather continual meditation of our
1.Pet.4. Sauiours life, and passion. And *S. Peter* in like maner. *Christo*, saith he, *passo in carne, & vos eadem cogitatione, armamini. Christ hauing suffred in his flesh, be yee also armed with the same cogitation*, that is to say, arme your selues with the continuall cogitation, or meditation of Christs passion.
S. Ephræm. tract. de natu. Dei curiose nō scrutanda. To.3. And therefore *S. Ephræm* a very ancient, and holly Father (of whome I haue sometimes spoken before) counselleth euery man diligentlie to ponder, and waigh euery action of our Sauiour, to accompanie him in cogitation, throughout the course of his life, to behould with the eyes of faith, the beauty & comelines of his holly face, to follow him from place to place, to see and note his miraculous workes, to contemplate all the persecutions, and contumelies that he suffred, to admire his humilitie, and patience, to attend vppon him to his passion, and to assist him vppon the crosse, like a faithfull seruant to adore, and glorifie him for his infinit bounty, and finallie this holly Father, hauing mentioned more particulers of his life, death, burial, and resurrection, saith in con-
Ibid. clusion. *Consider all these things prudently, perfectly, and faithfully, for except thou behould them all, with the eyes of thy faith, thou canst not be eleuated in spirit from earth to heauen*.

5 Thus teacheth he, who speaking also els where particulerly of his

his passion, saith. *Venite cuncti Ecclesiæ filij* &c. *Come all the children of the church, and let vs meditate vppon all the passions and suffrings of our Lord with teares and sobbs, and in our meditation let vs tremble &c. Distillent tibi frater lachrimæ &c. Let teares deare brother, distill from thee by the meditation of our Lords passion, for such teares are sweete, as flow from thence, and the soule which doth continualy ruminate vppon the same, is illuminated from aboue, and therefore let thy cogitation be alwaies fixed thereon.* Thus saith he. *S.Ephrem.de passione Do. to.3.*

6 *S.Bernard* also axpounding these wordes of the Canticles. *Fasciculus mirrhæ dilectus meus mihi &c. My beloued is to me as a posie of mirrhe, and shal remaine betwixt my pappes*, applieth the same notablie to the consideration of our Sauiours bitter passiõ, signified by the bitternes of the mirrhe, whereof he aduiseth euerie man to make a nosegay or posy, to sticke it in his breast, and there to weare it continually, *retaining alwaies in memorie all those bitter thinges which hee suffred for vs, and pondering them with continuall meditation.* *D.Ber.super. cant.ser. 43.*

7 Thus saith *S.Bernard*, and then declaring his owne practise thereof, hee affirmeth, that from the time of his first conuersion, he had euer an especiall care to carie in his breast, this posie gathred of all the paines, and sorrowes of our Saniour, and after a perticular declaration thereof (which for breuities sake I omit) he concludeth thus. *Hæc meditare &c. I hould it for true wisdome to meditate vppon these thinges, and in them haue I I placed the perfection of my iustice, or righteousnes, the plenitude of knowledge, the riches of saluation, and the copie and plentie of al merit, out of these I draw sometimes the houlsome drinke of sorrow, and some times againe, the sweete oyntement of consolation, these doe erect and comfort mee in aduersitie, these doe represse and moderate mee in prosperitie, and leade mee safelie as it were, in the kings high way, betwixt the weale and woe of this present life, these doe reconcile vnto me, the iudge of the world, whiles they represent him vnto me, not onlie meeke, humble, & placable, but also imitable, or to be followed (though he be dreadfull to all powre, & principalitie, and terrible to the kinges of the earth) and therefore I haue had these oft in my mouth, alwaies in my hart, and familiar in my stile, finallie this is my highest philosophy to know Iesus, and him crucified.* *Ibid.*

8 These are the words of this holy Father, shewing sufficiẽtly his continual practise of the meditation of our Sauiours passiõ, whereby he arriued to the hight of cõtemplation. And the like may be said of *S. Francis*, who in reward of his profoũd, & affectionat meditations of our Sauiours passiõ, had the similitud of his most glorious woũds miraculously printed in his handes, feete and side, as I haue signified elsewhere, so so that hee might iustlie say with the Apostle. *Stigmata Domini mei Iesu Christi, in corpore meo porto. I beare the marks, or prints of my Sauiour Iesus in m* *S. Bonauentura. in vita S. Francisci. num. 29. Chap. 27. Gal.6.*

Blosius. monile spirit.ca. 2. Bozius de sig eccl.to.1. sig.37.ca.12.

body. And we read also the like of *S.Katerin* of *Siena*, and of *S.Elizabeth* of *Spalbec*, and of a holie woman called *Lucia* of *Narni*, in the time of pope *Alexander* the sixt, whereby it hath pleased God to shew, how gratefull vnto him is the meditation of his passion, and how willinglie hee vniteth himselfe with those, that daylie, and dulie frequent the exercise thereof.

9 But now let vs consider, what vse or practise our aduersaries haue or can haue, of this speciall point of contemplatiue disciplin, and high way to perfection. And first to speake of their apostles (to wit *Luther*, *Caluin*, *Beza*, and other their euangelical progenitours) it is euident, that in all their writinges, and workes, there appeareth not so much as one worde of anie method, manner, or rules of meditation, either of our Sauiours life, or of his passion and death, and much lesse of the exercise of contemplation: whereas the bookes of our Catholikes, concerning meditations of all sorts, and perticularlie of the life, and passion of Christ, are so manie, not onlie in Latine, but also in the vulgar tongue of euerie Catholike countrie, that (as I signified before touching bookes of the practise of contemplation) no one man can presume to haue heard of them all, and much lesse to haue seene them all: whereby it appeareth, that the practise of such meditations, and contemplation, is familiar and vsual amongst Catholikes, and vnknowen, or at least not vsed, amongst Lutherans and Caluinists.

Cap.21. in fine.

10 Furthermore, it may easielie bee iudged, by the loose liues of their said masters, and teachers (whereof I haue spoken amplie before) that they neuer vsed (and much lesse deliuered to their disciples) any such notable meanes, and way to mortification, as is the due, and serious meditation of our Sauiours passion For if they had dulie practised the same, they could not possiblie haue benne so carnal, and sensual as they were, no more then it is possible for *a carnal, and sensual man to vnderstand*, and tast *those thinges which belonge to the spirit of God*. For the continuall vse of pious meditations, and the grace of contemplation, can no more stand with carnalitie and licentiousnes, *then ligh, with darknes, or Christ with Belial*, the owne being the fruite, and gift of the holie Ghost, and the other the workes of the flesh and the diuel.

1.Cor.2.

2.Cor.6.

11 Therefore *S.Bernard* speaking of the loue, which our Sauiour shewed towards vs in his passion, saith that the continual consideration thereof: *staieth and sustaineth the soule of man, ne inclinetur in carnalia, & secularia desideria, that it bee not inclined, and swayed to carnall, and secular desires.*

S. Bernar. tract. de diligendo. Deo.

12 But what neede I stand vppon coniectures in this matter, seeing

we

wee haue a verie autentical testimonie of *Luther* himselfe, concerning his owne meditations, whereby we may also take a skantling of the humour of his disciples and followers, who persisting in his doctrin, cannot bee thought to haue anie other, and especially a better spirit, then their master. He then saith of himself thus. *Ego Martinus Lutherus, vix vllam consolationem ex morte, & resurrectione Christi capere possum, ex bonis autem a deo acceptis, vt edere panem, & bibere ceruisiam, optimè possum. I Martin Luther, can hardlie receiue anie consolation of the death and resurrection of Christ, but I can take verie great pleasure in the goods, that I haue receiued of God, as in eating bread, and drinking beare.*

Luther. in colloq. latinis c. de chr. sta. nis fo. 1.

13 Thus saith this spirituall doctor, discouering notablie his spirit, in so much that if a horse, or a mule, or a blacke Iacke, or a barrel of beare could speake, they would shew as much good spirit as he: whereto if I add, what he saith he learned of his hostesse in *Isenack*, and knew also by his owne experience to bee true (as I haue noted before) to wit that, *nothinge is more louelie and sweete vppon earth, then the loue of a woman*, and further what he writeth of the delights of matrimonie, as that *it is most worthie to be called a spirituall, heauenlie, and a deuine state, and that it moueth, vrgeth, and inclineth men to the highest, and most spirituall worke*, if wee add I say, these thinges to his bread, and his beare, which was no doubt dooble, and not single, wee may easely perceiue, whereon he vsed most to meditate, and wee shal maruaile nothinge at al, that hee could receiue no comfort of the meditation of Christs death, and resurrection, seeing that as *S. Bernard* saith. *Quomodo ignis & aqua &c. As fire and water cannot bee together, so carnal and spirituall delights, cannot bee coupled in one soule.*

Chap. 30. nu 22. Annotatio. Lutheri. in ca. 31. prouer. Luther. to. 5. comment. in 1. Cor. 7. fo. 100. & 107.

14 Whereby wee may also iudge, what communication *Luther*, and such others could haue with the spirit of Christ, especially seeing that *S. Bernard* also saith, that *vbi Christus suæ, aut passionis gratiam, aut resurrectionis gloriam sedula inspicit cogitatione versari, ibi profecto adest libens*, that is to say, *Christ doth diligentlie and willinglie assist in a soule, which doth diligentlie meditate vppon the grace of his passion, or the glorie of his resurrection.* So that I leaue it to the iudgment of the prudent Reader, whether it was likelie that the spirit of Christ assisted in the soule of *Luther*, so possest with the dronken delight of dooble beare and carnal pleasures, that the meditation of his passion and resurrection, could (as he saith) skantlie giue him anie consolation.

S. Bernar. tract. de diligendo. Deo.

15 And therefore I conclude concerning him, that it is not possible that he could haue anie heauenlie visions, or deuine fauours, though

well he might be sometimes alienated from his sences, whē the dooble beare was good, and strong. yea, and be otherwaise also rauished in spirit (or rather by a spirit) when he was other whiles opprest with the wicked spirit that possest him: as it fell out once before he leaft his monastery, where being at masse, and the gospell being read of casting out the dumme deuil, he fell downe vppon the ground, crying out. *Non sum, non sum. I am not, I am not.* And what passed afterwards betwixt him, and his deuil, I shall haue further occasion to declare heareafter.

Surius in comment. An.1483.

16 And in the meane time (to ad somewhat more concerning all other sectaries, originallie deriued frō him) it is manifest, that although they treate, and speake much of the merits, and passion of Christ, and seeme highly to esteeme the same, yet they make no such vse thereof for contemplation, as may produce in them those admirable, & deuine effects, whereof I treate heere. And this, I say, is manifest, for that their opinion, and doctrin concerning the passion of Christ, is such, that it doth wholy exclude true mortification, and the perfect imitation of Christ, which is the speciall effect, that the due meditation of his passiō, ought to worke in a contemplatiue man, as the Apostle signified plainely, when hauing said (as I noted before) *absit mihi gloriari &c. God forbid that I should glory in any thing, but in the crosse of Christ*, he added (to shew the true and proper effect that should follow thereof) *per quem mihi mundus crucifixus est, & ego mundo. By whom the world is crucified, or dead to me, and I to the world.*

1. Pet. 4.

17 And *S. Peter*, hauing counselled vs to arme our selues, with the meditation of Christs passion, (as I haue also declared before) addeth immediately (to shew the end, and effect thereof.) *Quia qui passus est in carne, desiit a peccatis. For he which hath suffred in his flesh, hath ceased from sinne:* as who would say, arme your selues with the cogitation, or meditation of Christs suffring, to the end, that yow may also suffer, and be crucified with him, by the mortification, or chastisement of the flesh, *for he which suffreth in his flesh*) that is to say, whose flesh, or sensualitie is mortified by suffring) ceaseth from sinne. To which purpose *S. Leo* saith. *Per voluntarias afflictiones, caro concupiscentiis moritur &c. By voluntary afflictions, the flesh dieth to cōcupiscence, & the spirit or soule, is renewed with vertues.* Thus he.

S Leo sermo. de ieiunio decimi mensis.

18 Loe then to what end, we ought to meditate vppon the passion of Christ, to wit, to suffer voluntarie in our flesh by the example of Christ, that is to say, to chastise our bodies, thereby to mortifie our passions, & affections, to the end we may cease from sinne, To which doctrin, holly *Ephræm* the ancient, and great contemplatiue, saith thus. *Beatus homo &c. happy is the man, that hath alwais before his eyes, our heauenly Lord, and his passions,*

Ephræm. serm de passione Domini propè finē.

sions, crucifying himselfe to the world, withall his concupiscences, and other earthly things, whereby he becommeth the imitator, or follower of his Lord: and this is true prudence. This is the care, and affection of a good seruant to his master, to endeuour alwayes, to imitat, and follow him in his good workes. Thus saith he, giuing to vnderstand that we ought to meditate vppon our Sauiours passion, to the end we may imitate, and follow him as our Lord, and master, drawing from him documents, and examples, of humilitie, obedience, pouertie, patience, contempt of the world, mortification, and abnegation of our selues, *that suffring with him*, as *S. Paule* saith, *we may* 1. Corint. 4.
reigne with him. And therefore the same blessed Apostle being, as he himselfe testifieth, *imitator Christi, a follower of Christ*, did chastise his owne body, as he witnesseth, and bring it to seruitude, and all the holly seruants of God, and great contemplatiues, of whome I haue spoken before, in like sort, followed the same example of our Sauiour, suffring with him (as *S. Peter* aduised) in their flesh by voluntarie, and bodily penance, by fasting, watching, long prayer, haire cloth, disciplins, and such like, thereby to crucify, and mortify their flesh, withall the concupiscences thereof, and hereto specially tended all their meditations, of the passion of Christ, whereby they obtained so great fauours of God, as I haue declared before.

19 But doe our aduersaries trow you, ayme at any such marke? Do they euer so much as thinke of our Sauiours life, and passion, to the end to chastise their bodies, and to suffer in their flesh? No truly, for their meditation thereof can be no other, according to their owne doctrin, but to perswade themselues, that he so suffred, and satisfied for them, that their sufferings, chastisements, and mortifications of their bodies, should be superfluous, and vaine, in so much that they assure themselues of their saluation, if they doe but only apply his merits to themselues, by a liuelie, or a sauing faith, as they call it, or rather to say truly, by a vaine presumption, or a rechlesse, and false securitie, whereby the wickedst man amongst them houldeth himselfe, as sure to be saued (yea, and to be as great a Saint) with all his wickednes, as *S. Iohn Baptist*, *S. Paule*, or *S. Mary Magdalen*, withall their pennaunce and mortification. Wherein, what fruit they draw for the imitation of Christ, out of the consideration of his passion, it may easely be iudged, and I will make it most euident heereafter, when I shall treate of their iustifiing faith, in which respect, I haue thought good only to touch the same thus breefelie in this place, and therefore will conclude, that seeing our aduersaries haue no vse at all of the meanes, whereby all the great contemplatiues of Gods church,

haue arriued to a perfect vnion with him (I meane the serious, and deuout meditation vppon the life, and passion of Christ, with true mortification of the flesh, by penance, and carriage of the crosse:) it cannot be expected, that they should haue the effects thereof, to wit, Ecstases, or rapts, deuine reuelations, the gift of miracles, and other celestiall fauours.

20 And yet this wilbe more euident, if we consider the same more particulerlie, as what our aduersaries may challenge to themselues in euery one of these kinds. And first for rapts, I shall not neede to trouble my reader, to examin whether they haue had any or no, seeing, that none of them euer so much as pretended to haue any, for ought that I haue read, or heard, so that I may proceede, to treate of the other effects of our christian contemplation.

21 Therefore (to say some what touching their miracles, reuelations, and visions) it is to be vnderstood, that though in conclusion, they are faine for want of such, to deny the continuance of them in the church of God vntill this time, yet it is sufficientlie knowne, that some of their principall pastors, and doctors, haue sometimes attempted to doe thinges, which might seeme miraculous, and haue pretended to haue reuelations, and visions, for the confirmation of their doctrin: whereby it is euident inough, that they knew in their owne consciences, that the power of doing miracles, remaineth still in the church of God, though they had not the grace, or the good happ to doe any. I will therefore first, lay downe some what concerning their miracles, visions, and reuelations, and after examine what they can say against ours.

Freder. Staphil. in absoluta resp. one.

Surius. an. 1546.

22 *Fredericus Staphilus*, who was sometime one of *Luthers* disciples, writeth, that *Luther* attempted once, to cast a deuil, out of a woman, brought vnto him from *Misnia* for that purpose, and that as he exorcised her, in the reuestry of the church (after his owne fashion (saith he) and not after the manner of the Catholike church) he tooke such a fright, that he sought meanes to runne out of the doore, and finding it shut so fast by the deuil (as it seemed) that it could not be opened, either within, or without, he cried out for helpe, and at lenght some of his friends abroad, cast in a hatchet at the window, wherewith *Fredericus Staphilus* (being then present with him, as he writeth and the yongest, and strongest in the company) hewed downe the doore, but it was pitifull to see, in what case the poore man was all the while, who (as the same author testifieth) was noe lesse distempered in his belly, then in his mind, and went wringing, and wrigling vpp, and downe lik

like a yew, saith he, that is great with lambe, and ready to yeane.

23 Also *Cochlæus* witnesseth of him, that he went about once to reuiue one *VVilliam Nesen*, who was drowned in the riuer *Albis*, and that he lost both his labour, & his credit therein. Neuertheles though he could himselfe doe no miracles whiles he liued, yet it pleased God to shew a miraculous, or at least a strange euent vppon his body, after his death. For whereas he died in the middest of winter, to wit the *seauenteenth* of Februarie, and in a very cold climat, where dead bodies doe not so soone putrifie, as in hotter regions, yea, and that his body was also enclosed and shut vp very close in tinne, it cast forth notwithstanding such a horrible stinke, that no man was able to endure it, in so much that those who assisted the conuoy thereof, from *Islebium* where he died, to the vniuersitie of *wittenberg*, were forst to depart and leaue it by the way. By occasiō whereof I cannot forbeare to put thee in mind (good reader) of what I declared before in the 27. chapter, of the bodies of the blessed a *F. Xauerius* in the *East Indie*, and b mother *Teresa* in *Spaine*, whose liues, and deaths, are yet fresh in memorie, and their bodies knowne to haue remained vncorrupt, some yeares after their decease, breathing forth most sweete, & fragant odours, as they still doe for ought is yet knowne to the contrarie, which I say, I wish should be noted with the difference of the euents, to the end we may the better distinguish betwixt the different merits of the holly, chast, and religious life of the twoo latter, and the Apostacie of the former from religion, and from his vow of chastitie. And thus much concerning *Luther*.

Cochla. in actis Lutheri. Surius vbi supra.

An.1546. Historiola de morte Lutheri annex. libro cochlæi de vita eius.

a *Num. 37.*
b *Num. 40.*

24 As for *Caluin*, it is testified by *Hierome Bolsec*, *Surius*, and diuers graue authours, that to gett credit, and reputation to him selfe, and his ghospell, he procured a poore man in *Geneua* called *Brule*, with the consent of his wife, to faine himselfe dead, to the end, that *Caluin* might seeme to raise him to life, but when the matter came to execution, and *Caluin* in presence of the people, after solemme prayer, called often vppon him to rise, he was found to be starke dead, where with his wife was so afflicted, that shee cried out vppon *Caluin*, and detected all the cosenage: neuertheles he procured to stopp her mouth with rewards, and in his next sermon to the people, laid the fault one their want of faith, that he could not raise the dead man. The like is also related by *Lindanus* and others, of a minister in the confines of *Polonia*, and *Hungary*, who made the like couenant with one called *Mathew* to faine him selfe dead, in the yeare of our Lord, a thousand fiue hundreth, fifty eight, & so it fell out, that he was found dead in dede, when

Surius an. 1538.

Linda. in Dubitantio. Feliciap. Ninguard. li. cōtra Annam Burg.

it was

Alan.cop.6. Dialog. Bellar.li.4. cap. 14. de notis eccles. Tertullian. in lib de prescript.

it was expected he should aryse, at the call, and commaundement of the minister: so that we may truly say of these men, as *Tertullian* said of certaine heretikes in his time, who couterfeited in like maner the miracles of the Apostles. *Illi*, saith he, *de mortuis suscitabant, isti de viuis mortuos faciunt. The Apostles raised dead men to life, and these men make liue men dead.*

25 And if it be true, which I haue crediblie heard, there haue passed in *England*, some such cozening deuises amongst our ministers to grace their ghospell, with some shew of miracles, though not of reuiuing dead men, yet in seeming to expell deuils out of some, whome they procured to faine themselues to be possest, but because I wil affirme no more of such matters, but what I know my selfe to be true, or find written, and testified by graue authors, I leaue it to my reader, to informe himselfe of the truth of what was discouered in *Londō*, some Eight, or nine yeares agoe, to haue benne practised in that kind by certaine puritan ministers, whereof (I haue credibly heard) there was a relation printed with publike approbation, and some also imprisoned for the same. And the like opinion of cozenage, and deceit, was also conceiued many yeares before, concerning exorcismes vsed by *M. Foxe*, vppon a woman in *Lothbury* in *London*, who was thought to be possest with a wicked spirit, which I also leaue to the enquirie of the reader, and will only vpon this occasion, declare what I know my selfe to be true concerning him, and his talent in casting out deuils.

26 Yt fell out, whiles I once lay in *London*, that a gentleman of the middle temple was possessed with a deuil, or at least was presumed so to be, and *M. Foxe* was brought by his friendes to cure him, & after some dayes, and many written relations (which went about *London* of the conferences betwixt *M. Foxe* and *Satan*) it was crediblie reported, that the Gentleman was fully deliuered, and *M. Fox* was generallie held for a very holy, & apostolicall man. But within a few dayes after, it being my chaunce to passe by the Gentlemans lodging, I met a protestant of his acquaintance & mine comming from him, who tould me that he was worse troubled then euer he had benne before. I asked him why they did not send againe for *M. Fox*, and he answered, that they had sent for him, & that he could not come, because he was troubled himselfe, meaning with the deuil. The next day, being in the companie of some honourable personages, who were perswaded that the gentleman was dispossessed, I tould them what I vnderstood thereof the day before, & namely that *M. Fox* was also himselfe so troubled with the deuil, that it might be well said vnto him. *Medice cura te ipsum. Phisician heale thy selfe.*

Where

Where with a principall man in the companie, a great friend, and disciple of master *Fox*, was much offended, saying that it was but some false rumour giuen out by the Papists. And when I affirmed, that he was a zealous protestant who tould it to me, he replied, that no man knew *M. Fox* better then he, and that the truth was, that the goodman would some times so deepelie consider of his sinnes, that he would dispaire of the mercy of God, whereat diuers in the companie laughed in their sleeues, and all that I replied was, that it seemed therebie, that *M. Fox* had litle grace, and thus ended our conference. But herebie it may appeare, what an exorcist *M. Foxe* was, who needed to be exorcised himselfe, and had so litle faith, and confidence in Gods mercy, that he some times dispaired thereof, which I thinke was neuer read, nor heard of in any man, that had the grace of casting out deuils, or of doing miracles, except in *Iudas*, who neuertheles vsed not to dispaire whiles he had the gift of miracles, though *M. Foxe* was thought to haue a speciall gift to doe both. Thus much for their miracles.

27 And now to come to their reuelations, and visions, thou maist remember, good Reader, how many examples I haue laid downe before of the great fauours of almighty God, donne to religious persons of both sexes, by the spirit of prophesie, diuers sorts of reuelations, and apparitions of our Sauiour himselfe, of his mother, of his Angels, & saints: whereas all that the *Lutherans, Caluinists*, & other sectaries can pretend to haue had in that kind, are no other but familiaritie, and conferences with deuils, idle dreames, manifest illusions, or fained lies.

28 *Luther* is not ashamed himselfe, to lay downe large disputations, which he had with the deuil, about the masse, and to confesse, that he was in the end ouercome by him, and forced to change his opinion. And further, to signifie the great familiaritie, and friendship, that had benne betwixt them many yeares, he saith that they *had eaten a bushell of salt together*: so that it needeth not to be doubted, but he was not only obsest, but also really possessed by him, as appeareth by that which I recounted before, of his falling downe, when the ghospell of the expulsion of the dumbe deuill was read. And therefore how sound, and holesome doctrin for christians his may be, which he professeth to haue learned of the Father of lies, and capitall enemy of mankind, euery man that tendreth his owne saluation, hath reason well to consider.

Luther. de Missa angulari & consecratione Sacerdotum. To. 6. Ger. Ienensi. fo. 28. & To. 7. VVitemberg fo. 443. Surius Comment. an. 1517.

29 And the like good ground also had *Vldericus Zuinglius* (as it seemeth) to reiect the masse, who writeth himselfe, that he was admonished in a dreame to do it, but saith, that he cãnot tel whether he that perswaded

him thereto, *was black*, *or white*. And as wel might he haue said, or rather much better, that he knew not whether he was a good spirit, or a bad, or els whether it was not some vaine fancy, or friuolous dreame of his idle braine.

30 And no lesse idle was a reuelation which *M. Foxe* pretendeth to haue had concerning the exposition, and computation of the two, and forty moneths, mentioned in the *Apocalips*, whereof he glorieth not a litle, as hauing found out a notable secret. I will giue it thee good Reader, in his owne wordes, to the end thou maist the better discerne his foolery, which was notablie discouered by the worthy and learned autour of the *VVarneword*, in his second part of his excellent treatise, of *the three Conuersions of England*, where he setteth downe at large master *Foxe* his woords, which are these that follow.

F. Ro. Pars. li. of the 3. conuer. p. 2. c. 8.

31 Because the matter, saith he, being of no small importance, greately appartaineth vnto the publike vtilitie of the church, and least any should misdoubt me herein to follow any priuat interpretation of my owne, I thought good to communicate to the Reader, that which hath benne imparted to me, in the opening of these misticall numbers, in the foresaid booke of reuelation contained, by occasion as followeth &c.

32 As I was in hand with these histories &c. Being vexed, & turmoiled in spirit about the reckoning of these numbers, & yeares, it so happened vppon a sunday in the morning, lying in my bed, & musing about these numbers, that suddenly it was answered to my mind, as with a maiesty thus, in wardlie saying within me. *Thou foole, count these moneths by sabaoths, as the weekes of Daniel, are counted by sabaoths.* The Lord I take to witnesse, thus it was, where vppon being thus admonished, I began to reckon the forty twoo moneths by sabaoths, first of months, and that would not serue, and then by sabbaoths of yeares, and then I beganne to feele some probable vnderstanding, yet not satisfied therewith, eftsones I repaired to certaine merchants of my acquaintance, of whome one is departed, a true, and faithfull seruant of the Lord, the other two yet liue, and are witnesses hereof, to whome the number of these foresaid moneths being propounded, and examined by sabaoths of yeares, the whole somme was found to surmount to *twoo hundreth Ninety foure yeares*, containing the full, and iust time of the foresaid persecutions, neither more nor lesse &c.

33 Thus farr *M. Foxe*, wherein thou art to vnderstand, good Reader, that all his drift is to proue, that the diuel hauing benne tied vpp a thousand yeares (as is mentioned in the *Apocalipse*) was loosed at the same

ſame time, that pope *Bonifacius* the Eight be ganne to reigne, which was in the yeare of our lord, as he ſaith *a thouſand twoo hundreth, ninety foure,* at what time he imagineth, that *Antichriſt* beganne, becauſe Pope *Bonifacius* made the ſixt booke of the Decretalls, and confirmed the orders of Friars, geuing them great priuiledges. And to the end this his deuiſe may haue the more probabilitie, he ſeeketh to apply the ouerplus of a thouſand yeares, from Chriſts time vntill Pope *Bonifacius* (which were *twoo hundreth ninty foure* yeares) to the twoo and forty monethes mencioned in the *Apocalipſe*, and to that purpoſe, inuenteth his fond reuelation, counting the ſaid moneths by ſabaoths of yeares, allowing *ſeauen* yeares to euery moneth, by which account, he, and his merchants, found the number of *twoo hundreth Ninety foure* yeares, which ſaith he, was *the full, and iuſt time of their perſecution, neither more, nor leſſe.*

34 But this is euidentlie falſe, for the yeare of our Lord *twoo hundreth Ninety foure*, fell vppon the *Eleauenth* yeare of the Emperour *Dioclesian*, who raigned twentie yeares, and beſides his former perſecutions, raiſed one of the greateſt, that euer was in the *Nineteenth* yeare of his raigne, which was the yeare of our Lord, *three hundreth* and *twoo*, that is to ſay, *Eight* yeares after the time, that the perſecution should haue ceaſed, according to *M. Foxes* dreame: And after *Dioclesian*, and *Maximian* who raigned with him, ſucceeded *Galerius*, and *Conſtantius*, vnder whome alſo the perſecution continued ſome yeares, with great violence in the Eaſt partes. And after them againe, the church was perſecuted vnder *Maximinus*, and *Maxentius*, vntil *Conſtantin* the great ouerthrew *Maxentius*, and receiued the chriſtian faith which was (as *Euſebius* reckoneth) in the yeare of our Lord *three hundreth Eighteene*, though Cardinal *Baronius* aſſigneth it to the yeare *three hundreth* and *twelue*, neither did it then ceaſe generallie, but was continued in the Eaſte parts vnder *Licinius*, for *Eight*, or *Nine* yeares after.

Baron. an. 294.

35 So that though wee make the moſt fauourable reckoninge that may be, to iuſtifie *M. Foxes* reuelation, his count of moneths by ſabaoths of yeares, falleth at leaſt *Eighteene* yeares, short of the time that *Conſtantine* receiued the faith, and ceaſed the perſecution only in the weſt partes, which were then ſubiect vnto him, whereas it alſo continued longer (as I haue ſaid) vnder *Licinius* in the Eaſt. Wherebie his reuelation appeareth to haue proceeded, either from a falſe, or lying ſpirit, or from his owne fantaſticall braine, intoxicat

with heresie yoined with ignorance, of the true Chronologie of times, wherein no man can suppose that the holly Ghost (if it had bene his reuelation) could haue erred one minute of an hower, and so doth *M. Foxe* desire it should be also vnderstood of his computation, which he saith contained, *the full, and iust time of the persecution, neither more nor lesse*.

36 But what should I say of this vanitie in his præposterous application of the twoo, and forty moneths mentioned in the *Apocalipse*, to the first twoo hundreth Ninetie foure yeares of persecution after Christ, which as the Authour of the *warneword* signifieth, all the Ancient Fathers vnderstand to make the *three* yeares and a *halfe*, wherein *Antichrist* shall raigne, and persecute the church in the end of the world, before the generall iudgement, which also other places of the holly scriptures, as well in the *Apocalipse*, as in *Daniell* doe confirme, seeing the time of Antichrists raigne, is reckoned in the *Apocalipse*, aswell by *a thousand twoo hundreth sixty* dayes, as by

Apoc.11. *Forty twoo* moneths, both which accounts make iust *three* yeares, and a *halfe*, signified in like manner both in *Daniel*, and also in an other

Dan. 11. place of the *Apocalipse*, *by tempus, tempora, & dimidium temporis, a*

Apoc. 12. *time, times*, and *halfe a time*. And therefore I conclude concerning *M. Foxe*, with the authour of the *warnewoords* censure vppon this reuelation, who saith, no lesse pleasantlie, then truly, that he findeth nothing so true, or credible therein, as those wordes of the spirit to *M. Foxe*, *thou foole*, for that he is therebie sentenced to be a foole by reuelation, that is to say, a notable, and autenticall foole, and for such a one he hath registred himselfe. And thus much for their reuelations.

37 I will only add hereto a famous vision, or apparition, which, *Andreas Carolostadius* (one of Luthers first disciples) had in *Basilea*. This *Carolstadius*, being *Archdeacon* of *wittenberg*, and hauing embraced *Luthers* doctrin, was driuen thence by him after a while, vppon priuat quarrels betwixt them (worthy to be vnderstood, if I had time to relate them) and was so persecuted by him, that he was forced to flee to the Sacramentaries in *Basilea*, who receiued him willingly because he was an enemy of *Luther*, though in the matter of the sacrament he dissented from them. And one day as he was preaching, there came a huge tall man into the church, and stood hard by one of the magistrats, though he was seene of none but of *Carolostadius* himselfe, and departing thence after a while, he went to

Carolostadius his house, where he found his sonne, whom he tooke vp as though he would haue cast him against the ground, but in the end he sett him downe againe, and bad him tell his Father, that he within three dayes would come for him *Carolostadius* after his sermon was ended, and before he came home to his owne house, asked the magistrate (neere to whome he saw the huge greate man) who he was that stood by him at the sermon, describing him vnto him, but he told him, that he saw none such, and vnderstanding when he came home, what had passed there, he tooke such a fright, that he fell sicke, and died within three dayes, as the diuell (for so he was) had foretould. And thus it pleased God to shew his iudgement notoriouslie in this manner, rather vppon him, as it may be presumed, then vppon diuers others of his companions, for that he was the first priest of all the sectaries, that presumed to marry: which he did publikelie in the church of *VVittenberg*, with great solemnitie.

Epist. Basileensium de morte Carolostadij. vide Alanum Copum dialoga 6. c. 32.

Stanisla. Reschius in Euangelic. sectar. centur. parag. Carolstadiani.

38 This shall suffise concerning the rapts, miracles, reuelations, and visions of *Lutherans* and *Caluinists*, for other then these, and such of like qualitie, I haue not read, nor heard of, neither doe they challenge any other to them selues: so that it is most cleare, that they haue not those externall signes of Gods vnion, which it hath pleased him to shew in his seruants, in all ages, and times, but rather the cleane contrarie, to wit, familiaritie with wicked spirits, idle dreames, and other manifest illusions, or els foolish fictions of their owne, discouering both their vanitie, and their impietie.

39 Yt resteth now to examine, what exceptions they take against our miracles, and what reason they haue to doe it. First they say commonlie, that miracles are ceased in the church of God, and that they were necessarie only for the conuersion of Infidels, and to proue it, they shew, that some kind of miracles, which were ordinarie in the time of the Apostles, ceased many hundreth yeares a goe, as namely the gift of tongues, and some other whereof we read in the acts of the Apostles. Whereto I answer. First that if it be true, that miracles are vtterlie ceased in the church, why haue their owne cheefe doctors, attempted diuers times to doe miracles, as to raise dead men, and to expell diuels? Is it not manifest thereby, that they themselues beleeued, theat the power of doing miracles doth still continue in the church? Secondlie I say, that it litle importeth, that some of the miracles which were done in the Apostles time, are either now ceased or els are not so ordinarie, as then they were, for no man houldeth that a mi-

racle once donne, must be alwayes donne: besides that, it was necessarie then for the conuersion of Infidels, that miracles should be more frequent, then now at this time amongst the faithfull, though neuertheles it is now also conuenient, for the glorie of God, and confirmation of the weake in faith, yea, and for the conuersion, or confusion of heretikes, and secret Atheists amongst christians, that there be some times notorious miracles in the church of God: which also may be confirmed by the experience of Gods prouidence in that behalfe, whereby miracles haue benne donne in all ages, and christian countries, euer since our Sauiours time, as I haue shewed alreadie, aswell in the a first part of this treatise, by examples of miraculous victories, as also in the b twenty seuenth chapter of this second part, where amongest other externall signes, of Gods internall vnion with religious men, I haue exemplified the same by their operation of miracles in euerie age, euen vntill these our dayes, and the like may be seene in Cardinall *Bellarmin*, *Baronius*, and diuers others.

a *Chap.* 15. *per totum.*
b *Chap.* 27. *per totum.*

40 Yea but say they, those miracles were either fained, or wrought by the meanes of the diuell, as the Magicians of *Pharao*, and diuers other amongst the Gentills, did many thinges which seemed very miraculous to delude the people, and *Antichrist* also shall doe the like.

41 To this I say first, that the sectaries of our times, ascribing our miracles to the deceits of the diuell, imitate therein the Scribes, Pharisees, Painims, and ould Heretikes: for the Scribes, and Pharisees said, that Christ did cast out deuils in the power of *Belzebub*, the Painims attributed the miracles donne by the Martyres, to Negromancie. And the *Arrians*, *Eunomians*, and *Vigilantians*, said the like of the Catholikes, as testifie *S. Ambroise*, *S. Hierome*, and *Victor* in his historie.

Matth. 12. *D. Ambros. in ser.* 55. *de Ger. & Pro. Hieron. contra Vigilan. Victor li.* 2. *de Persecut. Vandall.*

42 Secondly I say, that it were no lesse then meere madnes to imagin, that the miracles testified by most graue historiographers, and most learned, and holly Fathers, haue beene all fained, for so should wee derogate from all humane credit, which whosoeuer should doe, he were not worthie to liue amongst men. For can any thing that relieth vppon the credit of men be counted true, if those thinges shalbe esteemed false, which the Saints of God (who haue benne the lights of the church in their ages) haue written, and reported vppon their owne sight, and knowledge?

43 And

43 And to omit manie others, what shal wee say of S. *Augustin*, who partlie for the confusion of the Painimes in his time, and partlie for the instruction of weake christians, recounteth verie particularlie, a greate number of euident miracles, wrought at *Millan, Carthage, Hippo*, and other places adioyning, which he either saw himselfe, or certainely knew to be true: as the recouerie of a blind mans sight, at the bodie of S. *Geruas* and *Protase* in *Millan*, whiles he was there, which holie bodies, hauing benne long vnknowne, were discouered as hee saith, to S. *Ambrose* by deuine reuelation. And S. *Ambrose* himselfe also maketh mention, not onlie of that miracle donne vppon the blind man, but also of diuers others, wrought by the merits of those twoo hollie Martyres.

S. Aug. de ciuitat. dei. li. 22. ca. 8.

Idem. li. 9. confes. ca. 7.

S. Ambros. li. 7. Epistolarum. epist. 2.

44 But to returne to *S. Augustin*, he saith, that this miracle was donne whiles the emperour was at *Milan. Immenso populo teste, & concurrente ad corpora Martirum. A number of people being wittnesse thereof, and flocking to the Martires!* And shal wee say, that *S. Augustin* fained this, or the rest that he relateth of sundrie disseases (and amongst them some most strange, and incurable by phisick) miraculouslie cured, diuers dead men, women and children reuiued, and possessed persons deliuered, partlie by holie men, and partlie at the memories, and monuments of Saints, and particularlie of *S. Stephen* the *Proto Martyr*, of which miracles some were most admirable, and donne in *S. Augustins* owne presence, in so much, that he saith, he caused them to be published in little bookes, or pamphlets, for the glorie of God. And such were the numbers of miracles donne at the same time, onlie at *Hippo*, where hee was Bishopp, that within two yeares space, they arriued almost to the number of seauentie, regestred in bookes (though manie were not written, whereof he saith, he was most assured) & in some other citties not farr from thence, he saith the number incomparablie exceeded the other, and in conclusion, hauing recounted verie particularly, a most miraculous cure, done at the memorie of *S. Stephen* vppon a man and a woman (brother and sister, who through their mothers malediction, were strooken by almightie God, with a most strange and terrible trembling of al their bodies) he sheweth the excessiue ioy of the people, saying thus. *They exulted and reioysed to the praise of God without wordes, with such a confused sound and cry, that our eares could scarse indure it, and what else was in their hartes, but the faith of Christ, for the which the bloud of Stephen was shed.*

S. Aug. de ciuit. Dei li. 22. c. 8.

8. Ideus ibid.

Ibid.

45 Thus saith *S. Augustin*, signifiyng not onlie the multitude of euident miracles wrought in his time, but also the notable effect thereof, in the confirmation of the Christian faith, to the greate glorie of God,

honour

honour of his Saints, and comfort of al his faithfull seruants. And shall we then say, that *S. Augustin* fained all this, and that he had so little care of his conscience, to lie wittinglie, or of his reputation to giue the Painimes, and enemies of christian religion (against whome he wrote) so great an aduantage, as to bee able to conuince him of manifest lies, in case he had forged, either al, or anie parte of those thinges which he affirmed? This is so incredible, that noe men of iudgemente can imagin it.

46 And it is no lesse incredible and absurd, to thinke that al the miracles, either of those times, or of these latter ages, were donne by the diuel, seing that verie manie of them did surpasse the powre of the diuel, or of the Angels them selues, who can doe nothinge aboue nature, without Gods special asistance, and therefore cannot giue sight to one that is borne blinde, or life to the dead, which not onlie Christ and his Apostles did, but also manie religious persons mencioned before, who amongst other miracles which they wrought, reuiued the dead, as *S.* [a] *Martin*, *S.* [b] *Benedict*, *S.* [c] *Dominick*, and lastlie Father [d] *Xauier* in our age, and manie other in former times, whome I haue not mencioned, so that it cannot with anie probabilitie bee said, either that all miracles are fained, or that they haue benne all donne by the diuel.

Chap. 27. nu. 15. 19. 30. & 37.
a *S. Sulpit. Seuer. in vita S. Martini.*
b *S. Greg. in vita S. Benedicti.*
c *S. Antonin hist. tit. 23. c. 4. paragr. 7. parte. 3.*
d *Horatius. Turselinus. in vita B. Fraunciſci Xauer. li. 2. ca. 7.*
S. Ber. in vita Malachiæ.

47 Therefore forasmuch as a true miracle, can haue no other authour but God himselfe, it is euident that God hath by miracles confirmed, not onlie the Roman Catholike religion in generall, but also monasticall or religious life in particular, seeing that Roman Catholikes, being withall religious men, haue in al ages wrought manie true miracles, testified by so manie graue authours, that it were impudencie to denie it. As now to speake, for examples sake, of some of these latter ages, who can be so shameles to denie, the testimonie of that most famous, learned, and holie *S. Bernard* of matters *de facto*, donne in his owne time, and by his owne familiar frindes, as that which hee writeth of *S. Malachias*, an Irish man, who was first a religious man, and after made bishopp, and the Pops Legat in *Ireland*. *Quo antiquorum genere miraculorum? &c. VVhat kind of ancient miracles* (saith S. *Bernard*) *was there wherein Malachias did not excell? He wanted not the spirit of prophesy, or reuelations, or power to punish wicked men, or the grace of healing and curing disseases, or of changinge the mindes of men, or of reuiuing the dead.* Thus saith *S. Bernard*, after hee had related manie particular miracles in those kindes, donne by *S. Malachias*.

48 And speaking afterwardes of his death (which was at *Clareualle*, where *S. Bernard* was then Abbot) he declareth that when the bodie of

of *S. Malachias* was brought in to the church to be buried, a boy, who was there by chance, and had his arme, and hand withered, and drye, that it serued to no vse, was cured by touching the hand of the holly man, with the cooperation of *S. Bernard* himselfe, who saith thus. *Et apprehensam aridam manum* &c. *I taking hould, of the withered, and dry hand, applied it to the hand of the Bishop, which reuiued it, and gaue it life. For there liued still the grace, and gift of healing in him, though he was dead, and his hand was to the dead hand, as Helizeus the prophet was to the dead man, in so much, that the boy, who was come thither with his hand lame, hanging vnprofitablie by his side, carried it home sound.* *Idem ibid.*

49 Thus saith *S. Bernard*, of a matter wherein he himselfe was an actor. And of what authoritie his testimonie may be, throughout the christian world, it may be iudged, by the reuerend respect which the very enimies of Catholike religion doe beare him, seeing, that *Luther* and *Melanchton* speaking of him, call him Saint, and *Caluin* tearmeth him, *pium scriptorem*, a pious, or godly writter, and truly whosoeuer readeth his workes, cannot but acknowledge that he was illuminated, and inspired by the holly Ghost. Besides that it appeareth, by all the histories that write of him, or of the time wherein he liued, that for his holly life, and very frequent miracles, he was held himselfe for a miracle: and amongst others, *Gotfridus* a graue authour who liued with him, testifieth, that in the Diocesse of *Constans*, he cured in one day, *tenne* persons that were lame handed, a *Eleuen* blynd, and *Eigteene* lame legged. Can it therefore be imagined, by any man of sence, and iudgement, that the miracles done by such holly men, were wrought by the diuell? For who shewed themselues throughout all the course of their liues, greater enemies of the diuell, then *S. Bernard*, *S. Malachias*, and such others, as they? How many soules conuerted they to God, and freed from the diuells power, by their preaching, inducing men from sinfull life to repentaunce, and from vice to all vertue? How many deuills expelled they from possessed persons, whereof *S. Bernard* relateth diuers notable examples, of *S. Malachias*, as others also recount the like of S. Bernard? In respect whereof they, and their miracles may be defended, and cleared from this calumniation, as our Sauiour defended, and cleared himselfe, and his miracles from the like, when he said, that if he did cast out diuells by the power of *Belzebub* (as the *Iewes* charged him to doe) it must neede follow, that the deuils kingdome was deuided in it selfe, and

Luther de abroganda missa. Melanch. Apolog. art. 5. Caluin. in institut. ca. 10. Gotfridus. li. 4. de vita Bernar. c. 4. S. Bernar. in vita Malachia Gulielm. Abbas in vita S. Bern. li. 2. 3. & 4. Matth. 12.

that the deuill was become his owne enemy.

50 This wilbe euident in the miracles of these holly men, if wee consider what the deuill could gaine by helping them to delude the people there with, for though it should be true, which our aduersaries say (to witt, that the Catholikes of those dayes, taught, together with the faith of Christ, diuers superstitions, neuertheles) they cannot with any reason deny, but that men were saued in that christian religion, especiallie in that time, when no other was knowne. For what soeuer our aduersaries, may thinke of the saluation of Catholikes, now, when the light of the ghospell (as they say) shineth, yet at that time, when their candle was vnder the bushell, and no other christian religion taught, and preached, nor other church of Christ seene, or knowne in the world, but the Roman Catholike church, they cannot be so absurd to say, that such holly men, yea, and all others professing the Catholike faith were damned, but must needes confesse, that those who professed the faith of Christ, in the manner that then it was taught, and liued well with all, were saued by the merits of Christs passion.

51 Therefore, I say, that seeing by those miracles of *S. Malachias, S. Bernard*, and such other as they, the faith of Christ was confirmed and established, and infinit numbers of men, moued to follow their dodoctrine, and example, in pennance, mortification, hate of sinne, and vice, and in the exercise of all vertue, to the saluation of their soules: it must needes follow, that the diuell could gaine nothing by furthering such miracles, but that he lost excedinglie therebie, aduancing the glory of Christ, and of christian religion, and helping to saue mens soules, whose perdition, aud damnation he desireth. So that if the diuel helped *S. Malachias, S. Bernard*, and such other religious men to doe miracles, it seemeth that he played booty with his enemies against himselfe.

52 Besides that, diuers of those miracles were such, that they surpassed the deuils power (as I haue already signified) and could not be donne by any, but by almightie God. *Qui facit mirabilia magna solus. VVho*
Psal. 71. *only doth great meruailes, or miracles*, that is to say, thinges aboue nature, and therefore the miracles which *Antichrist* shall doe, shalbe such only, as the deuil can worke, by naturall meanes, or by deception of the sight, and so they shall not be true miracles, though they shall seeme miraculous, to the common sort of people. In which respect the
2. Thessal. 2. Apostle calleth them, *Mendacia*, that is to say, miracles in apparence and

not in deede.

53 And here in I wish it to be noted, that one, and the selfe same effect, may be wrought both miraculouslie, and naturalie, and therefore may be in one man a miracle, and none in an other. As for example, some disease which is naturallie curable by medicin, may be cured without medicin, by deuine power giuen by almightie God to his saintes, either in heauen or on earth, who when they cure diseases, by prayer, or benediction without medicin, they doe a miracle, though the same might be neuer so easelie cured otherwaise: whereas the deuil working the same effect by some natural, though secret, & hidden meanes, doth no miracle, and this is the difference betwixt many miracles done by Gods seruantes, and the like strange effects wrought by the deuil.

54 But heere I would be glad to knowe, at what time true miracles ceased, and diabolicall illusions beganne in the church? For they neither can, or doe deny, that Christ gaue the Apostles and other his disciples, power to doe miracles, and it is also euident in the scripture, that he promised the same to those that should beleeue in him, *Mar. 16.* saying. *Signa autem eos qui crediderint, hæc sequentur* &c. *These signes shall follow them, which shall beleeue in me, they shall speake strange tongues, they shall take away serpentes, and if they drinke any deadly, or poisonfull thinge, it shall not hurte them, they shall lay their handes vppon the sick, and they shall recouer.* Thus said our Sauiour, giuing to vnderstand, not that euery christian should haue this grace or gift of miracles (for in the very Apostles time, there were infinit numbers of christians conuerted by them, which had it not) but that it should remaine in his church amongest the faithfull, & be exercised by some, from time to time, for his glory, and the edification of his seruantes, whereof wee haue seene continuall experience, euen vntill this day. And therefore, seeing our aduersaries say, that our miracles are illusions of the diuell, it is reason, that they tell vs, at what time the true miracles ceased, and if they cannot assigne vs the yeare of our Lord, let them assigne vs the age, and we will conuince them, with the experience of most manifest miracles donne afterwards, witnessed by the grauest authours, and hollyest men of the time wherein they liued yea, and we will shew them now in these last ages, as wonderfull miracles, as any in former times.

55 For what could be more stupendious, and more free from all suspicion, either of humane fraud, or of Diabolicall illusion, then a

miracle donne at the tombe of *S. Vincent Ferrer*, a *Dominican* frier, who died in the yeare of our Lord, *a thousand foure hundreth and Eighteene.*

56 The story breeflie is thus. A woman falling mad, and desiring greatelie to eate mans flesh, required some of her husband, and being denied it, killed a child of her owne, not past twoo yeares old, and deuiding him in to two partes, boiled the one halfe, which her husband, comming in shortly after, tooke out of the pott, and carried both the parts to *S. Vincents* tombe (who died latelie before, and was then famous for dayly miracles) and it pleased God for the merits of his seruant, to restore the child to life, and integritie of body, as it is testified by diuers graue men, and amongst others, by the most learned, and holly bishopp of *Florence*, Saint *Antoninus*, whose many notable workes, are witnesses of his learninge, piety, and great iudgement, besides that his holly life, and miracles were such, that he was canonized for a Saint.

S. Antoninus histor. par. 3. tit. 23. c. 8. paragr. 9.

57 This worthy bishop, speaking in his historie of *S. Vincent* (who liued in the same age) affirmeth of this miracle, that it was so famous in *Britany*, where it was donne, that the people flocked from farre, and neere, to see the child, *and all of them saw*, saith he, *a marke, or scarre, remaining in the body of the child in manner of a threed:* and he addeth further, that he himselfe had seene, the autenticall testimonies of notaries, witnessing that *Eight and thirty* dead men, had benne reuiued after the death of *S. Vincent* in diuers parts, by his merits, and intercession, and that the said testimonies were taken by commission, giuen by the Popes *Nicolas* the *fifth*, and *Calixstus* the third, to enquire of his life, and miracles. And lastly that the Pope *Calixstus*, after due examination of the whole processe, by Cardinals, and Bishops, canonized him for a Saint, with the consent, and approbation of all the court of *Rome*, which I haue thought good to note here, to the end it may appeare, that Neither. *S. Antoninus* reported these thinges vppon slender ground, nor that any man can with reason reiect his testimonie.

Idem Ibid.

58 But what neede we alleadge miracles of former ages, seeing that the age wherein we lyue, hath abounded with notable examples in diuers partes of christendome, as in *Rome*, *Loreto*, and *Luca* in *Italy*, *Mondeuy* in *Sauoy*. And to omit many other more ancient, at *Munich* in *Bauier*, at the body of *S. Benno*, not past twoo yeares agoe. At what time also it pleased our Sauiour to glorifie his owne name, in the blessed virgin *Mary* his Mother, by many admirable miracles donne at her

image,

image, at *Montague*, neere to *Sichen* in *Brabant*, and there (amongst diuers other cures of incurable, and inueterate diseases) to reforme, and rectifie the shape of a most mishapen, and deformed criple, borne with his knees so fast ioyned to his breast, that they could not be seperated, and his legges fastened to his theighs, and they to his belly with one skinne, whereby he was faine to goe vppon his handes with the helpe of two litle stilts, vntill he was 23. yeares ould, at what time he receiued his perfect shape, by the miraculous helpe of our blessed Lady.

59 The truth whereof, and of many wonderfull circumstances in his cure, hath benne so autenticallie proued, and the man himselfe so knowne, to many thousandes of people in the lowe countries, both before the miracle, and since, that no man that hath not a brazen face, can be so impudent to deny it, or can with any shew of reason ascribe it to the deuil, whose workes cannot exceede the power, and limits of nature, as this did, which any man must needes confesse, that shall read the story thereof, written aswell in Latin by *Iustus Lipsius*, as by others in *French*, and translated out of French into English, by *M. Chambers* a learned, and vertuous priest of our nation, who hath also præfixed thereto a learned epistle, and preface of his owne concerning miracles, in which respect, I may be the breefer touching that matter.

Iustus Lipsius in Diua Sichem ẽsi siue Aspricolli.

60 Neuerthelesse I cannot omit, to say some what of a famous miracle, donne the last yeare in the Diocesse of *Bisanson* in *Burgundy*, at a place called *Fauerney*, in the feast of *Pentecost*, or whitsontide, at what time the blessed Sacrament, being sett forth in a reliquarie within a tabernacle, vppon a table of wood which was couered with alter clothes of linnen, and enuironed with silke curtaines, vnder a canopie, with many candels, and lights burning about it, it chaunced that some snuffe of a candell, falling vppon the linnen clothes in the night, sett the same on fire, in such sort, that the tabernacle, and the table it selfe, and all the furniture about it was burned, and consumed to ashes, whereas the blessed Sacrament, with the reliquarie wherein it was placed, being safe, and vntouched, stood still suspended in the aire without any supporr, & so remained al whitsonday, and the munday following, during which time, not only al the people of *Fauerney*, but also thousandes of others, moued with the fame of the miracle, repaired thither to see it: And vpon the Tuesday, following, the curat of a parish not farre frõ *Fauerney*, being there, and saying Masse at the high aulter of the same

church, it pleased God, that at the time of the eleuation of the Masse, the reliquarie, which hanged in the aire, with the blessed sacrament in it, descended of it selfe, by litle and litle downe to a table, which was sett vnder it decētlie couered, and there placed it-selfe vppon a corporall, which was also spread vppon the same table: and this was donne in the presence and sight, of a great multitude of people, as is witnessed by a publike testimonie of Monseigneur de *Langut*, Archbishop of *Besanson*, and prince of the Empire, vppon autenticall information taken of the whole matter, exactlie and maturelie descussed (as he signifieth) in his Archipiscopall consistorie, with the assistance, and aduise of a great number of Deuines, Canonists, and Ciuilians, and the interuention of his sollicitour, and atturney generall, all which I say appeareth by his testimoniall letters, printed in *Bisanson*, and dated the 10. of *Iuly*, of the last yeare, *a thousand sixe hundreth* and eyght.

61 And if common fame may warrant the relation of matters not yet published in print, I may add also diuers notable miracles, hapned in our contry of late yeares whereof the fame hath benne, and is very publike, euen in forraine countries, as to omitt others, that the body of *Sr. Gerard Braybrooke* knight, buried twoo hundreth yeares agoe, was found the last yeare in *S. Faythes* Church in London, with the flowers very oderiferous, which were cast in to the graue with him, together with a *Breue* of *Pope Bonifacius* the Ninth. And because the curious Reader may desire perhaps to see the forme, and contents of the said *Breue*, which was so miraculouslie preserued, I haue thought good to lay downe the coppy of it here, which is as followeth.

Maij an. 1608.

62 *Bonifacius Episcopus seruus seruorum Dei, Dilecto filio nobili viro* Gerardo Braibrooke *iuniori Militi, & Dilectæ in Christo filiæ nobili Mulieri* Elizabethæ *eius vxori Lincoln. Diocesis salutem, & Apostolicam benedictionem. Prouenit ex vestræ deuotionis affectu, quo nos & Romanam Ecclesiam reueremini, vt petitiones vestras, illas præsertim, quæ animarum vestrarum salutem respiciunt, ad exauditionis gratiam admittamus. Hinc est quod nos vestris supplicationibus inclinati, vt confessor quem quilibet vestrum duxerit eligendum, omnium peccatorum vestrorum, de quibus corde contriti, & confeßi fueritis, semel tantum in mortis articulo, plenam remißionem vobis in sinceritate fidei, in vnitate sanctæ Romanæ Ecclesæ, ac obedientia, & deuotione nostræ, vel successorum nostrorum Romanorum Pontificum Canonicè intrantium persistenttbus, authoritate Apostolica concedere valeat, deuotioni vestræ tenore præsentiam indulgemus. Sic tamen, quod idem Confessor, de his de quibus fuerit alteri satisfactio*

impendenda

impendenda, eam vobis per vos, si superuixeritis, vel per hæredes vestros, si tunc forté transieritis faciendam, iniungat quam vos, vel illi facere teneamini, vt prefertur. Et ne (quod absit) propter huiusmodi gratiam, reddamini procliuiores ad illicita in posterum committenda, volumus, quod si ex confidentia remissionis huiusmodi aliqua forté committeretis, illa prædicta remissio vobis nullatenus suffagetur. Nulli ergo omnino hominum liceat hanc paginam nostram concessionis, & voluntatis infringere, vel ei ausa temerario contraire. Si quis autem hoc attentare præsumpserit, indignationem omnipotētis Dei, & B. Petri, & Pauli Apostolorum eius, se nouerit incursurum. D. Romæ apud Sanctum Petrum, nono Iunij. Pontificatus nostri, Anno Secundo.

63 Thus farre are the wordes of the *Breue*. The effect was, that Pope *Bonifacius*, gaue to Sir *Gerard Braibrooke* the younger, and the Lady *Elizabeth* his wife, licence to make choise of a ghostlie father, who might at the hour of their deathes, giue them plenary indulgence of their sinnes, vppon foure conditions. The first was, that they should be contrite in harte, and confessed. The second, that they should remaine in the vnion of the Roman Church, and in the obedience of the lawfull Bishopp therof. The third, that their ghostly father should enioyn them to make full satisfaction, either by themselues, or by their heires, to all such as they should haue anie way defrauded, or wronged, and that they, or their heires should performe it. The fourth was, that they should not presume in hope of this pardon, to commit anie vnlawful act, in the meane time, for in so doing, the said graunt of pardon, should bee vtterlie void, and of no effect.

46 This is the effect of the *Breue*, whereby it hath pleased almightie God, partlie to conuince a common calumniation of our aduersaries (who are wont to say, that Catholikes are licenced to sinne by the Popes pardons, whereof the contrarie is euident in this *Breue*:) and partlie to approue, not onlie our Catholike religion in generall, but also the Popes authoritie in perticular (namelie in the matter of indulgences) seeing it is euident by this miracle, that Sir *Gerard Braibrooke*, beinge a catholike, and vsing the benifit of the popes indulgences, at the hour of his death, was so acceptable to almightie God, that it hath pleased his deuine Maiestie, to giue such a publike testimonie thereof, as heere hath bene declared.

65 It beeing most manifest, that almightie God hath continued the powre and grace of miracles in the Roman Church, from the Apostles time, euen vntill this day, and that these miracles haue benne so testified, that there can be no doubt thereof, and manie of them so farr surpassinge all naturall meanes, that they could proceede from no other authour

authour but almightie God, it followeth that the same Catholike Roman Church, is the true church of Christ, seeing it hath alwaies had, and hath still, such an vndoubted testimonie of Gods assistance, and his approbation of the doctrin taught therein. And for asmuch, as those that haue excelled in this gift, and grace of miracles, haue benne for the most parte religious men, professing the obseruation of the euangelicall counsels, it also followeth, that religious and monastical life, is most gratefull to almightie God, & that the true professors thereof are vnited with him. And againe, seeing that one the other side, al the sectaries of our time are professed enemies, aswell of the Catholike Roman church, as of our religious life, and no way participant of the grace of miracles, it is euident, that they are noe lesse voyde of all vnion with allmightie God, then of the perfection, and truth of Christian religion.

66 But heere our aduersaries will say, that wee doe them wronge to exact miracles of them, seeing there were diuers greate prophets in the old testament, which did no miracles, and namelie *S. Iohn Baptist*, though he was (as the *Magdebergenses* say) held by the Pharisees for an heretick. Wheteto I answer, that neither the ould prophets which did no miracles, nor *S. Iohn Baptist*, taught anie thinge contrarie to the common doctrin, and much lesse deuided themselus schismatically from the pastors of the church at that time, as the sectaries now doe, and therefore the Pharisees being demaunded by our Sauiour, what they thought of *S. Iohns* Baptisme, did not disalow it, and *Iosephus* testifieth, that S. *Iohn Baptist* was a verie good man, and highlie esteemed of the Iewes for his great vertue: whereby it appeareth sufficientlie, that the *Magdeburgenses* abuse their readers shamefullie, when they affirme that he was held by the Priests and Pharises for an heriticke.

Magdebur. cent. 1. li. 1. c. 10.

Ioseph. li. 18. de antiq. c 7. Magdebur. vbi supra.

67 Besides that it is altogether needelesse, that hee should confirme his preaching by miracles, seeing his speciall commission was no other but to preach Christ who was then liuing, & confirmed both *S. Iohns* preaching, and his owne by infinit miracles. So that the example of *S. Iohn Baptist*, and some of the other prophets of the ould law, cannot excuse our aduersaries from our iust demaund of their miracles, seeinge they teach a new doctrin, without anie commission from the pastors of the church: for as the Apostle saith. *Quomodo prædicabunt, nisi mittantur? How shall they preach, except they bee sent? Et nemo sumit sibi honorem &c. And no man taketh honour vppon him in Gods Church, except hee bee caled of God, as Aron was.*

Rom. 11. Heb. 5.

68 Therefore there are two kindes of missions, and vocations, the one

ordinarilie by the authoritie of lawful superiours, and the other extraordinarie from God imediatlie, it is reason, that whosoeuer is sent to preach, either by the one, or by the other, he shew his commission, or els no man is bound to beleeue him: those that are sent to preach by their lawfull and ordinarie superiours, haue their warrant from them, which they are alwaies able to shew, as euerie preacher, and minister in *England*, can shew his authoritie to preach, and teach from his bishopp, but those that are sent immediatlie from God, must either proue their commission by miracle, or els they are not to bee beleeued. When God commaunded *Moyses*, to take the gouerment of the children of *Israel*, and to deliuer them out of the hands of *Pharao*, *Moyses* answered. *Non credent mihi, neque audient vocem meam &c. They will not beleeue me, nor heare my voyce, but will say, God hath not appeared vnto thee.* Wherevppon God gaue him powre to multiplie miracle vppon miracle. *Vt credant*, saith he, *quod apparuerit tibi Dominus. To the end they may beleeue, that God hath appeared vnto thee.* Exod. 4.

69 Also when our Sauiour came to preach the new law, hee proued his commission from his Father, by cõtinual miracles, notwithstanding that the scriptures of the ould testament, gaue sufficient testimonie of him, in so much that he said himselfe. *Si opera non fecissem in eis &c. If I had not donne workes amongst them, which no man els hath donne, they should not haue sinne*, that is to say, they should not offend, in refusing to receiue my doctrin. And in like manner, when he sent his disciples to preach, he gaue them power withal, to heale the diseased, to raise the dead, to cleanse lepers, & to cast out deuels, *and they preached euerie where*, saith the scripture, *Domino cooperante, & sermonem confirmante sequentibus signis. Our Lorde workinge with them, and confirminge their speech with signes, or miracles, which followed the same.* Ioan. 15. Matth. 10. Mar. vltimo.

70 Herevppon *S. Augustin*, teacheth that miracles were necessarie, for the conuersion of the world. And *Melancthon* himselfe (who was one of *Luthers* dearest dearlinges) affirmeth, that when there is greate darknes, and obscuritie in the world, God doth cal and send new teachers, or preachers, and add also miracles thereto, to the end, that their mission may be certainely knowne. D. Aug. li. 22. de ciuit. c. 8. Philip. Melan. in ca. 3. Matth.

71 For this cause I say, we iustlie exact miracles of our aduersaries, because they pretend their vocation from God himselfe imediatlie, not hauinge anie mission from the superiours of the Church, againste whome they haue rebelled, teachinge a new doctrine contrarie to theirs, and to that which hath benne generally receiued. And whereas they pretende to haue scripture for their warrante, and that

therefore they neede no miracles, they are to vnderstand, that in this their case of extraordinarie vocation, and mission which they pretend, it suffiseth not to alledge scriptures (for soe doe all heretickes, aswell as they) except they also shew by extraordinarie meanes (that is to say by miracles) that they haue the true sence thereof: and this may appeare by the proceedinges of our Sauiour himselfe, and his Apostles, for although the scriptures of the old testament, gaue ample testimonie of him, and that both he himselfe, and his Apostles alleadged them aboundantlie to the Iewes, according to their true sence, yet neuertheles because they deriued not their authoritie of preaching, from the ordinarie pastors, and gouernours, established by the law of *Moyses*, they confirmed their doctrin, and proued their mission by miracles, shewing euidentlie therebie, that their sence, and vnderstanding of the scriptures was true, which otherwaise might still haue benne in controuersie, betwixt the Iewes and them.

Ioan Sleidan histor. li. 5. vide Martin. Cromer. li. 1. colliquio.

72 Therefore *Luther* had reason when (as *Sleidan* reporteth) he wrote to the senate of *Mulhusium* (concerning a new preacher amongst them called *Muncerus*) requesting them to examine him, who gaue him commission to preach, *and if*, saith *Luther*, *he say, that God gaue it him, let him be vrged to proue it by some euident miracle, which if he cannot doe, them let him be reiected: for God alwayes vseth to shew his will by Miracles, when he will haue the ordinary custome, and course of doctrin to be changed.* This iudgement gaue *Luther* himselfe, against *Muncerus*, who being one of his owne brood (though then declined from him) and teaching other nouelties, alleadged scripture no doubt, as plentifully as *Luther* himselfe, which neuertheles *Luther* would not allow, except *Mnncer* could eyther shew an ordinarie vocation, or proue his extraordinarie, and secret commission, by miracles.

73 In like manner, I say to *Luther*, and all his progenie, with farre more reason, that seeing the Catholike Roman church, is deriued from Christ himselfe, and his Apostles, by a continuall succession of Bishops, without any interruption (which cannot be denied) and that they cannot shew, at what time the succession of Christs doctrin, ceased in the said succession of Bishops, we iustlie require of them, that if they will teach vs a new doctrin out of the scriptures, they eyther shew their commission from the superiours of the church, or els proue it by miracle, whereby we may know that they vnderstand the scriptures aright, for otherwise wee shall alwayes haue more reason to beleeue our pastors, then them.

74 For seeing that our pastors, are successiuelie descended from the Apostles,

Apostles, as I haue said, and haue had hitherto the possession of the scriptures, and conserued the same, wee are to presume, that they haue also had, and conserued the true sence thereof, especiallie seing our Sauiour promised to his church, his assistance *to the worldes end, and that* *Mat.16.*
hell gates shall not preuaile against it, yea, and commaundeth vs, *to hold* *Ibid.*
for Ethnicks, and publicans, all those, *that will not heare, and obay it.* In *Matth.18.*
which respect, S. *Paule* also calleth it, *the pillar and stay of truth.* And *1. Timoth.3.*
therefore, forasmuch as an inuisible church (such I meane as the protestants imagin) cannot be heard, and obayed, according to our Sauiours commaundement, his promise of continuall assistance, must needes be vnderstood of the visible church, that he, and his Apostles planted, from which we directlie deriue ours, prouing it inuincibly, to be the same church, not only because we haue had a continual succession, both of bishops, and doctrin, from the Apostles euen vntill this day, but also because otherwise it must needes follow, that the visible church of Christ hath failed, and lost his spirit and assistance, contrarie to his promise, which were blasphemous to say, and most absurd to imagine.

75 Therefore I conclude, that seeing our aduersaries, haue neither succession from the Apostles, nor lawfull mission from the superiours of the church, neither yet doe by miracle proue, or confirme their extraordinarie vocation, and sence of scriptures (which they pretend to haue from the holly Ghost) we haue iust cause, to hould them for those, of whom Christ forewarned vs, when he said, *that some should* *Ioan. 10.*
come in to the fould, not by the dore, which is the ordinarie way, *but by the windowe*, to kill, and destroy the flock.

76 Now then good Reader, I am to request thee seriously to ponder, & way with thy selfe, what a blindnes, or rather senceles stupiditie, hath seazed those men, which see not the cleare sunne shyne of Gods glory, manifest in all former ages, yea, and in these our dayes, by most notable, and euident miracles, but doe reiect them as diabolicall illusions. as though our Sauiour Christ, not with standing the bitter pasion, which he suffred for his spouse the church, and the promise of his holly Spirit, and asistance, had suffred the same to be abused, and deceiued by the deuil, for so many hundreth yeares together, euen vnder the maske, and pretence of his owne name, and faith, which is so absurd, and ridiculous to thinke, that when they laugh, and iest at our miracles (which they doe because they cannot tell with reason how to impugne them) they make themselues ridiculous, or rather to say truly, worthy of pity, and compasion, in that boasting so much

of faith, as they doe, they shew themselues neuertheles more incredulous, and faithlesse, then infinit numbers of Pagans, and Infidels, who by the like miracles, haue benne conuerted to the christian faith.

77 For what argument is there so potent to persuade, or so manifest to conuince in matter of religion, as a true miracle, surpassing the power of all creatures, which must needes be an vndoubted testimony, of a deuine operation for the confirmation of truth, and therefore it hath alwayes accompanied true religion, as wee may perceiue by the miracles, aswell in the ould testament, as the new. In which respect, also *S. Augustin* alleadgeth the authoritie of miracles in the Catholike church, for the confutation not only of Painimes, but also of all Heretikes, saying that the Catholike church hath euer preuailed, *hereticis miraculorum maiestate damnatis*, *heretikes being condemned by the maiestie of miracles.* And *S. Ambrose* also vrgeth notablie, the glory of miracles against the *Arrians*, so that we may say to our aduersaries, as our Sauiour said to the *Pharisees*, who being taxed by him of willfull blindnes, after his manifest miracle donne vppon the man that was borne blind, asked him. *Numquid & nos caci sumus? VVhat, and are we also blind?* whereto he answered. *Si caci essetis* &c. *Yf you were blind in deede, you should not haue sinne, but because you say, wee see, therefore your sinne remaineth.* Wherein our Sauiour gaue them to vnderstand, that if their blindnes had proceeded of meere ignorance, it had benne the more excusable, but forasmuch as it proceeded of willful obstinacie, flowing from an ouerweening of their owne knowledge, and wit, therefore their sinne could not be excused: and so I say, we may iustly say to our aduersaries, who presume so much of their owne knowledge, and are so bent to the defence of their conceits, and fancies, that they willfully shut their eyes, against the bright sunne beames of Gods most miraculous workes, donne in confirmation of the catholike Roman religion, whereby their willfull blindnes, and consequentlie their sinne is inexcusable, and they shew themselues, to be of those. *Qui vident, & caci fiunt. VVhich see, and become blind*, as our Sauiour said of the pharisees: our Lord open their eyes, with the light of his grace.

S. Aug. To. 6. de vtilitate credendi li. 17.
S. Ambros. Ser. in festo SS. Geruasij & Protasij.
Ioan. 9.
Ioan. 9.

For

For the finall conclusion of the question, concerning the Euangelicall Counsells, and religious life, the matter of religious vowes is debated, and defended against our aduersaries. Also, that the continencie of clergy men, is beneficiall to the common wealth, and that certaine wicked, Emperours, who haue sought by lawes to restraine, & to prohibit monasticall life, haue bene seuerelie punished by almighty God for the same. Finallie a breefe recapitulation is made of all the premisses, concerning the true imitation of Christ, and our aduersaries are thereby conuinced, to be vtterly void, aswell of all Christian perfection, as of the true felicitie of man, and common welth.

Chap. 33.

1 THough I haue sufficientlie proued our Catholike doctrin, and confuted the opinions of our aduersaries, and answered diuers of their obiections, concerning our practise of the euangelicall Counsels in monasticall disciplin, yet for the more aboundant manifestation of the truth, I thinke good before I fully conclude the discourse of this matter, to cleare some other doubts, and scruples, which perhaps may seeme to some, to be of more moment then they are, and to require particuler satisfaction.

2 One speciall reason, why the sectaries of these dayes, reiect the manner of our imitation of Christ, and obseruation of his counsells, is, because we doe bind our selues thereto by vow, which they hold to be superfluous and superstitious, for such reasons as shalbe declared, in the discourse and discussion of this question, when I shall haue first confirmed, and established the truth of our Catholike doctrin, concerning the same, and the practise of our church, out of the Scriptures, and Fathers, which I will doe with what breuitie I may, because I hast to treat of some other matters.

Luther de captiuit. Babilon. de vita cōiugali. Iean Caluin li. 4. instit. c.13. Philip. Melanch. disputat. 16. de iureiuran.

3 Yt cannot be with any reason denied, but that a good worke donne by obligation of vow, is more gratefull to God, then if it were donne at libertie. First, because it proceedeth of greater vertue, that is to say, of greater charitie, and loue to God, and of greater liberalitie. For he that doth offer to God, not only his worke, but also his liberty with all, sheweth himselfe farre more louing, and liberal towards him, then he that offreth the same worke, & reserueth his libertie to himselfe. As in like sort the seruant, who out of loue, and good wil to his master, doth bind himselfe voluntarilie to his seruice, doth deserue more fauour, & loue at his masters hands, then he that doth the like seruice with-

out

S. Anselmus li. de similitudinibus c. 84.

out obligation, and may leaue it when he will. And therefore *S. Anselme* saith very well. *Plus donat, qui arborem cum fructibus, quam qui solos fructus donat. He which giueth the tree with the fruit* (that is to say himselfe, with his woorke) *giueth more, then he which giueth the fruit alone.*

4 Secondlie, an act donne by vowe, is made therebie an act of religion, in which respect, it is more gratefull to God, then if it were only, an other vertuous good worke, and not religious with all. As for example, a man that liueth continentlie, doth an act of temperance, but he that is continent by obligation of vow, doth an act not only of temperance, but also of religion, because he doth it purposelie for the honour, and seruice of God, as *S. Augustin* teacheth, who speaking of vowed virginitie, saith that it *is not honoured, because it is virginitie, sed quia deo dicata est, but because it is dedicated to God, and kept in the flesh, religione & deuotione spiritus, with the religion, and deuotion of the spirit.* I haue cited the place before, vppon an other occasion, and therefore forbeare to repeate the whole heere.

S. August. de sancta virginit. c. 8.

5 Furthermore, the conueniencie of vowes may appeare, by that they doe greatlie incite, and vrge a man to Gods seruice, by reason of the obligation that groweth thereof, which wee may well vnderstand, if wee consider mans frailty, and mutabilitie in his good purposes, when he hath no obligation to performe them: and therefore wee see, that counsellors of princes, magistrats, souldiars, and such others, not withstanding their good will, and purpose to serue their princes faithfullie, are further moued, and incited thereto by obligation of oath. Herevppon *S. Augustin* saith to *Armentarius. Let it not repent thee to haue vowed, but rather be gladd, that it is not now lawfull for thee, to doe that which thou mightst haue donne before with thy owne detriment* &c. And againe afterwards. *Fœlix necessitas quæ ad meliora compellit. Happy is the necessity, which compelleth a man to be better.*

S. Aug. ep. 45. in circa finem.

6 Lastlie, the holly Ghost doth in the psalmes, and diuers other places of the scripture, exhort vs to vowe, saying. *Vouete, & reddite domino deo vestro. Vow, and render,* or pay it, *to your Lord God.* Whereto the holly Ghost would not aduise vs, if it were better to worke with out vow, as our aduersaries teach it to be.

Psalm. 75.

7 Heereto I add, that the vse of vowes, is most manifest in the ould testament, as the vowes of a *Iacob,* b *Iephthe,* c *Anna* mother to *Samuel,* d *Dauid,* and of all the people of e *Israell,* when they were to fight with the *Cananæans,* & in diuers places of the booke of f *Numeri.* As also the obligation of vowes, is no lesse euident in g *Deuteronomy,* where

a *Genes. 28.* b *Iudic. 11. ca.* c *1. Reg. 1.* d *Psalm. 21. & 65.* e *Num. 21.* f *Num. ca. 6. 30.* g *Deut. 23.*

wher *Moyses* said. *Cum votum voueris Domino Deo* &c. Whē thou shalt haue vowed a vow to thy Lord God, bee not slack to performe it, for thy Lord wil require it at thy hands, and if thou delay it, it shal be imputed vnto thee for a sinne, if thou wilt not promise at al, thou shalt be without sinne, but that which is once past out of thy mouth, thou shalt obserue and performe, as thou hast promised to thy Lord God, and spoken of thy owne will, and out of thy owne mouth. Thus saith *Moyses* in *Deuteronomy*, and the like also we read in the booke of *Numbers*, in the *Psalmist*, and in *Ecclesiastes*, which I omit to lay downe, as needles, for that our aduersaries denie not, either the vse, or obligation of vowes in the ould law.

Num.30. Psal.75. Eccles.5.

8 The question then betwixt vs and them, beeing not so much, whether vowes are lawful, & obligatorie in the new law (which al of them except *Peter Martire* doe graunt) as what manner of thinges may lawfullie be vowed, I wil for breuities sake, leaue generalities, and examin whether the euangelical counsells may be vowed to God or no, and to that purpose, I will treat particularlie of one of them, to wit of *Chastitie*, whereby the question wil be sufficientlie discussed, concerning the other two, the reason being alike in al three.

9 Therefore, to the end I may be the breefer, I omit the example of the blessed virgin *Maries* vow of chastitie, signified sufficientlie by her owne wordes, to the Angell. *Quomodo fiet istud, quoniam virum non cognosco? How can this be, seeing that I know not anie man?* That is to say, seing it is not lawfull for me to know anie man, by reason of my vow of continency, as *S. Gregory Nissen*, *S. Augustin*, *S. Bede*, *Rupertus*, & *S. Bernard* doe teach expressely. I omit also the arguments that may be made for our Catholike doctrin, vppon the wordes of our Sauiour, concerning three kindes of Eunuchs, where it is plaine inough, by the verie name of Eunuch, and the manner of our Sauiours speech, that he included a vow of chastity, seeing that no man can properlie be called an Eunuch, who may chose whether he will be continent or no, but he onlie which cannot but be continent by reason of his naturall impotencie, and therefore in like manner the voluntarie Eunuch, must needes be such a one, as hath of his owne free will depriued himselfe of the power of mariage, which also the wordes of our Sauiour that follow doe make more euident, for that he saith. *Qui se castrauerunt, who haue guilded themselues.* Signifiyng, that they haue by their voluntarie act, debarred them selues from al vse and knowledge of women, which they cannot otherwayse lawfullie doe, but by promise and vow to God, whereby they are morally, and in conscience disabled to contract mariage.

Luca.1.

S.Greg.Nissen.in orat. in natiuit Domini. post medium.

S.Aug. li.de sancta virginit.cap.4.

S.Beda. in com in Luc.

Ruper.3. in cantica .li.3. circa finem.

S.Ber.in verba Euangelij missus est Ang. homile 4. post initium.

Mat.19.

10 But

10 But I will not, I say, insist vppon the further proofe of this, or other arguments, which might bee deduced from other places of scripture, but will manifestlie shew, both the vse, and also the obligation of a vow of chastitie, out of *S. Pauls* words to *Timothy*, saying. *Adolescentiores viduas deuita, &c. Auoid, or eschew the yonger widdowes, for when they haue plaid the wantons in Christ, they will marry, hauing damnation, because they haue broken their first faith.* Thus saith the Apostle, meaning by their *first faith*, their vow of continencie.

11 For whereas some of our aduersaries, would haue it to be vnderstood of the faith of Baptisme, which they say, the young widowes broke by liuing licentiouslie, it cannot stand with the wordes of the Apostle, who giueth plainely to vnderstand, that they brooke their first faith, by hauing a will to marry, *nubere volunt*, saith he, *habentes damnationem, because they haue broken their first faith.* Yt being therefore euident, that no man promiseth in Baptisme to abstaine from mariage, it cannot be said that any man breaketh his faith of baptisme, by hauing a will to marry, for if it were soe it would also follow, that no christian man might marry. Neuerthelesse, presupposing a vow of chastitie in any man, it may truly be said of him, that by breaking his vow, he also breaketh his promise, and faith, giuen to God in Baptisme, wherein euery one promiseth to keepe the law of God, which law bindeth vs to obserue all lawfull vowes, as is the vow of chastity, and in this sence, I say (which maketh nothing against vs) it may be said, that the widowes brake their faith of Baptisme, and so incurred eternall damnation, for breaking their first faith.

12 But if we consider the vniforme consent of all the ancient Fathers, concerning the interpretation of this place, we may wonder at the bouldnes (I will not say impudencie) of such as deny the vse, and obligation of vowes of continencie, in the Apostles time.

Tertull. li. de monogamia cap. 13.

13 *Tertullian*, alleadging the same wordes of the Apostle, in his booke *de monogamia*, saith. *Habentes iudicium, quod primam fidem resciderunt illam scilicet, in qua in viduitate inuentæ, & professæ, eam noluerint perseuerare. Hauing iudgement, or damnation, because they brake their first faith, to wit, that faith, wherein they would not perseuer being found in widdowhood, and hauing professed it.* Thus saith *Tertullian* of the widdowes who being conuerted to the christian faith, in their widdowhood, made also a particular profession, and promise to perseuer therein, which promise, or profession he saith, the Apostle calleth *their first faith*, and is the same which wee call a vow of chastitie in widowes.

S. Epiphan. lib. 2. contra Hæreses Hæresi. 61. in fine.

14 Also *S. Epiphanius. Si qua vidua fuit*, saith he, *ac Deo dicata &c. Yf shee*

ſhee which was a widow, and dedicated to God, and afterwards maried, had iudgement, and condemnation, becauſe ſhee reiected her firſt faith, or promiſe, how much more ſhall ſhee haue iudgement, which was a virgin dedicated to God, & hath married, and played the wanton againſt Chriſt, and hath reiected a greater faith, or promiſe. Thus ſaith *S. Epiphanius*, teaching twoo thinges to be noted. The one, that the firſt faith whereof the Apoſtle ſpeaketh, is to be vnderſtood of a vow of continencie, in reſpect whereof he ſaith, that thoſe yong widowes were dedicated to God. The other is, that the virgins vow, is greater then the vow of the widow, and that her iudgement, and damnation, is alſo greater if ſhee breake it, the reaſon is, becauſe the merit of virginity, is greater thē the merit of widohood, & therefore, as the virgin ſhall haue a greater reward, then the widow, if ſhee keepe her vow of virginity, ſo alſo ſhee ſhalbe more ſeuerelie puniſhed, if ſhee breake it.

15 The like alſo ſaith *S. Chriſoſtome*, concerning both theſe points, who expounding the Epiſtle to the *Corinthians*, & particularly thoſe wordes of the Apoſtle, *ſi nupſerit virgo, non peccauit*, he ſaith. *Non de ea dicit* &c. *He doth not ſpeake of the virgin, which hath made choiſe of virginity, for ſhee hath ſinned* (if ſhee mary:) *for if the widowes haue iudgement, which after their choiſe of widdowhood doe marry againe, much more is the ſame to be vnderſtood of virgins.* And againe in his homilies, vppon the Epiſtle to *Timothy*, & vppon thoſe very wordes of the Apoſtle, whereof I treat here, he ſaith of the yong widowes thus. *VVhen they haue vowed themſelues to him*, (that is to ſay to Chriſt) *they haue damnation, becauſe they breake their firſt faith. Fidem pactum dicit, he calleth the couenant which they make, their faith.* Thus farre *S. Chriſoſtom*, of the yong widdowes, calling their ſolemne promiſe, or vow of continency, *a couenant.*

S. Chriſoſt. ho. 19. in 1. Cor. 7. ante finem.

S. Chriſoſt. in 1. ad Timoth. 5. ho. 15. initio.

16 In like maner *S. Auguſtin. Quid ait Apoſtolus*, ſaith he, *de quibuſdam quæ vouerunt* &c. *VVhat ſaith the Apoſtle, of ſome which did vow, and did not render, or pay their vow? Hauing*, ſaith he, *damnation, becauſe they haue broken their firſt faith. VVhat meaneth he by ſaying, that they haue broken their firſt faith? Vouerunt & non reddiderunt. They made a vow, and did not render, or pay it.* Thus ſaith *S. Auguſtin*, expounding the words of the pſalme, *vouete, & reddite domino deo veſtro, vow, and render, or pay it to your Lord God.*

S. Auguſt. in Pſal. 75.

1. Timoth. 5.

17 To theſe I will add a cannon of a counſell of *Carthage*, of two hundreth and foureteene Biſhops, celebrated about the yeare of our Lord, three hundreth ninetie fiue. Wherein it was decreed, that widowes, which haue vowed themſelues to God, and do after marry, ſhall not be admitted to the holly communion, neither yet to eate, & drinke, with chriſtians: *quoniam fidem caſtitatis, quam domino vouerunt, irritam facere auſæ*

Concil. Carthag. 4. can. 104.

 ſunt:

ſunt: becauſe they are ſo bould, to breake the faith, or promiſe of chaſtity which they vowed to God. And it is further ſignified in the ſame decree, that *ſecundum Apoſtolũ, damnationẽ habebunt, according to the Apoſtle, they ſhal haue dãnation.*

1.Timoth. 5.
Concil.Tolet 4.can.55.

18 Finally a Synod held at *Toleto* in *Spaine* by ſeauentie Biſhops, vnderſtandeth the ſame wordes of the Apoſtle, in the ſame ſort, and ſo doe *S. a Baſill, S. b Hierome, S. c Ambroſe, Primaſius, Theodoretus, Theophilactus, Oecumenius, S. Beda, Haymo, Sedulius, S. Anſelmus,* and al other ancient expoſitours, of that epiſtle of *S. d Paule* to *Timothy.*

a S.Baſil. ad Amphilo.epi- circa.mediũ.
b S.Hierom. li.7. contra Iouin. aliquot paull. poſt.initium. & in ca.44. Ezechiell. poſt.mediũ.
c.Ambroſ. in 1.Timo.5. in verba Adulocentulas vero viduas &c.
d 1.Timo.5.

19 And whereas ſome of the ſectaries, doe not vnderſtand by the word *damnation* (which *S. Paule* ſaith the young widdowes incurred) anie paine due to ſinne, but onlie reproch, and infamie before men, becauſe the Greeke word κρίμα, ſignifieth iudgment, and may bee taken (ſay they) for accuſation before men, whereby they would haue it to be vnderſtood, that men would iudge euel of ſuch young widowes, and condemne them of leuitie and follie, for leauing their profeſſion (though neuertheles before God they ſhould be excuſed, yea and ſhould do well to marrie, becauſe it is better to marrie then to burne:) whereas, I ſay, ſome of the ſectaries, as *Bucer*, and *Peter Martir,* make this gloſe, it is to bee vnderſtood, that this ſhameles ſhift and cauill, is not onlie contrarie to all the Fathers, but alſo to the vſual ſence of the worde *Crima* in the ſcripture, & namelie in the Apoſtle him ſelfe, who alſo els where vſeth the ſame word, for the iudgement of God condemning to eternall paine, in which reſpect, it is in our Latin verie properlie tranſlated *damnation*, as when the Apoſtle ſpeaketh of thoſe who did blaſphemouſly belie him, charging him to ſay, *let vs doe euel that good may come of it*, he vſeth the ſame worde, *to crima*, ſaying. *Quorum dãnatio iuſta eſt. VVhoſe damnation is iuſt*, meaning vndoudtedlie, Gods iuſt iudgment of eternall damnation. Alſo when he ſaith. *Qui reſiſtunt Dei ordinationi, ipſi ſibi damnationem acquirunt. Thoſe which reſiſt the ordinance of God, doe purchaſe to themſelues damnation*, he hath the ſame wordes in the Greeke, *to crima.* And the like may alſo be ſeene in other places of the holie ſcripture, as Cardinall *Bellarmin* hath verie learnedlie obſerued, thriſe in one chapter of *S. Iohns* Goſpell, againſt *Peter Martir*, and *Bucer*, who were the deuiſers & forgers of this falſe and counterfeit coyne.

Rom.1.
Ibid.cap.13.
Bell.de Monachis. ca. 24.
Iohan.3.

20 Furthermore, whereas they ſay, that the yong widdowes of whom *S. Paule* ſpeaketh, were to bee condemnded onlie by men, of leuitie and follie for leauing their profeſſion, I would gladlie know of them, whether this condẽnation, or iudgmẽt of man were iuſt, or vniuſt. If it were iuſt, how commeth it to paſſe, that it is no ſhame for *Luther* & al his fellow Monkes, and Friers (as they ſay it was not but a vertue) to breake their

their vowes of chaſtitie and to marrie? And one the other ſide, if they were vniuſtlie condemned (becauſe as the ſectaries ſay, ſuch vowes are vnlawfull, and therefore may lawfullie, yea, and commendablie be broken:) why did the Apoſtle ſo ſeuerelie reprehend them, as it appeareth by his owne wordes, who as *S. Chriſoſtom* ſaith. *Vehementer accuſat. Doth vehemently accuſe, or blame thoſe widdowes, which after their vow of continencie doe marrie.* Whereypon *S. Chriſoſtom* alſo inferreth in the ſame place. *Non his ergo &c. Therefore the Apoſtle ſaid not to theſe*, or ſuch as they, *but to others that are free, ſi ſe non continent, nubant: if they doe not liue chaſt, let them marrie.*

S. Chriſoſt. li de virginitate. ca. 30.

21 To conclude, al the holie Fathers of the church, followinge the doctrin of the Apoſtle in this place, doe with one voyce condemne, not onlie of leuitie or follie, but of greueous ſinne, al ſuch as breake vowes of chaſtitie, iudging them to incurre the paine of eternal damnation. In which reſpect *S. Epiphanius* ſaith. *Tradiderunt Apoſtoli &c. The Apoſtles haue deliuered vnto vs, that it is ſinne to marrie after a reſolution and decree made of virginitie.* And *S. Hierom* hauing ſaid, that virgins which marrie after their vow, ſhall haue damnation, addeth. *Virgines enim, quæ poſt conſecrationem nupſerint, non tam adulteræ, quam inceſtæ ſunt. For virgins which marrie after their conſecration, doe not commit adulterie, but inceſt.*

Hære. 16. *S. Hierom. l. 1. contra. Iouin loco notato ſupra.*

22 *S. Ambroſe* (as I haue ſignified before) ſaith alſo, that ſhee which marrieth after ſhee is veyled, committeth adulterie, and becommeth, *ancilla mortis the hand-maid of death.* S *Auguſtine* ſaith in like manner of ſuch, that *iure damnantur, they are worthilie, and iuſtlie condemned.* Not meaning that they are condemned by man, but by almightie God, for that he ſpeaketh of the breach of a vow made to him. *Quod niſi reddant*, ſaith hee, *iure damnantur. VVhich if they render, and pay not, they are iuſtlie condemned.* S. *Baſil* affirmeth that ſuch ſeeke to couer, *ſtupri ſcelus, honeſto coniugij nomine, the wickednes of whoredome, with the honeſt name of marriage*: and that, *dant manus nequitiæ, they giue their handes to wickednes*: and laſtlie that, *ſhee is worthylie counted an adultreſſe, who during the life of her immortal husband, hath for the vices of the fleſh introduced, or brought a mortal man into the bed of our Lord.*

S. Amb. ad virginem. lapſ. cap. 5. *S. Aug. de bono viduitat. cap. 8.* *S. Baſil. de vera virginitate. parũ á medio.*

23 *S. Chriſoſtome*, hauing aleadged the wordes of the Apoſtle, *habentes damnationem &c. hauing damnation*, &c, expoundeth them expreſſelie of deuine puniſhmẽt, ſaying, *that Chriſt doth alwaies puniſh thoſe, who do not liue honeſtly*, ſignifiing that thoſe which breake a vow of chaſtity, do not liue honeſtly, & therfore ſhalbe puniſhed by Chriſt with ſẽtẽce of dãnation.

S. Chriſoſt. l de virginit. cap. 36.

24 Thus then thou ſeeſt good Reader, how cleare it is by theſe wordes of the Apoſtle, accordinge to the vniforme, conſent of al the ancient

learned, and holly Fathers, that vowes of chastitie were vsuall in the Apostles time, and approued by them, and that the vowers were bound to the performance thereof, vnder paine of eternall damnation. Where vppon I inferre against our aduersaries, that all their gloses vppon this place, deuised by them to answer our arguments drawne from thence, are most false, and vaine, which I will shew particularlie by the circumstances of the text. And to beginne with *Luther*, he saith, that the faith which the yonge widowes broke, was the christian faith, *who,* saith he, returned to *Iudaisme, or Paganisme, to the end they might freely marry againe.* Whereas you see all the Fathers agree, that the faith, whereof the Apostle speaketh, was their vowe of chastitie, which is also cleare, by the text it selfe, by the which it appeareth, that they brooke their faith, by hauing a will to marry. Besides that it is manifest, that if those widdowes were not hindred from marriage by their vow, they had no cause to forsake the christian faith, to the end they might marry, amongst the Iewes, or Gentills, seeing that the marriage of widdowes (not hindred by vow of chastitie) was alwayes permitted amongst Christians, and allowed by the Apostle himselfe, as appeareth in this epistle, and his other to the *Corinthians*.

Lutherus in lib. de votis monasticis. Vide Bellar. de Monachis ca. 24.

1. Cor. 7.

25 In like manner the vanitie of the three cauiling gloses of *Caluin*, is no lesse euident. For first he saith, that the widowes faith, was their faith or promise, made in Baptisme, and that they brooke it by dissolute, and wanton life: wherein you see, he contradicteth, not only all the Fathers, but also the most naturall, and litterall sense of the text it selfe, which ascribeth their breach of vow, and their damnation, to their will, and desire of marriage, which desire is no way repugnant to the faith or promise made in baptisme, as I haue declared before.

Vide Bellar. loco citato.

26 His second shift is, that though the yong widdowes had promised and vowed to liue chast, yet their promise or vow, was of it selfe void, because they were not of that age, which the Apostle required for the admission of widowes, to the ministrie of the church, saying. *Vidua eligatur non minus sexaginta annorum. Let a widow be chosen, of no lesse, then threescore yeares.* But this cauill, is no way compatible, eyther with the interpretation of the Fathers, which you haue heard, or with the text it selfe, which sheweth plainelie, that though the Apostle to auoid inconueniences, did ordaine, that the yonger sort of widowes, should not be admitted to the office of *Diaconisse*, yet he vtterlie misliked, and condemned those that had broken their vow, iudging them to haue incurred, eternall damnation therebie, so that it is manifest, that their vow did still bind them. Wherein I also wish it to be no-

ted by the way, that whereas the Apostle ordaineth, that no widow shall be chosen vnder threescore yeares of age, he speaketh not of their admission to make a vow of continencie, but that they should not be admitted to the office of Diaconissa (as *Tertullian* saith) or to be of the number of those, who were susteined, and nourished by the church, as *S. Chrisostome*, *S. Ambrose*, and *S. Hierome* do expound it, and may be confirmed, by the greek text, where our Latin word *eligatur*, is *catalegésto*, which properlie signifieth to be *enrolled, registred*, or admitted, *to the catalogue, or number of others*: and the reason of the Apostles ordinaunce was (as *S. Hierome* noteth) partly because the yonger widdowes might gett their liuing by their labour, and partly because they were in more danger to fall to incontinencie, then the elder: and lastly, because it was very scandalous, and reprochfull to the christian faith, that any of those widdowes, which were nourished by the church, should be noted of lasciuiousnes, in which respect it was necessarie, that a very speciall care should be had in the choise, and admission of them, whereby neuer the lesse, the yonger sort were not prohibited to liue single, or to make a vow of continency, if they were so disposed.

Tertul. de veland virginis ca. 9. & li. 1. ad vxorem cap. 7.

S. Chris. & S. Ambros. in hunc locum S. Hieron. in ep. ad Saluinam circa medium.

S. Hieron. ibid.

27 For whereas our aduersaries, doe further vrge for that purpose, the wordes of the Apostle that follow. *Volo iuniores nubere, filios procreare* &c. *I will, that the yonger marry, and bringe forth children* (which they hould to be an absolute precept of marriage) it is to be vnderstood, that he no more commaunded young widowes to marry, then to bring forth children, which was not in their power to performe, depending vppon Gods benediction, and their naturall fertilitie: but his meaning was therebie, to aduise *Timothy*, to permit such widowes to marry, as were of them selues disposed thereto. For whereas the primitiue feruour of christian zeale, was such in the Apostles time, that all the faithfull tended to perfection, and those which were widowes, betooke themselues for the most part to perpetuall widowhood: therefore the Apostle foreseeing that this custome growing first of deuotion, would seeme in time to be obligatorie, in such sort, that many yong widowes more fraile then the elder, and forbearing marriage (rather to accommodat them selues to the custome and example of others, then of their owne deuotion) would commit scandale (as some already had donne) the Apostle, I say, to preuent this inconuenience, would haue it vnderstoode, that there was no obligation for widdowes to forbeare marriage, and to vow chastitie, & therefore he signified, that he would haue such of the younger sort, as were inclined, to marry and to take husbands.

1. Timot. 5.

1. Tim 5. S. Chrisost. in hunc locum.

28 This is conforme, to the doctrin, and sence of *S. Chrisostome*, who expounding the foresaid wordes of the Apostle: *Volo iuniores nubere. I will that the yonger marry Volo*, saith he, *quia & ipsæ volunt. I will, because they themselues will.* Meaning, that the Apostle did speake of no other, but such widdowes, as were themselues disposed to marry, whom he would not haue to be prohibited. Which also *S. Chrisostome* signifieth further afterwards, saying. *An vero matrimonium præcipit? Absit, sed neque prohibet. Doth he commaund mariage? God forbid, neither doth he prohibit it &c. Non quod adolescentulas viduas esse nolit, sed quod adulteras fieri vetet. Not that he would haue no young women to remaine widdowes, but because he forbiddeth them to be incontinent*, that is to say, he permitteth them to marry, for the remedie, and preuention of incontinencie. And the same is also taught expresselie by *S. Ambrose*, *S. Augustin*, and *S. Hierom*, who all affirme, that those wordes of the Apostle (*I will that the yonger marry*) were no precept, but a counsell, for the remedy of the infirmitie of the yonger sort.

S. Ambros. li. de viduis parum ab initio. S. August. li. de bono viduita. ca. 8. S. Hieron. ep. 11. ad Ageruchiã, statim ab initio. 1. Corint. 7.

29 Moreouer, it is also euident, that the Fathers doe vnderstand in like manner, that the same wordes of the Apostle did concerne those only, who were free from all vowes of continencie, as manifestlie appeareth, by that which they all say, concerning the like wordes of the same Apostle to the *Corinthians*, to wit, *those which doe not liue chast, let them marry, for it is better to marry then to be burnt*, which (as I haue amply shewed before) they seriouslie affirme, and teach, to belong only to those, who haue not bound themselues to continency by vow. Besides that, the Apostle should be contrarie to himselfe, if he should eyther commaund, or yet permit marriage, to those whome he reprehended, and iudged worthy of eternall damnation, for the only desire thereof. Thus much for *Caluins second glose.*

30 His third glose is, that the promise of continencie, which the yonge widdowes made, was not a vow to God, but only a bare promise to the church, to liue single, and chast, to the end they might serue with more freedome in the office of *Diaconissæ*: euen as, saith he, a woman that should desire to be entertained for a seruant, might promise not to marry, to the end shee might the more willingly be receiued, and serue with more libertie. But this euasion is as friuolous, as the former, both for that all the Fathers doe with one consent teach, that the yonge widowes vowed continencie to almightie God (as I haue shewed) and also for that the Apostle, himselfe signifieth the same sufficientlie, in that he giueth sentence of eternall damnation against them, for breaking their vow, as I haue proued, not only by

by the interpretation of the Fathers, but also by the vsuall sence, of the Latine, and Greeke text.

31 And whereas *Caluin* seeketh yet an other starting hole, saying that they were not reproued by *S. Paule*, for hauing a will to marry, but for their wanton, and lasciuious life (whereby they brooke, saith he, their faith or promise of chastitie, which they made to the church:) it is to be considered, that the Apostle condemned in them a present sinne, shewing them to be in state of damnation, at the same time that they had a will to marry. *Nubere volunt*, saith he, *habentes damnationem* &c. *They haue a will to marry, hauing damnation* &c. Which could not be if their marriage were lawfull, as *Caluin* houldeth it, seeing their lasciuious acts were past, and they desirous to amend the same by honest marriage (according to Caluins doctrin) which for that present (I meane for the state wherein they were then) deserued rather commendation, then condemnation, because they desired, and sought, a lawfull remedie, as *Caluin*, and his fellowes suppose: so that the Apostle should not in that case, haue had reason to condemne them for a present offence, as *Cardinall Bellarmin* noteth iudiciouslie, against this shift of *Caluin*.

1. Tim. 5.

Bellar. lo. cit.

32 Whereto I also add, that though it be graunted, that they brooke their vow by their wanton life, and therefore incurred damnation (as in deede they did) *Caluin* gaineth nothing therebie, seeing it doth not follow therefore, that vowes of chastitie, doe not bind in conscience vnder paine of eternall damnation. For though fornication, is of it selfe a deadlie sinne, yet when it is committed, with breach of vow, it is farr more greeueous, and deserueth farre greater damnation, as being both against the law, and against the vow, so that, a votarie committing fornication, deserueth damnation for twoo respects, the one for breaking the commaundement, and the other for breaking the vow.

33 And therefore, though the Apostle had not spoken, of the desire of marriage in the yong widowes, nor attributed their breach of vow thereto, as he doth expresselie, yet ascribing it (as *Caluin* saith he doth) to their vnchast, and lasciuious life, and adiudging them worthie of damnation, for breaking their vow therein, he sheweth euidentlie, that vowes of chastitie were vsuall in his time, and that they doe bind in conscience vnder paine of eternall damnation. Wherevppon I also inferre further, that forasmuch, as the younge widdowes promised to the church, not only to lyue chast, but also to liue single, and vnmarried (according to *Caluins* owne confession

fession in his last glose) it must needes follow, that they were condemned, aswell for their desire of marriage, as for their incontinencie, seeing that their first faith debarred them from both, and bound them, no lesse to remaine widdowes, then to liue chast.

34. Besides that, it seemeth a strange conceipt of *Caluin*, to distinguish betwixt a vow made to God, and a vow made to the church. Can ther any thing be donne to the church, pertaining to the seruice of God, that is not donne to God? For seeing the church is the misticall body of Christ, and he the head thereof, there must needes be an inseparable; and mutual communication betwixt the one, and the other. Therfore when *Saule* persecuted the church, our Sauiour said vnto him.
Act. 9. *Quid me persequeris? VVhy doost thou persecute me?* And to his disciples he
Luc. 10. said. *Qui vos audit, me audit, qui vos spernit, me spernit* &c. *He which heareth you, heareth me he which despiseth you, despiseth me.* And when *Ananias* and *Saphica* defrauded the church, in the price of their goods, S. *Peter* said, *they lyed to the holly Ghost.* Whereby it appeareth, that Christ
Act. 5. doth so communicat with his misticall body, and spouse the church, that what is donne to her, is donne to him, yea rather to him, then to her, he being the end, whereto shee, and all her actions are referred. Where vppon it followeth, that seeing by *Caluins* confession, the widowes promised not only chastitie, but also single life, to the church, they promised the same to Christ, rather then to the church, and therfore breaking their faith to the church, they brake it to Christ, and according to the sentence of the Apostle, they iustly incurred eternall damnation.

35 So that we see, these Archsectaries, can by no meanes auoid, or elude this euident testimonie of the Apostle, concerning the obligation of vowes of chast, and single life, whereby it may easely be iudged, that they and their fellowes, sought these cauilling shiftes, euen contrarie to their owne consciences, only to defend their licentious liues, and their breach of vowes, being most of them votaries, as *Lu-Luther, Bucer, Peter Martir, Pomeranus, Munsterus, Pellicanus, Musculus, Menius, Miconius, Ochinus*, and *Oecolampadius*, who were all of them Monkes, or Friers: and as for *Caluin*, and *Beza*, with diuers others of them, though they were not Monkes, Friers, or religious men, yet they were priestes, and consequentlie bound by their profession to chastitie: and therefore resoluinge themselues to breake their vowes, and to marry (as they all, or most of them did) it is no maruaile, though they busied their braines, and employed all their witts, to find out new gloses of the scriptures neuer heard, or dreamt of before,

thereby

thereby to cast a mist before the eyes of men, to obscure the truth, and shadowe their owne lasciuious impietie.

36 And out of the same fountaine, flowed their beastlie paradoxes, and detestable doctrin, whereof I haue spoken before in the 30. chapter, whereto may be added *Luthers* assertion concerning vowes, no lesse strange, and impious, then any of the former, affirming that a man can no more make a vow, that he will not haue the companie of a woman, and multiplie the earth, then that he will not be a man, *which saith he, were meere folly to vow*, and if it should be vowed, were of no validitie, wherefore he aduiseth, and counselleth his disciples, not to care, or be moued at all, *etiam si decies, iuraueris, voueris, mera ferrea, & adamantina pacta. Although thou hast*, saith he, *sworne tenne times, or vowed vowes of Iron, and made couenants of Diamond or adamant.*

Chap. 30. nu. 2. 3. 4. vsque ad nu. 20.

Luther de vita coniugali.

37 Behold the sound aduise of this holly doctor, how conforme it is to the doctrin of the Apostle, and of all the ancient Fathers, who teach as you haue heard, that the breach of vowes of chastitie, are damnable, and (as the Fathers say) *sacrilegious, and worse then adultery, or incest.* Where vppon I also inferr further, that seeing the euangelicall counsell of virginitie, and continencie, may not only be lawfullie vowed to God, but also being vowed, ought to be performed vppon paine of eternall damnation, it must needes follow, that the twoo other euangelicall counsells of pouerty, and obedience, being also most acceptable to God, and necessarie to the perfection of christian religion (as I haue amply proued) may in like manner be lawfullie vowed, and ought to be accomplished vppon the same penaltie. Where vppon also it yet followeth further, that the same vowes are not only lawfull, but also meritorious, for seeing the breach of them deserueth eternall damnation, as it appeareth in the Apostle, it cannot be denied, but that the obseruation thereof, meriteth eternall reward, for it pertaineth noe lesse to the iustice of God, to performe his promise, in the reward of good deedes, proceeding of his grace, then to punish euil: and such is his mercy, bounty, and liberalitie, that he inclineth farre more to reward, then to punish, promising reward for euery cupp of could water giuen in his name: how then will he reward those, who freely giue him the greatest good they haue, that is to say, their will and libertie, yea all they haue, by an irreuocable promise, couenant, and vow, making themselues a true Holocaust, or burnt Sacrifice, according to *S. Gregory*, who saith notablie thus. *Qui se per fidem &c. Those which by faith, doe vow themselues to God in holly*

S. Greg. ep. 20. in Ezechiel. Post medium.

Greg. ibid. Paulo post. Origin. super Numeros homi. 25. post mediū.

holly conuersation doe become, the Holocaust of God: and after a while. *Cum quis suum aliquid deo vouet* &c. *VVhen any man doth vow vnto God some part of that he hath, and not all, he is a sacrifice, but when he voweth to him, omne quod habet, omne quod sapit, all that he hath, all that he liueth, all that he knoweth, or vnderstandeth,* that is to say, he that giueth by vow to almightie God, all his wealth, his will, his vnderstanding, his iudgement, life, and all, *Holocaustum est,* saith S. *Gregory,* he is a *Holocaust, or burnt Sacrifice.*

38 And this doe the true religious performe, by the three vowes of *pouerty, chastity,* and *obedience.* For by the first, they irreuocablie giue to God, their wealth, and substance. By the second, their bodies. And by the third, their soules, not reseruing to them selues, so much as libertie of will, or iudgement, and consequentlie they doe, as it were sacrifice themselues, fully and wholy, and imitate our Sauiour Christ in great perfection, and therefore *Origen,* treating of diuers kindes of vowes, saith. *Semetipsum deo offerre* &c. *For a man to offer, or sacrifice himselfe to God, is more perfect, and eminent, then all other vowes, and he, that doth it, is the imitator of Christ.* Thus saith he. And S. *Augustin* maketh no doubt to affirme, that the Apostles bound themselues, to this imitation of Christ by vow, when they leaft all to follow, and obey him. *Dixerunt,* saith he, *potentes illi* &c. *Those mighty ones* (to wit the Apostles) said, *behould we haue forsaken all, and followed thee, hoc votum potentissimi vouerant* &c. *This vow those most potent, and mighty Apostles had vowed, but whence had they this* (that is to say, the grace to vow this) *but from him of whom it is said, that he giueth the vow, to the vower:* Thus saith S. *Augustin,* signifying notably by the example of the Apostles, as well the perfection of those, that bind themselues by vow, to the perfect imitation of Christ, as also that the same proceedeth from the speciall grace of God, *qui dat votum vouenti, who giues the vow to the vower,* and therefore is the only authour of all lawfull vowes, no lesse then of all other thinges that are acceptable to him.

S. Aug. li. 17. de ciuitate dei ca. 4. post medium.

39 No meruel then, that the vse of vowing the Euangelicall counsells, passed from the Apostles by their doctrin, and example, to other faithfull people in their time, as may appeare sufficientlie, not only by the vow of chastity, which the widowes made (as I haue declared alreadie) but also by the vow of pouerty, which the Fathers doe note, in those that sould their goods in the Apostles time to liue in common, namely in *Ananias,* and *Saphira,* whose fraude, and offence (for

Act. 5.

(for the which *S. Peter* punished them) did consist (as the Fathers vnderstand.) in breach of their vow, and therefore *S. Ciprian,* treating of the obligation to performe vowes made to God, alleadgeth the example of *Ananias* in the Acts of the Apostles. And *S. Chrisostome,* saith in the persone of *S. Peter, to Ananias. Quare hoc fecisti?* &c. *VVhy didest thou this? wouldest thou haue thy money? Thou shouldest haue had, or held it in the beginninge, before thou didest promise it, but now after thou hast consecrated it to God, thou hast committed a greater sacriledge,* &c. *It was lawfull for thee to hould thy owne goodes, therefore why hast thou made them holly, and after taken them.* Thus saith he. And *S. Hierome* in like sort, affirmeth, that *Ananias,* and *Saphira, were condemned, quia post votum obtulerunt, quasi sua* &c. *Because after their vow, they offred their goods, as though they had benne their owne, and not his, cui semel ea vouerant, to whome they had once vowed them. Also S. Basille,* S. *Augustin,* S. *Fulgentius,* S. *Gregorie, Oecumenius,* and S. *Beda* to omit others, doe teach the same expressélie.

S. Chrisost. ho. 12. in act in medio.

S. Hieron. ep. 8. ad Demetri. post medium.

S. Basill. ser. 1. de institut. monachorũ.

40 And as this custome of vowinge these Euangelicall concells seuerallie, was introduced in the Apostles time, approued, and authorised by them, and by their example: so also the vse of vowing the same iointlie in monasticall, or religious life, proceeded from the same ground, at the same time, as may appeare by that which I haue before declared, out of S. *Dionisius,* S. *Paules* disciple, who ascribeth the institution of monasticall disciplin, to the Apostles, and amongst other things which he relateth, concerning the profession of Monkes, he testifieth, that they made a solemne promise, and couenant before the aulter, to renounce the world, and to embrace the monasticall life, which (as I haue sufficientlie proued before) consisteth in the obseruation of the three Euangelicall counsells, of *pouerty chastity,* and *obedience.* And this publike, and solemne manner of monasticall profession by way of vow, hath benne continued in the church of God euer since: in respect whereof, it hath alwayes bene held vnlawfull, and damnable, for a professed religious man, not only to abandon his vocation, but also to haue the will, and determination to doe it, and therefore S. *Anthony* (as S. *Athanasius,* reporteth in his life) exhorting the Monks his brethren to perseuerance, compared those religious, that were weary of their profession, to *Lots* wife, who loking backwards, was turned in to an image of salt, and applied to them, the saying of our Sauiour. *Nemo ponit manum suam* &c. *No man that puts his hand to the plough, and looketh backwards, is fit for the kingdome of heauen. Respicere autem retrorsum,* saith he, *nihil aliud est* &c. *To looke*

S. Aug. ser. 25. de verb. Apostol.

S. Fulgent. ep. de debito coniugali c. 8

Oecumen. in hunc locum.

Arator li. 1. in act.

S. Athanas. in vita S. Antonij.

 backward

backward is nothing els, but to repent thee of that which thou hast begunne, and to tye, or entangle thy selfe againe with worldly desires. Thus saith *S. Athanasius*, or rather, both *S. Antony* and he, of the only desire to leaue a religious, or monasticall life, after it is once vndertaken, what then would they haue said of apostasie from the same?

41 *S. Basill*, who liued in the time of *S. Antony*, writing to a Monk that was fallen, putteth him in mind of his couenants made with God, *coram multis testibus, before many witnesses*: and in his rules of monasticall life, signifieth, that he which hauing vowed himselfe to God in religious professiõ, & passeth afterwards to any other state of life, *sacrilegij se scelere obstrinxit* &c. Is guilty of sacriledge, *because he hath*, saith he, *as it were stolne himselfe from God, to whome he had dedicated*, and *consecrated himselfe.* Thus saith *S. Basill.* Also S. *Augustin. Nemo*, saith he, *positus in Monasterio frater dicat* &c. *Let no brother, or religious man, that is in a monastery say, I will leaue, and forsake it, or that it is not to be thought that only those shalbe saued, who liue in monasteries, or that others which liue abroad, doe not pertaine to God, for to him, that should so say, it is to be answered. Illi non vouerunt, tu vouisti. They haue not vowed, but thou hast vowed.*

S. Basil. ep. 1. ad monachũ lapsum in fine.

Idem quæst. vel regula 14. fusius explicata.

S. August. in Psal. 75. ante finem.

42 Finallie *Iohannes Cassianus*, who wrote also a thousand twoo hundreth yeares agoe, treating of the perfection of religious men, and hauing said, that inestimable glory in heauen, is promised them for the obseruation of their rules, and most greueous paines, prepared for them, if they neglect them, concludeth. *Melius est enim* &c. *For it is better according to the sentence of the scripture, not to vow, then to vow, and not to performe it.* Thus saith he, whereto I might add diuers other testimonies of the Fathers of those times, if it were needefull, but herebie it sufficientlie appeareth, that such as vndertooke monasticall profession, in the primatiue church, tied themselues thereto by vow, no lesse then those of S. *Benedicts* order, which beganne in the next age after S. *Augustin*, and *Iohannes Cassianus*, to witt, about the yeare of our Lord, 500. from which time forward, I thinke our aduersaries make no doubt, but that the vse of vowes hath benne alwayes annexed, to the obseruation of the Euangelicall counsells in monasticall disciplin, as may appeare by the rules of S. *Benedict* still extant, both in writing, and in practise, amongst those of his holly order.

Circa an. 400.

Ioan. Cassian. de institutis renũciant. ca. 33.

Circa an. 500.

43 Seeing then I haue proued, that the Euangelicall counsells, haue benne practised vnder the obligation of vowes, euen from the time of the Apostles, and with their warrant, who seeth not the absurditie of

Luther, *Caluin*, and other of their crew, which teach, that we ought to vow nothing (especiallie for the seruice, and worshipp of God) but such thinges only as we are bound to doe by precept, as to keepe the commaundements, which euery christian man voweth in baptisme, though he be otherwaise bound thereto by precept? Whereas I haue shewed by the authoritie of Scriptures, Fathers, and the continuall practise of the Church, that chastitie, and single life (which is not commaunded in the Scriptures, but counselled) was vowed in the Apostles time, and throughout the primitiue Church, principallie for the worshipp and seruice of God.

Luther de vot. monast. Caluin li. 4. instit. ca. 13.

44 Besides that it is most manifest, that the vowes mentioned by me before out of the ould testament, were of thinges not commaunded, and *Moyses* himselfe speaking of the obligation of vowes in *Deuteronomy* saith. *Si nolueris polliceri, absque peccato eris. Yf thou wilt not promise thou shalt be without sinne*, that is to say, *thou shalt not be bound vnder paine of sinne, to doe that, which thou promisest*, which cannot be vnderstood of such thinges, as God hath commaunded, for they are to be performed vnder paine of sinne, whther they be vowed, or no.

Genes. 28. Leuit. 27. Numb. 6. & 30. Deuter. 12. & 23.

45 And no lesse euident is also the absurditie of *Peter Martyr*, who affirmeth, that the vse of vowes, belonged only to the ceremonies of the old law, whereof the contrarie appeareth most manifestlie, by all that which I haue proued in this chapter, out of the Scriptures, Fathers, & custome of the Church, which may be confirmed by the prophesie of *Isayas*, who foretould of the christians, that *colent eum in hostiis & muneribus, & vota vouebunt domino, & soluēt*. They shall worship *him in sacrifices, and giftes, and shall make vowes to our Lord, and performe them*. Which wordes, S. *Hierome*, & S. *Cyrill*, & others that comment vppon that place, doe expresselie expound of the christians, and is fulfilled by our sacrifice of the Masse, & all kind of religious vowes, vsed cōtinually in the church.

Petrus Mar. in li. de vot. & cælibat. contra Smitheum.

Isay. 19.

46 The like may be said of the vanitie, and absurditie of their obiections against our vowes. For what can there be said of any weight, or soliditie against such a manifest truth, grounded vppon such authoritye as I haue alleadged? This may appeare by their vaine, and friuolous cauills, absurdlie grounded vpon such places of scripture, as teach that our seruice to God, or good workes, ought to be volūtarie, or free, as when the psalmist saith. *Voluntàriè sacrificabo tibi. I will sacrifice to thee voluntary*. And that of the *Apostle*. *Ne veluti ex necessitate bonum tuum sit, sed voluntarium. That thy good deede may not be, as it were of necessitie, but voluntarie*, and such like: which signifie nothing els, but that

Psal. 53.

we should doe all our good workes (yea euen those, whereto we are bound eyther by precept, or vow) with a good will, and with alacritie and promptitude, for loue, and not for feare, with ioy, and mirth, and not with grudging, or heauines of hart, as the scripture testifieth of the chrildren of *Israell* saying. *Lætatus est populus cum vota sponte promitteret, quia corde toto offerebant ea domino. The people reioyced when they did of their owne free will promise, or make their vowes, because they offred them to their Lord with all their hartes.* Whereby yt appeareth, that the obligation that followeth of a vow, doth no more preiudicat the promptitude, & reddines in the execution, then doth the obligation of a precept, which though yt bindeth of necessity, yt may and ought to be freely, and promptly executed, and therefore though sacrifice was commaunded in the ould law, yet the psalmist said. *Voluntariè sacrificabo tibi. I will sacrifice voluntary vnto thee,* that ys to say, as freely and willingly, as though there were no necessity or commandement thereof at all, and the same ys also to be vnderstood of vowes.

1. Paralip. 29.

Psal. 53.

47 And no lesse vaine, and friuolous ys the argument, that they frame vppon their false conceit of christian libertie, which they say, ys impeached, and vterly ouerthrowne, by the obligation of vowes, and therefore they teach that Christ would haue all kindes and states of life, to be continually free for any man to choose, or leaue as he should thinke good. Whereas neuerthelesse they tye themselues to marriage, whereby they are no lesse restrayned from single life, then they should be debarred from marriage by a vow of chastity: and though they teach this freedome and Euangelicall liberty (as they call yt) when they impugne our vowes, yet at other times when they argue against our Euangelicall counsells, they hould, and teach, that nothing was leaft at our libertie, or indifferent, but that all thinges are eyther preciselie commaunded, or forbidden, wherein how they agree with themselues, I leaue it to the iudgement of others.

48 Finallie whereas they pretend such libertie of the ghospell, that they hold the obligation of vowes, to be no other then the seruitude of the law, from the which they say, Christ deliuered vs, it is to be vnderstood, that the true christian libertie, which we haue by the faith, and grace of Christ, is no other, but that wee are deliuered, first, frō the seruitude of sinne (*for liberati a peccato,* saith the Apostle, *serui facti estis iustitiæ, being deliuered from sinne, you are become the seruants or bondmen of righteousnes.*) Secondlie, we aree also freed from the manifould ceremonies of the ould law, which were but shadowes, and significa-

Rom 6.

tions

tions of those thinges, which wee now haue in veritie and truth. And lastlie, we are discharged of the feare and bondage of law, but not of the obligation of law, because wee doe by the helpe of charitie and grace, fulfill the commaundement of Gods law, willinglie and ioyfully, out of a filiall loue, and not for seruil feare, so that although wee are boundby the law, yet ar not, *sub lege, vnder the law*, & this is the true christian libertie, whereof the Apostle speaketh, as *S. Augustin* teacheth notablie, and this no more excludeth the obseruation of vowes, then the obligation of the tenne commaundements, whereto euerie christian man is bound, not with-standing anie libertie, or freedome from the law, that he may lawfullie pretend to haue from the merits of Christ.

49 Moreouer, the sectaries obiect particularlie against vowes of chastitie, that the Apostle haueing exhorted the *Corinthians* to virginitie, addeth. *Hoc ad vtilitatem vestram dico, not vt laqueum vobis inijciam. I say this for your profit, and not to intangle you, or to cast you into a snare*. By which words *Peter Martir* vnderstandeth, that vowes of chastitie are plainelie forbidden, as snares and intanglements of mens consciences: whereas the meaning of the Apostle is no other, but that he so exhorteth them to continencie, that he will not compell them vnto it, for so S. *Augustin* expoundeth it, saying. *Non vt laqueum vobis inijciam, id est non vt vos cogam, Not that I cast you into a snare*, that is to say, *not that I compell you*. And the like saith *S. Hierom* against *Iouinian*, and *Theodoretus*, *Theophilact*, and others, that haue writen commentaries vppon the same epistle, so that though the Apostle would not compell anie man, to bind himselfe by vow to chastitie, yet he leaft it to euerie mans election, vppon good, and mature deliberation, to bind himselfe if he were so disposed. This shall suffice touchinge the obiections of our aduersaries, against religious vowes. And what the Politikes obiect against the same, in regard of common welth, shal bee declared, and answered in the next Chapter.

1. Cor. 7

S. Aug. de bono. viduitat. cap. 5. S. Hierom. li. 1. contra Iouin. ante. medium Theodoret & Theophilac. in hunc locum.

Certaine obiections of the Politikes, out of the lawes of diuers Emperours and Kinges, against religious disciplin are ansuered, and the impietie of the said lawes is shewed, by the notable punishment of God vppon the lawe makers. VVith a breefe recapitulation, and conclusion of all the former chapters, concerning religious discipline.

CHAP 34.

Chap 34

1 It resteth now, good Reader, for the conclusion of that which I haue hetherto treated, concerning our euangelical perfection, and true imitation of Christ in religious disciplin, that I also cleare certaine other difficulties, proposed by the politikes against religious life, in regarde of common welth, which they suppose to be much preiudiced, not onlie by vowes of chastitie (whereby the increase, and multiplication of mankinde, they say is hindred) but also because the retired life of religious men, and spirituall occupations, debarre them from the temporal seruice of common wealth, in respect whereof, *Vitiza* king of *Spaine*, forced religious men and priestes to marrie, yea, and gaue them leaue to keepe concubins, for the increase of the common welth. And the emperour *Valens*, compelled monkes to serue in the warres, as I haue noted before. And *Mauritius* the emperour ordained, that no souldiar should enter into religion, except he were lame, and vnfit for the warres, or els had serued out the time discribed by the law. And *Isacius Comnenus* emperour of *Constantinople*, confiscated all the lands and goods of monasteries, allowinge them certaine stipends. Finally the emperour *Nicephorus Phocas*, not onlie pilled and spoyled monasteries, but also made a law, that noe more religious houses or monasteries should be built, prouiding thereby verie prudentlie (as these men thinke) for the seruice, defence, and benefit of the common wealth.

Baron. an. 701. Vasæus. in Chron, an 762. Baron. an. 373. Baron. an 1057. Baron. an. 969. Nicetas Choniates Annal. in Manuele. Comneno.

2 Here then it is to be considered, that the true ground of this obiection, can be no other but meere Athisme, denying the prouidence of God, in the affaires of men, and gouermente of common wealth. For no man who firmelie beleeueth, that common wealths, and princes states, doe principallie depend vppon the will, and prouidence of God, can imagin that those thinges which are most pleasant to God, and proceede from his holie inspiration (as I haue proued virginitie and religious life, to doe) can be in anie case hurtfull to common wealth. Therfore those which make anie doubt of this point, must for their better satisfaction, call to mind, that which I haue sufficientlie shewed, partlie in the first part of this treatise, and partlie in this, to witt, that almighty God is he, as the prophet saith, *that changeth times and ages, and translateth, constituteth and ordaineth kingdomes at his pleasure*: which I haue amplie proued, aswell by the euident successe of *Daniels* prophesies, concerning the foure Empyres, as also by verie manie examples of Gods instice

Chap. 17. num. 1. 2. 3. & sequent.

Chap. 18. 19. 21. & 22. per totum.

iustice, executed vppon princes and their states for sinne, besides diuers other proofes of Gods prouidence, in the conduct of mens affaires, both priuat, and publike: whereto is also to be added, the consideration of that which I haue also treated in this second part, concerning the end and cheefe good of common welth, which I haue proued to consist in mans vnion with God, by the meanes of religion.

3 This being so, were it not absurd to thinke, that religious life, which doth speciallie vnite man with God, can be damageable to man, or common wealth, which depend on the will and prouidence of God? I haue declared before, that religious perfection is so contrarie to mās sensual and corrupt nature, that it is not possible, that anie man, and much more manie men, should arriue vnto it, without Gods special vocation, and assistance. Can therefore anie man with reason imagin, that God should be so contrarie to himselfe, as hauing a care to maintaine and conserue common wealths, hee would cause and moue men to religious life, if the same were hurtfull and preiudiciall to common wealth? This cannot be imagined of the goodnes of almightie God, of whome it were extreame folly, and impietie to thinke, that he will suffer that state to perish, which florisheth in perfection of christian religion, and is thereby most acceptable, and deare vnto him, and most vnited with him,

4 Yea, but say the Pollitikes, if all men should be religious, how could common welth stand? Whereto I answer with the common prouerbe. *If the sky fall we shal ketch larkes.* As though there were anie danger, that either all men, or most men, will be religious? Therefore *S. Hierom* said wel to *Iouinian. Noli metuere ne omnes virgines fiant, difficilis res est virginitas, & idio rara, quia difficilis. Feare not that all will be virgins, or liue continent, virginitie is a hard and difficult thinge, and therefore rare because it is difficult.* And *S. Ambrose* saith to the same purpose: *Nonullos dixisse audiui &c. I haue heard manie say, that by religious life, the world goeth to wrack, mankind decaieth, and mariage is ouerthrowne. But I aske, who euer sought for a wife and could find none?* And againe, *if anie man,* saith he, *doth thinke that mankind is deminished by the consecration, or profession of virgins, let him consider, that where there are few virgins, there are also few men, and where there is more frequent profession of virginitie, there is also great number of men.* Thus saith these learned & holie Fathers, taxing the nedlesse feare, & idle doubts, that worldlinges cast of the decay of the world by religious perfectiō, as though almightie God, who both gouerneth the whole world by his prouidence, and moueth men to religious life, could not, or would not, out of his infinit bountie and goodnes, so accommodate his inspi-

S. Hieron cōtra Iouin. li. 1. post medium.

S. Ambros. li. 3 de virgin. ante medium.

Idem ibid.

tions, to the temporall necessitie of euery common welth, that the same shalbe conserued, and not endammaged thereby, and therefore we may well say with the prophet. *Trepidauerunt timore vbi non*
Psal. 13. *erat timor. They trembled for feare, where there was no cause of feare,* where as on the other side, it may be feared, or rather with great reason affirmed, that common welth should receiue farre more dammage, by the decay of religious continencie, then by the maintenaunce, and conseruation thereof.

5 For whatsoeuer may be thought, of countries newly inhabited, or falne to vtter desolation (where there can be no feare of any immoderat encrease of people for some time) yet in countries already peopled (as all christian countries are) it is euident, that the numerositie of people, if it grow to excesse, is dāgerous to the common welth, seeing that thereof may follow, extreame pouerty in very many, and consequently
2. Politico. c. 7. theftes, & robberies, yea seditions, & rebellions, which not only *Aristotle*, but also experience teacheth, to be many times effects of pouertie.

6 And if we consider, what hath followed in our owne country, of the free libertie of marriage in all men without exception, since the suppression of catholike religion, we shall haue litle cause to thinke, that the continencie of religious, and ecclesiasticall men, was euer preiudicial to our common welth, which appeareth sufficiently by the innumerable multitud of rogues, vagabounds, & idle persons, swarming euery where in *England*, more then euer, to the great detriment of the weale publike, in so much that the gallowes deuowreth more in these our dayes, about *London* only, then it did in times past, throughout all *England*: besids the multituds of poore people, that load, & ouerchardge euery parish, not withstanding the ordinary remedy of euacuation cōtinuallie vsed, in sending out infinit numbers to the warres of *Fraunce, Ireland, Holland,* and voyages by sea, without the which (and the great mortalitie, that hath benne, many times by plauges) it may well be supposed, that the encrease of our people, would haue benne insupportable, and farre exceeded the habilitie of our territorie, to maintaine them.

7 This was very well considered (as it seemeth) by a Burges of the Parliament, in the last Queenes time, who made a motion to the lower house (as I haue hearde) that it might bee enacted (that all the ministers, throughout *England*, shoulde either bee forced to liue single, and continent, or els be made Eunuchs, for that being married, as they are, and not hauing any other maintenaunce, then their benefices

fices (which cannot descend to their children, nor be leaft to their wiues) twoo great inconueniences, he said, must needes follow thereon, the one, that they cannot helpe to releeue the poore of the parish (as the curats did in Catholike times, and the monasteries much more) and the other that they must needes leaue beehind them, a race of rogues, and beggars, to be susteined by their parishes, to the great greauaunce thereof, and the generall oppression of the common welth.

8 And although I doe not allow, both the partes of this twoofould proposition, I meane the latter, yet I must needes say, that he had great reason in the former, to witt, that it were good, and necessarie for the common welth, that ministers should be bound to liue single, and continent for the same reasons that he yealded, which were so pregnant, and euident, that they cannot be denied. Where vppon it also followeth, that the chast and continent life of religious men, neither was in times past, nor could be, any way hurtfull to the common welth, but rather very behoofefull, and profitable thereto, for that the encrease of the people was thereby kept in such moderation, as it neither was redoundant to the surchargde, and oppression of the common welth, nor yet defectiue for the due defence thereof, as sufficientlie appeared in all occasions, aswell of forraine, as ciuil warres, wherebie it is also euident, how vaine, and friuolous is the doubt, mentioned in the obiection of the wante of souldiars, supposed to ensue of religious life.

9 To this purpose it is also to be considered, that the strẽgth of a country or an army, consisteth not so much in multitudes of men, as in a competent number well disciplined, for did not *Alexander* the great, ouerthrow *sixe hundreth thousand* men of *Darius*, yea, and conquer a great part of the world, with lesse then forty thousand men? Did not also the Romans propagate, and enlarge their empyre, rather by militarie discipline, then by number of souldiears? And who knoweth not, if he be a soldiear, that when twoo armies meete, of a hundred thousand men a peece, that the battaile is commonlie wonne or lost, before fortie thousand be slaine on both parties? And that great armies, are many times dissipated and defeated, rather by some stratageme, or inuention of warre, then ether by the force, or multitude of men? whereof proofe hath bene made in sondrie battailes, wherein it hath bene seene, that a handfull of men, in comparison, haue put to flight, infinit thousandes. Al which considered, it must needes be graunted, that the good successe thereof, could not so much depend vpon the

multitudes of people, as on Gods benediction, and assistaunce, for *nisi Dominus custodierit ciuitatem* &c. *Except our Lord doe keepe the citty, they labour in vaine, that defend it.* And as the valiant *Iudas Machabeus* said. *Non in multitudine exercitus victoria belli, sed de cælo fortitudo est. The victory in warre, doth not consist in the multitude, or greatenes of the army, but all fortitude, and strenght is from heauen.* Where vppon it followeth, that the more that any common welth is vnited with God, by religious perfection, the more victorious, it shalbe in warre, the more prosperous in peace, and the more happy in all occasions.

Machaba. li. 1. ca. 3.

10 Furthermore it is to be considered, that religious men, are not so wholy exempt from armes, but that they may, and ought in extremities, to vse them for the necessarie defence, of the citty, or country where they dwell, as it is manifest by the practise of the church, aswell in former times, as in this. *S. Gregory* the greate, gaue order to the bishopps of *Italy*, in time of the *Lumbards* warres, aboue a *thousand* yeares agoe, to commaund all ecclesiasticall persons, to assist in defence of their citties, and the like was ordained by the late Popes, in the time of the league in *Fraunce*, wherein some cleargie men did notable feates of armes, and amongst others, a *Iesuit* saued the citty of *Paris* from surprise, when it was one night assailed on that side where they kept their watch, neere to their owne colledge. So that as in cases of necessitie, they are not debarred from the vse of temporall armes, so also, at other times they vse the spirituall, for the defence, and prosperitie of the common wealth, appeasing with their penaunce, and prayers the wrath of God, which otherwise might destroy, or seuerelie punish the same, for the sinnes of men.

S. Greg. li. 7. Ep. 20. Indict. 1. Baron. an. 598.

11 Here vppon *S. Bernard* saith of religious men, that *ipsi pro toto ecclesiæ corpore viz. tam viuis, quam mortuis, orare sunt constituti.* They are ordained to pray, for the whole body of the church, as well the liuing, as the dead.

S. Bern. ser. breues. Ser. 63.

12 The truth of this may appeare, by many notable examples, which occurre in all histories, and times, of singular benefits donne to citties, countries, princes, and their states, by the merits and prayers of religious men, whereof I will alleadge some in diuers ages.

13 *S. Hilarion*, the holly Abbot, disciple to *S. Antony*, obtained of almighty God, abundaunce of raine, for the remedie of an extreame drought, which followed presentlie vppon *S. Antonies* death, and continued for *three* yeares together, in the countries adioining to the deserts of *Egipt*, where also infinit number of people, as S. *Hierome* witnesseth, being stroken, or bitten by venemous serpents, were cured by him

Obiit an. 372.

S. Hieron. in vita S. Hilarionis aliquantulum post medium.

him with holly oile, which he gaue them to apply to their woundes.

14 He deliuered also the citty of *Epidaurus*, in *Dalmatia*, from a monstrous serpent called *Boa*, so huge, that he deuoured, and swallowed vp both men, and beastes, which he drew to him, with the violent force of his breath, but the holly man hauing caused a great pile, and heape of woode to be laid together, forced the serpent by his prayers, to come foorth in presence of the people, and to clime vppon it, and to remaine there vntill fire was put vnder him, and he burned. *Idem. ibid. circa finem.*

15 Also the same citty of *Epidaurus*, being in extreame danger of a deluge, by a terrible inundation of the sea, was most miraculouslie deliuered by him. For the people, seeing the sea swell in such horrible manner, that mountaines of waues came rowling vppon the citty, they had such a confidence in his prayers, that they tooke him by force, and sett him on the shore, and after that he had made the signe of the crosse thrise in the sand, and stretched out his hands against the waues, *it is incredible*, saith *S. Hierome*, *to what a height the sea swelled*, and standing vp before him, and as it were raging for the opposition which he made against it, vntill at lenght it retired it selfe. *Hoc* (saith he) *Epidaurus, & omnis illa regio*, &c. *This the citty of Epidaurus, and all the country doth testifie vntill this day, and the mothers doe teach it to their children, to the end, it may be recommended to the memory of all posterity.* Thus writeth S. *Hierome*, who liued in the same age, and was borne in the same country of *Dalmatia*, where this happened.

16 The worthy and religious Emperour *Theodosius*, surnamed the *Great*, obtained a notable, and miraculous victorie, against his enimies, by the prayers and merits of a holly Monk, called *Senuphius*, whose staffe and scapular, he carried himselfe in the battaile, and so notorious was the miracle, that there was a feast, solemnized yearely, a long time after in *Alexandria*, in memorie of it. Besides that, there was also a statua, or image of *Theodosius* erected there, expressing the manner how he carried the staffe of *Senuphius* in his hand, and his scapular vppon his head in the battaile. *Glicas Anal. par. 4. Metaphrastes die 31. Ianuarij. Baron. an. 389.*

17 *Mascezil* hauing but *fiue thousand* men, and being accompanied, and assisted by the prayers of the holly Monks of the Iland of *Capraria*, ouerthrew his brother *Gildo*, the Tyrant of *Africk*, who had in his army, *seauenty thousand* souldiars, but afterwards forsaking the company, and counsell of those holly men, by whose meanes he had obtained that notable victorie, he fell to ruine, as testifieth *Orosius*, who liued in the same age. *An. 398. Orosius li. 7. c. 36. Baron. an. 398.*

18 a *Kericus*, or *Cipriacus*, a captaine of *Iustinian* the Emperour, obtai- *a An. 527. Ciril. in vita B. Theodos. To. 7. an. 527.*

ned a great victory againſt the *Perſians*, by the praiers and miraculous aſſiſtance, of S. *Theodoſius* the Abbot, as witneſſeth S. *Ciril* in the life of *S.Theodoſius*.

b *S.Greg. li. 6.ep.23. indict.15.* Baron. an. 596.

19 S.b *Gregory*, attributeth the deliuerie of *Rome*, from the ſeige & ſack of the *Lumbards*, to the holie life, merits, & interceſſion *of three thouſand* religious women, which were then maintained in the cittie,

c *Obijt.an. 613. Surius.To 2. Baron. an. 603.*

20 S. c *Theodorus Sicæota* an abbot, deliuered the people of *Hieruſaleme*, from a great drought by his praiers, & the country of *Caria*, from the inundation of the riuer *Copas*, by ſetting in the ſhoare a croſſe, which afterwardes it neuer paſſed.

d *An.982. Baron. eodẽ. an. & an. 961.To.10.*

21 S.d *Nicon* hauing liued *twelue* years in religion, & being then ſent by his abbot to conuert nations, deliuered the cittie of *Lacedæmon*, from a great plague by his praiers.

e *Circa an. 113.Surius li. 2. ca. 7. To. 4.& in vita S. Bernar. l. 2. c. 7.*

22 Duke e *Ranulph*, hauing obtained a great victorie againſt *Roger* king of *Sicily*, attributed it whollie to the merits and praiers of S.*Bernard* then liuing, and therefore meeting with a monke of his order, as he was in purſuit of his enemies, he fell at his feete.

f *Obiit an. 1189.Sur.to. 6.ca.7.invita S. Hugonis.*

23 *Henrie* f the ſecond, king of *England*, aſcribeth his eſcape from drowning in the ſea, to the merits and praiers of *S.Hugh*, towhome he recommended himſelfe, though he was then liuing, and prior of the *Carthuſians*, but afterwardes biſhop of *Lincolne*.

g *Obiit an. 1226. Sur. To.5. in vita S. Fran.*

24 *S.g Frauncis*, deliuered the cittie of *Aretium*, from a perillous ſedition, by commaunding the diuels, which cauſed it, to depart from thence, as witneſſeth *S.Bonauenture* in the life of *S.Francis*.

h *Obiit an. 1153. S. Antonin.inhiſt. par.3.tit.24. ca.6.Sur.12. Auguſt.*

25 Alſo about the ſame time, *S.*h *Clare* the holie virgin, deliuerd the cittie of *Aſſiſio*, from the ſack and ſpoyle, of a great armie of the Emperour *Frederick Barbaroſſa*, conducted by *Vitalis de Auerſa*, who had ſworne, that hee would neuer, raiſe his ſeige, vntill hee had taken it, and when it was brought to ſuch extremitie, that it could no longer reſiſt the enemie, S. *Clare* being then prioreſſe of a monaſterie there, aſſembled all her religious ſiſters, and cauſed them to ioyne with her in extraordinarie praier and penance, and ſo acceptable were their hollie indeuours to almightie God, that the verie next night, the armie of *Vitalis* was ſuddenlie diſſolued, and hee forced to depart thence.

i *Obiit an. 1292. Surius To. 4. 7. Auguſti.*

26 S.i *Albertus* a *Carmelit* Frier, miraculouſlie deliuered *Meſſina*, ſtronglie beſeiged by *Roger* king of *Naples*, from an extreame, and remediles famin, by three ſhipps furniſhed with prouiſion, which vppon a ſudden appeared in the hauen, and could not by anie human meanes arriue thither, which benifit the king, and people of *Meſſina*, attributed

to

the merits and prayers of *S. Albertus.*

27 k *S. Vincentius Ferrerius*, of *S. Dominicks* order, droue away a horrible storme in *Catalunia*, with the signe of the crosse, obtained raine in an extreame drought in *Carcassona* in *Fraunce*: and with holly water, and singing holy himmes, destroyed innumerable vermin, which wasted and ruined the fieldes, and vine yards, at *Murisia* in *Spaine*.

k *Obiit an.* 1418. *Petrus Ransanus in vita S. Vincentij li.* 3.

l *Platus de bono status religio. l.* 2. *c.* 30.

28 Many more examples might be added in this kind, of temporall blessinges, bestowed by almightie God vppon countries, and states, through the merits, & intercession of religious men, which I willingly pretermit, to say somewhat of farre greater benefits, I meane spirituall, and such as are most notorious, and euident to the world, to wit, the conuersion of nations to the christian faith, by the holly labours of religious men, which I will breefelie touch, for the satisfaction of the vnlearned, who doe not vnderstand the latine tongue, for that the learned, either are not ignorant of it, or at least may see it amply laid downe, by l Father *Platus* of the societie of *Iesus* in his booke, *de bono status religiosi*, and by *Bozius*, de signis ecclesiæ.

l *P. Platus de bono stat. religiosi li.* 2. *ca.* 30. *Bozius de sig. Eccle. li.* 4. *sig.* 6.

29 m *S. Remigius*, who was first a Monke from his childhood, and after bishop of *Rhemes* in *Fraunce*, conuerted king *Clodoue*, and all the French nation, from Paganisme to the faith of Christ, about the yeare of our Lord, *fiue hundreth*, and *thirtie*, and about the same time, or within *tenne* yeares after, n *S. Martin*, first a Monk, and after bishop, conuerted the *Sueuians*, from the *Arrian* heresie, to the Catholike faith.

m *Baro. an.* 499.

n *Baro. an.* 560.

30 o *S. Augustin*, with *Foure* other religious men, sent by *S. Gregory* the Pope (who was also religious, before he was Pope) conuerted king *Ethelbert* in *England*, and his subiects in *Kent*, to the Christian faith. And not long after, *Lambert* p of *Liege*, a religious man, conuerted also a part of *Germany*.

o *Baro. an.* 596.

p *Platus vbi supra.*

31 q *S. VVilfrid*, *S. VVillibrod*, *S. Swibert*, and *S. Boniface*, all of them english men, and religious by profession, though afterwards bishops, sowed the holy seede of christian religion, in the higher and lower *Germanie*, as *S. VVilfrid* first, and after *S. VVillibrod in Holland*, and *Friseland*, *S. Guibert* in *Saxony*, *S. Boniface* in *Thuringia*, *Hassia*, and in diuers other partes of *Germany*, in so much that he is euen vntill this day, accounted by the *Germans* their Apostle, being made bishop of *Mentz*, by Pope *Gregorie* the second, and afterwards martyred.

q *Ibidem & Bozius vbi supra. An.* 683. *Baro. an.* 723.

32 *Villeardus*, r *Ludgerus*, and *Ansgarius*, all three religious in *Fraunce*, conuerted also an infinit number of Infidells, to the christian faith,

r *P. Platus vbi supra.*

Circa an. 800. faith, the twoo first in *Franconia* in *Germany*, the third in *Denmarke*, *Suethland*, *Gothland*, and *Grouland*, and an other religious man, called ſ *Steuen*, succeding *Anſgarius*, in his labours in *Suethland*, and the countries adioining, conuerted all the prouince of *Helinga*, though he was martired in the end.

ſ *Bozius vbi ſupra.*

t *P. Plat. ibid.* Circa. an. 970.

33 *Albus* t the Abbot of *Fleuri* in *Fraunce*, was alſo martired in preaching the faith of Chriſt to the *Gaſcons*, after that he had conuerted very many of them.

u *Circa an. 980. Idem ibid. Cromer. li. 8. vide Bozium vbi ſupra.*

34 *Adalbertus* u firſt biſhop of *Prague*, and afterwards a profeſſed Monke of S. *Benits* order, in the monaſterie of *Caßinum* in *Italy*, went together with his brother *Gaudentius* (who was alſo a monke) into *Panonia*, now called *Hungary*, and brought all that nation (then moſt barbarous) to the fould of Chriſts church, and from thence went to preach to the *Sarmatians*, *Rußians*, *Lituanians*, *Moſcouits*, *Prußians*, and ſpeciallie to the *Polonians*, whoſe king *Boleſlaus* they made chriſtian; though afterwards, *Adalbertus* was martired in *Prußia*.

x *Circa an. 1025. Platus li. 2. c. 30.*

35 *Bruno*, x ſonne to *Lotarius* duke of *Saxony*, profeſſing religion in *Rome*, was ſent by Pope *Iohn*, the *Nineteenth* of that name, into *Rußia*, where hauing gained many to the chriſtian faith, he was crowned with martirdome: though not lõg after, an other religious man called *Bonifacius*, diſciple of S. *Romoaldus*, conuerted the king of *Rußia*, and all that nation, excepting only the kinges brother, who cauſed the ſaid *Bonifacius* to be cruellie murthered, or rather martyred..

y *Circa an. 1125. Idem ibid.*

36 *Otho*, y being ſent by Pope *Calixtus* the *ſecond*, from a monaſterie in *Germany* (where he profeſſed religious life) into *Pomerania*, baptized *Warceſlaus* the prince thereof, and his ſubiects. And within a while after, an other religious man, called *Vicelinus*, went with *foure* companions from *Fraunce*, to preach the chriſtian faith to the *Vandals*, whome after thirty yeares continuall labour, they conuerted, and founded amoungſt them many notable monaſteries.

z *An. 1245. Ibidem.*

37 Alſo in the age following the holly orders of z S. *Fruncis*, and S. *Dominicke*, being inſtituted, Pope *Innocentius* the *fourth*, ſent certaine *Franciſcans*, into ſome parte of *Tartary*, where they planted the chriſtian faith, and after ſome yeares, built many churches, and monaſteries there.

Circa an. Do. 1247. Ibidem.

38 About the ſame time, *Aſcelinus* a *Dominican*, was alſo employed with others of his order, by the ſaid Pope *Innocentius*, in the conuerſion of the *Tartars*, though with no other fruite at the firſt, but their owne meritorious labours, yet the miſſion being afterwards continued in thoſe partes, an infinit number of people was conuerted, and chriſtened

ſtened, amongſt whom no light nor knowledge of Chriſt had bene before, and that with ſo great fruite, as it is written, that the ſoules conuerted by them to the faith, could not be numbred, eſpeciallie amongſt the *Cumans*, wherupō the ſuperior there, writing to the general (which letters are yet extant) declareth, that many thouſands of men, not only of the comon people, but alſo of the nobilitie, receiued Baptiſme.

39 In the age enſuing, to witt the yeare of our Lord *a thouſand three* *An.* 1341.
hundred forty one, other miſſions were made of the *Franciſcans*, into thoſe
partes, by Pope *Benedict* the tenth, who ſent twoo of that order, as his
Apoſtolicall legats, to the Emperour of *Tartary*, with whoſe licence,
they greately propagated the chriſtian faith in thoſe countries, & about
the ſame time, a great learned man of the ſame order, called *Gonſalus*
Sauratus, was ſent into *Armenia*, as alſo an other called *Paſchalis* in to *Me-* *Platus ibid.*
dia, and *Gentilis* into *Perſia*, where they laboured many yeares, and wann
many ſoules to God, though not with ſuch publike, and general fruite,
as in other partes.

40 About theſe times alſo, an other *Franciſcan*, called *Odoricus Foroliuien-* *Circa an.*
ſis, being ſent into the Eaſt, & South partes, amongſt the Infidels, bapti- 1370.
zed *twenty thouſand* ſoules. *Ibidem.*

41 Alſo the king of *Hungary*, hauing ſubdued certaine nations of the
Infidels, adioyning *eight Frãciſcãs*, were ſent vnto him at his requeſt, & in
a few dayes, cõuerted *two hundreth thouſand* to the faith of Chriſt, where
vpon the ſaid king, ſent for *two thouſand* more of the ſame order, & the *Ibidem.*
general that then was, wrote publike letters (which are yet extant) to al
his order, encouraging them to vndertake that glorious enterpriſe.

42 In the next age, to witt, about the yeare of our Lord, *a thouſand* *Circa an.*
foure hundred and fiftie, *Iohannes Capiſtranus* a *Franciſcan*, in one voyage 1450.
which he made amongeſt the Infidells, baptized 12000. and reconciled *Ibidem.*
alſo many ſchiſmatikes vnto the church, in the ſame iourney.

43 Afterwards in the ſame age, the *Franciſcans*, not only aſſiſted *Chri-*
ſtophorus Columbus, in his ſuite to *Ferdinand*, the Catholike kinge of Spaine, by whoſe meanes he was ſent in the diſcouery of the weſt *Indiæ*, *An.* 1493.
but alſo ſome of the ſame order, preſentlie went thither themſelues, to preach the chriſtian faith. And about the ſame time, a way being alſo opened in to the eaſt *Indiæ*, by *Vaſco Gama*, eight of the ſame order, men excelling in learning and pietie, were ſent thither, who multiplied their owne order there in ſuch ſort, that their Couents were diſtributed into *thirteene* prouinces.

44 About the ſame time, to wit, the yeare of our Lord, *a thouſand fiue* *An.* 1500.
hundreth, the *Dominicãs* were alſo employed into thoſe countries, & after *Ibidem.*

them the *Augustins*, where they haue had euer since a glorious haruest, with great fruite and profitt of soules, and amplification of the christian religion.

An.1540. Ibidem. Bozius vbi supra.an. 1541. Horatius Tursellinus in vita B. Xaueriij li.1. ca.13. d *Chap. 27. Nu. 37. Obiit an. 1552.*

45 Lastly the *society of Iesus*, being instituted about the yeare of our Lord, *one thousand fiue hundreth, and fortie*, was sent shortly after to the East, and West *India*, where they gained infinit soules to God, and especially in the *East*, whither they went in the yeare, *a thousand, fiue hundreth, forty and one*, vnder the conduict of the famous, and holly Father *B. Francisco Zauerio*, of whom I haue spoken d before, as also of his glorious labours in spreading the ghospell, and faith of Christ in *Capo de Camorin* (where he built aboue *forty* churches) in *Mazane* (where he baptized two kinges, and a great number of their subiects) in *Malaca*, in the Ilandes of *Molucche* and *Moro*, and lastly in *Giapone*, in all which places, he exceedinglie dilated, and propagated the christian faith, which hath also benne much encreased there, and daily is, by the Fathers of the same societie, especiallie in the threescore kingdomes of *Giapone*, where the haruest, and labour, hath hetherto benne only theirs. Whereto I may also add, for Gods greater glory, that whereas it seemed in times past, that there was no hope of accesse or possible meanes, for the preaching of the christian faith, in the ample and rich kingdome of *China* (by reason of certaine penall, and capitall lawes, forbidding the entraunce thereof to all strangers) the Fathers of the societie, haue neuertheles, not only opened the passage thither, but also planted themselues in diuers partes thereof, and in the principal cittie called *Pachin*, where the kinges court resideth, where they haue also by his licence erected a colledge, as also many more in diuers other parts of his dominions.

S. Chrisost. hom. 56. ad populum antiochen. de monachor. vita. Euseb.li.1.de demonstra. ca.8.

46 Thus then thou seest, good Reader, how inestimable is the benefit, that the whole world hath receiued by religious men, no lesse in this very age, then in former times, seeing that they haue benne for so many hundreth of yeares, and still are, the speciall instruments, and meanes, to promulgate the law, and faith of Christ to the world, for the saluation of man: wherebie it well appeareth, how worthilie *S. Chrisostome* calleth them. *Luminaria mundi. The lights of the world.* And how truly also *Eusebius* saith, that they are consecrated to God. *Pro vniuerso genere.* For all mankind.

47 And therefore I cannot omit here by the way, to desire thee to reflect some what serioustlie vppon this point, and well to ponder twoo thinges. The one, what an euident testimonie this is, not only of the great worth, and merit of religious profession, but also of the veritie

of Catholike religion, which admiteth and teacheth it, seeing that there redoundeth thereof, so great glory to almightie God, and such notable fruit to the whole world, as hath here benne declared.

48 The other is, to consider, what benefit the world hath reaped, or may reape, by our aduersartes in this kind, I meane what nations they haue conuerted from Infidelitie, to the faith of Christ, or what endeuours, or yet good will, they haue shewed thereto, yea, or how it can stand with their profession to doe it, seeing they haue no exercise of the Euangelicall counsells (to wit of voluntarie pouertie, chastitie, and abnegation of themselues) but reiect them, partly as superstitious, temerarious, and a tempting of God, and partly as impossible (as I haue signified before) wherebie they vtterlie exclude themselues, from all practise of Apostolicall preachinge, for the conuersion of Infidells.

49 For he that is charged, and burdened with wife and children, and will be sure of his, and their prouision, before he stir his foote, how can he vndertake such long and dangerous voyages, and wholy depend vpon gods prouidence, as the Apostles did, in forsaking all to followe him, and as our religious still doe, and all others must doe, who meane to vndertake that heroicall labour?

50 This certainly is the woorke of God in ours, & performed by him in most strange and admirable manner, that is to say, to confounde the stronge by the weake, and to reduce all the strenght, power, and wisedome of the world, to his subiection, and obedience, not by force of armes, and powerfull meanes, but by infirmitie, and supposed folly, I meane by such instruments, and ministers, as being feble, weake, and simple in the sight of men, and yet practising the perfection of that which they preached, should not only perswade men the possibilitie of his law, but also induce them to the obedience of it by their example. For otherwaise, who would not haue expected, that those which preached, this strange, and rigorous law, should first practise it themselues? Can he be fitt to perswade men to contemne riches, who walloweth in wealth, and will himselfe endure no want? And he that cannot liue without a wife, and pampereth himselfe in ease, and pleasure, can he induce men to represse concupiscence, or *to gueld themselues*, as our Sauiour, counselled, for the kingdome of heauen, or to mortifie their owne passions, and affections for the loue of God? Would not euery man deride such a preacher, and bid him first practise his owne doctrin, and then preach it to others? And therefore I say, our Sauiour ordaining the publication of his law throughout the world, both practised, and taught the obseruation of the Euangelicall counsells, as

a ſpecial meanes to effect, and accompliſh it: whereof we haue alſo hitherto ſeene the admirable effect and experience, in the conuerſion of all nations, to the christian faith, by the Apoſtles, their diſciples, and laſtly by religious men, all of them obſeruinge the Euangelical counſells. Where vppon I conclude, that our aduerſaries, hauing no practiſe thereof at all, can neither conuert Infidells in forreine nations, or yet arriue to any perfection of vertue at home, and much leſſe induce others thereto, either by their example or inſtruction, as shall further appeare in the next chapter.

51 But to returne to our queſtion, concerning the notable fruite of religious perfection in common welth, what greater teſtimonie can be giuen thereof, then that the moſt prudent, valiant, and vertuous Emperours, Kinges, and Princes that euer were (whom it behoued to haue care, as well of their ſtate, as of religion) haue alwayes ſo greatly reuerenced, religious perſons, and ſo highly reſpected them for their holy merits?

*Bar.an.*388. *Glicas Anal.par.*4. *Metaphras. die* 31. *Ian. Baron. an.* 602.

52 This is manifeſt in *Theodoſius* the great, who laboured very much to haue *Senuphius*, a holly Monke, preſent with him in the battaile, which he was to fight with *Maximus* the Tyrant, for the great confidence he had in his prayers, and obteined a miraculous victory, by hauing only his ſtaffe, and his ſcapular, as I haue declared before. *Mauritius* the Emperour, being in diſtreſſe, and affliction of mind, wrote to all the monaſteries in the Eaſt part, as farre as *Hieruſalem*, to be releeued by their prayers, as I will further declared heareafter.

Baron. an. 1007.

53 *Henry*, the firſt Emperour of that name (who was no leſſe renowned for his prowes, and valour, then for his piety, and holly life, for the which he was after canonized:) ſo much honored, *S. Romoaldus* the Abbot, both aliue, and dead, that he helped to carry his body vppon his shoulders to his buriall, as I haue ſignified before vppon an other occaſion.

*Beda l.*3.*Hiſtor.c.* 24.

54 *Oſwy* king of *Northumberland*, in the time of our *Saxon* kinges (shortly after the conuerſion of that part of *England*, to the christian faith) shewed the great eſtimation he had of religious men, and their profeſſion, by a vow which he made to build a monaſterie, and to dedicat his daughter to religious life, if he ouerthrew *Penda* king of the *Mercians*, which he performed afterwards, as shall further appeare after a while.

*Chap.*28. *nu.*25.& 26

55 And the like may iuſtly be ſaid, not only of thoſe worthy Emperours, Kinges, and Princes, who became religious men (of whome I haue named many in the twenty eight chapter, and amongſt the reſt eight,

eight or nine in our owne country:) but also of an infinit number of others, who haue erected, and built monasteries, endowed them with ample possessions, and honoured them with great immunities prerogatiues, and priuiledges, whereof we haue also many domesticall examples, and those so notorious, that I shall not neede to borrow any from a broad, seeing that no man can be ignorant (if he haue read our chronicles) that the most worthy, and famous kinges, that euer wee had, either before the conquest, or since (from the first conuersion of the *Saxons*, and *English*, to the christian faith) haue benne founders of monasteries, and especiall patrons of religious men.

56 The first Christian English king *Ethelbert*, being conuerted, and baptised by *S. Augustin* the monke, and other religious men his companions, erected a monasterie, which he dedicated to *S. Peter* and *S. Paule* in *Canturbury*, and gaue it great possessions, as appeareth by his owne letters patents, or Charter, wherein he testified, that he did it with the consent of the venerable Archbishop *Augustin*, and of his princes. a He also founded an other monasterie in the Ile of *Ely*, which he did dedicat to our blessed Lady. b And shortly after, or at the same time, *Seibert*, king of the *East-Saxons* (who was baptised by *Melitus*, companion to S. *Augustin* aforesaid) built the famous monasterie of *westminster*.

An.605.

Guliel. Spina de Abbat. canobij S. Aug. vide Harpsfield in histo. eccl. seculo. 7. ca. 9.

a *Polidorus Virg. lib. 4. Angli. hist.*

b *Idem ibid. Harpsfield.*

57 A few yeares after, to wit, about the yeare of our Lord, *sixe hundreth, & thirty, Sigebertus*, king of the *East Angles* (who first planted learning in the famous vniuersity of *Cambridge*) so much honoured, & esteemed monastical, & religious life, that he built a monastery for himselfe, where he became religious, leauing his kingdome to his cosen *Egrick*.

c *Beda li. 3. hist. c. 18. an. 63.*

58 In the same age also, king *Ethelwald*, sonne to S. *Oswald* king of *Nothamberland* (where the faith of Christ was then newly receiued) gaue landes to the holly bishop S. *Ced*, to erect a monasterie there, *firmely beleeuinge, that he should be much helped, and assisted by the prayers of those, who were to serue God there*, for so saith, our venerable countriman, S. *Bede*, who wrote almost *nine hundreth* yeares agoe.

Circa an. 645.

d *S. Beda hist. eccles. li. 3. ca. 23.*

59 Within a while after, e *Egbert*, king of *kent*, built a monasterie of Nunnes in the Ile of *Tenet*.

e *Circa an. 655. vide Harpsfield.*

60 In like manner f *Cenoualchius* (or as *VVilliam* of *Malmesbury* calleth him, *Cheneuallus*) king of the west *Saxons*, about the same time, built a most famous monastery, at *winchester*, & endowed it with all the landes, that were within *seauen* miles compasse of it, and shortly after, a notable monasterie of Nunnes was founded at *witby* by *Oswy* g king of *Northũberland*, in dischardge of the vow, which he made to God before his

f *Circa an. 660. Ranul. li. 5. ca 13. vide Harpsfield vbi supra.*

Circa an. 664.

g *S. Beda li. 3. ca. 24.*

battaile, with kinge *Penda*, whereof I haue spoken before, and in the same monasterie, he placed his daughter *Edelfred*, to be brought vp in religious disciplin, as he had also vowed.

h *an.* 693. *Guliel. Malmesb. de pontific.*

61 h *Cissa* (who as some write, was Father to *Inas*, king of the west *Saxons*, and built the citty of *Chichester*) founded the Abbay of *Abington* in the same age.

i *an.* 705. *Idem de reg. Harpsf. secu.* 8. *c.* 23.

62 In the age following (to wit about the yeare of our Lord *Seauen hundred and fiue*) *Ethelred* i, king of the *Mercians* (who inhabited the middle part of *England*) built a monastery, at a place called *Bardoue*, and resigning his kingdome to his nephew *Chenred*, professed himselfe religious in the same monasterie, and was afterwards Abbot thereof.

k *ex Chron. Onuphrij Ioan. Capgraue Harpsf. sec.* 8. *c.* 8. *Pol. li.* 4.

63 And within *Fiue, or six* yeares after, not only his sonne *Chenred*, but also k *Offa*, king of the *East Angles*, gaue great possessions to the Abbay of *Esam*, and afterwads went both of them to *Rome* to Pope *Constantin*, and entred into religion.

l *an.* 740. *Polid. Ibid.*

64 The valiant, and Pious *Inas*, king of the *west Saxons*, in the same age, built the famous Abbay of *Glastonbury*, gaue landes to the Abbay of *Abington*, went to *Rome*, and made his kingdome tributarie to the sea Apostolike.

m *an.* 770. *Polid. l.* 4. *An.* 775.

65 And in that age also, m *Offa* king of the *Mercians*, founded an Abbay at *S. Albans*, in honour of our first martyr, S. *Alban*, and an other at *Bath*: he went also to *Rome*, and made his kingdome tributarie to Pope *Hadrian* the first.

n *An.* 810. *Polid. li.* 4.

66 *Chenulphus* n king also of the *Mercians*, in the age followinge, built the Abbay of *wimchelcomb*, about the yeare of our Lord *Eight hundreth* and *tenne*.

o *An.* 893. p *Apul. Polido. in Chron. l.* 5.

67 In the same age, the noble, and worthy *Alured*, king of the *Mercians* (who by the perswasion of *Neotus* Abbot of *Glastonbury*, did institute our famous o vniuersitie of *Oxford*) founded three monasteries, one at *winchester* (by the aduise of a holly french monke, called p *Grimbald*, (whose counsaile he vsed in all his affaires) an other for Nunnes at *Shafsbury*, whereof his daughter *Elfgrina* was afterwards Abbesse) and the third at a place called *Athelne*, or *Ethelinge*.

q *An.* 939. *Polid. l.* 6. r *An.* 964. *Guil. el. Malmesb. li.* 2. *ca.* 9. *Marian. in chron.*

68 His grandechild q *Adelstan* (who was the first of all our English kinges, that was monarke of all the *Iland* of *Britanny*) builded twoo monasteries in the age following (about the yeare *Nine hundreth thirty nyne*) the one at *Melton*, and the other at *Michilney*.

69 King r *Edgar*, who for his great valour, and vertue was not only called *Honor, & deliciæ Anglorum, the honour, and delight* or darling of *England*,

England, but was also greatlie honored, and esteemed by forreine nations, founded three monasteries in the same age, one at *wilton* (whereof his owne daughter s *Edith* was Abbesse) an other at *Ramsey*, and the third at a place called *Varuell*. s *Vide Harpsfield secu.* 10. c. 8.

70 *Canutus* t king of *England, Denmarke*, and *Norway*, reedified the famous monasterie of S. *Edmund*, at *Edmundsbury*, being decayed, & both gaue vnto it great landes, and possessions, and also honoured it with many priuiledges, and immunities. t *Circa an.* 1030. *Harpsf. sec.* 11. *ca.* 17.

71 The like did also the holly king, u S. *Edward* the confessor, to the Abbay of *westminster*, which in time of the *Danish* warres, had benne defaced, and almost vtterly ruined, and he not only repaired and amplified it with sumptuous buildinges (and namely with that magnificent church which yet standeth) but also procured a cõfirmation from the sea Apostolike, of certaine priuiledges which he gaue vnto it, and a decree, that the custome of crowninge, and annointing the kinges of *England* in that *Abbay*, should be perpetuall. u *Circa an.* 1063. *Ibid. ca.* 16. *Barro. an.* 1060.

72 And forasmuch, as I haue sufficientlie shewed, the great sanctity and hollines of this king, in the *three, and twentith* chapter, and also how the same was testified, and manifested to the world by almightie God, with many notable miracles, both in his life time, and after his death (whereof not only all our histories, but also the publike iudgement of the church in his canonization giueth sufficient testimonie) I will therefore speake no further thereof in this place, but only note by the way for a speciall argument, of the great merit of monasticall, and religious life, that such holly kinges, as this, and diuers others named before (who were great seruantes of God, and honoured as saintes by all the christian world) haue benne founders of monasteries, and principall patrons of religious men.

73 But to conclude this point, concerning the opinion of kinges, and Princes, seeing I haue now already deduced the former examples, from our first christian English kinges, to the time of *VVilliam* the *conquerer* (who also founded three Abbayes, one in *kent* called *Battaile Abbay*, an other in the suburbs of *London*, and the third at *Cane* in *Normandy*) I feare I should be ouer tedious, if I should prosecute the same in like manner through the ensuing ages (especiallie seeing there is much lesse doubt thereof, then of the former times) and therefore I will end, with one of our kinges since the conquest, who was no lesse victorious, then wise, and vertuous, I meane *Henry* the *fift*, who (as *Polidor Virgill* well noteth in the beginning of his life) knowing right well, that all thinges are gouerned, and guided by the prouidence of God, *Barro. An.* 1087. *Epito. Chronic. apud Polid.* *Polid. in Chro. l.* 22.

and that all humane power is to no purpose, be it neuer so great, if it be not supported and strengthned by the deuine, beganne his gouerment, with the erection of twoo famous monasteries, neere to *Richmond*, the one called *Bethlem*, and the other *Sion*, placing in the former the holy Chartrouse Monkes, and in the latter, the religious sisters of S. *Brigits* order, of both which orders, and monasteries, I haue spoken before in the *sixe and twenty* chapter, as also of the succession thereof, still remaining vntill this day, in twoo notable Couents of our countrifolkes, in *Flaunders*, and *Portugall*.

74 And one speciall reason which, besides the great merits of those twoo holly orders, moued that wise, and vertuous king, to make choice of them to people his twoo new monasteries, was (no doubt) that hauing learned out of our holly scriptures, that *multum valet assidua oratio iusti, the continuall prayer of the iust is of great valew, and force, in the sight of God*, he perswaded himselfe, that his prudence, and prowes being assisted with the continuall prayers, and merits of those great seruants of God, would produce no lesse notable effects in his gouerment, and state, then were after seene by experience, it being most euident, that he was not only most vertuous, and pious, but also one of the most victorious princes, that *England* euer had, as appeared by his famous battailes, and victories in *France*, where he was crowned king of that realme in *Paris*, and afterwardes leaft the possession of the greatest part thereof to his sonne, and the title of the whole to his posteritie.

75 And this shall suffise, concerning the reuerent respect, that christian kinges, and princes (especiallie ours) haue euer borne to monasticall, and religious profession. Whereby two thinges euidentlie appeare, the one, what opinion, and beleefe these princes had, of the benefit, that they and their states reaped, by the prayers, merits, and holly labours, of religious men. The other, that they sucked (as I may say) the same beleife, euen with the milke of christian religion, as appeareth not only in *Constantin*, the first christian Emperour, and his successors in the Empire, but also in our first christian English king *Ethelbert*, and others that liued in the same age, or haue since succeded them in our country, vntill king *Henry* the *eight*, father to the late Queene *Elizabeth*.

Beda in Histor. Anglic. l. 2. 6 2.

76 And although I haue made no mention here, of the christian kinges in *Brittany*, before the entrance of the *Saxons* and *English*, yet whosoeuer shall consider, what a famous monasterie the *Britans* had in *Bangor*, wherein there were two thousand monkes, at the entrance of S.

Augustin,

Augustin, and an other alſo in *Abington*, where, as ſome write, were ordinarilie aboue fiue hundred monkes (of whom ſixty liued retired in the monaſterie, and the reſt got their liuinge abroad by their labour, in the woods, and deſerts adioining, and repaired to the monaſtery euery ſunday) whoſoeuer I ſay shall conſider this, muſt needes cōceiue, that theſe ſo populous monaſteries, either were founded, and erected by the ancient British kinges, or at leaſt amplified, enriched, & patronized by them: which would be as eaſely proued, as the former, if the ancient hiſtories, and monuments of thoſe ages were extant, which perished, no doubt, with the whole ſtate of *Brittany*, in the cruel warres, and conqueſt made by the *Saxons*: ſo that in this alſo, our aduerſaries may note, a moſt manifeſt argument, not only of the antiquitie, and merit of religious life, but alſo of the great eſtimation, that our *British* kings had thereof. *Harpſf. Secu. 10. ca. 9. ex chron. Abindonenſi.*

77 But what doubt can be made of the benefit, that redoundeth to princes ſtates, by the prayers of religious men, ſeeing that it is euident in the holly ſcriptures, that almightie God preſerueth whole citties, prouinces, and ſtates, ſometimes for the regard he hath; to the interceſſion, and merits of ſome one man, which he ſignified euidentlie by the prophet *Ezechiell* when he ſaid of the *Iewes*. *Quæſiui de eis virum*, &c. *I ſought for ſome man amongſt them, who might put himſelfe betweene them, and me like a hedge, and ſtand oppoſit againſt me for the earth, to the end I might not deſtroy it, and I found none, & I powred my indignation vpon thē* &c. *Ezech. 22.*

78 Thus ſaid almighty God by the prophet, and the like he ſignified, when being moued with iuſt indignation agaiuſt the *Iewes*, & ready to deſtroy them for their wickednes, he not only pardoned them diuerstimes at the interceſſion of *Moyſes*, but alſo ſaid once vnto him. *Dimitte me, vt iraſcatur furor meus* &c. *Suffer me, or let me doe my will, that I may extend my wrath againſt them, and I will make thee prince of a great nation.* And when *Moyſes*, neuertheles perſiſted to pray for them, *placatus eſt dominus*, ſaith the ſcripture, *ne faceret malum, quod locutus eſt contra populum ſuum. Our Lord was appeaſed, or diuerted from executing the punishment, which he had threatned againſt his people.* *Exod. 32.*

79 Lo then, how much almighty God, reſpecteth good mens prayers, ſeeing that he ſuffreth his handes, as it were to be bound thereby, and held from the execution of his iuſtice vppon the wicked. To which purpoſe alſo we read in the ſcriptures, that if there had benne but *tenne* iuſt men in *Sodome*, God would for their ſakes, haue ſpared the whole citty, not with ſtanding all the abomination thereof, as I haue declared in the firſt part of this treatiſe, where I alſo shewed *Geneſ. 18.*

Zzz the

the notable effects of prayer, for the reliefe of all humane necessities, alleadging diuers examples thereof, in matters concerning princes, and their states, which therefore I omit here, and conclude, that hereby it sufficientlie appeareth, what exceeding benefit all common welths, and states of princes reape, by the prayers of good religious men, besides their other pious labours, whereby they conuert Infidels to the christian faith, and sinners to repentance, inducing wicked men to reforme their manners, no lesse by their holy example, then by their learned sermons, exhortations, and instructions. In which respect, *S. Chrisostome* in twoo of his homilies to the people, exhorted them most seriouslie, to visit oft times monasteries, and religious houses, and to frequent the company of religious men. *Adi*, saith he, *tales viros* &c. *Repaire to such men, use their conuersation, goe I say vnto them, and touch their holly feete, multo enim honestius* &c. *For it is much more honorable to embrace their feete, then the heades of other men.*

S. Chrisost. ho 59. ad populum.

80 Thus saith *S. Chrisostome*, of religious men, in respect of their holly example, and endeuoures, whereof the experience is also daily seene, euen vntill this day, in all Catholike countries, where the holly labours of religious men (I meane of those, that are both actiue & contemplatiue) doe tend to nothing els, but to draw euery man to liue in his state, and vocation, according to the perfection of christian religion, which perfection (as I signified before) the more it is practised in common welth, the more it vniteth the same with God, and consequentlie aduanceth it to true felicitie.

81 Thus then wee see, that religious life, is no way hurtfull to common welth, but most profitable, and necessarie thereto, which will yet appeare more manifestlie, by the answere of that other part of the former obiection, which concerneth the lawes of certaine Emperours, and Kinges, preiudiciall to religious profession. I will therefore beginne, with the law of *Mauritius* the Emperour.

82 This Emperour ordained, that no souldiar should enter in to religion, except he were lame, or otherwise vnfit for the warre, or els had serued out the time assigned by the law, as is signified before in the obiection, and forasmuch as the holly, and famous *Pope*, *S. Gregory* the great, who liued in the same time, gaue his opinion amply to the Emperour himselfe, concerning that constitution, it may suffise (in respect of his authoritie and antiquitie) that I lay downe the same, with his reasons. For although to mollifie the hard, and peruerse hart of that tyrannicall Emperour, the holly man wrote vnto him, a letter of great submission (signifying neuertheles that he wrote as a priuat person, and

Barro. an. 565.

and not as a bishop, to the end, that his humble manner of writtinge, might not preiudice the authoritie, and dignitie of his seat) yet he represented plainely vnto him, the absurditie, and impiety of his law, saying, that he was astonished to see it, seeing that the way to heauen was shut vp to many thereby; *for though there be diuers*, saith he, *that can ioyne religious life, with secular habit, yet there are many others, that cannot be saued, except they vtterly forsake the world.* S. Greg. l.2. ep.62. indict. 11.

83 Moreouer, he wisheth him to consider with himselfe, what he would answer to Christ, if he should aske him, why he was so vngratefull to debarre, and withould his souldiars from his seruice, seeing he had made him an Emperour, of a *Notary*, and then he addeth, that perhaps the Emperour would say, that it might be well thought, that none of those souldiars which became religious, were truly conuerted, wherto he answereth, that he himselfe had knowne in his owne dayes, conuerted souldiars in monasteries, men of such holly life, that they did miracles. *Sed per hanc legem*, saith he, *ne quisquam talium conuerti valeat, prohibetur. It is forbidden by this law of yours, that none should be conuerted.* Thus saith *S. Gregory*, to the Emperour *Mauritius*. And writting also at the same time to his phisician, to the end that he might communicate the same with him, he saith, that *Iulian*, the *Apostata*, did make the like law, & that if the Emperour did thinke, that his armies were diminished, and his forces decreased by reason that many souldiars entred in to religion, he wished he would consider, whether he had conquered the kingdome of *Persia*, by the force of his souldiars or no, or whether God had not giuen the same in to his handes, rather by his owne prayers, and teares, then by the meanes of his power, yea in such sort, as he himselfe, knew not how it was wrought. Idem ep. 65. Indict. 11. Baron. an. 593.

84 Thus did this holly man, notablie represent to *Mauritius*, the iniquitie of his law, shewing euidently vnto him, his ingratitude towards God, in that hauing receiued not only the Empire from his liberall hand, but also the kingdome of *Persia*, rather by miracle, then by his owne force and strength, he did neuertheles confide more in his armies, and pollicies, then in Gods assistaunce, yea, and withhould his souldiars and subiects from Gods seruice, for the which, both he, and they, and all the world, was created and ordained.

85 But so it pleased God afterwards to dispose, for the confusion of the Emperour, and all such pollitikes as he, that notwithstanding his contempt of religious life, he was faine, ere many yeares past, to haue recourse to religions men, for the remedy of his necessities, both priuate, and publike, for within *four* or *fiue* yeares, after that he had made Baron. an. 598.

Surius die 22. Aprilis to. 2.

this law, one of his sonnes was stroken with a leprosie, which no phisicke could cure, whereuppon, he and the Empresse, sent for *Theodorus* a monke, famous for miracles at that time, and humbly craued the helpe of his prayers, for the recouery of their sonne, whome he miraculouslie restored to perfect health. And within *three*, or *foure* yeares after, it pleased God to reueale, not only to the same *Therdorus*, but also to a monke in *Constantinople*, that *Mauritius* should shortly loose, both his Empire, and his life, which the Monke published very strangelie, running throughout all the citty, with a naked sword in his hand, cryinge. *Hoc ferietur* Mauritius. *With this Mauritius shalbe stroken.* Signifying that he should die violentlie with the sword (which was shortly after executed by *Phocas*, as I haue declared more particularly in the first part of this treatise,

Baron. an. 602. Annal. Cedreni. Baron. an. 602. Chap. 35. Num. 30.

86 And in the meane time, *Mauritius* being frighted with this, and certaine other ominous predictions, sought remedy by the meanes of religious men, writting to all monasteries, euen as farre as *Hierusalem*, to be assisted by their prayers. Whereby it appeareth, how true it is that, which th prophet saith. *Vexatio, dabit intellectum. Vexation, or affliction, will giue vnderstanding*, seeing that *Mauritius* in his aduersitie, acknowledged the merits of religious life, which in his prosperitie he contemned, shewing sufficientlie, that in the extremities of Princes, and their states, more confidence is to be reposed, in the prayers of religious, and good men, then in princelie power, or humane pollicie. Thus much concerning *Mauritius*, and his wicked law.

Isay. 28.

87 And whereas the Arrian Emperour *Valens*, king of *Spaine*, *Isacius*, and *Nicephorus Phoca*, Emperour of *Constantinople*, made also other lawes preiudiciall to monasticall, and religious life, as I haue signified in the obiection, it is to be considered, that as there were most wicked men, so also God did punish them most exemplarlie for the same.

Bar. an. 378. Vasaus in Chron. an. 710. Vasa; an. 714.

88 The Emperour *Valens*, being ouerthrowne, and pursued by the *Gothes*, was burned in a litle Cabin where he had hid himselfe. And *Vitiza*, was disposest of his kingdome, and depriued of his eyes, by *Roderic* his successour, and for as much as also the said *Roderic* continued, and kept in vre, the beastly lawes of *Vitiza*, ordaining that priestes, and religious men should marry &c. Yt pleased God to take a greater reuenge, not only vppon him, but also vppon all *Spaine*, giuing him, and them, in to the handes of the *Mores*, who slew him in bataile, and conquered *Spaine*, as I haue declared at lardge in the first part of this treatise, to shew a partly, how seuerelie God punisheth the sinnes of the flesh, and b partly, how he turneth the wicked pollicies of men, to their owne ruine, which

a Chap. 20. Num. 8. b Chap. 13. Nu. 14.

which latter point, being also very considerable in this matter, is there c handled at large, and confirmed by many examples. c *Chap. 3. nu. 4. & ch. 31. nu. 5 6. 7. 8. & 9.*

89 But in the Emperour *Isacius Commenus* (who confiscated all the goods of monasteries) it is very remarkeable, that he, being afterwards stroken from his horse with a thunderbolt, was so terrified with Gods iudgement vppon him, that after a whyle he gaue ouer his empire, and became not only a monke, but also porter of the monasterie where he liued, being also contented to doe all other base offices about the house, as occasion required, so that in recompence of the iniury which he did to monasteries, he was forced by Gods iustice, to end his dayes in the seruice of a monasterie. *Baron. an. 1060.*

90 And now, to say some what also of the Emperour *Nicephorus Phoca* (who got his empire with periurie, and adulterie, and was a man of insatiable auarice) it is nomeruaile, though such a wicked Tyrant as he, made lawes against the foundation, and erection of monasteries, seeing he also ordained, that no landes should be giuen to the church, and possest himselfe of bishopricks, and was otherwise so prophane, that he would haue ordained, that all souldiars dying in the field should be canonized, and honoured with hymnes, and holly ceremonies as martyrs, and had done it, if the Patriarke of *Constantinople*, had not stoutly resisted him, but in the end, Gods iustice fell vppon him, by the meanes of *Theophano* his owne wife, who caused him to be slaine, and married his murderer, *Iohn Zimisces*, and made him Emperour, *Baron. an. 969. Zonar. Annal. to. 3.*

91 And how pernitious to the Empire, those his wicked lawes were, it may appeare, by the constitutions of *Basilius*, the Emperour, who succeded *Iohn Zimisces*, and reuoked those lawes of *Nicephorus*, testifying, & affirming, that all the calamities fallen lately before vpon the Empire, were the iust punishment of God for the same, and that therefore he annulled, and abolished them. So that the example of these princes, & their lawes, proueth nothing els, but that the enemies of religious life, are wicked men, & that the lawes ordained against the same, are vniust, hatefull to almightie God, and pernitious to princes, and their states, drawing the wrath, and vengeance of almighty God vppon them, whereby also the great merit of religious life, and the conueniencie, and necessitie thereof in common welth, sufficientlie appeareth.

92 Though many other pointes belonging to this matter, doe offer themselues vnto me to be handled, neuerthelesse considering that I haue benne already much longer, then I was at first determined to be, I will conclude this chapter, and all the former concerning religious perfection, and the end of common wealth.

93 And first for the matter of vowes, which I haue handled in the last chapter, it appeareth sufficientlie, as I hope, that the vse of vowes of chastitie, and of the other euangelical counsels, obserued in religious discipline, is most conforme to the scriptures, and deriued from the doctrine, and practise of the Apostles, and from their time, continued in the church of God vntill ours: and finallie, that the obiections of the sectaries, against the same, are but meere shiftes, and cauils, proceeding only of a desire, to defend the breach of their owne vowes, to couer their shame, and excuse their Apostacy, from the Catholike faith.

94 And whereas, I vndertooke in the fiue and twentith chapter, to proue that the Catholike Roman religion, is not only the true religion, but also most conforme to true pollicie, and fit for gouerment of common wealth, and that the opinions of *Lutherans*, and *Caluinists* (wherein they dissent from vs) are contrarie, aswell to true religion, as to true pollicie, I haue for this purpose, allready proued in these former chapters. First, that the Roman Catholikes, haue amongest them the true imitation of our Sauiour Christ, by the obseruation of the Euangelicall counsels, and that therein consisteth, the highest perfection of Christian religion.

95 Secondly, that by the meanes of this religious perfection, they arriue to a perfect vnion with God, testified in all ages, by the externall signes of reuelations, visions apparitions of our Sauiour Christ, and his saintes, rapts, and most miraculous workes, accompanied with ineffable sweetenes, and spirituall consolations.

96 Thirdly, that the sectaries haue no true imitation of our Sauiour Christ, nor obseruation of the Euangelicall counsells, yea, and that they are open, and sworne enemies, of the true Euangelicall, and religious perfection. And lastly, that they haue no externall signes, of any internall vnion with God, as the Catholikes haue, by deuine rapts, reuelations, visions, or miracles, but are by the iustice of God, exposed to illusions of wicked spirits, fantasticall dreames, false, and fanaticall reuelations, as I haue signified in the last chapter, by all which it appeareth, that they haue not any perfection of Christian religion, and consequentlie no vnion with God.

97 And therefore, for as much as I haue also proued amply before, that the perfect vnion of man with God, is not only a most speciall, and assured effect of true christian religion, but also, that it is the end, and felicitie of man, and common welth, twoo thinges must needes follow thereon. The one, that the Roman Catholikes, hauing this vnion

vnion with God, haue aſwell the truth of Chriſtian religion, as the felicitie of man, and of common welth. The other, that the ſectaries, being enemies of true chriſtian perfection, and therefore void of all vnion with God, haue neither truth of religion, nor the true happines, which is the end of man, and common welth: whereuppon it is alſo to be inferred, that their religion is moſt pernicious to all princes ſtates, not only for that it depriueth them of Gods ſpeciall protection, and benediction (which can neuer concurre with falſe religion:) but alſo becauſe it draweth his wrath, and malediction vppon them ſooner, or latter, howſoeuer he may for a time ſuffer them to proſper, for ſuch cauſes, as I will declare amply heareafter, in the third part of this treatiſe. Beſides that, ſome of the cheefe and principall pointes of their religion, are of themſelues, ſo contrarie to true reaſon of ſtate, that the beleefe, and practiſe thereof, muſt needes ouerthrow the common welth in time, or at leaſt breede great inconuenience therein, as I haue shewed partly already in their abſurd, and beaſtly doctrine, of the impoſſibilitie to liue chaſt, and will now shew further, concerning ſome other pointes of their beleefe, in the next chapter.

To proue that the Catholike religion is conforme to true reaſon of ſtate, and the contrary doctrin repugnant thereto, ten points, controuerſed betwixt the Catholikes, and their aduerſaries, are debated by way of ſtate: and it is euidently shewed, that the doctrin of Catholikes, leadeth to all vertue, and is therefore moſt conuenient for ſtate, and that the doctrin of their aduerſaries, eyther withdraweth from vertue, or inciteth to vice, and conſequently is moſt pernicious to all ſtates. Finally, the bad frute of Lutheraniſme *and* Caluiniſme *in Common welth, is shewed by the experience thereof, ſufficiently acknowledged by* Luther, Caluin, *and others their fellowes.*

CHAP. 35.

1 HAuing hitherto shewed the neceſſitie, fruit, and dignitie of the Catholike Roman religion in common welth, aſwell by the end, and felicitie of common welth it ſelfe, as by the perfection of Chriſtian religion (both which I haue proued, to be proper only to the Roman Catholike church) I will now a litle further proſecute the ſame ſubiect in this chapter, and confront certaine important points of our Catholike doctrin, with the contrarie doctrin of our aduerſaries, whereby it shall euidentlie appeare, that our Catholike religion, tendeth wholy to the practiſe of

of perfect vertue, and is consequentlie most behouefull for common welth, and that the opposite doctrine of our aduersaries, either direectly draweth the professors of it to vice, or at least, withdraweth them from the practise of vertue, and so by a necessarie consequence, is most pernicious to common welth, which doth stand, and florish by vertue, and is ruined by vice, as I haue ampely proued before in the ninth Chapter. And for this purpose I meane to examine tenne seuerall pointes of religion, controuersed betwixt vs and our aduersaries, and to treat thereof in this chapter, only by way of state, reseruing their further discussion by way of religion, to the third part of this treatise, because otherwais this part would grow ouerlong, and to a greater volume then would seeme conuenient.

Chap. 9. per totum.

2 First then concerning our iustification by faith, and workes. The Catholike religion, teacheth two thinges, speciallie to be cōsidered for our purpose. The one is, that no man hauing the vse of reason, can be iustified, without the concurrence of *seauen* acts, declared by the councell of *Trent*, to witt, of *faith, the feare of God, hope, charity, repentaunce* of sinnes past, *intention to receiue the sacraments with full purpose to amend,* and finally, *to obserue the commandements of God.* The other point is, that good workes proceeding of Gods grace, doe increase our iustification, whereby it may be truly said, according to the expresse wordes of the scripture, that *we are iustified by workes, and not by faith only.*

Concil. Trident. Sessio. 6. ca. 6.

Iac. 2. d. 24.

3 Of these two points of Catholike doctrin, there followeth this euident benefit to common welth, that those which professe the same, and desire to be iustified, doe not only dispose themselues with all dilligent endeuour, to the loue of God, and their neighbours, to the hate of sinne and vice, and to the practise of all vertue, but also doe performe all kind of good workes, all which must needes redound to the publike good, in so much, that if this doctrin were beleeued, and followed of all men, there should neede no other, to make all the members of the common welth most vertuous, and the whole common welth most happy.

4 But the doctrine of our aduersaries, teaching iustification by only faith, must needes woorke a farre different, or rather a contrarie effect in common welth, and in euery member thereof. For although our aduersaries are forced sometimes, by the irrefragable veritie of our Catholike religion, to graunt (at least in words) the necessitie of charity and good workes to iustification, yet such are their groundes, and such is the whole course of their doctrin, that they doe in

deed

indeed, not only exclude good woorkes wholly from iustification, but also vtterly abase and decry them, treating of them so contemptuosly, and odiously that how soeuer they otherwise contradict themselues, they must needes induce their followers, to an extreame negligence, and contempt of well doing, to the vnspeakeable dammage of all the common wealths, where their religion ys embraced.

5 And to the end, that this may partly appeare (so farre forth as cōcerned this point whereof I presently treat) I will lay downe some of *Luthers* grounds, concerning iustification by only faith.

6 He teheth, a that *fides sine & ante caritatē iustificat. Faith iustifieth without, and before charity.* That b *fides, nisi sit sine vllis etiam minimis operibus, non iustificat, imo non est fides. Faith, except yt be without all kind of workes, yea without the least workes, that may be, doth not iustifie neither yet ys faith.* That c *opus, nn potest doceri* &c. *A worke cannot be taugh, with out the preiudice of faith seing that faith, and workes, are extreamely contrarie the one to the other, so that the doctrin of workes, must needes be the doctrin of deuills.*

7 That d *the highest art, and Christian wisdome, ys, not to know the law, and to be ignorant of workes, and of all actiue iustice.*

8 Also, f *Caueamus,* saith he, *a peccatis, caueamus ab operibus bonis. Let vs beware of sinnes, let vs beware of good workes, and let vs attend only to the promise of God, and to faith, for that ys a short, and compendious perfection.*

9 And in an other place, he saith. g *Vides quā diues sit homo Christiā⁹,* &c. *Thou seest how rich a Christiā mā ys who though he would, cannot loose his saluation, with any sinnes what soeuer, except he wil not beleeue: no sinnes can damne him, but only incredulity. There is no other way, whereby a man may agree, or deale with God, but by faith: he careth not for workes, neither dotht he neede them.*

10 And againe. h *Nullum opus,* saith he, *tam malum est* &c. *There ys no worke so euill, that yt can damne a man, neither any, so good, that can saue a man, but only faith saueth, and only incredulity damneth.* Also. i *nullum peccatum est* &c. *There ys no sinne but incredulity* or lack *of beleefe, no iustice* or righteousnes, *but faith* Also, k *erga Deum* saith he, *non operibus sed nuda fide indigemus.* &c. *Towards God we neede no workes but bare faith, for we must come with Isaac only, that ys to say with faith, we must dismisse our seruantes, and asses, that ys to say our workes, how much wickeder thou art, so much sooner will God infuse, or power his grace into thee.*

11 Finally, he peremptorily affirmeth, that *quando sic docetur, fides iustificat quidem sed simul seruare oportet* &c. *When any man teacheth thus, faith doth iustifie, yet we must also keepe the commandements of God (because yt ys written. Si vis ad vitam ingredi serua mandata. Yf thou wilt enter into life keepe the commandements.) There Christ ys presently denied, and faith abolished, because that*

a *Luther in ca. 2. ad Gal.*
b *Idem disput. an opera faciant ad iustificationem.*
c *vide Iodocuū Coccium in Thesau. To. 2. de iustificat. ar. 3.*
d *Luther de votis monast*
e *in argumē ep. ad Gala. editio. 1.*
f *Sermo de nouo testam. siue de missa*
g *De captiuitate Babylo. ca. de Baptismo.*
h *Ad euangeliū dominica. 8. post fest. trinitatis.*
i *Cōtra Ambrosium Catharinum.*
k *Sermo. de piscatura Petri.*
l *in ca. 2. ad Gala.*
Mat. 19. c. 17

which ys only Gods, ys attributed to the commandements of God, or the law.

12 Thus much I haue thought good to alledge out of *Luther* who teacheth these most impious, an absurd paradoxes, not only in the places here alleadged, but also in diuers other which I omit, thinking these sufficient, to shew his doctrin concerning only faith, to the end yt may appeare, that he excludeth all kinde of good workes from iustification, not only in respect of any operation they may haue therein, but also in regard of their verry concurrence, or presence with faith, abasing, contemning, and reiecting them, as you haue heard. And what maruaile, seing that he also affirmeth els where, m that euery good worke ys a sinne, which ys also taught expressely by n *Melancthon*, o *Caluin*, and other sectaries, who are sprong from *Luther*, in so much, that *Nicholaus Amsdorfius* a *Lutheran* writting against *Georgius Maior*, about the matter of iustification, intituled his booke. *Quod bona opera sint perniciosa ad salutem.* That good workes are pernicious to saluation, and amongst diuers other fond, and folish arguments, he produceth p, *Luthers* assertion, and doctrin in confirmation of his, citing for the same q *Luthers* owne wordes, out of diuers partes of his workes.

m *Luther in assertion. ar.* 31.32. & 36.
n *Melanch. in locis commũ. editio.* 1.
o *Caluin. li.* 3. *institu. ca.* 24. ss. 9. & *cap.* 11. ss. 554
p *Nicola. Amsdorf. cõtra Georgiũ Maior.*
q *Vide Iodoc Coccium in Thesauro vbi supra.*

13 And in a conference which was held at r *Altembourg*, in the yeare of our lord, a *thousand fiue, hundreth sixty eight*, and printed at *Iena* in the yeare a *thousand fiue hundred, seauenty*, the rigid *Lutherans*, insisting vpon the groundes and principles of their great master *Luther*, maintained (as I may say) with tooth, and naile, that *the good workes of the law and new obedience, doth not belong to the kingdome of Christ, but to the world*: that christians, with good *workes. belong to the diuel, and only faith, without good workes, doth performe all, wheter we respect the merit, or the presence of good workes.* And finally to omit others strange paradoxes.) they taught that this proposition, *opera sunt necessaria, workes are necessary*, ys a false proposition, and that *adeo illa necessaria non sunt, vt ad salutem incommodent, sintque perniciosa. They are so farre fom being necessary that they are hurtfull, and pernicious to saluation.*

r *Colloquiũ habitũ Altẽburgue an.* 1568.

14 Thus crowed they after their kind, discouering themselues, to be chickens of *Luthers* brood. But now yf we consider, what a holsome doctrine all this ys, which I haue related here, and how necessary, and profitable the same may be for the publike, or priuat weale of men, and for their spirituall good we shall easely see, that yf all the infernall spirites, had laid their heades together, to teach a doctrine to draw men to all impiety, and to make them most desperately wicked, they could not haue inuented more pernicious principles, or haue laid downe more pestilent groundes for that purpose.

15 For

15 For he which shal beleeue, and be perswaded in conscience, that *God regardeth not his workes whether they be good, or bad: And that no sinne but incredulity can damne him*: that *his best workes, are sinnes*: that *a iustifying faith, can not stand with good workes*: that *the doctrin of good workes, is the doctrine of deuils*: that *good workes, are pernicious to saluation*: and finally, that *the more wicked a man is, the nearer he is to Gods grace* (for al this doe *Luther* and his followers teach, as you haue heard before:) what wickednes wil such a one forbeare to commit, when occasion either of pleasure, or commoditie, shall inuite him thereto, in case he may hope to auoid the penaltie of temporall lawes, as not only princes, and great men, but also inferiour persons find meanes to doe many times, as experience teacheth? What then can be expected in a common welth, where this doctrine is currant, but that most men shall abandon themselues to all vice, and wickednes, relying only vppon their iustifying faith, and not only contemning, and reiecting all kind of good workes, but also hating them as pernicious impediments to their saluation? And therfore I conclude for the present, that as the doctrine of Catholikes, concerning iustification, containeth great motiues to vertue, and to all good workes, and is consequentlie most beneficiall to common welth: so on the other side the doctrin of our aduersaries (which looseth the bridle to all vice, and wickednes) is most pernicious thereto, and thus much for the first point.

16 Secondlie, the like may be said of the different doctrin of Catholikes, and sectaries, touching inherent, and imputatiue iustice. For the Catholikes hold, according to the holly scriptures, that it is necessarily required to the iustification of euery christian man, to haue not only, *remission of sinnes*, but also *innouation of spirit*, and the *infusion of charity, by the gift of the holly Ghost*, (that is to say a real, and true iustice inherent in him, giuen him by almightie God, through the merits of our Sauiour Christ) whereby he is not only reputed, but also made iust, which kind of iustice cannot possibly stand with any mortall sinne: wherevppon it must needes follow, that those which seeke to be iustified, according to this doctrin, doe labour to be truly vertuous, and to eschew all vice, and consequentlie to become notable members of the common welth.

Ephes. 4. Tit. 3.

Rom. 5. S. Aug. de spu. & litte. c. 9. & 11. Item tracta. 26. in Euãg. Ioan. & passim.

Caluin li. 3. institutio. ca. 11. ss. 2. 3.

17 But our aduersaries beleeue, on the other syde, that they are iustified without any real, or inherent iustice in themselues, by the imputation of the iustice of Christ only, which iustice is in him, and not in them, whereby they are not iust in deede, but reputed for iust, so that their iustification, may according to their opinion, stand with all wic-

kednes. For if it be true, which they teach, that not only, the a corruption in humane nature, and the very concupiſcence in man, but al the beſt b workes of the beſt men, are mortall ſinnes, though not imputed, for the merits of Chriſt (for ſo they teach:) yt ys euident, that they are alwayes truly impious, and wicked in the ſight of God, not withſtanding their imputatiue iuſtice. And therefore yt ys manifeſt, that they haue no cauſe, or motiue by this their doctrine, to labour to be truely vertuous (being as they hold alwaies damnably vicious, but may rather preſume to make the ſame a cloke to couer all kind of wickednes, ſeeing that their ſuppoſed iuſtice, doth not exclude mortall ſinne, but may be imputed to them, be they neuer ſo wicked, whereby yt appeareth, that the doctrin of Catholiks, ys in this point alſo very beneficiall, and theirs very preiudiciall to common welth.

18 Thirdly, the Catholikes teach out of the holly ſcriptures, *that no man knoweth* (without a ſpeciall reuelation) *utrum odio, vel amore dignus ſit.* Whether he be worthy of loue, or hate, neither yet (though he be in ſtate of grace) whether he ſhall haue the gift of perſeuerance, and that by euill life, he may alſo looſe Gods grace and be damned: where vppon yt followeth, that ſuch Catholikes, as labour to liue according to Catholike doctin, are moued hereby to ſtand continually vppon their gard, and by all meanes poſſible of prayer, penance, and good workes, to procede daily from vertue, to vertue, *operantes ſalutem*, as the apoſtle aduiſeth, *cum timore, & tremore, working their ſaluation with feare and tremblinge*, by which meanes they both liue moſt vertuouſly themſelues, and alſo geue good example to others, to the great benefit of the common welth.

19 But the ſectaries, hold that no man ys faithfull, and iuſt, exept he aſſure himſelfe, not only of his iuſtification, but alſo of his prædeſtination, and ſaluation, and that the faith which iuſtifieth, conſiſteth in this aſſurance, wherefore *Caluin* defineth *faith to be a firme, and certaine knowledge of Gods mercy and beneuolence towards vs which knowledge*, ſaith he, *being founded on the truth of the free promiſe made vs in Chriſt, is both reuealed to our mindes, and ſealed in our hartes, by the holly Ghoſt.* Whereuppon yt muſt needes follow, that ſuch, as are wicked men amongſt the ſectaries, and beleeue them ſelues to be iuſtified by only faith (as they all doe) cannot haue in their opiniõ, any neede at all to amẽd their liues in reſpect of their ſaluatiõ, ſeeing that they hold them ſelues already aſſured of yt. And I make no doubt, but that yf the wickedſt *Caluiniſt*, or *Lutheran* in *England*, (be he neuer ſo deſperat a malefactor) were demaunded, whether he be ſure of his ſaluation, or no, he would preſentlie anſwere,

yea

a *Luther. in articulis a Leo 10. damnat. art.* 2.
b *Idem in aſſertion. ar.* 31. 32. & 36. *vide Bellar. l.* 4. *de inſtit. c.* 1.
Caluin *in Antidoto cõcil. triden. ſſ* 6. *c.* 11. & *li.* 3. *inſtit. ca.* 11 *ſſ* 10. & 11. *Itẽ li.* 3. *ca.* 3 & *c.* 14. *ſſ.* 9.
Ecclaſ. *c.* 9.
Concil um *Trident ſeſſ.* 6 *ca.* 9. & 12.
Rom. 11. 22.
1. cor. 10. 12.
Philip. 2. 13.
Apoc. 3. 2. ep. 2. Io 8. Pſal. 2. 11.
Philip. 2.
Luth. *in art* 10. 11. & 12.
Melanch. *in locis com. tit. l. fide*
Caluin. *in Antido. conſilij. ſeſſ.* 6. & *in li.* 3. *inſtit. c.* 2. *ſſ.* 16. 17.
1-. Bucer *in li. con cor. ar. de iuſtificat.*
Petrus martir. *ad c.* 8. *ep. ad Rom.*
Ex Bellar. *li.* 3. *de iuſtif. c.* 3. & 12.

yea, for that he not only beleeueth, and assureth himselfe, that Christ died for him, but also applieth by faith, Gods promise vnto himselfe, and so is sure to be saued by Christs merits. And if the doctrine of the sectaries be true, it cannot be denied, but that hauing this faith and assurance, he shall vndoutedlie be saued: And this being soe, what needeth he to amend his life for feare of damnation?

20 And whereas *Caluin* to blind the eyes of the simple, affirmeth that a wicked man hath not this iustifying faith, he must needes confesse, that either the wickedst man in the world may haue it, or els, that no man knoweth when he hath it, where vppon it will follow, that no man can be sure of his saluation. For if a man can know when he hath it, who can better know it, then he that feeleth it in his hart (which is the most assured knowledge thereof, that any man can haue) and this no doubt, doth the wickedst *Caluinist* feele, if he beleeue according to the rules of his religion: and, as I haue said, if you aske him whether he feele it, or no, he will assure you, that he doth, yea, and that it is reuealed vnto him by the holly Ghost: so that wee must needes graunt, either that wicked men may haue this iustifying faith and securitie, which *Caluin* denieth, or els that those, which feele it them selues, cannot be assured of it, and consequentlie, that this doctrine of securitie is vaine, and false, and the most dangerous doctrin, both for body, and soule, that euer was taught in the world, as no doubt it is.

21 For how many may it be thought, that this presumptuous, and false securitie, carrieth headlong yearly first to the gallowes, and after to hel, whilest many that are most wicked, and sinfull in life, and yet withall hold themselues secure of their saluation, haue no feare of eternal punishment, & doe hope by some meanes, or other, to escape the temporal penalty of the law, whereby they are embouldened to commit all mischiefe? Besides that, it is euident, that this doctrin, not only confirmeth the wicked in their wickednes (as I haue said) but also impaireth those, that are otherwaife of thēselues wel disposed, making them careles, and negligent, in their manner of life, whereby they fall into infinit temptations, which no man can auoid, and much lesse resist without much prayer, continuall watch, great care, and diligent preuentions, all which must needes seeme needeles, to those that are alreadie secure of their saluation,

22 Therefore I conclude, that this doctrine of securitie, is not only an impediment to vertue, but also a prouocation to vice, and sinne, and therefore most pernicious to common welth, whether we respect the spiritual, or the temporall good thereof.

23 Fourthly, the Catholike church teacheth, that the morall part of Moyses his law, consisting in the commaundemẽts, was not takẽ away, but confirmed by Christ, and that the said cõmaundements, are not only possible to be kept, but also easy, sweete, and delectable with the helpe of Gods grace, and as the psalmist saith, *more to be desired then gold, or precious stone, and sweeter then the honny, or the honny combe.* Whereby Catholikes are moued, and encouraged, to doe their vttermost endeuour to obserue them, and consequentlie to liue in the exact practise of all vertue, to the great benefit of the common welth, but the sectaries teach, not only that the commaundements are vnpossible to be kept, but also that they are wholy abrogated by Christ: and to the end it shal not be said, that I slander them, with these opinions, I thinke good to lay downe some of their owne wordes, first concerning the impossibilitie to keepe the commaundements, and after touching the abrogation of them.

Psal. 18. 11. *Psal. 18. 11.*

24 *Luther* writing of the first against *Siluester Prieras*, saith thus. *Pessime façis* &c. *Thou doest very ill, that thou deniest, that God hath commaunded impossible thinges, and thou dost much worse, in that thou darest call this a falsity,* to wit, *we cannot fulfill the commaundements of God in this life.* So he. *Melancthon* saith, that whereas the law commaundeth, that God shall be loued &c. *it commaundeth as impossible a thing, as if it should bid vs fly ouer the hill Caucasus. Caluin* also determineth the same, as a matter out of doubt. *Sit,* saith he, *extra controuersiam* &c. *Let it be out of all controuersie, that the accomplishment of the law in this flesh, is impossible.*

Luther in respon ad dialog. Siluest. prieratis. Melanch. ad ca. 4. epi. ad Rom. editio Caluin li. 2. institut. ca. 7. Vide Io. Cocci lib. 3. art. 2. de Iustif. hominis.

25 Thus say they, concerning the impossibilitie to keepe the commaundements, but how impious, and absurd this their doctrin is, it may appeare by two consequents that must needes follow thereof. The first is, that they doe in effect taxe God of iniustice, not only for commaunding thinges impossible, but much more for ordaining punishment for the breach thereof, for no man can be iustly punished, for that which he cannot performe. The other consequent is, that they disanimate their followers, from endeuouring to obserue Gods commaundements, for no man can haue courage, or will to obserue that, which he shall hold to be impossible, and therefore how preiudiciall to common welth this doctrin is, any man may easely iudge.

26 But much more absurd, and preiudiciall is their opinion, concerning the abrogation of the Commaundements by Christ, which *Luther* teacheth euidently, when he reasoneth thus. *Sola fides, & verbum* &c. *Only faith and the word, doe reigne in the soule, whereby it is manifest, that only faith suffiseth a christian man for all thinges, and that he needeth no*

Luther de libertate Christiana.

workes

workes for his iustification, and if he neede no workes, he needeth no law, if he neede no law, he is free from the law, and it is true, that the law is not made for the iust. Thus argueth *Luther*, and vppon the same ground he affirmeth resolutelie els where. *Sola fides necessaria est* &c. *Only faith is necessary, that we may be iust, all other thinges are most free, neither commaunded any more nor prohibited.* And againe in an other place. *Nihil omnino*, saith he, *Deo es obligatus* &c. *Thou art bound to God in nothing, but to beleeue and confesse him, in all other thinges, he maketh thee free, that thou maiest doe according to thy owne will, without any offence of conscience* &c. So he.

Idem ad ca. 2. ad Galat.

Idem in ca. 7. ep. 1. ad Corinth.

27 And doth he not plainelie teach herein, that Christians are exempted from all obligation of Gods law, and commaundents? Where vppon his dearest darling *Philip Melancthon*, saith thus. *Necesse est, vt fateamur* &c. *VVe must needes confesse, that the commaundements are also abrogated, our sophisters* (he meaneth *the Catholikes*) *doe say, that the iudiciall, and ceremoniall part of the law is abrogated, and that the law of manners* (that is to say the morall part of the law, or the commaundements) *is encreased by Christ, so that they make of Christ twise Moyses.* Thus saith *Melancthon*, giuing to vnderstand, that the Catholikes in teaching that Christ did not abrogat the morall part of *Moyses* law, but confirme it, doe deny Christ, making him no other then a second *Moyses*.

Melanch. in locis comun. editio. 2. pa. 76.

28 To the same purpose also, the rigid *Lutherans*, of whome I made mention before taught, and mainteined in the foresaid conference at *Altemburg*, that *nihil ad nos Christianos præcepta decalogi pertinent: the precepts of the Decalogue*, or the tenne commaundements, *doe belong nothing at all to vs Christians.* And the reason, that they yeld thereof is, because the christian which beleeueth *is*, say they, *supra omnem obedientiam, & supra omnem legem, aboue all obedience, and aboue all law.* Thus they.

Colloquium Altemburg. habitum an. 1568. impres. Ienæ an. 1568. in 4.

29 Therefore, what marueile is it, that a sect of *Lutherans* called *Antinomi*, draw also out of these principles of *Luther*, these conclusions following. *Lex non est digna, vt vocetur* &c. *The law is not worthy to be called the word of God, if thou be a whoore, or a fornicator, or an adulterer, or any other sinner what soeuer, only beleeue, and thou art in the way of saluation, euen when thou stickest fast, in the very midest of thy sinne. The tenne commaundements belong to the court, but not to the Pulpit. VVhosoeuer haue any thinge to doe vvith Moyses, doe goe the right vvay to the diuell* &c. The saying of *Peter*. *Certam facite vocationem vestram per bona opera. Make sure your vocation by good workes, is vnprofitrble. VVhensoeuer thou hast any cogitation, that any meanes is to be vsed in the church that men may be good, honest, and holly, and chast, thou art already gone astray from the ghospell.* Thus they, teaching in truth nothing els, but the very quintessence of *Luthers* doctrin concerning

Confeßio Mansfeldés. in secta Antinomorum. Vide Iodocũ Coccium vbi supra. Et Stanislaũ Reschium de Euangelic. sect. centuriis tit. Antinomio.

cerning faith, and workes, or rather explicating the same, and extracting out of it, such necessarie consequences, as must needes follow of it, as it may be euident to any man, that shall consider his groundes, and principles aboue mentioned.

30 But to omit other thinges, and to touch only that which concerneth the abrogation of the commaundements, can any thing be more pestiferous to common welth, then this doctrin? For seeing, that all the tenne commaundements, except the keeping of the sabaoth (whereto christians are not bound as the Iewes were) are nothing els in effect, but the very explication of the law of nature, obserued by the Gentils, according to the light of naturall reason, can any reasonable man thinke, that Christ exempted his seruants from the obseruation thereof? Can any doctrin tend more directly then this, to ouerthrow all common welth, and to extinguish the very law of nature in men, and to make men litle better, then beastes?

31 For if euery man were persuaded, that he hath no obligation in conscience by the law of God, to honour, and obey his parents, nor to forbeare theft, periurie, fraud, and deceit, fornication, adulterie, and such other thinges, as the law of God, and nature forbiddeth, what a confusion would there follow amongst men within a while? Would not the shame, that men naturallie haue of sinne, be lost by litle, and litle, and so, humane nature become bestiall, and no other bridle be left to restraine men fron any enormitie, but only the feare of humane lawes? Which how litle it auaileth many times, experience showeth, and I haue sufficientlie signified in my first part? [*ar* 1. *ch.* 9. *nu.* 28. 29. 30.31.32. & 33.] And how preiudiciall this doctrin, is also to the authoritie of humane lawes, I will declare heareafter, in an article a part, and doe conclude for the present, that it sufficiently appeareth, by this which I haue here debated, that this doctrin of the sectaries, touching the abrogation of the commaundements, is no lesse absurd, beastly, and iniurious to God, and nature, then preiudiciall to common welth.

32 Fiftly, the Catholike doctrin concerning mans free will, aswell in morall, and ciuill, as in naturall actions, is a great motiue, to incite men to the practise of all morall vertue, for the publike good: for, he that considereth the excellencie and dignitie of vertue, and the benefit, both priuat, and publike, that may be reaped thereby, and beleeueth with all, that he may liue vertuouslie if he will, he cannot, but be much encouraged thereto. Besides that, vpon the consideration of mans free will, are grounded all pollitical lawes, precepts and prohibitions, paines, and rewardes: For if man had not free will, to doe at least ciuillie, and

and morally well, he could neither be iustly punished, nor rewarded neither yet admonished, counselled, or commaunded, as the very pagan philosophers argue out of the light of reason, so that if there were not free will in man for ciuill, and morall actions, all politicall gouerment (which proceedeth from the very law of nature, and reason) must needes be vtterly superfluous, and against reason.

Aristot. ethic l. 3. Plato. in Gorgia.

33 Whereby yt appeareth, not only that the catholike doctrin concerning mās free will, ys most cōforme to reason of state, but also that the contrary opinion of *Luther, Caluin*, and other sectaries, ys most repugnant thereunto and absurd, seeing yt cannot stand with that course of pollitical gouernment, which nature hath ordained, besides that, yt must needes hinder mens endeuour to be vertuous, and draw them to all kind of vice: for he which ys persuaded, that all humane actions are guided by an absolute necessity (as the Arch sectaries aboue named haue tanght) he must needes conceiue also, that yf God haue ordained him to be vertuous, he shalbe vertuous whether he wil, or no, yf to be vicious, he cannot doe withall. Where vppon yt must needes follow, that beleeuing this doctrin, and finding bad inclinations in himselfe (as euery man doth more or lesse) he will thinke yt very vayne and superfluous to resist them, and so will suffer himselfe to be transported there with, persuading himselfe, that he cannot helpe yt. So that yf this opinion were generally receiued, men would become no better then beastes, following their owne sensuall appetits in all thinges, as drawne thereto by an absolute necessity: and therefore how inconuenient this would be, either for common welth, or for mens particuler estates, euery man may iudge, seing that yt doth frustrate and euacuat, not only all politicall gouuerment and morall vertue (as I haue declared) but also all humane prouidence, discourse, deliberation, and consultation in mens priuat affaires, all which were needelesse and vaine, yf man had not free wil to make his choise and electiō: in which respect *Eusebius Cæsariensis*, shewing the absurdity of this opinion by many notable reasons, concludeth very wel, that those which hold yt, do peruert and ouerthow, *vniuersam vitam humanam, all the life of man.*

Luther in assert. art. 36 Caluin. li. 1. institut. ca 16. ss. 8. & li. 2. c. 4. ss. 6. Bucer. li. de. cōcordia ar. de libero arb. Melanch. in locis cōmun. editis an 1521

Euseb. de preparatione Euang. li. 1. ca. 7.

34 Sixtly no lesse absurd, and inconuenient for common welth ys the impious and blasphemous opinion of *Luther Melanchthon, Zuinglius, Caluin, Beza* and other sectaries, that God doth not only moue, and commaund men to sinne, but also worke yt in them. *Luther*, teacheth that *mala opera in impijs operatur deus. God worketh euill workes in wicked men*, and asketh this question. *Quis audet negare?* &c. *VVho dare deny, that he ys oft*

Luther in Assertionib⁹ impressis Vitenberg. an. 1520. art. 36.

times compelled in euill workes to doe otherwise, then he thought. And againe in his booke *de seruo arbitrio*, he affirmeth that, *Iudas did necessarily betray Christ*, and that *yt was not in his hand or power to doe otherwise, or to change his will* which, saith he, *God moued by his omnipotency, as he doth all other thinges.* Where vppon *Melancthon* making as yt were a glose, vppon this ground of his master teacheth, *that the treason of Iudas, was the proper worke of God, as wel as the vocation of Paule.*

Melanch. ad ca. 8. ep. ad Rom. edit. 1.

Zuinglius ser. de prouidentia ad Phillippum Cattor. principem an. 1530. ca. 6.

35 *Zuinglius* also, deliuereth the same doctrin, and amongst diuers other deuilish and blasphemous speches, he saith thus. *Vnum atque idem facinus puta adulterium &c. One and the selfe same wicked act, to wit adultery, or homicid, as it is the worke of God, the Author and mouer of it, is not an offence, or sinne, but as it is, the worke of man, it is a sinne* and a wicked act: and againe. *Numen ipsum auctor est eius, quod nobis est iniustitia, illi autem nullatenus est. God himselfe is the authour of that which is iniustice in respect of thvs, ough it is not so in respect of him.* Thus he, and affirmeth also further, that God not only moueth, but also *compelleth the theefe to kill the innocent*, and yet that the theefe is iustly punished for it, *because he sinneth against the law of God*, not as the author, but *as the instrument*, whome therefore, *Zuinglius* compareth to *a hammer, and a file* which a man may vse, as it pleaseth him, turning the hammer into a file, or the file, into a hammer.

Ibid. ca. 5.

Ibid. c. 6.

Vide Bellar. lib. 2. cap. 3. de Amiss. gratia a statu peccati. Iod. Cocciū. To. 2. de peccato hom. art. 1. libri. 2.

36 The very same doctrin, teacheth *Caluin* in diuers partes of his workes, as in his booke *de æterna dei prædestinatione*, printed at *Geneua* in the yeare 1552. fol. 905. 916. 906. 944. & 946. & li. 1. Institut. ca. 17. ss. 11. & ca. 18. ss. 1. & ss. 2. & *deinceps, & libro* 2. ca. 4. ss. 2. 3. & 4. & li. 3. ca. 23. ss. 4. 7. 8. & 9. in which places he affirmeth, that God not only permitteth all the sinnes of men, but also that he hath determined them from all æternity, that he commaundeth the diuell to draw men to sinne, and that he inclineth, moueth, and compelleth men thereto, yea, and that he worketh himselfe in the mindes of wicked men, as the first cause, vsing them as his instruments.

37 The same also is taught seriously by *Peter* a *Martyr*, and most amply by b *Beza*, whose wordes I willingly pretermit, not to rake vp further the chānel of such a filthy, and beastly doctrin, which the very Painims, would haue abhorred, who beleeued, and taught most constantly, that God c being goodnes it selfe, cannot possible be the cause, or author of sinne, no more then fire, being hott by nature, can refrigerat, or coole any thing.

a *Petrus martir ad. c. 2. li. 1. Samuel. & in ep. ad Rom.*
b *Beza in responsione ad Sebastianum.*
c *Castalionem de æterna dei prædestinat.*

38 But to let passe for the present the considerations belonging to religion, and to touch only, one, or twoo concerning reason of state, who seeth not what inconuenience must needes follow of this doctrin

in

in common welth? For what care will any man haue to auoid ſinne, when he shal be perſwaded that if he ſinne, he doth but fulfill the eternal decree of God, whoſe will he cannot reſiſt: and that God both moueth, and compelleth him thereto, yea, and worketh it in him. How can ſuch a one (I ſay) that is ſo perſwaded, either hate ſinne, or be ſorry for it, or yet beleeue, that he doth ſynne at all, or thinke any punishment to be iuſt, be it deuine, or humane, that shalbe inflicted vppon him for any offence what ſoeuer?

39 For whereas the maſters of this deteſtable doctrin teach, that euil acts are ſinne, not in reſpect of God (though they ſay he is the author and mouer of them) but in reſpect of vs, who are the inſtruments of God, and doe breake his eternal law, their abſurditie in this diſtinctiō is euident, for diuers reaſons. For firſt, who knoweth not that the authour, mouer, and worker of an euil act, vſing an inſtrument which cannot reſiſt his will, is in fault for the act, and not the inſtrument (no though it be an actiue inſtrument, as they ſay man is) eſpeciallie ſeeing they alſo teach (as appeareth in the former article) that man hath no vſe at all of free wil, but is drawne, and compelled to will, or doe euery thing that he doth by an abſolute neceſſitie, and an eternall decree of God: in which reſpect *Zuinglius* hath great reaſon (acording to this opinion) when he compareth man in this caſe, to a *hammer* or a *file*, ſeeing he hath no more libertie in his action, then thoſe or any other paſſiue, or dead inſtrumenrs: whereuppon it muſt needes follow, that God being both the mouer of mans euill will, and intention, and alſo the worker of the euil act in him, is the ſinner (if any ſinne be committed) and not man, who is but Gods inſtrument, and cannot chooſe but fulfill his will, which conſequent, how blaſphemous it is, euery man ſeeth.

40 Secondly, if the reaſon of mans ſinne be in this caſe, becauſe he breaketh the eternall law of God (for ſo ſay theſe doctors) I would gladly know of them, whether the abſolute will of God, and his eternal decrees, be not in all caſes to be held for his lawes, and ſo to be obeyed: which cannot be denied, for, whatſoeuer he eternallie decreeth, and abſolutelie willeth, the ſame is his law, and therfore ought to be performed. Whereuppon I inferre, that ſeeing God hath not only eternallie decreed the ſinnes of men (as theſe ſectaries teach) but alſo moueth, and compelleth men thereto, effecting, working, and executing his owne decree in them, and by them, it cannot with any reaſon be ſaid, that men ſinne, in concurring with his abſolut will, but rather that they doe their duty in obeying the ſame: ſo that, albeit God haue

eternallie decreed, that adulterie shall not be committed, and that all men are bound to obay this diuine law, and decree (as many doe) yet it must needes be vnderstood, that when he moueth, and forceth men to commit adulterie, he either contradicteth himselfe in breaking his owne law, or at least, dispenseth with his law, and maketh the breach thereof in such case, to be lawfull. As for example, if a prince hauing forbidden the transport of corne, or money out of his country, vpon paine of death, should neuerthelesse commaund, yea and compell some afterwards to breake his law, could any man beso absurd to say, that such a subiect so commaunded, and compelled by his prince, should thereby commit any offence against him? Or that the prince, did not in that case dispense, with his owne law? And if he should not, but would inflict the penalty vppon the party, would not all men iustly condemne such a prince, of monstrous iniustice, and tirannie?

41 Thus then it appeareth, that two notable, and blasphemous absurdities, doe necessarilie follow of this opinion of these sectaries. The one, that if any sinne be committed in the transgression of gods law, God is the sinner, being the author and worker of it, and not man, who is but Gods instrument, and cannot resist his will, and consequentlie cannot sinne therein, no more then a horse, or a beast, seing that according to the knowne, and common axiome. *Nullum est peccatum, quod non sit voluntarium. There is no sinne, which is not voluntarie.* The other absurditie is, that God doth daily, and hourelie, either breake, or at least dispense with his owne eternal lawes, mouing, and compelling men to the breach thereof, seeing that daily, and hourelie, men doe transgresse them by Gods owne motion, and compulsion, as these sectaries teach. Whereuppon there followeth also, an other notable absurditie, touching both religion, and state, to witt, that all penal lawes, deuine, and humane, ordained for the punishment of sinne, are vtterlie vniust, yea, and that there is no hell, or damnation for sinners, because there is no sinne committed by men, according to this ground.

S. Aug. li. de vera religione c. 14.

42 Therefore I appeale here, to the iudgement of any indifferent man, what a good Christian, and member of a common welth, he is like to be, that is thus perswaded, and how pernicious it would be to all states, that this doctrin of *Caluin*, and other sectaries should be taught, and receiued therein? Whereas the contrarie doctrin of Catholikes, as it is most pious, so is it also most political, teaching that God being infinitlie good, and iust, is so farr from mouing, or tempting any man to sinne, that *he hateth both the sinne, and the sinner*, and neither tempteth

Psalm. 72. Sap. 14. Iac. 1. 13.

pteth any man himselfe (for *Deus neminem tentat*, saith S. Iames. *God* 1. Cor. 10. 13.
tempteth no man) neither yet *suffreth* any man *to be tempted aboue his power*, as the apostle teacheth expressly: And therefore, although God concurre with man to the act of the sinne, as he doth to the actions of all his creatures (as an vniuersal cause, without whose concurrence, no creature what soeuer, could haue any operation:) yet he concurreth not to the deformitie of the act, wherein the sinne consisteth, which deformitie proceedeth from a particuler cause, that is to say, from the will of man: so that, albeit God may be said to be a cause of the action, yet he cannot be said to be a cause of the sinne.

43 As in like case, when a monster is borne of a woman, the monstruositie, or deformitie (which is a certaine sinne of nature) cannot be referred to the heauens, which are an vniuersal cause, but to the defect of the parents, who are the next cause: for, the influence of the heauens, which is vniuersal, and worketh in all creatures alike, would not produce, either man or horse, or plant, if it were not determined, by a particuler cause: and therefore man, who doth procreat the monster, is the cause of the deformitie, and not the heauen, which alwayes giueth such influence, that a perfect man might be produced thereby, if there were not some defect and hindrance in man himselfe, who is the next cause.

44 And the like is to be vnderstood in this question, concerning the cause of mans sinne, for that the concurrence of God, to the actions of man, is indifferent either to good, or bad, and may be vsed well, if man will, and therefore seeing that man doth abuse both it, and his owne free will, to the breach of Gods law, he is truly the cause of his owne sinne, and iustly deserueth to be punished. And here vpon it followeth, that all punishment for sinne, and the lawes that ordaine the same, are most iust, which whosoeuer beleeueth (as all Catholikes doe) he hath thereby a notable motiue to obay all good lawes, as well humane, as deuine, and to acknowledge euen his owne punishment to be most iust, in case he transgresse them. Whereby it appeareth how necessarie this Catholike doctrin is to be taught, and beleeued, in regard both of conscience, and of common welth, and how preiudiciall the contrarie doctrin of the sectaries is in both respects. And therefore no marueile, that *Plato* forbad it to be taught in his common welth, ordaining that *no man, either young, or ould,* Plato dialog. 2. de repub.
should be suffred to say, or heare, that God is the cause of euil, which saith he, *is neither holly to be spoken, nor profitable to vs.* Thus much for this point.

45 Seauenthly, who can deny, the great vtilitie, that groweth to common welth, by the Catholike doctrin, and practise of the sacrament of pennance, consisting in the *Confession* of sinnes, *Contrition*, and *Satisfaction?* What a notable, and potent remedie, is it against all sinne, and vice, seeing that thereby we are taught, and accustomed to examine our consciences, to discerne betwixt sinne, and sinne, to stirr vp in our selues acts of contrition, and sorrow for the same, to make full purpose of amendment (without the which, we know our confession to be fruitelesse:) and finallie to labour to doe satisfaction, not only to almightie God by pennance, but also to our neighbour in case of wronges, by restitution of goods, and fame, and to doe all kind of good workes, for the publike good? Besides that the very shame to confesse our owne sinnes and deffects, is a notable bridle to restraine vs from offending either God, or our neighbour.

46 And of these great benefits, we haue most manifest, and daily experience in the Catholike church. For besides the priuat, and particuler comfort that men receiue thereby in their owne soules, and the encrease of Gods grace, for the repression of sinne (which euery man, that duly frequenteth confession, trieth sufficientlie in himselfe) there follow also thereof many notable commodities to the publike, to wit, greate store of almes giuen to the poore, and many charitable workes daily done, the reconciliation of enemies, and composition of quarrels, restitution of stolne, or ill gotten goods, and the reformation of manners in seruants towards their masters, in children toward their parents, in maried folkes one towards the other, and in all sort of officers, and subiects towardes their princes: whereas the sectaries, hauing no vse of confession, are depriued aswell of the priuat, as of the publike benefit thereof, yea and liue in such a continual ignorance of the state of their owne soules, that it is a lamentable case to see.

47 For I may be bold to say, that very few of them (if there be any at all) doe so much as know, how to examine duly their owne consciences, or are able to discerne truly betwixt sinne, and sinne, in so much, that they know not many times, how, and when, they offend God, which we find daily by experience in such of them, as are conuerted to the Catholike religion, who no doubt, will alwayes testifie the same, as also, what light of soule, encrease of grace, and spirituall consolation they find by the vse of confession. And so notorious, is the dammage that followeth of the want thereof to the common welth, that the citty of *Noremberg* in *Germany*, hauing receiued *Luthers* new Ghospel, and banished confession, found such euident in-

conuience

conuenience thereby, that they sent a solenne embassage, and made great suit to the Emperour *Charles* the fift, to haue it restored againe in to their citty, by an imperiall law, as witnesseth *Dominicus Soto*, who was there present, and testifieth further, that the Embassadours were worthily laughed at for their paines, seeing they imagined, that men might be compelled, by an Imperiall law, to confesse their secret sinnes, without any obligation in conscience, or remission of sinnes, both which they denied according to *Luthers* doctrin which they professed.

Dominicus Soto in 4. Sentẽtia dist. 18. q. 1. ar. 1.

48 But if any of our aduersaries shall obiect here, as some are wont to doe, that our vse of confession, is rather an encouragement to sinne, then a restraint of it, by reason of the facilitie to obtaine absolution, and pardon at the priests handes, it may easely appeare how fond, and friuolous their conceit is, if wee consider twoo thinges.

49 The first is, that they haue no reason to imagine so great facilitie therein, seeing that the very repugnance, which all men naturallie haue to discouer their owne imperfections, and offences, might of it selfe, suffice to diuert vs from confession, were it not that the force of Gods grace, ouer commeth nature therein. For proofe whereof, we find by experience, that some wicked men, who stick not to brag, and vaunt of their wicked acts amongst themselues, yea in publike before others, are neuerthelesse so ashamed, to confesse them before Gods minister, in the sacrament of confession, that they are hardly drawne to doe it once a yeare, to satisfie the precept of the church.

50 But if we add to this natural repugnance, the contrition, and sorrow, that is requisit on our part: the full purpose (with the helpe of Gods grace) neuer to commit the same sinnes againe, or any other: the pennance enioined by the priest, and satisfaction to be donne (al which is of necessitie required to obtaine remission:) yea, and which is more, if we consider, that if the said pennance be not sufficient to satisfie Gods iustice, and that the defect thereof be not otherwaies supplied in this life, it is to be payed in purgatorie, *centupliciter*, saith a *S. Bernard*, a hundreth fold, *vsque ad* b *nouissimum quadrantem*, *euen to the last farthing* (which moueth vs also to add voluntarie penance of our owne part, to the iniunction, and ordonance of the priest:) if all this, I say, be well waighed, no man hath reason to say, that we are easely quit of our sinnes, or that the facilitie of pardon, doth encourage vs to sinne, the rather.

a S. Bernar. Ser. de obitu Humberti monachi & Concil Florent. in litteris vnionis b Matth. 5. S. Cyprian. ep. 52. ad Antonianum.

51 But now if we consider, on the behalfe of our aduersaries, how much more easely they cleare their skore, or rather (if I may so say) scape scot-free, with their only faith, and imputatiue iustice, it will

quickly

quickly appeare, how ridiculous this their obiection is against vs: for if wee Catholikes be animated to sinne, the rather (as they say we are) by the hope of an easy remission, at the priests handes (whereto neuerthelesse all the foresaid conditions are requisit on our part) what may be said of them, who neede not in their conceit, to doe any more, then only to beleue firmelie, that their sinnes are forgeeuen them for the meritts of Christ.

Luther in postil. dominica Reminiscere.

52 Therefore *Luther* saith. *Qui fortiter, & firmiter credit*, &c. He which *strongly, and firmely beleeueth, that his sinnes are forgiuen him, he may omit this confession, and confesse to him selfe alone.* So he. And of contrition he saith thus.

Idem sermo de penitent. an. Dom. 1517. & in Assertiõ art. 6.

53 *Contritio quæ paratur*, &c. *The contrition which is gott by the discußion, collection, and detestation of our sinnes, pondering their greeuousnes, filthines, multitud, and the losse of eternall blisse, and the purchase of eternall damnation, this contrition, I say, makes a man an hipocrit, and a greater sinner.* Thus he. Who also saith of satisfaction thus.

Idem sermo de penitentia. vide Iodocum Coccium lib. 7. de pœniten.

54 *Post peccata etiam grauißima* &c. *After the most greeueous sinnes, that may be, no satisfaction is to be done by vs, lest we derogat from the satisfaction of Christ.* Thus teacheth *Luther.*

Caluin in institut. ca. 4. ss. 25. 30. 31. & 32. Vide Io. Cocci. ibidem.

55 Also *Caluin*, vtterly reiecteth all the meanes, that Catholikes vse, for the satisfaction of their sinnes (as namely *Lachrimas, ieiunia, & officia charitatis. Teares, fastinges, and offices, or workes of charity.*) And addeth further. *Talibus mendaciis* &c. *To such lies I oppose, the franke, and free remißion of sinnes, so clearelie declared in the holy scripture, as nothing more.* So he. Fathering his loose, & wicked doctrin vpon the scriptures, though most falselie, as it will appeare most manifestlie in the next chapter, where I hall haue occasion to treate amply, of the continual practise of mortification and penance in the church of God,

Chap. 36. from num. 4. to nu. 49.

56 Now then, can any man inuent, or imagin, an easier way to the remission of his sinnes, then to lay all the pennance, satisfaction, and penaltie thereof vppon Christes backe, and to beare no part of the burthen himselfe? Or can any doctrin more animate men to sinne, then this? No truly, and therefore I may truly say, that it is most pernicious to common welth, as it may appeare euen in *Plato*, who in his lawes ordained, punishment for a certaine kind of wicked men, who liued in his time, and were of opinion, that God pardoneth the greatest offences, and sinnes of men, with all facilitie, as for a litle sacrifice, and prayer, which kind of men *Plato* numbreth with the *Atheists*, that deny the prouidence of God, and holdeth them to be no lesse hurtfull to the common welth, then they: and no meruaile, seeing that one of

Plato. de legib. dial. 11.

the

the speciall benefits of religion in common welth (to wit the feare of gods iustice in the chastisement of sinne) was vtterly frustrated by that opinion. And truly the like may wel be said, of the meanes prescribed at this day, by the sectaries for the remission of sinne, which they teach to be more facil, and easy, then that which *Plato* condemned, seeing that they escape, as they thinke, farr better cheape then with sacrifice, and prayer, to wit, with a franke, and free remission only, for the merits of Christ: Thus much for the seuenth point.

57 Eightly, the Catholike doctrin, and practise of prayer to Saints, and of their canonization, and the honour donne vnto them, is a great helpe, and furtherance, to good, and vertuous life, and consequentlie most consonant to reason of state, for what greater spurr, or prouocation to vertue can be imagined, then the notable example of the most vertuous liues of Saintes, and the honour which, wee see, is daily donne them in earth, euen by Emperours, Kinges, and Princes, besides the ineffable felicitie which wee beleeue they haue, and shall haue eternallie in heauen? Can any thing, I say, more potentlie moue vs to aspire to the perfection of vertue, then not only to see it so highly rewarded, and glorified euen in this world, but also to haue so many notable guides to lead vs to the practise of it by their example, represented vnto vs partly in the written histories of their liues, partly by our preachers, and lastly by their feastes, and solemnities, images, and pictures? So that though nothing els were to be respected in this point, but only this continuall incitation to vertue, & sanctitie, it must needs be graunted to be most politicall.

58 But who can sufficientlie expresse, the inestimable benefit, that not only priuat and particuler men, but also whole common welths, kingdomes, and states, receiue by the intercession, and prayers of Angels, and Saints, procured by our inuocation of them, whereof the experience is euident in all histories, by infinit examples in all ages, and times, which I shall not neede to relate here, seeing that I haue sufficientlie performed it, partly in the first [a] part of this treatise, and partly in the [b] *foure and twentith* chapter of this second part, where I answered certaine obiections of *Machiauel*, and therefore I remit my reader thereto, and conclude, that it is manifest hereby, that the doctrin of the sectaries, impugning the prayer to Saints, and the honour donne them here in earth, is preiudiciall to common welth, depriuing it, both of a great motiue to vertue, and also of the benefit of their protection? besides that, contening, & dishonoring the Saintes of God, whom his spouse the church, ordaineth to be reuerenced, & honoured,

[a] *Par. 1. ch. 15. per totum.*
[b] *Chap. 24. nu. 31.*

they contemne, and dishonour God himselfe, and thereby prouoke his iust iudgement, and wrath against the common welth, where their religion is generally embraced.

59 The ninth point, which I wish to be considered, is, our doctrin, concerning the fast of Lent, friday, saturday, and the vigils of our principall feastes, which how necessarie it is for common welth, it seemeth to be sufficientlie acknowledged in our country, euen at this day. For albeit our aduersaries hold it for superstitious, yet our wise magistrates, knowing the fast of Lent to be conuenient, for the encrease, and breede of all kind of cattell in the spring time, and that the other fasts also, doe helpe greatly, aswell to conserue all kind of flesh vittaile (which otherwaise might be ouer much wasted) as to maintaine, the fishing at sea, whereof resulteth the maintenance, and encrease of mariners, necessarie for our nauigation, (whereto may be added also, a consideration of good economy, to wit, frugalitie, and moderation of expence, in euery particuler familie:) for these causes, I say, and such like, our magistrats doe still retaine, some publike vse of those fasts, yea and haue added thereto, a kind of abstinence from flesh vppon the wensday, ordained by act of parlament, in the late Queenes time, though neuerthelesse it is no way obserued in *Englãd*, for ought I know, neither yet are the other fasts kept by our aduersaries, otherwise then for seruants only, to saue charges, for euery one, that can get flesh, eateth it freely without scruple, whereby the law is generallie broken, and the common wealth endammaged.

60 But besides these foresaid benefits, that grow to common welth, by the obseruation of our fasts, fiue other may be recounted, very important to be considered. The first is, the repression of vice, by the maceration, and extenuation of the flesh, whereby concupiscence, and lust is restrained, the flesh made subiect to the spirit, and many exorbitant sinnes, which grow of excesse auoided, to the publike good, wherefore *S. Ambrose* calleth fasting. *Fundamentum castitatis, & culpæ mortem. The foundation of chastitie, and the death of sinne.*

Ambros. in li. de Helia. & ieiunio. c. 3.

61 The second benefit is, the purification of the soule, whereby it is enabled the better to performe the act of contemplatiõ, wherein consisteth the end, and felicitie of common welth. For as the Apostle witnesseth. *Quanto externus homo noster corrumpitur, tanto internus innouatur.* By "how much more our outward man is corrupted, or weakened, so much more is our inward man renewed. And therefore also *S. Chrisostome* calleth fasting. *Alimentum animæ.* The meat or nurriture of the soule, and "addeth this reason: *sicut corporalis iste cibus* &c. As this corporall meate doth

2. Cor. 4. d. 16.

S. Chrisost. ho. 1. in Genes.

doth nourish and fatten the body, so doth fasting strenghtens the soule, and giueth it fethers and winges, whereby it may mount vp, and contemplat the highest thinges. For this cause also the old philosophers, prescribed great abstinence and fasting to their contemplatiues, as I haue declared before, in the *seauenthteene* chapter, when I treated of philosophicall contemplation.

Chap. 17. nu. 17.

62 The third benefit is, the health of the body which is greatly hindred and impaired by repletion, and plentiful diet, and therefore S. *Basill* calleth fasting, *matrem sanitatis the mother of health*, and addeth. *Interroga medicos & dicent tibi* &c. Aske the phisicans and they will tell thee, that there is nothing more dangerous then to haue thy body in too good a plight, in which respect those which are most skilfull in the art of phisick, doe by fasting abate the redundance of the body, lest other waise the waight of corpulency, may oppresse nature. So he.

S. Basil. de laudibus ieiunij ho. 2.

63 The fourth benefit is, the pacification of Gods wrath, by the affliction of our bodies, as appeareth in the *Niniuits*, who by their fasting, appeased the wrath of God, and scaped the destruction, threatned them by the prophet, and therefore S. *Ambrose* doth worthily call fasting. *Sacrificium reconciliationis. A sacrifice, whereby we are reconciled to God.* And S. *Basil* saith that, *pœnitentia sine ieiunio ociosa, & infrugifera est. Pennance without fasting, is idle, and fruteles*: and, *per ieiunium*, saith he, *satisfacito deo, satisfie God by fasting.*

Iona. 3. *S. Ambros. li. de Helia. & ieiu. ca. 9.* *S. Basil. de laude ieiunij ho. 1.*

64 The fift benefit is, the impetration or obteining at God handes, not only of all temporall good, necessary for common welth, but also Gods grace, whereby we are disposed to all vertue, aswell moral and politicall, as Theological, for which cause. S. *Ambrose* calleth fasting. *Radicem gratiæ, the roote of grace.* And S. *Chrisostome, matrem omnium bonorum. The mother of all good.* And *omnium virtutum magistram. The mistresse, or teacher of all vertue.* And saith in an other place. *Ieiuna quia peccasti*, &c. Fast because thou hast sinned, fast that thou maist not sinne, fast that thou maiest receiue gifts of God, and fast that thou maiest retaine and keepe his gifts which thou hast receiued. And S. *Basill*, shewing the notable effects and fruits of fasting, by many examples of the holly scripture, saith that *it giueth wisdome to lawmakers, fortitude in warre, and quiet or tranquillity in peace*, meaninge, that it obtaineth of God, those gifts and benefits for the common welth. And therefore S. *Chrisostome* also worthily termeth it, *bonorum, atque beneficiorum cardinem*, the very hinge whereon doe hang and depend all the good thinges, and benefits spiritual, and temporall, which wee haue of almighty God: whereby it sufficiently appeareth, how necessary and profitable fasting is to common welth.

S. Ambros. vbi supra ca. 3. *Chrisost. ho. 1. in Gen.* *S. Basil. hom 1. de laud. ieiunij,* *Chrisost. ser. 2. de ieiunio.*

65 But perhaps, our aduersaries will say, that all these commodities may follow also of their doctrin, seeing that they doe not condemne all fasting, but only the fasts ordained by the church at certaine times, and vppon sett daies, as also the prohibition of flesh, eggs, and other meates, and that they allow voluntary fastes, as good, and necessary for the ends aforesaid.

66 But how litle benefit, the common welth reapeth by their doctrin in this behalfe, experience sheweth sufficiently, euen in them selues of whom wee see how few there are, which fast voluntarily, besides that it is manifest, that a voluntary fast, not prescribed by lawes, and at certaine times, can neuer be generall to the publike good, and when there is no prohibition of flesh, neither the flesh vittailes are generally spared, nor the fishing, and nauigatiō thereby maintained, nor cōcupiscence in men sufficiently repressed, nor yet the act of penaunce well permed, and consequently the iustice of God not so fully satisfied, nor his grace, and gifts so aboundantly obtained, as by the vniuersal and more strict fastes, that are prescribed by the Catholike church, as *S. Leo* surnamed the great, teacheth notably in those words. *Exercitatio continentiæ* &c. The practise of continency, or temperance, which euery man imposeth vppon himselfe, doth belong to the commodity but only of some portion, or part, whereas the fast that the whole church ordaineth, excludeth no man from the benefit of the generall purification, and then is the people of God most mighty, and strong, when the hartes of all the faithfull, agreeing in the vnity of holly obedience, there is an vniforme preparation, and the selfe same munition, or defence throughout the whole campe, of our christian army. Thus farr *S. Leo.* Where vppon I conclude, that our Catholike doctrin and practise of prescribed, and generall fasts, are most behouefull to the commō welth, and that the contrary doctrin of our aduersaries, hindring such notable, and vniuersall benefits, as hath benne declared, is most preiudiciall thereto.

S. Leo. ser.3. de ieiunio 7. mensis.

67 The tenth and last point shalbe, the different doctrin of Catholikes, and sectaries, touching the christian liberty, which Christ purchased for vs with his precious bloud, which wee say, was no other but freedome from the thraldome, and bondage of the diuel, and sinne, and from the seruitude of the Mosaical law, and that therefore, our christian liberty is no way preiudicial to the obedience due to our magistrats, and superiors spirituall, or tēporall, but that we are still bound to obay them as the apostle teacheth. *Non propter iram, sed propter cōscientiā. Not for wrath* (that is to say) *for feare of punishment, but for conscience,* which how

how necessarie it is to be taught, beleeued, and practised for the good of common welth, any man may easely iudge.

68 But the sectaries teach, that wee are freed by our Sauiour Christ, not only from the bondage of sinne, and the *Mosaycal* law (yea and from the commaundements of God, as I haue declared before) but also from all obligation of humane lawes, or statutes, I meane obligation in conscience, for so teacheth *Luther* expreslie, saying. *Nulla lex nos obligat, neque captiuat apud Deum.* No law doth bind, or captiuat vs before God, *apud quem*, saith he, *omnia licent, liberaque sunt*, before whome, or in whose sight, all thinges are lawfull, and free, or indifferent. And here vppon he also inferreth, that which I haue in part alledged out of him before, to wit; *nihil omnino Deo es obligatus, nisi solum vt credas, & eum confitearis, in omnibus aliis* &c. Thou art bound to God in nothing at all, but only to beleeue & confesse him, in all other things he makes thee free, that thou maist doe according to thy owne will, with out any offence of conscience. Thus he. *Caluin* also teacheth the very same in effect, making our christian libertie to consist speciallie in three things. The first is, that there be no regard had of the law, or of woorks, when there is question of iustification by *faith* (which, *Caluin* calleth not *fidem*, but *fiduciam*, confidence.) The second is, that good woorks be not examined by the rule of the law, but as to be accepted of God assuredlie, of what sort soeuer they be. The third is, that the vse of all externall things, be held for indifferent in such sort, that no scruple be made, whether we vse, or leaue them. Thus teacheth *Caluin* in greate conformitie with *Luther*, most impiouslie destroying, not only all that part of religion, and woorship of god, which consisteth in external things, but also all common welth, freeing, and exempting men by this doctrin, from all obligation in conscience to obay human lawes, which concerne for the most part, the good vse, or abuse of externall things: besids that, *Caluin* teacheth also expressélie els where, that Christians are not bound in conscience to the obseruation of euery particuler law of princes (he meaneth iust lawes) but to the general præcept of God to honour princes, and to respect the end of the lawe, that is to say peace, and the loue of our neighbour.

Luther in ca. 7. ep. 1. Cor.

Vide Conradum kellim aduersus cauinas Lutheri nuptias li. 4. tractatu 2. ca. 1.

Caluin li. 3. Instit. ca. 19. ss. 2. 4. & 7.

Vide Bellarm. li. 2. de Iustifica. ca. 1.

Caluin li. 4. Instit. ca. 10. ss. 5.

69 But if this be true, how standeth it with the doctrin of the Apostle, who hauing taught that all power is of god, and that he which resisteth the same resisteth Gods ordonance, addeth, *necessitate subditi estote &c.* Be yee subiect of necessitie, not only for feare of punishment,

cc

Rom. 13.

" but also for conscience sake? Is it not euident that the meaning of the apostle is, that conscience bindeth, wheresoeuer punishment may be iustly feared? In which respect, he showeth the necessitie of our obedience, by the consideration, aswel of abond in conscience, as of the feare of punishment, extending the one as far as the other: to which purpose S. *Augustin* saith, that *omnis iusta pœna, peccati pœna est.* If then we iustly feare punishment, for the breach of euery iust law of our prince, we are also to acknowledge, an obligation in conscience to obserue the same, especiallie seeing the Apostle teacheth in the same place, that those which resist humane power, *damnationem sibi acquirunt*, " doe purchase damnation to them selues, and that our princes, and " gouuernours are, *ministri Dei*, the ministers of God, that is to say, his substituts, and, as it were liuetenants, where vppon it must needs follow, that our disobedience to their iust lawes, doth include a disobedience to God, whose place, and person they represent. And therefore *S. Bernard* saith notably well. *Siue Deus, siue homo vicarius Dei &c.* Whether God, or man being the vicar, or substitut of God, doe geue a " commaundment, it is to be obayed with like care, *vbi tamen Deo contraria non præcipit homo*, when neuertheles man doth not commaund things " contrarie to God. Thus saith *S. Bernard.* And this I haue said breefely, to show that the christian libertie which these archsectaries teach, is no lesse repugnant to the veritie, & truth of the holly scriptures, then preiudicial to common welth, which would be vtterly subuerted, if all respect of conscience in the obseruation of humane lawes were abolished, as it wold be if their doctrin were generally receiued, seeing that it woulde follow thereon, that to breake human lawes, would be held for nothing els but to vse, & practise the priuilege of our christian libertie, as shall further appeare in the third part of this treatise.

Vide Bellarmin. li. 4. de Romano Pōtif. ca. 16.

Retract. li. 1. c. 9.

S. Bernard tract. de præcepto & dispē.

70 And although *Luther* doe afterwards, in the place before alledged, acknowledge a kind of obligation, of one man to an other, affirming that there is no danger of conscience before God, but only when there is offence committed against our neighbour, yet it is euident, that he doth not acknowledge thereby any obligation to obay humane lawes, but only to performe couenants, and mutual offices of charitie, & ciuill conuersation, & therefore he concludeth. *In summa nemini quicquam debeamus nisi vt inuicem diligamus, & mutuò per charitatem inseruiamus.* In fine, let vs owe nothing to any man, but that we loue, and mutuallie serue one an other for charitie sake.

71 And

71 And that this (I say) is his sense, and meaning, and not to teach bedience to human lawes, it appeareth plainely, aswell by that which haue cited out of him before (where he saith, that no law bindeth vs ,, efore God) as also by his exposition in the same place, of these wor- es of the Apostle. *Pretio empti estis, nolite fieri serui hominum.* You are " earely bought, doe not become the slaues of men, which saith he, ,, he Apostle, without all doubt, doth say, as a common, or general sen- ence, *contra statuta hominum*, against the statutes of men, *quibus tàm li- ertas, quàm aequalitas ista fidei annihilatur, & conscientiae arctantur*, with the " which, aswell this libertie, as the equalitie of faith is annihilated, and nens consciences are streightned or entangled. And againe afterwards, " lleadging also the same text, he saith, that the Apostle speaketh there ,, f Christ, *qui proprio sanguine nos ab omnibus peccatis, legibusque redemit, at- ue liberos effecit:* who with his owne bloud, reedemed vs from all sin- es, and lawes, and made vs free. And then addeth, that neuerthelesse, tis redemption, doth not concerne, *humanos contractus*, &c. humane contracts, or bargaines, by the which men are bound one to an other, s the contracts of the slaue, or seruant with his Lord, or master, and of he wife with her husband, *hos contractus*, saith he, *Paulus non tollit, sed ult seruari*, these contracts *Paule* doth not take away, but will haue " hem to be kept. ,,

Luther. vbi supra.

72 Thus saith *Luther*, distinguishing plainelie, as you see, betwixt the bligation to performe bargaines, or charitable offices, and an obli- gation to obay humane lawes, admitting the former, and denying the atter, vppon pretence of our christian libertie.

73 I haue debated this, the more largelie out of *Luthers* owne wor- des, aswell to the end, I might truly, and manifestlie shew his opinion, concerning this point, as also, that by the same occasion, I may further discouer here, his notable folly and grosse ignorance: his folly, in the euident contradiction of himselfe: and his ignorance, in his absurd, and ridiculous doctrin.

74 As for the first, it is to be considered, that hauing laid downe his general rule, or ground of the indifferencie of all externall thinges, in the sight of God, he maketh an exception, against his owne rule, see- ming to admit an obligation in conscience, euen in our externall actions, when they are iniurious to our neighbour, as I haue signified before, to which purpose he saith thus. There is no danger of con- science before God, in eating, or drinking, or in apparell, or in liuing in this, or that manner, *nisi contra proximum sit quod agitur*, except when that, which is done is preiudiciall to our neighbour. Thus he.

Luther vbi supra vide Conrad. Kellin. li. 4. tracta. 2. ca. 3.

75 And the reason, which he yeeldeth for it is, that although man is not bound to God, further then to beleeue, and confesse him (as I haue declared before) yet one man hath obligation to an other, for the performance of the workes of charitie, and of ciuill conuersation, in which respect, he saith also, that albeit wee are free towards God, yet wee are not free towards our neighbour, and albeit God careth not for our externall actions, in regard of himselfe, yet he careth for them, in regard of our neighbour, where vppon he also inferreth, that in offending, or wronging our neighbour, in externall thinges, wee endanger our consciences.

nu. 64.

76 Thus teacheth he, and yet neuerthelesse, he contradicteth it presentlie after. For hauing said, that there is no danger of conscience, in externall actions, but only when our neighbour is wronged, he addeth immediatelie. *Contra Deum hic peccari non potest, sed contra proximum.* For here, or in this case, that is to say, in externall acts, *we cannot sinne against God, but against onr neighbour.* But if it be true, which he affirmeth before, to witt, that there is danger of conscience, when we wrong our neighbour, how can it be true, that, *contra Deum hic peccari non potest? wee cannot sinne in this case against God?* Doth he not teach, that in doing iniurie to our neighbour, we endanger our conscience? And how can our conscience be in danger, when wee cannot sinne, and offend God? And therefore what els saith he here in effect, but that wee cannot offend God, when wee doe offend him, which is a most strange, and ridiculous contradiction.

77 Aad no lesse strange, and ridiculous is his folly, and grosse ignorance, in affirming that no sinne, or offence to God, canbe committed in externall thinges, but when there is some offence to our neighbour: for who knoweth not, that euen in those examples which he alledgeth of eating, drinking, and apparell, God may be most hainouslie offended, by dronkennesse, surfets, and prodigall expences, when neuerthelesse, our neighbour is no way wronged, or offended, but perhaps pleasured, and benefited? And who seeth not, that by this his wicked position and ground, of the indifferencie of all external things (which is also *Caluines* doctrin, as you haue heard) the holy sacraments themselues, are made indifferent to be vsed, or leaft at our pleasure, and that we cannot offend God therein (according to *Luthers* opinion) when no offence of our neighbour concurreth?

78 Furthermore how absurd is he, in making humane acts sinfull, & offensiue to god, not in respect of God himselfe, but only in respect of our neighbour, as though any sinne could be committed against a creature,

but in respect of some law, or ordonance made by the creator, whereby the offence is principally, and in order of nature, first committed against him, whose law, and will is thereby infringed, and broken: And therefore wee see, that wee doe not offend God alwaise in doing hurt to our neighbour (as in killing him by order of iustice) but in doing it inordinatelie, that is to say, against iustice, because the hurt, and offence of our neighbour, in that case, is against the will, and law of God, who is iustice it selfe, and to whome all iniustice is opposit, and offensiue. Besides that, it is to be considered, that no humane law, or iustice hath force to bind, but only, as it is conforme to the eternal law, and iustice of God, and therefore seeing, that euery effect dependeth more on the first cause, then on the second, and receiueth more influence from it, it followeth, that whatsoeuer is against humane law, reason, or iustice (in matters touching either our neighbours, or our selues) is principallie against the iustice, and eternall law of God, and consequentlie is a sinne committed directlie against him.

79 Lastly, what an impious, and monstrous absurditie, was it in *Luther,* to teach that God careth not for our externall acts, in respect of himselfe, but only in respect of our neighbour? Did he not know, or was he so wicked, and absurd to thinke, that God is not the last end of man, and of all humane actions, as well, as of all other thinges, and that therefore the loue, honour, duty, respect, and obligation of one man to an other, is speciallie for God, and to be principallie referred to his glory? Doth not the scripture teach vs, that *Deus vniuersa operatus est, propter semetipsum. God made, and wrought all thinges for him selfe?* Wherevppon it must needes follow, that he also careth for all things, principally for him selfe: for although he neede not our goods, as the *Psalmist* saith, neither receiueth any benefit by any seruice, honour, or glory, that we yeld him, either in our workes, or in our faith, yet it is most iust, that he be glorified by vs in all our actions, whether they concerne him, our selues, or our neighbours, wee being all his slaues, and creatures, and he our Lord, creator, and last end, or felicitie, & therefore he respecteth the obligation, that we haue one to an other, both as it is iust, & dependant on his eternal law, & because it finally redoūdeth to his seruice, & glory, for the which he created vs, & al thinges els: And to say otherwise as *Luther* doth (to wit, that God careth not for humane actions, but only in respect of man) is rather to make man the end of God, then God the end of man, which is in effect to introduce *Atheisme*: whereby wee see, to what beastlie absurditie *Luther* is driuen, to maintaine his wicked pretence of christian

Prouerb. 16.

libertie, being nothing els in truth, but the ſeruitude, and bondage of

1. Pet. 2. ſinne, or (as *S. Peter* ſaith) *velamen nequitiæ, the veile, or couer of wickednes,* in which reſpect it is euidentlie pernicious to common welth.

80 And this shall ſuffiſe for the *Tenne* pointes, whereof I purpoſed to treat in this chapter, whereto I could, and would add many more, were it not, that I haue thought it conuenient to reſerue diuers for the third part of this treatiſe, both becauſe they more properlie belong to the ſubiect that I haue ſpeciallie deſigned to handle therein, and alſo becauſe, I am forced for diuers cauſes, to haſt to the concluſion of this part, which is now already growne to a iuſt volume, and therefore cannot well be much further extended.

81 Now then I hope, good Reader, thou haſt euidentlie ſeene, aſwell by theſe *Tenne* pointes laſtly debated, as alſo by certaine other handled before, touching the euangelicall counſells, that the doctrin, and practiſe of Catholike religion, leadeth directlie to the perfection of vertue, and to the true imitation of Chriſt by pennaunce, and good workes, by mortification of the flesh, by reſtraint of the paſſions, and affections of the mind, and by repreſſion of concupiſcence, and of all kind of vice, and conſequentlie, that it muſt needes be moſt neceſſarie, and beneficiall to common welth, as I haue euidentlie proued. Whereas on the other ſide, the contrarie doctrin of our aduerſaries, do admit no mortification of the flesh, no pennaunce, nor ſatisfaction for ſinne, on our part, but looſeth the raines, and bridle to all kind of vice, teaching as I shewed, a iuſtification by only faith, an impoſſibilitie to liue chaſt, and to keepe the commaundements, an abrogation of them by Chriſt, a contempt, and reiection of all good woorkes, a preſumptuous, and falſe ſecuritie of ſaluation, an abſolute neceſſitie, yea a deuine motion, temptation, and compulſion of man to ſinne, and laſtly a chriſtian libertie, admitting all libertie of the flesh, which muſt needes induce a ſeruitude, and bondage of the ſpirit, and breede a remedileſſe diſſolution, and corruption of life and manners, remediles I ſay, in ſuch as liue in the true profeſſion, and practiſe of this doctrin.

82 And although this is manifeſt inough, by that which I haue diſcourſed alreadie, yet for the more euident proofe thereof, I will here lay downe, what experience *Luther* himſelfe, and others his diſciples, and followers had of it, in the profeſſors of their new Ghoſpel, in their primitiue church, if I may ſo terme it. And this shall appeare by their owne confeſſion.

Luther in, ſermonibus cōuiual Germanicæ fo. 55

83 *Luther*, in certaine ſermons, which he wrote in the German tongue

gue saith thus. Yt is a wonderfull, and scandalous thinge, saith hee, that from the time that the pure doctrin of the Ghospel was first restored, & brought to light, the world hath euery day becōe worse & worse: euery man abuseth christian liberty at his pleasure, no otherwaise, then as though it were lawfull for euery man to doe euery thing that he listeth. And againe in the same sermons. Since that the ghospell, saith he, was reuealed, vertue is killed, iustice oppressed, temperance tied, or bound, truth rent and torne by doggs, faith shut vp, wickednes is become ordinary, deuotion banished, and heresie remaineth.

Ibid. fo.625 vide Thesaurum Iodoci. Coccij To. 1. de sig. eccles. ar.12

84 Also in an other place. *Nostrorum plerosque*, saith he, *septiceps illæ diabolus inuasit* &c. The seauen head diuel, hath inuaded or possesseth, the most part of our men, and hath made them worse then they were vnder the Pope. And againe: *vidimus*, saith he, *quod hoc tempore* &c. Wee see that at this time, men are much worse, more couetous, more licentious, thē euer they were before in the papalty. Thus saith *Luther*, of the professors of his ghospell, whom he also confessed (as *Surius*, testifieth) *decuplo Sodomitis peiores euasisse*: to be growne tenne times worse, then the *Sodomits*.

Idem præfat in postillam. Surius in cōment. an. 1537

85 But let vs heare one, or twoo witnesses more of his owne followers. *Andreas Musculus*, a famous Lutheran, saith thus of himselfe, and his fellowes. *Cum nobis Lutheranis hoc tempore ita agitur, vt si quis videre volet ingentem turbam nebulonum.* The case standeth so with vs Lutherans, at this day, that if a man, would see a huge multitude of knaues, and turbulent fellowes, let him goe to some citty where the ghospell is purely preached, and he shall find them there in heapes: for it is clearer then noone day, that of vnbridled, and disordered men (amongest whom all vertue is extinguished, and nothing reputed for sinne, and where the diuel hath his full swinge) there are no where more found, then amongst the professors of the ghopel. No not amongst Turkes Ethincks or other infidels. Thus farre *Musculus*.

Andreas. Msucul. Dominica1. aduent.

86 And that this excesse of wickednes, in these new ghospellers, proceeded principally from their very doctrin, it may appeare sufficiently by the testimony of *Ioannes Andreas* a *Lutheran* preacher, who reprehendinge the horrible Epicurian, and bestly life of the *German* ghospellers (in their quaffing, & drinking, their couetousnes, pomps, prophanation of the deuine name & their blaphemies) addeth as followeth. God, saith he, seriously commaundeth in his word, and requireth a serious and christian disciplin in his christiās, but that is now esteemed to be a new popery and a new monkery, for thus they say, wee haue learned now, to be saued by only faith in Christ, who satisfyed with his

" death for al our ſinnes, & we cannot ſatisfie for them with our faſting, " almes, prayer, and other workes, therefore permit, and ſuffer vs to lay a ſide ſuch workes, ſeeing wee may be ſaued otherwiſe by Chriſt, " and doe relie only vppon the grace of God, and vppon the merits of " Chriſt. And to the end, that all the world may acknowledge them to be no papiſts, nor to confide any thing at all in good workes, they " doe not exerciſe any of them. In ſteede of faſting, they ſpend both " night, and day in banketting, and quaffing, and whereas they should " doe good to the poore, they skinne, and flea them, they turne prayers into oathes, blaſphemies, and execrations of the name of God, yea " ſo deſperatelie, that Chriſt is not ſo much blaſphemed at this day by " the Turkes. Finallie in ſteede of humilitie, there raigneth euery where amongſt them pride, elation, and hautines of mind, with all ex- " ceſſe in coſtly apparell, which is wrought, and trimmed, either moſt " ſumptuouſlie, or moſt foolishlie, and all this kind of life, is called by them Euangelicall. In the meane while thoſe miſerable men, per- " ſwade themſelues, that they retaine in their minds a right, and true " faith in God, and that God is mercifull vnto them, yea they iudge themſelues to be better, or more vertuous, then the wicked and falſe " Apoſtolicall papiſts.

87 Thus ſaith *Iohn Andrew*, diſcouering not only the maladie, and diſeaſe of his fellow ghoſpellers, but alſo the true cauſe, and roote, frõ whence it proceeded, and this by their owne confeſſion, excuſing themſelues of their vices, and enormities (as you haue heard) by the groundes of their doctrin, and with great reaſon, ſeeing that the ſame being laid for the foundation, no other building can be raiſed vpon it, but ſinne, and wickednes.

88 Therefore no maruaile, that *Caluin* alſo reaped the like fruit of the like doctrin in his followers, whom in a French ſermon (which he wrote vppon *S. Paules* Epiſtle to the *Epheſians*) he called, *the moſt facinorous, and wicked of all mortall men*: and not finding wordes ſufficient to expreſſe their impietie, tearmed them, *horrible monſters, and euill ſpirits in the ſhape of men.* So that we neede no other witneſſes of the vile, and beaſtlie liues of the firſt goſpellers, then their owne maſters, and teachers, not treating of different ſects from theirs, but euerie one ſpeaking of thoſe of his owne crew, and therefore I hold it needeleſſe to lay downe the cenſures, and iudgements that one ſect gaue of an other, whereof I haue alſo giuen ſome litle taſt before in the 31. chapter, where I treated of the pride of the ſectaries.

Caluin concio 1. in ep. ad epheſ. V. de Coccio vbi ſupra.

89 But now our aduerſaries will ſeeke perhaps to anſwere all this

four

four wayes. First by the way of recrimination, ripping vp the faults, and bad liues of many Catholikes, to proue therebie, that our Catholike faith, hath no aduantage of theirs, in respect of the liues of the professors of it. Secondlie they will perhaps, produce examples of diuers of their profession, who liue vertuouslie, or at least morallie well in the sight of the world. Thirdlie, it may be, they will alledge the sermons, and exhortations of diuers of their writers and preachers, as of these aforenamed, reprehending vice, and exhorting to vertue. And lastly, they will say perhaps, that howsoeuer our Catholik religion may bee in these, or other points conforme to reason of state, yet it is repugnant to the holly scriptures, and consequentlie to the truth of Christian religion. Thus, I say, our aduersaries, may, or perhaps will answere to that which I haue discoursed in this, and all the former chapters, concerning the bad fruits, and effects of their religion, in the corruption of mens manners. Wherefore to the end that thou maist, good reader, receiue some satisfaction concerning this important matter, I will in the next chapter, handle three of the four points last mentioned, remitting the fourth to the third part of this treatise, for that it will require a more ample discourse, then can stand with the conuenient proportion of this present volume.

Three obiections are answered. The first, concerning the bad liues of some Catholikes. *The second touching the good liues of some* Lutherans, *and* Caluinists. *And the third concerning their exhortatiōs to vertue, and by occasion heereof, it is amply proued that the mortificatiō or chastisemēt of the flesh, is necessary to good life. Also that the worst, and most vicious* Catholiks, *are commonly those which become* Lutherans, *or* Caluinists. *Lastly that the exhortations, which* Luther, *and* Caluin *vsed to induce men to vertue, and to withdraw them from vice, were ridiculous in them, being wholy repugnant to their religion, and by the way they are fitly compared to* Epicurus, *& his followers, as well for their doctrin, as for their manner in the deliuery of it.*

CHAP. 36.

1. WHereas there is nothing more ordinarie, or common to all sectaries, then to seeke to obscure, and blemish the resplendant truth of Catholike religion, with odious exaggerations of the bad, and vicious liues of many Catholikes, vsing the same as an argument, to proue corruption in their doctrine, I wish it here to be considered, that although all were true, which they say in this kind (as a great parte of it is but meere fictions, and calumniations) yet it were litle to the purpose, for

the matter now in hand, seeing that the question is not here, whether all those which professe a true religion, be good men, or no (whereof there can be no doubt, seeing that our Sauiour himselfe affirmed, that there should sit wicked men, *euen vppon the chaire of Moyses*, whose do-
Matth. 23. ctrine neuerthelesse, he commaunded should be followed, and teacheth vs also, that the kingdome of heauen (that is to say his militant church)
Matth. 25. is like *to a sheepefould*, wherein there are both sheepe, and gotes: and *to*
Matth. 13. *a barne floore*, wherein there is cockell, or darnell, mixt with the good
Ibid. Cap. 13. corne, to *a nett*, in the which there are good fishes, and bad: and lastly
Matth. 25. to *tenne virgins*, of whom fiue were wise, and fiue folish: by all which similitudes he signifieth, that there are in his church, both good, and wicked men, that is to say, such as professe, one true faith, and yet doe many of them neuerthelesse liue wickedlie, as *S. Augustin* teacheth against the Donatists, out of these very similituds, and wordes of our Sauiour. Therefore, I say, our question is not now, concerning this point, (though the same be also controuersed betwixt our aduersaries, and vs) but whether the bad liues of Catholikes, do any way proceede from their religion.

2 To which purpose, it is to be vnderstood, that as amongst the twelue Apostles themselues, who receiued the Catholike religion immediately of Christ, there was a wicked *Iudas* (not because the religion which he professed, did induce him to wickednes, but because he obserued not the rules of his religion:) so also amongst Catholikes, there are many euill men, because they liue not according to the prescript of Catholike religion, which if they would doe, they must needes be vertuous, yea holly men: for that Catholike religion not only teacheth all perfection of vertue, but giueth also the true, and effectuall meanes to eschew vice (as to mortifie all inordinate passions, and affections, and to obtaine Gods grace for the reformation of manners:) whereas on the other side, *Lutheranisme*, and *Caluinisme*, worketh the contrarie effects, as I haue euidentlie shewed already: so that though there are wicked men in the profession of both religions, yet this difference is to be noted betwixt them, that the wickednes of the one, to wit of the sectaries, may, and doth many times, grow of the doctrin, and practise of their religion, but the bad life of the Catholikes, can haue no other ground, or reason, but because they doe not duly practise the precepts, and counsells of their religion.

3 For how is it possible, that he should be a wicked man, who following the rules, and prescript of Catholike religion, laboureth continuallie to subdue his sensualitie, and passions, by pennance, fasting, and all

all kind of mortifications, by prayer, meditation of our Sauiours life, and passion, daily examination of his conscience, frequent confession of his sinnes, and communion, with full purpose, and diligent endeuour to amend his life by such meanes as I haue declared particulerlie, when I treated of contemplation: whereto I add the obseruation of the euangelicall counsells, of voluntarie pouerty, perpetuall chastity, the perfect abnegation of his owne will, and the exercise of all kind of good workes (all which the Catholick religion partly commaundeth, and partly counselleth) how is it, I say, possible, that he who practiseth all this, can be otherwise then a good, and holly man? For by these meanes, all the dearest seruantes of God, and greatest Saints in his church, haue arriued to that perfection of holly life, which the whole world hath admyred in them: besides that experience teacheth, that those Catholikes which doe duly vse, and exercise the same meanes, are alwaies good, & vertuous men, and that on the other side, those which neglect, or omit them, are so much the worse, or more wicked, by how much more negligent they are in the practise thereof, and finally that those are alwaise the worst, and most vicious, who vse the least, or no practise thereof at all. *Chap. 18. 19. 20. & 21.*

4 But now for as much, as our aduersaries do reiect a great part of these meanes, houlding them for superfluous, and needeles to good life, yea for superstitious, and vnlawfull (as not only the practise of the Euangelicall counsells, and confession, whereof I haue spooken sufficientlie already, but also all the mortifications, and chastisement of the flesh vsed in the Catholike church) therefore I thinke good to prooue here, that the practise of mortification, and punishment of the flesh, is very important, and necessarie to represse concupiscence, to appease Gods wrath, and to obtaine his grace, and mercifull assistance to good life, whereby it will appeare, that the contempt, or omission thereof, is a cause of bad, and vicious life, aswell in many Catholikes, as in the *Lutherans*, and *Caluinists* themselues. And this I hope to make most euident, and cleare, not only by the scriptures of the ould, and new testament, but also by the examples of our Sauiour Christ himselfe, of his Apostles, and of all the holly men, no lesse in the primitiue church, then in these later ages.

5 In the ould testament, we reade, that the famous, and holly *Iudith*, after her husbands death intending to liue a widow, vsed to fast euery day except the saboaths and festiuall dayes, and to weare haire cloth, *super lumbos eius*, which shee did, no doubt, to the end to represse concupiscence, and the better to conserue herselfe in vidual chastity, & *Iudith ca. 8.*

afterwards

Ibid.cap.9 Afterwards being resolued to attempt her heroical enterprise against
Ibid.cap.4. *Holofernes, she intred into her oratory, put on hairecloth, cast ashes on her head, prostrated herselfe vpō the groūd,* to obtain Gods assistāce therein. And to the same end the people also *humbled their soules*, saith the scriptures, *in fasting and praire*, and *the priestes put one hairecloth*, whereby they obtained Gods fauour, for the good successe of *Iudiths* attempt.

Hestor. ca.4. 6 Also when king *Assuerus* published his cruel edict against the *Iewes*, vppon the wicked suggestion of wicked *Aman*, not onlie *Mardocheus did put one sackcloth and cast ashes vppon his head*, but also the *Iewes* abroad, throughout al the dominion of *Assuerus* fasted, *and manie of them vsed*, saitht he scripture, *sacco & cinere pro strato, sackcloth and ashes for their be d*, to moue the mercie of almightie God to deliuer them, which hee did by the meanes of *Hester*.

7 In like manner king *Dauid* to obtaine the life, and health of his
2. Reg. 12 sonne in the cradel, punished his bodie with fasting, and lying vppon
3. Reg. 21. tho ground seauen daies together. Also the wicked *Achab*, being threatned by the prophet *Elias*, for the death of *Naboth*. *Operuit carnem suam cilicio, ieiunanit, & dormiuit in sacco. Couered his flesh with haiercloth, fasted, and slept in sackloth*, by which meanes he inclined almightie God to mercy, & to differr the distruction of his house vntill after his death.

4. Reg. 6. 8 And when *Benadad* king of *Siria* inuaded *Samaria*, & the pople were miserablie afflicted with extreame famine, in so much that a woman did eate her owne child, their king *Ioram, tore his garments, and al the people* saith the scripture, *saw the hairecloth which the king ware inward vppon his flesh*. And the *Niniuites*, being threatned by *Ionas* the prophet, with a generall distruction of their cittie, obtained mercie at Gods handes
Iona. 3. by their repentance, and by fasting, sitting in the ashes, and wearinge sackcloth.

9 Finallie, when *Iudas Machabæus* was asayled by *Timotheus*, both hee
2 Macha:10 and al those which were with him, *cast ashes vppon their heades*, and praied vnto almightie God, *lumbos ciliciјs præcincti*, hauing their loynes gyrt with hairecloth, and thereby obtained a famous and miraculous victorie, being assisted by fiue Angels.

10 Thus then we see in the ould testament, the vse of mortification, by fasting, sackcloth, hairecloth next the skinne, lying one the ground, and sleeping in sackcloth and ashes, to afflict and punish the bodie, not onlie to the end to pacifie Gods wrath, and to doe penance for sinne, as the *Niniuits* and *Achas* did, or to obtaine Gods fauour, and assistance in temporall necessityes, as we see in *Dauid*, *Ioram*, *Mardocheus*, & *Iudas* but als to represse concupiscence, and to obtayne Gods grace, for the

the conseruation of chastity, as appeareth in the holly widow *Iudith*.

11 And this practise of mortification, is also no lesse euident in the new testament, where we read that *S. Iohn Baptist* (of whom our Sauiour him self testifyed, that *there neuer arose a greater amongst the sonnes of women*) in his tender yeares left his fathers house, and betooke himselfe to a solitary life in the desert, where *his garments were made of Camels hayre* (not soft, and delicat, or of fyne chambler, as the *Magdeburgenses. Bucer, Chytraeus*, and other sectaryes do idelly affirme, to maintayne theyr delicate doctryne) but as *S. Chrysostome* sayth. *Compunctioni, & penitentiae accommodata. Fit for compunction, and penance*, and *ad indicandum mundi contemptum, to shew his contempt of the world*. Which our Sauiour also insinuated, when he asked the *Iewes* concerning *S. Iohn*, whether they expected to see him, *vestitum mollibus, clad in soft garments*, adding that such were to be found in the howses of kinges: whereby hee gaue to vnderstand, that *S. Iohns* garments were of a cleane contrarie qualitie, and as farre from being delicat and soft, as the pouertie, and asperitie of the desert, differeth from the riches & delicasie of a kinges pallace, that is to say, that they were poore, homely, rough and vnpleasāt to the flesh, whereto also his diet was correspōdent, being such only as the desart yealded, to wit, *wylde honnie and locusts*, which were either little beastes, (that men vsed in that countrie to eate, dryed with smoke, or as some thinke the tops of hearbes) and not a delicat kind of shell fish called a *Lobster*, (as the daintie sectaries aforenamed would make men beleeue:) and therefore *S. Hierom* saith of *S. Iohn*. *Vestis aspera, zona pellicea, cibus locustae, melque siluestrae, omnia virtuti, & continentiae praeparata. His garment was rough, his girdle of haire, his meat locusts and wild honnie, all prepared and disposed for vertue, and continencie*. And our Sauiour himselfe, to declare the austeritie of *S. Iohns* abstinence, and fast, saide of him. *Venit Ioannes, non manducans panem, neque bibens vinum. Iohn came neither eating bread, nor drinking wine &c.*

Luc. 7. Luc. 1. Euseb. lib. 9 de demonst. euang. c. 5. S. Hiero. ad Rusticum. ep. 4. Magd ep. 1 li. 1. ca 6. Bucer, & Chytra in ca. 3. math. S. Chrysost. ho. 10 in matth. Luc. 7. Euthimi. in 3. Matth. Magdeb. vbi supra. & Melanchton. in concione de Ioh. Baptist. Hieron. ep ad Rusticum. l 2 Luc. 7. Math, 3. Acts. 1. Math. 4.

12 And this seuere life *S. Iohn* did lead, to moue others by his example, to doe the *worthy workes of penance*, which he preached, shewing him selfe therein a true prophet and forerunner of our Sauiour, who also practised himselfe, all the mortification which hee preached, as the scriptures doe aboundantlie testifie: and I haue sufficientlie signified, the same before, when I treated of christian contemplation, and of the euangelical councels, where I had occasion to speake of our Sauiours most rigorous fast in the desert, fortie dayes and nights, his voluntarie pouertie, liuing of almes, and going barefoote, his wearie labours, and trauells all one foote, and his watching and continual praier, whole

nights together: whereto I add, that being in the wild wildernes, *cum bestijs*, *with beastes*, as the euangelist saith, he had no better bed, then the ground, and it is also more then probable, that he vsed at other times not onlie to fast, but also to weare haire cloth, though it be not expressed in the gospell. And this I say, for that in the 68. psalme (which in six seueral places of the scripture, is applied to our Sauiour) he saith by the mouth of the prophet. *Operui in ieiunio animam meam &c. & posui vestimentum meum cilicium. I couered my soule with fasting &c. and I clad my selfe with haire cloth.* And al this our Sauiour did, to moue vs to the imitation of his patience, humilitie, and mortification, to the end, that suffring with him, we may raigne hereafter with him, and participate of the glorie of his kingdome, which, as he testifieth himselfe, can not be obtained, but by such as *vse violence*, and walke the *straight* and *narrow way*, which he went before vs, his whole life, and doctrin tendinge to nothinge els (as I haue oft signified, and cannot to oft repeat) but to teache vs the contempte, and hate of the worlde, abnegation of our selues, and the continual carriage of our crosse, praier, penance, and mortification of the flesh.

Mar. 1. *Ioan. 2. 15. 16. Rom. 11. & 14. Acts. 1.* *Math. 11.* *Math. 7.*

13 Wherein also his Apostles imitated him, leauinge vs the like example: In which respect S. *Paule* saith. *Imitatores mei estote, sicut & ego Christi, Be you followers of me, as I am of Christ.* And in what sort he imitated Christ, it is euident, in that he witnesseth of him selfe, that *he gloried in nothing, but in the crosse of Christ*, and that *the world was crucified to him, and hee to the world*, which he further explicateth, when he saith. *Qui Christi sunt* &c. *Those which are Christs, haue crucified their flesh, with al the vices, & concupiscences thereof*, that is to say (as S. *Thomas*, noteth verie wel) *they haue conformed themselues to Christ crucified, afflicting, & chastising their owne flesh* and therefore haue ouercome all their vices, and vitious inclinations. And herein is fulfilled the counsell of our Sauiour, concerninge the carriage of our crosse, when hee said. *If anie man will come after mee, let him take vp his crosse*, that is to say, lett him not onlie beare patientlie, such crosses as shal bee laid vppon him by me, or by my permission, but also willinglie take, vp or lay vppon himselfe, *crucem suam*, his owne crosse, by voluntarie affliction, and chastisment of him selfe: whereof the Apostle sheweth the practise in himselfe, when hee proposeth himselfe for an example of mortification, sayinge. *Castigo corpus meum, & in seruitutem redigo &c. I doe chastise my bodie and bringe it to subiection, least whiles I preach to other men, I become my selfe a reprobate* Vpon which wordes, the learned Greeke Doctor *Theophilactus*, noteth, that the greeke word *vpopiazo*, which in our latine translation is

1. Cor. 11. & 4. *Galat. 6.* *Galat. 5.* *D. Tho. in hunc locum.* *Math. 16. & Marc. 8.* *1. Cor. 9.* *Theophil. in ca. 9. ep. 1. ad. Corinth.*

is *castigo*, signifieth a chastisement by blowes, or stripes, which leaue behind them black, and blew markes, and therefore he saith, that when the Apostle said. *Castigo corpus meum*. I chastice my body, *plagis se illud affecisse arguit*, he gaue to vnderstand, that he did beate himselfe, with stripes or blowes: though other Fathers vnderstand the word *Castigo*, more generallie, as comprehending, Fasting, and all kind of bodily labours and afflictions.

14 And this the Apostle also signified (aswell concerning the rest of the Apostles, as himselfe) when he described the office and duty of Gods ministers, saying to the *Corinthians*. *Exhibeamus nosmetipsos sicut ministros Dei* &c. *Let vs shew our selues as the ministers of God*, and then specifying wherein, he addeth, not only *in multa patientia*, &c. *In much patience, tribulations, necessities, distresses, stripes, and prisons* (which kind of afflictions were imposed vppon the Apostles, by their persecutors) but also, *in laboribus, in vigiliis, in ieiuniis, in castitate* &c. *In labours, in watching, in fasting, in chastity* &c. Signifying the mortifications which they voluntarilie imposed vppon themselues, besides the voluntarie pouertie, wherein they liued, being sustained partly by almes, and partly by the labour of their owne handes.

2. Cor. 6.

2. Cor. 11.

15 And it is further testified, by most graue, and ancient authors, that *S. Iames* the Apostle, (who was bishop of *Hierusalem*, and called, *frater Domini*, the brother of our Lord) did neuer drink wine, nor eate flesh, but fasted continuallie with bread, and water, and that he went alwayes barefoote, and spent the greatest part, aswell of the night, as of the day, in prayer, in so much, that his knees grew to be as hard, as the knees of a camell, and the skinne of his forehead, became senselesse, by the continuall custome of kneeling with his forehead vppon the ground. So that we may easely iudge, that all the rigour which holly men haue vsed from time to time, vppon their owne bodies for the conquest of the flesh, proceeded from the doctrin, and example of our Sauiour, and his Apostles: which may also be confirmed by the great austeritie of the first Christians in *Alexandria*, vnder *S. Marke* the Euangelist, whereof I haue spoken amply in the 25. chapter, where among other remarkeable points of their perfection, I declared the most admirable abstinence, and fasts which some of them kept three dayes together, and some six, without eating, or drinking any thing at all, their refection being commonly no other, but bread and salt, and their drinke water, except that some (who were counted more delicat then the rest) did eate some times, hissop with their bread.

Egesip. li. 5. apud Euseb. li. 2. ca. 22. eccl. histor. Galat. 1. Metaphras. & Sur. 1. Maij. S. Io. Chrisost. ho. 5. in Matth.

vide Suriũ 17. Decemb.

16 It is written also of *S. Lazarus*, whom our Sauiour raised from death, that being banished by the *Iewes*, together with his sisters, *Mary Magdalen*, and *Martha*, and made bishop of *Marsels* in *France*, he grew admirable to all men for the austeritie of his life, going alwayes barefoote, neuer sleeping but in ashes, and hairecloth, with a hard stone vnder his head, and neuer eating any thing before sunne setting, and then nothing but barly bread, and drinking water.

Idẽ 22. Iulij

17 Also his sister, *S. Mary Magdalen*, spent thirty yeares, in continual mortification, and pennance vppon a montaine in a desert, not farr from *Marsells*, whereof the memorie and monuments remaine yet, and are yearely visited with great deuotion, aswell by strangers, as by the inhabitants of that cuntrie. And now to proceede to the ensuing ages in the primitiue church, we read, of the holly virgin *S. Cycilly* (who was martired within 230. yeares after our Sauiour Christ) that being nobly borne, and hauing dedicated her virginitie to almightie God, shee laboured to conserue it by prayer, fasting, and wearing of hairecloth next her skinne, vnder other costly, and sumptuos apparell, whereby shee obtained such grace of almighty God, that shee not only remained in her virginall puritie (not withstanding that her parents espoused her, against her will, to a yong noble man, called *Valerian*) but also conuerted him, and his brother *Tiburtius*, to the christian faith, and suffred a glorious martirdome shortly after them.

Idem & Lipoman . ex Metaphraste. 22 Nouemb.

18 I haue made mention of this blessed virgin, and martyr, the rather for the particuler deuotion I haue to her, and the glorious memory that remaineth of her heere, by reason that her body hath bene twise found whole and vncorrupt, first about 800. yeares agoe, when Pope *Paschalis*, the first of that name (hauing had a reuelation from her selfe) found it appareled with a garment of silke, imbrodered with gould, and couered ouer with a silk veil, and at her feete a linnen cloth embrued with her bloud, all which he translated, with great solemnitie vnto the church, which now beareth her name, where shee was martired (it being then her dwelling house:) and there it was also found againe the second time ten yeares ago (to wit, in the yeare of our Lord 1599.) within a coffin of Cypresse, and appareled in the same manner, that I haue declared, with the bloudy lynnen cloth lying also by it.

Sigebert. in chron. an. 821.

19 And of all this, the truth is so euident, that no man can with any shew of reason deny it. For, the first finding of it, by Pope *Paschalis*, is sufficientlie testified, not only by *Anastasius Bibliothecarius* (who liued

liued in the same time, and maketh very particuler relation of it) but also by the letters patents of Pope *Paschalis*, which are yet extant to be seene in the *Vatican*, in which letters he relateth her apparition, and speech to him, with all the circumstances before declared, and diuers others, which I omit for breuities sake, all which may be seene in the ninth tome of Cardinal *Baronius*, where he recounteth also the manner how it was found the second time, and how hee himselfe being sent by pope *Clement*, together with Cardinal *Sfondrato*, to see it, found it in such sort, as I haue declared, and that pope *Clement* vppon their relation repared thither, and was an eye witnesse of it, & did afterwards cause it to be reburied in the same place, and for the more solemne celebration of the feast, song himselfe a solemne masse, in *Pontificalibus*, being assisted with all the sacred colledge, of Cardinalls, and an infinit number of people.

Baron. to. 9 an. 821.

20 This I haue thought good to touch by the way, for the greater glory of God, and the honour of his Saints, and to shew with all, how gratefull those are to him, who vse to mortifie, and chastise themselues, which shall also further appeare by the examples of the most famous men in the church of God. Amongst all the glorious Saints, that haue benne since the Apostles time, there was none more Apostolicall, or whose memorie hath benne more celebrated by the pennes of learned, and holly men, then *S. Martin* bishop of *Tours*, in *Fraunce*, whose life was written by a *S. Sulpitius Seuerus* a bishop, and his disciple, by b *S. Gregory* also, bishop of *Towrs*, whom he miraculouslie restored to health, and by c *Venantius Fortunatus*, bishop of *Poitiers*, who being deliuered of a great paine in his eyes, by annointing with the oyle of his lampe, out of gratitude, made a Poeme in his praise, besides that other notable men haue recounted his great miracles and published his praises, as d *Herbenus*, likewise bishop of *Towrs*, e *Richerius Metensis*, f *Gibertus Gemblacensis* g *Honorius Augustudonensis* h *Odo* Abbot of *Cluny*, i *S. Bernard*, and (to omit diuers others) the historiographers k *Sozomenus*, and l *Nicephorus*.

21 And amongst other testimonies of the common opinion and publick fame, or rather of the whole churches iudgement concerning his holly life, I cannot omit, that he was honored for a Saint, and that there were churches built, and dedicated vnto him shortly after his death, namely in our country during our primitiue church, as appeareth in *S. Bede*, who testifieth, that when *S. Augustin*, and his companions came to conuert the *English*, to the christian faith, the church

a *S. Sulpitius Seuerus in vita S. Martini.*
b *Greg. Turon. de gloria confessor. ca. 4. & 20.*
c *Venãt. Fortunat. de vita S. Mart.*
d *Herbenus de laud. S. Mart.*
e *Richer. de vita S. Mart.*
f *Gibertus.*
g *Honorius*
h *Odo Cluniac. de vita & translat. S. Mart.*
i *S. Bern. ser. de S. Mart.*
k *Sozomen. li. 3. ca. 13.*
l *Niceph. li. 9. c. 16.*

where they beganne first to assemble themselues, to singe, to pray, to say masse, to teach, and to baptise (for so saith m *S. Bede*) *was made, antiquitus*, saith he, *in honorem sancti Martini, in ould time, in honour of S. Martin, dum adhuc Romani Britaniam incolerent, whiles the Romanes dwelt yet in Britany.*

m *S. Beda li. 1. histor. Angli. c. 26.*

22 Now then, this famous holly man, hauing benne a monk, before he was Bishop (as I signified, when I spoke of contemplation) practised his monasticall austeritie n euer after during his life, in fasting, watching, and wearing haire cloth, in so much, that he neuer did eate more, then of necessitie he must to maintaine life, and lay alwayes vpon the hard ground, in hairecloth, and vsed such continuall mortification, that his life seemed to be nothing els but a perpetuall penance. And this was so gratefull to almightie God, that he honoured this his seruant with the grace, and gift of miracles, which he did so aboundantlie, and in such stupendious manner (o raising dead men, curing all manner of disseases, casting out diuels, and hauing as it were, an absolute commaund ouer all kind of creatures) that he conuerted innumerable gentils to the christian faith, whereby it manifestlie appeareth, how acceptable to almightie god is the mortification, & chastisment of the flesh, when it concurreth with true faith, and other christian vertues.

n *S. Sulpitius Seuerus in vita S. Mar.*

o *S Bernar Ser. in Festo S. Mart. Nicephor. li. 9. ca. 16.*

23 The like also may be said of *S. German*, bishop of *Auxerre* in *Fraunce*, who hauing benne first a married man, and of great authority in that kingdome, liued all the time of his bishopricke in most seuere disciplin, and pennance, abstaining from all wine, oyle, vineger, salt, or what els soeuer might seazon or giue tast to his meat, which was no other but barly bread. And he vsed commonlie before his repast (which was neuer before night) to eate ashes, and sometimes forbare to eat or drink fiue, or six dayes together: Also his apparell was all one winter, and sommer, and next to his skinne he wore a shirt of haire, day and night, his bed was neuer other then bare bordes, without any bolster, or other thing to lay vnder his head, which kind of life he continued thirtie yeares together, as witnesseth *Constantius* a priest and notable writer of that time.

Vide Surium 31. Iulij.

24 And how acceptable to God this his mortification, and pennance was, it may appeare, not only in the same author, but also in our owne histories, namely in our venerable, and worthy contriman, *S. Bede*, who testifieth of him, that when our *Britany* was greatlie afflicted, with the Pelagian heresie (before the conquest thereof by the *Saxons*) he passed thither out of *France*, together with *S. Lupus* bishop of *Troys*, and wrought so many notable miracles (which *S. Bede* recounteth particulerly,

S. Beda li. 1. histor. eccl. Angl. ca. 17.

Ibid ca. 18. 19. 20. & 21.

particulerlie, and I omit for breuities sake, that the *Pelagians* were vtterly confounded thereby, and such of them as could not be conuerted, were, by common consent banished, and the whole Iland cleared of that pestilent infection of the *Pelagian* heresie. So that the good fruites of this holly Bishop in our country, and the notable miracles, which it pleased God to worke by him, both there, and els where (as appeareth in the historie of his life) doe giue sufficient testimonie to the world, how gratefull his mortification, and pennance, was to his deuine maiestie.

25 To these two precedent examples of these two holly Bishops, & Confessors, I will add two other, of two of the most famous doctors of Gods church, the one a grecian Bishop (to wit, *S. Gregory Nazianzen*, surnamed for his profound learning *Theologus*, the *Deuine*) and the other *S. Hierome*, who was, I may say, the oracle of the world in his time, for his exquisit knowledge, of all the learned tongues, and vnderstanding of the holly scriptures.

26 *S. Gregory Nazianzen*, testifieth of himselfe, by what meanes he vsed to quench the fire, and heate of concupiscence, and other passions in his youth: I did extenuat, saith he, my body, with continual laboures, for that my flesh did continuallie boile in the flower of my age: I ouercame the greedy, and gluttonous appetit of my belly, and the tiranny of the partes adioining thereto. I mortified my eyes, and repressed the fury of anger, and brideled, or restrained all the members, or partes of my body. My bed was the earth, my appparell was hairecloth, my sleepe was continuall watching, and my teares, my repose. In the day time I vsed continuall labour, & trauell. In the night I stood as still as an Image, writting Hymnes, not admitting any humane delight into my soule, no not so much, as to my thought. This was the stile, and course of my life, when I was yonge, for that flesh, and bloud like a fournace cast out continuall flames, and sought to withdraw me from the way of heauen.

S. Gregor. Nazianzen. ho. de ieiunio & silentio.

27 The like doth also *S. Hierome*, witnesse of himselfe, writting to the holly virgin *Eustochium*, of the temptations, which he passed, in the deserts of Syria. O how oft, saith he, did it seeme to me, that I was amidst the delicious dainties of Rome, whiles I liued in that hydeous wildernes, which being parched, with the excessiue heate of the sunne, striketh a horrour in to the monkes that dwell there. I sate me downe solitarie and full of greefe, hauing my weake, and feble body clad with sackcloth, and my flesh euen blacke, and consumed. I mourned all the day, and when sleepe ouercame me against my will, I prostrated

S. Hieron. ad Eustochium de virginit. custodia ep.

ſtrated my ſelfe vppon the cold ground, though my bones were ſkant able to hold together. I ſpeake not of what I did eate, and drinke, for the monkes (that dwell there) be they neuer ſo ſick do neuer drinke any thing but water, nor euer eat any thing that is ſodd, which they hould for ſenſualitie. In this baniſhment, and priſon of mine (whereto for the feare of hell I voluntarie condemned my ſelfe, hauing no other companie but ſcorpions, and wild beaſts) I found my ſelfe many times in my conceit, amids the danſes of the Roman dames, my face was pale with much faſting, and yet my will burned with bad deſires, and finding my ſelfe abandoned of all other helpe, I caſt my ſelfe at the feete of Ieſus, I waſhed them with my teares I ſubdued my rebellious fleſh with faſting whole weekes together.

28 Iam not aſhamed to recount my temptations, and conflicts, but rather I lament that I know not now, what then I was, but I remember, I continued ſighing, and crying day, and night, neuer ceaſing to ſtrike my owne breaſt, vntill at lenght this tempeſt, and ſtorme was ouerblowne, and the deſired calme returned, by the commaundement of my Lord &c. And I call him to witnes, that after all theſe ſighs, ſobbs, and teares, and that I had fixed my eyes, and cogitations wholy vppon heauen, with ſo great affliction, as I haue declared, I felt ſuch contentment, and heauenlie delights, that I was abſorpt, tranſported and rauiſhed out of my ſelfe, and thought my ſelfe to be amidſt the quyres of Angels, ioyfully, and merrilie ſinging, *poſt odorem vnguentorum tuorum curremus*, we will runne o Lord, after the fragant ſauour of thy ointments.

29 Thus ſaith *S. Hierome*, concluding further with theſe wordes (which *I* wiſh all men to note) if therefore the fleſh doe ſo terribly aſſault thoſe which doe afflict, and torment it, what doe they thinke they ſhall ſuffer, who doe pamper it with pleaſures, and delights: is it poſſible, that ſuch ſhall not haue very violent temptations? Though in ſuch caſe, *I* thinke there can be no greater temptation then not to be tempted.

30 All this *I* haue alleadged, out of this ancient, and learned Father, the more amply, to the end it may appeare thereby, that not only theſe mortifications, and aſperities, haue benne alwayes accuſtomed by the moſt holly, and learned men in Gods church (as neceſſarie for the repreſſion of humane paſſions and ſenſualitie) but alſo that the ſame are no leſſe acceptable to God, then fruitful to vs, ſeeing they wrought ſuch effect in this holly man, as hath benne declared, to wit, the conqueſt of concupiſcence, and peace of ſoule, yea aboundance of heauenlie delights,

delights, and consolations which almightie God vseth to impart to his seruants in the greater measure, by how much more they afflict, and chastise themselues for the loue of him.

31 But what doubt can there be, that this custome of mortification hath bene continual in Gods church, seeing that it is euident that monastical, and religious life (which of it selfe is nothing els but a continual mortification) hath benne deriued by a neuer ceasinge succession, from the Apostles time, vntill this verie day, though in different orders of religion, yet all communicatinge, and agreeinge in the chastisement of the flesh, by abstinence, and fastinge, watchinge, praier, and meditation, haireclоth, disciplines, and such like, some more, and some lesse, all tendinge to the perfect imitation of Christ, for the mortification of sensualitie, thereby to attaine to christian perfection, that is to say, to true sanctitie, and hollines of life.

32 And as for the deriuation of religious life from the Apostles time, I shall not neede to say any thing thereof in this place, for that I haue proued it at large in the 25. 26. and 27. chapters, where I haue also treated amply of the spirituall consolations, which God hath giuen to religious men in all ages, in the exercise of contemplation: and therefore I will now say some what only concerning the mortifications, and rigorous disciplin, practised by the ancient religious in the first *foure hundreth*, and *fiue hundreth* yeares, omitting neuertheles to speake of the first monkes in the Apostles time, vnder *Saint Marke* in *Alexandria*, because I haue touched it sufficientlie a litle before, and more amply in the 25. chapter.

33 I will therefore beginne with *S. Paule* the Hermit, whose life *S. Hierome* writteth, testifying of him, that in the cruell persecutions of the church vnder *Decius* the Emperour, which was about the yeare of our Lord, *two hundred, and fifty*, he retired himselfe to the desert, and liued there solitarie, without any humane companie, or comfort, almost a *hundreth* yeares, during which time, he clothed himselfe with the leaues of a Palme tree, and fedd vppon the fruit thereof, drinking water, without any other sustenance, for well neere *forty* yeares, at what time it pleased almightie God, to prouide him miraculouslie of a peece of bread, brought him by a crow euery day, for threescore yeares together, vntill *Sainct Anthony*, hauing benne also threescore yeares in the same wildernes, found him by reuelation, and was an eye witnesse, of Gods mercifull

S. Hieron. in vita Pauli.

mercifull prouidence towards him. For whereas the crow had benne alwayes accustomed, to bring to *S. Paule* halfe alofe for his repast, he brought him then a whole lofe for him, and his guest, as not only, S. *Hierome* in the life of S. *Paul*, but also S. *Athanasius*, witnesseth in the life of S. *Antony*, and this shall suffise for S. *Paul*.

34 And although I haue made mention diuers times alreadie of S. *Antony*, and spoken largely of his contemplation, and of Gods great fauours towards him in the exercise thereof, yet hauing hitherto said nothing of his mortifications, I will add here concerning him, that (as S. *Athanasius* testifieth in the famous historie, which he wrot of his life) he did neuer vse to eat vntill after sunne setting, & then his repast was no other but bread, and salt, with a litle water for his drinke, from the which he also abstained many times three dayes together, taking his refection only the fourth daye, & he vsed for his bed nothing els, but a matt of rushes, couered with hairecloth, and watched in prayer whole nights, and so liued closed vpp, in and ould ruinous castle *twenty* yeares, vntill an infinit number of people, being moued with the fame of his holly life, repaired to see him from all partes, & forced him to come forth, at what time it pleased God to giue testimonie to the great merits of this his mortification, by many notable miracles, which he did in the expulsion of deuils, and the cure of many sick, and diseased persons.

35 And what the opinion of all the learned, and good men, or rather of the whole world, was in the primitiue church concerning his sanctitie, and hollines, may appeare sufficientlie, not only by all ecclesiasticall histories, which write of his time, but also by that, which I recounted in the 16. chapter, to wit, how much S. *Augustin* was moued with the fame of his rare vertue, before he himselfe was conuerted to the Christian faith, & how *Potitianus* and his companion, were suddainelie drawne to forsake the world, only by reading the historie of his life, as S. *Augustin* also testifieth. Thus much of S. *Antony*.

36 S. *Hilarion* (of whom I haue also spoken before, though not of his mortifications) retiring himselfe, to the desert, when he was but *Fifteene* yeares of age (being as S. *Hierome* witnesseth, of a very tender, and delicat complection) became a mirrour of austeritie. For finding himselfe molested with temptations of the flesh, by reason of the heate of his youth, he resolued to quench the flame of concupiscence, by withdrawing from it all the matter, that might kindle, and nourish it, saying to himselfe (as S. *Hierome* also witnesseth.) O

S. Hieron. in vita hilarionis.

asse,

asse, I will shortly, bring thee so low, and hamper thee in such sort, that thou shalt not be able so much as to kicke. I will not feede thee with barley, but with straw, I will punish thee with hunger and thirst, I will lay such loade vppon thee, and so treate thee both with heate, and cold, that thou shalt haue somewhat els to thinke vppon, then fleshly pleasure.

37 Thus said hee, and presently beganne to put the same in practise, for he contented himselfe once in three, or foure dayes, to eate a few carrickes (which is a fruit in that country like to figgs) and to drinke the ioyce of herbes, and at such times, as he did not meditat, and pray, he also wearied his body with labour, digging the ground so long as he was able, and then made matts of rushes, in imitation of the monkes of *Egipt*, whom he had seene vnder S. *Antony*. Also he built him selfe a litle cabane, which was to be seene, in S. *Hieromes* time, not past *foure* foote broad, *fiue* in height, and some what longer then his body, so that it was more like a sepulcher, then a house. His bed was no other then a matt of rushes, laid vppon the bare ground, his apparell was of sackcloth, which he neuer changed, nor washed so long as it lasted: And this kind of life he ledd from *sixtenne* yeares of age, till he was *one and twenty*. And for *three* yeares after, he vsed to eate nothing but a few *Lentils*, stiped in cold water, and for as many yeares more, a litle dry bread, sopt in water with salt, and during other *three* yeares, he liued vppon herbes, and rootes, and then finding himselfe some what sickly, he vsed to eat euery day *six* ounces of barley bread, and a few sod herbes, with a litle oyle, which he continued till he was threescore and three yeares of age, and from that time, till he was foure skore, he did neuer eate bread, but a certaine pottage made with meale, and hearbes, shred very small, which serued him both for meat, and drinke, forbearing neuerthelesse to eate till the sunne was sett. And this kind of diett and fast, he neuer after altred, or broke, for any sicknes, or other occasion whatsoeuer,

38 All this, and much more S. *Hierome* testifieth, concerning the austeritie of S. *Hilarion*, which almighty God also approoued, with many wonderfull miracles, recounted by S. *Hierome*, whereof I haue already related some in the *seauen and twentith*, and *thirty fourth* chapters, vppon other occasions. *Chap. 27. nu.11. ch.34. nu.12. 13. & 14.*

39 And therefore whereas these great seruantes of God (whose vertue the Christian world admired) were speciall propagators of monasticall life, ouer all the east parts (as I haue declared in the *Fiue and*

chap.25. nu. 31. & 32. *twentith* chapter) let vs see, what was the practise of their disciples, and such as descended from them. This may appeare, by that which the historiographers, and authours of those times doe write, concerning the manner of life of the monks, and hermits of *Egipt*, *Armenia*, *Nitria*, and *Syria*, of whome *Palladius*, and *Theodoretus* (to omit diuers others) wrote particuler histories, relating their most admirable asperities, and mortifications, and the miracles, which it pleased God to worke by them: of all which, the said authors themselues, either had benne eye witnesses, or els had otherwaise most assured knowledge.

40 These then affirme of the hermits and monkes aforesaid, that (besides the ordinarie obligation of pouerty, chastitie, and other regular disciplin common to them all) some of them, for their further mortification, fasted without eating, or drinking *two*, or *three* dayes together, some *fiue*, and some *seauen*, and some did eate nothing during the lent time, but herbes, or dried pease, steeped in water, which abstinence some others also made some yeares together, and some vsed to eat stinking, and loathsome meate, to depriue themselues of all pleasure in eating. Others accustomed themselues, to stand on their feete al the night long in prayer. Other to goe barefoote through thornes, and briars, in the remembrance of the payne that our Sauiour suffred by the nailes, that pearced his handes, and feete, and also to stand whole nights with their armes spread, and stretched out in imitation of Christ crucified. Some afflicted their bodies with continuall labour in the sunne, during the extremitie of the Egiptian heates, which as *Palladius* saith, might be cōpared with the furnace of *Babilon*. Some lay both day, and night abroad, exposed aswell to the winters could of frost and snow, as to the sommers heat. Others wore chaines of Iron about their bodies, vnder their hayrecloth. Finallie to omit diuers other particulers, such was the rigour, and violence which some vsed vppon them selues, that it had not bene possible for humane nature to endure it, so many yeares as they did, if God had not miraculouslie assisted them, aswell for his owne glory, as also to inuite others by their example to penance, and mortification: which *Theodoretus* obserueth notably well in diuers religious hermits, and monkes of his time, but especiallie in one called *Symeon*, whom he tearmeth, *magnum orbis miraculum, the great miracle of the world*, in respect of his rare vertue, and holly life, knowne, as he saith, to all the *Romane* Empire, yea to the very *Ethiopians*, and *Indians*.

Palladius in Macario. Theodoretus in Marciani uita de Sabino sub. fine. Pallad. in Pachomio. Idem. in Isidoro presbitero. Idē in Paulo Simplici. Theodoretus in Macedonio. Iacobo. Theodosio Romano Eusobio.

Idem in Simeone.

41 This *Simeon*, being a shepheard, and hearing related out of the

gospell

gospell, that our Sauiour called them *happy, who weepe, and mourne,* *Ibidem.*
and those miserable, or *wretched, who laugh*, and are merry, was so *Math. 5.*
moued and stroken therewith, that he shortly after resolued to abandon the word; and repairing to certaine religious men in those partes, and being receiued amongst them, he so profited in feruour of spirit, and desire of true mortification, that within a while, he exceeded them all, fasting from all kind of sustenance, whole weekes together, and binding his body vnder his cloathes very strait, with a rough, and sharpe corde made of the Palme tree, which did so gaule, and exulcerat his fleshe, that the bloud dropped from him, whereby it was perceiued, and he forced to leaue it. And not contenting himselfe with the austeritie that others vsed, he retired himselfe to a litle cabane, where he liued three yeares alone in admirable manner, attempting to fast forty dayes,
as our Sauiour *Christ*, *Moyses*, and *Elias* did, with out meate, or *Matth. 4.*
drinke, which he also performed, and continued it euer after during *Exod. 24.*
the lent time, as long as he liued, which was aboue *thirty* yeares. *3. Regum. 19.*

42 And whereas it pleased God in the meane time, to giue him such a grace in the operation of miracles, that he was oppressed with the multitude of people which came partly to see him & partly to receiue health, and remedy by him (such being also their importunity, that they tore his very garments from him, to haue some relikes, and monument of him) he procured a piller to be made, first *six* cubits high, and after *twelue*, after *twenty*, and at last he caused it to be raised *six and thirty* cubits, and in the top thereof, a receptacle to be made for his body, not past *two* cubits broad, open to the aire without any doore, where he stode on his feete perpetuallie, *thirty* yeares together, eating only once a weeke a litle pittance, which was brought him vp by a ladder, and bestowing all the night, as also the greatest part of the day, in prayer, and contemplation, vntill it was three of the clocke in the after noone. And from that time forward vntill sunne setting, he either preached to the people (who were continually there in great numbers) or compounded quarrells, and controuersies, which were remitted to his iudgement from all parts, or gaue answeres to questions demaunded of him, or els cured the blind, lame, and disseased by his prayer, or benediction.

43 Furthermore, such was the fame of his life, that the most Christian, and worthy Emperour *Theodosius*, being reprehended by him, for an edict which he made in fauour of the *Iewes*, reuoked

FFff iij it,

it, and humbly craued the assistance of his prayers, and benediction. Besides that his very pictures, and Images, were sett vp in euery house, and shopp in *Rome*, and as *Theodoretus* also testifieth vppon his owne knowledg (who knew him well and frequented him often) the confluence, and concourse of people vnto him, was like a sea continually filled with supplies of riuers, on euery side, for that infinit numbers of men, and women, flocked vnto him from all parts, as from *Italy, Spaine, France*, and *Brittany*, besides *Ismalits, Persians, Armenians, Iberians, Homerits*, and other Eastern nations, though Infidels, and Pagans, of whom he conuerted (saith *Theodoretus*) an infinit number to the christian faith, and speciallie of the *Ismaelits*, or *Sarazins*, who came vnto him ordinarilie in great troopes, sometimes *twoo* hundred, or *three* hundred, and sometimes a *thousand* together. *Quos ego vidi, & audiui*, saith he, *patriam impietatem abnegantes*, &c. Whom I haue seene, and heard renounce the impietie of their contry, and receiue of him the euangelicall doctrin of Christ.

44 All this *Theodoretus* saith, to shew the manifest concurrence of almightie God with this holly man. Besides that he also answereth notablie the friuolous cauils of such, as may perhaps blame, and condemne this extraordinarie manner of life in him, to which purpose, he wisheth them to consider, that God hath often moued his seruants to doe thinges extraordinarie, to stirre and awake the slouthfull out of
Esa. 20. their drowsy sleepe, and *therefore*, saith he, *God commaunded the prophet*
Hierem. 28. Esay, *to goe naked, and barefoote, Hieremy to carry collers of wood, and Iron*
Osea. 1. *about his neck. Osee to marry a common queane. And Ezechiell* to lie *forty dayes*
Ezechiel. 4. *on his right side, and three hundred and 90. dayes on his left*, &c. And here vppon *Theodoretus* concludeth, that as almightie God, hauing care of those, which were sluggish, and slouthfull in his seruice in those times, commaunded his prophets to doe these strange, and extraordinarie thinges, *ita hoc nouum, & admirabile procurauit spectaculum*, &c, So he caused this new, and admirable spectacle, drawing all men to it, by the noueltie, and strangenes of it, to the end they might the rather beleue the admonitions, and doctrin of his seruant, for the good of their owne soules. So he.

45 I haue thought it conuenient (good reader) to lay downe al this, the more largelie out of this ancient, and approued author, to the end it may euidentlie appeare, not only what was his, and the generall opinion concerning the vse, and practise of mortification in his time (which was within the first *foure hundreth* yeares) but also how acceptable the same was to almighty God in this holly hermit: seeing

it pleased his deuine maiestie to approue it in him, with continuall miracles, and the conuersion of innumerable soules to the christian faith, which no man, that hath so much as common sense, can ascribe to anie deceyt, or illusion of the diuell, or anie other cause, then the omnipotent hand, and spirit of God, who to conuince the Epicurian worldlinges of sinnfull delicacy, and slought, stirred vp this, and other his seruāts, to the rigorous practise of these incredible asperities, assistinge them therein aboue the course of nature, to the end, that no man might be excused from doing the worthy fruits of penance, with the pretence of disability: for he which considereth, and seeth that God enableth his seruants, which confide in him, to doe, and suffer more then humane nature can beare, how can he with reason doubt of Gods assistance (if he will dulie implore, and seeke it) for the performance of such works, as doe not surpasse the ordinary power of man? I meane such moderat chastisement of the flesh, as wee see hath benne alwayes vsed by good, and holie men, in the church of God, and is most necessarie to good life.

46 And this shall suffice concerning the mortifications practised by the monkes and hermits of *Egipt, Pallestina, Siria*, and other countries in the East parts: who *shined*, saith *S. Chriostome, like Angels in mortall bodies*, in which respect he also calleth the deserts of *Egipt, a paradise of pleasure*, as I haue declared more amplie, in the *fiue and twentith* chapter, where I treated of monastical disciplin, and laid downe the opinions of S. *Chrisostome, S. Augustin, S. Hierome*, and *Sozomenus*, concerning the perfection of those who professed it. Whereby it may appeare, in what veneration the church of God held them at that time (which was the *fourth*, and *fift* age) and therefore I shall not neede to make a further deduction of mortification in monastical life, seeing from that time forwardes, our aduersaries doe not denie it, and if they should, they might bee easelie conuinced by the experience thereof, which is most manifest, euen at this day, in the ancient rules, and religious orders of S. *Basill*, S. *Augustin*, & S. *Benet*, who being al three religious men (the two former, within lesse then *foure hundreth* yeares after Christ, and the third in the age following) & liuing themselues in great austerity, intituled the strict rules, which haue bene euer since obserued in those of their orders, and haue serued also for patterns of perfection, and mortification to the latter orders of religion, al which doe imbrace, and practise the chastisement of the flesh, and true abnegation of themselues, in imitation of our Sauiour Christ, of his Apostles, and of the first christians in the primitiue church.

S. Chrisost. in ca. 2. Mat. ho. 8
Chap. 25. nu. 33. Ibid nu 32. & 35
S. Augustin. de moribus eccles.
S. Hiero. ep. 8. ad Marcel. li. 2.
Sozome. histor Tripart.

47 So

47 So that the continual custome of penitential life, and mortification, hath bene so euident in the church of God, euen from our Sauiours time to this, and not onlie approued, but also practised by all the learned Fathers, and Saints of God, yea so confirmed also by almightie God himselfe, with infinit miracles, that no man can denie the necessitie and merit of it, without extreme impudencie and follie, especially seeing that I may also boldlie affirme, that no one example can be produced of anie Saint, or holie man in Gods church (that hath benne famous for sanctitie and holines of life) who hath not also excelled in the practise of mortification, and austeritie, seeing that the exteriour mortification, and chastisement of the bodie, is the special and ordinarie meanes, to attaine to the interiour mortification of the minde, wherein consisteth the perfection of christian life: and therefore no meruel, that the enemies of austeritie and penance, are so farre from deseruinge the fame or reputation of sanctitie, that they are commonlie infamous for vice and wickednes, as experience sheweth, and may be exemplified in those, who were the cheefe and first impugners of mortification in our age, I meane, *Luther*, *Caluin*, *Beza*, and all the first sectaries, of whose beastlie and ambitious liues, I haue spoken amplie in the thirtie chapter.

Chap.30.nu 23. 24.&c.. vsque ad nu 30.

48 Therefore I conclude, that seeing the catholike church, carefully recommendeth to al her children, the vse and practise of diuers sorts of mortifications, and that the same are speciall meanes for the repression, & conquest of sensuality, and for the obtayning of Gods grace (in which respect they are most necessary to good life) yt ys no meruell yf those catholiks which contemne, and neglect them, are no lesse loose, dissolut, and vicious many tymes, then *Luther*, *Caluyn*, and others of theyr crew, giuing all liberty to the flesh, and neglecting the meanes whereby theyr vicious inclinations, and habits may be repressed, and reformed: And this wilbe much more euident, if wee consider what manner of men those catholikes commonly are, who forsake theyr religion, to become *Lutherans*, and *Caluinists*, whereby yt will also appeare, what are the special motiues which draw them thereto.

49 For who seeth not by experience (yf he list to note yt, as I wish thee good reader, to do) that the most dissolute, and licentious Catholikes, are alwayes those, which embrace the doctrin of *Luther* and *Caluin*, such Catholikes I meane, as seeking liberty of life, and yelding themselues, as yt were, captyues to worldly, and fleshly pleasures, wil no longer endure the straight disciplin of catholike religion: which *S. Ambrose* obserued notably in certayne loose Catholikes of his time, who

who beinge religious men, grew weary of their profession, and became flat heretikes, though they taught but some part of that carnall doctrin, which the sectaries of our dayes professe: & therefore marke, good reader, I beseech thee, how he painteth both the one, and the other in their proper collours, writting to the church of *Vercells*, thus as followeth.

50 *Audio*, saith he, *venisse ad vos* &c. I heare, that some are come vnto you, who teach, that there is no merit of abstinence, nor grace of virginitie, that all men are to be valued, or esteemed a like (that is to say, are of like merit,) and that those men are madd, or dote, who chastise their flesh to make it subiect to the spirit: which the Apostle *S. Paul* would neuer haue done himselfe, nor written for the instruction of others, if he had held it for dotage, or madnes. For he glorieth saying. *I chastise my body, and bring it into bondage, least whiles I preach to others, I may become, my selfe a reprobate.* Therefore they which preach to others, and do not chastise their owne bodies, are held for reprobats, and can any thing be more to be reproued, and reiected, then that which allureth to lasciuiousnes, to corruption, to wantõnes, and is an incitation to lust, a prouocation to pleasure and a nourishment of incontinencie? What new schole hath sent forth these *Epicurians*? No schole truly of philosophers, but of ignorant men, who preach pleasure, perswade delicacy, and say, that chastitie is to no vse or purpose. These were with vs, but they were not of vs &c. Yet whiles they were here, at first they fasted, they kept their cloisters, they had no place, or commoditie to liue riotouslie, or licence to iangle, or dispute idelly, but so delicat were they, that they could not endure this, and therefore they went from vs, &c. I admonished them, but I preuailed nothing, and they sowed abroad such doctrin, that being themselues inflamed, they became very fire brandes to kindle, and enflame other men to all kind of vice: Miserable men! who hauing lost all their former fasting, and continencie, doe now with a diuelish mind, enuy the good workes of others, whereof they themselues haue lost the fruit.

S. Ambros. ep. li. 3. ad Vercellens eccles.

1. Cor. 9.

50 Thus saith S. *Ambrose*, of certaine *Iouinian* heretikes in his time, whose Epicurian doctrin impugning chastitie, and mortification of the flesh, our late sectaries haue reuiued, and added thereto, many other heresies of their owne, tending all to the libertie of the flesh, as may appeare in those, whom I haue named in the *three and thirtith* chapter, to wit, *Luther, Carolstadius, Caluin, Beza, Oecolampadius, Bucer, Peter Martir, Ochinus, Miconius, Menius, Musculus, Pellicanus, Pomeranus*, and

Chap. 33. nu. 35.

GGgg *Munsterus,*

Munſterus, with diuers others, who being votaries (I meane religious men) or Catholike prieſts at leaſt, and therefore bound alſo by vow to liue ſingle, and chaſt) and not brooking the reſtraint that is vſed in Catholike religion, and eſpeciallie in monaſticall profeſſion, became renegats, or (as *S. Ambroſe* ſaith of thoſe in his time) very fire brandes, to incenſe other men to luſt and libertie, ſetting abroach that impure, and carnall doctrin, whereof I haue ſpoken before in the *thirty* chapter, to wit, a that it is as impoſſible to liue chaſt, as to liue with-
a *Ch.*30.*nu* out meat: b that *Poligamy* (or the hauing of many wiues at once) is not
2. 3. 4. & forbidden in the new law: c that it is not lawfull ſo much as to pray
b *nu.*16.17. for the gift of chaſtitie, no more, then for the ſpirit of propheſie,
& 18.
c *Idē .nu* 8. or the gift of miracles: d that a man may be diuorced from his
d *nu.* 15. wife, and marry an other for many cauſes: finallie that Chriſt ſo ſuf-
e *Chap.* 35. fred, e & ſatisfied for vs, that all our ſatisfaction, pennance, and
*nu.*54.& 55. mortification is ſuperfluous, and vaine: beſides all thoſe other moſt abſurd, and impious paradoxes, which I haue mentioned in the laſt chapter.

51 All which do giue ſo large a ſcope to ſenſualitie, and ſinne, that no man needeth to doubt, but that the authors thereof, came (as *S. Ambroſe* ſaith of their predeceſſors) out of the ſchoole of *Epicurus*, ſeeking nothing els but to liue in all libertie of the fleſh, and to colour their owne wickednes, and apoſtaſie, with ſome pretence of religion. In which reſpect, we may alſo with *S. Ambroſe*, woorthilie lament the caſe of all ſuch renegats and apoſtatats, as of moſt wretched, and miſerable men, who hauing loſt the fruit of their former holly labours, and endeuours (of faſting, pennance, chaſtitie, mortification, and good workes, which they exerciſed in the Catholike church) doe not only enuy the merits, and good workes of other men, as *S. Ambroſe* ſaith, but alſo ſeeke to draw all men with them to damnation, by their pernicious example, and doctrin, which being plauſible, and gratefull to fleſh, and bloud, doth eaſely inſinuat it ſelfe into the corrupt nature of man, no leſſe then the deteſtable doctrin of *Mahomet* did, which (as I haue noted in the 14. and in the 30. chapter)
*Chap.*14. & hath by the ſame meanes eaſely ouerflowed a great part of the world,
*Chap.*30. as alſo in like manner the ſenſuall, and beaſtly philoſophy of *Epi-*
num. 20.
*Cicero.li.*2. *curus*, not with ſtanding the abſurditie of it, found an infinit num-
de finib. ber of fauourers, and followers, not only in *Greece*, and *Italy* but alſo throughout all barbarous nations, as *Cicero* teſtifieth.

52 Therefore it is no wonder, that the worſt ſort of Catholikes, doe ſometimes become *Lutherans*, and *Caluiniſts*, ſuch Catholikes I meane,

I meane, as wholie abandon themselues, to sensual, and worldie pleasures, and so liue in the profession of catholike religion, that they reape no more benefit thereof, then *Lutherans*, or *Caluinists*, vseing no more deuotion, penance and mortification, then they, or at least (if they vse anie at al (they doe it not for deuotion, but onlie for feare of the penalties, ordained by the ecclesiastical lawes. Besides that, it is to be obserued, that these loose catholikes, of whome I speake here, are commonlie such as neuer frequent the holie sacraments of confession, and communion, except perhaps once a yeare, and then onlie for fashion sake.

53 And therefore whereas almightie God, doth not ordinarilie vse to giue his grace to men by miracle, but by the vsual, and ordinarie meanes prescribed in his church, that is to say, by praier, penance, and the holie sacraments, which hee hath ordained to supplie the benefit of his passion vnto vs, for otherwayes, *Turkes*, and *Infidels*, should bee saued, aswell as Christians, seeinge that hee died for al men alike, though all men doe not perticipate of the benefit, but those onlie, who vse the meanes which he hath leaft, & prescribed for that purpose, therefore I say, it is no meruel, that such catholikes, as vse no mortification, and doe not frequent the holie sacraments, with such diligence and deuotion, as is requisit, are not partakers of Gods grace, but fall into horrible sinnes, and manie times into schisme, heresie, and apostasie. And this will be most euident, when I shal treate of the admirable effects of the hollie Sacraments of Gods Church, which for diuers respects I doe remit to the third part of this treatise, where I am to handle the question of the church, and diuers controuersies belonginge thereto.

54 In the meane time, I conclude vppon the premisses two thinges. The one, that the worst, and most dissolute catholikes, are commonlie those, which become *Lutherans*, and *Caluinists*. The other, that the bad liues of catholikes, cannot be attributed, to anie demerit of their religion, , but to their owne negligence, in that they doe not obserue the rules thereof. And thus much for the first point, concerning the bad liues of catholikes.

55 And for the second point, touched by the way of obiection, in the end of the last chapter (to wit the laudable liues of some *Lutherãs*, or *Caluinists*) it is to be vnderstood, that as al those, who professe a true religion, are not good men, so neither are al the prefessors of false religions, scãdalous in life, though good christians they cãnot be, howsoeuer they may liue morally wel in the eye of the world. This I say for two

causes, the one, for that amongst such are found many times notable hipocrits, who by the very instigation of the deuil, doe seeke to authorize their bad, and hereticall doctrin, with the external shew of piety, and vertue, being (as *S. Hierome* saith of some such in his time) *Intus Nerones, & foris Catones, Neroes within, and Catoes without*, or rather, as our Sauiour said, *rauening wolues, clad in sheepes skinnes.* Such were *Arrius, Pelagius, Vigilantius, Nestorius*, and diuers other Arch heretickes, who by their pretence of piety, deluded the people wonderfully, in so much that many good, and holly men were abused with their dissembled modestie, grauitie, and counterfet vertue, as *S. Epiphanius* testifieth of *Arrius*, who, he saith, vsed to goe in the streetes, with a stole about his neck, and shewed such loue to religious chastity, that he assembled many virgins to liue together in religious disciplin, as also many priests, vntill he had infected them with his heresie, who therefore were afterwardes expelled out of the citty of *Alexandria*, together with him, assoone as his heresie was discouered.

Hieron. ep. li. 2. ep. 13. ad Rustic.
Matth. 7.
S. Epiphan. de heret. li. 2.

56 We read also, that very many, and amongst the rest, the holly bishop *S. Polinus*, were for a while greatly deceiued in the Archhereticks *Pelagius*, and *Vigilantius*, by reason of their hipocriticall, and pretended deuotion, in so much, that *Pelagius* had for some time, the reputation of a very holly man. And *Theodoretus* testifieth of the Archheretícke *Nestorius*, that he drew all men to the admiration of him, with an affected grauitie, and an hipocriticall abstinence. And the like hath benne obserued more, or lesse in the most part of sects, especiallie in their ringleaders, and first progenitours, though (to say truly) in none lesse then in those of our time, who were so farre from dissembling, or couering their impietie, that they deuised all their licentious doctrin to defend it, which neuertheles, others of their followers, may perhaps practise with more modestie, and art, in which respect it may be presumed, that hipocrisie which is common to all other heretikes, or sectaries, may be a cause that some *Lutherans*, or *Caluinists*, are lesse scandalous in life, then their doctrin of it selfe permitteth.

D. August. retract. li. 2. c. 33.
Baron. an. 411. to 5.
Baron. an. 406.
Theodore ep. ad Sporadiū.

57 An other cause, which I hould to be more ordinarie, is the good disposition, and inclination, that many men naturallie haue to vertue, which may be, and is, no doubt, such in many, that they lead a commendable life, (exteriorlie in the sight of the world) of what religion soeuer they be, being naturallie inclind to piety, iustice, liberalitie, temperance, modestie, clemencie, and mercy, whereby they

exercise

exercise the acts of these vertues, with great promptitude, and facilitie and are not easely corrupted in manners, especiallie in such sort, that they cast of the naturall bridle of modestie, and shame, or commit scandals, and publike offenses. And of these kind of men, I haue my selfe knowne very many in our country, and diuers of them my owne kinsfolks, and deare friends, who though they were no Catholikes, yet were (and are no doubt if they be still liuing) of such an honest, and vertuous disposition, and cariage, that they were, and are worthilie beloued, and respected, aswell of all other men, as of my selfe.

58 And it is no meruell, that there are such professing false religions, seeing that *Plato* obserued the like, amongst the very *Atheists* of his time. For where as he ordained seuere punishment for *three* sorts of *Atheists*, or impious men (as he tearmeth them) he maketh mention of some, who though they held, that there was no GOD, or deuine prouidence, in the gouerment of humane affaires, yet were so well, and vertuouslie disposed by nature, that they liued very ciuilly, and morallie well, without hurt to the common welth, as I haue signified before vppon other occasions.

Plato de legib. dial. 11.

59 And of this sort of morall men (yea, and such as did many good deedes for the benefit of the common wealth) there were alwayes very many a mongst the Paynims, as well *Greekes*, as *Romans*, and are now euen amongst the *Turkes*, not withstanding that their religion, I meane Paganisme and Mahometisme, are most absurd in it selfe, and replenished with motiues to all vice, and wickednes, as appeareth in the *seauenth*, *eight*, *ninth* and *fourteenth* chapters, where I haue handled that matter at large.

60 Also *Epicurus* (who placed mans felicitie in sensuall pleasures, and delights) was for his owne person very ciuill, and morallie honest, in so much that *Cicero*, reprouing, and reiecting his doctrin, confesseth neuertheles, that he was, *vir bonus, a good man*, and that many of his sect, were men of great modestie, and morall honestie, waighing all their actions in the balance of reason, and duty, and not of pleasure, *in so much*, saith he, *that their life confuteth their doctrin, and as some men are said to say better, then they doe, so they doe better then they say:* Thus said *Cicero* of some honest *Epicurians:* And the like may be said, of many honest sectaries, whose good nature, and disposition, seconded with the desire of a good name and fame, so farre ouerwaigheth the corruption of their doctrin, that they vse the libertie of it, with much moderation, and great respect of their reputation, and honour,

Cicero li. 2. de finibus.

whereas others of a malignant nature, and bad diſpoſition, are commonlie tranſported therewith, beyond all limits of modeſty, and ſhame, and runne headlong to the extremitie of vice, whereto it tendeth.

61 So that *Lutherans*, and *Caluiniſts*, haue not in this point (I meane for the good liues of ſome of them) any aduantage at all of the very *Turks*, *Paynimes Epicurians* and *Atheiſts*, nay I may bouldly ſay, that for ſome notable vertues, they come ſhort of many of them. For where haue we ſeene in any of their profeſſion, ſuch a notable contempt, of riches, honours, pleaſures, and delights of the world, as ſundry pagan philoſophers, both taught, and practiſed? Could euer any of them be compared for temperance, and abſtinence, with the *Phitagorians*, who neuer did eat fleſh or fiſh? Or for contempt of worldly welth, and honours, with *Antiſthenes*, who hauing heard *Socrates* teach philoſophy, ſould, and gaue away all his goods, leauing himſelfe nothing but a cloake? Or with *Crates* (who, as ſome write, caſt all his goods into the ſea, leaſt they might corrupt and ouerthrow him? Or as others affirme, ſould them and put the money into a bank, to the vſe of the poore, if his children ſhould become philoſophers, or other waiſe, to their vſe, leaſt wanting both vertue, and riches they might perhaps periſh? Or els with *Diogenes*, who dwelling in his tub, ſo litle eſteemed the large offers, which *Alexander* the great made him, that he deſired nothing of him, but to ſtand out of his light, and not to keepe the ſunne from him? And ſeeing a poore boy drinke in his hand, caſt away his diſh, as ſuperfluous? Or finallie, with all the other Cinick Philoſophers, who profeſſing a voluntarie and moſt exact pouerty, and liuing, as I may ſay, from hand to mouth, contented themſelues only with that, which might ſuffice nature? Who if they had made their election of pouertie, for the loue of God, referring it wholly, or principallie, to his ſeruice, as Catholick Chriſtians doe (I meane ſuch as profeſſe religious life) they had performed an act of ſinguler, and perfect Chriſtian vertue: And although their intention, was no other, but to auoide the diſtractions, and temptations, which accompanie worldly wealth, to the end they might more freely giue themſelues to the ſtudie and practiſe of Philoſophie, yet it cannot be denied, but that they farre excelled therein the *Lutherans*, and *Caluiniſts*, amongſt whom no ſuch practiſe of that morall vertue, (I meane the magnanimous contempt of the world) hath euer benne ſeene, for ought that I could euer heare, or read.

Suidas. *Dio. Laërtius.*

Philoſtrat. in vita Apollō. *Diocles.*

Plutar. in Apotheg.

62 But

62 But howsoeuer it may be sayd, that some of them doe lyue laudably, or morally wel, and consequently may be called good moral men (as I say manie *Painimes, Epicurians* & *Athists* were, and manie *Turkes* are at this day) yet I may boldlie affirme two thinges, which I wish they would consider. The one, that their good life, and moral vertue, be it neuer so commendable, shal auaile them nothing to their saluation, except they become members of the catholike church, as S. *Augustin* testifieth, saying. *Quisquis ab hac ecclesia catholica &c.* whosoeuer is seperat from this catholike church, how laudably soeuer he liueth, hee shal not haue life euerlasting, but the wrath of God remaineth vppon him, for this onlie sinne, that hee is deuided from the vnitie of Christ. And againe, in an other place. *Nemo,* saith he, *poterit esse iustus &c.* No man can be iust, so long as he is seperat from the vnitie of this bodie. And afterwardes declaring what bodie he meaneth, he saieth, *Sola ecclesia catholica, corpus est Christi* &c. The onlie catholike church, is the bodie of Christ, whereof he is the head, and Sauiour, and out of this bodie, the holie Ghost giueth life to none &c. Thus saith S. *Augustin*, with whome al the holie Fathers vniformelie agree, teaching, that there is no saluation out of the catholik church, though a man lyue neuer so wel, no, not though he suffer martirdome for Christ: for so say expressely *S. Ciprian, S. Augustyn, S. Chrisostome, S. Fulgentius,* and *Pacianus* in the places alleadged in the margent.

S. August. ea 152. ad Donatistas.
Idem. ep 50. ad Bonifacium comitẽ
Cyprian. de simplicit prel
August. ep 204 ad Donatum.
Chrysost. ho 11. in epist ad Ephes
Fulgent. li. de fide ca. 34.
Pacian. ep 2. ad Simpron.

63 And because some perhaps may doubt, what church is to be vnderstood by the Catholike church, I will add a word, or twoo concerning the same out of *S. Augustyn,* who sheweth it euidently, teaching that it is that visible church, which is called by the prophet *Esay*, the house of our Lord, set on the top of hills, whereto all nations shall flow: and by *Daniel*, a hill which shal fill the whole world: and by the roiall prophet, a tabernacle set in the sunn, *id est* saith *S. Augustyn, in manifestatione*, that is to say, in manifestation, or publike show to the world. And lastly by our Sauiour him selfe, it is compared to a candell, which is not sett vnder a bushell, but vppon a candlestick, and to a citty built vppon a hill, which cannot be hid. *Quam facile est tibi,* saith *S. Augustyn attendere, & videre.* Which it is easy for thee to see, and behold *Ipsa est enim ecclesia Catholica, vnde Catholice grece nominatur* &c, for that is the Catholick church where vppon it is called *Catholice* in greeke, because it is dispersed, ouer the whole world. *Hanc ignorare nulli licet, & ideo secundum verbum Domini, abscondi non potest,* Of this catholick church no man ought to be ignorant, and therefore according to the word of our Lord, it cannot be hid.

Esay. 2.
Daniel. 2.
Psalm. 18.
Mat. 5.
Idem. li de vnitate eccles. contra ep Petiliani
Idem. ep 170. ad Seuerinu

thus

64 Thus he: teaching expressely, as you see, out of the prophets, and our Sauiours owne wordes, that the Catholike church is so visible, and vniuersall, that it can neuer be hid, or vnknowne. Which *S. Chrisostome* also doth seriously vrge, and inculcat to the *Ethnicks* of his tyme, willing them to learne, *vim veritatis*, the force of truth, *quomodo facilius est solem extingui, quam ecclesiam obscurari*, that it is easyer for the sunne to be extinguished, then the church to be obscured, or hid: whereuppon it followeth euidently, that the Catholike church cannot possibly be the church of *Lutherans*, or *Caluinists*, which lay hid vnder the bushell, or rather was not extant at all, for many hundreth of yeares. Whereto I also add, that *S. Augustyn* sheweth in like manner, which is the Catholike church, by the continuall, and manifest succession of bishops in *S. Peters* chayre, saying to the *Donatists*. *Numerate sacerdotes* &c. Count the priests, euen from the very seat of *Peter*, and see who hath, *succeeded* one an other in that order of fathers. That is the rock, which the proud gates of hell shal not ouercome. So he, which I might confirme by other most manifest places, as well out of him, as also out of S. *Ireneus*, *S. Cyprian*, *S. Hierome S. Ambrose*, *Optatus Mileuitanus*, and diuers others, but that I touch this poynt only by the way (and therefore thus breefly as you see) to shew what *S. Augustin*, and other fathers meane, by the Catholike church, to wit, a visible, and vniuersall church, wherin there is a continuall and manifest succession of bishops, from *S. Peter*: And this I haue sayd, to the end it may also appeare, that (according to the doctrin of these fathers) out of this church there is no righteousnes, no sanctity, hollynes, nor saluation, how wel soeuer any man, that is out of it, man seme to liue, but that he is, *prophanus*, as saith *S. Hierom*, *a prophane man*, *quicunque extra hanc domum agnum comederit*, whosoeuer ea-
" teth the lambe out of this house, that is to say, out of the communion
" of *Peters* charie. Which I wish may be well pondered, not only by *Lutherans*, and *Caluinists*, but also by all others, who being out of the vnity of this visible, vniuersall, and catholike Roman church, doe vainelie flatter themselues, with their owne good liues, if there be anie such. And thus much for the first point.

S. Chrisost. ho.4.de.verb Esaia. vidi dominum.

Idē. in psalmo contra Partem. Donati.& ep. 160.& li.2. cōtra literas Petiliani.

Irena.li. 3. Cyprian. ep. 55 ad Cornel. & de simplicitate pralat. or. Ambros. in ca.ep.ad. Ti. Optat' lib.2. contra Donatis.

S.Hieron.ep. ad Damasū.

65 The other, which I wish also to be considered of *Lutherans* and *Caluinists*, is, that how well disposed, or vertuous soeuer anie of them, many seeme to be, yet they are not, neither can be counted trulie vertuous, that is to say, good, & perfect christians, being al of them, professed enimies of those christian vertues, in the which consisteth, the perfection of christian religion, I meane the true imitation of Christ, by the perfect abnegation of our selues, the mortification of the flesh, contēpt

of

of the world for the pure loue of God, and the obseruation of the euangelicall counsells taught, and practised by our Sauiour, and his apostles, & by infinit numbers of christians, euer since their time, vntill this day, though now reiected, and derided by *Lutherans*, and *Caluinists*: all which I haue amply proued before, when I treated of the euangelicall counsells in particuler, where, I hope, I made it most manifest, that *Lutheranisme*, and *Caluinisme*, is vtterly void of Christian perfection, and therefore I conclude, that the laudable, and good life of such as professe that religion, neither arriueth to the perfection of christian vertue in any of them, nor can be any iustification of their doctrin, which, as I haue also sufficientlie declared, inuiteth, & draweth men to vice. *Chap. 28. 29. 30. & 31.* *Chap. 28. 29. 30. & 31.*

66 But now, perhaps some will obiect further, & aske how it chanceth then, that in their bookes, and sermons, they exhort men to vertue, and greatly reprehend vice, as we see in the sermons before alleadged, of *Luther* himselfe, *Andreas Musculus*, and *Iohn Andrew*, besides many other which might be also alleadged? Whereto I answer, that I cannot in this more fitly compare them to any, then to *Epicurus*, with whom they simpathize notablie in the deliuery of their carnal doctrin: for although Epicurus taught that mans felicitie doth consist in sensuall, and corporall pleasures, and his cheefe misery in paine, and sorrow, yet he greatly praised vertue, and namely continency, and temperance, where vppon *Cicero* saith, *non id spectandum est, quid dicat* &c. *Yt is not so much to be regarded, what Epicurus saith, as what it is conuenient for him to say, who measureth all good with pleasure, and all euill with sorrow* &c. *For how can he praise temperance, who placeth his cheefe good in sensuall, and bodily pleasures, seeing that temperance is the enemy of sensuality, which hunteth after nothing els, but the pleasure of the body?* *Cicero li. 3. de offic. in fine.*

67 Thus he: who also in an other place saith, that *Epicurus saith many thinges notably well, sed quam constanter, conuenienterque dicat, non laborat, but he careth not how constantlie, or conuenientlie he speaketh, that* is to say, how well he agreeth with himselfe. And againe, *laudat* saith he, *sæpe virtutem* &c. *He praiseth vertue often, not vnlike to Caius Gracchus, who when he had spent all the treasure of the Romans, did in wordes defend the treasure, in so much*, saith *Cicero*, that *if you read his orations, you would take him to be a speciall patron of the treasure.* *Tusc. quæst. li. 5.* *Ibid. li. 3.*

68 Finally *Cicero* obserueth also, that very many were deceiued with the doctrin of *Epicurus*, and his disciples by many graue, and notable sentences contained in their workes: *Atque his*, saith he, *capiuntur imperiti, & propter huiusmodi sententias, istorum hominum est multitudo. Hereby* *Ibid. lib. 5.*

many are deceiued, and by meanes of such sentences, there is a great multitude of these men, that is to say, of *Epicurians*. Thus saith *Cicero*, discouering notably the deuelish sleight, that *Epicurus*, and his disciples vsed, to sophisticat their sensuall doctrin, not only with the collour, and name of philosophie, but also with some mixture of vertuous, and pious precepts, in so much, that (as *Cicero* also noteth els where) *Epicurus* wrote bokes, *de sanctitate, & pietate, of hollines, and piety*, with such shew of religion, that if *you read them*, saith *Cicero*, *you would think that they were written by Coruncanus, or Scæuola* (two famous high bishops) *and not by one that did vtterly destroy all religion.*

Idem de natura deorum li. 1.

69 Lo then, what was the infernall inuention, and deuelish deuise of *Epicurus*, to instill the poison of carnall pleasure, euen into the best disposed minds, with the pious prætext of religion, and vertue. And the like may be obserued in *Luther*, and *Caluin*, and other Archsectaries of our time, in the publication of their Epicurian doctrin, which they honoured with the title of the Ghospell, and resperſed with exhortations to vertue, reprehensions of vice, and frequent allegations of holly scriptures, as though it were wholly conforme to the word of God, and that they sought nothing els but to reforme mens errours, and manners, to extirpat vice, and to plant true religion, and vertue in the mindes of men. Therefore it may be said of their pious prætexts, as *Cicero* said of *Epicurus*, and his like proceeding, to wit, that it is not so much to be considered what they say, as what is conuenient for them to say, according to their owne groundes, and how they agree with themselues in their doctrin.

70 For to what purpose doe they exhort to vertue, & cry out against vice, when their doctrin vndermineth all vertue, and establisheth vice? Not only depriuing men, of the meanes whereby vice is to be repressed (to wit of all kind of mortification, and chastisement of the flesh, without the which the Apostle himselfe held not himselfe secure (as *S. Ambrose* noteth in the place before alleadged:) but also teaching all those points aboue mentioned, which as I haue declared, open a wide gappe to all sinne, and wickednes? For when men are persuaded, that only faith iustifieth, that good workes are not necessarie, but hurtfull to iustification, and saluation, that the best workes of the best men, are damnable sinnes: that mens actions proceede not of free will, but of an absolute necessitie: that God moueth, and compelleth men to synne: that our Christian libertie admitteth no obligation either of humane, or yet of deuine lawes: that therefore the tenne commaundements are abrogated by Christ: that all things but faith, are indiffe-

Cor. 9. S. Ambros. ep. li. 3. ad vercel. eccles.

rent to be vsed or left: that nothing can damne a man, but incredulitie: that chastity in the vnmaried, is neither possible, nor to be demaunded of God: that the more wicked a man is, the more neere he is to Gods grace: and finally, that whatsoeuer our workes are, we are iustified, & sure to be saued, if wee apply the merits of Christs passion to our selues by only faith: when men I say, shall be thus persuaded, to what purpose, shall they be exhorted to vertue, or reprehended for vice, seing that of this doctrin it followeth infalliblie, not only that vertuous, and good life is superfluous, fruitlesse, and impossible, when fate doth not force men to it, but also vice, and sinne, is gratefull to God, being his owne motion, and worke, yea fatall to all such as commit it, and therfore ineuitable, and remedilesse?

71 How ridiculous then, and absurd, are they, who teach this doctrin, and yet cry out against vice, and perswade men to vertue? Might they not keepe that wind (as men are wont to say) to coole their pottage, and not loose it vainelie with such a fruitles labour? For may not the wickedst man in the world, iustly answere them according to their owne groundes, that he can doe no otherwaise, then he doth, because he hath no free will, and that God moueth, and compelleth him to sinne, & therefore cannot of his iustice punish him for it, and that though it were in his power to amend his life, and to doe all the good workes in the world, yet it were needelesse, seeing that the best workes, are no better then the worst, being all damnable synnes in the sight of God: and finallie, that he is iustified by only faith, and sure to be saued, what soeuer he doth, if he trust wholly in Christs merits? May not, I say, the most desperat cutthroat in the world, stopp their mouthes with these their owne groundes?

72 Therefore the *Lutherans* in *Germany*, had great reason to excuse, & defend their bad liues (as you heard in the last chapter) by this very doctrin of their masters, which drew them, or rather droue them headlong, to all that liberty of the flesh, which *Luther*, *Musculus*, and *Iohn Andrew* so seuerely reproued in them. *Chap. 35. nu. 86.*

73 Haue we not then iust cause to say, that these their masters, and reprouers, are as ridiculous, as a phisitian should be, if he should counseil his patients, to vse all riot in diet, and yet still exhort them to haue care of their healths, yea, and chide them when they surfett? Or rather may they not be compared to one, that should cast a man headlong from the top of a tower, and not only call after him and bid him stay, but also exclaime, and cry out against him, for falling? For so doe they, who when they haue precipitated men by their doctrin, and example

to all synne, and wickednes, call vppon them to lyue vertuouslie, yea and be rate them, and rayle vppon them, for their vice.

74 This truly is so euident, that it cannot be denied, and therefore two probable, or rather most certaine causes, may be giuen, why they vsed in their bookes, and sermons, to exhort men to vertue, and dehort them from vice. The one is, that, which I haue already touched, when I spoke of the like proceeding of *Epicurus*, to wit, to make their doctrin more currant amongst wel disposed men. For if either *Epicurus*, had taught and published his licentious philosophy, or they their sensuall doctrin nakedly, without some cloake of religious piety, and of loue to vertue, and hate of vice, no honest mind would euer haue brooked, and much lesse embraced either the one, or the other, whereas now wee see, that many honest, and well disposed men, being deceiued with the honourable title of religion, and of the gospell of Christ, and with the plausible pretence of holly scriptures, and some shew of vertue, and promise of reformation, doe as it were, in a goulden cup, d:inke the poisoned dreggs of heresie, so much the more greedely, by how much more conforme, and agreable it is to mans corrupt nature, and sensualitie, by which meanes also, the carnall philosophie of *Epicurus*, and the beastly religion of *Mahomet*, were the more easely dispersed ouer the world, as I haue declared before.

75 The other reason that moued them, was also common to them with *Epicurus*, and his disciples, to wit, because they had iust cause to feare, that no wise prince, or magistrat, would admit, and endure their doctrin, if they should publish it without any maske, or visard of vertue, being otherwise of it selfe so licentious, and pernitious to common welth, as I haue signified: For which cause the Duke of *Saxony* (*Luthers* great patron) seeing after some time, the bad, and beastly fruites of *Luthers* new ghospell in his dominions, was forced to command a solemne visitation to be made, throughout all *Saxony*, where in it was ordained, that the ministers should preach pennance, the feare of God, and the necessitie of good workes: which was done with *Luthers* consent, though it were directly contrarie to that doctrin, which he had most constantly taught, in so many places of his workes, as you haue heard: so ready was he, to collour, dissemble, and contradict his owne principles, for the pleasure of a prince, and to saue the credit of his ghospell, when he saw it endangered: but of his contradictions, and other of his fellowes I shall haue occasion to speake more amply hereafter.

Surius in comment an 1528.

The

The conclusion of this treatise, deuided into two chapters. And first, in this, a breefe recapitulation of the whole, with certaine considerations resulting theron, concerning our vnion with God, christian perfection, & felicitie, woorthy to be well pondered of euery christian man: And next, certaine douts are cleared, touching christian perfection: & how farre it may extend it selfe in this life.

CHAP. 37.

1 BEING now, good Reader, to conclude this second part of my treatise, I haue thought good to add these two chapters following, as well to refresh in thee the memorie of that which hath benne hitherto treated, as also to represent vnto thee, certaine considerations resulting thereon, right worthy of thy due ponderation.

2 First then, I showed euidentlie (if I be not deceiued) the necessity of religion in common welth, by an argument deduced from the whole to the parts, prouing it to be so necessarie for the conseruation of the whole world (where of euery common welth is but a part) that the same could not stand with out it, in respect that the religion of man, is the special meanes whereby all creatures are reduced to their creator, receiuing perfection, & consummation by glorifiing him, for whose seruice, & glory they were created. So that religion is nothing els but, as I may say, a sacred & holly bond, or knot, whereby the world is tied, knit, & combined with God, and thereby conserued: in so much, that if this link, or knot were dissolued, the world, & consequentlie all common welths (as well, as all other worldly things) must needs fall to ruine, and vtterly perish: the which I showed speciallie in the first, second, and third chapter.

3 Secondlie, I proued the necessitie of religion in common welth, by a more particuler consideration of the proper end, and felicitie, as well of common welth, as of all mankind in general, and of euery particuler man, prouing their felicitie to be all one, and to consist in vnion with God, which is obtained by religion. And this I performed in the 4. and 5. chapter, confirming it with the doctrin as well of the ancient philosophers, as of our deuines, whereby I clearely deduced, not only the necessitie, but also the supereminent dignity of religion in common welth, yea & that it must needs be the true rule, and touchstone by the which all policy is to be tried, & examined. And by the

way, I breefely proued the natural ſubordination of the ciuil ſocietie, (that is to ſay of common welth) to the religious, or eccleſiaſtical ſocietie (which is the church) by the ſame reaſon & law of nature, that the body is ſubordinat, and ſubiect to the ſoule, earth to heauen, humane things to deuine, and man to God, by all which I conuinced the politikes of abſurditie, errour, ignorance, & impietie, in that they peruert the courſe of nature, preferring their falſe reaſon of ſtate before religion, and this I ſpeciallie debated in the 6. chapter.

4 Thirdlie I deſcended from the conſideration of religion in general, to the diſcuſſion, what religion in particuler is the end, and felicitie of common welth. And for as much, as there haue benne in the world, and yet are, 4. ſeueral religions profeſſed (all which, at leaſt, beare the name of religion) to wit *Paganiſme, Mahometiſme, Iudaiſme*, & the *Chriſtian religion*, I diſcuſſed which of them is moſt conuenient for ſtate, and proued that the chriſtian religion is truely political, not only becauſe the other three are moſt abſurd, & ridiculous in them ſelues, & in many reſpects pernicious to common welth (breeding contempt of religion, Atheiſme, vice, & all corruption of manners) but alſo becauſe the chriſtian religion being the law of grace, hath the only meanes to reforme mens manners, to repreſſe vice, to plant vertue, and to vnite man & common welth with God (wherein conſiſteth their true felicitie) and that therefore the ſame, is conforme as well to true reaſon of ſtate, as to the veritie of true religion.

5 And to the end this might more clearely appeare, I diſcourſed amply, as well of the admirable effects of chriſtian religion in the conuerſion of ſinners, and the reformation of mens manners, as alſo of the vnſpeakeable dignitie, and excellencie of chriſtian contemplation, and of the practiſe thereof, where by the ſoule of man is moſt admirablie vnited with God, & man beatified, or made happy euen in this life. And all this I treated from the 6. chapter, to the 25. And by the way, I not only showed how the prouidence of God in conſeruing the empire of the Romans, concurred with his iuſtice in puniſhing the ſame, throughout the courſe of the Roman hiſtorie (whiles their common welth and empire was pagan) but alſo I anſwered certaine friuolous obiections of *Macchiauel* againſt chriſtian religion, namely in the 24. chapter, where I diſcouered his abſurd ignorance, and malicious impietie.

6 Fourthly, whereas chriſtian religion is, now at this day, diuerſlie profeſſed in diuers parts, & cuntries of chriſtendome, as by *Catholikes, Lutherans, Caluiniſts, Anabaptiſts*, and many other ſectaries (in which

respect it may seeme doutfull to some which of these professions are most conforme not only to the veritie of religion, but also to reason of state) I haue therefore from the 24. chapter hitherto proued, that the catholike Roman religion is truelie political, & geeueth true happines to man, & common welth, and that the professions of the sectaries (& particularly *Lutheranisme*, & *Caluinisme*) are most absurd, in respect as well of true policie, & reason of state, as of the veritie of christian religion. And to this end I proued, that the catholike Roman religion only, hath the true imitation of Christ, the perfect practise of the Euangelicall counsels, & consequentlie the highest degree of christian perfection, vnion with God, and the true felicitie of man, and common welth: and that on the other side, the aduersaries of the catholyke religion, and Roman church, haue none of these at all, & consequently neither the true felicitie of man, & common welth, nor the veritie of christian religion.

7 And this, I hope, I haue made cleare, not only by the holly Scriptures, and the ancient Fathers, but also by all the external and euident signes, that almightie God hath at any time vsed to show his internal vnion with his seruants, which I haue euidentlie proued, to be most manifest in the catholikes of these dayes, as they also were in the saints, & holly men of the primitiue church, and of all the ensuing ages vntill this time, whereas I haue also showed, on the other side, that the sectaries haue no participation at all of such deuine fauours, nor any external signes, of Gods internal vnion with them.

8 Lastly I haue proued my intent in lyke manner, by the doctrin and fruits of both religions, hauing showed euidentlie in ten points of controuersie, that the Catholike Roman religion deliuereth the true meanes to mortifie the flesh, to restrayne the violence of the passions, to practise all vertues, to obtaine Gods grace, & consequentlie to make happy, as well the whole common welth, as euerie member thereof. And that on the other side, the religion of the Sectaries, namely of *Luther*, & *Caluin*, doth not only teach diuers absurd, impious, & blasphemous opinions and heresies, but also that it is an Epicurien doctrin, teaching all libertie of the flesh, fostering, & feeding sensualitie, withdrawing all men from vertue, and dryuing them headlong to vice, and sinne, to the ruine, as well of the whole common welth, as of euery particuler man that professeth it. And this I haue amply declared, as well in the 30. chapter (where I treated of the Euangelical counsel of *chastity*, and layed downe the absurd, and licentious doctrin of the Sectaries, with their loose, and lewed liues) as also in the two last

chapters, where of I hope, good Reader, the contents are yet so fresh in thy memorie, that I shall not neede to trouble thee with any further recapitulation thereof, and therefore I will now proceede to draw some considerations out of all the premisses, for thy further satisfaction.

9 The first consideration shalbe, that seeing I haue sufficientlie proued that the end, and felicitie of man, and common welth, consisteth in vnion with God, it infinitlie importeth euery man (be he priuat, or publik person) seriouslie to ponder, and waigh speciallie two things. The one, the woorth & valew of this end: The other by what meanes, and by whom the same is obtained. And therefore to say some what breefelie of both points, and first of the former: What is there in the world that can haue any kind of comparison therewith, whether we respect honour, & glory, proffit, and benefit, or els pleasure, swetenes, & delight? Is there any honour, & glory in the world comparable to that which we receiue by our vnion with God?

10 For put the case, that a man were the greatest friend, mignion, & fauorit of the greatest prince in the world, what were that in respect of friendship, and vnion with almightie God, who is Lord, of Lords, king of kings, and the authour and geuer of all true honour, glory, & happines? Where vppon *S. Bernard* saith. *Quam miseri sumus &c. How wretched are we, that hunt after the glory which we haue one of an other, and neglect that which is only of God, and hath continuance, yea & replenisheth, & filleth the soule with true contentment, & delight?* Where as the other depending only on the vaine conceits of men, is not only mixt with infinit corosiues, & disgusts, but also subiect to so many dangers, crosses, checks, & changes, by practises of enemies, ielosies, suspicions, the inconstancie, and mutabilitie of the princes themselues, that it is many times sooner lost then had, and endeth very oft with lamentable disgrace, and remediles ruine.

S. Bern. ser. 17. in psalm. qui habitat.

11 Besids that, if we consider what true honour & glory is, as that it is nothing els, but *the publik voice* (as *Cicero* saith) *of men, which iudge well and truely of excellent vertue*, it is euident that where there is not solid, and true vertue (which cannot be had without vnion with God) there can be no true honour, & glory, though mens titles, fauours, power, & pompe be neuer so greate: in which respect the glory of wicked men, is woorthilie tearmed in the holly scriptures, *stercus, & vermis, dung, & woormes*, being lyke to the gloworme, or to a kind of rotten wood, which shyneth in the dark, & being brought, to the light, appeareth to bee nothing els, but filth, and putrefaction: And euen so,

Cicero Tusculan. q. li. 3.

1. Macha. 2.

the honour, and glory of the world seeme neuer so glorious in the corrupt iudgement of worldly men (whose reason is obscured, and darkned with errour, & passion) yet being vewed and considered with a cleare vnderstanding, illuminated with Gods grace, it presently discouereth the abiection, & basenes of it selfe, as that it is nothing els in verity, but a most miserable seruitud and bondage, masked with a vaine, and false opinion of honour, and glory: for who is such a slaue, or so infamous, as he that is tiranised by his owne passions, by the deuil, and sinne, as all worldlings, and wicked men are, be they neuer so honorable, & glorious in the sight of men?

12 Whereas he that is vnited with almighty God, & thereby not only his familiar friend, and fauorit, but also *vnus spiritus* (as the A- 1.Cor. 6.
postle saith) *one spirit with him*, is truely honorable, and glorious, triumphing ouer the deuil his owne passions, and sinne, contemning all the vanities of the world, and becomming euen in this life, a heauenly and deuine creature, as I haue declared sufficiently in my tract of contemplation: and therefore such a one, I say, is truely honorable, how abiect soeuer he seeme to worldly men. The due consideration whereof, hath moued those wise, potent, and worthy Emperours, kings, and princes (of whome I haue spoken before) to reiect, and renounce all their earthly glory, power, and dominion, to the end they might the more assuredlie and freely, enioye this other honour consisting in perfect vnion with God, with out the which, they woorthilie esteemed all worldlie honour, to be no better then base bondage, and seruitud: Whereas on the other side, all worldlie contempt is to him that is truely vnited with God, the hyghest, and truest honour, & glory that may be, being that which our Sauiour Christ, the king of glory, chose for himselfe, & for his dearest frends: whome by that meanes he glorifieth, not only eternallie in heauen, but also temporallie euen heere on earth.

13 This may appeare, both by the greate respect, and reuerence which the greatest princes haue in all ages and times borne to holly men, whiles they liued) though in the eye of the world they were otherwayse most contemptible) and much more by the honour donne

to them after theyr deaths, on theyr feastiual dayes, & by the infinit miracles that haue benne from time to time and yet are wrought at their monuments, & memories, which are more triumphant then the thrones, & trophees of all earthly potentats, kings, & emperours, who become their suppliants, crouching, & kneeling vnto them, and reuerencing euery litle rag, or relick of them; so honorable, & glorious euen in this world is he, who contemneth worldly honour, & glory for the loue of God, to the end he may be vnited with him, and therefore the
Psal. 138. psalmist saith of such. *Mihi autem nimis honorificati sunt amici tui deus &c. They frends, o God, ar to me very honorable, and their principality is very strong,* or potent: and our sauiour also him self said of his seruants. *Si quis mihi*
Ioan. 12. *ministrauerit, &c. VVho soeuer shall serue me, my Father which is in heauen, will honour him,* or make him honorable. And finally, of such a one the
Eccli. 39. wise man saith in *ecclesiasticus. Collaudabunt multi sapientiam eius &c. Many shall praise his wisdome, and it shall neuer be abolished, the memory of him shall neuer faile, & his name shall be required or sought after from generation to generation, nations, & people shall speake of his wisdome, & the church shall show foorth, or declare his praise.*

14 Neuertheles I wish it heere to be noted, that I doe not so separate these two kinds of honours, spiritual, & temporal (I meane by spiritual, that which consisteth only in mans vnion with God, and contempt of the world) as though they were incompatible, or could not stand together, but to show how they are truely to be distinguished, & how they may concurre, & which of them is to be preferred: for there is no dout but temporal honours, & dignities are the gifts of God, & being well vsed, & referred to Gods glory, as to their end, may not only well stand with mans vnion with God, but also may some way be the fruits, & effects thereof, as when almighty God bestoweth temporal honours vppon his seruants, or conserueth them in honour, & dignitie, for his owne greater glory, & seruice: which may be exemplified in all those famous, & holly emperours, kings, & Princes, which haue benne either canonised by the church for saints, or otherwaise knowne to be greate seruants of God, though they still retained their dignitie, & states vntill their deaths, whose temporal honours receiuing soliditie, & stabilitie by their vnion with God, haue made their fame no lesse memorable to all posteritie, then theyr soules are, & euer shall be glorious in heauen: so that they may be counted truely honorable.

15 Whereas infinit other wicked princes, though no lesse potent in temporal dominion then they, yet are eyther buried in perpetual obliuion, or els remayne more infamous for their vices, then famous, or memorable

morable for their power, and dignity, whyles also their soules are plunged in to the perpetual miserie of euerlasting damnation, and therefore of such the booke of wisdome testifieth, that. *Illos deridebit Deus &c. God will deride them, and they shall fall with out honour, and be a very contumely, or shame amongst the dead for euer.* Whereby it appeareth that true honour, whether we respect it, as it is temporal only in this life, or as it is eternal, proceedeth from mans vnion with God. *Sap. 4.*

16 The like also is to be said of benefit, or proffit, which if it be considered as it auaileth, or helpeth to the true felicitie or happines of man, can grow from no other roote, but the blessing of almightie God the geeuer of all true happines (who as *Aristotle* himselfe teacheth) doth speciallie loue, benefit, & cherish those, which are most vnited with him, whome therefore, he concludeth to be most happy, as I haue signified diuers times before: Besids that if we take benefit, and proffit to consist in welth, & ritches, is there any so ritch, & welthy, as he that enioyeth God, who is all in all, and geeueth also abundance of welth, & all kind of temporal commodities to his friends, & seruants, when it is conuenient for them? In which respect the psalmist saith. *Diuites eguerunt, & esurierunt, &c. Ritch men haue wanted, and benne hungry, but those which seeke God shall want no good*, that is to say, not so much as any temporal good, when it is not preiudicial to their euerlasting good. *Arist. eth. li. 10.* *Psal. 33.*

17 Therfore we see that God hath blessed many of his seruants in all times, euen with temporal welth, to the end they may by the good vse thereof serue, & glorifie him, do good to others, and consequentlie encrease their owne merit: though otherwaise when he seeth in his deuine prouidence, that the same wold hinder the saluation of their soules, he eyther doth not geeue it them, or mercifullie depriueth them of it, euen for their benefit: for as our sauiour himselfe, most deuinelie said. *Quid prodest homini &c. VVhat doth it proffit a man to gaine all the world, if he loose his soule.* In which case ritches are so farre from being proffitable, or beneficial, that they are most pernicious, being, as *Salomon* saith. *Conseruatæ in malum Domini. Conserued, or keapt to the hurt of their maister,* & possessor, whereof also *S. Iames* admonisheth vs, saying, *your gold and siluer is rusted, and their rust, shalbe a testimonie to yow, and shall eate your flesh like fire.* *Matth. 16.* *Eccles. 5.* *Iac. 5.*

18 Furthermore it is euident that al the benefit, & proffit that groweth of worldly welth, & ritches, proceedeth of the good vse thereof, for, as the comical poet saith, *the goods of fortune ar* good, or bad, *according to the mynd of him, that possesseth them: Quæ vti scit, illi bona, illi, qui non vtitur recte, mala: they are good, or beneficial to him that vseth them well, but to him that abu-* *Terent.*

seth them they are pernicious, Whereof we daily see the experiēce in those, who vse their owne goods, & welth, no otherwise then as kniues to cut their owne throtes, purchasing to thēselues thereby, nothing els but infamy, hatred, & destruction both temporal, & eternal. And therefore seeing the good vse of all things in this world, principally dependeth on Gods grace, & direction (which inseparablie accompanieth his vnion with man) it is manifest that all temporal goods, & commodities are most beneficial, & proffitable to those who are vnited with God.

19 And what neede I speake of the incōparable pleasure, & delight that mans vnion with God doth yeeld him, I meane such a vniō, & in such a degree, as I require to the felicity of man in this life; whereby he liueth, & perseuereth in the grace, fauor, & frendship of God, free from the tyrannie of the deuil, & mortal sinne, enioying true repose & peace of cōscience, cōmanding his owne passiōs, & affectiōs, contēning the world, & al the vanities thereof, abounding in feruor of soule, swimming, as I may say, in a sea of swetnes, ioy, & exultation in the loue of God: & finally participating now & then of those extraordinarie visitations, and deuine consolations which almightie God, out of his infinit bounty, is wont euen in this life to impart sometimes to his dearest seruants, and frends, whom (as we read in the canticles) he leadeth. In *cellam vinariam.* In to his wine cellers, where *inebriātur ab vbertate domus Dei*, they are, out of the plenty of Gods house, made drōk as it were, with an inundation, & *torrent*, (as the psalmist saith) of heauenly pleasure & delight, hauing euen in this our mortal & miserable state, a true tast, or assay, of immortalitie, & eternal felicitie? what need I, I say, treat further of this, in this place seeing that I haue most amply discoursed vpon thesame in diuers parts of this treatise, not only out of the doctrin of our christian deuines, confirming it by the examples of holly men in all ages, & times, but also out of the opinion euen of the philosophers themselues, who though for want of Gods grace, & true vnion with him, they could neuer arriue to the experience of the true pleasure, & delectation of it, yet saw by reason, & seriously taught, that all earthly delites, & contentmēts, are but as it were, trash, & trumpery in respect thereof, for which cause they placed therein the end, and felicitie of man in this life, no lesse then the wisest, & most learned christians doe.

Cant. 1. & 2.
Psal. 35.
Ibid.

20 Therfore I cōclude, that whether we respect honour, proffit, or pleasure, nothing in this world is cōparable to mās vniō with God, in which respect the *Psalmist* saith. *Quid mihi est in cælo, & à te quid volui super terram?* &c. *What is there for me in heauen, or what wold I haue of thee*, ô Lord, *vppon the earth? my flesh, & my hart haue fainted, or failed in me*, for the feruent desire I

Psal. 72.

haue

haue to be vnited with thee. *Deus cordis mei pars mea Deus in æternũ. Thou,* ô Lord, who art *the God of my hart,* shalt be *my part, or portion for euer: for those which goe away frõ thee shall perish, & thou destroyest all those who following their owne lusts, & desires, doe deuide themselues from thee,* & therfore, *mihi adhærere Deo bonũ est &c. It is good for me to be vnited with God, & to put my hope in him.* Thꝰ said this royal prophet, who though he aboũded in all worldly honour, welth, power, & prosperity, yet placed his delite, & felicitie in nothing but in his vniõ with almightie God: which the Apostle also signified of himselfe when he said. *Omnia arbitror vt stercora, vt Christum lucrifaciam. I hold all things to be no better then dung, to the end I may gaine Christ.* *Philip.* 3.

21 And of this vnion with God, *S. Bernard* saith notably thus: *caro & sanguis, vas luteum quando &c. when is our flesh & blood, our vessel of clay partaker of this?* mary, *when the soule feeleth in it selfe such affection, that it is dronk with a deuine loue, and forgetting wholly it selfe, becommeth as a lost, & broken vessell to it self, & passeth wholly into God, & adhering, or cleauing fast to him, is made one spirit with him, saying with the psalmist, my flesh, and my hart haue failed. Thou ô Lord who art the God of my hart shalt be my part, or portion for euer: & I will count him,* saith S. Bernard, *a happy, & holly man, whosoeuer he is, to whome God hath granted the experiẽce of this, in this mortal life, though it be but seeldome, yea but once, & that for neuer so short a time, euen for one minut of an houre.* Thus saith this holly & contemplatiue Father, of the ineffable woorth, & delectation of mans vnion with God. *S. Bern. de diligendo Deo S. Felix qui.*

22 This thẽ is that *vnũ* which, as our sauiour said to *Martha*, is absolutly necessary, for that all other things doe by their, multiplicitie, rather distract, thẽ delite, rather deuid then vnite, rather encũber, then comefort: This is that *margarit*, or pretious stone, which the wise negotiatour, or marchant seeketh, & finding it, geeueth all he hath to buy it: this is that inestimable sweetenes, whereto the royal Prophet inuiteth vs, saying. *Gustate & videte quoniam suauis est Dominus. Tast and see, for our lord is sweete:* whereof the wise mã also speaketh, whẽ treating of a deuout soule, vnder the parable of a wise, & valiãt womã, he saith. *Gustauit, & vidit, quòd bona est negotiatio eius. She tasted, & saw, that she had made a good bargaine.* For so incomparable is the valew of this vnion with God, that no man can conceiue it, but he that possesseth it, & therfore when S. *Peter* enioyed it vpõ the mount with our sauiour, he said, *bonũ est nos hic esse*, it is good for vs to remaine heere: This is the goale whereto euery man ought to runne, & the marke whereat we all ought to shute, the treasure of treasures, the fountaine of all true honour, benefit, and pleasure, the heauenly reward of all our earthly labours, heauen on earth, and eternall happines in heauen: finallie, this is the end whereto all *Luc* 10. *Matth.* 13. *Psal.* 33. *Prouer.* 31. *Matth,* 17.

mankind was ordained, and consequentlie the true felicitie of man, & common welth. And therefore I leaue it to the consideration of any man, who tendereth, & desireth his owne good, how much it importeth him to seeke, & procure it by all possible meanes, & what an extreame folly it is, to preferre any worldly honour, proffit, or pleasure before it. Thus much concerning, the woorth and valew of the end of man consisting in his vnion with God.

23 And now to say some what also of the other point, to wit, of the meanes how it is to be obtained, & who they are that arriue vnto it, I haue made it manifest, as I think, through out all this discourse, that the only meanes to attaine to this end, & true felicitie, is the christian religion, wherein the true imitation of our Sauiour Christ is taught, & practised, by a perfect abnegation of our selues, the mortification of the flesh, and the exercise of all vertue: so that it is not to be vnderstood that all those which professe, and hold the christian faith, arriue to this felicitie, but those only who practise the same in perfection, as I haue showed amply in the 22. & 25. chapters, where I haue also declared, that although the hyghest perfection of Christian religion, consisteth in the perfect imitation of our sauiour Christ, by the obseruation of the Euangelicall counsels (which in their highest perfection, are not compatible with the profession of seculer men, such I meane as are maried, & haue proprietie in goods, lands, or possessions) yet euery christian man professing any lawful state, or condition of life, may be a perfect contemplatiue, & vnited with God in greate perfection, which I exemplified in many kings, & princes, who albeit they flowed in welth, honour, & prosperitie, yet were of such rare vertue, mortification, & contemplation, that they were hyghly fauored by almightie God, not only with internal graces, & vertues, but also with external, & euident signes of his internal vnion with them.

24 And this, I say, I haue sufficiently signified before: And therfore for as much as there are three sorts of christians, who neuer arriue to that happy vnion with God in this life whereof I treate heere, I think good first to say some what of them, as wel because the due consideration thereof, seemeth to me very necessarie, & important for euery christian man, as also because the same being declared, it will more clearelie appeare, who they ar that do attaine thereto.

25 The first sort of those, whom I exclude from it, ar such, as beleeuing all that which the christian religion teacheth, & being free from all heresie, or errour in matter of faith, doe neuertheles wholly abandon and geue ouer themselues to the world, the flesh, & the deuil, in such sort

that

that they haue no more practise of christian precepts for good life, then the very woorst sort of heretikes, or infidels haue.

26 These are they, whome our Sauiour himselfe compared to one, who being inuited to the banket of the greate king, at the mariage of his sonne, sate doune amongst the rest, without his wedding garment (that is to say with out charitie) whome therefore the king comaunded to be taken, & bound hand and foote, and cast in to the exteriour darknes. *Vbi est fletus, & stridor dentium. VVhere there is weeping, wayling, and gnashing of teeth.* *Matth. 22.* *Ibid.*

27 These are they of whome the Apostle spake, when hauing recommended that *faith which woorketh by charitie*, and afterwards declared the *woorks of the flesh*, he concluded that, *qui talia agunt, regnum Dei non consequentur. Those which doe such woorks, as these, shall not obtaine the kingdome of God.* Finallie, these are they of whom I spooke in the last chapter, who not brooking the restraint of Catholike religion, but hunting after a licentious libertie, doe many times become *Lutherans, Caluinists*, yea Turks, or Infidels: and therefore these are so farre from all vnion with God, that they are rather members of the deuil, not withstanding their faith, though it be neuer so greate, yea able to remoue mountaines, as the Apostle witnesseth. *Galat. 5.* *1. Cor. 13.*

28 The second sort of christians which doe not arriue to this vnion, is of those, who though they are not altogether careles of their liues, but willing to serue God, and to saue their soules, yet their care, & diligence commonlie extendeth no further, then to conserue themselues in one state, with out seeking to proffit, or proceede in vertue, and true mortification: and therefore, where as there are three degrees of good Christians, the first of beginners, the second of such as proffit in the way of vertue, and the third of those which arriue to perfection (to which three sorts of men, I applied the three waise of contemplation, whereof I haue amply treated before, to wit, the *purgatiue*, the *illuminatiue*, & the *vnitiue way*) these of whome I now treate, are to be ranked with the first sort, to wit, with beginners who neuer passe further then the *purgatiue way*.

29 For, al be it they doe many good deeds, and are now & then, yea perhaps for the most part, in the state of grace, & consequentlie vnited with God in some degree, yet for as much as their fall into mortal sinnes, is also frequent, whereby they loose all vnion with God, and become his enemies for the time (I meane vntill they ryse againe) therefore such men, vsing no other endeuour, then only to rise when they are fallen, & rather to purge, & cleanse themselues from sinne, then to furnish

and

and adorne themselues with vertue (seruing God rather for feare, then for loue, & louing him so, that they may also loue the world with all) such, I say, are so farre from being partakers of that happy vnion with God (wherein I place the felicitie of man in this life) that they are in more danger dayly to fall cleane a way from him, and to loose his grace altogether, then to receiue those fauours which he bestoweth vppon his deare seruants, and friends, who liue in continual mortification of the flesh, contemning, and hating the world, yea themselues for the loue of him, whom therefore he woorthilie loueth cherisheth, & espouseth, communicating himselfe vnto them in such sort, as I haue si-
Chap. 21. gnified a litle before, and much more at large when I treated of christian contemplation, and of the admirable effects thereof.

30 Therefore I wish these kind of men for their owne speciall good, to consider, how farre they are from performing the obligation, and duty of perfect christians, which what it is I showed amply in the 23. chapter, out of our sauiours owne doctrin of the 8. christian beatituds,
Matth. 5. and his other admirable precepts of *pouerty of spirit, mansuetud, patience,* the *loue of our enemies; contempt of the world abnegation of our selues,* and the *continual cariage of our crosse,* in imitation of him, from the which no man professing the faith of christ is exempted, as I declared at large in the place aboue mentioned, where vppon it followeth, that seeing all these vertues are most necessarie to the true imitation of Christ, and that noman can in this life arriue to such perfection therein, but that he ought to endeuour to be more perfect (in which respect *S. Iohn* saith in the
Apoc. 22. *Apocalips. Qui iustus est iustificetur adhuc: he which is iust, let him be iustified*
S. Bern. ep. 253. *still,* And *S. Bernard: Numquam iustus arbitratur se comprehendisse &c.* The iust man neuer thinketh he hath comprehended, he neuer saith he hath ynough, he is alwaise hungry, & thirsteth alwaise after iustice, so that if he shuld liue euer, he woold euer striue to be iuster, and endeuour with all his force to proceede from good to better: for that he is not bound to the seruice of God for a yeere, or for a certaine time, like a hyreling, but for euer:) heere vppon, I say, it followeth, that those which content themselues to arriue but to a certaine degree of vertue; & do not seeke daily to encrease, and proffit therein, do not performe the duty of perfect christians.

31 This may further appeare in the royal prophet, who foretold the continual progresse that christians should make in vertue through the
Psal. 83. grace of Christ, their law maker: *etenim benedictionem,* saith he, *dabit legislator &c. For their law maker shall geue them, his benediction, or grace, they shall goe from vertue to vertue, & so the God of Gods in Sion shall be seene.*

32 This

32 This is alſo ſignified in many places of ſcripture, where we are exhorted to vertu, by words importing mocion, & proceeding, or going forward, as *to goe, to comme, to walke, to runne: Qui vult venire poſt me,* ſaith Luc. 9.
our Sauiour, he which will come after me, let him deny himſelfe, and take vp his croſſe, and follow me: ſignifying that he which will be a perfect christian & follower of Chriſt, muſt ſtil goe forward in the imitation of Chriſt, that is to ſay, neuer ſtand at a ſtay: *Ambulate* ſaith he alſo, *dum lucem habetis,* walke whiles you haue light: & S. Iohn, Ioan 12.
to the ſame purpoſe, ſaith, that he which ſaith he remaineth in Chriſt, 1.Ioan.2.
ought to walke, as be walked.

33 In like manner the Apoſtle vſeth the ſame manner of ſpeech very Rom. 6.
oft, exhorting vs, to *walke in the newnes of life, to walke woorthy of our vo-* Ephes. 4.
cation, & to walke woorthy of God, which he expoundeth to the *Theſſalo-* 1.Theſ.4.
nians, ſaying. *VVe pray, & beſeech you, that as you haue receiued of vs, how you ought to walke, & pleaſe God: ſic & ambuletis, vt abundetis magis: you walke ſoe, that you may abound more.* And agayne to the *Coloßians* more plainely: *VVe doe not ceaſe* ſaith he, *praying for you, vt ambuletis dignè Deo, per omnia placentes, in omni opere bono fructificantes, & creſcentes in ſcientia Dei. That you* Coloſ. 1.
may walke woorthy of God, in all things pleaſing, fructifying in euery good woorke, & encreaſing in the knowledge of God &c. Geeuing to vnderſtand, that then we walke worthy of God, & our vocation to the faith of Chriſt, when we goe forward, & proceede ſtill fructifying, & encreaſing in good woorks, & the knowledge of God.

34 Therefore *S. Auguſtin* ſaith, *Quid eſt ambulare? &c. VVhat is it to* S. Aug. de verb. Apoſto. ſer.15.c.15.
walke, I ſay breefely, it is to proffit, leſt perhaps you doe not vnderſtand it, & walke more ſlowly then you ſhuld doe. So he.

35 This alſo the Apoſtle expreſſeth yet more fully to the *Corinthians,* comparing the courſe of a chriſtian mans life, to a race wherein we are to runne continuallie vntill we arriue at the goale: *An neſcitis,* ſaith he, *quod hi qui in ſtadio currunt &c. Doe yee not know that thoſe which runne in the race doo all runne, & yet but one winneth the prize? therefore ſo runne that you may obtaine.*

36 Here vppon *S. Bernard* maketh a notable diſcourſe, which I thinke Sanctus Bernard vbi ſupra.
good to ſett doune here, though it be ſome what long, for it containeth moſt excellent doctrin concerning this matter. *Ibi tu chriſtiane,* ſaith he, *fige tui curſus profectuſque metam* &c. O Chriſtian, fixe thou the bounds of thy courſe & progreſſe there, where Chriſt fixed, and ſetled his, who became obedient euen vntill death: therefore how much, or how well ſoeuer thou runneſt, if thou doe not runne vntill death, thou canſt not reach, or arriue at the goale, & winne the prize, which is

" Christ: for if whiles he runnes, thou standest still, thou dost not come
" neare to him, but goest further from him, & therefore art to feare that which *Dauid* said. *Ecce qui elongant se a te peribunt: Behold all those which*
" *doe separat themselues from thee,* ô Lord, *shall perish*: therefore if to proffit,
" or goe forward in vertue be to runne, thou ceasest there to runne, where thou dost cease to proffit, & where thou beginnest no longer to runne,
" there thou beginnest to faint, & faile: where vppon it is euidentlie to
" be gathered, that *nolle proficere, non nisi deficere est, not to seeke to proffit, is nothing els but to fayle,* or decay. *Iacob* saw the ladder & angels vppon it,
" of whome none appeared resting, or standing still, but all of them
" either going vp, or comming doune, to the end we may plainelie vn-
" derstand that in the state of this our mortal life, there is no meane to be found betwixt proffiting & decaying, but that as our bodies are alwaise
" either encreasing, or decreasing, so also of necessitie our spirit, or soule,
" doth either proffit or decay.

37 Thus farre *S. Bernard*, who also els where saith further thus. *Quis-*
" *quis in schola Christi non proficit &c.* Whosoeuer doth not proffit, or goe

Idem ep. 341. forward in the schoole of Christ, he is vnwoorthie of such a maister,
" especiallie seeing our case is such, that nothing remaineth in one state,
" & therefore let no man say vnto me, I will remaine as I ame, it suffiseth me to be this day, as I was yesterday: for such a one sitteth doune in
" the way, and stayeth vppon the ladder, where *Iacob* the Patriarck saw
" none but those, which either went vp, or came doune, and therefore I say, *qui existimat se stare, videat ne cadat, he which thinkes that he standeth, let*

1. *Cor.* 10. " *him take heede lest he fall*: the way is hard, and narrow, and the many mansions, or resting places (where of our sauiour spake) are not heere,

Ioan. 14. but in the house of his Father: therefore he which saith that he remai-
" nes, or rests in Christ, *ought to walke as Christ walked*, for Christ, as the

1. *Ioan.* 2. Euangelist witnesseth, *encreased, and proffited in wisdome, & age, & grace,*

Luc. 2. *both before God and men,* therefore he rested not, *sed exultauit vt gigas, ad*

Psalm. 18. " *currendam viam suam, but exulted like a gyant to runne his course,* & so also we, if we be not mad, will runne after him.

38 Thus he and addeth further after a while: *let vs be moued hereto with*
" *the* example of our owne seculer desires, for when doe we euer see an ambitious man content himselfe with the dignities that he hath got,
" and not aspire to hygher? Or when is the curious mans eye, and eare
" satisfied? And what shall I say of couetous, and voluptuous men, or of those that hunt after vayne praise? Doe not their insatiable desires ar-
" gue vs of negligence, and tepiditie? Therefore let vs hold it for an
" infamous thing to be lesse desirous of spiritual goods, then they are of temporal:

temporal: and let a soule that is conuerted to God be a shamed to seeke righteousnes with lesse affectiō, then it sought iniquitie, & sinne, seeing that the *reward of sinne is death, and the fruit of the spirit is life euerlasting:* Rom. 6. In which respect we may be a shamed, to goe now more negligentlie towards life, then before we went towards death, and now to seeke the encrease of our saluation with lesse diligence, then before we sought to augment our perdition, and damnation, wherein we shall be altogether inexcusable, considering that the faster we runne in the way of life, the more easilie we runne, and the greater that the light burden of our sauiour is, the more portable it is: Doe not the very number of fethers, rather ease, and lift vp the byrds that beare them, then burden, or depresse them? For take the fethers away, and the rest of the body falleth doune to the ground: euen so also the light burthen, the sweete yoke, & disciplin of Christ, doth rather beare vs, then is borne by vs, in so much that in laying it a syde, we presentlie fall to the ground.

39 Thus saith this holiy, and deuout Father: which is right woorthie to be duly considered of euery christian man (of what condition vocation, or state, or of what perfection soeuer he be) but speciallie of those, of whome I treate principallie at this present, I meane such idle, slouthfull, & vnproffitable seruants, as do not continuallie employ the talents, which their Lord, and maister hath geeuen them to be put to vse, and encrease, & therfore they may well feare, that when the dreadfull day of account, and reckoning shall come, they shal (as our sauiour himselfe testified of such) be worthilie, *cast in to the exteriour darkenes, where there is weeping, and gnashing of teeth.* Matth. 25.

40 For if the iustest, and most perfect man, be bound still to tend to perfection, or otherwayse fainteth (as *S. Bernard* saith) and faileth in the course of christian life, or rather (as he saith in an other place) goeth backward, for *non progredi in via vitæ,* saith he, *regredi est, not to goe forward, in the way of life is to goe back ward.* And if the Apostle himselfe, who gloried in nothing but in the crosse of Christ, & was crucified, & wholly dead to the world, and therefore had alreddy obtained an incomparable perfection of vertue, yet did not think that he might stay his course there, but saith: *Fratres, ego me non arbitror comprehendisse* &c. *Brethren I doe not thinke that I haue comprehended, yet one thing: forgetting the things which are behynd, & extending my selfe to those that are before, I doe still prosecut my course towards the marke:* If he, I say, not only said this of himselfe, but also seriouslie aduised it to all others, how perfect soeuer they be (adding, *Quicunque ergo perfecti sumus, hoc sentiamus, let vs therefore as many of vs, as are perfect think, or perswade our selues thus*) what shal

Vbi supra. S. Bernard serm. 2. de purificatio. B. Virg.

Philip. 3.

Ibid.

we say of those who soe litle care for perfection of vertue, that they either sit doune, and rest in the beginning of their race, or goe one steppe forward, & two or three backward, and get no ground of the enemy, but rather runne round about, (as the psalmist saith of wicked men, *Impij in circuitu ambulant*, *wicked men walke in a circle* as in a labirinth or a maze, ore els being entred in to the christian combat against such suttle, and potent enemies (as are the world, the flesh, and the deuil,) they fight so lasilie, & cowardlie, that they continuallie receiue many mortal wounds of them? Can such euer hope to arriue at the goale, to winne the prize, or to get the victorie, and croune, which is reserued for those that perseuer to the end, consummat their course, and fight manfully in the meane time? Nay, may not such cowardlie souldiars rather iustly feare, that they shall not only loose the croune of euerlasting life, which they might haue gained, but also die eternalie of the deadly wounds, which they receaue oft times, if God doe not extend extraordinarie mercy towards them?

Psal. 11.

41 And whereas, men are most commonlie the more negligent in this behalfe, for that they presume ouer much, either of themselues, or els of Gods mercy, I will breefely touch both kinds of presumptions, following *S. Bernard* in his notable treatise vppon the psalme. *Qui habitat in adiutorio altissimi*, &c. where he excludeth from Gods helpe, & protection three sorts of men: The first are those (saith *S. Bernard*) that *doe not hope*: The second, those *that despaire*: And the third, those that *hope in vaine*: of which three, the first, & last are those of whome I am to speake at this present.

S. Bernard in psal. qui habitat &c. Ser. 1.

42 Of the first, *S. Bernard* saith, that there are some which may well be saide not to hope in God, because they confide in themselues, who hauing had, saith he, greate feruour in deuotion, in watching, in fasting, and such like, or perhaps stored themselues (as it seemeth to them) with the ritches of many merits, become so confident therein, that they grow remisse, and slack in the feare of God, & being drawne awaye with pernicious securitie, doe decline to Idlenes, and curiosities, and soe by degrees fall at last in to greeuous sinnes: *These*, saith *S. Bernard, doe not dwell in the helpe of the heighest*, neither doe hope in him, because they trust to themselues, where as they ought soe much the more to feare, and to be the more solicitous, and carefull, by how much greater the gifts, and graces are which they haue receiued.

S. Bernard in psal. qui habitat in adiutorio. Ser. 1.

Ibidem.

43 And therefore, he which is timorous, careful, and feruorous for a while, vntill he haue made some good progresse in vertue, & haue had some tast of Gods goodnes, and then groweth more cold, and careles

when

when his care, and feruour shuld encreaſe: ſuch a one, ſaith *S. Bernard*, *dealeth no otherwaiſe, then as if he shuld ſaye, what neede I now ſerue God any longer, ſeeing I haue that alreddy which he was to geeue me:* But, ô *ſi ſcires*, ſaith he, *quàm parum eſt quod habes &c.* *ô I would thou kneweſt, how litle it is which thou haſt, and how ſoone thou shalt looſe it, if he who gaue it thee, doe not conſerue it in thee:* And after a whyle admonishing theſe kind of men of their folly, and danger, in that they make not their habitation in God, but in their owne merits, & ſtrength, he ſaith. *Quid ſtultius eſt* &c? What greater folly is there then to dwel in a houſe that is yet skant begunne? doſt thou think that thou haſt made an end? *At cum conſummauerit homo* (ſaith the ſcripture) *tunc incipit*, when a man hath made an end, then he beginnes. Finallie, it is a very ruinous habitation, or houſe which hath more neede to be vnder-propped, and vpholden, then inhabited. *Ibid.* *Eccleſ.* 18.

44 Thus diſcourſeth *S. Bernard* elegantlie, to moue thoſe, which haue begunne well, & receiued ſtore of Gods gifts, and graces, not to preſume ſoe much on their owne ſtrength, and merits, as to ſlacke their former care, and endeuour (as though they had any goodnes of themſelues, or could conſerue it with out Gods grace, who gaue it them) but ſtill to proceede and goe forward with humilitie, diligence, and feruour, acknowledging alwaiſe their owne infirmitie, & whence is all their ſtrength, and ſufficiencie, and to *woorke their ſaluation*, as the Apoſtle aduiſeth, *with feare, and trembling*, remembring alſo his other admonition. *Qui exiſtimat ſe ſtare, videat ne cadat: he which thinks that he ſtandeth, let him take heede leſt he fall:* And finallie to practiſe carefullie our ſauiours important precept, *vigilate, & orate, ne intretis in tentationem, watch, and pray, leſt you enter into temptation*, for, as *S. Bernard* ſaith, *magna virtus eſt, & ſumma ſecuritas* &c. It is a greate vertue, and the heigheſt or cheefe ſecuritie to liue well, and yet to be more attent to what thou wanteſt, then what thou ſeemeſt to haue gott, fogetting thoſe things which are behind, & extending thy ſelfe to thoſe, which are before. Thus much concerning thoſe wich preſume of them ſelues, and therefore doe not hope in God. *Philip.* 2. 1. *Cor.* 10. *Matth.* 26. *S. Bern. in pſal. qui habitat.* *Philip.* 3.

45 The other ſort of preſumptuous men, is, of thoſe *which hope in God* (ſaith *S. Bernard*,) *but in vayne*, becauſe they doe ſoe flatter themſelues with the confidence, or rather preſumption of his mercy, that they are the leſſe carefull to auoide ſinne: *And agaynſt theſe*, ſaith he, *the prophet pronounceth, maledictus homo qui peccat in ſpe, curſed is the man, who ſinneth in hope:* ſoe hee, and after a whyle he addeth further, *that he hopes in vaine, who by contempt reiecteth Gods grace, and by that meanes doth euacuat*, *Idem.* *Ibid.*

and fruſtrat his owne hope: and finallie he concludeth, that thoſe kind of men, *dwell not in the helpe of the higheſt, but in their owne ſinne.* Thus teacheth this holly Father.

46 Such therefore are to conſider, that God is no leſſe iuſt, then mercifull, and that as he extendeth his mercy to ſome, ſo alſo he executeth his iuſtice vppon others, forſaking many (moſt iuſtly no dout) for their negligence: And therefore ſeeing no man knoweth whether God will extend mercy, or iuſtice towards him: and that euery man maye iuſtly feare, that the more negligent he is, in hope of Gods mercy, the more he abuſeth the ſame, and deſerueth the rigour of his iuſtice, is it not extreame folly in men by their negligence, to put in hazard their eternal ſaluation, rather then *to redeeme* (as *S. Bernard* ſaith) *endles, and incomprehenſible torments, breuiſſimo, & leuiſſimo labore, with a moſt short, & eaſy labour?*

S. Bern. in Pſal. qui habitat in adiutorio &c.

47 And although God be mercifull to ſinners, yea and out of his infinit mercy, doth ſome times ſaue the woorſt, and moſt wicked men from euerlaſting damnation, yet we are not to think, that either they, or yet good men, shall be, by his mercy wholly exempt from his iuſtice (*qui iuſtitias iudicabit,* as the pſalmiſt ſaith, *who will iudge,* or examin *the righteouſnes of the iuſt*) but that they shall yeeld a ſtrait *account for euery idle woord,* and pay the penaltie, and dets of their negligences, *ad nouiſſimum quadrantem, euen to the laſt farthing,* either in this world, or in the next: *where* (ſaith *S. Bernard*) *all thoſe things, which haue benne heere negligentlie omitted, shall be payed in purgabilibus locis centupliciter, a hundreth fold, in places appointed for purgation:* ſoe that, although they be finallie ſaued, yet it shall be (as the apoſtle ſaith), *quaſi per ignem, as by fyre,* when all the *wood, hay,* and *ſtubble* which they haue built vppon, the foundation of the chriſtian faith, shall be conſumed: where vppon *S. Auguſtin* geeueth a notable aduertiſement, concerning the fire of purgatory, by occaſion of thoſe woords of the apoſtle. *Ipſe autem ſaluus erit, ſic tamen quaſi per ignem: he shall be ſaued, yet ſoe as by fyre.*

Pſal. 74. See S. Bern. ſer. 55. in cantica. Matth. 12. Matth. 5. S. Bern. in ſer. de obitu Humberti. 1. Cor. 3. S. Aug. in Pſal. 37.

" 48 Becauſe (ſaith *S. Auguſtin*) it is ſaid, he shall be ſaued, that fire is contemned: yea truely, though ſaued by fire, yet that fire shall be more " greeuous, then any thing that can be ſuffred in this life, and you know " how greate torments malefactors haue ſuffered, or may ſuffer, & yet they haue ſuffred no greater then goodmen haue alſo endured, for " what hath any malefactor ſuffred by the law, that martyrs haue not " ſuffred for the confeſſion of Chriſt? Thoſe euils therefore that are here in this world, be much more eaſy, and yet you ſee that men will doe " what ſoeuer you commaund them, rather then endure them: therefore

how

how much better doe they, in performing that which God commaundeth, to the end they maye auoide those torments which are greater. Soe he. And againe in an other place, he which will not, saith he, cultiuat his field, but will let it be filled with bryres, & thornes, shall feele the malediction of his ground here, and after this life, he shall either endure the fyre of purgation, or shall suffer eternal payne: for no man escapeth this sentence, therefore it behoueth vs soe to deale, that we maye feele paine only in this lyfe. Thus saith *S. Augustin*, & the lyke also he teacheth expressélie in [a] diuers other places, agreeing with al the Fathers of the church greeke, and latin concerning the paynes due after this lyfe for humane negligences, and sinnes vnsatisfied heere, as it may appeare by the places [b] cited in the margent: wherebie we may see, how vnaduised they are, who wil rather expose themselues to such vnspeakeable, though temporal torments, then take a litle paynes to doe their duty heere, being with all vncertaine, whether their negligence maye prouoke the iustice of almightie God, vtterlie to forsake them, and to cast them in to euerlasting fyre, as it falleth out with many, who hauing made greate progresse in the seruice of God, become negligent at the first, and after a whyle geue themselues ouer, to all wickednes.

Idem lib. 2. de Genes. cõt. Manich. c. 20.

[a] *li. 21. de ciuit. ca. 13. ser. 41. de sãctis & li. 50. homil. ho. 16*

[b] *Orig. ho. 6. in ca. 15. exod. ho. 14. in ca. 24. leuit. ho. 13. in Hierem. & ho. 25. in numer. Greg. Nissen. in orat. de mortuis. S. Ambros. in 1. Cor. & ser. 20. in Psal. 118 S. Greg. li. 4. Dialog. ca. 39. & in Psal. 3. pœnitent. Tertull. li de anima. ca. 35. S. Cyprian. ep. 52. S. Bernard. ser. de obitu Humberti.*

49 Therefore I wish all men, no lesse then my selfe (for I write this for my owne instruction, as well as for other mens) continuallie to remember a notable admonition, geeuen by *S. Chrisostome* to all christians. *Tu christiana*, saith he, *delicatus es miles*, &c. Thou ô christian, art a delicat souldiar, if thou thinkest to ouercome with out fight, or to triumph with out combat, show thy strength, & valour, fight manfully, & fircelie, consider the couenant, waygh the condicion, know the warrefare, the couenant that thow hast made, the condicion, which thou hast admitted, and the warrefare, where to thou hast bound thy selfe. So he, wherein he admonisheth vs of three things, which it importeth euery christian man to haue continuallie before his eyes.

S. Chris ser. de martyribus &c. To. 3.

50 The first our couenant with God, when we were made christians, to wit, the promise we made in our Baptisme, which was to renounce the world, the deuil, and the flesh, and to serue God in the profession of the christian faith, during our liues: in which couenant we promised, not only to beleeue in God, but also to obay and serue him, in keeping his commaundements, in which respect the apostle saith, that *factus est causa salutis æternæ omnibus obtemperantibus. Christ was made the cause of eternal saluation, to all those which doe obay him*, and therefore we ought dayly, & duly to consider, how well, or euill we performe this couenãt.

Hebra. 5.

51 The

51 The second point is, the condicion of this bargaine contracted betwixt God, and vs, which is no other, but eyther vnion with God, (first by grace in this world, and after eternallie in heauen) for the performance of the couenant, or els eternal damnation in hell for the breach of it: except we satisfy the Iustice of God, by doing the woorthy frutes of penance in this life: which if we duly ponder, and haue any care of our eternal good, or euil, we must needs be moued to looke a bout vs, and to endeuour to discharge our duty, if not for the loue of God, and regard of his benefits (or in hope of the euerlasting reward, which he on his part hath couenanted to geue vs) yet at least for feare of the vnspeakable torments, prepared for such as doe not accomplish the bargain on their parts.

52 The third point touched by *S. Chrysostome*, is the warrefare, whereto we haue geeuen, and enroled, our names: whereby we are to vnderstand, that the life of a christian man, is no other then, as *Iob* saith, *militia super terram, a warre fare vppon the earth*, that is to say, a continual fight against the three enemies before named, the world, the flesh, and the deuil, vnder the banner, and conduct of our captaine, and sauiour *Iesus Christ*, who guideth vs in the battaile, fighting together with vs, and for vs, and will assuredly geeue vs both the victorie, and the croune, if we follow him, and fight vnder him with perseuerance to the end: to which purpose it is to be considered that three qualities, or vertues are no lesse requisit in a christian to his victorie in this spiritual warre, then in a comon souldiar in his temporal, or seculer warre.

Iob. 7.

53 The first is, true christian valour, and magnanimitie in the contempt of the world, and of all the transitorie pleasures, and delites thereof, as of things vnwoorthie of him whome God hath ordained, and called to euerlasting ioyes, of ineffable, and incomprehensible valew, which therefore are obiects woorthy of the noble mynd of a true christian, who shuld say with the Apostle, *conuersatio nostra est in cælis, our conuersation is in heauen. quia sub cælo*, saith *S. Bernard*, *omnia labor &c. For vnder heauen all things are but a labour, sorrow, vanity, and affliction of spirit.*

Philip. 3.
S. Bern. in Psal. Qui habitat in adiutorio &c. Ser. 16.

54 The second vertue, requisit in a souldiar, as wel spiritual as temporal, is fortitud, and patience, not only in the valiant resistance of the assalts of his enemies, and in manfullie assailing them, as occasion shall require, but also in suffring, and enduring patientlie the labours, and trauailes incident to their profession, and necessarie to the obtaining of the victorie: for as the delicat carpet knight, who cannot endure hunger, cold, thirst, watching, hard lying, and such other bodilie afflictions,

ctions, is not fit for the temporall warre: so also he is vnfit for our christian campe, and vnwoorthy the name of a christian souldiar, who pampereth himselfe with pleasures, and delytes, and refuseth to carry his crosse, and to endure the afflictions of bodilie penance, which is the special meanes to ouerthrow his enemies, and especiallie his most domestical, and dangerous enemy the flesh, in which respect the apostle (as I haue signified diuers times before, and cannot repeat to oft) speaking of his owne fight, and combat, said, *non sic pugno tanquam aërem verberans* &c. *I doe not fight so, as a man that beateth the ayre, but I chastise my body, and bring it into seruitud, lest whyles I preach to others, I become my selfe a reprobat*: so that according to the doctrin of this holly apostle, the christian souldiar which doth not chastise his body, fighteth no otherwaise then he that shuld make warre with flyes, beating the ayre all the day: and which is more to be considered, is in danger to become a reprobat, as I haue more amply signified in the last chapter. *1. Cor. 9.*

55 The third condicion or qualitie in a christian souldiar, is an exact obedience to the commaundment, and will of his captaine, with a true conformitie to his actions, and imitation of his industrie, valour, and vertues: for euen as a temporal souldiar ought not (according to *Plutarks* rule and aduise) to haue any mocion at all of himselfe, but such only, as he receiueth from his captaine: so ought also the spiritual souldiar much more to be guided, and conducted wholly by the will of his captaine, and general, our sauiour *Iesus Christ*, who hath left vs sufficient direction for our conduct in his warrefare, not only by his woord, but also by his example, which therefore we ought exactlie to follow. For what a shame were it for a souldiar, to see or vnderstand that his captaine keepeth watch, and ward, that he lyeth all night in the trenches, that he endureth hunger, raine, and cold, and exposeth himselfe to all the dangers, and labours, that militarie profession requireth, and yet he (I meane the souldiar) in the meane time, to lie warme on a fetherbed, to feede well and delicatlie, and to take his ease, and pleasure: can such a souldiar hope for any other, but the vtter disgrace of his captaine, and to be casht for a cowardlie and lazy companion? *Plutar. in Galba.*

56 And so in like manner, seeing we haue before our eyes both the doctrin of our maister, and Captaine *Iesus Christ*, and also his example, inuiting, and leading vs to the abnegation of our selues, contempt of the world, and cariage of our crosse, as the only meanes to obtaine his fauour, and to subdue his, and our enemies in this our spiritual warrefare: were it not a shame for vs, not only to reiect his heauenlie counsel, and instructions, but also to be more dainty and delicat then he?

And what excuse can we haue for our sloth, seeing that besids his owne doctrin, and exemplar practise, we haue also the manifest example of an infinit number of his seruants in all ages, who haue exactlie followed his steps in the continual cariage of their crosse, and mortification of themselues (as I declared amply in the last chapter:) besids that he hath also geeuen vs sufficient assurance, that he will assist our endeuours, and not only enable vs to beare his yoke, and burthen, but also make the same light, and pleasant vnto vs: in so much that it may be truely said, that many souldiars, and men of diuers trades, and occupations, take more paines to earne a poore pay, or hyre, then many good men doe to obtaine an eternal croune, yea and which is more, many wicked men, endure more miserie many times to procure the accomplishment of their filthy pleasures, and consequentlie to purchase hell, and endles damnation, then we are bound to take for the purchase of heauen, and euerlasting saluation: and therefore what els can we expect, if we neglect our duties (not with standing all these considerations) but that we shall be depriued of the reward, and croune prepared for vs, and also punished eternallie for our disobedience, and ingratitude?

57 Thus then we see how necessarie it is for euery christian man duly to ponder, and considere those three things a boue mecioned by *S. Chrysostome* (to wit, his couenant with almightie God, the condicion, and the warrefare, or continual combat where to he is bound) to the end that the remembrance, and consideration thereof, may moue, and incite him to show his vallour, there by to winne the victorie, and crowne, which is in effect that vnion with God wherein consisteth mans end and felicitie, first to be obtained in part by grace in this life, and after fully to be enioyed in eternal glory. And thus much I haue thought good to say by the way of aduise, and admonition to such as doe not labour dayly to proffit in vertue, and good life, but hauing alreddie well, and comendablie played their first prize, in this spiritual combat, and behaued themselues valiantlie for a while, doe afterwards relent, and seeke not so much to obtaine the victorie, as only to maintaine the combat in some sort, and so weakelie, that they receiue many greeuous, and deadlie wounds, whome therefore I place in the second ranke of those that seeldome, or neuer arriue to that vnion with God, which I haue described before, to be the felicitie of man in this life, and consequentlie of common welth.

58 The third sort, is of those who are cut of from the church of Christ, be they heretikes, schismatikes, or excommunicated persons: for such

ſuch being ſeparated, and deuided from chriſts miſtical body, can haue no influence of his grace, nor participation of his holly ſpirit, and conſequentlie no vnion with him. And this being ſo euident, that no chriſtian man will deny it, of what religion ſoeuer he be, I ſhall not neede to produce an further proofes thereof in this place: (eſpeciallie, for as much at I haue made it manifeſt in the laſt chapter, out of the vniforme doctrin of the moſt learned, and ancient Fathers, that though they should liue neuer ſo well in the ſight of men, yet being out of this arke of *Noe*, and *houſe of God*, (that is to ſay, being ſeparated from the vnitie & communication of this Catholike Roman church) they cannot poſſiblie be ſaued: And this ſhall ſuffyſe concerning the 3. ſorts of *Chriſtians*, whome I affirmed neuer to arriue to perfect vnion with God.

59 Now therefore, I will next proceede to ſpeake of the other point, mentioned by me in the end of the 24. number, to wit, who they are that doe attaine to this vnion. For ſeeing thoſe only are excluded from it, who are either deuided from the vnitie of the Catholike Roman Church, or contaminated, and defiled with mortal ſinne, or els careles to proceede, and proffit in vertue, it followeth that ſuch as are members of the ſaid church, and with all doe not only liue in the obſeruation of the commaundments of God (that is to ſay free from mortal ſinne) but alſo daily tend to perfection (ſuch perfection I meane, as may ſtand at leaſt with their ſtate and vocation) thoſe, I ſay, do attaine to the perfection of Chriſtian religion, and conſequentlie to a perfect vnion with almightie God, and to the felicitie which God hath ordained for man in this life.

60 Wherein neuertheles it is to be obſerued, that although euery one, that is iuſtified, or in the ſtate of grace, is vnited with God, yet all ſuch doe not arriue to that degree of vnion with God, wherein I place the felicitie of man in this life, becauſe euery ſinner, be he neuer ſo wicked, if he truely repent, is preſently iuſtified, & in the ſtate of grace, though, being yet but in the firſt ſteppe, as I may ſay, towards chriſtian perfection, and felicity, he deſerueth not the name of a perfect, & happy chriſtian, except he perſeuer in iuſtice: it being requiſit to the chriſtian felicitie, and perfection, whereof I treate heere, not only to beleeue, and liue well for a whyle, but alſo to continue in true beleefe, and in the exerciſe of vertue, *eſuriendo & ſitiendo iuſtitiam, hungring, and thyrſting after iuſtice* (as our Sauiour ſpeaketh:) which who ſoeuer doth, he is a perfect chriſtian, and may truely be called a iuſt, yea, and a happy man, being continuallie vnited with God, and therefore dwelleth as the Pſalmiſt ſaith) *in adiutorio altiſſimi* &c. *in the helpe of the heygheſt, and* *Pſal. 90.*

Matth. 5.

in the protection of the God of heauen.

61 And no meruel though continuance, and perseuerance is requisit to our christian, and supernatural felicitie, seeing the philosophers required the same to theirs, which was only natural, consisting in the continual exercise of the moral vertues, as appeareth in *Aristotle*, who therefore defined it to be *an operation*, or woorking *according to vertue in a perfect life*, that is to say in a continual course, and progresse of vertue: for as one swallow, saith *Aristotle*, maketh no summer, so neither one, nor yet many iust, and vertuous acts, make a man truely happy, but the continuance thereof.

Arist. ethic. 1. c. 7. See S. Tho. vppon the ethicks li. 1. lec. 14. & in epito. ethic.

62 And the same is with much more reason required to the perfection of our christian felicitie: for though it be but temporal, and imperfect in respect of the eternal, yet being the high way, and special meanes to lead vs thereto, yea and a resemblance, or rather some beginning, and participation thereof in this life, it must needs be so much the more perfect, by how much more it resembleth, and approcheth to the eternitie, and perfection of that other, which is the end, and consummation of it: And therefore the more continual, and durable it is, the more perfect it is, and the more deserueth the name of felicitie: to which purpose it may also be noted, that when our sauiour taught the 8. Beatituds (consisting in *pouerty of spirit, mansuetud, purity of hart, mercy, hunger, and thirst of iustice*, and the rest) he meant not that those are happy who exercise the acts of those vertues for a daye, or two, or for a while, but those who hauing the habits of them infused by the holly ghost, doe conserue the same, and eagerlie prosecut, and performe the acts thereof, whensoeuer occasion requireth: for such doe truely enioye that repose, and peace of mynd, that light of soule, that feruour of spirit, that abundance of Gods grace, and sweetenes in his loue, and finallie those heauenlie visitations, and deuine fauours, by the which he maketh his seruants happy euen in this life, as I haue often signified before.

Matth. 5.

63 Therefore for as much as true iustice, or righteousnes, where in consisteth christian perfection, & felicitie, is lost, and extinguished by mortal sinne, (which maketh vs enemies of God, members of the deuil, and consequentlie most miserable) it followeth that our perfection, and felicitie, cannot stand with mortal sinne, but requireth perseuerance in vertue, and true iustice: whereby it may appeare, that I did not with out greate reason exclude from our christian felicitie, all those who doe not labour to proceede, and proffit in the waye of vertue, but content themselues with a certaine mediocritie thereof, and ayme at

no

other marke, but to ryse when they are fallen, and therefore goe continuallie stumbling, rysing, and falling, comitting many mortal sinnes: for although such be sometimes vnited with God (as I haue said) when they arrise from sinne, yet they are farre from that degree of vnion with God, which is requisit to Christian felicitie, seeing they are many tymes not only most wretched, and miserable for the present, but also in greate danger of eternal miserie, that is to say of euerlasting damnation, whereinto many such doe daily fall, as I haue sufficientlie declared before.

64 But heere now, there may be moued a dout which I thinke good to satisfie by the way, to wit, whether there is, or can be any christian perfection, seeing I haue made it euident before, that no man can be so perfect in this world, but that he may be more perfect, yea and that he ought still to tend to perfection, where vppon it seemeth to follow, that there is no true christian perfection, seeing that what soeuer is perfect, wanteth nothing to perfection, for if it doe, it is not perfect, and therefore if any christian man were perfect, he shuld not neede to seeke further perfection: Seeing then the most perfect christian, is still bound to tend to perfection, and consequentlie is vnperfect, it seemeth that there is no christian perfection.

65 For the satisfaction of this dout, and to show with all, how farre christian perfection may extend it self in this life, it is to be considered, in what it consisteth principallie (or essentiallie, as *S. Thomas* speaketh) *S. Tho. 2. 2.* as that it principallie consisteth, in the obseruation of the law of God, *q. 184. ar. 3.* as I haue signified before, where by man is truly made the seruant, fréd, and child of God, enheritour of his kingdome, and a perfect christian, wanting nothing that is necessarie to his saluatiō: for otherwaise *Christ* were not a good, and perfect law maker, and a sauiour, if his law being fully performed, suffized not to make vs perfect christians, and to saue vs by the helpe of his grace, and merits of his passion.

66 Now then this obseruation of the law of God, is true iustice, and righteousnes, where of *S. Iohn* speaketh, when he saith, *he which doth iustice, is iust, as he also* (that is to say Christ) *is iust, and the doers of the law,* *1. Ioan. 3.* *Rom. 2.* saith the Apostle, *shall be iustified before God: Also you are my friends,* saith our sauiour, *if you doe those things which I commaund you:* and againe: *he* *Ioan. 15.* *which loueth me,* saith he, *will keepe my commaundments, and my Father will* *Ioan. 14.* *loue him, and wee will come vnto him, and make our abode with him:* whereby our sauiour signifieth, that those which keepe his commaundments, are truely vnited with his Father, and him, which they could not be if they were not iust, and therefore he also said to the same puroose, *if thou wilt* *Matth. 19.*

 enter

enter into life keepe the commaundments, which in like manner the holly
Psal. 118. Ghost teacheth expresselie, by the royal prophet, saying, *beati immaculati*
Item psal. 1. *in via* &c. *happy are the immaculat*, or the vnspotted *in the way, who walke in the law of our Lord.*

67 Also the holly scripture testifying that *Zacharias*, and *Elizabeth were both iust before God*, showeth the cause, adding, *incedentes in omnibus mandatis, & iustificationibus domini, sine querela, going in all the commaundments, and iustifications of our Lord, without blame.* Finallie *Ecclesiastes* geeuing this golden lesson. *Time Deum, & mandata eius obserua, feare God, and keepe his commaundments*, addeth *hoc est omnis homo, this is euery man*; that is to say, this is the end, and perfection, of euery man. So that in the obseruation of the law, and commaundments of God, consisteth both mans iustice, and his perfection, in which respect it is sayde of *Noe* in the holly scripture, that he was *vir iustus, & perfectus, a iust, and perfect man*, and almightie God said to *Abraham, ambula coram me, & esto perfectus, walke before me, and be perfect.* And againe: king *Ezechias* praying to almightie God for health in his sicknes said, that *he had walked before him in veritate & in corde perfecto, in truth, and in a perfect hart*, which almightie God approued by granting him his request and restoring him to health. In all which I wish it to be noted by the way, not only that true iustice, and perfection consisteth in the performance of Gods law (whereof I speciallie treate for the present) but also that the commaundments, and law of God, are possible to be kept, which our aduersaries do absurdlie deny, as shall further appeare in the next chapter.

Luc. 1. Eccles. ca. vlt. Gen. 6. Ibid. 17. Isay. 38.

68 Of this perfection *Moyses* spoke, when he saide to the people, *perfectus eris, & absque macula, thou shalt be perfect, and with out spot.* And the Royal prophet, *perfectus ero coram te* &c. *I will be perfect before thee*, ô Lord, *and I will keepe my selfe from my iniquitie.* And our sauiour to his disciples, *perfecti estote*, &c. *be you perfect, as your heauenly Father is perfect.* Also the Apostle speaketh thereof in diuers places, as *Gaudete, perfecti estote* &c. *reioyce, be perfect, take exhortations, be of one mynd* &c. and *Quicunque perfecti sumus* &c. *let vs all that are perfect, be of this minde.* And againe, *all scripture*, saith he, *inspired of God is proffitable* &c. *vt perfectus sit homo Dei, ad omne opus bonum instructus, that the man of God may be perfect, instructed to euery good woork.* Also *S. Iames, patientia*, saith he, *opus perfectum habeat, vt sitis perfecti, & integri* &c. *let patience haue a perfect woorke, that you may be perfect, and entyre, fayling in nothing.* Finallie *S. Iohn* saith also of this perfection. *Qui seruat verbum eius in hoc verè charitas Dei perfecta est, he that keepeth his world* (or commaundment) *in him the charity*

Deut. 18. 2. Reg. 22. Matth. 5. 2. Cor. 13. Philip. 3. 2. Tim. 3. Iac. 1. 1. Ioan. 2.

of God is perfect in very deede.

69 Neuertheles I wish it to be vnderstood, that I doe not assigne here a perfection voide of all frailties, or imperfections, that is to say, free from all venial sinne, with out the which no man passeth the course of this our mortalitie (as *S. Iohn* witnesseth, saying, *Si dixerimus* &c. 1. *Ioan.* 1. *if we shall say that we haue no sinne, we seduce our selues, and the truth is not in vs, & S. Iames: in multis offendimus omnes, we doe all offend in many* *Iaco.* 3. *things*: and lastly Salomon, *septies in die*, saith he, *cadit iustus, & resurget,* *Prouer.* 24. *The iust man shall fall seuen times a day, and rise a gaine:*) but I exclude from our christian perfection al mortal sinnes, because they doe directlie impugne the law of God, in so much that our iustice, and righteousnes is lost, and abolished therebie, and we seperated from all vnion, & frendship with God, made members of the deuil, and deputed to eternal damnation, except we repent.

70 Whereas the other sort of sinnes, which I call venial, because in respect of their lightnes, and our frailty they deserue pardon, are not directlie *contra legem Dei*, against the law of God as *S. Thomas* teacheth, but *S. Thomas* 1. *prater legem*, besyd the law, not hauing (saith he) perfectlie and absolutly 2. *q.* 87. *ar.* 5. the nature of sinne, but being a disposition thereto, in which respect & *q.* 88. *ar.* he also compareth venial sinne to sicknes and mortal sinne to death, 1. *primũ* & and therefore such humane frailties, as the iustest men doe now, and 22. *q.* 105. 1. then commit, do not exclude charitie, nor deuide them from the vnion, & 1. 2. *q.* 72. and frendship of God, nor abolish their iustice, and perfection, but 5. 6. may well stand there with, according to the doctrin of *S. Augustin,* *S. Aug. li. de* who speaking of iust men in the law of nature, saith. *Quia sæpe in leuis-* *natura & simis &c. because sinne doth creepe in oft times in very light, or smale matters, &* *gratia ca.* 38. *sometimes at vnawares they were iust, and yet not with out sinne,* so he: teaching that light & litle sinnes, commonlie called venial, doe not exclude iustice, or righteousnes, where of there can be no dout, for other waise no man could be iust in this life, which were flat contrarie to the holly scriptures, as it may appeare by that which I haue alreddy touched a litle before, and shall appeare more amply in the next chapter, where I meane to confirme our Catholike doctrin concerning a true, real, and inherent iustice.

71 Therefore the Christian perfection, whereof I speak here (and whereto I doe so much exhort euery christian man) is to be vnderstood to be no other, but such, as God doth expect, and exact of vs in this life, *perfectio*, saith *S. Hierome, quam capere potest humana natura: a perfe-* *S. Hieron. in ction, which humane nature may receiue*, that is to say, such a perfection *Ezechiel li.* as may stand with our frailty: such I meane, as though it be grounded 14. *c.* 46.

vppon

vppon the obseruation of Gods law, through the helpe, and assistance of his grace, (with out the which no man *can think so much as a good thought*, and much lesse ariue to any degree of perfection) yet, it is not free or exempt from humane imperfections, and therefore it may be daily refined, encreased, and grow more perfect, vntil it come to be consummated, and perfited, in euerlasting glory, as the wise man signifieth, saying, *iustorum semita, vt lux splendens* &c. *The way of the iust, as a shyning light, proceedeth, and groweth continuallie, vntill it be perfect day,* meaning by *perfect day*, the perfection of the next life: where (saith the Apostle) *cum venerit quod perfectum est, euacuabitur quod ex parte est, when that shall come which is perfect, that which is of a part*, or vnperfect, *shall be euacuated*, or made voide.

2. Cor. 3. *Prouer. 4.* *1. Cor. 13.*

72 And therefore, as there are diuers degrees of iustice, or righteousnes (for no man is so iust in this life, but he may be more iust, as I haue [a] sufficientlie proued alreddy:) so also, there are diuers degrees of perfection, and in euery degree a man may be said to be both perfect, and vnperfect: perfect, in respect of those that are not soe perfect as he: and vnperfect, in respect of others that excell him imperfection: As for example, he that obserueth the commaundments, (that is to say liueth with out mortal sinne) is perfect, (hauing attained to the first degree of christian perfection) and yet not so perfect as he, who doth with all, obserue the Euangelical counsel of voluntarie pouertie, and therefore our sauiour saide to the yong man, who affirmed that he keapt the commaundments. *Si vis perfectus esse* &c. *If thou wilt be perfect, goe, and sell all thou hast, & geeue it to the poore*, and yet he that shuld soe doe, shuld not be so perfect, as he that shuld adde thereto continencie, and chastitie for the pure loue and seruice of God, as may appeare by that which I haue amply discoursed in the 29. chapter, to proue that virginitie, and chastitie is a special point of christian perfection.

a Supra. nu. 30. & sequent. *Matth. 19.*

73 Also such a one, as liueth out of mortal sinne, and with all obserueth those two Euangelical councels of pouertie, and chastitie, is not equal in perfection to him, who addeth thereto the third counsel of perfect obedience, and abnegation of himselfe in religious disciplin: where by he maketh a perfect sacrifice, and holocaust of himselfe to almightie God, as I haue amply proued in the 31. chapter, where I also showed the greate dignitie, and high perfection of religious life, out of the most ancient, holly, and learned Fathers, who call it *vitam perfectissimam, a most perfect life: perfectionis culmen, virtutisque fastigium, the heyght of perfection, and topp of vertue, a most hygh, and excellent profession, lyke to the purity of Angels, wherein is vowed not only all hollines, but also all perfe-*

S. Dionis. ecclesiasti Hierar. c. 6. par. 2. *S. Basil. de monast. constit. c. 18.* *S. Greg. Nazianz. de obitu. Basil.* *S. Chrisost. li. 3. aduers. vitup. vita monast.*

ction

ction of hollines, yea and the very end, and consummation of all perfection, for so saith *S. Bernard*, meaning only such a perfection as may be obteined and had in this life: which also may be continuallie augmented and encreased, as I haue signified before. *S. Bernard de vita solitar. ad fratres de mōte.*

74 For no man in religion is so perfect, but he may be more perfect, that is to saye, more feruent in the loue of God, more resined to his will, more humble, more patient, more meeke, and more pure of hart if he keepe continual watch vppon himselfe, duly examine his conscience, combatt daily with his passions, and bad inclinations, and mortify, or chastise his flesh to make it subiect to the spirit, whereby his *in ward man* as the Apostle speaketh, *may be renewed from daye to daye*. And yet when he hath all donne, he shall be vnperfect in respect of the Angels, and saints in heauen, in whome alsothere are degreese of perfection, no lesse then of glory, and therefore the Apostle saith that, *as one star differeth from another their in brightnes, so also shall it be in the resurrection of the dead*. Finally the most perfect angel, or saint or rather the perfections of all angels, saints, and other creatures, if they were all ioyned in one, yet shuld be vnperfect in respect of the infinit perfection of almighty God, who is perfection it selfe, and imparteth his owne excellencies, and perfections to his creatures, *diuidens singulis prout vult, deuiding the same to euery one as it pleaseth him*. *2. Cor. 4.* *1. Cor. 15.* *1. Cor. 12.*

75 Thus then we see, that there are diuers degrees of perfection, and that the best men, are both *perfect*, and *vnperfect*, which *S. Augustin* obserueth very well in the woords of the apostle, who hauing signified how much he contemned the world, *being configured*, (as he saith) *to the death of Christ*, acknowledged his owne imperfection, adding, *non quod iam acceperim, aut iam perfectus sim, not that I haue alreddy receiued, or that I am now perfect*; and yet neuertheles saith *S. Augustin*, he saith shortly after. *Quicunque ergo perfecti sumus, hoc sentiamus, let vs therefore, as many as are perfect, be thus minded*. *Philip. 3.* *Ibidem.*

76 Here vppon *S. Augustin* saith, that although the apostle was, *perfectus viator, a perfect trauailer*, yet he was not, *ipsius itineris perfectione peruentor, a perfect arriuer at the end of his iourney*; as also els where he saith to the same purpose that we may be heere, *perfecti viatores, nondum perfecti possessores, perfect trauaylers, but not yet perfect possessors*, geeuing to vnderstand, that all human perfection is no other, but, as it were, a continual iourney, or peregrination towards our cuntry, which is heauen, and that (if we proceede from vertue to vertue in this life) we shall haue there an eternal possession of true perfection in euerlasting glory: in which respect *S. Bernard* also saith, that the perfection of this life, is *S. Aug. li. 2. de peccator merit. & remiss. ca. 13. Idē de verb. Apost. ser. 15. ca. 15.* *S. Bernardi in psal. qui habitat.*

but *imperfecta perfectio, an imperfect perfection*, which ſhall be perfited in the life to come, and in the meane time (ſaith *S. Auguſtin*) *aliter non potes eſſe perfectus, niſi ſcias hic te non poſſe eſſe perfectum, thou canſt not otherwaiſe be perfect, except thou knoweſt, that heere thou canſt not be perfect*, ſignifying that nothing is more requiſit, on our partes, to chriſtian perfection, then a true, and profound humilitie, which can neuer be with out perfect charitie, from whence proceedeth the obſeruation of Gods law, and conſequently all chriſtian perfection, as ſhall further appeare in the next chapter.

S. Aug. in Pſal-38.

77 Therefore I conclude for the preſent concerning this point, with a breefe, and graue aduiſe of *S. Auguſtin*: *proficite* (ſaith he) *fratres mei* &c. *Goe forwards my brethren*, and proffit in the way of vertue, *diſcuſſe*, or examin *your ſelues, alwaiſe with out deceit, flattery, or partialitie*, &c. *let that which thou art diſpleaſe thee, if thou wilt attaine to that which thou art not: for if thou doſt pleaſe thy ſelfe*, or ſtand in thy owne conceit, *thou remaineſt by the way, if thou ſayeſt, it ſuffiſeth* (that is to ſay, if thou perſwadeſt thy ſelfe, that thou haſt ynough, or needeſt no more) *thou art vtterly loſt, therefore alwaiſe adde more, alwaiſe walke, alwaiſe goe forward*, or proffit, *doe not remaine*, or ſtay *by the way, doe not goe backward, doe not goe out of the way: he ſtayeth which doth not proffit; he goeth backward, which returneth to thoſe things, that he had left before: and he goeth out of the way, who becommeth an Apoſtata*, that is to ſay, who forſaketh his faith or his practiſe of perfection, *for better goeth the halt, or lame man in the way, then he that runneth out of the way*, Thus ſaith this holly Father.

Idē de verb. apoſt. ſer. 15. ca. 15.

78 And for as much, as I haue in my tract of contemplation, laid downe the particuler meanes, how a man may daily proffit in vertue, and arriue to that perfection, whereof I haue heere treated, I ſhall not neede to enlarge my ſelfe further therein: and therfore I remit thee, good reader, therto, deſiring thee to be mindfull thereof, for thy owne eſpecial good, ſeeing that our ſauiour Chriſt propoſed the perfection of his law to all men with out exception, (as I haue alſo ſignified before) and that therefore euery chriſtian man, is ſo bound to tend, yea and to attaine thereto (at leaſt according to his vocation, and ſtate) that what ſoeuer he ſhall want thereof, and leaue vnſatisfied at the houre of his death, it ſhall be ſupplied by the iuſtice of God, in the next life, with vnſpeakeable torments, either temporal, or eternal, *for no man*, ſaith, *S. Auguſtin, eſcapeth this ſentence*, as I haue declared out of him, and other Fathers, more particulerlie a before, which I leaue to thy pious, and ſerious conſideration.

S. Aug. de Geneſ. cōtra Manich. li. 2. c. 20.
a nu. 48.

An

An obiection of our aduersaries concerning christian perfection, is fully answered, whereby their doctrin of imputatiue iustice is confuted: with an application of all the former discourse to common welth, by the consideration of 4. notable effects of charitie, by the which it is proued, that the Catholike Roman Religion only, geeueth true felicitie to common welth.

CHAP. 38.

THOV hast seene good reader, in the last chapter what christian perfection is, to wit, that it is nothing els but true christian iustice, or righteousnes, whereby man remaineth vnited with God and most happy, according to the happines that may be had in this life.

1 But perhaps, our aduersaries will demaund heere, what perfection can be said, or imagined to be in our iustice? seeing that the same is (as they teach) continuallie a stained, and soiled with sinne: and that our iustice, or righteousnes is not in vs but in *Christ*, whose iustice is only b imputed vnto vs: & that our sinnes are not remitted, and taken a way thereby, but only couered, and hid: soe that we remaine alwaise not only vnperfect, but also wicked, and abominable before God, soe farre foorth as concerneth our owne actions, especially seeing that our very best woorks are impure sinfull, and damnable, for so teach our aduersaries. And if this be true, then all the christian perfection, (where to I haue soe seriously exhorted my reader) is but an Idle conceit, and needeles to be sought, or procured, and consequentlie all my former discourse, which hath speciallie tended thereto, hath benne built vppon a false foundation

a *Luther. in artic. à Leone 10. damnatis, art. 2. & in assert. ar. 31. 32. & 36. Caluin. in Antidoto Concil. sess. 5. & li. 4. Instit. c. 15. §. 10. & 11. Item libro secundo ca. 1. sect. 8.*

b *Caluin. li. 3. Instit. ca. 11. § 2. 3. 21. & 22. Item li. 3. ca. 3. & ca. 14. §. 9.*

2 Therefore, good reader, I must craue thy patience, whiles I extend my selfe a litle vppon this point, as well to confirme, and establish all my former discourse, and doctrin concerning christian iustice, and perfection, as also to discouer vnto thee, the absurditie of these opinions of our aduersaries, which are not only blasphemous against God, but also most pernicious to man, and common welth, as I haue alreddy showed in part, in the 35. chapter, where I haue debated this matter by way of state, and therefore this occasion being now offred, I can not forbeare to treate it also by way of religion, which neuertheles I will doe with as conuenient breuitie, as the importance of the matter may permit.

3 Now then: that which I vndertake heere to proue, is, that our iu-

stice or righteousnes, whereby we are iustified, is a gift of good communicated, and infused in to our soules, by the which we are inwardly, or in spirit changed, renewed, and sanctified, our sinnes truely remitted and we consequentlie of wicked men, made truely iust: This the apostle signifieth when he saith, *cum apparuit benignitas & humanitas saluatoris nostri* &c. *VVhen the benignitie, and humanitie of our sauiour appeared, not by the woorks of iustice which we did, but according to his mercy, he saued vs by the water of regeneration, & renouation of the holly ghost, whome he powred abundantlie in to vs by Iesus-Christ our sauiour, to the end that being iustified by his grace, we maye be heyres according to the hope of life euerlasting.* Thus farre the Apostle who describing the manner of our iustification, as you see, showeth with all as well the principal causes thereof, as the effect.

4 For he signifieth, that the efficient cause of our iustification, *is the benignitie, and mercy of God,* the meritorious cause, *our sauiour Iesus-Christ,* the instrumental cause, *the washing of baptisme,* the formal cause the *infusion of the holly ghost* abundadtlie communicated vnto vs: and finally that the effect resulting of these causes, is a *regeneration, and renouation,* which must needs import an inward change in our soules, wrought by the holly ghost, and not a bare imputation of an extrinsecal iustice: & therefore the apostle yeelding the reason why almigthie God doth regenerat, and renew vs by the infusion of the holly ghost, addeth, *vt iustificati gratia ipsius, heredes simus* &c. That is to saye, to the end that *being iustified by his grace, we may be heyres* &c. geeuing to vnderstand that our iustification consisteth in the *regeneration, and renouation,* which the holly ghost woorketh in vs by his grace.

5 This maye also be confirmed out of the same Apostle, when he saith to the Corinthians, *& hæc quidem fuistis* &c. *These you haue benne,* (to wit fornicators, and Idolaters,) *but you are washed, but you are sanctified, but you are iustified in the name of our Lord Iesus Christ, and in the spirit of God,* that is to saye, (as the ancient Fathers expound it) they were purged, and sanctified in baptisme, by the inuocation of the name of *Iesus Christ,* and by the operation of the holly ghost, in so much that *S. Chrisostome,* and *S. Hierome* doe proue out of these woords of the Apostle, that all sinnes are fully forgeeuen in baptisme: where vppon it followeth, that our iustification consisteth, not in that our sinnes are only couered, or hid, and Christs iustice imputed vnto vs, (as the sectaries teach) but in that they are washed away, and cleansed, yea and that we are (saith *S. Chrisostome*) made not only pure, and cleane, but also holly, and iust, *non enim dixit, lauati tantum estis* &c. *for the apostle said not only, you are wasshed, but you are also sanctified, and iustified:* behold then how

1. Cor. 6.

S. Chrisost. & S. Ambr. & Theophilact. in hunc locum.

S. Chrys. ho. ad Baptizan. S. Hieron. ep. ad Oceanum.

S. Chrisost. ho. ad Baptizan.

how this ancient, and learned Father vrgeth the woords of the apostle to the same purpose, that the catholikes now doe, to wit, to proue a real iustification, consisting in a true remission of sinnes, and a true sanctification whereby we are, saith he, *made holly, and iust*.

6 This the Apostle also proueth in his epistle to the Romans by an inuincible argument, grounded vppon the plenitud, and fulnes of Christs merits, and the abundance of grace, which we receue thereby. *Si enim vnius delicto*, saith he, *mors regnauit per vnum* &c. *if by one mans fault, death hath reigned by one, much more those which receiue abandance of grace, and of the gift, and of iustice, shall reigne in life by one Iesus Christ*: in which woords it is to be noted, that the Apostle speaking of iustification, doth plainelie exclude, and reiect the imputation of iustice, making expresse mention of a righteousnes, which we receiue abundantly with grace, and a gift geuen vs by almightie God: which abundance of grace, and iustice being geeuen vs, and receiued by vs, must needs be really in vs, and make vs truely iust: and this is much more euident by that which followeth. *Sicut enim*, saith the Apostle *per inobedientiam vnius hominis* &c. *for euen as by the disobedience of one man, many sinners were made, so by the obedience of one man, many iust shall be made.* *Rom. 5.* *Ibidem.*

7 Thus saith the Apostle, who as you see compareth, or rather opposeth *Christ*, to *Adam*, and our iustification geuen vs by *Christ*, to the death of the soule, or damnation purchased vs by *Adam*, concluding that we are made as truely iust by *Christ*, as we were truely sinners by *Adam*, yea and this he also enforceth further in the same place, saying *si enim vnius delicto multi mortui sunt* &c. *for if by one mans fault many haue died, much more the grace of God, and the gift in the grace of one man Iesus Christ hath abounded vnto more men*, whereby the apostle signifieth, not that more are iustified by *Christ*, then haue died, or benne condemned by *Adam*, (which in the greeke is manifest, wherein steede of *plures, more men*, we read *pollous, many men*,) but that Christs grace was more abundant, and of greater force to iustifie vs, then Adams sinne to make vs sinners, and to condemne vs: which he confirmeth also afterwards saying, *vbi abundauit delictum, superabundauit gratia, where the fault abounded, grace hath benne much more abundant.* *Ibidem.* *Ibidem.*

8 Wherevpon I inferre, with the blessed Apostle, that seeing the sinne of *Adam* was of force to make vs truelie sinners, the merits, and grace of *Christ* are of farre greater force to purge, and cleanse vs from our sinnes, and to make vs truely iust, for otherwaise we must needs say that our helpe is not equiualent to our harme, nor our remedy to our disseas, nor our rysing to our fall, nor our gaine to our losse, nor conse-

quently *Christ* to *Adam*, which were impietie to think, and blasphemy to say, and yet soe must our aduersaries say, contrarie to this expresse doctrin, of the Apostle, if they will maintaine this their opinion of *imputatiue iustice*.

9 This may further appeare if we add hereto, many other places of scripture, which euidentlie proue a true remission of sinnes in vs with purity, and cleanes of hart, and a real sanctification, and innouation of spirit: as when the psalmist saith. *Dele iniquitatem meam, blot out* ô Lord, *my iniquitie: Amplius laua me ab iniquitate mea* &c. *wash me more* ô Lord *from my iniquitie, and cleanse me from my sinne: thou wilt sprinkle me with hissop, and I shall be made cleane, thou wilt wash me, and I shall be made whiter then snow: creat or make in me, ô God, a new hart, and innouat a new spirit in my bowels* &c. and *confirme me with the principal spirit.* Thus prayed the royal prophet, demaunding nothing els but iustification, consisting, in true remission of sinnes, and purity of hart by the infusion of the holly ghost.

Psal. 50.

10 The same also may be confirmed out of the apostle, where he saith that *Christ* gaue himselfe for his church, *vt illam sanctificaret* &c. to the *end he might sanctifie it, cleansing it with the washing of water in the woord of life*, and *vt mundaret sibi populum acceptabilem, that he might make cleane, and pure for himselfe an acceptable people*, and againe *vt sanctificaret per suum sanguinem populum, that he might sanctifie his people by his blood.* And is not this sanctification, trow you, real, and true, but imputatiue? This may appeare by our sauiours owne woords, who in his prayer to his Father before his passion said, *&* *pro eis, ego sanctifico me ipsum, vt & ipsi sint sanctificati in veritate, I sanctifie my selfe for them, that they may be sanctified*, or made holly *in veritie*, or truth.

Ephes. 5. *Tit.* 2. *Hebr.* 15. *Ioan.* 17.

11 Thus saith our sauiour, but if we haue no true remission of sinnes, or sanctification, but only by imputation, and that we still remaine soiled with our sinnes, when we are iustified, and sanctified, then *Christ* either did not, or could not performe that by his passion which he desired, I meane he did not sanctify vs in verity, and truth neither shuld it be true which S. Ihon saith, *sanguis Iesu Christi emundat nos ab omni peccato, the blood of Iesus Christ doth make vs cleane, from all sinne*, nor that our Sauiour *Christ is, agnus Dei qui tollit peccata mundi, the lambe of God which taketh away the sinnes of world.*

1. *Ioan.* 1. *Ioan.* 1.

12 Loe then how blasphemous is the opinion of our aduersaries, which by a necessarie consequent, doth euacuat the merits of Christs passion, and death, depriuing it of the principal force and effect thereof, euen in that where in God is most glorified, the deuil most confounded,

founded, and we most honored, and benefited, to wit, in the perfect repaire of our wrack receiued by Adam, I meane our true iustification, and the full remission and abolition of our sinnes by the merits of Christ.

13 But let vs heare the doctrin of the ancient Fathers. *Iustitia*, saith *S. Augustin*, *virtus est animi magna præcipuéque laudabilis, Iustice, or righteousnes, is a greate vertue of the mind and highly commendable*: and presently after, *quis fecit in homine iustitiam* &c. *who made iustice, or righteousnes in man, but he which iustifieth the wicked, hoc est per gratiam suam, de impio facit iustum, that is to say, he which by his grace doth make a iust man of a wicked man.* Thus hee, where you see that righteousnes is a vertue of the mind, and therefore really inherent in vs as other vertues ar, and that God doth not only repute a man to be iust, but also *facit iustum ex impio, maketh him iust*, where he was wicked before. *S. Aug. in Psal. 118. Conc. 26. Ibidem.*

14 Againe: *quid est aliud iustitia*, saith he, *cum in nobis est* &c. *what els is iustice, when it is in vs, or any other vertue, wherebie we liue well and wiselie, but the beautie of the inward man?* so he: acknowledging righteousnes to be really in vs as other vertues are, and that it is the beauty of the soule: where vppon he also saith els where, that, when mans nature is iustified by his creator, *à deformi forma formosam transfertur in formam*, *it is transposed, or changed from a deformed vnto a beautifull forme.* Which is flat contrarie to the doctrin of *Luther*, and *Caluin*, who teacheth that a man being iustified remaineth still deformed with sinne, though *Christ* for his owne merits do hold, and repute him to be iust. *Idem ep. 85. ad consentium. Idem de Trinitate li. 15. c. 8.*

15 Furthermore, *legimus*, saith the same Father, *iustificari in Christo qui credunt in eum, we read that those are iustified in Christ which beleeue in him*, and then to show how they are iustified, he addeth *propter occultam communicationem, & inspirationem gratiæ spiritualis, by the meanes of a secret communication, and inspiration of a spiritual grace*, and this grace he saith els where, *is caritas diffusa in cordibus nostris per spiritum sanctum qui datus est nobis, charitie infused in to our harts by the holly ghost which is geeuen vs.* *Idem li. 1 de peccator. mer. & remiss. ca. 10. li. de spiritu & littera per totum.*

16 Whereby it is euident that he neither taught nor knew any other iustice, or righteousnes in man but a real, and inherent iustice, consisting in true remission of sinne, and infusion of faith, charity, and other vertues: and therefore no meruel that *Caluin* is forced flatly to reiect him in this question, though neuertheles he acknowledgeth him sometimes to be the most faithfull, and best witnes of antiquitie, but whether of them deserueth more to be beleeued, and followed, I remit it to the iudgement of any vnpassionat man, that hath care to saue his soule. *Et ser. 15 de verb. apostoli & de hæres. hær. 88. Caluin Instit. li. 3. c. 11. sect. 15. Idem li. 3. c. 3. sect. 10. & li 4. c. 14. sect. 26.*

17 Yet if *S. Augustin* had bene singuler in this point, or euer hetherto

noted

noted by any good christian man to haue erred therein, *Caluin* might seeme to haue more reason to reiect him: And therefore let vs heare one of the Fathers of the greeke church, to wit *S. Chrisostome.* who expounding the epistle of *S. Paul* to the *Ephesians*: and particulerly these woords, *Deus nos gratificauit in dilecto filio suo, God hath made vs gratious,* or acceptable *in his beloued sonne*, saith thus, *gratiosos nos reddidit, hoc est* &c. *he hath made vs gratious, that is to say, he hath not only deliuered vs from sinne, but also hath made vs his beloued friends: for as if a man shuld make one faire, and yong, who before was old, scabbed, disseased and pestiferous, and should beautifie him so, that his face, and eyes shuld cast out resplendant beames of light, and further cloth and adorne him with purple, and all kind of furniture, euen so hath God, as it were, curiouslie wrought our soule, and made it beautifull, woorthy to be desired, and beloued.*

Ephes. 1.

S. Chrysost. in Ep. ad Ephes. c. 1.

18 Thus farre *S. Chrisostome*, who yow see teacheth that God doth not only geeue vs remission of sinnes when he iustifieth vs, but also doth so renew, beautify, and deck our soules with his grace, that we are not esteemed only, and reputed to be acceptable in his sight, but also are in deede made gratious and acceptable vnto him, and adorned with an inward, and spiritual beauty. And I haue the rather alledged this place of *S. Chrisostome* expounding the woords of the Apostle, because our aduersaries abuse them, to the confirmation of their opinion of imputatiue iustice, pretending that the greeke woord *echaritosen*, (which in our latin translation is *gratificauit*) doth signifie *gratiosos habuit*, that is to say *hath held, or esteemed vs for gratious*, where as *S. Chrisostome*, (who may woorthily be presumed to haue vnderstood the greeke, and the meaning and drift of the apostle, some what better then any of our aduersaries) interpreteth it, *gratiosos reddidit*, hath made vs gratious, or acceptable, and vrgeth the same notablie, as you haue heard, for the proofe of our Catholike doctrin, of a true, and inherent iustice.

S. Ambros. li. 6. Hexamer. c. 8. & li. 6. in lucā. S. Hieron. li. 1. aduer. pelagian. Ibid. li. 3. S. Prosper. in respons. ad ca. 6. Gallorum. S. Basil. de baptis. ho. 1. par. 2. Nyssenus & Nazianz. orat. in sanct. Baptis.

19 I might add many other testimonies of the Fathers to proue inherent Iustice, and true remission of sinne, if I thought it needefull, but to auoide prolixitie, I remit my reader to the places cited in the margent, and to all those Fathers who treate of the effects of Baptisme, teaching not only a full remission, ablution, and abolition of our sinnes, (according to the promise of God by his prophet, saying *I will power vppon you a cleane water, and you shall be cleansed from all that filth, and corruption*) but also a perfect *regeneration, and renouation* of the soule, whereby we become *noua creatura*, as the Apostle saith, *a new creature*, and are made, saith S. Gregorie Nazianzen, *of old new*, and *of a humane deuine*, and as *S. Chrisostome* testifieth, b *mundiores solis radiis, cleaner then the beames*

Ezech. 36. *Clemens Alexand. li.* 1. *pædagog. ca.* 6. *Galat* 6. a *Orat. in sanct. baptis.* b *Hom. ad baptizan.*

beames of the sunne, being [c] the *children of God*, and [d] *temples of the holly ghost*, and therefore truely iust, not by the same iustice, whereby Christ is iust, (as our aduersaries absurdlie affirme) but by the iustice saith *S. Augustin,* [e] *qua iustos nos facit, wherebie he maketh vs iust, and* [f] *quam dat homini Deus, vt sit homo iustus per Deum: which God geeueth to man, to the end that man may be iust by God.* For, soe saith *S. Augustin.* Soe that our iustice being true iustice, may be called both Christs iustice, and ours, Christs, because he doth geeue it vs, and ours because we haue, and possesse it by his gift: And therefore I conclude with him, saying also els where, [g] *that the grace of Christ, doth woorke inwardlie our illumination, and iustification.*

c *Rom.* 8.
d 1.*Cor.* 4.
e *S. Aug. de spir. & lit. c.* 9. & 11.
f *Idē tract.* 2.6 *in Ioan. To.* 9.
g *Idem de peccat. merit. & remiss. li.* 1. *c.* 9.

20 But heere our aduersaries may perhaps demaund, why then the prophet *Isay* doth saye of all men, and of all their iustice, or righteousnes [h] *facti sumus vt immundi omnes, & quasi pannus menstruatæ, vniuersæ iustitiæ nostræ: we are all become as vncleane, and all our iustices, as a stayned clout.* which woords of the prophet our aduersaries doe commonly obiect against the true iustice, and righteousnes whereof I haue hitherto treated, to whome I answere: that the prophet in this place speaketh not of iust men, but only of the wicked *Iewes*, for whose greate sinnes, and wickednes, the citty of *Hierusalem* was to be geeuen ouer in to the hands of the king of *Babilon*, and therefore speaking in their person he saith, *we are all become as vncleane* &c. wherein it is also to be obserued, that when he speaketh of *all their iustices*, he doth not meane all the woorkes of those wicked men, (whereof some might be at least morally good, or indifferent,) and much lesse doth he meane the woorks of iust, or good men, but he vnderstandeth the woorks of the law, wherein they did put all their confidence, placing speciallie therein all their iustice, and righteousnes, though neuertheles they performed the same with so bad intention, and euil circumstances, that the prophet woorthily said, that they were all *vncleane, and like to a filthy stained clout.*

h *Isay.* 64.

21 And of those kind of woorkes, and to those wicked men the same prophet said also in the person of God, [i] *Ne offeratis vltrà sacrificium frustrà* &c. *doe not offer sacrifice any more in vaine, their incense is abomination to me, I will not endure their Neomenie, their Sabbats, and other feasts: your assemblies, are wicked: my soule hateth their Calends, and your solemnities* &c. whereby it cannot be vnderstood, that God hated all the sacrifices, feasts, and woorkes of the law, or held them to be vnpure, and vncleane, when they were well performed by good men, but when they were donne wickedly or by such as presumed so farre thereon, that they perswaded themselues to be iustified therebie, how badly soeuer they liued other-

i *Isay.* 1.

waise, in which respect the prophet speaking in the person of those wicked men, as I haue said, called those woorkes, and feasts of the law *iustitias nostras, our iustices*, because they placed all their righteousnes therein. Finallie those woords of the prophet, are soe farre from impugning the iustice of good woorkes, that both *Luther*, and *Caluin* doe confesse it in their commentaries vppon the same place, as a *Card. Bellarmin* noteth, though neuertheles *Luther* being allwaise most inconstant, and variable, doth els where absurdlie labour to proue therebie, that all the woorkes of the iustest, and best men are sinnes.

a *Bellar. de iustificat. li.* 4. *c.* 20.
Luther in assert. 31.
b *Rom.* 4.

22 Furthermore our aduersaries obiect against real, and inherent iustice those woords of the apostle, b *credidit Abraham Deo, & reputatum est ei ad iustitiam, Abraham beleeued God, and it was reputed to him for iustice*, where vppon they will needs gather, that *Abraham* was not iust in deede, in the sight of God, but only that God reputed, and esteemed, him to be soe. Whereto I answere, that the woords *reputatum est*, doe not signifie only an estimation, or imputation of a thing which is not in deede, but a true estimation of that which truely is: for almightie God, (whose iudgments are alwaise according to iustice, and veritie) reputeth, or esteemeth euery thing as it is in deede, and therefore as those whome he reputeth for euil men, are euil in deede, so also those whom he reputeth for good men, are truely good, because he hath made them good, and iust by his grace.

23 Besids that it is euident in the same epistle, and chapter of the Apostle that the woord *imputare, to impute*, doth signifie there a true esteemation of that which really is, as it is reputed to be, for we read in him, that *ei qui operatur, merces imputatur, non secundum gratiam, sed secundum debitum, to him that woorketh, the hyre, or wages is imputed, not according to grace, or fauour, but according to duty*, so that you see, *imputation* heere, doth not signifie a bare opinion of a thing to be due, when it is not due, but a true esteemation of a thing no lesse due, then is the hyre to the labourer, or woorke man; and in this sence we deny not but that it may be truely saide, that the iustice of *Christ* is imputed vnto vs, when it is truely communicated, and geeuen vnto vs by our sauiour *Christ*, and that we are truely reputed for iust, when God hath made vs iust by the remission of our sinnes, and infusion of his grace, in which sence neuertheles, our aduersaries will not admit it.

Rom. 4.

24 The like is also to be answered to an other obiection, which our aduersaries make out of the same chapter of the Apostle, and the 31. Psalme, where we reade. c *Beati quorum remissæ sunt iniquitates* &c. *happy are they whose iniquities are remitted, and whose sinnes are couered: blessed is the*

Rom 4.
c *Psal.* 31.

the man to whome God hath not imputed sinne : where vppon our aduersaries absurdlie inferre, that no sinnes are truely remitted, but only couered, and not imputed.

25 To which purpose it is to be noted, that they fly heere to their comon shift, to find out some few obscure texts of scripture to interpret
therebie a greate number of plaine, and euident places, which might
be exemplified in most controuersies betwixt them, and vs, and in this
is most manifest: for is there any thing in the holly scriptures, either
more plaine, or frequent then the mention of true remission, and abolition of sinne, which is expressed there so many waise, and by such different manner of speech, that nothing can be added to make it more
cleare, as when the prophet saith, a *if your sinnes shall be like skarlet they shall* a *Esay. c. 1.*
be made as whyte as snow, b *The iniquitie of the people shall be taken away.* c *I ame* b *c. 33.*
he who doe wipe, or blot out thy sinnes for my owne sake: d *I haue abolished thy ini-* c *c. 43.*
quitie like a cloud, and thy sinnes as a mist: & in an other prophet, e *I will power* d *c. 44.*
out a cleane water vpon you, and you shalbe cleanzed frō all your filth. And againe e *Ezechiel. 36.*
in an other, f *he will cast all our sinnes in to the bottome of the sea* : And in the f *Miche. 7.*
prouerbs, g *sinnes are purged by mercy, and faith.* Also in the Psalmist, h *he* g *Prou. 15.*
hath made our iniquities to be as farre from vs, as the east is from the west. And h *Psal. 102.*
againe : i *his sinne shalbe sought, and shall not be found* : whereto may be i *Psal. 9.*
added the prayers of the psalmist which I haue mentioned before, to
wit, that it might please God to k *blot*, or wipe *out his iniquitie, to make him* k *Psal. 50.*
cleane, and to wash him more, and more, that so he might be *whiter then snow.* *Ibid.*

26 Also in the new testament the like manner of speeches are most
frequent, which I haue partly alledged before, as that our sauiour l *was-*
shed our sinnes in his blood: m *shall cleanse our consciences from dead woorks*, n *ma-* l *Apoc. 1.*
ke a purgation of sinnes, o *purifie our harts*, p *take a way the sinnes of the world*, q m *Heb. 9.*
cancel our obligation of det, r *kill our enmities in him selfe*, s *exhaust or consume* n *Ibid. ca. 1.*
sinne, and finally *make vs* t *holly, immaculat, and irreprehensible coram ipso, be-* o *Act. 15.*
fore him, or in his sight, in all which you see, the holly ghost teacheth p *Ioan. 1.*
such a full, and perfect remission, and vtter abolition of sinne (to our ex- q *Colloss. 2.*
ceeding comefort) that if a man should studdy, and deuise woords, and r *Ephes. 2.*
phrases to signifie, and perswade the same, it were not possible to doe it s *Habr. 9.* t *Coloss. 1.*
more effectuallie.

27 And yet all these places being so euident, as you see, must be vnderstood, say our aduersaries, of couering, or hiding sinne, or not imputing it, because the scripture sometimes vseth such manner of speech
though reason would require, that the more rare and obscure phrases,
or manners of speech, should be expounded by the more frequent and
cleare, especiallie seeing they ar other whiles so conioined the one with

the other, that they must needs be vnderstood to signifie one and the selfe same thing in effect, or at least to be a consequent the one of the
2. *Esdra.* other, as for example we read in *Esdras, ne operias iniquitatem eorum, & peccatum eorum, coram facie tua non deleatur, do not couer,* ô Lord) *their iniquitie, and let not their sinne be blotted out before thy face*, and againe in the psal-
Psal. 50. mist: *auerte faciem tuam a peccatis meis, & omnes iniquitates meas dele, turne a way thy face from my sinnes, and blot out my iniquities,* and againe: *remisisti*
Psal. 84. *iniquitatem plebis tuæ, & operuisti omnia peccata eorum, thou hast remitted the iniquitie of thy people, and hast couered all their sinnes.* And so in like man-
Psal. 31. ner the same psalmist saith in the place before alleadged, *blessed are they whose iniquities are forgeeuen, and whose sinnes are couered,* geeuing to vnderstand that when sinnes are forgeeuen, they are so couered, that almighty
Hebr. 4. God himselfe to whose eyes, (*omnia nuda sunt, & aperta, all things are naked, and open*) seeth them not, because they are vtterly blotted out, and extinguished, as it may further appeare in the same place, where the
Psal. 31. psalmist hauing said, *blessed is the man to whome God hath not imputed sinne,* addeth immediatlie, *nec est in spiritu eius dolus, nor any deceit is in his spirit,* or soule, whereby he signifieth plainelie, that mans sinnes are couered, and not imputed, when his soule is cleare, or free from sinne.

28 But to decide this controuersie, lett vs heare the interpretation of some of the most ancient, and learned fathers of the church. *S. Iustin* the martir, who liued with in a 150. yeres after *Christ*, in his disputation with *Triphon* the Iew, alledgeth the same woords of the psalme, *beatus cui non imputabit Dominus peccatum, blessed is he to whome God shall not impute sinne,* and expoundeth them thus. *hoc est cui pænitenti Deus peccata remittit* &c. *that is to say* (saith he) *to whome being pænitent God shall remit his sinnes, not as you* (Iewes) *doe say deceiuing your selues, or as others like you doe affirme,* to wit, *that although they be sinners, yet if they know God, he will not impute their sinnes vnto them.* Thus farre *S. Iustin*, expresselie reiecting, as you see, this interpretation of our aduersaries, and coopling them with the *Iewes,* and other miscreants of that time, who held, as it seemeth, the same opinion, that they doe now, concerning this point.

S. Iustin in Dialogo Triphone in fine.

Orig. li. 4. in ep. ad Rom. 29 *Origen* also interpreteth the same verse of the psalme of true, and perfect remission of sinne, making three degrees therein, saying, that it is a greate benefit when God remitteth, or forgeeueth a mans sinnes: a greater when he coucreth them, and the greatest when he doth not impute them, for that then they are blotted out in such sort, that no appearance, or show thereof remaineth, as though a man had neuer sinned.

S. Aug. concio 2. in psal. 31. 30 *S. Augustin* expounding also the same woords of the psalmist saith,

saith, *non sic intelligatis* &c. *do not you vnderstand that which the psalmist saith,* (to wit that sinnes are couered,) *as though they remained there, and liued still*: and againe afterwards, *medicus,* saith he, *tegit vt curet, emplastro enim tegit, the phisician couereth the wound,* or sore, *to the end he may cure it, for he couereth it with a plaister*: and the same similitud is also vsed by *S. Gregory* the greate. *S. Greg. magnus in 2. Psal. penit.*

31 Thus then you see how farre these Fathers differ from *Luther Caluin* and other sectaries in the exposition of the psalmist, and of the Apostle, concerning the couering, and not imputing sinne, which the Fathers vnderstand to signifie a full, and perfect remission, whereas these other teach the contrarie, euacuating, as I haue said, the fruits of Christs merits, and establishing the kingdome, and tyrannie of the deuil.

32 For if it be true, which *S. Iohn* teacheth and no true Christian can deny, to wit, that the *Sonne of God appeared,* (that is to say came in to the world, and tooke our flesh,) *vt peccata tolleret,* to the end that he might take away sinnes, and, *vt dissoluat opera diaboli, to dissolue the woorks of the deuil,* and if the woorks of the deuil be sinne, and that *he which sinneth* (as *S. Iohn* also saith) *is of the deuil,* yea his bondman, and his slaue: and if *Christ* came to redeeme vs, and deliuer vs, from this bondage of the deuil, and sinne, and *to renew vs* in spirit, to make vs *new creatures*, to *cleanse vs,* to *sanctifie vs,* to *iustifie vs,* yea to make vs *immaculat*, and *irreprehensibile* in his sight, to make vs *his frends*, his *brethren*, his *children*, his *temples*, and his *kingdome*, in whome he might raigne, and rule as in his proper inheritance dearely purchased with his blood. If all this, I say be true, (as it must needs be, being the expresse doctrin of the scripture,) how is it performed, if notwith standing the merits of our sauious passion applied vnto vs by baptisme, and such other meanes as he hath appointed, we are only reputed by almightie God to be iust, and not so in deede: nor truely sanctified, but remaine still defiled with sinne, bondmen of iniquitie, and children of the deuil, as *S. Iohn* saith we are, whiles we are in sinne? *1. Ioan. 3. Ibidem. Ibidem. Coloss. 1. Tit. 3. 1. Cor. 3. Rom. 8. Galat. 6. 1. Cor. 6. Coloss. 1. Ioan. 15. Matth. 28. Luc 8. Matth. 5. Rom. 8. 2. Cor. 6. Apoc. 1. & 5. 1. Ioan. 3.*

33 Can we then be the children of God, and the children of the deuil both at once? or can we say that *Christ* conquered the deuil, and dissolued his woorks, (that is to say sinne) if it still remaine in our soules when we are iustified? can there *be any agreement betwixt Christ, and Belial?* any *participation betwixt light and darknes? my bed,* saith the holly ghost by the prophet, *is narrow, and two can not lie in it at once, but the one must fall to the ground,* whereby it is signified that God, and the deuil cannot dwell together in one soule, as they must needs doe, if mortal sinne still re- *2. Cor. 6. Isay. 28.*

maine in it, not with standing that it is sanctified by the infusion of the holly ghost. And much more if our best woorks are sinfull, and damnable, as *Luther*, *Caluin*, and others their followers teach, contrarie to the expresse doctrin of the holly scriptures, which testifie that good woorks, which proceede of Gods grace, are *spirituales hostiæ acceptabiles Deo*, *spiritual sacrifices acceptable to God*, and (as the Apostle saith of the almes of the *Philippians*,) *hostia accepta placens Deo, an acceptable sacrifice pleasing to God*, in which respect our Sauiour himselfe speaking of the good woorks of the faithfull, saith, *si oculus tuus fuerit simplex* &c. *if thy eye be simple, all thy body shall be light, and if all thy body be light, not hauing any part of darknes, the whole shall be light, and as a candle of brightnes shall illuminat thee.*

1. Pet. 2. Philip. 4. Matth. 6. Luc 11. See Bellarm. li. 4. de iustific. ca. 15.

34 Thus saith our sauiour, describing a perfect good woorke, meaning by the *eye*, the intention, and by the *light body*, the good woork, and therefore he saith els where, *let your light so shyne before men, that they may see your good woorks*: so that according to our sauiours similitud, and testimonie, good men may doe woorks which shall be *throughlie light, and cleare*, and *haue*, as he saith, *no part of darkenes*, that is to say, no mixture of sinne: so that such woorks, being the woorks of the holly Ghost in vs, are so farre from being sinfull, and damnable in Gods sight, that they may abyde the trial of Gods iustice, and iudgement, as the royal prophet signified of himselfe, saying, *Igne me examinasti & non est inuenta in me iniquitas: Thou hast tried me*, ô Lord, *with fire, and iniquitie hath not benne found in me*: and the Apostle much more clearely: *Si quis*, saith he, *superædificat supra fundamentum hoc* &c. *if any man build vpon this foundation gold, siluer, precious stones, wood hay, stubble* &c. *fire shall try euery mans woork, of what kind*, or quality *it is, if any mans woork, which he built thereupon, doe abide, he shall receiue reward, if any mans woorke burne, he shall suffer detriment, but himselfe shall be saued, yet so as by fire.*

Matth. 5. Psal. 6. 1. Cor. 3.

35 Thus saith the Apostle, signifing by *gold, siluer*, and *precious stones*, such woorks of good men, as proceede from the grace of God, and therefore are so good, and pure, that being tried by the fire of Gods iudgement, they doe suffer no detriment, but shall receiue reward, where as other woorks of theirs, to wit light, and venial sinnes (which he therefore compared to *wood, hay*, and *stuble*) shall not be able to abyde the like trial, and much lesse receaue any *reward*, but suffer *detriment*, that is to say punishment, yet so, as the party who did those woorks shalbe saued, *quasi per ignem, as by fire*: whereby it is euident, that these woorks of the latter sort, are not mortal, but venial sinnes, (as the ancient Fathers do also interpret the same) and that the other woorks

S. Aug. ser. 41. de sanct. S Greg. li. 4. dial. ca. 39.

woorks compared to *gold, siluer*, and *precious stones*, are good woorks proceeding from Gods grace, and so farre from being damnable, (as the sectaries would haue our best woorks to be) that Gods iudgement doth find them to be not only pure, but also woorthy of *reward*, in which respect the Apostle speaking els where of his owne fight, and course, and his perseuerance in the faith of *Christ*, did nothing dout to say, that the *croune of iustice was laid vp, or reserued* for him, *quam reddet* 2.Tim.4.
mihi dominus, saith he, *in illa die iustus iudex*, which (croune) *our lord the iust iudge, will render me in that day.*

36 And although the Apostle doe exclude from iustification, not only Rom. 3.
the woorks of infidels, which goe before faith, but also the moral woorks of the faithfull themselues, which doe not proceede from grace, yet he teacheth euidentlie, that the woorks which follow faith, and proceede of grace, doe iustifie before God, and therefore he saith, that *factores legis iustificabuntur apud Deum, the doers of the law shall be iusti-* Rom. 2.
fied before God, and not the hearers only, meaning by iustification, an encrease of iustice, that is to say, a iustification, of the iust, according to the saying of *S. Iohn, qui iustus est, iustificetur adhuc, he which is iust, let him be* Apoc. 22.
iustified still, to which purpose also the apostle saith of almes, *augebit in-* 2. Cor. 9.
crementa frugum iustitiæ vestræ, it shall augment the encrease of the fruit of your iustice, and *S. Iames* also witnesseth, that *factor operis beatus in suo facto* Iac. 1.
erit, the doer of the woork, shalbe blessed in his deed. and that *Abraham was* Iac. 2.
iustified by woorks, when he offred his sonne Isaac, &c. and after concludeth, that *man is iustified by woorks, and not by faith only*, as I will proue more largely in the third part.

37 Seeing then our good works which flow from the fountayne of Gods grace, are acceptable to him, yea so pure in his sight, that they may abyde the trial of his iudgement, and iustifie vs, that is to say, encrease our iustification, how false, and absurd is the contrarie doctrin of our aduersaries, teaching that such woorks are mortal sinnes? & whereto may they be thought to tend, but, as I haue saide, to establish the tyranny of the deuil, and to ouerthrow the kingdome of *Christ*, in our soules, not withstanding their pretence to patronize Christs merits against vs, charging vs most falselie to impugne the same by our Catholike doctrin of good woorks, and of the merit thereof, whereby they say we obscure the glory of *Christ*, attributing to our selues, and to our owne merits, that which *Christ* hath merited for vs: as though it could be any derogation to the merits of our sauiour to say, that he not only merited for vs himselfe and conquered the deuil, and sinne, but also made vs able to merit, & to conquer them both? or rather is it not farre more

more glorious to *Christ*, and a greater confusion to the deuil, that *Christ* conquereth him, and sinne daily in vs, & by vs, then if he had only once subdued them for vs? for by making such weake ones, as we are, daily to treade them vnder our feete, his conquest, and triumph is farre more glorious, his mercy to vs more manifest, his enemies, and ours, more confounded, and we infinitlie more obliged to him, in which respect we may truely say with the Apostle. *Deo gratias qui dedit nobis victoriam, thanks be to God, who gaue vs victorie*: but how by our selues? no, but *per Dominum Iesum Christum, by our lord Iesus Christ*, from whose grace, and merits proceed all our force, and habilitie, all our good woorks, our iustification, and saluation, in which respect *S. Augustin* saith, that *when Christ crowneth our merits, he crowneth his owne gifts.*

1. Cor. 1. 5

Ibid.

S. Aug. ep. 105. contra pelagian.

38 Threfore as our doctrin concerning the merits of works, remismission of sinne, and iustification, is glorious to our sauiour, (teaching that his merits were of sufficient force, with the helpe of his grace, to make vs merit, to cleanse, and wash away our sinnes, to renew vs in soule, and to make vs as truely iust, as before we were truely sinners) so the contrarie opinion of our aduersaries, is not only dishonorable to our sauiour *Christ*, yea blasphemous, (as I haue signified) but also pernicious to common welth, for that it serueth to no other end, but for a very couer, and cloke to sinne, yea for an incouragement thereto, seeing that whosoeuer is imbued with this doctrin, must needs thinke it bootelesse for him to labour either to cleanse his soule from sinnes past by repentance, and penance, or els to preserue it in puritie, for the time to come, perswading himselfe, that he is, and alwaise shall be polluted with damnable sinnes, doe he what he can, and yet not with standing that he shall be still iustified by the imputation of Christs iustice, and thereby be the child of God, the temple of the holly Ghost, and coheire with Christ? and therefore will any man that is thus perswaded, care greatelie what he doth? no truely, or at least he needeth not to care, if this doctrin be true, in which respect it is no lesse preiudicial to common welth, (as I declared more amply in the 35. chapter) then repugnant to the verity of our holly scriptures, and to the doctrin of all the ancient Fathers.

39 Herevppon I conclude, that seeing it is euident by all this discours concerning iustification, that when we are iustified our sinnes are through the merits of *Christ*, truely remitted, and our soules by the infusion of the holly Ghost, purified, renewed, illuminated, and sanctified, and that thereby we become temples of the holly Ghost, the children of God, heyres to his eternal kingdome, and are therefore most acceptable,

acceptable, and deare vnto him, it must needs follow, that whosoeuer liueth, and perseuereth in this state of Christian iustice, he is a perfect christian, and continuallie vnited with God, not with standing the humane frailties, and imperfections whereto the iustest man is subiect in this life: For although the said imperfections, (or venial sinnes) can not stand with the perfect puritie of the next life, forasmuch as they are not directlie a repugnant to the law of God, they doe not exclude vs either from the perfection of this life, or yet from b true iustice, as I declared in the last chapter, c besids that they are not alwaise committed, and being committed, they are (as *S. Augustin* teacheth) daily remitted through the repentance, penance, and prayers of the iust, so that then the soule, being both purged from those imperfections, and also adorned with grace, and the habits of all vertue, remaineth pure, immaculat, and irreprehensible before God, yea most faire, and beautifull in his sight, according to all those testimonies of the holly scriptures, and Fathers, which I haue alledged before to this purpose.

40 Now then to proceed, hauing declared in the last chapter in d what consisteth christian perfection, and felicitie, e who they are that arriue vnto it, and by what meanes it is obtained, I will now apply the same, and all my former discourse to common welth, showing how it is made no lesse happy, then particuler men who are members of it.

41 This may sufficientlie be gathered, and inferred of that which I haue alreddy discoursed: For seeing the felicitie, and happines of the whole common welth, and of euery member thereof, is all one, (as I proued in the fourth chapter) it cannot be denied, but that the meanes also to beatifie, or make happy the common welth, must needs be the same that geeueth happines to euery part thereof: for as when euery part of the boddy is sound, and healthfull, the whole boddy is sound, and well disposed: soe also the whole common welth must needs be happy, when euery member thereof (that is to say euery particuler man) is happy.

42 Seeing then I haue proued that no man can obtaine true vnion with God (which is the end, and felicitie of euery man) but by the perfect exercise, and practise of the Catholike Roman religion, it is consequentlie euident that common welth cannot be vnited with God, but by the same meanes, especiallie for two causes declared before, the one, because perfect vertue, (which is the stay, and principal piller to vphold common welth) cannot otherwaise be had but by the Catholike religion, and the other because true vnion with God, (wherein consisteth the end, & felicitie of common welth) is also the special effect thereof.

a *S. Tho. 1. 2. q. 87. ar. 5. & q. 88. ar. 1. primum & 22. q. 105. 1. 1.*
b *Chap. 37. nu. 88.*
c *S. Aug. li. de natu. & grat. ca. 38. S. Aug. ep. 108. & li. 50. hom. ho. 40.*
Chap. 37.
d *Nu 78. 79. & 80.*
e *Nu. 77.*

43 And to the end that this may be the more manifest, and that I may with all cleare a principal difficultie controuersed betwixt our aduersaries and vs, concerning the meanes whereby the christian religion doth vnit man with God, (they ascribing it to *only faith*, and we rather to *charity* then to *faith*, though in deede to the concurrence of both, and of all other vertues, yet in such sort, that faith is vnderstood to be the foundation, and charitie the consummation of the whole building,) to the end, I saye, that this may appeare, I will first proue that our vnion with God is properly the effect of perfect *charity*, and then I will euidently show, that the vertue of perfect *charity*, is proper only to the Catholike Roman church, and not to be found in the congregations of *Lutherans*, or *Caluinists*, or of any other sectaries of these dayes, where vppon it must needs follow, that the religion which the Catholike Roman church teacheth, vniteth man with God, and consequently geeueth true felicitie to comon welth.

44 Therefore for as much, as our vnion with God, and consequently the felicitie of common welth, is wrought by our iustification, which our aduersaries attribut wholly to *faith*, I will here show the excellencie, or rather the preeminence of *charity*, before *faith*, in the woorke of iustification, thereby to show also, how our vnion with God, and the true felicitie of common welth, is principally wrought by *charity*.

45 Let vs then consider how much the Apostle himselfe preferreth *charitie* before *faith* for iustification, seeing he saith, that though he should *haue all faith, yea such as might remoue mountaines, yet if he had not charitie, he were nothing*, & further comparing them together for woorth, and valew, he concludeth expressélie, that of *faith, hope*, and *charitie, maior horum charitas, the greatest of these is charitie*: and treating els where of iustification, he saith also, that the *faith* which is necessarie thereto, is, *fides quæ per dilectionem operatur, a faith which woorketh by loue*, or charitie wherein he signifieth plainely, that *charitie* is (as the schoolemen speake) the forme, or that which geeueth viuacitie, life, and operation to *faith* in the act of iustification; as the soule geeueth life, and operation to the boddy, which in the greeke text is more euident, then in our latin, for that the woord *operatur* in latin, is in the greeke *euergoumeny*, that is to saye, *mota*, or *acta*, *moued*, or *stirred*, geeuing to vnderstand, that *faith* when it iustifieth, is moued, or styrred by *charitie*, as the body is by the soule, whereuppon it followeth not only that *faith* with out *charitie* is (as S. *Iames* woorthilie tearmeth it) *inanis vaine* (so farre foorth as concerneth iustification, but also that *charitie* farre excelleth *faith* in woorth, and dignitie, as much as the forme excelleth the matter, and the soule

1. Cor. 13.

Ibid.

the

the boddy. Whereby two absurd heretical opinions of the sectaries are clearely confuted, the one of *Luther*, who teacheth, as you haue heard, in the 35. chapter, that *fides sine charitate, & ante charitatem iustificat, faith iustifieth with out, & before charitie*, whereas the Apostle teacheth, as you see, the flat contrary, to wit that the *faith* which iustifieth, must be such a *faith*, as shall woorke or be moued by *charitie*, and therefore it cannot possibly iustifie with out, and before *charitie*, no more then the boddy can doe the functions requisit thereto, or yet liue, with out the soule.

Chap. 35. nu. 5.

Luther. in ca. 2 ad Galat.

46 The other absurd opinion confuted by this place of *S. Paule*, is of *Caluin*, and all other sectaries at this day, who hold, that albeit *charitie* doe, and must needs concurre with *faith* to iustification, (because *faith* cannot be with out *charitie*, as they fondly affirme) yet the act of iustification, is to be attributed, say they, only to *faith*, and not all to *charitie*, wherein, they say as wisely, as if they shuld affirme that mans actions are to be attributed wholly, and only to the boddy, and not at all to the soule, where as it is euident in the Apostle, that, as all mens actions are principally to be ascribed to the soule, from whence proceedeth his life, and operation, soe also the act of *faith* in iustification is cheefely to be attributed to *charitie*, which geeueth life, and operation vnto it.

Caluin in Antidoto concil. ad art. 11. sess. 6 & li. 3. instit. c. 16. sect. 1.

47. Therefore *S. Augustin* saith, *fidem non facit vtilem nisi charitas, nothing maketh faith proffitable but charitie*, and in an other place, *sine amore fides nihil prodest, with out loue faith nothing proffiteth*, where vppon it followeth, that seeing *faith* doth iustifie, as the apostle teacheth by the meanes, and operation of *charitie*, much more doth *charitie* iustifie which geeueth life, and operation to *faith*, in which respect *S. Augustin* maketh no dout at all to saye thus, *caritas inchoata, inchoata iustitia est, caritas magna, magna iustitia est, caritas prouecta, prouecta iustitia est, caritas perfecta, perfecta iustitia est: charitie begunne*, (that is to saye vnperfect) *is vnperfect iustice, greate charitie, is greate iustice, charitie increated, is increased iustice, perfect charitie, is perfect iustice*. Thus saith this ancient, and most learned father, not denying iustification by *faith*, but geeuing to vnderstād whence proceedeth all the force, and efficacie of *faith* in the woorke of iustification: and therefore also in his treatise vppon *S. Iohn*, he proueth notably that all the summe of christian religion is reduced to *charitie*, because he which truely loueth God, must needs both beleeue, and hope in him, where as euery one which beleeueth, doth not hope in God, and loue him, to which purpose he saith also els where, *dilectio sola discernit inter filios Dei, & filios diaboli, only loue, or charitie, doth discerne, or distinguish betwixt the children of God, and the children of the deuil.*

S. Aug. de trinit. li. 15. ca. 18.

S. Aug. de natu. & gra. ca. vlt.

Idē in Ioan. tract. 83.

Idem in ep. 1. Ioan. tractatu 5.

48 Furthermore our Sauiour himselfe sufficiently signified the eminent excellencie of *charitie*, and the power it hath to iustifie, when he abridged the whole law, into the loue of God, and of our neighbour,
Matth. 22. saying, *in his duobus mandatis pendet vniuersa lex, & prophetæ: vppon these two commaundements dependeth the whole law, and the prophets:* where vp-
Rom. 13. pon the Apostle also saith, *plenitudo legis dilectio, the plenitud*, or accomplishment *of the law, is loue*, or charitie, and there vppon it also followeth that *charitie* doth iustifie, for he which fulfilleth the law, is iust,
Chap. 37. nu. 77. 84. 85. & 86. and a perfect christian (as I haue proued in the last chapter) and therefore seeing that he which hath true *charitie*, doth thereby fulfill the law, he must needs also therebie obtaine true iustice, and christian perfection: in which respect the Apostle calleth *charitie, vinculum perfectionis*,
Coloss. 3. *the bond of perfection*, saying, *induite vos* &c. *put vppon you the entrailes, or bowels of mercy, benignitie, humilitie, modestie, patience, bearing one with an other* &c. *super omnia autem hæc caritatem habete, quod est vinculum perfectionis, aboue all these, haue charitie which is the bond of perfection.* And *S. Pe-*
1. Pet. 4. *ter* also exhorteth vs to haue *mutuam caritatem ante omnia, mutual charitie aboue all other things*, and the reason is because *charitie* geeueth perfectiō, and connexion to all other vertues: for with out it, there is no true ver-
S. Aug. de verb. Domini ser. 53. ca. 6. tue, and where it is there are all vertues, *sola charitas est*, saith *S. Augustin, quæ vincit omnia* &c. *It is only charitie which ouercommeth all things, with out the which all things are nothing woorth, and which draweth all things vnto it, wheresoeuer it is.*

49 More ouer such is the prerogatiue of charitie a boue all other vertues, that no other but it can make a man truely good, and ver-
Aug. ep. 52. tuous, and therefore *S. Augustin* saith, *non faciunt bonos vel malos mores, nisi boni vel mali amores, nothing but good, or euil loues, maketh good, or euil manners*, and in an other place he affirmeth, *that charitie is the precious mar-*
Idem tractatu 5. in ep. Ioan. *garit, with out the which, nothing can proffit vs, and which alone, if we haue it suffiseth*: and againe in an other place, speaking of the righteousnes of
S. Aug. de natura, & gratia. ca. 38. *Abel the iust*, he ascribeth the same to *charitie* only, saying, *qua vna verè iustus est, quicunque iustus est, by the which* (charitie) *alone, he is truly iust whosoeuer is iust*, not meaning, that charitie can euer iustifie, or yet be alone with out *faith*, and other vertues, but that it only hath this preeminence aboue all other, to consummat and perfect the rest, and that when it is once had in perfection, there needeth no more to be added to perfect iustification, nor consequentlie to true vnion with God, for he that is iustified, is truely vnited with God, and the more iust he is, the greater is his vnion with God, and therefore seeing *charitie* doth consummat, & perfect our iustification, it doth principallie woorke our vnion with

GOD.

God, in which respect *S. Dionisius Areopagita* calleth it *virtutem vnificam, connexiuam, adunatiuam, & commiscentem, a vertue which combineth, vniteth, knitteth, and mingleth together*, whereby he signifieth the force it hath to vnit, and conioine man with God in such sort, that they become, as it were both one, as I haue showed amply when I treated of contemplation, and particulerly of the *vnitiue waye*. S. Dionis. Areop. li. de diuinis nom. ca. 4. par. 1. & 2. Chap. 20. & 21.

50 This the Apostle signifieth when he saith, *qui adhæret Deo, vnus spiritus est, he which adhæreth*, that is to saye is vnited *with God, is one spirit* with him, and that this is wrought principallie by *charitie*, *S. Iohn* signifieth plainely, when he saith, *Deus est charitas* &c. *God is charitie, he that dwelleth in charitie, dwelleth in God, and God in him*, and againe: *si diligamus inuicem, Deus in nobis manet, if we loue one an other, God remaineth in vs.* Also our Sauiour himselfe witnesseth the same, saying, *qui diligit me, sermonem meum seruabit* &c. *he which loueth me will keepe my commaundments, and my father will loue him, and we will come vnto him, and make our abode with him.* Thus saith our sauiour, teaching as you see, that not only the obseruation, & keeping of his commaundments, but also his, and his fathers vnion with vs, is the speciall effect of our true loue of him, that is to saye of perfect *charitie*. 1. Ioan. 4. Ibid.

51 Whereby it may appeare how absurdly *Luther*, and his followers doe ascribe all our vnion with God, *to only faith*, alledging for that purpose the woords of the prophet *Osee* to the people of the *Iewes*, speaking of their last conuersion, *sponsabo te mihi in fide, I will espouse thee vnto me in faith*, in which woords of the prophet, *fides*, is not of necessitie to be vnderstood, to signify the *faith* whereby we beleeue, and are iustified, (as *Card. Bellarmin* noteth very well) but the fidelitie which God vseth in performance of his promises towards vs, in which sence he promised to espouse his people *in fide, in faith*, that is to say *fideliter, faithfully*, or assuredly, as he saide immediatlie before, *sponsabo te mihi in iustitia, iudicio, & in misericordia, I will espouse thee vnto me in iustice, iudgement, and in mercy*, which may very well be vnderstood to signifie *iustly*, and *mercifullie*. Osee 2. Bellar. de iustific. li. 1 ca. 23. Osee 2.

52 But though *fides* shuld there signifie beleefe, or a iustifying *faith*, yet our aduersaries shuld gaine nothing thereby, seeing that *faith* doth not otherwaise conioine vs with God, then as it iustifieth, to wit *per dilectionem, by loue, or charitie*, by the meanes, and force whereof, it woorketh both those effects, and therefore howsoeuer it may be saide, that *faith* doth make the espousal, or contract betwixt God, and our soule, yet, it is charitie which maketh the matrimonie, and perfect Vnion betwixt him, and vs, as it is sufficientlie expressed throughout all the canticles, where the coniunction of *Christ*, with his church, or with a faithfull 1. Cor. 13.

ſoule,is ſignified by a continual allegorie of two paſſionat louers, or of the bridegroome, or the ſpouſe languiſhing, as it were, with the loue one of the other, in which reſpect *S. Bernard* calleth the canticles *Epitalamij carmen*, or *carmen nuptiale*, a *wedding, or mariage ſong*, (betwixt the bridegroome, and his ſpouſe) *exprimens*, ſaith he, *caſtos iucundoſque complexus animorum* &c. *expreſſing the chaſt, and pleaſant coniunction of their minds, and the mutual charitie of their affections one to an other.*

S. Bern. in in cant. ſerm.1.

53 Thus then we ſee, what is the ſpecial force, and effect of *charitie*, to wit, to conioine, and vnite vs with God, whereby it appeareth that although faith is woorthily eſteemed to be the foundation of our iuſtification and vnion with God, (for as the Apoſtle ſaith, *accedentem ad Deum oportet credere* &c. *whoſoeuer commeth to God muſt beleeue* &c. and *ſine fide impoſſibile eſt placere Deo, with out faith is is impoſſible to pleaſe God*) yet *charitie* is the conſummation, and perfection thereof, which the moſt ancient, & learned fathers of Gods church doe teach expreſſelie.

Habr. 11.

54 *Puto*, ſaith *Origen*, *quod prima ſalutis initia* &c. *I think that the firſt beginning*, or the very foundation *of our ſaluation is faith, the augmentation*, or *encreaſe of it hope, and the perfection, and toppe of the building, charitie*. The like ſaith *S. Ignatius* diſciple to *S. Iohn* the *Euangeliſt*, *principium vitæ*, ſaith he, *eſt fides* &c. *The beginning of life is faith, the end of it loue, or charitie, and both ioyned, and vnited together doe perfit the man of God.*

Origen. in in cap. 4. ep. ad Rom.

S. Ignat. ad ad Philippens.

55 Alſo *Clemens Alexandrinus* ſaith, *præcedit fides*, &c. *faith goeth before, feare raiſeth the building, and loue doth conſummat*, or end it. Finally to omit diuers others for breuities ſake, *S. Auguſtin* ſaith, *Domus Dei credendo fundatur* &c. *The houſe of God is founded by beleefe, erected, or raiſed by hope, and perfited, or finished by charitie.*

Clemens. Alexand. li. 2. ſtromat.

S. Aug. ſer. 20.

56 Loe then how vniforme is the doctrin of theſe moſt learned, and ancient fathers, and conforme to the holly ſcriptures before alledged, all teaching that our iuſtification, and conſequentlie our vnion with God, is perfited by *charitie*, in which reſpect, we doe truely ſay, that *charitie* doth iuſtifie, yet not ſoe, that we deny iuſtificatiō by *faith*, but rather eſtablish it, ſignifying wherein conſiſteth the life, and efficacie of *a iuſtifying faith, quæ per dilectionem operatur*, (as the Apoſtle ſaith) *which woorketh*, or rather is moued, and made to woorke *by charitie*. And therefore, whereas the Apoſtle ſpeaketh oft times of iuſtification by faith, he neuer ſaith, or euer meaneth, that *faith* iuſtifieth *alone*, without *charitie* and other vertues, but that it iuſtifieth, as the beginning and firſt diſpoſition to iuſtification, and the meanes to obtein all other things neceſſarie thereto, as *S. Auguſtin* teacheth expreſslly *ſaying*. *Ideo dicit Apoſtolus iuſtificari hominem*, &c. *Therfore the Apoſtle ſaith that man is iuſtified by faith, not by woorks,*

1. Cor. 13.

S. Auguſt. de prædeſtinat. ſancto. c. 7.

woorks, because faith is geuen first, by the which the rest are obteined, which ar properlie called woorks, wherein we liue iustly. So he.

57 And this shall suffise for this time, for so much as concerneth iustification, whereof I meane to treate more amply in the third part, and to declare further, how faith, and woorkes doe iustifie, and what works are excluded from iustification, with diuers other things pertaining to this question, contenting my selfe for the present, breefely to haue showed the excellent dignitie, and efficacie of charitie in working our iustification, and vnion with God, wherein consisteth the felicitie of man, and common welth. I will therefore now proceede to show that this most excellent vertue of *charitie* is proper to the Roman Catholikes, and not to their aduersaries, whereby it will euidentlie appeare, that the common welth cannot attaine to true felicitie, but by the Catholike Roman religion.

58 It is therefore to be vnderstood that some of the woorthyest, and highest fruits of perfect *charitie*, or the loue of God, are those most excellent points of perfection, which our sauiour recommended vnto vs, no lesse by his example, then by his doctrin, to wit, the continual cariage of our crosse, the contempt of the world, and the mortification, or chastisement of our owne bodies for the pure loue of God. For soe deepe, and firme is the roote that our selfe loue hath taken in our corrupt nature, that nothing is able to extirp and root it out, and to plant in vs a true christian contempt of the world, and a holly hate of our selues, but *charitas Dei, diffusa in cordibus nostris, per spiritum sanctum qui datus est nobis, The charitie,* or loue of God *spread in our harts by the holly ghost, which is geeuen vs,* whereof the power, and force, exceedeth all natural power, and therefore the Apostle saith, *neither death, nor life, nor Angels, nor principalities, nor powers, nor things present, nor things to come, neither might nor hyght, nor depth, nor other creature, shall be able to seperate vs from the charitie of God, which is in Christ Iesus our Lord.* Also the spouse of Christ in the Canticles, feeling in her selfe the admirable force, and power of his loue, woorthily compared it to death, saying *fortis vt mors dilectio, loue is as strong as death,* geeuing to vnderstand that euen as death killeth, & destroyeth the body, depriuing it of all sence, mocion, and operation, soe also true loue of God, suppresseth, and conquereth all the inordinat affections of the soule of man, in such sort that he dieth wholly to the world, and himselfe, & liueth only to God, saying with the Apostle, *I liue not now, but Christ liueth in me.*

Rom 5. *Rom. 8.* *Cant 8.* *Galat. 2*

59 The experience hereof hath benne sufficientlie seene in those holly men, of whose admirable austerities, (surpassing the power, and

ſtrength of humane nature) I treated amply in the laſt chapter, in whome *Theodoretus* (who wrote the liues of many of them, aboue a 11. hundreth yeres agoe) showeth notably the ſtupendious force, of Gods loue, prouing euidentlie that the voluntarie aſperities, of hunger, cold, faſting, watching, and other mortifications which they endured, excelled all the labours, and trauailes that any ſort of men what ſoeuer, vndergoe in any ſtate, or condicion of life in this world, which he attributeth wholly to the force of a deuine loue, where with they were enflamed, deſcribing the notable effects thereof in a large diſcourſe, whereof I thinke it not amiſſe to lay downe ſome part here, as well for our edification, as for our better inſtruction in this point.

Theodoret. hiſtor. religioſa, orat. de charitate.

60 Therefore this ancient father hauing exemplified the greate force of charity, firſt in *Moyſes*, and after in *S. Paule*, alledgeth his woords to the Romans, *Quis nos ſeparabit à charitate Chriſti?* &c. *who ſhall be able to ſeperat vs from the loue of Chriſt? ſhall afflictions, anguish of mind,* &c. And then (ſaith *Theodoretus*) the Apoſtle showeth the cauſe of this ſufferance, ſaying, *in his omnibus ſuperamus propter Deum, qui dilexit nos, in all theſe we ouercome for God, who loued vs, for conſidering who we are, and what benefits we haue receiued, and that we did not preuent God with our loue, but were preuented by him, yea and were beloued of him, whiles we hated him, and were reconciled to him, when we were his enemies, not by any ſute, or petition of ours, but by his owne ſonne, whom he ſent as embaſſadour vnto vs, (in ſo much that we, who had donne the iniurie were inuited, and allured by him which had receiued it) and furthermore pondering with our ſelues, the croſſe, paßion, and death, that the ſonne of God ſuffred for vs, and the hope of reſurrection that he hath geeuen vs thereby, we ouercome all difficulties, and comparing the memorie of our benefits, with our corporal afflictions, which are but tranſitorie, and short, we doe willinglie endure them: for when we ballance, and waigh all the troubles of this life with our loue to God, we find them very light, and though we collect, and gather in our minds all the pleaſures, and delites of the world, and conſider on the other ſide, the loue that we owe to God, they doe appeare more vaine and vanishing then a shaddow, and more fraile then the fading flowers of the ſpring.*

Rom. 8.

61 Thus he, and after a while proſecuting ſtill the ſame matter he addeth. *Qui ergo diuinum accepit amorem,* &c, *he therefore that hath receiued the loue of God, contemneth all earthlie things, treadeth vnder his feete all the pleaſures of the boddy, he deſpiſeth ritches, glory, and all honour of men, he eſteemeth the Imperial purple no more then cobwebs: and precious ſtones to be no better then peble ſtones in the ſea coaſt: he holdeth not bodilie health for any happines, nor ſicknes for calamitie, nor pouertie for miſerie, neither doth he meaſure felicitie by ritches, and delites, but thinketh all theſe things to be moſt like to the fleeting water*

of a riuer, which passeth a long by the trees planted on the banks, and stayeth not at any of them.

62 Finally this graue, and learned authour hauing after many other notable sentences, and aduises, concerning the effects of charity, alledged the examples of the greate torments that the Apostles, and innumerable martires of Gods church, being inflamed with this heauenlie fire, most willingly suffred, he returneth to those holly men of whose voluntarie penances, and austerities he had treated before, saying, *Huius quoque pulchritudinis amore capti, noui Athletæ* &c. *These late, or new champions being also surprised with the beauty of this loue, undertooke those greate combats, which exceeded the nature of men.* Thus farre *Theodoretus*: showing, as you see, the admirable force, and notable fruits of charitie in those holly hermits, monks, and religious men who being inflamed with the feruent loue of God, serued for patterns, and examples to the world of true mortification, and Christian perfection in his dayes: And therefore to the end we may now discerne, and discusse in what church, and profession of Christians, these, and other true frutes of perfect charity are practised, it shall suffise that we only consider, what I haue alreddy treated concerning the same, which may also serue for a recapitulation thereof, and euidentlie show that they abound, and florish in the Catholike Roman church, and that *Lutherans*, and *Caluinists*, cannot claime to themselues so much as any shadow thereof.

63 For this purpose I will touch only 4. principal effects, or fruits of charitie, whereof the first shall be that which I haue now lastly mentioned, and was practised in greate perfection by these holly men of whome *Theodoretus* treateth: to wit, a true, & holly hatred of themselues, showed by the continual cariage of their crosse in the exercise of penance, and mortification, or chastisement of their flesh.

64 Now then, that this effect of perfect charitie is no lesse manifest at this day, then it alwaise hath benne in our Catholike Roman church, it is cleare both by our Catholik doctrin cõcerning the necessitie therof, and also by the continual practise of it, euident in infinit numbers, as well of seculer, and lay men, as of religious and cleargy men, exemplar euen at this day in all kind of mortification, I meane not only such mortification as the Catholik church ordaineth, and enioineth to be generally vsed at certaine times, but also many particuler, and priuat penances, as frequent, and rigorous fasts, disciplins, haire cloth, laborious peregrinations, watching, and diuers other austerities partly prescribed by the ancient rules of religions with in the first 400. and 500. yeres, (as I haue signified before in the 36. chapter,) and partly enioined in

ſome caſes by ghoſtly fathers, and partly voluntarilie vndertaken, and practiſed by particuler men of all ſtates to ſatisfie the iuſtice of God for ſinnes paſt, (through the merits of our ſauiours ſuffrings, and ſatisfaction) to preuent future ſinnes, by the repreſſion of concupiſcence, to obtaine Gods mercy towards other men, as well for the conuerſion of ſinners, as for the releefe of their temporal neceſſities, and finally to conforme their liues to the liues of our ſauiour, of *S. Iohn Baptiſt*, of the Apoſtles, & of all the holly men of the primatiue church, of whoſe ſeueritie, and rigour in all kind of penances, and mortifications, I treated amply in the aforeſaid 36. chapter, where I alſo declared the continual practiſe thereof from our ſauiours time to theſe our dayes, by a continual ſucceſſion of ages, and times, ſo that it cannot be denied, but that the vſe and cuſtome thereof, and conſequently this notable fruit, and effect of charitie, both is, and alwaiſe hath benne euident in the Catholike Roman church.

65 But now on the other ſide, if we conſider either the doctrin, or yet the practiſe of our aduerſaties, we ſhall find them to be vtterly voide thereof, as it hath appeared ſufficiently in diuers parts of this treatiſe, eſpeciallie in the 35. chapter, where I layed downe diuers points of their doctrin, wholly repugnant to all mortification of the fleſh; teaching ſuch a free remiſſion of ſinne by the merits of *Chriſt*, that all our voluntarie penances are in their opinion derogatorie to Chriſts merits, and ſatisfaction: beſids that theire doctrin alſo of iuſtification by only faith, and of a Chriſtian liberty, exempting vs from all obligation of external woorks, doth wholly exclude all penance, and chaſtiſement of the fleſh, as needeles and ſuperfluous: And therefore no meruel that they haue no exerciſe amongſt them at all of mortification, whereof they are ſuch open aduerſaries, that they exclaime againſt nothing more then the practiſe thereof in the Catholik church.

See the 35. chap.

Ibidem.

66 So that of this moſt notable effect of charitie they haue not ſo much as any pretence, whereby the common welth is infinitly endammaged both ſpirituallie, and temporallie, for as the reſtraint, and mortification of the fleſh, doth notablie repreſſe vice and aduance the vertue of temperance, which (as I haue declared in the ninth chapter out of *Plato*,) is a moſt political vertue: ſoe alſo the general libertie of the fleſh muſt needs foſter, and nouriſh all kind of vice, and breede generallie greate intemperance, and enormitie of ſinne, to the greate offence of God, & breach of political lawes, and conſequentlie to the greate preiudice of common welth: and thus much for the firſt fruit of perfect charitie.

67 An

67 An other ſpecial fruit, and effect thereof is, the obſeruation of the
commaundments of God, and of the Euangelical counſels: and firſt
touching the commaundments, the ſame appeareth euidentlie by our
ſauiours owne woords alledged before, to wit, *Si quis diligit me, ſermo-*
nem meum ſeruabit &c. *if any man loue me, he will keepe my commaund-* 1. *Ioan.* 14.
ments &c. as alſo in that he abridged the whole law into the two pre- *Matth.* 22.
cepts of *charitie*, to which purpoſe alſo the Apoſtle ſaith, *plenitudo legis*
dilectio, the fulnes or *accompliſhment of the law is loue*, or charitie, and fi- *Rom.* 13.
nallie *S. Iohn* teacheth that. *Hæc eſt charitas Dei vt mandata eius cuſtodiamus*,
This is the charitie, or the loue of God, *that we keepe his commaundments.* 1. *Ioan.* 5.

68 Now then heere we are to conſider whether this fruit of charitie
be to be found in the Catholike Roman church, or amongſt the ſectaries, and firſt concerning them, it is manifeſt that they are in this point
as I may ſay *rei confitentes, ſo guilty that they confeſſe their fault*, teaching that
the commaundments are impoſſible to be kept: yea *Luther Melanchthon*, *See chap.* 35.
the *Antinoni*, and the rigid *Lutherans* affirme, that the commaundments
are abrogated by *Chriſt*, as appeareth in the 35. chapter, whereto tendeth alſo all their doctrin concerning iuſtification by only faith, and
our Chriſtian libertie, which *Luther* teacheth to be ſuch, that we are *Luther de*
bound to nothing but only to beleeue, and confeſſe God, and that in *chriſtia. li-*
all other things, we are free, and left to our owne libertie, as I haue alſo *bert.*
declared more at large in the 35. chapter: and therefore it is euident by *Item ad c.* 2.
the doctrin of theſe Archſectaries, that they neither kept the com- *ad Galat.*
maundments, nor thought it needefull to doe it, no nor yet, as it may *Item in ep.*
be preſumed, euer ſo much as endeuored to keepe them: for no man is *c.* 7. *ep.* 1. *ad*
ſoe ſimple to take paines, to doe that, which he thinketh to be but nee- *Cor.*
deles, and impoſſible.

69 The like may alſo be ſaid with greate reaſon of all *Lutherans Cal-*
uiniſts, and other ſectaries who beleeue, and follow this doctrin of their
maiſters: ſo that I may well conclude that this moſt excellent effect of
perfect charitie, to wit the obſeruation of the commaundments, or
law of God, is not to be found amongſt theſe aduerſaries of the Catholike Roman church, where vppon it alſo followeth that their congregations can not be the true church of *Chriſt*, ſeeing that almighty God
promiſed in the old teſtament, to geeue his holly ſpirit to his ſeruants in
the new teſtament, whereby they ſhuld obſerue his commaundments,
as appeareth in the prophet *Ezechiel*, who ſpeaking of the church of
Chriſt, ſaith in the perſon of almightie God, *Spiritum meum ponam in me-* *Ezech. c.* 36.
dio veſtri &c. *I will place*, or put *my ſpirit in the midſt of you, and I will*
make, or cauſe that *you ſhall walke in my precepts, and keepe my iudgements.*

 Thus

Thus saith the prophet, whereby it is euident that the commaundments of God shall be fully obserued in the church of *Christ*.

70 And if this be denied it must neede follow that the church of God had greater priuiledge, and assistance of his grace, and holly spirit vnder the law of *Moyses*, then it hath now in the law of grace: And this I say, for that it is euident, that in *Moyses* his law the commaundments, and law of God were exactly fulfilled, as the scripture testifieth of diuers holly men in that time, as namely of *Iosue*, saying, *non præteriit de vniuersis mandatis, ne vnum quidem* &c. *he did not let passe, or transgresse so much as one of all the commaundments which God commaunded to Moyses.*

Iosue ca. 11.

71 Also of *Dauid* we read in the booke of kings, that *fecit rectum in oculis Domini* &c. *he did that which was right,* (or iust) *in the sight of God, and did not decline from all those things* (that is to say from any of those things) *which God commaunded him all the dayes of his life, except in the matter of Vrias.* besids that he signifieth of himselfe, that he performed the commaundments of God with all facilitie by the helpe of his grace, and therefore he saith *viam mandatorum tuorum cucurri* &c. *I ranne the way of thy commaundments when thou didest dilate my hart.* In life manner the Euangelist witnesseth of *Zacharias*, and *Elizabeth*, (as I haue signified in the last chapter) *that they were both iust before God, walking in all the commaundments, or iustifications of our Lord with out blame.*

3. Reg. c. 15. *Psal.* 118. *Luc.* 1.

72 Seeing then these, and many others no dout, kept the commaundments of God vnder the law of *Moyses*, it were very absurd, and iniurious to *Christ*, to say that the commaundments are impossible to be obserued in his church, which hath receiued of him the law of grace, and aboundance of his spirit, and a promise of his continual assistance vntill the end of the world, besids that he himselfe also witnesseth that his *yoke is sweete, and his burden light*, and S. *Iohn* saith that *mandata eius grauia non sunt, his commaundments are not heauy*, yea and the psalmist testifieth that they are *dulciora super mel, & fauum, sweeter then hunny, and hunny combe.* what meruel then that good, and holly men being assisted with gods grace, and holly spirit, doe not only receiue infinit sweetenes and consolation in the obseruation and performance of the commaundments, but also doe excede, or goe beyond them, performing much more then is commaunded? as I haue alreddy proued before when I treated of the Euangelical counsels, and will also proue more particulerly after a while.

Math. 11. *1. Ioan.* 5. *Psal.* 18.

73 In the meane time I inferre herevpon that the comaundments of god are not impossible, but easy, and sweete by the helpe of gods grace which I could confirme by infinit places of Scriptures, and Fathers but

that

that for breuities sake I must remit all this question to be handled more at large in the third part of this treatise: therefore for the present, I wish it to be noted, that the fathers abhorred this opinion of the sectaries, as impious, and blasphemous, and therefore *S. Basil* saith, *impium est dicere impossibilia esse spiritus præcepta, it is a wicked thing to say that the precepts of the holly ghost are impossible to be kept* and *S. Chrisostome* in like manner, *nequaquam*, saith he, *dominum accuses*, &c. *doe not thou accuse our Lord, he doth not commaund impossible things, multi ipsa superant præcepta, many doe surpasse, or goe beyond the præcepts themselues*: and *S. Paulinus* to the same purpose saith *nec sufficit quod iusta non facimus* &c. *neither doth it suffise vs, that we doe not those things which are commaunded, except we also pronounce him to be vniust, who commaunded them, whiles we complaine that the very authour of equitie did commaund things not only difficult, and hard, but also impossible.* Finallie to omit others *S. Augustin* saith thus, *eo ipso quo firmissimè creditur* &c. *for as much as it is most firmelie beleeued that God being iust, and good, could not commaund impossible things, we are heereby admonished both what to doe in those things that are easy, and also what to craue of God in those things which are hard, or difficult: for all things ar easy to charitie, whereto alone the burden of Christ,* (that is to say Christs law, or commaundment,) *is light.*

S. Basil in orat. in illud Attende tibi. non longè à principio. S. Chrisost. ho. 8. de pœnitent. circa medium. S. Paulin ep. ad Celantiã inter ep. S. Hieron. li. 1 ep. 14. S. Aug. li. de natura & gratia ca. 69.

74 Thus saith this holly father geeuing to vnderstand two things, the one that to affirme God to haue commaunded things impossible, were to accuse him to be neither good, nor iust, which is no lesse then meere blasphemy, and impiety: and the other is, that the hardest commaundments are easyly performed with the helpe of charitie, which therfore he saith we ought to craue of God in our prayers, whereby he also teacheth that the obseruation of the commaundments, or law of God, is an effect, or frute of charitie, as I haue showed before.

75 And now to say some what particulerlie of the Roman church, it is euident that in it is the true obseruation of Gods law, and commandments not only because it is the true church, and spouse of *Christ*, and practiseth all the meanes that God hath ordained for the performance of his law, (as I haue proued sufficientlie before) but also because the Euangelical counsels of *Christ* (which include the commaundments) are fully and exactly obserued therein, as appeared in the 25. 28. 29. 30. and 31. chapters, where I haue manifestlie showed, that the Roman Catholikes only, haue the true imitation of *Christ*, by the obseruation of the Euangelical counsels, besids that it is no lesse manifest, that the counsels doe both include the commaundements, and also in some sort exceede them in perfection: for although Christian perfection doth consist in the obseruation of the precepts, (as I haue declared in the last chapter,

and that the counsels are referred thereto as to their end,(being proposed,and taught by our sauiour to the end that the præcepts may be the more perfectlie obserued) yet they doe excell the precepts three waise.

See Bellarmin li. 2. de monachis c. 6.

76 The first is if we compare together those counsels, and precepts, which concerne one,and the selfe same matter, as for example the precepts forbidding couetousnes,are, *non concupisces rem proximi*, *Thou shalt not couet thy neighbours goods*; and *non furaberis*, *thou shalt not steale*, and the Euangelical counsel, that concerneth that matter, is *voluntarie pouertie*, but to forbeare to steale,or not to couet the goods of our neighbour, is not of such excellencie,and merit, as to forsake or geeue away all that we haue to the poore for the loue of God,whereto our sauiour promiseth a hundreth fold in this life, and an euerlasting kingdome in the next.

77 The like also may be said of the councel of virginitie, as that it is more excellent, and perfect then the precept *non mæchaberis*,*thou shalt not commit adulterie*, for he which doth, for the loue of God conserue himselfe in perpetual virginitie,and chastitie, is no dout more perfect then he, that only forbeareth to commit adultery,or fornication, as maried folks may easily doe.

78 Secondly it is also euident,that a farre greater measure of charitie is necessarie to the keeping of the counsels (which require a perfect renuntiation of our goods, and pleasures) then to the obseruation of the precepts only,which may be kept,and yet our goods, and moderat pleasures retained:in which respect S. Augustin saith of virgins, *maior amor*,*maius onus imposuit*,*a greater loue laide a greater burthen vppon them*,therfore where there is greater charitie,or loue of God,there is also greater perfection.

S. Aug. ser. 18. de verb. Apostoli.cap. 11.

79 Thirdly if we compare the state of those that keepe the counsels, with those that keepe the precepts only, the former no dout are of farre greater merit,and perfection,because the counsels being perfectly obserued,doe include the precepts,and ad more thereto, in which respect our sauiout answered to the yong man, who said that he had kept the commaundments, *adhuc vnum tibi deest* &c. *Thou yet wantest one thing*, *if thou willt be perfect*, *goe and sell all thou hast and geeue it to the poore*, *and follow me*, whereuppon S. Augustin saith, *magister bonus mandata legis ab ista excellentiore perfectione distinxit* &c. *Our good maister* (Christ) *distinguished the commaundments of the law*, *from this more excellent perfection*, *for he said there*, *if thou wilt enter into life keepe the commaundments*: and *heere* (he saith) *if thou wilt be perfect sell all thou hast* &c. So he, who also in the same place calleth this aduise of our Sauiour to the yong man, *grande & præclarum prrfectionis*

Mar. 10. Luc. 18. Matth. 19. S. August. ep. 89. q. 4. ad Hilarium.

perfectionis consilium, a greate, and notable counsel of perfection, as may be seene more at large before in the 28. chapter, where I treated of the counsel of *voluntarie pouertie* in particuler. *Ibid.*

80 For these respects the ancient fathers of the church doe affirme, that the Euangelical counsels doe surmount, or goe beyond the precepts. *Origen* saith, that they are *supra debitum*, and *supra præceptum*, *aboue*, or beyond *our duty*, and *aboue the præcept*, or commaundment of God: and *S. Ambrose* speaking of virginitie, saith *non enim præcipitur quod supra legem est* &c. *That which is aboue the law is not commaunded, but is rather perswaded by the way of councell*: and not only *S. Paulinus*, but also *S. Augustin*, doe geeue to vnderstand that virginitie, (which is one of the Euangelical counsels) is a *woork of supererogation*: to which purpose *S. Paulinus* alluding to the parable of our Sauiour concerning the good *Samaritan*, who cured the wounded man, saith, that he which doth adde the counsel of virginitie to the præcepts, *dé suo supererogat*, doth *lay out of his owne more then is commaunded*, and shall be rewarded for it, when our Lord returneth, as the good *Samaritan* promised to the innekeeper, to render, or repay him at his returne whatsoeuer he shuld lay out of his owne, more then the 2. pence which he gaue him for the cure of the wounded man.

Orig. in ca. 15 ad Romã.
S. Ambrosius ad Vercel. eccles. li. 3. ep. 25.
S. Paulin. Nolan. ad Sulpit. Seuerum. ep. 4.

81 And the very same application of that parable is vsed by *S. Augustin* not only concerning virginitie in his booke *de virginitate* but also els where concerning the other counsels, mentioned in the holly scriptures, whereof he saith thus. *Hæc sunt quæ amplius erogantnr saucio* &c. *These are those things, which are laid out ouer and aboue*, that which was ordained) *for the cure of the wounded man, whome the Samaritan out of his mercy, and compassion caused to be caried to the inne to be cured. And therefore they are said not to be commaunded by our Lord, although they are by him aduised to be offred, to the end we may vnderstand that they are so much the more gratefull, by how much more they are vndue*, that is to say, by how much lesse wee are bound to vndertake them. Thus teach these two holly fathers, wherein I wish our aduersaries to note, that the tearme *of supererogation* applied to woorks, is not a late inuention of ours, but vsed 1200. yeres a goe, and deriued out of the holly scripture, by the ancient fathers.

S. August de virginitate ca. 30.
Idem li. 2. quæst. Euãg. q. 19.
Idem li. 1. de Adulterinis coniugiis. c. 14.

82 *S. Chrisostome* also testifieth that *multi & ipsa superant mandata, many doe passe* or goe beyond the *commauudments*, as appeareth in the place, which I haue alledged out of him a before, to proue the possibilitie to keepe the commaundments. And *S. Gregory* affirming also the same, saith, *Alij non iudicantur, & regnant, qui etiam præcepta legis perfectione virtutum transcendunt* &c. *some are not iudged, and doe reigne, who do transcend, or mount*

S. Chrisost. ho. 8 de pœnitent.
a Nu. 75.
S. Greg. li. 26. Moral. ca. 20.

mount aboue the præcepts of vertue, not being contented, only to fulfill that which the law of God commaundeth to all men, but endeuoring also with a more excellent desire to exhibit more, then they could heare in the general præcepts. Thus saith *S. Gregory* in conformitie with all the other fathers, concerning the counsels of our sauiour.

83 Finally for as much as the heyghest perfection of Christian life, consisteth in the true imitation of *Christ*, and in the perfect obseruation of his commaundments (as I haue often signified before) and that *Christ* is truely imitated, and the commaundmẽts perfectly obserued, (so farre foorth as is required in this life) by the meanes of the Euangelical counsels (which cannot be perfectly practised, and performed, with out a most excellent, and eminent charitie) Therefore all the ancient, and holly fathers of the church do with vniforme consent, attribute the heyghest perfection of Christian life, to the performance of the counsels, in religious disciplin, as I haue signified breefely in the last chapter, and proued more at large in the 28. 29. 30. and especiallie in the 31. chapters; whereuppon I conclude, that seeing the Catholike Roman church hath the true imitation of *Christ*, by the exact practise of the Euangelical counsels, it hath also that most excellent fruit, and effect of charity, whereof I now treate, to wit the perfect obseruation of the commaundments of God, and consequentlie the heyghest, and all the perfection of Christian religion: and that on the other side, the aduersaries of the Roman church, being professed enemies of the Euangelical counsels, and not obseruing the commaundments by their owne confession, (seeing they teach them tobe impossible to be kepte) are therefore vtterly voide, not only of the true imitation of *Christ*, and of Christian perfection, but also of perfect charity, which (as I haue
Coloss. 3. showed before) the Apostle calleth *vinculum perfectionis, the bond of perfection.*

84 And to the end thou maist, good reader, the better call to mind what I haue discoursed, and proued before concerning this point, it may please thee to remember, that hauing deduced the doctrin, and practise of these counsels of our sauiour out of expresse scriptures, and the ancient fathers, not only in general, but also of euery counsel in particuler, I showed that the saide sectaries haue no vse, or practise thereof at all: as first concerning voluntarie pouerty, I made it maninifest, that albeit there hath benne in all ages, and times from our sauiour *Christ* vntill this day, infinit numbers who haue followed his counsel, and example of *voluntarie pouertie*, abãdoning all their worldly welth, substance, and honours for the loue of God, and amongst them

many emperours, kings, princes, and most eminent personages, (eminent I say for their temporal power, dignitie, and riches,) yet it was neuer heard that any *Lutheran*, or *Caluinist* would leaue the valew of sixe pence, and much lesse all his temporal commodities, and dignities, to become poore, needy, and contemptible for Christs sake.

85 In like manner I showed also the same touching the Euangelical councel of *chastitie*, as that notwithstanding the expresse doctrin and practise thereof deliuered vnto vs by our Sauiour, and his Apostles and that innumerable holly men, and women in all succeeding ages vntill this day, haue voluntarily consecrated themselues to the seruice of God, by vow of perpetual chastity, newertheles the *Lutherans*, and *Caluinists*, haue not so much practise of this Angelical, and heauenly vertue, as painimes had, amongst whome it was heyghly esteemed, and practised by many, (as I showed euidently in the 30. chapter) whereas these professors of the new Ghospell, and pretended reformers of the world doe with might, and maine impugne it, teaching a most carnal and absurd doctrin, contrary to experience, and comon sence, to wit, *that it is no more possible to liue chast, then to liue with out meate*, besids that, to exclude, and debarre men from the special meanes to attaine vnto it (I meane from Gods grace and assistance) they teach also, that it is no more lawfull to craue of God the gift of *chastitie*, then the gift, or grace of prophesie, or of doing miracles: also that a man may be diuorced from his wife, and marry againe for many causes, and that *Poligamie*, or the hauing of many wiues at once, is not forbidden in the new testament, but indifferent to be vsed, or left at our pleasure, for so teacheth *Luther*, and other of the sectaries his followers, opening a wide gappe to Mahomets beastly *Alcoran*, as I haue declared in the 30. chapter, where I also showed that their liues were sutable to their doctrin, being most impure, carnal, and scandalous, as I will declare further after a whyle.

See the 3 chap.

86 Moreouer, touching the third Euangelical counsel of *obedience*, or abnegation of our selues, (whereto our sauiour most seriously inuited euery christian man,) I also made it manifest, that although the practise thereof hath benne alwaise euident in Gods church in religious disciplin, from the time of the Apostles vntill this day, yet the sectaries aboue named, haue not soe much as any pretence, or shadow thereof, hauing no practise of the abnegation of themselues any way in the world, no, not so much as in captiuating theyr reason, and vnderstanding to faith, seeing they reduce all matters of faith, and the sence of holly scriptures (as all heretikes haue euer donne) to their owne vnderstanding, and priuat iudgement, which they ridiculously call the

ſpirit of God, euery one of them pretending to haue the infalible aſſiſtance of Gods ſpirit,though they be neuer ſo different in opinion, and doctrin of moſt important points of diuinitie, condemning one an other of abſurd, and damnable hereſies: beſids the luciferian, pride which *Luther*, *Caluin*,and others of them show in their owne writings, and with moſt odious exprobrations, doe caſt in the teeth one of an other, as I declared amply in the 31. chapter: ſoe that, it is more cleare then the ſunne,that they haue no collour, or pretence at all of that true chriſtian humilitie,and abnegation of themſelues, which our ſauiour required in his ſeruants,and followers,wherevppon I haue inferred diuers times before, and now conclude that their congregations being vtterly deſtitut of all exerciſe, or practiſe of the Euangelical counſels, haue no participation of that notable fruite of charity,whereof I now treate, nor any true imitation of *Chriſt*, nor perfection of Chriſtian religion, nor finally that felicitie which is the end of man, and common welth: and that on the other ſide the Catholike Roman church exerciſing, and performing exactly theſe counſels of our ſauiour, and conſequentlie obſeruing the law, and commaundments of God (as I haue declared before) excelleth in all chriſtian perfection, and geeueth true felicitie to the common welths where it floriſheth.

87 And this may appeare, ſo farre foorth as concerneth the Euangelical counſels, by the greate benefits that redound to the comon welth by the obſeruation thereof. For although the perfect practiſe of them cannot ſtand with the ſtate of euery member of the political body, (I meane, ſuch as are maried men, and haue proprietie in goods,or poſſeſſions) yet it is neceſſarie for the perfection of the whole common welth, that they be exactly obſerued in ſome part thereof, and therfore I showed by diuers inſtances,and examples in the 31. chapter, that ſome things are neceſſarie for the whole, that are not needefull to be found in euery part: and this, I ſay, is euident in the Euangelical counſels in regard of comon welth.

88 To which purpoſe it is to be conſidered, that whereas there are three things eſpecially which doe corrupt, and ruin not only the ſoules of men, but alſo whole comon welths, (to wit, *concupiſcentia carnis*, *concupiſcentia oculorum*, and *ſuperbia vitæ, the concupiſcence of the fleſh, the concupiſcence of the eyes, and the pride of life*) our ſauiour, intending to cure theſe moſt dangerous and inueterat diſſeaſes of mankind, to the benefit as well of all men in general, (that is to ſay of whole common welths) as of euery man in particuler, propoſed, like to a wiſe, skilfull, and pious phiſition,three remedies of a contrarie qualitie, to wit the three

1. *Ioan.* 2.

notable

notable vertues of *single*, and *chast life*, *voluntarie pouertie*, *and obedience*, or abnegation of our selues, practising also the same himselfe most exactly for our example, and encouragement.

89 Therefore whosoeuer doth duly follow his counsel, and example in the exercise of these three vertues, must needs be not only a good and perfect christian, (sacrifizing himselfe wholy *soule, body, goods*, and *liberty* to almighty God) but also an excellent member of his common welth, liuing therein most laudably with out the iniury, or offence of any, louing euery man as himselfe, benefiting all men to his power, practising profound humilitie, pacience, remission of iniuries, and all kind of vertue, and finally abounding in perfect charitie, which is the fountaine from whence floweth all perfection as well political, or ciuil, as Euangelical, and Christian.

90 And although it is not necessarie, or conuenient, as I haue said, that euery member of the comon welth, doe exactly obserue these counsels, yet it is requisit that some doe performe them in perfection, for where as most men that are transported with vice, and sinne, doe commonly measure all others by their owne infirmitie, and therefore would easily suppose, that the perfection of vertue were impossible to be obtained, if they shuld not see the perfect practise of it in some men at least, it cannot be denied, but that the example of such as performe Euangelical counsels, is an euident argument to all men that those vertues are possible, yea and helpeth to dispose, and notably moue, and incite many to the exercise thereof, if not in the heyghest perfection, yet at least in some sort, according to their state, and vocation. And therefore the couetous rich man, seeing riches abandoned for the loue of God, is moued thereby at least, lesse to affect his welth, and to vse the same well without the offence of God, or of his neighbour; and the incontinent man, be he maried, or single, is by the example of the virgin, the sooner induced to liue continent in his vocation. Lastly the proud, and ambitious man learneth lesse to esteeme the world, and the vanities thereof, by the profound humilitie of those that doe wholly contemne it, and deny themselues for the loue of God: so that vertue is notably furthered, and aduanced in the common welth by the example of such as practise the Euangelical counsels, and not only by their example, but also by their other good endeuours of admonitions, fraternal correptions, and exhortations.

91 For; the excellent, and singular charitie, or loue of God, which moueth them to practise perfect vertue themselues, inciteth them also to further the same in others, by all possible meanes, and to ioyne the

actiue with the contemplatiue life in the heyghest perfection; whereby the common welth is exceedingly benefited, as may appeare by all that which I haue amply laid doune before, concerning the gaining of infinit numbers of soules to God, and the conuersion of innumerable nations to the Christian faith, by such only, as haue practised the Euangelical counsels: and therefore when our sauiour determined to employ his disciples in the promulgation of his law, and the conuersion of the world, he taught them the Euangelical councels, knowing in his deuine wisdome, that none could be fit instruments to induce other men to Christian perfection, (which is repugnant to flesh and bloud) if they did not perfectlie practise it themselues; wherevppon I inferred, that our aduersaries being enemies to the Euangelical counsels, can neither themselues arriue to christian perfection, nor perswade other Christians to embrace it, and much lesse conuert infidels to the Christian faith: All which I haue largely debated in the 34. chapter, where I haue also declared what greate benefits, spiritual, and temporal God hath in all ages bestowed vppon princes, and their states by the prayers, and endeuours of religious men obseruing the Euangelical counsels. Finally I haue also shewed, in the same chapter, how much the first christian Emperours, and kings, as well in our cuntry, as els where haue esteemed, and honored such men, and laboured to aduance their profession: by all which it euidently appeareth, how necessarie, and beneficial the exercise of the Euangelical counsels is, not only to euery common welth in particuler, but also generally to the whole world. Thus much concerning the second effect of charitie, consisting in the performance of the commaundments, and of the Euangelical counsels of our sauiour.

Chap. 34.

92 The third fruite of perfect charity (whereof I determined to treate) is all kind of good woorks, for, although our aduersaries do attribute the same wholly to faith, as the proper fruite thereof, yet they are to vnderstand, that good woorks are no otherwaise the frutes of faith, then as faith woorketh, or is made to woorke by charitie, from whence they doe immediatlie proceede, and therefore are the proper frutes, and effects thereof, in which respect *S. Augustin* saith, that the Apostle commending faith vnto vs, doth recommend no other, but an *holsome* and *Euangelical faith*, *cuius opera ex dilectione procedunt*, *the woorks whereof doe proceede from loue*, or charity: and againe (*si fides*, saith he, *sine dilectione sit* &c. *if faith be with out charity, it shall be with out woorks, adde to it hope, and loue, and take no thought for thy woorking, for charity can not be idle.* Also in the same place, *quod credit*, saith he, *fidei est*, *quod operatur charitatis*,

S. Aug. de fide & operib. c. 14.

Idem præfat. in psal. 13.

Ibidem.

tatis, that a man beleeueth, it is of faith, that he worketh, it is of charity. Thus he.

93 And this may be confirmed out of the Apostle, who attributeth to charitie all the effects, and fruites of vertue, saying, *charitas patiens est, benigna est* &c. *charity is patient, is benigne, or meeke, charitie enuieth not, dealeth not peruersely, is not puffed vp, is not ambitious, seeketh not her owne, is not prouoked to anger, thinketh not euil, reioyseth not vppon iniquitie, but reioyseth with the truth, suffereth all things, beleeueth all things, hopeth all things, beareth all things* &c. So saith the Apostle, signifying that charity is the mother of all vertue. *1. Cor. 13.*

94 Now then, it resteth to be considered, where this notable effect of charity is to be found, whether in the congregations of the sectaries, or in the Catholike Roman church, to which purpose I shall not neede to trouble thee, good reader, with any further discourse, then with a breefe recapitulation, of what I haue treated alreddy concerning the doctrin, and liues of the sectaries, and Roman Catholikes.

95 First, for the sectaries: I haue declared at large in the 35. chapter what an absurd, pernicious, and pestilent doctrin they teach touching charitie, and woorks, as that faith only iustifieth before charitie, and with out charity, (for so teacheth *Luther*) that good woorks are neither meritorious, nor necessarie to saluation, but hurtfull thereto: that the best woorks of the best men are damnable sinnes: that nothing can damne a man but incredulitie, or lack of faith: that the more wicked a man is, the nearer he is to Gods grace: that whatsoeuer our woorks are, we are sure to be saued, if we apply to our selues the merits of *Christ* by faith: that mens actions proceede nor of free will, but of absolut necessitie: that God moueth, and compelleth men to sinne: besids those other absurd, and impious paradoxes, mencioned a litle before in this chapter touching the abrogation of the commaundments by *Christ*, the impossibilitie to keepe them, and our Christian liberty admitting no obligation of law humane, or deuine: wherevppon it must needs follow, (as I haue signified before diuers times, and speciallie in the 36. chapter) that all vertuous, and good life is superfluous, yea impossible, (when fate doth not compell men vnto it,) and that vice, and sinne is acceptable to God, seeing that according to their doctrin, it proceedeth of his owne mocion, and compulsion, and is his owne woorke, and therefore by a necessarie consequent must needs be good, and commendable, ineuitable, and remediles to man. *See chap. 35.* *Nu. 68.*

96 What then can be expected of those which teach, or beleeue this doctrin, but al wickednes, vice, and sinne? especiallie seeing they also reiect all the meanes that may bridle lust, & concupiscence in man, as all

QQqq iij kind

kind of penance, mortification, and chastisement of the flesh, as I haue sufficiently declared in the 35. and 36. chapter: where I also inferred vp- Chap. 35. & 36.
pon the premisses, that their exhortations to vertue, and reprehensions of vice, are not only booteles, and fruitles, but also ridiculous in them, being contrarie to their owne grounds, and of no other force, or effect, then a weake antidote, geeuen after a strong poison, especiallie seeing that also the liues of their cheefe maisters, and doctors, (*Luther, Caluin, Beza*, and others) were conforme to their doctrin, and so beastly as I described in the 30. chapter, and therefore no meruel though their first disciples practising their doctrin, and imitating their example, loosed the bridle to all vice, and wickednes in such sort, that their maisters themselues were ashamed of them, and exceedinglie lamented and complained thereof, as euidently appeareth by that which I haue alled-
Chap. 35. ged before out of the writings of *Luther, Caluin, Andreas Musculus*, and *Iohn Andrewes*, which last signified plainely that the Ghospellers in *Germany* excused all their wickednes, by the doctrin of only faith, whereuppon they wholly relied, holding good woorks, and all good christian disciplin for nothing els, but for a new popery, and monkery, (for so saith *Iohn Andrewes*) as may be seene more at large in the 35. chapter, whereto may also be added the testimonies not only of *Villagagnon* (first a *Caluinist*, and after a Catholike) concerning the brutish bestiality of the Geneuian ministers, and others sent by the magistrats of *Geneua* to *Noua Francia* in *America*, but also of *Czecanonius*, and *Wigandus* protestant writers in *Germany*, witnessing the greate excesse of enormities, that grew in all those parts by reason of *Luthers* loose, and dissolut doctrin, to the exceeding dammage of the comon welth, as I haue signified more amply in the 30. chapter: by all which it appeareth most ma-
Chap. 30. nifestly, what frute of good woorks their ghospell yeldeth, and what benefit the common welth may reape therebie.

97 But perhaps some will say that howsoeuer *Luther*, and his followers the *Lutherans* ouerlashed in their doctrin concerning good woorks, excluding them from iustification, yet *Caluin* admitteth them thereto in some sort, at least as frutes, or signes of a good faith, affirming that faith can not be void of good woorks, & therefore he exclaimeth greatly against those, that charge him to teach that iustification may be without them.

98 Whereto I answere, that although *Caluin*, and the milder sort of *Lutherans* are more modest in woords, then *Luther*, and his followers, not speaking so outragiouslie against good woorks as they, yea seeming to admit them in some sort to iustification, yet for as much, as they doe

euacuat

euacuat the ſpeciall frute, and effect thereof, denying their merit, (contrary to the doctrin of our ſauiour, and his Apoſtles) whereby they alſo impaire the reputation of good woorks, and hinder mens deſire, and dilligence to performe them, Therefore, I ſay, their doctrin is impious, and pernitious to common welth, eſpecially if *Caluins* opinion be well examined, what he meaneth when he requireth good woorks with faith to our iuſtification.

99 For although he ſeemeth ſometymes to admit them, (as I haue ſaid) yet in truth he holdeth them to be altogeather needeles on our part: I ſay on our part: for, expounding his owne opinion what he meaneth, when he ſaith, that faith can not be with out good woorks, he ſignifieth plainely, that the good woorks which he requireth to our iuſtification, are not ours, but the woorks of *Chriſt* imputed to vs: but let vs heare his owne woords, in the ſame place where he cryeth out againſt his calumniators, as he calleth them.

100 *Non ſomniamus*, ſaith he, *fidem bonis operibus vacuam, aut iuſtificationem qua ſine illis conſtet* &c. *we doe not ſo much as dreame of a faith voide of good woorks, or of a iuſtification which may ſtand with out them: this only difference there is, that where as we confeſſe that faith, and good woorks do neceſſarilie concurre together, we place iuſtification in faith, and not in woorks: and in what manner this is donne, it is eaſy to declare, if we turne our ſelues to Chriſt, to whom faith is directed, and from whom it receiueth all the force it hath. wherefore, we are iuſtified becauſe we apprehend by faith the iuſtice of Chriſt (by which only we are reconciled to God,) and this thou canſt not apprehend, but thou doſt alſo apprehend his ſanctification, for he was geeuen vs for our iuſtice, wiſdome, ſanctification, and redemption: and therefore he iuſtifieth no man, but he doth withall ſanctifie him, for theſe benefits are conioined together with a perpetual, and indiuiſible bond* &c. And after a while hauing added more to the ſame purpoſe, he concludeth, *cum ergo hæc beneficia* &c. *Seeing therfore our lord doth not grant vs the fruition of theſe benefits,* (of iuſtification, and ſanctification) *but by geeuing himſelfe vnto vs, he doth geeue vs them both together, and neuer geueth the one with out the other: and ſo it is manifeſt how true it is, that we are not iuſtified with out woorks, neither yet by woorks: becauſe ſanctification is no leſſe contained then iuſtice, in the participation of Chriſt, whereby we are iuſtified.* So he, explicating his owne opinion, how good woorks muſt needs concurre with faith in our iuſtification: wherein neuertheles yow ſee he doth not ſo much as mencion our woorks, but geueth to vnderſtand that the woorks of *Chriſt* (which are comprehended in his ſanctification) are imputed to vs together with his iuſtice, for it is euident that Caluins conſtant opinion and doctrin concerning our iuſtification, is that

Caluin inſtit. li. 3 c. 16. §. 1.

Caluin li. 3. inſtit. ca. 11. §. 2. & 3.

that it consisteth in the remission of sinne, & the imputation of Christs iustice vnto vs, *vt pro iustis,* saith he, *in Christo censeamur, qui in nobis non sumus, that we may be held for iust in Christ, who are not* (iust) *in our selues:* So that when he teacheth that we are not iustified, with out woorks, and declareth his meaning to be no other, but because we apprehend the sanctification of *Christ* by faith together with his iustice, it is manifest by his owne interpretation, that the good woorks which he requireth together with faith in our iustification, are Christs, and not ours, I meane no otherwaise ours, then Christs iustice and sanctification is ours, that is to say, not really, and in deede, but only by imputation, according to his opinion, which I haue sufficiently confuted in the beginning of this chapter.

Caluin li. 3. institut. c. 14. sect. 9.
Ibidem li. 3. c. 11. sect. 13. & 17.
Idem de eter. Dei praedestina. printed at Geneua an. 1552. fol. 905. 906 916. 944. & 945.
Item li. 1. instit. ca 17. §. 11. & ca. 18. §. 1. & §. 2. & § 4.
Itē ibid li. 2. ca 4 §. 2. & §. 3. & 4.
Item li. 3. c. 23. §. 4. 7. 8. & 9.
** Chap. 35. & 36.*

101 And this is also most conforme to his doctrin in other points, seeing he teacheth expressely, as I haue declared in the 35. chapter, that our best woorks are mortal sinnes, and that our iustification by faith, is *soluta conditionibus legis, free from the conditions of the law:* Besides his other blasphemous opinion, that God is the authour of sinne, inclining, mouing, ad compelling men thereto, yea and woorking it himselfe in their minds, as the first cause, vsing them as his instruments, which how absurd, and impious it is, I haue alreddy showed sufficientlie before: where by it is euident, that his doctrin concerning woorks being well sifted, and examined, is no lesse preiudicial to good life, & consequently no lesse pernicious to common welth then *Luthers,* though it be sometimes more cunningly shrowded with some more shaddow, and colour of piety.

102 Whereas on the other side, I haue manifestly showed in diuers parts of this treatise, and especiallie in the *35. and 36. chapters, that the doctrin, and practise of the Catholike church, is most behoouefull, and beneficial to common welth, inuiting, encouraging, and leading men to all kind of good woorkes, vertue, and christian perfection, teaching out of the holly scriptures, and fathers, that good woorks are necessary to iustification, and saluation: that they are most acceptable to almighty God, and meritorious: that contrition, confession, and satisfaction, is requisit to the remission of sinne: that the chastisement of the body is not only gratefull, and pleasing to almighty god, and satisfactory for sinnes past, but also needefull to the repression of concupiscence, and preuention of future sinnes: that the meditation of our sauiours life, passion, death, and resurrection, is necessarie to the true imitation of him, and geeueth singular contentment, and comefort to a deuout soule (though *Luther* saith, that he had more gust, and pleasure in bread and

beare,

beare, then in such meditations, as I declared out of his owne dronken confession in the 32. chapter:) finally that the practise, and performance of the Euangelical counsels of *Christ*, is necessarie to the perfection of Christian religion: all which doctrin tending directly to vertuous and good life, to the repression of vice, to the reformation of manners, and to Christian perfection, and being most exactly practised in the Catholike Roman church, must needs bring foorth plenty, and abundance of all good woorks, to the incredible benefit of comon welth. *Chap. 32.*

103 And to this purpose I haue also further proued in the 36. chapter, that although there are very many who professe Catholike religion, and are with all very vicious, and wicked, yet their vice, and wickednes, neither doth, nor can proceede of the Catholike faith which they professe, but of their owne negligence, in not following and obseruing the prescript, and rules thereof: And againe on the other side, I also showed in the same place, that the bad life of such as professe *Lutheranisme*, or *Caluinisme*, both may, and commonly doth spring of their doctrin, and beleefe, and that the good deeds, or commendable liues of some of them, are not the fruits of their religion, but to be ascribed to the hypocrisie of some, and to the good natural disposition of others, yea and that therein also they haue no aduantage of *Epicurians*, *Pagans*, *Turks*, or *Atheists*, amongst whome there haue benne, & are many as morally good, and vertuous as any of them. Finallie that amongst the old philosophers there were diuers who in moral vertue excelled the best of them: whereas all those that euer haue benne famous and admirable in gods church for sanctitie, and hollines of life, and haue attained to the perfection of Christian religion, haue benne Roman Catholiks, and liued in the exercise of the Catholike Roman doctrin, as appeareth at large in the 36. chapter aforesaid. So that there is nothing more euident, then that this notable frute of charity, (consisting in good woorks, and true Christian vertue) doth no way belong to the profession of sectaries, but to the Catholike Roman Religion, which therefore is most conuenient, and necessary to the happy state of common welth, as well temporal, as spiritual. *Chap. 36.* *Ibidem.*

104 There remaineth yet the fourth effect, or frute of charitie, wherof I promised to speake heere, to wit our vnion with God, which I haue proued to be a special effect of charity, as well in my tract of contemplation, when I treated of the *vnitiue way*, as also in this chapter, where I haue showed the eminent dignitie, and excellent operation of charity in the woork of iustification, and in vniting the soule of man with God: in which respect it is called by the ancient, and learned Fa- *Chap. 10 & 21.*

S.Dionisi.li. de diuinis nomin. c 4. par. 1. & 2. ther *S. Dionysius, virtus vnifica, connexiua, concretiua, commiscens* &c. As I haue signified before, in this a chapter.

a Num. 49.

105 And now to show that this effect of charitie is euident in the Catholike Romar church, the same appeareth by the euident experience, and manifest demonstration of all the external signes, of Gods internal vnion with his seruants: which I haue showed to be no lesse manifest in Roman Catholikes at this day, then it alwaise hath benne in other seruants of God in former times. To which purpose I haue laid doune in the 27. chapter, examples of Gods extraordinary fauours, graces, and gifts bestowed vppon his saints in this life, not only in the old, but also in the new testament, and euer since continued in all ages successiuely from the Apostles vntill this day, I meane the admirable, and stupenduous effects of a contemplatiue, and extatical loue, as abundance of spiritual sweetenes, and heauenly consolations in prayer, extases, and rapts, the spirit of prophesie, reuelations, visions apparitions, of our sauiour, Angels, and Saints, the operation of miracles, and such other euident signes of Gods vnion with holly men: of all which the Catholike Roman church only, hath euer had, and still hath the special priuiledge, as by the examples aforesayde is more cleare then the sunne, especiallie seeing I haue also euidently showed that *Lutherans*, and *Caluinists*, and other aduersaries of the Roman church, haue not, nor euer had any participation of those deuine fauours, and external signes of Gods internal vnion with them, but rather manifest tokens of the contrarie by fained miracles, false reuelations, fanatical dreames, and manifest illusions of wicked spirits, such as I showed in *Luther, Caluin, Zuinglius, Carolstadius, Foxe*, and others, as it may be seene in the 32. chapter.

Chap. 27.

Chap. 32.

106 Besids that I also made it manifest partly in the same chapter, and partly in the 27. that those deuine graces, and gifts whereof I speake, haue benne alwaise most euident in such Roman Catholikes, as haue not beene subiect to the least suspicion of any deceit, or illusion, in respect of their admirable sanctitie, and hollynes of life, manifest to the Christian world; and approued in diuers of them, with such stupendious miracles as passed the deuils power to doe, or counterfet.

Ibid. & Chap. 27.

107 Finally I showed this effect of charity not only in the greatest seruants of God for the 600. yeres last past, to wit in *S. Bernard, S. Francis, S. Dominick, S. Thomas, Aquinas S. Catherin of Siena, S. Brigit*, and diuers others (besides many holly men, and women of this age) but also in the old religious monks, and hermits of the first 600. yeeres after *Christ*, as *S. Paule* the first hermit, *S. Antony, S. Hilarion, S. Ephram, S. Basil, S.*

Hierome, S. Martin, S. Augustin, S. Benet, S. Gregory, and others, of whom I haue produced notable examples in this kind, and by them haue deriued a continual succession from the primitiue church vntill this day, as well of these spiritual graces, and miraculous gifts, as also of religious, and monastical life which they all professed.

08 So that it being euident, that God hath testified, and manifestly showed his internal vnion with holly men, by such external fauours euen from the time of his Apostles, to this our age, and that the same hath benne alwaise, and is still most manifest in Roman Catholiks, yea and that no *Lutheran*, *Caluinist*, or other Sectarie can, or euer could challenge to themselues, any true participation thereof, it must needs be granted that this effect of perfect charitie, (to wit Gods vnion with man,) is proper to the Catholike Roman church only, and to that religion which she professeth, and deliuereth toher children.

109 Whereuppon I conclude that for as much as it appeareth by the whole discourse of this treatise, that the end, and felicitie of man, and of commou welth, consisteth in mans vnion with God, and that this vnion is wrought by perfect charitie, which is found only in the Catholike Roman church and religion, therefore it must needs follow, that the said Catholike Roman religion, and church hath the only meanes to vnite man with God, and consequentlie to make a happy common welth, both spirituallie, and temporallie: spirituallie, for that the members thereof liuing in the perfect practise of the Catholike Roman religion, shall abound in all the frutes of the spirit mentioned by the Apostle, who saith, *Fructus autem spiritus sunt charitas, gaudium, pax* &c. *The fruits of the spirit are charitie, ioye, peace, patience, longanimitie, bounty, benignitie, mansuetud, faith, modestie, continencie, chastitie*, and that these are proper to Roman Catholikes, it appeareth sufficiently by all those effects of Catholik religion whereof I haue treated as well in diuers parts of this treatise, as now lastly in this chapter: Of these the Apostle also addeth further in the same place, *aduersus huiusmodi non est lex., against such as these, there is no law*, signifying that those which haue these vertues infused by the spirit of God, doe not neede any written law, humane, or deuine, to diuert or with hold them from doing euil, or to a compel thē to discharge their duty, towards God or man, because (as he saith of such els where) *sibi ipsi sunt lex, they are a law to themselues*, hauing the law of God written in their harts by the holly Ghost: whereby they are also *ciues sanctorum, & domestici Dei, fellow cittizens of saints, and houshold seruants of God*, & finally do enioye true peace, comefort, and ioye of soule, which farre excelleth, al bodily or wordly pleasures, and contentments.

5. Gal.

a D. Tho. 1. 2. q. 96. ar. 5.

Rom. 2.

Hierem. 31.

Psal. 36.

Ephes. 2.

110 And the more general this spiritual felicitie is in the members of the common wolth, the greater also is the temporal happines that redoundeth thereof to the whole state, which being spirituallie vnited with God in all the parts, and members thereof, must needs *dwell* (as the psalmist saith) *in the helpe of the heyghest, and in the protection of the God of heauen*, and florish in all plenty, tranquilitie, peace, prosperitie, and securitie. According to the promise made by allmighty God to his people, saying. *Si in præceptis meis ambulaueritis. & mandata mea custodieritis* &c. If you walke in my præcepts, and keepe my commaundments, I will geeue you, raine in due season, and the earth shall bring foorth her spring, and your trees shall be filled with frutes: the thrasshing of your haruest shal reach to the vintage: and the vintage shall continue vntill the sowing time, you shall eate your bread to your fill: and you shall dwell in your land with out feare, I will geeue you peace in your coasts, you shall sleepe, and there shall be no man to afright you: I will take away noysome beasts, and the swoord shall not passe ouer your bounds: you shall pursue your enemies, and they shall fall before you: fiue of yours shal pursue a hundreth strangers, and a hundreth of you ten thousand: your enemies shall fall by the swoord in your sight: I will respect you, and make you encrease: you shall be multiplied, and I will ratifie my couenant with you: you shall eate the eldest of their old store, and shall cast away the old vppon the coming in of the new: I will sett my tabernacle in the midst of you, and my soule will not reiect you: I will walke a mongst you, and will be your God, and you shall be my people.

Leuit. 26.

111 Thus said almighty God to the *Iewes*, promising them all the temporal felicitie that could be imagined, if they would inuiolablie obserue his law. And the same is no dout to be vnderstood of any other people, or common welth, liuing in the profession of true religion and the obseruation of the commaundments of God: wherein neuertheles I wish it to be vnderstood, that for as much as temporal prosperitie, being considered in it selfe, is common, as well to bad common welths, as to good, at least for a time: it is neuer to be taken for any part of true happines but only when it cōcurreth with the spiritual felicitie before mēcioned, or rather redoundeth thereof, as a benediction, and blessing of almighty God bestowed vppon his particuler people: for otherwaise it may rather be counted an infelicitie, and malediction, for such reasons, as I haue signified partly in the 9. chapter, and much more at large in the first part of this treatise, where I laid downe the causes why God prospereth wicked men, and showed euidently that their sinfull prosperity, doth not only pronosticat, but also accelerat their ruin, and is, as

Chap. 26.

S. Augustin ſaith, a iuſt punishment of God for their ſinne, ſeruing for no other end ſometimes then, as it were, a lightning before death, and other while, for a pleaſant paſture to feede, and fatten them for the ſlaughter, yea being many times an aſſured token, & argument of their reprobation, or an earneſt penny of their eternal damnation, and therefore the greater, and more general is ſuch proſperity of the wicked, the greater is their infelicitie, and miſery, as shall further appeare in the third part of this treatiſe, when I shall treate of the notable punishments of almighty God extended vppon princes, and their ſtates, for hereſie, and ſchiſme, whereby alſo the eminent dignitie, and excellent fruit of Catholike religion in common welth, shall be yet much more manifeſt.

S. Aug. in Pſal. 9.

See the firſt part. chap. 26. nu. 25. 26. &c. vnto the end of the chapter.

112 And this being as much as I haue thought good to repreſent vnto thee, good reader, in this ſecond part, I will heere make an end, remitting thee to the third, as well for the complet accomplishment of my whole proiect, as alſo for ſome things which I haue particulerly promiſed in my firſt part, and not yet performed. In the meane time, I beſeech almighty God to inſpire thee, to make no leſſe vſe, and benefit of theſe my labours, then I hartely wish thee, to Gods greater glory, and thy owne eternal good.

Laus Deo qui dedit velle
& perficere.

The principall faults escaped are thus to be amended. The letter p. signifieth the page, The letter n. the number, and the letter l. the line.

PAg. 59. l. 10. for, in the yeare after the foundation of Rome, reade in the yeare 415. after the foundation of Rome, p. 61. n. 8. l. 8. For esteenning, esteeming. p. 67. l. 16. for hould, should p. 68. l. 10 for here, how p. 71 n. 24 l. 8 for aloustruse, abstruse, p. 73. n. 28. l. 2. for others, oathes p. 74 l. 9. for hem, them. ibid. n. 32. l. 2. for *cum profundum, cum in profundum* p. 82 n. 24. l. 3 for attended, attend. p. ibid. n. 31. l. 1. for, labour to, labour to be like to p. 84 n 39. l. 1. for emplified, exemplified p. 88. n. 47. l 12. for stade, stoode p. 91. l. 4 for laudes, landes p. 92. n. 10. l. 13. for with, which. p. 95. l. 2. for intigate, mitigate. p. 94. n. 13. l 6. for Liuij Liuy. And the like correct in more places hard by p. 97 n. 21. l. 3. for *Turius, Furius*. p. 100. n. 32. l. 1. for *Madonie, Macedonie*, p. 184. l. 1. for hebctat, hebetat p. 290. n. 11. l. 2. for asaxe, as are p. 318. l. 4. for treate, treated p. 329. n. 27. l. 8. for cast, case. Ibid. n. 28. l. 5 for *icta, ista*. p. 353 n 25. l. 12 for diuinitions, difinitions p. 354 l. last, for cruell, crueltie p. 357. n. 32. l. last, for not, nor. p. 360. n. 7. l. 6. for held, geld p. 446. n. 21. l. 16. for monarie, monasterie.

If there be some other litle faults which I haue ommitted, and thou shalt chance to finde in the readinge, I pray thee of thy gentlenes to correct them.

A TABLE SHEVVING BRIEFLY THE PRINCIPALL POINTS THAT ARE HANDLED IN the Second part of this Treatise.

A

A TABLE SHEVVING BRIEFLY THE PRINCIPALL POINTS THAT ARE HANDLED IN the Second part of this Treatise.

A

D

Notable

THE TABLE.

I

L

a million

very

An

FINIS.